# ENVIRONMENTAL REGULATION

ASPEN CASEBOOK SERIES

# ENVIRONMENTAL REGULATION
## LAW, SCIENCE, AND POLICY

### NINTH EDITION

**ROBERT V. PERCIVAL**
ROBERT F. STANTON PROFESSOR OF LAW
DIRECTOR, ENVIRONMENTAL LAW PROGRAM
UNIVERSITY OF MARYLAND CAREY SCHOOL OF LAW

**CHRISTOPHER H. SCHROEDER**
CHARLES S. MURPHY PROFESSOR EMERITUS OF LAW AND PROFESSOR
EMERITUS OF PUBLIC POLICY
DUKE UNIVERSITY SCHOOL OF LAW

**ALAN S. MILLER**
FORMER GEF AND CLIMATE CHANGE COORDINATOR
THE INTERNATIONAL FINANCE CORPORATION

**JAMES P. LEAPE**
FORMER DIRECTOR GENERAL
WORLD WILDLIFE FUND INTERNATIONAL

Wolters Kluwer

Published by Wolters Kluwer in New York.

Wolters Kluwer Legal & Regulatory U.S. serves customers worldwide with CCH, Aspen Publishers, and Kluwer Law International products. (www.WKLegaledu.com)

To contact Customer Service, e-mail customer.service@wolterskluwer.com, call 1-800-234-1660, fax 1-800-901-9075, or mail correspondence to:

Wolters Kluwer
Attn: Order Department
PO Box 990
Frederick, MD 21705

Printed in the United States of America.

1 2 3 4 5 6 7 8 9 0

ISBN 978-1-5438-2616-6

**Library of Congress Cataloging-in-Publication Data**

Names: Percival, Robert V., author. | Schroeder, Christopher H., author. |
    Miller, Alan S., author. | Leape, James P., author.
Title: Environmental regulation : law, science, and policy / Robert V.
    Percival, Robert F. Stanton Professor of Law Director, Environmental Law
    Program, University of Maryland School of Law; Christopher H. Schroeder,
    Charles S. Murphy Professor of Law and Public Policy Studies, Duke
    University School of Law; Alan S. Miller, Former GEF and Climate Change
    Coordinator, The International Finance Corporation; James P. Leape,
    Former Director General World Wildlife Fund International.
Description: Ninth edition. | New York : Wolters Kluwer, 2021. | Series:
    Aspen casebook series | Includes index. | Summary: "Casebook on
    environmental law for upper level law students"– Provided by publisher.

Identifiers: LCCN 2021023488 (print) | LCCN 2021023489 (ebook) |
    ISBN 9781543826166 (hardcover) | ISBN 9781543826173 (ebook)
Subjects: LCSH: Environmental law–United States. | LCGFT: Casebooks (Law)
Classification: LCC KF3817 .E548 2021 (print) | LCC KF3817 (ebook) |
    DDC 344.7304/6–dc23
LC record available at https://lccn.loc.gov/2021023488
LC ebook record available at https://lccn.loc.gov/2021023489

# About Wolters Kluwer Legal & Regulatory U.S.

Wolters Kluwer Legal & Regulatory U.S. delivers expert content and solutions in the areas of law, corporate compliance, health compliance, reimbursement, and legal education. Its practical solutions help customers successfully navigate the demands of a changing environment to drive their daily activities, enhance decision quality and inspire confident outcomes.

Serving customers worldwide, its legal and regulatory portfolio includes products under the Aspen Publishers, CCH Incorporated, Kluwer Law International, ftwilliam.com and Medi-Regs names. They are regarded as exceptional and trusted resources for general legal and practice-specific knowledge, compliance and risk management, dynamic workflow solutions, and expert commentary.

To my family, Barbara, Marita, Richard, and Zoey.

R.V.P.

To Kate, Emily, Ted, and Lily, and to my parents, Jane and Herb,
for their unqualified support and love.

C.H.S.

To Sue, Joanna, and my parents, Ruth and Ralph Miller.

A.S.M.

To Suki, Benjamin, and Jonathan.

J.P.L.

# SUMMARY OF CONTENTS

# CONTENTS

Public concern for the environment has been a catalyst for profound changes in American law. During the past half century, environmental law has grown from sparse common law roots into a vast system of public law that lies at the heart of the modern regulatory state. Environmental law has generated an immense and fiercely complex web of regulations that affects the way we live, work, and do business. Environmental regulation has profoundly affected so many other areas of legal practice, including real estate and commercial transactions, corporate law, criminal law, torts, contract law, and bankruptcy. This book seeks to provide a comprehensive introduction to environmental law.

The ninth edition of this book goes to press after more than a year of turmoil due to profound public health, environmental and economic crises. The deadly COVID-19 pandemic has infected more than one hundred million people in every corner of the world, killing millions. The severity of the global climate crisis has become even more apparent with wildfires, storms, and coastal flooding unprecedented in severity. Efforts to slow the spread of infection have shrunk economies and caused unemployment to soar to levels not seen since the Great Depression. The pandemic's disproportionate impacts on people of color, combined with a cascade of public concern for racial justice, have made issues of environmental justice more important than ever.

But there are profound signs of hope. The development of COVID-19 vaccines in record time has slowed the spread of the disease and help start an economic revival. Fossil fuel companies that long fought climate action are now telling a skeptical public that they will change their ways. A U.S. president who waged a relentless campaign against the environment was decisively defeated at the ballot box. Hours after taking office in January 2021 a new president committed to environmental justice and climate action rejoined the Paris Climate Accord and repealed a host of his predecessor's anti-environmental actions. Thus, this new edition of the casebook appears at a particularly eventful time in the development of environmental law.

The first edition of this casebook appeared nearly three decades ago. Subsequent editions repeatedly added new material to keep pace with developments in the field. The end product was a book that repeatedly grew in size with layers of new material that became somewhat unwieldy. With the ninth edition it was time to take a fresh look at the casebook, to pare down dated material, and to focus on the essentials. Thus, the 9th edition is more user friendly and compact even as it comprehensively updates material in the casebook. Previous adopters will be pleased that this was accomplished while retaining the same basic structure as the 8th edition.

The authors particularly would like to thank Professors Carmen Gonzalez, Helen Kang, Amy Sinden, and Cliff Villa, for their very helpful suggestions concerning how to incorporate more materials on environmental justice throughout the casebook. This edition of the casebook places more emphasis on environmental justice issues than in previous editions, just as the Biden administration is making such issues a top priority. As in the previous editions, the text seeks to broaden students' vision by inviting them to explore how law relates to the larger problems society seeks to solve through collective action. It approaches environmental law through a regulatory policy focus that explores the full range of forces that shape the way law affects human behavior. By focusing on regulation—viewed expansively as embracing all forms of collective action to protect the environment—the text seeks to enhance understanding of the way law affects the behavior of institutions and individuals. This requires far more than mastery of "black letter" law; it also demands an appreciation of the complex processes by which political, economic, and ethical concerns shape regulatory policy. Thus, the text consistently focuses not only on the substance of environmental statutes, but also on how they are translated into regulations and on the factors that affect how they influence real-world behavior.

Despite its comprehensiveness, the book seeks at every turn to make environmental law and policy accessible to the non-specialist. Among the key features it employs to accomplish this goal are charts and diagrams mapping the structure of each of the major environmental statutes, problems and questions based largely on real-world environmental controversies, "pathfinders" explaining where to find crucial source materials for every major subject area, an extensive glossary of environmental terms, and a list of environmental acronyms. The casebook's website is located at a site whose URL is easy to remember because it is the acronym for *Environmental Regulation: Law, Science & Policy*: *www.erlsp.com*. The site will provide chapter-by-chapter updates of material in the casebook and links to the rich array of environmental information available through the Internet. Each year a statutory and case supplement to the text is published (*Environmental Law: Statutory and Case Supplement*), which provides both the updated text of the principal environmental statutes and recent judicial decisions in the field.

The chapters are organized in a manner that gives teachers considerable flexibility in deciding what to cover and in what order. Because each chapter is designed to be self-contained, the material may be covered in a variety of sequences, depending on the length of the course and the teacher's desired areas of emphasis. The teacher's manual identifies several alternative coverage options.

The authors appreciate the numerous comments received from faculty and students who have used previous editions of this text. These comments and suggestions have been invaluable in helping us improve the ninth edition, as we hope you will notice. We hope you will continue to give us such useful feedback on this edition as well.

*Robert V. Percival*
*Christopher H. Schroeder*
*Alan S. Miller*
*James P. Leape*

June 2021

The authors are enormously grateful to the many talented professionals at Aspen/Wolters Kluwer Legal & Regulatory U.S. who helped make this eighth edition possible, in particular John Devins. We have been particularly fortunate to work with the finest editors in the business at The Froebe Group, including Dena Kaufman and Sara Nies. Professor Percival, who prepared the ninth edition, expresses his appreciation to the many student research assistants who have helped him update this book over the years including for the ninth edition Samuel Boden, Madeleine Dwyer, Miles Light, and Zoe Rydzewski.

The authors gratefully acknowledge the permissions granted to reproduce the following materials.

Andreen, William L. "Success and Backlash: The Remarkable (Continuing) Story of the Clean Water Act," *4 J. Energy & Env. L. 25* (Winter 2013). The George *Washington* University Law School. Reprinted with permission.

Dreher, Robert G. *NEPA Under Siege: The Political Assault on the National Environmental Policy Act.* Georgetown Environmental Law and Policy Institute. Copyright © 2005.

EPA's Assessment of Top Environmental Concerns and the Public's Ranking (chart), in Counting on Science at EPA, 249 Science 616 (1990). Copyright ©1990 by the AAAS. Reprinted with permission of Science.

Esty and Chertow, *A Vision for the Future, Thinking Ecologically, The Next Generation of Environmental Policy* (1997). Copyright 1997 by the Yale University Press. Reprinted by permission.

Fortuna and Lennett, Hazardous Waste Regulation: The New Era (chart), p. 67. Copyright ©1986. Material is reproduced with permission of McGraw-Hill, Inc.

Fredriksson, Per G. *Trade, Global Policy, and the Environment.* International Bank for Reconstruction and Development/The World Bank. Copyright © 1999. Licensed under CC BY 3.0 IGO.

Goodstein, Eban S. *Economics and Environment (2nd edition).* John Wiley & Sons, Inc. Copyright © 1995.

Hamilton, James T. *Regulation through Revelation: The Origin, Politics, and Impacts of the Toxics Release Inventory Program* (2005). Cambridge University Press. Reprinted with permission from author.

Horta, Korinna. "In Focus: Global Environment Facility," Foreign Policy in Focus (December 1998). Institute for Policy Studies. Reprinted with permission.

Magat, Wesley, et al. "The Industrial Water Pollution Standard-Setting Process" (chart). *Rules in the Making: A Statistical Analysis of Regulatory Agency Behavior.* Resources for the Future. Copyright © 1986.

Pope Francis, *Laudato Si — On Care for Our Common Home* (2015). Libreria Editrice Vaticana. Copyright © 2015.

Rechtschaffen, Clifford. "How to Reduce Exposures with One Simple Statute: The Experience of Proposition 65," *29 Env. L. Rep. 10581* (1999). The Environmental Law Reporter. Copyright © 1999.

Salzman, James. "Creating Markets for Ecosystem Services: Notes from the Field," *80 N.Y.U. L. Rev.* 870 (2005). New York University School of Law. Reprinted with permission.

Schmieder, Randy. Illustration of a Delhi Sands flower-loving fly, from *Life on the Edge: A Resource Guide to California's Endangered Plants and Wildlife* (1994). Heyday Books. Reprinted with permission from the artist.

Toles, Tom. "The Unwritten Contract" (cartoon). The Buffalo News. Copyright ©1995. Reprinted with permission of Andrews McMeel Universal. All rights reserved.

Zaelke, Stilwell, and Young, What Reason Demands: Making Laws Work for Sustainable Development in Making Law Work: Environmental Compliance & Sustainable Development (Zaelke, Kaniaru, and Kruzikova eds., 2005). Reprinted with permission.

Percival, Robert. "The Poison Poor Children Drink: Six Lessons from the Flint Tragedy," JURIST – Academic Commentary (February 11, 2016). http://jurist.org/forum/2015/11/robert-percival-six-lessons.php. JURIST Legal News & Research Services, Inc. Copyright © 2016.

Percival, Robert. "Looking Backward, Looking Forward: The Next 40 Years of Environmental Law," *43 Env. L. Rep. 10492* (June 2013). The Environmental Law Reporter®. Copyright © 2013.

# CHAPTER 1

# ENVIRONMENTAL VALUES AND POLICIES: AN INTRODUCTION

All ethics so far evolved rest upon a single premise: that the individual is a member of a community of interdependent parts. The land ethic simply enlarges the boundaries of the community to include soils, waters, plants and animals, or collectively the land. . . .

A thing is right when it tends to preserve the integrity, stability and beauty of the biotic community. It is wrong when it tends otherwise.

*— Aldo Leopold*

I urgently appeal, then, for a new dialogue about how we are shaping the future of our planet. . . . We can no longer speak of sustainable development apart from intergenerational solidarity. Once we start to think about the kind of world we are leaving to future generations, we look at things differently; we realize that the world is a gift which we have freely received and must share with others. Since the world has been given to us, we can no longer view reality in a purely utilitarian way, in which efficiency and productivity are entirely geared to our individual benefit. Intergenerational solidarity is not optional, but rather a basic question of justice, since the world we have received also belongs to those who will follow us.

*— Pope Francis*

The desire to ensure that present and future generations enjoy the benefits of both a prosperous economy and a healthy environment has become a universal aspiration that can provide common ground between remarkably diverse interests. The path for achieving this goal is often referred to as "sustainable development," a concept that has broad public support, despite sharp disagreements over specific policies for pursuing it.

Since the late 1960s, spectacular growth in public concern for the environment has had a profound impact on the development of American law. During this period, U.S. environmental law has grown from a sparse set of common law precedents and local ordinances to encompass a vast body of state and federal legislation. Numerous federal and state agencies now implement these laws through complex regulations that affect virtually every aspect of our lives. In addition, as environmental concerns increasingly transcend national boundaries, environmental law has now become an urgent priority around the globe.

U.S. environmental law has roots in many traditional fields of law, including torts, property, and constitutional law. Much of its continued evolution has been a response to perceived deficiencies of the common law as a vehicle for responding to new problems and new knowledge about the environmental effects of human activity. Chapter 2 explores the major sources of environmental law and provides an overview of the contemporary structure of the field. Throughout its development, environmental law has faced continual criticisms for not changing quickly enough. Such criticism comes both from those who think environmental law responds too weakly and too slowly to environmental problems as well as from those who think its requirements are unnecessarily burdensome and restrictive, forcing the public and private sectors to devote resources to problems that are either imaginary or overstated.

The United States and the world are now at a crucial moment in the development of environmental law and public health protection policy. In 2015 the Worldwatch Institute warned of the increasing threat that, as "human activities disrupt ecological systems worldwide, . . . infectious disease will spread from animals to humans." Worldwatch Institute, *State of the World 2015*, at 16 (2015). This phenomenon is known as zoonosis, and the diseases it spawns can be deadly. Emerging zoonotic diseases then included Ebola and the coronavirus that produced severe acute respiratory syndrome (SARS). The Worldwatch report noted that "despite rising attention to high-profile pandemics like Ebola, neither governments nor publics appreciate that such outbreaks are emblematic of a systemic, global problem." This warning proved prescient. The COVID-19 pandemic, believed to have originated in animal to human transmission in China, swept the world in 2020 and 2021. In little more than a year it infected more than 160 million people in virtually every country in the world, causing more than three million deaths. The United States, which has less than 4.3 percent of the world's population, accounted for one-fifth of global COVID-19 infections and one-sixth of all deaths. Johns Hopkins Coronavirus Resource Center, *https://coronavirus.jhu.edu/map.html*. These deaths and the enormous economic toll of lockdowns to combat the virus were disproportionately concentrated among the poor, minorities, the elderly, and those exposed to higher levels of pollution.

The global pandemic occurred even as the devastating effects of the climate crisis have become shockingly apparent. During the summer of 2020 several parts of the world experienced all-time record temperatures above 50 degrees Celsius (122 degrees Fahrenheit). In 2020 Death Valley, California established a global temperature record of 130 degrees Fahrenheit. Devastating wildfires, unprecedented in number and scope, swept through the western United States in 2020 after devastating Australia during its summer six months before. Unusually extreme weather phenomena, including fire tornadoes, appeared, and the melting of the Greenland and Antarctica ice caps accelerated, hastening sea level rise. As of 2020, the ten warmest years on record have all occurred since 1998, and 9 of the 10 have occurred since 2005. The Centers for Disease Control and Prevention (CDC) notes that due to climate change some "existing health threats will intensify and new health threats will emerge." CDC, Climate Effects on Health, *https://www.cdc .gov/climateandhealth/effects/default.htm* (2020). By disrupting physical, biological, and ecological systems, climate change can produce "increased respiratory and cardiovascular disease, injuries and premature deaths related to extreme weather events," as well as "changes in the prevalence and geographical distribution of food- and water-borne illnesses and other infectious diseases." Id.

The climate crisis poses daunting challenges because it is inextricably linked to the carbon fuel cycle on which the economies of the world depend. Even as we continue to grapple with long-standing problems of ground-level air pollution, toxic waste generation, and water pollution, other problems have emerged. These include plastic pollution and ubiquitous contamination from toxic per- and polyfluoroalkyl substances (PFAS) that have eluded regulation for decades. Thus, environmental law faces two simultaneous problems. One involves reforming the tools at hand, to make them stronger and more effective. The other involves building structures, institutions, and rules sufficient for the more transformative demands of the climate crisis. This casebook explores the current regulatory instruments of environmental law and the criticisms that have been leveled against those instruments from different perspectives. It also examines the possibility that these instruments, while essential, have to be supplemented in significant ways if we are to meet the environmental demands of the twenty-first century.

This chapter begins by exploring some of the fundamental traditions of thought and attitude that form contemporary views regarding the environment. There is broad agreement that some forms of collective action are necessary to address some environmental problems. At the same time, the diversity of diagnoses about how environmental law needs to change intimates that there are also areas of fundamental disagreement about the concrete form such collective action should take.

## A.  ENVIRONMENTAL PROBLEMS AND PROGRESS

The domain of environmental law and policy extends to any place where the earth is modified by human action. Some of today's environmental problems have been around for centuries. Lead poisoning from wine goblets affected the Roman Empire. The Ancestral Pueblo peoples of the American Southwest intensively used and eventually depleted the natural resources of the mesas upon which they built their cliff dwellings.

Others are new. Synthetic organic compounds and nuclear power did not exist prior to World War II. Still others are old problems with new consequences caused by great increases in scale. In the past 50 years we have added more people and more pollutants to the planet than in the preceding 10,000 years. As just one illustration, the amount of carbon emissions from fossil fuel burning—a major contributor to the climate crisis—grew from practically nothing at the start of the Industrial Revolution to 500 million tons at the start of the twentieth century to 1.6 billion in 1950 and to nearly 10 billion in 2011. Ecologist Eugene F. Stoermer and Nobel prize–winning atmospheric chemist Paul Crutzen argue that human impact on Earth's ecosystems has been so extensive that we have entered a new geologic epoch that should be called the anthropocene. This epoch would signify a time when humans became the dominant influence on the planet's natural systems.

Some scientists believe the anthropocene should date from the Industrial Revolution of the late eighteenth century; others maintain that it should start much earlier, with the rise of human agriculture.

John Holdren and Paul Ehrlich are credited with first suggesting that the impact (I) that human behavior has on the environment results from the combined effect of population size (P), the level of affluence (A), and the type of technologies (T) that enhance our abilities to consume resources. Paul Ehrlich & John Holdren, Impact of Population Growth, 171 Science 1212-1217 (1971). This I = PAT formula ignores interdependencies and other complicating factors, but it does identify three significant elements that give rise to environmental issues.

Global population has increased from 3.85 billion in 1972 to 7.71 billion at the end of 2020, U.S. Census Bureau, U.S. and World Population Clocks, *http://www.census.gov/popclock*, and the United Nations Population Division estimates it is growing at the rate of 75 million people per year. Increases in population change land use patterns, consume more nonrenewable natural resources such as fossil fuels, intensify land uses such as agriculture, and produce more pollution. The group of individuals adversely affected by health-related environmental factors also increases as total population increases. For example, despite the fact that the percentage of the world's population served with water supplies that have been treated or improved grew from 79 percent in 1972 to 90 percent in 2015, hundreds of millions of people still lack access to safe drinking water and adequate sanitation. As a consequence, nearly 300,000 children under the age of five die every year from water, sanitation, and hygiene-related causes. Air pollution from particulate matter and ozone causes millions of premature deaths annually.

The impacts of technological change on the environment have been substantial. The automobile, which barely existed at the turn of the twentieth century, now contributes about one-third of global greenhouse gases and is a major source of some of the most harmful air pollutants. Technological improvements such as sonar and vast drift nets give fishing fleets the ability to wipe out ocean fisheries—a real concern in light of the fact that two-thirds of the world's marine fisheries are currently considered overexploited by the Food and Agriculture Organization of the United Nations (FAO). The development of plastics has facilitated growth in the throwaway economy, increasing per capita waste generation significantly.

The role of affluence can be illustrated through the idea of an Ecological Footprint. Developed by the World Wildlife Fund (WWF) and others, the Ecological Footprint provides a measure of the human pressures being placed on global ecosystems. It estimates how much productive land is required to produce food and wood, to build and maintain human infrastructure, and to absorb the carbon dioxide people generate from energy production, expressing that estimate in terms of a "global hectare," or a hectare of land with biological productivity equal to the global average. The per capita footprint for the United States was 7.19 in 2011 compared to 2.13 for China. Both figures then exceeded the global "break-even" standard of 1.78. WWF, 2012 Living Planet Report at 142, 144. By 2017 the U.S. footprint had increased to 8.0 and China's to 3.7. Global Footprint Network, data.footprintnetwork.org. Figure 1.1 maps the ecological footprints of each country.

### Figure 1.1 Global Map of Ecological Footprint of Consumption

**Consumption around the world**

Both human demand and natural resources are unevenly distributed across the Earth. The pattern of human consumption of these resources differs from resource availability, since resources are not consumed at the point of extraction. The Ecological Footprint per person, across countries, provides insights into countries' resource performance, risks and opportunities[17, 18, 19].

Varying levels of Ecological Footprint are due to different lifestyles and consumption patterns, including the quantity of food, goods and services residents consume, the natural resources they use, and the carbon dioxide emitted to provide these goods and services.

*Figure 14: Global map of the Ecological Footprint of consumption per person in 2016*
*The Ecological Footprint per person is a function of both total population and rates of consumption within a country. A country's consumption includes the Ecological Footprint it produces, plus imports from other countries, minus exports[20].*

**Key**
- > 5 gha/person
- 3.5 - 5 gha/person
- 2 - 3.5 gha/person
- 1.6 - 2 gha/person
- < 1.6 gha/person
- Insufficient data

WWF LIVING PLANET REPORT 2020   58

59

Source: World Wildlife Fund for Nature, Living Planet Report 2020 at 59 (2020).

Society and government have not been silent in the face of increasing human pressures on the global ecosystem. Since the early 1970s, national, international, state, and local governments have been responding to the increased human pressure on the environment in a wide variety of ways. At the international level, agreements and programs aimed at reducing adverse environmental impacts of human activity have proliferated. Beginning in 1972, a series of once-a-decade environment summits have provided a focal point for these efforts. These summits began with the United Nations Conference on the Human Environment in Stockholm in 1972 and now extend through to the United Nations Conference on Sustainable Development held in Rio de Janeiro in June 2012, also known as Rio+20 because it occurred 20 years after the Rio Earth Summit in 1992.

National and local environmental efforts have been equally impressive. Again, the early 1970s were a catalytic period, with the first Earth Day, April 22, 1970, symbolically marking the beginning of the modern environmental era. In the United States, a structure of national legislation sprang into place in a remarkably short period of time, and the Environmental Protection Agency (EPA) was established to administer many of the new laws and regulations. For an overview of these developments, see Mary Graham, The Morning After Earth Day (1999) and Richard J. Lazarus, The Making of Environmental Law (2004). Today, we have a complex array of rules and regulations aimed at mitigating adverse environmental effects, the implementation of which now annually costs the private sector hundreds of billions of dollars per year.

The world's policy responses have had positive effects. For example, air quality in the United States has generally improved, notwithstanding increases in population and Gross National Product. EPA reports that emissions of carbon monoxide,

60 percent of which come from automobiles, fell by 85 percent from 1980 to 2019, even though vehicle miles traveled increased by 94 percent during the same time period. EPA, Air Trends (*https://www.epa.gov/air-trends/carbon-monoxide-trends*). Controls on the use of lead additives have been even more successful: Emissions of lead fell 98 percent between 1981 and 2019. Internationally, global average life expectancy has been extended by more than ten years since 1972, with some of this improvement clearly due to reduction in environmental health risks.

The Ecological Footprint proves a helpful summary statistic for our current environmental situation. The good news is that the global per capita footprint is now growing at a slower rate than population growth — 1.6 percent per year since 1985 versus 1.8 percent per year before then. We have begun, it would seem, to take steps to reduce the pressures that population growth puts on the global ecosystem. More disturbing, however, is news that the World Wildlife Fund and others believe that our present levels of use exceed the maximum footprint that the earth can sustain indefinitely. According to the WWF, we have been overshooting the capacity of the world to sustain existing population levels since 1980. "Through changes in technology and land management practices, biocapacity has increased about 28% in the past 60 years." But it has not kept pace with human consumption: "humanity's Ecological Footprint has increased about 173% over the same time period and now exceeds the planet's biocapacity by 56%." WWF, 2020 Living Planet Report, at 56. Continued ecological deficits of this kind will lead to a gradual depletion of the earth's capital stock and are inconsistent with the objective of sustainable development that is now embraced in one form or another by almost all environmental organizations.

The concept of "sustainable development" is widely embraced, but poorly defined. Worldwatch observed in 2015 that "we now find ourselves in a world of sustaina*babble*—marked by wildly proliferating claims of sustainability." State of the World 2015, at 4. In 2015 the United Nations adopted 17 Sustainable Development Goals (SDGs) as part of its 2030 Agenda for Sustainable Development. In 2019, the United Nations Environment Programme (UNEP) published its sixth edition of the Global Environmental Outlook (GEO6). The report assessed progress that had been made in addressing 93 environment-related indicators of the UN's Sustainable Development Goals. It found that good progress had been made over the last 15 years in responding to 22 of them. "For example, there has been an increase in terrestrial, mountain and marine protected areas; there has been an increase in the effort to combat invasive species; there has been significant progress towards renewable energy; there has been an increase in sustainability reporting and mainstreaming in policy; and there has been an increase in development assistance for climate change and the environment." But the report found negative trends with respect to indicators for forests, fisheries, endangered species, and materials consumption and a lack of data precluding an assessment of progress toward other SDG indicators.

In December 2020 UNEP reported that the nations of the world are not on track to meet even their weak initial nationally determined contributions (NDCs) to reducing greenhouse gas emissions (GHGs) pursuant to the Paris Agreement. UNEP Emissions Gap Report 2020, at xxi (2020). Thus, if current policies continue, global temperatures are likely to rise by at least 3 degrees Celsius by the end of the century, which will have catastrophic consequences for the planet's environ-ment. "Emissions from the richest 1 percent of the global population account for more than twice the combined share of the poorest 50 percent." Id. at xxv. The global COVID-19 pandemic has reduced the growth of global GHG emissions in the short-term, but it will not contribute significantly to emissions reductions by 2030 unless economic recovery policies emphasize strong decarbonization. "The state of the planet is broken," declares UN Secretary General Antonio Guterres. While the development of vaccines eventually may curb the COVID-19 pandemic, there is no vaccine for the damage global warming is causing.

But there are hopeful signs. A total of 126 countries, accounting for 51 per-cent of global GHG emissions, have announced net-zero GHG emissions goals by around mid-century. Japan has pledged to be net-zero by 2050, China by 2060, and President Biden is pursuing his campaign promise to make the United States net-zero by 2050. But to be credible these promises must be fleshed out by strong near-term policies and actions. Global oil prices have plummeted, placing the fos-sil fuel industry in an unprecedented decline, while renewable energy's prospects are brightening. In August 2019 the CEOs of 181 of America's largest corpora-tions declared that corporations should serve not just their shareholders, but also their customers, employees, suppliers, and communities, including protecting "the environment by embracing sustainable practices across our businesses." Business Roundtable, Statement on the Purpose of a Corporation (2019), *https://opportunity .businessroundtable.org/ourcommitment/*. Whether this is "sustaina*babble*" or a true breakthrough remains to be seen.

Environmental problems share one or more of a set of characteristics that makes them important and difficult problems. Many involve potentially cata-strophic and often irreversible adverse effects that can be spread across large areas, populations, and time periods in ways that make collective action to solve them essential. At the same time, there is great uncertainty about the mechanisms and effects of actions affecting the environment, so that debate over whether or not activities are actually causing substantial harm is often intense. There is also great resistance to actions aimed at solving them, sometimes because the economic costs are concentrated among a powerful few, sometimes because the costs involve life-style changes among the many.

There are reasons to think that further environmental progress will be increas-ingly difficult. For one thing, we have taken a number of steps that lay along the path of least resistance, going after obvious environmental problems where reme-dial steps were relatively manageable. Rivers literally on fire because of the oil and chemical film on their surface, lakes suffocating from massive algae blooms, dense clouds of smog over cities, and odors from open solid waste dumps cried out for attention. Improving environmental quality by picking off such "low-hanging" fruit was clearly the correct first step, but by and large the actions taken to redress such obvious problems have proven insufficient to bring the quality of our environment to where we wish it to be. Progress from here on confronts tougher problems.

In the United States, environmental policy has become an intensely partisan political issue unlike it was in the 1970s, when the major environmental laws passed Congress with wide bipartisan support. Although Congress in 2016 passed consen-sus legislation (the Frank Lautenberg Chemical Safety for the 21st Century Act) to comprehensively overhaul regulation of toxic substances, such legislative compromises are extraordinarily rare. After the Trump administration took office in 2017 it aggressively pursued more than 125 regulatory changes to weaken environmental protection measures. Many of these actions were stymied in the courts, and the Biden administration is swiftly reversing many policies that caused substantial damage to the environment.

The increasingly partisan nature of environmental debate marks the current political landscape despite the fact that public opinion surveys throughout the modern environmental era have registered strong support for environmental protection. President Richard Nixon once described the environment as "a cause beyond party" and "a common cause of all the people of this country." Although a Pew Research Center report in February 2020 found rising support among the public for more aggressive government action to protect the environment and to respond to the climate crisis, only 21 percent of Republicans named it as a top priority compared to 78 percent of Democrats. Pew Research Center, As Economic Concerns Recede, Environmental Protection Rises on the Public's Policy Agency, *https://www.pewresearch.org/politics/2020/02/13/ as-economic-concerns-recede-environmental-protection-rises-on-the-publics-policy-agenda/.*

Partisanship over the environment does not typically express itself as disagreement about whether or not environmental quality is an important goal. Instead, the battles over further environmental initiatives focus on whether they are effective, as well as whether or not they come at too high a cost to other values, including private property rights, economic growth, and individual freedom. The costs and benefits of environmentally damaging behavior frequently fall on quite distinct groups of people; the beneficiaries of a cement factory's production and profits are typically distinct from the downwind communities affected by the plant's air pollution, for example. Similarly, the costs and benefits of environmental improvements typically create different groups of winners and losers. This makes for difficult political decision making, especially as proposals for further improvement become more and more expensive.

## B.   *ENVIRONMENTAL ETHICS AND VALUES*

Humans interact with the world in two ways relevant to environmental policy. Their physical actions alter the world in measurable ways, and they also organize, categorize, and evaluate that world through the conceptual schemes and value perspectives they inhabit. This understanding of the role of values in interpreting the world suggests that terms like "adverse environmental impacts" and "environmental problems" are concepts constructed by and of human beings. Different value perspectives may construct a term differently, and hence different worldly phenomena may be included within it.

Indeed, American environmentalism comprises a mix of value systems, beliefs, and perspectives, and draws on a complex of historical, philosophical, and religious traditions. This diversity will not always be apparent. In the policy context, differences in perspective may often be masked from view by a shared consensus that a certain state of affairs deserves attention. After proposals to dam the Grand Canyon surfaced in the 1960s, for example, opposition to the idea was waged on economic grounds, on conservationist grounds, on cultural-historical grounds, on Deep Ecological grounds, as well as others. Because consensus existed at the programmatic level of opposition to the dam, dissecting differences in the underlying rationale for that opposition was superfluous to the process of building a political coalition to fight the project; indeed, such dissection might actually inhibit such coalition-building.

Such consensus will not always exist, however. The economic perspective on environmental value, the conservationist perspective, and the Deep Ecological perspective strenuously disagree about the nature of the environmental problem posed by logging old-growth forest in the Pacific Northwest, for instance. Consensus among environmentalists often falls apart over the question of remedy: Should the country's response to toxic air pollutants consist of efforts to reduce emissions to their optimal level—the point at which further reduction costs more than the human health and welfare gains from such reduction—or should it consist of strategies aimed at achieving zero emissions, and if the latter, how quickly? Should animal experimentation be permitted when the information gained will serve human needs, only when it will serve vital human needs, or not at all? Remedial questions often expose underlying value disagreements because they press advocates to articulate their vision of a properly functioning economy or society. Many of the issues joined in this text can be better understood by seeing how different perspectives within environmentalism urge different solutions to problems.

Environmental values can be distinguished in many ways. One fundamental division separates perspectives depending on whether their main object of moral or ethical concern is humankind, living things (with a further division between approaches that place high value on all living things versus some smaller set of living things, such as all mammals or all animals capable of experiencing pain), or entire ecosystems. These are referred to as human-centered (or anthropocentric), bio-centered, and eco-centered, respectively. Economics supplies the human-centered perspective most influential in contemporary policy debates. The scientific discipline of ecology provides the intellectual framework for some of the most influential bio-centered and eco-centered approaches. We will return to each of these in more detail after canvassing the large landscape of values influencing environmental thinking today.

A great deal of writing about environmental philosophy views all human-centered approaches to ethics or morals as seriously insufficient. Some rule out classifying a human-centered ethic as an environmental ethic at all, preferring to reserve the latter name for any "ethic which holds that natural entities and/or states of affairs are intrinsically valuable, and thus deserve to be the object of our moral concern," irrespective of whether they are useful or valuable to us in meeting our needs. Thompson, A Refutation of Environmental Ethics, 12 Envtl. Ethics 147, 148 (1990). Defined this way, only bio-centered or eco-centered ethics qualify.

Consider, for example, Aldo Leopold's land ethic. Building on an understanding of humanity as but one part of a dynamic ecosystem, Leopold wrote that "a thing is right when it tends to preserve the integrity, stability, and beauty of the biotic community. It is wrong when it tends otherwise." A. Leopold, A Sand County Almanac 201, 224-225 (1968). Much of Leopold's work was devoted to expressing the value of aspects of the environment that had no obvious economic value. "To sum up," he wrote, "a system of conservation based solely on economic self-interest is hopelessly lopsided. It tends to ignore, and thus eventually to eliminate, many elements in the land community that lack commercial value, but that are (as far as we know) essential to its healthy functioning. It assumes, falsely, I think, that the economic parts of the biotic clock will function without the uneconomic parts." Id. at 213. Leopold plainly thought that polluting discharges may "tend otherwise" at levels well below those that are optimum from the economic perspective. For Leopoldians, the environmental problem of pollution can arise in situations in which the economic perspective would see no problem.

In particular, Leopold and other ecologists tend to believe that the scale of man's actions constitutes its most destructive quality. "The combined evidence of history and ecology seems to support one general deduction: the less violent the man-made changes, the greater the probability of successful readjustment in the [ecosystem]. Violence, in turn, varies with human population density; a dense population requires a more violent conversion. In this respect, North America has a better chance for permanence than Europe, if she can contrive to limit her density." Id. at 220. From the economic perspective, in contrast, large-scale disruptions of natural order are not necessarily to be avoided; it all depends on what costs and benefits to human beings are associated with those disruptions.

The science of ecology has had a growing influence on both human-centered and bio-centered systems of environmental values. The National Environmental Policy Act (NEPA)'s call for "systematic, interdisciplinary" analysis of "the profound impact of man's activity on the interrelationships of all components of the natural environment" is very much a call with ecological origins. Ecology's central orientation is to view "living organisms and this nonliving (abiotic) environment [as] inseparably interrelated and interact[ing] upon each other." E. Odum, Fundamentals of Ecology 10 (2d ed. 1959). Ecological study provides a warning that if humans want to retain the relatively hospitable surroundings the earth has so far provided, we must become much more cognizant of the ecological ramifications of our actions. Leopold's land ethic evolved from his reflections as an applied ecologist studying the diversity and resilience of local ecosystems.

Perhaps most significant, seen as a way of understanding the human-environment relationship, ecology serves as a unifying thread for a number of different biocentric and ecocentric points of view. Its stress on relationships among mutually dependent components lends itself to an emphasis on harmony and cooperation that a variety of perspectives have found congenial. Leopold's land ethic is the starting point for many contemporary efforts to develop a picture of ethical behavior that is not centered on humans. For an investigation of the land ethic's meaning and its influence, see Companion to A Sand County Almanac (J.B. Callicott ed., 1987).

Religious values also play significant roles in environmental perspectives. The relationship between Western religions and the environment has been particularly controversial. In 1967, Lynn White wrote an influential essay in which he argued that much of the blame for our current situation rests with the biblical account of the Creation, in which God set humankind apart from the rest of creation, gave men and women dominion over creation, and instructed them to subdue it. White, The Historical Roots of Our Ecological Crisis, 155 Science 1203 (Mar. 10, 1967). White's analysis was supported soon thereafter in John Passmore's Man's Responsibility for Nature (1974). For a detailed review of the emergence of the religious environmental movement, see Stephen Ellingson, To Care for Creation (2016).

Among the world's religions, the Judeo-Christian tradition has often seemed to fare the worst in terms of its alleged association with beliefs inhospitable to environmental protection. The dominion tradition, however, has been responded to by others who retrieve the biblical tradition of stewardship as a counterweight to the views of White and Passmore. In January 1990, for example, Pope John Paul II issued a message entitled "Peace with All Creation." In it he explained that alongside the arms race, regional conflicts, and domestic injustice, world peace is threatened "by a lack of due respect for nature, by the plundering of natural resources and by a progressive decline in the quality of life." Throughout the message, the Pope employed the vocabulary of ecology.

On June 18, 2015, Pope Francis issued an encyclical entitled *Laudato Si* (Praise Be to You) On Care for Our Common Home. The encyclical was published in eight languages. A copy in English is available online at *http://www.vatican .va/content/dam/francesco/pdf/encyclicals/documents/papa-francesco_20150524 _enciclica-laudato-si_en.pdf*. The encyclical reviews the history of the Catholic Church's concern for the environment, noting Pope John XXIII's concern over the testing of nuclear weapons in 1963, Pope Paul IV's condemnation of environmental degradation in 1971, and statements of environmental concern by their successors. Declaring that God has entrusted the world to humans, Pope Francis states that nature is misused when it is viewed as property we use for ourselves alone. He notes that many religious traditions properly view activity that harms the environment as a sin. The Pope urgently appeals "for a new dialogue about how we are shaping the future of our planet."

Pope Francis argues that the most significant victims of environmental degradation are the poor, and he maintains that humans have a moral responsibility to protect the environment for future generations. He emphasizes that the climate crisis is an enormously serious problem, and he urges the nations of the world to reach a new global agreement to control emissions of greenhouse gases. In preparation for issuance of the encyclical, which is considered one of the most authoritative statements of Roman Catholic doctrine, the Vatican convened a summit meeting on the environment in April 2015 where then UN Secretary-General Ban Ki-moon delivered the keynote address. Consider the value perspectives reflected in the Pope's encyclical, reproduced in part below.

Pope Francis

*Laudato Si* — On Care for Our Common Home

(*2015*)

## WHAT IS HAPPENING TO OUR COMMON HOME

### I. Pollution and Climate Change

#### Climate as a Common Good

25. Climate change is a global problem with grave implications: environmental, social, economic, political and for the distribution of goods. It represents one of the principal challenges facing humanity in our day. Its worst impact will probably be felt by developing countries in coming decades. Many of the poor live in areas

particularly affected by phenomena related to warming, and their means of subsistence are largely dependent on natural reserves and ecosystemic services such as agriculture, fishing and forestry. They have no other financial activities or resources which can enable them to adapt to climate change or to face natural disasters, and their access to social services and protection is very limited. For example, changes in climate, to which animals and plants cannot adapt, lead them to migrate; this in turn affects the livelihood of the poor, who are then forced to leave their homes, with great uncertainty for their future and that of their children. There has been a tragic rise in the number of migrants seeking to flee from the growing poverty caused by environmental degradation. They are not recognized by international conventions as refugees; they bear the loss of the lives they have left behind, without enjoying any legal protection whatsoever. Sadly, there is widespread indifference to such suffering, which is even now taking place throughout our world. Our lack of response to these tragedies involving our brothers and sisters points to the loss of that sense of responsibility for our fellow men and women upon which all civil society is founded. . . .

### V.  Global Inequality

51. Inequity affects not only individuals but entire countries; it compels us to consider an ethics of international relations. A true "ecological debt" exists, particularly between the global north and south, connected to commercial imbalances with effects on the environment, and the disproportionate use of natural resources by certain countries over long periods of time. The export of raw materials to satisfy markets in the industrialized north has caused harm locally, as for example in mercury pollution in gold mining or sulphur dioxide pollution in copper mining. There is a pressing need to calculate the use of environmental space throughout the world for depositing gas residues which have been accumulating for two centuries and have created a situation which currently affects all the countries of the world. The warming caused by huge consumption on the part of some rich countries has repercussions on the poorest areas of the world, especially Africa, where a rise in temperature, together with drought, has proved devastating for farming. There is also the damage caused by the export of solid waste and toxic liquids to developing countries, and by the pollution produced by companies which operate in less developed countries in ways they could never do at home, in the countries in which they raise their capital: "We note that often the businesses which operate this way are multinationals. They do here what they would never do in developed countries or the so-called first world. Generally, after ceasing their activity and withdrawing, they leave behind great human and environmental liabilities such as unemployment, abandoned towns, the depletion of natural reserves, deforestation, the impoverishment of agriculture and local stock breeding, open pits, riven hills, polluted rivers and a handful of social works which are no longer sustainable." [Bishops of the Patagonia-Comahue Region (Argentina), Christmas Message (Dec. 2009), 2.]

## INTEGRAL ECOLOGY

159. The notion of the common good also extends to future generations. The global economic crises have made painfully obvious the detrimental effects of disregarding our common destiny, which cannot exclude those who come after us.

We can no longer speak of sustainable development apart from intergenerational solidarity. Once we start to think about the kind of world we are leaving to future generations, we look at things differently; we realize that the world is a gift which we have freely received and must share with others. Since the world has been given to us, we can no longer view reality in a purely utilitarian way, in which efficiency and productivity are entirely geared to our individual benefit. Intergenerational solidarity is not optional, but rather a basic question of justice, since the world we have received also belongs to those who will follow us.

## NOTES AND QUESTIONS

1. The gist of *Laudato Si* is that mankind has a strong moral obligation to protect the environment that has not been honored despite repeated global environmental summits. As a result we face an "ecological crisis" that particularly harms the poorest and most vulnerable. We must pursue intergenerational equity and hear "both the cry of the earth and the cry of the poor." The encyclical emphasizes "how everything is interconnected" and that various factors such as loss of freedom, violence, and corruption can undermine the effectiveness of legal institutions ("Laws may be well framed yet remain a dead letter. Can we hope, then, that in such cases, legislation and regulations dealing with the environment will really prove effective?"). The encyclical presents a solid discussion of the causes and consequences of climate change, and it stresses the importance of shifting away from highly polluting fossil fuel energy sources to renewable energy, something that has caused great distress to the fossil fuel industry and the climate deniers it promotes. It stresses that access to safe drinking water should be considered a fundamental human right, and it strongly emphasizes the importance of protecting wetlands and preserving biodiversity. Importantly, the encyclical declares that the biblical reference in the book of Genesis to man having "dominion" over the earth has been incorrectly interpreted to permit unbridled development ("the Bible has no place for a tyrannical anthropocentrism unconcerned for other creatures"). Rather, it argues that "our 'dominion' over the universe should be understood more properly in the sense of responsible stewardship" and that the right to private property is "not inviolable," but rather subject to a "social mortgage."

2. In other portions of *Laudato Si*, Pope Francis stresses the importance of developing effective national environmental laws and regulations ("Society, through non-governmental organizations and intermediate groups, must put pressure on governments to develop more rigorous regulations, procedures and controls. Unless citizens control political power — national, regional and municipal — it will not be possible to control damage to the environment."). He also notes the importance of continuity ("policies related to climate change and environmental protection cannot be altered with every change of government. Results take time and demand immediate outlays which may not produce tangible effects within any one government's term. That is why, in the absence of pressure from the public and from civic institutions, political authorities will always be reluctant to intervene, all the more when urgent needs must be met. To take up these responsibilities and the costs they entail, politicians will inevitably clash with the mindset of short-term gain and results which dominates present-day economics and politics.").

Pope Francis argues that laws, even when enforceable, will not alone bring about the necessary changes without ecological education that motivates individuals to change their behavior.

3. Pope Francis's encyclical was part of a diplomatic initiative by the Vatican to persuade other countries to reach a global agreement on measures to reduce greenhouse gas emissions. In December 2015, 195 nations signed the Paris Agreement establishing a new regime to govern global action to respond to the climate crisis.

4. What obligations for environmental protection do current humans owe to future generations? Does the concept of "sustainable development" imply that we must at least leave the natural environment in as good a shape as it is today?

5. The Pope's encyclical makes a powerful case that global warming and climate change will have the greatest impact on poor communities in developing countries that have played little or no role in creating the problems. Should developed countries compensate developing countries for the costs of responding to the climate crisis?

### Preservationist Perspectives

Another distinctive value system whose influence you will see in American policy and law is that of the preservationist. Preservationists may emphasize historical continuity, within our culture, our traditions, and our relationships with the natural environment. They may, however, also demand the preservation of certain places because they provide the context and catalyst for contemporary revelation and self-understanding. "Why should we not also enjoy an original relation with the universe?" asks Emerson.

> Why should not we have a poetry and philosophy of insight and not of tradition, and a religion by revelation to us, and not the history of theirs? Embosomed for a season in nature, whose floods of life stream around and through us, and invite us, by the powers they supply, to action proportioned to nature, why should we grope among the dry bones of the past. . .? The sun shines today also. There is more wool and flax in the fields. There are new lands, new men, new thoughts. Let us demand our own works and law and worship.

Where are these insights found? By communing with nature itself, for "[u]ndoubtedly, we have no questions to ask which are unanswerable."

> We must trust the perfection of creation so far as to believe that whatever curiosity the order of things has awakened in our minds, the order to things can satisfy. . . . [N]ature is already, in its forms and tendencies, describing its own design. Let us interrogate the great apparition that shines so peacefully around us. Let us inquire, to what end is nature?. . .
> In the woods, we return to reason and faith. There I feel that nothing can befall me in life—no disgrace, no calamity (leaving me my eyes), which nature cannot repair. Standing on the bare ground—my head bathed by the blithe air and uplifted into infinite space—all mean egotism vanishes. I become a transparent eyeball; I am nothing; I see all; the current of the Universal Being circulates through me; I am part or parcel of God. [R.W.

Emerson, Nature (1836), reprinted in New World Metaphysics 171, 171-174 (G. Gunn ed., 1981).]

The writings of Emerson, Thoreau, and other Transcendentalists firmly graft into American literary history the connection between spiritual renewal and nature, so that one recurring argument for wilderness preservation urges doing so "because our lives and our conception of ourselves will be enhanced—in a spiritual sense—if we learn to appreciate [nature] for what it is and we learn how to live in harmony with it." J. Thompson, Preservation of Wilderness and the Good Life, in Environmental Philosophy (R. Elliot & A. Gare eds., 1983).

These thoughts may misleadingly suggest that preservationists are necessarily human-centered thinkers, valuing nature for what it provides for the human spirit. For many in this tradition, nature is to be valued first for itself; it then turns out that human contemplation of nature proves a source of inspiration as well. This biocentric idea is well expressed by the naturalist John Muir, founder of the Sierra Club:

> The world, as we are told, was made especially for man—a presumption not supported by the facts. . . . Now it never seems to occur to [many people]. . .that Nature's object in making animals and plants might possibly be first of all the happiness of each of them, not the creation of all for the happiness of one. Why should man value himself as more than a small part of the one great unit of creation?

Some argue that the kind of intrinsic value Muir attributes to nonhumankind supports the conclusion that those nonhumans possess rights that environmental policy ought to respect. David Brower, when he was chairman of the Sierra Club, expressed his agreement with Muir by announcing, "I believe in the rights of creatures other than man." However, animal rights advocates disagree over the precise source of those rights. Peter Singer and others argue for an animal welfare ethic, basing their views on the capacity of animals to experience pleasure and pain, and on that basis extending a human-centered ethic, Benthamite utilitarianism, to cover nonhuman species. See P. Singer, Animal Liberation (2d ed. 1990). Tom Regan, on the other hand, rejects the utilitarian approach and instead finds support for animal rights in the idea that living beings who have the capacity to experience life in certain qualitative ways (including having beliefs and desires, perceptions, memory, and a sense of the future) possess inherent value that gives them a right to respect, independent of the pleasures or pains they may experience. See T. Regan, The Case for Animal Rights (1983).

However wide the internal disagreements among these and other bio-centered or eco-centered ethics, they remain distinguishable from economics and other human-centered views in that they seek to articulate "not an ethic for the *use* of the environment, a 'management ethic,' but an ethic *of the* environment." J.B. Callicott, The Case Against Moral Pluralism, 12 Envtl. Ethics 99, 99 (1990). Professor Callicott, a University Distinguished Research Professor at the University of North Texas, predicted in 2013 that as climate change becomes more apparent, people in the future will wonder, "What were they thinking back at the turn of the century driving those CO2-belching hunks of metal around, often just for the hell of it?"

# Environmental Philosophy: A Pathfinder

For those wishing to explore more of the historical development and diversity of American environmental thought, see S.P. Hays, Conservation and the Gospel of Efficiency: The Progressive Conservation Movement, 1890-1920 (1959); S. Udall, The Quiet Crisis (1963); R. Nash, Wilderness and the American Mind (1967); J. Petulla, American Environmental History (2d ed. 1988); R. Nash, The Rights of Nature (1989); P. Shabecoff, A Fierce Green Fire: The American Environmental Movement (1993); and E. Freyfogle, A Good That Transcends (2017).

A classic statement of the economic perspective on environmental issues is J.H. Dales, Pollution, Property, and Prices (1968). This perspective is also outlined in simplified form in W. Baxter, People or Penguins: The Case for Optimal Pollution (1974); R. Posner, The Economics of Law (1987); and A.M. Polinsky, An Introduction to Law and Economics (1983). Mark Sagoff has done some of the most interesting work critiquing the economic perspective on environmental issues. Much of his work is summarized in M. Sagoff, The Economy of the Earth (1988). J. Baird Callicott is the leading expositor of Leopold's land ethic. See his In Defense of the Land Ethic (1989) as well as his edited collection of essays, Companion to a Sand County Almanac: Interpretive and Critical Essays (1987).

Useful collections of essays in environmental philosophy include: D. Scherer ed., Upstream/Downstream: Issues in Environmental Ethics (1990); F. Ferre & P. Hartel eds., Ethics and Environmental Policy (1994); R. Attfield & A. Belsey eds., Philosophy and the Natural Environment (1994); M. Zimmerman et al., Environmental Philosophy (1998); M. Smith, Thinking Through the Environment (1989); S.M. Gardner & Allen Thomson, The Oxford Handbook of Environmental Ethics (2017). Bill McKibben's books stress the significance of the loss of nature on the human spirit as well as on nature itself. B. McKibben, The End of Nature (1990) and Enough (2004).

Many scholars have put forward their own approach to environmental philosophy. For good reviews and extensive bibliographies, see R. Attfield, The Ethics of Environmental Concern (2d ed. 1991); A. Dobson, Green Political Thought, chs. 1 & 2 (1998); N. Carter, The Politics of the Environment, ch. 2 (2001); Holmes Rolston III, A New Environmental Ethics (2d ed. 2020).

Much of the important literature in this field is contained in Environmental Ethics, a journal published quarterly by the Center for Environmental Philosophy at the University of North Texas. The journal's website can be found at *https://www.pdcnet.org/enviroethics*.

## C.   ENVIRONMENTAL JUSTICE

For four decades the environmental justice movement has challenged environmental policy to shift to a paradigm that would emphasize preventing vulnerable populations from being exposed to environmental risks, rather than simply managing, regulating, and distributing such risks. Connecting environmental issues to a larger agenda of social justice, this movement focuses on the connections between discrimination, poverty, and the distribution of environmental risks. It argues that "low-income communities and communities of color bear a disproportionate burden of the nation's pollution problem" because the "environmental laws, regulations, and policies have not been applied fairly across all segments of the population." R. Bullard, Unequal Protection: Environmental Justice and Communities of Color xv (1994). In a relatively short period of time, environmental justice concerns emerged as major ethical considerations in modern environmentalism. An outpouring of global concern over racial justice following the senseless murder of George Floyd by police in Minneapolis in May 2020 has given renewed impetus to the environmental justice movement.

### 1. History of the Environmental Justice Movement

The historical roots of the environmental justice movement usually are traced to protests that arose in 1982 over the siting of a landfill for disposal of polychlorinated biphenyls (PCBs) in the poor community of Afton, North Carolina, a town with an 84 percent Black population in Warren County, North Carolina. Decrying "environmental racism," protesters laid down in a road to block delivery of 6,000 truckloads of PCB-contaminated soil. Although the protests failed to stop the disposal, they brought national attention to the disproportionate siting of hazardous waste disposal facilities in poor and minority communities. In 1983 the General Accounting Office (GAO) released a study finding that three out of every four major hazardous waste disposal facilities in the southeastern United States were located in poor communities with majority African American populations. GAO, Siting of Hazardous Waste Landfills and Their Correlation with Racial and Economic Status of Surrounding Communities, *https://www.gao.gov/assets/150/140159 .pdf.* In 1987 the United Church of Christ Commission on Racial Justice released a report entitled *Toxic Wastes and Race* confirming the disproportionate concentration of hazardous waste disposal facilities in minority communities.

In March 1990 a group of more than 100 grassroots activists sent a letter to the leaders of the top ten national environmental groups arguing that "[r]acism is the root cause of your inaction around addressing environmental problems in our communities." Noting that very few people of color were on the staff of the environmental groups, the letter demanded that they cease fundraising and operations in communities of color until leaders from those communities "make up between 35-40 percent of your entire staff." Southwest Organizing Project, Letter to leaders of national environmental organizations, March 16, 1990.

In October 1991 the First National People of Color Environmental Leadership Summit was held in Washington, DC. Participants in this summit endorsed a set of 17 Principles of Environmental Justice that are reproduced below. In September 1992 the National Law Journal published an extensive study of EPA enforcement cases finding that penalties for violations of nearly every major federal environmental statute were much greater in white neighborhoods than in minority communities. Marianne Lavelle & Marcia Coyle, Unequal Protection—The Racial Divide in Environmental Law, Nat'l L. J. Sept. 21, 1992, at S1.

Studies of the causes of environmental justice problems showed that they involve far more than simply decisions concerning the siting of locally undesirable land uses (LULUs). A study analyzing census data from St. Louis metropolitan areas from 1970 to 1990 found that "[i]ndustrial facilities that were originally sited in white areas often became surrounded by minority residents who are attracted to these neighborhoods by falling housing prices." T. Lambert & C. Boerner, Environmental Inequity: Economic Causes, Economic Solutions, 14 Yale J. on Reg. 196, 197, 206-207 (1997). Others have found that a better predictor of LULU location than either race or class is the degree to which a local community is politically organized. Jay Hamilton, Politics and Social Costs: Estimating the Impact of Collective Action on Hazardous Waste Facilities, 24 RAND J. Econ. 101, 104-105 (1993).

In September 1993, EPA created a National Environmental Justice Advisory Council (NEJAC) to provide independent advice to the agency on environmental justice issues. In February 1994, President Bill Clinton issued Executive Order 12,898, requiring every federal agency to make "environmental justice part of its mission by identifying and addressing, as appropriate, disproportionately high and adverse human health or environmental effects of its programs, policies, and activities on minority populations and low-income populations." Each agency was required to develop an "agency-wide environmental justice strategy" to achieve these ends.

EPA has been widely criticized for its failure to implement Executive Order 12,898 as vigorously as it might. The Government Accountability Office concluded that EPA failed to take environmental justice considerations adequately into account when developing rules under the Clean Air Act. For instance, in developing a rule to reduce the sulfur content of gasoline, EPA analysis determined that pollution near oil refineries would be increased as a result of the rule, because the process of removing the sulfur generates some air emissions, while the amount of pollution being emitted by automobiles would be decreased. This raises potential environmental justice issues, because minority and low-income communities are disproportionately located near such facilities. Yet in responding to comments that raised this environmental justice concern, "specifically, EPA did not publish its estimate that potentially harmful emissions would increase in 26 of the 86 counties with refineries affected by the rule." GAO, EPA Should Devote More Attention to Environmental Justice When Developing Clean Air Rules, p. 4 (July 2005).

Executive Order 12,898 prompted all federal agencies to undertake a review of their internal decision-making procedures to incorporate consideration of environmental justice issues into those procedures, pursuant to guidance published by EPA's Environmental Justice Office in 1995. The Nuclear Regulatory Commission (NRC) was among the agencies who revised its procedures accordingly. (As an independent agency, the NRC is not directly covered by Executive Order 12,898, but it voluntarily promulgated an environmental justice strategy for internal decisions.)

A license application by Louisiana Energy Services (LES) to build a uranium enrichment plant in Homer, Louisiana, an almost entirely African-American town located in economically depressed northern Louisiana, provided a major test of the NRC's strategy. The draft environmental impact statement (EIS) for the application, issued prior to the executive order, did not include an analysis of environmental equity, but the final one, issued after the order, did. It described the neighborhoods surrounding the proposed facility, the site selection process, possible discrimination, and possible disproportionate impacts. The EIS concluded that there was no evidence of discrimination and no significant disproportionate impacts.

In May 1997, the NRC's Atomic Safety and Licensing Board (ASLB) rejected LES's permit application on environmental justice grounds. The Board found that NRC staff had failed to comply with the executive order by conducting only a cursory review of the site selection process. On appeal, the full NRC Board agreed that NRC staff had failed to delve sufficiently into disparate impacts that might be caused by the new facility, but it rejected the ASLB's additional instructions to the staff to inquire into whether racial discrimination influenced the process, ruling that the National Environmental Policy Act was not a tool for addressing racial discrimination. LES subsequently abandoned its plans and terminated the licensing process.

The George W. Bush administration deemphasized environmental justice issues at the national level, but it did not repeal Executive Order 12,898. Many state and local governments adopted laws emulating the executive order by requiring decision makers to take environmental justice concerns into account when making permitting decisions. For example, Virginia law contains a Commonwealth Energy Policy designed to "[e]nsure that development of new, or expansion of existing, energy resources or facilities does not have a disproportionate adverse impact on economically disadvantaged or minority communities." Va. Code Ann. §67-102(A)(11). One of the "[e]nergy objectives" of the Commonwealth Energy Policy is to "[d]evelop[ ] energy resources and facilities in a manner that does not impose a disproportionate adverse impact on economically disadvantaged or minority communities." Id. §67-101(12). As discussed below, these provisions played a significant role in Friends of Buckingham v. State Air Pollution Control Board, 947 F.3d 68 (4th Cir. 2020), which rejected issuance of a permit for a pipeline compressor station in a Virginia community that is 84 percent non-white.

In 2004 the state of North Carolina completed detoxification of the PCB landfill in Warren County that had become an early symbol of the lack of class- and race-related justice in environmental policy. "State and federal sources spent $18 million to detoxify or neutralize contaminated soil stored at the Warren County PCB landfill. A private contractor hired by the state dug up and burned 81,500 tons of oil-laced soil in a kiln that reached more than 800 degrees Fahrenheit to remove the PCBs (polychlorinated biphenyls). The soil was put back in a football-size pit, re-covered to form a mound, graded, and seeded with grass." Robert Bullard, Environmental Racism PCB Landfill Finally Remedied But No Reparations for Residents, *https://blackcommentator.com/74/74_reprint_environmental_racism_pf.html*.

Subsequent studies repeatedly have confirmed the disproportionate exposure to environmental risks of low-income and minority communities. On the twentieth anniversary of its initial environmental justice report, the United Church of Christ performed a new study finding that 56 percent of the population living within 3 kilometers of a hazardous waste site are people of color, whereas minority communities make up only 30 percent of the population outside of these areas. Toxic Wastes and Race at Twenty 1987-2007, A Report Prepared for the United Church of Christ Justice & Witness Ministries.

EPA's 2008 Report on the Environment reported an infant mortality rate—considered to be a particularly useful measure of health status because it indicates both current health status of the population and predicts the health of the next generation—to be 14.0 in 2003 for Black infants and 6.8 for white infants. A number of other indicators reflect significant disparities, including rates of cancer, cardiovascular disease, asthma, birth defects, and levels of mercury and lead in the blood, all of which have some linkage to environmental contaminants. See EPA, Report on the Environment (2008).

National attention to environmental justice issues was renewed during the Obama administration, but it was marred by the Flint, Michigan lead poisoning scandal. For more than a year, from 2014 to 2015, impoverished residents of Flint, Michigan were drinking lead-laden tap water that poisoned their children. The Flint tragedy originated with the appointment by Michigan governor Rick Snyder of Darnell Earley as emergency manager for Flint. To save money, Earley decided in April 2014 to shift the source of the city's water supply to the polluted Flint River. Because Flint River water is highly corrosive, lead from pipes in Flint's water supply system leached into the drinking water, poisoning Flint residents. Shockingly, after test data revealed the lead contamination, state and federal officials failed to inform Flint residents. Officials initially denounced private groups who tried to publicize test results. Yet when General Motors complained that the water was corroding parts at a plant in Flint, government officials quietly reconnected the plant to its former water supply.

The Flint tragedy dramatically highlighted an environmental justice problem—environmental risks continue to be disproportionately concentrated in poor and minority communities. Flint is a majority African-American community with more than 40 percent of the population living below the poverty line. Government officials in Flint responded promptly to GM's complaints about the water, but its poor residents were not warned of the hazard.

Studies continue to confirm that other low-income and minority communities are disproportionately exposed to environmental risks. Using EPA data on air pollution, a study published in 2018 found significant disparities in exposure to the deadliest particulate air pollution—particulate matter of 2.5 micrometers in diameter (PM2.5). The study found that "those in poverty had 1.35 times higher burden [of exposure] than did the overall population, and non-Whites had 1.28 times higher burden. Blacks, specifically, had 1.54 times higher burden than did the overall population." Ihab Mikati, Disparities in Distribution of Particulate Matter Emission Sources by Race and Poverty Status, 108 Am. J. Public Health 480 (2018). These "disparities held not only nationally but within most states and counties as well." Exposure to PM2.5 is associated with respiratory and heart diseases, increasing the risk of premature death. Studies also are finding a relationship between exposure to such pollution and higher death rates from COVID-19.

Although President Trump did not repeal President Clinton's environmental justice executive order, he proposed to dismantle the agency's Office of Environmental Justice. In March 2017, Mustafa Ali, leader of this office, resigned in protest of the Trump administration's proposal, which Congress did not adopt. In November 2017 the NAACP and the Clean Air Task Force released a report finding that Blacks are 75 percent more likely than other Americans to live in "fence-line communities" located in close proximity to oil and gas facilities. NAACP & Clean Air Task Force, Fumes Across the Fence Line (2018), *https://www.catf.us/wp-content/uploads/2017/11/CATF_Pub_FumesAcrossTheFenceLine.pdf.*

One of those fence-line communities is the Grays Ferry neighborhood of South Philadelphia, located near a massive 150-year-old oil refinery owned since 2012 by Philadelphia Energy Solutions (P.E.S.). Residents of the community experienced an unusual incidence of life-threatening health conditions, including gall-bladder and other cancers. EPA data revealed that the refinery was responsible for "the bulk of toxic air emissions" in Philadelphia. The refinery was "out of compliance with the Clean Air Act nine of the past 12 quarters through 2019 with little recourse." Between 2014 and 2019, it was fined almost $650,000 for violating air, water, and waste-disposal rules. Linda Villarosa, Pollution Is Killing Black Americans. This Community Fought Back, N.Y. Times Magazine, July 28, 2020. On June 21, 2019, a series of explosions caused by corroded pipes set off massive fires at the P.E.S. refinery, releasing 5,000 pounds of deadly hydrofluoric acid. P.E.S. went bankrupt and was sold to a developer who plans to demolish the refinery despite efforts by Trump administration officials to have the refinery reopened.

On January 27, 2021, President Biden signed Executive Order 14,008, 86 Fed. Reg. 7619, which directs federal agencies to take an "all of government" approach to environmental justice. The order directs federal agencies to develop programs, policies, and activities to address the disproportionate health, environmental, economic, and climate impacts on disadvantaged communities. It establishes a White House Environmental Justice Interagency Council and a White House Environmental Justice Advisory Council to address current and historical environmental injustices. The order establishes a goal of delivering 40 percent of the overall benefits of relevant federal investments to disadvantaged communities. It also initiates the development of a Climate and Environmental Justice Screening Tool, building off EPA's EJSCREEN, to identify disadvantaged communities and inform equitable decision making across the federal government.

## 2.  *Principles of Environmental Justice*

Initially EPA used the term "environmental equity" to refer to the notion that environmental risks should be equitably distributed across income and population groups. It later changed to "environmental justice," the term used in President Clinton's Executive Order 12,898. EPA's current definition of environmental justice is as follows: "Environmental justice is the fair treatment and meaningful involvement of all people regardless of race, color, national origin, or income, with respect to the development, implementation, and enforcement of environmental laws, regulations, and policies." EPA defines "fair treatment" to mean that "no group of people should bear a disproportionate share of the negative environmental consequences resulting from industrial, governmental and commercial operations or policies."

The concept of "meaningful involvement" was not contained in EPA's initial definition of environmental justice. After it was added, EPA explained that "meaningful involvement" means "[p]eople have an opportunity to participate in decisions about activities that may affect their environment and/or health," that "[c]ommunity concerns will be considered in the decision-making process" and that "[t]he public's contribution can influence the regulatory agency's decision." EPA, Learn About Environmental Justice, *https://www.epa.gov/environmentaljustice/ learn-about-environmental-justice.*

Participants in the First National People of Color Environmental Leadership Summit in 1991 endorsed a declaration of 17 principles of environmental justice, which are reproduced below.

## First National People of Color Environmental Leadership Summit

## Principles of Environmental Justice

(1991)

**WE, THE PEOPLE OF COLOR**, gathered together at this multinational People of Color Environmental Leadership Summit, to begin to build a national and international movement of all peoples of color to fight the destruction and taking of our lands and communities, do hereby re-establish our spiritual interdependence to the sacredness of our Mother Earth; to respect and celebrate each of our cultures, languages and beliefs about the natural world and our roles in healing ourselves; to ensure environmental justice; to promote economic alternatives which would contribute to the development of environmentally safe livelihoods; and, to secure our political, economic and cultural liberation that has been denied for over 500 years of colonization and oppression, resulting in the poisoning of our communities and land and the genocide of our peoples, do affirm and adopt these Principles of Environmental Justice:

1. **Environmental Justice** affirms the sacredness of Mother Earth, ecological unity and the interdependence of all species, and the right to be free from ecological destruction.

2. **Environmental Justice** demands that public policy be based on mutual respect and justice for all peoples, free from any form of discrimination or bias.

3. **Environmental Justice** mandates the right to ethical, balanced and responsible uses of land and renewable resources in the interest of a sustainable planet for humans and other living things.

4. **Environmental Justice** calls for universal protection from nuclear testing, extraction, production and disposal of toxic/hazardous wastes and poisons and nuclear testing that threaten the fundamental right to clean air, land, water, and food.

5. **Environmental Justice** affirms the fundamental right to political, economic, cultural and environmental self-determination of all peoples.

6. **Environmental Justice** demands the cessation of the production of all toxins, hazardous wastes, and radioactive materials, and that all past and current producers be held strictly accountable to the people for detoxification and the containment at the point of production.

7. **Environmental Justice** demands the right to participate as equal partners at every level of decision-making, including needs assessment, planning, implementation, enforcement and evaluation.

8. **Environmental Justice** affirms the right of all workers to a safe and healthy work environment without being forced to choose between an unsafe livelihood and unemployment. It also affirms the right of those who work at home to be free from environmental hazards.

9. **Environmental Justice** protects the right of victims of environmental injustice to receive full compensation and reparations for damages as well as quality health care.

10. **Environmental Justice** considers governmental acts of environmental injustice a violation of international law, the Universal Declaration on Human Rights, and the United Nations Convention on Genocide.

11. **Environmental Justice** must recognize a special legal and natural relationship of Native Peoples to the U.S. government through treaties, agreements, compacts, and covenants affirming sovereignty and self-determination.

12. **Environmental Justice** affirms the need for urban and rural ecological policies to clean up and rebuild our cities and rural areas in balance with nature, honoring the cultural integrity of all our communities, and provided fair access for all to the full range of resources.

13. **Environmental Justice** calls for the strict enforcement of principles of informed consent, and a halt to the testing of experimental reproductive and medical procedures and vaccinations on people of color.

14. **Environmental Justice** opposes the destructive operations of multi-national corporations.

15. **Environmental Justice** opposes military occupation, repression and exploitation of lands, peoples and cultures, and other life forms.

16. **Environmental Justice** calls for the education of present and future generations which emphasizes social and environmental issues, based on our experience and an appreciation of our diverse cultural perspectives.

17. **Environmental Justice** requires that we, as individuals, make personal and consumer choices to consume as little of Mother Earth's resources and to produce as little waste as possible; and make the conscious decision to challenge and reprioritize our lifestyles to ensure the health of the natural world for present and future generations.

## NOTES AND QUESTIONS

1. As reflected in the Principles, environmental justice concerns extend far beyond concerns about inequality in the distribution of environmental risks. They emphasize the importance of including communities in decision-making processes for "a wide range of decisions affecting the environment, including standard setting, program design, enforcement, the cleanup of contaminated properties, and exclusionary regulatory processes." Center for Progressive Reform, Perspective on Environmental Justice (2005). The EJ 2020 Action Plan, released by EPA during the Obama administration, reflects this broad scope in outlining how environmental justice concerns should be integrated into EPA rulemaking, permitting, compliance and enforcement, and science during the 2016-2020 period. *https://www.epa.gov/environmentaljustice/ ej-2020-action-agenda-epas-environmental-justice-strategy.*

2. Professor Robert Kuehn notes that Dr. Robert Bullard has distilled the 17 principles of environmental justice into five basic characteristics: "(1) protect all persons from environmental degradation; (2) adopt a public health prevention of harm approach; (3) place the burden of proof on those who seek to pollute; (4) obviate the requirement to prove intent to discriminate; and (5) redress existing inequities by targeting action and resources." Kuehn notes that in Bullard's view, environmental justice seeks to make environmental protection more democratic and asks the fundamental ethical and political questions of "who gets what, why and how much." Robert Kuehn, A Taxonomy of Environmental Justice, 30 Envt'l L. Rep. 10681, 10683 (2000).

3. Professor Kuehn has identified four classic dimensions of environmental justice: (1) distributive justice, (2) procedural justice, (3) corrective justice, and (4) social justice. Id. Distributive justice, which has received the most attention in environmental justice debates, means "addressing the disproportionate public health and environmental risks borne by people of color and lower incomes." Id. at 10644. Procedural justice refers to "the perceived fairness of the process leading to an outcome." Id. at 10688. "Corrective justice involves not only the just administration of punishment to those who break the law, but also a duty to repair the losses for which one is responsible." Id. at 10693. Social justice involves "integrating environmental concerns into a broader agenda that emphasizes social, racial, and economic justice." It means expanding the concept of environmental justice to address larger societal problems such as "housing discrimination, residential segregation, and education and employment policies that compel minority populations to live, work, and play in more polluted areas." Id. at 10700. Can you identify which of the 17 principles address each of these four dimensions of this taxonomy?

4. Principle 4 refers to nuclear testing, which left a legacy of some of the worst environmental justice problems, including displacement of communities and devastation of the environment where testing occurred. This legacy is documented by the Nuclear Free Future Foundation in Uranium Atlas: Facts and Data about the Raw Material of the Atomic Age (2020). During the nuclear arms race in the 1950s testing of nuclear weapons in the atmosphere occurred on almost a weekly or monthly basis. Responding to the warnings of scientists concerning the buildup of radioactive materials in the food chain around the world, the United States and the Soviet Union signed a Test Ban Treaty in 1963. France continued atmospheric testing until 1974, and China until 1980. Underground testing was banned in 1996 in the Comprehensive Nuclear-Test-Ban Treaty, though North Korea has continued to conduct underground tests.

5. Although national environmental organizations have improved the diversity of their staff and leadership, whites still dominate, constituting 85 percent of their staff and 80 percent of their board members.

### 3.  Legal Responses to Environmental Justice Problems

Efforts to invoke the equal protection clause of the Fourteenth Amendment of the Constitution to challenge discriminatory official action have been stymied by the difficulty of proving intentional discrimination, as required by Washington v.

Davis, 426 U.S. 229 (1976). Thus, most efforts to redress disproportionate environmental impacts have focused on convincing officials to exercise permitting discretion to combat such disproportionate effects.

A non-environmental statute, section 601 of Title VI of the Civil Rights Act of 1964, prohibits discrimination on the basis of race, color, or national origin under any program or activity receiving federal funding. Section 602 authorizes agencies to issue implementing regulations tailored to agencies' individual programs. Administrative complaints under these Title VI regulations have become a main avenue for environmental justice advocates to challenge agency decisions they claim impose disproportionate burdens on disadvantaged communities. Under these regulations, complainants do not have to prove a discriminatory intent, which would be their burden if they sued in court claiming a violation of section 601. The Supreme Court has ruled that section 602 authorizes regulations designed to avoid disparate impact alone. Guardians Ass'n v. Civil Serv. Comm'n, 463 U.S. 582 (1983). EPA has issued such disparate impact regulations, and on February 5, 1998, it issued further Interim Guidance describing how it would investigate environmental justice complaints in order to "accommodate the increasing number of Title VI complaints that allege discrimination in the environmental permitting context."

Title VI complaints based on environmental justice concerns are handled by EPA's Office of Civil Rights (OCR), which has been receiving complaints regarding siting of facilities, such as hazardous waste facilities, under programs administered by EPA. Under the cooperative federalism design of many of our environmental laws, qualifying states actually administer the day-to-day decisions concerning many of our federal statutes, and the Title VI complaint process extends to state decisions under those statutes.

Private parties can seek declaratory or injunctive relief under section 601 of Title VI. Cannon v. University of Chicago, 441 U.S. 677 (1979). Success in such actions requires proof of discriminatory intent. In situations where such intent is absent or difficult to prove, environmental justice advocates have sought to establish a similar private right of action to enforce agency implementing regulations issued under section 602, which would only require proof of disparate impact. In a non-environmental case, the Supreme Court foreclosed that option by denying an implied right of action to enforce agency regulations issued to implement Title VI. Alexander v. Sandoval, 532 U.S. 275 (2001).

In September 2016, the U.S. Commission on Civil Rights released a report critical of EPA's environmental justice efforts. The report found that EPA had largely failed to protect communities of color from the effects of pollution. It noted that "EPA has never made a formal finding of discrimination and has never denied or withdrawn financial assistance from a recipient in its entire history, and has no mandate to demand accountability within the EPA." The report concluded that when EPA is faced with environmental justice concerns it does not act until it is forced to do so. U.S. Commission on Civil Rights, Environmental Justice: Examining the Environmental Protection Agency's Compliance and Enforcement of Title VI and Executive Order 12,898 (Sept. 2016).

On January 19, 2017, the last full day of the Obama administration, EPA's External Civil Rights Compliance Office made its first ever finding of discrimination. The Office concluded that evidence showed that "African Americans were treated less favorably than non-African Americans" during permit hearings for the Genesee Power Station—which burns wood waste and other debris—from 1992 through 1994. A "preponderance of the evidence in EPA's record would lead a reasonable person to conclude that race discrimination was more likely than not the reason . . .". The quarter-century delay in making this finding was widely viewed as reflecting the abysmal state of civil rights enforcement at EPA.

Despite the lack of success of Title VI complaints, environmental justice (EJ) claims do occasionally become the object of litigation when agencies incorporate EJ considerations into their normal administrative procedures, as instructed by the executive order. For example, environmental justice analysis has been held subject to judicial review under NEPA and the Administrative Procedure Act (APA) when an agency has included such analysis in its environmental impact statement. E.g., Communities Against Runway Expansion, Inc. v. FAA, 355 F.3d 678 (D.C. Cir. 2004); Sierra Club v. Federal Energy Regulatory Commission, 867 F.3d 1357 (D.C. Cir. 2017).

State laws addressing environmental justice concerns may provide more promising alternatives as illustrated by Friends of Buckingham v. State Air Pollution Control Board, 947 F.3d 68 (4th Cir. 2020). In that case, the Virginia State Air Pollution Control Board granted a permit to construct a compressor station for the Atlantic Coast Pipeline in Union Hill, Virginia, a predominantly African American community. Plaintiffs argued that the board failed to comply with state law requiring consideration of the potential for disproportionate health impacts on a minority community. The Fourth Circuit agreed, holding that the board (1) failed to make findings regarding Union Hill's demographics, (2) failed to consider the potential air pollution impacts even if there was no violation of applicable air emissions standards, and (3) relied on an incomplete factual record in assessing suitability of the site. The court vacated the issuance of the permit and remanded the matter back to the board. The decision is particularly significant because it holds that environmental justice concerns cannot be dismissed simply by finding that air quality regulations will not be violated in the aggregate. The Fourth Circuit explained that "environmental justice is not merely a box to be checked, and the Board's failure to consider the disproportionate impact on those closest to the Compressor Station resulted in a flawed analysis."

In September 2020 New Jersey Governor Phil Murphy signed what is considered to be the strongest state environmental justice legislation in the nation. The legislation requires New Jersey's Department of Environmental Protection (DEP) to maintain a list of "burdened communities," defined as census tracts in the lowest third of median income or with a 40 percent or more non-English-speaking population. The bill requires permit applicants to conduct environmental justice impact assessments that will be presented at public hearings. It authorizes DEP to deny permits for facilities that would expose burdened communities to unreasonable risks and it requires DEP to consider community sentiment.

Along with problems that raise the other environmental values reviewed in this introduction, environmental justice issues will come up and be reviewed in more detail in subsequent chapters of this text that deal with siting controversies, the exposure of sensitive populations to toxic substances, regulatory priority-setting, enforcement, and environmental impact statements. The pathfinder below provides a guide to the literature on environmental justice.

## Environmental Justice: A Pathfinder

Important resources on environmental justice include C. Villa et al., Environmental Justice: Law, Policy and Regulation (3d ed. 2020) and Cliff Villa's website of environmental justice resources at: *https://environmentaljusticebook.org*. Other books include Barry E. Hill, Environmental Justice: Legal Theory and Practice (4th ed. 2018); and Michael B. Gerrard & Sheila R. Foster eds., The Law of Environmental Justice: Theories and Procedures to Address Disproportionate Risks (2d ed. 2009). Dr. Robert Bullard is one of the pioneers in studying the disparate impact of environmental risks. His books *Dumping in Dixie: Race, Class and Environmental Quality* (1990), and *Unequal Protection, Environmental Justice and Communities of Color* (1994) are classics in the field. Among his many other books are *The Quest for Environmental Justice: Human Rights and the Politics of Pollution* (2005).

Environmental justice issues have been the subject of many law review articles, including: Clifford J. Villa, Remaking Environmental Justice, 66 Loyola L. Rev. 469 (2020); Helen H. Kang, Respect for Community Narratives of Environmental Injustice, 25 Widener L. Rev. (2019); Foster, Justice from the Ground Up: Distributive Inequalities, Grassroots Resistance, and the Transformative Politics of the Environmental Justice Movement, 86 Cal. L. Rev. 775 (1998); Been, Locally Undesirable Land Uses in Minority Neighborhoods: Disproportionate Siting or Market Dynamics?, 103 Yale L.J. 1383 (1994); Lazarus, Pursuing "Environmental Justice": The Distributional Effects of Environmental Protection, 87 Nw. U. L. Rev. 101 (1993); Foster, Race(ial) Matters: The Quest for Environmental Justice, 20 Ecology L.Q. 721 (1993).

A discussion of the state of environmental justice at the end of the Obama administration by top environmental practitioners, The State of Environmental Justice: An Obama Administration Retrospective, can be found at 47 Envtl. L. Rep. 10385 (2017). The Trump administration's change of course is reviewed in Uma Outka & Elizabeth Kronk Warner, Reversing Course on Environmental Justice Under the Trump Administration, 54 Wake Forest L. Rev. 393 (2019).

President Clinton's Executive Order 12,898, Federal Actions to Address Environmental Justice in Minority Populations and Low-Income Communities, appears at 59 Fed. Reg. 7,629 (1994). Regulations issued by EPA to implement Title VI of the Civil Rights Act of 1964, 42 U.S.C. §2000d, can be found at 40 C.F.R. §§7.10-7.35. EPA's External Civil Rights Compliance Office webpage contains copies of key documents regarding implementation of the agency's Title VI compliance program, *https://www.epa.gov/ogc/external-civil-rights-compliance-office-title-vi*. Information on EPA's environmental justice program, including reports by the National Environmental Justice Advisory Committee, is at *http://www.epa.gov/compliance/environmentaljustice*. EPA's Plan EJ 2020, concerning how to integrate environmental justice into the agency's activities, is described at *https://www.epa.gov/environmentaljustice/about-ej-2020*. During the Obama administration, EPA maintained a blog on "Environmental Justice in Action" at *http://blog.epa.gov/ej/*. A memorandum of understanding signed by the heads of 17 federal agencies on August 4, 2011, now requires every agency to finalize and publicize its environmental justice strategy annually and to provide the public with annual implementation reports.

## D.  ECONOMICS AND THE ENVIRONMENT

Each of the value systems we have briefly canvassed has associated with it a distinctive discourse and set of concepts within which its problems are formulated and debated. In recent years, economics has become increasingly the lingua franca in government policy discussions about the environment. The late William Baxter, writing in the language of economics, argued that "to assert that there is a pollution problem or an environmental problem is to assert, at least implicitly, that one or more resources is not being used so as to maximize human satisfactions. Environmental problems are economic problems, and better insight can be gained by the application of economic analysis." W. Baxter, People or Penguins: The Case for Optimal Pollution 17 (1974).

Users of other value systems relevant to environmental policy disagree with this statement. They object to the value premises implicit in the economic approach, they reformulate environmental problems in their own discourses, and they engage in technical criticisms of economic methods to show that those methods are incomplete, misleading, or inaccurate. Because economic concepts and terminology are so prevalent in this field, it is vital that everyone approaching environmental law be conversant with those concepts and terminology—if only so that criticism of them can be informed and astute.

The readings in this section serve to introduce the economic approach to environmental problems.

### 1.   The Role of Prices and Markets

Eban S. Goodstein

Economics and the Environment
_____

33-39 (1995)

From an economist's point of view, market systems generate pollution because many natural inputs into the production of goods and services such as air and water are "underpriced." Because no one owns these resources, in the absence of government regulation or legal protection for pollution victims, businesses will use them up freely, neglecting the external costs imposed on others. For example, suppose the Stinky Paper Co. discharges polluted water into a stream, which kills the fish that downstream people enjoy eating. If Stinky were forced to compensate these people for the damages it imposed (**internalize the externality**), the firm would in effect be paying for the water it used up. Water would no longer be "underpriced." As a result, Stinky would conserve its use of water and would seek out ways to clean up its discharge. This, in turn, would raise the production costs of the firm. . . .

Because the river water is commonly owned and thus a "free" good, Stinky overexploits it and the fisherfolk downstream are exposed to a negative externality of the paper production process. From an economic point of view, many pollution problems arise because by their nature environmental resources such as water and air are commonly owned. . . .

Because all resources in an economy cannot be privately owned, market systems will generate too much pollution by either of the standards considered in this book — efficiency or safety. There are two related reasons for this. The first is the **free-access problem** which can arise when property is commonly held. The free-access problem can be stated simply: If people weigh private benefits against private (as opposed to social) costs, they will overexploit common resources when given free access. This idea was popularized in the late 1960s by a social ecologist named Garrett Hardin, who called it "The Tragedy of the Commons." [See page 47.] . . .

The free-access problem may explain why there is a tendency for commonly held resources such as clean air and water or fisheries to be overexploited. But why does the government have to decide what to do about it? Instead, why don't the victims of negative externalities simply band together on their own to prevent pollution? As we noted earlier, this was the response to environmental degradation of common grazing and fishing grounds in traditional societies. Informal social pressure and tradition were relied on to prevent overexploitation. The modern American equivalent would be to sue an offending company or individual for damages. Indeed, a few so-called **free-market environmentalists** have advocated eliminating many environmental regulations, then relying on lawsuits by injured parties to "internalize" externalities.

Such private remedies to environmental degradation run into what economists call the **public goods problem**. Public goods are goods which are enjoyed in common. The provision of public goods is a problem for the free market due to the existence of two factors: free-riding and transactions costs. To illustrate, consider a good that is enjoyed in common such as, for example, the noise level after 11 o'clock at night in Axl's neighborhood. Now suppose that neighbor Tipper cranks her sound system. Axl could go to the considerable trouble of obtaining signatures from all of his neighbors, getting money from them to hire a lawyer, file a lawsuit, and possibly obtain a legal injunction requiring her to turn the music down. The costs of undertaking this action are known as **transaction costs**, and they are particularly high because of the public nature of the injury.

If Axl does undertake the effort, he will benefit not only himself but also the entire neighborhood. Some of the neighbors might refuse to help out and instead **free-ride** on Axl's provision of the public good. Instead, Axl decides it's not really worth organizing a lawsuit and tosses and turns in bed, hoping that someone else will make the effort. The result is that although there may be considerable total demand for a quiet evening in the neighborhood, it doesn't get expressed. It is not worth it to any one individual to overcome the transaction costs and the possibility of free-riding required to provide the public good of the lawsuit though, if he did, the social benefits might far outweigh the cost.

In most towns, the response to noise pollution is a government regulation called a nuisance law. With such a regulation in place, Axl can just call the police, greatly reducing the costs associated with stopping the noise. The general principle is that without government intervention, public goods—in this case, a quiet evening—will be undersupplied. . . .

To summarize. . . , in contrast to private goods, public goods are goods which are consumed in common. The true demand for public goods will not be satisfied in pure market economies due to high transaction costs and free-riding. Free-market environmentalists who advocate relying solely on the court system to internalize environmental externalities recognize these twin hurdles. But they believe these obstacles are not really that large, especially considering the costs associated with regulation. Most economists, however, argue that as a result of transaction costs and free-riding, public goods such as clean air or water, rain forests, wilderness parks, and other environmental amenities will be undersupplied in a laissez-faire market system.

## NOTES AND QUESTIONS

1. **"Polluter Pays" Principle.** Markets limit resource use to activities valued in the market more highly than its value when used in other ways. If the resource, e.g., clean air, is not sold in a market, it will be used for waste disposal (pollution) even if clean air is valued more. Having the polluter pay for the externalities or damages caused by its pollution ensures that the costs of production reflect the costs of environmental damage. If this "polluter pays" principle were carried through to all factors of production, the result would be an efficient allocation of resources. The difficulties of internalizing externalities by implementing the "polluter pays" principle are well explored in F. Anderson et al., Environmental Improvement Through Economic Incentives (1982).

2. **"Beneficiary Pays" Principle.** Some situations do not lend themselves to implementation of the "polluter pays" principle. Especially significant, international environment problems, such as global warming, do not, because international agreements operate under a rule of voluntary assent by nation-states. If treaties sought to impose net costs on a country because that country imposed more pollution costs on other countries than they imposed on it, the country "will simply decline to participate. . . . Under the rules of international law, where each country must give consent, regulatory instruments must instead follow a 'Beneficiary Pays Principle.' The beneficiaries of global environmental protection must attract non-beneficiary sources to participate, because the former cannot compel the latter to comply." Wiener, Global Environmental Regulation: Instrument Choice in Legal Context, 108 Yale L.J. 677, 752 (1999).

3. **The Coase Theorem.** In an important article, Ronald Coase argued that polluter pays and beneficiary pays would, if bargaining were costless, each lead to efficient allocation of resources. Under either approach, the pollution will be abated only if controlling it is cheaper than the damage it causes its victims. For example, if the peace of mind of the residents who live near a nuclear reactor currently shut down for repairs was worth more than the value of operating the plant, then the plant would not be restarted either because the residents could gain by paying the plant not to operate (under beneficiary pays) or because it would not be economical for the plant to compensate residents for their fears (under polluter

pays). In principle, either solution will result in solving the environmental problem, economically viewed, because it will eliminate the undesirable externality aspects of the situation. See Coase, The Problem of Social Cost, 3 J.L. & Econ. 1 (1960).

Coase's views have been particularly influential in the privatization movement, because one application of Coase's argument is to urge that sometimes pollution problems can be left to private market solutions, where polluter and pollutee can bargain for the appropriate level of polluting activity relatively free from governmental interference. See, e.g., T.L. Anderson & D.R. Leal, Free Market Environmentalism (rev. ed. 2001). One of the earliest, and still among the most valuable, essays on the advantages of markets for pollution rights is H. Dales, Pollution, Property and Prices (1968).

4. **Are the Two Really Equivalent?** Whether polluter pays or beneficiary pays can be viewed as a question of who has been assigned an initial entitlement. If the polluter can continue polluting until she is paid to stop, she has a right to pollute; if the polluter must pay the beneficiaries (who you might think of as victims, were the pollution not stopped), they have a right to be free of pollution. In addition to noting the obvious unreality of the zero-transaction-cost assumption, critics of Coase's Theorem are quick to point out that the initial allocation of such rights can have a significant impact on the distribution of income. The distribution of income in turn affects tastes and alters the ultimate outcomes produced by market economies. In addition, one's thinking about the initial allocation may be affected by ethical or moral considerations.

While extolling the importance of efficiency, economists have tried to dismiss distributional concerns by arguing that they should be dealt with by general tax and welfare policies or by assuming that winners and losers are approximately the same when more efficient policies are pursued. Noting that Coase himself emphasized that all market transactions have costs (Coase argued that the very existence of firms illustrated that nonmarket mechanisms can be cheaper in some circumstances than market ones), Judge Guido Calabresi maintains that "distributional issues cannot, even in theory, be avoided." Calabresi, The Pointlessness of Pareto: Carrying Coase Further, 100 Yale L.J. 1211, 1215 (1991). Calabresi argues that transaction costs, "no less than existing technology, define the limits of what is currently achievable in society," id. at 1212, and that "there is no difference, in theory or in practice, between the reduction or elimination of these impediments and any other innovation in knowledge or organization which might make us all better off." Id. at 1218. Thus, he maintains that the real challenge for social policy is to decide which impediments to invest in removing, which inevitably requires explicit consideration of distributional concerns.

5. **Economic Efficiency as a Policy Objective.** The economic approach to environmental problems treats the environment as a resource that is underpriced. Were it priced properly, markets would ensure it was used by whoever valued it most, as measured by persons' willingness to pay for it. Ideally, markets produce efficient outcomes—resources move to the users who value them most highly, and no voluntary exchange among potential users is left unexecuted. Many of the value systems introduced earlier in this chapter challenge whether this is the appropriate way to approach environmental issues. Some have questioned whether efficiency in the sense just described has any justification as a public policy objective.

If the efficiency criterion had a normative basis in the ethical theory of utilitarianism, it would have a demonstrable connection with happiness or a related normative conception of the good, and it would judge the value of actions and decisions according to their consequences. The efficiency criterion and the theory of welfare economics from which it is developed possess neither of these attributes, however, and they therefore have no justification in the ethical theory of utilitarianism.

Sophisticated economic analysts do not try to connect the efficiency norm with the classical [utilitarian goal] of maximizing pleasure or happiness. . . . As Richard Posner correctly points out, "The most important thing to bear in mind about the concept of value in the welfare economist's sense is that it is based on what people are willing to pay for something rather than the happiness they would derive from it."

Some policy analysts, however, believe that the satisfaction of consumer and other personal preferences has a moral foundation as a policy goal because it leads to or produces satisfaction in the sense of pleasure or happiness. This belief rests on nothing more than a pun on the word "satisfaction." Preferences are *satisfied* in the sense of "met" or "fulfilled"; this is also the sense in which conditions and equations are satisfied. "Satisfaction" of this sort has no necessary connection with "satisfaction" in the sense of pleasure or happiness.

The evidence indicates, in fact, that the satisfaction of preferences does not promote or cause satisfaction in the sense of happiness. Empirical research confirms what ordinary wisdom suggests: happiness depends more on the quality and pursuit of preferences than on the degree to which they are satisfied.

It is useful to recognize, moreover, that the contemporary "utilitarianism" represented by current welfare economic theory is not concerned with what happens to people as a result of their choices. Instead, it is concerned with the beliefs and expectations revealed in those choices. The focus is on the amount people are willing to pay for things rather than on the consequences of those decisions, except insofar as those consequences are defined tautologically in terms of willingness to pay. [M. Sagoff, The Principles of Federal Pollution Control Law, 71 Minn. L. Rev. 19, 55-57 (1986).]

Is the economic approach to environmental issues a sound one? How would you defend it or criticize it?

## 2.  *Cost-Benefit Analysis and the Social Cost of Carbon*

When markets for environmental resources do not exist, welfare economics suggests that government can sometimes legitimately intervene. In order to test whether any proposed governmental policy actually improves overall welfare, welfare economics recommends that such policy be subjected to a cost-benefit analysis (CBA), which seeks to compare the "social benefit" of the policy to its "opportunity cost—the social value foregone when the resources in question are moved away from alternative economic activities into the specific project" contemplated by the policy. E.J. Mishan, Cost-Benefit Analysis xii (1976).

To incorporate climate impacts into government policy making, in 2009 President Obama convened an Interagency Working Group (IWG) to estimate the social cost of carbon emissions, an estimate of the monetized damage of incremental increases in greenhouse gas (GHG) emissions. Members of the IWG included experts from a dozen agencies. The IWG used three peer-reviewed models translating GHG emissions into changes in atmospheric carbon concentrations, temperature changes and economic damages, including the Dynamic Integrated Climate Economy (DICE) model developed by William Nordhaus. Applying three different discount rates and five different emissions trajectories to each model, the IWG produced 45 different distributions of the social cost of carbon. It then selected a central value using a 3 percent discount rate (to account for the lower value of costs and benefits occurring later than sooner). The U.S. Department of Energy's use of the IWG's social cost of carbon estimate in issuing energy efficiency rules for commercial refrigeration equipment was upheld in Zero Zone, Inc. v. U.S. Department of Energy, 832 F.3d 654 (7th Cir. 2016).

After several updates between 2010 and 2016, the Obama administration in 2016 settled on a social cost of carbon of $52/ton for 2020, rising to $62/ton in 2030, $74/ton in 2040, and $85/ton in 2050, all in 2019 dollars. The rising estimates over time reflect the expectation that future emissions will "produce more damage as the effects of climate change become more serious." Michael A. Livermore & Richard L. Revesz, Reviving Rationality: Saving Cost-Benefit Analysis for the Sake of Our Environment and Our Health 159 (2020). Livermore and Revesz note that these should be considered to be lower bound estimates because they do not include significant categories of climate-induced damage such as "catastrophic climate events, climate-induced migration and conflict, certain human health costs, natural disturbances . . . damages to ecosystem services and biodiversity," including the catastrophic 2020 California wildfires.

Shortly after taking office in 2017, President Trump abolished the IWG and ordered that all its supporting documents be withdrawn as "no longer representative of governmental policy." Executive Order 13,783, 82 Fed. Reg. 16,093 (2017). EPA then began using a social cost of carbon estimates of $1 to $6/ton by using a 7 percent discount rate and excluding all consideration of climate impacts outside of the United States. On January 20, 2021, the day of his inauguration, President Biden issued the following executive order.

## Protecting Public Health and the Environment and Restoring Science to Tackle the Climate Crisis

Executive Order 13,990, 86 FR 7037 (2021)

**Section 1.** *Policy.* Our Nation has an abiding commitment to empower our workers and communities; promote and protect our public health and the environment; and conserve our national treasures and monuments, places that secure our national memory. Where the Federal Government has failed to meet that commitment in the past, it must advance environmental justice. In carrying out this charge, the Federal Government must be guided by the best science and be protected by processes that ensure the integrity of Federal decision-making. It is, therefore, the policy of my Administration to listen to the science; to improve public health and protect our environment; to ensure access to clean air and water; to limit exposure to dangerous chemicals and pesticides; to hold polluters accountable, including those who disproportionately harm communities of color and low-income communities; to reduce greenhouse gas emissions; to bolster resilience to the impacts of climate change; to restore and expand our national treasures and monuments; and to prioritize both environmental justice and the creation of the well-paying union jobs necessary to deliver on these goals.

To that end, this order directs all executive departments and agencies (agencies) to immediately review and, as appropriate and consistent with applicable law, take action to address the promulgation of Federal regulations and other actions during the last 4 years that conflict with these important national objectives, and to immediately commence work to confront the climate crisis. . . .

**Sec. 5.** *Accounting for the Benefits of Reducing Climate Pollution.* (a) It is essential that agencies capture the full costs of greenhouse gas emissions as accurately as possible, including by taking global damages into account. Doing so facilitates sound decision-making, recognizes the breadth of climate impacts, and supports the international leadership of the United States on climate issues. The "social cost of carbon" (SCC), "social cost of nitrous oxide" (SCN), and "social cost of methane" (SCM) are estimates of the monetized damages associated with incremental increases in greenhouse gas emissions. They are intended to include changes in net agricultural productivity, human health, property damage from increased flood risk, and the value of ecosystem services. An accurate social cost is essential for agencies to accurately determine the social benefits of reducing greenhouse gas emissions when conducting cost-benefit analyses of regulatory and other actions.

(b) There is hereby established an Interagency Working Group on the Social Cost of Greenhouse Gases (the "Working Group"). The Chair of the Council of Economic Advisers, Director of OMB, and Director of the Office of Science and Technology Policy shall serve as Co-Chairs of the Working Group.

(i) Membership. The Working Group shall also include the following other officers, or their designees: the Secretary of the Treasury; the Secretary of the Interior; the Secretary of Agriculture; the Secretary of Commerce; the Secretary of Health and Human Services; the Secretary of Transportation; the Secretary of Energy; the Chair of the Council on Environmental Quality; the Administrator of the Environmental Protection Agency; the Assistant to the President and National Climate Advisor; and the Assistant to the President for Economic Policy and Director of the National Economic Council.

(ii) Mission and Work. The Working Group shall, as appropriate and consistent with applicable law:

(A) publish an interim SCC, SCN, and SCM within 30 days of the date of this order, which agencies shall use when monetizing the value of changes in greenhouse gas emissions resulting from regulations and other relevant agency actions until final values are published;

(B) publish a final SCC, SCN, and SCM by no later than January 2022;

(C) provide recommendations to the President, by no later than September 1, 2021, regarding areas of decision-making, budgeting, and procurement by the Federal Government where the SCC, SCN, and SCM should be applied;

(D) provide recommendations, by no later than June 1, 2022, regarding a process for reviewing, and, as appropriate, updating, the SCC, SCN, and SCM to ensure that these costs are based on the best available economics and science; and

(E) provide recommendations, to be published with the final SCC, SCN, and SCM under subparagraph (A) if feasible, and in any event by no later than June 1, 2022, to revise methodologies for calculating the SCC, SCN, and SCM, to the extent that current methodologies do not adequately take account of climate risk, environmental justice, and intergenerational equity.

(iii) Methodology. In carrying out its activities, the Working Group shall consider the recommendations of the National Academies of Science, Engineering, and Medicine as reported in Valuing Climate Damages: Updating Estimation of the Social Cost of Carbon Dioxide (2017) and other pertinent scientific literature; solicit public comment; engage with the public and stakeholders; seek the advice of ethics experts; and ensure that the SCC, SCN, and SCM reflect the interests of future generations in avoiding threats posed by climate change.

## NOTES AND QUESTIONS

1. In response to President Biden's executive order, on February 26, 2021, the newly reconstituted Interagency Working Group on the Social Cost of Greenhouse Gases announced that it was returning to the social cost of carbon estimates used previously during the Obama administration. It issued interim estimates of the social cost of carbon (SCC) of $51/ton, the social cost of nitrous oxide (SCN) of $1,800/ton, and the social cost of methane (SCM) of $1,500/ton. The costs estimated for nitrous oxide and methane are much higher because they have much greater heat-trapping ability than carbon dioxide.

2. Does the fact that the Trump administration was able to slash the social cost of carbon used by agencies in cost-benefit analysis to only a small fraction of the estimate used during the Obama administration suggest that cost-benefit analysis is prone to political manipulation? In California v. Bernhardt, 472 F.Supp.3d 573 (N.D. Calif. 2020), a court struck down an attempt by the Trump administration to repeal a Bureau of Land Management (BLM) regulation to prevent methane leaks from oil drilling on public lands. The court stated that while President Trump's "Executive Order 13783 may have withdrawn the relevant technical support documents [for the IWG's estimate of the social costs of

methane] for political reasons, it did not and could not erase the scientific and economic facts that formed the foundation for that estimate—facts that BLM now ignores." The court found the use of the Trump administration's interim estimates to be arbitrary and capricious, and it excoriated BLM's "unmitigated fervor to abolish" the rule by "engineer[ing] a process to ensure a preordained conclusion."

3. The Biden administration's interim estimate of the social cost of carbon dioxide emissions is reproduced in Figure 1.2. With a 3 percent discount rate, the average estimate of the social cost of carbon is $51/ton, but with a 5 percent discount rate it is only $14/ton. Why is the SCC much lower with a higher discount rate? The Trump administration used a 7 percent discount rate in preparing its estimates of the SCC. Which discount rate is more appropriate to use? For more than a decade interest rates of government bonds have been extraordinarily low, even negative in some parts of the world. Should this dictate that a lower discount rate be used?

**Figure 1.2   Biden Administration's Estimate of the Social Cost of Carbon for 2020**

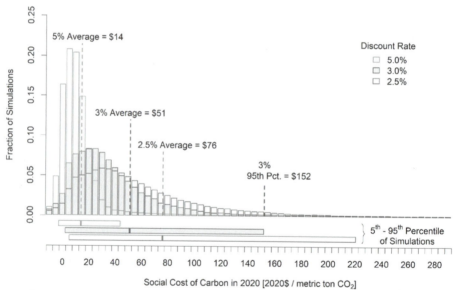

Source: Interagency Working Group on Social Cost of Greenhouse Gases, Technical Support Document: Social Cost of Carbon, Methane, and Nitrous Oxide Interim Estimates under Executive Order 13990 7 (February 2021).

## Cost-Benefit Analysis and the Value of Human Life

Cost-benefit and risk-benefit analyses have become a standard part of environmental policy discussions. They were at the heart of the controversy surrounding EPA's decisions to ban certain products that contain asbestos, discussed in Chapter 3 (see *Corrosion Proof Fittings*, 947 F.2d 1201 (5th Cir. 1991)) and EPA's crucial decision to ban lead additives from gasoline. The success of the U.S. ban in reducing the incidence of lead poisoning in children helped inspire virtually every country in the world to ban lead additives in gasoline. Robert Percival, Getting the lead out: the phase-out of gasoline lead additives—a global environmental success story, in The Impact of Environmental Law: Stories of the World We Want 8 (Eisma-Osorio & Kirk, eds. 2020). A cost-benefit analysis by economists Peter Tsai and Thomas Hatfield estimated in 2011 that this global lead phaseout had generated $2.45 trillion in net benefits per year, approximately 4 percent of global gross domestic product. Peter L. Tsai and Thomas H. Hatfield, Global Benefits from the Phase-out of Leaded Fuel, 74 J. Envt'l Health (Dec. 2011).

One of the most controversial issues raised by cost-benefit analysis concerns how to value human life. Many object to the exercise of "placing a value on human life" in a cost-benefit assessment. See W.K. Viscusi, Strategic and Ethical Issues in the Valuation of Life, in Strategy and Choice (R. Zeckhauser ed., 1991). However controversial the idea might be, the Administrative Conference of the United States has recommended that, except where costs and benefits are "highly conjectural" or unquantifiable, agencies should "disclose the dollar value per statistical life" used to reach determinations that the costs of regulations are cost-benefit justified. ACUS, Valuation of Human Life in Regulatory Decision-Making, Recommendation 88-7. Using some of the shadow price methodologies, economists initially estimated people's willingness to pay to save a human life at anywhere from $200,000 to $7 million, in 1990 dollars.

In 1991, Lawrence Summers, then the World Bank's chief economist, wrote a memorandum supporting the export of toxic wastes from industrialized countries to the developing world. He noted that "the economic logic behind dumping a load of toxic waste in the lowest wage country is impeccable" because lost earnings caused by a given amount of health damage would be lower there. Arguing that "underpopulated countries in Africa are vastly *under* polluted," the memo maintained that cancer risks should be of less concern there because life expectancy already is low. Weisskopf, World Bank Official's Irony Backfires, Wash. Post, Feb. 10, 1992, at A9. Brazil's environmental minister dubbed this reasoning "perfectly logical but totally insane." Cockburn, "Earth Summit" Is in Thrall to the Marketeers, L.A. Times, Mar. 1, 1992, at M5.

Cass Sunstein notes that 1995 the Second Assessment Report on Climate Change by the Intergovernmental Panel on Climate Change (IPCC) used a value of $1.5 million for saving a life in the developed world but only a value of $150,000 for saving a life in a developing country. Cass R. Sunstein, Valuing Life: Humanizing the Regulatory State 133 (2014). He notes that "under this approach, an American life is worth ten or twenty Indian lives, a result that philosopher John Broome deemed 'absurd.'" In the face of such criticism, the IPCC now uses a uniform value of a statistical life (VSL) of $1 million, a choice that Sunstein deems "quite arbitrary and potentially harmful to people in rich and poor nations alike."

In their book Priceless: On Knowing the Price of Everything and the Value of Nothing (2004) Frank Ackerman and Lisa Heinzerling, who are prominent critics of cost-benefit analysis, have written:

> The basic problem with narrow economic analysis of health and environmental protection is that human life, health, and nature cannot be meaningfully described in monetary terms; they are priceless. When the

question is whether to allow one person to hurt another, or to destroy a natural resource . . . when harms stretch out over decades or even generations . . . —then we are in the realm of the priceless, where market values tell us little about the social values at stake.

There are hard questions to be answered about protection of human health and the environment, and there are many useful insights about these questions from the field of economics. But there is no reason to think that the right answers will emerge from the strange process of assigning dollar values to human life, human health, and nature itself, and then crunching the numbers.

Id. at 8.

Columnist George Will has described the concept that life is priceless as "useful nonsense." He observes that "[i]t is useful to talk that way, thereby inclining our minds to place high value on life, precisely because we constantly must act in ways that cause that value to be jostled and compromised by competing values." George Will, Suddenly: The American Idea Abroad and at Home, 1986-1990, at 206 (1990).

## NOTES AND QUESTIONS

1. The moral outrage that greeted the Summers's memo and the IPCC's use of different VSL estimates for people in rich countries and people in poor countries resulted in the authors of having to disavow differential valuations of life. What consequences is it likely this will have for environmental policy? When damages are awarded to the survivors of victims of tortious actions, their compensation usually is calculated on the basis of the value of the victim's expected lifetime stream of future income. Is this approach morally offensive?

2. Sunstein argues that cost-benefit analysis "is the best way we have of accounting for the consequences of regulation." However, he suggests that it "should be humanized in four different ways." First, costs and benefits should not be viewed "as arithmetic abstractions, but as efforts to capture qualitatively diverse goods and to promote sensible trade-offs among them." Second, nonquantifiable benefits like human dignity should not be ignored. Third, because human intuition can misfire, with people holding unrealistic fears, cost-benefit analysis should be willing to reject such intuitions. "Fourth, policies and regulations need to benefit from the dispersed information of a wide variety of human beings."

3. Is cost-benefit analysis inherently biased against environmental values? It usually is easier to measure the costs of regulation (though ex-ante estimates of them are likely to be highly exaggerated if the cost estimates come from regulatory targets) than their environmental benefits. Yet cost-benefit analysis has become a staple of environmental policy analysis. As you encounter it in various settings throughout the book, consider whether it is an appropriate basis for deciding what to do—because it supplies the "right answer"—or whether the elements that make it up—rigorous efforts to estimate the costs of correcting some harmful environmental stressor and to identify the magnitude of the health or environmental benefits to be gained—are better considered "useful insights" for a decision that cannot in the final analysis be made solely on economic grounds.

### 3. *Valuing Ecosystem Services*

In recent years, ecologists have been attempting to place monetary values on the services that entire ecosystems perform for the benefit of humankind. One of their premises is that hard-to-quantify values of such services, as well as benefits that emerge from the interaction and interdependency of ecosystems, may be lost when project-specific cost-benefit analyses are being performed. See, e.g., Gretchen Daily ed., Nature's Services: Societal Dependence on Natural Ecosystems (1997). One controversial attempt to place a global value on everything that the world's ecosystems do for humans came up with a central estimate of $33 trillion per year. Costanza et al., The Value of the World's Ecosystem Services and Natural Capital, 387 Nature 253 (May 1997). Global gross national product then was estimated to be $18 trillion per year; it now is several times that.

This "value of everything" project has attracted a great deal of criticism, in part because it is meaningless to develop a global estimate of all ecosystem services when the relevant questions almost always relate to more specifically defined ecosystems and more narrowly defined capital projects that might compete with leaving ecosystems in place. A greater appreciation of the value of ecosystem services has been working its way into the smaller, but considerably more realistic, analyses as well, as the following excerpt describes.

James Salzman

## Creating Markets for Ecosystem Services

80 N.Y.U. L. Rev. 870 (2005)

Largely taken for granted, healthy ecosystems provide a variety of such critical services. Created by the interactions of living organisms with their environment, these "ecosystem services" provide both the conditions and processes that sustain human life — purifying air and water, detoxifying and decomposing waste, renewing soil fertility, regulating climate, mitigating droughts and floods, controlling pests, and pollinating plants. Although awareness of ecosystem services is certainly not new, efforts to identify and calculate these services' valuable contributions to social welfare are. Recent research by ecologists and economists has demonstrated the extremely high costs of replacing many of these services if they were to fail, on the order of many billions of dollars in the United States for pollination alone. Such estimates are inherently uncertain, of course, but the extraordinary costs required to substitute for many important services by artificial means are beyond dispute.

One cannot begin to understand flood control, for example, without realizing the impact that widespread wetland destruction has had on the ecosystem service of water retention; nor can one understand water quality without recognizing how development in forested watersheds has degraded the service of water purification. The costs from degradation of these services are high, and suffered in rich and poor countries alike. One might therefore expect that ecosystem services would be prized by markets and explicitly protected by the law. Despite their economic value and central role in provision of important public benefits, however, ecosystem services are only rarely considered in cost-benefit analyses, preparation of environmental impact assessments, or wetlands mitigation. Nor, in the past, have significant markets arisen that capitalize on the commercial value of these services. This is starting to change, however. From their origins as an obscure phrase just nine years ago, "ecosystem services" have gone mainstream, with new initiatives and markets for provision of services blossoming around the world. The United States Environmental Protection Agency (EPA), for example, has created a Science Advisory Board on Valuing the Protection of Ecological Systems and Services. In Australia, a high-level advisory body, known as the Wentworth Group, has called for a new approach to environmental protection that focuses on provision of ecosystem services. In Costa Rica, the government is administering a nationwide scheme of payments for services. The international climate change negotiations are closely focusing on policy instruments that encourage carbon sequestration. And this is just the tip of the iceberg. A recent study documented 287 cases of payments for forest ecosystem services from around the world and an international marketplace website for services has just been launched (available at http://www.ecosystemmarketplace.com). . . .

The first insight of an ecosystem services perspective is that investing in natural capital can prove more efficient than using built capital to deliver key services. . . . A well-known example in the water quality field makes the point in a concrete setting. In the early 1990s, a combination of federal regulation and cost realities drove New York City to reconsider its water supply strategy. New York City's water system provides about 1.5 billion tons of drinking water to almost nine million New Yorkers every day. Ninety percent of the water is drawn from the Catskill/Delaware watershed, which extends 125 miles north and west of the city. Under amendments to the federal Safe Drinking Water Act, municipal and other water suppliers were required to filter their surface water supplies unless they could demonstrate that they had taken other steps, including watershed protection measures, to protect their customers from harmful water contamination.

Presented with a choice between provision of clean water through building a filtration plant or managing the watershed, New York City easily concluded that the latter was more cost effective. It was estimated that a filtration plant would cost between $6 billion and $8 billion to build. By contrast, watershed protection efforts, which would include not only the acquisition of critical watershed lands but also a variety of other programs designed to reduce contamination sources in the watershed, would cost only about $1.5 billion. Acting on behalf of the beneficiaries of the Catskills' water purification services, New York City chose to invest in natural rather than built capital. Nor is New York City alone. As of 1996, the EPA had indicated that over 140 municipalities qualified to use watershed conservation as a means of ensuring high drinking water quality. . . .

If ecosystem services clearly provide valuable services, then why don't more payment schemes exist? Why are markets so hard to set up? The answer is three-fold—ignorance, institutional inadequacy, and the problems inherent in public goods.

Perhaps the most basic reason we do not pay more attention to the provision of ecosystem services is that we take them for granted. . . . This lack of knowledge is due both to the lack of relevant data and to the multivariate complexity of the task. Analysis of how ecosystems provide services has proceeded slowly not only because ecosystem level experiments are difficult and lengthy, but also because research to date has focused much more on understanding ecosystem processes than determining ecosystem services. And how an ecosystem works is not the same as the services it provides. . . .

[It] is [also] fair to say that our laws were not designed with ecosystem services in mind. Legal protection of ecosystems was not a primary objective when the relevant laws were drafted over two decades ago. Generally speaking, our pollution laws (e.g., the Clean Air Act and Clean Water Act) rely on human health-based standards. Our conservation laws (e.g., the Endangered Species Act and Marine Mammal Protection Act) are species-specific. And planning under our resource management laws (e.g., the National Forest Management Act and Federal Land Policy and Management Act) must accommodate multiple and conflicting uses. Of course, parts of these laws, such as the Clean Water Act's Section 404 wetlands permit program and use of water quality standards, the Endangered Species Act's critical habitat provisions, and the National Forest Management Act's use of indicator species such as the spotted owl, clearly can help to conserve ecosystem services. The point, though, is that these laws were not primarily intended to provide legal standards for conservation of natural capital and the services that flow from it and, as many authors have pointed out, in practice they usually don't. . . .

The last reason there are so few markets, and perhaps the most important, concerns the role of markets and public goods. . . . We have no shortage of markets for most ecosystem goods (such as clean water and apples), but the ecosystem services underpinning these goods (such as water purification and pollination) are free. The services themselves have no market value for the simple reason that no markets exist in which they can be bought or sold. As a result, there are no direct price mechanisms to signal the scarcity or degradation of these public goods until they fail (at which point their hidden value becomes obvious because of the costs to restore or replace them). This might not be critically important if most lands providing services were public property that could be set aside for conservation, but they are not. Private lands are vital not only for biodiversity conservation, but also for provision of most other services. . . .

Such circumstances make ecosystem services easy to take for granted. Because it is difficult to prevent someone who did not pay for an ecosystem service from benefiting from it, it is equally difficult to get such people to pay for provision of these services. Why pay for something when you have always gotten it for free? As a result, a key challenge in implementing an ecosystem services approach lies in creating a market where none exists — in capturing the value of the service by compensating the providers. This approach, notably unlike that of traditional regulatory or tax instruments, views environmental protection much as a business transaction between willing parties.

## NOTES AND QUESTIONS

1. The "value of everything" project derived its total value for ecosystem services by using data from studies of discrete resource allocation issues such as those discussed in the Salzman excerpt and then extrapolating to a world scale.

Economists have criticized this extrapolation as "a serious error." "Values estimated at one scale cannot be expanded by a convenient [multiplier] to another scale, nor can two separate value estimates simply be added together. When we estimate a compensation measure of one element of an ecosystem, we assume that other aspects of the constraints influencing human well-being are unchanged. For example, we might compute a compensation measure for the elimination of a specific wetland. In another analysis, a compensation measure for the elimination of a different wetland might have been estimated, holding the first at its initial level. But the two compensation measures are *not* additive. . . ." Bockstael et al., On Valuing Nature, 34 Env't Sci. & Tech. 1384 (2000).

2.  There has been considerable interest in incorporating the value of ecosystem services into an increasing variety of environmental programs, from wetlands loss mitigation programs to emissions trading programs and beyond. See, e.g., J.B. Ruhl, S. Kraft & C.L. Lant, The Law and Policy of Ecosystem Services (2007). Using incentive- or market-based plans to maintain or preserve ecosystem services also has become a hot topic in natural resource management circles. Ecosystem services cannot be marketed, however, until the functional linkages between different elements of the environment and valuable services are well enough understood so that realistic values can be assigned to them with sufficient reliability to give investors confidence that they are getting their money's worth. The ecosystem services idea is stimulating significant progress in ecological studies to fill these gaps. See the National Research Council, Valuing Ecosystem Services 2 (2004).

3.  For an assessment of the development of the ecosystem services concept during the last two decades see R. Costanza et al., Twenty Years of Ecosystem Services: How Far Have We Come and How Far Do We Still Need to Go?, 28 Ecosystem Services 1 (2017). The authors review the history and development of the ecosystem services concept, the research and controversy it has triggered, and efforts to apply it to improve environmental policy. They argue that the concept highlights some fundamental changes that need to be made in economic theory and practice to promote sustainability. Rough estimates of the impact of alternative environmental policies on the future global value of ecosystems have been made in I. Kubiszewski et al., The Future Value of Ecosystem Services: Global Scenarios and National Implications, 26 Ecosystem Services 289 (2017).

## E.   *ECOLOGICAL PERSPECTIVES*

The science of ecology seeks to understand the functioning of ecosystems, both on a small scale (such as the ecosystem of a small freshwater wetland) and on a grand scale (such as the global oxygen-carbon dioxide-water cycle, which plays a vital role in world climate and climate changes). Through studying ecosystems, ecologists seek knowledge about the entire process of life by synthesizing chemical, geological, and meteorological information about the environment and biological and chemical information about living organisms and combining them into a single system.

This drive to comprehensiveness derives from the overarching idea of interde-pendence, which is further reflected in such ecological slogans as "you can never do just one thing" and "everything is connected to everything else." This idea lies close to the heart of many bio-centered or eco-centered philosophies. Aldo Leop-old, for instance, wrote that "all ethics rest upon a single premise: that the individ-ual is a member of a community of interdependent parts. . . . The land ethic simply enlarges the boundaries of the community to include soils, plants, and animals, or collectively: the land." A Sand County Almanac 203 (1968). A major portion of the ecological research agenda concerns tracing the consequences of actions through successively widening sequences of effects.

The first generation of ecologists believed that most ecosystems will exhibit *homeostasis,* or the quality of returning to a self-sustaining equilibrium after being disturbed, unless the disturbance is too great. Homeostasis, which is often referred to as the balance of nature, is a dynamic equilibrium, with prey and predator, com-petition and coexistence within the system; nevertheless, over the system as a whole and over time, the diversity and complexity of functioning ecosystems produce a stability, or balance. In any ecosystem, the "presence and success of an organism depend upon the completeness of a complex of conditions, while in turn indi-vidual organisms contribute to the stability of the system itself by occupying an ecological 'niche'—performing a function that contributes to the stability of the system." See E. Odum, Fundamentals of Ecology (3d ed. 1971). This traditional homeostatic understanding has recently been challenged by the "new," or "non-equilibrium" ecology. The extent of disruption an ecosystem could absorb and still maintain homeostasis was defined as its "carrying capacity," and this concept played an important role in debates surrounding the environmental laws passed in the early 1970s.

Because ecosystem interconnections can be complex and multifarious, an eco-logical rule of thumb is that seemingly simple actions typically will have non-ob-vious and unintended consequences that may culminate in a threat to ecosystem stability. Introduce a new organism into an ecosystem and it may function as a virulent pathogen, like the measles that decimated the Eskimos and South Sea Islanders following their first contacts with Western civilization. Bioaccumulation provides another mechanism through which seemingly discrete actions can have unintended consequences. Chemicals, such as the pesticide DDT, accumulate in the tissue of animals that consume other animals, plants, or water containing the chemical. When these animals are consumed in their turn by still others, the chemicals can continue to accumulate or concentrate until they reach dangerous, even fatal proportions. Both the American condor and the bald eagle populations have suffered because plants and insects sprayed with pesticides were consumed by rodents and snakes that were then consumed by the predator birds, eventually pro-ducing pesticide contamination in them sufficient to weaken their egg membranes so that their young died before birth.

A second rule of thumb for ecologists is that smaller actions have less dras-tic consequences on functioning ecosystems than do larger actions. As Leopold expressed it: "The combined evidence of history and ecology seems to support one general deduction: the less violent the man-made changes, the greater the proba-bility of successful readjustment in the [ecosystem]. Violence, in turn, varies with human population density; a dense population requires a more violent conversion: In this respect, North America has a better chance for permanence than Europe, if she can contrive to limit her density." A Sand County Almanac, at 220.

One of the first pieces of modern-era environmental legislation, the National Environmental Policy Act, was partly premised on the idea that interdisciplinary ecological study ought to precede major federal actions in order that the unintended environmental effects of actions could be better represented in an overall cost-benefit assessment of the action. See, for example, section 102(2)(A)-(B), requiring federal agencies to "utilize a systematic, interdisciplinary approach which will insure the integrated use of the natural and social sciences and the environmental design arts in planning . . . [and to] insure that presently unquantified environmental amenities and values may be given appropriate consideration in decisionmaking. . . ."

Preferring small actions to large ones combines a counsel of caution with an underlying judgment that the ways of nature ought to be respected. The methodological principle of ecology, seeing humans as one constituent member of ecosystems composed of many interdependent parts rather than as a dominant, qualitatively distinct member, combines with an admiration for the homeostatic qualities of "natural" systems to produce a prescription for humans: Live in harmony with nature, not at odds with it. Do not maximize, but rather harmonize. The natural equilibrations of functioning ecosystems come to constitute a norm, and to provide a sense of normality, that humans are urged to respect. A good collection of essays touching on some of ecology's broader implications is The Subversive Science: Essays Toward an Ecology of Man (P. Shepard & D. McKinley eds., 1969).

The preference for smallness blossomed into an entire worldview in the late 1960s and 1970s, stimulated by the publication of E.F. Schumacher's Small Is Beautiful (1973) and I. Illich's Tools for Conviviality (1973). As described by Schumacher,

> To strive for smallness means to try to bring organizations and units of production back to a human scale. . . . There are many reasons for favoring smallness. Small units of production can use small resources — a very important point when concentrated, large resources are becoming scarce or inaccessible. Small units are ecologically sounder than big ones: the pollution or damage they may cause has a better chance of fitting into nature's tolerance margins. Small units can be used for decentralized production, leading to a more even distribution of the population, a better use of space, the avoidance of congestion and of monster transport. Most important of all: small units, of which there can be a great number, enable more people "to do their own thing" than large units of which there can only be a few. Smallness is also conductive to simplicity. Simplicity . . . is a value in itself. [E.F. Schumacher, The Age of Plenty: A Christian View, in Economics, Ecology and Ethics 126, 133 (H. Daly ed., 1980).]

The following reading illustrates how the principles of ecology have been combined with ecocentric strands of environmental ethics to produce a distinctive approach to organizing society to respond to environmental problems.

Robert Paehlke

## Environmentalism and the Future of Progressive Politics

(1989)

[E]nvironmentalism as a set of values has an autonomous logical validity apart from the political process, and it ought to be set out separately from environmentalism as an ideology. More important, since politics itself rests on values—it has been defined as "the authoritative allocation of values"—one cannot see clearly the political implications of environmentalism without delineating first its value priorities.

What, then, are the central value assertions of environmentalism? The following have consistently been emphasized in the writing of environmentalists and are implicit in their actions.

1. An appreciation of all life forms and a view that the complexities of the ecological web of life are politically salient.
2. A sense of humility regarding the human species in relation to other species and to the global ecosystem.
3. A concern with the quality of human life and health, including an emphasis on the importance of preventative medicine, diet, and exercise to the maintenance and enhancement of human health.
4. A global rather than a nationalist or isolationist view.
5. Some preference for political and/or population decentralization.
6. An extended time horizon—a concern about the long-term future of the world and its life.
7. A sense of urgency regarding the survival of life on earth, both long-term and short-term.
8. A belief that human societies ought to be reestablished on a more sustainable technical and physical basis. An appreciation that many aspects of our present way of life are fundamentally transitory.
9. A revulsion toward waste in the face of human need (in more extreme forms, this may appear as asceticism).
10. A love of simplicity, although this does not include rejection of technology or "modernity."
11. An aesthetic appreciation for season, setting, climate, and natural materials.
12. A measurement of esteem, including self-esteem and social merit, in terms of such nonmaterial values as skill, artistry, effort, or integrity.
13. An attraction to autonomy and self-management in human endeavors and, generally, an inclination to more democratic and participatory political processes and administrative structures.

## NOTES AND QUESTIONS

1. Needless to say, not all environmentalists accept all of these values. Most environmentalists find many of these values central to their outlook on life, but the list is not a catechism. One recurring criticism that Deep Ecology levels at the "problem-solving" approach that typifies much environmental law is that it does

not address directly ways in which consumption contributes to environmental problems. Gus Speth argues that "consumer spending has been a leading driver of environmental decline. . . . In the modern environmental era, there has been too little environmental focus on consumption. This situation is changing, but most mainstream environmentalists have not wanted to suggest that the position they advocate would require serious lifestyle changes." The Bridge at the End of the World, 147-148 (2009). Does the idea of a Conserver Society provide a perspective for environmentalists to employ that avoids the pitfall of advocating serious lifestyle changes, or is such advocacy inevitable to get beyond the limitations of the problem-solving approach?

2. In his book Ecology and the Politics of Scarcity, William Ophuls provides the following statement of "the essential message of ecology."

> [A]lthough it is possible in principle to exploit nature rationally and reasonably for human ends, man has not done so. Because he has not been content with the portion naturally allotted him, man has invaded the biological capital built up by evolution. Moreover, due to man's ignorance of nature's workings, he has done so in a peculiarly destructive fashion. . . . We must learn to work with nature and to accept the basic ecological trade-offs between protection and production, optimum and maximum, quality and quantity. This will necessarily require major changes in our life, for the essential message of ecology is limitation: there is only so much the biosphere can take and only so much it can give, and this may be less than we desire. [W. Ophuls, Ecology and the Politics of Scarcity 43 (1977).]

3. Perhaps the ultimate objective of environmental policy is to answer the question Christopher Stone poses: "What sort of planet will this be?" Stone argues that while technology and resource constraints define the range of future options that we realistically can seek, environmental ethics seek to tell us which of these alternative futures we ought to select. Environmental law, then, seeks to determine how we can arrange our social institutions in order to achieve the future that we want. C. Stone, Earth and Other Ethics 15-16 (1987). What obligation do we have toward future generations when making choices concerning what sort of planet this will be? Do we have an obligation to leave future generations at least the same range of choices that we have? Or do we owe them some lesser obligation because they depend on us for their existence and their values will be influenced by the state of the world we choose to leave them? How would proponents of the economic perspective approach these questions? The ecological perspective?

## F.   COMMON POOL RESOURCES

Previous discussions have already explained how we tend to overuse our environmental resources because they are available without cost to us, so that the price mechanism does not make us aware of the harm we are causing to other humans or the environment. That harm is thus external to our private calculations concerning how much of the resource we should use. A good many environmental issues present this problem of external costs in ways that share a common structure. In his classic article "The Tragedy of the Commons," Garrett Hardin argues that if common pool resources (such as a common grazing area) may be used without charge by anyone, individually rational behavior will become collectively deficient. The desire to feed their herd for free will produce overgrazing, destroying the commons. In the excerpt below Hardin extends this analogy to pollution.

Garrett Hardin

## The Tragedy of the Commons

168 Science 1243 (1968)

In a reverse way, the tragedy of the commons reappears in problems of pollution. Here it is not a question of taking something out of the commons, but of putting something in — sewage, or chemical, radioactive, and heat wastes into water, noxious and dangerous fumes into the air; and distracting and unpleasant advertising signs into the line of sight. The calculations of utility are much the same as before. The rational man finds that his share of the cost of the wastes he discharges into the commons is less than the cost of purifying his wastes before releasing them. Since this is true for everyone, we are locked into a system of "fouling our own nest," so long as we behave only as independent, rational, free-enterprisers.

The tragedy of the commons as a food basket is averted by private property, or something formally like it. But the air and waters surrounding us cannot readily be fenced, and so the tragedy of the commons as a cesspool must be prevented by different means, by coercive laws or taxing devices that make it cheaper for the polluter to treat his pollutants than to discharge them untreated. We have not progressed as far with the solution of this problem as we have with the first. Indeed, our particular concept of private property, which deters us from exhausting the positive resources of the earth, favors pollution. The owner of a factory on the bank of a stream — whose property extends to the middle of the stream — often has difficulty seeing why it is not his natural right to muddy the waters flowing past his door. The law, always behind the times, requires elaborate stitching and fitting to adapt it to this newly perceived aspect of the commons.

## NOTES AND QUESTIONS

1. Hardin's story of the commons is a "tragedy" because a dynamic is at work within the story that is leading to eventual disaster, disaster for all. What is that dynamic? Insofar as the dynamic relates to the desire of "each herdsman to maximize his gain," is the tragedy unavoidable? Many who disagree with the economic approach to environmental problems do so because they believe humans ought not, and need not, pursue their own "gain" single-mindedly. Aldo Leopold, for one, claimed that anyone approaching the environment as exclusively an object for personal gain in effect treated it as a piece of property, "entailing privileges but not obligations." In arguing for a "land ethic," he argued for a change in humanity's disposition toward the environment, one that "changes the role of Homo sapiens

from conqueror of the land-community to plain member and citizen of it. [This] implies respect for his fellow-members, and also respect for the community as such." A. Leopold, A Sand County Almanac 204 (1968). This idea has been widely influential among environmentalists.

2.  Surely the tragedy of commons is not inevitable, as other studies have shown, because some commons have existed for centuries, and continue to exist. E. Ostrom, Governing the Commons: The Evolution of Institutions for Collective Action (1990). As one study suggests, "Perhaps what existed in fact was not a 'tragedy of the commons' but rather a triumph: that for hundreds of years—and perhaps thousands, although written records do not exist to prove the longer era—land was managed successfully by communities." Cox, No Tragedy of the Commons, 7 Envtl. Ethics 49, 60 (1985). Small communities are likely to be more successful at avoiding the tragedy through informal controls so long as there are no external markets for the resources. Cultural anthropologists, including especially students of Native American cultures, have identified cultural and ideological explanations for husbanding commons resources. Moreover, as Carol Rose points out, the tragedy occurs only when use of the commons reaches a level where congestion develops or where the resources are used so intensively that it exceeds the carrying capacity of the commons. Rose, Rethinking Environmental Controls: Management Strategies for Common Resources, 1991 Duke L.J. 1.

3.  The type of situation exemplified by Hardin's article is often called a "common pool resource" problem (CPR). CPRs are sometimes analyzed through a model of behavior known as the Prisoner's Dilemma, named for the story used to illustrate the behavior. In that story, two persons suspected of a serious crime are isolated from each other and told that if either testifies against her colleague she will go free, so long as the other suspect doesn't also turn state's evidence, in which case each will receive a moderate sentence. If neither suspect testifies, then each will be convicted of a lesser crime, for which there already is sufficient evidence. Each will then receive a light sentence for the lesser crime. However, if one suspect keeps quiet while the other testifies, the silent suspect will receive a harsh sentence. From the perspective of any single suspect, each gets a shorter sentence by testifying against the other, regardless of what the other one does. Thus the strategy of testifying "dominates" any other strategy that the suspect could choose, and any suspect interested in minimizing his or her sentence should adopt it. However, the final result of both actors following this strategy is that they each get moderate sentences, which is worse for each than if they had both kept silent, in which case each would have received a light sentence.

The result of the prisoner's dilemma is an outcome that is "individually rational and collectively deficient." B. Barry & R. Hardin, Rational Man and Irrational Society? 25 (1982). It is individually rational because each player chooses her dominant strategy, which is the rational thing to do. It is collectively deficient because there exists another outcome that would leave each suspect better off than the all-testify outcome. Thus individual rationality and collective deficiency identify the problem of collective action, namely that "it may be in everyone's individual interest not to cooperate in a collective effort even though everyone would be better off if everyone cooperated." Id.

4. Some have urged that organizing collective action to prevent tragedies of the commons should constitute a primary function of government. The late Mancur Olson, for instance, wrote that "[a] state is first of all an organization that provides public goods for its members, the citizens." M. Olson, The Logic of Collective Action 15 (1965). Long before the problem of collective action became identified as such, theorists had observed that such cases were ones in which government might legitimately intervene, and even writers not otherwise associated with interventionist views about government have concluded that prisoner's dilemma cases provide a legitimate occasion for intervention. For example, John Stuart Mill wrote:

> There are matters in which interference of law is required, not to overrule the judgment of individuals respecting their own interest, but to give effect to that judgment; they being unable to give effect to it except by concert, which concert again cannot be effectual unless it receives validity and sanction from the law. [J.S. Mill, Principles of Political Economy, Bk. V., Chap. XI, Sec. 12.]

Mill suggested that "I would rather cooperate than welch, but only if you cooperate" is an individually rational judgment in some circumstances, and that it may require legal sanction to ensure universal cooperation, which all seem to desire.

5. Others have argued that privatizing the commons by creating property rights in common resources is a solution superior to government regulation of access. Jim Krier cautions that there are difficulties with either approach. Given that the root of the tragedy of the commons is the difficulty of coordinating human behavior, Krier questions whether proponents of these approaches are "implicitly arguing that a community plagued by noncooperation can improve its condition by cooperating." Krier, The Tragedy of the Commons, Part Two, 15 Harv. J.L. & Pub. Pol'y 325, 338 (1992). Krier claims that because the public must organize in order to get the government to intervene to protect the commons, the problems of free riders and factional influence persist. Because "markets themselves depend on an active governmental role," Krier finds no reason to believe that the same governmental failures that plague regulatory programs will not plague the establishment and oversight of new natural resources markets. Id. at 341-342.

6. Despite the popularity of his essay, Garrett Hardin has come under harsh criticism for repugnant racial and social views. Political Science professor Matto Mildenberger of UC-Santa Barbara declares that "Hardin was a racist, eugenicist, nativist and Islamophobe. He is listed by the Southern Poverty Law Center as a known white nationalist. His writings and political activism helped inspire the anti-immigrant hatred spilling across America today. And he promoted an idea he called 'lifeboat ethics': since global resources are finite, Hardin believed the rich should throw poor people overboard to keep their boat above water." Matto Mildenberger, The Tragedy of the Tragedy of the Commons, Scientific American, April 23, 2019. The Southern Poverty Law Center notes that Hardin "began calling for the United States to reject the UN Declaration of Human Rights, explicitly arguing that the government should adopt coercive measures to prevent women (especially, as he argued elsewhere, non-white women) from reproducing. According to Hardin, certain racial groups have 'adopt[ed] overbreeding as a policy to secure [their] own aggrandizement,' and because of this, he argued, 'the freedom to breed is intolerable.'"

## PROBLEM EXERCISE: ENERGY EXTRACTION AND TRANS-PORT: ANWR, PIPELINE, AND FRACKING CONTROVERSIES

The National Environmental Policy Act (NEPA), analyzed in depth in Chapter 8, directs federal agencies to prepare detailed environmental impact statements (EISs) before taking any major action "significantly affecting the quality of the human environment." 42 U.S.C. §4332(C). NEPA declares it to be "the continuing policy of the Federal government . . . to use all practicable means and measures . . , to create and maintain conditions under which man and nature can exist in productive harmony, and fulfill the social, economic, and other requirements of presents and future generations of Americans." This is the closest U.S. federal environmental law comes to enshrining as national policy a particular set of environmental values. NEPA long has been an important legal tool for environmental interests challenging energy and infrastructure projects, as illustrated in the problem exercise below.

### The Arctic National Wildlife Refuge

For decades a fierce controversy has been waged over whether or not the U.S. government should permit oil drilling in the Arctic National Wildlife Refuge (ANWR), a pristine wilderness area along the northeast coast of Alaska. Sometimes called North America's Serengeti, the area is home to a vast herd of porcupine caribou whose migratory range extends over 96,000 square miles. It is the kind of place most Americans encounter only in the pages of National Geographic, which describes it as "a land of mountains and broad, lake-filled plains, where caribou have worn trails in rock and geese have traced paths in the sky over millennia of rhythmic wandering; where ice holds the sea and frost the land until a brief, glorious burst of flowering summer; . . . a roadless land, a part of the North little touched by the 20th century, or the 19th, or the first." Lee, Oil in the Wilderness: An Arctic Dilemma, National Geographic, Dec. 1988, at 858. The late Alaska Governor Wally Hickel, who pushed to open ANWR to oil drilling, described it instead as "a barren, marshy wilderness in the summer, infested with uncountable mosquitoes, and locked in temperatures of 60 and 70 degrees below zero for up to nine months of the year."

ANWR was established by Congress in 1960 when it set aside 19 million acres of land, half of it as wilderness area. But Congress also designated 1.5 million acres along the coast ("section 1002 lands," named after the section of the statute creating the category) for further study for possible oil exploration. Located 40 miles east of North America's largest oil field at Prudhoe Bay, these section 1002 lands represent "the chance of a lifetime to search for 'elephants'—oil fields with more than a hundred million barrels of producible reserves—in perhaps the last major hunting ground on North America's mainland." Id. at 863. The U.S. Geological Survey initially estimated the amount of recoverable oil in ANWR as ranging from 5.7 to 16 billion barrels of oil (BBO), with a mean value of 10.4 BBO.

The Department of the Interior (DOI) has performed numerous assessments of the environmental impact of drilling in ANWR. One forecast negative "widespread, long-term changes in wildlife habitats, wilderness environment, and Native community activities," and possibly a "major population decline" in the caribou herd. Another forecast only that "there is a risk that a decline could occur" in the caribou population, but it anticipated "no appreciable population decline."

A study by the U.S. Fish and Wildlife Service found that the environmental impact of oil drilling in nearby Prudhoe Bay had been far greater than estimated in the environmental impact statements prepared when the project was considered 15 years before. It noted that 11,000 acres of wildlife habitat had been destroyed, nearly twice what had been predicted, and that the populations of bears, wolves, and other predators, and most bird species had declined. Although caribou had increased in number, the report attributed this increase to a decline in the numbers of bears and other caribou predators. It noted that more than 200 million gallons of fresh water unexpectedly were being withdrawn from lakes and streams by oil operations each year and that erosion, sedimentation, and oil spills had done far more damage to water quality than anticipated.

Nine months before the *Exxon Valdez* oil spill occurred in Prince William Sound, the New York Times published an editorial supporting the opening of ANWR to oil exploration. Risks Worth Taking for Oil, N.Y. Times, June 2, 1988, at A26. While conceding that "drilling is certain to disrupt the delicate ecology of the Arctic tundra," the editorial opined that "the likely value of the oil far exceeds plausible estimates of the environmental cost." The editorial concluded: "If another oil field on the scale of Prudhoe Bay is discovered, developing it will damage the environment. That damage is worth minimizing. But it is hard to see why absolutely pristine preservation of this remote wilderness should take precedence over the nation's energy needs." The political winds supporting opening ANWR to oil drilling shifted abruptly in March 1989 with the massive *Exxon Valdez* oil spill in Alaska.

During the Clinton administration, which opposed drilling, the Department of Interior forecast more environmental damage than previously, concluding that drilling would result "in a major, adverse impact on the [caribou] herd" and damage to water supplies and fragile tundra vegetation. Kenworthy, Study Condemns Arctic Oil Drilling, Wash. Post, Aug. 27, 1995, at A4. Proponents of drilling argued instead that new drilling technologies permit drilling to be done with a "dramatically reduced . . . footprint on the tundra, minimiz[ing] waste produced, and protect[ing] the land for resident and migratory wildlife. . . . Estimates indicate that no more than 2,000 will be disturbed." Bush Administration National Energy Plan 5-9 (2001).

Native Americans living in remote villages near ANWR have a very different perception of what the ANWR battle is about. To Sarah James, a Gwich'in from Arctic Village, Alaska, it "is not just an environmental issue." Rather,

> [i]t is about the survival of the ancient culture that depends on the caribou. It is about the basic tribal and human rights to continue [our] way of life. For thousands of years we have lived with the caribou right where we are today. We are talking about an Indian nation that still lives on the land and depends on the herd. In my village 75 percent of protein comes from caribou. It's not just what we eat. It is who we are. Caribou are our life. It's in our stories and songs and the whole way of the world. [S. James, Testimony before a Subcomm. of the Senate Environment and Public Works Comm. (Mar. 1991).]

In contrast to the Gwich'in, Inupiat Eskimos argue that ANWR should be opened to oil exploration because of the economic benefits development will provide. The Arctic Slope Regional Corporation, which represents the Inupiat of the North Slope, owns 92,000 acres of land that they wish the oil companies to develop. An Inupiat representative argues that as a result of development at Prudhoe Bay,

> [r]evenues from the only economy we have—the oil industry—have provided high schools in each of our eight villages for the first time in our history. We now have health clinics, utilities, a local senior citizens' home and other basic public services that most Americans take for granted. [Letter from Brenda Itta-Lee, Vice President for Human Resources, Arctic Slope Regional Corporation, to the editors, Wash. Post, Aug. 28, 1991.]

In March 2003, a committee of the National Research Council of the National Academy of Sciences released a report on the "Cumulative Effects of Oil and Gas Activities on Alaska's North Slope." The report, which had been requested by congressional proponents of opening ANWR, confirmed that oil companies have reduced the "footprint" of their drilling technologies, but it also found that oil exploration in Alaska has produced "a steady accumulation of harmful environmental and social effects that will probably grow as exploration expands." Andrew C. Revkin, Experts Conclude Oil Drilling Has Hurt Alaska's North Slope, N.Y. Times, Mar. 5, 2003, at A15.

**Question One.** If it in fact is true that there is far more recoverable oil available in the Arctic than previously estimated and that new technologies will minimize environmental damage, should oil drilling in ANWR proceed?

**Question Two.** How much confidence in projections of environmental impact should be required before a decision concerning a major development project is based on them? Should it depend on the likely magnitude of the consequences? On their reversibility? Is the source of such predictions relevant to assessing their credibility?

**Question Three.** In light of the different perspectives on Arctic drilling by the Gwich'in and Inupiat tribes, does Arctic oil drilling raise environmental justice concerns? How should such concerns be factored into the decision-making calculus?

The Obama administration opposed drilling in ANWR, but it supported drilling in the Outer Continental Shelf (OCS) off the north coast of Alaska as part of its "all-of-the-above approach" to achieving energy independence. Chastened by its experience in the more temperate Gulf of Mexico, BP stated that it did not plan to drill in Arctic waters because the company believed it to be too risky. After receiving conditional approval for exploratory drilling in the Beaufort Sea, Royal Dutch Shell encountered severe problems. Despite spending more than $7 billion on the project, Shell announced in September 2015 that it would stop drilling for oil off the Alaskan coast "for the foreseeable future."

In December 2016, President Obama indefinitely banned offshore oil and gas drilling in 115 million acres (98%) of federally owned Arctic waters in the Chukchi and Beaufort Seas off Alaska's north shore. He took this action under a provision of the 1953 Outer Continental Shelf Lands Act. Prime Minister Justin Trudeau simultaneously announced that Canada also will designate "all

Arctic Canadian waters as indefinitely off limits to future offshore Arctic oil and gas licensing, to be reviewed every five years through a climate and marine science-based life-cycle assessment."

Economists Robert Hahn and Peter Passell believe that the question whether to drill in ANWR and the OCS can be informed through the use of cost-benefit analysis. They believe that 7 billion barrels of oil could be extracted from ANWR and 11 billion from the OCS. At crude oil prices of $100/barrel, they calculated that this oil would be worth $2.1 trillion while costing less than $400 billion to develop (even including the cost of cleaning up oil spills). Hahn and Passell concede that this expanded production would have a barely discernible impact on global oil prices (reducing them by just 1.3%), but they argue that the $1.7 trillion in net benefits presents a "compelling" case for expanded drilling. They argue that the value of keeping ANWR and the OCS unspoiled by oil drilling cannot possibly be this great, and they suggest cutting a deal with environmentalists. Environmentalists should be willing to accept such drilling if they were promised that the government would use hundreds of billions of dollars of the net benefits of drilling to restore environmental treasures like the Everglades and Louisiana coastal wetlands. See Robert Hahn & Peter Passell, Save the Environment: Drill, Baby, Drill, N.Y. Times, Sept. 14, 2008.

**Question Four.**  Should oil drilling on the OCS off the north shore of Alaska be permitted? Whose assessment of the risks of such drilling should be accepted? Would it be better to allow drilling in ANWR rather than on the OCS because it would be easier to contain an oil spill on land?

**Question Five.**  How would you respond to the analysis by economists Hahn and Passell? Do you perceive any flaws in their calculations of net benefits from drilling? Should environmentalists be willing to accept a deal where a significant portion of the enormous value of the additional oil is reinvested in projects that would benefit the environment?

On December 22, 2017, President Trump signed into law the Tax Cuts and Jobs Act of 2017, which contains a provision opening ANWR to oil drilling. The provision was added at the behest of Republican Senator Lisa Murkowski of Alaska, a long-time supporter of drilling ANWR in order to increase royalties to be received by the state of Alaska. The bill passed the Senate by a vote of 51-48 under a "reconciliation" procedure that avoided the need to obtain 60 votes to overcome a filibuster. It was argued that because the measure would raise revenue from oil royalties it was germane to the tax bill.

On September 12, 2019, the Interior Department's Bureau of Land Management released its final environmental impact statement (EIS) for holding an oil and gas lease sale for ANWR. BLM announced that its preferred option was to lease nearly the entire 1.6 million-acre coastal plain for drilling. The EIS reported that climate change could have "catastrophic consequences" for birds on the coastal plain, whether or not oil drilling was allowed, potentially leading to the extinction of 69 of the 157 bird species during the next 85 years. The EIS stated that "the large magnitude of climate change effects" would be "likely to overshadow smaller magnitude impacts of oil development." On the day the EIS was released, the U.S. House of Representatives by a vote of 225-193 voted to repeal the provision in the

Tax Cut and Jobs Act of 2017 that allowed drilling in ANWR. Steven Mufson & Juliet Eilperin, Trump administration opens huge reserve in Alaska to drilling, Washington Post, Sept. 13, 2019.

On January 6, 2021, two weeks before leaving office, the Trump administration conducted a sale of leases to drill in ANWR. No large oil company bid and most of the few leases awarded went to the Alaska Industrial Development and Export Authority (AIDEA), a public corporation owned by the state government. On his first day in office, President Biden placed a moratorium on drilling in ANWR and mandated a review of the potential environmental impacts of the leasing program. See Executive Order 13,990, Protecting Public Health and the Environment and Restoring Science to Tackle the Climate Crisis, Sec. 4.

## The Keystone XL and Dakota Access Pipelines

For years environmentalists opposed construction of the Keystone XL pipeline that would carry crude oil from tar sands deposits in the Canadian province of Alberta more than 1,100 miles south to an existing pipeline terminal in Steele City, Nebraska. In January 2012, President Obama rejected the first route proposed for Keystone XL because it crossed through the environmentally sensitive Sandhills region of Nebraska and above the Ogallala Aquifer, a precious source of water for agriculture. TransCanada, the company seeking to build the pipeline, then proposed a new route that would skirt around the Sandhills. In January 2013, the new route was endorsed by the state of Nebraska, which previously had opposed the pipeline.

Environmentalists vehemently objected to Keystone XL because the oil it would carry is unusually carbon-intensive. The State Department's draft Supplemental Environmental Impact Statement (SEIS), released on March 1, 2013, reports that lifecycle greenhouse gas (GHG) emissions from tar sands crude could be 81 percent greater than emissions from the average crude refined in the United States in 2005.

Despite the GHG-intensive nature of the tar sands oil, the draft SEIS argued that Keystone XL would not have a significant impact on the environment because the oil will be extracted even if the pipeline is not approved. The oil could be transported by rail or through an alternative pipeline that would extend west from Alberta to the Pacific Ocean. Environmentalists argued that if President Obama vetoed the Keystone XL it would make it much more difficult and expensive for tar sands oil to be exported. Proponents of the pipeline argued that it would create numerous construction jobs in the United States while reducing U.S. dependence on supplies of crude oil from the volatile Middle East. President Obama announced in November 2015 that he was denying a permit for the pipeline to cross into the United States because the oil it would carry would exacerbate the climate crisis. "America is now a global leader when it comes to taking serious action to fight climate change, and frankly, approving this project would have undercut that leadership," Obama stated.

After taking office in January 2017, President Donald Trump announced a new policy goal of U.S. "energy dominance." In March 2017, President Trump reversed President Obama's decision to veto the Keystone XL Pipeline. However, pipeline construction was halted in April 2020 when a federal district court in Montana ruled that the nationwide general permit used to authorize the pipeline's crossing of federal waterways had been issued in violation of the Endangered Species Act. Although the judge tried to halt all pipeline projects that relied on this permit, on July 6, 2020, the U.S. Supreme Court modified the injunction so that it only applied to the Keystone XL project.

**Question Six.** Should President Obama have approved the Keystone XL pipeline? How should the apparent tradeoff between jobs and the environment be reconciled? If it proves true that the tar sands crude will be extracted by Canada regardless of whether the pipeline is built, was the draft SEIS correct in saying that the approval of Keystone XL would not have a significant effect on the environment?

In fall 2016, vigorous protests erupted in North Dakota as environmentalists and Native American groups sought to block completion of a pipeline to transport oil from North Dakota's Bakken formation. The Standing Rock Tribe of Native Americans argued that the U.S. Army Corps of Engineers should not approve an easement to allow the pipeline to pass under Lake Oahe, a source of drinking water for their communities. The "Leave It in the Ground" movement opposed the pipeline because it would make it easier to transport fossil fuels. The movement's slogan is "Leave fossil fuels in the ground and learn to live without them." Proponents of the pipeline maintain that it will be a safer means of transportation than using rail tank cars, which have been prone to accidents. Despite finding no legal obstacles to approval of the pipeline, called Dakota Access, the Obama administration asked the companies to pause the project so additional environmental reviews could be completed.

As noted above, after taking office in January 2017 President Trump announced a new goal of U.S. "energy dominance." He quickly instructed the U.S. Army Corps of Engineers to grant an easement allowing the pipeline to be built under Lake Oahe. Three months later the pipeline was finished and running. However, Judge Boasberg of the federal district court in the District of Columbia ultimately ruled that a full-blown environmental impact statement (EIS) was required because the Corps "failed adequately to consider the impacts of an oil spill on Standing Rock's fishing and hunting rights and on environmental justice." In June 2020 he ordered the Dakota Access pipeline to be shut down and drained of oil until the EIS is completed, a process expected to take more than a year. The D.C. Circuit upheld the order to complete an EIS and to revoke the easement for the pipeline to pass under Lake Oahe, but it reversed the order directing that the pipeline be shut down pending completion of the EIS. Standing Rock Sioux Tribe v. U.S. Army Corps of Engineers, 985 F.3d 1032 (D.C. Cir. 2021). On his first day in office, President Biden revoked the March 2019 permit for the Keystone XL Pipeline. See Executive Order 13,990, Protecting Public Health and the Environment and Restoring Science to Tackle the Climate Crisis, Sec. 6. However, the Biden administration has decided to continue to allow the Dakota Access Pipeline to operate even though it no longer has a legal easement to pass below Lake Oahe.

**Question Seven.** Since the purpose of performing an EIS is to inform a federal agency's decision concerning whether or not to approve a project, is it ever appropriate to allow a project that had been completed in violation of NEPA to continue operating while the EIS is being developed?

## Hydraulic Fracturing for Oil and Natural Gas

Although the United States has only 2 percent of the world's oil reserves, it has one of the world's largest technically recoverable reserves of shale gas. In a few short years, the U.S. energy supply mix has been dramatically altered by a surge in extraction of natural gas from shale formations. This phenomenon is the result of a dramatic expansion in the use of hydraulic fracturing, commonly referred to as "fracking." Fracking is a technique involving underground injection of a mix of chemical fluids under high pressure to fracture and hold open shale formations to release hydrocarbons held within them. Due to expanded use of fracking, U.S. natural gas production rose from 20.2 trillion cubic feet in 2007 to 34.4 trillion cubic feet in 2020. Production from shale gas wells rose between 2007 and 2011 from less than 2 trillion cubic feet to more than 8.5 trillion cubic feet. As a result of this huge expansion in domestic supply, natural gas prices in the United States plunged from more than $9 per million Btus in 2008 to less than $3 per million Btus. Plunging natural gas prices have encouraged U.S. electric utilities to shift away from coal-fired generation in favor of natural gas. This has helped reduce U.S. emissions of greenhouse gases to their lowest level since 1994. Fracking also has increased domestic oil production from 5.0 million barrels per day (bpd) in 2008 to 6.5 million bpd in 2012. U.S. Energy Information Administration, Annual Energy Outlook 2013 (April 2013). U.S. crude oil production reached a peak of 12.8 million barrels/day in January 2020 before declining to 11.3 million b/d as oil prices declined in 2021.

Despite its immense economic benefits, fracking raises a host of serious environmental concerns. Fracking fluids include many toxic chemicals that can pollute underground aquifers that are sources of drinking water through surface spills or poor well casing and/or cementing. These chemicals are mixed with huge volumes of water—in some cases up to 7 million gallons per well. Special care is required to dispose of wastewater generated by fracking operations. Often this is injected deep below the water table and in a few cases underground injection has been associated with small earth tremors. Fracking operations also release toxic air pollutants, including benzene and methane, a potent greenhouse gas. Fracking operations also are noisy and require a procession of heavy vehicles and equipment that industrialize rural areas and quickly deteriorate rural roads.

Companies that use fracking to increase gas and oil production acknowledge that it poses environmental risks, but they maintain that the risks are not great and are outweighed by its enormous benefits. They note that fracking fluids are injected into wells lined with steel casings that are cemented together. They also maintain that the surface footprint of fracking operations has been greatly reduced due to technology that allows drilling horizontally for up to two miles from eight wells located together on a three-acre pad.

Many members of the public find it disquieting that most fracking operations are exempt from federal environmental regulation. The Safe Drinking Water Act directs EPA to regulate underground injection to protect public water supplies, but fracking operations that do not use diesel fuel as an additive are excluded from the definition of "underground injection." This provision, contained in section 322 of the Energy Policy Act of 2005, 42 U.S.C. §300h(d), is often called the "Cheney exclusion" because it was quietly slipped into the Act at the behest of Vice President

Cheney. In 2010, Congress directed EPA to study the environmental impact of fracking. In December 2016, shortly before the Obama administration left office, EPA released its report. The report found that fracking "can impact drinking water resources under some circumstances." These include:

- water withdrawals for hydraulic fracturing in times or areas of low water availability, particularly in areas with limited or declining groundwater resources;
- spills during the handling of hydraulic fracturing fluids and chemicals or produced water that result in large volumes or high concentrations of chemicals reaching groundwater resources;
- injection of hydraulic fracturing fluids into wells with inadequate mechanical integrity, allowing gases or liquids to move to groundwater resources;
- injection of hydraulic fracturing fluids directly into groundwater resources;
- discharge of inadequately treated hydraulic fracturing wastewater to surface water; and
- disposal or storage of hydraulic fracturing wastewater in unlined pits resulting in contamination of groundwater resources.

EPA, Hydraulic Fracturing for Oil and Gas: Impacts from the Hydraulic Fracturing Water Cycle on Drinking Water Resources in the United States (2016).

With fracking largely exempt from the federal regulation, states have employed a diverse array of approaches to regulating fracking. Fracking is now employed in dozens of states, but only a handful have regulated it stringently. Fracking has been used extensively in Pennsylvania, and operators are required to obtain a permit from the state Department of Environmental Protection, but state law preempts local zoning and land use control laws from blocking fracking operations. Shawna Bligh & Chris Wendelbo, Hydraulic Fracturing: Drilling into the Issue, 27 Nat. Resources & Env't 7 (Winter 2013).

Alaska and Florida have no laws governing fracking. Vermont, New York, and Maryland have banned all fracking activities. Some states require disclosure of chemicals used in fracking fluid, but the gas and oil industry has resisted such requirements, claiming that the composition of fracking fluid is a trade secret.

**Question Eight.**   Fracking has split the environmental community. Some groups support a complete ban on fracking because of what they perceive as serious risks to the environment. A few groups, emphasizing the environmental benefits of a shift away from coal toward natural gas, believe that fracking can be done safely if properly regulated. Should fracking be banned? How should the environmental benefits of increased use of natural gas instead of coal (reduced greenhouse gas emissions and reduced pollution from coal combustion) be factored into this decision?

**Question Nine.**   Should fracking be exempt from federal environmental laws, such as the Safe Drinking Water Act that is intended to protect underground sources of drinking water by regulating underground injection? What are the benefits of leaving regulation of fracking to the states? In the absence of transboundary harm, is there any justification for federal regulation of fracking?

# CHAPTER 2

# ENVIRONMENTAL LAW: A STRUCTURAL OVERVIEW

Most of today's environmental law violates the basic principles of ecology. Nature teaches the connectedness of all activities, but most current-generation law regulates separate pollutants with little consideration of ecosystems as a whole. The continuums of nature generally adapt gradually, but today's environmental law makes sharp distinctions between safe and unsafe, attainment versus nonattainment areas, permissible versus impermissible levels of pollution.[*]

*— Donald Elliott*

If you have traveled in the remote parts of the Deep South, I am sure you have seen the architecture of Tobacco Road—shacks built of whatever materials were available at the time, often by a series of owners. Maybe the roof is corrugated tin, but one wall is made from a billboard and the door step is a cinder block. No part matches any other part, and there are holes here and there. Still, it provides a measure of basic shelter, and there comes a point where it is easier to tack a new board over a gap that appears than to redesign the entire structure.[**]

*— Ronald Outen*

Although U.S. environmental law often is portrayed as if it were invented by Congress during the 1970s, its roots run much deeper. Environmental law is an outgrowth of centuries of common law doctrines that seek to protect people and property from harm caused by the actions of others. Its common law roots help explain both the complexity of environmental law and the difficulties it confronts in seeking to preserve natural resources and to prevent harm that often is far removed in space and time from the actions that cause it.

Environmental law's structural complexity is a product of centuries of evolving common law doctrine, federal and state statutes that direct agencies to issue a vast array of regulations, and even agreements between sovereign states. Most environmental statutes respond to particularly visible manifestations of broader ecological

---

    [*] Toward Ecological Law and Policy, in Thinking Ecologically (M.R. Chertow & D.C. Esty eds., 1997).

    [**] Environmental Pollution Laws and the Architecture of Tobacco Road, in National Research Council, Multimedia Approaches to Pollution Control: Symposium Proceedings 139 (1987).

problems. Considered together, environmental statutes and common law principles provide regulatory authority that is at once piecemeal and overlapping. Thus, even though the environmental law articulates some of society's noblest aspirations, its legal architecture may resemble more closely a shack on Tobacco Road than a Gothic cathedral. Ronald Outen, Environmental Pollution Laws and the Architecture of Tobacco Road in National Research Council, Multimedia Approaches to Pollution Control: Symposium Proceedings 139 (1987).

The complex architecture of environmental law reflects not only the circumstances of its birth, but also the complexity of the problems it addresses and the difficulty of reconciling the competing values environmental policy implicates. Although there is a remarkable cross-disciplinary consensus in favor of collective action to address problems caused by "individually rational but collectively deficient" behavior, often there is sharp disagreement concerning the precise form that action should take. The diverse philosophies that animate environmental concerns and the immense uncertainties that surround forecasts of likely policy outcomes provide ample opportunity for controversy.

This chapter is designed to introduce the "big picture" of environmental law by providing a roadmap of sorts to help you navigate this legal labyrinth. After reviewing the roots of environmental law, it explores the principal federal environmental statutes and the wide range of alternative regulatory strategies they employ. The chapter concludes with an introduction to the process by which statutes are translated into regulations.

## A.  SOURCES OF ENVIRONMENTAL LAW

What is environmental law? Dan Tarlock argues that environmental law, "as now defined, is primarily a synthesis of pre-environmental era common law rules, principles from other areas of law, and post-environmental era statutes which are lightly influenced by the application of concepts derived from ecology and other areas of science, economics, and ethics." A. Dan Tarlock, Is There a There There in Environmental Law?, 19 J. Land Use & Envtl. L. 213, 222 (2004). Tarlock notes that environmental law lacks not only an internal set of rules, but also a clear constitutional foundation. He acknowledges that environmental law "looks like and is positive law." However, Tarlock argues that it actually could be viewed as representing "a radical break with the Western legal tradition," including both the common law and constitutionalism, because much of it seeks to protect natural systems and future generations that traditionally are not recognized as having legal personalities. Id. at 235. Ricardo Lorenzetti, President of the Supreme Court of Argentina, argues that the environmental paradigm challenges established thought in many areas of law. He describes the impact of environmental law on other areas of law as like a party to which the host has invited other areas of law, but told them to come wearing different clothing than they normally do. Ricardo Lorenzetti, *Teoria del Derecho Ambiental* (2008).

There is broad agreement that environmental law cannot be reduced to a simple set of decision rules that can dictate how policy makers should act in the face of uncertainty. Tarlock maintains that "for the foreseeable future, environmental law will be a law about the process of decision rather than a process of evolving decision rules." Tarlock, supra at 219-220. It will "be a messy process of adapting the contingencies and limitations of science to 'wicked' problems informed by rebuttable principles." Tarlock, supra at 253-254. Continued controversy over environmental policy seems a given, even as the environmental law field has matured to the point where it is possible to outline fundamental principles described in this chapter. Because environmental regulation inevitably creates winners and losers, it always will provide ample incentive for pushback by regulatory targets. While Professor Huffman assures us that "[e]nvironmental law is here to stay," he foresees growing tensions between decentralization and internationalization, the ascendance of market mechanisms, and the rise of "unexpected political alliances," fueled in part by the environmental justice movement. James L. Huffman, The Past and Future of Environmental Law, 30 Envtl. L. 23 (2000). Professor Lazarus questions "whether environmental law can maintain the passion and commitment needed to rebuff the never-ending efforts to make it more responsive to the concerns of the here and now at the expense of those in seemingly distant places and future times." Lazarus, supra at 254.

Environmental law today is a complex combination of common law, legislation, regulations, international agreements, and even quasi-public/quasi-private initiatives. After centuries of wrestling with environmental conflicts, the common law now has been supplemented, and in some cases supplanted, by regulatory statutes that declare broad environmental goals while delegating to administrative agencies responsibility for developing specific policies to achieve them. Despite the ascendance of regulatory legislation, understanding of the common law roots of environmental law remains important for several reasons. The common law articulates foundational principles that have shaped the development of regulatory programs and it retains considerable vitality as a safety net when unregulated activities cause environmental harm. Common law notions also retain considerable influence, for better or worse, on courts reviewing environmental regulations and efforts to enforce compliance with them.

## 1. Common Law Roots

Prior to the explosion of environmental legislation in the 1970s, the common law was the legal system's primary vehicle for responding to environmental problems. For centuries common law courts had wrestled with what is perhaps the quintessential question of environmental law: how to harmonize conflicts that inevitably occur when human activity interferes with the interests of others in the quality of their physical surroundings. The common law relied largely on nuisance law doctrines to resolve environmental controversies, although conduct that resulted in a physical invasion of property could be addressed as a trespass. Nuisance law is designed to protect against invasions of interests in the use and enjoyment of land, while trespass protects against invasions of interests in the exclusive possession of land.

A leading treatise's declaration that nuisance law is an "impenetrable jungle," W. Prosser, Handbook of the Law of Torts §86, at 571 (4th ed. 1971), no doubt reflects, in some respects, the difficulties courts face in attempting to harmonize the competing interests at stake in environmental controversies. The history of nuisance law illustrates the tension between competing perspectives on environmental problems that can be characterized as "moral outrage" and "cool analysis." The early common law of nuisance held actors strictly liable when their actions interfered with property rights held by others. This common law version of moral outrage focused largely on whether certain interests had been invaded, not on the utility of the conduct that produced the invasion. As the Industrial Revolution intensified environmental conflicts, the common law more frequently employed balancing approaches, reflecting the cool analysis perspective, that considered not only the nature of the interference with property rights but also the nature and utility of the conduct that generated the interference.

While applicable to related problems, private and public nuisance actions have distinct legal roots. Private nuisance actions focus on invasions of interests in the private use and enjoyment of land. Public nuisances were common law crimes that involved offenses against the state arising from actions that interfered with public property (e.g., obstruction of the king's highway, encroachment on the royal domain) or that endangered the health or property of large numbers of people. Actions to abate private nuisances could be brought by private parties damaged by them. Public nuisances were subject to abatement actions by governmental authorities or by private parties who suffered special injury.

## A.   Private Nuisance

Non-trespassory invasions of another's interest in the private use and enjoyment of land are actionable as *private nuisances*. Unlike intentional trespass, where liability attaches even in the absence of a showing of harm, private nuisance liability requires a showing of significant harm. Moreover, the interference with property rights must be intentional and unreasonable or actionable under rules imposing strict liability on those engaging in abnormally dangerous activities as in Fletcher v. Rylands, L.R. 3 H.L. 330 (1868). As the Restatement of Torts explains, these requirements reflect a recognition that some conflicts are inevitable in a modern society:

> Life in organized society, and especially in populous communities, involves an unavoidable clash of individual interests. Practically all human activities unless carried on in a wilderness, interfere to some extent with others or involve some risk of interference, and these interferences range from the mere trifling annoyances to serious harms. It is an obvious truth that each individual in a community must put up with a certain amount of risk in order that all may get together. The very existence of an organized society depends upon the principle of "give and take, live and let live," and therefore the law of torts does not attempt to impose liability or shift the loss in every case where one person's conduct has some detrimental effect on another. Liability is imposed only in those cases where the harm or risk to one is greater than he ought to be required to bear under the circumstances at least without compensation. [Restatement of Torts (Second) §822 comment g (1978).]

Nuisance law has long wrestled with the difficult question of how to determine the level of harm or risk that requires compensation.

Actions for private nuisance evolved from the ancient assize of nuisance, which was designed to secure the free enjoyment of property. In the early fifteenth century the assize of nuisance was displaced by an action on the case for nuisance. While procedurally simpler than the assize, actions on the case provided only a damages remedy. Suits in equity were necessary in order to obtain injunctions ordering the abatement of private nuisances; such actions were rarely brought prior to the mid-nineteenth century.

An influential early case in the development of nuisance law was a seventeenth-century decision involving a pig sty built adjacent to William Aldred's property. In Aldred's Case, 77 Eng. Rep. 816 (1611), the pig sty was held to be a private nuisance because the wretched stench that it generated interfered with Aldred's enjoyment of his property. While the decision did not imply that all unpleasant odors emanating from the property of others were actionable, it established that if a non-trespassory invasion of property rights was sufficiently great, air pollution was actionable as a private nuisance. As Lord Holt explained in declaring the failure to repair a wall separating a privy from a neighbor's property to be a nuisance, "every man must so use his own as not to damnify another." Tenant v. Goldwin, 92 Eng. Rep. 222 (1702). This principle—that no one has the right to use their property in a manner that causes harm to another—has come to be known as the "*sic utere*" principle because it is derived from a Roman law maxim ("*sic utere tuo ut alienum non laedas*").

Early nuisance law performed a kind of zoning function by initially encouraging noxious activities to move away from populated areas. As the Industrial Revolution progressed, environmental insults became more difficult to avoid simply by relocating noxious activities. This created a tension between common law notions of strict liability and approaches that would balance the value of activities that generated pollution against the rights of victims. The clearest example of this tension is the 1858 decision of the Court of Common Pleas in Hole v. Barlow, 4 C.B.N.S. 334 (1858). Citing fears that nuisance actions could bring industry to a halt in England's great manufacturing towns, the court refused to hold a brickmaking operation liable as a private nuisance despite the pollution it produced. The court upheld a jury instruction that "no action lies for the use, the reasonable use, of a lawful trade in a convenient and proper place even though some one may suffer annoyance from its being carried on." While this sharp departure from precedent threatened to eviscerate private nuisance doctrine, it was soon overruled. The decision in Bamford v. Turnley, 122 Eng. Rep. 27 (1862), returned to the strict liability premise that private property may not be used to cause harm to another. The court held that pollution from a brick kiln erected by a defendant while constructing a house was actionable as a nuisance. The court rejected the defendant's argument that operation of the brick kiln was justified because of its convenience for the defendant. But it left open the prospect that pollution caused by factories might not be held to a similarly strict standard.

While not deviating from the black-letter principle of *Aldred's Case*, the common law gradually tempered private nuisance doctrines by increasing the severity of harm required and by adjusting notions of reasonableness. As industrialization changed the conditions of urban environments, courts expected individuals to become more tolerant of discomfort produced by industrial activity. To qualify as a private nuisance, the degree of interference with a plaintiff's "comfortable and convenient enjoyment" of land had to be substantial. Because the standards of substantiality and reasonableness could vary with the location and circumstances of the pollution, nuisance law became a kind of zoning device. As Lord Thesiger explained in Sturges v. Bridgman, L.R. 11 Ch. D. 852 (1879): "What would be a nuisance in Belgrave Square would not necessarily be one in Bermondsey." Judges observed that plaintiffs were not entitled to pollution-free air, but rather to "air not rendered to an important degree less compatible, or at least not rendered incompatible, with the physical comfort of human existence." Walter v. Selfe, 4 De G. & Sm. 315, 322 (1851).

In St. Helens Smelting Co. v. Tipping, 11 H.L.C. 642 (1865), the owner of a large estate one and one-half miles from a copper smelter alleged that the smelter's emissions had damaged his trees, crops, and animals and caused him substantial personal discomfort. The area around the smelter had been singled out in a report by the Lords Select Committee on Noxious Vapors in 1863 as a "scene of desolation" caused by pollution from heavy industry. The report had stated that "[f]arms recently well-wooded, and with hedges in good condition, have now neither tree nor hedge left alive; whole fields of corn are destroyed in a single night, especially when the vapours fall upon them while in bloom; orchards and gardens, . . . have not a fruit tree left alive. . . ." Brenner, Nuisance Law and the Industrial Revolution, 3 J. Legal Stud. 403, 416 (1974). The court rejected the company's argument that smelting may be carried on with impunity if the smelter is in a suitable location. As the lord chancellor explained: "The word 'suitable' unquestionably cannot carry with it this consequence, that a trade may be carried on in a particular locality, the consequence of which trade may be injury and destruction to the neighboring property." The court held the company liable only for damage to the property that could be shown "visibly to diminish [its] value," and not for mere personal discomfort that the pollution may have caused Tipping.

American courts followed the English common law's rejection of the notion, reflected in *Hole v. Barlow*, that activities causing substantial harm can be tolerated if they are conducted in a lawful and convenient place. Like the British courts, many American courts rejected the "coming to the nuisance" doctrine, which would have barred recovery to victims who complained about conditions that existed prior to their moving into an area. Relying on the principle that any unreasonable use of property to the injury of others is a nuisance, the Maryland Court of Appeals in 1890 explained its rejection of balancing approaches in the following terms:

> The law, in cases of this kind, will not undertake to balance the conveniences, or estimate the difference between the injury sustained by the plaintiff and the loss that may result to the defendant from having its trade and business, as now carried on, found to be a nuisance. No one has a right to erect works which are a nuisance to a neighboring owner, and then say he has expended large sums of money in the erection of his works, while the neighboring property is comparatively of little value. The neighboring owner is entitled to the reasonable and comfortable enjoyment of his property, and, if his rights in this respect are invaded, he is entitled to the protection of the law, let the consequences be what they may. [Susquehanna Fertilizer Co. v. Malone, 73 Md. 268, 20 A. 900, 902 (1890).]

Thus, Maryland's highest court upheld a judgment that noxious vapors from a large fertilizer factory that damaged the health and property of a neighboring family were actionable as a nuisance, even though several other fertilizer plants were located in the area.

This did not mean that U.S. courts would issue injunctions to shut down nuisances caused by economically important activities, particularly if they could afford to compensate their victims. In determining what relief to award, American courts generally were more inclined to balance environmental damage against the value of polluting activities than English courts. This has been interpreted by some legal historians as reflecting the American legal system's efforts to promote industral growth in the nineteenth century, L. Friedman, A History of American Law (1973); M. Horwitz, The Transformation of American Law, 1780-1860 (1977), though others have found a more mixed picture. Schwartz, Tort Law and the Economy in Nineteenth-Century America: A Reinterpretation, 90 Yale L.J. 1717 (1981). In any event, it is clear that courts increasingly were confronted by conflicts caused by the environmental impact of industrial activity.

In a society that encouraged industrial growth, many judges were reluctant to award injunctions against private nuisances if they involved activities that had considerable economic value. Despite the strong language used by the Maryland Court of Appeals in its *Susquehanna Fertilizer* decision, the court only awarded damages to the plaintiffs, rather than granting injunctive relief. The same pattern is reflected in the decision below. The case arose from a series of lawsuits brought by landowners who lived in the vicinity of two copper smelters located in Ducktown, Tennessee, near the Georgia-Tennessee border. Copper had been discovered near Ducktown in 1843 by a prospector disappointed in the search for gold. Copper mines were developed in the early 1850s, and the area thrived for a time. An economic downturn and the absence of a rail link for transporting the ore caused the mines to close in 1879. After the bankruptcy of the Union Consolidated Mining Company, thousands abandoned Ducktown, leaving it a virtual ghost town. A remarkable engineering feat permitted construction of a railroad spur to Ducktown, and in 1891, the Ducktown Sulphur, Copper & Iron Company, a British corporation, purchased the assets of Union and reopened the mines. In 1893 and 1894, it opened copper smelters. In 1899, a group of New York investors formed the Tennessee Copper Company which began smelting copper in the Ducktown area in 1901. Charging that the smelters were private nuisances, nearby landowners filed three lawsuits against the companies seeking damages and an injunction to stop pollution from the smelters. In each case, the court of chancery appeals had directed that operation of the smelters be enjoined, reversing the trial court's refusal to issue an injunction. Appeals were then heard by the Tennessee Supreme Court.

## Madison v. Ducktown Sulphur, Copper & Iron Co.

113 Tenn. 331, 83 S.W. 658 (1904)

MR. JUSTICE NEIL delivered the opinion of the Court.

The bills are all based on the ground of nuisance, in that the two companies, in the operation of their plants at and near Ducktown, in Polk county, in the course of reducing copper ore, cause large volumes of smoke to issue from their roast piles, which smoke descends upon the surrounding lands, and injures trees and crops, and renders the homes of complainants less comfortable and their lands less profitable than before. The purpose of all the bills is to enjoin the further operation of these plants. . . .

Ducktown is in a basin of the mountains of Polk county, in this State, not far from the State line of the States of Georgia and North Carolina. This basin is six or eight miles wide. The complainants are the owners of small farms situated in the mountains around Ducktown.

The method used by the defendants in reducing their copper ores is to place the green ore, broken up, on layers of wood, making large open-air piles, called "roast piles," and these roast piles are ignited for the purpose of expelling from the ore certain foreign matters called "sulphurets." In burning, these roast piles emit large volumes of smoke. This smoke, rising in the air, is carried off by air currents around and over adjoining land. . . .

The general effect produced by the smoke upon the possessions and families of the complainants is as follows, viz.:

Their timber and crop interests have been badly injured, and they have been annoyed and discommoded by the smoke so that the complainants are prevented from using and enjoying their farms and homes as they did prior to the inauguration of these enterprises. The smoke makes it impossible for the owners of farms within the area of the smoke zone to subsist their families thereon with the degree of comfort they enjoyed before. They cannot raise and harvest their customary crops, and their timber is largely destroyed. . . .

The court of chancery appeals finds that the defendants are conducting and have been conducting their business in a lawful way, without any purpose or desire to injure any of the complainants; that they have been and are pursuing the only known method by which these plants can be operated and their business successfully carried on; that the open-air roast-heap is the only method known to the business or to science by means of which copper ore of the character mined by the defendants can be reduced; that the defendants have made every effort to get rid of the smoke and noxious vapors, one of the defendants having spent $200,000 in experiments to this end, but without result.

It is to be inferred from the description of the locality that there is no place more remote to which the operations referred to could be transferred.

It is found, in substance, that, if the injunctive relief sought be granted, the defendants will be compelled to stop operations and their property will become practically worthless, the immense business conducted by them will cease, and they will be compelled to withdraw from the State. It is a necessary deduction from the foregoing that a great and increasing industry in the State will be destroyed, and all of the valuable copper properties of the State become worthless. . . .

While there can be no doubt that the facts stated make out a case of nuisance, for which the complainants in actions at law would be entitled to recover damages, yet the remedy in equity is not a matter of course. Not only must the bill state a proper case, but the right must be clear, and the injury must be clearly established, as in doubtful cases the party will be turned over to his legal remedy; and, if there is a reasonable doubt as to the cause of the injury, the benefit of the doubt will be given to the defendant, if his trade is a lawful one, and the injury is not the necessary and natural consequence of the act; and, if the injury can be adequately compensated at law by a judgment for damages, equity will not interfere. . . .

A judgment for damages in this class of cases is a matter of absolute right, where injury is shown. A decree for an injunction is a matter of sound legal discretion, to be granted or withheld as that discretion shall dictate, after a full and careful consideration of every element appertaining to the injury. . . .

The question now to be considered is, what is the proper exercise of discretion, under the facts appearing in the present case? Shall the complainants be granted, in the way of damages, the full measure of relief to which their injuries entitle them, or shall we go further, and grant their request to blot out two great mining and manufacturing enterprises, destroy half of the taxable values of a county, and drive more than 10,000 people from their homes? We think there can be no doubt as to what the true answer to this question should be.

In order to protect by injunction several small tracts of land, aggregating in value less than $1,000, we are asked to destroy other property worth nearly $2,000,000, and wreck two great mining and manufacturing enterprises, that are engaged in work of very great importance, not only to their owners, but to the State, and to the whole country as well, to depopulate a large town, and deprive thousands of working people of their homes and livelihood, and scatter them broadcast. The result would be practically a confiscation of the property of the defendants for the benefit of the complainants—an appropriation without compensation. The defendants cannot reduce their ores in a manner different from that they are now employing, and there is no more remote place to which they can remove. The decree asked for would deprive them of all of their rights. We appreciate the argument based on the fact that the homes of the complainants who live on the small tracts of land referred to are not so comfortable and useful to their owners as they were before they were affected by the smoke complained of, and we are deeply sensible of the truth of the proposition that no man is entitled to any more rights than another on the ground that he has or owns more property than that other. But in a case of conflicting rights, where neither party can enjoy his own without in some measure restricting the liberty of the other in the use of property, the law must make the best arrangement it can between the contending parties, with a view to preserving to each one the largest measure of liberty possible under the circumstances. We see no escape from the conclusion in the present case that the only proper decree is to allow the complainants a reference for the ascertainment of damages, and that the injunction must be denied to them. . . .

## NOTES AND QUESTIONS

1. Despite the damage caused by the smelters, the Tennessee Supreme Court in *Madison* refused to issue an injunction to control their harmful emissions because they had considerable economic value to the community. Is this tantamount to allowing the smelters to condemn the plaintiffs' property? By refusing to stop pollution that affects less valuable properties is the court contributing to environmental justice problems? Recall the statement by Lord Thesiger in Sturges v. Bridgman, L.R. 11 Ch. D. 852 (1879): "What would be a nuisance in Belgrave

Square would not necessarily be one in Bermondsey." Belgrave Square was (and is) one of the wealthiest areas in London where many embassies are located, while Bermondsey has long been a poorer neighborhood of industrial activity. Does this raise environmental justice problems?

2. The Tennessee Supreme Court's decision in *Madison* demonstrates that landowners at least could recover damages in private nuisance actions when pollution caused sufficient harm to their property. In *Madison*, there was virtually no discussion of the issue that has proved to be the most substantial obstacle to common law recovery in modern environmental cases today: proof of causal injury. Why was the causation issue not litigated more vigorously by the defendants in *Madison*?

3. While private nuisance actions offered some prospect of redress for pollution damage, their promise had been largely illusory at the time of the *Madison* litigation, particularly when the damage was caused by substantial industrial establishments. A study of private nuisance actions in late nineteenth-century England concluded that the law simply "was not being applied in industrial towns." Brenner, Nuisance Law and the Industrial Revolution, 3 J. Legal Stud. 403, 419 (1974). Several factors diminished the practical value of nuisance law. Recovery generally was only permitted for actual, physical damage to property that caused a decline in its market value. Property values generally increased with industrialization even in contaminated areas, making recovery difficult. Lawsuits were prohibitively expensive for the average British worker. Environmental conditions in most factory towns were so bad that the requirement that nuisances be evaluated in light of the "state of the neighborhood" actually "militated against the recognition by the common law of minimum standards of comfort and health." Id. at 420. Fearful of discouraging industrialization, courts held factories liable only in rare cases where the pollution was so devastating that it produced a "scene of desolation" for miles around, as in *Tipping's Case*. Id. at 416. Moreover, many of the largest polluters were public or quasi-public enterprises that were protected from liability because their actions were authorized by statute.

4. There is evidence that nuisance actions against polluting facilities were much more common in the United States than in Britain in the late nineteenth and early twentieth centuries. In addition to the *Madison* litigation, dozens of other private nuisance actions were filed against the Ducktown smelters during this period. While courts in the United States often awarded damages, instead of issuing injunctions to shut down polluting facilities, private parties occasionally succeeded in shutting down polluters in cases where environmental damage was quite severe. See, e.g., McClung v. North Bend Coal & Coke Co., 1 Ohio Dec. 187 (C.P. Hamilton 1892), aff'd, 9 Ohio C.C. 259 (1895) (injunction obtained against coking operations that destroyed more than 200 evergreen trees and impaired the health of persons on the ancestral estate of President William Henry Harrison).

5. The early common law did not provide much protection against pollution of groundwater. Only in the rare cases where landowners could prove that a specific source of pollution caused groundwater to reach their land in a polluted condition were nuisance principles applied. Ballard v. Tomlinson, 29 Ch. D. 115 (1885) (common law liability for sewage discharged into well that resulted in pollution of the well of another). For similar reasons, the common law has not proved adequate for redressing nonpoint source pollution. See Columbia Avenue Saving Fund Co.

v. Prison Commission of Georgia, 92 F. 801 (W.D. Ga. 1899) and cases cited therein (refusing to enjoin prison construction because the damage it would cause to nearby streams would be the product of nonpoint source pollution); United States v. Brazoria County Drainage District No. 3, 2 F.2d 861 (S.D. Tex. 1925) (drainage ditch that contributed to erosion not a common law nuisance).

6.  The Restatement of Torts (Second) defines private nuisance as "a non-trespassory invasion of another's interest in the private use and enjoyment of land." Restatement of Torts (Second) §821D (1978). Only those who have property rights and privileges with respect to the use and enjoyment of the land may recover, and only if the harm they suffer is significant. Why does nuisance law require a showing of significant harm, while trespass law does not? The Restatement provides that to constitute a private nuisance the invasion of property rights must be either "intentional and unreasonable; or unintentional and otherwise actionable under the rules governing liability for negligent, reckless or ultrahazardous conduct." §822. Why do intentional invasions of property rights that cause significant harm have to be unreasonable in order to be actionable as a private nuisance?

7.  The traditional common law requirement for a private nuisance is a substantial and unreasonable interference with the private use and enjoyment of land. Is a decline in property values caused by proximity to a polluted site actionable at common law even if there is no proof that the pollution has seeped onto plaintiffs' property? In Adkins v. Thomas Solvent Company, 487 N.W.2d 715 (Mich. 1992), the Michigan Supreme Court held that 22 property owners who lived near a contaminated site could not recover for the diminution of their property values because no contaminants actually had migrated to their property and a hydrogeological barrier precluded such migration in the future. The court reasoned that

> [i]f any property owner in the vicinity of the numerous hazardous-waste sites that have been identified can advance a claim seeking damages when unfounded public fears of exposure cause property depreciation, the ultimate effect might be a reordering of the polluter's resources for the benefit of persons who have suffered no cognizable harm at the expense of those claimants who have been subjected to a substantial and unreasonable interference in the use and enjoyment of property. [Id. at 727.]

Two dissenting Justices argued that depreciation of property values can constitute an actionable interference with the use and enjoyment of property when it can be shown to be the normal consequence of a defendant's conduct. Cf. Livingston v. Jefferson County Board of Equalization, 640 N.W.2d 426, 10 Neb. App. 934 (2002) (proximity to a confined animal feed operation (CAFO) should be considered when assessing the value of property for tax purposes).

8.  When pollutants do physically invade the property of another, liability also may be premised on a theory of trespass. In Martin v. Reynolds Metals Co., 221 Or. 86, 342 P.2d 790 (Or. 1959), the Oregon Supreme Court affirmed an award of $91,500 in damages to farmland due to fluoride emissions from a nearby aluminum plant that settled on the land and poisoned cattle. The court held that the intrusion of fluoride particles constituted a trespass because the particles invaded the property owner's interest in exclusive possession. In *Martin*, the plaintiffs opted to pursue a trespass theory because the statute of limitations for trespass was more

favorable than that applicable in nuisance actions. See also Borland v. Sanders Lead Co., 369 So. 2d 523 (Ala. 1979) (lead pollution constituting a trespass) and Bradley v. American Smelting & Refining Co., 104 Wash. 2d 677, 709 P.2d 782 (1985) (allowing a trespass claim based on the deposit of airborne pollutants from a copper smelter but only where "actual and substantial damage" can be shown).

9. In defining what constitutes an intentional invasion of property rights, the Restatement focuses on the foreseeability of harm. For certain kinds of activities that result in environmental harm, this may have important consequences. For example, the Restatement deems pollution of groundwater to be far less foreseeable than surface water pollution. It notes that invasions of property rights that result from discharges to lakes, streams, and surface waters ordinarily should be considered intentional, because such discharges are substantially certain to cause such an invasion, particularly if the pollution is continued for any length of time. However, invasions resulting from the pollution of groundwater "are ordinarily not intentional since the course of such waters is usually unknown and the actor can thus foresee no more than a risk of harm in most cases." Restatement of Torts (Second), §832 comment f.

10. While groundwater contamination is more readily foreseeable than in the past, the foreseeability requirement can be a formidable obstacle to using the common law to recover for contamination caused by past dumping practices. In Cambridge Water v. Eastern Counties Leather, 1 All ER H.L. 53 (1994), a British leather company's repeated spillage of perchloroethene (PCE) over a period of several decades resulted in contamination of an aquifer used by Cambridge Water to supply drinking water. Due to the contamination, the water company had to discontinue use of the aquifer and develop an alternative water supply. The water company sued and was awarded a judgment of approximately £1 million by a court of appeal. The court held the leather company strictly liable for the damage it had caused. Citing Ballard v. Tomlinson, 29 Ch. D. 115 (1885), the court deemed it unimportant whether the leather company could foresee that its accidental spillages would cause groundwater contamination in violation of modern water quality standards. The House of Lords then allowed an appeal and reversed the court of appeal's decision. After noting that *Ballard v. Tomlinson* involved harm that was foreseeable (sewage discharged into a well polluted another well), Lord Goff concluded that "foreseeability of harm is indeed a prerequisite of the recovery of damages in private nuisance, as in the case of public nuisance." Id. at 72. He then considered whether the leather company could be held liable under the rule in Rylands v. Fletcher, 3 H.L. 330 (1868), imposing strict liability for harm caused by abnormally dangerous activities. However, he found that "foreseeability of damage of the relevant type should be regarded as a prerequisite of liability in damages under the rule" in *Rylands. Cambridge Water*, at 76. Finding that the leather company could not reasonably have foreseen the damage that it caused the water company, Lord Goff concluded that the leather company could not be held liable. Although Cambridge Water argued that the leather company should at least be held liable for releases of PCE that continued after the discovery of the aquifer contamination, Lord Goff rejected this argument, noting that the PCE that actually had reached the groundwater probably had been released at a time when the contamination was not foreseeable.

### Harmonizing Conflicting Interests: To Balance or Not to Balance in Fashioning Remedies for Nuisances?

The early common law assessed nuisance claims by focusing almost exclusively on the nature of the interference pollution caused to the property rights of its victims. Yet defendants continued to press courts to balance the hardship of pollution abatement against the damage to victims when considering requests for equitable relief. By 1927, this debate had reached the point where Judge Learned Hand described the state of nuisance law as one of "great confusion" with U.S. courts split over whether or not to balance comparative hardships between polluters and victims. Smith v. Staso Milling Co., 18 F.2d 736 (2d Cir. 1927). In *Staso Milling*, Judge Hand explained why he believed that the balancing approach was reasonable, particularly when courts were considering whether to grant injunctions against private nuisances:

> The very right on which the injured party stands in such cases is a quantitative compromise between two conflicting interests. What may be an entirely tolerable adjustment, when the result is only to award damages for the injury done, may become no better than a means of extortion if the result is absolutely to curtail the defendant's enjoyment of his land. Even though the defendant has no power to condemn, at times it may be proper to require of him no more than to make good the whole injury once and for all. [Id. at 738.]

Yet a balancing approach does not necessarily preclude injunctions against nuisances. In *Staso Milling*, Judge Hand affirmed an injunction barring a slate processing mill from polluting a stream. Even though construction of the plant had altered "the balance of convenience" in a manner that might normally preclude an injunction, Hand noted that prior to building the plant the plant's owners specifically had promised nearby property owners that it would not pollute the stream. Noting that no similar promise had been made with respect to air pollution, Hand indicated that an injunction barring the plant from releasing dust could be modified if the plant could demonstrate that no better technology was available for controlling emissions of dust.

The doctrine of anticipatory nuisance allows plaintiffs who can persuade a court that an activity about to be undertaken would constitute a nuisance to obtain an injunction blocking the activity. While it can be very difficult to prove a nuisance *ex ante*, filing such an action can generate the kind of assurances the *Staso Milling* court relied upon to enjoin water pollution in that case.

While many American courts have enthusiastically embraced the balancing approach, some tension between strict liability and balancing has persisted in private nuisance cases. The evolution of the Restatement of Torts' position illustrates this tension. The First Restatement adopted an explicit balancing approach for determining whether an interference with property rights was unreasonable. Section 826 of the First Restatement provided that intentional invasions of another's interest in the use or enjoyment of land are unreasonable unless the utility of the actor's conduct outweighs the gravity of the harm. This encouraged courts to balance the social value of a polluting activity against the damage it caused. After criticism of the First Restatement's formulation, the Second Restatement added an alternative criterion of unreasonableness in section 826(b). It states that an intentional invasion is unreasonable if *either* the gravity of the harm outweighs the utility of the actor's conduct *or* "the harm caused by the conduct is serious and the financial burden of compensating for this and similar harm to others would not make the continuation of the conduct not feasible." This has supplemented what appeared to be a kind of risk-benefit calculus of reasonableness with an alternative test focusing on the financial feasibility of damages. A further embellishment was added by section 829 of the Second Restatement. It states that even in cases where compensation is beyond the financial capacity of an enterprise, an invasion should be deemed unreasonable if the harm it causes "is severe and greater than the other should be required to bear without compensation." As a result, the Second Restatement's definition of unreasonableness now embraces notions of fairness or moral outrage as well as feasibility and risk-benefit balancing. Each of these three notions is represented in current regulatory approaches for controlling pollution, as we will see in subsequent chapters.

Economists emphasize that because environmental problems involve interactions between polluters and victims, efficient solutions to nuisance problems involve remedies that minimize the joint costs or maximize the joint value of the interacting activities. If only the polluters determine the extent of harm, then a rule holding polluters strictly liable for the damages they cause is efficient because it will induce them to take the efficient amount of care while ensuring that the prices of their goods reflect their full social costs. However, if the victim's behavior can affect the extent of damage (e.g., by moving away or by investing in measures that shield her from the effects of pollution), economists argue that strict liability is only efficient if a defense of contributory negligence is recognized, because victims otherwise will have no incentive to take actions that can avoid damage more cheaply. These arguments are explained in clear and nontechnical terms for the noneconomist in A.M. Polinsky, An Introduction to Law and Economics 92-93 (1983).

William Landes and Judge Richard Posner argue that the common law is best understood as an attempt by judges to promote efficient resource allocation. They argue that efficiency dictates that liability for private nuisances be imposed only "where the nuisance causes substantial damage that exceeds the cost of eliminating it and where, moreover, the defendant (injurer) can eliminate the nuisance at a lower cost than the plaintiff (victim)." W. Landes & R. Posner, The Economic Structure of Tort Law 49 (1987). Landes and Posner conclude that nuisance law generally, but not always, conforms to this principle, particularly now that courts frequently balance the value of competing land uses, the suitability of the conduct to the character of the locality, and the relative costs of avoiding harm. They note that the requirement that harm be substantial serves to screen out cases in which damage is too small to warrant resort to the legal system for abating the nuisance. Id. Landes and Posner criticize as inefficient the alternative test of unreasonableness articulated in section 826(b) of the Second Restatement, but they note that few American courts have adopted it.

As noted in Chapter 1, the Coase Theorem states that if bargaining is costless and cooperative then any choice of an entitlement or remedy will lead to an efficient outcome. This observation is premised on the notion that parties can engage in exchanges that will lead to efficient outcomes. Ours, however, is not a world of zero transaction costs; imperfect information and strategic behavior make it difficult to reach efficient outcomes. Estimates of the damages caused by pollution, the benefits of polluting activity, and the costs of control alternatives are fraught with uncertainty. Polluters and their victims can gain strategic advantages by misrepresenting these parameters or by providing estimates that fall at different ends of the range of uncertainty. Moreover, as Judge Hand noted in *Staso Milling*, if victims always are entitled to injunctions against pollution they could use this entitlement as "a means of extortion" to hold out for more than the efficient level of compensation. In theory the common law offers a flexible, case-by-case assessment of liability that could permit courts to overcome some of the problems of strategic behavior. Economists argue that the common law can promote efficient outcomes by placing liability on the party that is the cheapest cost avoider. See Michelman, Pollution as a Tort: A Non-Accidental Perspective on Calabresi's Costs, 80 Yale L.J. 647 (1971). This approach, however, may require courts to obtain accurate estimates of the damages and benefits of polluting activities, information that is not always readily available. For suggestions concerning how courts can minimize the impact of such uncertainty, see A.M. Polinsky, An Introduction to Law and Economics 24 (1983).

One approach for coping with imperfect information is for courts to structure flexible remedies that take advantage of market forces to determine which party can control pollution most efficiently. See Calabresi & Melamed, Property Rules, Liability Rules and Inalienability: One View of the Cathedral, 85 Harv. L. Rev. 1089 (1972); Rabin, Nuisance Law: Rethinking Fundamental Assumptions, 63 Va. L. Rev. 1209 (1977). The conditional injunction approach has been recommended on these grounds. It was used by the New York Court of Appeals in the famous decision of Boomer v. Atlantic Cement Co., 26 N.Y.2d 219, 257 N.E.2d 870 (1970). The court in *Boomer* issued a conditional injunction barring the operation of a cement plant whose air emissions had caused substantial damage to nearby property until the plant paid surrounding residents the full value of their permanent damages if the plant continued operation. The theory behind this approach was that the plant would opt to continue operations only if the operations had more economic value than the cost of the damage they produced. Further background information on the *Boomer* case can be found in Daniel A. Farber, The Story of *Boomer*: Pollution and the Common Law in Environmental Law Stories 7 (R. Lazarus & O. Houck eds., 2005). Farber reports that the plaintiff landowners ultimately recovered substantially more in damages than would have been expected from the appellate decision and that the plant remains the second largest cement facility in the United States. Id. at 21, 25.

The notion that rights and liabilities should be allocated in a manner that promotes efficiency can be controversial because of its distributional consequences. Viewed from the moral outrage perspective, the Tennessee Supreme Court's refusal to enjoin the Ducktown smelter's emissions and the New York court's decision to permit the cement plant in *Boomer* to purchase the right to continue operation may seem outrageous to the victims of the pollution, even though they ultimately may receive damages. After all, as Judge Hand noted in *Staso Milling*, the polluter "has no power to condemn" the victim's property, but a damage award that allows the pollution to continue produces virtually the same result. Despite courts' concern for achieving efficient outcomes, distributional concerns also play a significant role in shaping environmental policy, as we will see throughout this casebook.

### Private Nuisance Actions Against Industrial Hog Farms

As discussed above, odors from a pig sty more than four centuries ago provoked the private nuisance litigation that produced the landmark decision in *Aldred's Case*. Today massive concentrated animal feeding operations (CAFOs) are the modern-day equivalent of the Ducktown smelter whose uncontrolled pollution spawned nuisance litigation a century ago. Between 1989 and 1995 large agribusinesses and their contractors built 700 CAFOs holding 8.2 million pigs in poor North Carolina counties with predominately Black populations. The pigs "produced twice as much manure as the population of New York City without a sewage treatment plant in sight." D. Lee Miller & Ryke Longest, Reconciling Environmental Justice with Climate Change Mitigation: A Case Study of NC Swine CAFOs, 21 Vt. J. Envtl. L. 523, 524 (2020). Using the lagoon and spray field system, the hog waste was "flushed from containment barns into uncovered and unlined earthen pits" the effluent from which was sprayed on nearby croplands. The CAFOs caused "air pollution, noxious odors, groundwater contamination, surface water pollution," while putting independent family farms out of business. Id. at 526. Studies have documented that people who live near these CAFOs suffered from "higher rates of all-cause mortality, infant mortality, mortality from anemia, kidney disease, tuberculosis, septicemia, and low birth weight." Id. at 525.

In 1997 the North Carolina Legislature imposed a moratorium on new hog waste lagoons, and it added permitting and inspection requirements that ultimately proved to be ineffectual. In 2000 Smithfield Foods, the world's largest pork producer, signed an agreement with the attorney general of North Carolina to fund research on new environmentally superior waste treatment technologies (ESTs) to "substantially eliminate" discharges, emissions, and odors from animal waste. Smithfield agreed that its growers would install the technology within three years of it being proved to be "technically, operationally, and economically feasible." Although an EST was developed, the swine companies refused to adopt it, claiming that any technology that was more expensive was not economically feasible. With the nuisance unabated, in 2014 more than 500 neighbors of the North Carolina swine CAFOs filed private nuisance actions in federal court using diversity jurisdiction against Smithfield and its livestock production division Murphy-Brown, Virginia corporations wholly owned by WH Group, a Chinese company. A federal jury awarded both compensatory and punitive damages to the plaintiffs. On appeal, the Fourth Circuit reached the following decision, which featured an unusually candid concurring opinion from Judge Wilkinson.

## McKiver v. Murphy-Brown LLC

980 F.3d 937 (4th Cir. 2020)

Before WILKINSON, AGEE and THACKER, Circuit Judges.

THACKER, Circuit Judge:

Murphy-Brown, LLC ("Appellant") challenges a jury verdict against it awarding compensatory and punitive damages to neighbors of its hog production facilities. Those neighbors, residents of rural Bladen County, North Carolina, sought relief under state nuisance law from odors, pests, and noises they attribute to farming practices Appellant implemented at an industrial-scale hog feeding farm. Having heard evidence of those harms and Appellant's role in creating them, a jury returned a verdict in favor of the neighbors, to the tune of $75,000 in compensatory damages per plaintiff, along with a total of $5 million in punitive damages, which was subsequently reduced to $2.5 million due to North Carolina's punitive damages cap. . . .

### APPELLANT'S POLICIES

Pursuant to North Carolina law, "[a] corporation may be subject to punitive damages based on a theory of direct liability where the corporation's acts or policies constitute the aggravating factor." . . . [A] reasonable jury here could conclude that Appellant's own policies reflected conscious and intentional disregard of the safety and wellbeing of others in the interest of protecting the company's bottom line, rendering direct liability applicable.

Here, Appellees advanced evidence that Appellant's own corporate policies—as opposed to a separate policy of Kinlaw Farms—prescribed the lagoon-and-sprayfield system, waste and carcass management, and all-hours truck traffic underlying the complaints. As a result, in contrast to vicarious liability for acts of its contractor, Appellant's liability is premised on the corporation's *own* act of maintaining a set of policies it knew perpetuated the effects of hog farming that (i) caused the state to outlaw such operations within a mile of homes, except where neighbors came to the nuisance and (ii) resulted in well-documented complaints and study results that applied to Kinlaw Farms, since the policies mandated uniform conditions across Appellant's grower sites.

### OFFICERS & MANAGERS CONDONING CONDUCT

Furthermore, the evidence demonstrates that Appellant's officers and managers had notice of the harms caused by its operations, based on studies, community meetings, and political engagement. Yet Appellant's leadership persisted in mandating the culpable practices and participated in political efforts aimed at minimizing regulation of harms known to be associated with Appellant's chosen farming methods. This evidence is sufficient to support punitive damages. . .

WILKINSON, Circuit Judge, concurring:
. . . I write separately . . . to acknowledge the full harms that the unreformed practices of hog farming are inflicting. . . .

In this case, the ancient tort of nuisance, which has long refereed disputes between neighbors, *see e.g., Tenant v. Goldwin* (1705), 92 Eng. Rep. 222, is claimed to have a very contemporary application. Plaintiffs, almost all of modest means and minorities, live in close proximity to Kinlaw Farms, the hog farm at issue in this case. They have brought suit contending that Murphy-Brown, which by virtue of contract directed Kinlaw's operations, "substantially" and "unreasonabl[y]" interfered—in a "willful and wanton" manner—with the "use and enjoyment of their property." The industry counters that such suits pose "a dire threat to hog farming" in North Carolina, and—even more urgently—"an existential threat to the livelihoods of farmers and the food security of our Nation." . . . I fully recognize the essential contributions of the pork industry in general, and of North Carolina's hog farms in particular. I am also not so naive as to imagine that hog farming could ever be an antiseptic enterprise. But the record here reveals outrageous conditions at Kinlaw Farms—conditions that, when their effects inevitably spread to neighboring households, violated homeowners' rights to the healthful enjoyment of their property. All this the jury recognized, and its verdict, once capped, was essentially a just one.

How did it come to this? What was missing from Kinlaw Farms—and from Murphy-Brown—was the recognition that treating animals better will benefit humans. What was neglected is that animal welfare and human welfare, far from advancing at cross-purposes, are actually integrally connected. The decades-long transition to concentrated animal feeding operations ("CAFOs") lays bare this connection, and the consequences of its breach, with startling clarity. Once, most hogs were raised on "smaller, pasture-based hog farms." Now, the paradigm has shifted: "large numbers of hogs, often many thousands" crowd together in each of the many cramped "confinement structures" that comprise the typical hog CAFO. The following illustrates how Kinlaw, an endpoint of this pasture-to-CAFO transition, created serious ecological risks that, when imprudently managed, bred horrible outcomes for pigs and humans alike.

The warp in the human-hog relationship, and the root of the nuisance in this suit, lay in the deplorable conditions of confinement prevailing at Kinlaw, conditions that there is no reason to suppose were unique to that facility. Confinement defined life for the over 14,000 hogs—all of which Murphy-Brown owned—that Kinlaw Farms had crammed into its twelve confinement sheds. Consistent with Kinlaw's role as a "finishing" facility, hogs arrived at around forty pounds, to be fattened to over seven times their starting weight. The one thing that never grew with the hogs, though, was the size of their indoor pens. Even though "[h]ogs grow bigger now," the pens' design has not changed a whit in twenty-five years. The sad fate of Kinlaw's hogs was, therefore, to remain in these densely packed pens from the time they arrived to the time they were shipped for slaughter, straining in vain as their increasing girth slowly but surely reduced them to almost suffocating closeness.

To manage waste under such conditions, the concrete floors of Kinlaw's sheds were partially slatted. These slats were supposed to allow the hogs' feces and urine to fall through to a gutter system below. But due to the close confinement just described, hogs were often packed too tightly to defecate over the slats. As a result, waste built up and as photos of Kinlaw's facilities show, hogs ended up covered in feces.

The waste that did make it through the slats to the gutter system was flushed four to six times a day to one of three nearby open-air "lagoons"—essentially three uncovered, 8 million-gallon cesspools. From there, the waste material was sprayed into the air, to fertilize nearby crops—a waste disposal method known as the lagoon-and-sprayfield system.

The dangers endemic to such appalling conditions always manifested first in animal suffering. Ineluctably, however, the ripples of dysfunction would reach farm workers and, at last, members of the surrounding community. To start, take the basic issue of air quality. When pigs defecated, gases accumulated in their sheds. But at certain concentrations—only possible under conditions of overcrowded, indoor confinement—these gases could become toxic, even fatal, to the hogs. To prevent its hogs from dying in their own wind, Kinlaw ventilated their sheds by opening curtains that released these noxious fumes unfiltered into the air outside.

Viewing the sheds' diminished air quality solely as a "hog problem" misses the very real hazard it represented for workers. Workers, after all, breathe the same air as the hogs they tend. Given that these gases could kill pigs, it is entirely unsurprising that "approximately 50 percent of [CAFO] workers experience one or more of the following health outcomes: bronchitis, toxic organic dust syndrome, hyper-reactive airway disease, chronic mucous membrane irritation, occupational asthma and hydrogen sulfide intoxication."

What may seem surprising, but should not, is the gaseous spiral's final arc: the air quality threat posed to Kinlaw's neighbors. Like workers, neighbors living within two miles of hog CAFOs suffer from elevated rates of respiratory problems. Nearby residents may also suffer from aggravated rates of high blood pressure, depression, and infant mortality. One study has even shown that children attending schools as far as three miles away from a hog CAFO face an increased likelihood of presenting asthma-related symptoms. . . .

. . . Up to "ten percent of pigs die in confinement most likely due to complications from their overcrowded environment and lack of individualized veterinary care." The hogs at Kinlaw faced a slightly lower, but still significant, mortality rate of around seven percent. This figure assumes that Kinlaw operated at full capacity. There is some suggestion that Kinlaw operated above capacity to account for the fact that "some [hogs] are going to die."

Dying hogs imperil human well-being in other ways. As Judge Thacker has noted, the problem lies in Kinlaw's method of storing and disposing of the numerous dead hogs. Kinlaw piled carcasses into uncovered storage containers that plaintiffs call "dead boxes." Unfortunately for Kinlaw's neighbors, exposed hog carcasses attracted buzzards and flies, which range with scant concern for property rights. A sorely unwelcome buzzard startled one neighbor's little girl so badly that she slammed a door on her foot. Other homeowners detailed their distress at finding flies in their hair and food, and suffering invasions of "more gnats than you've ever seen in your life." These unwelcome visitations were not minor inconveniences. They were hazardous to health and vectors of disease. And they originated with the mistreatment of Kinlaw's hogs.

The plentiful hog carcasses of Kinlaw Farms also posed a nuisance to neighbors when they were carted away daily in "dead trucks," which caused the worst of the odors. Other Kinlaw trucks created noise and dust ceaselessly. As part of the initial design, Murphy-Brown placed a private service road leading to Kinlaw Farms within feet of nearby homes when an alternate route would have impacted neighbors far less. Instead, neighbors suffered from trucks constantly entering and leaving Kinlaw Farms—the truck delivery schedule, set by Murphy-Brown, showed eleven deliveries between 12:30 A.M. and 5:30 A.M. during a single morning. Again, Murphy-Brown cut corners and its neighbors suffered for it.

At the risk of replaying this theme *ad nauseum*, it should be observed that these interlocking dysfunctions were characteristic not just of close confinement but of the lagoon-and-sprayfield system as well. The negative effects on animals, workers, and homeowners are here all visible in a single glance. As with any large, uncovered cesspool, it should come as no surprise that "[e]nvironmental and health concerns with the lagoon technology include emissions of ammonia, odors, pathogens, and water quality deterioration." The waste in these lagoons almost "certainly" contained "pathogenic microorganisms and bacteria," including antibiotic-resistant bacteria. When this waste material is sprayed into the air, everything around, including nearby homes, is at the mercy of the prevailing winds. While the odor potential from spraying untreated hog waste high into the air—where it then drifts toward nearby homes—is self-evident, Murphy-Brown also knew of odor complaints from neighbors of hog farms with setups similar to Kinlaw. Nevertheless, it persisted in requiring the system for Kinlaw.

Even setting dispersion aside, the existence of lagoons maintained like Kinlaw's tends to compromise local water quality. Studies have shown that many lagoons leach waste material into both surface water and groundwater. In surface water, leakage can produce toxic algae blooms inimical to local wildlife and their habitat. And waste that enters groundwater creates a health hazard, particularly for any nearby residents who drink or bathe with well water. Water quality concerns are especially pressing here because Kinlaw—like many eastern North Carolina hog facilities—sits in a floodplain. Similarly situated lagoons have overflowed during hurricanes, and even under less dramatic weather conditions, recently sprayed waste material at Kinlaw can easily flow into the nearby Cape Fear River. Needless to say, deterioration in the local water quality is a grievous blow to both animal and human welfare. Here as elsewhere, these two values are not orthogonal, but integrally connected.

At the end of all this wreckage lies an uncomfortable truth: these nuisance conditions were unlikely to have persisted for long—or even to have arisen at all—had the neighbors of Kinlaw Farms been wealthier or more politically powerful. Indeed, North Carolina's ban on building new lagoon-and-sprayfield systems arose after CAFOs threatened to expand into a General Assembly member's home district of Moore County, a popular destination for golfers and tourists. In 1997, residents of Bladen County suffered from a poverty rate almost twice that of Moore County—by 2018, the poverty rate grew to nearly three times that of Moore County. And a substantial proportion of residents near Kinlaw Farms are people of color.

It is well-established—almost to the point of judicial notice—that environmental harms are visited disproportionately upon the dispossessed—here on minority populations and poor communities. *See* Brief of the North Carolina Environmental Justice Network and the Rural Empowerment Association for Community Help (noting that "[Industrial hog operations are] disproportionately concentrated in communities of color" and "that African Americans, Latinos, and Native Americans are 1.54, 1.39, and 2.18 times (respectively) more likely than whites to live within three miles of one or more [operations]."). But whether a home borders a golf course or a dirt road, it is a castle for those who reside in it. It is where children play and grow, friends sit and visit, and a life is built. Many plaintiffs in this suit have tended their hearths for generations—one family for almost 100 years. They are exactly whom the venerable tort of nuisance ought to protect. Murphy-Brown's interference with their quiet enjoyment of their properties was unreasonable. It was willful, and it was wanton. The record fully supports the jury's finding that punitive damages were warranted.

Moreover, plaintiffs' suffering—stemming from Murphy-Brown's mistreatment of its hogs—was avoidable. The scale of industrial hog farming is no warrant to ride roughshod over the property rights of neighbors, the health of workers and community members, and the lives of the hogs themselves. In fact, not one of the above problems is insuperable. Many can be mitigated using "[s]imple management and manure handling controls." For example, facilities could decrease the number of hogs penned in each shed, install covers on lagoons to lessen air and water pollution, or implement available controls to remove pollutants from the air prior to ventilation. Moreover, "[i]f Smithfield paid for more labor, [it] may be able to keep the swine houses cleaner, which would also keep the hogs cleaner, reduce the dust, and reduce the odor." This suggestion appears particularly apt for Kinlaw, where a single employee managed all twelve hog sheds—over 14,000 hogs—largely by himself. . . .

All this and more this nuisance lawsuit has laid bare. Courts may take note when an industry has "unduly lagged in the adoption of new and available devices." While it is obviously not our job to displace corporate decision-making with our own, improvements in technology may bear relevance at trial to a company's remediation efforts and options. . . .

## NOTES AND QUESTIONS

1. While affirming the jury's compensatory damages award and the right of plaintiffs to receive punitive damages, the court held that the amount of the punitive damages award should be reconsidered. During their closing argument, plaintiffs' lawyers had emphasized the enormous size of the salaries of the executives who run the Chinese corporation that purchased Smithfield in 2007. The court viewed this as too prejudicial. After several food safety scandals had rocked China, the purchase of a major U.S. pork producer by a Chinese company was widely viewed as a way of assuring Chinese consumers that imported pork from the U.S. would meet the highest safety standards.

2. Hours after this decision was released, Smithfield announced that it had reached a settlement with the plaintiffs. The terms were not disclosed, but both sides expressed satisfaction with the result.

3. As the court notes, swine CAFOs have been disproportionately located near low-income and minority communities. In 2014 community groups in North Carolina filed an environmental justice complaint with EPA under Title VI of the federal Civil Rights Act. The complaint alleged that communities of color were disproportionately impacted by the CAFOs. After EPA issued a Letter of Concern to the North Carolina Department of Environmental Quality (DEQ) in 2017, state officials agreed to settle the case by updating the state's general permit for swine and broadening community participation in the permit issuance process.

4. A major part of the industry pushback against the nuisance suits was a successful effort to get the North Carolina Legislature to enact a Right-to-Farm law in 2017. The law prohibits nuisance lawsuits against agricultural operations. The Fourth Circuit panel confirmed that the lawsuit filed by the plaintiffs would now be barred, but it held that the Right-to-Farm law was not retroactive. The panel concluded that "policy and justice concerns weigh against allowing retroactive amendments to alter

the damages available in pending suits. A decision in Appellant's favor as to the effect of the 2017 RTFA amendments would reward powerful defendants who, faced with a possible judgment against them, could escape responsibility."

## B.   Public Nuisance

While the common law is most useful for addressing conflicts between a single source of pollution and a few neighbors, there is wide agreement that private nuisance actions alone are grossly inadequate for resolving the more typical pollution problems faced by modern industrialized societies. When numerous and diverse pollutants emanating from widely dispersed sources affect large populations, the common law is a poor vehicle for providing redress. R. Posner, Economic Analysis of Law 46-47 (2d ed. 1977). The difficulty plaintiffs face is well described in the Report of the Lords Select Committee on Noxious Vapours in 1862, which noted that "partly in consequence of the expense such actions occasion, partly from the fact that where several works are in immediate juxtaposition, the difficulty of tracing the damage to any one, or of apportioning it among several, is [so] great as to be all but insuperable." H.L. Select Committee on Noxious Vapours at v, quoted in Brenner, Nuisance Law and the Industrial Revolution, 3 J. Legal Stud. 403, 425 (1974). Even when the *aggregate* damage caused by pollution is quite large, the damage to any individual victim may be insufficient to make a lawsuit worthwhile. While the class action device provides a mechanism for dealing with such problems, it has not played a significant role in redressing environmental damage. In cases where pollution interferes with rights held in common by the public, the common law's response has been to rely on public nuisance actions, to which we now turn.

The common law offers somewhat greater promise for protecting the environment when used by governmental entities to protect their citizens against *public* nuisances. The Second Restatement defines a public nuisance as "an unreasonable interference with a right common to the general public." Restatement of Torts (Second) §821B (1978). As with the doctrine of private nuisance, with public nuisance not all invasions of rights are actionable, only unreasonable ones. In determining whether interference with a public right is unreasonable, the Restatement directs courts to consider whether the conduct: (1) involves a significant interference with the public health, safety, comfort, or convenience; (2) is illegal; or (3) is of a continuing nature or has produced a long-lasting effect on the public right that the actor has reason to know will be significant.

The doctrine of public nuisance was used most frequently in the early common law to prosecute those who obstructed public highways or encroached on the royal domain. The doctrine later expanded to embrace actions against those who fouled public waters or emitted noxious fumes. Following the Industrial Revolution, public nuisance actions were rarely prosecuted to abate pollution. When such actions were brought, courts were not "eager to find large enterprises guilty of public nuisances, because they feared the economic consequences of a policy of strict enforcement." Brenner, Nuisance Law and the Industrial Revolution, 3 J. Legal Stud. 403, 421 (1974). It is not surprising that many of the public nuisance actions that were brought by governmental authorities targeted nonresident polluters, as illustrated in the decisions below.

Two early Supreme Court decisions involved public nuisance actions brought by state authorities against out-of-state polluters. The first grew out of the burgeoning sewage disposal problem faced by many rapidly expanding American cities. In the late nineteenth century, most cities disposed of their sewage by simply dumping it untreated into the nearest lake or stream. As one American court had noted, "the history of sewers shows that from time immemorial the right to connect them with navigable streams has been regarded as part of the jus publicum." Newark v. Sayre Co., 60 N.J. Eq. 361, 45 A. 985 (1900). Not surprisingly, with rapid urbanization, sewage disposal became a major source of environmental conflict among cities and states that shared public waterways.

Chicago disposed of its raw sewage by dumping it into the Chicago River, which flowed into Lake Michigan, the source of the city's drinking water. When a cholera epidemic killed more than 1,400 Chicago residents in 1854 (more than 2 percent of the city's population), polluted drinking water was viewed as a likely culprit. To improve the quality of its drinking water, Chicago in 1867 built a water tunnel two miles out into Lake Michigan. However, this provided only temporary relief, as the lake became more contaminated with the city's sewage and diseases believed to be associated with contaminated drinking water increased to frightening levels. In 1891, the death rate from typhoid fever in Chicago reached 174 per 100,000 persons.

To resolve the city's sewage disposal problem, in 1892 the Illinois Drainage and Water Supply Commission began construction of a 28-mile canal to reverse the flow of the Chicago River. This ambitious project would link the river with the Des Plaines River, which drained into the Mississippi River. Chicago's raw sewage no longer would flow into Lake Michigan; it would empty into the Mississippi River instead.

Though hundreds of miles away, residents of St. Louis, Missouri became upset when they learned that the Mississippi River, their source of drinking water, would now become the recipient of the raw sewage from more than one million Chicago residents. Missouri filed a common law nuisance action against Illinois in the United States Supreme Court. Arguing that the sewage would endanger the health of its citizens, Missouri asked the Supreme Court to enjoin Illinois and the Sanitary District of Chicago from discharging sewage through the canal.

Illinois tried to have the case dismissed on jurisdictional grounds, arguing that it was not really a dispute between states subject to the Supreme Court's original jurisdiction. The Supreme Court rejected Illinois's arguments and held that it had jurisdiction. Missouri v. Illinois, 180 U.S. 208 (1901). As Justice Holmes later explained:

> The nuisance set forth in the bill was one which would be of international importance—a visible change of a great river from a pure stream into a polluted and poisoned ditch. The only question presented was whether as between the States of the Union this court was competent to deal with a situation which, if it arose between independent sovereignties, might lead to war. Whatever differences of opinion there might be upon matters of detail, the jurisdiction and authority of this court to deal with such a case is not now open to doubt. [Missouri v. Illinois, 200 U.S. 496, 518 (1906).]

The Supreme Court appointed a special commissioner to hear evidence in the case, which dragged on for years as Chicago's sewage poured through the canal and on to the Mississippi. Missouri's lawyers argued that disease-producing bacteria contained in Chicago's sewage had caused a 77 percent increase in typhoid fever deaths in St. Louis after the canal was opened in January 1900. Illinois argued that any increase in deaths from typhoid fever was an artifact of a change in reporting practices that for the first time had consolidated a host of fever-related deaths under the classification of typhoid fever. Illinois's lawyers argued that the drainage canal actually had improved water quality in the Mississippi's tributaries by increasing their volume and rate of flow. They maintained that any injury caused by bacteria in the Mississippi was the product of sewage dumped by other Missouri cities upriver from St. Louis. Missouri responded that any increase in the volume or rate of flow of the river's tributaries served only to hasten the delivery of Chicago's sewage and its accompanying bacteria.

## Missouri v. Illinois

200 U.S. 496 (1906)

Mr. Justice Holmes delivered the opinion of the court.

This is a suit brought by the State of Missouri to restrain the discharge of the sewage of Chicago through an artificial channel into the Desplaines River, in the State of Illinois. That river empties into the Illinois River, and the latter empties into the Mississippi at a point about forty-three miles above the city of St. Louis. It was alleged in the bill that the result of the threatened discharge would be to send fifteen hundred tons of poisonous filth daily into the Mississippi, to deposit great quantities of the same upon the part of the bed of the last-named river belonging to the plaintiff, and so to poison the water of that river, upon which various of the plaintiff's cities, towns, and inhabitants depended, as to make it unfit for drinking, agricultural, or manufacturing, purposes. . . .

Before this court ought to intervene the case should be of serious magnitude, clearly and fully proved, and the principle to be applied should be one which the court is prepared deliberately to maintain against all considerations on the other side. See Kansas v. Colorado, 185 U.S. 125.

As to the principle to be laid down the caution necessary is manifest. It is a question of the first magnitude whether the destiny of the great rivers is to be the sewers of the cities along their banks or to be protected against everything which threatens their purity. To decide the whole matter at one blow by an irrevocable fiat would be at least premature. If we are to judge by what the plaintiff itself permits, the discharge of sewage into the Mississippi by cities and towns is to be expected. We believe that the practice of discharging into the river is general along its banks, except where the levees of Louisiana have led to a different course. The argument for the plaintiff asserts it to be proper within certain limits. These are facts to be considered. Even in cases between individuals some consideration is given to the practical course of events. In the back country of England parties would not be expected to stand upon extreme rights. St. Helen's Smelting Co. v. Tipping, 11 H.L.C. 642. See Boston Ferrule Co. v. Hills, 159 Massachusetts, 147, 150. Where, as here, the plaintiff has sovereign powers and deliberately permits discharges similar to those of which it complains, it not only offers a standard to which the defendant has the right to appeal, but, as some of those discharges are above the intake of St. Louis, it warrants the defendant in demanding the strictest proof that the plaintiff's own conduct does not produce the result, or at least so conduce to it that courts should not be curious to apportion the blame.

We have studied the plaintiff's statement of the facts in detail and have perused the evidence, but it is unnecessary for the purposes of decision to do more than give the general result in a very simple way. At the outset we cannot but be struck by the consideration that if this suit had been brought fifty years ago it almost necessarily would have failed. There is no pretence that there is a nuisance of the simple kind that was known to the older common law. There is nothing which can be detected by the unassisted senses — no visible increase of filth, no new smell. On the contrary, it is proved that the great volume of pure water from Lake Michigan which is mixed with the sewage at the start has improved the Illinois River in these respects to a noticeable extent. Formerly it was sluggish and ill smelling. Now it is a comparatively clear stream to which edible fish have returned. Its water is drunk by the fishermen, it is said, without evil results. The plaintiff's case depends upon an inference of the unseen. It draws the inference from two propositions. First, that typhoid fever has increased considerably since the change and that other explanations have been disproved, and second, that the bacillus of typhoid can and does survive the journey and reach the intake of St. Louis in the Mississippi.

We assume the now prevailing scientific explanation of typhoid fever to be correct. But when we go beyond that assumption everything is involved in doubt. The data upon which an increase in the deaths from typhoid fever in St. Louis is alleged are disputed. The elimination of other causes is denied. The experts differ as to the time and distance within which a stream would purify itself. No case of an epidemic caused by infection at so remote a source is brought forward, and the cases which are produced are controverted. The plaintiff obviously must be cautious upon this point, for if this suit should succeed many others would follow, and it not improbably would find itself a defendant to a bill by one or more of the States lower down upon the Mississippi. The distance which the sewage has to travel (357 miles) is not open to debate, but the time of transit to be inferred from experiments with floats is estimated at varying from eight to eighteen and a half days, with forty-eight hours more from intake to distribution, and when corrected by observations of bacteria is greatly prolonged by the defendants. The experiments of the defendants' experts lead them to the opinion that a typhoid bacillus could not survive the journey, while those on the other side maintain that it might live and keep its power for twenty-five days or more, and arrive at St. Louis. Upon the question at issue, whether the new discharge from Chicago hurts St. Louis, there is a categorical contradiction between the experts on the two sides.

The Chicago drainage canal was opened on January 17, 1900. The deaths from typhoid fever in St. Louis, before and after that date, are stated somewhat differently in different places. We give them mainly from the plaintiff's brief: 1890, 140; 1891, 165; 1892, 441; 1893, 215; 1894, 171; 1895, 106; 1896, 106; 1897, 125; 1898, 95; 1899, 131; 1900, 154; 1901, 181; 1902, 216; 1903, 281. It is argued for the defendant that the numbers for the later years have been enlarged by carrying over cases which in earlier years would have been put into a miscellaneous column (intermittent, remittent, typho-malaria, etc., etc.), but we assume that the increase is real. Nevertheless, comparing the last four years with the earlier ones, it is obvious that the ground for a specific inference is very narrow, if we stopped at this point. The plaintiff argues that the increase must be due to Chicago, since there is nothing corresponding to it in the watersheds of the Missouri or Mississippi. On the other hand, the defendant points out that there has been no such enhanced rate of typhoid on the banks of the Illinois as would have been found if the opening of the drainage canal were the true cause.

Both sides agree that the detection of the typhoid bacillus in the water is not to be expected. But the plaintiff relies upon proof that such bacilli are discharged into the Chicago sewage in considerable quantities; that the number of bacilli in the water of the Illinois is much increased, including the *bacillus coli communis*, which is admitted to be an index of contamination, and that the chemical analyses lead to the same inference. To prove that the typhoid bacillus could make the journey, an experiment was tried with the *bacillus prodigiosus*, which seems to have been unknown, or nearly unknown, in these waters. After preliminary trials, in which these bacilli emptied into the Mississippi near the mouth of the Illinois were found near the St. Louis intake and in St. Louis in times varying from three days to a month, one hundred and seven barrels of the same, said to contain one thousand million bacilli to the cubic centimeter, were put into the drainage canal near the starting point on November 6, and on December 4 an example was found at the St. Louis intake tower. Four others were found on the three following days, two at the tower and two at the mouth of the Illinois. As this bacillus is asserted to have about the same length of life in sunlight in living waters as the *bacillus typhosus*, although it is a little more hardy, the experiment is thought to prove one element of the plaintiff's case, although the very small number found in many samples of water is thought by the other side to indicate that practically no typhoid germs would get through. It seems to be conceded that the purification of the Illinois by the large dilution from Lake Michigan (nine parts or more in ten) would increase the danger, as it now generally is believed that the bacteria of decay, the saprophytes, which flourish in stagnant pools, destroy the pathogenic germs. Of course the addition of so much water to the Illinois also increases its speed.

On the other hand, the defendant's evidence shows a reduction in the chemical and bacterial accompaniments of pollution in a given quantity of water, which would be natural in view of the mixture of nine parts to one from Lake Michigan. It affirms that the Illinois is no better or no worse at its mouth than it was before, and makes it at least uncertain how much of the present pollution is due to Chicago and how much to sources further down, not complained of in the bill. It contends that if any bacilli should get through they would be scattered and enfeebled and would do no harm. The defendant also sets against the experiment with the *bacillus prodigiosus* a no less striking experiment with typhoid germs suspended in the Illinois River in permeable sacs. According to this the duration of the life of these germs has been much exaggerated, and in that water would not be more than three or four days. It is suggested, by way of criticism, that the germs may not have been of normal strength, that the conditions were less favorable than if they had floated down in a comparatively unchanging body of water, and that the germs may have escaped, but the experiment raises at least a serious doubt. Further, it hardly is denied that there is no parallelism in detail between the increase and decrease of typhoid fever in Chicago and St. Louis. The defendants' experts maintain that the water of the Missouri is worse than that of the Illinois, while it contributes a much larger proportion to the intake. The evidence is very strong that it is necessary for St. Louis to take preventive measures, by filtration or otherwise, against the dangers of the plaintiff's own creation or from other sources than Illinois. What will protect against one will protect against another. The presence of causes of infection from the plaintiff's action makes the case weaker in principle as well as harder to prove than one in which all came from a single source. . . .

We might go more into detail, but we believe that we have said enough to explain our point of view and our opinion of the evidence as it stands. What the future may develop of course we cannot tell. But our conclusion upon the present evidence is that the case proved falls so far below the allegations of the bill that it is not brought within the principles heretofore established in the cause.

## NOTES AND QUESTIONS

1. Why did Missouri fail to convince the Supreme Court that Chicago's sewage discharges constituted a public nuisance? Did the discharge of raw sewage into a canal that eventually flows into the Mississippi affect the quality of drinking water in St. Louis? If so, was it an unreasonable interference with the rights of Missouri's citizens? Should it make any difference that Chicago's sewage would not have reached the Mississippi but for construction of the canal?

2. What is the relevance of Justice Holmes's statement that "[e]ven in cases between individuals some consideration is given to the practical course of events. In the back country of England parties would not be expected to stand upon extreme rights"? Does this suggest that some balancing of interests is appropriate in public nuisance cases?

3. Following the opening of the canal, the death rate from typhoid fever in Chicago fell from more than 80 per 100,000 to less than 10 per 100,000. But Missouri claimed that the canal had improved public health in Chicago only at the expense of citizens of St. Louis. How persuasive was the statistical evidence Missouri presented to demonstrate that the sewage discharges had caused a substantial increase in typhoid fever deaths in St. Louis? What other evidence could Missouri have presented to demonstrate that the sewage discharges had harmed its residents? Suppose that Missouri had been successful in proving that the opening of the canal had caused a substantial increase in the incidence of typhoid fever in St. Louis, but that Illinois was able to prove that it produced an even larger decrease in typhoid fever deaths in Chicago. Would Missouri be entitled to the injunction that it sought?

4. As Chicago continued to grow, it had to divert ever larger amounts of water from Lake Michigan to flush out the increased volumes of sewage in the drainage canal. In 1924, Wisconsin, Michigan, and New York invoked the Supreme Court's original jurisdiction to sue Illinois and the Sanitary District for diverting too much water from Lake Michigan. They successfully argued that Illinois's diversions had lowered the levels of Lakes Michigan, Huron, Erie, and Ontario, their connecting

waterways, and the St. Lawrence River more than six inches, causing serious injury to their citizens and property. Ironically, Illinois was joined as a defendant by the state of Missouri, which intervened because of its interest in keeping as much water as possible flowing through the drainage canal to the Mississippi River. Former Justice Charles Evans Hughes, who had just finished serving as Secretary of State in the Harding and Coolidge administrations, was appointed by the Court to serve as special master. Based on his findings confirming the allegations of the upstream states, the Court ruled against Illinois in January 1929. The Court concluded that the upstream states were entitled to equitable relief, Wisconsin v. Illinois, 278 U.S. 367 (1929), and it ultimately issued an injunction requiring Chicago to build sewage treatment plants to reduce its need to divert water from Lake Michigan. Wisconsin v. Illinois, 281 U.S. 179 (1930) and 281 U.S. 696 (1930).

5. Justice Holmes notes that Missouri's own cities, including cities upstream of St. Louis, routinely discharged raw sewage into the Mississippi. What is the significance of this observation? Would the outcome of this case have been any different if Missouri had required its cities to employ more sophisticated treatment technology to protect the Mississippi from pollution? Thomas Merrill describes the decision in *Missouri v. Illinois* as an endorsement of "the reverse golden rule: in a transboundary pollution case, the affected state cannot demand that the source state adhere to a higher standard than the affected state applies to its own citizens." Thomas W. Merrill, Golden Rules for Transboundary Pollution, 46 Duke L.J. 931, 1000 (1997).

6. In a subsequent case, the Court denied relief to New York when it sought an injunction to prevent New Jersey from discharging raw sewage into New York Bay. The Court declared that before it would act "to control the conduct of one state at the suit of another, the threatened invasion must be of serious magnitude and it must be established by clear and convincing evidence." New York v. New Jersey, 256 U.S. 296, 309 (1921). The Court emphasized that New York had failed to prove that there were visible suspended particles, odors, or a reduction in the dissolved oxygen content of the Bay sufficient to interfere with aquatic life. It also observed that New York itself discharged sewage from 450 sewers directly into adjacent waters.

7. New Jersey was more successful when it sued to stop New York City from ocean dumping of garbage. A special master found that New York City had caused enough garbage to wash upon New Jersey shores to fill 50 trucks, damaging fish nets and making swimming impracticable. The Supreme Court issued an injunction prohibiting the city from dumping garbage off the coast of New Jersey effective June 1, 1933. New Jersey v. City of New York, 284 U.S. 585 (1931). The Court subsequently extended this deadline for a year to give the city more time to build garbage incinerators. New Jersey v. City of New York, 290 U.S. 237 (1933).

8. Is the judiciary an appropriate institution for formulating pollution control policy, or is such a task better left to administrative agencies with more specialized expertise? As we will see, a major obstacle to effective pollution control has been the reluctance of politically accountable officials to implement policies that may adversely affect local industries. Could judges, who are more insulated from political forces, do a more effective job of formulating environmental policy?

9. Governmental entities have themselves been among the most persistent violators of environmental regulations. Efforts to force them to comply with the environmental laws perennially come up against the argument that there isn't

enough money to do so. Confronted with this argument in a public nuisance action in 1858, a British court said of local authorities: "If they have not funds enough to make further experiments, they must apply to Parliament for power to raise more money. If, after all possible experiments, they cannot [dispose of their sewage] without invading the Plaintiff's rights, they must apply to Parliament for power to invade his rights." A.G. v. Birmingham Borough Council, 70 Eng. Rep. 220, 4 K. J. 528, 541 (Vice Ch. Ct. 1858). See also Wisconsin v. Illinois, 289 U.S. 395, 406 (1933) (holding the state of Illinois responsible for providing the necessary funds to complete construction of sewage treatment works for Chicago).

10.  A year after it decided *Missouri v. Illinois*, the Supreme Court was again confronted with a common law nuisance action involving interstate pollution. This time the controversy involved a source of pollution already familiar to us — sulfur dioxide emissions from the very Ducktown, Tennessee copper smelters involved in *Madison v. Ducktown Sulphur, Copper & Iron Co.* Invoking the Court's original jurisdiction, the state of Georgia brought a common law nuisance action against the smelters, which, as you may recall, were located directly across the Georgia-Tennessee border. In 1904, the year that the Tennessee Supreme Court had decided not to enjoin operation of the smelters, Georgia filed suit in the Supreme Court, complaining that the smelters' emissions crossed the border and caused considerable property damage in Georgia. Georgia asked the Supreme Court to enjoin operation of the smelters. In response to Georgia's lawsuit, the companies pledged to change their method of operation to reduce their emissions. Georgia then agreed to dismiss its lawsuit without prejudice. But after the smelters installed tall smokestacks that simply transported the pollution across a wider swath of territory, Georgia again filed suit.

## Georgia v. Tennessee Copper Co.

206 U.S. 230 (1907)

MR. JUSTICE HOLMES delivered the opinion of the court.

This is a bill in equity filed in this court by the State of Georgia in pursuance of a resolution of the legislature and by direction of the Governor of the State, to enjoin the defendant Copper Companies from discharging noxious gas from their works in Tennessee over the plaintiff's territory. It alleges that in consequence of such a discharge a wholesale destruction of forests, orchards, and crops is going on, and other injuries are done and threatened in five counties of the State. It alleges also a vain application to the State of Tennessee for relief. A preliminary injunction was denied, but, as there was ground to fear that great and irreparable damage might be done, an early day was fixed for the final hearing and the parties were given leave, if so minded, to try the case on affidavits. This has been done without objection, and, although the method would be unsatisfactory if our decision turned on any nice question of fact, in the view that we take we think it unlikely that either party has suffered harm.

The case has been argued largely as if it were one between two private parties; but it is not. The very elements that would be relied upon in a suit between fellow-citizens as a ground for equitable relief are wanting here. The State owns very little of the territory alleged to be affected, and the damage to it capable of estimate in money, possibly, at least, is small. This is a suit by a State for an injury to it in its capacity of quasi-sovereign. In that capacity the State has an interest independent of and behind the titles of its citizens, in all the earth and air within its domain. It has the last word as to whether its mountains shall be stripped of their forests and its inhabitants shall breathe pure air. It might have to pay individuals before it could utter that word, but with it remains the final power. The alleged damage to the State as a private owner is merely a makeweight, and we may lay on one side the dispute as to whether the destruction of forests has led to the gullying of its roads.

The caution with which demands of this sort, on the part of a State, for relief from injuries analogous to torts, must be examined, is dwelt upon in Missouri v. Illinois, 200 U.S. 496, 520, 521. But it is plain that some such demands must be recognized, if the grounds alleged are proved. When the States by their union made the forcible abatement of outside nuisances impossible to each, they did not thereby agree to submit to whatever might be done. They did not renounce the possibility of making reasonable demands on the ground of their still remaining quasi-sovereign interests; and the alternative to force is a suit in this court. Missouri v. Illinois, 180 U.S. 208, 241.

Some peculiarities necessarily mark a suit of this kind. If the State has a case at all, it is somewhat more certainly entitled to specific relief than a private party might be. It is not lightly to be required to give up quasi-sovereign rights for pay; and, apart from the difficulty of valuing such rights in money, if that be its choice it may insist that an infraction of them shall be stopped. The States by entering the Union did not sink to the position of private owners subject to one system of private law. This court has not quite the same freedom to balance the harm that will be done by an injunction against that of which the plaintiff complains, that it would have in deciding between two subjects of a single political power. Without excluding the considerations that equity always takes into account, we cannot give the weight that was given them in argument to a comparison between the damage threatened to the plaintiff and the calamity of a possible stop to the defendants' business, the question of health, the character of the forests as a first or second growth, the commercial possibility of reducing the fumes to sulphuric acid, the special adaption of the business to the place.

It is a fair and reasonable demand on the part of a sovereign that the air over its territory should not be polluted on a great scale by sulphurous acid gas, that the forests on its mountains, be they better or worse, and whatever domestic destruction they have suffered, should not be further destroyed or threatened by the act of persons beyond its control, that the crops and orchards on its hills should not be endangered from the same source. If any such demand is to be enforced this must be, notwithstanding the hesitation that we might feel if the suit were between private parties, and the doubt whether for the injuries which they might be suffering to their property they should not be left to an action at law.

The proof requires but a few words. It is not denied that the defendants generate in their works near the Georgia line large quantities of sulphur dioxid[e] which becomes sulphurous acid by its mixture with the air. It hardly is denied and cannot be denied with success that this gas often is carried by the wind great distances and over great tracts of Georgia land. On the evidence the pollution of the air and the magnitude of that pollution are not open to dispute. Without any attempt to go into details immaterial to the suit, it is proper to add that we are satisfied by a preponderance of evidence that the sulphurous fumes cause and threaten damage on so considerable a scale to the forests and vegetable life, if not to health, within the plaintiff State as to make out a case within the requirements of Missouri v. Illinois, 200 U.S. 496. Whether Georgia by insisting upon this claim is doing more harm than good to her own citizens is for her to determine. The possible disaster to those outside the State must be accepted as a consequence of her standing upon her extreme rights.

It is argued that the State has been guilty of laches. We deem it unnecessary to consider how far such a defense would be available in a suit of this sort, since, in our opinion, due diligence has been shown. The conditions have been different until recent years. After the evil had grown greater in 1904 the State brought a bill in this court. The defendants, however, already were abandoning the old method of roasting ore in open heaps and it was hoped that the change would stop the trouble. They were ready to agree not to return to that method, and upon such an agreement being made the bill was dismissed without prejudice. But the plaintiff now finds, or thinks that it finds, that the tall chimneys in present use cause the poisonous gases to be carried to greater distances than ever before and that the evil has not been helped.

If the State of Georgia adheres to its determination, there is no alternative to issuing an injunction, after allowing a reasonable time to the defendants to complete the structures that they now are building, and the efforts that they are making, to stop the fumes. The plaintiff may submit a form of decree on the coming in of this court in October next.

*Injunction to issue.*

## NOTES AND QUESTIONS

1.  Why did Georgia succeed in getting an injunction from the United States Supreme Court when plaintiffs in *Madison v. Ducktown Sulphur, Copper & Iron Co.* had been refused such relief by the Tennessee Supreme Court? Justice Holmes suggests that in fashioning a remedy for a public nuisance, the Court has less latitude to balance the equities because the plaintiff is a sovereign state. What is his rationale for this conclusion? Is this why the Court ultimately held that Georgia was entitled to an injunction? As discussed below, pages 122-125, a century later in 2007, a sharply divided Supreme Court cited *Georgia v. Tennessee Copper* in upholding the standing of states to challenge EPA's decision not to regulate emissions of greenhouse gases (GHGs) that cause climate change.

2.  Why did Georgia succeed in the *Tennessee Copper* case when Missouri failed to get the Supreme Court to enjoin Chicago's discharge of sewage in *Missouri v. Illinois*? Did Georgia simply have better evidence than Missouri that the pollution had caused damage to its citizens? Did it make any difference that the defendants in *Tennessee Copper* were two private companies rather than another sovereign state?

3.  In *Tennessee Copper*, Justice Holmes warned: "Whether Georgia by insisting upon this claim is doing more harm than good to her own citizens is for her to determine. The possible disaster to those outside the State must be accepted as a

consequence of her standing upon her extreme rights." What did he mean by this? Recall Justice Holmes's comment in *Missouri v. Illinois* that if Missouri had won the case many other suits would follow, and Missouri might find itself a defendant in cases brought by downstream states.

4. In a separate opinion, Justice John Marshall Harlan argued that the Court should apply the same standard in nuisance cases brought by public authorities as it would in private nuisance actions. He wrote: "If this were a suit between private parties, and if, under the evidence, a court of equity would not give the plaintiff an injunction, then it ought not to grant relief, under like circumstances, to the plaintiff, because it happens to be a state, possessing some powers of sovereignty." However, he concurred in the majority's decision, explaining that "Georgia is entitled to the relief sought, not because it is a state, but because it is a party, which has established its right to such relief by proof." Do you agree that courts should apply the same standard in deciding nuisance cases regardless of whether or not the plaintiff is a public entity? Why do you think the common law developed different standards to govern public and private nuisances?

5. In addition to actions by governmental authorities, public nuisance actions can be brought by private parties if they can demonstrate that the nuisance has harmed them in a manner not shared with the general public. William Prosser notes that the traditional "special injury" requirement for private actions derived from the ancient notion that private parties should not be able to vindicate the rights of the sovereign and from a desire to prevent a multitude of actions to redress the same nuisance. Prosser, Private Action for Public Nuisance, 52 Va. L. Rev. 997 (1966). As courts and legislatures broadened citizen rights of action to redress environmental damage, the special injury requirement has come under fire. As Professor Denise Antolini notes, the "traditional doctrine presents a paradox: the broader the injury to the community and the more the plaintiff's injury resembles an injury also suffered by other members of the public, the less likely the plaintiff can bring a public nuisance lawsuit." Denise E. Antolini, Modernizing Public Nuisance: Solving the Paradox of the Special Injury Rule, 28 Ecology L.Q. 755, 761 (2001). While the Restatement (Second) of Torts suggested that the special injury requirement should not bar actions seeking equitable relief or class actions brought against public nuisances by private individuals, Restatement (Second) of Torts §821C and comment j (1978), this approach has not been embraced by courts. "Although courts still struggle with application of the different-in-kind test (often bending the rule to avoid unfair results), the traditional doctrine is nonetheless repeated like a mantra in virtually every public nuisance case." Antolini, supra at 861. Professor Antolini argues that courts should adopt an "actual community injury" standard that would permit recovery of damages or injunctive relief in a private action for a public nuisance, if the plaintiff "suffered an actual or threatened injury in common with the community that was the subject of the nuisance," with "injury" defined as "substantial interference with community values," which would not be limited to pecuniary loss and could include environmental and aesthetic injury. Id. at 862-863.

6. Faced with the threat of an injunction, the Tennessee Copper Company eventually settled with the state of Georgia by setting up a fund to compensate those injured by its emissions and by agreeing to restrict its operations during the

growing season (April to October). The other smelting company, the Ducktown Sulphur, Copper & Iron Company, refused to restrict its operations, claiming that it already had spent $600,000 constructing "purifying works" to reduce the percentage of sulfur emitted from the ores from 85.5 percent to 41.5 percent. Despite this investment, Ducktown released more than 13,000 tons of sulfur emissions in 1913. In 1914, Georgia applied to the Supreme Court for a final injunction against Ducktown. While noting that it could not determine precisely how much of a reduction in Ducktown's emissions would be necessary to prevent harm to property in Georgia, the Court issued a final injunction on June 1, 1915. Georgia v. Tennessee Copper Co., 237 U.S. 474 (1915). The Court specified that no more than 20 tons of sulfur per day could be emitted during the period from April to October and no more than 40 tons per day during the rest of the year. 237 U.S. at 478. The Court appointed an inspector to monitor Ducktown's operations. A year later, in response to the inspector's report, the Court modified the injunction to permit releases of 25 tons of sulfur per day from April to October, and 50 tons per day during the rest of the year. 240 U.S. 650 (1916). In light of the Court's conclusion that it could not determine what level of emissions reduction would prevent harm to property in Georgia, what basis do you think it had for specifying emissions limits in its injunction?

7.  Both the Tennessee Copper and Ducktown companies ultimately settled with the State of Georgia by agreeing to participate in an administrative compensation system where a board of arbitrators would rule on claims of damage caused by the smelters' emissions. The companies and the State each appointed one arbitrator to rule on claims of injury, with an umpire designated by the two arbitrators to resolve disagreements between the other two. While the companies posted bonds to ensure that they could provide $25,000 per year in compensation, review of the records of the arbitral tribunal reveals that it actually awarded only a tiny amount of compensation. Between 1921 and 1928, it approved 140 out of 203 claims filed (approximately 69 percent), but it awarded only an average of $189 per year in damages, approximately 10 percent of the total amount of claims made annually. Percival, *Resolución de Conflictos Ambientales: Lecciones Aprendidas de la Historia de la Contaminación de las Fundiciones de Minerales*, in *Prevención y Solución de Conflictos Ambientales: Vías Administrativas, Jurisdiccionales y Alternativas* 399 (Lexis Nexis 2004).

8.  Causation was not a significant issue in the litigation because the environmental effects of the open roast-heap smelting process were strikingly visible. The smelter emissions destroyed virtually all vegetation over a vast swath of land, transforming the Ducktown area into a bizarre moonscape of barren red hills that is apparent even today after decades of intensive reforestation efforts. Although the Supreme Court's injunction ultimately was relaxed in 1918 with Georgia's consent due to unusual demand for copper during World War I, fear of liability helped advance the development of a new pollution control technology, the lead chamber process, that permits sulfur to be reclaimed and used to produce sulfuric acid. Indeed, the technology proved so successful that the production of sulfuric acid eventually replaced copper as the area's major product. While all copper mining in the area ceased in 1987, the area's largest employer today is a Swiss chemical company that continues to use the old Tennessee Copper production facilities to produce sulfuric acid.

9. Interstate pollution remains a serious problem, but the Supreme Court no longer is in the business of establishing emissions limits in federal common law nuisance actions. Why would the Supreme Court be reluctant to hear such actions? Consider the following comment by the Court in refusing the injunction sought by New York against New Jersey's sewage disposal practices:

> We cannot withhold the suggestion, inspired by the consideration of this case, that the grave problem of sewage disposed presented by the large and growing populations living on the shores of New York Bay is one more likely to be wisely solved by cooperative study and by conference and mutual concession on the part of the representatives of the States so vitally interested in it than by proceedings in any court however constituted. [New York v. New Jersey, 256 U.S. 296, 313 (1921).]

Do you agree with the Court's conclusion?

10. In Illinois v. City of Milwaukee, 406 U.S. 91 (1972) (*Milwaukee I*), the Supreme Court confirmed that federal common law nuisance actions could be brought against polluting governmental entities, but it reversed its previous willingness to hear such actions under its original jurisdiction. The Court held that the federal district courts were the proper forum for hearing a nuisance action by Illinois charging four Wisconsin cities with polluting Lake Michigan. While rejecting the argument that new federal environmental legislation had preempted federal common law, the Court noted:

> It may happen that new federal laws and new federal regulations may in time pre-empt the field of federal common law of nuisance. But until that comes to pass, federal courts will be empowered to appraise the equities of the suits alleging creation of a public nuisance by water pollution. While federal law governs, consideration of state standards may be relevant. Thus, a State with high water-quality standards may well ask that its strict standards be honored and that it not be compelled to lower itself to the more degrading standards of a neighbor. There are no fixed rules that govern; these will be equity suits in which the informed judgment of the chancellor will largely govern. [406 U.S. at 107-108.]

Not long after this decision, the explosion of federal environmental protection legislation led the Court to slam the door on most federal common law actions, as we will see below.

11. Even in cases of public nuisance, the common law has proved to be a crude mechanism at best for controlling the onslaught of modern-day pollution. An excellent account of the history and shortcomings of common law actions to redress air pollution problems is provided by Noga Morag-Levine, Chasing the Wind: Regulating Air Pollution in the Common Law State (2003). Most of what we study today as environmental law consists of federal and state statutes, which often create elaborate regulatory schemes implemented by administrative agencies. Common law principles, however, have had an important impact on many current regulatory programs. And as scientific advances make it easier to measure pollutants and to trace their impacts on the environment, common law actions may become

more popular (as already seems to be occurring in certain areas). Thus, although most of our attention will be focused on the large and complex body of environmental statutes, it is important not to lose sight of the big picture that includes the common law, which can still serve as an important tool for addressing regulatory gaps left by public law.

## 2. Regulatory Legislation

### A. Environmental Statutes: A Historical Perspective

The federal statutes that dominate environmental law today are the product of a remarkable burst of legislative activity that began in 1970, the year of the first Earth Day celebration. But, as noted above, the historical roots of environmental law extend much further back in time. The historical evolution of environmental law in the United States can be divided into roughly nine major phases, as indicated below.

---

## Nine Stages in the History of U.S. Environmental Law

1. The Common Law and Conservation Era: Pre-1945
2. Federal Assistance for State Problems: 1945-1962
3. The Rise of the Modern Environmental Movement: 1962-1970
4. Erecting the Federal Regulatory Infrastructure: 1970-1980
5. Extending and Refining Regulatory Strategies: 1980-1994
6. Regulatory Recoil and Reinvention: 1994-2009
7. The Obama Administration Tackles Climate Change: 2009-2017
8. The Trump Administration Rolls Back Environmental Regulations: 2017-2021
9. The Biden Administration Focuses on Climate and Environmental Justice 2021-

---

Until the end of World War II, environmental law was largely a product of common law, as discussed above, with federal legislative efforts concentrated on the development and later the conservation of public resources. We call this period the *Common Law and Conservation Era.*

In nineteenth-century America, regulatory legislation was left largely to state and local governments. State laws and local ordinances to protect public health and to require the abatement or segregation of public nuisances were common, although they were poorly coordinated and rarely enforced in the absence of a professional civil service. Like the early English antipollution laws, American smoke abatement ordinances did not clearly specify what levels of emissions were proscribed. See, e.g., Sigler v. Cleveland, 4 Ohio Dec. 166 (C.P. Cuyahoga 1896) (holding that an ordinance outlawing "dense smoke" was unconstitutionally over-broad because it was so vague that it could ban all smoke).

Most federal legislation that affected the environment did so by promoting development of natural resources. The Homestead Act of 1862 and the Mining Act of 1872 unabashedly encouraged rapid development of public resources by authorizing private parties to lay claim to public land and the mineral resources on it. Land grants to encourage railroad construction turned over up to 180 million acres of public lands to private developers. R. Robbins, Our Landed Heritage: The Public Domain, 1776-1970 (1976). While the concerns of preservationists and conservationists helped spur establishment of the first national park in 1872, support also came from the railroads, which were seeking to promote tourism and to further the development of western lands. The establishment of the national forest system in 1891 marked a turning point of sorts, for it withdrew forest lands from development under the Homestead Act.

During this period, Congress did adopt some regulatory legislation, including the Rivers and Harbors Act of 1899 and the Pure Food and Drug Act of 1906. However, these statutes were not motivated primarily by concern over public health or environmental protection, but rather by a desire to promote commerce. Congress banned discharges of refuse to navigable waters not out of concern for water quality, but rather to prevent obstructions to the free flow of commerce, which at that time was largely conducted on waterways. When it enacted the Pure Food and Drug Act in 1906 and the Federal Insecticide Act of 1910, Congress's primary concern was not to protect public health, but rather to prevent consumers from being defrauded by products that were not what they were advertised to be.

Congress was not entirely oblivious to public health concerns during this period. In an unusual case when a public health problem was particularly visible and obvious, Congress was capable of acting. For example, in 1838 Congress acted to impose safety regulations to prevent steamship boilers from exploding. Several decades later, when it was discovered that the use of white phosphorus in match manufacturing caused many workers to be inflicted with a horribly disfiguring disease called phossy-jaw, because it literally ate away that area of the face, Congress acted again. The Esch-Hughes Act of 1912 sought to eliminate the use of white phosphorus in match manufacturing to prevent this disease. Because Congress did not believe at the time that it had the constitutional authority to directly prohibit such an activity, it imposed a federal excise tax to make it prohibitively expensive to use white phosphorus in match manufacturing.

The period from 1945-1962 coincides with the second phase in the history of U.S. environmental law, the period of *Federal Assistance for State Problems*. Although federal law imposed few regulations on private industry that were animated by environmental concerns, after World War II the federal government became involved in encouraging the states to adopt pollution control measures of their own. The Water Quality Act of 1948 provided grants to states for water pollution control. In 1956, over President Eisenhower's veto, Congress provided funding for the construction of sewage treatment plants by municipalities. This funding was premised on the notion that cities otherwise would be reluctant to build sewage treatment plants that would primarily benefit downstream cities. While this eventually became a major program of federal financial assistance, it did not create any system of federal regulation. Instead, the federal government sought to encourage the states to regulate on their own.

The federal programs in the 1950s and 1960s were premised on the notion that environmental problems were the responsibility of state and local governments. The primary federal role was to assist with research and funding while letting the states decide how to control pollution. With expanding economic activity in the post–World War II era, the interstate character of pollution became increasingly apparent. The notion that pollutants do not respect state or even national boundaries was brought home by scientists' warnings that the entire planet was being dangerously poisoned by radiation from nuclear tests in the atmosphere. The premise that the federal role in pollution control should be a nonregulatory one became increasingly tenuous.

When Congress adopted legislation in 1955 directing the Department of Health, Education, and Welfare (HEW) to conduct a five-year program of research on the effects of air pollution, it continued to emphasize that pollution control was primarily a state responsibility. By 1960, Congress had begun to appreciate the national dimensions of the air pollution problem. Recognizing that a large percentage of the pollution came from products marketed nationwide, Congress mandated a federal study to determine what levels of automobile emissions were safe. In 1963, when it enacted an early version of the Clean Air Act, Congress acknowledged the need for federal involvement in efforts to protect interstate air quality. The Act directed HEW to publish national air quality criteria, and it also authorized a cumbersome conference procedure for dealing with interstate air pollution problems.

The third phase in the history of U.S. environmental law, the period from 1962-1970, constitutes the *Rise of the Modern Environmental Movement*. This is often traced from the publication of Rachel Carson's *Silent Spring*, which alerted the public to the possibility that pesticides could be accumulating in the food chain in a way that could cause severe, long-term environmental damage. In 1967, the Environmental Defense Fund was formed by a group of scientists who sought to have DDT banned on the ground that it was precisely that kind of pesticide. Another group, the Natural Resources Defense Council, was the product of efforts to force the Federal Power Commission to consider environmental concerns when licensing an electric power project that would have destroyed a particularly scenic and historic stretch of the Hudson River at Storm King Mountain. At the time, no federal agencies shouldered primary responsibility for responding to concerns about environmental protection. The new environmental groups went to court to try to require government agencies to be more responsive to environmental concerns.

The growing popularity of outdoor recreation and increased concern over the environmental impact of public works produced landmark legislation during this period. In 1960, Congress adopted the Multiple-Use Sustained-Yield Act, which directs federal agencies to manage the national forests to serve the multiple uses of "recreation, range, timber, watershed, and wildlife and fish purposes." Growing concern for the preservation of natural areas was reflected in the subsequent enactment of the Wilderness Act in 1964 and the Wild and Scenic Rivers Act in 1968. Other federal laws reflected public interest in protecting social and cultural values from the impact of public works programs. For example, section 4(f) of the Department of Transportation Act of 1966 required that special effort be made to prevent federally funded construction projects from damaging parks, recreation areas, wildlife refuges, and historic sites.

To the extent that federal law was regulatory in character prior to 1970, most targets of environmental regulation were government agencies rather than private industry. In legislation like the National Historic Preservation Act of 1966, Congress sought to ensure that government agencies respected social and cultural values when pursuing development projects. These laws laid the groundwork for the subsequent enactment of the landmark National Environmental Policy Act (NEPA), which was signed into law on January 1, 1970. NEPA required federal agencies to take environmental concerns into account when taking any action with a significant impact on the environment. This served as a catalyst for forcing federal agencies that previously had been unresponsive to environmental concerns to incorporate them in their decision-making processes.

The fourth phase of the history of U.S. environmental law encompasses the decade of the 1970s, which has been called "the environmental decade" because it marked the period when virtually all the major federal regulatory legislation to protect the environment was first enacted. While environmental issues had hardly been mentioned by either candidate during the 1968 presidential campaign, by 1970 "the environment[al] cause had swollen into the favorite sacred issue of all politicians, all TV networks, all goodwilled people of any party." Theodore White, The Making of the President 45 (1973). President Nixon's embrace of environmental causes may have been motivated more by political opportunism than genuine environmental concern, but his administration's environmental accomplishments were considerable, including the creation of EPA and the establishment of major federal regulatory programs, including the Clean Air Act and Clean Water Act. For a description of this history, see Richard J. Lazarus, The Making of Environmental Law 67-97 (2005). Further perspective on this extraordinary period is provided in an entertaining memoir by Russell Train, who served as the second administrator of EPA. Russell E. Train, Politics, Pollution, and Pandas (2003).

We call this fourth phase in the history of U.S. environmental law *Erecting the Federal Regulatory Infrastructure* because it featured an explosion of federal regulatory legislation adopted between 1970 and 1980. These statutes established the ground rules for environmental protection efforts by mandating that environmental impacts be considered explicitly by federal agencies, by prohibiting actions that jeopardize endangered species, and by requiring the establishment of the first comprehensive controls on air and water pollution, toxic substances, and hazardous waste. The rapid growth of environmental legislation in the 1970s was accompanied by a parallel opening up of the courts to judicial review of agency decisions that affected the environment and to citizen suits to force implementation and enforcement of the new laws. This gave concerned citizens sorely needed tools for challenging agency action and for ensuring that previously unresponsive agencies implemented the ambitious new legislative directives.

A chronology of the major federal environmental statutes is presented below. While the statutes listed are among the principal statutes covered in this casebook, they are by no means a comprehensive catalog of all federal environmental legislation.

# Chronology of Significant Federal Environmental Legislation

1. *National Environmental Policy Act* (NEPA): Signed into law on January 1, 1970; establishes broad national environmental policy goals; requires federal agencies to assess environmental impacts of significant actions; establishes Council on Environmental Quality.

2. *Clean Air Act*: Clean Air Amendments of 1970 establish a basic framework for federal regulation of air pollution; replace Clean Air Act of 1963 and Air Quality Act of 1967, which had authorized HEW to publish air quality criteria to be used by states in setting standards; set deadlines for EPA to promulgate national ambient air quality standards to be implemented by the states, national emission standards for hazardous air pollutants, and auto emission standards; authorized citizen suits. The Act was substantially amended in 1977 and 1990 to require implementation of more stringent controls in areas that had failed to attain national standards, to address the acid rain problem (in 1990), and to make other substantial changes in the framework for federal regulation of air pollution.

3. *Federal Water Pollution Control Act* (Clean Water Act): Enacted in 1972, it bans the unpermitted discharge of pollutants into surface waters, requires application of technology-based controls on dischargers, and establishes a national permit program, the National Pollutant Discharge Elimination System (NPDES), which is implemented by states subject to EPA supervision; authorized grants for construction of sewage treatment plants; authorized citizen suits. Reauthorized and substantially amended by the Clean Water Act Amendments of 1977 and the Water Quality Act of 1987.

4. *Federal Insecticide, Fungicide, and Rodenticide Act* (FIFRA): 1972 Federal Environmental Pesticide Control Act, which amended 1947 legislation, establishes basic framework for pesticide regulation; requires registration of pesticides and authorizes EPA to ban unreasonably dangerous pesticides. Amended in 1988 to require more expeditious review of pesticides previously registered and in 1996 by the Food Quality Protection Act to strengthen protections against pesticide residues on food.

5. *Marine Protection, Research, and Sanctuaries Act of 1972* (Ocean Dumping Act): Prohibits ocean dumping of wastes except with a permit at sites designated by EPA.

6. *Endangered Species Act* (ESA): Enacted in December 1973, this legislation prohibits federal action that jeopardizes the habitat of species in danger of extinction and prohibits the taking of any such species by any person.

7. *Safe Drinking Water Act* (SDWA): Enacted in 1974; requires EPA to set limits for maximum allowable levels of contaminants in public drinking water systems. Amended in 1986 to require more expeditious promulgation of standards and in 1996 to provide more flexibility in standard-setting.

8. *Toxic Substances Control Act of 1976* (TSCA): Provides EPA with comprehensive authority to regulate or prohibit the manufacture, distribution, or use of chemical substances that pose unreasonable risks; requires premanufacture

notification of EPA for new chemicals or significant new uses of existing chemicals. Amended in 2016 to require tiered chemical testing and to eliminate a requirement that regulations employ the "least burdensome means."

9. *Resource Conservation and Recovery Act of 1976* (RCRA): Directs EPA to establish regulations ensuring the safe management of hazardous waste from cradle to grave. Reauthorized and substantially amended by the Hazardous and Solid Waste Amendments of 1984 (HSWA), which impose new technology-based standards on landfills handling hazardous wastes, require phaseout of land disposal for certain untreated hazardous wastes, and increase federal authority over disposal of nonhazardous solid wastes.

10. *Comprehensive Environmental Response, Compensation, and Liability Act of 1980* (CERCLA): Establishes strict liability system for releases of hazardous substances and creates a "Superfund" to finance actions to clean up such releases. Amended in 1986 to increase the size of the Superfund, impose numerical goals and deadlines for cleanup of Superfund sites, and specify standards and procedures to be followed in determining the level and scope of cleanup actions, and in 2002 to encourage redevelopment of brownfields sites.

11. *Emergency Planning and Community Right-to-Know Act* (EPCRA): Enacted in 1986, this statute requires corporations to provide local authorities with detailed information concerning their use of any of several hundred toxic substances and to report annually the quantities of such chemicals released into the environment.

The federalizing of environmental law began with President Nixon signing the National Environmental Policy Act (NEPA), 42 U.S.C. §§4321-4370a, on national television on January 1, 1970. Declaring that "each person should enjoy a healthful environment," the statute established as "the continuing policy of the Federal Government . . . to use all practicable means and measures . . . to create conditions under which man and nature can exist in harmony. . . ." NEPA revolutionized environmental policy making not by imposing any substantive environmental controls, but rather by mandating changes in the decision-making process of federal agencies. The statute requires agencies to incorporate environmental concerns into their decision making by requiring them to perform detailed assessments of the environmental impacts of, and to consider alternatives to, any "major Federal actions significantly affecting the quality of the human environment." While NEPA only mandated *consideration* of environmental impacts, Congress soon declared certain impacts to be presumptively unacceptable when it forbade the taking of endangered species of fish, wildlife, or plants by enacting the Endangered Species Act in 1973. Once it became clear that citizens could enforce these requirements in court, they became a powerful new tool for challenging development projects.

Following the enactment of NEPA, Congress launched a succession of far-reaching regulatory programs to control pollution. In December 1970, Congress adopted the Clean Air Act, 42 U.S.C. §§7401-7642, and in October 1972 the Federal Water Pollution Control Act, 33 U.S.C. §§1251-1376, subsequently renamed the Clean Water Act. These statutes replaced what had been relatively modest federal research and financial assistance programs with comprehensive regulatory schemes to control air and water pollution throughout the nation. The Environmental Protection Agency (EPA), established by executive order in 1970, was directed to identify air pollutants that threatened public health or welfare and to establish national ambient air quality standards to be implemented by the states. In the Clean Water Act, Congress prohibited all unpermitted discharges of pollutants into the waters of the United States, it required EPA to implement technology-based effluent limits on dischargers, and it established a national permit system to be implemented by EPA or states subject to EPA supervision. Both acts spawned breathtakingly complex national regulatory programs. These programs have grown even more complicated over time as Congress, EPA, and state regulators have made adjustments in them in response to problems with their implementation.

While the first federal environmental statutes focused on control of conventional pollutants, growing public concern over toxic substances spurred enactment of a series of additional statutes that focused on protection of public health. Congress enacted the Safe Drinking Water Act (SDWA) in 1974, and in 1976 it enacted both the Toxic Substances Control Act (TSCA), 15 U.S.C. §§2601-2629, and the Resource Conservation and Recovery Act (RCRA), 42 U.S.C. §§6901-6987. The Safe Drinking Water Act requires EPA to establish regulations to protect public health from contaminants in public water supplies. TSCA authorizes the most explicitly far-reaching regulatory controls, which can be imposed on any chemical substance found by EPA to present an unreasonable risk to health or the environment. RCRA (which is a part of legislation also known as the Solid Waste Disposal Act) requires EPA to establish controls ensuring the safe management of hazardous waste from "cradle to grave."

Although EPA was formed in 1970 to consolidate environmental protection responsibilities in a single federal agency, EPA is not the only regulatory agency with substantial responsibilities for protecting public health and the environment. The Food and Drug Administration, which is now under the direction of the Department of Health and Human Services, has long been responsible for ensuring the safety of food, drugs, and cosmetics under the federal Food, Drug, and Cosmetic Act. In 1970, Congress created the Occupational Safety and Health Administration as part of the Department of Labor and charged it with ensuring the safety of the workplace. The Nuclear Regulatory Commission and the Department of Energy are responsible for protecting the public from risks posed by atomic material under the Atomic Energy Act. While the laws administered by these agencies usually are referred to as health and safety laws rather than environmental legislation, they are extremely important for the control of substances, products, and activities that pose environmental risks. Other agencies with substantial environmental responsibilities include the Department of the Interior, which is responsible for managing most public lands; the Department of Transportation, which regulates the transport of hazardous materials under the Hazardous Materials Transportation Act; the Council on Environmental Quality, charged with coordinating federal environmental policy and assisting federal agencies with NEPA compliance; the U.S. Army Corps of Engineers, which operates a permit program for dredge and fill activities under section 404 of the Clean Water Act; and the Department of Energy, which administers the National Energy Policy and Conservation Act.

### Figure 2.1   Legislative Authorities Affecting the Lifecycle of a Chemical

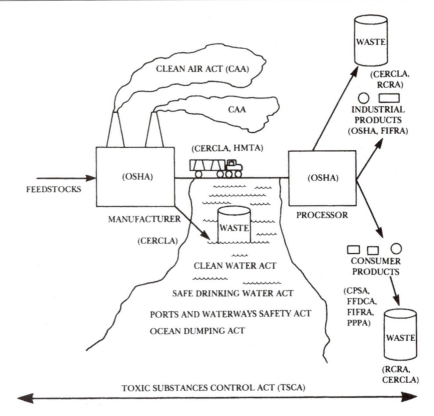

CERCLA: Comprehensive Environmental Response, Compensation, and Liability Act
FFDCA: Federal Food, Drug, and Cosmetic Act
RCRA: Resource Conservation and Recovery Act
FIFRA: Federal Insecticide, Fungicide, and Rodenticide Act
CPSA: Consumer Product Safety Act
OSHA: Occupational Safety and Health Act
HMTA: Hazardous Materials Transportation Act
PPPA: Poison Prevention Packaging Act

One of the final steps in the erection of the federal regulatory infrastructure was the enactment in 1980 of the Comprehensive Environmental Response, Compensation, and Liability Act, known as CERCLA or the Superfund law. This legislation went beyond the traditional command-and-control regulatory approach to controlling pollution and established a system of strict joint, and several liability for broad classes of parties associated with the release of hazardous substances. CERCLA creates powerful incentives for businesses to prevent releases of hazardous substances to avoid future liability.

Figure 2.1 provides a crude illustration of the jurisdictional reach of the major federal environmental laws. It illustrates that the regulatory authorities available for responding to an environmental problem generally depend on its location or the medium affected by the problem or the characteristics of the pollutant or product thought to be the source of the problem. For example, the Occupational Safety and Health Administration has jurisdiction over workplace hazards; the Consumer Product Safety Commission has authority to regulate hazards in consumer products; foods, drugs, and cosmetics are regulated by the federal Food and Drug Administration (FDA).

The regulatory authorities available to EPA to control pollution are largely dependent on where pollutants are discharged and the nature and source of each pollutant. The Clean Air Act authorizes the use of ambient air quality standards to control pollutants that come from numerous or diverse sources and that threaten public health or welfare. The types of controls that can be imposed depend on whether the source is a mobile or a stationary source of pollution; more stringent controls are imposed on new sources than on existing sources. EPA's jurisdiction under the Clean Water Act covers virtually all discharges of pollutants into the "waters of the United States," although the Army Corps of Engineers is given jurisdiction under the Act over the discharge of dredged or fill material into navigable waters. The Ocean Dumping Act gives EPA jurisdiction over the transport and dumping in ocean waters of materials other than dredged material. The Safe Drinking Water Act gives EPA jurisdiction over contaminants in public water supply systems, while FIFRA allows EPA to regulate the licensing and use of pesticides.

In theory, the Toxic Substances Control Act (TSCA) is the broadest source of EPA's regulatory authority because it authorizes EPA to ban or to restrict the manufacture, marketing, use, or disposal of any "chemical substance or mixture" (with the exception of pesticides and products regulated by the FDA). TSCA thus authorizes EPA to regulate chemicals through all phases of their "lifecycle," from manufacture through use and disposal in any environmental medium. Thus it appears to cover all of the activities shown in the diagram. While RCRA's coverage is somewhat more narrowly confined to solid wastes that are deemed hazardous by EPA, it too authorizes extensive controls. RCRA mandates regulation of hazardous wastes from "cradle to grave," including controls on disposal of it in any environmental medium (e.g., land disposal, incineration).

Complaints are often heard that the fragmented structure of environmental law makes it difficult to pursue coordinated regulatory responses to cross-media contamination. Often there is considerable overlap among the various laws that may be used to address a particular environmental problem. Congress has not laid out a single grand scheme or unifying principle that establishes priorities for regulation under the various statutes. Rather, it has directed that agencies implement a variety of programs under several statutes, while urging them to try to coordinate their actions with other agencies and within themselves.

From 1980 to 1994, the fifth phase in the history of environmental law featured Congress *Extending and Refining Regulatory Strategies* it had launched to protect the environment during the 1970s. As the initial environmental laws were reauthorized by Congress, they were broadened, strengthened, and made more specific. Comprehensive amendments to RCRA were adopted in 1984, to CERCLA and the Safe Drinking Water Act in 1986, to the Clean Water Act in 1987, and to the Clean Air Act in 1990.

Many of the amendments enacted during this period tried to force the federal environmental agencies to implement the environmental laws in a more expeditious fashion. Faced with an executive branch less sympathetic to environmental concerns, Congress imposed new deadlines for agencies to act and it established specific sanctions for agencies which failed to carry out the laws. "Hammer" provisions written into some laws specified regulations that would take effect automatically if an agency failed to adopt regulations of its own by a particular date. For example, the Hazardous and Solid Waste Amendments of 1984 said that all land disposal of hazardous waste would be banned by certain dates unless a specific determination was made that certain levels of treatment were sufficient to avoid future environmental problems. Sanctions for violating the environmental laws also were increased dramatically, with substantial criminal penalties imposed on those who intentionally violate the laws.

During this period there also was a move toward more innovative forms of regulation. The Emergency Planning and Community Right-to-Know Act, 42 U.S.C. §§11001-11050, enacted in 1986, requires industries to report annually the volume of their releases of hundreds of toxic substances. The Act creates a national inventory of toxic releases that must be made accessible to the public, using information as a tool for mobilizing public pressure to reduce toxic emissions. The Clean Air Act Amendments of 1990 provide the first large-scale experiment with emissions trading approaches long advocated by economists as a more efficient means for reducing pollution. While mandating significant reductions in sulfur dioxide emissions, the law creates emissions allowances that may be bought and sold to ensure that the reductions are obtained in the cheapest manner possible. During this period Congress also amended several environmental statutes to broaden the role of Native American tribes in environmental policy. EPA is now authorized to treat tribes in the same manner as it treats states under the Clean Air Act, the Clean Water Act, the Comprehensive Environmental Response, Compensation and Liability Act, and the Safe Drinking Water Act.

Beginning with the midterm election of 1994, the pendulum that swung so powerfully toward environmental protection during the 1970s and 1980s appeared to be moving in the other direction with a Congress and a judiciary decidedly more skeptical about environmental regulation. We call this a period of *Regulatory Recoil and Reinvention*.

The 1994 congressional elections gave the Republicans control of both houses of Congress under a leadership decidedly antagonistic toward environmental regulation. However, their aggressive efforts to repeal major provisions of the federal environmental statutes backfired, as demonstrated in 1995 when legislation to dramatically weaken the Clean Water Act passed the House but was killed because of public outcry and President Clinton's veto threat.

Unable to directly repeal the environmental statutes, the congressional leadership concentrated on measures to make it more difficult to adopt new regulations or to enforce existing laws. These included appropriations riders that temporarily prevented the listing of new endangered species and that suspended environmental safeguards for timber harvesting on federal lands. They also included legislation to make it more difficult to regulate state and local governments and small businesses. In March 1995, Congress enacted the Unfunded Mandates Reform Act, which makes it procedurally more difficult to impose new regulatory requirements on state and local governments in the absence of federal funding for compliance. In March 1996, Congress enacted the Small Business Regulatory Enforcement Fairness Act (SBREFA), which makes it more difficult for EPA to issue regulations that affect small businesses.

**Figure 2.2**

To defuse pressures to weaken the environmental laws, the Clinton administration launched a series of initiatives to "reinvent regulation" to make it more flexible and less costly. Efforts to find common ground between industry and environmental groups over legislative reforms were successful in August 1996 when food safety reform legislation (the Food Quality Protection Act of 1996) and legislation to reauthorize the Safe Drinking Water Act were enacted by overwhelming margins in Congress. Each piece of legislation was the product of significant compromises between industrial and environmental interests that produced consensus legislation with broad support from traditionally antagonistic groups.

The administration of President George W. Bush was generally hostile toward environmental regulation. Shortly after taking office, President Bush in March 2001 repudiated the Kyoto Protocol and his own campaign pledge to regulate emissions of carbon dioxide that contribute to climate change. While significant amendments to CERCLA to encourage cleanup and redevelopment of brownfields were adopted unanimously by Congress in 2001 and signed into law in January 2002, Small Business Liability Relief and Brownfields Revitalization Act, Pub. L. No. 107-118, the Bush administration pressed Congress unsuccessfully to open ANWR to oil drilling (discussed in Chapter 1) and to weaken other environmental laws. After the Democrats recaptured both houses of Congress in the 2006 elections, they pushed for legislation to increase energy efficiency and to promote renewable energy. In December 2007, Congress enacted the Energy Independence and Security Act of 2007, which raised automobile fuel economy standards to 35 miles per gallon by 2020 and mandated increased production of biofuels, and a phaseout of the use of inefficient incandescent light bulbs by 2014.

The seventh phase in the history of U.S. environmental law began as soon as President Barack Obama took office in 2009. Obama acted quickly to *Tackle Climate Change.* Less than a week after taking office, President Obama moved to strengthen fuel economy standards and to reconsider the Bush administration's veto of California's request to adopt its own controls on greenhouse gases (GHGs) from motor vehicles. In June 2009, the House of Representatives narrowly passed comprehensive legislation to control GHG emissions, but the legislation never came to a vote in the Senate. In the 2010 midterm election, Republicans gained control of both houses of Congress. In the 112th session of Congress in 2011-2012, the Republican-controlled House of Representatives approved more than 300 bills to roll back or restrict environmental regulation. Nearly all of these measures failed to win approval in the Senate.

After winning reelection in 2012, President Obama vowed in his 2013 State of the Union Address that if Congress did not act to respond to climate change, he would take executive action to do so. In 2015, EPA adopted the Clean Power Plan to regulate GHG emissions from existing power plants, but these regulations were stayed by the U.S. Supreme Court in January 2016 before any court had a chance to rule on their merits. In June 2016 Congress overwhelmingly adopted the Frank S. Lautenberg Chemical Safety for the 21st Century Act, a comprehensive overhaul of the Toxic Substances Control Act.

The eighth phase began after the surprise election victory of President Donald Trump. From 2017-2021 the Trump administration made determined efforts to roll back federal environmental regulations. Although many of its actions were invalidated by courts, the administration attempted to roll back 125 environmental regulations. President Trump withdrew from the Paris Climate Agreement, making the United States the only country in the world not participating in it. Trump's EPA tried to shrink federal Clean Water Act jurisdiction by replacing the Obama administration's Water of the U.S. (WOTUS) rule with a much narrower Navigable Waters Protection Regulation (NWPR). It replaced the Clean Power Plan's (CPP) restrictions on greenhouse gas emissions with a toothless Affordable Clean Energy (ACE) regulation. Even after President Trump was defeated in the November 2020 election, his administration rushed to grant leases for oil drilling in the Arctic National Wildlife Refuge before leaving office.

In August 2020 a bipartisan group of six former EPA administrators released a report providing a blueprint for restoring EPA. Entitled "Resetting the Course of EPA," *https://www.environmentalprotectionnetwork.org/wp-content/uploads/2020/08/Resetting-the-Course-of-EPA-Report.pdf,* the report anticipated President Trump's defeat in the 2020 presidential election. Beginning on inauguration day, President Biden moved swiftly to cancel Trump administration rollbacks and to place renewed focus on environmental justice and the climate crisis. See Executive Order 13,990, Protecting Public Health and the Environment and Restoring Science to Tackle the Climate Crisis.

## B.   The Impact of Regulatory Legislation on Common Law Actions

With the advent of comprehensive federal regulatory statutes, courts soon faced questions concerning the impact of public law on common law actions. While statutes may supplant common law if legislative bodies so intend, legislative intent is often deliberately left murky because legislators are loath to disturb the products of decades of judicially developed doctrine. Thus, the relationship between environmental statutes and the common law can be a complicated one.

As noted above, the Supreme Court in Illinois v. City of Milwaukee, 406 U.S. 91 (1972) (*Milwaukee I*), delegated jurisdiction over federal common law nuisance actions between states to the federal district courts. Thus, following the Supreme Court's decision in *Milwaukee I*, Illinois pursued its common law nuisance action in federal district court. While this action was pending, the federal Clean Water Act was enacted. This legislation established a comprehensive regulatory scheme to control water pollution by requiring all dischargers of pollutants into surface waters to obtain a permit, usually from a state environmental agency operating under federal oversight. Milwaukee ultimately obtained a permit limiting the discharges from its sewage treatment plants. While Milwaukee argued that the permit precluded Illinois's nuisance action, Illinois maintained that the permit limits were too lax and that the discharges remained a nuisance at common law.

In 1977, the district court rejected Milwaukee's defense, ruling that Milwaukee's discharge of inadequately treated sewage was a nuisance under federal common law and ordering the city to control its discharges more stringently than required by its Clean Water Act permit. The Seventh Circuit affirmed the district court's holding that the Clean Water Act had not preempted the federal common law of nuisance, but it held that the district court should not have required more stringent limits on discharges of treated sewage than required by the city's permit. The case then returned to the Supreme Court, which addressed the impact of the Clean Water Act's regulatory scheme on federal common law nuisance actions in City of Milwaukee v. Illinois, 451 U.S. 304 (1981) (*Milwaukee II*).

In *Milwaukee II*, the Supreme Court held that Illinois's federal common law nuisance action had been preempted by the federal Clean Water Act. Writing for the Court, Justice Rehnquist noted that legislative preemption of *federal* common law did not implicate the same federalism concerns that require clear expressions of congressional intent before state law may be preempted. Illinois had argued that there was clear evidence that Congress had not intended to preempt federal common law based on the savings clause in the citizen suit provision of section 505(e) of the Clean Water Act, which provides: "Nothing in this section shall restrict any right which any person (or class of persons) may have under any statute or common law to seek enforcement of any effluent standard or limitation or to seek any other relief (including relief against the Administrator or a State agency)." However, the Supreme Court read this language narrowly to mean "that nothing *in §505*, the citizen-suit provision, should be read as limiting any other remedies which might exist. . . .[I]t means only that the provision of such suit does not revoke other remedies. It most assuredly cannot be read to mean that the Act as a whole does not supplant formerly available federal common-law actions but only that the particular section authorizing citizen suits does not do so." 451 U.S. at 328-329 (emphasis in original).

Citing the comprehensive nature of the Clean Water Act's regulatory scheme and the technical complexities courts would have to confront to formulate pollution control standards, Justice Rehnquist concluded that Congress implicitly had supplanted federal common law by adopting a comprehensive regulatory scheme for water pollution control. "Congress' intent in enacting the Amendments was clearly to establish an all-encompassing program of water pollution regulation. *Every* point source discharge is prohibited unless covered by a permit, which directly subjects the discharger to the administrative apparatus established by Congress to achieve its goals." Justice Rehnquist concluded that "[t]he establishment of such a self-consciously comprehensive program by Congress, which certainly did not exist when *Illinois v. Milwaukee* was decided, strongly suggests that there is no room for courts to attempt to improve on that program with federal common law." *Milwaukee II*, 451 U.S. at 318-319 (emphasis in original). He went on to note that application of federal common law would be "peculiarly inappropriate in areas as complex as water pollution control. . . . Not only are the technical problems difficult—doubtless the reason Congress vested authority to administer the Act in administrative agencies possessing the necessary expertise—but the general area is particularly unsuited to the approach inevitable under a regime of federal common law. Congress criticized past approaches to water pollution control as being 'sporadic' and 'ad hoc,' S. Rep. No. 92-414, p. 95 (1971), 2 Leg. Hist. 1511, apt characterizations of any judicial approach applying federal common law, see Wilburn Boat Co. v. Fireman's Fund Ins. Co., 348 U.S. 310, 319 (1955)." *Milwaukee II*, 451 U.S. at 325.

Justice Rehnquist noted that Illinois was free to pursue its case for more stringent controls on Milwaukee's discharges before the Wisconsin state agency responsible for issuing Milwaukee a permit under the Clean Water Act. But he maintained that "[i]t would be quite inconsistent with this scheme if federal courts were in effect to 'write their own ticket' under the guise of federal common law after permits have already been issued and permittees have been planning and operating in reliance on them."

The Court soon confronted the question whether the Clean Water Act pre-empted *state* common law actions in International Paper Company v. Ouellette, 479 U.S. 481 (1987). The *Ouellette* litigation commenced when Harmel Ouellette, a Vermont resident, appeared in the office of Peter Langrock, a country lawyer in a two-person firm. Ouellette complained that he and his wife, who owned property in Vermont fronting on Lake Champlain, no longer could tolerate the stench generated by pollution from a paper mill located across the lake in New York. Langrock filed a private nuisance action in Vermont state court on behalf of 150 lakeshore property owners. The defendant, International Paper Company (IPC), removed the action to federal court, where it maintained that the Clean Water Act preempted state common law in light of the Supreme Court's *Milwaukee II* decision. The case ultimately went to the U.S. Supreme Court, which rendered the following decision.

## International Paper Co. v. Ouellette

479 U.S. 481 (1987)

JUSTICE POWELL delivered the opinion of the court. . . .

[W]e turn to the question presented: whether the Act pre-empts Vermont common law to the extent that law may impose liability on a New York point source. We begin the analysis by noting that it is not necessary for a federal statute to provide explicitly that particular state laws are pre-empted. Hillsborough County v. Automated Medical Laboratories, Inc., 471 U.S. 707, 713 (1985). Although courts should not lightly infer pre-emption, it may be presumed when the federal legislation is "sufficiently comprehensive to make reasonable the inference that Congress 'left no room' for supplementary state regulation." Ibid. In addition to express or implied pre-emption, a state law also is invalid to the extent that it "actually conflicts with a. . .federal statute." Ray v. Atlantic Richfield Co., 435 U.S. 151, 158 (1978). Such a conflict will be found when the state law "stands as an obstacle to the accomplishment and execution of the full purposes and objectives of Congress." Hillsborough County v. Automated Medical Laboratories, Inc., supra, at 713. . . .

Given that the Act itself does not speak directly to the issue, the Court must be guided by the goals and policies of the Act in determining whether it in fact preempts an action based on the law of an affected State. After examining the CWA as a whole, its purposes and its history, we are convinced that if affected States were allowed to impose separate discharge standards on a single point source, the inevitable result would be a serious interference with the achievement of the "full purposes and objectives of Congress." See Hillsborough County v. Automated Medical Laboratories, Inc., supra, at 713. Because we do not believe Congress intended to undermine this carefully drawn statute through a general saving clause, we conclude that the CWA precludes a court from applying the law of an affected State against an out-of-state source.

. . . In this case the application of Vermont law against IPC would allow respondents to circumvent the NPDES permit system, thereby upsetting the balance of public and private interests so carefully addressed by the Act. . . .

An interpretation of the saving clause that preserved actions brought under an affected State's law would disrupt this balance of interests. If a New York source were liable for violations of Vermont law, that law could effectively override both the permit requirements and the policy choices made by the source State. The affected State's nuisance laws would subject the point source to the threat of legal and equitable penalties if the permit standards were less stringent than those imposed by the affected State. Such penalties would compel the source to adopt different control standards and a different compliance schedule from those approved by the EPA, even though the affected State had not engaged in the same weighing of the costs and benefits.

Our conclusion that Vermont nuisance law is inapplicable to a New York point source does not leave respondents without a remedy. The CWA precludes only those suits that may require standards of effluent control that are incompatible with those established by the procedures set forth in the Act. The saving clause specifically preserves other state actions, and therefore nothing in the Act bars aggrieved individuals from bringing a nuisance claim pursuant to the law of the source State. By its terms the CWA allows States such as New York to impose higher standards on their own point sources, and in *Milwaukee II* we recognized that this authority may include the right to impose higher common-law as well as higher statutory restrictions. 451 U.S., at 328 (suggesting that "States may adopt more stringent limitations . . . through state nuisance law, and apply them to in-state dischargers").

An action brought against IPC under New York nuisance law would not frustrate the goals of the CWA as would a suit governed by Vermont law. First, application of the source State's law does not disturb the balance among federal, source-state, and affected-state interests. Because the Act specifically allows source

States to impose stricter standards, the imposition of source-state law does not disrupt the regulatory partnership established by the permit system. Second, the restriction of suits to those brought under source-state nuisance law prevents a source from being subject to an indeterminate number of potential regulations. Although New York nuisance law may impose separate standards and thus create some tension with the permit system, a source only is required to look to a single additional authority, whose rules should be relatively predictable. Moreover, States can be expected to take into account their own nuisance laws in setting permit requirements.

## NOTES AND QUESTIONS

1. *Ouellette* preserves the ability of plaintiffs to bring state common law actions against polluters so long as the law of the source state, rather than the receiving state, is applied. As Dan Farber observes in discussing *Ouellette*, "after hanging by its fingernails from a cliff in *Milwaukee II*, the common law came roaring back in the final episode." Farber, The Story of *Boomer*, Environmental Law Stories 40 (2005). Preemption of state common law remedies by state regulatory statutes remains extremely rare.

2. The requirement that the state common law of the source state be applied did not significantly disadvantage the plaintiffs in *Ouellette*. On remand, New York nuisance law proved no more favorable to the paper company than Vermont's would have been. International Paper hired an engineering firm, which conducted extensive "smell test" experiments in an effort to show that the plant's air emissions were not a nuisance. Langrock countered with the testimony of tolltakers working at the Crown Point Bridge who said out-of-state drivers persistently asked, "What the hell is that awful smell?" when they arrived at the tollbooth. With evidence showing that International Paper had violated its air and water permits more than 1,000 times, plaintiffs pressed for punitive damages. The company ultimately settled with the plaintiffs for $5 million, including the establishment of a trust fund for environmental projects in the Lake Champlain area. The colorful story of this litigation is recounted by Peter Langrock, the plaintiffs' lawyer, in P. Langrock, Addison County Justice: Tales from a Vermont Courthouse (1997).

3. For a discussion of the difficulty the Court had in developing a defensible rationale for the result in *Ouellette*, as revealed in the papers of the late Justice Thurgood Marshall, see Percival, Environmental Law in the Supreme Court: Highlights from the Marshall Papers, 23 Envtl. L. Rep. 10606, 10618 (1993). The history of the interstate nuisance litigation over water pollution is described in more detail in Percival, The Clean Water Act and the Demise of the Federal Common Law of Interstate Nuisance, 55 Ala. L. Rev. 717 (2004).

4. Two months after it decided *Milwaukee II*, the Supreme Court held that neither the Clean Water Act nor the Marine Protection, Research, and Sanctuaries Act of 1972 (Ocean Dumping Act) created an implied private right of action for damages. The Court in Middlesex County Sewerage Authority v. National Sea Clammers Ass'n, 453 U.S. 1 (1981) further concluded that the federal common law of nuisance has been fully preempted in the area of water pollution by the Clean Water Act and, to the extent that ocean waters not covered by the Clean Water

Act are involved, by the Ocean Dumping Act. In the litigation following the *Exxon Valdez* oil spill, Exxon claimed that the Clean Water Act preempted private claims for punitive damages for water pollution caused by reckless conduct. The Supreme Court rejected this position in Exxon Shipping Co. v. Baker, 554 U.S. 471 (2008). The Court stated that: "All in all, we see no clear indication of congressional intent to occupy the entire field of pollution remedies, nor for that matter do we perceive that punitive damages for private harms will have any frustrating effect on the CWA remedial scheme, which would point to preemption." Id. at 489. In a footnote the Court then distinguished *Milwaukee II* and *National Sea Clammers* as cases "where plaintiffs' common law nuisance claims amounted to arguments for effluent-discharge standards different from those provided by the CWA." Id. at 489 n.7. The "private claims for economic injury" in the *Exxon Valdez* litigation "do not threaten similar interference with federal regulatory goals," the Court explained.

5.  In January 2009, a federal district judge ruled in favor of an interstate nuisance claim brought by the state of North Carolina against the Tennessee Valley Authority (TVA) for transboundary air pollution. After a lengthy trial the court required three coal-fired power plants operated by TVA in eastern Tennessee and one in Alabama to adopt stricter pollution control measures to abate a nuisance their pollutants caused in North Carolina. But the court rejected the state's efforts to require new controls on seven other, more distant power plants. North Carolina v. Tennessee Valley Authority, 593 F. Supp. 2d 812 (W.D.N.C. 2009), rev'd, 615 F.3d 291 (4th Cir. 2010). The court cited the Clean Air Act's savings clause, 42 U.S.C. §7604(e), in ruling that compliance with the Clean Air Act did not preclude nuisance liability. North Carolina v. Tennessee Valley Authority, 549 F. Supp. 2d 725, 729 (W.D.N.C. 2008). On appeal the U.S. Court of Appeals for the Fourth Circuit reversed, stating that the decision "would encourage courts to use vague public nuisance standards to scuttle the nation's carefully created system for accommodating the need for energy production and the need for clean air. The result would be a balkanization of clean air regulations and a confused patchwork of standards, to the detriment of industry and the environment alike." North Carolina v. Tennessee Valley Authority, 615 F.3d 291, 296 (4th Cir. 2010). After North Carolina sought Supreme Court review, TVA in April 2011 settled both this case and parallel litigation charging it with violating the Clean Air Act by agreeing to close 18 old coal-fired generating units at three power plants. The settlement, which included eight units that had been required to install scrubbers by the district judge's order, is expected to reduce TVA's emissions of sulfur dioxide by 97 percent below 1977 levels and nitrogen oxides by 95 percent.

6.  In Bell v. Cheswick Generating Station, 734 F.3d 188 (3d Cir. 2013), the Third Circuit held that a power plant's compliance with the Clean Air Act does not insulate it from liability for nuisance, negligence, and trespass under Pennsylvania common law. The decision reversed a lower court that had dismissed a class action by 1,500 people living within a mile of a coal-fired power plant. The plaintiffs initially filed suit in Pennsylvania state court, alleging that emissions from the plant had caused ash and other contaminants to land on their property. The company that owned the plant, GenOn Power Midwest, L.P., then removed the case to federal court and filed a motion to dismiss, arguing that the Clean Air Act preempted the lawsuit because it imposed extensive regulations on the plant's operations. In support of its decision, the Third Circuit cited the Clean Air Act's "savings clauses"

in both the citizen suit provision, 42 U.S.C. §7604(e), and the provision for retention of state authority, 42 U.S.C. §7416. While noting that the plant's federal permit mandates that it prevent emissions from harming others, the court also noted that the permit itself has a savings clause providing that it shall not be construed as impairing state common law remedies. The court concluded that its decision was mandated by the Supreme Court's decision in *International Paper Co. v. Ouellette* (1987), which cited similar savings clause provisions in holding that the Clean Water Act did not preempt state tort litigation based on the law of the source state. Rejecting the company's arguments that this could cause conflicting state regulatory standards, the Third Circuit concluded that, like the Clean Water Act, the Clean Air Act serves "as a regulatory floor, not a ceiling, . . . that states are free to impose higher standards on their own sources of pollution, and that state tort law is a permissible way of doing so." See also Merrick v. Diageo Americas Supply, Inc., 805 F.3d 685 (6th Cir. 2015) and Freeman v. Grain Processing Corp., 848 N.W. 2d 58 (Iowa 2014) (both holding that the Clean Air Act does not preempt state common law tort claims when brought under the law of the source state).

7. In July 2004 eight states (Connecticut, New York, California, Iowa, New Jersey, Rhode Island, Vermont, and Wisconsin) and the City of New York filed a federal and state common law nuisance action against six of the largest electric utilities in the United States. The suit alleged that power plants operated by the defendant utilities account for 10 percent of U.S. emissions of carbon dioxide ($CO_2$), a greenhouse gas that contributes to global warming and climate change. Claiming that global warming already has begun to alter the climate of the United States, the plaintiffs sought an injunction requiring the utilities to cap their $CO_2$ emissions and then to reduce them by a specified percentage each year for at least a decade. On September 15, 2005, federal district Judge Loretta Preska dismissed the states' lawsuit by holding that it presented a nonjusticiable political question. Connecticut v. American Electric Power Co., 406 F. Supp. 2d 265 (S.D.N.Y. 2005). In September 2009 the U.S. Court of Appeals for the Second Circuit reversed Judge Preska's decision and held that the lawsuit could go forward. 582 F.3d 309 (2d Cir. 2009). The Supreme Court then agreed to review the case, resulting in the unanimous decision below.

## American Electric Power Co. v. Connecticut

564 U.S. 410 (2011)

JUSTICE GINSBURG delivered the opinion of the Court.

We address in this opinion the question whether the plaintiffs (several States, the city of New York, and three private land trusts) can maintain federal common law public nuisance claims against carbon-dioxide emitters (four private power companies and the federal Tennessee Valley Authority). As relief, the plaintiffs ask for a decree setting carbon-dioxide emissions for each defendant at an initial cap, to be further reduced annually. The Clean Air Act and the Environmental Protection Agency action the Act authorizes, we hold, displace the claims the plaintiffs seek to pursue.

. . . [T]he Second Circuit held that all plaintiffs had stated a claim under the "federal common law of nuisance." For this determination, the court relied dominantly on a series of this Court's decisions holding that States may maintain suits to abate air and water pollution produced by other States or by out-of-state industry. See, *e.g.*, Illinois v. Milwaukee, 406 U.S. 91, 93 (1972) (*Milwaukee I*) (recognizing right of Illinois to sue in federal district court to abate discharge of sewage into Lake Michigan).

The Court of Appeals further determined that the Clean Air Act did not "displace" federal common law. In Milwaukee v. Illinois, 451 U.S. 304, 316-319 (1981) (*Milwaukee II*), this Court held that Congress had displaced the federal common law right of action recognized in *Milwaukee I* by adopting amendments to the Clean Water Act, 33 U.S.C. §1251 et seq. That legislation installed an all encompassing regulatory program, supervised by an expert administrative agency, to deal comprehensively with interstate water pollution. The legislation itself prohibited the discharge of pollutants into the waters of the United States without a permit from a proper permitting authority. At the time of the Second Circuit's decision, by contrast, EPA had not yet promulgated any rule regulating greenhouse gases, a fact the court thought dispositive. "Until EPA completes the rulemaking process," the court reasoned, "we cannot speculate as to whether the hypothetical regulation of greenhouse gases under the Clean Air Act would in fact 'spea[k] directly' to the 'particular issue' raised here by Plaintiffs." . . .

## IV

### A

"There is no federal general common law," Erie R. Co. v. Tompkins, 304 U.S. 64, 78 (1938), famously recognized. In the wake of *Erie*, however, a keener understanding developed. See generally Friendly, In Praise of *Erie*—And of the New Federal Common Law, 39 N.Y.U. L. Rev. 383 (1964). *Erie* "le[ft] to the states what ought be left to them," *id.*, at 405, and thus required "federal courts [to] follow state decisions on matters of substantive law appropriately cognizable by the states," *id.*, at 422. *Erie* also sparked "the emergence of a federal decisional law in areas of national concern." *Id.*, at 405. The "new" federal common law addresses "subjects within national legislative power where Congress has so directed" or where the basic scheme of the Constitution so demands. *Id.*, at 408, n.119, 421-422. Environmental protection is undoubtedly an area "within national legislative power," one in which federal courts may fill in "statutory interstices," and, if necessary, even "fashion federal law." *Id.*, at 421-422. As the Court stated in *Milwaukee I*: "When we deal with air and water in their ambient or interstate aspects, there is a federal common law."

Decisions of this Court predating *Erie*, but compatible with the distinction emerging from that decision between "general common law" and "specialized federal common law," Friendly, *supra*, at 405, have approved federal common law suits brought by one State to abate pollution emanating from another State. See, *e.g.*, Missouri v. Illinois, 180 U.S. 208, 241-243 (1901) (permitting suit by Missouri to enjoin Chicago from discharging untreated sewage into interstate waters); New Jersey v. City of New York, 283 U.S. 473, 477, 481-483 (1931) (ordering New York City to stop dumping garbage off New Jersey coast); Georgia v. Tennessee Copper Co., 240 U.S. 650 (1916) (ordering private copper companies to curtail sulfur dioxide discharges in Tennessee that caused harm in Georgia). See also *Milwaukee I*, 406

U.S., at 107 (post-*Erie* decision upholding suit by Illinois to abate sewage discharges into Lake Michigan). The plaintiffs contend that their right to maintain this suit follows inexorably from that line of decisions. . . .

The defendants argue that considerations of scale and complexity distinguish global warming from the more bounded pollution giving rise to past federal nuisance suits. Greenhouse gases once emitted "become well mixed in the atmosphere"; emissions in New Jersey may contribute no more to flooding in New York than emissions in China. The plaintiffs, on the other hand, contend that an equitable remedy against the largest emitters of carbon dioxide in the United States is in order and not beyond judicial competence. And we have recognized that public nuisance law, like common law generally, adapts to changing scientific and factual circumstances. *Missouri*, 200 U.S., at 522 (adjudicating claim though it did not concern "nuisance of the simple kind that was known to the older common law").

We need not address the parties' dispute in this regard. For it is an academic question whether, in the absence of the Clean Air Act and the EPA actions the Act authorizes, the plaintiffs could state a federal common law claim for curtailment of greenhouse gas emissions because of their contribution to global warming. Any such claim would be displaced by the federal legislation authorizing EPA to regulate carbon-dioxide emissions.

### B

"[W]hen Congress addresses a question previously governed by a decision rested on federal common law," the Court has explained, "the need for such an unusual exercise of law-making by federal courts disappears." *Milwaukee II*, 451 U.S., at 314 (holding that amendments to the Clean Water Act displaced the nuisance claim recognized in *Milwaukee I*). Legislative displacement of federal common law does not require the "same sort of evidence of a clear and manifest [congressional] purpose" demanded for preemption of state law. *Id.*, at 317. "'[D]ue regard for the presuppositions of our embracing federal system . . . as a promoter of democracy,'" *id.*, at 316 (quoting San Diego Building Trades Council v. Garmon, 359 U.S. 236, 243 (1959)), does not enter the calculus, for it is primarily the office of Congress, not the federal courts, to prescribe national policy in areas of special federal interest. The test for whether congressional legislation excludes the declaration of federal common law is simply whether the statute "speak[s] directly to [the] question" at issue. Mobil Oil Corp. v. Higginbotham, 436 U.S. 618, 625 (1978).

We hold that the Clean Air Act and the EPA actions it authorizes displace any federal common law right to seek abatement of carbon-dioxide emissions from fossil-fuel fired power plants. *Massachusetts* made plain that emissions of carbon dioxide qualify as air pollution subject to regulation under the Act. And we think it equally plain that the Act "speaks directly" to emissions of carbon dioxide from the defendants' plants.

Section 111 of the Act directs the EPA Administrator to list "categories of stationary sources" that "in [her] judgment . . . caus[e], or contribut[e] significantly to, air pollution which may reasonably be anticipated to endanger public health or welfare." §7411(b)(1)(A). Once EPA lists a category, the agency must establish standards of performance for emission of pollutants from new or modified sources within that category. §7411(b)(1)(B); see also §7411(a)(2). And, most relevant here, §7411(d) then requires regulation of existing sources within the same category. For existing sources, EPA issues emissions guidelines, see 40 C.F.R. §60.22, .23 (2009); in compliance with those guidelines and subject to federal oversight, the States then issue performance standards for stationary sources within their jurisdiction, §7411(d)(1)....

If EPA does not *set* emissions limits for a particular pollutant or source of pollution, States and private parties may petition for a rulemaking on the matter, and EPA's response will be reviewable in federal court. As earlier noted, EPA is currently engaged in a §7411 rulemaking to set standards for greenhouse gas emissions from fossil-fuel fired power plants. To settle litigation brought under §7607(b) by a group that included the majority of the plaintiffs in this very case, the agency agreed to complete that rulemaking by May 2012. The Act itself thus provides a means to seek limits on emissions of carbon dioxide from domestic power plants — the same relief the plaintiffs seek by invoking federal common law. We see no room for a parallel track.

### C

The plaintiffs argue, as the Second Circuit held, that federal common law is not displaced until EPA actually exercises its regulatory authority, *i.e.*, until it sets standards governing emissions from the defendants' plants. We disagree.

The sewage discharges at issue in *Milwaukee II*, we do not overlook, were subject to effluent limits set by EPA; under the displacing statute, "[e]very point source discharge" of water pollution was "prohibited unless covered by a permit." As *Milwaukee II* made clear, however, the relevant question for purposes of displacement is "whether the field has been occupied, not whether it has been occupied in a particular manner." Of necessity, Congress selects different regulatory regimes to address different problems. Congress could hardly preemptively prohibit every discharge of carbon dioxide unless covered by a permit. After all, we each emit carbon dioxide merely by breathing.

The Clean Air Act is no less an exercise of the legislature's "considered judgment" concerning the regulation of air pollution because it permits emissions *until* EPA acts. The critical point is that Congress delegated to EPA the decision whether and how to regulate carbon-dioxide emissions from power plants; the delegation is what displaces federal common law. Indeed, were EPA to decline to regulate carbon-dioxide emissions altogether at the conclusion of its ongoing §7411 rulemaking, the federal courts would have no warrant to employ the federal common law of nuisance to upset the agency's expert determination.

EPA's judgment, we hasten to add, would not escape judicial review. Federal courts, we earlier observed, can review agency action (or a final rule declining to take action) to ensure compliance with the statute Congress enacted. As we have noted, the Clean Air Act directs EPA to establish emissions standards for categories of stationary sources that, "in [the Administrator's] judgment," "caus[e], or contribut[e] significantly to, air pollution which may reasonably be anticipated to endanger public health or welfare." §7411(b)(1)(A). "[T]he use of the word 'judgment,'" we explained in *Massachusetts*, "is not a roving license to ignore the statutory text." "It is but a direction to exercise discretion within defined statutory limits." EPA may not decline to regulate carbon dioxide emissions from power plants if refusal to act would be "arbitrary, capricious, an abuse of discretion, or otherwise not in accordance with law." §7607(d)(9)(A). If the plaintiffs in this case are dissatisfied with the outcome of EPA's forthcoming rulemaking, their recourse under federal law is to seek Court of Appeals review, and, ultimately, to petition for certiorari in this Court.

Indeed, this prescribed order of decisionmaking — the first decider under the Act is the expert administrative agency, the second, federal judges — is yet another reason to resist setting emissions standards by judicial decree under federal tort law. The appropriate amount of regulation in any particular greenhouse gas-producing sector cannot be prescribed in a vacuum: as with other questions of national or international policy, informed assessment of competing interests is required. Along with the environmental benefit potentially achievable, our Nation's energy needs and the possibility of economic disruption must weigh in the balance. . . .

It is altogether fitting that Congress designated an expert agency, here, EPA, as best suited to serve as primary regulator of greenhouse gas emissions. The expert agency is surely better equipped to do the job than individual district judges issuing ad hoc, case-by-case injunctions. Federal judges lack the scientific, economic, and technological resources an agency can utilize in coping with issues of this order. Judges may not commission scientific studies or convene groups of experts for advice, or issue rules under notice-and-comment procedures inviting input by any interested person, or seek the counsel of regulators in the States where the defendants are located. Rather, judges are confined by a record comprising the evidence the parties present. Moreover, federal district judges, sitting as sole adjudicators, lack authority to render precedential decisions binding other judges, even members of the same court.

## NOTES AND QUESTIONS

1. What is it about the Clean Air Act that convinces the Court that it displaces the federal common law of interstate nuisance in the context of greenhouse gas (GHG) emissions? If EPA had not commenced a rulemaking to regulate GHG emissions from power plants, would the nuisance litigation still be displaced?

2. The Court holds that the Clean Air Act displaces the *federal* common law of nuisance with respect to this lawsuit, but in another portion of the opinion the Court expressly reserved judgment on the question of whether *state* nuisance law is preempted, noting that the issue had neither been briefed nor argued. In light of *International Paper Co. v. Ouellette*, should the Clean Air Act be held to preempt *state* common law nuisance suits for emissions that contribute to climate change?

3. More than 20 cities, counties, and states have brought separate climate suits in state courts asserting state law fraud claims against more than 20 companies that produce or sell fossil fuels. These cases allege that the fossil fuel industry knew about the dangers of climate change but acted to deceive the public in order to promote their products. Unlike the plaintiffs in *American Electric Power (AEP)*, the governments bringing these cases do not seek orders requiring reductions in greenhouse gas emissions; instead they seek damages to compensate them for some of their costs of responding to climate change. The fossil fuel industry defendants have sought to remove each of these cases to federal courts, but they have been largely unsuccessful. In BP p.l.c. v. Mayor and City Council of Baltimore,

141 S. Ct. 1532 (2021), the Supreme Court held that appellate courts can consider all grounds for removal when district court remand orders are appealed. But the Court declined to address the oil industry's argument that all climate litigation, because it deals with a global problem, should be deemed to arise under federal common law and be displaced by the *AEP* decision. In a case filed initially in federal court under federal common law, the Second Circuit has ruled that *AEP* should displace both federal *and* state nuisance actions. City of New York v. Chevron Corp., 993 F.3d 81 (2d Cir. 2021).

4. The first post-*AEP* decision involving a claim of displacement of federal nuisance law involved the very Chicago Sanitary Canal that spawned the *Missouri v. Illinois* decision. Today Great Lakes states are highly concerned that the canal may serve as a conduit for invasive species of Asian carp to reach the Great Lakes from the Mississippi River. Michigan, joined by four other Great Lakes states, brought a federal nuisance action against Illinois in an effort to force the closing of the canal to block the carp from reaching Lake Michigan. The states argued that the potential economic damage to commercial and recreational fishing and tourism from an Asian carp invasion of the Great Lakes would be far greater than the losses to Illinois caused by halting shipping on the canal. In August 2011, the U.S. Court of Appeals for the Seventh Circuit upheld a district judge's refusal to issue a preliminary injunction to require the Army Corps of Engineers to close the canal. Michigan v. U.S. Army Corps of Engineers, 667 F.3d 765 (7th Cir. 2011). But the court agreed with the states that the federal common law of nuisance had not been displaced in the context of invasive species. The court concluded that *American Electric Power* "did not establish a new test based solely on Congress's delegation of regulatory power; it simply pointed out that delegation is one type of congressional action that is evidence of displacement." 667 F.3d at 777-778. The court stressed that the Supreme Court had emphasized the comprehensive nature of the Clean Air Act even with respect to regulation of greenhouse gas emissions and the multiple avenues for public and private enforcement as well as the right of the public to seek judicial review of denials of petitions for rulemakings. In contrast to the Clean Air Act's provisions, "congressional efforts to curb the migration of invasive species, and of invasive carp in particular, have yet to reach the level of detail one sees in the air or water pollution schemes." Id. at 778-779. The court noted that "neither the Corps nor any other agency has been empowered actively to regulate the problem of invasive carp, and Congress has not required any agency to establish a single standard to deal with the problem or to take any other action." It also emphasized that no enforcement mechanism has been created by Congress that would provide recourse in the courts for parties adversely affected by invasive carp. Thus, it concluded that federal nuisance law had not been displaced.

5. In September 2012, the U.S. Court of Appeals for the Ninth Circuit dismissed a public nuisance suit seeking damages to relocate an Alaskan village disappearing due to sea level rise. Residents of the village of Kivalina sued 22 oil, energy, and utility companies, alleging that they had contributed to global warming and climate change that caused the sea level rise. In 2009, federal district judge Saundra V. Armstrong dismissed the case as a nonjusticiable political question. On appeal the Ninth Circuit affirmed the dismissal, but on the narrower ground that the Clean Air Act had displaced the federal common law of nuisance concerning emissions

of greenhouse gases based on the *American Electric Power* decision. Native Village of Kivalina v. ExxonMobil Corp., 696 F.3d 849 (9th Cir. 2012). Writing for the panel, Judge Sidney R. Thomas stated that "the Supreme Court has held [in *AEP*] that federal common law addressing domestic greenhouse gas emissions has been displaced by Congressional action. That determination displaces federal common law public nuisance actions seeking damages, as well as those actions seeking injunctive relief." Thus, "the solution to Kivalina's dire circumstance must rest in the hands of the legislative and executive branches of our government, not the federal common law." 696 F.3d at 858.

## C.   Standing to Sue to Enforce the Environmental Laws

A fundamental question confronting courts early in the development of modern environmental law was who would have standing to seek judicial redress to enforce the new laws. This question reached the Supreme Court in the following classic case that arose when the U.S. Forest Service agreed to allow the Disney Corporation to develop a large ski resort in a national wildlife refuge adjacent to Sequoia National Park. After failing to persuade the Forest Service to at least hold a public hearing on the proposal, the Sierra Club filed suit under the judicial review provisions of the Administrative Procedure Act. A federal district court granted a preliminary injunction to halt the project, but the Ninth Circuit reversed, holding that the Sierra Club had not alleged a sufficient interest to qualify for standing. The U.S. Supreme Court then granted review and issued the following decision.

## Sierra Club v. Morton

405 U.S. 727 (1972)

Mr. Justice Stewart delivered the opinion of the Court.

The Mineral King Valley is an area of great natural beauty nestled in the Sierra Nevada Mountains in Tulare County, California, adjacent to Sequoia National Park. It has been part of the Sequoia National Forest since 1926, and is designated as a national game refuge by special Act of Congress. Though once the site of extensive mining activity, Mineral King is now used almost exclusively for recreational purposes. Its relative inaccessibility and lack of development have limited the number of visitors each year, and at the same time have preserved the valley's quality as a quasi-wilderness area largely uncluttered by the products of civilization.

. . . The final Disney plan, approved by the Forest Service in January 1969, outlines a $35 million complex of motels, restaurants, swimming pools, parking lots, and other structures designed to accommodate 14,000 visitors daily. This complex is to be constructed on 80 acres of the valley floor under a 30-year use permit from the Forest Service. Other facilities, including ski lifts, ski trails, a cog-assisted railway, and utility installations, are to be constructed on the mountain slopes and in other parts of the valley under a revocable special-use permit. To provide access to the resort, the State of California proposes to construct a highway 20 miles in length. A section of this road would traverse Sequoia National Park, as would a proposed high-voltage power line needed to provide electricity for the resort. Both the highway and the power line require the approval of the Department of the Interior, which is entrusted with the preservation and maintenance of the national parks.

. . . The petitioner Sierra Club sued as a membership corporation with "a special interest in the conservation and the sound maintenance of the national parks, game refuges and forests of the country," and invoked the judicial-review provisions of the Administrative Procedure Act, 5 U.S.C. §701 et seq. . . .

The first question presented is whether the Sierra Club has alleged facts that entitle it to obtain judicial review of the challenged action. . . .

The injury alleged by the Sierra Club will be incurred entirely by reason of the change in the uses to which Mineral King will be put, and the attendant change in the aesthetics and ecology of the area. Thus, in referring to the road to be built through Sequoia National Park, the complaint alleged that the development "would destroy or otherwise adversely affect the scenery, natural and historic objects and wildlife of the park and would impair the enjoyment of the park for future generations." We do not question that the type of harm may amount to an "injury in fact" sufficient to lay the basis for standing under §10 of the APA. Aesthetic and environmental well-being, like economic well-being, are important ingredients of the quality of life in our society, and the fact that particular environmental interests are shared by the many rather than the few does not make them less deserving of legal protection through the judicial process. But the "injury in fact" test requires more than an injury to a cognizable interest. It requires that the party seeking review be himself among the injured.

The impact of the proposed changes in the environment of Mineral King will not fall indiscriminately upon every citizen. The alleged injury will be felt directly only by those who use Mineral King and Sequoia National Park, and for whom the aesthetic and recreational values of the area will be lessened by the highway and ski resort. The Sierra Club failed to allege that it or its members would be affected in any of their activities or pastimes by the Disney development. Nowhere in the pleadings or affidavits did the Club state that its members use Mineral King for any purpose, much less that they use it in any way that would be significantly affected by the proposed actions of the respondents. . . .

The trend of cases arising under the APA and other statutes authorizing judicial review of federal agency action has been toward recognizing that injuries other than economic harm are sufficient to bring a person within the meaning of the statutory language, and toward discarding the notion that an injury that is widely shared is ipso facto not an injury sufficient to provide the basis for judicial review. We noted this development with approval in *Data Processing*, 397 U.S., at 154, in saying that the interest alleged to have been injured "may reflect 'aesthetic, conservational, and recreational' as well as economic values." But broadening the categories of injury that may be alleged in support of standing is a different matter from abandoning the requirement that the party seeking review must himself have suffered an injury.

Some courts have indicated a willingness to take this latter step by conferring standing upon organizations that have demonstrated "an organizational interest in the problem" of environmental or consumer protection. Environmental Defense Fund v. Hardin, 428 F.2d 1093, 1097. It is clear that an organization whose members are injured may represent those members in a proceeding for judicial review.

See, e.g., NAACP v. Button, 371 U.S. 415, 428. But a mere "interest in a problem," no matter how longstanding the interest and no matter how qualified the organization is in evaluating the problem, is not sufficient by itself to render the organization "adversely affected" or "aggrieved" within the meaning of the APA. The Sierra Club is a large and long-established organization, with a historic commitment to the cause of protecting our Nation's natural heritage from man's depredations. But if a "special interest" in this subject were enough to entitle the Sierra Club to commence this litigation, there would appear to be no objective basis upon which to disallow a suit by any other bona fide "special interest" organization, however small or short-lived. And if any group with a bona fide "special interest" could initiate such litigation, it is difficult to perceive why any individual citizen with the same bona fide special interest would not also be entitled to do so.

The requirement that a party seeking review must allege facts showing that he is himself adversely affected does not insulate executive action from judicial review, nor does it prevent any public interests from being protected through the judicial process. It does serve as at least a rough attempt to put the decision as to whether review will be sought in the hands of those who have a direct stake in the outcome. That goal would be undermined were we to construe the APA to authorize judicial review at the behest of organizations or individuals who seek to do no more than vindicate their own value preferences through the judicial process. The principle that the Sierra Club would have us establish in this case would do just that.

As we conclude that the Court of Appeals was correct in its holding that the Sierra Club lacked standing to maintain this action, we do not reach any other questions presented in the petition, and we intimate no view on the merits of the complaint. The judgment is affirmed.

Mr. Justice Douglas, dissenting.

I share the view of my Brother Blackmun and would reverse the judgment below.

The critical question of "standing" would be simplified and also put neatly in focus if we fashioned a federal rule that allowed environmental issues to be litigated before federal agencies or federal courts in the name of the inanimate object about to be despoiled, defaced, or invaded by roads and bulldozers and where injury is the subject of public outrage. Contemporary public concern for protecting nature's ecological equilibrium should lead to the conferral of standing upon environmental objects to sue for their own preservation. See Stone, Should Trees Have Standing? — Toward Legal Rights for Natural Objects, 45 S. Cal. L. Rev. 450 (1972). This suit would therefore be more properly labeled as Mineral King v. Morton.

Inanimate objects are sometimes parties in litigation. A ship has a legal personality, a fiction found useful for maritime purposes. The corporation sole — a creature of ecclesiastical law — is an acceptable adversary and large fortunes ride on its cases. The ordinary corporation is a "person" for purposes of the adjudicatory processes, whether it represents proprietary, spiritual, aesthetic, or charitable causes.

So it should be as respects valleys, alpine meadows, rivers, lakes, estuaries, beaches, ridges, groves of trees, swampland, or even air that feels the destructive pressures of modern technology and modern life. The river, for example, is the living symbol of all the life it sustains or nourishes—fish, aquatic insects, water ouzels, otter, fisher, deer, elk, bear, and all other animals, including man, who are dependent on it or who enjoy it for its sight, its sound, or its life. The river as plaintiff speaks for the ecological unit of life that is part of it. Those people who have a meaningful relation to that body of water—whether it be a fisherman, a canoeist, a zoologist, or a logger—must be able to speak for the values which the river represents and which are threatened with destruction. . . .

The voice of the inanimate object, therefore, should not be stilled. That does not mean that the judiciary takes over the managerial functions from the federal agency. It merely means that before these priceless bits of Americana (such as a valley, an alpine meadow, a river, or a lake) are forever lost or are so transformed as to be reduced to the eventual rubble of our urban environment, the voice of the existing beneficiaries of these environmental wonders should be heard.

## NOTES AND QUESTIONS

1. The Sierra Club's complaint contained the following allegations concerning the Club's interest in the dispute:

> Plaintiff Sierra Club is a non-profit corporation organized and operating under the laws of the State of California, with its principal place of business in San Francisco, California since 1892. Membership of the club is approximately 78,000 nationally, with approximately 27,000 members residing in the San Francisco Bay Area. For many years the Sierra Club by its activities and conduct has exhibited a special interest in the conservation and the sound maintenance of the national parks, game refuges and forests of the country, regularly serving as a responsible representative of persons similarly situated. One of the principal purposes of the Sierra Club is to protect and conserve the national resources of the Sierra Nevada Mountains. Its interests would be vitally affected by the acts hereinafter described and would be aggrieved by those acts of the defendants as hereinafter more fully appears.

Why was this allegation insufficient to establish the Sierra Club's standing? What would they have had to allege concerning their interests and activities in order to have had standing to bring their action?

2. The government argued before the Supreme Court that if the Sierra Club had standing on the basis of their allegation, then "anyone who asserts an interest in a controversy has standing." Do you agree?

3. While *Sierra Club v. Morton* was before the Supreme Court, the Wilderness Society and other environmental groups filed an amicus brief that described in more detail the specific nature of the Sierra Club's interest in Mineral King. It recited the Club's long efforts to include the area in Sequoia National Park, that the Club regularly conducted camping trips in the area, and that its individual members used the area for recreational purposes and would be damaged by its development. In its reply brief, however, the Sierra Club expressly declined to rely on this as a basis for standing. Why, do you think, did they refuse to do so?

The papers of the late Justice Thurgood Marshall indicate that the Court was well aware that the Sierra Club's use of Mineral King was more direct than reflected in the complaint's allegations. Justice Brennan sought to have the Court dismiss the case as improvidently granted because the Club's members did actually use the area. While he was unsuccessful in this effort, Justice Stewart did agree to modify the majority opinion one week before it was released to add a crucial footnote specifying that the Sierra Club was free to amend its complaint on remand. Percival, Environmental Law in the Supreme Court: Highlights from the Marshall Papers, 23 Envtl. L. Rep. 10,606, 10,620 (1993).

4. Although he did not join in Justice Douglas's very personal dissent, Justice Blackmun also dissented. Noting that the case involved "significant aspects of a wide, growing, and disturbing problem, that is, the nation's and the world's deteriorating environment," Justice Blackmun questioned whether the law must "be so rigid and our procedure so inflexible that we render ourselves helpless when the existing methods and the traditional concepts . . . do not prove to be entirely adequate for new issues." Both Justice Douglas and Justice Blackmun felt so strongly about their dissents that they took the unusual step of reading them from the bench when the decision was announced.

5. Should trees have standing? U.S. courts have consistently rejected the viewpoint of Justice Douglas's dissent. How convincing is his claim that in other areas of law courts recognize legal representatives for entities incapable of representing their own interests? Many environmentalists argue that a basic problem with our legal and political processes is that they are incapable of taking into account the interests of future generations. For an ambitious proposal by the Climate Legal Initiative to redress this problem in the context of shaping climate change policy, see Burns H. Weston & Tracy Bach, Recalibrating the Laws of Humans with the Laws of Nature: Climate Change, Human Rights, and Intergenerational Justice (2009).

6. The Supreme Court's recognition that injury to aesthetic and environmental values may be sufficient to confer standing even if the injury is shared by many remains the case's most significant legacy. While the Court ruled against the Sierra Club on the standing issue, it noted in a footnote that the decision did not bar the Sierra Club from seeking to amend its complaint when the case returned to the district court. On remand, the Sierra Club amended its complaint to allege that its members used the area and it added as co-plaintiffs nine individuals who regularly visited Mineral King and a group that owns property nearby. The Club also added a new claim that the National Environmental Policy Act, which had been enacted after the original lawsuit had been filed, required the preparation of an environmental impact statement (EIS). The draft EIS was released in January 1975. By then Mineral King had become a national environmental *cause célèbre*. When the final EIS was released in 1976, the Mineral King project had essentially died a natural death. The EIS found severe environmental impacts from the proposed development and recommended that the project be scaled down significantly. The ski resort was never built. The Sierra Club's lawsuit eventually was dismissed without prejudice in 1977. Mineral King was made part of Sequoia National Park in October 1978. It remains spectacularly beautiful and largely off the beaten path today. The narrow, winding road into the secluded canyon has not been improved and trailers and RVs are prohibited from tackling its 639 curves, which are a challenge to motorists.

### Standing Doctrine in Environmental Cases After Sierra Club v. Morton

*Sierra Club* confirmed a shift in standing logic. Previously, standing doctrine in effect conceived of the government as being just like a private party, and standing could be determined by the following test. Hypothetically substitute "Jones" for the government agency as defendant in the case. If the complaint stated a cause of action in tort, or for breach of contract, or for violation of a property right against Jones, the plaintiff had standing. This became known as the "legal wrong" test of standing. The government agency could then invoke its alleged statutory authority for the action, and thus the issue of the validity of the statute or the propriety of the action under the statute would be joined.

This legal wrong test, which has also been termed a "private law" model of standing, was modified somewhat as the regulatory state expanded. The Supreme Court began to acknowledge standing in situations where specific statutory language suggested that Congress had intended to give additional parties the right to sue. For instance, in FCC v. Sanders Brothers Radio Station, 309 U.S. 470 (1940), the Court permitted a competitor of an FCC licensee to sue on the basis of the competitor's alleged economic injury, even though the common law did not protect against competitively caused economic loss, because the Federal Communications Act allows anyone "aggrieved or whose interests are adversely affected" to seek judicial review, 47 U.S.C. §402(b)(6), and the competitor had suffered a traditionally recognized type of injury, economic damage.

When the Administrative Procedure Act (APA) was passed in 1946, it provided that "a person suffering legal wrong because of agency action, or adversely affected or aggrieved by agency action within the meaning of a relevant statute, is entitled to judicial review thereof." 5 U.S.C. §702. In his influential manual on the APA, the attorney general stated that this language codified then-existing law.

In the 1960s, lower courts pushed standing doctrine to the limits of section 702, largely under the influence of citizen and environmental groups — the presumed beneficiaries of many of the statutes Congress had enacted — who were dissatisfied with agency interpretations and actions. The details of these doctrinal developments are told in Stewart, The Reformation of American Administrative Law, 88 Harv. L. Rev. 1669 (1975), and Sunstein, Standing and the Privatization of Public Law, 88 Colum. L. Rev. 1432 (1988).

*Sierra Club* and contemporary cases seemed to recognize a general right of citizens to challenge government action as long as they had suffered "injury in fact" and raised claims "arguably" within the "zone of interests" that Congress sought to protect. *Sierra Club* was followed in the Court's next term by United States v. Students Challenging Regulatory Agency Proceedings, 412 U.S. 669 (1973) (*SCRAP*). Plaintiffs were law students challenging the ICC's approval of a freight rate they alleged would discourage the use of recycled materials. As injury-in-fact, they alleged that the rate change would lead to increased litter, as well as an increase in consumption of natural resources, in the forests, parks, and mountain areas around Washington, D.C., which the students used for hiking, fishing, and backpacking. Although the Court thought this an "attenuated line of causation," it held the plaintiffs' allegations sufficient for standing.

*SCRAP* was a high-water mark for environmental standing. Although it has never overruled *SCRAP*, the Court has issued decisions suggesting that it has drawn back from it. This is especially so in one recurring pattern of cases in which the plaintiff's injury is not directly caused by the complained-of agency action but is mediated by the actions of third parties. In such cases, the Court has expressed concern over whether a ruling in the plaintiff's favor will actually redress the plaintiff's injury; otherwise, it has said, "exercise of its power . . . would be gratuitous and thus inconsistent with the Art. III limitation" limiting federal jurisdiction to "cases and controversies." Simon v. Eastern Kentucky Welfare Rights Organization, 426 U.S. 26, 38 (1976) (*EKWRO*).

In the case that follows, EPA's decision not to regulate emissions of greenhouse gases that cause climate change was challenged by a group of NGOs, cities, and states, with Massachusetts as the lead plaintiff. EPA argued that any harm caused by climate change was too remote and too diffuse to give plaintiffs standing to sue.

## Massachusetts v. EPA

549 U.S. 497 (2007)

JUSTICE STEVENS delivered the opinion of the Court.

. . . EPA maintains that because greenhouse gas emissions inflict widespread harm, the doctrine of standing presents an insuperable jurisdictional obstacle. We do not agree. At bottom, "the gist of the question of standing" is whether petitioners have "such a personal stake in the outcome of the controversy as to assure that concrete adverseness which sharpens the presentation of issues upon which the court so largely depends for illumination." *Baker v. Carr*, 369 U.S. 186, 204 (1962). . . .

To ensure the proper adversarial presentation, *Lujan* [*v. Defenders of Wildlife*] holds that a litigant must demonstrate that it has suffered a concrete and particularized injury that is either actual or imminent, that the injury is fairly traceable to the defendant, and that it is likely that a favorable decision will redress that injury. However, a litigant to whom Congress has "accorded a procedural right to protect his concrete interests," *id.*, at 572, n.7—here, the right to challenge agency action unlawfully withheld, §7607(b)(1) — "can assert that right without meeting all the normal standards for redressability and immediacy," *ibid.* When a litigant is vested with a procedural right, that litigant has standing if there is some possibility that the requested relief will prompt the injury-causing party to reconsider the decision that allegedly harmed the litigant. *Ibid.* . . .

Well before the creation of the modern administrative state, we recognized that States are not normal litigants for the purposes of invoking federal jurisdiction [in *Georgia v. Tennessee Copper*]. . . .

Just as Georgia's "independent interest . . . in all the earth and air within its domain" supported federal jurisdiction a century ago, so too does Massachusetts' well-founded desire to preserve its sovereign territory today. That Massachusetts does in fact own a great deal of the "territory alleged to be affected" only reinforces the conclusion that its stake in the outcome of this case is sufficiently concrete to warrant the exercise of federal judicial power.

When a State enters the Union, it surrenders certain sovereign prerogatives. Massachusetts cannot invade Rhode Island to force reductions in greenhouse gas emissions, it cannot negotiate an emissions treaty with China or India, and in some circumstances the exercise of its police powers to reduce in-state motor-vehicle emissions might well be pre-empted.

These sovereign prerogatives are now lodged in the Federal Government, and Congress has ordered EPA to protect Massachusetts (among others) by prescribing standards applicable to the "emission of any air pollutant from any class or classes of new motor vehicle engines, which in [the Administrator's] judgment cause, or contribute to, air pollution which may reasonably be anticipated to endanger public health or welfare." 42 U.S.C. §7521(a)(1). Congress has moreover recognized a concomitant procedural right to challenge the rejection of its rulemaking petition as arbitrary and capricious. §7607(b)(1). Given that procedural right and Massachusetts' stake in protecting its quasi-sovereign interests, the Commonwealth is entitled to special solicitude in our standing analysis.

With that in mind, it is clear that petitioners' submissions as they pertain to Massachusetts have satisfied the most demanding standards of the adversarial process. EPA's steadfast refusal to regulate greenhouse gas emissions presents a risk of harm to Massachusetts that is both "actual" and "imminent." *Lujan*, 504 U.S., at 560. There is, moreover, a "substantial likelihood that the judicial relief requested" will prompt EPA to take steps to reduce that risk. Duke Power Co. v. Carolina Environmental Study Group, Inc., 438 U.S. 59, 79 (1978).

## THE INJURY

The harms associated with climate change are serious and well recognized. Indeed, the NRC Report itself—which EPA regards as an "objective and independent assessment of the relevant science," 68 Fed. Reg. 52930—identifies a number of environmental changes that have already inflicted significant harms, including "the global retreat of mountain glaciers, reduction in snow-cover extent, the earlier spring melting of rivers and lakes, [and] the accelerated rate of rise of sea levels during the 20th century relative to the past few thousand years. . . ." NRC Report 16.

Petitioners allege that this only hints at the environmental damage yet to come. According to the climate scientist Michael MacCracken, "qualified scientific experts involved in climate change research" have reached a "strong consensus" that global warming threatens (among other things) a precipitate rise in sea levels by the end of the century, "severe and irreversible changes to natural ecosystems," a "significant reduction in water storage in winter snowpack in mountainous regions with direct and important economic consequences," and an increase in the spread of disease. He also observes that rising ocean temperatures may contribute to the ferocity of hurricanes.

That these climate-change risks are "widely shared" does not minimize Massachusetts' interest in the outcome of this litigation. According to petitioners' unchallenged affidavits, global sea levels rose somewhere between 10 and 20 centimeters over the 20th century as a result of global warming. These rising seas have already begun to swallow Massachusetts' coastal land. Because the Commonwealth "owns a substantial portion of the state's coastal property," it has alleged a particularized injury in its capacity as a landowner. The severity of that injury will only increase over the course of the next century: If sea levels continue to rise as predicted, one Massachusetts official believes that a significant fraction of coastal property will be "either permanently lost through inundation or temporarily lost through periodic storm surge and flooding events." Remediation costs alone, petitioners allege, could run well into the hundreds of millions of dollars.

### CAUSATION

EPA does not dispute the existence of a causal connection between man-made greenhouse gas emissions and global warming. At a minimum, therefore, EPA's refusal to regulate such emissions "contributes" to Massachusetts' injuries.

EPA nevertheless maintains that its decision not to regulate greenhouse gas emissions from new motor vehicles contributes so insignificantly to petitioners' injuries that the agency cannot be haled into federal court to answer for them. For the same reason, EPA does not believe that any realistic possibility exists that the relief petitioners seek would mitigate global climate change and remedy their injuries. That is especially so because predicted increases in greenhouse gas emissions from developing nations, particularly China and India, are likely to offset any marginal domestic decrease.

But EPA overstates its case. Its argument rests on the erroneous assumption that a small incremental step, because it is incremental, can never be attacked in a federal judicial forum. Yet accepting that premise would doom most challenges to regulatory action. Agencies, like legislatures, do not generally resolve massive problems in one fell regulatory swoop. . . . That a first step might be tentative does not by itself support the notion that federal courts lack jurisdiction to determine whether that step conforms to law.

And reducing domestic automobile emissions is hardly a tentative step. Even leaving aside the other greenhouse gases, the United States transportation sector emits an enormous quantity of carbon dioxide into the atmosphere—according to the MacCracken affidavit, more than 1.7 billion metric tons in 1999 alone. That accounts for more than 6% of worldwide carbon dioxide emissions. To put this in perspective: Considering just emissions from the transportation sector, which represent less than one-third of this country's total carbon dioxide emissions, the United States would still rank as the third-largest emitter of carbon dioxide in the world, outpaced only by the European Union and China. Judged by any standard, U.S. motor-vehicle emissions make a meaningful contribution to greenhouse gas concentrations and hence, according to petitioners, to global warming.

### THE REMEDY

While it may be true that regulating motor-vehicle emissions will not by itself *reverse* global warming, it by no means follows that we lack jurisdiction to decide whether EPA has a duty to take steps to *slow* or *reduce* it. Because of the enormity of the potential consequences associated with man-made climate change, the fact that the effectiveness of a remedy might be delayed during the (relatively short) time it takes for a new motor-vehicle fleet to replace an older one is essentially irrelevant. Nor is it dispositive that developing countries such as China and India are poised to increase greenhouse gas emissions substantially over the next century: A reduction in domestic emissions would slow the pace of global emissions increases, no matter what happens elsewhere.

We moreover attach considerable significance to EPA's "agree[ment] with the President that 'we must address the issue of global climate change,'" 68 Fed. Reg. 52929 (quoting remarks announcing Clear Skies and Global Climate Initiatives, 2002 Public Papers of George W. Bush, Vol. 1, Feb. 14, p. 227 (2004)), and to EPA's ardent support for various voluntary emission-reduction programs, 68 Fed. Reg. 52932. As Judge Tatel observed in dissent below, "EPA would presumably not bother with such efforts if it thought emissions reductions would have no discernable impact on future global warming." 415 F.3d, at 66.

In sum—at least according to petitioners' uncontested affidavits—the rise in sea levels associated with global warming has already harmed and will continue to harm Massachusetts. The risk of catastrophic harm, though remote, is nevertheless real. That risk would be reduced to some extent if petitioners received the relief they seek. We therefore hold that petitioners have standing to challenge the EPA's denial of their rulemaking petition.

[Chief Justice Roberts filed a dissent, joined by Justices Scalia, Thomas, and Alito arguing that plaintiffs lacked standing because any harm caused by climate change was too speculative, remote, and diffuse and unlikely to be remedied by judicial action. The Chief Justice argued that responding to any problems caused by climate change was the proper function of Congress and the president and not the federal courts.]

## NOTES AND QUESTIONS

1. Does this decision represent a relatively fact-specific disagreement between the Justices in the majority and the dissent unlikely to affect standing law generally, or do the opinions reflect a basic division on the Court that may greatly affect the law of standing? Both the majority and dissent employ the modern, three-part framework for addressing issues of standing: injury, causation, and redressability. To the majority, injury is established by rising sea levels that, according to affidavits from plaintiffs' experts, already are swallowing up coastal lands. But in his dissent Chief Justice Roberts dismisses this as modeling the prediction of future damage from climate change as "pure conjecture" that would render "utterly toothless" a requirement that injury be "imminent." With respect to the redressability prong of standing, the majority and dissent could not be further apart. Justice Stevens stresses that redressability does not require that the problem of climate change be solved "in one fell regulatory swoop." Incremental progress to slow or reduce the injury is all that is required. The Chief Justice deems the plaintiffs' affidavits suggesting that U.S. action could be a catalyst for broader regulation of GHG emissions by other countries to be "conclusory" and "fanciful." He describes the majority's approach as "every little bit helps, so Massachusetts can sue over any little bit." Massachusetts v. EPA, 549 U.S. at 546 (Roberts, C.J., dissenting).

2. Most fundamentally, the disagreement between the majority and dissent seems to center over their divergent views concerning the proper role of the judiciary in deciding issues of environmental policy. Criticizing the Court's 1973 standing decision in the *SCRAP* case, the Chief Justice writes: "Over time, *SCRAP* became emblematic not of the looseness of Article III standing requirements, but of how utterly manipulable they are if not taken seriously as a matter of judicial

self-restraint. *SCRAP* made standing seem a lawyer's game, rather than a fundamental limitation ensuring that courts function as courts and not intrude on the politically accountable branches. Today's decision is *SCRAP* for a new generation." Id. at 548 (Roberts, C.J., dissenting). In response Justice Stevens deems it "quite wrong" to denigrate the claims of plaintiffs as analogous to a "lawyers game." Quoting verbatim from *SCRAP* and supplying his own emphasis, Stevens writes: "*To deny standing to persons who are in fact injured simply because many others are also injured, would mean that the most injurious and widespread Government actions could be questioned by nobody.*" Id. at 526 n.24.

3. A superb book that focuses in detail on the legal strategy behind the *Massachusetts v. EPA* litigation is Richard Lazarus, *The Rule of Five* (2020). The book reveals that the plaintiffs deliberately pitched the case as a standard administrative law case rather than a groundbreaking environmental one.

4. In his dissent Chief Justice Roberts also argues that the decision "changes the rules" of standing by creating a special rule of standing for states. Although the majority opinion, citing *Georgia v. Tennessee Copper*, emphasizes that the Court owes "special solicitude" for the interests of states, it then finds that they meet each of the normal requirements for establishing standing—injury, causation, and redressability. Some observers believe that Justice Stevens's discussion of *Georgia v. Tennessee Copper* and the special status of states was inserted to get Justice Kennedy's crucial fifth vote, particularly since Justice Kennedy raised *Tennessee Copper* at oral argument even though it had not been cited in any briefs. Will *Massachusetts v. EPA* be treated as a relatively narrow "sovereign-state" standing decision or will it make it easier for private plaintiffs to establish standing, particularly to litigate climate change issues? For lower court decisions favoring the former, see, e.g., Public Citizen v. NHTSA, 489 F.3d 1279, 1294 n.2 (D.C. Cir. 2007), Canadian Lumber Trade Alliance v. United States, 517 F.3d 1319 (Fed. Cir. 2008), and Washington Environmental Council v. Bellon, 732 F.3d 1131 (9th Cir. 2013).

5. Justice Breyer is the only Justice from the *Massachusetts v. EPA* majority who is still on the Court. Three of the four dissenters who rejected standing for climate litigation—Chief Justice Roberts and Justices Thomas and Alito—remain on the Court. Now that the Court has a solid 6-3 conservative majority, it is possible that it will restrict environmental standing in the future. Environmental standing is explored in more detail in Chapter 10.

6. In November 2016, federal district judge Ann Aiken in Portland, Oregon, rejected a motion to dismiss a novel "future generations" climate change lawsuit against the federal government. Juliana v. United States, 217 F. Supp. 3d 1224 (D. Or. 2016). The plaintiffs, who included 21 people who were between the ages of 8 and 19 when the case was filed, allege that the federal government knew about the dangers of climate change for more than 50 years, but failed to take action to protect them and continued to promote fossil fuel use. They claimed that this violated their substantive due process rights to life, liberty, and property as well as the government's public trust obligations to hold natural resources in trust for future generations. The plaintiffs sought a declaration that their rights have been violated and an order requiring federal officials to develop a plan to control emissions of greenhouse gases. Days before the case was scheduled to go to trial in October 2018, Chief Justice John Roberts granted an emergency motion by the federal

government to stay the trial. Judge Aiken then certified an interlocutory appeal to the Ninth Circuit of her denial of the motion to dismiss. All three judges on the Ninth Circuit panel hearing the appeal—Andrew D. Hurwitz, Mary H. Murgia, and Josephine Staton—had been appointed by President Barack Obama.

## Juliana v. United States

947 F.3d 1159 (9th Cir. 2020)

HURWITZ, Circuit Judge:

In the mid-1960s, a popular song warned that we were "on the eve of destruction." The plaintiffs in this case have presented compelling evidence that climate change has brought that eve nearer. A substantial evidentiary record documents that the federal government has long promoted fossil fuel use despite knowing that it can cause catastrophic climate change, and that failure to change existing policy may hasten an environmental apocalypse.

The plaintiffs claim that the government has violated their constitutional rights, including a claimed right under the Due Process Clause of the Fifth Amendment to a "climate system capable of sustaining human life." The central issue before us is whether, even assuming such a broad constitutional right exists, an Article III court can provide the plaintiffs the redress they seek—an order requiring the government to develop a plan to "phase out fossil fuel emissions and draw down excess atmospheric $CO_2$." Reluctantly, we conclude that such relief is beyond our constitutional power. Rather, the plaintiffs' impressive case for redress must be presented to the political branches of government. . . .

The government . . . argues that the plaintiffs lack Article III standing to pursue their constitutional claims. To have standing under Article III, a plaintiff must have (1) a concrete and particularized injury that (2) is caused by the challenged conduct and (3) is likely redressable by a favorable judicial decision. A plaintiff need only establish a genuine dispute as to these requirements to survive summary judgment.

### 1.

The district court correctly found the injury requirement met. At least some plaintiffs claim concrete and particularized injuries. Jaime B., for example, claims that she was forced to leave her home because of water scarcity, separating her from relatives on the Navajo Reservation. Levi D. had to evacuate his coastal home multiple times because of flooding. These injuries are not simply " 'conjectural' or 'hypothetical;'" at least some of the plaintiffs have presented evidence that climate change is affecting them now in concrete ways and will continue to do so unless checked.

The government argues that the plaintiffs' alleged injuries are not particularized because climate change affects everyone. But, "it does not matter how many persons have been injured" if the plaintiffs' injuries are "concrete and personal." And, the Article III injury requirement is met if only one plaintiff has suffered concrete harm.

**2.**

The district court also correctly found the Article III causation requirement satisfied for purposes of summary judgment. Causation can be established "even if there are multiple links in the chain," as long as the chain is not "hypothetical or tenuous." The causal chain here is sufficiently established. The plaintiffs' alleged injuries are caused by carbon emissions from fossil fuel production, extraction, and transportation. A significant portion of those emissions occur in this country; the United States accounted for over 25% of worldwide emissions from 1850 to 2012, and currently accounts for about 15%. See *Massachusetts*, 549 U.S. at 524–25 (finding that emissions amounting to about 6% of the worldwide total showed cause of alleged injury "by any standard"). And, the plaintiffs' evidence shows that federal subsidies and leases have increased those emissions. About 25% of fossil fuels extracted in the United States come from federal waters and lands, an activity that requires authorization from the federal government. . . .

The more difficult question is whether the plaintiffs' claimed injuries are redressable by an Article III court. . . . To establish Article III redressability, the plaintiffs must show that the relief they seek is both (1) substantially likely to redress their injuries; and (2) within the district court's power to award. Redress need not be guaranteed, but it must be more than "merely speculative."

The plaintiffs first seek a declaration that the government is violating the Constitution. But that relief alone is not substantially likely to mitigate the plaintiffs' asserted concrete injuries. A declaration, although undoubtedly likely to benefit the plaintiffs psychologically, is unlikely by itself to remediate their alleged injuries absent further court action.

The crux of the plaintiffs' requested remedy is an injunction requiring the government not only to cease permitting, authorizing, and subsidizing fossil fuel use, but also to prepare a plan subject to judicial approval to draw down harmful emissions. . . . The plaintiffs concede that their requested relief will not alone solve global climate change, but they assert that their "injuries would be to some extent ameliorated." Relying on *Massachusetts v. EPA*, the district court apparently found the redressability requirement satisfied because the requested relief would likely slow or reduce emissions. That case, however, involved a procedural right that the State of Massachusetts was allowed to assert "without meeting all the normal standards for redressability;" in that context, the Court found redressability because "there [was] some possibility that the requested relief [would] prompt the injury-causing party to reconsider the decision that allegedly harmed the litigant." The plaintiffs here do not assert a procedural right, but rather a substantive due process claim.

We are therefore skeptical that the first redressability prong is satisfied. But even assuming that it is, the plaintiffs do not surmount the remaining hurdle—establishing that the specific relief they seek is within the power of an Article III court. There is much to recommend the adoption of a comprehensive scheme to decrease fossil fuel emissions and combat climate change, both as a policy matter in general and a matter of national survival in particular. But it is beyond the power of an Article III court to order, design, supervise, or implement the plaintiffs' requested remedial plan. As the opinions of their experts make plain, any effective plan would necessarily require a host of complex policy decisions entrusted, for better or worse, to the wisdom and discretion of the executive and legislative branches. . . .

The dissent correctly notes that the political branches of government have to date been largely deaf to the pleas of the plaintiffs and other similarly situated individuals. But, although inaction by the Executive and Congress may affect the form of judicial relief ordered when there is Article III standing, it cannot bring otherwise nonjusticiable claims within the province of federal courts.

The plaintiffs have made a compelling case that action is needed; it will be increasingly difficult in light of that record for the political branches to deny that climate change is occurring, that the government has had a role in causing it, and that our elected officials have a moral responsibility to seek solutions. We do not dispute that the broad judicial relief the plaintiffs seek could well goad the political branches into action. We reluctantly conclude, however, that the plaintiffs' case must be made to the political branches or to the electorate at large, the latter of which can change the composition of the political branches through the ballot box. That the other branches may have abdicated their responsibility to remediate the problem does not confer on Article III courts, no matter how well-intentioned, the ability to step into their shoes.

STATON, District Judge, dissenting:

In these proceedings, the government accepts as fact that the United States has reached a tipping point crying out for a concerted response — yet presses ahead toward calamity. It is as if an asteroid were barreling toward Earth and the government decided to shut down our only defenses. Seeking to quash this suit, the government bluntly insists that it has the absolute and unreviewable power to destroy the Nation.

My colleagues throw up their hands, concluding that this case presents nothing fit for the Judiciary. On a fundamental point, we agree: No case can single-handedly prevent the catastrophic effects of climate change predicted by the government and scientists. But a federal court need not manage all of the delicate foreign relations and regulatory minutiae implicated by climate change to offer real relief, and the mere fact that this suit cannot alone halt climate change does not mean that it presents no claim suitable for judicial resolution.

Plaintiffs bring suit to enforce the most basic structural principle embedded in our system of ordered liberty: that the Constitution does not condone the Nation's willful destruction. So viewed, plaintiffs' claims adhere to a judicially administrable standard. And considering plaintiffs seek no less than to forestall the Nation's demise, even a partial and temporary reprieve would constitute meaningful redress. Such relief, much like the desegregation orders and statewide prison injunctions the Supreme Court has sanctioned, would vindicate plaintiffs' constitutional rights without exceeding the Judiciary's province. For these reasons, I respectfully dissent.

## NOTES AND QUESTIONS

1. Why did the Ninth Circuit find that it was incapable of redressing the plaintiffs' claims? Is this part of the decision consistent with the Supreme Court's finding of redressability in *Massachusetts v. EPA*, which also challenged the federal government's failure to control greenhouse gas emissions? Judge Staton in

dissent read *Massachusetts* to hold that "a perceptible reduction in the advance of climate change is sufficient to redress a plaintiff's climate change-induced harms." But the majority noted that "*Massachusetts* 'permitted a State to challenge EPA's refusal to regulate greenhouse gas emissions,' finding that as a sovereign it was 'entitled to special solicitude in [the] standing analysis.' Here, in contrast, the plaintiffs are not sovereigns, and a substantive right, not a procedural one, is at issue." Is this rationale for distinguishing Massachusetts's finding of redressability persuasive to you?

2. Recall the statement by the late Justice Ginsburg in *American Electric Power v. Connecticut* that EPA "is surely better equipped" to "serve as primary regulator of greenhouse gas emissions . . . than individual district judges issuing ad hoc, case-by-case injunctions." She noted that "judges lack the scientific, economic, and technological resources an agency can utilize in coping with issues of this order." Does the rationale of *American Electric Power* support the majority's finding of lack of redressability in *Juliana*?

3. In her dissent Judge Staton argues that "[i]t is as if an asteroid were barreling toward Earth and the government decided to shut down our only defenses." Is this an appropriate analogy? Would a more appropriate one be a frog in a slowing boiling pot, which Al Gore used in his movie classic *An Inconvenient Truth*?

## D.  Environmental Federalism: Three Models of Federal-State Relations

While the growth of environmental regulation largely has been driven by federal legislation, states and Native American tribes continue to play an important role in the development and implementation of environmental policy. Even though the federal environmental laws often require states to meet minimum national standards, they generally do not preempt state law except in narrowly defined circumstances. State common law remains an important tool for seeking compensation for environmental damage. Some of the most innovative environmental protection measures are the product of state legislation, such as California's Proposition 65 (see Chapter 3), New Jersey's Environmental Cleanup and Responsibility Act (discussed in Chapter 4), and Michigan's Environmental Protection Act.

The federalization of environmental law was a product of the concern that state and local authorities lacked the resources and political capability to control problems that were becoming national in scope. Congress has employed three general approaches for accomplishing its environmental protection objectives. The first approach is to *provide federal financial assistance* to encourage states to adopt environmental standards on their own. While this approach proved largely ineffective for controlling air and water pollution, it remains the principal federal approach to issues such as land use management where political opposition to federal regulation is particularly acute. Federal programs encourage state and local planning for land use and solid waste management under the Coastal Zone Management Act, the Clean Water Act, and Subtitle D of the Resource Conservation and Recovery Act. The power of this tool for motivating states to act depends largely on the amount of federal financial assistance involved. As federal funding for such programs has declined, this approach has become a less significant vehicle for promoting state action.

The second model, which currently is the predominant approach to federal-state relations under the environmental statutes, can be called a *"cooperative federalism" approach*. Under this model, federal agencies establish national environmental standards and states may opt to assume responsibility for administering them or to leave implementation to federal authorities. The Clean Air Act, the Clean Water Act, RCRA, and the Safe Drinking Water Act require EPA to establish minimum national standards, while authorizing delegation of authority to implement and administer the programs to states that demonstrate that they can meet minimum federal requirements. In states that choose not to seek program delegation, the programs are operated and enforced by federal authorities. Federally recognized Native American tribes also may qualify for EPA approval to be treated "in the same manner as a state" to manage delegated programs under the Clean Air Act, Clean Water Act, and Safe Drinking Water Act, but not under the Resource Conservation and Recovery Act. See D. Pingaro, Tribal Environmental Protection Activity Under EPA-Administered Programs, 8 Envtl. L. News 11 (Summer 1999).

Statutes requiring the establishment of minimum federal standards have long been thought to be necessary to prevent regulatory competition among states from undermining environmental quality. Professor Richard Revesz challenged the "race-to-the-bottom" rationale in Rehabilitating Interstate Competition: Rethinking the "Race-to-the-Bottom" Rationale for Federal Environmental Regulation, 67 N.Y.U. L. Rev. 1210 (1992). Based on economic models positing that state regulatory standards would be set at levels where the benefits of increased employment would at least offset the costs of increased environmental degradation, Revesz argued that there is no theoretical basis for believing that regulatory competition would induce states to set suboptimally low standards. He also noted that there is little empirical support for the notion that environmental standards have a substantial effect on industry location decisions. Revesz, Federalism and Regulation: Some Generalizations, in Regulatory Competition and Economic Integration: Comparative Perspectives (D. Esty & D. Geradin eds., 2000). Professor Kirsten Engel responded that even if regulatory standards have little effect on industrial location, a "race-to-the-bottom" would occur because state officials believe that they do based on the results of a survey of state regulators. K. Engel, State Environmental Standard-Setting: Is There a "Race" and Is It "To the Bottom"?, 48 Hastings L.J. 271 (1997).

A third approach to environmental federalism eschews state administration of federal standards in favor of federal control. *Preemption of state law* has been employed sparingly in the federal environmental laws. It usually is reserved for regulation of products that are distributed nationally, as businesses favor nationally uniform regulation to avoid having to comply with balkanized regulatory standards. Examples include regulation of chemicals under the Toxic Substances Control Act (TSCA), pesticide registration under the Federal Insecticide, Fungicide, and Rodenticide Act (FIFRA), provisions of the Clean Air Act governing vehicle emissions, regulation of nuclear materials under the Atomic Energy Act (AEA), and regulation of hazardous materials transportation under the Hazardous Materials Transportation Act. While these laws generally provide that federal regulation preempts inconsistent state standards, the question of whether state standards are inconsistent with federal regulations can be a difficult one.

In Engine Manufacturers Association v. South Coast Air Quality Management District, 541 U.S. 246 (2004), the Court held that regulations by the South Coast Air Quality Management District requiring operators of public and private fleets of more than 15 vehicles to buy only low-emission or alternative fuel vehicles were preempted by the federal Clean Air Act. In Silkwood v. Kerr-McGee Corp., 464 U.S. 238 (1984), the Court held that an award of punitive damages under state law for exposure to nuclear material was not preempted by the Atomic Energy Act (AEA). In Pacific Gas & Elec. v. California Energy Comm'n, 461 U.S. 190 (1983), the Court upheld a California state initiative that blocked licensing of new nuclear power plants pending development of a facility for disposal of high-level nuclear waste because it was an economic measure rather than a safety regulation in conflict with the AEA.

In Virginia Uranium v. Warren, 139 S.Ct. 1894 (2019), the Supreme Court held that the Atomic Energy Act, which gives exclusive jurisdiction to the federal Nuclear Regulatory Commission (NRC) to regulate the safety of nuclear materials, did not preempt a Virginia moratorium on uranium mining. A company that owns land on which a large uranium deposit had been discovered argued that the state moratorium was preempted because it had "the purpose and effect of regulating the radiological safety hazards of activities entrusted to the NRC (here, the milling of uranium and the management of the resulting tailings)." Three dissenting Justices (Chief Justice Roberts, Justice Breyer, and Justice Alito) believed the company should be allowed to prove this allegation at trial. Six other Justices disagreed and held that the moratorium was not preempted, but they split into two camps. Justices Gorsuch, Thomas, and Kavanaugh stated that it was clear that the AEA did not preempt the moratorium on mining and that the Court should not inquire into the state's motivation for it. Justices Ginsburg, Sotomayor, and Kagan agreed that the moratorium should be upheld but did not join Justice Gorsuch's opinion because they did not agree with its discussion of the perils of inquiring into legislative motive.

A separate set of federalism issues involve claims that state environmental regulations violate the dormant Commerce Clause by discriminating against interstate commerce. These issues are introduced in Chapter 4E, which discusses challenges to state laws restricting disposal of out-of-state wastes. They also arise in other contexts. See, e.g., Rocky Mountain Farmers Union v. Corey, 730 F.3d 1070 (9th Cir. 2013) (holding that California's Low Carbon Fuel Standard that requires a 10 percent reduction in the carbon intensity of fuels used in the state does not violate the dormant Commerce Clause despite using the distance the fuel must be transported as a factor in calculating carbon intensity). California regulations restricting air emissions from ocean-going vessels when located within three miles of the coast were upheld in Pacific Merchant Shipping Ass'n v. Goldstene, 639 F.3d 1154 (9th Cir. 2011). The court held that California's "exceptionally powerful interest in controlling the harmful effects of air pollution" outweighed any countervailing federal interests under the Commerce Clause.

Claims that federal environmental regulation has been too intrusive on state and local prerogatives have become a prominent part of the current political ferment over federalism. There has been considerable debate over how responsibility for environmental protection should be divided in our federal system and how to improve relations between federal agencies and the states. State officials have lobbied for devolution of greater authority from federal to state authorities. EPA has sought to be more responsive to state concerns, but it finds itself in a difficult position. As the National Academy of Public Administration describes the problem: "EPA's paradox is that it must maintain national programs and seek national consistency while simultaneously attempting to make its programs and standards fit an incredibly diverse and dynamic nation." Resolving the Paradox of Environmental Protection: An Agenda for Congress, EPA & the States xii-xiii (1997).

Those who challenge calls to devolve more responsibility for environmental protection to the states cite several reasons for their opposition. First, there are economies of scale in having national regulatory programs. Professor Daniel Esty questions whether "we really want every state or hamlet to determine for itself whether polychlorinated biphenyls create additional cancer risks greater than $10^{-6}$, and if so, at what cost these risks are worth worrying about." Esty, Revitalizing Environmental Federalism, 95 Mich. L. Rev. 570, 573 (1996). Second, national programs are better able to deal with transboundary pollution. "[I]nsofar as the central reason for environmental regulation is to mitigate the impact of market failures that emerge from uninternalized externalities, drawing more lines on the map only multiplies the potential for transboundary spillovers." Id. Third, fairness and equal protection concerns may support "the establishment of baseline national standards so that Americans are not exposed to fundamentally unequal levels of environmental risk." Steinzor, Unfunded Environmental Mandates and the "New (New) Federalism": Devolution, Revolution, or Reform?, 81 Minn. L. Rev. 101, 172 (1996). Professor Peter Swire notes that it may be easier to focus public attention on environmental problems and enact legislation at the national level so that citizen preferences can overcome the concentrated interests of regulated industry. Swire, The Race to Laxity and the Race to Undesirability: Explaining Failures in Competition Among Jurisdictions in Environmental Law, 14 Yale L. & Pol'y Rev./Yale J. Reg. 167 (1996).

State and local officials often chafe at the cost of implementing federal requirements, such as regulations implementing the Safe Drinking Water Act. Arguing that it is unfair for the federal government to impose "unfunded mandates," state and local officials lobbied Congress to restrict this practice. In March 1995, Congress overwhelmingly approved legislation making it more difficult to impose federal mandates on state and local governments. The legislation, known as the Unfunded Mandate Reform Act of 1995, Pub. L. No. 104-4, 109 Stat. 48 (1995), requires that more detailed cost estimates be provided for federal mandates and makes it easier for opponents of such provisions to defeat them in Congress. The law requires the Congressional Budget Office (CBO) to provide estimates of the future cost of legislative mandates if they may exceed $50 million annually for state or local governments or the private sector. Any member of Congress can raise a point of order demanding that mandates estimated to cost state or local governments more than $50 million annually be stricken from legislation unless federal funding is provided or the mandate is specifically approved by a majority vote. Mandates for which future federal funding is promised are to expire if the funding is not subsequently provided.

The legislation also imposed new requirements on agencies issuing regulations that impose federal mandates. The law requires federal agencies, prior to publishing a notice of proposed rulemaking, to prepare assessments of the anticipated costs and benefits of any mandate that may cost state or local governments or the private sector more than $100 million annually. It also prohibits federal agencies from issuing regulations containing federal mandates that do not employ the least costly method or that do not have the least burdensome effect on governments or the private sector unless the agency publishes an explanation of why the more costly or burdensome method was adopted. These provisions are subject to judicial review if the underlying agency action already is reviewable in court.

States have become more aggressive at challenging federal mandates in court. In New York v. United States, 505 U.S. 144 (1992), the state of New York argued that the federal government infringed on its Tenth Amendment rights when it directed in the Low-Level Radioactive Waste Policy Act that states that failed to make arrangements to dispose of low-level radioactive wastes by January 1, 1993, must "take title" to all such waste generated within their borders. The Court agreed, holding that Congress may not commandeer the legislative processes of the States by directly compelling them to enact and enforce a federal regulatory program. Justice O'Connor, writing for the Court majority, justified this conclusion in terms of electoral accountability. "Where the Federal Government directs the States to regulate, it may be state officials who will bear the brunt of public disapproval, while the federal officials who devised the regulatory program may remain insulated from the electoral ramifications of their decision." She explained that Congress still can persuade states to regulate in a particular way by (1) using their spending power to attach conditions on the receipt of federal funds so long as the conditions "bear some relationship to the purpose of the federal spending" and (2) offering states the choice of regulating that activity according to federal standards or having state law preempted by federal regulation.

The "anti-commandeering" doctrine of New York v. United States has not had a major impact on the federal environmental laws because these laws usually offer states a choice between regulating according to federal standards or having state standards preempted by federal ones. A rare exception was ACORN v. Edwards, 81 F.3d 1387 (5th Cir. 1996), a case in which the Fifth Circuit held that a provision in the Safe Drinking Water Act requiring states to establish programs for removal of lead contamination from school and day care drinking water systems violated the Tenth Amendment principles outlined in New York v. United States. The court held that the requirement "is an attempt by Congress to force States to regulate according to Congressional direction." Id. at 1394. While noting that Congress is free to regulate directly drinking water coolers that move in interstate commerce, the court held that it could not force the states to establish a regulatory program under penalty of civil sanctions without violating the Tenth Amendment.

In Printz v. United States, 521 U.S. 898 (1997), the Supreme Court, by a 5-to-4 vote, held that the Brady Handgun Violence Protection Act's requirement that state and local law enforcement officers conduct background checks of handgun purchasers was unconstitutional. Citing New York v. United States, the Court majority reiterated the notion that the federal government may not compel the states to enact or administer a federal regulatory program. While the four dissenters attempted to distinguish the Brady law as not requiring state or local officials to make policy, the Court majority concluded that the entire object of the law was to direct the functioning of the state executive, which would compromise the dual sovereignty structure of federalism established by the Constitution.

In National Federation of Independent Business v. Sebelius, 567 U.S. 519 (2012), the Supreme Court for the first time struck down an attempt to condition receipt of federal funds as unduly coercive of states. While upholding the constitutionality of the Affordable Care Act, the Court held that a requirement that states substantially expand their Medicaid programs or lose all federal Medicaid funds was unconstitutionally coercive in violation of the Tenth Amendment. Noting that this condition threatens states with the loss of 10 percent of a state's overall budget, Chief Justice Roberts, writing for the majority, described it as "a gun to the head" and "economic dragooning that leaves the States with no real option but to acquiesce in the Medicaid expansion." Id. at 581. While this decision has not had immediate consequences for environmental regulations, states challenging the Obama administration's Clean Power Plan cited it in arguing that the regulations unconstitutionally coerced them by effectively requiring them to eschew new coal-fired power plants.

## NOTES AND QUESTIONS

1. Which environmental problems are appropriate subjects for federal regulation and which should be left to state, tribal, or local authorities? Economist Wallace Oates argues that responsibility "should be assigned to the smallest jurisdiction whose geographical scope encompasses the relevant benefits and costs" of the problem. W. Oates, Thinking About Environmental Federalism, 130 Resources 14 (Winter 1998). Do you agree? Because ecosystem boundaries rarely conform to political boundaries, problems that involve interstate externalities clearly warrant federal intervention.

2. How strong is the federal interest in establishing minimum national standards for the quality of drinking water municipalities provide, as Congress has done in the Safe Drinking Water Act? In June 2003, the D.C. Circuit rejected arguments that the Safe Drinking Water Act exceeded Congress's constitutional authority under the Commerce Clause. The state of Nebraska challenged EPA's regulations setting maximum contaminant levels for arsenic in drinking water by arguing that Congress had no authority to regulate intrastate distribution and sale of drinking water. Noting that this was a facial challenge to the Act, the court stated that to succeed it would require a showing that under "no set of circumstances" could the Act be constitutional. Because a number of water utilities sell substantial volumes of drinking water across state lines, the court concluded that "the Act is a valid exercise of power under the Commerce Clause," without addressing whether intrastate sales of drinking water had a sufficiently substantial impact on interstate commerce to justify federal regulation. Nebraska v. EPA, 331 F.3d 995 (D.C. Cir. 2003).

3. Professor Thomas Merrill argues that when states have more experience than EPA regulating a particular industry they are likely to do a better job of regulation. He maintains that this explains why hydraulic fracturing has boomed in traditional oil states while being sharply restricted in states with little experience dealing with the industry. Thomas W. Merrill, Federalism and the Fracking Revolution, Wash. Times, July 14, 2015. But are state regulators more likely than EPA to be "captured" by economically powerful local industries?

**E.   The Commerce Clause and Constitutional Authority to Protect the Environment**

In 1995, the Supreme Court for the first time in nearly 60 years overturned a federal law for exceeding Congress's authority under the Commerce Clause. In United States v. Lopez, 514 U.S. 549 (1995), the Court held, by a bare 5-to-4 majority, that Congress does not have the authority under the Commerce Clause to prohibit the possession of firearms in the vicinity of schools. The Court stated that Congress has the authority to regulate three broad classes of activities under the Commerce Clause: (1) "the use of the channels of interstate commerce"; (2) intrastate activities that threaten "the instrumentalities of interstate commerce, or persons or things in interstate commerce"; and (3) "activities having a substantial relation to interstate commerce." The Court added that the "proper test" for the third category is "whether the regulated activity 'substantially affects' interstate commerce." Id. at 558-559.

While it now has become routine to raise *Lopez* challenges whenever federal regulatory authority is asserted, the decision has had scant impact on environmental law. The *Lopez* majority emphasized that the Gun-Free School Zones Act had "nothing to do with 'commerce' or any sort of economic enterprise, however broadly one might define those terms." Id. at 561. Citing with approval Hodel v. Virginia Surface Mining & Reclamation Association, Inc., 452 U.S. 264 (1981), which upheld federal regulation of intrastate coal mining under the Surface Mining Control and Reclamation Act, the Chief Justice stated that "[w]here economic activity substantially affects interstate commerce, legislation regulating that activity will be sustained." *Lopez*, supra, 514 U.S. at 560. Significantly, the Chief Justice did not question the validity of even Wickard v. Filburn, 317 U.S. 111 (1942), which he described as "the most far reaching example of Commerce Clause authority over intrastate activity," because it "involved economic activity in a way that the possession of a gun in a school zone does not." Id. In *Wickard*, the Court upheld federal regulation of the production and consumption of home-grown wheat because of its effect on the price and market for wheat sold in interstate commerce. Because *Wickard* remains good law, *Lopez* should not significantly restrict federal authority to regulate businesses or individuals when they engage in virtually any activity that can be deemed economic. For an analysis of the likely implications of *Lopez* and *Morrison* on the environmental laws, see Schroeder, Environmental Law, Congress and the Court's New Federalism, 78 Ind. L.J. 413-457 (2003).

*Lopez* has generated several challenges to other federal environmental laws. A challenge to the constitutionality of the federal Superfund legislation (the Comprehensive Environmental Response, Compensation and Liability Act, also known as CERCLA) on *Lopez* grounds was rejected in United States v. Olin Corp., 107 F.3d 1506 (11th Cir. 1997). The Eleventh Circuit reversed a district court decision declaring that CERCLA exceeded Congress's authority under the Commerce Clause. The court found that regulation of intrastate, on-site waste disposal was an appropriate element of a broader attempt by Congress to protect interstate commerce from pollution. In National Association of Home Builders v. Babbitt, 130 F.3d 1041 (D.C. Cir. 1997), a divided panel of the D.C. Circuit rejected a *Lopez*-based challenge to Congress's constitutional authority to apply section 9 of the Endangered Species Act to prohibit the taking of an endangered fly that was located entirely within a small area.

The one area in which the Court has addressed the effect of *Lopez* on environmental law, albeit somewhat obliquely, is with respect to the jurisdictional reach of the Clean Water Act. Solid Waste Agency of Northern Cook County v. U.S. Army Corps of Engineers (*SWANCC*), 531 U.S. 159 (2001), which is discussed in Chapter 6, raised the question whether Congress has the constitutional authority to regulate isolated wetlands because they are used by migratory birds. Relying on *Lopez*, a county agency argued that Congress could not require it to obtain a federal permit under section 404(a) of the Clean Water Act to fill wetlands in an abandoned sand and gravel pit. Deciding *SWANCC* by the same 5-to-4 lineup that prevailed in *Lopez*, the Court ducked the constitutional issue by construing section 404(a) narrowly. The Court found that Congress had not expressed a clear intent to apply section 404(a) to isolated wetlands visited by migratory birds, which "would result in a significant impingement of the states' traditional and primary power over lands and water use." To avoid what it described as "significant constitutional and federalism questions," the Court held that section 404(a)'s jurisdictional predicate—"waters of the United States"—did not include isolated wetlands where migratory birds are present. Thus, *SWANCC* narrows the jurisdictional reach of the Clean Water Act, while leaving the ultimate effect of *Lopez* on federal constitutional authority to protect the environment unresolved.

In June 2005, the Supreme Court decided Gonzales v. Raich, 545 U.S. 1 (2005), which upheld federal authority to prohibit the cultivation and use of marijuana for medical purposes. In an opinion by Justice Stevens that was joined by four other Justices, the Court held that Congress had a rational basis for concluding that the personal cultivation and use of marijuana would substantially affect interstate commerce because failure to regulate intrastate cultivation and use would leave a gaping hole in the comprehensive federal scheme for regulating illicit drugs. The Court majority emphasized that Congress clearly acted rationally in deciding that regulation of intrastate cultivation and use of marijuana was an essential part of the larger regulatory scheme. Justice Scalia, who did not join the majority opinion, filed a separate opinion concurring in the judgment. Scalia argued that Congress's authority to regulate intrastate activities that substantially affect interstate commerce derives from the Necessary and Proper Clause. "Where necessary to make a regulation of interstate commerce effective, Congress may regulate even those intrastate activities that do not themselves substantially affect interstate commerce," Scalia stated.

In 2017 a panel of the U.S. Court of Appeals for the Tenth Circuit unanimously reversed a district court decision holding that Congress did not have the constitutional authority to protect the endangered Utah prairie dog when it is found on private land. Citing *Gonzales v. Raich*, the court in People for the Ethical Treatment of Property Owners (PETPO) v. U.S. Fish and Wildlife Service, 852 F.3d 990 (10th Cir. 2017), held that even a purely intrastate species could be protected by Congress against non-commercial takes because it was necessary to preserve the integrity of a larger federal regulatory scheme. As a result of this decision, all nine circuits of the U.S. Courts of Appeals that have considered the issue have upheld the constitutionality of the Endangered Species Act.

## NOTES AND QUESTIONS

1. While no federal environmental law has been found to exceed Congress's authority to regulate activities that substantially affect interstate commerce, there has been considerable uncertainty concerning the proper rationale for upholding federal authority under the Commerce Clause to protect endangered species. One source of confusion is the uncertainty concerning the proper focus for analyzing whether interstate commerce is substantially affected. Should the focus be on: (1) the commercial value of the resource or species sought to be protected—in which case the more endangered a species is the lesser may be the federal authority to protect it, or (2) the commercial nature of the prohibited activity that threatens the species—which would make it possible to ban commercial construction that threatens a species, but perhaps not actions by hikers or dirt-bikers, or (3) the effect of the overall regulatory program on interstate commerce—which would permit consideration of the potentially enormous economic benefits of protecting biodiversity? Which of these is the proper focus for analyzing the constitutional authority of Congress to protect the environment under the Commerce Clause?

2. Does Gonzales v. Raich, 545 U.S. 1 (2005), effectively lay to rest any doubt concerning the constitutionality of individual applications of the Endangered Species Act to noneconomic, intrastate activity because they can be viewed as necessary to preserve the integrity of a larger regulatory program that clearly satisfies Commerce Clause requirements? The *PETPO* decision by the Tenth Circuit clearly endorses this notion.

3. The *Lopez* decision has spawned numerous challenges to federal regulatory authority based on the argument that Congress has exceeded the bounds of its Commerce Clause authority. Virtually all of these challenges have failed, though a few arsonists were released from prison because of the Supreme Court's decision in Jones v. United States, 529 U.S. 848 (2000), construing the federal arson statute as not applying to residential properties. This may suggest that the Court's efforts to revive limits on federal authority have been primarily a symbolic "shot across the bow" to encourage Congress to articulate more clearly the connection between activities it seeks to regulate and interstate commerce. For a discussion of how Congress's Commerce Clause authorities can be harnessed to protect environmental values, see Robert V. Percival, "Greening" the Constitution—Harmonizing Environmental and Constitutional Values, 32 Envtl. L. 809 (2002).

# B.  APPROACHES TO REGULATION: ASSESSING THE OPTIONS

## 1.  Regulation and Its Alternatives

Regardless of the philosophic perspective one brings to environmental policy, there is broad agreement that some form of collective action should be undertaken to address environmental problems for reasons explored in Chapter 1. While this can provide a powerful rationale for government regulation, it is important to bear in mind that collective action can assume a wide variety of forms, not all of which involve centralized action by government. Some communities are able to avoid the depletion of common resources without government involvement by using informal and private means to discourage overuse. These may include efforts to discourage outsiders from using the commons, see, e.g., To Protect Resources, Many Communities Use Informal Regulations, Wash. Post, July 17, 1989, at A2 (noting that lobster trappers avoid depletion of the lobster stock by using surreptitious violence to keep outsiders away), or community norms that regulate its use by neighbors. See Ellickson, Of Coase and Cattle: Dispute Resolution Among Neighbors in Shasta County, 38 Stan. L. Rev. 623 (1986) (study of cattle grazing patterns). Natural resources also can be protected from environmental damage by privatizing them — by creating enforceable property rights owned by someone with an incentive to protect the resource. The Nature Conservancy, for example, has been enormously successful in buying environmentally significant properties in order to preserve them.

Informal, community-based controls are most likely to protect common resources where such resources are concentrated in a small area and there is strong community support for limiting exploitation. If entry into the commons is difficult to control or community support is lacking, informal controls are unlikely to work. Privatization is more likely to succeed in protecting resources such as land (in which property rights can be easily defined) than in protecting the quality of air or water. Thus, one should be cautious about drawing the simplistic conclusion that government regulation is always the appropriate response to the circumstances described by Hardin's "Tragedy of the Commons." One need not quarrel with the problem Hardin identifies — that truly unrestricted use of the commons will tend to deplete common resources — to appreciate the diversity of approaches, both governmental and nongovernmental, that can be used to combat it.

Kip Viscusi has identified four institutional mechanisms that may be used to control environmental risk: market forces, government regulation, liability, and social insurance. Viscusi, Toward a Diminished Role for Tort Liability: Social Insurance, Government Regulation, and Contemporary Risks to Health and Safety, 6 Yale J. on Reg. 65 (1989). These categories provide a useful framework for organizing our discussion of society's options for responding to environmental problems when informal controls fail. Each of the institutions Viscusi identifies plays a role in environmental policy with varying emphasis depending on the nature of the problem to be addressed.

While most of the focus of environmental policy has been on government regulation, nonregulatory alternatives are becoming increasingly important complements to regulatory policy. Indeed, government now frequently uses regulation to enhance the effectiveness of the other institutional mechanisms for protecting the environment. For example, some regulatory legislation now requires information disclosure to harness the market power of informed consumers as a means to prevent environmental damage. Other regulations require that insurance be purchased by those engaging in activities that create environmental risk to ensure that the liability system can provide compensation for environmental damage. Thus, these four institutional mechanisms are best viewed not as discrete alternatives, but rather as part of a web of societal responses to environmental problems.

As illustrated in Figure 2.3, each of the four institutions has its own strengths and weaknesses as a vehicle for controlling environmental risks. Market forces can respond more quickly and flexibly than government regulation to discourage consumption of products that cause environmental damage, but markets are likely to be effective only when consumers are sufficiently well-informed about the link between a product and environmental damage to induce the marketing of less damaging substitutes. Unlike regulation, the liability system can provide compensation

**Figure 2.3   Comparison of Institutional Mechanisms for Controlling Environmental Risks**

| Institutional mechanism | Advantages | Drawbacks |
| --- | --- | --- |
| Market Forces | Can control risks rapidly and efficiently when consumers are well informed and have a choice of alternatives | Inadequate incentives to generate and disclose accurate information to consumers; many risks not tradeable in markets due to absence of transferable property rights |
| Common Law Liability | Can provide compensation to victims of environmental damage; more efficient than regulation when private parties have better information than government about nature of risks and how to control them | Inadequate incentives to control risks due to difficulties of proving causal injury and recovering for harm that is widely dispersed or in excess of source's capacity to provide compensation |
| Government Regulation | Can efficiently prevent environmental harm by internalizing external costs of risky activity; can be used to respond to equity concerns by altering the distribution of risks and benefits; can be used to generate better information about risks | Does not provide compensation to victims of environmental damage; difficult to tailor regulation to take into account relevant differences within classes of regulatory targets; can be counterproductive in the absence of accurate information about the nature of risks and control options |
| Insurance | Helps ensure that compensation will be available for victims of environmental damage | Can reduce incentives to prevent environmental damage |

to victims of environmental damage. This provides an incentive for potentially liable parties to prevent harm, the goal regulation seeks to pursue more directly by requiring or prohibiting certain conduct. The effectiveness of the liability system, both in providing compensation and deterring harm, is limited by the financial capability of parties, which can be expanded through the purchase of insurance. The availability of insurance may tend to reduce the insured's incentives to prevent harm, though premiums priced to reflect differences in the riskiness of insured activity provide some incentive for investments in preventive measures.

When consumers are well informed and free to choose, market forces can generate remarkably effective pressure to stop practices that cause environmental damage. For example, although the Marine Mammal Protection Act limits the number of dolphins that tuna fishers can kill each year, environmentalists had long complained that the law was poorly enforced, particularly on foreign boats. They launched a boycott of tuna that succeeded when major seafood processors announced that they would no longer purchase tuna that had been captured using fishing practices that result in harm to dolphins.

In the absence of informed consumers, seafood processors who used "dolphin-safe" methods would be placed at a competitive disadvantage because it is more expensive to catch tuna using methods that avoid harm to dolphins that swim nearby. Indeed, the company that first announced the new policy stated that tuna prices would rise by 2 to 10 cents a can because of the higher costs of purchasing tuna caught using dolphin-safe methods. Because of their higher cost, companies could not be expected to employ dolphin-safe fishing methods in the absence of consumer pressure. To attract environmentally conscious consumers, firms that purchase only dolphin-safe tuna began labeling their products as dolphin-safe (see Figure 2.4).

### Figure 2.4 Tuna Label Logo

Monitoring compliance with corporate pledges of voluntary action can be difficult when highly visible practices are not involved. To monitor compliance with "dolphin-safe" claims, an international monitoring program inspects tuna facilities and sends monitors out with fishing vessels. Congress has enacted the Dolphin Consumer Protection Information Act, 16 U.S.C. §1385, which prohibits companies from making false "dolphin-safe" claims. Concerned that some "green advertising" has been deceptive, the Federal Trade Commission (FTC) has adopted guidelines governing the use of environmental claims in advertising and marketing.

The guidelines, which apply to any claims about the environmental attributes of products or packaging, are designed to offer guidance to companies and are not enforceable regulations. 57 Fed. Reg. 36,363 (1992).

Many states have laws that regulate "green marketing" claims. California's statute is the most detailed. The law prohibits the use of terms such as "recycled," "ozone friendly," and "biodegradable" unless products meet certain specifications. For example, to be identified as "recycled," a product must contain at least 10 percent of post-consumer material. Advertisers challenged the California law on grounds that it violated their First Amendment rights. But an appellate court held that the state's interests in preventing deceptive advertising sufficed to justify the burden on commercial speech rights. Association of National Advertisers v. Lungren, 44 F.3d 726 (9th Cir. 1994).

Several countries now have government-sponsored eco-labeling programs. Germany's Blue Angel program awards environmental seals of approval to products based on lifecycle analysis of their environmental impacts. The European Union has established an ambitious eco-labeling program modeled on the German approach. Products deemed environmentally superior are identified with a flower logo containing an "E" in the flower's pistil. In the United States, private organizations, including Green Seal, Inc. and Scientific Certification Systems, have established environmental certification programs. For a critique of government involvement in eco-labeling, see Menell, Structuring a Market-Oriented Federal Eco-Information Policy, 54 Md. L. Rev. 1435 (1995).

In July 2016, President Obama signed legislation requiring labeling of products containing genetically modified organisms (GMOs). The law requires food packages to display an electronic code or other symbol to signify whether or not they contain GMOs. The law was supported by the food industry, which wanted a national standard rather than separate state laws. After waging expensive campaigns to defeat state referenda to require GMO labeling in California, Colorado, and Oregon, the industry changed its position following the enactment of GMO labeling legislation in Vermont. Opponents of GMO labeling, which is widely required outside the United States, argued that because GMOs are safe, labeling requirements would unnecessarily alarm consumers.

Common law liability has been the principal alternative to government regulation for protecting the environment. Even the staunchest supporters of market mechanisms for controlling risk, who describe themselves as "free market environmentalists," emphasize the importance of liability standards for defending property rights against environmental insults. As discussed at the beginning of this chapter, the difficulties involved in proving a causal link between a particular action and damage to a particular plaintiff have limited the effectiveness of common law liability as a mechanism for controlling environmental risk. One strength of liability approaches is that they offer some prospect of compensating victims after damage is done, which the regulatory system does not. And the prospect of having to pay compensation can serve as a powerful deterrent to spur investment in efforts to prevent environmental harm.

Economists argue that the decision concerning the relative emphasis to place on liability and regulation is analogous to a choice between letting the market regulate the price of outputs and organizing a firm to control inputs into the production process. Liability rules establish the price of environmental damage (the output), while regulations seek to control the activities (inputs) that create such damage. While the former approach might seem more appealing to market enthusiasts, regulation of inputs is not as unusual as it might seem. Indeed, the very reason why firms are organized is that resort to markets has its own costs, and companies find it is cheaper to control inputs into the production process by resorting to a nonmarket substitute, the formation of firms. Calabresi, The Pointlessness of Pareto: Carrying Coase Further, 100 Yale L.J. 1211 (1991). In some circumstances it is simply more efficient to resort to nonmarket mechanisms to achieve our goals. Of course, in the environmental arena the choice is not really between free markets and government regulation. Instead, as Judge Richard Posner notes, "the choice is between two methods of public control, the common law system of privately enforced rights and the administrative system of direct public control." R.A. Posner, Economic Analysis of Law 271 (2d ed. 1977). The question of how to find the proper mix of liability and regulation is one of the fundamental challenges facing environmental policy makers.

Economist Steven Shavell argues that four factors should be considered in assessing the relative efficiency of liability and regulation as mechanisms for controlling risk. Shavell, Liability for Harm Versus Regulation of Safety, 13 J. Legal Stud. 357 (1984). The first is the *relative knowledge of private parties and the public* concerning the benefits of risky activities and the costs of reducing risks. Shavell argues that liability tends to be more efficient than regulation in controlling risk when a private actor is in a better position than the government to assess the risks of an activity and to determine the level of care to exercise. Regulation is favored when the government is in a better position than a private actor to assess risks and to determine what precautions to employ.

The second factor Shavell identifies is *the capacity of private parties to provide compensation* for the full amount of harm their actions produce. If an activity can cause more damage than the actor is capable of repaying, fear of liability will not provide sufficient incentive for private investment in an efficient level of precautions. Shavell's third consideration is the *chance that some private parties will escape suit* for the harm that they cause. Parties unlikely to be held liable for harm they produce, such as those who cause harm that is widely dispersed or difficult to trace, will not have adequate incentive to reduce risks to an efficient level in the absence of regulation.

The fourth consideration Shavell identifies is the *relative administrative costs* of the tort system and of direct regulation. Despite complaints about the administrative costs of the tort system, he notes that the liability system's administrative costs usually are incurred only if harm occurs, while the administrative costs of regulation are incurred regardless of the occurrence of harm. Applying these factors, Shavell advocates using regulation to prevent environmental harms where the government has a superior capability to assess risks and private parties are likely to escape liability for the harm their actions cause. He also suggests liability may be superior to regulation where private parties have better access to information about the true costs of prevention and neither governmental nor private parties are systematically better at estimating harm. Kaplow & Shavell, Property Rules Versus Liability Rules: An Economic Analysis, 109 Harv. L. Rev. 713, 750 (1996).

We now turn to a contemporary case study to illustrate the choices available to policy makers in determining the relative emphases to place on liability and regulation in preventing environmental damage.

---

## CASE STUDY: LIABILITY, REGULATION, AND THE PREVENTION AND REMEDIATION OF OIL SPILLS

Until 1990, liability for oil spills in U.S. waters was governed by a confusing patchwork of five federal laws, three international conventions, three private international agreements, and dozens of state laws. The federal laws and international agreements were designed largely to limit the liability of shipowners in the event of a major spill, with the precise liability limits depending on where the oil came from (e.g., the Trans-Alaska Pipeline Act) or where it was spilled (e.g., the Deepwater Port Act, the Outer Continental Shelf Lands Act). The most extreme of these Acts, the aptly named Limitation of Liability Act of 1851, limited liability to the value of the vessel after the casualty occurred. Courts strained to interpret this pre–Civil War relic expansively because of its potentially extreme consequences. For example, in the case of the wreck of the *Torrey Canyon*, which spilled 100,000 tons of crude oil into the English Channel in 1967, liability under this statute would have been just $50—the value of the sole lifeboat that survived the wreck.

Proposals to rationalize this patchwork of oil spill laws were bottled up in Congress for nearly two decades. This legislative gridlock finally was overcome only after the *Exxon Valdez* disaster. Not surprisingly, the legislation Congress adopted—the Oil Pollution Act of 1990 (OPA 90), 33 U.S.C. §§2701-2761—focused largely on prevention of spills from oil tankers even as multinational oil companies increasingly were undertaking riskier offshore drilling operations in deeper waters. On April 20, 2010, a massive explosion and fire at the Deepwater Horizon oil drilling rig in the Gulf of Mexico killed 11 workers and resulted in massive releases of crude oil from the bottom of the Gulf that continued for nearly three months. It is estimated that an average of 53,000 barrels of oil were released daily for a total release of 4.9 million barrels of oil, the worst oil spill in U.S. history. The following questions ask you to consider what the proper mix of liability and regulation should be in order to prevent various kinds of oil spills and to facilitate remediation and compensation when they do occur.

**Question One: Who Should Be Held Liable for Oil Spills?**   When OPA 90 was being debated in Congress, environmentalists argued that both shipowners and the oil companies that own the cargo should be held strictly liable for oil spills to deter oil companies from shipping their oil in "rust buckets" manned by untrained crews. (Because Exxon happened to be the owner of the *Exxon Valdez*, this would not have made any difference with respect to liability for that spill.) Oil companies argued that only the owners and operators of vessels should be held strictly liable for spills. The oil companies maintained that holding cargo owners liable for oil spills would be akin to making persons who ship something by Federal Express responsible for damages in the event a Federal Express cargo plane crashed. With whom do you agree? Is the Federal Express analogy an apt one? Should the nature of the cargo make any difference?

During the debate leading to enactment of OPA 90, the Royal Dutch/Shell Group announced that it would stop using its own tankers to carry oil to the United States except for an offshore terminal near Louisiana. The company explained that it took this move because a "shipowner who is involved in a pollution incident in the U.S.A., even when he has behaved properly, responsibly and without negligence, may face claims which far outweigh the potential commercial reward from such trade." Wald, Oil Companies Rethink Risk of Having Tankers, N.Y. Times, June 13, 1990, at A26. Does this reinforce the case for extending liability to cargo owners? By contrast, Arco Marine, a subsidiary of Atlantic Richfield, announced that it would ship oil only in its own ships. "We think we have better control that way, and therefore, have some control over the liability," explained Jerry Aspland, president of Arco Marine. Id. Which decision is more likely to expose the company to liability—Royal Dutch/Shell's or Arco Marine's? Which decision is likely to reduce the chances that the company's oil would be involved in a spill?

**Question Two: What Role Should Regulation Play in Prevention of Oil Spills?** Regulation seeks to prevent damage that fear of liability alone will not deter. What mix of regulation and liability should be employed to ensure that the appropriate amount of care is exercised? Liability will not be much of a deterrent for those who believe they can escape liability for their actions because of the difficulty of proving causation under the common law. Large oil spills are another matter, however, because their source is usually obvious, although precise assessments of the damage they wreak can be difficult. Professor Shavell notes that regulation is more efficient than liability for deterring accidents that cause more damage than responsible parties are capable of repaying. Except in circumstances where major multinational oil companies are the responsible parties, large oil spills certainly are capable of causing damage that exceeds the capacity of private parties to provide compensation. Indeed, arguments in favor of limited liability are premised on the notion that spills may be so expensive to clean up that it will be impossible to get adequate insurance to pay the full costs of a spill. In these circumstances, what regulations, if any, should be imposed to prevent oil spills or to minimize the damage they cause? From an economist's perspective, regulation should be used to stimulate investment in safety to the point where further investment would cost more than the reduction in damage it would produce. How would you apply this principle to regulations designed to prevent oil spills?

**Question Three: Should Oil Tankers Be Required to Have Double Hulls?** Congress previously had directed the Secretary of Transportation to consider whether or not to require oil tankers operating in U.S. waters to have double hulls. The oil and shipping industries fiercely resisted a double hull requirement, and no action was taken to impose one. Proponents of a double hull requirement argued that had the *Exxon Valdez* been equipped with a double hull, far less oil would have been spilled. Shipowners argued that the cost of outfitting ships with double hulls would be prohibitive, particularly if existing ships had to be retrofitted. Understandably more enthusiastic, the Shipbuilders Council of America claimed that double bottoms could be added to the entire American fleet for less than $2 billion, less than the amount Exxon spent cleaning up the Alaskan spill. They admitted that retrofitting existing ships with double hulls would be far more expensive than installing them on new vessels. Lowey, In '88, 6 Oil Spills Every 7 Days, N.Y. Times, June 22, 1990, at A27. In the wake of the *Valdez* spill, one major oil company stunned the industry by announcing that it was ordering double hulls for all its new tankers. Should double hulls be required? If so, should they be required only on new ships, or should existing ships be retrofitted?

After a long and bitter legislative struggle, Congress in 1990 enacted OPA 90, whose provisions are outlined below.

## The Oil Pollution Act of 1990 (OPA 90)

**Parties Liable.** OPA 90 makes owners and operators of vessels or facilities that discharge oil strictly liable for cleanup costs and damages caused by such discharges. Liability was not extended to cargo owners. §1002, 33 U.S.C. §2702.

**Limitation of Liability.** Section 1004 of OPA 90 increases the federal liability limit to $1,200 per gross ton, an eight-fold increase over the cap formerly provided in section 311 of the Clean Water Act. OPA 90 also creates a new $1 billion Oil Spill Liability Trust Fund, funded by a five-cent-per-barrel tax on oil, to pay for cleanup costs in excess of the liability limit. The entire $1 billion fund can be paid out for a single spill, with up to $500 million available for payments for damage to natural resources. (Section 311 of the Clean Water Act formerly had authorized a $35 million compensation fund, but the fund contained only $4 million at the time of the *Exxon Valdez* spill.)

**State Liability Laws.** OPA 90 expressly disavows any intent to preempt state liability requirements with respect to oil spills and removal activities. §1018, 33 U.S.C. §2718.

**Regulations to Prevent Oil Spills.** Congress ultimately opted to impose a double hull requirement on virtually all oil tankers operating in U.S. waters. For existing ships, the double hull requirement is to be phased in over the next 20 years on a schedule that varies based on tankers' size and age. The older and larger the ship, the sooner the requirement phases in. For example, beginning on January 1, 1995, single-hull tankers of at least 30,000 gross tons that were at least 28 years old had to be retrofitted or retired, as did smaller tankers that were at least 40 years old. Barges of less than 5,000 tons operating on inland waterways and ships that transfer their oil to smaller ships more than 60 miles offshore are exempt from the requirements.

## NOTES AND QUESTIONS

1. The Oil Pollution Act of 1990 is widely viewed as an enormous success. It is credited with improving the safety of oil tankers operating in U.S. waters and its double hull requirement has now been adopted internationally. Two years after

the legislation was enacted, a study by the Petroleum Industry Research Foundation found a "sea change" in the shipping industry's safety practices, including improved operational procedures and new inspection regimes. Solomon, U.S. Oil Spills Have Declined Sharply, Study Says; Stiffer Federal Law Is Cited, Wall St. J., Aug. 24, 1992, at A5. A 1998 study by the National Research Council (NRC) of the National Academy of Sciences noted that there has been a substantial reduction in the amount of oil spilled in U.S. waters. The study concluded that this decline

> was the result of a number of actions that are in process or emerging, notably: an increased awareness among vessel owners and operators of the financial consequences of oil spills and a resulting increase in attention to policies and procedures aimed at eliminating vessel accidents; actions by port states to ensure the safety of vessels using their ports; increased efforts by ship classification societies to ensure that vessels under their classification meet or exceed existing requirements; improved audit and inspection programs by charterers and terminals; and the increased liability, financial responsibility, and other provisions of OPA 90.

National Research Council, Double-Hull Tanker Legislation: An Assessment of the Oil Pollution Act of 1990 (1998). The NRC study concluded that "complete conversion of the maritime oil transportation fleet to double hulls will significantly improve protection of the marine environment." The committee estimated that the cost of this conversion worldwide will total approximately $30 billion over a 20-year period. This represents an additional cost of approximately 10 cents per barrel of oil transported. The capital costs of double-hull tankers are estimated to be 9 to 17 percent higher than single hulls' and their operating and maintenance costs are expected to be 5 to 13 percent greater.

2. As noted above, it had been argued that because OPA 90 does not extend liability to cargo owners "there is no incentive to charter safer, but perhaps more expensive tankers," Anderson, Oil Pollution Act Fouls the Regulatory Waters, Wall St. J., Feb. 20, 1992, at A14. Thus, many predicted that the market would not support investments in safer tankers and that OPA 90 could prove counterproductive. The NRC study found that there has been a decline in the percentage of oil shipped in tankers owned by oil companies, a trend it attributed to "a decision by some major oil companies to leave the tanker business, in large part to avoid high-liability exposure as well as for other economic reasons." Greenpeace International was sharply critical of the decision by ExxonMobil in January 2001 to charter two single-hulled tankers for five years each despite the availability of double-hulled alternatives. A London tanker broker expressed surprise at ExxonMobil's decision. "I find it strange that such a profitable company can't afford a double-hulled tanker," given their record profits. The broker noted that double-hull tankers cost only a few thousand dollars more per day to charter. Pete Harrison, Galapagos Oil Spill Renews Tanker Safety Debate, Reuters News Wire, Jan. 26, 2001.

3. The regulatory provisions of OPA 90 have been influential throughout the world. The International Maritime Organization adopted regulations that required all new oil tankers to have double hulls or equivalent safety features beginning in July 1993. The regulations were adopted after the organization released a study showing that double hulls would prevent any oil spillage in 80 percent of cases

where tankers ran aground. Hudson, Tanker Safety Plans Are Mulled as Oil Spill Threatens Shetlands, Wall St. J., Jan. 8, 1993, at A7. The international community has generally adopted the MARPOL regulations, which also require all existing oil tankers to be double hulled (or to use some approved alternative) by no later than 2023. As double hull requirements are gradually being phased in, the percentage of tankers in the world fleet with double hulls increased from 4 percent in 1990 to 10 percent in 1994, and 30 percent in 2001. More than 50 percent of very large crude oil carriers (VLCCs) (carriers of 200,000 tons or more) now have double hulls. As of January 2010, single-hull vessels (with a few exceptions) cannot operate in U.S. waters.

4. Is the key to the success of OPA's double hull requirement the fact that it was phased in on a strict schedule over time? Contrast the success of the Oil Pollution Act's scheduled phase-in of the double hull requirement with the sorry record of the Clean Air Act's new source review program. In the Clean Air Act, Congress did not specify a schedule for phasing in new pollution control technology—it simply required all new sources (or old sources making major modifications) to install the new pollution control technology. This created an incentive to continue to operate older, much dirtier sources far longer than initially anticipated and to try to disguise major modifications of those sources as routine maintenance activities that would not trigger new source review. See the discussion of new source review in Chapter 5.

5. In response to the *Exxon Valdez* oil spill, Exxon spent $2.1 billion in cleanup costs, paid a civil fine of $900 million to the federal government, and settled private damages actions for $303 million. A jury hearing other claims against Exxon by a class of 32,000 plaintiffs awarded $507.5 million in compensatory damages and assessed $5 billion in punitive damages for reckless conduct by Exxon. After years of post-trial litigation, the U.S. Court of Appeals for the Ninth Circuit reduced the punitive damages award to $2.5 billion. In Exxon Shipping Co. v. Baker, 554 U.S. 471 (2008), the U.S. Supreme Court held that federal maritime law limits punitive damages to the amount of compensatory damages, slashing the $2.5 billion punitive damages award to $507.5 million.

6. BP first set aside $42 billion to pay compensation and penalties for the Deepwater Horizon spill. Under pressure from President Obama, BP quickly agreed to set up a $20 billion compensation fund called the Gulf Coast Claims Facility (GCCF), initially administered by lawyer Kenneth Feinberg. In a little more than a year the GCCF paid $5 billion to settle 200,000 claims. BP subsequently reached a settlement for damages with more than 100,000 private plaintiffs who had filed suit instead of seeking compensation from the GCCF. Under the settlement the GCCF was replaced by a court-supervised process that includes no specific limit on the compensation to be paid. Plaintiffs are to be paid for their demonstrated losses plus a "risk transfer premium" that reflects possible future losses, inconvenience, aggravation, and emotional distress. In November 2012, BP agreed to plead guilty to 14 federal criminal charges and to pay the U.S. government more than $4 billion for the spill. BP agreed to plead guilty to 12 felonies—11 cases of manslaughter for each of the workers killed in the explosion and one felony count of lying to Congress about the amount of oil spilled. The settlement included a criminal fine of $1 billion, $525 million to settle civil securities fraud charges by the Securities and Exchange Commission, $2.4 billion

for environmental restoration in the Gulf states, and $350 million for research to improve oil spill prevention and response efforts.

In February 2013, a trial to determine civil penalties and natural resource assessment damages for the 2010 Deepwater Horizon oil spill opened in federal district court in New Orleans. The first phase of the trial focused on whether BP, Transocean, and/or Halliburton were simply negligent or grossly negligent in their actions that resulted in the spill. In September 2014, federal district judge Carl Barbier ruled that BP was guilty of gross neglect and willful misconduct. Judge Barbier held that BP had acted with "conscious disregard of known risks." If BP had been determined to have been simply negligent, the Clean Water Act specifies a civil penalty of $1,100 per barrel of oil spilled. However, because the company was found to be grossly negligent, the penalty could have been up to $4,300 per barrel. The second phase of the trial focused on how much oil was spilled. The U.S. government argued that 4.9 million barrels were spilled, but BP claimed that only 3.1 million barrels were spilled. In April 2016, Judge Barbier approved a nearly $20 billion settlement between BP and the federal government. The settlement, first announced in July 2015, includes $12.8 billion in fines and natural resource damages under the Clean Water Act, plus $4.9 billion to states affected by the spill. Combined with the cleanup costs of the spill and its settlement with private parties, BP reported in July 2016 that it expected to spend $61.6 billion to cover the costs of the spill.

7. Several investigations were undertaken of the causes and consequences of the Deepwater Horizon oil spill. President Obama's National Commission on the BP Deepwater Horizon Oil Spill released a staff report noting that in the two decades since the 1989 *Exxon Valdez* spill and the enactment of the Oil Pollution Act there had been scant development of oil spill response technology even as oil exploration technology changed rapidly. The report concluded that "industry and government underfunded response R&D, and, as a result, the clean-up technology used" to respond to the spill was "dated and inadequate." Another Commission staff report that examined efforts to kill the Macondo well found that BP had no proven technology for stopping such a deepwater spill and that government agencies were unprepared to oversee the efforts to stop it. On January 11, 2011, the Commission released its final report. The report called for "fundamental reform" to produce dramatic improvements in oil industry safety practices. The Commission recommended that an independent safety agency be created to regulate offshore oil drilling and it called for significantly increased funding for oil spill response planning. The Commission expressed "serious concerns" about offshore drilling in Arctic waters off the northern coast of Alaska because of very limited industry response capabilities there. A copy of the report is available online at *https://www.gpo.gov/ fdsys/pkg/GPO-OILCOMMISSION/pdf/GPO-OILCOMMISSION.pdf.* In April 2013, members of the President's Commission that investigated the spill lambasted Congress for failing to adopt any legislation to prevent future spills and for failing to provide adequate funding for regulatory oversight of offshore drilling. On April 28, 2017, President Trump signed Executive Order 13,795 on "Implementing an America-First Offshore Energy Strategy." It directed federal agencies to promote offshore oil drilling in the outer continental shelf off Alaska, in the Gulf of Mexico, and in the Atlantic. The executive order was revoked by President Biden on his first day in office. See Executive Order 13,990, Protecting Public Health and the Environment and Restoring Science to Tackle the Climate Crisis.

## 2.  The Regulatory Options

Despite increasing interest in nonregulatory strategies, there is wide agreement that some form of regulation is essential to prevent environmental degradation. We now turn to the question of what form that regulation should take. This has become a topic of considerable controversy in recent years as proponents of regulatory approaches that employ economic incentives harshly criticize command-and-control regulation.

Once it has been determined that a problem deserves some form of collective response, three important issues must be confronted: (1) What conduct or activity should be targeted for collective action? (2) On what basis should judgments be made about how that conduct should be altered? (3) What form of collective action should be employed in an effort to alter that conduct? These issues are not an exhaustive catalog of all the components of regulation, and decisions concerning them need not be made in any particular sequence. But the classifications can serve as a useful starting point for study of environmental regulation by isolating some of the major points of dispute over the strengths and weaknesses of various regulatory alternatives. Thus, for present purposes we can think of an environmental regulation as a government directive given to a particular *regulatory target* based on some finding (*basis for controls*) that prohibits or requires some type of action (depending on the *type of regulation* employed).

Regulation can assume many forms, and it can be implemented through a wide array of instrumentalities. To understand how environmental regulation works it is useful to outline the range of possible options for each of the three components of regulation identified above.

### A.  Regulatory Targets

The environmental statutes generally define what activities, products, pollutants, or entities (industrial facilities, individuals, government agencies) can be regulated. The categories listed below are all well-represented within the current universe of environmental regulation, as shown in Figure 2.5.

**Products.**  Legislation aimed at products ranges from the very broad, such as the Toxic Substances Control Act (TSCA), under which EPA can regulate virtually any aspect of the lifecycle of "any chemical substance or mixture" (manufacture, processing, distribution, use, or disposal); to the rather specific, such as the Federal Insecticide, Fungicide, and Rodenticide Act (FIFRA), governing just the substances mentioned in the Act's title; to the very specific, such as the Lead-Based Paint Poisoning Prevention Act or the provisions of TSCA directed at particular substances (e.g., asbestos or PCBs).

**Pollutants.**  Virtually all damaging residuals from industrial, commercial, and some domestic activities fall within the jurisdiction of some federal environmental statute, although it also seems that regulation never quite covers the entire universe of residuals, as illustrated by periodic outcries when a heretofore unregulated substance or activity causes widely publicized environmental damage.

**Figure 2.5    The Principal Federal Environmental Laws Classified by Type of Statute and Regulatory Targets**

| *1. Waste management and pollution control laws* | *Regulatory targets* |
|---|---|
| Clean Air Act | Emissions of air pollutants |
| Clean Water Act | Discharges of pollutants into the navigable waters of the United States |
| Resource Conservation and Recovery Act | Generation, transportation, treatment, storage, and disposal of hazardous wastes |
| Comprehensive Environmental Response, Compensation, and Liability Act | Liability for responses to releases of hazardous substances and damage to natural resources |
| Safe Drinking Water Act | Contaminants in public drinking water supplies, underground injection of hazardous wastes |
| Ocean Dumping Act | Ocean dumping of material |
| Surface Mining Control and Reclamation Act | Surface coal mining operations on nonfederal lands |

| *2. Health and safety laws* | *Regulatory targets* |
|---|---|
| Occupational Safety and Health Act | Workplace hazards |
| Toxic Substances Control Act | Manufacture, processing, use, or disposal of any chemical substance or mixture except for pesticides, tobacco, food, and drugs |
| Federal Insecticide, Fungicide, and Rodenticide Act | Distribution, sale, and use of pesticides |
| Emergency Planning and Community Right-to-Know Act | Storage and release of hazardous substances |
| Hazardous Materials Transportation Act | Transportation of hazardous materials |
| Consumer Product Safety Act | Dangerous consumer products |
| Food, Drug, and Cosmetic Act | Food additives, drugs, and cosmetics |
| Atomic Energy Act | Atomic materials |

| *3. Resource management laws* | *Regulatory targets* |
|---|---|
| National Environmental Policy Act | Major federal actions significantly affecting the environment |
| Endangered Species Act | Actions that threaten endangered species |
| Federal Land Policy and Management Act | Management of federal lands |
| Coastal Zone Management Act | Development in coastal zones |
| Multiple-Use Sustained-Yield Act | Management of national forests |
| Wild and Scenic Rivers Act | Wild and scenic rivers |
| Wilderness Act of 1964 | Wilderness areas |

**Industrial Facilities.**   Federal regulation targeted at industrial facilities is perhaps the best known, and seemingly the easiest, form of regulation to enforce, for facilities are fewer in number than individuals. Consider the difference, for example, between the EPA's requirement that the automobile industry install emission control devices at the factory and a regulation imposing no obligation on automobile manufacturers but requiring each car owner to install a comparable device. Industrial facilities may be a more attractive target for federal regulators because enforcement against them raises none of the federalism concerns that arise when the federal government tries to coerce state and local government into action. As environmental regulation becomes more comprehensive, small businesses frequently are becoming regulatory targets (e.g., gas station owners whose underground storage tanks are now regulated by RCRA subtitle I, dry cleaners affected by both RCRA and the 1990 Clean Air Act Amendments).

**Government Agencies.**   In some cases, government entities are regulated because they own certain kinds of facilities that have become part of the pollution problem (e.g., public water supply systems, sewage treatment plants, nuclear weapons production plants, schools with asbestos-containing materials). Regulations aimed at government *qua* government are best represented by NEPA, which requires federal agencies to change their decision-making processes to incorporate environmental concerns.

**Individuals.**   There are few extant examples of federal regulation of private individuals who are not doing business as firms. Among the important exceptions are federal prohibitions generally applicable to all persons, such as the ban on unpermitted dredging and filling of wetlands and the federal prohibition on the taking of endangered species. Regulation of individual conduct is less popular than regulation of corporations for both political and practical reasons. Early attempts by EPA to solve some of the air pollution problem by imposing transportation control plans on cities in ways that would directly affect individual driving habits were barred by Congress after vehement protests. For a strong argument that environmental law needs to rethink its aversion to regulating the behavior of individuals, who now contribute a substantial share of many pollution problems, see Michael P. Vandenbergh, From Smokestack to SUV: The Individual as Regulated Entity in the New Era of Environmental Law, 57 Vand. L. Rev. 515 (2004).

**Land Uses.**   The major pieces of federal lands legislation establish rules governing the management of public lands. While most private land use decisions are regulated only at the local level, some of the federal environmental laws contain provisions that affect land use decisions, such as the Clean Water Act's requirements that permits be obtained before dredge-and-fill operations are conducted in wetlands.

The choice of regulatory target can be a crucial determinant of the success of a regulatory scheme. A program that seeks to regulate a few easily identified targets will be much easier to implement and to enforce than one that attempts to regulate numerous, poorly identified, or widely dispersed entities. Environmental regulation inevitably creates winners and losers based on how the costs and benefits of regulation are distributed. This has important political and practical consequences. Politically powerful regulatory targets are more likely to be successful in lobbying against environmental regulation that will affect them.

## B.  Bases for Controls

Although environmental regulations ultimately are aimed at improving environmental quality, the terms of each specific regulation are founded on methodologies that have different starting points, or bases. The environmental statutes employ three major approaches for determining how far to go in controlling a regulatory target.

**Health (or Environment).**   Some statutes direct that controls be established on the basis of what is required to achieve a goal stated exclusively in health- or environment-related terms. For example, section 109 of the Clean Air Act instructs EPA to set ambient air quality standards at a level requisite to protect human health with an "adequate margin of safety." At least the first part of that instruction — requisite to protect human health — takes EPA on a search for a level of ambient air quality based on a medical assessment of the effects of air pollution on human health. In setting that level, EPA is not supposed to examine other issues that might be germane to setting a standard, such as how much it will cost to achieve that level of control or whether technology exists to do so. The Delaney Clauses of the federal Food, Drug, and Cosmetic Act also impose controls on a purely health-related basis by directing that no food or color additives be approved if they have been found to induce cancer in man or in animals.

**Technology (or Feasibility).**   Other statutes tie the ultimate regulatory standard to the capabilities of technology. These might be viewed as the opposite of health-based standards, because instead of asking what is needed to protect health they ask what it is possible to do. For example, under the Clean Air Act (CAA), EPA issues performance standards for new sources that are based on the best control technology that has been adequately demonstrated (CAA §111(a)(1)(C)). Other statutes employ a hybrid approach that directs that health be protected to the extent feasible. For example, the Occupational Safety and Health Act directs OSHA to ensure "to the extent feasible" that no worker "will suffer material impairment of health or functional capacity." Since it limits health-based regulation to what is feasible, this approach is best described as a feasibility-limited, health-based approach.

**Balancing.**   While this category can capture a variety of values that may serve as bases for controls, they all share the common attribute of requiring some comparison of the gains of a proposed standard with its costs. For example, the Toxic Substances Control Act requires EPA to protect against "unreasonable risks" to be determined by balancing the environmental and health effects of chemicals against the economic consequences of regulation.

Consider how the three bases for controls relate to one another. Figure 2.6 supplies a rough schematic representation that facilitates comparison of how each of the three options operates when used to control a pollutant that harms human health.

The figure shows two graphs, the right-hand one of which has been flipped on its y-axis so that the two curves drawn can be shown intersecting. The line descending from left to right is the Health curve. It indicates that the adverse health effects of pollution generally decline as emissions are reduced. A line from any point on

**Figure 2.6    Bases for Controls: Health-Based, Technology-Based, and Balancing Approaches**

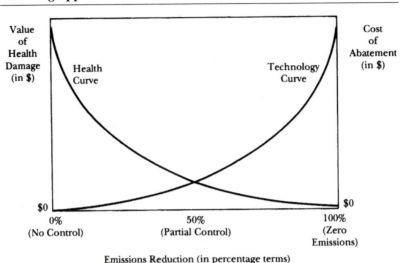

the Health curve to the left-hand *y*-axis identifies the monetary value of the "marginal" health benefits, those gained by further emissions controls. The shape of the curve as drawn is suggestive only; many other configurations are possible. In the toxics field, one particular aspect of the curve as drawn is, however, salient. Current federal policy assumes that there is no safe level of exposure to most toxic air pollutants. Accordingly, you cannot get to zero health effects until you get to zero emissions.

In depictions of this kind, the line emanating from the left-hand origin, labeled "Technology," is frequently designated "Costs of Abatement." Costs are determined by the underlying technologies available for abating, so it is fair to designate this the Technology curve. Each point on this curve implies an underlying technology, which produces the incremental pollution reduction at that point on the curve, and at the marginal cost indicated by extending a line to the right-hand *y*-axis, but the same technology need not underlie each point. A rudimentary and inexpensive technology may suffice to eliminate 80 percent of emissions, for example, but after that point this becomes ineffective and another must be selected.

The Health and Technology curves are employed in health-based (H-based) and technology-based (T-based) regulation, respectively. H-based regulation is concerned with controlling emissions until a certain level of health-related safety is achieved. The process can be understood graphically as long as one understands this is an idealized simplification of the actual standard-setting procedures. An H-based regulator would first determine how much health protection is required. This determination could be represented as a point on the Health curve. A line from here down to and perpendicular to the *x*-axis then establishes the emissions reduction necessary to achieve the desired level of health protection. In a pure H-based system, costs are not examined.

Conversely, a T-based regulator works with the Technology curve. Over the years of refining environmental pollution regulation, we have formulated a variety of T-based requirements that pick out different points along the Technology curve. The Clean Water Act of 1972, for instance, imposed a two-phased set of controls on discharges into water: a standard of "best practicable technology" (BPT), to be achieved by 1977, and a tougher one of "best available technology economically achievable" (BAT) by 1983. The BAT process can be described for illustrative purposes, again bearing in mind this is an oversimplification.

BAT requires EPA to select the best technology that it concludes will work effectively. Then EPA estimates the emissions reduction that technology could achieve (which could be represented on the chart by locating that technology on the Technology curve and finding the level of emissions reduction associated with it). Finally, the Agency determines whether bearing those costs is "economically achievable" by industry. If they are, the level of control corresponding to the chosen technology (represented, again, by extending a line through the correct point on the Technology curve, perpendicular to the horizontal axis) becomes the regulatory standard; if not, EPA must proceed leftward along the Technology curve until an economically achievable point is reached.

Other T-based regulations use the Technology curve in different ways, but they all share the essential feature of ignoring the Health curve, just as H-based regulations ignore the Technology curve. In contrast, regulations based on balancing approaches are concerned with both curves, particularly where they intersect. The central idea behind balancing approaches is to determine, at least approximately, where to set emission controls so that any stricter control is not justified, because the incremental costs of control are greater than the incremental value of the health gains, and any more lenient controls are likewise unjustified, because the health losses would be greater than the savings in control costs. This point can be represented as the point where the two curves intersect.

## C. Types of Regulation

Regulations must be expressed in directives that are specifically understandable by the regulatory target and enforceable by subsequent government intervention, if necessary. Among the major types of regulation (not all of them germane to all the categories of regulated activity) are:

**Design Standards or Technology Specifications.** These specify how a certain plant, piece of machinery, or pollution control apparatus should be designed. OSHA has written numerous design standards, such as the standard of 36 inches' clearance between library shelves in law libraries. EPA writes fewer of them, although some of its performance standards become de facto technology specifications. This can occur when EPA has written a regulation on the assumption that a particular technology exists whose performance can meet the regulation. A regulatory target may prudently decide its safest course to compliance is to install that technology. Then, should the target fail to comply, it can defend by attempting to place responsibility on EPA.

**Performance Standards or Emission Limits.** These set an objective, or performance level, for the regulatory target to meet, without specifying how. These include emission limits that specify the rate, amount, and kind of pollutants that may be emitted from a given source over a specific period of time. EPA's new-source performance standards under the Clean Air Act and its various effluent limitations under the Clean Water Act are simply a few of the many environmental regulations that are nominally performance standards—but bear in mind that some of these routinely devolve into de facto design standards.

**Ambient or Harm-Based Standards.**    A very different type of performance standard than emissions limits, these play a significant enough role in regulatory decision making to merit separate mention. These establish a level of environmental quality to be achieved or maintained in some environment, be it a lake or stream, an airshed or an underground aquifer. As such, ambient standards are incomplete, because they are not directed at a particular regulatory target. Typically, federal ambient standards are contained in legislation that instructs the states to achieve those levels within a certain time period, but without specifying how the states are to do this—this is why ambient standards can be viewed as performance standards (whose target is the states). Of course, under *New York v. United States*, such legislation cannot compel states to comply, but states frequently do cooperate with such legislation. The option in case of non-compliance is for the federal government to make choices of pollution levels for individual sources, choices that states themselves prefer to make.

**Product Bans or Use Limitations.**    These prohibit a product or activity or limit its use. They typically involve products such as chemicals, pesticides, or food additives. They also may include a land use strategy, as when the National Park Service bans autos in Yosemite National Park during certain times or bans off-road vehicles from specified wilderness areas. In occupational settings, use limits can be directed at workers.

**Marketable Allowances.**    Economists have long advocated marketable allowances, which permit companies to buy and sell emission rights, using market forces to ensure that pollution is reduced in the least costly manner. The 1990 Amendments to the Clean Air Act embrace this approach by providing electric utilities with tradeable allowances to emit sulfur dioxide. These allowances are based on the theory that companies that can reduce emissions most cheaply will do so and sell their allowances to companies for whom such reductions would be more expensive.

**Challenge Regulation or Environmental Contracting.**    While not widely employed in the United States yet, there is considerable interest in these tools. With challenge regulation, the government establishes a clear environmental performance target, while the regulated community designs and implements a program for achieving it. Unlike purely voluntary programs, such as EPA's 33/50 program, specific regulatory responses take effect if the target is not met. Environmental contracting, used in EPA's Project XL, involves an agreement between a government agency and a source to waive certain regulatory requirements in return for an enforceable commitment to achieve superior performance.

**Pollution Taxes or Emissions Charges.**    Economists also have supported pollution taxes or emissions charges to internalize the social costs of activities damaging public health or the environment. One early example was the Esch-Hughes Act of 1912, which imposed a tax on white phosphorus to induce manufacturers of matches to use a safer, but more expensive, substitute. Congress in 1989 imposed an escalating tax on CFC production to accelerate both the phaseout of these chemicals and the development of substitutes. Emissions charges are based on the "polluter pays" principle, to provide added incentive for emissions reductions. For example, the 1990 Clean Air Act Amendments finance a new national permit program by imposing an emissions charge of at least $25 per ton on sources needing permits.

**Subsidies.** Subsidies are the converse of taxes. Corporate investments beneficial to the environment can be encouraged by providing companies with public funds, tax breaks, or other benefits to subsidize such activity. In the past, subsidies frequently promoted environmentally destructive activities, such as the development of wetlands or logging on public lands. Elimination of such subsidies can be a means to promote environmental protection.

**Deposit-Refund Schemes.** Combining elements of both taxes and subsidies, deposit-refund schemes impose a fee that later can be refunded when a product is returned for recycling or disposal in an environmentally responsible manner. Several states have enacted "bottle bills" that impose a refundable deposit on beverage containers. Deposit-refund schemes help reduce litter and can serve as a disincentive for "midnight dumping," which taxes on waste disposal otherwise might encourage.

**Liability Rules and Insurance Requirements.** Some statutes strengthen common law rules imposing liability for environmental damage. CERCLA imposes strict, joint, and several liability for environmental cleanup costs and natural resource damages. Regulations issued under other statutes seek to increase the effectiveness of liability rules by requiring that facilities seeking permits to handle hazardous materials have sufficient insurance or other resources to pay for potential damage caused by their activities. In return for limiting liability for nuclear accidents, the Price Anderson Act requires utilities to purchase $150 million of private insurance per reactor and to contribute to a second-tier federal compensation fund totaling $7 billion.

**Planning or Analysis Requirements.** Beginning with NEPA's directive that federal agencies prepare environmental impact statements, environmental regulation occasionally requires that certain information be gathered and analyzed or that certain plans be prepared prior to undertaking environmentally significant decisions. Efforts to encourage states to control nonpoint source pollution and to improve the management of nonhazardous solid waste have relied largely on requirements for more comprehensive planning.

**Information Disclosure (Labeling) Requirements.** These require the regulatory target to disseminate information. Their usual objective has been to inform persons of hazards they can avoid through proper conduct, such as wearing ear protection in noisy areas or avoiding foods containing sodium when on a low-sodium diet. Disclosure requirements may be subdivided into design and performance categories. Congress has specified the precise wording of cigarette warning labels (a design standard). California's Proposition 65 requires businesses employing toxic chemicals to give "clear and reasonable warning" to exposed individuals (a performance standard). Informational regulation also is being used to generate public pressure for emissions reductions, as illustrated by the EPCRA's requirement that facilities report annual releases of toxic substances.

The choice of what mix of controls to employ is likely to be influenced by the nature of the regulatory targets and the chosen basis for control. Some types of controls are better suited for certain regulatory targets and bases for control than are others. For example, information disclosure and labeling requirements are more likely to be effective when the regulatory target is a product that informed consumers can decline to purchase than when it is widely dispersed sources of air pollution. Statutes that require that controls be based on the capabilities of a certain level of technology leave little room for choice concerning the type of control to employ. While regulators can set performance standards that reflect the capabilities of a given level of technology, regulatory targets may play it safe by simply installing the particular technology used to derive the standard. Unless regulators are extraordinarily prescient in determining appropriate levels of emissions charges or environmental taxes, they cannot ensure that pollution will be limited to any specific level, such as that required by health-based standards.

Like the choice of regulatory targets, the choice of which type of control to impose will create winners and losers because it will not affect every member of the regulated community in the same way. By requiring companies to pay for emissions they previously could discharge for free, emissions charges may transfer wealth from polluters to regulators. Yet these same polluters may be winners under a marketable permit scheme because the scheme would allow them to sell rights to pollute that previously were not transferable. Advocates of marketable permits claim this is a virtue because it creates an incentive for emission reductions beyond what otherwise would be required by regulation. Opponents note that because the source of this incentive is the ability to transfer rights to pollute, aggregate levels of pollution will not be any lower and pollution actually may increase around facilities purchasing pollution rights.

### 3.   Comparing Regulatory Strategies

The choice of which regulatory strategy to employ usually is a matter for Congress. The environmental statutes generally identify regulatory targets by defining the jurisdictional reach of the authorities they delegate to agencies. Congress also usually specifies the bases for control and types of regulation agencies may employ to implement the environmental laws. For example, when air pollution became politically salient, Congress chose to regulate by establishing *health-based performance standards*, the national, uniform *ambient air standards* (see sections 108 and 109 of the Clean Air Act), through an instruction *targeted at the states* instructing each state to develop a plan outlining how it would achieve those standards. When it enacted the Clean Water Act, Congress required EPA to impose *technology-based effluent standards* targeted directly at the *industrial facilities* that discharge pollutants into surface waters.

Dissatisfaction with the performance of executive agencies in implementing the environmental laws has encouraged Congress to write regulatory legislation with increasing specificity. Congress now often specifies deadlines for implementing action by agencies, and occasionally it spells out precise regulatory consequences should an agency fail to meet a deadline. For example, the 1984 amendments to the Resource Conservation and Recovery Act (RCRA) provided that the land disposal of broad classes of hazardous wastes would be banned automatically after certain deadlines unless EPA specified levels of treatment that would render such disposal safe.

Despite the increasing specificity with which Congress writes the environmental statutes, executive agencies inevitably have considerable discretion in defining the precise contours of the regulatory strategy used to implement statutory commands. Thus, both legislators and executive officials face important choices in choosing among the available regulatory options. Given the high stakes of these choices (for both the regulated community and the environment) and the rich mix of available options, it is not surprising that assessments of regulatory alternatives can be highly controversial. Indeed, dissatisfaction with existing regulatory strategies has ignited a lively debate between proponents of approaches that rely on economic incentives and defenders of the traditional command-and-control approach. Before exploring this debate, it is important to identify the various criteria available for assessing regulatory options.

Many criteria can be used to evaluate alternative regulatory strategies. Professor Thomas McGarity suggests six such criteria: (1) administrative feasibility, (2) survivability (under existing conditions of judicial and political review), (3) enforceability, (4) efficiency, (5) fairness and equity, and (6) ability to encourage technological advance. McGarity, Media-Quality, Technology, and Cost-Benefit Balancing Strategies for Health and Environmental Regulation, 46 Law & Contemp. Probs. 159 (Summer 1983). McGarity concludes that each regulatory strategy scores high under some of these six criteria but not under others. Similar conclusions were reached in an OTA report, Environmental Policy Tools: A User's Guide 23 (1995). OTA found that the best mix of regulatory tools depends on the relative importance of each criterion. For example, because efficiency is enormously important to most economists, they are harshly critical of command-and-control regulations that generally do not vary regulatory standards to take into account differences in compliance costs. Proponents of command-and-control regulation may recognize its inefficiency, but believe that it scores high on administrative simplicity, enforceability, and equity, which they may view as more important values than efficiency.

Given the pervasive uncertainty that surrounds environmental problems and the enormous diversity of regulatory targets encompassed by the environmental laws, the task confronting regulators is indeed a difficult one. The legal system seeks to formulate general rules to be applied to certain classes of activities and enterprises. Yet the diversity of regulatory targets implies that it will be virtually impossible to design regulations that take into account relevant differences between individual targets.

There are several strategies available for adjusting regulations to account for the diversity of regulated entities. Consider the following possibilities. Uniform regulations can be issued with a procedure for granting variances. Regulations can be designed to apply to a smaller class of activities or entities that have similar characteristics or regulations can rely on case-by-case decision making to permit consideration of individual circumstances. While case-by-case review can be valuable if the number of regulatory targets is small, it is likely to prove extremely cumbersome if there are large numbers of regulated firms. Another possibility is enforced self-regulation, which directs individual firms to draft their own rules, subject to some form of certification. See I. Ayres & J. Braithwaite, Responsive Regulation: Transcending the Deregulation Debate (1992). These privately written rules can then be publicly enforced, e.g., under the Clean Water Act EPA can penalize firms for violating their privately drafted oil spill prevention rules. In an effort to increase regulatory flexibility, EPA has begun experimenting with environmental contracting through its Project XL. The project gives selected companies more flexibility to meet environmental standards if they enter into contracts with EPA that promise greater reductions in pollutant discharges than would be achieved through existing standards.

The tension between flexibility and complexity and its implications for enforcement of environmental regulations is explored in the following case study.

## CASE STUDY: OIL SPILL LIABILITY AND SECTION 311 OF THE CLEAN WATER ACT

The tradeoff between regulatory flexibility and complexity is well illustrated by the history of federal regulation of discharges of oil spills and hazardous substances under section 311 of the Clean Water Act. This experience, on which the strict liability provisions of the Superfund legislation (CERCLA) are modeled, began in 1970 with the precursor of today's Clean Water Act. In 1970 Congress established a national policy that "there should be no discharges of oil or hazardous substances into or upon the navigable waters of the United States." As originally written, section 311 of this Act prohibited and required the reporting of all discharges of "harmful quantities" of oil. While this sounds like a relatively straightforward prohibition, it required the Secretary of the Interior, who at the time administered the statute, to determine what constituted "harmful quantities" of oil. Given the enormous uncertainties that surround assessments of the impact of pollutants on aquatic life, any regulation that required actual proof of harm would be extremely difficult to enforce. For small discharges of oil or hazardous substances, the costs of demonstrating harm surely would exceed any likely recovery. As a result, the Secretary of the Interior opted for a simpler, but less flexible, interpretation of section 311. He promulgated what came to be known as the "sheen test" for oil discharges. Under that test, any oil spill that caused "a film or sheen upon or discoloration of the surface of the water or adjoining shorelines" was deemed a harmful quantity prohibited by the statute.

The sheen test was challenged by dischargers, who argued that section 311 required evidence that small spills actually had caused harm. In United States v. Boyd, 491 F.2d 1163 (9th Cir. 1973), the Ninth Circuit held that the "harmful quantities" language in the statute meant that de minimis discharges were not illegal if they were not actually harmful. As a result, defendants charged with spilling oil could contest whether the discharges actually had caused harm. In a subsequent case, United States v. Chevron Oil Co., 583 F.2d 1357 (5th Cir. 1978), the Fifth Circuit held that the sheen test was only a rebuttable presumption of harm to the environment. The court emphasized that Congress had not chosen to prohibit *all* discharges of oil, but rather only discharges in "harmful quantities." Under the Fifth Circuit's approach, defendants were free to contest whether their discharges had caused harm, but they bore the burden of showing that the discharge had not actually been harmful.

In 1978, Congress amended section 311 to provide that environmental officials could prohibit any discharge of oil or hazardous substances that they found "may be harmful to the public health or welfare of the United States." After extensively considering alternative approaches for determining what discharges may be harmful, EPA in 1987 again promulgated the sheen test. The sheen test again came under judicial scrutiny when challenged by defendants charged with releasing oil. After the Coast Guard assessed civil penalties ranging from $250 to $1,000 against Chevron for 12 discharges of oil that created oil sheens, the company successfully argued in court that the discharges were not illegal under section 311 because any impact of the spills on the ecosystem was de minimis. On appeal, the Fifth Circuit reversed. The court held that the 1978 amendments had authorized EPA to prohibit spills that "may be harmful" regardless of whether or not they caused actual harm. In holding that spills that violated the sheen test violated the statute regardless of whether or not they caused harm, the court explained that EPA could adopt a less flexible approach to regulation in order to avoid the administrative expense of a more complicated inquiry: "In sum, the agency may both proscribe incipient injury and measure its presence by a test that avoids elaborated inquiry. While it is apparent that such an approach sometimes over-regulates, it is equally apparent that this imprecision is a trade-off for the administrative burden of case-by-case proceedings." Chevron U.S.A., Inc. v. Yost, 919 F.2d 27 (5th Cir. 1990).

---

## NOTES AND QUESTIONS

1. Why do you suppose that Congress did not simply prohibit *all* discharges of oil in section 311? What was to be gained by prohibiting only discharges in harmful quantities? Does the use of the sheen test effectively sacrifice these ends by prohibiting even discharges that may not be harmful?

2. If you determined that only discharges of oil or hazardous substances that are harmful should be prohibited, who should bear the burden of proof concerning the impact of the discharge: the discharger or enforcement officials? What effect is the allocation of the burden of proof likely to have on the enforceability of the prohibition?

3. Should it matter whether the discharger believed that the discharge would be harmful? Criminal prohibitions generally require some element of intentional conduct, though it need not necessarily be an intent to cause harm to the environment. By contrast, strict liability provisions impose liability without regard to fault. What impact would an intent requirement have on incentives to prevent discharges? What impact would a strict liability standard have on such incentives?

4. In April 1994, the Coast Guard announced a pilot program to issue "tickets" to dischargers who spill less than 100 gallons of oil. The tickets can be served on violators immediately by Coast Guard officials. The alleged violators then have the option of paying the fine within 30 days or seeking an administrative hearing to contest the charges. 59 Fed. Reg. 16,558 (1994).

### Assessing Regulatory Strategies and Their Effect on Technological Innovation

Each regulatory strategy places its own informational demands on regulators, and each has its own practical and political consequences. Uniform, technology-based controls initially were thought to be easier to develop and monitor. Thus, it is not surprising that nationally uniform, technology-based controls, in some form, are essential features of the regulatory approach employed in the Clean Air Act, the Clean Water Act, and RCRA. Risk-balancing and health-based standards were thought to be more difficult to implement and administer because they require considerable information about health effects and economic impacts that are difficult to assess with precision.

Experience with environmental regulation has demonstrated that industry estimates of prospective compliance costs often prove to be far too pessimistic. EPA Assistant Administrator William G. Rosenberg notes: "Historically, actual costs are generally much lower than projections because of improved technology. For example, in 1971 the oil industry estimated that lead phase-out would cost 7 cents a gallon, or $7 billion a year. In 1990, with 99 percent of lead phase-out accomplished, actual costs are only $150 million to $500 million a year, 95 percent less than earlier estimates." Rosenberg, Clean Air Amendments, 251 Science 1546, 1547 (1991).

Industry estimates of the costs of complying with the acid rain control program in the 1990 Clean Air Act Amendments quickly proved to be substantially overstated. By 1992, EPA had reduced its cost estimate of the acid rain control program to $3 billion per year from the $4 to $5 billion it employed when the legislation was adopted. EPA then estimated that emissions allowances would trade for only $275 per ton instead of its previous estimates of $500 to $750 per ton and industry estimates of as much as $1,500 per ton. EPA Issues Final Rules for Utilities on Acid Rain, Wall St. J., Oct. 27, 1992, at A18. In fact, allowances sold for far less, at prices ranging from $75 to $225 per ton between 1997 and 1999.

Several studies have confirmed that pollution control regulations tend to be substantially less costly than expected before regulations are adopted. One reason for this phenomenon is that new technologies that lower control costs are developed in response to regulation. Goodstein & Hodges, Polluted Data, 35 The American Prospect 64 (1997). Another factor may be that regulations do not achieve as much pollution control as expected. See Harrington, Morgenstern & Nelson, Predicting the Costs of Environmental Regulations, 41 Environment 10 (Sept. 1999).

## NOTES AND QUESTIONS

1. Technology has proved to be remarkably adaptable once regulation has created the proper incentives. The chemical industry publicly denied the availability of reasonable substitutes for chlorofluorocarbons (CFCs), chemicals that damage the ozone layer, until regulation became imminent after the discovery of the Antarctic ozone hole and the development of an international consensus that CFCs should be phased out. Since regulations were announced, substitutes have become available at a remarkable rate. Miller, Policy Responses to Global Warming, 14 S. Ill. L. Rev. 187 (1990).

2. The economic and political risks are such that Congress has only rarely chosen to threaten the shutdown of an entire industry should emissions standards

prove unachievable. The issue is more often what form of regulation is most conducive to innovation. In particular, fixed emissions standards based on current assessments of technology are widely faulted for the absence of incentives for further innovation. An industry regulated by a "best available technology" standard may rightly question the benefits of research on new pollution control methods knowing that the costs could increase. Moreover, once the required level of emissions reduction has been achieved, there is no remaining incentive for efforts to go still further. See Dudek & Palmisano, Emissions Trading: Why Is This Thoroughbred Hobbled?, 13 Colum. J. Envtl. L. 217, 234-236 (1988).

3.  Advocates of increased reliance on economic incentive approaches to regulation argue that they are better suited to stimulating technological innovation than the "game of chicken" approach Congress employed in dealing with the auto industry in the early 1970s. Pollution taxes and emissions trading schemes create a continuous incentive for innovations that reduce emissions while giving companies flexibility to meet emissions limits however they can, including process changes and other alternatives to conventional end-of-pipe technology. Others are more skeptical of the impact of economic incentive approaches on technological innovation. They argue that such approaches are best suited for stimulating cost savings rather than improvements in pollution control. Should this matter? A study of emissions trading under the Clean Air Act suggests that flexibility has led to innovation in the form of cost-saving modifications as opposed to new hardware or exotic technologies. Dudek & Palmisano, supra at 235-236.

4.  While renewed interest in economic incentive approaches to environmental regulation makes them appear to be a recent invention, they actually have been the subject of high-level debate from the start of the federalization of environmental law. In 1965, the Economic Pollution Panel of the President's Science Advisory Committee discussed pollution taxes in their report Restoring the Quality of the Environment. In 1966, the President's Council of Economic Advisers (CEA) proposed the use of effluent charges to create incentives for dischargers to reduce pollution, with the revenue raised to be used to pay for municipal treatment plants. CEA, Economic Report of the President, 1966, at 124 (1966). In his Environmental Message of 1971, President Nixon proposed that Congress impose a charge on sulfur dioxide emissions, and he pushed for a stiff tax on gasoline lead additives to encourage their rapid phaseout. These proposals were not given serious consideration by Congress.

5.  One of the most important reasons why Congress did not quickly embrace incentive-based approaches to regulation was its awareness that a shift to such policies would create losers as well as winners. As Figure 2.7 indicates, each of the principal incentive-based approaches has advantages and drawbacks that reflect, at least in part, how they alter the distribution of the costs and benefits of regulation. In addition, a study of congressional staff discovered that neither proponents nor opponents of effluent charges really understood the theory behind them. S. Kelman, What Price Incentives? Economists and the Environment 100-101 (1981).

6.  A report issued by the World Resources Institute (WRI) estimates that a strategy of shifting the revenue burden of taxation from economic "goods" to environmental "bads" could raise between $100 to $180 billion per year. "Congestion tolls on urban highways could generate $40 to $100 billion, carbon taxes would

**Figure 2.7   Comparison of Uniform, National Regulatory Approaches with Incentive-Based Approaches to Regulation**

|  | *Pros* | *Cons* |
|---|---|---|
| 1. *Uniform, National Regulation* | Arguably easier to establish | Inefficient since ignores differences in marginal control costs |
|  | Assures protection of health | Provides no incentive to reduce emissions beyond maximum permitted |
|  | Precludes relocation to avoid controls |  |
| 2. *Effluent Charges* | Creates incentives for dischargers to reduce emissions in the most cost-effective manner | No guarantee sufficiently protective levels of control will be achieved |
|  | Provides funds to cover social costs of pollution | Difficult to determine socially efficient level of such charges |
|  |  | Increases cost of production |
|  |  | Creates incentive for midnight dumping |
| 3. *Marketable Permits* | Creates incentives for dischargers to reduce emissions in the most cost-effective manner | Can result in less equitable distributions of pollutants |
|  | Overall allowable level of pollution can be determined in advance by allocation of permit rights | Some believe it is unfair to permit polluters to profit from sale of rights to pollute |
| 4. *Deposit-Refund Schemes* | Reduces incentive for midnight dumping | Administrative costs of collecting and refunding deposits reduce attractiveness |
| 5. *Provision of Subsidies for Investments in Pollution Controls* | Assists small and less profitable firms in bearing costs of compliance | Penalizes firms that already have invested in compliance technology |
|  |  | Redistributes income from taxpayers to polluting activities |

Source: Adapted from Congressional Research Service, Pollution Taxes, Effluent Charges and Other Alternatives for Pollution Control 2-8 (May 1977).

yield $30 to $50 billion, and solid-waste charges could raise another $5 to $10 billion." R. Repetto, R. Dower, R. Jenkins & J. Geoghegan, Green Fees: How a Tax Shift Can Work for the Environment and the Economy 11 (1992). These additional revenues could permit the government to reduce marginal tax rates on economically productive activities like labor, producing $45 to $80 billion in net economic benefits annually. Id. The WRI estimated that effluent charges, charges on environmentally damaging activities or products, and the reduction of tax benefits and subsidies for resource exploitation could generate nearly $40 billion in extra revenue each year. Id. at 83.

---

## PROBLEM EXERCISE: DESIGNING A NATIONAL GREENHOUSE GAS CONTROL PROGRAM

As the Obama administration pressed Congress to adopt a national program to control emissions of greenhouse gases, the question of whether a carbon tax or a cap-and-trade approach should be used was debated. Consider the advantages and drawbacks of each of these approaches as described by the Congressional Research Service:

> Market-based mechanisms that limit greenhouse gas (GHG) emissions can be divided into two types: quantity control (e.g., cap-and-trade) and price control (e.g., carbon tax or fee). To some extent, a carbon tax and a cap-and-trade program would produce similar effects: Both are estimated to increase the price of fossil fuels, which would ultimately be borne by consumers, particularly households. . . .
>
> If policymakers had perfect information regarding the market, either a price (carbon tax) or quantity control (cap-and-trade system) instrument could be designed to achieve the same outcome. Because this market ideal does not exist, preference for a carbon tax or a cap-and-trade program ultimately depends on which variable one wants to control—emissions or costs. Although there are several design mechanisms that could blur the distinction, the gap between price control and quantity control can never be completely overcome.
>
> A carbon tax has several potential advantages. With a fixed price ceiling on emissions (or their inputs—e.g., fossil fuels), a tax approach would not cause additional volatility in energy prices. A set price would provide industry with better information to guide investment decisions: e.g., efficiency improvements, equipment upgrades. Economists often highlight a relative economic efficiency advantage of a carbon tax, but this potential advantage rests on assumptions—about the expected costs and benefits of climate change mitigation—that are uncertain and controversial. Some contend that a carbon tax may provide implementation advantages: greater transparency, reduced administrative burden, and relative ease of modification.
>
> The primary disadvantage of a carbon tax is that it would yield uncertain emission control. Some argue that the potential for irreversible climate

change impacts necessitates the emissions certainty that is only available with a quantity-based instrument (e.g., cap-and-trade). Although it may present implementation challenges, policymakers could devise a tax program that allows some short-term emission fluctuations, while progressing toward a long-term emission reduction objective. Proponents argue that short-term emission fluctuations would be preferable to the price volatility that might be expected with a cap-and-trade system.

Although a carbon tax could possibly face more political obstacles than a cap-and-trade program, some of these obstacles may be based on misunderstandings of the differences between the two approaches or on assumptions that the tax would be set too low to be effective. Carbon tax proponents could possibly address these issues to some degree, but there remains considerable political momentum for a cap-and-trade program. [Jonathan L. Ramseur & Larry Parker, Carbon Tax and Greenhouse Gas Control: Options and Considerations for Congress (Feb. 23, 2009).]

**Questions:**   Which approach do you favor and why? Why do you think most politicians favor a cap-and-trade program? Why do most economists prefer a carbon tax?

## C.   THE REGULATORY PROCESS

The regulatory process is the arena in which law is translated into policy. This occurs in large part through the actions of administrative agencies operating under the watchful eye of the judiciary. By increasing the authority of administrative agencies, regulatory legislation has helped transform "the system of shared powers created by the constitution" into "a system of shared influence over bureaucratic decision-making." Strauss, Legislative Theory and the Rule of Law, 89 Colum. L. Rev. 427, 428 (1989), quoting M. McCubbins & T. Sullivan eds., Congress: Structure and Policy 403 (1987). A wide range of interests seek to influence how agencies implement the environmental statutes, including environmental groups, regulated industries, powerful congressional committees, and the Executive Office of the President. The umpire lurking in the background is the judiciary, whose intervention routinely is sought by parties disappointed by agency decisions.

### 1.   Law, Policy, and Agency Decision Making

Whenever Congress decides to confront an environmental issue, its options can be visualized as a "policy space," in the parlance of our policy sciences colleagues. Each point within that space represents a discrete, defined program for action, including the action of doing nothing. The statutes Congress enacts seldom point to a single unique location within the policy space, however. Instead, Congress identifies a target area, a subset of all the available options, and instructs an administrative agency to implement the statute by resolving all the remaining issues necessary to produce a definitive governmental decision.

To translate the environmental laws into regulations, administrative agencies must choose a regulatory alternative within the policy space established by law and develop, propose, and promulgate regulations. The Administrative Procedure Act and the environmental laws under whose authority the agency acts outline the ground rules for agency action, but agencies generally have considerable discretion over both the substance of regulatory policy and the procedures used to formulate it. How agency discretion is exercised within the policy space identified by the environmental statutes determines the precise contours of environmental policy and, presumably, the level of environmental protection the laws actually provide. Thus, study of the rulemaking process and agency decision making is critical to understanding environmental policy.

Dissatisfied with administrative implementation of the environmental laws, Congress has incorporated increasingly detailed regulatory directives into the environmental laws, coupled with provisions designed to force agencies to act. The classic agency-forcing device is a provision that authorizes a citizen suit against agency officials who fail to take certain action.

Virtually all of the major federal environmental statutes authorize citizens to bring action-forcing litigation against EPA when the EPA administrator has failed to perform a nondiscretionary duty. Most citizen suit provisions are patterned on section 304(a)(2) of the Clean Air Act, which authorizes "any person" to sue the administrator of EPA "where there is alleged a failure of the Administrator to perform any act or duty under this chapter which is not discretionary with the Administrator." 42 U.S.C. §7604(a)(2). Virtually identical provisions are contained in the Clean Water Act (§504(a)(2)), 33 U.S.C. §1365, the Resource Conservation and Recovery Act (§7002(a)(2)), 42 U.S.C. §6972(a)(2), the Safe Drinking Water Act (§1449), 42 U.S.C. §300j-8, the Toxic Substances Control Act (§20(a)(2)), 15 U.S.C. §2619, the Comprehensive Environmental Response, Compensation, and Liability Act (§310), 42 U.S.C. §9654, and other statutes. Because these statutes also authorize court awards of attorneys' fees to prevailing parties, plaintiffs can recover their legal costs when they successfully sue officials who fail to act.

During the 1980s, Congress often amended the environmental statutes to require agencies to issue regulations by certain deadlines. Agencies who missed these deadlines usually became the targets of citizen suits, called "deadline litigation," alleging that the agency had failed to perform a nondiscretionary duty. While such lawsuits are not the only avenue for persuading agencies to initiate regulatory proceedings, they have been one of the most effective ones. The Administrative Procedure Act and most federal environmental laws require agencies to give citizens the right to petition for the initiation of rulemaking proceedings. See 5 U.S.C. §553(e). A study performed for the Administrative Conference of the United States found that citizen petitions were used relatively infrequently. Most administrative practitioners indicated that there "were more effective ways to influence agency action, such as informal contacts or litigation, and that they would be loath to file a petition for rulemaking because of the delay they expect in the final disposition of their requests." Luneberg, Petitions for Rulemaking: Federal Agency Practice and Recommendations for Improvement 140 (1986).

Although agencies generally are not required to respond to citizen petitions by a certain date, one unusual exception to this rule is provided by section 21 of the Toxic Substances Control Act, 15 U.S.C. §2620. Section 21 of TSCA requires EPA within 90 days to grant or deny citizen petitions to initiate rulemaking actions under TSCA to control chemicals that may present "unreasonable risks" to public health or the environment. If EPA fails to act on such a petition within 90 days, or denies the petition, the petitioners may file suit in federal district court seeking de novo review of such failure or denial. If a court determines that the action sought by the petition meets the requisite statutory standard, "the court shall order the [EPA] Administrator to initiate the action requested by the petitioner." 15 U.S.C. §2620(b)(4)(B). The combination of a tight deadline for EPA to respond to petitions and a cause of action to challenge petition denials in court provides petitioners with a potentially significant tool to stimulate agency action.

## 2.   *Rulemaking Procedures*

In the late 1960s, when the fledgling environmental movement launched an assault on the use of DDT, a formal adjudicatory hearing was held to consider cancelling the registration of DDT. The hearing took more than 8 months and produced 9,312 pages of testimony from 125 expert witnesses. Charles F. Wurster, DDT Wars 155 (2015). After environmental concerns stimulated an avalanche of federal environmental legislation in the early 1970s, agencies relied increasingly on informal rulemaking proceedings to make regulatory decisions. Today most environmental regulations are promulgated through informal rulemaking, although pesticide cancellation proceedings under FIFRA still involve formal adjudicatory hearings.

The procedural requirements for informal rulemaking are relatively straightforward. Informal rulemaking proceedings are governed by section 4 of the Administrative Procedure Act (APA), 5 U.S.C. §553, which requires that agencies provide (1) public notice in the Federal Register of proposed rulemaking actions, (2) an opportunity for the public to submit written comments, and (3) publication of final rules in the Federal Register accompanied by a concise statement of their basis and purpose. Agencies are permitted to formulate rules through informal rulemaking unless an enabling statute requires that hearings be conducted on the record.

Agencies undertake to develop rulemaking proposals prior to issuing a notice of proposed rulemaking. In some cases, agencies may publish an advance notice of proposed rulemaking (ANPR) to solicit input from the public when the agency need not act quickly or to defuse pressure for faster action by indicating that the agency is considering the issue.

For EPA rulemaking proceedings, draft rulemaking documents usually are prepared by a work group of EPA staff who represent offices likely to be affected by the initiative. Draft notices of proposed rulemaking and supporting documents, which may be prepared with the help of outside consulting firms in more complex rulemakings, generally are reviewed by a steering committee composed of representatives from the major EPA offices. The final step in EPA's internal review procedures is "red border" review by top-level management and the EPA administrator.

Some of the federal environmental laws specify additional rulemaking procedures, but these procedures generally are consistent with those of the informal rulemaking model. For example, section 307(d) of the Clean Air Act, 42 U.S.C. §7607(d), provides extensive requirements for maintenance of a rulemaking docket by EPA for rulemakings under the Clean Air Act. It also specifies a standard for judicial review of agency action, which generally tracks the judicial review provisions of APA section 706 (although it provides that courts may invalidate rules for procedural errors only if the errors were so serious that "there is a substantial likelihood that the rule would have been significantly changed if such errors had not been made").

Other environmental statutes require that public hearings be held before certain major regulatory decisions are made (see, e.g., §§3001(a) and 3004(a) of RCRA, 42 U.S.C. §§6921(a) and 6924(a), which also require "consultation with appropriate Federal and State agencies"). Section 6(c) of the Toxic Substances Control Act, 15 U.S.C. §2605(c), specifies detailed procedures for informal rulemaking under section 6(a) of TSCA. It requires that EPA provide an opportunity for oral testimony and authorizes the submission of rebuttal testimony and cross-examination if the EPA administrator determines that it is necessary to resolve disputed issues of material fact. The Occupational Safety and Health Act also requires OSHA to hold a public hearing if written objections are filed to a proposed rule by any interested parties, and it gives such parties the right to conduct cross-examination when it conducts hearings on proposed rules.

---

# The Regulatory Process: A Pathfinder

The Administrative Procedure Act (APA), 5 U.S.C. §§551 et seq., establishes the basic procedural requirements agencies must follow in conducting informal rulemaking. Its basic requirements—that agencies provide public notice and an opportunity to comment prior to promulgating regulations—are implemented through notices published daily in the Federal Register describing agency actions and how to comment on them. The Federal Register can be accessed online at *www.archives.gov/federal_register/*. Public comments and background documentation for agency actions are usually kept in rulemaking dockets referenced in the Federal Register notices. Information concerning EPA's rulemaking dockets is available online at *https://www.epa.gov/dockets* and comments on rules proposed by any federal agency may be submitted electronically at *www.regulations.gov*.

Some environmental statutes supplement the APA by specifying additional procedures agencies must follow before taking certain actions. See, e.g., §6(c) of TSCA or §307(d) of the Clean Air Act. The Negotiated Rulemaking Act of 1990 generally codifies agency practices for conducting negotiated rulemaking. The Freedom of Information Act, 5 U.S.C. §552, provides an important tool for obtaining information from agencies that may assist citizens in participating in rulemaking proceedings.

Other statutes require agencies to consider certain factors when undertaking rulemaking. The Regulatory Flexibility Act (RFA), 5 U.S.C. §601, requires agencies to consider the impact of regulations on small businesses, and the Small Business Regulatory Enforcement Fairness Act (SBREFA) authorizes judicial review of an agency's compliance with the RFA.

Executive Order 12,866 requires federal agencies to submit significant rulemaking actions to OMB's Office of Information and Regulatory Affairs (OIRA) for review prior to publication in the Federal Register. Each agency publishes a summary of its rulemaking plans and a description of the status of existing rulemakings in an Agenda of Regulatory and Deregulatory Actions that appears in the Federal Register at the end of April and October. See, e.g., 86 Fed. Reg. 16952 (2021).

A useful introduction to the regulatory process that highlights important legal and procedural issues is Jeffrey S. Lubbers, A Guide to Federal Agency Rulemaking (6th ed. 2019). The Administrative Law Review, published by the ABA's Section of Administrative Law and Regulatory Practice, features articles on the regulatory process and an annual review of administrative law cases.

Despite the relatively minimal procedural requirements imposed by the APA, it has become enormously difficult for regulatory agencies to issue regulations through informal rulemaking. Agencies face several constraints on their ability to complete complex rulemakings efficiently and expeditiously. These include budgets that rarely provide sufficient resources to conduct more than a handful of major rulemakings in any given year, frequent turnover of technical staff, and the difficulty of obtaining critical information that typically is more readily available to the regulated community than to the regulators. As a result of these and other constraints, "[n]o health and safety agency has been able to promulgate regulations for more than three controversial chemicals in any given year." Shapiro & McGarity, Reorienting OSHA: Regulatory Alternatives and Legislative Reform, 6 Yale J. on Reg. 1, 6-7 (1989).

Although the procedural requirements for informal rulemaking remain remarkably simple, fear of judicial reversal has caused agencies to bend over backwards to supply detailed justifications for their actions. For example, Thomas McGarity notes that when EPA issued the initial national ambient air quality standards in 1971, the APA-required "concise general statement of basis and purpose" for the rules occupied a single page in the Federal Register. By 1987, "revision of a single primary standard consumed 36 pages in the Federal Register and was supported by a 100-plus-page staff paper, a lengthy Regulatory Impact Analysis that cost the agency millions of dollars, and a multi-volume criteria document." T. McGarity, Some Thoughts on "Deossifying" the Rulemaking Process, 1992 Duke L.J. 1385, 1387.

The seemingly innocuous requirement of a concise statement of basis and purpose "has blossomed into a requirement that agencies provide a 'reasoned explanation' for rules and that they rationally respond to outside comments passing a 'threshold requirement of materiality.'" Id. at 1400. As McGarity notes, while these additional analytic requirements are "not especially burdensome in theory," in practice they "invite abuse by regulatees who hire consultants and lawyers to pick apart the agencies' preambles and background documents and launch blunderbuss attacks on every detail of the legal and technical bases for the agencies' rules." Id. As a result, agencies seeking to avoid judicial reversals must go to great lengths to provide exceedingly thorough responses to comments.

Agencies also must comply with requirements for presidential and congressional review of rulemaking actions, as discussed below. These include the provisions of Executive Order 12,866, which specifies that significant regulatory actions must be reviewed by the Office of Management and Budget before they can be published in the Federal Register, and the Small Business Regulatory Enforcement Fairness Act (SBREFA), Pub. L. No. 104-121. SBREFA requires EPA and OSHA to give representatives of small businesses an opportunity to review and comment on certain rules that may affect them before the rules are even proposed publicly. SBREFA also authorizes judicial review of agency compliance with the Regulatory Flexibility Act (RFA), 5 U.S.C. §§601 et seq. The RFA requires agencies to prepare "regulatory flexibility analyses" when proposed or final rules are issued that "have a significant economic impact on a substantial number of small entities." Modeled on NEPA's environmental impact statement requirement, regulatory flexibility analyses require EPA to analyze alternatives to any regulatory action likely to have a substantial effect on small entities.

In December 2000, Congress enacted the Information Quality Act (IQA), section 515 of Title V of Pub. L. No. 106-554, also sometimes called the Data Quality Act, as part of the FY 2001 Treasury and General Government Appropriations Act. The IQA requires the Office of Management and Budget (OMB) to issue "guidelines ensuring and maximizing the quality, objectivity, utility, and integrity of information (including statistical information) disseminated by Federal agencies." The OMB published government-wide guidelines for complying with the IQA in February 2002 (67 Fed. Reg. 8,452). These and other requirements piled by the executive branch on top of the APA's seemingly simple statutory provisions have contributed to ossification of the regulatory process and the ability of regulated industries to successfully forestall the adoption of new regulatory standards. See McGarity, Shapiro & Bollick, Sophisticated Sabotage (2004), for a description of how regulatory targets are able to use procedural gambits to sabotage the adoption of regulations.

### 3. The Congressional Review Act

SBREFA also requires that all rules issued by federal agencies be sent first to Congress for review before taking effect. The legislation creates special fast-track procedures for Congress to enact a resolution disapproving the rules. This provision, known as the Congressional Review Act, 5 U.S.C. §§801 to 808, provides that if Congress enacts a joint resolution disapproving a regulation, the regulation shall not take effect or continue in effect. If a regulation is disapproved by Congress, the Act prohibits the agency that issued it from issuing any new rule that is "substantially the same as" the disapproved rule unless specifically authorized by subsequent legislation. 5 U.S.C. §801(b)(2).

In Immigration and Naturalization Service v. Chadha, 462 U.S. 919 (1983), the Supreme Court held that a legislative veto of regulations is unconstitutional because it bypassed the president's role in approving or disapproving legislation. The Congressional Review Act (CRA) avoids this constitutional problem by providing that joint resolutions of disapproval must be signed by the president or enacted over his veto. In March 2001, Congress used the CRA for the first time to repeal a regulation. The regulation repealed by Congress was the Occupational Health and Safety Administration's ergonomics standard to protect workers from repetitive stress injuries. The regulation, which had been under development by OSHA for a decade, finally had been issued in the closing days of the Clinton administration. OSHA expected that the rule would prevent 500,000 worker injuries per year from carpal tunnel syndrome, back strains, and other ailments. OSHA acknowledged that the rule would be expensive for businesses, estimating that it ultimately could cost $4.5 billion to implement, but it projected that it would save $9 billion per year by reducing worker injuries. On March 1, Congressional Republicans introduced a resolution of disapproval, which was approved by the Senate on March 6, 2001, by a vote of 56-44. On March 7, the House of Representatives adopted the joint resolution by a vote of 223-206. Using the fast-track procedures of the Congressional Review Act, the joint resolution was adopted without any hearings or committee action, with no opportunities for amendments, and with floor debate limited to ten hours. President Bush endorsed the disapproval effort and signed the joint resolution repealing the rule.

Because it requires either the president's signature on a disapproval resolution or its enactment by super-majorities in both Houses of Congress, the CRA, as a practical matter, is only used when a new administration seeks to repeal regulations issued by an outgoing one. Prior to the Trump administration taking office, the March 2001 veto of the OSHA ergonomics rules had been the only time it was used successfully.

When President Trump took office in 2017, Republicans had control of both Congress and the White House. A total of 14 resolutions of disapproval passed both houses of Congress pursuant to the CRA and were signed into law. Three environmental regulations were vetoed by these resolutions: the Interior Department's "stream protection rule" governing disposal of debris from mountaintop coal removal, a BLM rule governing land use plans under the Federal Land Policy and Management Act, and Interior Department regulations governing the "Non-Subsistence Take of Wildlife, and Public Participation and Closure Procedures on National Wildlife Refuges in Alaska." In Center for Biological Diversity v. Bernhardt, 946 F.3d 553 (9th Cir. 2019), the court upheld the veto of the Alaska regulation. After passing the House, a resolution to veto BLM regulations governing methane emissions from oil and gas operations on federal lands surprisingly was defeated in the Senate on May 10, 2017, when three Republican Senators joined all 48 Democrats in voting against the resolution.

## 4.  Presidential Oversight of Rulemaking

When decisions are being made about environmental regulations that affect important constituencies, few government officials are purely disinterested observers of the rulemaking process. No official has more clout with executive agencies than the president, who appoints agency officials who serve at the president's plea-sure. In the exercise of this "clout" over executive agencies, the president is sup-posed to be guided by a constitutional duty to "take Care that the Laws be faithfully executed." U.S. Const., art. II, §3.

Every president since Richard Nixon has established some sort of regulatory review program. The programs operated during the Reagan and Bush adminis-trations were the targets of harsh criticism by environmentalists who argued that they were used to block implementation of the laws. President Clinton's regula-tory review program was established by Executive Order 12,866, which provides that only significant regulatory actions are subject to OMB review. Executive Order 12,866 also establishes time limits on OMB review, and it provides for public disclo-sure of information concerning the review process.

The Clinton administration also sought to use its executive oversight author-ity to require agencies to incorporate environmental justice concerns in their actions. In 1994, President Clinton issued Executive Order 12,898, 59 Fed. Reg. 7,629 (1994). The executive order directs each federal agency to "make achieving environmental justice part of its mission by identifying and addressing, as appropri-ate, disproportionately high and adverse human health or environmental effects of its programs, policies, and activities on minority and low-income populations." The executive order directs agencies to consider the impact of environmental and human health risks on minority and poor communities. Each agency is required to develop an environmental justice strategy and to revise agency rules or policies to promote environmental justice. Other executive orders require agencies to consult and coordinate with Indian Tribal Governments (E.O. 13,084) and to respect prin-ciples of federalism (E.O. 13,132).

The president is not the only source of pressure exerted on agencies. Its law-making and appropriations powers give Congress formidable tools for influencing agency decision making. Although the Supreme Court's decision in INS v. Chadha, 462 U.S. 919 (1983), removed the "legislative veto" from Congress's arsenal, Con-gress has not hesitated to exercise other oversight authority to influence agency action and to contest presidential efforts to exert greater control over regulatory decisions. As noted above, congressional dissatisfaction with EPA's performance has resulted in the enactment of increasingly specific statutory directives designed to serve as agency-forcing mechanisms. These provisions effectively dictate what agency priorities should be and establish timetables for agency action enforceable in court.

Congress has been far more than a disinterested observer of the regulatory process. Members of Congress often seek to influence agency decisions, and con-gressional pressure can have a significant impact on agency decision making. The legal bounds on executive and congressional oversight of the rulemaking process were addressed in Sierra Club v. Costle, 657 F.2d 298 (D.C. Cir. 1981). The D.C. Circuit was faced with a challenge to EPA's promulgation of new source perfor-mance standards for coal-fired power plants. Environmental groups claimed that the standards had been weakened significantly at the eleventh hour after President Carter summoned EPA Administrator Douglas Costle to the White House where he was lobbied by Senator Robert Byrd of West Virginia, a state heavily dependent on high-sulfur coal. The court held that the meeting was proper in light of "the basic need of the President and his White House staff to monitor the consistency of executive agency regulations with Administration policy. . . . The authority of the President to control and supervise executive policy-making is derived from the Constitution; the desirability of such control is demonstrable from the practical realities of administrative rulemaking." The court concluded that except for adjudicatory or quasi-adjudicatory proceedings or specific docketing requirements imposed by statute, it was legal "for EPA not to docket a face-to-face policy session involving the President and EPA officials during the post-comment period, since EPA makes no effort to base the rule on any 'information or data' arising from that meeting."

Upon taking office, President Obama announced plans to take a fresh look at the process for presidential review of rulemaking. However, on January 18, 2011, he signed Executive Order 13,563, 76 Fed. Reg. 3,821 (2011), which largely reaffirmed the regulatory review process that operated during the Clinton administration governed by E.O. 12,866. In addition, this executive order directed agencies to conduct a retrospective review of their existing regulations to determine if they "should be modified, streamlined, expanded or repealed" to make them more effective or to reduce regulatory burdens. In July 2011, President Obama issued Executive Order 13,579, 76 Fed. Reg. 41,587 (2011), which calls upon independent agencies (those, such as the Federal Trade Commission, whose commissioners are not removable at will by the president) to perform retrospective analyses of their existing regulations. On August 23, 2011, OMB's Office of Information and Regulatory Affairs (OIRA) released the results of the retrospective reviews. The 800-page report listed more than 500 regulations that were being revised or eliminated. EPA reported that it was shifting from paper-based to electronic reporting by hazardous waste generators that it claimed would save up to $126 million annually. Neither industry groups nor environmentalists were particularly impressed with the agency plans, with the former arguing that they were mainly cosmetic and the latter arguing that they focused only on relaxing regulations rather than improving their effectiveness.

For sharply contrasting views concerning how well review of EPA rules by the Office of Management and Budget's Office of Information and Regulatory Affairs functioned during the Obama administration, see Cass R. Sunstein, The Office of Information and Regulatory Affairs: Myths and Realities, 126 Harv. L. Rev. 1838 (2013), and Lisa Heinzerling, Inside EPA: A Former Insider's Reflections on the Relationship Between the Obama EPA and the Obama White House, 31 Pace Envt'l. L. Rev. 325 (2014).

Ten days after taking office, President Trump signed Executive Order 13,771 on Reducing Regulation and Controlling Regulatory Costs. President Trump described it as mandating "the largest cut by far, ever in terms of regulation" and as the key to "cutting regulations massively" for businesses. The order required federal agencies to repeal two existing regulations for each new regulation they issued, and it gave each agency a regulatory budget of zero for the imposition of aggregate costs on industry during the current fiscal year. On his first day in office, President Biden revoked Executive Order 13,771 and other Trump executive orders on federal regulation, describing them as "harmful policies and directives that threaten to frustrate the Federal Government's ability to confront [. . .] problems." Executive Order 13,992, 86 Fed. Reg. 7049 (2021).

On his first day in office, President Biden issued a presidential memorandum on "Modernizing Regulatory Review," 86 Fed. Reg. 7223 (2021). The memo reaffirmed the basic principles that have governed regulatory review since the Clinton administration issued Executive Order 12,866, and it directed OMB to make recommendations concerning how to "modernize and improve the regulatory review process." Consistent with the Biden administration's focus on environmental justice, it directed OMB to take into account the distributional consequences of regulations and "to ensure that regulatory initiatives appropriately benefit and do not inappropriately burden disadvantaged, vulnerable, or marginalized communities."

## NOTES AND QUESTIONS

1. Does *Sierra Club v. Costle* lay to rest any questions concerning the legality of regulatory review? Does it suggest that the president can lawfully dictate to an agency head the substance of a regulatory decision Congress has directed the agency to make?

2. Regardless of who ultimately is responsible for an administrative decision, that decision must conform to applicable requirements of the underlying regulatory statute and the Administrative Procedure Act in order to withstand judicial review. If OMB directs agencies to make decisions arbitrarily or capriciously or to base them on factors inconsistent with the requirements of the underlying regulatory statute, such decisions are likely to be reversed. Suppose, however, that the administrative record and the appropriate statutory criteria would support *either* a decision favored by the agency or a different decision favored by OMB. Should a decision directed by the president be upheld in these circumstances even if it differs from that which the agency would have reached independent of presidential input?

3. Some statutory limits on executive oversight may be inferred from the environmental statutes themselves. In Environmental Defense Fund v. Thomas, 627 F. Supp. 566 (D.D.C. 1986), the Reagan administration OMB blocked EPA from issuing regulations governing the storage of hazardous waste in underground tanks, even though the statutory deadline for issuing such regulations had passed. EDF filed a deadline suit against EPA, but it took the unusual step of also joining OMB as a defendant. The court held that OMB had no authority to block EPA from promulgating regulations beyond the date of a statutory deadline. While noting that "[a] certain degree of deference must be given to the authority of the President to control and supervise executive policymaking," the court declared that efforts by OMB to block regulations after deadlines have expired are "incompatible with the will of Congress and cannot be sustained as a valid exercise of the President's Article II powers." Id. at 570. "Thus, if a deadline already has expired, OMB has no authority to delay regulations subject to the deadline in order to review them under the executive order." Id. at 571. Does this decision mean that EPA effectively could avoid OMB's regulatory review simply by waiting until after a statutory deadline has expired before issuing proposed regulations?

4. Prior to joining the Supreme Court, Elena Kagan wrote an article noting that President Clinton assumed directive authority over agency heads by issuing an unprecedented 107 presidential directives to them. She argues that the president

should be viewed as having the authority to direct decision making by agency heads, not as a result of a constitutional imperative, but rather as an appropriate rule of interpretation in circumstances where Congress has not expressly indicated to the contrary. Elena Kagan, Presidential Administration, 114 Harv. L. Rev. 2245 (2001). However, this interpretive rule would be contrary to the understanding of Congress at the time it adopted the regulatory statutes, an understanding reinforced by the pre-Clinton regulatory review programs that expressly disavowed such directive authority. See Percival, Presidential Management of the Administrative State: The Not-So-Unitary Executive, 51 Duke L.J. 963 (2001). Percival argues that such authority cannot be derived from the president's appointment and removal powers, even though as a practical matter they give him considerable ability to influence decisions by executive officers. He argues that the constitutionally required confirmation process envisions that agency heads will have some degree of independence from the president and that the political cost of the president firing an agency head serves as an important check on abuses of presidential power.

5. The APA's judicial review provisions direct courts to strike down agency actions that are "arbitrary, capricious, an abuse of discretion, or otherwise not in accordance with law." If an agency's only justification for repealing a rule had been to comply with President Trump's directive to repeal two rules for every new one that is promulgated, would it have been possible to convince a reviewing court that the action is arbitrary enough to be struck down? In December 2019, a lawsuit challenging the 2-for-1 executive order was dismissed by federal district judge Randolph Moss for lack of standing. The judge held that the public interest groups and a union bringing the lawsuit lacked standing because they could not show that it led to specific regulations that affected their members being derailed or repealed. Public Citizen v. Trump, 435 F.Supp.3d 144 (D.D.C. 2019).

## 5.   *Judicial Review and the Regulatory Process*

The major federal environmental statutes specifically authorize judicial review of agency action taken pursuant to them, and they also specify the procedures for obtaining judicial review. See, e.g., RCRA §7006(a), 42 U.S.C. §6976; TSCA §19, 15 U.S.C. §2618; CWA §509(b), 33 U.S.C. §1369(b); CAA §307(b), 42 U.S.C. §7607(b). These statutes, coupled with the judicial review provisions of the APA, 5 U.S.C. §§701-706, lay out the ground rules for challenging agency decisions in the federal courts. They generally permit suits challenging final agency action (as distinguished from "preliminary, procedural, or intermediate agency action," which may be reviewed only when the final action is taken, APA §704) as long as it is not "committed to agency discretion by law" (such as a decision whether or not to initiate enforcement action, Heckler v. Chancy, 470 U.S. 821 (1985)), §701(a)(2). Plaintiffs seeking judicial review also must have exhausted administrative remedies by raising objections in the rulemaking proceeding before the agency. The agency's action also must be deemed sufficiently "ripe for review" by courts, who seek to avoid premature adjudication of issues that have not crystallized to the point at which they are having more than a hypothetical impact on prospective litigants.

Virtually all of the federal environmental statutes also authorize *citizen suits* (FIFRA is the principal exception) against governmental agencies who fail to perform their statutory duties and against those who violate the statutes. It is important not to confuse the citizen suit provisions of the environmental statutes with the statutes' judicial review provisions. The citizen suit provisions generally authorize two types of lawsuits: action-forcing lawsuits against the agency for failure to perform a nondiscretionary duty and citizen suits against anyone who violates the environmental laws. The *judicial review* provisions of the environmental statutes authorize courts to review agency actions, such as the issuance or repeal of environmental regulations. We now turn to a brief history of judicial review and its impact on the regulatory process.

When the Supreme Court in Citizens to Preserve Overton Park v. Volpe, 401 U.S. 402 (1971), reversed a decision to authorize the expenditure of federal funds to build an interstate highway through a park, the decision was a surprise for two reasons: it indicated that courts were willing to review a wider range of agency actions and to scrutinize more carefully the rationale behind agency decisions. The plaintiffs in *Overton Park* alleged that the Secretary of Transportation had violated a provision of the Department of Transportation Act of 1966 that prohibited him from approving any project that required public parkland unless he determined that no feasible and prudent alternative to the use of the land existed and that all possible planning had been done to minimize harm to the park from such use. Relying on the judicial review provisions of section 706 of the APA, the plaintiffs argued that the Secretary's decision was an abuse of discretion and contrary to law.

In response to the lawsuit, the government argued that the Secretary's decision was not reviewable by a court because it was "committed to agency discretion by law" and thus exempt from review pursuant to the judicial review provisions of the APA, 5 U.S.C. §701(a). Because the Secretary had not made any specific findings at the time he made the decision, the Agency submitted affidavits to the court to support the Secretary's claim that he had indeed balanced the cost of other routes and safety considerations against the environmental impacts of the project. Although the court held that the Secretary did not need to make formal findings, it remanded the case to the district court for review based on reconstruction of the record actually before the Secretary at the time the decision was made. The court indicated that the Secretary had an obligation under the statute to do more than simply articulate a universally applicable rationale (i.e., that considerations of costs, the directness of the route, and community disruption favor use of the parkland) and that courts had an obligation to ensure that agency officials exercise their discretion properly.

With the enactment of the National Environmental Policy Act, which declared the importance of environmental values in national policy and required agencies to prepare environmental impact statements, environmentalists gained a powerful tool for challenging agency decisions. Courts began a period of greater scrutiny of agency actions characterized as the "hard look" doctrine, as Judge Leventhal referred to it in Greater Boston Television Corp. v. FCC, 444 F.2d 841, 851 (D.C. Cir. 1970), cert. denied, 403 U.S. 923 (1971).

This burst of judicial activism featured greater scrutiny of agency actions not only at the behest of environmentalists, but also in response to challenges by regulated industries. The courts struck down several EPA regulations in response to lawsuits by affected industries, even after the Agency began to develop detailed administrative records to support its rules. See, e.g., Kennecott Copper Corp. v. EPA, 462 F.2d 846 (D.C. Cir. 1972) (national secondary air quality standard for sulfur dioxide struck down as inadequately justified by agency); International Harvester Co. v. Ruckelshaus, 478 F.2d 615 (D.C. Cir. 1973) (denial of waiver for new motor vehicle emissions reduction standards invalidated); Portland Cement Association v. Ruckelshaus, 486 F.2d 375 (D.C. Cir. 1973) (new source performance standard for Portland cement plants struck down).

The movement by reviewing courts to require agencies to go beyond the minimum procedures required by the APA was brought to an abrupt halt by the Supreme Court in Vermont Yankee Nuclear Power Corp. v. Natural Resources Defense Council, 435 U.S. 519 (1978). *Vermont Yankee* involved a challenge to a decision by the Atomic Energy Commission to grant a license to a nuclear power plant. Although the license had been granted only after extensive licensing hearings, the hearings did not consider the environmental effects of the uranium fuel cycle, deferring that issue for a subsequent informal rulemaking proceeding. NRDC argued that NEPA required the AEC to employ additional factfinding procedures when considering the environmental impact of nuclear waste disposal, beyond those explicitly required by the APA. The D.C. Circuit agreed and held that such issues must be considered in individual licensing proceedings employing more formalized factfinding procedures. Natural Resources Defense Council v. Nuclear Regulatory Commission, 547 F.2d 633, 653 (D.C. Cir. 1976). The Supreme Court then reversed.

In an opinion by Justice Rehnquist, the Court held that the APA "established the maximum procedural requirements which Congress was willing to have the courts impose upon agencies in conducting rulemaking procedures." While noting that "[a]gencies are free to grant additional procedural rights in the exercise of their discretion," the Court held that "reviewing courts are generally not free to impose them if the agencies have not chosen to grant them." Vermont Yankee Nuclear Power Corp. v. Natural Resources Defense Council, 435 U.S. 519 (1978). Sternly admonishing the lower courts that "our cases could hardly be more explicit in this regard," Justice Rehnquist warned:

> [I]f courts continually review agency proceedings to determine whether the agency employed procedures which were, in the court's opinion, perfectly tailored to reach what the court perceives to be the "best" or "correct" result, judicial review would be totally unpredictable. And the agencies, operating under this vague injunction to employ the "best" procedures and facing the threat of reversal if they did not, would undoubtedly adopt full adjudicatory procedures in every instance. Not only would this totally disrupt the statutory scheme, through which Congress enacted "a formula upon which opposing social and political forces have come to rest," Wong Yang Sung v. McGrath, 339 U.S., at 40, but all the inherent advantages of informal rulemaking would be totally lost. [435 U.S. at 546-547.]

*Vermont Yankee* repudiated attempts by reviewing courts to require agencies to provide more complete rulemaking records encompassing a wider range of issues that might be deemed relevant on judicial review. The decision had important

implications for judicial review of agency compliance with the procedural obligations established by the National Environmental Policy Act (NEPA), an issue we will
examine when we study NEPA in Chapter 8. But it had even broader implications,
sending the lower courts a message that they should be more deferential to agency
rulemaking procedures.

While *Vermont Yankee* mandated greater judicial deference to agency procedural decisions, the Court did not abandon judicial review as a check on the substance of agency decisions. Even though the APA specifies a relatively deferential
standard of review (section 706 provides that courts are to overturn agency action
only if it is "arbitrary, capricious, an abuse of discretion, or otherwise not in accordance with law"), the Court has not made the standard a toothless one. In Motor
Vehicle Manufacturers Association v. State Farm Mutual Auto Insurance Co., 463
U.S. 29 (1983), the Supreme Court affirmed a D.C. Circuit decision striking down
the Reagan administration's rescission of a regulation requiring automobile manufacturers to install passive restraint systems in cars. The Court held that the agency
had failed to offer an adequate explanation of its decision in light of the extensive
evidence in the record that passive restraint systems could prevent substantial numbers of deaths in automobile accidents.

Shortly after the *State Farm* decision, the Supreme Court substantially
expanded judicial deference to agency decisions in the case that follows. The case
involved a challenge to another agency effort to change policy abruptly.

## Chevron U.S.A. v. Natural Resources Defense Council

467 U.S. 837 (1984)

JUSTICE STEVENS delivered the opinion of the Court.
In the Clean Air Act Amendments of 1977, Pub. L. 95-95, 91 Stat. 685, Congress enacted certain requirements applicable to States that had not achieved the
national air quality standards established by the Environmental Protection Agency
(EPA) pursuant to earlier legislation. The amended Clean Air Act required these
"nonattainment" States to establish a permit program regulating "new or modified
major stationary sources" of air pollution. Generally, a permit may not be issued
for a new or modified major stationary source unless several stringent conditions
are met. The EPA regulation promulgated to implement this permit requirement
allows a State to adopt a plantwide definition of the term "stationary source." Under
this definition, an existing plant that contains several pollution-emitting devices
may install or modify one piece of equipment without meeting the permit conditions if the alternative will not increase the total emissions from the plant. The
question presented by these cases is whether EPA's decision to allow States to treat
all of the pollution-emitting devices within the same industrial grouping as though
they were encased within a single "bubble" is based on a reasonable construction of
the statutory term "stationary source."

The EPA regulations containing the plantwide definition of the term stationary source were promulgated on October 14, 1981. 46 Fed. Reg. 50766. Respondents filed a timely petition for review in the United States Court of Appeals for
the District of Columbia Circuit pursuant to 42 U.S.C. §7607(b)(1). The Court of

Appeals set aside the regulations. National Resources Defense Council, Inc. v. Gorsuch, 222 U.S. App. D.C. 268, 685 F.2d 718 (1982).

The court observed that the relevant part of the amended Clean Air Act "does not explicitly define what Congress envisioned as a 'stationary source,' to which the permit program . . . should apply," and further stated that the precise issue was not "squarely addressed in the legislative history." Id., at 273, 685 F.2d, at 723. In light of its conclusion that the legislative history bearing on the question was "at best contradictory," it reasoned that "the purposes of the nonattainment program should guide our decision here." Id., at 276, n.39, 685 F.2d, at 726, n.39. Based on two of its precedents concerning the applicability of the bubble concept to certain Clean Air Act programs, the court stated that the bubble concept was "mandatory" in programs designed merely to maintain existing air quality, but held that it was "inappropriate" in programs enacted to improve air quality. Id., at 276, 685 F.2d, at 726. Since the purpose of the permit program—its "raison d'être," in the court's view—was to improve air quality, the court held that the bubble concept was inapplicable in these cases under its prior precedents. Ibid. It therefore set aside the regulations embodying the bubble concept as contrary to law. We granted certiorari to review that judgment, 461 U.S. 956 (1983), and we now reverse.

The basic legal error of the Court of Appeals was to adopt a static judicial definition of the term "stationary source" when it had decided that Congress itself had not commanded that definition. Respondents do not defend the legal reasoning of the Court of Appeals. Nevertheless, since this Court reviews judgments, not opinions, we must determine whether the Court of Appeals' legal error resulted in an erroneous judgment on the validity of the regulations.

When a court reviews an agency's construction of the statute which it administers, it is confronted with two questions. First, always, is the question whether Congress has directly spoken to the precise question at issue. If the intent of Congress is clear, that is the end of the matter; for the court as well as the agency must give effect to the unambiguously expressed intent of Congress. If, however, the court determines Congress has not directly addressed the precise question at issue, the court does not simply impose its own construction on the statute, as would be necessary in the absence of an administrative interpretation. Rather, if the statute is silent or ambiguous with respect to the specific issue, the question for the court is whether the agency's answer is based on a permissible construction of the statute.

"The power of an administrative agency to administer a congressionally created . . . program necessarily requires the formulation of policy and the making of rules to fill any gap left, implicitly or explicitly, by Congress." Morton v. Ruiz, 415 U.S. 199 (1974). If Congress has explicitly left a gap for the agency to fill, there is an express delegation of authority to the agency to elucidate a specific provision of the statute by regulation. Such legislative regulations are given controlling weight unless they are arbitrary, capricious, or manifestly contrary to the statute. Sometimes the legislative delegation to an agency on a particular question is implicit rather than explicit. In such a case, a court may not substitute its own construction of a statutory provision for a reasonable interpretation made by the administrator of an agency. . . .

In light of these well-settled principles it is clear that the Court of Appeals misconceived the nature of its role in reviewing the regulations at issue. Once it determined, after its own examination of the legislation, that Congress did not actually have an intent regarding the applicability of the bubble concept to the permit program, the question before it was not whether in its view the concept is "inappropriate" in the general context of a program designed to improve air quality, but whether the Administrator's view that it is appropriate in the context of this particular program is a reasonable one. Based on the examination of the legislation and its history, which follows, we agree with the Court of Appeals that Congress did not have a specific intention on the applicability of the bubble concept in these cases, and conclude that the EPA's use of that concept here is a reasonable policy choice for the agency to make. . . .

In these cases, the Administrator's interpretation represents a reasonable accommodation of manifestly competing interests and is entitled to deference: the regulatory scheme is technical and complex, the agency considered the matter in a detailed and reasoned fashion, and the decision involves reconciling conflicting policies. Congress intended to accommodate both interests, but did not do so itself on the level of specificity presented by these cases. Perhaps that body consciously desired the Administrator to strike the balance at this level, thinking that those with great expertise and charged with responsibility for administering the provision would be in a better position to do so; perhaps it simply did not consider the question at this level; and perhaps Congress was unable to forge a coalition on either side of the question, and those on each side decided to take their chances with the scheme devised by the agency. For judicial purposes, it matters not which of these things occurred.

Judges are not experts in the field, and are not part of either political branch of the Government. Courts must, in some cases, reconcile competing political interests, but not on the basis of the judges' personal policy preferences. In contrast, an agency to which Congress has delegated policymaking responsibilities may, within the limits of that delegation, properly rely upon the incumbent administration's views of wise policy to inform its judgments. While agencies are not directly accountable to the people, the Chief Executive is, and it is entirely appropriate for this political branch of the Government to make such policy choices — resolving the competing interests which Congress itself either inadvertently did not resolve, or intentionally left to be resolved by the agency charged with the administration of the statute in light of everyday realities. . . .

We hold that the EPA's definition of the term "source" is a permissible construction of the statute which seeks to accommodate progress in reducing air pollution with economic growth. "The Regulations which the Administrator has adopted provide what the agency could allowably view as . . . [an] effective reconciliation of these twofold ends. . . ." United States v. Shinier, 367 U.S., at 383.

The judgment of the Court of Appeals is reversed.

## NOTES AND QUESTIONS

1. The judicial review provisions of the Administrative Procedure Act provide that reviewing courts are to "decide all relevant questions of law, interpret constitutional and statutory provisions, and determine the meaning or applicability of the terms of an agency action." 5 U.S.C. §706. Is this consistent with the notion that courts should defer to agency interpretations of statutes?

2. Judicial deference to the decisions of administrative agencies stems in part from notions of agency expertise. To what extent are such notions relevant when the agency is not making complicated technical or scientific judgments, but rather is engaging in statutory interpretation? Who should be more "expert" at divining the intent of Congress—courts or agencies?

3. *Chevron* was decided by a unanimous Supreme Court, though only six Justices participated in the decision. The papers of the late Justice Thurgood Marshall provided no evidence that the six Justices appreciated that *Chevron* would work any significant change in administrative law. Within a week of its initial circulation, Justice Stevens's first draft opinion was joined by the other five Justices without any substantive comment or suggested changes. Percival, Environmental Law in the Supreme Court: Highlights from the Marshall Papers, 23 Envtl. L. Rep. 10606, 10613 (1993). Release of the papers of the late Justice Harry A. Blackmun shed further light on this mystery because they contained notes taken by Justice Blackmun during conference. These notes indicate that the Justices initially were badly split when they voted in conference. Justice Stevens, who ultimately authored the unanimous opinion for the six Justices who participated in the final vote is recorded as stating, "When I am so confused, I go with the Agency." His statement appeared to reflect frustration expressed by several Justices at the difficulty of understanding the workings of complex, new regulatory programs like the Clean Air Act, which may have influenced their ultimate directive to afford agencies greater deference. See Robert V. Percival, Environmental Law in the Supreme Court: Highlights from the Blackmun Papers, 35 Envtl. L. Rep. 10637, 10644 (2005).

4. *Chevron*'s two-step framework leaves reviewing courts considerable wiggle room because they still must determine whether a statute is ambiguous (Step One)—and statutory ambiguity often is in the eye of the beholder, as decisions subsequent to *Chevron* quickly made clear. In Chemical Manufacturers Association v. Natural Resources Defense Council, 470 U.S. 116 (1985), the Supreme Court split 5-4 on the question whether or not the word "modified" in the Clean Water Act was ambiguous. In Board of Governors v. Dimension Financial Corp., 474 U.S. 361 (1986), the Supreme Court unanimously rejected the Federal Reserve Board's interpretation of the term "bank" by concluding that the term was clear and unambiguous.

5. How, if at all, do you think *Chevron* has affected judicial review of decisions by administrative agencies? *Chevron* has been the most frequently cited decision in administrative law cases. By its sixth birthday, *Chevron* had been cited more than 1,000 times, Sunstein, Law and Administration After *Chevron*, 90 Colum. L. Rev. 2071, 2074-2075 (1990), and it is now the most cited administrative law decision in history. Yet *Chevron* does not seem to have insulated agency interpretations of statutes from effective judicial review. In the first four years after *Chevron* was decided, the Supreme Court rejected an administrative agency's interpretation of a statutory provision in six cases. See, e.g., Immigration and Naturalization Service v. Cardoza-Fonseca, 408 U.S. 421 (1988) (rejecting INS's interpretation of the term "well founded fear" of persecution for purposes of determining when asylum may be granted to refugees).

6. In a study of the Supreme Court's use of *Chevron*, Thomas Merrill finds it "clear that *Chevron* is often ignored by the Supreme Court." Merrill, Judicial Deference to Executive Precedent, 101 Yale L.J. 969, 970 (1992). Statistics compiled

by Professor Merrill indicate that *Chevron*'s two-step framework has been used in only about half of the cases in which the Court has recognized that a question of deference to an agency interpretation is presented. In contrast to the Supreme Court itself, the courts of appeals have treated *Chevron*'s two-step approach as controlling whenever the agency is entitled to heightened deference, as in cases of agency rulemaking. In a study of all the courts of appeals decisions in the 1990s involving EPA rulemaking, Schroeder and Glicksman found *Chevron* to be universally applied. The agency prevailed in 75 percent of those challenges. Interestingly, when the court concluded that the Congress had clearly spoken (*Chevron* Step One), the agency success rate was much lower: 41 percent. When the agency was able to get past Step One to Step Two, where the question is whether the agency's construction of the statute was reasonable, it prevailed in 93 percent of the cases. Schroeder & Glicksman, Chevron, State Farm and the EPA in the Courts of Appeals During the 1990s, 31 Envtl. L. Rep. 10371 (2001).

7. *Chevron*'s scope has been further diminished by the Supreme Court's decision in United States v. Mead Corp., 533 U.S. 218 (2001). In *Mead*, the Court held, over a lone, but vigorous dissent by Justice Scalia, that "administrative implementation of a particular statutory provision qualifies for *Chevron* deference when it appears that Congress delegated authority to the agency generally to make rules carrying the force of law, and that the agency interpretation claiming deference was promulgated in the exercise of that authority." 533 U.S. at 226-227. *Mead* moves judicial review of agency interpretations in the direction of Skidmore v. Swift & Co., 323 U.S. 134 (1944), which stated that the degree of deference owed an agency interpretation of a statute should depend on several factors, including the thoroughness of the agency's deliberations and the persuasiveness of its reasoning. *Mead* has clarified that the *Chevron* doctrine is grounded in congressional intent, rather than notions of separation of powers. To determine when *Chevron* deference is due, *Mead* makes the threshold questions whether Congress intended to give the agency authority to make rules with the force of law and whether the agency interpretation in question was issued in the exercise of such authority. As Professor Thomas Merrill observes, the post-*Mead* landscape of judicial review now encompasses three different degrees of deference to agency interpretations:

> *Chevron*—a rule-like doctrine that requires courts to accept reasonable agency interpretations of ambiguous statutes; *Skidmore*—a standard that requires courts to consider agency interpretations under multiple factors and defer to the interpretation if it is persuasive; and no deference—a rule that applies when independent judicial review is required, for example, where the agency action is alleged to violate the Constitution, or where statutes designed to constrain agency discretion like the Administrative Procedure Act (APA) are at issue. [Thomas W. Merrill, The *Mead* Doctrine: Rules and Standards, Meta-Rules and Meta-Standards, 54 Admin. L. Rev. 807, 812-813 (2002).]

Although Professor Merrill criticizes the Court for leaving unclear how to determine when Congress has given an agency the power to act with force of law, he concludes that *Mead* actually will strengthen *Chevron*, by diminishing the need to water it down in cases that fall within its now narrower scope.

8. Another deference doctrine, which proved decisive in the *Coeur Alaska* case discussed in Chapter 6, is called *Auer* deference. It provides for reviewing courts to defer to government agencies' interpretations of their own regulations. Auer v. Robbins, 519 U.S. 452 (1997). In June 2019, a 5-4 majority of the Court specifically refused to overrule it in *Kisor v. Wilkie*, 139 S.Ct. 2400 (2019), but it remains on shaky grounds, as does *Chevron*. Prior to joining the Supreme Court, Judge Neil Gorsuch criticized the *Chevron* doctrine as inconsistent with the duty of courts to declare what the law is. Gutierrez-Brizuela v. Lynch, 834 F.3d 1142, 1149 (10th Cir. 2016) (Gorsuch, J., concurring). Since joining the Court, Justice Gorsuch has been a fierce opponent of *Chevron* deference. In April 2020, Justice Thomas, in a dissent joined by Justice Gorsuch in *County of Maui v. Hawaii Wildlife Fund*, 140 S. Ct. 1462 (2020), opined that *Chevron* deference is unconstitutional because it "likely conflicts with the Vesting Clauses of the Constitution." While *Chevron* has not yet been overruled, it may well be overruled in the future because a majority of Justices on the Court have expressed their disagreement with it. For now, as a practical matter, *Chevron* deference seems to be a bit of a dead letter because advocates now rarely cite it when arguing before the Court. In the *Maui* case, the majority noted that "neither the Solicitor General nor any party has asked us to give [*Chevron* deference] to EPA's interpretation of the statute." It then went on to emphasize that it would not have given EPA *Chevron* deference even if the agency had asked for it because EPA's interpretation "is neither persuasive nor reasonable."

9. Judicial review played a major role in stymieing efforts by the Trump administration to roll back environmental regulations. In its zeal to deregulate, the administration frequently cut corners and violated the Administrative Procedure Act, leading to losses in court. A study by the Institute for Policy Integrity of the outcome of 189 policy decisions by the administration found that only 37 were successful while 152 failed, a success rate of less than 20 percent. Institute for Policy Integrity, Roundup: Trump-Era Agency Policy in the Courts, Feb. 2021, *https://policyintegrity.org/trump-court-roundup.*

# CHAPTER 3

# PREVENTING HARM IN THE FACE OF UNCERTAINTY

Where a statute is precautionary in nature, the evidence difficult to come by, uncertain, or conflicting because it is on the frontiers of scientific knowledge, the regulations designed to protect the public health, and the decision that of an expert administrator, we will not demand rigorous step-by-step proof of cause and effect. Such proof may be impossible to maintain if the precautionary purpose of the statute is to be served.

—*Ethyl Corp. v. EPA, 541 F.2d 1 (D.C. Cir. 1976)*

Undoubtedly, reformers are correct to note that no society should flatly ignore foregone benefits and other negative effects of precautionary regulation. But this is a trivial observation, for no serious proponent of the precautionary principle disagrees with it. Despite frequent caricaturing of the precautionary principle as a crudely absolutist doctrine, its proponents actually regard the principle as merely one aspect of a much more elaborate regulatory process in which the precautionary principle is applied with a view toward proportionality of response and adaptability over time. . . . [T]he precautionary approach focuses on particular categories of harm and separates them out for special treatment. . . . [Its] asymmetry represents a procedurally rational attempt to catalyze empirical investigation, redress political imbalance, and respond with prudence to threats of a potentially catastrophic or irreversible nature.

—*Douglas A. Kysar, Regulating from Nowhere (2009)*

This chapter covers two of the central questions of environmental law: (1) how to determine what risks require regulatory intervention, and (2) how stringently to regulate them. The first question implicates techniques for characterizing harm-causing potential that have been given the general label "risk assessment." The second focuses on the issue of acceptability and attempts to determine how much of that harm-causing potential ought to be eliminated. We refer to the latter as the question of "how safe is safe?," which involves questions of "risk management" and is the subject of Section B. Humans voluntarily expose themselves to some risks by engaging in risky activities, such as mountain climbing. But we usually have little choice over the air that we must breathe to stay alive. Some modern regulatory approaches seek to minimize involuntary exposure to environmental risk by better informing the public about risks. Section C of this chapter focuses on "regulation by revelation," information disclosure approaches to improve the public's ability to choose to avoid particular risks.

## A. UNCERTAINTY, RISK ASSESSMENT, AND THE PRECAUTIONARY PRINCIPLE

Toxic substances are characterized by the potential for causing serious harm or death at relatively low exposure levels, levels at which further preventative action can sometimes be very costly. The harm that low exposures will cause is also very hard to predict and impossible to predict with certainty. Thus, the regulation of toxic substances vividly exposes some of the hardest problems in risk assessment and risk management when the harm-causing potentials of human activities are shrouded in uncertainty, difficult to assess, and expensive to reduce. Even when public policy has endorsed precautionary regulation in the face of uncertainty, it has been largely reactionary, acting to prevent harm only after substantial damage has been done.

Courts asked to enjoin some activity as a nuisance due to its harm-causing potential must engage in a form of risk assessment, aimed at determining whether the defendant's activity poses risks or causes harm that warrants judicial intervention. If intervention of some kind seems warranted, the court must then address risk management issues when it sets the terms of an injunction. For illustrations, see the nuisance cases studied in Chapter 2.

### 1. Identifying What Risks Should Be Regulated

Before an agency or court is authorized to regulate any substance or product, typically some threshold finding must be made, and typically that finding relates to the harmful potential of the substance or product to be regulated. For instance, the agency implementing a statute might be instructed to issue a preventative regulation only when it has definitive proof that a substance or product will in fact cause harm if exposure continues. Section 108 of the Clean Air Act, for example, originally ordered EPA to issue ambient air quality standards for certain pollutants "which, in [the] judgment [of the administrator], [have] an adverse effect on public health or welfare." This language was interpreted to require proof of actual harm before agency action could be taken. Ethyl Corp. v. EPA, 541 F.2d 1, 14 (D.C. Cir. 1976) (en banc). One implication of such a threshold requirement when dealing with toxic substances is that the regulatory process may end up waiting until it is possible to "count the dead bodies," because definitive evidence of harm to humans typically comes only when actual deaths or serious illnesses can be linked to past exposures.

A striking characteristic of modern statutes regulating toxic substances is precisely their unwillingness to wait for such definitive proof. Instead, they instruct agencies and courts to act in advance of such proof; in other words, when either the harmful nature of a substance or the magnitude of the harm that it will cause, or both, are still doubtful. The crucial question then is: Short of certainty of serious harm, what must be known before it is appropriate to regulate?

Historical experience—as opposed to regulatory theory—indicates that even though the manifest language of modern statutes has authorized regulation prior to definitive proof of harm, the regulatory system still frequently continues to wait for such proof before implementing strict regulation because of the enormous pressures to avoid imposing regulatory burdens in doubtful cases. This is well illustrated by a class of per- and polyfluoroalkyl substances, known as PFAS, one of which — perfluorooctanoic acid (PFOA) — was linked to severe health problems in humans who ingested it in heavily contaminated drinking water. Despite the discovery of widespread contamination of water supply systems with PFAS, they have been largely unregulated at the federal level.

Most of the chemicals that have been stringently regulated became the focus of regulatory attention only after highly publicized incidents in which high-level, acute exposures caused visible and substantial harm. For a review of this history, see Robert V. Percival, Who's Afraid of the Precautionary Principle?, 23 Pace Envtl. L. Rev. 21, 36-75 (2006). For example, early regulatory action to restrict mercury discharges was undertaken only after the discovery that children in Minimata, Japan, had suffered severe birth defects from mercury that had accumulated in fish from waste discharges between 1953 and 1960. Similarly, EPA signaled its intent to regulate two PFAS chemicals — PFOA and perfluorooctane sulfonic acid (PFOS) — only in early 2020, long after PFAS contamination entered mainstream policy debates through high-profile publicity, including the 2019 feature film *Dark Waters*.

In other cases, opportunities to prevent significant, chronic health damage were missed even though there had been highly publicized incidents involving acute exposures. In October 1924, the use of lead additives in gasoline became a source of considerable public controversy after several workers in a tetraethyl lead processing plant in Elizabeth, New Jersey, died from acute lead poisoning. Some cities banned the use of tetraethyl lead, which was taken off the market while a panel convened by the Surgeon General studied the health effects of lead additives. After a study was quickly prepared showing that gas station attendants where leaded gasoline was sold did not have higher levels of lead in their blood, tetraethyl lead returned to the market. The Surgeon General recognized that the study was inadequate for assessing the long-term effect of lead additives on human health and recommended follow-up studies that never were undertaken. It was not until several decades later that regulatory attention focused on the effects of lead emissions on children's health. The early story of lead (non)regulation is told in Gerald Markowitz & David Rosner, Deceit and Denial 12-138 (2002).

Discovery of the deadly threat that asbestos poses to human health was made due to the large number of workers who died of respiratory diseases in occupations that exposed them to asbestos. Yet for decades the asbestos industry covered up the dangers of its products, as discussed in detail in Paul Brodeur's book *Outrageous Misconduct* (1985). Because asbestos causes certain "signature injuries" — asbestosis and mesothelioma — that are uniquely related to asbestos exposures, it ultimately became possible for workers with such diseases to prove who caused them, even though they typically appear only decades after initial exposure. Dr. Irving J. Selikoff of Mt. Sinai School of Medicine, who became the world's leading expert on asbestos diseases, accurately predicted that hundreds of thousands of Americans occupationally exposed to asbestos eventually would die of asbestos-related cancer. After the industry coverup was revealed, large punitive damages were awarded to workers harmed by asbestos exposure, leading to the 1982 bankruptcy of the Johns Manville Corporation, the world's largest asbestos company.

In the 1970s the discovery that a mining company was dumping tailings containing asbestiform fibers nearly identical to those known to cause cancer when inhaled generated one of the early, important cases addressing the issue of how much must be known before regulatory action is justified. In that case, Reserve Mining was discharging 67,000 tons of taconite tailings daily into the otherwise pristine water of Lake Superior, the source of drinking water for the city of Duluth, Minnesota. The federal government, joined by Minnesota, Wisconsin, Michigan, and several environmental groups, brought suit under the Clean Water Act, the Rivers and Harbors Act, and the federal common law of nuisance against Reserve for discharging the tailings. The district court entered an order, later stayed by an Eighth Circuit panel, that required the company immediately to cease discharging tailings into the water and air around its iron ore processing plant. Reserve Mining Co. v. United States, 498 F.2d 1073 (8th Cir. 1974). The district court found that both air and water discharges were "substantially endanger[ing]" the surrounding population, despite the inconclusiveness of evidence concerning their effects on human health. Sitting en banc, the Eighth Circuit addressed Reserve's claim that its discharges posed no legally cognizable risk to public health because there was no evidence that ingestion of the fibers in drinking water would increase the incidence of diseases.

## Reserve Mining Company v. EPA

514 F.2d 492 (8th Cir. 1975) (en banc)

BRIGHT, Circuit Judge:
[On appeal from the district court's injunction of further discharges by Reserve Mining into Lake Superior, the Eighth Circuit addressed] first, whether the ingestion of fibers, as compared with their inhalation, poses any danger whatsoever; and second, should ingestion pose a danger, whether the exposure resulting from Reserve's discharge may be said to present a legally cognizable risk to health.

### 1.   Ingestion of Fibers as a Danger to Health

All epidemiological studies which associate asbestos fibers with harm to health are based upon inhalation of these fibers by humans. Thus, although medical opinion agrees that fibers entering the respiratory tract can interact with body tissues and produce disease, it is unknown whether the same can be said of fibers entering the digestive tract. If asbestos fibers do not interact with digestive tissue, they are presumably eliminated as waste without harmful effect upon the body.

The evidence bearing upon possible harm from ingestion of fibers falls into three areas: first, the court-sponsored tissue study, designed to measure whether asbestos fibers are present in the tissues of long-time Duluth residents; second, animal experiments designed to measure whether, as a biological phenomenon, fibers can penetrate the gastrointestinal mucosa and thus interact with body tissues; third, the increased incidence of gastrointestinal cancer among workers occupationally exposed to asbestos, and the hypothesis that this increase may be due to the ingestion of fibers initially inhaled. [All three yielded inconclusive results.]

## CONCLUSION

The preceding extensive discussion of the evidence demonstrates that the medical and scientific conclusions here in dispute clearly lie "on the frontiers of scientific knowledge." The trial court, not having any proof of actual harm, was faced with a consideration of 1) the probabilities of any harm and 2) the consequences, if any, should the harm actually occur. . . .

In assessing probabilities in this case, it cannot be said that the probability of harm is more likely than not. Moreover, the level of probability does not readily convert into a prediction of consequences. On this record it cannot be forecast that the rates of cancer will increase from drinking Lake Superior water or breathing Silver Bay air. The best that can be said is that the existence of this asbestos contaminant in air and water gives rise to a reasonable medical concern for the public health. The public's exposure to asbestos fibers in air and water creates some health risk. Such a contaminant should be removed.

As we demonstrate in the following sections of the opinion, the existence of this risk to the public justifies an injunction decree requiring abatement of the health hazard on reasonable terms as a precautionary and preventive measure to protect the public health. . . .

The district court found that Reserve's discharge into Lake Superior violated §§1160(c)(5) and (g)(1) of the Federal Water Pollution Control Act. (FWPCA). These two provisions authorize an action by the United States to secure abatement of water discharges in interstate waters where the discharges violate state water quality standards and "endanger . . . the health or welfare of persons." §1160(g) (1). . . .

In the context of this environmental legislation, we believe that Congress used the term "endangering" in a precautionary or preventive sense, and, therefore, evidence of potential harm as well as actual harm comes within the purview of that term. We are fortified in this view by the flexible provisions for injunctive relief which permit a court "to enter such judgment and orders enforcing such judgment as the public interest and the equities of the case may require." 33 U.S.C. §1160(c) (5). . . . The record shows that Reserve is discharging a substance into Lake Superior waters which under an acceptable but unproved medical theory may be considered as carcinogenic.

Concededly, the trial court considered many appropriate factors in arriving at a remedy, such as a) the nature of the anticipated harm, b) the burden on Reserve and its employees from the issuance of the injunction, c) the financial ability of Reserve to convert to other methods of waste disposal, and d) a margin of safety for the public.

An additional crucial element necessary for a proper assessment of the health hazard rests upon a proper analysis of the probabilities of harm.

With respect to the water, these probabilities must be deemed low for they do not rest on a history of past health harm attributable to ingestion but on a medical theory implicating the ingestion of asbestos fibers as a causative factor in increasing the rates of gastrointestinal cancer among asbestos workers. With respect to air, the assessment of the risk of harm rests on a higher degree of proof, a correlation between inhalation of asbestos dust and subsequent illness. But here, too, the hazard cannot be measured in terms of predictability, but the assessment must be made without direct proof. But, the hazard in both the air and water can be measured in only the most general terms as a concern for the public health resting upon a reasonable medical theory. Serious consequences could result if the hypothesis on which it is based should ultimately prove true.

A court is not powerless to act in these circumstances. But an immediate injunction cannot be justified in striking a balance between unpredictable health effects and the clearly predictable social and economic consequences that would follow the plant closing.

In addition to the health risk posed by Reserve's discharges, the district court premised its immediate termination of the discharges upon Reserve's persistent refusal to implement a reasonable alternative plan for on-land disposal of tailings. . . . During these appeal proceedings, Reserve has indicated its willingness to deposit its tailings on land and to properly filter its air emissions. At oral argument, Reserve advised us of a willingness to spend 243 million dollars in plant alterations and construction to halt its pollution of air and water. Reserve's offer to continue operations and proceed to construction of land disposal facilities for its tailings, if permitted to do so by the State of Minnesota, when viewed in conjunction with the uncertain quality of the health risk created by Reserve's discharges, weighs heavily against a ruling which closes Reserve's plant immediately.

Indeed, the intervening union argues, with some persuasiveness, that ill health effects resulting from the prolonged unemployment of the head of the family on a closing of the Reserve facility may be more certain than the harm from drinking Lake Superior water or breathing Silver Bay air.

Furthermore, Congress has generally geared its national environmental policy to allowing polluting industries a reasonable period of time to make adjustments in their efforts to conform to federal standards. . . .

We believe that on this record the district court abused its discretion by immediately closing this major industrial plant. In this case, the risk of harm to the public is potential, not imminent or certain, and Reserve says it earnestly seeks a practical way to abate the pollution. A remedy should be fashioned which will serve the ultimate public weal by insuring clean air, clean water, and continued jobs in an industry vital to the nation's welfare. . . .

Reserve must be given a reasonable opportunity and a reasonable time to construct facilities to accomplish an abatement of its pollution of air and water and the health risk created thereby. In this way, hardship to employees and great economic loss incident to an immediate plant closing maybe avoided. See *Georgia v. Tennessee Copper Co.* Reserve shall be given a reasonable time to stop discharging its wastes into Lake Superior. A reasonable time includes the time necessary for Minnesota to act on Reserve's present application to dispose of its tailings at Milepost 7 . . . or to come to agreement on some other site acceptable to both Reserve and the state. Assuming agreement and designation of an appropriate land disposal site, Reserve is entitled to a reasonable turn-around time to construct the necessary facilities and accomplish a changeover in the means of disposing of its taconite wastes.

## NOTES AND QUESTIONS

1.  In announcing its initial stay, the three-judge panel had stated:

> The discharges may or may not result in detrimental health effects, but, for the present, that is simply unknown. The relevant legal question is thus what manner of judicial cognizance may be taken of the unknown.
>
> We do not think that a bare risk of the unknown can amount to proof in this case. Plaintiffs have failed to prove that a demonstrable health hazard exists. This failure, we hasten to add, is not reflective of any weakness which it is within their power to cure, but rather, given the current state of medical and scientific knowledge, plaintiffs' case is based only on medical hypothesis and is simply beyond proof. [498 F.2d at 1083-1084.]

Did the en banc opinion reverse course on this point?

2.  The en banc court concluded that the negative results of the effort to find asbestiform fibers in Duluth residents could not be "deemed conclusive in exonerating the ingestion of fibers in Lake Superior as a hazard," but that it had to be "weigh[ed] heavily in indicating that no emergency or imminent hazard to health exists." Do you agree with the latter conclusion? If fibers were there that the study simply failed to identify because of its small scope, how does the failure to find them suggest the absence of an imminent hazard?

3.  Federal and state environmental officials responded to this decision with alarm. A bill was introduced in Congress to shift the burden of proof to polluters to prove the safety of their discharges once it was shown that they presented "a reasonable risk of being a threat to public health." Supporting this proposed legislation, then-chairman of the Council on Environmental Quality Russell W. Peterson explained the problem in the following terms:

> Because of the latent health effects of carcinogens it will be more than 10 years before the magnitude of the health risk to the people of Duluth and Silver Bay will be fully realized, and unfortunately it will be based upon the fate of over 200,000 people. Even a few more days of additional exposure pose an unnecessary and unacceptable risk to the residents of the area. [Peterson, letter to Hon. Wallace H. Johnson, reprinted in Burdens of Proof in Environmental Litigation, Hearing before the Subcomm. on Environment of the Senate Commerce Comm., 93d Cong., 2d Sess. 8 (1974).]

4.  The full story of the battle and litigation over Reserve Mining's taconite dumping has proven so compelling that it has been the subject of a number of books and articles exploring the case's background, the colorful characters involved, and its implications. See, e.g., John Applegate, The Story of Reserve Mining: Managing Scientific Uncertainty in Environmental Regulation in Environmental Law Stories 44 (Houck & Lazarus eds., 2005). In 2003, Minnesota Public Radio presented a retrospective on the *Reserve Mining* case that is available online at *http://news.minnesota.publicradio.org/features/2003/09/29_hemphills_reservehistory/*.

5.  *The Aftermath of* **Reserve.** Reserve converted to land-based disposal of its taconite tailings in 1980, at a cost of about $200 million. It closed temporarily in 1982, reopened in six months, and then closed again. Since then, it has gone through several owners and has operated sporadically, but never on anything approaching the

scale of its operation in the early 1970s, when it accounted for 10 percent of the nation's iron. By 1977, Duluth had installed a water filtration system that removed 99.9 percent of the asbestos fibers from its drinking water. See Daniel A. Farber, Eco-pragmatism 124 (1999). No epidemiological follow-up has been done on Duluth residents, so it is unknown whether their exposure to Reserve's tailings resulted in a heightened incidence of gastrointestinal cancer. However, "it is worth noting that the general view in the public health community today is that ingestion of asbestos fibers in drinking water is not a significant hazard to human health." Applegate, supra at 74.

### The *Ethyl Corp.* Decision

A second influential early decision was Ethyl Corp. v. EPA, 541 F.2d 1 (D.C. Cir. 1976) (en banc). *Ethyl Corp.* involved part of the Clean Air Act that at the time of the decision authorized EPA to regulate gasoline additives if their emissions "will endanger the public health or welfare" (§211(c)(1)(A)). The EPA reviewed a number of suggestive, but inconclusive, studies on the effects of lead emissions from gasoline exhausts on urban populations, especially children. The administrator concluded that lead in gasoline presented "a substantial risk of harm," and on that basis ordered reductions in the lead content of gasoline.

Like *Reserve, Ethyl Corp.* also highlights the uncertainty that dogs risk analyses. It was impossible for the EPA to demonstrate conclusively that lead was harmful at the levels being considered for regulation; nor could EPA determine precisely the probability that lead at such levels was harmful.

The lead additive manufacturers sought judicial review of EPA's decision. They claimed the statute required EPA to have "proof of actual harm" from auto emissions of lead before it could order limits on the amount of lead in gasoline. In December 1974, a three-judge panel of the D.C. Circuit, with one dissent, struck down the regulations. The panel held that there was insufficient evidence to prove that lead emissions "will endanger the public health or welfare," as required by the Clean Air Act. Emphasizing that EPA could not prove that specific cases of lead poisoning had been caused by gasoline emissions, despite the fact that leaded gasoline had been on the market for 50 years, the majority concluded that "the case against auto lead emissions is a speculative and inconclusive one at best."

EPA sought a rehearing en banc, and the full court agreed to hear the case. In March 1976, the court reversed the panel decision in a 5-4 decision. The majority's decision was written by the late Judge J. Skelly Wright, the dissenting judge in the panel decision. The en banc opinion is over 100 pages long. The following brief excerpt addresses the question of whether the "will endanger" standard of the statute required the EPA to demonstrate that actual harm would occur if the lead content of gasoline was not reduced.

## Ethyl Corp. v. EPA

541 F.2d 1 (D.C. Cir. 1976) (en banc)

WRIGHT, Circuit Judge:

. . . Case law and dictionary definition agree that endanger means something less than actual harm. When one is endangered, harm is *threatened*; no actual injury need ever occur. Thus, for example, a town may be "endangered" by a threatening plague or hurricane and yet emerge from the danger completely unscathed. A statute allowing for regulation in the face of danger is, necessarily, a precautionary statute. Regulatory action may be taken before the threatened harm occurs: indeed, the very existence of such precautionary legislation would seem to *demand* that regulatory action precede, and, optimally, prevent, the perceived threat. . . .

The Administrator read [section 211(c)(1)(A)] [as a precautionary statute], interpreting "will endanger" to mean "presents a significant risk of harm." We agree with the Administrator's interpretation. . . .

While the dictionary admittedly settles on "probable" as its measure of danger, we believe a more sophisticated case-by-case analysis is appropriate. Danger, the Administrator recognized, is not set by a fixed probability of harm, but rather is composed of reciprocal elements of risk and harm, or probability and severity. . . . That is to say, the public health may properly be found endangered both by a lesser risk of a greater harm and by a greater risk of a lesser harm. Danger depends upon the relation between the risk and harm presented by each case, and cannot legitimately be pegged to "probable" harm, regardless of whether that harm be great or small. . . .

Where a statute is precautionary in nature, the evidence difficult to come by, uncertain, or conflicting because it is on the frontiers of scientific knowledge, the regulations designed to protect the public health, and the decision that of an expert administrator, we will not demand rigorous step-by-step proof of cause and effect. Such proof may be impossible to obtain if the precautionary purpose of the statute is to be served. Of course, we are not suggesting that the Administrator has the power to act on hunches or wild guesses. . . . [H]is conclusions must be rationally justified. . . . However, we do hold that in such cases the Administrator may assess risks. He must take account of available facts, of course, but his inquiry does not end there. The Administrator may apply his expertise to draw conclusions from suspected, but not completely substantiated, relationships between facts, from trends among facts, from theoretical projections from imperfect data, from probative preliminary data not yet certifiable as "fact," and the like. We believe that a conclusion so drawn — a risk assessment — may, if rational, form the basis for health-related regulations under the "will endanger" language of Section 211.[58]

## NOTES AND QUESTIONS

1. *Reserve* and *Ethyl Corp.* differ in several respects. For one thing, in *Reserve* a federal court was asked in the first instance to regulate potentially harmful behavior, while in *Ethyl Corp.* an administrative agency had taken the initial step, which then came before the court for judicial review.

Second, *Reserve* involved a substance, taconite mill tailings, that had not yet been shown to cause adverse health effects, although it was judged physically indistinguishable at the fiber level from asbestos fibers, which had been. The medical

---

58. It bears emphasis that what is herein described as "assessment of risk" is neither unprecedented nor unique to this area of law. To the contrary, assessment of risk is a normal part of judicial and administrative fact-finding. Thus EPA is not attempting to expand its powers; rather, petitioners seek to constrict the usual flexibility of the factfinding process.

concern in *Reserve* was based on a medical opinion, found by the district court to be "reasonable," that such similarity was enough to raise a public health concern. *Ethyl Corp.*, in contrast, involved lead, an element known to be "toxic, causing anemia, severe intestinal cramps, paralysis of nerves, fatigue, and even death." 541 F.2d at 8. The question for the EPA administrator, however, was not whether lead was toxic; rather it was whether "the automotive emissions caused by leaded gasoline present 'a significant risk of harm' to the public health." 541 F.2d at 7. The answer to this question was much less clear than the question of whether lead was toxic, because inhalation of airborne lead was only one of several significant sources of lead exposure for urban children (diet, ingestion of lead-based paint, ingestion of lead in dirt and dust were others), because it was unclear how much inhaled lead contributed to the total body burden of lead, and because it was uncertain at what level of total body burden it became appropriate to conclude lead was having an adverse health effect.

2.  In *Ethyl*, EPA had based its decision to require reductions in lead additives on three conclusions: (1) based on a preliminary determination that a level of 40 μg/dl of lead in blood is indicative of a danger to health, a significant part of the population was currently experiencing a dangerous condition because blood lead levels in excess of 40 μg/dl existed to a small but significant extent in the general adult population and to a very great extent among children; (2) airborne lead is directly absorbed in the body through respiration to a degree that constitutes a significant risk to public health; and (3) airborne lead falls to the ground, where it mixes with dust and poses a significant risk to the health of urban children. The court observed that while no specific blood lead level could be identified as the threshold for danger, the 40 μg/dl level was a conservative standard, and that studies of the blood lead levels of workers who work outside and whose only exposure to lead is through the ambient air justified EPA's second conclusion. The court found that theoretical, epidemiological, and clinical studies also supported the second conclusion, and it upheld the third conclusion as a hypothesis consistent with known information about the behavior of children and the presence of high lead concentrations in urban soil and dust.

3.  By comparison, consider the government's case in *Reserve*:

> The government's case . . . had several steps, virtually all of which were debatable. The first step was to show that Reserve's tailings were in fact present in Duluth's water supply. The second was to demonstrate that [the taconite tailing] were asbestos or its functional equivalent. . . . Third, while the carcinogenicity of inhaled asbestos was well known, the effects of the ingestion of asbestos were unknown. Lacking direct evidence, the government sought to infer a hazard from epidemiological studies of asbestos workers, animal studies on the movement of fibers within mammalian bodies, and a study of number of fibers found in residents of Duluth. . . . Epidemiological studies of gastrointestinal cancer among Duluth residents did not show a higher than expected rate, however, given the long latency of the disease, the worst effects could have been yet to come. Finally, the government had to show that there were enough asbestos fibers in Duluth's water to have toxic effects. [Applegate, supra at 60-61.]

If you were a government attorney at the time, would you have thought your chances were better in defending EPA's lead decision in *Ethyl Corp.* or in prosecuting the case in *Reserve?*

4.  Shortly after the *Ethyl Corp.* decision, Congress amended the Clean Air Act to change the standard for regulating fuel additives from "will endanger public health or welfare" to "may reasonably be anticipated to endanger the public health or welfare." Is the new statutory standard more consistent with what the EPA administrator actually found in support of the lead phasedown decision than the "will endanger" standard is?

## 2.  *Uncertainty and the Precautionary Principle*

Regulatory decisions invariably must be made in the face of considerable uncertainty. The idea that danger or risk is a composite of the probability of harm occurring and the magnitude of the harm that might occur has proved widely influential. The greater the potential harm, the more likely it is that public policy will take precautions to avoid it even in the face of considerable scientific uncertainty. This is consistent with what has come to be known as the Precautionary Principle, which is widely embraced throughout the world. As endorsed unanimously by the nations of the world in the 1992 Rio Declaration, the principle states: "Where there are threats of serious or irreversible damage, lack of full scientific certainty shall not be used as a reason for postponing cost-effective measures to prevent environmental degradation."

As explained earlier, a federal agency must make some threshold finding about a toxic substance before regulation is appropriate. Very often that finding will be related to the danger posed by the substance — sometimes that the substance poses a "significant risk" or an "unreasonable risk," sometimes that the substance "will endanger public health," as in *Ethyl Corp.*, sometimes that the substance "may reasonably be anticipated to endanger public health," as section 211 was subsequently amended to read.

Whatever the threshold level of risk happens to be, the idea that danger is composed of reciprocal elements of probability and severity has the implication that two exposures might both satisfy the threshold finding, even though the probability of one causing harm is much less than the probability of the other one causing harm, as long as the severity of the harm associated with the first is correspondingly greater than that associated with the second. In an article published shortly after *Ethyl Corp.*, Talbot Page employed the image of a seesaw to depict the underlying concept. See Page, A Generic View of Toxic Chemicals and Similar Risks, 7 Ecology L.Q. 207 (1978). We will adopt the same imagery here.

In Figure 3.1, the Threshold Finding can represent some level of risk, whether it be a "will endanger" standard, a "may reasonably be anticipated to endanger" standard, or some other formulation. What *Ethyl Corp.* acknowledges is that the concept of risk gives us at least two variables, magnitude of harm and probability of it occurring. In Figure 3.1, the other rectangular figure represents the probability that a substance under review will actually cause harm, and the distance the rectangle is from the fulcrum, "O," represents the magnitude of that harm, should

**Figure 3.1    Threshold Finding**

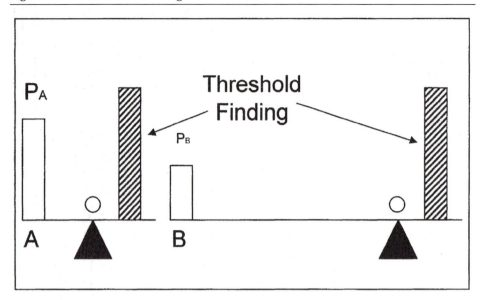

it occur. The regulator's initial task is to decide whether risk associated with the substance under review exceeds that threshold level of concern or, in seesaw terms, whether the left side pushes the right side down because the left side weighs more. Because there are two variables, the threshold finding might be satisfied either by a high probability of a lesser harm occurring (the seesaw on the left) or by a lower probability of a greater harm occurring (the seesaw on the right).

Straightforward as this idea may initially seem, it has powerful implications. One of the most dramatic arises with substances that exceed the relevant threshold even though they have fairly low probabilities of causing harm, because that harm would be catastrophic should it occur. Suppose, for example, that the harm that might occur because of some exposure was 10 times greater than a harm that we would want to prevent if we were certain the smaller harm would occur. Then the seesaw concept of risk or danger would urge us to regulate that exposure even though we thought it only 10 percent likely that the harm would actually occur, because the lower probability of harm occurring would be offset by the greater magnitude of that harm, should it occur.

Now suppose that we have a number of substances that may cause substantial harm, but as to which we are relatively uncertain whether they will. Will following the advice of the seesaw make sensible policy? In terms statisticians (and environmental lawyers) use, this policy tolerates a number of "false positives," chemicals regulated that turn out not to cause the anticipated harm, in order to reduce "false negatives," chemicals not regulated that turn out to cause harm. This is so because the policy regulates such substances when there is only a small chance that the exposure will prove harmful in the feared way. Using the numbers from our example, regulating when there is a 10 percent chance the harm will occur means that over a number of different regulatory decisions we will actually expect to be wrong 90 percent of the time. Over time, in other words, the ratio of "guilty" chemicals to "innocent" chemicals should approach 1 to 9.

This is just the opposite of the criminal law, where many believe that it is better that 10 guilty persons go free (false negatives) than to have a single innocent person convicted (a false positive). Talbot Page argues that these contrasting policies are justified by the different values at stake in each case:

> Limiting false positives is the guiding principle of criminal law. The objective is to limit the chance of a false conviction. . . . A principal reason for this is that liberty is a primary good, i.e., a good for the deprivation of which there is no adequate compensation. The asymmetrical results achieved by the criminal justice system are intentional and follow from the exceptional value placed on liberty. . . .
>
> The costs of false negatives and false positives are asymmetrical for environmental risk [that is, the feared harm greatly exceeds the benefits of the risky activity] as well, but the asymmetry is in reverse order. For environmental risk, the asymmetrically high cost arises from a false negative: in criminal law from a false positive. Similarly, just as a primary good, liberty, is an important concern in criminal law, so another primary good, health, is an important concern in environmental risk management, but again the roles are reversed.
>
> The analogy between criminal risk and environmental law requires that the roles of negatives and positives be reversed. [Page, A Generic View of Toxic Chemicals and Similar Risks, 7 Ecology L.Q. 207, 233-234 (1978).]

### The Aftermath of *Ethyl Corp.*

EPA's lead phasedown regulations ultimately generated the best evidence concerning the impact of lead emissions from gasoline on lead levels in children's blood. After long delays, the phasedown produced a significant reduction in levels of lead emissions from gasoline. Epidemiologists investigating changes in levels of lead in children's blood discovered an astonishingly high degree of correlation between these changes and changes in gasoline lead emissions, as indicated in Figure 3.2. They found that when gasoline lead use peaked sharply each summer, blood lead levels peaked sharply as well. They concluded that this could only be explained by changes in the levels of lead emissions from gasoline because other major sources of lead (lead paint and food) are roughly constant year-round. This and other evidence that had developed subsequent to the *Ethyl Corp.* decision proved so striking that the D.C. Circuit subsequently stated, in a case reviewing even stricter lead limits imposed by EPA in 1982, that "the demonstrated connection between gasoline lead and blood lead, the demonstrated health effects of blood lead levels of 30 μg/dl or above, and the significant risk of adverse health effects from blood lead levels as low as 10-15 μg/dl, would justify EPA in banning lead from gasoline entirely." Small Refiner Lead Phasedown Task Force v. EPA, 705 F.2d 506, 531 (D.C. Cir. 1983). In 1985, EPA went almost that far by requiring reductions in levels of lead in gasoline to one-fifteenth the level upheld in the *Ethyl Corp.* decision. EPA's decision virtually to eliminate lead additives from gasoline relied heavily on the results of a cost-benefit analysis made possible by the initial precautionary action upheld in *Ethyl Corp.* This is one of the reasons that

**Figure 3.2    Lead Used in Gasoline Production and Average NHANES II Blood
Lead Levels (Feb. 1976-Feb. 1980)**

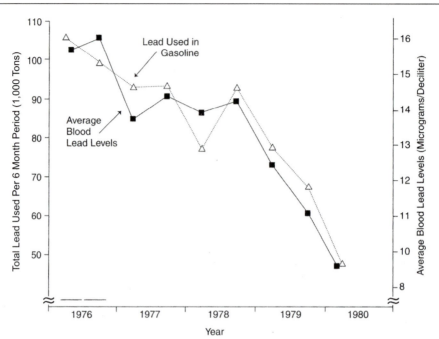

*Source:* Small Refiner Lead Phasedown Task Force v. EPA, 705 F.2d 506, 528
(D.C. Cir. 1983).

the case "is considered a landmark in U.S. environmental law because it established
that EPA could act in a precautionary fashion rather than wait for scientific certainty
about the harmfulness of a substance before acting." Ackerman & Heinzerling, Priceless—On Knowing the Price of Everything and the Value of Nothing 4 (2004).

The 1990 Amendments to the Clean Air Act completed the phaseout of gasoline lead additives by entirely prohibiting the sale of leaded gasoline for highway use, effective January 1, 1996. CAA §211(n). The phaseout of lead additives
has produced a dramatic reduction in average levels of lead in children's blood.
Thus, it is widely viewed as one of the greatest environmental success stories, even
by those otherwise critical of environmental regulation, as noted in Chapter 1.

The use of risk assessments that quantify the amount of risk associated with different environmental exposures has become routine in the modern regulatory state.
The next section examines the ascendancy of quantitative risk assessment techniques.

### 3.    Assessing the Significance of Risks

While the *Reserve* and *Ethyl Corp.* decisions stand as powerful endorsements
of the concept of precautionary regulation, neither they nor the "precautionary
principle" provide a ready answer for the question of how precautionary regulatory

policy should be. See Percival, Who Is Afraid of the Precautionary Principle? 23 Pace Envtl. L. Rev. 801, 808 (2006). The *Ethyl Corp.* majority stated that regulations could not be based "on hunches or wild guesses," and it expressly endorsed the notion that regulators should engage in risk assessment. Four years later, an influential Supreme Court decision provided even greater momentum toward development and use of quantitative risk assessment techniques. The decision reviewed regulation of toxic exposures in the workplace by the Occupational Safety and Health Administration (OSHA) of the Department of Labor.

The Occupational Safety and Health Act requires OSHA to establish standards to control workplace exposures to toxic substances. Section 6(b) of the OSH Act directs OSHA to "set the standard which most adequately assures, to the extent feasible, on the basis of the best available evidence, that no employee will suffer material impairment of health or functional capacity even if such employee has regular exposure to the hazard dealt with by such standard for the period of his working life," 29 U.S.C. §655(b)(5). The OSH Act initially authorized OSHA to set exposure limits based on previously established national consensus standards. Thus, in 1971 OSHA adopted the threshold limit values (TLVs) recognized by the American Council of Government Industrial Hygienists (ACGIH) and approximately 20 consensus standards established by the American National Standards Institute (ANSI). To assist OSHA in promulgating permanent exposure limits, the OSH Act established the National Institute for Occupational Safety and Health (NIOSH), a research agency charged with recommending occupational safety and health standards to OSHA.

In October 1976, NIOSH strongly recommended that OSHA promulgate an emergency temporary standard (ETS) to protect employees from "grave danger" from exposure to benzene. NIOSH based this recommendation on epidemiological studies showing that workers exposed to benzene were suffering an unusually high incidence of cases of leukemia. After OSHA issued an ETS of 1 ppm effective May 1977, the standard was invalidated by the U.S. Court of Appeals for the Fifth Circuit. OSHA then conducted a rulemaking to promulgate a permanent permissible exposure limit (PEL) for benzene of 1 ppm, which again was struck down by the Fifth Circuit.

The Fifth Circuit held that OSHA had not demonstrated that the costs of the standard bore a reasonable relationship to its benefits. OSHA sought Supreme Court review to consider whether such cost-benefit balancing was required under the OSH Act. A badly divided Supreme Court then surprised the parties by deciding the case on other grounds.

## Industrial Union Dep't, AFL-CIO v. American Petroleum Institute

448 U.S. 607 (1980) (the *Benzene* decision)

Mr. Justice Stevens announced the judgment of the Court and delivered an opinion, in which The Chief Justice and Mr. Justice Stewart joined and in Parts I, II, III-A, III-B, III-C and III-E of which Mr. Justice Powell joined.

[Justice Stevens set forth the facts of the case at some length, reciting the studies upon which OSHA had relied, and the industries' criticisms of them. Although studies associated benzene with a variety of adverse health effects, including non-malignant blood disorders, chromosomal aberrations, and leukemia, all studies were at levels of exposure higher than 10 ppm. The Court found the record evidence of adverse effects at that level "sketchy at best."]

In the end, OSHA's rationale for lowering the permissible exposure limit to 1 ppm was based, not on any finding that leukemia has ever been caused by exposure to 10 ppm of benzene and that it will *not* be caused at 1 ppm, but rather on a series of assumptions indicating that some leukemias might result from exposure to 10 ppm and that the number of cases would probably be reduced by reducing the exposure level to 1 ppm. In reaching this result, the Agency first unequivocally concluded that benzene is a human carcinogen. Second, it concluded that industry had failed to prove that there is a safe threshold level of exposure to benzene.

[Having made these findings and conclusions, OSHA determined that 1 ppm was the lowest feasible level of exposure that could be achieved. Estimated compliance costs included $266 million in capital investments, $200 million in first-year, startup costs, and $34 million in annual costs. About 35,000 employees would benefit from the regulation.

As Justice Stevens framed the issues, there were two arguably relevant sections of the Occupational Safety and Health Act, section 3(8), which defines an "occupational safety and health standard," and section 6(b)(5), which instructs the secretary to set a standard based on feasibility. The two provisions read as follows:

> The term "occupational safety and health standard" means a standard which requires conditions, or the adoption or use of one or more practices, means, methods, operations, or processes, reasonably necessary or appropriate to provide safe or healthful employment and places of employment. §3(8), 29 U.S.C. §652(8).
>
> The Secretary, in promulgating standards dealing with toxic materials or harmful physical agents under this subsection, shall set the standard which most adequately assures, to the extent feasible, on the basis of the best available evidence, that no employee will suffer material impairment of health or functional capacity even if such employee has regular exposure to the hazard dealt with by such standard for the period of his working life. Development of standards under this subsection shall be based upon research, demonstrations, experiments, and such other information as may be appropriate. In addition to the attainment of the highest degree of health and safety protection for the employee, other considerations shall be the latest available scientific data in the field, the feasibility of the standards, and experience gained under this and other health and safety laws. §6(b)(5), 29 U.S.C. §655(b)(5).]

## III

. . . In the Government's view, §3(8)'s definition of the term "standard" has no legal significance or at best merely requires that a standard not be totally irrational. It takes the position that §6(b)(5) is controlling and that it requires OSHA to promulgate a standard that either gives an absolute assurance of safety for each and every worker or reduces exposures to the lowest level feasible. The Government interprets "feasible" as meaning technologically achievable at a cost that would not impair the viability of the industries subject to the regulation. The respondent industry representatives, on the other hand, argue that the Court of Appeals was correct in holding that the "reasonably necessary and appropriate" language of §3(8), along with the feasibility requirement of §6(b)(5), requires the Agency to quantify both the costs and the benefits of a proposed rule and to conclude that they are roughly commensurate.

In our view, it is not necessary to decide whether either the Government or industry is entirely correct. For we think it is clear that §3(8) does apply to all permanent standards promulgated under the Act and that it requires the Secretary, before issuing any standard, to determine that it is reasonably necessary and appropriate to remedy a significant risk of material health impairment. Only after the Secretary has made the threshold determination that such a risk exists with respect to a toxic substance would it be necessary to decide whether §6(b)(5) requires him to select the most protective standard he can consistent with economic and technological feasibility, or whether, as respondents argue, the benefits of the regulation must be commensurate with the costs of its implementation. Because the Secretary did not make the required threshold finding in these cases, we have no occasion to determine whether costs must be weighed against benefits in an appropriate case.

Under the Government's view, §3(8), if it has any substantive content at all, merely requires OSHA to issue standards that are reasonably calculated to produce a safer or more healthy work environment. Apart from this minimal requirement of rationality, the Government argues that §3(8) imposes no limits on the Agency's power, and thus would not prevent it from requiring employers to do whatever would be "reasonably necessary" to eliminate all risks of any harm from their workplaces. With respect to toxic substances and harmful physical agents, the Government takes an even more extreme position. Relying on §6(b)(5)'s direction to set a standard "which most adequately assures. . .that no employee will suffer material impairment of health or functional capacity," the Government contends that the Secretary is required to impose standards that either guarantee workplaces that are free from any risk of material health impairment, however small, or that come as close as possible to doing so without ruining entire industries.

If the purpose of the statute were to eliminate completely and with absolute certainty any risk of serious harm, we would agree that it would be proper for the Secretary to interpret §§3(8) and 6(b)(5) in this fashion. But we think it is clear that the statute was not designed to require employers to provide absolutely risk-free workplaces whenever it is technologically feasible to do so, so long as the cost is not great enough to destroy an entire industry. Rather, both the language and structure of the Act, as well as its legislative history, indicate that it was intended to require the elimination, as far as feasible, of significant risks of harm.

**B**

By empowering the Secretary to promulgate standards that are "reasonably necessary or appropriate to provide safe or healthful employment and places of employment," the Act implies that, before promulgating any standard, the Secretary must make a finding that the workplaces in question are not safe. But "safe" is not the equivalent of "risk-free." There are many activities that we engage in every day—such as driving a car or even breathing city air—that entail some risk of accident or material health impairment; nevertheless, few people would consider these activities "unsafe." Similarly, a workplace can hardly be considered "unsafe" unless it threatens the workers with a significant risk of harm.

Therefore, before he can promulgate *any* permanent health or safety standard, the Secretary is required to make a threshold finding that a place of employment is unsafe—in the sense that significant risks are present and can be eliminated or lessened by a change in practices. This requirement applies to permanent standards promulgated pursuant to §6(b)(5), as well as to other types of permanent standards. For there is no reason why §3(8)'s definition of a standard should not be incorporated by reference into §6(b)(5). . . .

This interpretation of §§3(8) and 6(b)(5) is supported by the other provisions of the Act. Thus, for example, §6(g) provides in part that

> [i]n determining the priority for establishing standards under this section, the Secretary shall give due regard to the urgency of the need for mandatory safety and health standards for particular industries, trades, crafts, occupations, businesses, workplaces or work environments.

The Government has expressly acknowledged that this section requires the Secretary to undertake some cost-benefit analysis before he promulgates any standard, requiring the elimination of the most serious hazards first. If such an analysis must precede the promulgation of any standard, it seems manifest that Congress intended, at a bare minimum, that the Secretary find a significant risk of harm and therefore a probability of significant benefits before establishing a new standard.

Section 6(b)(8) lends additional support to this analysis. That subsection requires that, when the Secretary substantially alters an existing consensus standard, he must explain how the new rule will "better effectuate" the purpose of the Act. If this requirement was intended to be more than a meaningless formality, it must be read to impose upon the Secretary the duty to find that an existing national consensus standard is not adequate to protect workers from a continuing and significant risk of harm. Thus, in this case, the Secretary was required to find that exposures at the current permissible exposure level of 10 ppm present a significant risk of harm in the workplace.

In the absence of a clear mandate in the Act, it is unreasonable to assume that Congress intended to give the Secretary the unprecedented power over American industry that would result from the Government's view of §§3(8) and 6(b)(5), coupled with OSHA's cancer policy. Expert testimony that a substance is probably a human carcinogen—either because it has caused cancer in animals or because individuals have contracted cancer following extremely high exposures—would justify the conclusion that the substance poses some risk of serious harm no matter how minute the exposure and no matter how many experts testified that they regarded the risk as insignificant. That conclusion would in turn justify pervasive regulation limited only by the constraint of feasibility. In light of the fact that there are literally thousands of substances used in the workplace that have been identified as carcinogens or suspect carcinogens, the Government's theory would give OSHA power to impose enormous costs that might produce little, if any, discernible benefit.

If the Government were correct in arguing that neither §3(8) nor §6(b)(5) requires that the risk from a toxic substance be quantified sufficiently to enable the Secretary to characterize it as significant in an understandable way, the statute would make such a "sweeping delegation of legislative power" that it might be unconstitutional under the Court's reasoning in A.L.A. Schechter Poultry Corp. v. United States, 295 U.S. 495, 539, and Panama Refining Co. v. Ryan, 293 U.S. 388. A construction of the statute that avoids this kind of open-ended grant should certainly be favored.

The legislative history also supports the conclusion that Congress was concerned, not with absolute safety, but with the elimination of significant harm. The examples of industrial hazards referred to in the Committee hearings and debates all involved situations in which the risk was unquestionably significant. For example, the Senate Committee on Labor and Public Welfare noted that byssinosis, a disabling lung disease caused by breathing cotton dust, affected as many as 30% of the workers in carding or spinning rooms in some American cotton mills and that as many as 100,000 active or retired workers were then suffering from the disease. It also noted that statistics indicated that 20,000 out of 50,000 workers who had performed insulation work were likely to die of asbestosis, lung cancer, or mesothelioma as a result of breathing asbestos fibers. . . .

### D

Given the conclusion that the Act empowers the Secretary to promulgate health and safety standards only where a significant risk of harm exists, the critical issue becomes how to define and allocate the burden of proving the significance of the risk in a case such as this, where scientific knowledge is imperfect and the precise quantification of risks is therefore impossible. The Agency's position is that there is substantial evidence in the record to support its conclusion that there is no absolutely safe level for a carcinogen and that, therefore, the burden is properly on industry to prove, apparently beyond a shadow of a doubt, that there *is* a safe level for benzene exposure. The Agency argues that, because of the uncertainties in this area, any other approach would render it helpless, forcing it to wait for the leukemia deaths that it believes are likely to occur before taking any regulatory action.

We disagree. As we read the statute, the burden was on the Agency to show, on the basis of substantial evidence, that it is at least more likely than not that long-term exposure to 10 ppm of benzene presents a significant risk of material health impairment. Ordinarily, it is the proponent of a rule or order who has the burden of proof in administrative proceedings. See 5 U.S.C. §556(d). In some cases involving toxic substances, Congress has shifted the burden of proving that a particular substance is safe onto the party opposing the proposed rule.[61]

---

61. See Environmental Defense Fund, Inc. v. EPA, 548 F.2d 998, 1004, 1012-1018 (1977), cert. denied, 431 U.S. 925, where the court rejected the argument that the EPA has the burden of proving that a pesticide is unsafe in order to suspend its registration under the Federal Insecticide, Fungicide, and Rodenticide Act (FIFRA). The court noted that Congress [in FIFRA] has deliberately shifted the ordinary burden of proof under the APA, requiring manufacturers to establish the continued safety of their products.

The fact that Congress did not follow this course in enacting the Occupational Safety and Health Act indicates that it intended the Agency to bear the normal burden of establishing the need for a proposed standard. In this case OSHA did not even attempt to carry its burden of proof. The closest it came to making a finding that benzene presented a significant risk of harm in the workplace was its statement that the benefits to be derived from lowering the permissible exposure level from 10 to 1 ppm were "likely" to be "appreciable." The Court of Appeals held that this finding was not supported by substantial evidence. Of greater importance, even if it were supported by substantial evidence, such a finding would not be sufficient to satisfy the Agency's obligations under the Act. . . .

Contrary to the Government's contentions, imposing a burden on the Agency of demonstrating a significant risk of harm will not strip it of its ability to regulate carcinogens, nor will it require the Agency to wait for deaths to occur before taking any action. First, the requirement that a "significant" risk be identified is not a mathematical straitjacket. It is the Agency's responsibility to determine, in the first instance, what it considers to be a "significant" risk. Some risks are plainly acceptable and others are plainly unacceptable. If, for example, the odds are one in a billion that a person will die from cancer by taking a drink of chlorinated water, the risk clearly could not be considered significant. On the other hand, if the odds are one in a thousand that regular inhalation of gasoline vapors that are 2% benzene will be fatal, a reasonable person might well consider the risk significant and take appropriate steps to decrease or eliminate it. Although the Agency has no duty to calculate the exact probability of harm, it does have an obligation to find that a significant risk is present before it can characterize a place of employment as "unsafe."

Second, OSHA is not required to support its finding that a significant risk exists with anything approaching scientific certainty. Although the Agency's findings must be supported by substantial evidence, 29 U.S.C. §655(f), §6(b)(5) specifically allows the Secretary to regulate on the basis of the "best available evidence." As several Courts of Appeals have held, this provision requires a reviewing court to give OSHA some leeway where its findings must be made on the frontiers of scientific knowledge. Thus, so long as they are supported by a body of reputable scientific thought, the Agency is free to use conservative assumptions in interpreting the data with respect to carcinogens, risking error on the side of overprotection rather than underprotection.

Finally, the record in this case and OSHA's own rulings on other carcinogens indicate that there are a number of ways in which the Agency can make a rational judgment about the relative significance of the risks associated with exposure to a particular carcinogen.

[In a concurring opinion, Justice Powell indicated that although he would not rule out the possibility that OSHA's regulation of benzene could have been upheld on the basis of a properly promulgated generic cancer policy, OSHA had not adopted such a policy at the time it established its revised PEL for benzene. Justice Powell indicated that he agreed with the Fifth Circuit's decision below that the "reasonably necessary" language of §3(8) required OSHA to establish that the costs of its regulations were not disproportionate to their benefits.]

Mr. Justice Rehnquist, concurring in the judgment. . . .

I believe that this litigation presents the Court with what has to be one of the most difficult issues that could confront a decision-maker: whether the statistical possibility of future deaths should ever be disregarded in light of the economic costs of preventing those deaths. I would also suggest that the widely varying positions advanced in the briefs of the parties and in the opinions of Mr. Justice Stevens, the Chief Justice, Mr. Justice Powell, and Mr. Justice Marshall demonstrate, perhaps better than any other fact, that Congress, the governmental body best suited and most obligated to make the choice confronting us in this litigation, has improperly delegated that choice to the Secretary of Labor and, derivatively, to this Court. . . .

Read literally, the relevant portion of §6(b)(5) is completely precatory, admonishing the Secretary to adopt the most protective standard if he can, but excusing him from that duty if he cannot. In the case of a hazardous substance for which a "safe" level is either unknown or impractical, the language of §6(b)(5) gives the Secretary absolutely no indication where on the continuum of relative safety he should draw his line. Especially in light of the importance of the interests at stake, I have no doubt that the provision at issue, standing alone, would violate the doctrine against uncanalized delegations of legislative power. . . .

[Justice Rehnquist then discussed why he believed that additional constraints on OSHA's authority cannot be ascertained from the legislative history or context of §6(b)(5). He termed that section's feasibility requirement "a legislative mirage" that could assume "any form desired by the beholder." He then concluded that this was not a question of whether such an unconstrained delegation was necessary.]

. . .It is difficult to imagine a more obvious example of Congress simply avoiding a choice which was both fundamental for purposes of the statute and yet politically so divisive that the necessary decision or compromise was difficult, if not impossible, to hammer out in the legislative forge. Far from detracting from the substantive authority of Congress, a declaration that the first sentence of §6(b)(5) of the Occupational Safety and Health Act constitutes an invalid delegation to the Secretary of Labor would preserve the authority of Congress. If Congress wishes to legislate in an area in which it has not previously sought to enter, it will in today's political world undoubtedly run into opposition no matter how the legislation is formulated. But that is the very essence of legislative authority under our system. It is the hard choices, and not the filling in of the blanks, which must be made by the elected representatives of the people. When fundamental policy decisions underlying important legislation about to be enacted are to be made, the buck stops with Congress and the President insofar as he exercises his constitutional role in the legislative process. . . .

Accordingly, for the reasons stated above, I concur in the judgment of the Court affirming the judgment of the Court of Appeals.

MR. JUSTICE MARSHALL, with whom MR. JUSTICE BRENNAN, MR. JUSTICE WHITE, and MR. JUSTICE BLACKMUN join, dissenting. . . .

[T]oday's decision represents a usurpation of decision making authority that has been exercised by and properly belongs with Congress and its authorized representatives. The plurality's construction has no support in the statute's language, structure, or legislative history. The threshold finding that the plurality requires is the plurality's own invention. It bears no relationship to the acts or intentions of Congress, and it can be understood only as reflecting the personal views of the plurality as to the proper allocation of resources for safety in the American workplace. . .

In this case the Secretary found that exposure to benzene at levels [of] about 1 ppm posed a definite, albeit unquantifiable, risk of chromosomal damage, non-malignant blood disorders, and leukemia. The existing evidence was sufficient to justify the conclusion that such a risk was presented, but it did not permit even rough quantification of that risk. Discounting for the various scientific uncertainties, the Secretary gave "careful consideration to the question of whether th[e] substantial costs" of the standard "are justified in light of the hazards of exposure to benzene," and concluded that "these costs are necessary in order to effectuate the statutory purpose . . . and to adequately protect employees from the hazards of exposure to benzene," 43 Fed. Reg. 5941 (1978). In these circumstances it seems clear that the Secretary found a risk that is "significant" in the sense that the word is normally used. There was some direct evidence of chromosomal damage, nonmalignant blood disorders, and leukemia at exposures at or near 10 ppm and below. In addition, expert after expert testified that the recorded effects of benzene exposure at higher levels justified an inference that an exposure level above 1 ppm was dangerous. The plurality's extraordinarily searching scrutiny of this factual record reveals no basis for a conclusion that quantification is, on the basis of "the best available evidence," possible at the present time. If the Secretary decided to wait until definitive information was available, American workers would be subjected for the indefinite future to a possibly substantial risk of benzene-induced leukemia and other illnesses. It is unsurprising, at least to me, that he concluded that the statute authorized him to take regulatory action now.

Under these circumstances, the plurality's requirement of identification of a "significant" risk will have one of two consequences. If the plurality means to require the Secretary realistically to "quantify" the risk in order to satisfy a court that it is "significant," the record shows that the plurality means to require him to do the impossible. But regulatory inaction has very significant costs of its own. The adoption of such a test would subject American workers to a continuing risk of cancer and other serious diseases; it would disable the Secretary from regulating a wide variety of carcinogens for which quantification simply cannot be undertaken at the present time.

There are encouraging signs that today's decision does not extend that far. My Brother Powell concludes that the Secretary is not prevented from taking regulatory action "when reasonable quantification cannot be accomplished by any known methods." The plurality also indicates that it would not prohibit the Secretary from promulgating safety standards when quantification of the benefits is impossible. The Court might thus allow the Secretary to attempt to make a very rough quantification of the risk imposed by a carcinogenic substance, and give considerable deference to his finding that the risk was significant. If so, the Court would permit the Secretary to promulgate precisely the same regulation involved in these cases if he had not relied on a carcinogen "policy," but undertaken a review of the evidence and the expert testimony and concluded, on the basis of conservative assumptions, that the risk addressed is a significant one. Any other interpretation of the plurality's approach would allow a court to displace the agency's judgment with its own subjective conception of "significance," a duty to be performed without statutory guidance.

The consequences of this second approach would hardly be disastrous; indeed, it differs from my own principally in its assessment of the basis for the Secretary's decision in these cases. It is objectionable, however, for three reasons. First, the requirement of identification of a "significant" risk simply has no relationship to the statute that the Court today purports to construe. Second, if the "threshold finding" requirement means only that the Secretary must find "that there is a need for such a standard," the requirement was plainly satisfied by the Secretary's express statement that the standard's costs "are necessary in order to effectuate the statutory purpose . . . and to adequately protect employees from the hazards of exposure to benzene." 43 Fed. Reg. 5941 (1978). Third, the record amply demonstrates that in light of existing scientific knowledge, no purpose would be served by requiring the Secretary to take steps to quantify the risk of exposure to benzene at low levels. Any such quantification would be based not on scientific "knowledge" as that term is normally understood, but on considerations of policy. For carcinogens like benzene, the assumptions on which a dose-response curve must be based are necessarily arbitrary. To require a quantitative showing of a "significant" risk, therefore, would either paralyze the Secretary into inaction or force him to deceive the public by acting on the basis of assumptions that must be considered too speculative to support any realistic assessment of the relevant risk. It is encouraging that the Court appears willing not to require quantification when it is not fairly possible. . . .

In passing the Occupational Safety and Health Act of 1970, Congress was aware that it was authorizing the Secretary to regulate in areas of scientific uncertainty. But it intended to require stringent regulation even when definitive information was unavailable. In reducing the permissible level of exposure to benzene, the Secretary applied proper legal standards. His determinations are supported by substantial evidence. The Secretary's decision was one, then, which the governing legislation authorized him to make.

In recent years there has been increasing recognition that the products of technological development may have harmful effects whose incidence and severity cannot be predicted with certainty. The responsibility to regulate such products has fallen to administrative agencies. Their task is not an enviable one. Frequently no clear causal link can be established between the regulated substance and the harm to be averted. Risks of harm are often uncertain, but inaction has considerable costs of its own. The agency must decide whether to take regulatory action against possibly substantial risks or to wait until more definitive information becomes available—a judgment which by its very nature cannot be based solely on determinations of fact.

Those delegations, in turn, have been made on the understanding that judicial review would be available to ensure that the agency's determinations are supported by substantial evidence and that its actions do not exceed the limits set by Congress. In the Occupational Safety and Health Act, Congress expressed confidence that the courts would carry out this important responsibility. But in these cases the plurality has far exceeded its authority. The plurality's "threshold finding" requirement is nowhere to be found in the Act and is antithetical to its basic purposes. "The fundamental policy questions appropriately resolved in Congress . . . are *not* subject to re-examination in the federal courts under the guise of judicial review of agency action." Vermont Yankee Nuclear Power Corp. v. NRDC, 435 U.S. at 558 (emphasis in original). Surely this is no less true of the decision to ensure safety for the American worker than the decision to proceed with nuclear power.

## NOTES AND QUESTIONS

1. What did OSHA fail to do in promulgating a revised PEL for benzene that in the Court's view was necessary for the regulation to withstand judicial review? As a result of the Court's decision, what must OSHA do differently in the future?

2. In light of the *Benzene* decision, who bears the burden of proving that the risk to be regulated is "significant"? How does Justice Stevens justify this allocation of the burden of proof? How can this burden be discharged?

3. Why did OSHA fail to prepare quantified dose-response estimates for benzene prior to promulgating the revised PEL? Did OSHA believe that its revised PEL for benzene would have significant benefits? Must OSHA prepare quantitative dose-response estimates in the future?

4. In most cases involving the regulation of potentially toxic substances there is considerable uncertainty over the magnitude and nature of the substance's impact on health. One means of coping with uncertainty is to use default assumptions or a "safety factor" approach that errs on the side of caution to protect health. Is OSHA free to use such conservative assumptions after *Benzene*? How much confidence must OSHA have in its finding that a risk is significant before it will withstand judicial review?

5. What is the principal point of disagreement between Justice Stevens's plurality opinion and Justice Marshall's dissent? In cases in which a substance is known to pose a risk but it is impossible to quantify the *magnitude* of the risk, what would happen under Justice Stevens's approach? Under Justice Marshall's?

6. How "significant" must a risk be in order to satisfy Justice Stevens? His plurality opinion notes that "safe" does not mean "risk free." He later states that a risk of one in a billion of dying from drinking chlorinated water is "clearly not significant," while a risk of one in a thousand that benzene inhalation might be fatal might well lead a reasonable person to consider the risk "significant." Where is the line between "significant" and "insignificant" risks to be drawn and by whom? Does Justice Marshall advocate a zero risk approach? Would he permit OSHA to regulate truly trivial risks? We will return to the question of "how safe is safe?" in Section C of this chapter.

7. Only three other Justices (Chief Justice Burger, Justice Stewart, and Justice Powell) joined in Justice Stevens's plurality opinion. Justice Powell did not join Part III-D of Justice Stevens's opinion, which discussed how to define and allocate the burden of proving the significance of a risk. In a concurring opinion, Justice Powell noted that he "would not rule out the possibility that the necessary findings [of significant risk] could rest in part on generic policies properly adopted by OSHA." Justice Powell, however, also expressed the view that OSHA was required "to determine that the economic effects of its standard bear a reasonable relationship to the expected benefits." As a result of the unusual 4-4-1 split, what is the actual "holding" in this case?

8. Justice Stevens's plurality opinion bases the requirement that OSHA determine that risks to be regulated are "significant" on an interpretation of section 3(8) of the OSH Act, 29 U.S.C. §652, which defines the term "occupational safety and health standard." What impact, if any, is the Court's decision likely to have on the regulation of toxic substances by EPA and other agencies operating under different statutory authorities?

9. Justice Rehnquist argues that section 6(b)(5) of the OSH Act is an unconstitutional delegation of legislative power to OSHA, a position that is not accepted by any other member of the Court. What do you think Congress would have to do to satisfy his concern? Compare Justice Rehnquist's position with that of the Court in Whitman v. American Trucking Ass'ns, 531 U.S. 457 (2001), discussed in Chapter 5.

### OSHA Regulation of Benzene After the *Benzene* Decision

Justice Marshall's prediction that the plurality decision would "eventually be abandoned" proved inaccurate. In fact, Justice Stevens's opinion provided considerable further impetus to a direction in which federal agencies were already heading—toward greater use of quantitative risk assessment as part of an overall approach to rulemaking. Partly as a result of *Benzene*, quantitative risk assessments (QRAs) became part of the standard procedures for toxics regulation. OSHA itself already had completed a risk assessment for the cotton dust standard, which meant that it did not have to be withdrawn following the *Benzene* decision.

Justice Marshall's dissent was prescient in one respect. He argued that the outcome in the *Benzene* decision could subject American workers to continuing exposure to substances that increased risks of cancer and other serious diseases. In the years that followed, OSHA performed several assessments of the risks of benzene exposure to humans. These assessments, which were based on a wealth of new epidemiological data, confirmed that benzene posed extremely serious risks to workers. In 1982, the International Agency for Research on Cancer concluded that workers exposed to 10 to 100 ppm of benzene faced excess leukemia risks of 170 per 1,000. Based on the results of five risk assessments, OSHA eventually concluded that workers exposed to 10 ppm of benzene faced excess leukemia risks ranging from 44 to 152 per 1,000, and that even workers exposed to 1 ppm of benzene faced excess leukemia risks ranging from 5 to 16 per 1,000.

OSHA noted that these estimates were among the most conservative of the estimates that could be derived from studies of benzene exposure. Studies performed by the Chemical Manufacturers Association, Dow Chemical, and NIOSH all found substantial excess leukemia risks from benzene exposure (88 per 1,000 at 10 ppm and 9.5 per 1,000 at 1 ppm). Experimental bioassays also revealed that benzene induces multiple site cancers in both sexes of two species of rodents, evidence that had not been available when the *Benzene* decision was decided. New studies showed that benzene was associated with chromosomal aberrations in exposed workers.

Despite all this data, OSHA took several years to promulgate a new PEL for benzene. OSHA held hearings on its proposed PEL in March and April 1986 and compiled a 36,000-page record prior to promulgating a new PEL in September 1987. The new standard, effective December 1987, lowered the benzene PEL from 10 ppm to 1 ppm as an 8-hour average, while lowering the short-term exposure limit (STEL) from 25 ppm to 5 ppm as a 10-minute average.

OSHA based its new PEL on risk assessments showing that exposure to 10 ppm of benzene posed a risk of 95 additional leukemia deaths per 1,000 workers, a level greatly in excess of both other toxic substance risks OSHA had deemed significant (including arsenic, ethylene oxide, and ethylene dibromide) and the risk of accidental death in high- and average-risk industries (where death risks ranged from 30 to 3 in 1,000). OSHA estimated that the new PEL would prevent at least 326 deaths from leukemia and other blood diseases and that the actual number of deaths prevented would be considerably greater. What OSHA left unsaid was that, due to judicial intervention, it had taken ten years to lower the benzene PEL to the very levels the agency had sought to adopt on an emergency basis in May 1977. The PEL ultimately promulgated by OSHA was at the same level as the PEL vacated by the Supreme Court in 1980 in the *Benzene* decision.

### Consideration of Costs After *Benzene*: *American Textile* and *Michigan v. EPA*

The Fifth Circuit had struck down OSHA's benzene PEL largely because OSHA had failed to demonstrate that the benefits of the standard bore a reasonable relationship to its costs. When the case was briefed and argued in the Supreme Court, it was widely expected that the Court would determine whether or not some form of cost-benefit balancing was required by the OSH Act, but the Court did not reach this issue. One year after deciding *Benzene* the Court again was faced with the question whether the OSH Act required some balancing of costs and benefits. In American Textile Manufacturers Institute, Inc. v. Donovan, 452 U.S. 488 (1981) (the *Cotton Dust* case), the Court held that the OSH Act did not require cost-benefit balancing. The vote was 5-3, with Justice Stevens joining the four *Benzene* dissenters. For an account of this case and the court's unusual efforts to muster a majority in *Benzene*, see Percival, Environmental Law in the Supreme Court: Highlights from the Marshall Papers, 23 Envtl. L. Rep. 10606, 10614-10616 (1993). For an in-depth discussion of the Benzene story, see Thomas O. McGarity, The Story of the *Benzene* Case: Judicially Imposed Regulatory Reform Through Risk Assessment, in Environmental Law Stories 141 (Houck & Lazarus eds., 2005).

In the 1990 Clean Air Act Amendments Congress mandated that EPA establish limits on emissions of hazardous air pollution that are based on the maximum achievable control technology (MACT). In 2008 the D.C. Circuit ruled that EPA erred in removing mercury from the list of chemicals that must be regulated under the tough MACT standards. New Jersey v. EPA, 517 F.3d 574 (D.C. Cir. 2008). In December 2012, EPA finalized new national standards to limit emissions of mercury and other toxic pollutants from U.S. power plants. EPA estimated that the standards would save more than 8,000 lives each year while preventing 5,100 heart attacks annually. While conceding that compliance with the standards would be costly, EPA estimated that they would generate benefits 13 to 29 times their cost.

EPA's regulations were challenged in the case below.

## Michigan v. EPA

576 U.S. 743 (2015)

Justice Scalia delivered the opinion of the Court.

The Clean Air Act directs the Environmental Protection Agency to regulate emissions of hazardous air pollutants from power plants if the Agency finds regulation "appropriate and necessary." We must decide whether it was reasonable for EPA to refuse to consider cost when making this finding.

**I**

The Clean Air Act establishes a series of regulatory programs to control air pollution from stationary sources (such as refineries and factories) and moving sources (such as cars and airplanes). 69 Stat. 322, as amended, 42 U.S.C. §§7401-7671q. One of these is the National Emissions Standards for Hazardous Air Pollutants Program—the hazardous-air-pollutants program, for short. Established in its current form by the Clean Air Act Amendments of 1990, this program targets for regulation stationary-source emissions of more than 180 specified "hazardous air pollutants." §7412(b).

For stationary sources in general, the applicability of the program depends in part on how much pollution the source emits. A source that emits more than 10 tons of a single pollutant or more than 25 tons of a combination of pollutants per year is called a major source. §7412(a)(1). EPA is required to regulate all major sources under the program. §7412(c)(1)-(2). A source whose emissions do not cross the just-mentioned thresholds is called an area source. §7412(a)(2). The Agency is required to regulate an area source under the program if it "presents a threat of adverse effects to human health or the environment . . . warranting regulation." §7412(c)(3).

At the same time, Congress established a unique procedure to determine the applicability of the program to fossil-fuel-fired power plants. The Act refers to these plants as electric utility steam generating units, but we will simply call them power plants. Quite apart from the hazardous-air-pollutants program, the Clean Air Act Amendments of 1990 subjected power plants to various regulatory requirements. The parties agree that these requirements were expected to have the collateral effect of reducing power plants' emissions of hazardous air pollutants, although the extent of the reduction was unclear. Congress directed the Agency to "perform a study of the hazards to public health reasonably anticipated to occur as a result of emissions by [power plants] of [hazardous air pollutants] after imposition of the requirements of this chapter." §7412(n)(1)(A). If the Agency "finds . . . regulation is appropriate and necessary after considering the results of the study," it "shall regulate [power plants] under [§7412]." . . .

EPA completed the study required by §7412(n)(1)(A) in 1998 and concluded that regulation of coal- and oil-fired power plants was "appropriate and necessary" in 2000. In 2012, it reaffirmed the appropriate-and-necessary finding, divided power plants into subcategories, and promulgated floor standards. The Agency found regulation "appropriate" because (1) power plants' emissions of mercury and other hazardous air pollutants posed risks to human health and the environment and (2) controls were available to reduce these emissions. It found regulation "necessary" because the imposition of the Act's other requirements did not eliminate these risks. EPA concluded that "costs should not be considered" when deciding whether power plants should be regulated under §7412.

In accordance with Executive Order, the Agency issued a "Regulatory Impact Analysis" alongside its regulation. This analysis estimated that the regulation would force power plants to bear costs of $9.6 billion per year. The Agency could not fully quantify the benefits of reducing power plants' emissions of hazardous air pollutants; to the extent it could, it estimated that these benefits were worth $4 to $6 million per year. The costs to power plants were thus between 1,600 and 2,400 times as great as the quantifiable benefits from reduced emissions of hazardous air pollutants. The Agency continued that its regulations would have ancillary benefits—including cutting power plants' emissions of particulate matter and sulfur dioxide, substances that are not covered by the hazardous-air-pollutants program. Although the Agency's appropriate-and-necessary finding did not rest on these ancillary effects, the regulatory impact analysis took them into account, increasing the Agency's estimate of the quantifiable benefits of its regulation to $37 to $90 billion per year. EPA concedes that the regulatory impact analysis "played no role" in its appropriate-and-necessary finding.

. . . Congress instructed EPA to add power plants to the program if (but only if) the Agency finds regulation "appropriate and necessary." §7412(n)(1)(A). One does not need to open up a dictionary in order to realize the capaciousness of this phrase. In particular, "appropriate" is "the classic broad and all-encompassing term that naturally and traditionally includes consideration of all the relevant factors." 748 F.3d, at 1266 (opinion of Kavanaugh, J.). Although this term leaves agencies with flexibility, an agency may not "entirely fai[l] to consider an important aspect of the problem" when deciding whether regulation is appropriate.

Read naturally in the present context, the phrase "appropriate and necessary" requires at least some attention to cost. One would not say that it is even rational, never mind "appropriate," to impose billions of dollars in economic costs in return for a few dollars in health or environmental benefits. In addition, "cost" includes more than the expense of complying with regulations; any disadvantage could be termed a cost. EPA's interpretation precludes the Agency from considering *any* type of cost—including, for instance, harms that regulation might do to human health or the environment. The Government concedes that if the Agency were to find that emissions from power plants do damage to human health, but that the technologies needed to eliminate these emissions do even more damage to human health, it would *still* deem regulation appropriate. No regulation is "appropriate" if it does significantly more harm than good.

There are undoubtedly settings in which the phrase "appropriate and necessary" does not encompass cost. But this is not one of them. Section 7412(n)(1)(A) directs EPA to determine whether "*regulation* is appropriate and necessary" (emphasis added). Agencies have long treated cost as a centrally relevant factor when deciding whether to regulate. Consideration of cost reflects the understanding that reasonable regulation ordinarily requires paying attention to the advantages *and* the disadvantages of agency decisions. It also reflects the reality that "too much wasteful expenditure devoted to one problem may well mean considerably fewer resources available to deal effectively with other (perhaps more serious) problems." Against the backdrop of this established administrative practice, it is unreasonable to read an instruction to an administrative agency to determine whether "regulation is appropriate and necessary" as an invitation to ignore cost. . . .

Our reasoning so far establishes that it was unreasonable for EPA to read §7412(n)(1)(A) to mean that cost is irrelevant to the initial decision to regulate power plants. The Agency must consider cost—including, most importantly, cost of compliance—before deciding whether regulation is appropriate and necessary. We need not and do not hold that the law unambiguously required the Agency, when making this preliminary estimate, to conduct a formal cost-benefit analysis in which each advantage and disadvantage is assigned a monetary value. It will be up to the Agency to decide (as always, within the limits of reasonable interpretation) how to account for cost.

Some of the respondents supporting EPA ask us to uphold EPA's action because the accompanying regulatory impact analysis shows that, once the rule's ancillary benefits are considered, benefits plainly outweigh costs. The dissent similarly relies on these ancillary benefits when insisting that "the outcome here [was] a rule whose benefits exceed its costs." As we have just explained, however, we may uphold agency action only upon the grounds on which the agency acted. Even if the Agency *could* have considered ancillary benefits when deciding whether regulation is appropriate and necessary—a point we need not address—it plainly did not do so here. In the Agency's own words, the administrative record "utterly refutes [the] assertion that [ancillary benefits] form the basis for the appropriate and necessary finding." The Government concedes, moreover, that "EPA did not rely on the [regulatory impact analysis] when deciding to regulate power plants," and that "[e]ven if EPA had considered costs, it would not necessarily have adopted . . . the approach set forth in [that analysis]."

\* \* \*

We hold that EPA interpreted §7412(n)(1)(A) unreasonably when it deemed cost irrelevant to the decision to regulate power plants. We reverse the judgment of the Court of Appeals for the D.C. Circuit and remand the cases for further proceedings consistent with this opinion.

JUSTICE KAGAN, with whom JUSTICE GINSBURG, JUSTICE BREYER, and JUSTICE SOTOMAYOR join, dissenting.

The Environmental Protection Agency placed emissions limits on coal and oil power plants following a lengthy regulatory process during which the Agency carefully considered costs. At the outset, EPA determined that regulating plants' emissions of hazardous air pollutants is "appropriate and necessary" given the harm they cause, and explained that it would take costs into account in developing suitable emissions standards. . . .

The Agency acted well within its authority in declining to consider costs at the opening bell of the regulatory process given that it would do so in every round thereafter—and given that the emissions limits finally issued would depend crucially on those accountings. Indeed, EPA could not have measured costs at the process's initial stage with any accuracy. And the regulatory path EPA chose parallels the one it has trod in setting emissions limits, at Congress's explicit direction, for every other source of hazardous air pollutants over two decades. The majority's decision that EPA cannot take the same approach here—its micromanagement of EPA's rulemaking, based on little more than the word "appropriate"—runs counter to Congress's allocation of authority between the Agency and the courts. Because EPA reasonably found that it was "appropriate" to decline to analyze costs at a single stage of a regulatory proceeding otherwise imbued with cost concerns, I respectfully dissent. . . .

## IV

Costs matter in regulation. But when Congress does not say how to take costs into account, agencies have broad discretion to make that judgment. Far more than courts, agencies have the expertise and experience necessary to design regulatory processes suited to "a technical and complex arena." And in any event, Congress has entrusted such matters to them, not to us.

## NOTES AND QUESTIONS

1. In light of the Court's decision, what kind of consideration must EPA give to the prospective costs of regulating mercury emissions from power plants? Justice Scalia states that "[w]e need not and do not hold that the law unambiguously required the Agency, when making this preliminary estimate, to conduct a formal cost-benefit analysis in which each advantage and disadvantage is assigned a monetary value." He leaves it "up to the Agency to decide (as always, within the limits of reasonable interpretation) how to account for cost." How can the agency determine what the costs of regulation are likely to be until it decides how stringent the regulations should be?

2. In her dissent Justice Kagan notes that "costs matter in regulation." She "agree[s] with the majority—let there be no doubt about this—that EPA's power plant regulation would be unreasonable if '[t]he Agency gave cost no thought *at all*.' " But she maintains "that is just not what happened here." Precisely how do the majority and dissent differ on the issue of EPA's consideration of costs?

3. What is the relevance of the "ancillary benefits" or "co-benefits" EPA claimed that the rule would produce? Technologies to control mercury emissions also have the benefit of reducing other pollutants, such as particulates, that cause substantial harm to public health. The majority reserves judgment on the question whether these benefits count. Should EPA be able to take these benefits into account in deciding whether or not to regulate mercury emissions?

4. During oral argument in the Supreme Court, it was noted that because it had been 15 years since EPA first decided to regulate mercury emissions from power plants and because the mercury regulations had not been stayed during the litigation, more than 90 percent of sources subject to the regulation already were in compliance. Thus, the Court's decision primarily benefited the few power plants that were planning to shut down rather than to comply with the regulations. This later proved to be of great significance when it was cited by industry counsel in their shockingly successful effort in January 2016 to persuade the Supreme Court to stay the Obama administration's Clean Power Plan, as discussed in Chapter 5.

5. In response to the *Michigan v. EPA* decision, EPA on April 25, 2016 issued a final supplemental finding that it is necessary and appropriate to regulate coal- and oil-fired generating units under section 112 of the Clean Air Act. The agency stated that cost is "one of several factors that must be considered," but not "the predominant or overriding factor." It concluded that it was appropriate to regulate mercury emissions because they "pose hazards to public health" and that it was necessary to regulate them because these hazards would remain after implementation of other provisions of the Clean Air Act. Supplemental Finding That It Is Appropriate and Necessary to Regulate Hazardous Air Pollutants from Coal- and Oil-Fired Electric Utility Steam Generating Units, 81 Fed. Reg. 24,420 (Apr. 25, 2016). However, in May 2020 the Trump administration withdrew this finding and found that it was not necessary and appropriate to regulate mercury emissions from power plants because their direct benefits did not exceed their direct costs. 85 Fed. Reg. 31286 (2020). Deviating from its standard approach to cost-benefit analysis, the agency refused to consider the substantial co-benefits of controls on mercury emissions reducing emissions of particulate matter and sulfur dioxide. Joseph Goffman & Laura Bloomer,

Disempowering the EPA: How Statutory Interpretation of the Clean Air Act Serves the Trump Administration's Deregulatory Agency, 70 Case Western L. Rev. 929, 961 (2020). The agency claimed that the Court's decision in *Michigan v. EPA* prohibits consideration of co-benefits, which "is flatly contradicted by the majority opinion, which made it absolutely clear that it did not decide the question of how co-benefits should be treated." Michael A. Livermore, Polluting the EPA's Long Tradition of Economic Analysis, 70 Case Western L. Rev. 1063, 1076 (2020).

### 4. Chemical Testing and Information About Chemical Risks

Aided by the impetus of *Benzene*, modern regulation of toxics has come to rely increasingly on quantitative risk assessments as important ingredients to any regulatory decision. The aim of a risk assessment is to provide an adequate understanding of how human beings react to exposure to a substance as well as an adequate understanding of how much human exposure is occurring or likely to occur. Given their crucial importance to the risk assessment enterprise, it is perhaps surprising to realize just how little information we have about the toxicity of chemicals and the extent of exposure to them. The chemicals for which the most toxicity data are available are those used in pesticides and therapeutic drugs because extensive testing is required before they can be licensed for marketing.

### A. Information About Chemical Risks

In 1987, the Conservation Foundation published a report that identified major deficiencies in our knowledge base in several areas. "Distressingly little is known about the toxic effects of many chemicals. . . . If little is known about the toxicity of chemical substantives, even less is known about the extent of human and environmental exposure." Conservation Foundation, State of the Environment: A View Toward the Nineties 136-138 (1987).

Industrialized society produces a large quantity and a large variety of chemicals. EPA lists more than 86,000 chemicals in its Toxic Substances Control Act (TSCA) Chemical Substances Control Inventory, but little remains known about many of them. Section 5 of TSCA does require that EPA be notified before any new chemicals are marketed and before existing chemicals are processed for a significant new use. TSCA requires manufacturers to submit whatever toxicity and exposure data they have when filing a pre-manufacture notice (PMN), but until 2016 TSCA did not require any certification of safety or any mandatory battery of tests prior to manufacture. It was estimated that only 6 percent of the PMNs received annually by EPA had toxicity test data at all. While TSCA gave EPA authority to order additional testing under limited circumstances, this authority produced little information because it required EPA to have individualized information suggesting that a chemical may pose an unreasonable risk before it could order testing. GAO, Toxic Substances Control Act: EPA's Limited Progress in Regulating Toxic Chemicals, May 17, 1994. In this regard, TSCA differed markedly from the Food, Drug and Cosmetic Act (FDCA) and the Federal Insecticide, Fungicide and Rodenticide Act (FIFRA), which place the burden of proof on the manufacturer to demonstrate safety and require extensive testing, as well as express approval, before food additives, therapeutic drugs, and pesticides can be licensed and placed on the market. It also differed from the approach to commercial chemicals employed by the European Union. Similar to the FDCA, the EU's REACH program adopts a policy of "no data, no market."

In 1997, the Environmental Defense Fund (EDF) issued a report highlighting how little was known about the toxicity of chemicals used in the United States in great volumes (more than 1 million pounds per year). EDF, Toxic Ignorance (1997). Based on review of a sample of 100 of these chemicals, EDF found that only 29 percent met the minimum data requirements for health hazard screening established by the Organization for Economic Cooperation and Development (OECD). A year later, EPA's own analysis found that "no basic toxicity information, i.e., neither human health nor environmental toxicity, is publicly available for 43% of the high-volume chemicals manufactured in the US and that a full set of basic toxicity information is available for only 7% of these chemicals." EPA, Chemical Hazard Data Availability Study (1998). In the same report, EPA estimated that the full battery of basic SIDS screening tests costs about $205,000 per chemical. It further estimated that "it would cost the chemical industry approximately 0.2% of the total annual sales of the top 100 US chemical companies to fill all of the basic screening gaps" for the entire set of HPV chemicals, or approximately $427 million compared with 1996 industry sales figures of $231 billion.

EPA launched a voluntary program, the High Production Volume Chemical Challenge Program, and by 2004, EPA had commitments from over 400 companies to voluntarily test approximately 2,150 chemicals for potential health and environmental effects. In 2007, EDF issued a report critical of the HPV effort. EDF, High Hopes, Low Marks: A Final Report Card on the High Production Volume Chemical Challenge (July 2007). Noting that the Program was by then two and a half years beyond its own final deadline for completion, EDF concentrated on the fact that data for some 700 chemicals remained incomplete and that 10 percent—the "orphans"—did not even have a sponsor. There are still more than 20,000 chemicals currently in use for which no toxicity testing has been done.

The European Union's approach to risk analysis and ascertaining the hazards associated with commercial chemicals has been more effective. Through the Registration, Evaluation and Authorization of Chemicals (REACH) program, the EU pursued a "no data, no market," approach. Enacted in 2003, the program entered into force on June 1, 2007. See *https://echa.europa.eu/regulations/reach/understanding-reach*. In the European Commission's words, REACH is "based on the principle that it is up to manufacturers, importers and down-stream users of substances to ensure that they manufacture, place on the market, import or use such substances that do not adversely affect human health or the environment." Under REACH, the burden is placed on all manufacturers, importers, and exporters of chemicals to register such chemicals and to supply basic toxicological information about those chemicals as a precondition to registration. Applicable to chemicals with sales over 1 ton/year (by comparison, the HPV Challenge Program's 1 million pounds per year is equivalent to 454 metric tons/year), REACH affects some 30,000 chemicals, and its informational requirements can cost between $200,000 to $2.2 million per chemical (the requirements are tiered by tons sold per year, as well as by the toxicity of the chemical). Implementation of REACH has almost completely phased out the harmful chemical perfluorooctanoic acid (PFOA), a prevalent and persistent compound. Under the REACH scheme, PFOA was deemed a substance of high concern for its negative effects on human health, and no "authorized use" has been found important enough to override the risk that it poses. Thus, the chemical has almost no market in the EU.

The EU's REACH program, which applies to U.S. chemical companies selling products in the EU, generated pressure on the United States to reform its approach to chemical regulation. As discussed below, this eventually resulted in enactment in June 2016 of the Frank R. Lautenberg Chemical Safety for the 21st Century Act, which comprehensively amended the Toxic Substances Control Act. As amended, TSCA now requires EPA to review the safety of all existing chemicals in active commerce in the United States and to regulate them as necessary to prevent unreasonable risk. EPA is to do so through a three-step process. First, using risk-based screening, EPA is required, within 9 to 12 months, to designate chemicals on its inventory as either "high priority" or "low priority." A formal risk evaluation then must be conducted for chemicals designated as "high priority" to determine if they present an "unreasonable risk." These decisions generally must be made within three years of the "high priority" designation. If a chemical is found to present an "unreasonable risk," EPA must issue regulations within two years to reduce the risk to levels that no longer are unreasonable. To assist the agency in making risk evaluations, the amendments now give EPA broad, new authority to issue administrative orders to require manufacturers to develop chemical hazard and exposure information without first making any finding of risk.

### B.  Information About Environmental Releases of Toxic Substances

The second deficiency noted by the 1987 Conservation Foundation report was the inadequacy of information about human or environmental exposures. Here, we have since learned some useful information due to provisions of the Emergency Planning and Community Right to Know Act (EPCRA), 42 U.S.C. §§11001-11050, enacted in 1986, which requires firms annually to report chemical releases into the environment, initially of some 329 chemicals and, by 2000, more than 650 chemicals. While the amount released into the environment and the amount to which humans are exposed are two quite different things, information about releases can be pivotal in helping to determine the extent to which controls of human-generated environmental risks might be able to ameliorate an identified exposure problem.

The first Toxics Release Inventory (TRI) reports, published in 1989, stunned EPA officials. The 18,500 companies that reported disclosed that they had released 10.4 billion pounds of the listed toxic chemicals in 1987: 3.9 billion pounds into landfills, 3.3 billion pounds were sent to treatment and disposal facilities, 2.7 billion pounds into the air, and 550 million pounds discharged into surface waters. EPA Assistant Administrator Linda Fisher described the totals as "startling," "unacceptably high," and "far beyond" EPA's expectations. Weisskopf, EPA Finds Pollution "Unacceptably High," Wash. Post, Apr. 13, 1989, at A33. Corrections to the data, including eliminating some reports filed by companies not required to do so, lowered the total figure to 7 billion pounds.

Releases went down in 1988 to 4.5 billion pounds, then up to 5.7 billion in 1989. Some viewed this as progress compared with 1987, because the number of firms reporting had increased to 22,650, and industrial production had risen 7 percent. Release of Toxic Chemicals in 1989 Reached 5.7 Billion Pounds, EPA Reports, 22 Envtl. Rep. 223 (1991). Environmental organizations disagreed, arguing that the chemicals reported under the TRI omitted 95 percent of the actual total, due to non-compliance and limitations of the types of chemicals and facilities that must report. NRDC, The Right to Know More (1991).

TRI reporting requirements have evolved over the years. Major additions to the list of industries who must report were made effective in 1998, including mining, utilities operating coal-fired power plants, RCRA Subtitle C facilities, and solvent recovery services. Chemicals also have been added to the list, including a major addition of persistent bioaccumulative toxics (PBTs), which became effective in 2000. In addition, minimum threshold reporting amounts have changed. For these reasons, year-to-year comparisons are complicated. In addition to providing current year data with regard to all the current reporting requirements, EPA's annual reports also provide some data for comparative purposes that pertain just to the "original" industries and chemicals—those required to report and to be reported in 1988. For this original grouping, total releases of TRI chemicals stood at 1.901 billion pounds in 1995, 2.067 in 1997, 1.636 in 2000, and 1.240 in 2006. Total releases in 2015 for all reporting industries stood at 3.4 billion pounds, down 24 percent from 2005. For more about TRI, see Section D2 of this chapter.

## NOTES AND QUESTIONS

1. Is it surprising to you that such a large volume of toxic materials continues to be released into the environment despite the growth of federal regulatory programs?

2. Compare the pros and cons of the EPA's HPV Challenge Program and the EU's REACH program. Why has the United States chosen not to adopt a program similar to REACH? Will the REACH program provide any benefits in the United States?

3. Is it surprising that we still know so little about the adverse health effects of so many toxic chemicals? What explains the difference between the form of regulation established by FDCA compared to TSCA?

4. How would you characterize the seriousness of the toxics "problem"? Is it a result of society's fear of the unknown, is it the product of unpleasant surprises that have been discovered only after substantial damage has been done, or something else? What additional information would you wish to obtain before deciding whether or how to allocate additional resources to toxic chemical regulation?

### 5.  Risk Assessment

In 1983, the National Research Council issued an influential study, Risk Assessment in the Federal Government: Managing the Process (1983), that continues to feature prominently in how government and others approach the risk assessment process. The NRC Report identified four principal steps in the risk assessment process:

- *Hazard identification:* Is the item under study (e.g., a chemical) causally linked to particular health (or public welfare) effects?
- *Dose-response assessment:* What is the relationship between the magnitude of exposure and the probability that the health (or public welfare) effects will occur?
- *Exposure assessment:* What is the level of exposure of humans (or the environment) to the hazard?
- *Risk characterization:* What is the overall magnitude of the risk?

Each of the first three steps in the risk assessment process requires the use of research data to estimate the types of hazard posed (hazard identification), the probability a hazard will occur (dose-response assessment), and the number of people exposed and their levels of exposure (exposure assessment). These three elements are then combined in the process of risk characterization.

Risks can be characterized in either quantitative or qualitative terms. *Quantitative* risk assessments generally specify either the total numbers of people likely to experience the adverse effect or the likelihood that any one individual exposed to the hazard would suffer the adverse effect. The former is referred to as "population risk" (e.g., 100 additional cases of cancer in the exposed population), the latter "individual risk" (e.g., an exposed individual faces a 1-in-10,000 chance of developing cancer). *Qualitative* risk assessments characterize risks in nonquantitative terms (e.g., the risk is small or large). They are used occasionally to provide rough rank orderings of the seriousness of different risks, a practice referred to as *comparative* risk assessment (which also is used at times to compare quantitative estimates to assess their significance).

An excellent nontechnical introduction to risk assessment is Conservation Foundation, Risk Assessment, and Control (1985). Also useful is a joint report by the American Chemical Society and Resources for the Future, Understanding Risk Analysis (1998). As one might expect from the previous material on the paucity of toxics information that is available, the Conservation Foundation study, at page 4, notes that "almost all risk assessments are plagued by inadequate data." The joint ACS/RFF study, at page 7, concludes that "the current state of scientific understanding has often been found to be incomplete, indecisive and controversial."

> Virtually all elements of risk assessment are clouded with uncertainty, basically of two kinds. First, the various scientific disciplines involved in assessing risk are not sufficiently developed either to explain the mechanisms by which particular causes produce particular effects or to provide good quantitative estimates of cause-and-effect relationships. Second, the data needed to analyze particular risks are usually not available. [Conservation Foundation at 5.]

**Hazard Identification.**   Regulatory agencies today have a far more difficult task than the first federal safety agency, the Steamboat Inspection Service, which was charged with preventing boilers on steamships from exploding. Cancer, far and away the most studied and feared health hazard, is better understood than it was decades ago but there remain significant gaps in knowledge, especially as they relate to the important issue of whether any specific carcinogen has a safe, or "no effects," threshold. Furthermore, it is sometimes difficult even to tell whether a given chemical is actually a human carcinogen. All the potential sources of information have their deficiencies and uncertainties.

**Epidemiologic Data.**   After incidences of disease are noted in a given segment of the population, well-conducted epidemiologic studies of that segment can sometimes find an association between a causative agent and that disease. Because epidemiology would provide direct evidence in human beings of the hazard, in theory this would be a most valuable source of reliable information. Such evidence, however, is extremely limited. Except in occupational exposure settings, it is extremely difficult to identify population subgroups whose characteristics are virtually identical save for their exposure to a substance being investigated. Even when such groups can be identified, historic levels of exposure actually experienced by each group are difficult to determine with precision. High background levels of common diseases like cancer mask all but the most catastrophic associations between diseases and particular causative agents. There may simply be too many variables—potential causes of the disease—in the population's history to sort out relative influences. Epidemiologic analysis, furthermore, requires that a disease manifest itself, yet the ideal function of environmental protection is to prevent disease.

**Experimental Data.**   Experimental data have significant advantages over epidemiologic data in that they permit scientists to assess environmental hazards in carefully controlled circumstances before widespread human exposure has occurred. Because ethical considerations preclude human exposure to substances that threaten health, most experimental data are derived from short-term tests or animal bioassays.

**Short-Term Studies and Molecular Comparisons.**   Certain short-term tests of chemicals (e.g., for mutagenicity) have been shown to be highly correlative to carcinogenicity; thus, performing such tests can provide some evidence of whether the suspected hazard is a carcinogen. However, scientists now know that not all mutagens are carcinogens and that many nonmutagenic substances may play an important role in the complex process by which cancer develops. Short-term screening tests thus have proved more useful for identifying cancer initiators than for screening cancer promoters or receptors. Scientists also have sought to infer that certain chemicals may be carcinogens by analyzing their molecular structure to determine if it is similar to that of known carcinogens. This is called inference from structure-activity relationships and has been used for limited purposes such as determining whether to require additional testing of certain chemicals for carcinogenicity. Neither of these sources of information assists in estimating the potency of the hazard.

**Toxicological Experiments on Laboratory Animals.**   Exposure of animals under controlled conditions to a suspected hazard allows researchers to control for other variables and thus isolate the hazard potential of the suspect chemical. Bioassay data are necessarily skimpy, however, because of the enormous sample sizes that are required to detect the risks posed by low-level exposures to toxic substances. Hazard identification frequently relies on just one or two experiments in a single species of rodent. Furthermore, while the validity of translating animal findings into conjectures of human reactions is widely accepted (indeed, fundamental to the entire toxicological research effort), the precise formulae for translating such findings remain disputed and depend on inferences that cannot be scientifically validated. Moreover, there are occasions when observations in animals are of very limited relevance to humans. Still, such studies remain the backbone of governmental and industry research in hazard identification. They are expensive and time-consuming — two years and $2.5 million is typical for a single rodent bioassay — so we should expect such data to be limited.

The Screening Information Data Set that was compiled under the High Production Chemical Challenge Program on a voluntary basis and under the EU's REACH program on a mandatory basis are primarily aimed at providing a standard set of hazard identification information, to determine whether the chemical is associated with one or more adverse health effects, such as cancer, birth defects, neuro-developmental abnormalities, and the like.

**Dose-Response Assessment.**   Experimental or epidemiologic data very seldom exist for the relatively low levels of exposure that must be examined when regulatory intervention is being considered. Scientists therefore must extrapolate from the available data the relationship between the doses relevant to regulation and the human health or environmental effects (the response) to assess the potency of a hazard.

Uncertainties in dose-response assessment come from a variety of sources. With epidemiologic data, the population as a whole typically contains subpopulations that are likely to be more susceptible to disease than the population studied, for instance, children, pregnant women, fetuses, and the elderly. It is often unclear how to translate epidemiologic data to predict the effects of exposure on such groups.

Toxicological studies present further problems, as noted above. There is no scientific consensus on how to transfer information about animal reactions to suspected hazards and human reactions, even holding the dose constant. Because body weight, body metabolism, differences in immune systems, and other variables are thought to be relevant to the study of how an organism responds to exposures, responses of humans and laboratory animals are likely to differ, but scientists are unsure as to how.

Toxicological studies also present the problem of extrapolating from higher doses to regulation-relevant, lower doses. In order to induce laboratory responses, animals are exposed to extremely high doses. There is disagreement about whether high-dose responses in animals provide an accurate basis for predicting low-dose responses even in the same animals, let alone a basis for drawing conclusions about humans exposed to low levels. Cancer-causing substances cause special problems, because the precise mechanisms through which specific carcinogens operate are still not completely understood, and therefore what effect extremely low levels of exposure will have cannot be known and hence must be estimated.

**Exposure Assessment.**   Often the weakest data link in the chain of steps in the risk assessment process is meaningful exposure data. Samples of the concentrations of a chemical in the blood or other organs can be taken, but this does not answer the question of the extent to which individuals have been exposed to that chemical because of environmental factors. Exposure assessments usually require the use of fate and transport models, which attempt to predict concentrations in the ambient air or water by starting with some estimates of the amount of chemicals being put into the environment by human and other sources. These models then take into account weather patterns, movements of water bodies, and any other environmental features that affect the transport of those chemicals. These models, needless to say, are imperfect. They also must take into account the fact that many chemicals interact with other chemicals in the presence of sunlight or other catalysts, forming new chemicals. These parts of the models also are imperfect because neither the precise quantities of other chemicals, nor the identity of all the chemicals present, nor the precise environmental conditions can be known, and chemical reactions can be significantly affected by these factors. Multiple pathways (e.g., the concentration of the chemicals in the air, in the water, in the soil, in products or foods consumed by the public) may sometimes need to be estimated. Finally, the characteristics of population groups potentially exposed to certain substances also may have a significant impact on risk assessment because some types of people are more susceptible than others to certain hazards.

At times, the hazard identification process has been subject to the whims of EPA administrators. For example, under the 2016 TSCA reforms, EPA was required to analyze the health risks of perchloroethylene (PERC), a chemical used in refrigerants and dry cleaning. However, EPA's draft evaluation of PERC looked at risks from the chemical either when it is exposed to the skin or breathed in, but not from both sources together. EPA's final risk evaluation found that perchloroethylene posed unreasonable risks to workers, occupational non-users, consumer and bystanders from 59 condition of use, but no unreasonable risk to the environment for any conditions of use."

Hazard identification and dose-response assessment attempt to answer the questions of whether a substance is hazardous and, if so, how hazardous it is. Gaps in scientific knowledge with which to determine the answers to these questions must be bridged by assumptions or default conclusions.

In its work leading up to the *Benzene* litigation, OSHA concluded that the gaps that needed to be bridged in producing a quantitative risk assessment argued against trying to generate a QRA at all. After *Benzene*, agencies generally have chosen the option of bridging the gaps with default assumptions. Much of the controversy over whether agencies are employing "sound science" in their work focuses on the choice of defaults, but also on other decisions agencies must make in evaluating available data. Those who wish to see government being more preventative in its approach to exposures to toxic materials worry that quantitative risk assessments contribute to the problem of "paralysis by analysis" that agencies increasingly confront.

Agencies are caught in a squeeze by opposing forces. They know they cannot act precipitously because the courts will strike down rules and regulations that lack an adequate evidentiary basis. Yet they also know that, however much they analyze and refine, the realities of science and the available evidence dictate that they will never eliminate all the major assumptions and judgments from their decision making, either. As much as regulatory foes assert that we can never achieve a risk-free society, so it also seems that an agency can never write an assumption- and judgment-free regulation.

When all is said and done, agencies appear to be doing their work carefully enough so that courts have generally deferred to agency decisions regarding how to fill in the analytical gaps in risk assessments. In International Fabricare Institute v. EPA, 972 F.2d 384 (D.C. Cir. 1992), representatives of a group of chemical companies raised what the court termed "a general challenge to the EPA policy of rejecting the existence of safe threshold levels for carcinogens in the absence of contrary evidence." Id. at 387. The court rejected their claim that it was arbitrary and capricious for EPA not to consider "new scientific evidence" questioning the appropriateness of assuming no safe thresholds of exposure to carcinogens.

The court concluded that new evidence offered amounted to "the opinion of a few scientists who, however qualified, are in their own words at odds with what is 'generally thought' about the subject." Id. at 391. EPA had previously considered these and other dissenting views and had declined to change its working assumptions. The court concluded that the agency need not "undertake a more detailed re-justification of its prior position" simply because of the "submission of comments consisting of little more than assertions that in the opinion of the commenters the agency got it wrong." Id. See also Synthetic Organic Chem. Mfrs. Ass'n v. Secretary, Dep't of Health & Human Servs., 720 F. Supp. 1244 (W.D. La. 1989) (rejecting claims that risk assessment methodologies are arbitrary and capricious). A study of court cases challenging EPA selection among conflicting scientific findings or among different modeling assumptions or other choices of inferential bridges found that EPA had never been reversed when addressing these questions, which stand on "the frontiers of scientific knowledge." Christopher H. Schroeder & Robert L. Glicksman, Chevron, State Farm, and EPA in the Courts of Appeals During the 1990s, 31 Envtl. L. Rep. 10371 (2001).

Risk assessments involving cancer-causing materials have sparked a particularly significant number of disputes, because agencies have invested considerable resources in identifying and regulating carcinogens, and because the assumptions employed in QRAs for carcinogens employ cautious default assumptions, such as the assumption that there is no safe level of exposure to a carcinogen, as well as the assumption that toxicological studies on laboratory animals that have been given massive doses of a chemical provide valid bases for extrapolating to effects in humans who are exposed to much lower doses of the chemical.

One focal point of the "sound science" criticisms of QRAs rests on the opinion of some scientists that we have acquired enough knowledge about the mechanisms of cancer causation in humans to question the relevance of the MTD and no-safe-threshold assumptions, at least in some cases. The challenge to EPA's approach that was rejected in the International Fabricare decision was a broad-scale attack on EPA's approach. Theories and evidence about mechanisms of action, and about pharmacokinetics (the analysis of how an organism processes a toxic substance—the rate of uptake, distribution within the body, excretion, metabolites formed in response) form the basis of such criticisms.

EPA generally has heeded the advice of the NAS and others and in formulating policy has continued to monitor and analyze advances in the scientific understanding of how particular substances cause or promote cancer. In incorporating new science, EPA's challenge is to define what must be shown when and by whom to warrant deviation from the default assumptions about the relevance of animal test data. For example, water is deliberately chlorinated by public health authorities to eliminate microbial pathogens (germs). Chloroform is a chemical byproduct of the chlorination of water. In regulating chloroform under the Safe Drinking Water Act, EPA acknowledged and credited studies providing reason to believe that chloroform did exhibit a no-effects threshold below which it did not pose a cancer risk to humans, and hence was unnecessary to remove the substance from drinking water. Yet, EPA nonetheless issued a standard of zero when it regulated chloroform in drinking water pursuant to a provision of the Safe Drinking Water Act (SDWA) requiring maximum contaminant level goals to be set on the basis of the "best available . . . science." 42 U.S.C. §300g-1(b)(3)(A). Litigation challenging EPA's decision produced one of the infrequent cases in which a court has reversed an EPA choice among different scientific conclusions. Chlorine Chemistry Council v. EPA, 206 F.3d 1286 (D.C. Cir. 2000).

*Chlorine Chemistry Council* arose in unusual circumstances. EPA had reached a fairly firm conclusion that the best available science justified concluding that chloroform had a no-effects threshold and yet it declined to use that science in issuing a regulation under a statute requiring the use of the best available science. The more typical disputes over "sound science" involve cases in which scientific findings are less conclusive, some pointing in one direction, others in different directions, and EPA resolves the disagreement and draws inferences that industry or other challengers argue to be unjustified.

Regulators are acutely aware of the uncertainties of risk assessments. Nonetheless, in justifying decisions regarding toxic exposures, EPA and other health agencies rely heavily upon such risk assessment. Science has such a powerful influence in modern society that Wendy Wagner suggests agencies engage in a "pervasive 'science charade,' where [they] exaggerate the contributions made by science in setting toxic standards in order to avoid accountability for the underlying policy decisions." Wagner, The Science Charade in Toxic Risk Regulation, 95 Colum. L. Rev. 1613, 1617 (1995).

Disputes over cancer mechanisms dominate debate over what constitutes good science in regulatory proceedings, but there are numerous other complicating factors. Analysts grow increasingly aware of the interactive, or synergistic, effects of multiple numbers of chemicals. Nonetheless, EPA has developed very little capability to assess synergistic effects. Likewise, non-carcinogenic effects have received less attention than cancer effects have, and yet these effects are increasingly a primary object of concern. When California performed a statewide comparative risk analysis, for example, its human health valuation committee concluded that many of its final rankings

> were driven by the extent and severity of noncancer impacts. The relative importance of noncancer impacts suggests that comparative risk projects must be cautious about rankings based on assessment methods that provide quantitative risk estimates for carcinogens and that the development and validation of noncancer risk assessment methods should be a higher priority. [California Comparative Risk Project, Toward the 21st Century: Planning for the Protection of California's Environment 85 (1994).]

Amidst growing concern over noncancer health effects, carcinogenicity still continues to receive the lion's share of attention. As suggested by EPA's stance in

*Chlorine Chemistry Council,* federal environmental health regulators take seriously our growing knowledge of the causal mechanisms of carcinogenic chemicals. Over the years, EPA's policies with respect to its fundamental premises for assessing risk from carcinogens have been embodied in Agency Guidelines and draft Guidelines. *Chlorine Chemistry Council* references EPA's 1996 Proposed Guidelines for Carcinogen Risk Assessment, which were intended to update Guidelines that had been issued in 1986. In March 2005, the agency finalized the process begun in 1996 by issuing new Guidelines for Carcinogen Risk Assessment, EPA/630/P-03/001B (March 2005), 70 Fed. Reg. 17,765 (Apr. 7, 2005). These Guidelines signal a greater Agency willingness to accept pharmacokinetic and mechanism of action evidence for nonlinearity than the prior Guidelines had:

> As an increasing understanding of carcinogenesis is becoming available, these cancer guidelines adopt a view of default options that is consistent with EPA's mission to protect human health while adhering to the tenets of sound science. Rather than viewing default options as the starting point from which departures may be justified by new scientific information, *these cancer guidelines view a critical analysis of all of the available information that is relevant to assessing the carcinogenic risk as the starting point from which a default option may be invoked if needed to address uncertainty or the absence of critical information.* [U.S. EPA, Guidelines for Carcinogen Risk Assessment, §1.3.1., EPA/630/P-03/001B (April 2005) (emphasis in original), 70 Fed. Reg. at 17,771.]

Initial hazard characterization and dose-response assessments are often the most visible and widely publicized features of a controversial risk assessment. Yet the components of a QRA that estimate the amount of human and environmental exposure are equally critical in determining how much harm an activity is actually causing. A chemical can be the most toxic in the world, but if it is also being completely contained it may not warrant further regulation. Even if exposure is occurring, in order to justify regulating an activity there must be some reason to believe that the activity is contributing to that exposure. High degrees of exposure may not justify regulating an activity if the exposure is coming from somewhere else. So exposure assessment is critical to a risk assessment, as are the hazard identification and dose-response assessment components, and such assessments similarly raise the issue of how much one needs to know about these exposure-related questions before regulation is justified. In *Ethyl Corp.,* for instance, there were gaps in the exposure assessment because the relationship between the lead that was being emitted from auto exhausts and the lead content in human blood was not well understood.

### PFAS, TSCA, and Chemical Testing

The lack of toxicity data for most chemicals is illustrated by the fact that the public became aware of the dangers of a family of per- and polyfluoroalkyl chemical substances called PFAS only as a result of tort litigation. In 1998 Robert Bilott, a lawyer, began investigating unusual deaths of cattle on the farm of his grandmother's neighbor in West Virginia. Nathaniel Rich, The Lawyer Who Became DuPont's Worst Nightmare, N.Y. Times Magazine, Jan. 6, 2016. Bilott filed suit against DuPont, which had disposed chemicals from its Washington Works plant in a landfill next to the neighbor's farm. After insisting that discovery be limited to regulated or listed chemicals, DuPont eventually was compelled to turn over records revealing that the stream from which the cattle drank was heavily contaminated with perfluorooctanoic acid (PFOA), an unregulated chemical used by DuPont in the production of Teflon. Also known as C-8, PFOA is part of a family of PFAS that were widely used to make Teflon, Scotchgard, and aqueous film-forming fire-fighting foams (AFFF). Invented by 3M and widely used by DuPont, these chemicals often are called "forever chemicals" because they spread easily in the environment, do not readily degrade, and bioaccumulate in people and animals exposed to them.

Bilott discovered that during the late 1970s and early 1980s DuPont and 3M had done studies finding adverse effects of PFOA exposure on test animals. The companies also discovered higher rates of serious health problems in their employees who worked with the chemical. Alarmed by the results of these studies, 3M announced in May 2000 that it voluntarily would cease production of PFOS and PFOA. DuPont then built its own PFOA production facility in Fayetteville, North Carolina. After Bilott informed EPA of the studies, EPA accused DuPont of violating section 8(e) of the Toxic Substances Control Act by failing to report the studies to EPA. Section 8(e) of TSCA requires chemical manufacturers to "immediately inform" the EPA administrator if they obtain information "which reasonably supports the conclusion" that a chemical "presents a substantial risk of injury to health or the environment." In December 2005 DuPont settled the violations by agreeing to pay a fine of $10.25 million and to contribute an additional $6.25 million to supplemental environmental projects.

DuPont ultimately agreed to a settlement to compensate the farmer for the deaths of his cattle. However, Bilott discovered that thousands of residents of nearby Parkersburg, West Virginia had been drinking water contaminated by high levels of PFOA. In August 2001, Bilott brought a lawsuit against DuPont in state court on behalf of 70,000 people who had been exposed to 0.05 ppb or more of PFOA in drinking water contaminated from the company's Washington Works plant. Leach v. E.I. Du Pont de Nemours & Co., Civil Action No. 01-C-608. Bilott relied on a 1999 decision by the Supreme Court of Appeals of West Virginia permitting plaintiffs to sue for medical monitoring expenses if they had substantial exposure to a substance that significantly increases their risk of developing a serious disease. He ultimately settled the *Leach* litigation for $70 million in September 2004. DuPont agreed to clean up Parkersburg, West Virginia's drinking water and to install a water treatment system with state-of-the-art technology. It also agreed to fund an independent "Science Panel" to determine what adverse health effects, if any, PFOA is capable of causing in class members.

Pursuant to the settlement, Bilott and DuPont jointly selected three of the nation's top epidemiologists to form the panel that would conduct a "C-8 Study" to determine what adverse health effects, if any, PFOA was capable of causing. In an unusual provision, DuPont agreed that it would not dispute whether PFOA was capable of causing any adverse health effects that the Science Panel found had a "probable link" to PFOA exposure. However, only class members with such health problems could continue their personal injury actions against DuPont. Most of the 70,000 class members provided medical histories and blood samples to assist the panel in performing the study. This created one of the largest and most complete data sets in the history of epidemiology, but it also meant that the C-8 Study took seven years to complete.

Shortly after the Science Panel's C-8 Study was launched, in January 2006 EPA announced a PFOA Stewardship Program that asked industry voluntarily to reduce PFOA production by 95 percent by 2010 and to eliminate it by 2015. The 3M Corporation already had announced that it would stop making PFOS and PFAS, and prior to 2010 it also stopped making aqueous fire-fighting foam (AFFF). DuPont stopped producing PFOS and PFOA in the United States, but it continued to produce them in China. However, Bilott concludes that EPA's Stewardship Program unfortunately caused a decade-long halt in the agency's own efforts to develop a regulatory program.

The Science Panel's work took seven years and cost $35 million. It released its findings in a series of reports between December 2011 and July 2012. The Panel ultimately found "probable links" between exposure to PFOA and six adverse health effects: high cholesterol, ulcerative colitis, thyroid disease, testicular cancer, kidney cancer, and pregnancy-induced hypertension. More than 3,500 members of the class who were diagnosed with any of the six linked diseases then came forward to file new personal injury actions against DuPont. Bilott agreed with DuPont that the cases should be tried in federal court using procedures for consolidating multi-district litigation (MDL). In April 2013 a DuPont "C8 Personal Injury Litigation" MDL was created in the Southern District of Ohio. Trial of the first of three "bellwether" cases commenced on September 15, 2015. Joining DuPont as a defendant was a new company, the Chemours Company. Chemours had been spun off from DuPont in July 2015 to enable DuPont to rid itself of the Teflon business, a move widely viewed as an attempt by DuPont to shield itself from PFOA liability.

The plaintiff in the first trial was Carla Bartlett, a secretary whose kidney cancer required her to undergo painful surgery. On October 7, 2015, the jury awarded Bartlett $1.6 million in compensatory damages after less than a day of deliberations. DuPont and Chemours asserted that the verdict actually was a victory for them because the jury had not awarded any punitive damages. However, in the second bellwether case, tried in the summer of 2016, the jury awarded $500,000 in punitive damages and $5.1 million in compensatory damages to a plaintiff with testicular cancer. The third trial, also a case of testicular cancer, resulted in a verdict of $2 million in compensatory damages and $10.5 million in punitive damages. After initially vowing to appeal all of the verdicts and to require trials in the thousands of remaining cases, DuPont and Chemours agreed in February 2017 to settle all of the personal injury claims for $671 million. The two companies agreed to split the cost of the settlement equally, though DuPont stated that Chemours eventually would have to bear nearly all future PFOA liability.

As companies phased out the production and use of PFOA and PFOS they have replaced them with thousands of structurally similar PFAS chemicals that have not been extensively tested. For example, GenX, DuPont's replacement for PFOA, has two fewer carbon atoms than PFOA, but otherwise is almost identical in structure. DuPont claims that it will degrade in the environment much faster than PFOA. PFAS have been discovered, usually in small concentrations, in drinking water serving 110 million people in virtually every state. PFAS have contaminated drinking water near military bases where AFFFs were used. But the thousands of chemical varieties of PFAS now on the market have not been extensively tested. To address the risks of these chemicals, Bilott filed a new class action on October 4, 2018 against DuPont, Chemours, 3M, and six other companies using or producing PFAS. The case was filed in the same Ohio federal court that heard the C8 litigation. The lead plaintiff is Kevin Hardwick, an Ohio firefighter exposed to PFAS through firefighting foams and retardants. Bilott's plaintiff class is far broader than in the C8 litigation. It is a nationwide class of U.S. residents who "have a detectable level of PFAS materials in their blood serum," which could include more than 100 million people. Building on the model Bilott used in the *Leach* litigation, the *Hardwick* plaintiffs request the formation of a PFAS Science Panel to conduct a nationwide study of the health effects of these chemicals. In October 2019 the judge hearing the *Hardwick* case denied an initial motion to dismiss by the defendant companies.

## B.   *HOW SAFE IS SAFE?—MODERN APPROACHES TO MANAGING RISK*

Up to this point, this chapter has focused on the issues raised by the first line of inquiry prompted by the preventative ambition—trying to determine what activities warrant regulatory attention due to their potential to cause harm. The second line of inquiry asks just "how safe is safe?" What constitutes acceptable risk? What should be done to reduce the harm-causing potential? The issues raised are no less complex or controversial.

This section focuses on the issues raised by this second line of inquiry. It is often said that the question of "how safe is safe?" raises primarily questions of social policy, as a society must negotiate the conflict between the values served by preventing harm and the values served by the harmful activity, which often advance social interests as well. This is then contrasted with the nature of the first line of inquiry, which is characterized as primarily scientific. It is largely due to this difference that the influential National Academy of Sciences report on risk regulation urged federal agencies to segregate these two activities as much as possible, assigning the resolution of risk assessment issues to science panels and the resolution of risk management issues to the regulatory agencies. National Research Council, Risk Assessment in the Federal Government: Managing the Process 5-8 (1983). The preceding section has suggested some of the ways in which this distinction is misleading. Risk assessment involves heavy elements of social policy and cannot be considered a matter of "pure science," especially when inferential bridges are required to fill gaps or where science is uncertain. The NAS Report urges explicit identification of the options available at each point where an assumption must be made or an inferential bridge built to span a data gap so that the policy makers can address those questions. However, critics doubt that such complete explicitness can ever be achieved in practice; thus, isolating the risk assessment process from the policy-making process inevitably will result in some, possibly important, policy decisions being made by scientists and other "experts" without public scrutiny. See Latin, Good Science, Bad Regulations, and Toxic Risk Assessment, 5 Yale J. on Reg. 89 (1988).

The question of how much information we need to have before it is appropriate to manage risk at all is also a question of assessing risk that is heavily policy-laden. For instance, in issuing the regulation that led up to the *Ethyl Corp.* litigation, EPA decided to regulate the lead content of gasoline even though the harm that the lead was causing was "impossible to forecast." Thus EPA "assessed" the risk of lead without performing a quantitative risk assessment at all. The decision that lead posed enough of a public health concern to justify regulation was an assessment based on policy, not pure science, even though of course science informed the decision. EPA in effect was operating on a version of the Precautionary Principle. That Principle, which is much more frequently invoked in international environmental disputes than it is domestically, has become a lightning rod because it endorses regulatory intervention based on less information than those who wish to avoid regulation would prefer. The *Reserve* court necessarily answered similar policy questions, and also adopted a precautionary stance.

So long as the interpenetration of science and policy into both risk assessment and risk management issues is not forgotten, there is value in distinguishing the two for analytical purposes because it enables exploration of the issues that Congress and regulatory agencies frequently face in choosing among the different regulatory responses to potentially harmful activity.

### 1. Introduction: Remedial Approaches in Reserve and Ethyl Corp.

As they did with the first line of inquiry, the early *Reserve* and *Ethyl Corp.* decisions provide useful introductions into the issues raised in determining "how safe is safe?"

First, *Reserve.* After finding that the air and water pollution from Reserve's plant posed a reasonable medical concern, the district court had ordered the facility closed immediately. The Eighth Circuit first stayed the injunction and then modified it. The court concluded "the evidence is insufficient to support the kind of demonstrable danger to the public health that would justify the immediate closing of Reserve's operations." Reserve Mining Co. v. EPA, 514 F.2d 492, 507 (8th Cir. 1975). While the appellate court referred approvingly to Judge Wright's analysis of risk in *Ethyl Corp.*, the court also concluded that "it cannot be said that the probability of harm is more likely than not" and that "it cannot be forecast that the rates of cancer will increase" as a result of the air and water pollution. 514 F.2d at 520. The court continued:

> In fashioning relief in a case such as this involving a possibility of future harm, a court should strike a proper balance between the benefits conferred and the hazards created by Reserve's facility. In its pleadings Reserve directs our attention to the benefits arising from its operations. [Reserve represented a $350 million capital investment with an annual payroll of $32 million, which supported 3,367 employees. Its production of taconite was 12 percent of the U.S. total.] [On the other side], the hazard in both the air and water can be measured in only the most general terms as a concern for the public health resting on a reasonable medical theory. Serious consequences could result if the hypothesis on which it is based should ultimately prove true. [514 F.2d at 535-536.]

In speaking of the need to balance "the benefits conferred and the hazards created" by *Reserve*, did the court explain how to strike such a balance? How can one strike a balance if one "cannot . . . forecast" the amount of harm that might occur? In fact, what did the court mean when it said that an increase in cancer rates cannot be forecast? Does it imply that a court must be *certain* that harm will occur before it can enjoin? Would that be consistent with Judge Wright's approach assessing and responding to risk? What is the implication of the court's conclusion that harm was less than likely? Is it that the probability of harm must be greater than 50 percent before a court should enjoin? Would that be consistent with Judge Wright's approach to assessing and responding to risk?

Suppose villagers living in a valley below an earthen dam convince a court that there is a one-in-ten chance that the dam would fail. Would the court be justified in enjoining the dam owner *either* to drain the dam completely *or* to reinforce the dam, and to do so immediately? Is your answer consistent with *Reserve?* With *Ethyl Corp.?* Suppose the dam operator complained that fixing or draining the dam immediately would cause it grievous financial loss, whereas a phased, three-year improvement and reinforcement plan could be accomplished at much lower costs. Would that influence your answer?

Next, *Ethyl Corp.* EPA's rule had ordered a graduated phasedown of the lead content in gasoline, beginning with a refinery average of 1.7 grams per gallon as of January 1, 1975, down through five steps to a final average of 0.5 grams after January 1, 1979. 38 Fed. Reg. 33,734 (1973). The court upheld EPA's phasedown order without closely examining its details or the agency rationale for choosing this particular phasedown instead of any of the counterproposals of industry. (Industry protested the rule's use of a refinery average instead of a company average; they also protested EPA's requirement that averages be computed quarterly, preferring semiannual or annual averaging.) Not only did the court not scrutinize the details of the phasedown, it also did not deliberate over the final target figure, 0.5 grams per gallon, that EPA issued. In its proposal for the phasedown rule, EPA had stated:

> Based on the available evidence, the Administrator has concluded that airborne lead levels exceeding 2 micrograms per cubic meter, averaged over a period of 3 months or longer, are associated with a sufficient risk of adverse physiologic effects to constitute endangerment of public health. . . . [A]ttainment of a 2-microgram level will require a 60 to 65 percent reduction in lead from motor vehicles. [37 Fed. Reg. 3,882 (1972).]

Does EPA seem to be saying here that 2 micrograms or less is not an "endangering" level of exposure? If so, it was initially justifying the phasedown from 1.7 to 0.5 (a 70 percent reduction) as necessary to achieve nonendangering exposure. In issuing its final rule, EPA appeared to shift ground:

> [I]t is difficult, if not impossible, to establish a precise level of airborne lead as an acceptable basis for a control strategy. . . . [However,] [s]trong evidence existed which supported the view that through these routes [air and dust] airborne lead contributes to excessive lead exposure in urban adults and children. In light of this evidence of health risks, the Administrator concluded that it would be prudent to reduce preventable lead exposure. [38 Fed. Reg. 33,734 (1973).]

To buttress its determination that a 70 percent reduction in the amount of lead used in gasoline was possible, EPA lengthened its initial reduction schedule from 4 to 5 years, so as to "moderate the economic and technological impacts of the regulations during the period over which the reduction would be accomplished." That done, EPA wrote that "though the benefits associated with the . . . lead reductions have not been quantified, the Administrator has concluded that this approach is not unreasonably costly and will prudently prevent unnecessary exposure to airborne lead." Costs, in fact, were projected to be less than 0.1 cent per gallon refined, adding only between $82 million and $133 million to the total of $1.5 billion the industry was to invest in refining capacity through the year 1980. 38 Fed. Reg. 33,734, 33,739 (1973).

Thus, EPA appeared to switch from justifying its decision on the basis of achieving a level of exposure that would not pose an endangering risk to one based on what technology and economic considerations would "prudently" permit. What considerations could have contributed to the shift? If 70 percent were "preventable," would 80 or 90 percent have been? EPA did not examine this question. Instead, it expressed the aim of determining the most cost-effective approach to the reduction of lead exposure from any source, whether airborne or not. Unfortunately, EPA had previously conceded that because the relative contribution of lead exposure from any one source could not be precisely quantified, "the most cost-effective approach to the aggregate prevention of excessive lead exposure has not been defined." 38 Fed. Reg. 1,258, 1,259 (1973). EPA continued, "the lead in gasoline issue presents particular difficulties regarding the cost-effectiveness of reducing lead contents below the level of 0.5 grams per gallon." So apparently EPA used its misgivings about whether removing lead from gasoline below 0.5 grams was cost-effective, when compared to other techniques for reducing the total body burden of lead, as a reason to stop at that point. Under its regulatory statutes, cost-effectiveness is occasionally a requirement, such as in the case of CERCLA's requirement that remedial measures be "cost-effective," 42 U.S.C. §9621(b) but more often it is not.

If EPA thought it "difficult, if not impossible" to determine an acceptable level of airborne lead, should it have ordered an immediate removal of all lead from gasoline? This would have been akin to the district court injunction in *Reserve*, whereas what EPA actually did more nearly resembled the court of appeals' decision there. If EPA had ordered immediate removal, should the court of appeals have reversed?

Recall, finally, that the decision to phase down lead content in gasoline that was sustained by *Ethyl Corp.* subsequently assisted EPA in both demonstrating the connection between lead exposure and adverse health effects and in quantifying those effects. Subsequently, EPA's decision to eliminate lead from gasoline entirely was supported by a risk assessment and then a cost-benefit analysis — based on data available because the decision to phase down lead had permitted scientists to understand the health effects of removing lead from the atmosphere.

### 2.  *Statutory Authorities for Regulating Risks*

A complex array of statutory authorities addresses the risks presented by toxic chemicals. The Toxic Substances Control Act (TSCA), which gives EPA authority over any chemical substance or mixture (other than pesticides regulated by FIFRA and food products, drugs, and cosmetics, regulated by the Food and Drug Administration), appears to provide the most comprehensive regulatory authority, although until it was amended in 2016 the procedural and evidentiary demands of the statute sapped it of much of its effectiveness. The Federal Insecticide, Fungicide, and Rodenticide Act (FIFRA) governs EPA's regulation of pesticides; the Safe Drinking Water Act (SDWA) governs EPA regulation of contaminants in public drinking water systems; section 112 of the Clean Air Act requires EPA to regulate emissions of hazardous air pollutants; and sections 304($l$) and 307 of the Clean Water Act require EPA to regulate toxic water pollutants. Agencies other than EPA also have significant authority to regulate toxic substances. The Food and Drug Administration (FDA), which is part of the Department of Health and Human Services, has jurisdiction over foods, drugs, cosmetics, and medical devices under the federal Food, Drug, and Cosmetic Act (FDCA). The Labor Department's Occupational Safety and Health Administration (OSHA) is responsible for protecting workers against toxic chemical hazards in the workplace pursuant to the Occupational Safety and Health Act (OSH Act). Workers in mines are protected separately under the federal Mine Safety and Health Act (MSHA), which is administered by the Department of Labor and its National Institute of Occupational Safety and Health. The Consumer Product Safety Commission (CPSC) regulates hazardous consumer products pursuant to the Consumer Product Safety Act (CPSA) and it also administers the Federal Hazardous Substances Act and the Poison Prevention Packaging Act, which require labeling of hazardous and poisonous substances. The Nuclear Regulatory Commission is responsible for regulating radioactive substances under the Atomic Energy Act.

This is by no means an exhaustive list. Several other statutes address specific aspects of the toxic substances problem. In 1985, the Office of Science and Technology Policy identified 21 different statutes that may be used by 12 different agencies just to regulate carcinogens.

Statutory authorities for regulating toxics differ greatly in the extent to which they require review or approval prior to the manufacture or use of such substances. The federal Food, Drug, and Cosmetic Act requires FDA approval prior to the marketing of new food additives, drugs, and cosmetics. EPA similarly must approve the registration of new pesticides under FIFRA prior to marketing. TSCA, however, is not a licensing statute. Under it, EPA must be notified 90 days prior to the manufacture of a new chemical or the application of an old chemical to a significant new use, and the EPA can intervene to require further information, but no specific approval is required unless EPA does intervene. Another class of statutes, "standard-setting laws," requires agencies to establish standards limiting toxic emissions, controlling worker exposure to toxics, or mandating warning labels on products. These include the OSH Act, the Safe Drinking Water Act, the Consumer Product Safety Act, TSCA, and the provisions of the Clean Air and Clean Water Acts that deal with toxic substances.

The early EPA actions regarding lead, as well as the various judicial opinions in *Ethyl Corp.* and *Reserve*, took differing approaches to the "how safe is safe?" question, and these modern statutes regulating toxic substances do so as well. Three general types capture most of the statutory approaches. Some statutes (e.g., FIFRA and TSCA before it was amended in 2016) require that regulators balance the threat to public health against the cost of regulation when setting regulatory standards — thus, they are risk-benefit balancing statutes. Others (e.g., the OSH Act and the Safe Drinking Water Act) direct that threats to health be regulated as stringently as is feasible. Such statutes are a special case of technology-based standards. Because the concern with toxics exposure at any level is so great that Congress frequently expresses the desire to eliminate exposure if only it were feasible, such standards as those of the OSH Act and the SDWA can be termed *feasibility-limited* standards. A third approach, which is embodied in the national ambient air quality standards of the Clean Air Act as well as in the original toxic air pollutants provisions of the Clean Air Act and the Delaney Clauses of the FDCA, requires that standards be based exclusively on concerns for protecting public health (health-based statutes). As amended in 1990, section 112 now requires that technology-based controls (reflecting the maximum achievable control technology, or MACT) be applied initially to control hazardous air pollutants, supplemented with purely health-based controls if the "residual risk" remaining after MACT has been applied is sufficiently great.

Sometimes specific types of risk-creating activities have been singled out for distinctive treatment within a broader regulatory regime. For instance, the Delaney Clause applies a health-based standard of zero to food additives, originally including pesticide residues in raw or processed foods, and to color additives if the additives caused cancer in laboratory animals. The Food Quality Protection Act (FQPA) of 1996 now exempts pesticide residues from the food additives covered by Delaney and makes them subject to a standard of "reasonable certainty of no harm." The legislative history of the Act suggests that many members of Congress anticipated this being interpreted as exposing individuals to no greater than a 1-in-1-million risk of cancer, but the degree of certainty required under FQPA is undefined in the statute itself.

These statutes also differ in the amount and kind of evidence that must be shown before a substance can be regulated and in the type of controls that they authorize regulators to impose. Some laws authorize outright prohibitions on the manufacture or use of certain chemicals (e.g., TSCA, FIFRA, FDCA), while others authorize the establishment of emission standards or ambient concentration limits (CAA, CWA, OSH Act), restrictions on use, and labeling, warning, or reporting requirements (TSCA). Figure 3.3 offers a rough comparison of the statutory authorities for regulating toxics.

### 3.  The Toxic Substances Control Act

For four decades the Toxic Substances Control Act (TSCA) served as the classic example of a law that required EPA to balance costs against benefits prior to regulating toxic substances. In fact, the term "unreasonable risk" appeared 35 times in 33 pages of the statute. Rodgers, The Lesson of the Owls and the Crows: The Role of Deception in the Evolution of the Environmental Statutes, 4 J. Land Use & Envtl. L. 377, 379 (1989). This proved to be enormously problematic and may explain why only five chemicals were regulated by EPA under TSCA prior to

**Figure 3.3    Summary of Federal Laws Authorizing Regulation of Toxic Substances**

BALANCING STATUTES

| Law | Type of controls | Threshold finding | Basis for controls |
|---|---|---|---|
| Food, Drug, and Cosmetic Act (FDCA) | controls levels of natural components of foods | "poisonous or deleterious . . . unless the quantity does not ordinarily render it injurious to health" | balances risk against need for plentiful and affordable food |
| FDCA | controls levels of environmental contaminants in foods | "poisonous or deleterious . . . unless the quantity does not ordinarily render it injurious to health" | balances risk against whether required, unavoidable, or measurable |
| FDCA | regulates introduction of new drugs and biologics | "substantial evidence that [it is] safe and effective"; "no imminent hazard to public health" | balances risk against efficacy and impact on health |
| Federal Insecticide, Fungicide, and Rodenticide Act | prohibits use of pesticides unless registered by EPA; EPA may restrict or condition usage | "will not generally cause any unreasonable risk to man or the environment" | balances adverse impacts of pesticide on human health and the environment against benefits of pesticide |
| Toxic Substances Control Act | can ban or restrict production, use, or disposal of existing chemicals (§6); can require testing of chemicals where data are inadequate to assess risk (§4); requires 90-day notice to EPA before introduction into commerce of new chemicals (§5) | "presents or will present an unreasonable risk of injury to human health or the environment" | "determination whether risk is 'unreasonable . . . without considering cost or other nonrisk factors' " |
| Consumer Product Safety Act | authorizes bans of unreasonably dangerous consumer products | "an unreasonable risk of injury" | balances risk against product utility, cost, and availability |

TECHNOLOGY- or FEASIBLITY-LIMITED STATUTES

| Law | Type of controls | Threshold finding | Basis for controls |
|---|---|---|---|
| Occupational Safety and Health Act | can limit worker exposure to toxic substances in the workplace | existence of a significant risk that can be reduced appreciably by regulation | ensure that no worker suffers material impairment of health or functional capacity to the extent feasible |
| Safe Drinking Water Act | limits contaminants in public drinking water supplies | "may have an adverse effect on the health of persons" | reduces contaminants as closely as feasible to levels where no adverse health effects will occur and which allow an adequate margin of safety |

| *Law* | *Type of controls* | *Threshold finding* | *Basis for controls* |
|---|---|---|---|
| Clean Water Act | sets effluent standards for discharges of toxic pollutants into surface waters | "identifiable effects on health and welfare" | uses best available technology to control discharges with health-based water quality standards as backstop |

HEALTH-BASED STATUTES

| | | | |
|---|---|---|---|
| §112 of the Clean Air Act | establishes emission standards for hazardous air pollutants | substance is one of 189 chemicals on initial list specified in statute or added to list on finding that it may present "a threat of adverse human health effects" | sets limits that "provide an ample margin of safety to protect the public health" if technology-based controls fail to do so after 8 years |
| FDCA | controls levels of added substances in food | "any poisonous or deleterious substance which may render it injurious to health" | reasonable certainty of no harm |
| FDCA | controls levels of added substances in food | "induce[s] cancer in laboratory animals" | reasonable certainty of no harm |

its amendment in 2016 by the Frank S. Lautenberg Chemical Safety for the 21st Century Act. Faced with uncertainties of data, the necessity of making assumptions linking data to policy-related conclusions, and decision making on the "frontiers of scientific knowledge," TSCA was one of the regulatory statutes that "eat up heroic amounts of money, remain information-starved, feature shameless manipulation of the data, face crippling political pressure, and produce little abatement." Oliver A. Houck, Tales from a Troubled Marriage: Science and Law in Environmental Policy 163, 169-170 (2003).

TSCA grants EPA broad authority to regulate the manufacture, processing, distribution, use, or disposal of any chemical substance on a finding that there is a "reasonable basis to conclude" that such an activity "presents or will present an unreasonable risk of injury to health or the environment," TSCA §6(a), 15 U.S.C. §2605(a). Prior to 2016, TSCA explicitly required EPA to determine whether a substance poses an "unreasonable risk," considering findings concerning not only health and environmental effects, but also the benefits of various uses of the substance, the availability of substitutes for it, and "the reasonably ascertainable economic consequences" of regulation. As amended in 2016 by the Frank R. Lautenberg Chemical Safety for the 21st Century Act, TSCA requires EPA to "consider and publish a statement based on reasonably available information with respect to . . . the costs and benefits of the proposed and final regulatory action and of the 1 or more primary alternative regulatory actions considered by the Administrator." TSCA §6(c)(2), 15 U.S.C. §2605(c)(2). But the initial decision whether the chemical poses an "unreasonable risk" and must therefore be regulated is to be made "without consideration of costs or other nonrisk factors." TSCA §6(b)(4), 15 U.S.C. §2605(b)(4).

Until it was amended in 2016, TSCA directed EPA to regulate "to the extent necessary to protect adequately against such risk using the least burdensome requirements." TSCA §6(a), 15 U.S.C. §2605(a). Although the legislative history of TSCA indicated that Congress did not envision that EPA would be required to perform quantitative risk assessments followed by formal cost-benefit analyses, this is how it was interpreted in the crippling *Corrosion Proof Fittings* decision. The House Committee report on the 1976 TSCA legislation explained that the balancing required by section 6 "does not require a formal benefit-cost analysis" because "such an analysis would not be very useful" given the difficulty of assigning monetary values to benefits and costs of chemical regulation. Toxic Substances Control Act, Report by the Comm. on Interstate and Foreign Commerce, U.S. House of Representatives, H.R. Rep. 94-1341, 94th Cong., 2d Sess. 14 (1976). The Senate Committee report emphasized that while section 6(c) required some balancing, "it is not feasible to reach a decision just on the basis of quantitative comparisons" because "[i]n comparing risks, costs, and benefits . . . one is weighing noncommensurates." It stressed that EPA also must give "full consideration" to the extraordinary "burdens of human suffering and premature death." Toxic Substances Control Act, Report of the Senate Comm. on Commerce, S. Rep. 94-698, 94th Cong., 2d Sess. 13 (1976).

Despite this legislative history, EPA's most aggressive use of its broad authority under section 6 of TSCA was struck down in court in the decision below. Acutely aware of the enormous difficulty of protecting the public from asbestos in schools and buildings, EPA announced in 1979 that it would consider banning all remaining uses of asbestos. 44 Fed. Reg. 60,061 (1979). It took EPA nearly ten years to promulgate a rule prohibiting, at staged intervals, the future manufacture, importation, processing, and distribution in commerce of asbestos in almost all products. EPA, Asbestos: Manufacture, Importation, Processing and Distribution in Commerce Prohibitions, 54 Fed. Reg. 29,460 (1989). The rule was based on a 45,000-page record. EPA "concluded that exposure to asbestos during the life cycles of many asbestos-containing products poses an unreasonable risk of injury to human health." It also found "that section 6 of TSCA is the ideal statutory authority to regulate the risks posed by asbestos exposure." EPA determined that

> only the staged-ban approach employed in this final rule will adequately control the asbestos exposure risk posed by the product categories affected by this rule. Other options either fail to address significant portions of the life cycle risk posed by products subject to the rule or are unreasonably burdensome. EPA has, therefore, concluded that the actions taken in this rule represent the least burdensome means of reducing the risk posed by exposure to asbestos during the life cycles of the products that are subject to the bans.

The asbestos industry challenged EPA's asbestos ban in the following case. The court's decision crippled TSCA and was the major reason its approach to regulation was changed so substantially by Congress when it enacted the Lautenberg Act in 2016.

## Corrosion Proof Fittings v. EPA

947 F.2d 1201 (5th Cir. 1991)

JERRY E. SMITH, Circuit Judge:

### 1. LEAST BURDENSOME AND REASONABLE

TSCA requires that the EPA use the least burdensome regulation to achieve its goals of minimum reasonable risk. This statutory requirement can create problems in evaluating just what is a "reasonable risk." Congress' rejection of a no-risk policy, however, also means that in certain cases, the least burdensome yet still adequate solution may entail somewhat more risk than would other, known regulations that are far more burdensome on the industry and the economy. The very language of TSCA requires that the EPA, once it has determined what an acceptable level of non-zero risk is, choose the least burdensome method of reaching that level.

In this case, the EPA banned, for all practical purposes, all present and future uses of asbestos—a position the petitioners characterize as the "death penalty alternative," as this is the *most* burdensome of all possible alternatives listed as open to the EPA under TSCA. TSCA not only provides the EPA with a list of alternative actions, but also provides those alternatives in order of how burdensome they are. [TSCA §6(a)(1)-(7); 15 U.S.C. §2605a(1)-(7).] Total bans head the list as the most burdensome regulatory option.

By choosing the harshest remedy given to it under TSCA, the EPA assigned to itself the toughest burden in satisfying TSCA's requirement that its alternative be the least burdensome of all those offered to it. . . . [T]he EPA's regulation cannot stand if there is any other regulation that would achieve an acceptable level of risk as mandated by TSCA. . . .

The EPA considered, and rejected, such options as labeling asbestos products, thereby warning users and workers involved in the manufacture of asbestos-containing products of the chemical's dangers, and stricter workplace rules. EPA also rejected controlled use of asbestos in the workplace and deferral to other government agencies charged with worker and consumer exposure to industrial and product hazards, such as OSHA, the CPSC, and the Mine Safety and Health Administration (MSHA). The EPA determined that deferral to these other agencies was inappropriate because no one other authority could address all the risks posed "throughout the life cycle" by asbestos, and any action by one or more of the other agencies still would leave an unacceptable residual risk.

Much of the EPA's analysis is correct, and the EPA's basic decision to use TSCA as a comprehensive statute designed to fight a multi-industry problem was a proper one that we uphold today on review. What concerns us, however, is the manner in which the EPA conducted some of its analysis. TSCA requires the EPA to consider, along with the effect of toxic substances on human health and the environment, "the benefits of such substance[s] or mixture[s] for various uses and the availability of substitutes for such uses," as well as "the reasonably ascertainable economic consequences of the rule, after consideration for the effect on the national economy, small business, technological innovation, the environment, and public health." Id. §2605(c)(1)(C-D).

The EPA presented two comparisons in the record: a world with no further regulation under TSCA, and a world in which no manufacture of asbestos takes place. The EPA rejected calculating how many lives a less burdensome regulation would save, and at what cost. Furthermore the EPA, when calculating the benefits of its ban, explicitly refused to compare it to an improved workplace in which currently available control technology is utilized. This decision artificially inflated the purported benefits of the rule by using a baseline comparison substantially lower than what currently available technology could yield. . . .

This comparison of two static worlds is insufficient to satisfy the dictates of TSCA. While the EPA may have shown that a world with a complete ban of asbestos might be preferable to one in which there is only the current amount of regulation, the EPA has failed to show that there is not some intermediate state of regulation that would be superior to both the currently-regulated and the completely-banned world. Without showing that asbestos regulation would be ineffective, the EPA cannot discharge its TSCA burden of showing that its regulation is the least burdensome available to it.

Upon an initial showing of product danger, the proper course for the EPA to follow is to consider each regulatory option, beginning with the least burdensome, and the costs and benefits of regulation under each option. The EPA cannot simply skip several rungs, as it did in this case, for in doing so, it may skip a less-burdensome alternative mandated by TSCA. Here, although the EPA mentions the problems posed by intermediate levels of regulation, it takes no steps to calculate the costs and benefits of these intermediate levels. Without doing this it is impossible, both for the EPA and for this court on review, to know that none of these alternatives was less burdensome than the ban in fact chosen by the agency. . . .

## 2. THE EPA'S CALCULATIONS

Furthermore, we are concerned about some of the methodology employed by the EPA in making various of the calculations that it did perform. In order to aid the EPA's reconsideration of this and other cases, we present our concerns here. . . .

In performing its calculus, the EPA only included the number of lives saved over the next thirteen years, and counted any additional lives saved as simply "unquantified benefits." The EPA and intervenors now seek to use these unquantified lives saved to justify calculations as to which the benefits seem far outweighed by the astronomical costs. For example, the EPA plans to save about three lives with its ban of asbestos pipe, at a cost of $128-227 million (i.e., approximately $43-76 million per life saved). Although the EPA admits that the price tag is high, it claims that the lives saved past the year 2000 justify the price.

Such calculations not only lessen the value of the EPA's cost analysis, but also make any meaningful judicial review impossible. While TSCA contemplates a useful place for unquantified benefits beyond the EPA's calculation, unquantified benefits never were intended as a trump card allowing the EPA to justify any cost calculus, no matter how high.

The concept of unquantified benefits, rather, is intended to allow the EPA to provide a rightful place for any remaining benefits that are impossible to quantify after the EPA's best attempt, but which still are of some concern. But the allowance for unquantified costs is not intended to allow the EPA to perform its calculations over an arbitrarily short period so as to preserve a large unquantified portion.

Unquantified benefits can, at times, permissibly tip the balance in close cases. They cannot, however, be used to effect a wholesale shift on the balance beam. Such a use makes a mockery of the requirements of TSCA that the EPA weigh the costs of its actions before it chooses the least burdensome alternatives.

We do not today determine what an appropriate period for the EPA's calculations would be, as this is a matter better left for agency discretion. We do note, however, that the choice of a thirteen-year period is so short as to make the unquantified period so unreasonably large that any EPA reliance upon it must be displaced. . . .

### 3. REASONABLE BASIS

In addition to showing that its regulation is the least burdensome one necessary to protect the environment adequately, the EPA also must show that it has a reasonable basis for the regulation, 15 U.S.C. §2605(a). . . .

Most problematical to us is the EPA's ban of products for which no substitutes presently are available. In these cases, the EPA bears a tough burden indeed to show that under TSCA a ban is the least burdensome alternative, as TSCA explicitly instructs the EPA to consider "the benefits of such substance or mixture for various uses and the availability of substitutes for such uses." [15 U.S.C. §2605(c)(1)(C).] These words are particularly appropriate where the EPA actually has decided to ban a product, rather than simply restrict its use, for it is in these cases that the lack of an adequate substitute is most troubling under TSCA. . . .

Considering that many of the substitutes that the EPA itself concedes will be used in the place of asbestos have known carcinogenic effects, the EPA not only cannot assure this court that it has taken the least burdensome alternative, but cannot even prove that its regulations will increase workplace safety. Eager to douse the dangers of asbestos, the agency inadvertently actually may increase the risk of injury Americans face. The EPA's explicit failure to consider the toxicity of likely substitutes thus deprives its order of a reasonable basis.

Our opinion should not be construed to state that the EPA has an affirmative duty to seek out and test every workplace substitute for any product it seeks to regulate. TSCA does not place such a burden upon the agency. We do not think it unreasonable, however, once interested parties introduce credible studies and evidence showing the toxicity of workplace substitutes, or the decreased effectiveness of safety alternatives such as non-asbestos brakes, that the EPA then consider whether its regulations are even increasing workplace safety, and whether the increased risk occasioned by dangerous substitutes makes the proposed regulation no longer reasonable. In the words of the EPA's own release that initiated the asbestos rulemaking, we direct that the agency consider the adverse health effects of asbestos substitutes "for comparison with the known hazards of asbestos," so that it can conduct, as it promised in 1979, a "balanced consideration of the environmental, economic, and social impact of any action taken by the agency."

In short, a death is a death, whether occasioned by asbestos or by a toxic substitute product, and the EPA's decision not to evaluate the toxicity of known carcinogenic substitutes is not a reasonable action under TSCA. Once an interested party brings forth credible evidence suggesting the toxicity of the probable or only alternatives to a substance, the EPA must consider the comparative toxic costs of each. Its failure to do so in this case thus deprived its regulation of a reasonable basis, at least in regard to those products as to which petitioners introduced credible evidence of the dangers of the likely substitutes.

## 4.  UNREASONABLE RISK OF INJURY

The final requirement the EPA must satisfy before engaging in any TSCA rulemaking is that it only take steps designed to prevent "unreasonable" risks. . . .

That the EPA must balance the costs of its regulations against their benefits further is reinforced by the requirement that it seek the least burdensome regulation. While Congress did not dictate that the EPA engage in an exhaustive, full-scale cost-benefit analysis, it did require the EPA to consider both sides of the regulatory equation, and it rejected the notion that the EPA should pursue the reduction of workplace risk at any cost. Thus, "Congress also plainly intended the EPA to consider the economic impact of any actions taken by it under . . . TSCA."

Even taking all of the EPA's figures as true, and evaluating them in the light most favorable to the agency's decision . . . the agency's analysis results in figures as high as $74 million per life saved. For example, the EPA states that its ban of asbestos pipe will save three lives over the next thirteen years, at a cost of $128-277 million ($43-76 million per life saved), depending upon the price of substitutes; that its ban of asbestos shingles will cost $23-34 million to save 0.32 statistical lives ($72-106 million per life saved); that its ban of asbestos coatings will cost $46-181 million to save 3.33 lives ($14-54 million per life saved); and that its ban of asbestos paper products will save 0.60 lives at a cost of $4-5 million ($7-8 million per life saved).

While we do not sit as a regulatory agency that must make the difficult decision as to what an appropriate expenditure is to prevent someone from incurring the risk of an asbestos-related death, we do note that the EPA, in its zeal to ban any and all asbestos products, basically ignored the cost side of the TSCA equation. The EPA would have this court believe that Congress, when it enacted its requirement that the EPA consider the economic impacts of its regulations, thought that spending $200-300 million to save approximately seven lives (approximately $30-40 million per life) over thirteen years is reasonable.

As we stated in the OSHA context, until an agency "can provide substantial evidence that the benefits to be achieved by [a regulation] bear a reasonable relationship to the costs imposed by the reduction, it cannot show that the standard is reasonably necessary to provide safe or healthful workplaces." Although the OSHA statute differs in major respects from TSCA, the statute does require substantial evidence to support the EPA's contentions that its regulations both have a reasonable basis and are the least burdensome means to a reasonably safe workplace.

The EPA's willingness to argue that spending $23.7 million to save less than one-third of a life reveals that its economic review of its regulations, as required by TSCA, was meaningless. As the petitioners' brief and our review of EPA case-law reveals, such high costs are rarely, if ever, used to support a safety regulation. [The court then reviewed each of four subcategories of product bans included in the rulemaking—friction products (where EPA had determined that three-fourths of the anticipated asbestos-related cancer benefits would be achieved); asbestos-cement pipe products; gaskets, roofing, shingles, and paper products; and products produced outside the United States—and found each of them legally unjustified, in each case substantially on the basis of the general deficiencies reviewed in the first part of the opinion. However, the court upheld EPA's decision to ban products that once were, but no longer are, being produced in the United States, noting that "sections 5 and 6 of TSCA allow the EPA to ban a product that presents or will present a *significant* risk" (emphasis the court's).]

## NOTES AND QUESTIONS

1. **TSCA and Multimedia Regulation.** Why did the court strike down the asbestos ban? Note that the court states that "EPA's basic decision to use TSCA as a comprehensive statute designed to fight a multi-industry problem was a proper one that we uphold today on review." What then was wrong with EPA's decision to ban asbestos? The *Corrosion Proof Fittings* decision served as a major impetus for adoption of the Frank R. Lautenberg Chemical Safety for the 21st Century Act, discussed below. As you read the materials on the new legislation, consider whether or not it would change the result in *Corrosion Proof.*

2. **Sufficiency of Evidence.** The court held that EPA had presented insufficient evidence to justify its asbestos ban. In what respects was EPA's evidence lacking? Note that EPA's decision to ban asbestos had not been undertaken lightly. It was the product of ten years of Agency activity that included an advance notice of proposed rulemaking in 1979 and a data collection rule promulgated under section 8(a) of TSCA in 1982. EPA had held 22 days of public hearings, taken thousands of pages of testimony, and received 13,000 pages of comments from more than 250 interested parties. The agency and its contractors had prepared ten major regulatory analysis documents in support of the rule. What additional information would EPA need and what additional analysis would it have to undertake to justify an asbestos ban?

3. **Reasonableness of Risk.** Did the court believe that the risks posed by asbestos were not unreasonable in light of the cost of the asbestos ban? EPA had estimated that the quantifiable benefits from the rule included the prevention of at least 202 cases of cancer at a total cost of $459 million over 13 years. Did the court think that this was too much for society to spend to prevent asbestos risks, did it simply disagree with EPA's calculations of costs and benefits, or both? Do you think that a risk that costs more than $2 million per life saved to eliminate is reasonable?

4. **Nonquantified Benefits.** EPA's benefit estimates did not attempt to quantify certain benefits including the prevention of asbestosis and certain other diseases and the avoided costs of treating asbestos diseases and lost productivity. EPA also stated that if it had followed the normal practice of using "upper bound" estimates, its risk assessment could have projected 10 times more lung cancer deaths and 20 times more mesothelioma deaths due to asbestos exposure. Recall the concern that cost-benefit analysis exhibits a tendency to "downgrade" unquantified benefits. How does the court of appeals treat the unquantified benefits of EPA's ban? Is its treatment appropriate? Do you believe that unquantified benefits should only be used as a "tie-breaker" in cost-benefit analyses?

5. **The Risks of Substitutes.** The data available to EPA concerning the health risks posed by asbestos were far better than the data available for virtually any other toxic substance. Unlike many other substances, scientific understanding of the

dangers of asbestos is based on the results of numerous epidemiological studies that have documented scores of thousands of deaths from asbestos exposure. The court faulted EPA for not giving more serious consideration to the potential risks posed by other substances that might be substituted for asbestos. For example, vinyl chloride is used to make PVC pipe, a likely substitute for asbestos-cement pipe. Under what circumstances did the court think EPA must assess the risk of substitutes? How extensively must EPA analyze such products?

6. **Technology-Forcing Regulation.** The court criticized EPA's assumption that the availability of a waiver would reduce the costs of replacing products for which no adequate substitutes for asbestos currently were available. Is the court suggesting that EPA should not be able to use TSCA to force the development of safer technology? Would a better approach for forcing technology be to impose a tax on asbestos products that increases over time?

7. **Risk Disaggregation.** EPA had found that 102 of the deaths avoided came from its ban of asbestos in friction products—primarily brake drums. The cost of this ban was estimated to be between $31 million and $85 million. The court indicated that it might have been inclined to uphold this part of the asbestos ban if that had been the only part of the rule challenged. As long as the court was remanding, however, it found that it was "impossible to ignore" EPA's failure to study the effect of nonasbestos brakes on automotive safety, "despite credible evidence that non-asbestos brakes could increase significantly the number of highway fatalities." Was EPA's failure to conduct further study of the highway fatality issue justified? To what extent does the court's decision hinge on disaggregating the overall risks posed by asbestos in order to analyze risk and cost estimates for each type of product containing it?

8. **"Cleanup" Ban on Future Products.** The one aspect of the asbestos ban that the court upheld was a ban on asbestos products not currently being produced. How could EPA determine that the benefits of such a ban would outweigh its costs? Such products pose no current risks. The court stated that although "EPA cannot possibly evaluate the costs and benefits of banning unknown, uninvented products, we hold that the nebulousness of these future products, combined with TSCA's language authorizing the EPA to ban products that 'will' create a public risk, allows the EPA to ban future uses of asbestos even in products not yet on the market." This portion of the decision represents a strong endorsement of a precautionary approach to regulation that upholds a vital part of EPA's ban that prevents the asbestos industry from introducing new products in the United States.

### The Frank R. Lautenberg Chemical Safety for the 21st Century Act

While the *Corrosion Proof Fittings* decision derailed EPA's efforts to ban asbestos in the United States, most developed countries have now banned asbestos. In September 2000, the World Trade Organization (WTO) rejected a challenge by Canada to France's decision to ban imports of chrysotile asbestos. The WTO panel ruled that because the dangers of asbestos are so substantial, countries could ban its import entirely as a necessary step to protect the health of their citizens. As of January 2021, 55 countries had adopted national asbestos bans, including the members of the European Union, Australia, Argentina, Chile, Israel, Japan, Saudi Arabia, Switzerland, and Turkey. China and India remain the two largest consumers of asbestos, while Russia and China are the two largest producers.

By preventing EPA from banning asbestos, the *Corrosion Proof Fittings* decision illustrated how toothless TSCA had become. This, coupled with the success of the EU's pre-market testing requirements, convinced EPA, environmental groups, and even the chemical industry that TSCA required legislative reform. On June 7, 2016, the U.S. Senate by a voice vote passed the Frank R. Lautenberg Chemical Safety for the 21st Century Act. The legislation passed the U.S. House by a vote of 403-12 on May 24, 2016. President Obama signed the legislation into law on June 22, 2016. This is the first comprehensive updating of TSCA since it was first adopted in 1976. The legislation is the product of a bipartisan agreement initially announced in May 2013 by Democratic Senator Frank Lautenberg and Republican Senator David Vitter. The legislation is named in honor of Lautenberg, who died suddenly less than two weeks after reaching the agreement. The legislation requires EPA to review and make a risk determination for all new chemicals. It establishes risk-based priorities for testing and evaluation of chemicals, and it requires the chemical industry to contribute funding to support such efforts. Significantly, it repeals the requirement that EPA impose the "least burdensome requirement" that adequately controls the risk.

The Lautenberg Act was supported by both the chemical industry and major environmental groups, including the Environmental Defense Fund. A few environmentalists and some state officials complained that the legislation was not stringent enough and could preempt state regulations. However, it is widely agreed that the legislation was far better than the existing law, which put too great a burden on EPA to use cost-benefit analysis to justify regulation and preempted state regulation of chemicals regulated by EPA.

In addition to repealing the mandate to adopt only the "least burdensome requirement" that adequately controls the risk, the other most significant change made by the Lautenberg Act is to bar the consideration of costs and other nonrisk factors when assessing whether a chemical poses an "unreasonable risk" to health or the environment. Thus, no cost-benefit balancing is to be used in making an unreasonable risk determination. Chemicals found to pose unreasonable risks are to be regulated to ensure that they no longer pose such risks. This applies both to new chemicals for which pre-manufacture notifications are received pursuant to TSCA section 5 and to existing chemicals reviewed under section 6. EPA still must determine the "reasonably ascertainable economic consequences" of regulations to eliminate unreasonable risks from existing chemicals. Regulations must be sufficient to ensure protection of "susceptible and highly exposed populations" including but not limited to children, pregnant women, workers, and the elderly.

The Lautenberg Act also changes section 5 of TSCA to require EPA to make affirmative determinations concerning the risks of new chemicals or significant uses of existing chemicals before they can be marketed. EPA must designate existing chemicals as high-priority substances for risk evaluations or low-priority substances. Risk evaluations are to be completed as soon as practicable, but not later than three years after their initiation, though the agency may extend this period for up to six months.

In November 2016 EPA designated the first ten existing chemicals for risk evaluation, a group that included trichloroethylene (TCE), N-methylpyrrolidone (NMP), carbon tetrachloride, methylene chloride, perchloroethylene (PERC), and asbestos. However, with the change of administration in January 2017, EPA shifted gears on its interpretation of the Lautenberg Act. In June 2017 EPA adopted final rules for prioritization and risk evaluation that interpreted its mandate under the Lautenberg reforms as narrowly as possible. For example, existing chemicals are now deemed "low priority" as a default, rather than after a finding that there is not an unreasonable risk, and the EPA administrator is allowed to determine what conditions of use are appropriate for review, instead of considering the whole lifecycle of the chemical. For example, in its scoping documents for risk evaluation of TCE, EPA concluded that it need not consider exposure pathways that could be regulated under other laws, interpreting these laws as reflecting Congress's judgment concerning the reasonableness of risk. Similarly, EPA's draft risk evaluations were narrower in scope than EPA's Scientific Advisory Committee on Chemicals thought appropriate. The Risk Evaluation Rule changed between proposal and finalization in response to industry commenters who claimed that EPA retained discretion under the new TSCA to limit risk evaluations to certain conditions of use, thereby narrowing EPA's regulatory power.

In August 2017, several environmental groups challenged EPA's rules to implement the Lautenberg Act. In *Safer Chemicals v. United States EPA*, 943 F.2d 397 (9th Cir. 2019), the Ninth Circuit ruled that some of the challenges were premature, while noting that: "If EPA does, in the future, fail to consider all conditions of use together in completing a risk evaluation, and if Petitioners are harmed by that failure, then Petitioners may, under TSCA, seek review of EPA's 'no unreasonable risk' determination." The court further found that TSCA's definition of "conditions of use" includes broader uses than EPA's proposed definition, but narrower than petitioners' definition, which included "legacy uses." This was considered a success for environmental groups as it left the door open for future litigation.

In March 2019 EPA did ban the use of methylene chloride in consumer paint and coating removal products, finding that it posed unreasonable risks. However, it did not ban the substance itself, instead deferring on the unreasonable risk determination for commercial uses of the substance. The Trump EPA also abandoned or deferred acting on two other proposals to ban chemicals made after passage of the Lautenberg Act: TCE and N-methylpyrrolidone (NMP). For new chemicals, due to backlogs in the required pre-manufacture notifications (PMNs), EPA has accelerated the PMN approval process. This process is worrisome to observers, who believe a faster process will make EPA less discriminating in its definition of unreasonable risk under TSCA 5(B)(3)(C). President Biden has asked agencies to review this and other EPA decisions made during the Trump administration. See Executive Order 13,990, Sec. 2, directing agencies to review actions taken between January 20, 2017, and January 20, 2021, that are inconsistent with the Biden administration's policy of "limiting exposure to dangerous chemicals and pesticides."

## NOTES AND QUESTIONS

1. Would the *Corrosion Proof Fittings* decision have been decided differently if the Lautenberg Act reforms had been in place when EPA tried to ban asbestos? Consider in particular the impact of dropping the "least burdensome means" requirement and the exclusion of cost and other nonrisk considerations from the risk determination.

2. As of June 2020 EPA had 32 existing chemicals under review, but it also had more than 32,000 active chemicals in its Chemical Registry. The agency had not taken a single action to use the revised provisions of section 4 of TSCA that make it easier to require chemical testing.

3. The most contentious issue with the Trump administration's implementation of the Lautenberg Act is that its risk evaluation procedures do not consider the totality of risks from chemicals to which workers and the public are exposed. Risks to workers are deemed adequately controlled by the Occupational Safety and Health Act, while public exposure to chemicals in the air and drinking water are deemed to have been handled by the Clean Air and Safe Drinking Water Acts. As the problem of exposure to PFAS demonstrates, many chemical exposures are not adequately controlled by these laws.

4. After receiving a critical review of the Trump administration risk evaluation policies from the National Academies of Science, NAS, The Use of Systemic Reviews in EPA's Toxic Substances Control Act Risk Evaluations (2021), the Biden administration's EPA announced on February 16, 2021, that it will no longer follow the Trump policies. The agency announced that it has "begun to develop a TSCA systemic review protocol in collaboration with the agency's Office of Research and Development to incorporate approaches from the Integrated Risk Information System (IRIS) Program, which the Academies' report strongly recommends." EPA, EPA Commits to Strengthening Science Used in Chemical Risk Evaluations, Feb. 16, 2021. In April 2021, EPA finalized an updated toxicity assessment for perfluorobutane sulfonic acid (PFBS), a member of a larger group of per- and polyfluoroalkyl substances (PFAS) that was developed to replace PFOS. PFBS has been found widely in the environment and consumer products. Although EPA's assessment found that PFBS "is less toxic than PFOA and PFOS," it is only a small part of the thousands of chemical variations that have been made to PFAS. Given that these toxicity assessments can take years to complete, how can TSCA keep pace with all the thousands of chemical variations of PFAS?

---

## Principal Provisions of the Toxic Substances Control Act

*Section 4* authorizes the EPA administrator to require the testing of any chemical substance or mixture on finding that such testing is necessary because there are insufficient data from which the chemical's effects can be predicted and the chemical either "may present an unreasonable risk of injury to health or the environment" or the chemical is produced in substantial quantities or may result in substantial human exposure. The Lautenberg Act expanded EPA's authority by authorizing the agency to issue unilateral orders requiring "the development of new information relating to a chemical substance if the Administrator determines that the information is necessary."

*Section 5* prohibits any person from manufacturing any new chemical substance or from processing any existing chemical substance for a significant new use unless the person notifies the EPA administrator at least 90 days in advance and submits any data that the person believes show that the chemical will not present an unreasonable risk. Before the new chemical can be marketed or significant new use can be made EPA must make an affirmative risk determination concerning the chemical. The EPA administrator may prohibit or limit the manufacturing, processing, distribution, use, or disposal of any chemical if he or she determines that the information is insufficient to permit a reasoned evaluation of the effects of the chemical and that it either may present an unreasonable risk or that it may result in significant human exposure.

*Section 6* requires the EPA administrator to prohibit the manufacture, processing, or distribution in commerce of a chemical substance; to limit the amounts, concentrations, or uses of it; to require labeling or record-keeping concerning it; or to prohibit or otherwise regulate any manner or method of disposal of it, upon a finding that the chemical "presents or will present an unreasonable risk of injury to health or the environment." The Lautenberg Act specifies that the administrator's risk evaluation is to be made "without consideration of costs or other nonrisk factors." It also requires that EPA establish a "risk-based screening process" to evaluate existing and new chemicals to determine if they are "high priority substances" or "low priority substances" and it sets deadlines for completing risk evaluations of high priority substances.

*Section 7* authorizes the EPA administrator to sue to seize or to obtain other relief to protect against imminently hazardous chemical substances.

*Section 8* authorizes the EPA administrator to require record-keeping or the submission of reports concerning the manufacture or processing of chemical substances.

*Section 9* requires the EPA administrator to refer chemicals to other federal agencies for regulation or to use other laws administered by EPA to regulate the chemical if he or she determines that the risks posed by the chemical may be sufficiently prevented or reduced by action taken under other laws.

*Section 18* preempts state and local regulations of chemicals regulated under TSCA, but it gives EPA authority to grant preemption waivers to states and it exempts actions taken pursuant to a state law in effect on August 31, 2003, which includes California's Proposition 65 and Massachusetts' Toxics Use Reduction Act.

*Section 19* authorizes judicial review of EPA regulations issued under TSCA.

*Section 20* authorizes citizen suits against any person alleged to be in violation of TSCA or against the EPA administrator for failure to perform nondiscretionary duties.

*Section 21* authorizes citizen petitions for the commencement of rulemaking proceedings.

## 4. The Occupational Safety and Health Act

In most of the environmental statutes regulating toxic substances, Congress has not explicitly endorsed cost-benefit or risk-benefit balancing in setting standards to control pollution or to protect public health. Rather, it has instructed agencies to control potentially dangerous substances by using technology-based standards usually up to the point at which further reductions in exposures are no longer "feasible." The Occupational Safety and Health Act is a classic example of such legislation.

Because of the nature of the adverse health effects associated with toxics, when Congress employs a technology-based approach to manage toxics, it generally mandates that technology be used up to the point at which it becomes infeasible to reduce emissions any further. At least, that is the theory. This feasibility-limited type of technology-based approach bases the level of control on the capabilities of technology rather than on the degree of risk or the results of risk-benefit balancing. The degree of risk is not entirely irrelevant to feasibility-limited statutes, for they require that some threshold level of risk, sufficient to satisfy the statute's regulatory trigger, be found, as illustrated by the interpretation of OSHA in *Benzene*, requiring OSHA to make a "significant risk" determination prior to issuing a regulation. Once that trigger has been satisfied, feasibility-limited approaches to regulation then instruct the agency to eliminate as much of the health risk as can feasibly be done.

Feasibility has two components: the technological and the economic. Something may be strictly possible given the current state of technology, e.g., a trip to the moon or to Mars, but so expensive that it could force an entire industry to shut down if mandated by regulators. Most feasibility-limited regulation is so limited precisely to avoid causing such massive dislocations. Thus, regulatory authorities implementing feasibility-limited standards have had to give consideration to both technological and economic factors, as we will see below.

In the *Benzene* decision, Justice Rehnquist argued that the term "feasible" in the statute was unconstitutionally vague. Subsequent decisions, however, have given the standard greater definition. In the only other Supreme Court decision addressing the authority of OSHA to regulate toxics in the workplace, the Court held that feasible meant "capable of being done, executed, or effected," both technologically and economically. American Textile Manufacturers Institute, Inc. v. Donovan, 452 U.S. 490, 508-509 (1981). To show that a standard is technologically feasible, OSHA must demonstrate by substantial evidence "that modern technology has at least conceived some industrial strategies which are likely to be capable of meeting the PEL, and which the industries are generally capable of adopting." AFL-CIO v. OSHA, 965 F.2d 962, 980 (11th Cir. 1992). Economic feasibility requires a showing, again by substantial evidence, of a "reasonable likelihood that the[] costs [of implementation] will not threaten the existence or competitive structure of an industry, even if it does portend disaster for some marginal firms." Id. at 982.

One of the major difficulties with implementing feasibility-based regulation is that it can require complicated engineering assessments that are difficult and expensive to make, particularly when most relevant information is controlled by the regulated industry. OSHA notes that it "spends an average of $500,000 and takes one year of study to determine the lowest feasible level for a *single* substance" and that it "does not have the resources to engage in that kind of analysis for more than a few substances."

Industry has a clear incentive to engage in strategic behavior to convince OSHA that stringent standards are infeasible. Because industry has better access to cost data, it sometimes has convinced OSHA that certain standards are far more expensive than they actually prove to be. For example: "OSHA predicted the cotton dust standard would cost $500 million in 1977 dollars whereas industry predicted twice the cost and anticipated substantial technical problems. As a matter of fact, a later detailed study indicated that the standard cost only $250 million in 1983 dollars, improved industry competitiveness and productivity as well, and improved health more than predicted." 50 FR 51,121, 51,164-167 (Dec. 13, 1985).

OSHA's contractor predicted that the OSHA vinyl chloride standard could not generally be achieved with engineering controls and the attempt would cost $1.5 billion. As a matter of fact, compliance was achieved within three years at a cost of less than 10 percent of that predicted. 49 FR 5,001, 5,253 (Jan. 22, 1980). [54 Fed. Reg. 2,366 (1989).]

## NOTES AND QUESTIONS

1. Will statutes that regulate to the limits of feasibility always be more protective of the safety of the exposed population than statutes that regulate on the basis of a risk-benefit balance? Usually? What factors contribute to making feasibility-limited regulations more stringent than risk-benefit based-regulations? If you are a union member, do you prefer the OSH Act's approach to the sort of risk-benefit regulatory regime established by TSCA?

2. Some U.S. industries are in economic decline as a result of market forces or a failure to invest in research and development and capital improvements. If investments in modern engineering controls to protect workers from exposure to toxic substances are far more economically damaging to declining industries, does feasibility-limited regulation imply that workers in such industries must be exposed to greater risks?

3. Other industries are growing rapidly due to market forces but face stiff foreign competition. They argue that requirements that they invest in expensive engineering controls will cause them substantial economic harm. How would you respond to these concerns in the context of the OSH Act's definition of feasibility? Should the evidence of strategic behavior by industry lead regulatory agencies in the future to discount industry cost estimates by some factor?

### 5.   *The Safe Drinking Water Act*

The Safe Drinking Water Act (SDWA) is designed to ensure that drinking water from public water supply systems throughout the United States will be safe. It authorizes EPA to limit contaminants in public drinking water supply systems that have at least 15 service connections or that regularly serve at least 25 individuals. It also requires EPA to set standards for state underground injection control programs to prevent underground injection from endangering sources of drinking water. The principal provisions of the SDWA are described below.

As amended in 1996, the SDWA incorporates the most recent refinements in the development of a feasibility-limited regulatory regime. The statute sets up a three-step process that EPA must complete. The EPA is instructed to establish health-protective goals for contaminants in drinking water, which are termed maximum contaminant level goals (MCLGs). These are to be set at the level at which "no known or anticipated adverse effects on the health of persons occur and which allows an adequate margin of safety." MCLGs are not enforceable standards, however. EPA next determines the level that is as close "as is feasible" to the MCLGs. 42 U.S.C. §300g-1(b)(4)(B). This "maximum contaminant level" (MCL) becomes the enforceable standard unless EPA analyzes the "quantifiable and nonquantifiable" costs and benefits with respect to any MCL it proposes, 42 U.S.C. §300g-1(b)(3)(C), and determines that the strictest feasible standard "would not justify the costs of complying with the level," in which case EPA can back away from the maximum feasible standard to a lesser standard.

MCLGs are to be set at a level at which "no known or anticipated adverse effects on the health of persons occur and which allows an adequate margin of safety." Under this standard, EPA has quite often set the MCLG at zero. This is especially true when the contaminant under review is a known or suspected carcinogen. Consequently, SDWA goal-setting has become one of the frequent battlegrounds over whether EPA is justified in using this no-threshold default assumption.

EPA has also set nonzero MCLGs for suspected carcinogens when the evidence of carcinogenicity is considered to be rather weak. For example, in November 1985, EPA established final recommended maximum contaminant levels (the term for MCLGs prior to the 1986 Amendments) for eight volatile organic compounds. While EPA established zero as the health-based goal for those compounds that were known or probable carcinogens, it established a nonzero goal for vinylidene chloride because the evidence of its carcinogenicity was weak. To take into account the possibility that vinylidene chloride was a carcinogen, EPA reduced the level of its nonzero health-based goal by a factor of ten from the level that it would have set based solely on consideration of noncancer health effects. This approach was upheld in NRDC v. EPA, 824 F.2d 1211 (D.C. Cir. 1987). The court described EPA's decision to compromise in the face of uncertainty as "neither an unreasonable interpretation of the statute nor an unwise choice of policy." The court rejected the argument that EPA had violated its obligation to resolve uncertainty on the side of protecting public health with the following explanation:

The Act defines "feasible" to mean "feasible with the use of the best technology, treatment techniques and other means which the Administrator finds, after examination for efficacy under field conditions and not solely under laboratory conditions, are available (taking cost into consideration)." 42 U.S.C. §300g-1(b)(5).

The 1996 Amendments contain refinements designed to improve upon EPA's slow record of implementation. As enacted in 1974, the SDWA directed EPA to establish national interim primary drinking water standards within 90 days, and to revise those standards after a National Academy of Sciences study recommended MCLs for various substances. EPA promulgated 16 interim standards, based on the recommendations of a 1962 U.S. Public Health Service study. Although the NAS issued its report, Drinking Water and Health, in 1977, by 1986 EPA had proposed final MCLs for only 8 chemicals, all volatile organic compounds. Amendments in 1986 instructed EPA to regulate 83 chemicals by 1989 and to add 25 chemicals to the list every 3 years after 1989. These same Amendments contained a statutory stipulation that any MCL set for synthetic organic chemicals had to be at least as stringent as the levels achieved by granulated activated carbon filtration.

By January 1991, EPA had promulgated MCLs for 67 of the 83 mandated chemicals and pledged to set new standards for 108 contaminants by 1995, 56 Fed. Reg. 3,526, 3,528 (1991), a goal it did not meet. The 1996 Amendments rescinded the provision for regulating 25 chemicals every 3 years. In its place, EPA was directed to publish a list of contaminants not now subject to regulation but that are known to occur in public water systems. Every 5 years thereafter, EPA is required to decide whether or not to regulate at least 5 contaminants on the list. Once EPA decides to regulate, it has 24 months to propose an MCLG and an MCL, and 18 months from then to promulgate the proposal. MCLs must be reviewed every 5 years. The 1996 Amendments also required EPA to review the 68 standards that it had issued prior to 1997. On July 1, 2003, the EPA announced completion of that review. 68 Fed. Reg. 42,907.

The SDWA's regulatory regime also permits the relaxation of its standards if the benefits to be achieved from regulating as much as feasible cannot justify the costs of regulating that stringently. Such a provision acknowledges that the primary objective of all toxics statutes is to advance public health, in this case by employing an assessment of adverse health effects to relax a regulatory standard. Most statutes are not structured in this way, but even when they are not, health-based considerations have sometimes been raised as an argument for relaxing a regulatory standard or not regulating at all. Suppose, for example, that a particular application of a feasibility-based or even a health-based standard resulted in extremely low levels of remaining risk, so low as to be in some sense almost unnoticeable, and a less stringent regulation would still result in extremely low risk. Even if risk-benefit balancing is not required by statute, should the agencies relax regulations in such cases? Achieving the final small degrees of pollution reduction is often very expensive, so that substantial economic consequences can turn on whether the agency imposes the strict demands of a statute or whether it recognizes the "common sense" proposition that an activity poses risks "too small to be regulated."

---

## Principal Provisions of the Safe Drinking Water Act

*Section 300g-1* requires EPA to promulgate national drinking water regulations (MCLGs and MCLs) for public water systems. Regulations are to be issued for each contaminant that may have any adverse effect on health and that is known or anticipated to occur in such systems. MCLGs are to be set "at the level at which no known or anticipated adverse effects on the health of persons occur and which allows an adequate margin of safety." MCLs are to be set as close to the MCLGs "as is feasible," unless after weighing the "quantifiable and nonquantifiable costs and benefits," the EPA determines that the benefits of that level would not justify the costs, in which case the MCL is to be set to "maximize[] health risk reduction benefits at a cost that is justified by the benefits."

*Section 300g-2* authorizes states to assume primary enforcement responsibility under the Act.

*Section 300g-3* requires EPA to notify states of violations of national primary drinking water regulations and to take enforcement action against public water systems if the states fail to do so. Owners or operators of public water systems are required to notify customers of violations.

*Sections 300g-4 & 5* authorize states to grant variances and exemptions under certain conditions.

> *Section 300g-6* prohibits the use of lead in pipes, solder, or flux in public water systems or in plumbing used to provide water for human consumption that is connected to such a system.
>
> *Section 300h* requires EPA to establish minimum requirements for state underground injection control programs to prevent underground injection that endangers drinking water sources, but exempts from regulation the injection of non-diesel fluids used in hydraulic fracturing operations related to oil, gas, or geothermal production.
>
> *Section 300i* grants EPA emergency powers to act against contamination of drinking water that may present an imminent and substantial endangerment to public health.
>
> *Section 300j-4* directs EPA to promulgate regulations requiring monitoring of drinking water and authorizes EPA to establish recordkeeping requirements.
>
> *Section 300j-7* authorizes judicial review of national primary drinking water regulations in the D.C. Circuit and of any other EPA action under the Act in the U.S. Courts of Appeal where the petitioner resides or transacts business.
>
> *Section 300j-8* authorizes citizen suits against any person alleged to be in violation of the Act and against the EPA administrator for failure to perform any nondiscretionary duty.
>
> *Sections 300j-21 to 26* codify the Lead Contamination Control Act of 1988, which requires recall of drinking water coolers with lead-lined tanks.

Like the OSH Act, the SDWA requires feasibility-limited reductions in risk. In implementing these statutes, costs must be given some consideration in determining the limits of feasibility.

Difficulties that EPA faced in regulating lead in drinking water under SDWA's feasibility standard as originally formulated played a role in the proviso added in 1996 that authorizes EPA to set the MCL at the level that "maximizes health risk reduction benefits at a cost that is justified by the benefits," if the EPA concludes that the "quantifiable and nonquantifiable benefits" of the feasibility-limited level do not justify the "quantifiable and nonquantifiable costs" of that level.

In 1991, EPA promulgated standards for controlling lead in drinking water, 56 Fed. Reg. 26,460 (1991). Because of its potentially severe health effects at even low levels of exposure, EPA established an MCLG of zero for lead. In order to promulgate the MCL for lead, EPA had to determine how close to zero the standard could feasibly be set. Although the use of lead pipes and lead solder in drinking water systems was prohibited in the 1986 Amendments to the SDWA, an enormous number of homes have such plumbing or are served by water distribution systems with such plumbing. While it would be technologically possible to reduce levels of lead in drinking water to "safe" levels, it could cost tens of billions of dollars to remove all lead service pipes.

Although the SDWA then appeared to require EPA to establish MCLs if "it is economically and technologically feasible to ascertain the level" of contaminants in water, §300f(1)(C), 42 U.S.C. §1401(1)(C), EPA decided not to promulgate an MCL for lead. The agency argued that Congress had not anticipated the problem of drinking water contamination occurring as a byproduct of pipe corrosion and that public water systems should not be responsible for contamination from portions of the distribution system beyond their control. 56 Fed. Reg. 26,460, 26,476 (1991).

Because of the source of the lead, measurements of lead in water at the tap vary widely within a single system. Compounding the issue of regulatory solutions, chemicals that might be added to the water system to reduce corrosion have the deleterious effect of increasing the levels of other chemicals subject to their own MCLs. EPA therefore adopted a "treatment technique" approach that requires water suppliers to employ corrosion control measures if more than 10 percent of water samples exceed 15 ppb lead at the tap. Corrosion control requirements took effect between 1996 and 1999 depending on the size of the water supply system. If corrosion control fails to reduce the percentage of samples exceeding this action level, water suppliers eventually may have to replace lead service lines on a schedule that stretches to the year 2014.

EPA's lead regulations were attacked by environmental groups as well as state and local officials. Environmentalists argued that the absence of an MCL, the 90th percentile action level approach, and the lengthy compliance deadlines made the regulations virtually impossible to enforce while leaving hundreds of thousands of children potentially exposed to high levels of lead in drinking water. Arguing that section 300f(1)(C) required EPA to establish an MCL because it is feasible to measure lead levels in water, environmental groups sued EPA. EPA countered by asserting that the term "feasible" encompasses the concept of "capable of being accomplished in a manner consistent with the Act." In EPA's view, the SDWA permitted EPA to decide that it could eschew a fixed MCL where the monitoring for and achievement of that MCL would not be conducive to overall water quality, because the levels of other controlled contaminants would be raised in the process. Environmentalists challenged the rule in the D.C. Circuit, which issued the following ruling.

## American Water Works Ass'n v. EPA

40 F.3d 1266 (D.C. Cir. 1994)

GINSBURG [DOUGLAS], Circuit Judge:

### I. BACKGROUND

The Safe Drinking Water Act requires the EPA to promulgate drinking water regulations designed to prevent contamination of public water systems. 42 U.S.C. §300g-1(b). A national primary drinking water regulation (NPDWR) is one that specifies for a contaminant with an adverse effect upon human health either an MCL or a treatment technique, and establishes the procedures and criteria necessary to ensure a supply of drinking water that complies with that MCL or treatment technique. 42 U.S.C. §300f(1). An NPDWR is an enforceable standard applicable to all public water systems nationwide. In most of the NPDWRs promulgated to date the EPA has set an MCL for the particular contaminant being regulated. The

EPA has the authority, however, to specify a treatment technique in lieu of an MCL if the Administrator finds that it is not "economically or technologically feasible" to determine the level of the particular contaminant in a public water system. 42 U.S.C. §300f(1)(C)(ii).

It is particularly difficult to determine the level of lead in a public water system. Less than one percent of all public water systems draw source water containing any lead. Instead, most lead enters a public water system through corrosion of service lines and plumbing materials containing lead, such as brass faucets and lead solder connecting copper pipes, that are privately owned and thus beyond the EPA's regulatory reach under the Act. System-wide measurement is made still more difficult because the degree to which plumbing materials leach lead varies greatly with such factors as the age of the material, the temperature of the water, the presence of other chemicals in the water, and the length of time the water is in contact with the leaded material. Indeed, lead levels in samples drawn consecutively from a single source can vary significantly. Measurement difficulties aside, treatment is made problematic because chemicals added to the drinking water supply in order to reduce the corrosion of pipes can increase the levels of other contaminants subject to MCLs.

Recognizing the peculiar difficulty of establishing an MCL for lead in public water systems, the EPA proposed regulations that distinguish between control of lead in source water and control of lead due to corrosion. First, the EPA proposed an MCL for lead in source water, to be measured at the point where the water enters the distribution system. Second, the EPA proposed to require a treatment technique — an "optimal corrosion control treatment" supplemented with a program of public education — to be tailored specifically by each public water system in such a way as to minimize lead contamination in drinking water without increasing the level of any other contaminant to the point where it violates the NPDWR for that substance.

The EPA solicited comments on this two-part monitoring and treatment proposal and on several alternatives that it was not then proposing. One such alternative was to require each public water system to replace the lead service lines it owns or controls that, after treatment to reduce corrosion, still contribute a significant amount of lead to tap water. Under this approach the EPA would erect a "rebuttable presumption" that the public water system "owns or controls and therefore can replace, the lead components up to the wall of the building served."

In the final rule the EPA abandoned its two-part monitoring and treatment proposal in favor of a rule under which all large water systems must institute corrosion control treatment, while smaller systems must do so only if representative sampling indicates that lead in the water exceeds a designated "action level." The agency also adopted a schedule that allows a public water system five or more years to comply with the regulation, depending upon the number of persons it serves. The EPA required larger systems to come into compliance sooner than smaller systems because they are generally more sophisticated technically and have a greater impact upon the purity of drinking water; also the states, which are responsible for implementing the regulation, would benefit from experience gained with larger systems before reviewing treatment plans for smaller systems. The EPA exempted from the rule all transient noncommunity public water systems, such as those in restaurants, gas stations, and motels.

Unlike the proposed rule, the final rule requires each public water system to replace each year at least 7% of the lead service lines it controls that when tested exceed a designated action level. A public water system is said to "control" a service line if it has authority to set standards for construction, repair, or maintenance of the line, authority to replace, repair, or maintain the service line, or ownership of the service line. The rule establishes a presumption that the public water system controls every service line up to the wall of the building it serves; the system can rebut the presumption only by demonstrating that its control is limited by state statute, local ordinance, public service contract, or other legal authority. A public water system that controls only part of a service line must replace the portion under its control and must offer to replace the remaining portion, although not necessarily at the system's expense.

### A. MCL for Lead at the Tap

The NRDC first contends that, because it is economically and technologically feasible to ascertain the level of lead in water, the Safe Drinking Water Act requires that the EPA set an MCL for lead. See 42 U.S.C. §300f(1)(C); 42 U.S.C. §300g-1(b)(7). Further, because the tap is the delivery point to the user of a public water system, the NRDC concludes that the MCL must be set at the tap.

At bottom the NRDC and the EPA disagree over the meaning of the word "feasible" as it applies to ascertaining the level of lead in drinking water. The NRDC argues that the Congress clearly expressed its intent that "feasible" be understood to mean "physically capable of being done at reasonable cost"; accordingly it argues that the EPA's rule is contrary to the plain meaning of the statute. For its part, the EPA does not dispute that it is "feasible" to monitor lead under the definition advanced by the NRDC; instead the agency interprets "feasible" to mean "capable of being accomplished in a manner consistent with the Act." The agency argues that if public water systems were required to comply with an MCL for lead, they would have to undertake aggressive corrosion control techniques that might reduce the amount of lead leached from customers' plumbing but would also increase the levels of other contaminants. The EPA argues that because the Congress apparently did not anticipate a situation in which monitoring for one contaminant, although possible, is not conducive to overall water quality, it impliedly delegated to the agency the discretion to specify a treatment technique instead of an MCL.

We agree with the EPA that the meaning of "feasible" is not as plain as the NRDC suggests. Although we generally assume that the Congress intends the words it uses to have their ordinary meaning, case law is replete with examples of statutes the ordinary meaning of which is not necessarily what the Congress intended. Indeed, where a literal reading of a statutory term would lead to absurd results, the term simply "has no plain meaning . . . and is the proper subject of construction by the EPA and the courts." If the meaning of "feasible" suggested by the NRDC is indeed its plain meaning, then this is such a case; for it could lead to a result squarely at odds with the purpose of the Safe Drinking Water Act.

The Congress clearly contemplated that an MCL would be a standard by which both the quality of the drinking water and the public water system's efforts to reduce the contaminant could be measured. See 42 U.S.C. §300g-1(b)(5). Because lead generally enters drinking water from corrosion in pipes owned by customers of the water system, an MCL for lead would be neither; ascertaining the level of lead in water at the meter (i.e. where it enters the customer's premises) would measure the public water system's success in controlling the contaminant but not the quality of the public's drinking water (because lead may still leach into the water from the customer's plumbing), while ascertaining the level of lead in water at the tap would accurately reflect water quality but effectively hold the public water system responsible for lead leached from plumbing owned by its customers.

We must defer to the EPA's interpretation of "feasible" if it is reasonable and we think that it is. A single national standard (i.e., an MCL) for lead is not suitable for every public water system because the condition of plumbing materials, which are the major source of lead in drinking water, varies across systems and the systems generally do not have control over the sources of lead in their water. In this circumstance the EPA suggests that requiring public water systems to design and implement custom corrosion control plans for lead will result in optimal treatment of drinking water overall, i.e. treatment that deals adequately with lead without causing public water systems to violate drinking water regulations for other contaminants.

Viewing the Act as a whole, we cannot say that the statute demonstrates a clear congressional intent to require that the EPA set an MCL for a contaminant merely because it can be measured at a reasonable cost. In light of the purpose of the Act to promote safe drinking water generally, we conclude that the EPA's interpretation of the term "feasible" so as to require a treatment technique instead of an MCL for lead is reasonable.

## NOTES AND QUESTIONS

1. In its decision, the D.C. Circuit also held that EPA had failed to provide adequate notice before adopting its novel definition of "control" of water service lines. It also held that EPA had failed adequately to explain why it had exempted non-community public water supply systems. In December 1999, EPA made minor revisions to its Lead and Copper Rule to clarify that corrosion controls must be optimized and to require that lead and copper samples be taken at the tap once every three years. It also provided that systems subject to lead service line replacement requirements must replace the portion of the lead service line that they own.

2. In 2004, EPA began a review of the implementation of its Lead and Copper Rule. Based on the results of this review, EPA released a Drinking Water Lead Reduction Plan in March 2005. In 2007, EPA promulgated new regulations that required water supply systems to provide advance notification and to obtain approval from state authorities of intended changes in treatment or source water that could increase corrosion of lead. The new regulations also required water suppliers to notify their customers of tap water monitoring results for lead. These changes were not enough to prevent the lead poisoning of residents of Flint, Michigan.

3. In January 2016, a federal state of emergency was declared in Flint, Michigan after it was revealed that thousands of residents had been exposed to high levels of lead in their drinking water following a shift in the source of their water supply in 2014. Below is a discussion of some lessons that can be learned from this tragedy.

Robert Percival

## The Poison Poor Children Drink: Six Lessons from the Flint Tragedy

*Jurist, Feb. 11, 2016*

Americans who visit China quickly notice one significant difference from travel in the US. Even if they are staying in luxury five-star hotels, they are told not to drink tap water because in China it is not safe to drink. By contrast, no matter where one travels in the US tap water should be safe to drink because of a federal law called the Safe Drinking Water Act (SDWA), 42 U.S.C. §300f et seq. Since its enactment in 1974, the SDWA has required tap water in the US to meet minimum federal standards to protect public health.

Thus it was shocking to learn that for more than a year impoverished residents of Flint, Michigan were drinking lead-laden tap water that poisoned their children. How could this happen in the 21st century in the most developed country in the world despite the SDWA and the now well-known dangers of exposure to lead? It seems astonishing that government officials violated the SDWA and failed promptly to inform Flint residents that their water was poisoned.

The Flint tragedy originated with the appointment by Michigan Governor Rick Snyder of Darnell Earley as emergency manager for Flint. To save money Earley decided in April 2014 to shift the source of the city's water supply to the polluted Flint River. Because Flint River water is highly corrosive, lead from pipes in Flint's water supply system leached into the drinking water, poisoning Flint residents. Shockingly, after test data revealed the lead contamination, state and federal officials failed to inform Flint residents. Officials initially denounced private groups who tried to publicize test results. Yet when General Motors complained that the water was corroding parts at a plant in Flint, government officials quietly reconnected the plant to its former water supply.

Behind these shocking events are dark realities that require reassessment of our current system for protecting public health. First, history demonstrates that it is easier to muster political will to control health risks that are highly visible. Long before the US had national environmental laws, Congress in 1912 imposed a prohibitive excise tax on the use of white phosphorous in match manufacturing because it inflicted a horribly disfiguring disease on workers exposed to it. Because lead exposure causes neurological damage that is less apparent to the naked eye, it took much longer for environmental policy to respond to it. While much of the rest of the world banned lead-based paint at the beginning of the 20th century, the US did not do so until 1978, more than a half-century later. Lead additives in gasoline were banned only in the 1990s after a prolonged struggle that extended for decades more than the effort to ban lead-based paint.

A second lesson from Flint is the folly of changing policy simply to [reduce] costs without considering the impact on public health. Incredibly in 1982 the Reagan administration proposed to allow more lead to be added to gasoline simply to reduce costs to oil refiners. Even as it was touting a new executive order requiring agencies to balance costs against benefits before taking regulatory action, the administration said only cost reductions need to be considered when proposing to relax existing rules. It was self evident to Reagan's minions that any measure saving industry money was desirable regardless of its effect on public health. Fortunately public outcry forced Reagan's Environmental Protection Agency (EPA) not only to abandon this disastrous proposal but eventually to eliminate gasoline lead additives entirely. Leaded gasoline now has been banned in virtually all the world. This is probably the most successful public health measure in the history of environmental law with economists estimating that it generates more than trillions of dollars in net benefits to society each year.

Third, the Flint tragedy dramatically highlights an environmental justice problem—environmental risks continue to be disproportionately concentrated on poor and minority communities. Flint is a majority African-American community with more than 40 percent of the population living below the poverty line. In 1982, columnist George Will wrote a remarkable column opposing the Reagan administration's effort to allow more lead in gasoline. Entitled "The Poison Poor Children Breathe," Will observed that "the problem of lead in the environment . . . is a childhood health problem that illustrates how society's hazards are often distributed regressively — persons lowest on the social ladder have special handicaps for climbing." Will noted that "[a]ny childhood disease that threatened affluent children as lead poisoning threatens poor children would produce public action faster than you can say 'swine flu.'" The same is true today, as illustrated by the Flint tragedy. Government officials in Flint responded promptly to GM's complaints about the water, but its poor residents were not warned of the hazard.

Fourth, Flint exposes fundamental inadequacies in how lead in drinking water currently is regulated under the SDWA. When EPA first regulated lead in drinking water in 1991, 56 Fed. Reg. 26,460 (1991), it knew that there is no safe level of exposure to lead. Because of lead's potentially severe health effects at even low levels of exposure, EPA established a health-based goal of zero lead in drinking water. The SDWA directs EPA to set limits on contaminants in drinking water as close as is feasible to the health-based goal. Thus EPA had to determine how close to zero the standard could feasibly be set.

Although the use of lead pipes and lead solder in drinking water systems was prohibited in 1986, an enormous number of homes still have such plumbing or are served by lead service lines. EPA concluded that Congress had not anticipated the problem of drinking water contamination occurring as a byproduct of pipe corrosion. It argued that public water systems should not be responsible for contamination from portions of the distribution system beyond their control. 56 Fed. Reg. 26,460, 26,476 (1991). Because a requirement that all lead service lines be removed would cost cities many billions of dollars, EPA instead required water suppliers to employ relatively inexpensive corrosion control measures to prevent lead from the pipes leaching into the water. Under the regulations EPA adopted, if more than 10 percent of a city's water samples exceed 15 ppb lead at the tap, the city water supplier is required to add a chemical to the water to inhibit corrosion. If these corrosion control measures failed to reduce the percentage of samples exceeding this action level, water suppliers were required to replace lead service lines on a schedule stretching to 2014.

When it shifted to the corrosive Flint River water, Flint failed to use corrosion controls, even though a March 2015 consultant's report urged it to do so. This clearly would have reduced levels of lead in Flint's water, though it would not have completely eliminated lead contamination. It is well known that levels of lead in tap water can vary widely within a single system. Some cities gamed the system by choosing to do most of their testing at locations where they knew they would be less likely to find lead contamination. Environmentalists argued that EPA's regulations were inadequate because they could leave up to one-tenth of a city's population exposed to unlimited levels of lead. Faced with legal challenges from environmentalists attacking the rules as too weak and cities attacking the rules as too stringent, a reviewing court upheld EPA's regulations. American Water Works Ass'n v. EPA, 40 F.3d 1266 (D.C. Cir. 1994).

Fifth, the Flint tragedy illustrates the difficulty of remediating environmental harm once toxic materials are incorporated into the infrastructure of urban areas. More than a decade ago high concentrations of lead were found in Washington, D.C.'s drinking water as a result of testing by Marc Edwards, the very Virginia Tech professor who blew the whistle on Flint's contamination. In addition to employing corrosion control measures D.C. began replacing lead service lines. Like the widespread use of asbestos and lead paint in homes and buildings, lead in water supply systems can continue to pose severe risks to public health long after use of the toxic materials is banned. Many cities like Flint and Washington, D.C. have lead pipes and plumbing in their water supply systems that eventually must be removed and replaced at great expense.

Sixth, Flint illustrates the importance of civil society groups serving as a backstop when government officials fail to implement or obey the law. Private parties were the first to publicize the lead contamination in Flint. Predictably they initially were dismissed as alarmists by the very government officials who failed to ensure that Flint's drinking water was safe. In 1882 the Norwegian playwright Henrik Ibsen wrote An Enemy of the People, a play about a community's demonization of a local doctor who exposes contamination of the town's economically vital baths. The play captures a timeless pattern that has been repeated for more than a century. Fortunately environmental laws in the US encourage private parties to hold government officials accountable when they fail to protect public health. This now appears to have happened, at least belatedly, in Flint. One can only hope that the lessons embodied in the Flint tragedy will make it less likely to be repeated in the future.

## NOTES AND QUESTIONS

1. EPA scientists reportedly had identified potential problems with Flint's drinking water in February 2015. After confirming the problem, they alerted agency officials in a memorandum circulated in June 2015. EPA requested that Michigan officials adopt corrosion controls for Flint's water supply, but the state resisted in favor of conducting additional water sampling over a six-month period. In the meantime, EPA and state officials failed to notify residents of Flint of the problem. After this was revealed, EPA Regional Administrator Susan Hedman was forced to resign. State criminal charges were brought against several employees of Michigan's Department of Environmental Quality and the Michigan Department of Health and Human Services. Class action lawsuits have been filed on behalf of Flint residents against state and local officials.

2. On December 22, 2020, EPA promulgated a new regulations to control lead and copper contamination in drinking water, *https://www.epa.gov/sites/production/files/2020-12/documents/lcrr_prepublicationnotice_frl-10019-23-ow.final_.pdf*. The rule was published in the Federal Register on January 15, 2021. 86 Fed. Reg.

4198 (2021). The new regulations still fail to establish an at-the-tap MCL for lead in drinking water, and they were harshly criticized for extending the time required for replacing lead service pipes to up to 33 years in many areas.

3. Financially strapped localities often argue that they lack the resources to implement SDWA regulations. In the 1996 Amendments, Congress provided some flexibility for EPA to address cost concerns of small water distribution systems, by permitting variances for such systems if they cannot afford to comply with the MCL and if they otherwise comply with "treatment technology, treatment technique[s] or other means" that the administrator finds "ensure adequate protection of human health." 42 U.S.C. §300g-4(e)(2), (3). MCLs promulgated prior to 1986 and MCLs for microbial contamination are excluded from the variance provisions.

4. EPA regulations require thousands of communities with unfiltered drinking water to install filtration systems unless EPA approves an alternative watershed protection program. Since the early 1990s, New York City has received a Filtration Avoidance Determination (FAD) from EPA. Instead of constructing an enormously expensive filtration system, the city relies on purchases of open space and strict controls on land use to prevent contamination of the city's watershed.

5. Enforcement of the SDWA has been a chronic problem, particularly because the Act's regulatory targets usually are agencies of state and local government. To enhance enforcement Congress in 1996 added provisions that require water systems to notify their customers within 24 hours if violations are discovered that have potentially serious health effects. For other violations, the supplier must notify its customers within one year of the violation. Water suppliers also must provide the public with an annual report of the levels of various contaminants found in their system. These reports, which are to be called "Consumer Confidence Reports," must explain in layperson's terms the health concerns that resulted in the regulation of each regulated contaminant and they must provide a toll-free hotline number for consumers to use to seek more information.

6. Despite promising for many years to promulgate an MCL for PFAS, the Trump administration EPA failed to do so before leaving office. It is widely expected that the Biden administration EPA will finally establish an MCL to regulate PFAS under the Safe Drinking Water Act. An important question is whether only a few PFAS, such as PFOA and PFOS that are no longer produced, will be regulated or whether the regulation will extend to much broader classes of PFAS. On March 1, 2021, a report by the Government Accountability Office found that EPA was making slow progress on regulating PFAS. It noted that EPA planned to promulgate a national drinking water monitoring standard for PFAS by December 2021 and that it had issued an advance notice of proposed rulemaking to designate the two PFAS believed to be most dangerous as hazardous substances under CERCLA. GAO, Manmade Chemicals and Potential Health Risks: EPA Has Completed Some Regulatory-Related Actions for PFAs (2021).

### 6. The Delaney Clauses of the Federal Food, Drug, and Cosmetic Act

In a number of regulatory settings, the regulated community has promoted the notion that regulators should recognize the concept of a de minimis risk level in establishing health-based standards. The idea of de minimis risk differs from risk-benefit balancing because risks are not compared with benefits. Instead, an activity's risks are compared with a relatively low level of risk, the de minimis level. The notion is that de minimis levels pose risks that ought to be acceptable to society; thus, the idea of de minimis risk is also sometimes advanced as one way to interpret the objective of statutes that seek to "protect public health" or to ensure that a substance is "safe."

The de minimis principle has been litigated in a variety of contexts, including the Delaney Clauses of the Federal Food, Drug, and Cosmetic Act. Enacted in the 1950s and 1960s, these provisions, all named after Congressman James Delaney (D-NY) who introduced them, prohibit the marketing or use of any food additive, color additive, or animal drug that is "found . . . to induce cancer in man or animal" 21 U.S.C. §376(b)(5)(B) (color additives), regardless of how small that risk of cancer might be. When the FDA sought to authorize the marketing of two color additives, Orange No. 17 and Red No. 19 (for use in cosmetics) on the grounds that the risk of cancer they posed was de minimis, Public Citizen sued to enforce the Delaney Clause's absolute bar. Public Citizen v. FDA, 831 F.2d 1108 (D.C. Cir. 1987).

Using QRAs, the FDA had estimated the risk of cancer from Orange No. 17 to be one in 19 billion at worst, and for Red No. 19 one in 9 million at worst. The FDA explained that it had used conservative assumptions in deriving these figures, and it characterized the risks as "so trivial as to be effectively no risk." It concluded that the two dyes were safe. 51 Fed. Reg. at 28,344, 28,360. The court of appeals agreed with the FDA that the risks were extremely small, relying in part on comparative risk assessments:

> Assuming that the quantitative risk assessments are accurate, as we do for these purposes, it seems altogether correct to characterize these risks as trivial. . . . A consumer would run a one-in-a-million lifetime risk of cancer if he or she ate one peanut with the FDA-permitted level of aflatoxins once every 250 days (liver cancer). . . . Another activity posing a one-in-a-million lifetime risk is spending 1,000 minutes (less than 17 hours) every year in the city of Denver—with its high elevation and cosmic radiation levels—rather than in the District of Columbia. Most of us would not regard these as high-risk activities. Those who indulge in them can hardly be thought of as living dangerously. Indeed, they are risks taken without a second thought by persons whose economic position allows them a broad range of choice.
>
> According to the risk assessments here, the riskier dye poses one ninth as much risk as the peanut or Colorado hypothetical; the less risky one poses only one 19,000th as much.
>
> It may help put the one-in-a-million lifetime risk in perspective to compare it with a concededly dangerous activity, in which millions nonetheless engage, cigarette smoking. Each one-in-a-million risk amounts to less than one 200,000th the lifetime risk incurred by the average male smoker. J.A. 536, citing E. Crouch & R. Wilson, "Inter-Risk Comparisons," in J. Rodricks & R. Tardiff, eds., Assessment and Management of Chemical Risks 97, 105, 108 (1984). Thus, a person would have to be exposed to more than 2,000 chemicals bearing the one-in-a-million lifetime risk, at the rates assumed in the risk assessment, in order to reach 100th the risk

involved in smoking. To reach that level of risk with chemicals equivalent to the less risky dye (Orange No. 17), he would have to be exposed to more than 40 million such chemicals. [831 F.2d 1108, 1111.]

The court went on to note that the law does recognize as a general principle the idea of "the de minimis doctrine, shorthand for *de minimis non curat lex* ('the law does not concern itself with trifles')":

> The doctrine . . . serves a number of purposes. One is to spare agency resources for more important matters. But that is a goal of dubious relevance here. The finding of trivial risk necessarily followed not only the elaborate animal testing, but also the quantitative risk assessment process itself; indeed, application of the doctrine required additional expenditure of agency resources.
>
> More relevant is the concept that "notwithstanding the 'plain meaning' of a statute, a court must look beyond the words to the purpose of the act where its literal terms lead to 'absurd or futile results.'" . . . Imposition of pointless burdens on regulated entities is obviously to be avoided if possible, especially as burdens on them almost invariably entail losses for their customers: here, obviously, loss of access to the colors made possible by a broad range of dyes.
>
> We have employed the concept in construing the Clean Air Act's mandate to the Environmental Protection Agency to set standards providing "an ample margin of safety to protect the public health," 42 U.S.C. §7412(b)(1) (1982). That does not, we said, require limits assuring a "risk-free" environment. Rather, the agency must decide "what risks are acceptable in the world in which we live" and set limits accordingly. . . .
>
> Moreover, failure to employ a de minimis doctrine may lead to regulation that not only is "absurd or futile" in some general cost-benefit sense but also is directly contrary to the primary legislative goal. In a certain sense, precisely that may be the effect here. The primary goal of the Act is human safety, but literal application of the Delaney Clause may in some instances increase risk. No one contends that the color additive Amendments impose a zero-risk standard for noncarcinogenic substances; if they did, the number of dyes passing muster might prove minuscule. As a result, makers of drugs and cosmetics who are barred from using a carcinogenic dye carrying a one-in-20-million lifetime risk may use instead a noncarcinogenic, but toxic, dye carrying, say, a one-in-10-million lifetime risk. The substitution appears to be a clear loss for safety.
>
> Judge Leventhal articulated the standard for application of de minimis as virtually a presumption in its favor: "Unless Congress has been extraordinarily rigid, there is likely a basis for an implication of de minimis authority to provide [an] exemption when the burdens of regulation yield a gain of trivial or no value." But the doctrine obviously is not available to thwart a statutory command; it must be interpreted with a view to "implementing the legislative design." Nor is an agency to apply it on a finding merely that regulatory costs exceed regulatory benefits. [831 F.2d 1108, 1112.]

Notwithstanding these considerations, the court invalidated FDA's decision, finding that the Delaney Clause permitted no de minimis exception. The question, said the court, is ultimately one of what Congress meant in the statute. The language of the Delaney Clauses did not acknowledge any exception and was absolute in its language. The legislative history also supported the idea that Congress intended an absolute bar. "[S]hort of an explicit declaration in the statute barring use of a de minimis exception, this is perhaps as strong as it is likely to get. Facing [during congressional debate over the Clause] the explicit claim that the Clause was 'extraordinarily rigid,' [SN3] . . . 'Congress persevered.'"

Moreover, our reading of the legislative history suggests some possible explanations for Congress' apparent rigidity. One is that Congress, and the nation in general (at least as perceived by Congress), appear to have been truly alarmed about the risks of cancer. . . . This concern resulted in a close focus on substances increasing cancer threats and a willingness to take extreme steps to lessen even small risks. . . .

A second possible explanation for Congress' failure to authorize greater administrative discretion is that it perceived color additives as lacking any great value. For example, Congressman Delaney remarked, "color additives provide no nutrient value. They have no value at all, except so-called eye appeal." Color Additives Hearings at 108. Representative Sullivan said, "we like the bright and light [lipstick] shades but if they cannot safely be produced, then we prefer to do without these particular shades.". . . [T]here is evidence that Congress thought the public could get along without carcinogenic colors, especially in view of the existence of safer substitutes. Thus the legislators may have estimated the costs of an overly protective rule as trivial.

So far as we can determine, no one drew the legislators' attention to the way in which the Delaney Clause, interacting with the flexible standard for determining safety of noncarcinogens, might cause manufacturers to substitute more dangerous toxic chemicals for less dangerous carcinogens. . . . But the obviously more stringent standard for carcinogens may rest on a view that cancer deaths are in some way more to be feared than others.

Finally, as we have already noted, the House committee (or its amanuenses) considered the possibility that its no-threshold assumption might prove false and contemplated a solution: renewed consideration by Congress. Considering these circumstances—great concern over a specific health risk, the apparently low cost of protection, and the possibility of remedying any mistakes—Congress' enactment of an absolute rule seems less surprising. . . . [831 F.2d at 1117-1118.]

*Public Citizen v. Young* dealt only with the Delaney Clause applicable to color additives in section 706 of the FDCA, 21 U.S.C. §376(B)(5)(B), and not with the separate Delaney Clause applicable to food additives in section 409, 21 U.S.C. §348(c)(3)(A). The court noted that while "the clauses have almost identical wording, the context is clearly different" given the potentially greater social costs of banning certain food additives. 831 F.2d at 1117. Citing this statement, EPA interpreted the food additives Delaney Clause to permit a de minimis exception when it estab-lishes tolerances for pesticide residues on processed foods under section 409. 56 Fed. Reg. 7,750 (1991). EPA argued that since FIFRA contains no Delaney Clause and no Delaney Clause applies to pesticide residues on nonprocessed foods under section 408 of the FDCA, it would be irrational to apply the Clause strictly to pro-cessed foods.

The Ninth Circuit rejected EPA's argument. It held that the interpretation of the color additives Delaney Clause in *Public Citizen v. Young* was "equally appli-cable" to the statutory language in section 409. Les v. Reilly, 968 F.2d 985, 989 (9th Cir. 1992). Finding the statutory language to be "clear and mandatory," the court explained that the legislative history indicates that "Congress intended the very rigidity that the language it chose commands." Id. at 988-989. The court refused EPA's invitation to distinguish between the color additives Del-aney Clause and the clause governing food additives. It found that "Congress intended to ban all carcinogenic food additives, regardless of amount or signif-icance of risk, as the only safe alternative." Id. at 989. Yet the court recognized that strict application of the Delaney Clause might not accomplish Congress's goal. It noted that consumers might switch to raw foods with pesticide residues that actually pose greater risks than the residues on processed foods that were at issue in the case.

### 7.   *FIFRA, Pesticide Residues on Food, and the Food Quality Protection Act*

The Clinton administration announced in May 1993 that it would seek to develop new food safety legislation in response to the *Les* decision. In June 1993, EPA, FDA, and the Department of Agriculture announced a major policy shift to promote reduced use of pesticides in food production. The agencies pledged a coordinated effort to remove high-risk pesticides from the market, and they endorsed integrated pest management, which emphasizes nonchemical pest-con-trol alternatives. The new policy coincided with the release of a National Academy of Sciences report finding that existing regulatory policies failed to protect children adequately in light of their greater sensitivity to pesticide risks. National Research Council, Pesticides in the Diets of Infants and Children (1993). EPA had begun to consider reforms in the process for registering pesticides under FIFRA in July 1992 when the agency requested public comment on how to structure regulatory incentives to encourage the development of safer pesticides. 57 Fed. Reg. 32,140 (1992). EPA indicated that it was considering accelerating the registration process for lower-risk pesticides and the possible restriction or removal of higher-risk pesti-cides for which safer substitutes become available. EPA policy that prohibits safety claims for pesticides also could be reconsidered in order to harness market forces to encourage the development of safer alternatives.

Concerned that EPA was not implementing the *Les* decision, NRDC subse-quently sued EPA to force the elimination of carcinogenic residues on processed foods. In October 1994, EPA settled the lawsuit by agreeing to conduct an expe-dited review of previously approved uses for 36 pesticides believed to contain carcinogens. Cushman, EPA Settles Suit and Agrees to Move Against 36 Pesticides, N.Y. Times, Oct. 13, 1994, at A24. In February 1995, EPA announced that it would require that 34 pesticides be phased out of processed foods within two years and that it would review data on 87 other pesticides during the next five years. EPA's decision increased pressure in Congress to reform the Delaney Clause. McCoy, EPA Agrees to Ban Pesticides, Comply with Rule in Food Act, Wall St. J., Feb. 9, 1995, at B16.

In deciding *Les v. Reilly*, the court noted the cogency of the arguments for the EPA's position but held that the Delaney Clause was clear, categorical, and dispositive. "If there is to be a change," the court added, "it is for Congress to direct." 968 F.2d at 990. The prospect that numerous high-volume pesticides would be removed from the market prompted the consensus enactment of the Food Quality Protection Act (FQPA) in 1996.

The FQPA amended the food additives Delaney Clause to specify that it does not include pesticide chemical residues in raw or processed foods. 21 U.S.C. §321(s). Such residues are now governed by a new, health-based standard of "reasonable certainty of no harm," and this standard is extended to raw foods on which a much wider range of pesticides typically are used than the 80 to 100 chemicals used on processed foods. Advocates of strict tolerances for pesticides on foods were willing to forgo the application of Delaney to pesticide residues on processed foods in return for the application of the new standard for pesticide residues on both raw and processed foods. The new standard requires "a reasonable certainty that no harm will result from aggregate exposure to the pesticide chemical residue, including all dietary exposures and all other exposures for which there is reliable information." Language in the legislative history, but not in the statute, suggests this reflects a policy to limit individual cancer risks to the exposed population to no greater than 1-in-1-million additional lifetime risk, although industry representatives are urging a more flexible interpretation.

The FQPA also provides for a less onerous, expedited registration process for "minor use" pesticides, defined as those that are used on commercial crops where the crop is smaller than 300,000 acres, for which no alternative pesticides are available, and where other requirements are met. It also establishes some tolerance setting flexibility for such pesticides, which expose a smaller population to risk than higher-volume pesticides do. As of August 2006—the statutory date established for EPA to finish its work—EPA had reassessed 9,637 tolerances out of a total of 9,721. These reviews resulted in recommendations to revoke 3,200 tolerances, modify 1,200, and leave 5,237 unchanged.

## NOTES AND QUESTIONS

1. The FDA's de minimis policy is but one of a variety of measures that the agency has taken through the years, in an effort to breathe some flexibility into an extremely rigid piece of legislation. Richard Merrill has depicted the policy as part of the "FDA's decade-long efforts to reconcile Congress's language with circumstances Congress may not have foreseen and for which it surely did not provide." He summarizes the factors that have induced FDA to seek escape from Delaney's literal meaning:

Improvements in analytic chemistry have enlarged the universe of compounds that FDA regulates as food (and color) additives. More extensive testing of chemicals and more sensitive protocols have enhanced toxicologists' ability to identify substances capable of producing tumors, including several substances adopted for food use years ago [e.g., saccharin, which had been in use since the early 1900s, but was not found to be carcinogenic in animals until the early 1970s]. Some of these substances gained market acceptance long before their carcinogenicity was discovered. In addition to these science-driven pressures on regulators, the public health community's concerns about the relationship between diet and cancer have shifted focus. A consensus has emerged that dietary patterns influence cancer incidence. Investigators have also revealed that the human food supply is full of substances (most occurring naturally) that have been, or may be, shown to cause cancer in laboratory animals. [Merrill, FDA's Implementation of the Delaney Clause: Repudiation of Congressional Choice or Reasoned Adaptation to Scientific Progress?, 5 Yale J. on Reg. 1, 2-3 (1988).]

2. What is the relevance of the last two points Professor Merrill makes? On these points, see also Gold, Slone, Stern, Manley & Ames, Rodent Carcinogens: Setting Priorities, 258 Science 261 (1992); Ames, Dietary Carcinogens and Anticarcinogens: Oxygen Radicals and Degenerative Diseases, 221 Science 1256 (1983); Committee on Diet, Nutrition, and Cancer, Commission on Life Sciences, National Research Council, National Academy of Sciences, Diet, Nutrition and Cancer: Directions for Research (1982). Professor Bruce Ames has argued that it is a serious mistake to focus regulatory attention and economic resources on removing extremely low risks of cancer associated with man-made chemicals because humans are exposed to much greater cancer risks from their dietary patterns and the consumption of natural carcinogens and anticarcinogens. See Ames, Ranking Possible Carcinogenic Hazards, 236 Science 271 (1987). How did *Public Citizen v. Young* address these comparative risk considerations?

3. Ames's suggestion that naturally occurring substances are consistently riskier than man-made substances has been challenged by some researchers. Two researchers from the Columbia University School of Public Health reexamined Ames's data by including allegedly more representative examples of synthetic chemicals and more consistent measures of exposure. Their results suggest that risks ranging from large to small are presented by both natural and synthetic substances. See Perera & Boffetta, Perspectives of Comparing Risks of Environmental Carcinogens, 80 J. Nat'l Cancer Inst. 1282 (1988). They argue that few natural substances have been tested for carcinogenesis and that Ames has exaggerated the risks of exposure to naturally occurring carcinogens.

4. How persuasive were the reasons for applying the Delaney Clause to food additives, as opposed to color additives, in the first place? Is the FQPA an improvement over the Delaney Clause approach to carcinogens in food additives?

5. In addition to the de minimis argument to which the court devoted most of its attention in *Public Citizen v. Young*, the Justice Department also argued that the two color additives did not "induce cancer within the meaning of the Delaney

Clause," despite the FDA's previous finding to the contrary. This position, which "is difficult to reconcile with FDA's historical view, shared by other agencies, that high-dose animal tests are a reliable means for identifying human cancer hazards," Merrill, FDA's Implementation of the Delaney Clause: Repudiation of Congressional Choice or Reasoned Adaptation to Scientific Progress?, 5 Yale J. on Reg. 1, 85 (1988), was not taken seriously by the court.

### 8. Hazardous Air Pollutants and Section 112 of the Clean Air Act

The Delaney Clauses administered by the FDA are rare instances of a "zero-risk" regulatory scheme under current environmental laws. Until the Clean Air Act was amended in 1990, the section of the Clean Air Act regulating hazardous air pollutants, section 112, had been interpreted as another example of a zero-risk statute because it required EPA to provide an "ample margin of safety to protect the public health."

In Natural Resources Defense Council v. EPA, 824 F.2d 1146 (D.C. Cir. 1987) (*Vinyl Chloride*), a unanimous U.S. Court of Appeals sitting en banc addressed the meaning of section 112. It held that to determine what constitutes an "ample margin of safety" the EPA "Administrator [must] make an initial determination of what is 'safe.' This determination must be based exclusively upon the Administrator's determination of the risk to health at a particular emission level." The court emphasized that "the Administrator's decision does not require a finding that 'safe' means 'risk-free,'" citing Justice Stevens's observation in the *Benzene* decision that few people consider many daily activities that entail risk (such as driving a car or breathing city air) to be unsafe. Instead, the court found only that "the Administrator's decision must be based upon an expert judgment with regard to the level of emission that will result in an 'acceptable' risk to health" and that "[t]his determination must be based solely upon the risk to health."

The *Vinyl Chloride* case indicated that EPA must decide what constitutes an "ample margin of safety" through a two-step process. In the first step, EPA must determine what is a safe level of emissions without considering costs or technological feasibility. In the second step, EPA may then consider costs and feasibility in determining how far to go beyond mere "safety" in providing an "ample margin" of same. Because EPA had not applied this two-step approach in two other pending regulations involving hazardous air pollutants—a standard for radionuclides promulgated only after EPA had been held in contempt of court and a standard for benzene emissions—it withdrew them as well as the vinyl chloride standard. EPA's first opportunity to respond to the *Vinyl Chloride* decision came when it reproposed the benzene standard in July 1988.

The D.C. Circuit's *Vinyl Chloride* decision forced EPA to confront the "how safe is safe?" question head on, and when it announced its reproposed benzene standard it requested public comment on four possible approaches for determining what constitutes an "acceptable risk." 53 Fed. Reg. 28,496 (1988). Approach A, called the "Case-by-Case Approach," proposed to base acceptable risk decisions on case-by-case consideration of levels of individual risk (probability of an exposed individual's getting cancer), population risk (number of predicted cases of cancer when average individual risk is multiplied by the number of exposed individuals), the distribution of risks among exposed populations, and the uncertainties involved, without establishing any hard-and-fast rules. Approach B, called the "Incidence" or "Population Risk Approach," would deem acceptable one case of cancer per year per source category. Approach C would deem an individual risk of 1 in 10,000 to be acceptable, while Approach D would accept an individual risk of 1 in 1 million.

Three of these four approaches are represented in Figure 3.4, which is adapted from a figure in EPA's Federal Register notice. The *x*-axis represents the size of the exposed population (ranging from 1 to 70 million); levels of individual risk (ranging from 1 in 1 million to 1 in one thousand) appear on the *y*-axis. The one-cancer-per-year "Incidence" or "Population Risk" approach (Approach B) appears as the line descending from left to right, while the "Individual Risk" approaches of 1 in 10,000 (Approach C) and 1 in 1 million (Approach D) appear as the horizontal lines.

In 1989, EPA reached a final decision on its proposed standards for controlling benzene emissions under section 112, which it announced in the following Federal Register notice. The General Counsel of EPA at the time described the contents of the final rule as representing the state-of-the-art thinking on how to determine acceptable or significant risk. What follows is an excerpt from EPA's final rule.

## EPA, National Emission Standards for Hazardous Air Pollutants; Benzene Emissions from Maleic Anhydride Plants, Ethylbenzene/ Styrene Plants, Benzene Storage Vessels, Benzene Equipment Leaks, and Coke By-Product Recovery Plants

54 Fed. Reg. 38,044 (1989)

### SELECTION OF APPROACH

Based on the comments and the record developed in the rulemaking. EPA has selected an approach, based on Approaches A and C but also incorporating consideration of incidence from Approach B and consideration of health protection for the general population on the order of 1 in 1 million from Approach D. Thus, in the first step of the *Vinyl Chloride* inquiry, EPA will consider the extent of the estimated risk were an individual exposed to the maximum level of a pollutant for a lifetime ("MIR"). The EPA will generally presume that if the risk to that individual is no higher than approximately 1 in 10 thousand, that risk level is considered acceptable and EPA then considers the other health and risk factors to complete an overall judgment on acceptability. The presumptive level provides a benchmark for judging the acceptability of maximum individual risk ("MIR"), but does not constitute a rigid line for making that determination.

The Agency recognizes that consideration of maximum individual risk ("MIR") — the estimated risk of contracting cancer following a lifetime exposure at the maximum, modeled long-term ambient concentration of a pollutant—must take into account the strengths and weaknesses of this measure of risk. It is an estimate of the upperbound of risk based on conservative assumptions, such as continuous exposure for 24 hours per day for 70 years. As such, it does not necessarily

**Figure 3.4   Approaches for Determining Acceptable Risk: Population Risk & Individual Risk**

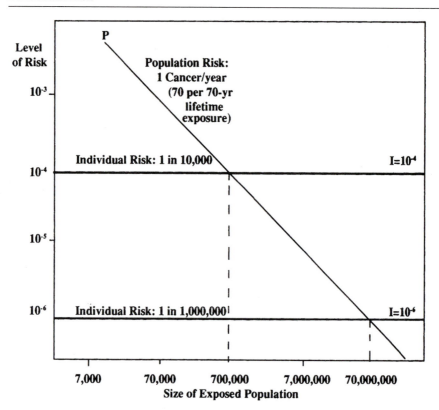

reflect the true risk, but displays a conservative risk level which is an upperbound that is unlikely to be exceeded. The Administrator believes that an MIR of approximately 1 in 10 thousand should ordinarily be the upper end of the range of acceptability. As risks increase above this benchmark, they become presumptively less acceptable under section 112, and would be weighed with the other health risk measures and information in making an overall judgment on acceptability. Or, the Agency may find, in a particular case, that a risk that includes MIR less than the presumptively acceptable level is unacceptable in the light of other health risk factors.

In establishing a presumption for MIR, rather than a rigid line for acceptability, the Agency intends to weigh it with a series of other health measures and factors. These include the overall incidence of cancer or other serious health effects within the exposed population, the numbers of persons exposed within each individual lifetime risk range and associated incidence within, typically, a 50 km exposure radius around facilities, the science policy assumptions and estimation uncertainties associated with the risk measures, weight of the scientific evidence for human health effects, other quantified or unquantified health effects, effects due to co-location of facilities, and co-emission of pollutants.

The EPA also considers incidence (the number of persons estimated to suffer cancer or other serious health effects as a result of exposure to a pollutant) to be an important measure of the health risk to the exposed population. Incidence measures the extent of health risk to the exposed population as a whole, by providing an estimate of the occurrence of cancer or other serious health effects in the exposed population. The EPA believes that even if the MIR is low, the overall risk may be unacceptable if significant numbers of persons are exposed to a hazardous air pollutant, resulting in a significant estimated incidence. Consideration of this factor would not be reduced to a specific limit or range, such as the 1 case/year limit included in proposed Approach B, but estimated incidence would be weighed along with other health risk information in judging acceptability.

The limitations of MIR and incidence are put into perspective by considering how these risks are distributed within the exposed population. This information includes both individual risk, including the number of persons exposed within each risk range, as well as the incidence associated with the persons exposed within each risk range. In this manner, the distribution provides an array of information on individual risk and incidence for the exposed population.

Particular attention will also be accorded to the weight of evidence presented in the risk assessment of potential human carcinogenicity or other health effects of a pollutant. While the same numerical risk may be estimated for an exposure to a pollutant judged to be a known human carcinogen, and to a pollutant considered a possible human carcinogen based on limited animal test data, the same weight cannot be accorded to both estimates. In considering the potential public health effects of the two pollutants, the Agency's judgment on acceptability, including the MIR, will be influenced by the greater weight of evidence for the known human carcinogen.

In the *Vinyl Chloride* decision, the Administrator is directed to determine a "safe" or "acceptable" risk level, based on a judgment of "what risks are acceptable in the world in which we live." 824 F.2d at 1165. To aid in this inquiry, the Agency compiled and presented a "Survey of Societal Risk" in its July 1988 proposal (53 FR 28512-28513). As described there, the survey developed information to place risk estimates in perspective, and to provide background and context for the Administrator's judgment on the acceptability of risks "in the world in which we live." Individual risk levels in the survey ranged from $10^{-1}$ to $10^{-7}$ (that is, the lifetime risk of premature death ranged from 1 in 10 to 1 in 10 million), and incidence levels ranged from less than 1 case/year to estimates as high as 5,000 to 20,000 cases/year. The EPA concluded from the survey that no specific factor in isolation could be identified as defining acceptability under all circumstances, and that the acceptability of a risk depends on consideration of a variety of factors and conditions. However, the presumptive levels established for MIR of approximately 1 in 10 thousand is within the range for individual risk in the survey, and provides health protection at a level lower than many other risks common "in the world in which we live." And, this presumptive level also comports with many previous health risk decisions by EPA premised on controlling maximum individual risks to approximately 1 in 10 thousand and below.

In today's decision, EPA has selected an approach based on the judgment that the first step judgment on acceptability cannot be reduced to any single factor.

The EPA believes that the level of the MIR, the distribution of risks in the exposed population, incidence, the science policy assumptions and uncertainties associated with the risk measures, and the weight of evidence that a pollutant is harmful to health are all important factors to be considered in the acceptability judgment. The EPA concludes that the approach selected best incorporates all of this vital health information, and enables it to weigh them appropriately in making a judgment. In contrast, the single measure Approaches B, C, and D, while providing simple decisionmaking criteria, provide an incomplete set of health information for decisions under section 112. The Administrator believes that the acceptability of risk under section 112 is best judged on the basis of a broad set of health risk measures and information. As applied in practice, the EPA's approach is more protective of public health than any single factor approach. In the case of the benzene sources regulated here, more than 99 percent of the population living within 50 km would be exposed to risks no greater than approximately 1 in 1 million; and, the total number of cases of death or disease estimated to result would be kept low.

Under the two-step process specified in the *Vinyl Chloride* decision, the second step determines an "ample margin of safety," the level at which the standard is set. This is the important step in the standard-setting process of which the actual level of public health protection is established. The first step consideration of acceptability is only a starting point for the analysis, in which a floor for the ultimate standard is set. The standard set at the second step is the legally enforceable limit that must be met by a regulated facility.

Even though the risks judged "acceptable" by EPA in the first step of the *Vinyl Chloride* inquiry are already low, the second step of the inquiry, determining an "ample margin of safety," again includes consideration of all of the health factors, and whether to reduce the risks even further. In the second step, EPA strives to provide protection to the greatest number of persons possible to an individual lifetime risk level no higher than approximately 1 in 1 million. In the ample margin decision, the Agency again considers all of the health risks and other health information considered in the first step. Beyond that information, additional factors relating to the appropriate level of control will also be considered, including costs and economic impacts of controls, technological feasibility, uncertainties, and any other relevant factors. Considering all of these factors, the Agency will establish the standard at a level that provides an ample margin of safety to protect the public health, as required by section 112.

## NOTES AND QUESTIONS

1. Recall the four approaches to answering the "how safe is safe?" question that EPA initially had proposed. Which of these approaches do you think the public favored? Which approach would be favored by industry? By regulators? Why?

2. One result of employing the Incidence Approach (Approach B) would be that the level of protection for any individual would depend on how densely populated the surrounding area is. As can be seen from Figure 3.4, very high levels of individual risk (e.g., 1 in 1,000) could be tolerated for (e.g., a community of 70,000) while far lower levels (e.g., less than 1 in 100,000) would be required in large metropolitan areas (e.g., New York City). Would this approach unfairly discriminate against individuals living in rural areas?

3. Why do you think EPA chose a combination of the four approaches for making "ample margin of safety" determinations rather than adhering to a single approach? Does EPA's policy provide adequate guidance concerning how the agency will make ample margin of safety determinations in the future, or does it simply confirm existing ad hoc practices? Would it be desirable for EPA to follow a less flexible, but more certain, policy for making such decisions?

4. How flexible do you think EPA will be in determining what levels of individual risk constitute an "ample margin of safety"? In applying its new approach to regulation of benzene source categories, EPA determined not to tighten controls on ethylbenzene-styrene process vents. EPA's decision left some individuals exposed to a maximum individual risk of 1 in 50,000 from this source, because the total numbers of such people were small enough that the incidence of cancer produced by this source category was estimated to be 1 case of cancer every 300 years. EPA decided to reduce emissions from benzene storage vessels by 20 to 60 percent to lower the estimated maximum individual risk from this source from a range of 1 in 2,500 to 1 in 25,000 to a level of 1 in 33,000, reducing the estimated incidence of cancer from this source from 1 case every 10 to 20 years to 1 case every 25 years. For coke byproduct recovery plants, EPA promulgated a standard that it estimated would reduce benzene emissions from this source by 97 percent. However, even at this reduced level the maximum individual risk would be 1 in 5,000, a risk greater than the 1 in 10,000 benchmark of EPA's overall approach. EPA sought to justify this decision by noting that it reflected a significant reduction in MIR from current levels and by stressing uncertainties in emissions estimates. EPA noted that the standard for coke byproduct recovery plants would reduce MIR from an estimated current level of 7 in 1,000 (which is estimated to be responsible for 2 cases of cancer per year) to 1 in 5,000 and a cancer incidence of 1 case every 20 years. The agency described this as "comparable" to the 1 in 10,000 benchmark in light of "estimating uncertainties in this case," which it believed to have resulted in an overestimation of actual levels of benzene emissions from this source. Id. EPA also determined not to tighten controls on benzene equipment leaks, despite previous estimates that emissions from this source category presented an MIR of 6 in 10,000 and 1 case of cancer every five years. EPA concluded that actual emissions levels were substantially lower than its previous estimates. Although the agency was not able to calculate actual emissions levels, it expressed the view that "the resulting MIR would be comparable to the benchmark of approximately 1 in 10,000."

5. When EPA interpreted the food additives Delaney Clause of section 409 of the FDCA to contain a de minimis exception, the agency stated that it would consider three factors in deciding what constitutes a "trivial risk": "the weight of the evidence regarding carcinogenicity, the size of the population exposed to the risk, and the level of the risk." EPA stated that "the risk comparisons most relevant to such an exercise are the prior decisions of the regulatory agencies" because they are the products of a public process. After reviewing how the "how safe is safe?" issue had been addressed in other contexts, EPA concluded that when the entire U.S. population is exposed to a probable human carcinogen, "the agency consensus appears to be that risks less than 1 in 1 million generally can be found to be acceptable without consideration of other factors while risks greater than that level require further analysis as to their acceptability." Is this approach consistent with the policy articulated in EPA's NESHAP for benzene?

### The 1990 Amendments to the Clean Air Act and Section 112

In 1990, Congress substantially revised section 112, shifting from a risk-based approach to regulation to a technology-based one. As discussed above in the *Michigan v. EPA* decision, the 1990 Amendments require EPA to establish technology-based controls on an initial list of 189 toxic air pollutants specified in section 112(b)(1). These standards are to reflect use of the maximum achievable control technology (MACT). Congress gave EPA ten years to write all the MACT standards. EPA has confronted a number of difficult issues in implementing section 112, and it has often been challenged by both industry and environmental organizations. Although it issued a number of MACT standards (there are currently 120 MACT categories) within the 10-year statutory deadline, EPA's failure to finish all of them by 2000 triggered section 112's "hammer" provision, requiring any source emitting a section 112 toxic for which a categorical MACT had not been issued to apply to its state air quality agency for a "case-by-case" MACT determination by May 15, 2002. §112(j). EPA and industrial groups reached a settlement in an industry suit challenging EPA's interpretation of the hammer that effectively extended its effective date until May 2004, which was the date EPA anticipated finishing writing the MACT standards. The Sierra Club then challenged EPA's rules as inconsistent with the plain language of the Act and EPA, fearful that its 2002 rules might be vacated, entered into a series of complex negotiations and settlement agreements with the Sierra Club. These agreements covered issues in MACT implementation beyond the deadline issues. One of the more contentious of these issues has been how to interpret the so-called MACT floor provisions of section 112. Those provisions provide that the technology-based standard EPA issues for existing sources in any industrial category or subcategory cannot be less stringent than the "best performing 12%" of that category, and that the standard for new sources cannot be less stringent than the control achieved in practice by the single best-controlled similar plant.

Besides issues such as these that affect the entire MACT process, EPA has also faced legal challenges when it has issued individual MACTs, including those for industrial boilers, hazardous waste combustors, brick kilns, and electric utilities. Several cases have litigated EPA's decision to form subcategories. Because of the MACT floor provision for existing sources, this is often a critical decision, affecting what plants will be included in the performance-based determination of the MACT for that subcategory. In 2007, the D.C. Circuit decided Sierra Club v. EPA, 479 F.3d 875 (D.C. Cir. 2007) ("Brick MACT"), a challenge to EPA's emission standards for brick and ceramics kilns. EPA had initially proposed a subcategory of kilns operating without any air pollution control technology, with a "no emissions reductions" MACT for them. In the final rule, EPA replaced the "no emission reductions" floors with a "work practice standard" for use of clean-burning fuels—essentially the same as no emissions reductions, as the kilns were already operating with clean fuels. The D.C. Circuit, rejecting the proposed standard, ruled that "EPA has a 'clear statutory obligation to set emission standards for each listed HAP,' which does not allow it to 'avoid setting standards for HAPs not controlled with technology.'" The court further noted that work practice standards are a legitimate substitute for emission floors only if EPA determines that it is impracticable to measure emissions from the kilns, which it had not.

Once the MACTs were issued, EPA had to move to the second phase of section 112 implementation. This requires it to make a "residual risk" determination to see if the emissions remaining after the MACT has been applied warrant further regulation. When EPA issued rules for the first six of the eight Phase I residual risk standards, it determined that no further controls were required, despite a finding that the most exposed individuals face more than a 1-in-1-million lifetime cancer risk. Section 112(f)(2) also refers to this benchmark. Environmental groups challenged EPA's interpretation of 112, resulting in the following decision.

## Natural Resources Defense Council v. EPA

529 F.3d 1077 (D.C. Cir. 2008)

SILBERMAN, Senior Circuit Judge.

Petitioners, the Natural Resources Defense Council and the Louisiana Environmental Action Network, challenge EPA's residual risk rulemaking under subsection 112(f) of the Clean Air Act for facilities that use or produce synthetic organic chemicals ("the industry"). We deny the petition.

### I

EPA initially promulgated technology-based emission standards for the industry in 1994 (there are 238 facilities in the United States that produce or use synthetic organic chemicals). Those standards required the use of control technologies such as recovery devices, thermal oxidizers, carbon absorbers, and steam strippers. After submitting the required report to Congress in 1999, the agency commenced residual risk rulemaking, apparently because . . . the industry's emissions pose lifetime excess cancer risks of greater than one-in-one million.

EPA determined that under the existing technology-based standard, no individual would face an excess lifetime cancer risk of greater than 100-in-one million, which EPA regards as the "presumptively acceptable" level under its precedents. . . . Petitioners . . . contend that the statute obliged EPA, in the residual risk rulemaking, to tighten the standards for the industry so that the lifetime excess cancer risk to exposed persons would be no greater than one-in-one million.

### II

### A

Petitioners contend that subsection 112(f)(2)(A) obliged EPA to revise industry standards to reduce lifetime excess cancer risk to one-in-one million. Petitioners rely primarily on the last sentence of that subsection, whereas EPA looks to the whole subsection. That provision states in full:

> If Congress does not act on any recommendation submitted under paragraph (1), the Administrator shall, within 8 years after promulgation of standards for each category or subcategory of sources pursuant to subsection (d) of this section, promulgate standards for such category or subcategory if promulgation of such standards is required in order to provide an ample margin of safety to protect public health in accordance with this section (as in effect before November 15, 1990) or to prevent, taking into

consideration costs, energy, safety, and other relevant factors, an adverse environmental effect. Emissions standards promulgated under this subsection shall provide an ample margin of safety to protect public health in accordance with this section (as in effect before November 15, 1990), unless the Administrator determines that a more stringent standard is necessary to prevent, taking into consideration costs, energy, safety, and other relevant factors, an adverse environmental effect. If standards promulgated pursuant to subsection (d) of this section and applicable to a category or subcategory of sources emitting a pollutant (or pollutants) classified as a known, probable or possible human carcinogen do not reduce lifetime excess cancer risks to the individual most exposed to emissions from a source in the category or subcategory to less than one in one million, the Administrator shall promulgate standards under this subsection for such source category. 42 U.S.C. §7412(f)(2)(A).

It is undisputed that facilities that produce or use synthetic organic chemicals emit carcinogens and are, therefore, within the reach of the last sentence. It is also undisputed that, in light of the fact that existing technology-based standards do not reduce the risk to less than one-in-one million, EPA was obliged to "promulgate standards" under subsection 112(f). Petitioners contend that the third sentence obviously means that residual risk standards must meet the threshold test — *i.e.*, EPA must reduce such risks to one-in-one million. That may well be a possible interpretation, but the sentence contains a glaring omission; it does not say what petitioners would like us to infer. Rather, that sentence instructs the Administrator to "promulgate standards," but it says nothing about the substantive content of those standards. If Congress had wished to set a "bright line" standard, it would have been rather easy for the draftsmen to say just that. The failure to do so could not have been accidental. In light of the rest of the subsection's language (and other provisions), it seems to us that the subsection was drafted as a deliberately ambiguous compromise.

We reach that conclusion because the second sentence, which sets forth the substantive standard to be applied, simply calls for standards that "provide an ample margin of safety to protect public health.". . . No distinction is drawn between carcinogens and non-carcinogens. The third sentence, on which petitioners rely, not only lacks the language that petitioners ask us to infer; it also specifically states that if the one-in-one million trigger is met, the Administrator must promulgate standards "under this subsection," which, perforce, takes us back to the second sentence.

EPA's construction of the subsection is bolstered by another paragraph, 112(f)(2)(B), which states:

Nothing in subparagraph (A) or in any other provision of this section shall be construed as affecting, or applying to the Administrator's interpretation of this section, as in effect before November 15, 1990, and set forth in the Federal Register of September 14, 1989 (54 Federal Register 38044). 42 U.S.C. §7412(f)(2)(B).

The cited item in the Federal Register is EPA's emission standard for benzene, which is a carcinogenic hazardous air pollutant. . . . [T]he *Benzene* standard established a maximum excess risk of 100-in-one million, while adopting the one-in-one million standard as an aspirational goal. This standard, incorporated into the amended version of the Clean Air Act, undermines petitioners' assertion that EPA *must* reduce residual risks to one-in-one million for all sources that emit carcinogenic hazardous air pollutants.

Petitioners respond that subsection 112(f)(2)(B) is a savings clause that only preserves EPA's specific regulations regarding benzene. But the text belies this contention. . . . The word "interpretation" indicates that the savings clause is not limited to EPA's benzene-specific determinations, but applies broadly to the agency's construction of the Clean Air Act in the *Benzene* standard. . . .

The parenthetical clause in the second sentence of subsection 112(f)(2)(A) lends further support to EPA's position. . . . EPA interprets the parenthetical as a "shorthand reference" to the *Benzene* standard, given that subsection (B) uses almost identical language, incorporating "the Administrator's interpretation of this section, as in effect before November 15, 1990, and set forth in the Federal Register. . . ." The phrase "this section (as in effect before November 15, 1990)" is certainly broad enough to encompass EPA's prior *interpretations* of "this section" as well as the text itself. In fact, the operative provision of the pre-1990 version of section 112 uses the exact same "ample margin of safety" language as subsection 112(f)(2) (A) currently uses. Thus, the parenthetical must refer to something more than the bare text of "this section," or else it would be surplusage.

Petitioners insist that EPA's interpretation renders the third sentence effectively meaningless. To be sure, the third sentence, as EPA interprets it, seems relatively anodyne; it lacks substantive force. But, at least as EPA reads it, the word "promulgate" means the agency is obliged to conduct a rulemaking to consider residual risks for sources that emit carcinogens. That extra procedural step is not a trivial obligation. Congress often imposes procedural requirements without dictating substantive outcomes. We also disagree with petitioners' argument that EPA did not "promulgate standards" under subsection 112(f)(2) because it simply readopted the initial standards. This position finds no support in the text of the statute. Subsection 112(f)(2) only mandates that residual risk standards "provide an ample margin of safety to protect public health." If EPA determines that the existing technology-based standards already provide an "ample margin of safety," then the agency is free to readopt those standards during a residual risk rulemaking.

Finally, petitioners argue that EPA unlawfully considered cost while setting the "ample margin of safety" in the residual risk standards. Petitioners are correct that the Supreme Court has "refused to find implicit in ambiguous sections of the [Clean Air Act] an authorization to consider costs that has elsewhere, and so often, been expressly granted." Whitman v. Am. Trucking Ass'n, 531 U.S. 457, 467, 121 S. Ct. 903, 149 L. Ed. 2d 1 (2001). In this case, however, we believe the clear statement rule has been satisfied. As explained above, subsection 112(f)(2)(B) expressly incorporates EPA's interpretation of the Clean Air Act from the *Benzene* standard, complete with a citation to the Federal Register. In that rulemaking, EPA set its standard for benzene "at a level that provides 'an ample margin of safety' in consideration of all health information . . . as well as other relevant factors *including costs and economic impacts*, technological feasibility, and other factors relevant to each particular decision." 54 Fed. Reg. at 38,045 (emphasis added). . . .

In sum, we conclude that EPA's interpretation of subsection 112(f)(2), although not an inevitable one, certainly is, at least, a reasonable construction of the statute.

## NOTES AND QUESTIONS

1. At the same time as it issued its residual risk determination, EPA also determined that its statutorily mandated review of the MACT standards did not require their revision at this time. NRDC challenged that determination on the ground that EPA had impermissibly considered compliance costs, when the consideration of costs is impermissible in establishing the initial MACT floors. The court ruled that it need not reach that issue because, although EPA did discuss costs, the record reflected that it had relied upon statutorily permissible criteria, and that its discussion of costs did not impermissibly "taint" that determination.

2. Implementing the revised section 112 was controversial and slower than the ambitious statutory timeline, but EPA has now finalized the required MACTs, which are being implemented. In contrast, EPA's track record in implementing health-based standards is less encouraging. Under the original section 112, EPA promulgated national emissions standards for only seven hazardous air pollutants in the first 20 years after enactment. One interpretation of this history is that EPA's difficulties were the result of its reluctance to implement what was perceived to be an unreasonably stringent statutory standard. EPA argues that some balancing of cost and economic considerations against protection of public health is inevitable in making regulatory decisions for controlling toxic substances.

While EPA would prefer statutory authorities that permit a more explicit balancing of risks against costs, EPA's track record for implementing TSCA, which requires such balancing, is also no better than its record for implementing section 112. EPA regulated only a few toxic substances under section 6 of TSCA, just as under section 112 of the Clean Air Act. EPA's most comprehensive regulation under section 6 of TSCA—the phaseout of commercial uses of asbestos—took a decade for EPA to complete and then was struck down by the Fifth Circuit in *Corrosion Proof Fittings*.

3. Why has EPA had such a dismal track record in implementing statutes to control toxic substances? Does the problem lie with the way EPA's statutory authorities are structured, or is it simply a result of the way EPA has chosen to implement these authorities? Do the statutes that EPA must implement place impossible informational demands on the agency? Wendy Wagner calculates that EPA and OSHA issued less than 15 percent of the standards Congress required them to promulgate during the 1970s and 1980s under science-based statutory mandates. Wagner, The Science Charade in Toxic Risk Regulation, 95 Colum. L. Rev. 1613, 1614-1615 (1995). Is the implementation of the revised section 112 a success story or not?

4. When EPA chose to adopt a multi-factor approach to acceptable risk, it might have drawn on the field of cognitive psychology to have identified even more relevant factors. Research in this area suggests that when people think about risk, many qualitative factors are relevant to their evaluation, in addition to the quantitative measures that are the exclusive focus of QRAs. Among the important distinctions, people have been found to accept voluntary risks more readily than

involuntarily imposed risks, dispersed risks more readily than concentrated risks, and risks that have received little media coverage more than risks that have been heavily covered in the news. Figure 3.5 captures some of the significant risk traits that influence people's evaluations of risk.

5. The fact that people incorporate these qualitative elements of risk into their assessments of risk situations is undeniable, and it sets up a tension between the way experts tend to view risk and the way laypersons do. "To the experts, risk means expected annual mortality. But to the public . . . risk means much more than that. Let's redefine terms. Call [population risk] 'hazard.' Call all the other factors, collectively, 'outrage.' Risk, then, is the sum of hazard and outrage. . . . We have two decades of data indicating that voluntariness, control, fairness, and the rest are important components of our society's definition of risk. When a risk manager continues to ignore these factors—and continues to be surprised by the public's response of outrage—it is worth asking whose behavior is irrational." Peter M. Sandman, Risk Communication: Facing Public Outrage, EPA J. 21-22 (Nov. 1987). Do these considerations help explain why EPA refused to settle on a one-dimensional definition of risk? Do they help explain some of the reactions to risk and risk regulation decisions discussed in this chapter?

## Figure 3.5    Qualitative Elements of Risk

| Risk Traits | Aggravating | Mitigating |
|---|---|---|
| Familiarity | New | Old |
| Personal control | Uncontrollable | Controllable |
| Voluntariness | Involuntary | Voluntary |
| Media attention | Heavy media coverage | No media coverage |
| Equity | Unevenly distributed | Evenly distributed |
| Impact on children | Children at special risk | Children not at risk |
| Impact on future generations | Future generations at risk | Future generations not at risk |
| Reversibility | Irreversible | Reversible |
| Identifiability of victims | Victims known | Victims unknown |
| Accompanying benefits | Benefits invisible | Benefits clear |
| Source | Human-generated | Natural origins |
| Trust in relevant institutions | Low trust in institutions | High trust in institutions |
| Immediacy of adverse effects | Adverse effects immediate | Adverse effects delayed |
| Understanding | Mechanisms poorly understood | Mechanisms well understood |
| Precedents | History of accidents | No past accidents |

Note: The first column lists certain important risk traits. The second lists the conditions that make the risk more threatening and, hence, less acceptable, holding all else constant. The third lists the conditions that reduce the threat of the risk, making it more tolerable.

Source: Timur Kuran and Cass Sunstein, Availability Heuristics and Risk Regulation, 51 Stanford Law Review 683, 709 (1999).

## PROBLEM EXERCISE: REGULATION OF TOXIC SUBSTANCES

Assume that the U.S. Department of Health and Human Services determines on the basis of the results of animal bioassays that chemical *X* is a probable human carcinogen. HHS lists the chemical as a substance reasonably anticipated to be a carcinogen in its Annual Report on Carcinogens.

**Question One.** Under which statutory authority could chemical *X* be regulated when it is used as: (a) an industrial solvent, (b) a pesticide, (c) a food or color additive, (d) a contaminant in drinking water, and (e) an air pollutant?

**Question Two.** What additional information, if any, would EPA, OSHA, or PDA need in order to be able to regulate chemical *X* under each of the statutes that authorize regulation of it for each of the five uses listed above? Why?

**Question Three.** How stringently could chemical *X* be regulated under each of the statutes that authorize regulation of it?

---

Close analysis of EPA decisions has found that "[a]fter more than [30] years of vigorous public health and safety regulation . . . there are surprisingly few examples of EPA using unreliable science or using science inappropriately to support a final regulation." Wendy Wagner, The "Bad Science" Fiction: Reclaiming the Debate over the Role of Science in Public Health and Environmental Regulation, 66 Law & Contemp. Probs. 63, 72 (2003). This suggests that the point of contention in sound science debates is more frequently a policy or political disagreement. Sometimes it is prompted by wanting to impose a higher burden of proof on government to demonstrate a clear causal connection between exposure and human health effects. This essentially recapitulates the debate over a precautionary approach to regulatory action embodied in decisions like *Ethyl Corp.* Sometimes it is prompted by the belief that giving a different priority to different scientific methods or recognizing different scientific theories will systematically produce better regulatory outcomes for the regulated community. None of these disagreements can be resolved purely as a matter of science, but science is the battlefield upon which they are often fought.

## Regulation of Toxic Substances: A Pathfinder

*Risk assessment* is explained in several useful studies. An influential early report is the National Research Council study, Risk Assessment in the Federal Government: Managing the Process (1983). A helpful introduction to risk assessment for nonscientists is the Conservation Foundation's 1985 monograph, Risk Assessment and Control. The National Academy of Sciences' comprehensive review of EPA's use of risk assessment is National Research Council, Science and Judgment in Risk Assessment (1994). Also useful are the reports of the Presidential/Congressional Commission on Risk Assessment and Risk Management, Framework for Environmental Health Risk Management (1997) and Risk Assessment and Risk Management in Regulatory Decision-Making (1997), which are available from the Government Printing Office. Before disbanding, the Commission, which was created by the Clean Air Act Amendments of 1990, made scores of recommendations for improving the use of risk assessment in regulatory decision making.

*Regulations* implementing TSCA are found at 40 C.F.R. pts. 700-799. FIFRA regulations appear at 40 C.F.R. pts. 150-189, and regulations implementing EPCRA are at 40 C.F.R. pts. 355-372. FDA regulations appear at 21 C.F.R. pts. 1-1299. OSHA's occupational safety and health standards can be found at 29 C.F.R. pt. 1910.

Comprehensive *practitioner's guides* to the Toxic Substances Control Act as amended by the Lautenberg Act include Lynn L. Bergeson & Charles M. Auer, New TSCA: A Guide to the Lautenberg Chemical Safety Act and Its Implementation (ABA 2017) and Miriam V. Gold & Jean Warshaw, Guide to the Toxic Substances Control Act (Nexis/Lexis 2020). An excellent critique of EPA's implementation of the Lautenberg Act is contained in Kevin McLean, Three Years After: Where Does Implementation of the Lautenberg Act Stand?, *http://eelp.law.harvard.edu/wp-content/uploads/McLean-TSCA.pdf.*

A superb free podcast on chemical regulation is "All Things Chemical," produced by Bergeson & Campbell, the leading Washington, D.C. law firm specializing in chemical regulation. The episodes, which appear every few weeks, feature interviews with a wide range of experts. The podcast is available online at *https://podcasts.apple.com/us/podcast/all-things-chemical/id1439928193.*

EPA's Office of Prevention, Pesticides and Toxic Substances makes *chemical release data* from the agency's Toxics Release Inventory (TRI) available to the public on its website at *https://www.epa.gov/toxics-release-inventory-tri-program/tri-data-and-tools.*

## C. REGULATION THROUGH REVELATION

People voluntarily engage in many activities—driving a car, skiing, mountain climbing—that subject them to risks, sometimes significant ones. Yet people resent being exposed involuntarily to even relatively modest risks and demand that society act to minimize such exposure. See Mark Sagoff, On Markets for Risk, 41 Md. L. Rev. 755 (1982). If the goal of toxic substance regulation is to minimize involuntary exposure to risks, it can be pursued not only by regulations that reduce toxic emissions, but also by providing individuals with information that will enable them to choose to avoid certain risks. Even when the incidence of toxics exposure does not directly affect them, consumers may desire to avoid purchasing products that have environmental or human health effects that they consider undesirable.

> [A]t least with regard to some areas of choice . . . consumer preferences may be heavily influenced by information regarding the manner in which goods are produced. Such information . . . can include the labor conditions of workers who produce a consumer good, the environmental effects of a good's production, the use of controversial engineering techniques such as genetic modification to create a good, or any number of other social, economic, or

environmental circumstances that are related causally to a consumer product, but that do not necessarily manifest themselves in the product itself. [A]
lthough such factors generally do not bear on the functioning, performance,
or safety of the product, they nevertheless can, and often, influence the
willingness of consumers to purchase the product. [Douglas Kysar, Preferences for Processes: The Process/Production Distinction and the Regulation
of Consumer Choice, 118 Harv. L. Rev. 525, 529 (2004).]

Either or both of these mechanisms that inform consumers of risks associated
with products can provide incentives to producers to reduce those risks.

The distinction between risks borne voluntarily and those borne involuntarily is
not always an easy one to make. Some risks are easier to avoid than others, and some
individuals are more capable than others of taking steps to avoid risks. We have no
choice about breathing, although in theory we could all wear space suits that filter toxic
pollutants out of the air we breathe. But few would be comfortable with the notion
that this makes such exposures a risk that we bear voluntarily, even if we were provided
with comprehensive information about what pollutants were in each batch of air we
encounter. Opportunities for voluntary avoidance of risks are greater when the risks
involve products that informed consumers can choose not to purchase. Thus, as discussed in Chapter 2, when individuals are informed and have choices, market forces
can serve as a powerful complement to regulation to prevent environmental damage.

But it is not easy to keep consumers with limited attention spans informed of the
risks they may choose to avoid. Information is not gathered and distributed without
cost. Yet approaches that inform consumers of risks may often be far cheaper than
traditional regulatory approaches for controlling risks. The latter often place significant burdens on regulators to demonstrate that certain substances or activities pose
risks worth regulating in the face of scientific uncertainty. Thus, considerable effort
is being devoted to developing new informational approaches to regulation as well as
approaches that shift the burden of gathering information to respond to uncertainty.

Some federal environmental regulations already require the disclosure of risk
information to workers and consumers. For example, OSHA requires that workers
be informed of the presence of hazardous chemicals in the workplace through a
regulation called the hazard communication standard. As a result of a decision by
the U.S. Court of Appeals for the Third Circuit, OSHA expanded its initial hazard
communication standard to cover all industries it regulates. United Steelworkers of
America v. Auchter, 763 F.2d 728 (3d Cir. 1985). The federal Emergency Planning
and Community Right-to-Know Act, discussed below, is designed to provide the
public with information on the presence of toxic chemicals in their communities.
It requires that companies publicly disclose their annual emissions of more than
600 different toxic chemicals and that local authorities be notified about hazardous
substances stored or used by the companies.

Informational approaches also may assist in the enforcement of environmental laws. For example, the Safe Drinking Water Act requires that public water suppliers inform their customers when they violate the Act either by failing to monitor
drinking water or by detecting contaminants in it at levels that exceed the maximum contaminant levels promulgated under the Act. By requiring that potential
victims be informed of violations, this kind of informational regulation can contribute to public pressure to correct violations. For example, the editor of a small newspaper in Washington, North Carolina, became curious when he noticed a cryptic

sentence on the back of his water bill. When he inquired further, he discovered information that led to his writing a Pulitzer Prize–winning series of articles. The articles revealed that for eight years local authorities had sought to conceal the fact that enormously high levels of carcinogenic chemicals had contaminated the town's drinking water. Within a month of the first article informing residents of the danger, the town's water supply system was shut down and the incumbent mayor was defeated in a bid for reelection. A new filtration system ultimately was installed to remove the chemicals from the drinking water. David E. Pitt, Town Gets Clean Water as Paper Gets a Pulitzer, N.Y. Times, Apr. 16, 1990, at A10.

Informational regulations have not always proved successful. In 1983, EPA decided an informational approach was the best way to respond to the widespread presence of asbestos hazards in schools. Rather than issuing regulations requiring that asbestos hazards be abated, EPA required school authorities to undertake a one-time inspection of their buildings to determine if friable asbestos was present and to inform parents and school employees if such materials were found. EPA officials believed that if parents were informed that their children were exposed to a potential hazard, they would ensure that action would promptly be taken to abate it. The regulation, however, proved to have unfortunate consequences. Despite EPA's efforts to provide guidance, school officials generally had a poor understanding of asbestos hazards and the proper means for abating them. Many inspections were poorly performed. Discoveries of asbestos often produced panicked reactions from parents and school authorities that actually may have exacerbated the risks to children. In 1987, Congress responded to this debacle by enacting the Asbestos Hazard Emergency Response Act, which required EPA to issue regulations requiring periodic inspections for asbestos and specifying abatement actions that must be undertaken when asbestos hazards are found.

As we have seen, a critical issue environmental regulation attempts to address is how to respond to uncertainty. Regulations that increase incentives for gathering and disseminating information may help improve society's response to environmental risk by reducing uncertainties concerning the presence and significance of risks. While regulatory authorities generally bear the burden of proving that risks are significant enough to warrant regulation, some new approaches to regulation have sought to shift this burden by requiring persons who generate risks to demonstrate that the risks are significant enough to warrant regulation. Licensing schemes such as FIFRA and the Food, Drug and Cosmetic Act already shift the burden to the manufacturers of pesticides, therapeutic drugs, and food additives to demonstrate the safety of their products. But society generally has not required that manufacturers of other products or dischargers of toxic pollutants make similar demonstrations, perhaps because they would be deemed too burdensome. A California citizens' initiative called Proposition 65, which was adopted in 1986, represents the most innovative effort to change the traditional burden of proof in a manner that would generate incentives for reducing public exposure to involuntary risk.

## *1.   California's Proposition 65: A Burden-Shifting Approach to the Information Problem*

On November 4, 1986, California voters overwhelmingly approved an innovative new approach to regulation of toxic substances. The law, adopted as voter initiative Proposition 65, is titled the "Safe Drinking Water and Toxic Enforcement Act of 1986." It combines a duty-to-warn approach with a shifting of the burden of demonstrating the safety of exposures to carcinogens and reproductive toxins. The simple concept articulated in Proposition 65 is that no one should knowingly expose another without warning to chemicals known to cause cancer or reproductive toxicity unless the discharger can demonstrate that the risk is not significant. This concept had so much political appeal that the initiative's opponents thought it could be defeated only by convincing voters that it had too many loopholes. Noting that Proposition 65 did not apply to pollution from government agencies, oil companies, and agribusinesses waged a $5.7 million advertising campaign against the initiative with the official slogan: "No on 65. It's Full of Exemptions." Proponents responded that they would be happy to work to remove any loopholes after Proposition 65 was approved. Voters approved the initiative by nearly a 2-1 margin. (Ironically, a subsequent voter initiative to extend Proposition 65 to government agencies was narrowly defeated in 1990 after fierce opposition from local governments concerned that it would require extensive warnings about drinking water contamination.)

The operative provisions of Proposition 65 are remarkably simple. First, the law prohibits the discharge into sources of drinking water of any chemical that is a carcinogen or reproductive toxin except in amounts that the discharger can prove are insignificant. The law states:

> No person in the course of doing business shall knowingly discharge or release a chemical known to the state to cause cancer or reproductive toxicity into water or onto or into land where such chemical passes or probably will pass into any source of drinking water, notwithstanding any other provisions or authorization of law except as provided in Section 25249.9. [Ch. 6.6 Cal. Health & Safety Code §25249.5.]

Section 25249.9 exempts discharges that the discharger shows "will not cause any significant amount of the discharged or released chemical to enter any source of drinking water" and that also are in compliance with all applicable regulations.

The second major provision of Proposition 65 is a prohibition on exposing anyone to carcinogens or reproductive toxins without warning unless the person responsible for the exposure can show that it poses no significant risk assuming lifetime exposure. The law provides:

> No person in the course of doing business shall knowingly and intentionally expose any individual to a chemical known to the state to cause cancer or reproductive toxicity without first giving a clear and reasonable warning to such individual, except as provided in Section 25249.10. [Ch. 6.6 Cal. Health & Safety Code §25249.6.]

Section 25249.10 exempts both exposures "for which federal law governs warning in a manner that preempts state authority" and:

> [a]n exposure for which the person responsible can show that the exposure poses no significant risk assuming lifetime exposure at the level in question for substances known to the state to cause cancer, and that the exposure will have no observable effect assuming exposure at one thousand (1,000) times the level in question for substances known to the state

to cause reproductive toxicity, based on evidence and standards of comparable scientific validity to the evidence and standards which form the scientific basis for the listing of such chemical [as a substance known to cause cancer or reproductive toxicity]. [Ch. 6.6 Cal. Health & Safety Code §25249.10.]

Not surprisingly, the initial implementation of Proposition 65 created considerable controversy. Bowing to industry pressure, California governor George Deukmejian placed only substances that had been demonstrated to cause cancer and reproductive toxicity in *humans* on the list of chemicals "known to the state to cause cancer." Thus, the state's original list of carcinogens and reproductive toxins subject to the law contained only 29 substances. Arguing that the law also required the listing of all substances that cause cancer or reproductive damage in animal tests, the supporters of Proposition 65 sued the governor. In AFL-CIO v. Deukmejian, 260 Cal. Rptr. 479 (Cal. Ct. App. 1989), the California Court of Appeal held that chemicals found to be carcinogens or reproductive toxins as a result of animal testing had to be included in the minimum list of chemicals "known to the state to cause cancer or reproductive toxicity" as defined by Proposition 65.

Following the decision in *AFL-CIO v. Deukmejian*, the list of chemicals known to the state of California to cause cancer or reproductive toxicity has been substantially expanded beyond the governor's initial list. By 1995, 542 chemicals were on the list. Some products containing these substances have been exempted by regulation.

In response to a petition from the Grocery Manufacturers of America, the California Health and Welfare Agency, the agency designated by the governor to implement Proposition 65, exempted food products containing naturally occurring carcinogens and reproductive toxins from the requirements of the legislation. The exemption applies to chemicals that are natural constituents of food or that can be shown to be present "solely as a result of absorption or accumulation of the chemical" from "the environment in which the food is raised, or grown, or obtained." 22 Cal. Code Reg. §12501. However, producers and distributors of food are required to use quality control measures that reduce natural chemical contaminants to the "lowest level currently feasible." In Nicolle-Wagner v. Deukmejian, 230 Cal. App. 3d 652, 281 Cal. Rptr. 494 (1991), this exemption was upheld by a California court of appeals which found that Proposition 65 was directed only at controlling exposure to toxics added to the environment by human activity.

While Proposition 65 does not specify what constitutes a "significant risk" for purposes of exposure to substances subject to the law, the law authorizes the California Health and Welfare Agency to issue regulations implementing its provisions. Because Proposition 65 placed the burden of disproving that a risk was significant on the discharger, California businesses discharging listed substances pressed for swift enactment of regulations specifying what exposure levels posed "significant risk." The shift in the burden of proof reversed the normal incentive for the regulated community to seek delay in the issuance of implementing regulations. Toxicologists from all over the country swarmed to California to participate in regulatory proceedings implementing the Act. Acting far more rapidly than federal regulators ever had, the Health and Welfare Agency issued regulations specifying "significant risk" levels for nearly 300 carcinogens, defining "significant risk" for carcinogens as a risk greater than 1 in 100,000. For reproductive toxins, Proposition 65 specifies that exposure at a level of one-thousandth the no-observed-effects level or above constitutes a "significant risk."

The key to its rapid and comprehensive regulatory implementation was that Proposition 65 reversed the usual incentive for industry to prolong the regulatory process with endless debates over "how safe is safe?" As David Roe, a co-author of the law, observes, "California managed to draw bright lines for more chemicals in the first twelve months of the Proposition 65 era than the federal government had managed to accomplish, under the supposedly omnibus Toxic Substances Control Act, in the previous twelve years." Roe notes that "much of the scientific information on which the California lines were based came directly from federal regulatory agencies, which had long since completed their assessment of the relevant research results; the difference was that, for once, there was a premium on getting to the bottom line." Roe, An Incentive-Conscious Approach to Toxic Chemical Controls, 3 Econ. Dev. Q. 179, 181 (1989).

In November 2017, California's Office of Environmental Health Hazard Assessment (OEHHA) added perfluorooctanoic acid (PFOA) and perfluorooctane sulfonate (PFOS) to the list of chemicals known to the state to cause reproductive toxicity for purposes of Proposition 65. OEHHA based this decision on EPA's 2016 Drinking Water Heath Advisories for both chemicals. Thus, even though EPA has delayed regulating these chemicals under the Safe Drinking Water Act, despite years of study, California businesses manufacturing or selling these chemicals have been subject to the requirements of California's Safe Drinking Water and Toxic Enforcement Act.

Businesses that discharge a listed substance at levels in excess of those defined to constitute a "significant risk" can escape liability (unless the substance passes into a source of drinking water) by providing a "clear and reasonable warning" to persons exposed. The question of what constitutes such a warning has been a subject of some dispute. A trade association of grocers initially responded to Proposition 65 by establishing a toll-free telephone number that consumers could call to find out if certain products contained carcinogens or reproductive toxins in significant amounts. Callers were not permitted to request a list of products containing carcinogens or reproductive toxins, but they were warned if they happened to ask about a specific product that did. Although the hotline received 28,000 calls in the first 14 months, only 488 warning messages were issued. Grocers maintained that the availability of the toll-free number made it unnecessary for warning labels to be displayed in their stores. Proponents of Proposition 65, who dubbed the system "800-BALONEY," filed suit, maintaining that the toll-free number was an attempt to circumvent the law. In August 1989, a California Superior Court ruled that the toll-free number "does not provide clear and reasonable warnings" as required by the law.

This decision was affirmed on appeal. Ingredient Communication Council, Inc. v. Lungren, 4 Cal. Rptr. 2d 216 (1992). The court explained why the use of a toll-free number was insufficient to meet the law's requirement to provide "a clear and reasonable warning":

> The major conceptual problem was that the system proceeded on the assumption [that] most consumers before shopping sit down with the food section of the newspaper each week, see the advertised 800 number,

make a list of the specific brand names of products they intend to buy, and then call to check whether these products carry a warning. This assumption is contradicted by the fact that about two-thirds of the buying decisions made by grocery consumers are made in the store on impulse. In addition, few consumers are willing to spend time researching and calling about those relatively inexpensive products they frequently buy in a grocery store; such purchases differ from those of automobiles or computers. [Id. at 225.]

California repealed a regulation that had exempted from Proposition 65 products regulated under the federal Food, Drug, and Cosmetic Act. However, a court ruled that Proposition 65's warning requirements could not be applied to dental mercury because they were preempted by the Medical Devices Amendments to the federal Act. Committee of Dental Amalgam Alloy Mfrs. v. Henry, 871 F. Supp. 1278 (S.D. Cal. 1994).

Regulations implementing Proposition 65 initially created a safe harbor for companies discharging airborne carcinogens if they took out a small newspaper ad stating: "WARNING: This area contains a chemical known to the state of California to cause cancer." 22 Cal. Code Reg. §12601. After a successful court challenge to this regulation, a new warning requirement was proposed that would include signs stating: "WARNING: Emissions or effluents from this facility will expose you to chemicals known to the state of California to cause cancer, including the following. . . ." Pease, Chemical Hazards and the Public's Right to Know: How Effective Is California's Proposition 65?, 33 Environment 13 (Dec. 1991).

Shortly after enactment of Proposition 65, the chairman of the Chemical Manufacturer's Association predicted that the law would have "a significant and detrimental effect on the agricultural and manufacturing business in the state." CMA Chairman Urges Renewal of Clean Air Act. Voluntary Steps on Air Toxics by Industry, 17 Envtl. L. Rep. 220 (1986). Yet little evidence has developed to suggest that the Act has had such an impact. Fear of adverse consumer reactions to warning labels has encouraged some manufacturers to reformulate their products to remove carcinogens and reproductive toxins. Kiwi Brands, Inc., a division of Sara Lee, removed a carcinogenic chemical from its Kiwi waterproofing spray for shoes. Pet, Inc. accelerated the removal of lead solder from cans used for several of its products including Old El Paso tamale/chili gravy and Progresso tomatoes. It is impossible to tell how frequently products have been reformulated. While some companies have released products with "new formulas they can now tout as safer—and sometimes even more effective, . . . [o]ther companies are reformulating quietly to avoid calling attention to chemicals in their old products." Randolph B. Smith, California Spurs Reformulated Products, Wall St. J., Nov. 1, 1990, at B1. Sears, Roebuck and Company reports that several of its suppliers have reformulated scores of products including carburetor cleaners and car wax.

One concern voiced by critics of Proposition 65 is that products containing weak carcinogens will be replaced with more dangerous substances that have not been identified as carcinogens or reproductive toxins because they have not been fully tested. When threatened with a lawsuit in September 1989, the Gillette Company removed Liquid Paper correction fluid from the California market because it contained trichloroethylene (TCE), a carcinogenic substance. Four months later, it introduced a "New Improved" Liquid Paper reformulated with the solvent 1,1,1-tri-chloroethane (TCA) instead of TCE. Yet an official of the Consumer Product Safety Commission has expressed "great concern" that TCA could be carcinogenic because of its structural similarity to the solvents it replaced. Smith, supra, at B7. In fact, Liquid Paper's leading competitor, Wite-Out Products, Inc., which originally had switched to TCA, has introduced a new correction fluid without TCA because of concern that TCA is toxic and likely to be banned as an ozone-depleting chemical.

Significant lawsuits continue to be brought under Proposition 65, although many firms who received notice of an intention to sue have chosen to alter their practices so as to avoid the need to produce warning labels. In 2005, the California Attorney General and environmental groups did bring suit against McDonalds, Frito-Lay, and other manufacturers or sellers of French fries or potato chips, on the basis of acrylamide being found in those foods. Acrylamide has been shown to cause cancer in laboratory animals and has been on California's Prop. 65 list since 1990, but it was only found in food in 2002. It is a byproduct of cooking starchy foods, high in trans-fats, at high temperatures. Firms, including McDonalds, are investigating means of altering the production processes. Press Release, Attorney General Lockyer Files Lawsuit to Require Consumer Warnings About Cancer-Causing Chemical in Potato Chips and French Fries (Aug. 26, 2005).

The following excerpt describes the success of Proposition 65 in reducing the exposure of Californians to lead.

Rechtschaffen

## How to Reduce Lead Exposures with One Simple Statute: The Experience of Proposition 65

*29 Envtl. L. Rep. 10581 (1999)*

Since 1988, California's Proposition 65, a right-to-know initiative, has achieved some noteworthy successes in reducing public exposures to lead in media as diverse as calcium supplements, brass kitchen faucets, water well pumps, ceramicware, hair dyes, wine capsules, and factory emissions. These sources all were subject to regulation by the federal government, but Proposition 65 has spurred faster and more significant lead reductions than federal law by prompting companies to reformulate products and change their manufacturing processes. . . . Thus, the success of Proposition 65, in particular its technology-forcing character, provides important lessons for the ongoing national debate about how best to reform environmental regulation. . . .

Federal law . . . has left significant gaps with respect to important sources of lead exposure. . . . Federal regulation . . . has been slow to address exposures from lead in drinking water from faucets and other plumbing hardware, lead in ceramicware, and lead in calcium supplements, among other products. These sources also can contribute significant, unhealthy levels of lead to the public. For example, in 1991, EPA found that lead in drinking water contributes 20 percent of total lead exposure for an average person, and possibly as much as 85 percent of lead for infants whose diets consist mainly of formula. Researchers estimated that approximately 30 percent of this drinking water contamination was due to lead leaching from brass faucets. Lead-glazed ceramicware is the largest source of lead in the diet. In the early 1990s, the ceramicware industry itself estimated that ceramicware could be the source of up to one-quarter of the "acceptable" lead exposure for adults in this country. Similarly, calcium supplements are widely used by the public to meet dietary requirements; over 50 percent of pregnant and lactating women regularly take calcium supplements. Until recently, almost all calcium supplements contained lead at levels of concern to public health officials. . . .

Proposition 65 has had . . . a striking effect on some of these . . . important gaps left by federal law. . . . In part, Proposition 65 prohibits a person in the course of doing business from "knowingly" discharging or releasing any listed chemical "into water or onto or into land where such chemical passes or will probably pass into any source of drinking water.". . . The statute also imposes a far-reaching warning requirement: businesses must provide a "clear and reasonable" warning prior to "knowingly and intentionally" exposing any individual to a listed chemical. This includes consumer product exposures, occupational exposures, and environmental exposures.

Proposition 65 only exempts exposures or discharges below a de minimis level, defined by the statute as exposures or discharges that pose "no significant risk" of cancer or that are below 1/1,000th of the no observable effect level (NOEL) for reproductive toxicants. The state has set a de minimis level for lead of 0.5 micrograms/day.

Proposition 65 has caused substantial reductions in public exposures to lead by triggering fundamental shifts in long-standing means of production to avoid or minimize the use of lead. In the case of consumer goods, most companies have reformulated their products nationwide, giving Proposition 65 a national effect. . . .

[Pipes, solder, faucets, valves, and other fittings in household plumbing all can contain lead that dissolves into water coming through a building's plumbing system. The Safe Drinking Water Act only requires the public water system to deliver water of a certain quality up to the household; lead that is added to the water after it enters the house is not regulated.] Thus, the best efforts of public drinking water systems can be completely undermined by lead leaching at the very last points of the distribution system. . . .

In 1992, the California Attorney General's office along with two environmental organizations, the Environmental Law Foundation and the Natural Resources Defense Council (NRDC), sued 14 major faucet manufacturers for violating Proposition 65's warning and discharge provisions. Five years earlier, the plumbing industry had begun working with EPA and NSF International, an industry standard-setting organization, to develop a voluntary standard for lead leaching from faucets. The Proposition 65 litigation quickened what had been a protracted negotiation process, and NSF established a voluntary standard in 1994. In 1995, the plumbing manufacturers settled the Proposition 65 suit, agreeing to manufacture faucets that are close to lead-free. Under the agreement, kitchen faucets must leach less than 5 micrograms/liter/day of lead, which is the level the state of California determined that the Proposition 65 exposure limits translates into when normalized to 1 liter. Bathroom and other faucets must meet the less stringent, voluntary NSF standard of 11 micrograms of lead/liter. The companies have until the end of 1999 to bring 95 percent of their products into compliance. (The voluntary NSF standard for faucets was made mandatory by the 1996 amendments to the SDWA.)

The Proposition 65 litigation, as well as the new NSF standard, has prompted significant changes in how faucets are made. Faucets are manufactured by three general methods, used alone or in combination: (1) fabrication, a technique in which extruded and drawn brass rod is machined into component parts, which are then welded together; (2) permanent mold casting (employed far less in the United States than in Europe), in which brass is poured into metal molds or dies; and (3) sand casting, in which brass is poured into sand molds. [Compliance with the Proposition 65 settlement has caused substantial modifications in all three production techniques, with some manufacturers dropping the sand-casting technique, which required the most fundamental alterations, in favor of mold casting and fabrication. Similar manufacturing modifications are occurring for submersible water pumps, water meters, ceramicware (china), calcium dietary supplements, and lead foil capsules on wine bottles—all of which can contribute noticeable amounts of lead to a person's total blood lead levels. Used in conjunction with TRI data, Proposition 65 has also enabled environmental organizations to sue a number of existing sources of lead air emissions, obtaining a number of significant settlements on terms that have produced significant reductions in lead air emissions in California.] . . .

In contrast to the fragmented approach of federal law, Proposition 65 covers a very broad range of activities and environmental media with a single law. The warning requirement applies without limitation to any exposure to a listed chemical, encompassing everything from kitchen faucets, ceramicware, water coolers, food and wine, lead-based paint, miniblinds, crystal decanters, water niters, hair dyes, bullets, and galvanized nails to factory emissions and workplace exposures. The discharge provision proscribes discharges to a "source of drinking water," but this applies broadly to surface water, groundwater, and tap water, and includes direct releases to water bodies or indirect releases onto land likely to migrate to sources of drinking water.

Second, unlike federal law, Proposition 65 is self-executing. Once a chemical is listed by the state as causing cancer or reproductive harm and the relevant statutory grace periods expire, Proposition 65's provisions take effect without specific administrative standards that specify acceptable levels of exposure. This contrasts with federal statutes, where private activity causing lead exposures is permitted until and unless the government sets a restrictive standard. Proposition 65 also is more "enforcement-friendly" than federal provisions. The statute can be enforced by public prosecutors or citizen groups acting in the public interest. There are extremely limited defenses available under the statute; the most important is that an exposure or discharge is below the de minimis level. Moreover, in an enforcement action, the defendant bears the burden of proving this. Violations of the statute result in penalties of up to $25,000 per day per violation, and 25 percent of the penalties go to the plaintiff initiating the enforcement action. Thus, enforcement actions are relatively easy to bring, face few defenses, and can result in enormous penalties—creating considerable incentives for groups outside of the government to search for violations. Moreover, both the California Attorney General's office and many environmental groups and private parties bringing cases have been willing to forego civil fines on defendant companies in exchange for product reformulations. Faced with the prospect of large penalties, many companies have consented to reformulate their products in order to reduce their potential liability; other manufacturers have done so to avoid the possibility of a lawsuit entirely. As a result, enforcement actions have prompted many product reformulations over the past 10 years.

Third, the Proposition 65 de minimis lead standard of 0.5 micrograms is stricter than federal requirements. The state health and welfare agency derived this standard by using OSHA's permissible exposure limit for daily exposure to airborne lead of 500 micrograms/day as the NOEL for lead. The use of this OSHA standard as the NOEL, as well as the conservative requirement in Proposition 65 of a thousand-fold safety factor for reproductive toxicants such as lead, has been heavily criticized by industry. This standard was never challenged, however, almost certainly because given the emergent consensus that there is no safe level of exposure to lead, the standard is scientifically justifiable.

Federal regulatory standards for lead exposure vary depending on the context, but no enforceable federal limits are as stringent as the state standard. As noted, EPA has set an MCLG of zero for lead in drinking water, but this is a nonenforceable health goal. In some cases, the federal government has set specific limits that exceed the Proposition 65 levels, such as action levels set by the FDA for ceramicware. In other contexts, such as calcium supplements, leaded crystal, and other products, there are no specifically enforceable limits on human exposure to lead.

Finally, Proposition 65 differs from most federal requirements by primarily relying on information disclosure to prompt lead reductions. This approach has been especially effective in the consumer marketplace. Because consumer demand can be extremely sensitive to disclosure of adverse health and safety information, particularly with respect to food products, many businesses have elected to reformulate their products rather than provide warnings and risk significant sales losses. By contrast, federal regulation largely relies on traditional, direct regulatory approaches, such as setting lead limits in a particular product. While more prescriptive, these federal requirements trigger far less consumer demand for product changes than information disclosure mandates. . . .

Proposition 65 has been able to quickly and efficiently fill in important gaps in the regulation of lead exposures left by federal law. In 10 short years, the statute's stringent lead limits have forced the development of new technology and substantially reduced pollution across a wide range of media and products. In the plumbing industry, Proposition 65 accelerated the search for new brass alloys, new production methods, and better manufacturing processes. Proposition 65 also prompted the ceramic industry to develop new lead-free glazes and improve its firing techniques, and calcium suppliers to find cleaner sources of calcium deposits. These and other experiences over the past decade illustrate that a simple, multimedia, self-executing statute like Proposition 65 can be more powerful than a host of complex regulatory programs in achieving actual reductions of pollutants in our environment.

## NOTES AND QUESTIONS

1. Apparently Proposition 65 has not had the dire economic effects forecast by those who opposed its adoption. Does this suggest that companies can readily find non-carcinogenic substitutes for substances subject to the Act, or could it indicate that the legislation has had little impact except on products targeted in lawsuits?

2. How do the levels that define "significant risk" for purposes of Proposition 65 compare with EPA's answer to the "how safe is safe?" question under section 112 of the Clean Air Act?

3. An unusual provision of the law is section 25180.7, which requires government employees to report within 72 hours to local health officers and to the local Board of Supervisors any information they receive about the illegal discharge of hazardous waste that is likely to cause injury to public health. Why do you think such a provision was included in the law?

4. Critics of Proposition 65 note that it does not distinguish between the relative levels of risk posed by different products that contain substances subject to the law. Concerns have been expressed that Proposition 65 could saturate consumers with warnings about a bewildering array of relatively minor risks, over-warning consumers to the point that they will abandon risk-avoidance efforts. Proposition 65's impact could be severely diluted if industry groups include warning labels on virtually all products to avoid any potential liability under Proposition 65. How realistic is this fear?

5. Rechtschaffen notes that some of the effects of Proposition 65 are being felt nationwide, because the adjustments that manufacturers make in order to reduce or eliminate chemicals covered by its requirements apply to a manufacturer's goods produced by that adjusted process, wherever they are sold. Is this because of the size of the California market? Would a Proposition 65-type law in the state of Montana, for example, have the same impact?

6. In November 2012, California voters rejected Proposition 37, which would have required retailers and food companies to label products that contained genetically modified organisms (GMOs). The proposition initially had been expected to pass easily. It was vigorously opposed by chemical and food companies who contributed mightily to the $44 million spent by the measure's opponents, dwarfing the $7.3 million spent by proponents. The final vote was 51.4 percent opposed and 48.6 percent in favor. Many countries, including members of the EU, Australia, China, India, Japan, New Zealand, Russia, and South Korea, require GMO foods to be labeled. What explains the defeat of Proposition 37? Are Californians weary of warning labels or are they convinced that GMOs pose no health risks?

## 2.   The Emergency Planning and Community Right-to-Know Act

In December 1984, an accidental release of methyl isocyanate at a chemical plant owned by the Union Carbide Corporation in Bhopal, India killed more than 3,000 people and severely injured scores of thousands of others. In response to this tragedy, several bills were introduced into Congress to strengthen regulation of toxic air pollutants. While arguing that a similar accident could not happen in the United States, the chemical industry pledged to reexamine its safety practices. On August 11, 1985, an accidental release of aldicarb oxime at a Union Carbide plant in Institute, West Virginia, resulted in the brief hospitalization of scores of residents, severely damaging the credibility of the industry shortly after it had assured the public that such accidents could not happen here.

Congress ultimately responded not by enacting new controls on toxic emissions, but rather by adopting legislation requiring comprehensive emergency planning and the reporting of chemical releases. This legislation, which was adopted at the same time as the Superfund Amendments and Reauthorization Act of 1986, is known as the Emergency Planning and Community Right-to-Know Act of 1986 (EPCRA),

Pub. L. No. 99-499, 100 Stat. 1613 (1986), 42 U.S.C. §§11001-11050. The principal provisions of the Act are outlined below. Section 301 of EPCRA requires the establishment of state emergency response commissions and local emergency planning committees, which must develop comprehensive emergency response plans required by section 303. Section 304 of EPCRA requires companies to notify these officials if any chemicals placed by EPA on a list of extremely hazardous substances pursuant to section 302 are released in amounts greater than certain designated thresholds.

## Principal Provisions of the Emergency Planning and Community Right-to-Know Act

*Section 301* requires the establishment of state emergency response commissions and local emergency planning committees.

*Section 302* requires EPA to publish a list of extremely hazardous substances and threshold planning quantities for these substances. Requires facilities where substances on the list are present in an amount in excess of the threshold quantities to notify the state emergency response commission and the local emergency planning committees.

*Section 303* requires local emergency planning committees to prepare a comprehensive emergency response plan and specifies minimum requirements for such plans.

*Section 304* requires owners and operators of facilities to notify community emergency response coordinators of releases of extremely hazardous substances.

*Sections 311 & 312* require owners and operators of facilities required by OSHA to prepare material safety data sheets (MSDSs) to submit MSDSs and an emergency and hazardous chemical inventory form to the local emergency planning committee, the state emergency response commission, and the local fire department.

*Section 313* requires owners and operators of facilities that have ten or more full-time employees and that were in SIC Codes 20 through 39 as of July 1, 1985 to complete a toxic chemical release form reporting the releases of each of more than 650 toxic chemicals used in quantities that exceed established threshold quantities during the preceding calendar year. These forms must be submitted to EPA and state officials by July 1 of each year to report data reflecting releases during the preceding calendar year. EPA is required to establish and maintain in a computer database a national toxic release inventory (TRI), based on data submitted on these forms, which must be accessible by the public through computer telecommunication.

*Section 325* provides for civil, administrative, and criminal penalties for certain violations of the Act and authorizes enforcement actions by EPA.

*Section 326* authorizes citizen suits against owners and operators of facilities that fail to comply with the Act and against the EPA administrator and state officials for failure to perform certain duties required by the Act.

To facilitate emergency planning, sections 311 and 312 of EPCRA require companies to report annually to local emergency planning authorities information concerning the identities, locations, and amounts of hazardous chemicals used at the facilities. Perhaps the most significant new requirement added by EPCRA is contained in section 313, which for the first time requires annual reporting of releases of toxic chemicals. This provision covers companies that employ ten or more full-time employees in a wide variety of industries if they manufacture, process, or otherwise use more than certain threshold quantities of listed chemicals. These companies must file Toxic Chemical Release Forms or Emissions Inventories with EPA and the states by July 1 of every year. The reports must include estimates of the "annual quantity of the toxic chemicals entering each environmental medium." The reports are to be based on readily ascertainable data; no additional monitoring or measurement requirements are imposed. Citizen suits can be brought under section 326 of EPCRA against companies that fail to comply with the reporting requirements imposed by the legislation.

Results of the first Toxic Release Inventory (TRI) were summarized earlier in this chapter. EPA was shocked by the large volume of reported releases. Community organizations and environmental groups used the data to support calls for stronger regulation. During the first week after the TRI became available through the National Library of Medicine, the Library received 225 requests for subscriptions, most from community groups and ordinary citizens. Roberto Suro, Grass-Roots Groups Show Power Battling Pollution Close to Home, N.Y. Times, July 2, 1989, at A1. On August 1, 1989, USA Today published a two-page list of "The Toxic 500," the U.S. counties with the most pollution from industrial chemicals as reported in the TRI. The National Wildlife Federation published a book identifying the 500 largest dischargers, who released more than 7.5 billion pounds of toxics, including 39 known or probable carcinogens. See G. Poje, The Toxic 500 (1988). NRDC used the data to prepare "A Who's Who of American Toxic Air Polluters," identifying more than 1,500 major sources of toxic air emissions. Subsequent updates of the TRI have continued to receive wide publicity, Holusha, The Nation's Pollution: Who Emits What, and Where, N.Y. Times, Oct. 13, 1991, at F10, and many community groups have used the TRI to issue reports publicizing local polluters. Schneider, For Communities, Knowledge of Polluters Is Power, N.Y. Times, Mar. 14, 1991, at D5.

The Environmental Defense Fund (EDF) created an interactive pollution locator called "Scorecard" that used TRI data to permit individuals to obtain information on the Internet about sources of pollution in their communities. By entering their zip code, individuals could find out what chemicals were being released by what sources in their neighborhoods, information about what is known concerning the potential health effects of the chemicals, and how the emissions rank relative to facilities in other parts of the country. The website also allowed visitors to send a free fax to companies who were emission sources demanding that they reduce their emissions (something that the companies soon grew tired of). The Scorecard website is no longer in operation, but beginning in January 2015, EPA made the TRI data available in a new web-based format (*https://www.epa.gov/trinationalanalysis*) that features interactive maps showing the data at state, county, municipal, and zip code levels. This was facilitated by a final rule adopted in August 2013 that requires facilities to submit their annual data electronically.

On the 30th anniversary of EPCRA in October 2016, EPA issued a report reviewing key events in the implementation of the statute. EPA, 30 Years of EPCRA (2016) (*https://www.epa.gov/toxics-release-inventory-tri-program/30th-anniversary-toxics-release-inventory-tri-program*). It includes videos with inspiring stories concerning how TRI data has been used by communities, universities, and industries to reduce the use of toxic chemicals.

The TRI has proven invaluable in providing information to inform public policy and public debate over those policies. For instance, Congress relied heavily on TRI data in specifying the 189 toxic chemicals required to be regulated as hazardous air pollutants in the 1990 Clean Air Act Amendments. EPA has used the TRI as the cornerstone of its pollution prevention strategy and as a means for improving the effectiveness of existing regulatory programs. Based on data from the TRI, EPA asked 600 dischargers to reduce voluntarily their emissions of 17 of the most dangerous toxics by 1995. The TRI has helped EPA adjust its regulatory priorities by revealing that some chemicals are released in far greater quantities than the agency had anticipated. For example, epichlorohydrin, a chemical used in the production of epoxy resins, solvents, plastics, and other products, is classified as a probable human carcinogen, but EPA had not considered regulating it until the TRI revealed that 70 facilities in 24 states discharged 363,000 pounds of it in 1987. EPA previously had only been aware of 20 sources of epichlorohydrin emissions. Charles L. Elkins, EPA Has Varied Plans for Use of Toxic Release Inventory Database, Hazardous Waste Management 42 (Aug. 1989). Congress subsequently placed this chemical on the list of 189 substances that must be regulated as hazardous air pollutants. EPA's Water Office has used the TRI data to identify potential violations of NPDES permits, to help in reviewing permit requests, and to establish water quality standards. The agency's Office of Toxic Substances has screened TRI data to determine what existing chemicals should be subjected to regulatory investigations and to verify production estimates for regulated chemicals.

TRI data also assists efforts to study the impact of other policy instruments. For instance, TRI data on chlorinated solvent wastes from 1987 to 1990 has been used to analyze the impact of state taxes on the generation or management of hazardous wastes. Hilary Sigman, The Effect of Hazardous Waste Taxes on Waste Generation and Disposal, 30 J. Envtl. Econ. & Mgmt. 199 (1996). TRI data also has figured prominently in the debates over environmental justice, helping researchers employ an array of tools to identify the extent to which environmental exposures may be visited in a disproportionate fashion on certain segments of the population.

These benefits from TRI are above and beyond the main reason that advocates pushed for enacting TRI in the wake of Bhopal. TRI backers believed first, that providing information about toxic releases from facilities to the communities nearby those facilities was a good idea in itself and second, that the disclosure of this information would prompt firms to change their behavior in ways that reduced the amount of those releases. The evidence to date bears out this latter expectation. TRI has been extensively studied, with many studies concentrating on the years 1988 through 1992, when TRI was producing heretofore unavailable information on releases and hence might be anticipated to have its greatest effect on firm behavior. Beyond its initial impacts, however, there continues to be evidence that the annual TRI reports affect firm behavior. Of course, TRI reports also continue to inform public debate and provide a valuable source of information against which to evaluate the impact of other environmental policies. Many of the research results are summarized in a book by James Hamilton, an excerpt of which is presented below.

James Hamilton

## Regulation Through Revelation

(2005)

[One group of researchers] views some firm voluntary actions to reduce emissions as strategic efforts to preempt more costly regulations. They analyzed changes in . . . TRI releases between 1988 and 1992 and conclude "that states with higher initial levels of toxic emissions and larger environmental group membership [in the neighboring communities] reduced toxic emissions more rapidly. . . . Since the threat of mandatory regulation is high while the marginal cost of self-regulation is relatively low, it makes good sense for firms to engage in voluntary emissions reductions.". . . [Other researchers] find that states with higher conservation group membership per 1,000 residents and states with less ideologically polarized politics had higher ratios of plants reducing toxic releases. This would be consistent with plants in these states facing (or anticipating) more pressure from environmentalists to reduce their TRI releases. . . .

[Investors are influenced by TRI data.] [O]n the first day the TRI data were released by the EPA to the public (June 19, 1989), the average abnormal return in the stock market for companies with TRI reports was negative and statistically significant. Companies listed in the TRI lost on average $4.1 million in stock value on the first day the data were released. . . . [Other researchers] point out that stock prices may drop upon the release of TRI data if relatively high emissions per dollar of firm revenue signal inefficient production, attract the attention of community activists, drive away green consumers, or generate scrutiny (and potential fines) from regulators. . . . [Still others] show that repeated provision of the TRI can provide new information to investors each year, because comparisons across years allow investors to see how firms change over time and relative to each other. . . . They find that "repeated provisions of the TRI information causes . . . negative returns to be statistically significant in the years 1990-1994, particularly for firms whose environmental performance worsened over time and relative to other firms."

[Community groups use TRI data to engage in environmental politics.] [Researchers] conducted a survey of active TRI users that included 67 responses from public interest groups. Among the citizen groups, 85% reported using the data to exert public pressure on facilities, 79% to educate affected residents, and 75% to lobby for legislative or regulatory changes. . . . 87% of the citizen group respondents [in a different survey] said their efforts had generated media coverage. Fifty-eight percent of the citizen groups indicated that "source reduction efforts were effected at plants" because of their work. . . .

An unanticipated and growing impact of the U.S. TRI is the adoption of pollution disclosure programs by other countries. After the initial years of the TRI demonstrated how emissions inventories and public data provision could work, in

1992 the United Nations Conference on Environment and Development (UNCED) developed an action plan that encouraged countries to create emission inventories and to allow the public access to the data. . . . Countries with versions of a [TRI-like program] include Australia, Canada, Japan, Mexico, Norway, the United Kingdom, and the United States. [Other countries such as Indonesia, also have variants of information disclosure programs.] . . .

The list of what we do not know about the impact of the TRI is . . . long. How accurate are the estimates reported by the facilities? Do plants lower their TRI figures by switching to chemicals not tracked on the list, and what impact on risks might this have? What are the exact mechanisms of information transmission in firms and communities that lead to changes in decision making? What percentage of reductions in reported TRI emissions is the result of information provision alone, and what percentages are the result of factors such as the impact of traditional command-and-control regulations or changes in firms' output levels? What factors are most important in amplifying or diminishing the influence of TRI on facility-level decisions?

[As TRI was being implemented, EPA] could not tell how widely the information would be used. Yet the first 15 years of public data releases (1989-2004) show that the TRI did bring new information to the public, did generate learning in many quarters, did change behavior in the private and public sectors, and did alter many policy debates.

## NOTES AND QUESTIONS

1. Numerous anecdotal reports also attest to TRI's impact. After Monsanto Corporation found that its 35 plants released more than 374 million pounds of toxic substances, more than 20 million of which went into the air, Monsanto's chairman pledged to reduce air emissions of hazardous chemicals by 90 percent by the end of 1992. Charles L. Elkins, Toxic Chemicals, the Right Response, N.Y. Times, Nov. 13, 1988, at F3. As Monsanto worked toward this goal, it updated the press on its progress, announcing in July 1991 that it had cut TRI air emissions by 58 percent from the 1987 TRI baseline. J. Hamilton, Regulation Through Revelation 225 (2005). In July 1993, Monsanto declared that it had met its goal by reducing emissions by 92 percent. Id. Some environmental groups worried that much of these were phantom reductions, but a U.S. Public Interest Research Group researcher said, "They have done some truly good things." Id.

2. A 2003 EPA study, How Are the Toxics Release Inventory Data Used? Government, Business, Academic and Citizen Uses, collects a large and diverse list of case studies of TRI uses. It summarizes its findings:

> Communities use TRI data to begin dialogues with local facilities and to encourage them to reduce their emissions, develop pollution prevent[ion] (P2) plans, and improve safety measures. Public interest groups, government, academicians, and others use TRI data to educate the public about toxic chemical emissions and potential risk. Industry uses TRI data to identify P2 opportunities, set goals for toxic chemical release reduction, and demonstrate its commitment to and progress in

reducing emissions. Federal, state, and local governments use TRI data to set priorities and allocate environmental protection resources to the most pressing problems. Regulators use TRI data to set permit limits, measure compliance with those limits, and target facilities for enforcement activities. Public interest groups use TRI data to demonstrate the need for new environmental regulations or improved implementation and enforcement of existing regulations. Investment analysts use TRI data to provide recommendations to clients seeking to make environmentally sound investments. Insurance companies use TRI data as one indication of potential environmental liabilities. Governments use TRI data to assess or modify taxes and fees based on toxic emissions or overall environmental performance. Consultants and others use TRI data to identify business opportunities, such as marketing P2 and control technologies to TRI reporting facilities. Id. at 1.

3. Concern about the accuracy of the TRI data has been ongoing. The first year's data is generally considered quite unreliable. Annual data quality reports generated by EPA in the mid-1990s suggest that "facilities generally determine thresholds correctly over 90 percent of the time," and hence are reporting the chemical releases that they should be. "Analyzing the EPA's data studies, Susan Dudley of the Mercatus Center noted they suggest that, 'while in the aggregate, the TRI reflects the number of pounds of listed chemicals released, releases reported on a facility basis may contain such large errors that make them unreliable for site-specific analysis.'" Hamilton, supra at 221. A 1998 paper reports results from a phone survey aimed at determining the cause of a substantial reduction in TRI figures for one chemical between 1991 and 1994. It found that "one type of paper change [in reporting requirements] redefining on-site recycling activities as in-process recovery, which does not have to be reported, accounted for more than half of these facilities' 1991-1994 reported reductions." Id. at 222.

4. TRI reporting has been significantly expanded three times, each through EPA-initiated action. In 1994, EPA added 286 chemicals to the reporting requirements. In April 1997, EPA expanded the number of facilities required to file annual TRI reports by nearly 25 percent by subjecting to EPCRA's requirements seven additional industries—metal and coal mining, electric utilities, petroleum bulk terminals, chemical wholesalers, solvent recovery services, and commercial hazardous waste treatment operations. As a result of this decision, more than 31,000 facilities are now covered by EPCRA. In 1999, it lowered the size of the releases that trigger the reporting requirement for 18 chemicals, including aldrin, mercury, chlordane, and dioxin, out of a concern that these chemicals are persistent in the environment and bioaccumulate. Hamilton, supra at 136-142. In one of the last actions of the Clinton EPA, the agency also lowered the reporting threshold for lead on January 17, 2001, something that it had been studying for years and proposed formally in August 1999. In 2019, Congress added a provision to the National Defense Authorization Act requiring certain PFAS chemicals to be added to the Toxics Release Inventory. EPA has added 172 PFAS to this inventory, though many of these are the long-chain versions of PFAS that are being phased out and not the thousands of other shorter-chain PFAS variations that are still widely used today.

5. EPCRA does not require that any warning labels be placed on products or that the public be informed prior to toxics discharges. Data on toxic releases are reported once a year, after the releases have occurred. Thus, unlike Proposition 65, which has the potential to mobilize the market forces of consumer purchasing decisions, EPCRA's effectiveness will turn on the extent to which the public uses the TRI to lobby for emissions reductions. Which approach do you think is more effective in reducing exposures to toxics, Proposition 65 or EPCRA—or are the two approaches more properly viewed as complementary? How could the TRI data help plaintiffs seeking to enforce Proposition 65's requirements?

### EPCRA Reporting Requirements and the Prevention of Terrorism

More than 10,000 facilities in the United States produce, use, or store chemicals in hazardous amounts. It is estimated that at least 100 of these could harm more than a million people in a worst-case chemical release and that more than 7,300 could harm more than 1,000 people. Jonathan Kalmuss-Katz, Eco Anti-Terrorism: EPA's Role in Securing Our Nation's Chemical Plants, 31 New York Envtl. Lawyer 63 (2011). In the late 1990s, hearings on the possible misuse of TRI information—the reporting of "worst case" scenarios for reporting facilities—were used as a vehicle to restrict some TRI information disclosure. U.S. House of Representatives, Committee on Commerce, Subcommittee on Health and Environment and Subcommittee on Oversight and Investigations, Joint Hearings on Internet Posting of Chemical "Worst Case" Scenarios: A Roadmap for Terrorists. Responding to concern over terrorism, Congress enacted the Chemical Safety Information, Site Security and Fuels Regulatory Relief Act, Pub. L. No. 106-40. Information about possible "worst case" chemical accidents is now available to the public only in limited-access reading rooms where it is easier to monitor who is accessing the information and for what purpose. The legislation also removed flammable fuels used as fuel from coverage under the risk management plan program.

As a result of the September 11, 2001 terrorist attacks, several federal agencies removed information about hazardous chemicals from their websites. EPA removed information about general risk management plans from its website and the Department of Transportation removed maps of pipelines and a study describing risk profiles for certain chemicals. The U.S. Centers for Disease Control removed a "Report on Chemical Terrorism" that described the chemical industry's vulnerabilities to a terrorist attack. The reading rooms that contain information about "worst case" chemical accidents did not experience any suspicious activity in the months immediately following September 11. Guy Gugliotta, Agencies Scrub Web Sites of Sensitive Chemical Data, Wash. Post, Oct. 4, 2001, at A29.

Environmental groups argue that rather than restricting disclosure of information about chemical risks, the government and the public should use this information to encourage companies to shift to the use of inherently safer chemicals as a means for reducing inviting targets for terrorists. An illuminating case study involves not a chemical plant, but rather the sewage treatment facility that serves Washington, D.C. The Blue Plains Wastewater Treatment Plant that serves Washington, D.C. is located only four miles south of the U.S. Capitol. Following the 9/11 terrorist attacks, reporters for the Washington Post disclosed that the plant was storing liquid chlorine in 90-ton tanker cars parked on-site. It was estimated that a single terrorist firing a rocket-propelled grenade at a tanker car could have released a toxic cloud of chlorine over the District of Columbia, quickly killing 38,000 residents. The Washington Suburban Sanitary Commission, which operates Blue Plains, quickly announced that it would no longer use liquid chlorine in its sewage treatment process. Carol D. Leonnig & Spencer S. Hsu, Fearing Attack, Blue Plains Ceases Toxic Chemical Use, Wash. Post, Nov. 20, 2001, at A1.

# CHAPTER 4

# WASTE MANAGEMENT AND POLLUTION PREVENTION

The Congress hereby declares it to be the national policy of the United States that pollution should be prevented or reduced at the source whenever feasible; pollution that cannot be prevented should be recycled in an environmentally safe manner, whenever feasible; pollution that cannot be prevented or recycled should be treated in an environmentally safe manner whenever feasible; and disposal or other release into the environment should be employed only as a last resort and should be conducted in an environmentally safe manner.

*— Pollution Prevention Act of 1990, 42 U.S.C. §13101(b)*

CERCLA's liability provisions have caused a virtual revolution in industry's approach to hazardous waste, providing a strong incentive for pollution prevention and waste minimization efforts that have reduced dramatically the amount of hazardous waste that is generated in this country. The effectiveness of the liability and enforcement provisions of the Superfund statute is no doubt a primary cause of the attack that is now being made upon it.[*]

*— Then-Assistant Attorney General Lois J. Schiffer*

Because all pollution is a form of waste, whatever affects the generation and management of waste affects the nature and scope of pollution problems. This chapter examines how regulatory policy has sought to influence waste management practices and to remediate environmental contamination. It begins by reviewing the sources of waste management and pollution problems and the broad array of regulatory authorities that have been enacted to respond to them. It then focuses on two federal laws—the Resource Conservation and Recovery Act (RCRA), which regulates how hazardous wastes are managed, and the Comprehensive Environmental Response, Compensation and Liability Act (CERCLA), often referred to as "the Superfund program," which governs remediation of hazardous substance contamination. The chapter concludes by examining constitutional limits on measures restricting interstate waste disposal and environmental justice concerns raised by the siting of waste disposal facilities.

---

[*] Envtl. Forum, Sept./Oct. 1995, at 25.

## A.   *WASTE MANAGEMENT AND POLLUTION PROBLEMS*

Waste is generated by virtually every entity at nearly every stage of extraction, production, and consumption processes. Much of this waste poses little environmental concern — nearly half is agricultural waste, primarily crop residues that are simply plowed under. Other waste streams can be highly dangerous. Chemical wastes that contain carcinogens and other toxic substances can harm human health when they seep through the ground and contaminate underground aquifers that supply drinking water. Mining and ore processing operations cause other environmental problems because they generate enormous quantities of overburden (soil and rock cleared away) and mineral tailings that may severely pollute streams with acidic runoff. Even common household wastes contain some dangerous constituents, though in concentrations much lower than industrial waste. Household garbage also contains organic matter that can form methane gas when decomposing in landfills.

Waste streams have changed over time in response to changes in production techniques, transportation technologies, consumption patterns, and energy use. In nineteenth-century America, horse droppings were a major part of the municipal waste stream. In 1840, New York was able to sell its street sweepings for $38,711 because they were two-thirds horse manure. The other third was dirt and dust. By 1860, better sources of fertilizer had become available and the city received less than $18,000 for its street sweepings; shortly after that it had to begin paying to dispose of them. Ash from domestic coal burning was a significant part of the early twentieth-century municipal waste stream. Manhattan alone produced nearly 1.2 million tons of coal ash in 1910.

The volume and composition of domestic waste streams have changed dramatically over time. In 1910, Americans produced about a half-pound of municipal garbage per person per day, twice the per capita amount produced in Europe. By 1960, the volume of municipal waste in the United States had grown to more than 88 million tons per year, 2.7 pounds of waste per person per day. Waste volumes continued to grow during the next six decades, reaching approximately 267.8 million tons in 2017, 4.51 pounds per person per day. Paper and paper products are the largest elements in the municipal waste stream (25%), followed by food waste (15.2%), plastics (13.2%), yard waste (13.1%), metals (9.4%), wood (6.7%), textiles (6.3%), glass (4.2%), and rubber and leathers (3.4%).

Waste management practices have changed substantially over time. In the nineteenth century, valuable products were reclaimed from domestic waste where possible, whether it was horse droppings used for fertilizer, uncombusted coal in ash, scrap metal, rubber, paper, or glass collected by junk cart men. Some coastal cities dumped their garbage at sea, a practice that is prohibited today; other cities built incinerators or sent their garbage to landfills.

In 2013, most of municipal solid waste (52.8%) still was sent to landfills, but this represented a significant decline from the 94 percent sent to landfills in 1960. As environmental standards have tightened, the number of operating landfills that dispose of municipal waste has declined sharply from 8,000 in 1988 to only 1,908 in 2013. Approximately 13 percent of the municipal waste stream is incinerated. A total of 80 municipal incinerators have the capacity to generate electricity, while burning a total of up to 95,300 tons of municipal solid waste each day. In recent years there has been a substantial resurgence of recycling and composting of waste. Only 6.4 percent of the municipal waste stream was recycled or composted in 1960, but this number increased to 16.8 percent in 1990 and 34.3 percent in 2013. A total of 87.2 million tons of waste was recycled in 2013, more than double the 34 million tons recycled in 1990. Auto batteries were the materials recycled most regularly (96%), followed by newspapers (72%), steel cans (67%), yard trimmings (60%), and aluminum beer and soda cans (50%).

Concern over the rising volume of municipal solid waste helped persuade Congress to adopt the Solid Waste Disposal Act of 1965 (SWDA). This legislation funded federal research and provided financial assistance to states to improve their waste management planning. It was not until more than a decade later, in 1976, that Congress responded to the growing problem of hazardous waste management by adopting the Resource Conservation and Recovery Act (RCRA) as an amendment to the SWDA. With the expansion of the petrochemical industry after World War II, the volume and toxicity of industrial waste streams had increased dramatically. At the end of World War II, U.S. industry was generating approximately 500,000 tons of hazardous waste per year. During the next 50 years the volume of this waste increased more than 500-fold. Despite the highly toxic compounds contained in this waste, much of it simply was dumped on land with virtually no concern for its potential to cause long-term environmental harm.

Many people may have assumed that the ground could act as a kind of bottomless sponge, absorbing without consequences any chemical compounds poured into it. The prevailing philosophy throughout the 1950s and 1960s was "out of sight, out of mind." This mentality was irrevocably jarred in 1978 by the discovery of a toxic soup bubbling up into the basements of homes in the community of Love Canal, New York, following heavy rains. The homes had been constructed on the site of a former industrial dump that had been deeded to the city for $1. While Love Canal became the focus of national attention, similar problems were being discovered throughout the nation. A childhood leukemia cluster was discovered in Woburn, Massachusetts, where the municipal drinking water wells were found to be heavily contaminated with industrial toxins.

In 1979 alone, more than 300 incidents of groundwater contamination were discovered; private and public water supply wells were capped in 25 states. House Comm. on Gov't Operations, Interim Report on Groundwater Contamination: Environmental Protection Agency Oversight, H.R. No. 96-1440, 3 (1980). EPA determined that 50 billion gallons of liquid wastes were placed in industrial surface impoundments every day; 70 percent of these impoundments were unlined and 2,600 of these were sitting directly on top of groundwater sources within one mile of a water supply well. Id. at 6 (as corrected by errata sheet). This put new pressure on EPA to implement the "cradle-to-grave" regulatory program for hazardous wastes mandated by RCRA. While RCRA authorized EPA to bring lawsuits against anyone contributing to conditions that "may present an imminent and substantial endangerment to health or the environment," its primary purpose was not to remediate past contamination. Congress addressed this problem in 1980 when it created the Superfund program in the Comprehensive Environmental Response, Compensation, and Liability Act (CERCLA).

While the Superfund program concentrates on remediating contamination problems caused by past waste management practices, contemporary management of hazardous waste is regulated under RCRA. In 2017, 25,596 entities reported that they generated almost 35 million tons of RCRA hazardous waste. EPA, The National Biennial RCRA Hazardous Waste Report (2017). In 2017, 1,168 facilities managed RCRA hazardous wastes. More than half of this waste was managed by facilities in two states—Texas and Louisiana. Most waste was managed by generators on site. Over 6 million tons of hazardous waste were shipped; almost 3.5 million tons of this crossed state lines.

Deepwell or underground injection is the principal method for managing hazardous waste, accounting for more than 69 percent of waste management in 2017. Only 1.3 million tons of hazardous waste were managed in landfills or surface impoundments in 2013; 1.1 million tons were incinerated.

Not all discarded toxics are regulated as hazardous waste. Household waste is exempt from federal hazardous waste regulations even though it may contain toxic constituents such as those found in paint, cleaners, oils, batteries, and pesticides. Several industries also have succeeded in winning special treatment for their wastes. The mining and petroleum industries generally have not been subjected to federal hazardous waste regulations despite the fact that their wastes have contributed to numerous incidents of environmental damage. Surface mining operations are regulated under the Surface Mining Control and Reclamation Act (SMCRA), while underground storage tanks that contain hazardous substances are regulated under RCRA.

Pollution controls imposed by the Clean Air Act and the Clean Water Act generate their own wastes including sludges from wastewater treatment plants and air pollution control equipment. In 1980, Congress temporarily exempted ash generated by coal combustion from regulation as hazardous waste under RCRA pending an EPA study that was required to be completed by October 1982. RCRA §8002(n), 42 U.S.C. §6982(n). EPA agreed to complete this study only after a lawsuit to require completion of the study was filed in 1991. After the EPA study finally was completed in March 1999, EPA considered regulating some coal combustion wastes as hazardous under Subtitle C of RCRA because they often contain arsenic, lead, mercury, and selenium and had been the cause of several incidents of environmental damage. However, after vigorous lobbying from the utility industry, EPA decided not to regulate the waste as hazardous. The issue came to national attention on December 22, 2008 when the collapse of an earthen containment wall at the Kingston power plant in Tennessee buried 400 acres of eastern Tennessee in coal ash sludge to a depth of six feet. The utility industry generates more than 130 million tons of this ash annually and much of it is stored in unlined ponds at 1,300 sites across the United States. Shaila Dewan, Hundreds of Coal Ash Dumps, with Virtually No Regulation, N.Y. Times, Jan. 7, 2009, at A1. In December 2014, EPA issued regulations governing disposal of coal combustion residuals in landfills and surface impoundments under Subtitle D of RCRA. The Coal Ash Rule regulated the disposal of coal combustion residuals (CCR) in landfills and surface impoundments. In 2018 the D.C. Circuit held that several provisions of the rule were insufficiently protective of the environment because they allowed "open dumps" that are prohibited under RCRA Subtitle D. Utility Solid Waste Activities Group v. EPA, 901 F.3d 414 (D.C. Cir. 2018).

As end-of-the-pipe pollution controls shifted some pollution from one medium to another, Congress recognized the importance of controlling pollution at its source. There is now broad agreement, reflected in the Pollution Prevention Act of 1990, that environmental policy should shift its focus from controlling discharges at the end of the pipe to encouraging process changes that prevent pollution by reducing the volume and toxicity of waste streams. Source reduction is now the preferred strategy, followed by recycling, and then treatment.

As the volume of discarded electronic products escalates, concern has grown over the environmental impact of toxic materials contained in this "e-waste." By 2013, 25 states and New York City had adopted e-waste recycling legislation. Most of these laws require product manufacturers to develop plans to collect and recover their products from consumers. While EPA does not have any regulations specifically covering e-waste, it has encouraged manufacturers of electronic products to establish "take-back" programs to recycle used electronics. These and other policy initiatives reflect the evolution of waste management policy from end-of-the-pipe controls to measures that create incentives for source reduction and recycling.

## NOTES AND QUESTIONS

1. The task of gathering data on waste generation and management is complicated by the difficulty of defining what material should be considered "waste." Are materials that are generated by production and extraction processes waste if they are not immediately used for some purpose? Are they wastes if they may be used at some time in the future as material inputs into other production processes?

2. Average per capita generation of municipal solid waste remains about twice as high in the United States as in Europe. Why is substantially more waste per capita generated by residents of the United States than by residents of other developed countries?

3. While RCRA and CERCLA are the most comprehensive statutory responses to the waste management problem, they are not the only laws that affect waste disposal practices. Before we examine the RCRA and CERCLA programs, it is useful to consider briefly the wide variety of other statutes that are used to regulate waste management practices.

## B. STATUTORY AUTHORITIES AFFECTING WASTE MANAGEMENT

Congress has long recognized that the best strategy for preventing pollution is to reduce the generation of waste while encouraging recycling. Yet environmental regulations have focused almost exclusively on waste *disposal* practices, influencing waste *reduction* only indirectly by raising disposal costs. Wastes are generated at many stages in the production process by the extraction of raw materials as well as during refining and fabrication. Some wastes generated during manufacturing are recycled as scrap that is fed back into the crude materials refining process to be transformed into a form usable in further product manufacturing. The rest become industrial waste. Manufactured products are themselves sources of waste when capital goods are demolished and when consumer goods and packaging are discarded as litter or household and commercial wastes. Although the design of production processes and finished products determines the volume and composition of waste streams, waste disposal considerations often have not been incorporated into product design decisions.

The variety and complexity of activities that generate and dispose of wastes are reflected in the patchwork way in which the environmental laws control various waste management activities. Nearly a dozen major federal statutes control some aspect of waste disposal. These include not only the principal pollution control laws, listed previously, but also other statutes designed to control radioactive wastes and uranium mill tailings. The extent of regulatory authority over waste management practices varies depending on the activity or product that generates the waste, the characteristics of the waste, and the location or method of waste disposal. For example, wastes burned or vented into the air may be subject to regulation under the Clean Air Act. Wastes discharged into inland or coastal waters are regulated under the Clean Water Act, while wastes dumped into the open ocean are controlled by the Marine Protection, Research, and Sanctuaries Act (MPRSA, also known as the Ocean Dumping Act). Radioactive wastes and uranium mill tailings are covered by their own separate statutes: The Nuclear Waste Policy Act regulates the most highly radioactive wastes generated by nuclear power plants; the Low-Level Radioactive Waste Policy Act controls other radioactive wastes, such as those generated by hospitals and laboratories; the Uranium Mill Tailings Radiation Control Act sets standards for the cleanup of wastes from uranium mines. The Safe Drinking Water Act regulates contaminants that are found in public drinking water supplies as well as hazardous wastes disposed of through underground injection in deep wells.

The nature of the activity that generates a waste also may have a significant influence on the way the waste is regulated. For example, wastes generated by households have been exempted from RCRA's hazardous waste regulations because of concern over the difficulty of extending the federal regulatory system into everyone's backyard. Because mineral extraction operations generate wastes in such large volumes, Congress temporarily exempted them from federal hazardous waste regulations pending further study. Recycling activities also have been exempted from hazardous waste regulation in order to encourage efforts to reduce the volume and toxicity of waste streams.

Solid waste disposal was not regulated at the federal level until relatively recently. Garbage disposal and other forms of waste management have traditionally been the exclusive concern of local and state governments, especially municipalities. Indeed, virtually all of the other major federal environmental legislation antedates the enactment of the principal federal laws regulating waste disposal. But concern over the environmental damage caused by improper waste disposal has rapidly produced in RCRA and CERCLA two of the most far-reaching federal environmental laws. RCRA provides for cradle-to-grave regulation of hazardous waste, while CERCLA imposes strict liability for the cleanup of releases of hazardous substances. While the two statutes have complementary objectives—RCRA to prevent releases of hazardous wastes and CERCLA to clean up releases of a broader class of hazardous substances—they each employ very different means to pursue their goal. RCRA employs a regulatory approach, while CERCLA is founded on a strict liability scheme.

## Regulation of Waste Management: A Pathfinder

The principal statutory authorities that regulate waste management practices are contained in the Resource Conservation and Recovery Act (RCRA), codified at 42 U.S.C. §§6901-6992k, and the Comprehensive Environmental Response, Compensation, and Liability Act (CERCLA), codified at 42 U.S.C. §§9601-9675. Because RCRA was originally enacted as an amendment to the largely nonregulatory Solid Waste Disposal Act, it is sometimes referred to by that name, though practitioners and courts generally use the RCRA acronym. Because CERCLA creates the federal Superfund, it is often referred to as the Superfund legislation. RCRA was substantially revised in 1984 by the Hazardous and Solid Waste Amendments (HSWA). Minor revisions were made in 1992 by the Federal Facility Compliance Act and in 1996 by the Land Disposal Program Flexibility Act. CERCLA was substantially amended in 1986 by the Superfund Amendments and Reauthorization Act (SARA). Amendments were added to CERCLA in 1996 by the Asset Conservation, Lender Liability and Deposit Insurance Protection Act (ACLLDIPA), in 1999 by the Superfund Recycling Equity Act, and in 2002 by the Small Business Liability Relief and Brownfields Revitalization Act (SBLRBRA). Because disposal of nonhazardous solid waste is largely governed by state law and municipal ordinances, it is important to consult sources of such law and to pay attention to the policies of state (and local) environmental officials.

EPA waste management regulations are codified at 40 C.F.R. pts. 239-282. Regulations governing management of hazardous waste begin at 40 C.F.R. pt. 260. Regulations covering underground storage tanks are found at 40 C.F.R. pts. 280-282. While CERCLA has largely been a nonregulatory program, it is beginning to generate a substantial body of regulations contained in 40 C.F.R. pts. 300-312. The list of reportable quantities of CERCLA hazardous substances appears at 40 C.F.R. pt. 302. Significant regulatory interpretations often are found in EPA guidance documents rather than in the Federal Register, which makes it difficult to monitor significant changes in EPA policy. The American Bar Association regularly sponsors satellite seminars to update practitioners on RCRA and CERCLA developments.

EPA maintains dockets containing important information about sites eligible for cleanup under CERCLA. These include a Federal Facilities Docket, a National Priorities List (NPL) Docket, and Superfund Administrative Records, which include Records of Decision (RODs) concerning site cleanups. EPA maintains a "RCRA Online" database at *www.epa.gov/rcraonline*, which enables users to locate documents covering a wide range of RCRA topics. A particularly useful guide to RCRA is EPA's RCRA Orientation Manual (2014), available at *https://www.epa.gov/sites/production/files/2015-07/documents/rom.pdf.*

Despite differences in their initial purposes and approaches, the RCRA and CERCLA programs are closely linked. Section 7003 of RCRA, 42 U.S.C. §6973, authorizes government actions to enjoin anyone who has contributed to waste-handling practices that may present an "imminent and substantial endangerment to health or the environment." This authority foreshadowed the enactment in 1980 of CERCLA's cleanup authorities. As congressional dissatisfaction with EPA's implementation of these programs produced major legislative revisions of each program (RCRA in 1984 and CERCLA in 1986), their interrelationship has become more important. Congress has recognized that the success or failure of RCRA's preventative regulations could have a major effect on the number of dump sites that the CERCLA program will have to clean up in the future. Thus, Congress directed that RCRA's regulatory program be used to phase out the most dangerous land disposal practices while requiring operating RCRA facilities to clean up prior releases of hazardous substances as a condition for obtaining an RCRA permit.

In addition to the regulatory authorities mentioned above, Congress has acted to encourage voluntary efforts to reduce the generation of waste. The Pollution Prevention Act of 1990 represents a step in this direction. The Act declares it "to be the national policy of the United States that pollution should be prevented at the source whenever feasible." In cases where pollution cannot feasibly be prevented, it declares recycling to be the preferred alternative, followed by treatment, and only then disposal. The Act requires EPA to establish a Pollution Prevention Office and a Source Reduction Clearinghouse to facilitate source reduction. The Act also required EPA to develop a Pollution Prevention Strategy, which EPA announced in January 1991. As part of this strategy, EPA targeted 17 high-risk chemicals, and it established a voluntary goal of reducing total environmental releases of these chemicals by 33 percent by the end of 1992 and by 50 percent by the end of 1995. EPA, Pollution Prevention Strategy (Jan. 1991). The 33/50 program was highly successful. More than 1,300 companies participated in the program, which reached its interim 33 percent reduction goal a year ahead of schedule. The 1995 goal of 50 percent reduction actually was achieved by 1994 when reductions totaled 757 million pounds.

EPA has emphasized that voluntary pollution prevention programs are not intended to substitute for strong regulatory and enforcement programs. Indeed, the agency has indicated that it is investigating more creative use of its existing regulatory authorities to encourage source reduction, and it has used the adoption of source reduction plans as a means for settling some enforcement cases.

The Pollution Prevention Act is designed mainly to create an improved information base that can facilitate future decisions about regulatory action to prevent pollution. The Act requires companies that already must file annual reports on environmental releases pursuant to the Emergency Planning and Community Right-to-Know Act to include in these reports descriptions of their source reduction and recycling activities. This information, which is made available to the public, includes estimates of the amount of source reduction each company expects to achieve during the next two years.

## C. *THE RCRA REGULATORY PROGRAM*

### 1. *RCRA: An Introduction*

#### A. History of the RCRA Program

The Solid Waste Disposal Act of 1965 had established a modest program of research on solid waste management centered in the old Department of Health, Education, and Welfare. In 1970, this legislation was expanded to authorize federal grants to support the development of new technology for solid waste management. Congress concluded that solid waste management was primarily a local responsibility, and it continued to define the federal role as a nonregulatory one.

By 1976, this had changed. RCRA was enacted after congressional committees had received estimates that the volume of solid waste generated in the United States was much greater than previously imagined. An estimated 3 to 4 billion tons of solid waste were reportedly being generated annually, and the amount was growing at an estimated 8 percent per year. The House committee report accompanying the legislation noted that each year Americans discarded 71 billion cans, 38 billion jars and bottles, 35 million tons of paper, 7.6 million televisions, 7 million cars and trucks, and 4 million tons of plastics. H.R. Rep. 94-1491, 94th Cong., 2d Sess., at 10-11 (1976).

After 1980, the history of RCRA became tightly intertwined with that of CERCLA. Mounting evidence of lax disposal practices prompted Congress to become actively involved in cleaning up the mistakes of the past and preventing their recurrence. By and large, RCRA has become the locus of Congress's prevention concerns, while CERCLA tackles the problems of cleaning up past mistakes, although there are important areas of overlapping responsibility. Under section 7003 of RCRA, for instance, the government can sue to enjoin activities causing "imminent and substantial endangerment," and thus can compel some cleanups. In addition, RCRA's "corrective action" requirements impose cleanup responsibilities as a condition for maintaining a current operating permit. In this section we concentrate on the predominant prevention aspects of the statute. RCRA's corrective action authorities are found in §§3004(u) & (v), 42 U.S.C. §§6924(u) & (v).

The 1976 Act established a basic statutory structure, which continues to the present: a system for identifying and listing hazardous wastes, a cradle-to-grave tracking system, standards for generators and transporters of hazardous wastes and for operators of treatment, storage, and disposal (TSD) facilities, a permit system to enforce these standards, and a procedure for delegating to states the administration of the permitting program. This complicated structure reflects RCRA's distinct, though interrelated, objectives.

First, RCRA aimed at making land disposal of wastes far safer than it had been previously. The "overriding concern" of Congress in enacting RCRA, as expressed in the House committee report accompanying the legislation, was "the effect on the population and the environment of the disposal of discarded hazardous wastes—those which by virtue of their composition or longevity are harmful, toxic, or lethal." The report noted that "[w]ithout a regulatory framework, such hazardous waste will continue to be disposed of in ponds or on the ground in a manner that results in substantial and sometimes irreversible pollution of the environment."

The RCRA structure provided such a regulatory framework. The identification and listing system would notify generators, transporters, and operators as to which wastes came under the Act's safeguards for hazardous wastes; the tracking system would ensure that compliance could be monitored and responsibility for future problems fixed; the standards, especially for TSD operators, would minimize the environmental costs of disposal, while the permitting system would put operators on clear notice of those standards.

RCRA represented a significant departure from the approach of end-of-the-pipe pollution control statutes such as the Clean Air Act and Clean Water Act by regulating the entire lifecycle of hazardous waste management activities. Congress recognized that environmental regulations should do more than simply transfer pollution from one medium to another. As the House committee that reported out the RCRA legislation explained:

> At present the federal government is spending billions of dollars to remove pollutants from the air and water, only to dispose of such pollutants on the land in an environmentally unsound manner. The existing methods of land disposal often result in air pollution, subsurface leachate, and surface run-off, which affect air and water quality. This legislation will eliminate this problem and permit the environmental laws to function in a coordinated and effective way.

Indeed, the committee optimistically declared that RCRA "eliminates the last remaining loophole in environmental law, that of unregulated land disposal of discarded materials and hazardous wastes." H.R. Rep. 94-1491, 94th Cong., 2d Sess., at 4 (1976). While the RCRA regulatory program has focused on protecting groundwater from contamination by hazardous wastes leaching from land disposal facilities, RCRA requires regulation of all avenues for treatment, storage, and disposal of hazardous waste, including incinerators and air emissions from hazardous waste landfills.

Second, RCRA aimed at technology forcing. The statute, through the regulations that EPA was instructed to promulgate, requires TSD operators to employ technologies for landfill disposal "as may be necessary to protect human health." §3004(a). Beyond this, however, RCRA evinces a concern that landfills were being used excessively because they were far cheaper than alternative disposal techniques. As one analyst notes: "It is not difficult to see why firms and others faced with the costs of incineration to render wastes less harmful (estimated to range from $300 to $1,000 per ton) or of burying the wastes in landfills (perhaps as little as $50 per ton) would choose the latter." R. Dower, Hazardous Wastes, in Public Policies for Environment Protection 154 (P. Portney ed., 1990). Imposing stricter safety requirements on landfills would raise the costs of such disposal; Congress believed that this would force the development of superior alternative technologies.

The desire to promote alternative disposal techniques became even more apparent as Congress has revisited the 1976 legislation, first in 1980 and again in 1984. For instance, as the late Senator John Chafee (R-RI) explained during debate on the 1984 Amendments:

> [L]and disposal is extremely cheap when compared with the available alternatives such as incineration or chemical-physical treatment. Therefore, we should not be surprised to find that land disposal and treatment

in land disposal facilities such as surface impoundments are being utilized much more frequently than the newer, high-tech options. . . . What we do not have, and will not have as long as cheap land disposal options are available, is a viable market to support the development and expansion of new, safer treatment and disposal technologies. [130 Cong. Rec. S30697 (daily ed. Oct. 5, 1984).]

The 1984 Amendments reflected a new level of congressional effort to force technological change because Congress was no longer relying on market forces to express the increased costs of land disposal and hence to stimulate that change. As Representative Norman Lent (R-NY) said, "I believe it is appropriate for the Congress to intervene at this time and to establish a new policy which calls for a review of known hazardous wastes and a determination whether these wastes are appropriate for land disposal." 130 Cong. Rec. H29490 (daily ed. Oct. 3, 1984). The most dramatic such interventions are the 1984 Amendments' land disposal ban provisions, analyzed later in this section.

Third, RCRA aimed at waste reduction. "Waste reduction" encompasses any techniques that adjust basic manufacturing processes so that waste is not generated in the first place. One incentive for waste reduction is provided by increasing the costs of waste disposal. Beyond this, initial elements of a waste reduction program were rudimentary at best and, in the process of implementing the regulatory aspects of RCRA, essentially ignored. There are signs this situation is changing following enactment of the Pollution Prevention Act of 1990.

One reason waste reduction was not more directly addressed by the 1976 statute involves the fourth objective of RCRA: Congress wanted to minimize direct regulation of American production processes. As the committee report accompanying the House version of the 1976 Act explained the provisions applicable to generators of hazardous wastes, "rather than place restrictions on the generation of hazardous waste, which in many instances would amount to interference with the production process itself, the committee has limited the responsibility of the generator for hazardous waste to one of providing information." H.R. Rep. No. 94-1491, 94th Cong., 2d Sess., at 26 (1976). The jurisdictional trigger of the statute reflects this intention, in that the statute defines "solid wastes" as "discarded material." §1004(27).

*American Mining Congress v. EPA*, excerpted below, involves some of the interpretational and implementational issues created by the desire of Congress to steer EPA away from direct regulation of normal production processes. As that decision suggests, some of the most significant problems arise with respect to the fifth objective of the statute: encouraging recycling. As a method for addressing the solid waste problem, recycling or resource recovery can be seen as standing between waste reduction and treatment, storage, and disposal. While waste reduction adjusts primary production processes so that waste is eliminated before it is generated, and TSD facilities dispose of or otherwise care for the generated wastes that remain, recycling takes generated wastes and returns all or part of them to primary production processes. Congress understood that increased recycling was yet another way to minimize environmental and public health damage from waste disposal and meant to encourage it. As the House report said, "an increase in reclamation and reuse practices is a major objective of the Resource Conservation and Recovery Act." H.R. Rep. No. 94-1491 at 2.

Although the desire to encourage recycling has been clear from the beginning, the status of recycling activities under RCRA's regulatory authorities has been problematic. Many of the problems relate to the distinction between "the production process itself" and "discarded material." If they are awaiting processing through a recycling facility, are piles of industrial residue from manufacturing "discarded materials" or are they part of "the production process itself"? Does it matter whether or not the recycling processes actually employed were being employed as part of production processes before RCRA was enacted (even if not employed as extensively as we would like)? From time to time, EPA has said that it "did not believe [its] authority extends to certain types of recycling activities that are shown to be similar to normal production processes. . . ." 50 Fed. Reg. at 614. In other places, however, it has been more aggressive, interpreting RCRA as "providing authority over hazardous wastes being used, reused, recycled, or reclaimed." 48 Fed. Reg. at 14,502. The line-drawing exercise here is important, because regulated firms have a substantial interest in being exempt from governmental regulation. This is precisely what was at stake in *American Mining Congress*. That litigation is also typical of a fair amount of litigation under RCRA. Because being caught by the RCRA regulatory net is financially onerous, and because the statute contains so many definitions and exemptions, we have witnessed considerable litigation about its jurisdictional boundaries.

Finally, RCRA sought to maintain substantial state responsibility for the solid waste problem. The legislation explicitly acknowledged that "the collection of solid wastes should continue to be primarily the function of State, regional and local agencies," §1002(a)(4). While it mandated comprehensive federal regulation of "hazardous wastes," it provided for the delegation of permitting responsibilities to qualifying state agencies. Thus, RCRA reflected the tendency of 1970s environmental legislation to leave politically divisive implementation of federal substantive legislation to the states. Some of this divisiveness emerges during controversies surrounding the siting of hazardous waste–related facilities.

While keeping the basic structure of the 1976 Act intact, Congress revisited RCRA with major amendments in 1984 called the Hazardous and Solid Waste Amendments (HSWA). HSWA sought to strengthen EPA's regulatory hand in accomplishing RCRA's primary objectives. Congress made more apparent its conviction that land disposal should be the disposal option of last resort and expressed its dissatisfaction with the slow pace of RCRA implementation.

Defining which of the myriad chemical waste streams are hazardous and what management practices will ensure that no damage is done to the environment proved to be far more difficult than anyone had imagined. These inherent difficulties were exacerbated in 1981 when the Reagan administration's regulatory relief program brought RCRA implementation to a temporary standstill. EPA's promulgation of final permitting standards for TSDs was delayed for years while existing TSDs were allowed to continue in operation as RCRA "interim status" facilities with minimal environmental controls. To qualify for "interim status," facilities were only required to notify EPA of their existence and to conduct minimal groundwater monitoring.

The 1984 Amendments mandated a major shift in the philosophy behind RCRA regulation. EPA previously had recognized that all landfills eventually leak, but it had focused most of its regulatory attention on measures to contain such leakage. The 1984 Amendments sought not only to speed EPA's development of regulatory standards and to close certain loopholes in EPA's existing regulations, but also to fundamentally change waste disposal practices by phasing out land disposal and by forcing the development and use of improved technology to detoxify hazardous wastes.

To speed EPA's implementation of RCRA, Congress imposed scores of new statutory deadlines for the promulgation of regulations by the agency. EPA had failed to meet most such deadlines in the original RCRA legislation. Indeed, most of the significant RCRA regulations, such as permitting standards for TSDs, were issued under court orders as a result of citizen suits brought by environmental groups. To ensure that the most significant new deadlines established by the 1984 Amendments were met, Congress coupled them with "hammer" provisions specifying what regulations would automatically take effect if EPA failed to act.

The principal thrust of the 1984 Amendments was to shift hazardous waste disposal away from the land and to encourage the development of more sophisticated treatment technologies. To minimize the land disposal of untreated wastes, Congress directed that such disposal be banned in stages unless EPA determined that there would be "no migration" of hazardous constituents as long as the waste remains hazardous. Recognizing that severe contamination already had occurred at many TSDs, Congress required facilities obtaining RCRA permits to take corrective action to clean up all prior releases of hazardous wastes and their constituents. To hasten the closing of interim status facilities that would not qualify for final permits, Congress required all TSDs to apply for final RCRA permits by October 1986 and to certify compliance with groundwater monitoring and financial responsibility requirements. As a result of these provisions, a majority of the existing treatment and storage facilities and incinerators opted to close, as did the vast majority of land disposal facilities.

Congress made minor amendments to RCRA in both 1992 and 1996. In 1992 it enacted the Federal Facility Compliance Act, which made it easier to enforce RCRA at federal facilities. In 1996, Congress enacted the Land Disposal Program Flexibility Act that amended RCRA to provide EPA with more flexibility in regulating the land disposal of certain wastes.

## B.  Structure of the RCRA Program

To understand how the RCRA program operates, it is useful to begin by sketching in greater detail the basic structure of the regulatory scheme the statute creates, rather than plunging headlong into what one court has called a "mind-numbing journey" (American Mining Congress v. EPA, 824 F.2d 1177, 1189 (D.C. Cir. 1987)) through EPA's complicated RCRA regulations. The structure of RCRA is outlined below. When studying RCRA, bear in mind what targets EPA generally may regulate under the statute (those who generate, transport, treat, store, or dispose of hazardous solid waste) and the basis for controls specified in the statute ("as may be necessary to protect human health or the environment").

---

# Structure of the Resource Conservation and Recovery Act

*§1002. Goals:* outlines statutory goals, including the principle that land disposal should be the least favored method for managing hazardous wastes.

## Subtitle C: Hazardous Waste Management (§§3001-3020)

*§3001:*        *Identification and Listing of Hazardous Waste:* requires EPA to develop criteria for determining what is a hazardous waste and to list wastes determined to be hazardous.

*§3002:*        *Regulation of Generators of Hazardous Waste:* requires EPA to establish recordkeeping requirements and a manifest system to be used to track shipments of hazardous waste from point of generation.

*§3003:*        *Regulation of Transporters of Hazardous Waste:* requires transporters of hazardous waste to use the manifest system.

*§3004:*        *Regulation of Facilities that Treat, Store, or Dispose of Hazardous Waste (TSDs):* requires EPA to set standards for TSDs to ensure safe handling of hazardous waste, sets minimum requirements for such standards, prohibits the land disposal of untreated wastes unless EPA specifically determines that such disposal is protective of human health and the environment, establishes minimum technology requirements for certain facilities, and requires corrective action for all releases of hazardous wastes or constituents.

*§3005:*        *Permit Requirements for TSDs:* requires TSDs to obtain a permit from EPA or states that incorporate the requirements of section 3004.

## Subtitle D: State or Regional Solid Waste Plans

*§§4001-4010:*    require EPA to establish guidelines for state solid waste management plans and to set minimum requirements for state plans including a ban on new open dumps, require EPA to establish criteria for classifying facilities as sanitary landfills, prohibit open dumping of solid waste except in sanitary landfills, and require EPA to establish minimum regulatory standards for municipal landfills to be implemented by the states.

### Enforcement, Citizen Suit, and Judicial Review Provisions

| | |
|---|---|
| *§3008:* | provides federal enforcement authorities including criminal, civil, and administrative penalties. |
| *§7002:* | authorizes citizen suits against those who violate RCRA regulations or permits, against anyone who has contributed or is contributing to the past or present handling of any solid or hazardous waste that may present an imminent and substantial endangerment to health or the environment, and against the EPA administrator for failure to perform any nondiscretionary duty. |
| *§7003:* | authorizes suits by EPA to restrain anyone who has contributed or is contributing to the past or present handling of any solid or hazardous waste that may present an imminent and substantial endangerment to health or the environment. |
| *§7006:* | authorizes judicial review of RCRA regulations in the D.C. Circuit. |

### Subtitle I: Regulation of Underground Storage Tanks

| | |
|---|---|
| *§9002:* | requires owners of underground storage tanks to notify state authorities. |
| *§9003:* | requires EPA to issue regulations governing detection, prevention, and correction of leaks from underground storage tanks, including financial responsibility requirements and new tank performance standards. |

RCRA is divided into two major parts: (1) subtitle C, a regulatory program covering *hazardous* solid wastes, and (2) subtitle D, a largely nonregulatory program to encourage states to improve their management of *nonhazardous* solid waste. Subtitle C of RCRA requires EPA to regulate generators of hazardous waste (§3002), transporters (§3003), and facilities that treat, store, or dispose of hazardous waste (§3004). Operating standards for TSD facilities are to be implemented through a permit system (§3005).

RCRA's subtitle C regulations are contained in 40 C.F.R. pts. 260-272. Generators are responsible for determining if their wastes are hazardous. Those who accumulate more than 100 kilograms of hazardous waste per month — an estimated 200,000 firms — are subject to regulation under subtitle C. These generators must obtain an identification number for their hazardous waste. To ensure that shipments of hazardous waste can be traced, generators must complete a multiple-copy manifest form to accompany the waste to its ultimate destination at a licensed TSD. The generator must notify authorities if a copy of the manifest form is not returned certifying that the waste reached its intended destination. 40 C.F.R. pt. 262.

Transporters also must use the manifest system, and they must mark and label their shipments of hazardous waste. 40 C.F.R. pt. 263. Transporters of hazardous waste must comply not only with EPA's manifest requirements, but also with regulations on hazardous materials transportation established by the Department of Transportation pursuant to the Hazardous Materials Transportation Act.

Facilities that treat, store, or dispose of hazardous waste must obtain a permit that incorporates minimum national standards established in EPA's regulations. 40 C.F.R. pt. 270. See Figure 4.1. These include not only general administrative requirements for recordkeeping, personnel training, and emergency preparedness, but also specific design, performance, and operating requirements for each category of facility. New units, replacement units, and lateral expansions of existing landfills and surface impoundments must meet certain minimum technology requirements. (For example, landfills must have double liners and a leachate collection system.) Facilities also must prepare closure plans describing how the facilities ultimately will be closed, and they must demonstrate that they have sufficient financial resources to compensate third parties for damages as well as to undertake safe closure and to conduct postclosure monitoring and maintenance.

Another significant requirement of the 1984 Amendments is that RCRA permits must require facilities to take "corrective action for all releases of hazardous waste or constituents from any solid waste management unit" at the facility. Thus, TSD facilities that wish to continue operation must clean up any prior contamination at their facility regardless of when or where it occurred. TSDs also must conduct regular groundwater monitoring and take corrective action if contamination is detected. When closing, TSDs must take precautions designed to ensure that their facilities will not leak in the decades to come, and they must ensure their financial responsibility to clean up releases that occur during postclosure care. Generators, transporters, and TSDs must all train their personnel in waste management and emergency response procedures, and they must notify the authorities of releases of hazardous substances.

The regulatory program established by RCRA can be viewed as essentially a two-tiered scheme: "hazardous wastes" are to be regulated stringently under subtitle C (from generation through transport to disposal), while all other solid wastes are subject to subtitle D and left largely untouched by federal regulation (although municipal solid waste landfills are now subject to minimum federal standards under subtitle D). Rather than attempting to vary the degree of regulation to match the degree of hazard posed by a particular waste, the RCRA program with few exceptions leaves only two regulatory options: comprehensive regulation with little regard for cost considerations, or no federal regulation at all. If a facility is found to be treating, storing, or disposing of a hazardous waste, it generally must comply with all permit requirements regardless of the degree of hazard its waste poses. Thus, RCRA properly can be viewed as mandating a form of health-based regulation, but one that does not vary once the regulatory threshold of "hazardousness" has been crossed.

To be sure, there is another provision in RCRA that gives EPA more discretion to tailor the extent of regulation to the degree of hazard involved. Section 7003 of RCRA authorizes EPA to sue to enjoin any person who has contributed to, or is contributing to, any solid or hazardous waste management practices that "may present

## Figure 4.1 A Capsule Description of RCRA's Subtitle C Program

EPA and the states share the responsibility for regulating newly generated hazardous waste under RCRA. RCRA was created to minimize the risks from hazardous wastes at all points in their life cycle, from their generation to their disposal. It was also designed to require safeguards; to encourage the proper disposal of municipal, commercial, and industrial waste; to eliminate or reduce waste; and to conserve energy and natural resources.

### Hazardous Waste and "Cradle to Grave" Management

RCRA involves a "cradle to grave" effort covering the generation, transportation, storage, treatment, and disposal of newly generated hazardous waste. EPA's system includes five basic elements:

- **Identification**—Generators and the types of waste that they produce must be initially identified.
- **Tracking**—A uniform "manifest" describing the waste, its quantity, the generator, and receiver, must accompany transported hazardous waste from the point at which it is generated to its final off-site destination and disposal.
- **Permitting**—All hazardous waste treatment, storage, and disposal facilities will be issued permits to allow EPA and the states to ensure their safe operation. There are about 7,000 facilities that must receive permits in order to continue operating.

- **Restrictions and controls**—Hazardous waste facilities must follow EPA's rules and guidance specifying acceptable conditions for disposal, treatment, and storage of hazardous wastes.
- **Enforcement and compliance**—Generators, transporters, and facilities are penalized if they do not comply with the regulations.

The cradle to grave system works through requirements for hazardous waste treatment, storage, and disposal facilties. Key to this system are RCRA operating permits. Basic operating permits identify administrative and technical standards with which facilities must comply. For example, the permits require operators of hazardous waste landfills to keep thorough records of the types and quantities of wastes they manage.

## Hazardous Waste Manifest Trail

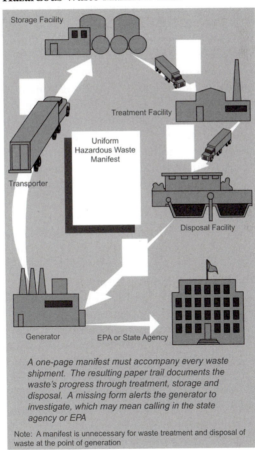

*A one-page manifest must accompany every waste shipment. The resulting paper trail documents the waste's progress through treatment, storage and disposal. A missing form alerts the generator to investigate, which may mean calling in the state agency or EPA*

Note: A manifest is unnecessary for waste treatment and disposal of waste at the point of generation

*Source:* EPA, Environmental Progress and Challenges: EPA's Update 88 (Aug. 1988).

an imminent and substantial endangerment to health or the environment." This was used extensively by the government to address the need to clean up abandoned dump sites prior to the enactment of CERCLA in 1980.

EPA's implementation of the land disposal ban provisions of the 1984 Amendments to RCRA has moved the RCRA program much closer to technology-based regulation. While the land ban appears to be a health-based standard on paper (it prohibits the disposal of untreated hazardous wastes unless it can be shown with a reasonable degree of certainty that there will be no migration of the waste as long as it remains hazardous), EPA has chosen to implement it by requiring that facilities use the best demonstrated available treatment technology (BDAT) before disposing of wastes on land.

Most of the dump site cleanup problem is a legacy of the inadequacy of controls on waste disposal practices in the past. But few people are confident that even new, tougher controls on hazardous waste disposal can ensure that existing facilities regulated under subtitle C of RCRA will not eventually become Superfund sites. This lack of confidence stems not only from the fact that a certain amount of illegal dumping undoubtedly occurs, but also from gaps in subtitle C's coverage. As a result, HSWA amended subtitle D of RCRA, which covers nonhazardous solid wastes, to require EPA to establish minimum regulatory standards to be used by the states in regulating municipal landfills. While these regulations subjected management practices for nonhazardous solid wastes to their first significant dose of regulation, subtitle C's regulations remain far stricter, particularly in light of the land disposal ban.

In the sections that follow we consider how far RCRA's jurisdiction extends by exploring the meaning of the terms that are the crucial jurisdictional triggers for RCRA regulation: "solid waste" and "hazardous waste." To be regulated under RCRA a substance must be a *solid waste*; only solid wastes that are *hazardous* are subject to regulation under the onerous subtitle C.

## 2.  What Substances Are "Solid Wastes"?

RCRA's jurisdiction extends to "solid waste." A waste does not have to be in solid form in order to be considered a "solid waste" for purposes of RCRA jurisdiction. Section 1004(27) of RCRA defines "solid waste" as including "any garbage, refuse, sludge from a waste treatment plant, water supply treatment plant, or air pollution control facility and other discarded material, including solid, liquid, semisolid or contained gaseous material, resulting from industrial, commercial, mining, and agricultural operations, and from community activities." 42 U.S.C. §6903(27).

Certain categories of waste have been exempted from RCRA by EPA or Congress by excluding them from the definition of solid waste. As illustrated in Figure 4.2 on page 317, Congress has exempted domestic sewage, industrial wastewater discharges that are subject to regulation as point sources under section 402 of the Clean Water Act, irrigation return flows, mining wastes not removed from the ground, and certain nuclear materials covered by the Atomic Energy Act. EPA by regulation also has exempted other categories of waste including household wastes (i.e., the garbage we generate at home), fertilizer used in agricultural operations,

**Figure 4.2 Statutory and Regulatory Exclusions from Definition of Solid Waste**

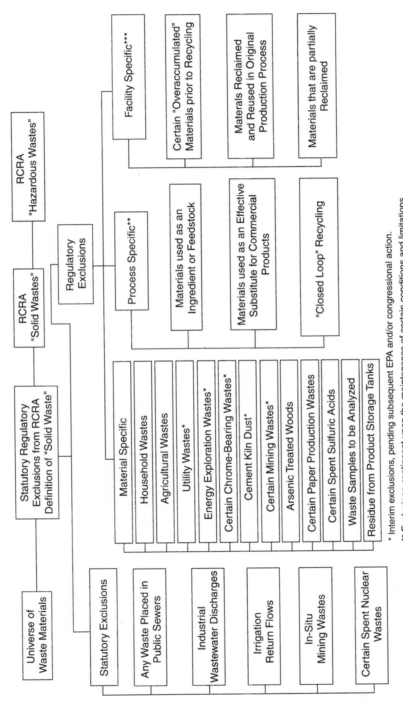

* Interim exclusions, pending subsequent EPA and/or congressional action.

** Exclusions contingent upon the maintenance of certain conditions and limitations.

*** Require prior approval of EPA regional administrator or authorized state on case-by-case basis.

*Source:* D. Lennett and R. Fortuna, Hazardous Waste Regulations: The New Era 67 (1987).

and certain categories of high-volume wastes that Congress had directed EPA to study (e.g., certain mining wastes). These exclusions can have significant environmental consequences because the wastes removed from the RCRA regulatory program include millions of gallons of hazardous materials whose disposal is largely unregulated.

A particularly troublesome issue for EPA has been the extent to which RCRA covers recycled materials. If material that otherwise would be discarded is recycled, can it be considered a solid waste? If a generator maintains that materials that otherwise would be considered wastes are being stored for future recycling, should the materials be covered by RCRA's regulations?

On January 4, 1985, EPA issued a definition of "solid waste" that required 54 pages of explanation in the Federal Register, 50 Fed. Reg. 614. Under EPA's definition, materials are considered solid wastes if they are abandoned by being disposed of, burned, or incinerated; or stored, treated, or accumulated before or in lieu of those activities. EPA determined that certain materials used in recycling also might fall within RCRA's jurisdiction depending on the nature of the material and the recycling activity involved. This resulted in a legal challenge by representatives of the mining and petroleum industries. They argued that EPA's jurisdiction under RCRA could not extend to materials that eventually would be reused because such materials were not wastes. The D.C. Circuit decided this challenge to EPA's definition of solid waste in the case that follows.

## American Mining Congress v. EPA

824 F.2d 1177 (D.C. Cir. 1987)

Before STARR and MIKVA, Circuit Judges, and McGOWAN, Senior Circuit Judge.

STARR, Circuit Judge:

These consolidated cases arise out of EPA's regulation of hazardous wastes under the Resource Conservation and Recovery Act of 1976 ("RCRA"), as amended, 42 U.S.C. §§6901-6933 (1982 & Supp. III 1985). Petitioners, trade associations representing mining and oil refining interests, challenge regulations promulgated by EPA that amend the definition of "solid waste" to establish and define the agency's authority to regulate secondary materials reused within an industry's ongoing production process. In plain English, petitioners maintain that EPA has exceeded its regulatory authority in seeking to bring materials that are not discarded or otherwise disposed of within the compass of "waste."

### I

RCRA is a comprehensive environmental statute under which EPA is granted authority to regulate solid and hazardous wastes. . . .

Congress' "overriding concern" in enacting RCRA was to establish the framework for a national system to insure the safe management of hazardous waste. H.R. Rep. No. 1491, 94th Cong., 2d Sess. 3 (1976), U.S. Code Cong. & Admin. News 1976, pp. 6238, 6240, 6241. . . .

RCRA includes two major parts: one deals with nonhazardous solid waste management and the other with hazardous waste management. Under the latter, EPA is directed to promulgate regulations establishing a comprehensive management system. EPA's authority, however, extends only to the regulation of "hazardous waste." Because "hazardous waste" is defined as a subset of "solid waste," §6903(5), the scope of EPA's jurisdiction is limited to those materials that constitute "solid waste." That pivotal term is defined by RCRA as

> any garbage, refuse, sludge from a waste treatment plant, water supply treatment plant, or air pollution control facility *and other discarded material,* including solid, liquid, semisolid or contained gaseous material, resulting from industrial, commercial, mining, and agricultural operations, and from community activities. . . .

42 U.S.C. §6903(27) (emphasis added). As will become evident, this case turns on the meaning of the phrase, "and other discarded material," contained in the statute's definitional provisions.

EPA's interpretation of "solid waste" has evolved over time. On May 19, 1980, EPA issued interim regulations defining "solid waste" to include a material that is "a manufacturing or mining by-product and sometimes is discarded." This definition contained two terms needing elucidation: "by-product" and "sometimes discarded." In its definition of "a manufacturing or mining by-product," EPA expressly *excluded* "an intermediate manufacturing or mining product which results from one of the steps in a manufacturing or mining process and is typically processed through the next step of the process within a short time."

In 1983, the agency proposed narrowing amendments to the 1980 interim rule. The agency showed especial concern over *recycling* activities. In the preamble to the amendments, the agency observed that, in light of RCRA's legislative history, it was clear that "Congress indeed intended that materials being recycled or held for recycling can be wastes, and if hazardous, hazardous wastes." The agency also asserted that "not only can materials destined for recycling or being recycled be solid and hazardous wastes, but the Agency clearly has the authority to regulate recycling activities as hazardous waste management."

While asserting its interest in recycling activities (and materials being held for recycling), EPA's discussion left unclear whether the agency in fact believed its jurisdiction extended to materials recycled in an industry's on-going production processes, or only to materials disposed of and recycled as part of a waste management program. In its preamble, EPA stated that "the revised definition of solid waste sets out the Agency's view of its jurisdiction over the recycling of hazardous waste. . . . Proposed section 261.6 then contains exemptions from regulations for those hazardous waste recycling activities that we do not think require regulation." The amended regulatory description of "solid waste" itself, then, did not include materials "used or reused as effective substitutes for raw materials in processes, using raw materials as principal feedstocks." EPA explained the exclusion as follows:

> [These] materials are being used essentially as raw materials and so ordinarily are not appropriate candidates for regulatory control. Moreover, when these materials are used to manufacture new products, the processes generally are normal manufacturing operations. . . . The Agency is reluctant to read the statute as regulating actual manufacturing processes.

This, then, seemed clear: EPA was drawing a line between discarding and ultimate recycling, on the one hand, and a continuous or ongoing manufacturing process with one-site "recycling," on the other. If the activity fell within the latter category, then the materials were not deemed to be "discarded."

After receiving extensive comments, EPA issued its final rule on January 4, 1985. Under the final rule, materials are considered "solid waste" if they are abandoned by being disposed of, burned, or incinerated; or stored, treated, or accumulated before or in lieu of those activities. In addition, certain recycling activities fall within EPA's definition. EPA determines whether a material is an RCRA solid waste when it is recycled by examining both the material or substance itself and the recycling activity involved. The final rule identifies five categories of "secondary materials" (spent materials, sludges, by-products, commercial chemical products, and scrap metal). These "secondary materials" constitute "solid waste" when they are disposed of; burned for energy recovery or used to produce a fuel; reclaimed; or accumulated speculatively. Under the final rule, if a material constitutes "solid waste," it is subject to RCRA regulation *unless* it is directly reused as an ingredient or as an effective substitute for a commercial product, or is returned as a raw material substitute to its original manufacturing process. In the jargon of the trade, the latter category is known as the "closed-loop" exception. In either case, the material must not first be "reclaimed" (processed to recover a usable product or regenerated). EPA exempts these activities "because they are like ordinary usage of commercial products."

## II

Petitioners, American Mining Congress ("AMC") and American Petroleum Institute ("API"), challenge the scope of EPA's final rule. Relying upon the statutory definition of "solid waste," petitioners contend that EPA's authority under RCRA is limited to controlling materials that are *discarded or intended for discard*. They argue that EPA's reuse and recycle rules, as applied to in-process secondary materials, regulate materials that have not been discarded, and therefore exceed EPA's jurisdiction. . . .

## III

Because the issue is one of statutory interpretation, the principles enunciated in Chevron, U.S.A., Inc. v. NRDC, 467 U.S. 837 (1984), and its progeny guide our inquiry. In *Chevron*, a unanimous Supreme Court laid out a now familiar, general framework for analyzing agency interpretations of statutes. First, the reviewing court is to consider whether Congress "has directly spoken to the precise question at issue." This inquiry focuses first on the language and structure of the statute itself. If the answer is not yielded by the statute, then the court is to look to secondary indicia of intent, such as the measure's legislative history. As the *Chevron* court emphatically declared: "[I]f the intent of Congress is clear, that is the end of the matter; for the court, as well as the agency, must give effect to the unambiguously expressed intent of Congress."

. . . Congress, it will be recalled, granted EPA power to regulate "solid waste." Congress specifically defined "solid waste" as "discarded material." EPA then defined "discarded material" to include materials destined for reuse in an industry's *ongoing* production processes. The challenge to EPA's jurisdictional reach is founded, again, on the proposition that in-process secondary materials are outside the bounds of EPA's lawful authority. Nothing has been *discarded,* the argument goes, and thus RCRA jurisdiction remains untriggered.

The first step in statutory interpretation is, of course, an analysis of the language itself. In pursuit of Congress' intent, we "start with the assumption that the legislative purpose is expressed by the ordinary meaning of the words used." These sound principles governing the reading of statutes seem especially forceful in the context of the present case. Here, Congress defined "solid waste" as "discarded material." The ordinary plain-English meaning of the word "discarded" is "disposed of," "thrown away," or "abandoned." Encompassing materials retained for immediate reuse within the scope of "discarded material" strains, to say the least, the everyday usage of that term. . . .

RCRA was enacted in response to Congressional findings that the "rising tide of scrap, discarded, and waste materials" generated by consumers and increased industrial production had presented heavily populated urban communities with "serious financial, management, intergovernmental, and technical problems in the disposal of solid wastes." . . .

The question we face, then, is whether, in light of the National Legislature's expressly stated objectives and the underlying problems that motivated it to enact RCRA in the first instance, Congress was using the term "discarded" in its ordinary sense — "disposed of" or "abandoned" — or whether Congress was using it in a much more open-ended way, so as to encompass materials no longer useful in their original capacity though destined for immediate reuse in another phase of the industry's ongoing production process.

For the following reasons, we believe the former to be the case. RCRA was enacted, as the Congressional objectives and findings make clear, in an effort to help States deal with the ever-increasing problem of solid waste *disposal* by encouraging the search for and use of alternatives to existing methods of disposal (including recycling) and protecting health and the environment by regulating hazardous wastes. To fulfill these purposes, it seems clear that EPA need not regulate "spent" materials that are recycled and reused in an *ongoing* manufacturing or industrial process. These materials have not yet become part of the waste disposal problem; rather, *they are destined for beneficial reuse or recycling in a continuous process by the generating industry itself.*

The situation in this case thus stands in sharp contrast to that in *Riverside Bayview,* another post-*Chevron* case. There, the Corps of Engineers had defined "the waters of the United States" within the meaning of the Clean Water Act, to include "wetlands." Recognizing that it strained common sense to conclude that "Congress intended to abandon traditional notions of 'waters' and include in that term 'wetlands' as well," the Court performed a close and searching analysis of Congress' intent to determine if this counterintuitive result was nonetheless what Congress had in mind. The Court based its holding (that the agency's expansive definition of "waters of the United States" was reasonable) on several factors: Congress' acquiescence in the agency's interpretation; provisions of the statute expressly including "wetlands" in the definition of "waters"; and, importantly, the danger that forbidding the Corps to regulate "wetlands" would defeat Congress' purpose since pollutants in "wetlands" water might well flow into "waters" that were indisputably jurisdictional. Thus, due to the nature of the water system, the very evil that Congress sought to interdict—the befouling of the "waters of the United States"—would likely occur were the Corps of Engineers' jurisdiction to stop short of wetlands.

EPA's regulation of in-process materials . . . seems to us an effort to get at the same evil (albeit, very broadly defined) that Congress had identified by extending the agency's regulatory compass, rather than, as with the regulation of wetlands, an attempt to reach activities that if left unregulated would sabotage the agency's regulatory mission. We are thus not presented with a situation in which Congress likely intended that the pivotal jurisdictional term be read in its broadest sense, detached from everyday parlance; instead, we have a situation in which Congress, perhaps through the process of legislative compromise which courts must be loathe to tear asunder, employed a term with a widely accepted meaning to define the materials that EPA could regulate under RCRA. And it was that term which the Congress of the United States passed and the President ultimately signed into law. . . .

## IV

We are constrained to conclude that, in light of the language and structure of RCRA, the problems animating Congress to enact it, and the relevant portions of the legislative history, Congress clearly and unambiguously expressed its intent that "solid waste" (and therefore EPA's regulatory authority) be limited to materials that are "discarded" by virtue of being disposed of, abandoned, or thrown away. While we do not lightly overturn an agency's reading of its own statute, we are persuaded that by regulating in-process secondary materials, EPA has acted in contravention of Congress' intent. Accordingly, the petition for review is granted.

MIKVA, Circuit Judge, dissenting:

. . . In my opinion, the EPA's interpretation of solid waste is completely reasonable in light of the language, policies, and legislative history of RCRA. Congress had broad remedial objectives in mind when it enacted RCRA, most notably to "regulat[e] the treatment, storage, transportation, and disposal of hazardous wastes which have adverse effects on the environment." 42 U.S.C. §6902(4). The disposal problem Congress was combatting encompassed more than just abandoned materials. RCRA makes this clear with its definition of the central statutory term "disposal":

> the discharge, deposit, injection, dumping, spilling, leaking, or placing of any solid waste or hazardous waste into or on any land or water so that such solid waste or hazardous waste or any constituent thereof may enter the environment or be emitted into the air or discharged into any waters, including ground-waters.

42 U.S.C. §6903(3). This definition clearly encompasses more than the everyday meaning of disposal, which is a "discarding or throwing away." Webster's Third International Dictionary 654 (2d ed. 1981). The definition is *functional*: waste is disposed under this provision if it is put into contact with land or water in such a way as to pose the risks to health and the environment that animated Congress to pass RCRA. Whether the manufacturer subjectively intends to put the material

to additional use is irrelevant to this definition, as indeed it should be, because the manufacturer's state of mind bears no necessary relation to the hazards of the industrial processes he employs.

Faithful to RCRA's functional approach, EPA reasonably concluded that regulation of certain in-process secondary materials was necessary to carry out its mandate. The materials at issue in this case can pose the same risks as abandoned wastes, whether or not the manufacturer intends eventually to put them to further beneficial use. As the agency explained, "[s]imply because a waste is likely to be recycled will not ensure that it will not be spilled or leaked before recycling occurs." The storage, transportation, and even recycling of in-process secondary materials can cause severe environmental harm. Indeed, the EPA documented environmental disasters caused by the handling or storage of such materials. It also pointed out the risk of damage from spills or leaks when certain in-process secondary materials are placed on land or in underground product storage. . . .

. . . [I]n this case the EPA has interpreted solid waste in a manner that seems to expand the everyday usage of the word "discarded." Its conclusion, however, is fully supportable in light of the statutory scheme and legislative history of RCRA. The agency concluded that certain on-site recycled materials constitute an integral part of the waste disposal problem. This judgment is grounded in the EPA's technical expertise and is adequately supported by evidence in the record. The majority nevertheless reverses the agency because it believes that the materials at issue "have not yet become part of the waste disposal problem." This declaration is nothing more than a substitution of the majority's own conclusions for the sound technical judgment of the EPA. The EPA's interpretation is a reasonable construction of an ambiguous statutory provision and should be upheld.

## NOTES AND QUESTIONS

1. Do you agree with EPA that the definition of "solid waste" should employ a functional approach that focuses on whether or not a substance poses a risk warranting regulation? If such judgments are relevant for definitional purposes, who should make them — EPA or the courts? Note that in his dissent Judge Mikva challenged the majority's statement that materials stored on-site for possible future reclamation "have not yet become part of the waste disposal problem." What basis did he have for questioning their statement? Did the majority give sufficient deference to EPA's conclusion that such materials are an integral part of the waste disposal problem? Should EPA's judgment on this factual issue make any difference to a court reviewing the scope of EPA's regulatory authority? Is the court's decision consistent with *Chevron*?

2. Should EPA be able to define "solid waste" broadly to encompass materials that it believes need to be regulated to prevent deliberate evasion of RCRA regulations? Five months after the D.C. Circuit's *AMC* decision, EPA proposed a new definition of "solid waste" in response to the court's decision. 53 Fed. Reg. 519 (Jan. 8, 1988). While EPA proposed to exclude from the definition materials reclaimed in a "closed loop," it concluded that the court's decision did not affect its authority to regulate materials "recycled in ways where the recycling activity itself is characterized by discarding." Thus, EPA indicated that it would consider

several factors in deciding whether materials recycled without passing through "a continuous, ongoing manufacturing process" were solid wastes. These factors include: (1) whether the material is typically discarded on an industry-wide basis, (2) whether the material replaces a raw material when it is recycled and the degree to which its composition is similar to that of the raw material, (3) the relation of the recovery practice to the principal activity of the facility, (4) whether the material is handled prior to reclamation in a secure manner that minimizes loss and prevents releases to the environment, and (5) other factors, such as the length of time the material is accumulated. How are each of these factors relevant to the question whether a material should be considered a solid waste?

3. As a result of the *AMC* decision, industry representatives argued that a number of substances that EPA has regulated under subtitle C of RCRA are not "solid wastes." For example, can EPA regulate sludge from wastewater stored in a surface impoundment if the sludge may at some time in the future be reprocessed for metals recovery? EPA said yes because it is the product of wastewater and it is stored in an impoundment that can threaten harm to the environment. The D.C. Circuit agreed in American Mining Congress v. EPA (*AMC II*), 907 F.2d 1179 (D.C. Cir. 1990). The court distinguished *AMC* in the following terms:

> *AMC's* holding concerned only materials that are "destined for *immediate reuse* in another phase of the industry's ongoing production process," id. at 1185 (emphasis added), and that "have not yet become part of the waste disposal problem," id. at 1186. Nothing in *AMC* prevents the agency from treating as "discarded" the wastes at issue in this case, which are managed in land disposal units that *are* part of wastewater treatment systems, which *have* therefore become "part of the waste disposal problem," and which are *not* part of ongoing industrial processes. Indeed, [we have] explicitly rejected the very claim that petitioners assert in this case, . . . namely, that under RCRA, potential reuse of a material prevents the agency from classifying it as "discarded." [907 F.2d at 1186 (emphasis in original).]

4. Can materials that are in fact recycled be considered wastes at the time of recycling? Citing *AMC*, EPA determined that materials inserted into a metals reclamation process cease to be solid wastes for purposes of RCRA regulation at the time they arrive at a reclamation facility because they are no longer "discarded materials." 53 Fed. Reg. 11,753 (1988). The materials involved were wastes that EPA had required to be treated through metals reclamation. Environmentalists successfully challenged this interpretation in American Petroleum Institute v. EPA, 906 F.2d 729 (D.C. Cir. 1990). The court explained that

> *AMC* is by no means dispositive of EPA's authority to regulate [such waste]. Unlike the materials in question in *AMC*, [the waste] is indisputably "discarded" *before* being subject to metals reclamation. Consequently, it *has* "become part of the waste disposal problem"; that is why EPA has the power to require that [it] be subject to mandatory metals reclamation. See 53 Fed. Reg. 11,752-53 (recognizing this point). Nor does anything in *AMC* require EPA to cease treating [the material] as

"solid waste" once it reaches the metals reclamation facility. [The material] is delivered to the facility not as part of an "*ongoing* manufacturing or industrial process" within "the generating industry," but as part of a mandatory waste treatment plan prescribed by EPA. [906 F.2d at 741 (emphasis in original).]

Noting that Congress consciously had decided not to regulate the *generation* of waste when it adopted RCRA due to concerns about interfering with production processes, EPA had maintained that it could not regulate material undergoing metals reclamation because that would interfere with an ongoing production process. Regulating furnaces used to recover metals from zinc-laden waste "would be like directly regulating the industrial production of zinc from ore," EPA argued. Rejecting this argument, the court explained: "The two forms of regulation might be 'like' each other, but they are by no means one and the same." 906 F.2d at 741 n.15. The court emphasized that even if the treatment process produced something of value—reclaimed metals—the important distinction for purposes of RCRA jurisdiction was whether the material being processed had been discarded, not whether the process extracted valuable products from the discarded material. 906 F.2d at 741 n.16.

5. Two ex-EPA officials formerly in charge of solid waste programs have commented:

[T]he regulatory distinction between wastes and products has led to discrepancies that are not defensible from an environmental standpoint. For example, certain pesticides that can be applied directly to the land at high concentrations cannot be legally disposed in state-of-the-art hazardous waste landfills until they have been pretreated. . . . Similarly, chemical treatment processes that are part of chemical production are relatively unregulated compared with chemical waste processes that are part of waste disposal. . . .

[These discrepancies] grow even more problematic as recycling becomes a desirable component of waste management.

Historically, a facility performing "legitimate" recycling has been exempt from many of the environmental management standards that apply to facilities deemed to be managing hazardous waste. . . . Yet a long list of recycling facilities, including oil refiners, battery recyclers, and scrap metal recyclers, have ended up as Superfund sites. Moreover, some facilities that claimed the recycling exemption (e.g., certain thermal facilities) look amazingly similar to hazardous waste treatment facilities, yet the same recycling facilities are allowed to reuse their ash as product while the hazardous waste incinerator must continue to treat it as hazardous waste, regardless of how clean that ash is. [Williams & Cannon, Rethinking RCRA for the 1990s, 21 Envtl. L. Rep. 10063, 10067 (1991).]

Are there any legitimate justifications for these discrepancies?

6. In United States v. Ilco, Inc., 996 F.2d 1126 (11th Cir. 1993), the Eleventh Circuit held that lead parts reclaimed from spent car and truck batteries for recycling purposes are solid wastes subject to regulation under RCRA. While the recycler

argued that it had never discarded the lead plates and groups removed from old batteries it had purchased, the court emphasized that the fact that "[s]omebody has discarded the battery in which these components are found . . . does not change just because a reclaimer has purchased or finds value in the components." 996 F.2d at 1131 (emphasis in original). In Owen Electric Steel Company v. Browner, 37 F.3d 146 (4th Cir. 1994), the Fourth Circuit held that slag produced by a steel mill which is "cured" on the ground for six months prior to being sold for use as a road base material is, despite its ultimate reuse, "discarded material" subject to regulation under RCRA. The court observed that "the fundamental inquiry in determining whether a by-product has been 'discarded' is whether the by-product is *immediately* recycled for use in the same industry; if not, then the by-product is justifiably seen as 'part of the waste disposal problem,'" *AMC I*, 824 F.2d at 1186, and therefore as a "solid waste." 37 F.3d at 150 (emphasis in original).

7. In 2000, the U.S. Court of Appeals for the D.C. Circuit issued two decisions that focused on the question whether material had been "discarded," subjecting it to regulation as waste under RCRA. In Association of Battery Recyclers v. EPA, 208 F.3d 1047 (D.C. Cir. 2000), the court held that EPA improperly classified secondary and residual materials generated in mining and mineral processing operations as solid waste for purposes of RCRA. The agency had done so when it promulgated Phase IV of its regulations limiting land disposal of hazardous waste. EPA argued that the materials could be regulated as wastes because they were not immediately reintroduced into the production process. However, the court rejected the notion that temporary storage of the materials even "for a few minutes" subjected them to regulation as solid waste. Referring to its 1987 decision in *AMC I*, the court asserted that "[l]ater cases in this court do not limit AMC," noting that none of the decisions subsequent to *AMC I* undermined the notion that material must be discarded before it can be regulated as a waste. The court distinguished American Petroleum Institute v. EPA, 906 F.2d 729 (D.C. Cir. 1990), as involving the taking of waste from one industry for reclamation in another. It distinguished *AMC II* as involving a situation where it was not clear whether or not the waste ultimately would be recycled because the defendants had asserted only that they "may" reclaim the material at some time in the future. In American Petroleum Institute v. EPA, 216 F.3d 50 (D.C. Cir. 2000), the court vacated part of an RCRA regulation that sought to subject oil-bearing wastewaters generated by the petroleum refining industry to regulation as a solid waste. While recognizing that wastewaters eventually become waste as they progress through later phases of treatment, the court held that EPA had not adequately explained why it had determined that wastewaters should be considered discarded even before they had received primary treatment.

8. One idea for determining whether a material is a waste would focus on its market value. Recycled material would be considered a waste if a producer had to pay someone to dispose of it. But if a recycler would pay the producer for the material, it would not be considered a waste. EPA believes that such an approach would not be enforceable because of frequent shifts in market prices and the ability of parent and subsidiary corporations to manipulate the price of transfers in ways that disguise their true value. 50 Fed. Reg. 614, 617 (1985). For an argument that EPA should reconsider this decision, despite the difficulties of applying a value-based standard, see Smith, The Solid Waste Definitional Dilemma, 9 Nat. Resources & Env't 3 (Fall 1994).

### 3. Distinguishing "Legitimate Recycling" from "Sham Recycling"

EPA has been bedeviled by the problem of sham recycling. Fly-by-night companies have sought to avoid RCRA regulation by claiming that they are recycling hazardous waste when they actually are simply disposing of it while avoiding RCRA regulation. The classic example of this is Marine Shale Processors (MSP), which operated an incinerator in Louisiana from 1985 to 1996. The company claimed it was exempt from RCRA because it was "recycling" hazardous waste by burning it in a 275-foot rotary kiln and then mixing the ash residue into construction materials. In June 1990, the U.S. government sued the company for violations of various environmental statutes including RCRA for treating hazardous waste without a permit. After lengthy trials, the court declared a mistrial in 1994 on the United States' RCRA claim for unpermitted operation of an incinerator after the jury was unable to answer whether MSP was engaged in "legitimate" or "sham" recycling. The court eventually awarded the United States and the Louisiana civil penalties against MSP totaling $8 million for violations of the CAA, CWA, and RCRA.

In October 2008, EPA adopted new regulations amending its definition of solid waste to address when recyclable materials are subject to regulation under RCRA. 73 Fed. Reg. 64,668 (2008). The regulations created two new exclusions from RCRA — the "Generator Controlled Exclusion" and the "Transfer-Based Exclusion." To qualify for either, secondary materials have to be recycled "legitimately," a term defined by reference to various "legitimacy factors" to distinguish true recycling from sham recycling. The Generator Controlled Exclusion excludes hazardous secondary materials that are legitimately reclaimed under the control of the generator. The exclusion covers materials generated and reclaimed on-site in the same facility, materials generated in one facility and reclaimed at a different facility under the control of the generator, and materials reclaimed by a contractor who certifies that it retains ownership of and liability for the materials. The Transfer-Based Exclusion exempts materials transferred to a third party for recycling or reclamation. To qualify for this exclusion, generators have to show that the materials will not be part of a sham recycling operation. This requires a showing: (1) "that hazardous secondary materials being recycled provide a useful contribution to the recycling process or to the product of the recycling process" and (2) "that the product of the recycling process is valuable." Generators also have to (3) consider whether the hazardous secondary material is managed like a normal feedstock for the manufacturing process, and (4) compare concentrations of the hazardous constituents found in the product made from the materials with "concentrations of hazardous constituents in analogous products."

EPA's 2008 regulations defining solid waste were criticized in Jeffrey M. Gaba, Rethinking Recycling, 38 Envtl. L. 1053 (2008). Professor Gaba concludes that they perpetuate many of the existing flaws in EPA's approach to regulation of recyclable materials. He criticized the regulations as "incoherent," "poorly drafted and confusing," and argues that they "may unnecessarily include materials involved in legitimate recycling within the coverage of Subtitle C." Reviewing the prior caselaw, Gaba concludes that: (1) "EPA may not regulate materials as solid wastes if they are still part of a continuous process within the generating industry itself" (*AMC I* and *Ass'n of Battery Recyclers*), and (2) "once generated, a material may be a statutory solid waste regardless of any subsequent act of recycling" (*American Petroleum Institute* and *AMC II*). Noting that in Safe Food & Fertilizer v. EPA, 350 F.3d 1263 (D.C. Cir. 2003), the court approved EPA's exclusion of certain wastes from Subtitle C regulation based on the agency's assessment of the likely environmental harm, Gaba makes the following proposal. "First, materials that are recycled through activities involving land application or burning of wastes should be classified as solid wastes and subject to Subtitle C regulation" because this activity "involves the same environmental harms as direct disposal of hazardous wastes. Second, EPA should classify all materials involved in 'sham' recycling as solid wastes." Gaba, supra at 1100. Gaba proposes that EPA should issue new criteria defining what constitutes "sham recycling," require generators to bear the burden of establishing that recycling of their byproducts is not a sham, and create a set of "safe harbor" provisions for discharging this burden similar to the provisions contained in CERCLA section 127's exemption from liability for recycling.

In response to such criticisms and litigation from both industry and environmental groups, EPA in July 2011 proposed once again to modify its definition of "solid waste" to encourage recycling of hazardous materials and to discourage sham recycling. 76 Fed. Reg. 44,094 (2011). On December 10, 2014, EPA adopted a revised definition of "solid waste," 80 Fed. Reg. 1694 (2015). The new definition expanded the scope of the legitimacy factors to cover all recycling. The four "legitimacy factors" it adopted to distinguish between legitimate recycling and sham recycling were: (1) the recycling involves a hazardous secondary material that provides a useful contribution to the recycling process or to a product; (2) the recycling process must produce a valuable product; (3) the hazardous secondary material must be managed as a valuable commodity; and (4) the product must be comparable to a legitimate product. EPA also replaced the Transfer-Based Exclusion with a "Verified Recycler Exclusion," a new standard governing when transferred materials qualify as solid waste. To oversimplify, the Transfer-Based Exclusion had required generators to satisfy themselves, based on several criteria, that the facilities they were sending their materials to were not sham recyclers. The Verified Recycler Exclusion would instead have required that the receiving facilities have an RCRA permit or a variance prior to the transfer.

On July 7, 2017, a three-judge panel of the D.C. Circuit split 2-1 in striking down some portions of the new definition. The court majority vacated most of the Verified Recycler Exclusion and reinstated the Transfer-Based Exclusion. It upheld EPA's requirement that secondary materials be handled as "valuable commodities." The court stated that "the imposition of a requirement of advance administrative approval cannot be justified merely on the differences that EPA has identified between on-site and third-party reclamation. EPA must explain why the risk that purported third-party recyclers will in reality 'discard' the materials is so high that reclamation under the Verified Recycler Exclusion may only proceed on the basis of prior agency approval." American Petroleum Institute v. EPA, 862 F.3d 50, 70 (D.C. Cir. 2017). In dissent, Judge Tatel wrote, "[T]he fundamental problem with the court's conclusion—that the Administrator needs more proof that off-site recycling is unsafe before requiring a variance—is that the court decides for itself a policy question Congress left to the Administrator." Id. at 81.

## 4. Identifying "Hazardous Waste"

In order to be subject to the cradle-to-grave regulations of RCRA's subtitle C, a material must be not only a "solid waste" but also a "hazardous" one. We now turn to the question of what solid wastes are hazardous for purposes of RCRA.

Although Congress required EPA to regulate hazardous waste under subtitle C of RCRA, it did not specify how the agency was to determine what wastes were hazardous. "Hazardous waste" is defined by section 1004(5) of RCRA as

> (a) solid waste, or combination of solid wastes, which because of its quantity, concentration, or physical, chemical, or infectious characteristics may—
>
> (A) cause or significantly contribute to an increase in mortality or an increase in serious irreversible, or incapacitating reversible, illness; or
>
> (B) pose a substantial present or potential hazard to human health or the environment when improperly treated, stored, transported, or disposed of, or otherwise managed.

Section 3001 of RCRA requires EPA to promulgate regulations identifying the characteristics of hazardous waste and listing particular wastes as hazardous "taking into account toxicity, persistence, and degradability in nature, potential for accumulation in tissue, and other related factors such as flammability, corrosiveness, and other hazardous characteristics."

EPA has implemented these provisions (40 C.F.R. pt. 261) by establishing two principal avenues for solid waste to be deemed "hazardous": by exhibiting one of four hazardous characteristics ("characteristic wastes") or by being specifically listed as a hazardous waste in EPA's regulations ("listed wastes"). Waste streams can be specifically listed as hazardous if EPA determines that they routinely contain hazardous constituents or exhibit hazardous characteristics. As indicated in Figure 4.3, EPA has established four general categories of listed wastes (the "F," "K," "P," and "U" lists). By the end of 1999, EPA had listed more than 860 types of wastes as hazardous by placing them in one of these four categories.

To prevent generators from evading hazardous waste regulations by diluting or otherwise changing the composition of listed waste streams, EPA in 1980 adopted two important rules: the "mixture rule" and the "derived-from" rule. The mixture rule provides that any mixture of a listed waste with another solid waste is itself considered to be a hazardous waste. The derived-from rule provides that wastes derived from the treatment, storage, or disposal of a listed waste (such as the ash residue from incineration of a listed waste) are deemed to be hazardous wastes. 40 C.F.R. §261.3(c)(2)(i). Thus, listed wastes are deemed to remain hazardous unless they are specifically "delisted" by EPA.

Although some industry groups maintained that the mixture and derived-from rules unlawfully expanded EPA's jurisdiction under RCRA, the rules became an important part of the RCRA program while legal challenges to the rules were held in abeyance for more than a decade. When the D.C. Circuit finally addressed the issue in December 1991, it struck down the mixture and derived-from rules without deciding whether they exceeded EPA's authority. Surprisingly, the court held

**Figure 4.3    RCRA Hazardous Waste Classifications**

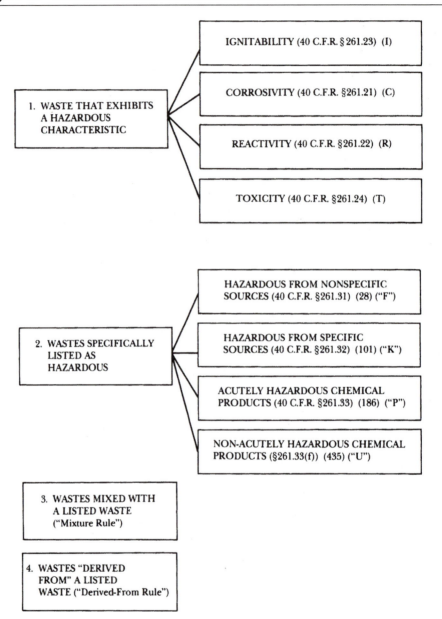

that EPA had not provided adequate notice and opportunity for comment when it proposed the rules in 1978. Shell Oil Co. v. EPA, 950 F.2d 741 (D.C. Cir. 1991). The court rejected EPA's argument that industry had suffered no prejudice from this 13-year-old procedural defect, even though the agency maintained that it had considered and rejected the very criticisms industry would have made had adequate notice been provided. Noting "the dangers that may be posed by a discontinuity in the regulation of hazardous wastes," the court suggested that EPA reenact the rules on an interim basis under the "good cause" exception to the Administrative Procedure Act, 5 U.S.C. §553(b)(3)(B). EPA then reinstated the rules, 57 Fed. Reg. 7,628 (1992), and it ultimately adopted a final rule that largely retains them while expanding certain exclusions. 66 Fed. Reg. 27,266 (May 16, 2001). The agency expanded an exclusion for mixtures and/or derivatives of wastes listed solely for the ignitability, corrosivity, and/or reactivity characteristics and it established a new conditional exemption for mixed wastes (that is, wastes that are both hazardous and radioactive).

Figure 4.3 identifies the different classifications of hazardous waste and the places where EPA regulations pertaining to them appear in the Federal Register. Wastes not specifically listed as hazardous must be managed as hazardous wastes if they exhibit one of the four hazardous characteristics (ignitability, corrosivity, reactivity, or toxicity). These "characteristic wastes" are considered hazardous only until they no longer exhibit the hazardous characteristic. Unlike listed wastes, characteristic wastes are not subject to the mixture or derived-from rules. If they are mixed with a substance other than a listed waste they need to be managed as a hazardous waste only as long as they continue to exhibit a hazardous characteristic. Substances derived from a characteristic waste are considered hazardous only if they continue to exhibit a hazardous characteristic.

Thus, the extensive regulatory standards prescribed by subtitle C of RCRA are applicable to solid wastes that are hazardous, which include: (1) wastes specifically listed as hazardous, (2) wastes that exhibit any of the four hazardous characteristics, and (3) wastes mixed with or derived from a listed waste.

During the first decade of RCRA implementation, EPA's slow progress in identifying and listing hazardous wastes was criticized frequently. Although EPA studied more than a dozen other potential characteristics that could be used to classify a waste as hazardous (including carcinogenicity, infectiousness, and organic toxicity), it did not adopt any of these other characteristics because it was unable to identify suitable tests for them. In 1981, EPA instead focused on studying 1,100 industrial production processes to expand its category of "listed wastes." But the agency promulgated new waste listings for only five wastes, finding that it had insufficient information to determine whether other waste streams should be listed. In 1986, EPA abandoned its plan to do more studies and shifted its focus to revising its hazardous characteristics. EPA based this decision on its conclusion that the industry study process was too expensive and had resulted in few waste listings.

The 1984 Amendments to RCRA directed EPA to identify additional hazard characteristics by November 1986 and to improve the existing toxicity characteristic test by March 1987. EPA missed these deadlines by three years. On March 5, 1990, the agency promulgated far-reaching revisions to its procedures for identifying toxic characteristic wastes. EPA added 25 organic chemicals (including benzene, vinyl chloride, and chloroform) to the 8 metals and 6 pesticides on its existing list of substances which if found as constituents in waste in certain concentrations render the waste hazardous under the toxicity characteristic. EPA also promulgated a new, more sensitive test, known as the toxicity characteristic leaching procedure, or TCLP, to be used to determine whether a solid waste contains these hazardous constituents. It estimated that these changes subjected more than 17,000 additional waste generators to regulation under subtitle C of RCRA, including many companies in the pulp and paper, petroleum refining and marketing, organic chemicals, pharmaceuticals, plastics, rubber, lumber, and textile industries. EPA estimated that the cost of complying with the new rules would range from $250 to $400 million per year, largely because the rules increased the volume of material considered to be hazardous waste by some 1.8 million metric tons. 55 Fed. Reg. 11,798 (1990).

Former EPA staffer William Pedersen has argued that the RCRA system is both overinclusive and underinclusive. Pedersen argues that RCRA is overinclusive because the mixture and derived-from rules result in the regulation of many wastes that are far less toxic than wastes excluded from the system. Pedersen, The Future of Federal Solid Waste Regulation, 16 Colum. J. Envtl. L. 109, 120 (1991). While EPA has acknowledged problems with the mixture and derived-from rules, prior to the *Shell Oil* decision it had been reluctant to propose any de minimis exception for fear that this would simply encourage dilution of wastes. See Gaba, The Mixture and Derived-From Rules Under RCRA: Once a Hazardous Waste Always a Hazardous Waste?, 21 Envtl. L. Rep. 10033 (1991). Pederson maintains that RCRA is underinclusive because more truly hazardous waste is excluded from the RCRA system than is included. He notes that while data on hazardous waste generation are notoriously unreliable, only a small fraction of the waste that is generated is listed as hazardous and that special exemptions (such as those for mining waste, household waste, and waste placed in public sewers) exclude more waste that possesses a hazardous characteristic than is included in the RCRA system. Id. at 118-119.

Pedersen maintains that the RCRA program's failure to provide more comprehensive coverage of hazardous waste is a result of the "stigma and drastic regulatory burden that attend listing a waste." Although the D.C. Circuit has held that concern over the stigma attached to a waste's being listed as hazardous is an insufficient basis for refusing to list an otherwise hazardous waste, Hazardous Waste Treatment Council v. EPA, 861 F.2d 270 (D.C. Cir. 1988) (rejecting argument that used oil should not be listed as a hazardous waste because it would discourage recycling), EPA has resisted efforts to expand the coverage of RCRA listings except when expressly required by Congress. EPA still has not listed discarded PFAS chemicals as hazardous wastes under RCRA despite the demonstrated toxicity of PFOA to humans and animals confirmed in the massive Ohio River Valley epidemiological study conducted in 2005-2006.

## NOTES AND QUESTIONS

1. Despite the decision in Hazardous Waste Treatment Council v. EPA, 861 F.2d 270 (D.C. Cir. 1988), EPA ultimately decided not to list used oil as a hazardous waste. 57 Fed. Reg. 21,524 (1992). The agency based its decision on the conclusion that gasoline-powered engine oils already are subject to regulation under subtitle C as characteristic wastes and that other oils are not hazardous with sufficient frequency to warrant listing. In Natural Resource Defense Council v. EPA, 25 F.3d 1063 (D.C. Cir. 1994), EPA's decision was upheld by the D.C. Circuit. The court stated that "Congress intended the agency to have substantial room to exercise its independent expertise in determining the appropriate grounds for listing." It concluded that RCRA did not require "EPA to promulgate its [listing] criteria in a

manner that would trigger automatic listing whenever certain technical conditions are met." Id. at 1070.

2. EPA's derived-from rule provides that "any solid waste generated from the treatment, storage, or disposal of a hazardous waste, including any sludge, spill residue, ash, emission control dust, or leachate (but not including precipitation run-off) is a hazardous waste." 40 C.F.R. §261.3(c)(2)(i). Why do you think EPA promulgated this regulation? As a result of the derived-from rule, would the residue left over after hazardous waste is treated to reduce its toxicity itself be a hazardous waste? Would soil, groundwater, or any other environmental medium become a hazardous waste when it comes into contact with a listed waste? See Chemical Waste Management, Inc. v. EPA, 869 F.2d 1526 (D.C. Cir. 1989).

3. Do you agree with Pedersen that the mixture and derived-from rules are likely to require that many nonhazardous materials be managed as a hazardous waste? How could EPA narrow the scope of these rules without encouraging dilution? Should EPA exempt waste that does not have a certain threshold concentration of hazardous constituents?

4. EPA has struggled mightily to develop a new Hazardous Waste Identification Rule (HWIR) that would tailor regulatory requirements more closely to the degree of hazard posed by a waste without creating the kind of loopholes the mixture and derived-from rules are designed to avoid. In 1992, EPA proposed two alternative approaches that quickly were withdrawn after a flurry of criticism. 57 Fed. Reg. 21,450 (1992). After EPA's action temporarily reinstating the mixture and derived-from rules was upheld in Mobil Oil Corp. v. EPA, 35 F.3d 579 (D.C. Cir. 1994), EPA signed a consent decree requiring the agency to propose a new HWIR. In December 1995, EPA proposed a new HWIR that would allow listed wastes and wastes subject to the mixture or derived-from rules to escape subtitle C regulation when the specific hazardous constituents they contain fall below certain levels. 60 Fed. Reg. 66,344 (1995). EPA's Science Advisory Board and industry groups heavily criticized the risk assessments the agency had been using to develop the HWIR proposal. Municipalities also were very concerned that the proposed rule might result in much larger volumes of hazardous materials ending up in municipal landfills subject only to subtitle D. As a result of the controversy surrounding its HWIR proposal, EPA reconsidered its proposal. In 2001, the agency adopted a final rule retaining the mixture and derived-from rules with revisions that expanded an exemption for mixtures and/or derivatives of characteristic waste that was hazardous solely for exhibiting a characteristic other than toxicity. 66 Fed. Reg. 27,266 (May 16, 2001). EPA also indicated that it would continue to work on developing a concentration-based HWIR. EPA's re-promulgation of the mixture and derived-from rules was upheld in American Chemistry Council v. EPA, 337 F.3d 1060 (D.C. Cir. 2003).

5. Note that the derived-from rule includes leachate (except for precipitation runoff). Leachate is produced when liquids (including rainwater) seep through wastes buried in landfills, producing a fluid that contains constituents of the original waste. But the effectiveness of the derived-from rule is limited if EPA does not have adequate knowledge. When the dangers of PFAS were first discovered by the public, it was from leachate in unlined landfills in West Virginia. That particular chemical, PFOA, was not regulated under RCRA because it was not

deemed hazardous by EPA, and the manufacturer of PFOA, DuPont, withheld its data about PFOA's toxicity. However, new state-of-the-art landfills have liners and leachate collection systems to keep hazardous constituents from escaping in the form of leachate. Would leachate collected from a hazardous waste landfill have to be managed as a hazardous waste under the derived-from rule? See Chemical Waste Management, Inc. v. EPA, 869 F.2d 1526 (D.C. Cir. 1989). What about rainwater runoff?

## 5.   *The Household Waste Exclusion and Incinerator Ash*

Wastes that have been listed as hazardous must be managed in accordance with subtitle C unless EPA grants a petition to delist a waste generated at a particular facility pursuant to §3001(f) of RCRA. Wastes that are not listed as hazardous are subject to subtitle C regulation only when they exhibit a hazardous characteristic, which usually requires some form of testing, as with the TCLP.

As landfill space tightened, many cities built incinerators to dispose of municipal garbage. In the year 2000, approximately 160 municipal waste incinerators burned about 16 percent of the more than 200 million tons of garbage generated in the United States that year. These incinerators generated more than 8 million tons of ash (approximately 25 percent by volume of the original waste stream). Ash residues include fly ash captured by emission control equipment, bottom ash, and the products of incomplete combustion. Heavy metals are present in the ash residues and occur in particularly large quantities in the fly ash.

As noted above, one of the four characteristics that can make a waste "hazardous" for purposes of subtitle C regulation is toxicity. Toxicity is determined by a procedure designed to measure the potential for a waste to leach hazardous constituents. The test procedure, formerly called the "extraction procedure" and now called the "toxicity characteristic leaching procedure" (TCLP), analyzes the extract from a sample of the waste for any of 40 chemical contaminants. If the extract has any of these substances in concentrations above specified levels (generally 100 times greater than levels allowed under the Safe Drinking Water Act), the waste is considered to be toxic and must be managed as a hazardous waste.

EPA's regulations require a person who generates a solid waste to "determine if that waste is a hazardous waste." 40 C.F.R. §262.11. If a waste is not a hazardous waste specifically listed in subpart D of 40 C.F.R. pt. 261, the person must determine whether the waste is hazardous because of its characteristics by either testing the waste or "[a]pplying knowledge of the hazard characteristic of the waste in light of the materials or the processes used." 40 C.F.R. §262.11(c)(2).

In 1987, the Environmental Defense Fund (EDF), a private environmental group, reviewed the results of tests performed on ash residues from more than 20 incinerators around the country. EDF discovered that fly ash and bottom ash from municipal waste incinerators often "flunked" EPA's toxicity test by leaching lead and cadmium at concentrations greater than the 5 and 1 milligram per liter cutoff levels for the toxicity characteristic. Fly ash failed the test 80 to 90 percent of the time, bottom ash failed 20 to 25 percent of the time, and combined ash failed about 50 percent of the time. At the time, few municipal incineration facilities tested their ash regularly.

Representatives of incinerator owners and operators argued that incinerator ash should be exempt from subtitle C of RCRA pursuant to §3001(i), which had been added by the 1984 Amendments. EPA initially did not agree. In July 1985, EPA interpreted § 3001(i) to clarify that incinerators were not managing hazardous waste when they incinerated municipal solid waste, but that such residues "would be hazardous under present EPA regulations if they exhibited a [hazardous waste] characteristic." 50 Fed. Reg. 28,725. But after EDF sued two incineration facilities, EPA changed its position and argued that section 3001(i) of RCRA does exempt incinerator ash from regulation under subtitle C. The Supreme Court ultimately decided the issue in the following decision.

## City of Chicago v. Environmental Defense Fund

511 U.S. 328 (1994)

JUSTICE SCALIA delivered the opinion of the Court.

We are called upon to decide whether, pursuant to §3001(i) of the Solid Waste Disposal Act (Resource Conservation and Recovery Act of 1976 (RCRA)), 42 U.S.C. §6921(i), the ash generated by a resource recovery facility's incineration of municipal solid waste is exempt from regulation as a hazardous waste under Subtitle C of RCRA. . . .

### II

RCRA is a comprehensive environmental statute that empowers EPA to regulate hazardous wastes from cradle to grave, in accordance with the rigorous safeguards and waste management procedures of Subtitle C, 42 U.S.C. §§6921-6934. (Nonhazardous wastes are regulated much more loosely under Subtitle D, 42 U.S.C. §§6941-6949.) . . .

RCRA does not identify which wastes are hazardous and therefore subject to Subtitle C regulation; it leaves that designation to EPA. 42 U.S.C. §6921(a). When EPA's hazardous waste designations for solid wastes appeared in 1980, they contained certain exceptions from normal coverage, including an exclusion for "household waste," defined as "any waste material . . . derived from households (including single and multiple residences, hotels and motels)," codified as amended at 40 CFR §261.4(b)(1) (1992). Although most household waste is harmless, a small portion—such as cleaning fluids and batteries—would have qualified as hazardous waste. The regulation declared, however, that "[h]ousehold waste, including household waste that has been collected, transported, stored, treated, disposed, recovered (e.g., refuse derived fuel) or reused" is not hazardous waste. Moreover, the preamble to the 1980 regulations stated that "residues remaining after treatment (e.g., incineration, thermal treatment) [of household waste] are not subject to regulation as a hazardous waste." By reason of these provisions, an incinerator that burned only household waste would not be considered a Subtitle C TSDF, since it processed only nonhazardous (i.e., household) waste, and it would not be considered a Subtitle C generator of hazardous waste and would be free to dispose of its ash in a Subtitle D landfill.

The 1980 regulations thus provided what is known as a "waste stream" exemption for household waste, i.e., an exemption covering that category of waste from generation through treatment to final disposal of residues. The regulation did not, however, exempt MWC ash from Subtitle C coverage if the incinerator that produced the ash burned anything *in addition to* household waste, such as what petitioner's facility burns: nonhazardous industrial waste. Thus, a facility like petitioner's would qualify as a Subtitle C hazardous waste generator if the MWC ash it produced was sufficiently toxic, see 40 CFR §§261.3, 261.24 (1993), though it would still not qualify as a Subtitle C TSDF, since all the waste it took in would be characterized as nonhazardous. (An ash can be hazardous, even though the product from which it is generated is not, because in the new medium the contaminants are more concentrated and more readily leachable, see 40 CFR §§261.3, 261.24, and pt. 261, App. II (1993).)

Four years after these regulations were issued, Congress enacted the Hazardous and Solid Waste Amendments of 1984, Pub. L. 98-616, which added to RCRA the "Clarification of Household Waste Exclusion" as §3001(i). The essence of our task in this case is to determine whether, under that provision, the MWC ash generated by petitioner's facility—a facility that would have been considered a Subtitle C generator under the 1980 regulations—is subject to regulation as hazardous waste under Subtitle C. We conclude that it is.

Section 3001(i), 42 U.S.C. §6921(i), entitled "Clarification of household waste exclusion," provides:

> A resource recovery facility recovering energy from the mass burning of municipal solid waste shall not be deemed to be treating, storing, disposing of, or otherwise managing hazardous wastes for the purposes of regulation under this subchapter, if—
>     (1) such facility—
>         (A) receives and burns only—
>             (i) household waste (from single and multiple dwellings, hotels, motels and other residential sources), and
>             (ii) solid waste from commercial or industrial sources that does not contain hazardous waste identified or listed under this section, and
>         (B) does not accept hazardous wastes identified or listed under this section, and
>     (2) the owner or operator of such facility has established contractual requirements or other appropriate notification or inspection procedures to assure that hazardous wastes are not received at or burned in such facility.

The plain meaning of this language is that so long as a facility recovers energy by incineration of the appropriate wastes, *it* (the *facility*) is not subject to Subtitle C regulation as a facility that treats, stores, disposes of, or manages hazardous waste. The provision quite clearly does not contain any exclusion for the *ash itself.* Indeed, the waste the facility produces (as opposed to that which it receives) is not even mentioned. There is thus no express support for petitioners' claim of a waste-stream exemption.[1]

Petitioners contend, however, that the practical effect of the statutory language is to exempt the ash by virtue of exempting the facility. If, they argue, the facility is not deemed to be treating, storing, or disposing of hazardous waste, then the ash that it treats, stores, or disposes of must itself be considered non-hazardous. There are several problems with this argument. First, as we have explained, the only exemption provided by the terms of the statute is for the *facility*. It is the facility, *not the ash*, that "shall not be deemed" to be subject to regulation under Subtitle C. *Unlike* the preamble to the 1980 regulations, which had been in existence for four years by the time §3001(i) was enacted, §3001(i) does not explicitly exempt MWC ash generated by a resource recovery facility from regulation as a hazardous waste. In light of that difference, and given the statute's express declaration of national policy that "[w]aste that is . . . generated should be treated, stored, or disposed of so as to minimize the present and future threat to human health and the environment," 42 U.S.C. §6902(b), we cannot interpret the statute to permit MWC ash sufficiently toxic to qualify as hazardous to be disposed of in ordinary landfills.

Moreover, as the Court of Appeals observed, the statutory language does not even exempt *the facility* in its capacity as a *generator* of hazardous waste. RCRA defines "generation" as "the act or process of producing hazardous waste." 42 U.S.C. §6903(6). There can be no question that the creation of ash by incinerating municipal waste constitutes "generation" of hazardous waste (assuming, of course, that the ash qualifies as hazardous under 42 U.S.C. §6921 and its implementing regulations, 40 CFR pt. 261 (1993)). Yet although §3001(i) states that the exempted facility "shall not be deemed to be treating, storing, disposing of, or otherwise managing hazardous wastes," it significantly omits from the catalogue the word "generating." Petitioners say that because the activities listed as exempt encompass the full scope of the facility's operation, the failure to mention the activity of generating is insignificant. But the statute itself refutes this. Each of the three specific terms used in §3000(i) — "treating," "storing," and "disposing of" — is separately defined by RCRA, and none covers the production of hazardous waste. The fourth and less specific term ("otherwise managing") is also defined, to mean "collection, source separation, storage, transportation, processing, treatment, recovery, and disposal," 42 U.S.C. §6903(7) —just about every hazardous waste-related activity *except* generation. We think it follows from the carefully constructed text of §3001(i) that while a resource recovery facility's management activities are excluded from Subtitle C regulation, its generation of toxic ash is not. . . .

---

1. The dissent is able to describe the provision as exempting the ash itself only by resorting to what might be called imaginative use of ellipsis: "even though the material being treated and disposed of contains hazardous components before, during, and after its treatment[,] that material shall not be deemed to be . . . hazardous." In the full text, quoted above, the subject of the phrase "shall not be deemed . . . hazardous" is *not* the material, but the *resource recovery facility*, and the complete phrase, including (italicized) ellipsis, reads "shall not be deemed to be *treating, storing, disposing of, or otherwise managing* hazardous *wastes*." Deeming a facility not to be engaged in these activities with respect to hazardous wastes is of course quite different from deeming the output of that facility not to be hazardous.

Petitioners contend that our interpretation of §3001(i) turns the provision into an "empty gesture," since even under the pre-existing regime an incinerator burning household waste and nonhazardous industrial waste was exempt from the Subtitle C TSDF provisions. If §3001(i) did not extend the waste-stream exemption to the product of such a combined household/nonhazardous industrial treatment facility, petitioners argue, it did nothing at all. But it is not nothing to codify a household waste exemption that had previously been subject to agency revision; nor is it nothing (though petitioners may value it as less than nothing) to *restrict* the exemption that the agency previously provided which is what the provision here achieved, by withholding all waste-stream exemption for waste processed by resource recovery facilities, even for the waste stream passing through an exclusively household-waste facility.

We also do not agree with petitioners' contention that our construction renders §3001(i) ineffective for its intended purpose of promoting household/nonhazardous-industrial resource recovery facilities, see 42 U.S.C. §§6902(a)(1), (10), (11), by subjecting them "to the potentially enormous expense of managing ash residue as a hazardous waste." It is simply not true that a facility which is (as our interpretation says these facilities are) a hazardous waste "generator," is also deemed to be "managing" hazardous waste under RCRA. Section 3001(i) clearly exempts these facilities from Subtitle C TSDF regulations, thus enabling them to avoid the "full brunt of EPA's enforcement effort under RCRA."

RCRA's twin goals of encouraging resource recovery and protecting against contamination sometimes conflict. It is not unusual for legislation to contain diverse purposes that must be reconciled, and the most reliable guide for that task is the enacted text. Here that requires us to reject the Solicitor General's plea for deference to the EPA's interpretation, which goes beyond the scope of whatever ambiguity §3001(i) contains. Section 3000(i) simply cannot be read to contain the cost-saving waste stream exemption petitioners seek.

For the foregoing reasons, the judgment of the Court of Appeals for the Seventh Circuit is *Affirmed.*

JUSTICE STEVENS, with whom JUSTICE O'CONNOR joins, dissenting.

The statutory provision in question is a 1984 amendment entitled "Clarification of Household Waste Exclusion." To understand that clarification, we must first examine the "waste exclusion" that the amendment clarified and, more particularly, the ambiguity that needed clarification. . . .

# I

When Congress enacted the Resource Conservation and Recovery Act of 1976 (RCRA), it delegated to the Environmental Protection Agency (EPA) vast regulatory authority over the mountains of garbage that our society generates. The statute directed the EPA to classify waste as hazardous or nonhazardous and to establish regulatory controls over the disposition of the two categories of waste pursuant to Subtitles C and D of the Act. 42 U.S.C. §6921(a). To that end, the EPA in 1980 promulgated detailed regulations establishing a federal hazardous waste management system pursuant to Subtitle C.

Generally, though not always, the EPA regulations assume that waste is properly characterized as hazardous or nonhazardous when it first becomes waste. Based on that characterization, the waste is regulated under either Subtitle C or D. Household waste is regarded as nonhazardous when it is first discarded and, as long as it is not mixed with hazardous waste, it retains that characterization during and after its treatment and disposal. Even though it contains some materials that would be classified as hazardous in other contexts, and even though its treatment may produce a residue that contains a higher concentration of hazardous matter than when the garbage was originally discarded, such waste is regulated as nonhazardous waste under Subtitle D. Thus, an incinerator that burns nothing but household waste might "generate" tons of hazardous residue, but as a statutory matter it still is deemed to be processing nonhazardous waste and is regulated as a Subtitle D, rather than Subtitle C, facility.

Section 261.4(b)(1) of the EPA's 1980 regulations first established the household waste exclusion. See 45 Fed. Reg. 33120 (1980). The relevant text of that regulation simply provided that solid wastes derived from households (including single and multiple residences, hotels and motels) were "not hazardous wastes." The regulation itself said nothing about the status of the residue that remains after the incineration of such household waste. An accompanying comment, however, unambiguously explained that "residues remaining after treatment (e.g., incineration, thermal treatment) are not subject to regulation as hazardous waste." Id., at 33099. Thus, the administrative history of the 1980 regulation, rather than its text, revealed why a municipal incinerator burning household waste was not treated as a generator of hazardous waste.

The EPA's explanatory comment contained an important warning: If household waste was "mixed with other hazardous wastes," the entire mixture would be deemed hazardous. Yet neither the comment nor the regulation itself identified the consequences of mixing household waste with other wastes that are entirely *nonhazardous*. Presumably such a mixture would contain a lower percentage of hazardous material than pure household waste, and therefore should also be classified as nonhazardous — assumptions that are not inconsistent with the EPA's warning that mixing household waste "with other *hazardous* wastes" would terminate the household waste exemption. The EPA's failure to comment expressly on the significance of adding 100 percent nonhazardous commercial or industrial waste nevertheless warranted further clarification.

Congress enacted that clarification in 1984. Elaborating upon the EPA's warning in 1980, the text of the 1984 amendment — §3001(i) of RCRA, 42 U.S.C. §6921(i) — made clear that a facility treating a mixture of household waste and "solid waste from commercial or industrial sources that does not contain hazardous waste," §6921(i)(1)(A)(ii), shall not be deemed to be treating hazardous waste. In other words, the addition of nonhazardous waste derived from other sources does not extinguish the household waste exclusion.

The parallel between the 1980 regulation and the 1984 statutory amendment is striking. In 1980 the EPA referred to the exclusion of household waste "in all phases of its management." Similarly, the 1984 statute lists *all phases* of the incinerator's management when it states that a facility recovering energy from the mass burning of a mixture of household waste and other solid waste that does not contain hazardous waste "shall not be deemed to be treating, storing, disposing of, or otherwise managing hazardous wastes." See 42 U.S.C. §6921(i). Even though that text only refers to the exemption of the facility that burns the waste, the title of the section significantly characterizes it as a *waste* exclusion. Moreover, the title's description of the amendment as a "clarification" identifies an intent to codify its counterpart in the 1980 regulation. . . .

## II

The relevant statutory text is not as unambiguous as the Court asserts. There is substantial tension between the broad definition of the term "hazardous waste generation" in §1004(6) of the Act and the household waste exclusion codified by the 1984 amendment: both provisions can be read to describe the same activity. The former "means the act or process of producing hazardous waste." 90 Stat. 2799; 42 U.S.C. §6903(6). Read literally, that definition is broad enough to encompass the burning of pure household waste that produces some hazardous residue. The only statutory escape from that conclusion is the 1984 amendment that provides an exemption for the activity of burning household waste. Yet that exemption does not distinguish between pure household waste, on the one hand, and a mixture of household and other nonhazardous wastes, on the other. It either exempts both the pure stream and the mixture, or it exempts neither.

Indeed, commercial and industrial waste is by definition nonhazardous: in order for it to fall within the exclusion created by the 1984 amendment, it must not contain hazardous components. As a consequence, the only aspect of this waste stream that would ordinarily be regulated by Subtitle C of RCRA is the ash residue. EPA could reasonably conclude, therefore, that to give any content to the statute with respect to this component of the waste stream, the incinerator ash must be exempted from Subtitle C regulation.

The exemption states that a facility burning solid waste "shall not be deemed to be treating, storing, disposing of, or otherwise managing hazardous wastes for the purposes of regulation under this subchapter" if two conditions are satisfied. As long as the two conditions are met — even though the material being treated and disposed of contains hazardous components before, during, and after its treatment — that material "shall not be deemed to be . . . hazardous." By characterizing both the input and the output as not hazardous, the 1984 amendment excludes the activity from the definition of hazardous waste generation that would otherwise apply. For it is obvious that the same activity cannot both subject a facility to regulation because its residue is hazardous and exempt the facility from regulation because the statute deems the same residue to be nonhazardous.[8]

---

8. The Court characterizes my reading of the text as "imaginative use of ellipsis," because the subject of the predicate "shall not be deemed to be . . . hazardous" is the recovery facility rather than the residue that is disposed of after the waste is burned. That is true, but the reason the facility is exempted is because it is not "deemed to be . . . disposing of . . . hazardous wastes." Thus it is the statutorily deemed nonhazardous character of the object of the sentence — wastes — that effectively exempts from Subtitle C regulation the activity and the facility engaged in that activity. If, as the statute provides, a facility is not deemed to be disposing of hazardous wastes when it disposes of the output of the facility, it must be true that the output is deemed nonhazardous.

Thus, if we are to be guided only by the literal meaning of the statutory text, we must either give effect to the broad definition of hazardous waste generation and subject all municipal incinerators that generate hazardous ash to Subtitle C regulation (including those that burn pure household waste) or give effect to the exclusion that applies equally to pure household waste and mixtures that include other nonhazardous wastes. For several reasons the latter is the proper choice. It effectuates the narrower and more recently enacted provision rather than the earlier more general definition. It respects the title of the 1984 amendment by treating what follows as a "clarification" rather than a repeal or a modification. It avoids the Court's rather surprising (and uninvited) decision to invalidate the household waste exclusion that the EPA adopted in 1980, on which municipalities throughout the Nation have reasonably relied for over a decade. It explains why the legislative history fails to mention an intent to impose significant new burdens on the operation of municipal incinerators. Finally, it is the construction that the EPA has adopted and that reasonable jurists have accepted.

The majority's decision today may represent sound policy. Requiring cities to spend the necessary funds to dispose of their incinerator residues in accordance with the strict requirements of Subtitle C will provide additional protections to the environment. It is also true, however, that the conservation of scarce landfill space and the encouragement of the recovery of energy and valuable materials in municipal wastes were major concerns motivating RCRA's enactment. Whether those purposes will be disserved by regulating municipal incinerators under Subtitle C and, if so, whether environmental benefits may nevertheless justify the costs of such additional regulation are questions of policy that we are not competent to resolve. Those questions are precisely the kind that Congress has directed the EPA to answer. The EPA's position, first adopted unambiguously in 1980 and still maintained today, was and remains a correct and permissible interpretation of the Agency's broad congressional mandate.

## NOTES AND QUESTIONS

1. If household waste can contain hazardous constituents, why would EPA have sought to grant it a waste-stream exemption from regulation as hazardous waste under subtitle C?

2. In light of the Court's decision, would ash produced by an incinerator that burned *only* household waste and *no* other materials be exempt from subtitle C regulation? Would it have been prior to the 1984 Amendment that added section 3001(i) to RCRA? What did the addition of section 3001(i) accomplish, according to Justice Scalia?

3. Justice Scalia notes that municipal incinerators whose ash becomes a hazardous waste will be subject only to the subtitle C regulations applicable to generators and not to subtitle C's more onerous requirements for TSDs. Does this mean that the Court's decision will not impose substantial additional costs on incinerators?

4. In May 1994, EPA issued guidance stating that incinerator ash be tested for hazardous constituents four times a year beginning in August 1994, using the Toxicity Characteristic Leaching Procedure (TCLP). In January 1995, EPA announced

that incinerator operators could combine fly ash and bottom ash prior to testing to determine if the waste exhibits a hazardous characteristic. The agency based this decision on the notion that ash does not become a waste until it leaves the combustion facility. Because bottom ash usually is less toxic than fly ash, the decision is expected to mean that most incinerator ash will not exhibit a hazardous characteristic when tested. EPA Says Municipal Incinerator Owners Can Combine Fly, Bottom Ash for Testing, 25 Envtl. Rep. 1841 (1995). If ash does not become a waste until it leaves the combustion facility, could incinerator operators treat ash that flunks the TCLP to render it nonhazardous prior to shipping it off-site without having to comply with subtitle C of RCRA?

5. In an article "Coping with the RCRA Hazardous Waste System: A Few Practical Points for Fun and Profit," 1 Envtl. Hazards 6 (July 1989), environmental lawyer Richard Stoll advises companies on avenues for escaping RCRA Subtitle C regulation. These include: (1) redirecting waste streams to public sewer systems or point source discharges to navigable waters, (2) changing manufacturing processes so that characteristic hazardous waste will no longer exhibit the hazardous characteristic, (3) petitioning EPA to delist your waste, (4) exporting hazardous waste to Canada pursuant to a treaty between the two countries, and (5) reclaiming non-listed sludges and by-products so that it no longer is considered waste.

6. Stoll notes that EPA has exempted from TSD status large generators who accumulate hazardous waste in tanks or containers for no more than 90 days. Even if each batch of hazardous waste in the containers is emptied at least once every 90 days, the containers can contain hazardous waste almost continuously. Does it make any difference from the standpoint of environmental risk whether each batch of waste has been there for no more than 90 days?

7. Wastes listed as hazardous can be delisted if a generator can demonstrate to EPA's satisfaction that the waste stream is not in fact hazardous at a particular facility. To obtain a delisting, a generator must petition EPA. To correct perceived abuses in the delisting process, section 3001(f) was added to RCRA by the 1984 Amendments. This section requires EPA, when evaluating delisting petitions, to consider any other factors that could cause the waste to be hazardous in addition to those for which the waste originally was listed. EPA must publish in the Federal Register a proposal to grant or deny a delisting petition within a year of receiving the petition; final action must be taken within two years.

8. Exports of hazardous waste to another country are regulated under section 3017 of RCRA, which was added by the 1984 Amendments. This section prohibits the export of hazardous waste unless the consent of the receiving country's government has been obtained. Persons who intend to export hazardous waste must give EPA advance notice. The secretary of state then must inform the government of the recipient country and request its consent to accept the waste. Canada has entered into an agreement with the United States that governs the export of hazardous waste. What impact does this agreement have on exporters' obligations under section 3017 of RCRA? See §3017(f).

### 6. Subtitle D, Coal Ash, and the Regulation of "Nonhazardous" Waste Disposal

Subtitle D of RCRA applies to solid wastes that are not regulated as hazardous. While nearly 280 million tons of wastes are regulated as hazardous under subtitle C each year, more than 20 times more solid waste falls under the jurisdiction of subtitle D. Subtitle D prohibits "open dumping" of such waste, but it allows for its disposal in "sanitary landfills." 42 U.S.C. §6944(a). Subtitle D provides that "a facility may be classified as a sanitary landfill only if there is no reasonable probability of adverse effects on health or the environment from disposal of solid waste at such facility." Id.

When RCRA was amended in 1980, Congress adopted the Bevill and Bentsen Amendments that temporarily exempted from Subtitle C regulation many potentially dangerous waste streams because they are generated in such large quantities. These included wastes generated from the exploration and production of crude oil or natural gas, cement kiln dust, mining and mineral processing waste, and waste from the combustion of coal and other fossil fuels at electric utilities and industrial facilities. EPA was required to study these "special wastes" and then to determine how they should be regulated. After missing the deadlines for completing these studies, EPA eventually completed them and generally decided not to regulate them as hazardous wastes under Subtitle C.

When Congress adopted the 1984 Amendments to RCRA, it recognized that even municipal dumps that managed solid waste not regulated under subtitle C could pose serious environmental hazards. Thus the 1984 Amendments added section 4010(c), which required EPA to revise its subtitle D criteria for sanitary landfills that may receive hazardous household wastes or hazardous wastes from small-quantity generators. The revised criteria must require that such facilities at least perform groundwater monitoring and undertake corrective action as appropriate. Congress also required states to adopt "a permit program or other system of prior approval and conditions" to assure compliance with the revised subtitle D criteria. RCRA §4005(c), 42 U.S.C. 6945.

The final rule adopted by EPA established standards for siting, design, operation, and closure of municipal landfills. Landfills are required within five years to conduct regular groundwater monitoring and to take corrective action to clean up contamination. The rules provide a flexible menu of design standards that states may elect based on their hydrogeological and other characteristics. States are required to establish permit programs to incorporate the subtitle D standards. If a state approves a landfill that has less stringent design standards than required by the federal criteria, the regulation gives EPA only 30 days in which to object. EPA is authorized to impose federal standards directly in states that fail to submit acceptable state programs.

EPA's subtitle D standards for municipal landfills were generally upheld by the D.C. Circuit in Sierra Club v. EPA, 992 F.2d 337 (D.C. Cir. 1993). The court held that EPA had the discretion not to set numeric limits for toxics in sewage sludge when it is co-disposed with municipal waste even though the Clean Water Act imposes such limits when sludge alone is disposed. But the court agreed with environmental groups that RCRA required all municipal landfills, regardless of their size or location, to conduct groundwater monitoring. This part of the decision was partially overturned by legislation adopted in 1996. The Land Disposal Program Flexibility Act provides EPA with express statutory authority to exempt certain small municipal solid waste landfills from groundwater monitoring requirements. The exemption applies to landfills that dispose of less than 20 tons of municipal solid waste daily, provided there is no evidence of groundwater contamination from the municipal waste unit. It applies to such landfills only if they serve a community that has no practicable waste management alternative and that receives less than 25 inches of precipitation a year or that does not have year-round access to a regional waste management facility. The legislation gives states the option to forgo the exemption and require groundwater monitoring by such landfills if necessary. It also authorizes states to suspend groundwater monitoring requirements for landfills upon a demonstration that there is no potential for migration of hazardous constituents into the uppermost aquifer during the landfill's operating life and its post-closure care period.

The by-products of coal combustion at power plants contain numerous carcinogens and neurotoxins including arsenic, boron, cadmium, hexavalent chromium, lead, lithium, mercury, molybdenum, selenium, and thallium. Exposure to these contaminants increases the risks of a variety of cancer and non-cancer health effects in humans and kills plants and wildlife. Most coal-fired power plants dump this coal ash in massive dry landfills or mix it with water and place it in surface impoundments. As of 2012 there were 310 of these landfills and 735 surface impoundments still receiving coal ash. Most of these are unlined and leaking hazardous constituents to groundwater or nearby surface waters. On December 22, 2008, a catastrophic collapse of a dike at an unlined coal ash surface impoundment in Kingston, Tennessee released 1.1 billion gallons of coal ash slurry into the Emory River in Tennessee, forcing its closure for nearly two years and spawning a $1.2 billion cleanup. In February 2014, a burst pipe spilled 39,000 tons of coal ash from a Duke Energy power plant into North Carolina's Dan River.

These disasters helped spur EPA to issue a final rule regulating disposal of coal combustion residuals (CCRs) in December 2014. 80 Fed. Reg. 21,302 (2015). The rule regulated the ash as a nonhazardous waste under Subtitle D of RCRA. It set requirements for the structural integrity of coal ash impoundments including groundwater monitoring and the use of liners for new impoundments. Existing impoundments were to be retrofitted with composite liners. The rule did not require facilities to receive a permit, and it is not federally enforceable. States were not required to regulate the wastes, though EPA encouraged states with solid waste management plans (SWMPs) to address CCRs in them.

This rule was struck down by the U.S. Court of Appeals for the D.C. Circuit in Utility Solid Waste Activities Group v. EPA, 901 F.3d 414 (D.C. Cir. 2018). The court held that the 2015 regulations did not adequately protect human health or the environment because the rule allowed continued operation of unlined impoundments. The court also rejected industry arguments that inactive coal ash dumps could not violate Subtitle D's prohibition on open dumping because they no longer received waste. EPA promulgated new regulations that were published in August 2020. 85 Fed. Reg. 53516 (2020). In November 2020, EPA finalized a rule that allows some facilities with impoundments classified as unlined to continue to operate by demonstrating that their impoundments are safe. Owners and operators who believe an unlined surface impoundment meets the RCRA standard for sanitary landfills can continue to use those impoundments. The rule provides a process for owners and operators to demonstrate that an engineered liner and/or naturally occurring soil will remain protective, such that the continued use of an unlined surface impoundment will "present no reasonable probability of adverse effects to human health or the environment."

## 7.  RCRA's "Imminent and Substantial Endangerment" Provisions

RCRA contains two important provisions that can be used to require responsible parties to bear the cost of cleaning up environmental contamination. Sections 7003 and 7002(a)(1)(b) of RCRA authorize lawsuits to require the cleanup of wastes that "may present an imminent and substantial endangerment to health or the environment." Section 7003 of RCRA authorizes the EPA administrator to sue any person "who has contributed or who is contributing" to "handling, storage, treatment, transportation or disposal of any solid waste or hazardous waste" that meets the "imminent and substantial endangerment" standard. Section 7002(a)(1) (b) authorizes citizen suits to be brought in the same circumstances. The statute specifies that eligible defendants may include "any past or present generator, past or present transporter, or past or present owner or operator" of a facility that treats, stores, or disposes of waste.

Prior to the enactment of CERCLA in 1980, section 7003 was one of the few authorities available to EPA to respond to dumpsite contamination problems. As initially enacted in 1976, section 7003 imposed liability on a defendant who "is contributing" to contamination that "is presenting" the requisite "imminent and substantial endangerment." When Congress amended RCRA in 1980 it changed this language to clarify that it also applied to past actions that "may present" such endangerment, easing the government's burden of proof. Section 7003 specifies that defendants may be restrained from contributing to endangerment, ordered "to take such other action as may be necessary, or both." This has enabled the government to obtain a wide range of equitable relief, including orders to defendants to remediate contamination. See, e.g., United States v. Price, 688 F.2d 204 (3d Cir. 1982).

When it amended RCRA in 1984, Congress added a parallel "imminent hazard" provision to the citizen suit provisions in section 7002. Section 7002(a)(1) (b) authorizes "any person" to bring such an "imminent and substantial endangerment" action, tracking the same language used in section 7003. Section 7002 also authorizes courts to issue the same broad equitable relief as section 7003. While courts generally have interpreted section 7002(a)(1)(b) coextensively with section 7003, citizens suing under the former must comply with additional requirements before filing suit, such as providing 90 days of notice of intent to sue (unless a violation of RCRA subtitle C is alleged). Citizen suits under section 7002(a)(1)(b) also can be precluded if federal or state authorities are diligently prosecuting their own enforcement actions or using CERCLA authorities to clean up the contamination.

Although the "imminent and substantial endangerment" language may suggest that actions under sections 7003 and 7002(a)(1)(b) can be used only to respond to the most serious contamination problems, courts have broadly interpreted the "imminent hazard" provisions to provide relief in a wide range of situations. Focusing on the "may present" language, courts have held that these provisions need not be confined to emergency situations. Proof of actual or immediate harm is not required, but rather only a showing of a risk of harm. United States v. Waste Industries, Inc., 734 F.2d 159 (4th Cir. 1984); Interfaith Community Organization v. Honeywell Int'l, Inc., 399 F.3d 248 (3d Cir. 2005). To be held liable for "contributing" to waste management that gave rise to the risk of harm, it has been held to be sufficient for a landowner to have been aware of contamination and to have failed to abate it. United States v. Price, 688 F.2d 204 (3d Cir. 1982). However, the mere sale of an industrial property that contains asbestos insulation has been held not to be the "handling, storage, treatment, transportation or disposal" of waste that could give rise to liability. Sycamore Industrial Park Associates v. Ericsson, Inc., 546 F.3d 847 (7th Cir. 2008).

Because sections 7002 and 7003 apply to activity involving not only hazardous waste, but also "any solid waste," they can be used to respond to contamination problems involving nonhazardous wastes and substances that are excluded from CERCLA's coverage. However, in Meghrig v. KFC Western, Inc., 516 U.S. 479 (1996), the Supreme Court unanimously held that section 7002(a) does not authorize a private cause of action under RCRA to recover the costs of past efforts to clean up a petroleum leak because the "may present" and "imminent" language clearly exclude waste that already has been cleaned up. The plaintiffs had sought to use RCRA, rather than CERCLA, to recover for the cleanup costs because petroleum is excluded from the list of hazardous substances whose release or threat of release can trigger CERCLA liability. Unlike CERCLA, which expressly authorizes contribution actions under section 113(f), RCRA has no express contribution provision. For an argument that RCRA should be construed to authorize an implied private right of action for contribution, see Kenneth K. Kilbert, Re-Exploring Contribution Under RCRA's Imminent Hazard Provisions, 87 Neb. L. Rev. 420 (2008).

An effort to use RCRA's "imminent and substantial endangerment" provisions to redress particulate pollution from diesel exhaust emitted by trains in a railyard was rejected by the Ninth Circuit in Center for Community Action v. BNSF Railway Co., 764 F.3d 1019 (9th Cir. 2014). The court held that emission of diesel particulate matter does not constitute "disposal" of solid waste under RCRA. Environmental plaintiffs argued that the defendant railroads disposed of solid waste — the diesel particulate matter — by allowing the waste to be "transported by wind and air currents onto the land and water near the railyards." The court noted that although RCRA's definition of "disposal" in section 7003(3) is quite broad, it does not include the word "emitting," indicating that it does not apply to waste first emitted into the air.

In another effort to expand the reach of the "imminent and substantial endangerment" provisions of RCRA, an environmental group sued the U.S. Forest Service for its alleged failure to regulate the disposal of spent lead ammunition in a national forest. In Center for Biological Diversity v. United States Forest Service, 640 Fed. Appx. 617 (9th Cir. 2016), the plaintiff alleged that the Forest Service had "contributed" to the poisoning of condors, which consume lead in animal carcasses. While the Ninth Circuit described the merits of the RCRA claim as "fairly debatable," it upheld the standing of the plaintiff and allowed the case to go forward. On remand the district court again dismissed the case, this time for seeking a nonjusticiable advisory opinion. The Ninth Circuit again reversed, Center for Biological Diversity v. United States Forest Service, 925 F.3d 1041 (9th Cir. 2019), remanding for the district court to consider "whether owning or managing land on which disposal of solid waste by third parties is ongoing, known, and unabated can be a sufficiently active role to permit contributor liability." Id. at 1053.

## D. CERCLA LIABILITY

### 1. CERCLA's Basic Principles

The Comprehensive Environmental Response, Compensation and Liability Act (CERCLA) was enacted four short years after Congress thought it had closed the "last remaining loophole" in environmental law through the passage of RCRA. The reconsideration was prompted by the Love Canal disaster, which came to light shortly after RCRA was enacted. In 1953, the Hooker Chemical and Plastics Corporation had transferred title to a 16-acre site to the Niagara Falls Board of Education for the sum of one dollar. The company acknowledged that it had buried chemicals on the site, which it had covered with a layer of clay, and the deed of sale stated that the company would not be responsible for any injuries that might occur. A school and 100 homes were built on the site. Following heavy rains in 1978, a chemical soup began seeping into residential basements. More than 80 chemical compounds were found, including many known carcinogens. Ultimately, 1,000 families were relocated and homes along the canal were demolished.

Love Canal became a national media event that crystallized a festering problem in terms that provoked an emotional response from the public. Love Canal highlighted the consequences of decades of poor waste management. Evidence began to appear that suggested billions of tons of hazardous waste had been dumped onto the land, into lakes, ponds, and lagoons, and scattered in 55-gallon drums that were slowly leaking contaminants or being ignited and causing toxic fires.

The public response contributed to a political climate that produced CERCLA, the most comprehensive new federal approach to environmental protection since the enactment of NEPA. Even though the story of Love Canal will forever be associated with CERCLA, it is important to understand that in many respects CERCLA represents a natural adaptation of centuries of common law developments as extended by modern environmental statutes.

CERCLA is a direct extension of common law principles of strict liability for abnormally dangerous activities and was modeled on a prior extension of those principles contained in the 1972 Clean Water Act's oil spill liability program. As discussed in Chapter 2, section 311 of the Clean Water Act applies the principle of strict liability to persons responsible for releases of "harmful quantities" of oil.

This provision, coupled with emergency response authorities contained in section 504(b) of the Act, established a national oil spill response program that made persons responsible for the spills strictly liable for response costs. In 1978, Congress broadened section 311 to encompass not only oil spills, but also releases of other hazardous substances in navigable waters. Congress also made dischargers liable not only for cleanup costs but also for damages to natural resources.

The core of CERCLA is its liability provisions and its authorization to EPA to spend monies from the Superfund for *removal* operations — short-term action to address immediate hazards — and for *remediation* operations — targeted at longer-term solutions, including decontamination. EPA is authorized to incur expenses responding to imminent threats to health and the environment under its removal authorities, but it can only spend money on remediation for sites that it has placed on the *National Priorities List* (NPL). §§104, 105. Section 105 instructed EPA to place at least 400 sites needing cleanup on the initial NPL and also to revise the *National Contingency Plan*, originally prepared to respond to oil spills, to deal with hazardous waste cleanup. State governments and federal authorities can engage in joint cleanup operations. EPA also has authority under section 106 to order private parties to abate actual or potential releases of hazardous substances in order to prevent imminent and substantial endangerment. Parties that fail to comply with these "unilateral administrative orders" (UAOs) without sufficient cause can be held liable to the federal government under section 107(c)(3) for three times the costs incurred by the Superfund as a result of the non-compliance. For more than a decade, the General Electric Company, which had been issued a UAO by EPA to clean up PCBs in the Hudson River, claimed that section 106 was an unconstitutional denial of due process. The D.C. Circuit rejected this claim in General Electric Company v. Jackson, 610 F.3d 110 (D.C. Cir. 2010).

For its response and remediation costs, the federal government draws on the Superfund, which was funded initially through a tax on chemical feedstocks, and later amended to include a small tax on petroleum. §111. This tax expired in 1995 and has not been reauthorized, requiring that greater and greater portions of the Superfund program be funded out of general revenues, appropriated annually by the Congress. The lack of reauthorization of the tax has been slowly starving the program for funds for cleanups that are not paid for by potentially responsible parties. See Section D6 for more discussion.

Section 107 identifies four classes of potentially responsible parties who bear cleanup liability under Superfund's cost recovery provisions: current owners and operators, owners and operators at the time waste was disposed of at the facility, generators of the waste, and persons who transported waste to the facility. These liability provisions are the engine driving Superfund, and the vast bulk of the substantial volume of litigation under the statute has involved the scope and implications of the Act's cost recovery provisions. In studying this comprehensive liability scheme, bear in mind that imposing liability has forward-looking deterrent effects in addition to its providing a method to finance cleanup of existing sites. Philip Cummings, the chief counsel of the Senate Environment Committee when CERCLA was drafted, has written that this deterrent effect is at the heart of the reasons for passage: "CERCLA," he writes, "is not primarily an abandoned dump cleanup program, although that is included in its purposes." Instead,

> [t]he main purpose of CERCLA is to make spills or dumping of hazardous substances less likely through liability, enlisting business and commercial instincts for the bottom line in place of traditional regulation. It was a conscious intention of the law's authors to draw lenders and insurers into this new army of quasi-regulators, along with corporate risk managers and boards of directors. [Cummings, Completing the Circle, Envtl. Forum 11 (Nov./Dec. 1990).]

The enormous publicity directed at CERCLA's remediation provisions (examined below) has obscured the fact that CERCLA's liability provisions also are designed to serve preventive ends. While some have argued that the CERCLA cleanup process is so bureaucratic as to make the program resemble a traditional command-and-control regulatory program, Coalition on Superfund, Coalition on Superfund Research Report ix (1989), CERCLA's liability provisions remain the heart of the statute. By imposing strict liability on broad classes of parties, Congress intended to create a powerful new incentive for waste reduction and more careful management of waste. As the Senate committee report on the original CERCLA legislation stated, "By holding the factually responsible person liable, [the bill] encourages that person — whether a generator, transporter, or disposer of hazardous substances — to eliminate as many risks as possible." S. Rep. No. 848, 96th Cong., 2d Sess. 33 (1980).

Thus, CERCLA pursues dual goals: to prevent environmental contamination and to ensure that it is cleaned up when it occurs. While some argue that CERCLA's liability scheme has delayed the cleanup of dump sites and wasted resources on litigation, any evaluation of CERCLA's liability provisions should be done in the context of the Act's dual objectives. Regardless of how rapidly EPA proceeds with dump site cleanups, the CERCLA program could still be a success if its liability provisions are effective in deterring environmental releases. Fear of CERCLA liability is likely to stimulate reductions in the volume and toxicity of waste, an increase in recycling, and an increase in the care with which waste is managed. As a report for the Rand Corporation noted:

> By exposing firms to unlimited liability for prior waste handling, Superfund sets up strong signals that equally stringent regulations will operate in the future as well. This should lead to more conservative waste-handling practices both today and in the future and may lead business to reduce its use of toxic materials — and to increase recycling of these substances. [Acton, Understanding Superfund: A Progress Report 19 (1989).]

While it is not known precisely how significant CERCLA's liability provisions have been in stimulating such behavior, it is clear that they have had a significant impact. A survey of industrial generators of hazardous materials published by EPA in 2006 concluded that the threat of liability for cleanup costs under CERCLA was of "primary importance" in influencing how they managed their hazardous materials. EPA Office of Solid Wastes, An Assessment of Good Current Practices for Recycling of Hazardous Secondary Materials 6 (2006). In the sections that follow, we consider how CERCLA's liability provisions operate.

# Principal Provisions of CERCLA

*§101. Definitions:* the term "hazardous substance" is defined in section 101(14); "release" is defined in section 101(22).

*§103. Notification Requirements:* requires reporting of releases of hazardous substances to the National Response Center.

*§104. Response Authorities:* authorizes the president to undertake removals or remedial actions consistent with the National Contingency Plan to respond to actual or potential releases of hazardous substances.

*§105. National Contingency Plan:* requires establishment of a National Priorities List (NPL) of facilities presenting the greatest danger to health, welfare, or the environment based on a hazard ranking system (HRS) and requires revision of National Contingency Plan (NCP).

*§106. Abatement Orders:* authorizes issuance of administrative orders requiring the abatement of actual or potential releases that may create imminent and substantial endangerment to health, welfare, or the environment and to issue such orders as may be necessary to protect public health and welfare and the environment. Any person who fails without sufficient cause to properly provide removal or remedial action pursuant to a §106 order can be held liable under §107(c) for punitive damages in an amount at least equal to, and not more than three times, the amount of costs incurred by the Fund as a result of the failure to take proper action.

*§107. Liability:* imposes liability on (1) current owners and operators of facilities where hazardous substances are released or threatened to be released, (2) owners and operators of facilities at the time substances were disposed, (3) persons who arranged for disposal or treatment of such substances, and (4) persons who accepted such substances for transport for disposal or treatment. These parties are liable for: (a) all costs of removal or remedial action incurred by the federal government not inconsistent with the NCP, (b) any other necessary costs of response incurred by any person consistent with the NCP, (c) damages for injury to natural resources, and (d) costs of health assessments. Creates exemptions for innocent purchasers, bona fide prospective purchasers, and *de micromis* contributors.

*§111. Superfund:* creates a Superfund which can be used to finance governmental response actions and to reimburse private parties for costs incurred in carrying out the NCP.

*§113. Judicial Review and Contribution:* bars pre-enforcement judicial review of response actions and abatement orders, and authorizes private actions for contribution against potentially responsible parties.

*§116. Cleanup Schedules:* establishes schedules for evaluating and listing sites on NPL, commencement of remedial investigation and feasibility studies (RI/FSs), and commencement of remedial action.

*§121. Cleanup Standards:* establishes preference for remedial actions that permanently and significantly reduce the volume, toxicity, or mobility of hazardous substances and requires selection of remedial actions that are protective of health and the environment and cost-effective, using permanent

solutions to the maximum extent practicable; requires cleanups to attain level of "legally applicable or relevant and appropriate standard, requirement, criteria or limitation" contained under any federal environmental law or more stringent state law.

§122. *Settlements:* sets standards for settlements with potentially responsible parties.

## 2. Liability Provisions of CERCLA

CERCLA makes a broad class of parties liable for the costs of responding to the release, or the substantial threat of a release, of "any hazardous substance." It authorizes responses to such releases (or to releases of "any pollutant or contaminant which may present an imminent and substantial danger to the public health or welfare") in section 104, and then specifies in section 107 the parties liable for the costs of responding to hazardous substance releases.

The term "hazardous substance" is broadly defined by section 101(14) to include hazardous wastes subject to regulation under subtitle C of RCRA, toxic water pollutants regulated under section 307 of the Clean Water Act, hazardous air pollutants listed under section 112 of the Clean Air Act, imminently hazardous chemicals regulated under section 7 of TSCA, substances other than oil that have been designated as hazardous pursuant to section 311(b)(2)(A) of the Clean Water Act (governing oil and hazardous substance spills in navigable waters), and additional substances designated by EPA. Thus, it is considerably broader than the universe of hazardous wastes regulated under subtitle C of RCRA. Petroleum, including crude oil, and natural gas, are specifically exempted from CERCLA's definition of hazardous substances, ostensibly because oil spills already were governed by section 311 of the Clean Water Act. As a result, CERCLA could not be used to respond to the problem of leaking underground storage tanks at gasoline stations. (In 1986, Congress created a separate program to control leaking underground storage tanks by adding subtitle I to the Resource Conservation and Recovery Act.) Because PFAS have escaped regulation under other federal environmental statutes, they are not currently CERCLA hazardous substances. Even if EPA regulates them as a contaminant under the Safe Drinking Water Act, as it has promised to do, they would not automatically become CERCLA hazardous substances because the SDWA is not one of the statutes cross referenced in section 101(14). However, there is strong support in Congress to require PFAS to be listed as hazardous substances.

While the definition of "hazardous substance" encompasses just about any toxic substance other than petroleum, section 104 also provides CERCLA jurisdiction over substances not listed in any of the categories of "hazardous substances" if it is a "pollutant or contaminant which may present an imminent and substantial danger to the public health or welfare." Thus, the release of a substance that does not happen to fall within CERCLA's broad definition of "hazardous substances" can still generate a CERCLA response if it presents "an imminent and substantial danger."

"Release" is broadly defined in section 101(22) to mean:

any spilling, leaking, pumping, pouring, emitting, emptying, discharging, injecting, escaping, leaching, dumping, or disposing into the environment (including the abandonment or discarding of barrels, containers, and other closed receptacles containing any hazardous substance or pollutant or contaminant). [§101(22).]

Not all releases of hazardous substances fall within CERCLA's broad jurisdiction. Section 107(i) of CERCLA exempts the application of pesticides registered under FIFRA, and section 107(j) exempts "federally permitted releases." The latter are defined in section 101(10) to include discharges authorized by permits issued under the Clean Water Act, RCRA, the Ocean Dumping Act, the Safe Drinking Water Act, the Clean Air Act, and the Atomic Energy Act, and certain fluid injection practices for producing oil or natural gas.

As a threshold matter, consider some constitutional challenges to CERCLA. In the years after CERCLA's enactment, litigants fighting its liability provisions routinely attacked the legislation on constitutional grounds, principally because it imposed tough liability standards for cleaning up hazardous wastes that had often been deposited many years before the statute was enacted. CERCLA thus raised an issue of impermissible retroactive legislation. One court summarized the challenges and its replies:

> The generator defendants raise numerous constitutional challenges to the district court's interpretation and application of CERCLA. They contend that the imposition of "disproportionate" liability without proof of causation violated constitutional limitations on retroactive statutory application and that it converted CERCLA into a bill of attainder and an *ex post facto* law. They further assert, along with the site-owners, that the trial court's construction of CERCLA infringed their substantive due process rights.
>
> The district court held that CERCLA does not create retroactive liability, but imposes a prospective obligation for the post-enactment environmental consequences of the defendants' past acts. Alternatively, the court held that even if CERCLA is understood to operate retroactively, it nonetheless satisfies the dictates of due process because its liability scheme is rationally related to a valid legislative purpose. We agree with the court's latter holding, and we find no merit to the generator defendants' bill of attainder and *ex post facto* arguments. . . . While the generator defendants profited from inexpensive waste disposal methods that may have been technically "legal" prior to CERCLA's enactment, it was certainly foreseeable at the time that improper disposal could cause enormous damage to the environment. CERCLA operates remedially to spread the costs of responding to improper waste disposal among all parties that played a role in creating the hazardous conditions. Where those conditions are indivisible, joint and several liability is logical, and it works to ensure complete cost recovery. We do not think these consequences are "particularly harsh and oppressive," United States Trust Co. v. New Jersey, 431 U.S. 1, 17 (1977) (retrospective civil liability not unconstitutional unless it is particularly harsh and oppressive), and we agree with the Eighth Circuit that retroactive application of CERCLA does not violate due process.

United States v. Monsanto Co. 858 F.2d 160, 173-174 (4th Cir. 1988) (citations omitted). The various constitutional challenges were uniformly unsuccessful in other courts as well. See, e.g., United States v. Northeastern Pharmaceutical & Chemical Co., Inc., 810 F.2d 726, 732-734 (8th Cir. 1986); United States v. Hooker Chemicals & Plastics Corp., 680 F. Supp. 546 (W.D.N.Y. 1988); United States v. Shell Oil Co., 605 F. Supp. 1064, 1069-1073 (D. Colo. 1985). Constitutional challenges gradually subsided, and litigation concentrated on questions of statutory interpretation.

The Supreme Court's decision in United States v. Lopez, 514 U.S. 549 (1995), that the Gun-Free School Zones Act exceeded Congress's authority under the Commerce Clause spawned some additional challenges to the constitutionality of federal regulatory statutes. When asked to approve a CERCLA consent decree for cleanup of a contaminated site, a federal district judge *sua sponte* asked the parties to brief whether Congress had the constitutional power to require cleanup of the closed industrial property. The judge then ruled that Congress had exceeded its authority under the Commerce Clause of the Constitution. On appeal, this decision was reversed in United States v. Olin Corp., 107 F.3d 1506 (11th Cir. 1997). The court held that "although Congress did not include in CERCLA either legislative findings or a jurisdictional element [connecting it to interstate commerce], the statute remains valid as applied in this case because it regulates a class of activities that substantially affects interstate commerce. . . . Because the legislative history of CERCLA documents how the unregulated management of hazardous substances, even strictly within individual states, significantly impacts interstate commerce, we conclude the statute can be applied constitutionally under the circumstances of this case. . . . CERCLA reflects Congress' recognition that both on-site and off-site disposal of hazardous waste threaten interstate commerce." While the company argued that "the record contains no evidence that its on-site disposal has caused off-site damage, much less harmed interstate commerce," the court did not deem this dispositive. "Olin's claim fails because . . . the regulation of intrastate, on-site waste disposal constitutes an appropriate element of Congress' broader scheme to protect interstate commerce and industries thereof from pollution."

## 3.  Responsible Parties

CERCLA embodies a liability approach to regulation. Rather than directing EPA to specify through regulations what actions persons must take to prevent environmental damage, CERCLA specifies the potential consequences if hazardous substances are released or if conditions posing a substantial threat of such a release are created. CERCLA's approach is intended not only to provide a means for financing the cleanup of environmental damage, but also to deter mismanagement of hazardous substances. Crucial to CERCLA's value as a deterrent is how the Act defines potentially liable parties. Section 107 of CERCLA broadly defines the parties potentially liable for response costs.

### A.  Owners

The case that follows is an early interpretation of CERCLA's liability provisions that has proven very influential. As you read it, consider what impact it is likely to have on incentives to prevent releases of hazardous substances in the future.

Consider also whether its strict interpretation of CERCLA could lead to unfair results in other circumstances.

## New York v. Shore Realty Corp.

759 F.2d 1032 (2d Cir. 1985)

Before FEINBERG, Chief Judge, OAKES and NEWMAN, Circuit Judges.

OAKES, Circuit Judge:. . .
On February 29, 1984, the State of New York brought suit against Shore Realty Corp. ("Shore") and Donald LeoGrande, its officer and stockholder, to clean up a hazardous waste disposal site at One Shore Road, Glenwood Landing, New York, which Shore had acquired for land development purposes. At the time of the acquisition, LeoGrande knew that hazardous waste was stored on the site and that cleanup would be expensive, though neither Shore nor LeoGrande had participated in the generation or transportation of the nearly 700,000 gallons of hazardous waste now on the premises. . . .

[LeoGrande controlled, directed, and made all decisions for Shore.] By contract dated July 14, 1983, Shore agreed to purchase the 3.2 acre site, a small peninsula surrounded on three sides by the waters of Hempstead Harbor and Mott Cove, for condominium development. Five large tanks in a field in the center of the site hold most of some 700,000 gallons of hazardous chemicals located there, though there are six smaller tanks both above and below ground containing hazardous waste, as well as some empty tanks on the property. The tanks are connected by pipe to a tank truck loading rack and dockage facilities for loading by barge. Four roll-on/roll-off containers and one tank truck trailer hold additional waste. And before June 15, 1984, one of the two dilapidated masonry warehouses on the site contained over 400 drums of chemicals and contaminated solids, many of which were corroded and leaking.

It is beyond dispute that the tanks and drums contain "hazardous substances" within the meaning of CERCLA §101(14). The substances involved—including benzene, dichlorobenzenes, ethyl benzene, tetrachloroethylene, trichloroethylene, 1,1,1-trichloroethylene chlordane, polychlorinated biphenyls (commonly known as PCBs) and bis (2-ethylhexyl) phthalate—are toxic, in some cases carcinogenic, and dangerous by way of contact, inhalation, or ingestion. . . . The purchase agreement provided that it could be voided by Shore without penalty if after conducting an environmental study Shore had decided not to proceed. LeoGrande was fully aware that the tenants, Applied Environmental Services, Inc., and Hazardous Waste Disposal, Inc., were then operating—illegally, it may be noted—a hazardous waste storage facility on the site. Shore's environmental consultant, WTM Management Corporation ("WTM") . . . found that there had been several spills of hazardous waste at the site, including at least one large spill in 1978. Though there had been some attempts at cleanup, the WTM testing revealed that hazardous substances, such as benzene, were still leaching into the groundwater and the waters of the bay immediately adjacent to the bulkhead abutting Hempstead Harbor. . . . The report concluded that if the current tenants "close up the operation and leave the material at the site," the owners would be left with a "potential time bomb." WTM estimated that the cost of environmental cleanup and monitoring would range from $650,000 to over $1 million before development could begin. After receiving this report Shore sought a waiver from the State Department of Environmental Conservation ("DEC") of liability as landowners for the disposal of the hazardous waste stored at the site. Although the DEC denied the waiver, Shore took title on October 13, 1983, and obtained certain rights over against the tenants, whom it subsequently evicted on January 5, 1984.

Nevertheless, between October 13, 1983, and January 5, 1984, nearly 90,000 gallons of hazardous chemicals were added to the tanks. And during a state inspection on January 3, 1984, it became evident that the deteriorating and leaking drums of chemicals referred to above had also been brought onto the site. Needless to say, the tenants did not clean up the site before they left. Thus, conditions when Shore employees first entered the site were as bad as or worse than those described in the WTM report. As LeoGrande admitted by affidavit, "the various storage tanks, pipe lines and connections between these storage facilities were in a bad state of repair." While Shore claims to have made some improvements, such as sealing all the pipes and valves and continuing the cleanup of the damage from earlier spills, Shore did nothing about the hundreds of thousands of gallons of hazardous waste standing in deteriorating tanks. In addition, although a growing number of drums were leaking hazardous substances, Shore essentially ignored the problem until June, 1984. [In October 1984, the district court held Shore liable under CERCLA for the state's response costs and issued an injunction under state nuisance law directing that Shore and LeoGrande remove the remaining hazardous waste stored on the property.]

### CERCLA

. . . CERCLA was designed "to bring order to the array of partly redundant, partly inadequate federal hazardous substances cleanup and compensation laws." It applies "primarily to the cleanup of leaking inactive or abandoned sites and to emergency responses to spills." And it distinguishes between two kinds of response: remedial actions—generally long-term or permanent containment or disposal programs—and removal efforts—typically short-term cleanup arrangements.

CERCLA authorizes the federal government to respond in several ways. EPA can use Superfund resources to clean up hazardous waste sites and spills. §111. The National Contingency Plan ("NCP"), prepared by EPA pursuant to CERCLA §105, governs cleanup efforts by "establish[ing] procedures and standards for responding to releases of hazardous substances." At the same time, EPA can sue for reimbursement of cleanup costs from any responsible parties it can locate, §107, allowing the federal government to respond immediately while later trying to shift financial responsibility to others. Thus, Superfund covers cleanup costs if the site has been abandoned, if the responsible parties elude detection, or if private resources are inadequate. . . . In addition, CERCLA authorizes EPA to seek an injunction in federal district court to force a responsible party to clean up any site or spill that presents an imminent and substantial danger to public health or welfare or the environment. §106(a). In sum, CERCLA is not a regulatory standard-setting statute such as the Clean Air Act. Rather, the government generally undertakes pollution abatement, and polluters pay for such abatement through tax and reimbursement liability. . . .

Congress intended that responsible parties be held strictly liable, even though an explicit provision for strict liability was not included in the compromise. Section 9601(32) provides that "liability" under CERCLA "shall be construed to be the standard of liability" under section 311 of the Clean Water Act, 33 U.S.C. §1321, which courts have held to be strict liability, and which Congress understood to impose such liability, see S. Rep. No. 848, 96th Cong., 2d Sess. 34 (1980). Moreover, the sponsors of the compromise expressly stated that section 9607 provides for strict liability. . . . Strict liability under CERCLA, however, is not absolute; there are defenses for causation solely by an act of God, an act of war, or acts or omissions of a third party other than an employee or agent of the defendant or one whose act or omission occurs in connection with a contractual relationship with the defendant. §107(b). . . .

**Covered Persons.**    CERCLA holds liable four classes of persons:

(1) the owner and operator of a vessel (otherwise subject to the jurisdiction of the United States) or a facility,

(2) any person who at the time of disposal of any hazardous substance owned or operated any facility at which such hazardous substances were disposed of,

(3) any person who by contract, agreement, or otherwise arranged for disposal or treatment, or arranged with a transporter for transport for disposal or treatment, of hazardous substances owned or possessed by such person, by any other party or entity, at any facility owned or operated by another party or entity and containing such hazardous substances, and

(4) any person who accepts or accepted any hazardous substances for transport to disposal or treatment facilities or sites selected by such person.

107(a). As noted above, section 107 makes these persons liable, if "there is a release, or a threatened release which causes the incurrence of response costs, of a hazardous substance" from the facility, for, among other things, "all costs of removal or remedial action incurred by the United States Government or a State not inconsistent with the national contingency plan."

Shore argues that it is not covered by section 107(a)(1) because it neither owned the site at the time of disposal nor caused the presence or the release of the hazardous waste at the facility. While section 107(a)(1) appears to cover Shore, Shore attempts to infuse ambiguity into the statutory scheme, claiming that section 107(a)(1) could not have been intended to include all owners, because the word "owned" in section 107(a)(2) would be unnecessary since an owner "at the time of disposal" would necessarily be included in section 107(a)(1). Shore claims that Congress intended that the scope of section 107(a)(1) be no greater than that of section 107(a)(2) and that both should be limited by the "at the time of disposal" language. By extension, Shore argues that both provisions should be interpreted as requiring a showing of causation. We agree with the State, however, that section 107(a)(1) unequivocally imposes strict liability on the current owner of a facility from which there is a release or threat of release, without regard to causation.

Shore's claims of ambiguity are illusory; section 107(a)'s structure is clear. Congress intended to cover different classes of persons differently. Section 107(a)(1) applies to all current owners and operators, while section 107(a)(2) primarily covers prior owners and operators. Moreover, section 107(a)(2)'s scope is more limited than that of section 107(a)(1). Prior owners and operators are liable only if they owned or operated the facility "at the time of disposal of any hazardous substance"; this limitation does not apply to current owners, like Shore. . . .

Shore's causation argument is also at odds with the structure of the statute. Interpreting section 107(a)(1) as including a causation requirement makes superfluous the affirmative defenses provided in section 107(b), each of which carves out from liability an exception based on causation. Without a clear congressional command otherwise, we will not construe a statute in any way that makes some of its provisions surplusage. . . .

Furthermore, as the state points out, accepting Shore's arguments would open a huge loophole in CERCLA's coverage. It is quite clear that if the current owner of a site could avoid liability merely by having purchased the site after chemical dumping had ceased, waste sites certainly would be sold, following the cessation of dumping, to new owners who could avoid the liability otherwise required by CERCLA. Congress had well in mind that persons who dump or store hazardous waste sometimes cannot be located or may be deceased or judgment-proof. See, e.g., Senate Report, supra, at 16. We will not interpret section 107(a) in any way that apparently frustrates the statute's goals, in the absence of a specific congressional intention otherwise. . . .

**Release or Threat of Release.** We reject Shore's repeated claims that it has put in dispute whether there has been a release or threat of release at the Shore Road site. The state has established that it was responding to "a release or a threatened release" when it incurred its response costs. We hold that the leaking tanks and pipelines, the continuing leaching and seepage from the earlier spills, and the leaking drums all constitute "releases." §101(22). Moreover, the corroding and deteriorating tanks, Shore's lack of expertise in handling hazardous waste, and even the failure to license the facility, amount to a threat of release. . . .

**Affirmative Defense.** Shore also claims that it can assert an affirmative defense under CERCLA, which provides a limited exception to liability for a release or threat of release caused solely by

> an act or omission of a third party other than an employee or agent of the defendant, or than one whose act or omission occurs in connection with a contractual relationship, existing directly or indirectly, with the defendant (except where the sole contractual arrangement arises from a published tariff and acceptance for carriage by a common carrier by rail), if the defendant establishes by a preponderance of the evidence that (a) he exercised due care with respect to the hazardous substance concerned, taking into consideration the characteristics of such hazardous substance, in light of all relevant facts and circumstances, and (b) he took precautions against foreseeable acts or omissions of any such third party and the consequences that could foreseeably result from such acts or omissions.

§107(b)(3).

We disagree. Shore argues that it had nothing to do with the transportation of the hazardous substances and that it has exercised due care since taking control of the site. Who the "third part(ies)" Shore claims were responsible are difficult to fathom. It is doubtful that a prior owner could be such, especially the prior owner here, since the acts or omissions referred to in the statute are doubtless those occurring during the ownership or operation of the defendant. Similarly, many of the acts and omissions of the prior tenants/operators fall outside the scope of section 107(b)(3), because they occurred before Shore owned the property. In addition, we find that Shore cannot rely on the affirmative defense even with respect to the tenants' conduct during the period after Shore closed on the property and when Shore evicted the tenants. Shore was aware of the nature of the tenants' activities before the closing and could readily have foreseen that they would continue to dump hazardous waste at the site. In light of this knowledge, we cannot say that the releases and threats of release resulting from these activities were "caused solely" by the tenants or that Shore "took precautions" against these "foreseeable acts or omissions."

## NOTES AND QUESTIONS

1. Why do you think Congress chose to extend CERCLA liability to current owners and operators of facilities where hazardous substances had been deposited? If the court had accepted Shore's argument that section 107(a)(1) covered only owners and operators at the time of disposal, what impact would it have had on the government's ability to obtain reimbursement for Superfund response costs? What impact is the court's decision likely to have on future purchasers of property containing hazardous substances?

2. *Shore Realty* rejected Shore's efforts to take advantage of the defense to liability provided by section 107(b)(3). Which of the conditions for eligibility for that defense did Shore fail to meet?

3. At the time Shore Realty purchased the property at issue in this case, Shore was aware that the tanks and drums on the site contained hazardous substances. Suppose Shore had known only that there were tanks and drums on the site, but not that they contained hazardous substances. Would this have made any difference for Shore's liability under CERCLA? Would it have made any difference if the tanks and drums had been buried on the property and Shore had not even been aware of their existence? Is it fair to hold persons who were not involved in the creation of environmental hazards liable for the costs of cleaning them up? Should innocent purchasers be absolved from CERCLA liability? If they are, what impact would this have on incentives for investigating potential contamination of property?

4. *Innocent Purchaser Defense.* After the passage of CERCLA and decisions like *Shore Realty*, owners of properties where improper disposal had occurred in the past continued to press for relief from liability, primarily on grounds of fairness. In 1986, when Congress enacted extensive amendments to CERCLA in the Superfund Amendments and Reauthorization Act (SARA), it responded to some of these fairness concerns. The SARA revisions created a defense for so-called innocent land purchasers. Congress did this by amending the third-party defense of section 107(b)(3) to make it available to innocent purchasers of contaminated property who can establish (1) they did not have actual or constructive knowledge of the presence of hazardous substances at the time the land was acquired, (2) they are government entities acquiring the property through involuntary transfer, or (3)

they acquired the land by inheritance or bequest. To establish lack of constructive knowledge of the presence of hazardous substances, SARA further provided that a purchaser "must have undertaken at the time of acquisition, all appropriate inquiry into the previous ownership and uses of the property consistent with good commercial or customary practice in an effort to minimize liability." §101(35)(B).

In determining whether a purchaser had made "all appropriate inquiry" ("AAI") courts were directed to consider the purchaser's specialized knowledge or experience, the relationship of the purchase price to the value of uncontaminated property, reasonably ascertainable information about the property, the obviousness of the likely presence of contamination, and the ability to detect such contamination by inspection. By creating a defense to liability for purchasers who undertake the appropriate inquiry, these provisions encourage more thorough inspections of property at the time of purchase.

This innocent purchaser defense, set forth in section 101(35)(B), has been virtually impossible to satisfy. The defense has been rejected by courts for a variety of reasons, including a landowner's failure to inquire about the disposal practices of a business that previously operated on the property, United States v. A & N Cleaners & Launderers Inc., 854 F. Supp. 229 (S.D.N.Y. 1994), actual knowledge that a lessor discharged waste on the property; United States v. Broderick Investment Co., 862 F. Supp. 272 (D. Colo. 1994), and failure to take precautions to prevent damage from hazardous substances known to be present on the site; Kerr-McGee Chem. Corp. v. Lefton Iron & Metal Co., 14 F.3d 321 (7th Cir. 1994).

Although a number of cases have found that on the facts presented the defendant failed to make an appropriate inquiry, the lack of a good definition of what satisfies this requirement initially was an ongoing complaint of prospective purchasers. In November 2005, EPA published a final rule establishing standards and practices for AAI to satisfy sections 101(35)(B)(ii) & (iii). 70 Fed. Reg. 66,070 (2005). These standards are codified at 40 C.F.R. §312. A key element of the rules is that purchasers typically will need to retain the services of an "environmental professional," an individual with training in conducting environmental audits (the regulations specify a variety of alternative combinations of education and experience that may qualify some as an environmental professional). They also require interviews with past and present owners, and a number of other due diligence measures. The environmental professional must submit a written report of his or her findings. The federal rules do not protect against liability under state Superfund statutes, which may impose differing requirements.

5. If *Shore Realty* had been decided after the innocent purchaser exemption had been added, what would have been the result in the case?

6. **Protection of Bona Fide Prospective Purchasers.** In 2002, Congress again revisited the issue of holding liable owners who purchase the property after all disposal has occurred. In the most fundamental change in liability since CERCLA was originally enacted, a new section 107(r) now exempts bona fide prospective purchasers from owner or operator liability, if they satisfy all the requirements of section 107(r). Review those requirements and compare them to the requirements for innocent purchaser status. The earlier innocent purchaser exemption has generally been argued for on the basis of fairness, but can such fairness reasons apply to purchasers who know the property is contaminated before purchasing? What other

reasons might Congress have had in mind in enacting section 107(r)? If section 107(r) had been in place when *Shore Realty* was decided, what result? Have the concerns expressed by the court in *Shore Realty* about the undesirable consequences of exempting such current owners been adequately addressed in section 107(r)?

7. ***Interim Owners and Passive Migration.*** In addition to current owners and operators, CERCLA imposes liability on owners and operators "at the time of disposal." CERCLA defines disposal very broadly, to include "the discharge, deposit, injection, dumping, spilling, leaking, or placing of any solid waste or hazardous waste into or on any land or water." §101(29). PRPs and EPA have disagreed over whether this language sweeps in owners who engaged in no active conduct relating to disposal themselves but who owned the land at a time when wastes deposited on the land before their ownership continued to leak or spill onto the land. The leading case upholding so-called passive interim owner liability is Nurad v. William E. Hooper & Sons, 966 F.2d 837 (4th Cir. 1992). The leading case rejecting such liability is United States v. CDMG Realty, 96 F.3d 706 (3d Cir. 1996). *Nurad* stressed that not recognizing passive owner liability would mean that "an owner could avoid liability simply by standing idle while an environmental hazard festers on his property." 966 F.2d at 845. *CDMG* claimed that its contrary interpretation made more sense in light of the active words used to define disposal and that to acknowledge passive owner liability would vitiate the innocent purchaser defense that only applies to purchases occurring *after* disposal. 96 F.3d at 715-716. More courts have followed *CDMG.* See ABB Indus. Sys. Inc. v. Prime Tech., 120 F.3d 351 (2d Cir. 1997); United States v. 150 Acres of Land, 204 F.3d 698 (6th Cir. 2000); Carson Harbor Village, Ltd. v. Unocal Corp., 270 F.3d 863 (9th Cir. 2001) ("disposal" does not include passive soil migration, but it may include other passive migration, such as from leaking tanks). But see United States v. Waste Industries, 734 F.2d 159 (4th Cir. 1984) (in a RCRA section 7003 action, passive current owner can be "contributing to . . . [the] disposal" of hazardous wastes).

### A Note on Property Transfer Statutes

Some states have pursued a different strategy than the innocent purchaser defense to assist purchasers who do not wish to acquire contaminated property. Instead, they have required sellers to disclose the status of the property or to certify that it is free of contamination. Indeed, the federal government has also used this approach in specific circumstances. For instance, in order to ensure that the federal government did not itself dupe innocent purchasers, SARA added section 120(h) to CERCLA. Section 120(h) requires federal agencies to notify purchasers of federal property of the type and quantity of any hazardous substance known to have been stored (for one year or more), released, or disposed on the property. Federal agencies are required to disclose such information to the extent that it is "available on the basis of a complete search of agency files." Notice must be included not only in the contract for the sale, but also in the deed to the property. Section 120(h), however, provides even more protection to purchasers than simply disclosing environmental hazards. It also requires federal agencies to enter into covenants warranting that remedial action has been taken to clean up the property and promising that the government will undertake further remedial action if necessary after the property is transferred.

In 1990, EPA promulgated regulations applying section 120(h)'s notice requirements only to properties on which hazardous substances were stored, released, or disposed when the property was owned by the federal government. EPA believed that Congress had enacted section 120(h) largely out of concern for property, such as former military facilities, on which the government itself had placed hazardous substances, and it sought to "avoid imposing unfair and unmanageable obligations on federal agencies that had no role" in bringing the hazardous substances to the property. 55 Fed. Reg. 14,210. In Hercules, Inc. v. EPA, 938 F.2d 276 (D.C. Cir. 1991), the D.C. Circuit held that EPA's interpretation was contrary to the express terms of the statute, which requires that the federal government disclose what it knows about hazardous substances on the property regardless of when the substances were placed there. The court dismissed EPA's concern about imposing unfair and unmanageable obligations on federal agencies by noting:

> CERCLA explicitly supports the imposition of remediation obligations on parties who were not responsible for contamination and who have no experience in the handling or remediation of hazardous substances, as when it imposes liability on the sole basis that a party is the current owner or operator of a site contaminated by some previous owner or operator. [938 F.2d at 281.]

Moreover, the court observed that section 120(h) limits agencies' obligations to the disclosure of information contained in agency files.

In 1992, Congress enacted two laws that expand required environmental disclosures when property is transferred. The Community Environmental Response Facilitation Act, Pub. L. No. 102-426, amends section 120(h) of CERCLA to require federal agencies to identify uncontaminated portions of federal property that is for sale in order to facilitate transfers to private parties. While retaining the requirement that the federal government remediate environmental contamination on such properties, the Act provides that property transfers may occur before the completion of long-term remedial action once cleanup plans have been approved and initiated.

The Residential Lead-Based Paint Hazard Reduction Act, Pub. L. No. 102-550, enacted as Title X of the Housing and Community Development Act of 1992, requires sellers or lessors of residential property to disclose to purchasers or lessees "the presence of any known lead-based paint" on the property. Sellers and lessors also have to provide purchasers with an informational pamphlet on lead paint hazards and give them up to ten days to conduct a lead paint inspection.

Several states have statutes requiring sellers to disclose information about known or suspected contamination on property being sold. Connecticut requires that sellers certify that any hazardous wastes discharged on the property have been cleaned up. New Jersey's statute is the most far-reaching because it requires an environmental assessment and a cleanup, if necessary, as conditions for property transfer. New Jersey's Environmental Cleanup Responsibility Act (ECRA) took effect on December 31, 1984. ECRA requires that an environmental assessment be made when industrial property is being sold and that a cleanup plan be implemented if the property is found to be contaminated. The Act requires that the seller transfer to the buyer either (1) a "No Further Action" letter from the state Department of Environmental Protection that declares either that no hazardous substances have been released on the site or that any discharge has been cleaned up or (2) an approved cleanup plan accompanied by financial assurances that the plan will be implemented. If a seller fails to comply with ECRA, the buyer may void the transaction, and the seller is strictly liable for response costs and damages for failure to implement the cleanup.

New Jersey officials maintain that ECRA produced significant environmental benefits, including far more dump site cleanups in that state than the Superfund program produced. By the end of 1991, a total of 1,759 remedial actions costing more than $478 million had been undertaken pursuant to New Jersey's ECRA. New Jersey officials attribute ECRA's success to the fact that it avoids expensive disputes over who is at fault for contamination by internalizing the cost of cleanup in the property transfer transaction. As the New Jersey Supreme Court noted, "the statute focuses on the environmental wrong, not the wrongdoer. Identification of the polluter plays no part in the ECRA process, which imposes a 'self-executing duty to remediate.'" In re Adoption of N.J.A.C. 7:26B, 608 A.2d 288, 291 (N.J. 1992).

In 1993, New Jersey amended ECRA to relax cleanup standards, streamline the remediation process required by the Act, and codify the administrative rules that allowed remediation to take place after transfer. This legislation, the Industrial Site Recovery Act (ISRA), allows parties to defer remediation of industrial property if the new owner plans to use it for substantially the same purpose. It permits soil cleanups to proceed without prior state approval in most cases and authorizes transfers of partial interests in property without requiring cleanup of an entire site. The law permits the use of substantially lower exposure estimates in calculating cleanup levels required to reduce residual risk, depending upon the expected future use of the land, and it authorizes the use of institutional controls that restrict access to a site as an alternative to permanent remediation.

The ISRA applies only to certain industrial properties where hazardous substances have been deposited. See N.J.S.A. 13:1K-8. Buyer and seller are permitted to transfer the property prior to remediation, in which case the parties would enter into an agreement specifying how remediation would be completed and a "No Further Action" letter obtained from the New Jersey Department of Environmental Protection. In the absence of contractual arrangements, however, when the seller and buyer enter into a contract with the knowledge that ISRA applies, the statute imposes absolute liability for cleanup upon the seller.

In 2009, the New Jersey legislature passed the Site Remediation Reform Act (SRRA). The SRRA creates an affirmative obligation for responsible parties to remediate any discharge for which they would be liable. It requires that all site remediations in the state be conducted under the supervision of a licensed site remediation professional (LSRP), and it creates a licensing board for LSRPs.

## NOTES AND QUESTIONS

1. If you were a prospective purchaser of property, which approach to property transfer laws would you prefer—a pure disclosure approach or ECRA/ISRA's mandatory cleanup approach? Which would you prefer if you owned contaminated

property that you wished to sell? Which if you owned property that you were certain was free of contamination?

2.  Which approach is more likely to protect truly innocent purchasers—CER-CLA's or ECRA's? If you are purchasing property in a state without any of the kinds of property transfer laws described above, how much investigation do you need to undertake to ensure that you will escape future CERCLA liability? Who bears the cost of this investigation? If you are purchasing property in New Jersey, how much investigation do you need to undertake? Who bears the cost?

3.  The U.S. Defense Department has complained that the requirement that it clean up toxic contamination before selling federal property makes it difficult to close military bases. Schneider, Toxic Cleanup Stalls Transfer of Military Sites, N.Y. Times, June 30, 1991, at A1. In 2005, Defense Department officials estimated that more than $940 million had been spent on remediation of contamination at the 33 military bases recommended for closure in 2005 and that more than $1.54 billion in additional costs would be necessary to complete the cleanup. Congressional Research Service, Military Base Closures: Role and Costs of Environmental Cleanups, June 27, 2005, at 6.

## B.  Operators

Even a party who does not own a facility can be held liable as an "operator" under CERCLA section 107. In FMC Corp. v. United States Dep't of Commerce, 29 F.3d 833 (3d Cir. 1994), the U.S. government was held liable for contamination caused by a rayon manufacturing plant that had been operated during World War II at the direction of the government's War Production Board. The Third Circuit, sitting en banc, decided by an 8 to 4 vote that the government was liable as an "operator" of the facility under CERCLA. The court noted that it previously had adopted a "substantial control" test to determine when a corporation should be held liable for the environmental violations of another.

In *FMC*, the en banc court found that the government clearly had exercised substantial control over FMC's rayon plant "as the government determined what product the facility would produce, the level of production, the price of the product, and to whom the product would be sold." 29 F.3d at 843. The court distinguished this situation from cases involving "governmental regulatory activities undertaken solely with the purpose of cleaning up hazardous materials. . . ." 29 F.3d at 841. But it rejected the government's argument that regulatory activities can never constitute the basis for CERCLA liability, finding that "the government can be liable when it engages in regulatory activities extensive enough to make it an operator of a facility or an arranger of the disposal of hazardous wastes even though no private party could engage in the regulatory activities at issue." 29 F.3d at 840. The dissenting judges argued that the company that profited from production of the rayon should bear the costs of cleanup, rather than "society as the ultimate beneficiary of the war effort. . . ." 29 F.3d 854 (Sloviter, C.J., dissenting).

In United States v. Brighton, 153 F.3d 308 (6th Cir. 1998), the court held that a township must have exercised "actual control" over the activities at a privately owned dump as opposed to merely possessing the "ability to control." "[M]ere regulation does not suffice, but actual operation does." The court instructed the trial court to consider "the government's expertise and knowledge of the environmental dangers posed by hazardous waste, establishment and design of the facility, participation in the opening and closing of the facility, hiring or supervising employees involved in activities related to pollution, determination of the facility's operational plan, monitoring of and control over hazardous waste disposal, and public declarations of responsibility over the facility and/or hazardous waste disposal." 153 F.3d at 327.

In United States v. Gurley, 43 F.3d 1188 (8th Cir. 1994), the Eighth Circuit also adopted an actual control test for determining when individuals can be held liable as operators under section 107(a)(2) of CERCLA. The court held that two elements were required for such liability: (1) that the individual "had the authority to determine whether hazardous wastes would be disposed of and to determine the method of disposal and (2) actually exercised that authority, either by personally performing the tasks necessary to dispose of the hazardous wastes or by directing others to perform those tasks." 43 F.3d at 1193.

One of the most frequently litigated operator liability issues concerns the liability of a parent corporation for a facility owned by a subsidiary, an issue the Supreme Court addressed in the following case.

## United States v. Bestfoods

524 U.S. 51 (1998)

JUSTICE SOUTER delivered the opinion of the Court.

The United States brought this action for the costs of cleaning up industrial waste generated by a chemical plant. The issue before us, under the Comprehensive Environmental Response, Compensation, and Liability Act of 1980 (CERCLA), is whether a parent corporation that actively participated in, and exercised control over, the operations of a subsidiary may, without more, be held liable as an operator of a polluting facility owned or operated by the subsidiary. We answer no, unless the corporate veil may be pierced. But a corporate parent that actively participated in, and exercised control over, the operations of the facility itself may be held directly liable in its own right as an operator of the facility. . . .

In 1957, Ott Chemical Co. (Ott I) began manufacturing chemicals at a plant near Muskegon, Michigan, and its intentional and unintentional dumping of hazardous substances significantly polluted the soil and ground water at the site. In 1965, respondent CPC International Inc. [which recently changed its name to Bestfoods] incorporated a wholly owned subsidiary to buy Ott I's assets in exchange for CPC stock. The new company, also dubbed Ott Chemical Co. (Ott II), continued chemical manufacturing at the site, and continued to pollute its surroundings. CPC kept the managers of Ott I, including its founder, president, and principal shareholder, Arnold Ott, on board as officers of Ott II. Arnold Ott and several other Ott II officers and directors were also given positions at CPC, and they performed duties for both corporations.

In 1972, CPC sold Ott II to Story Chemical Company, which operated the Muskegon plant until its bankruptcy in 1977. Shortly thereafter, when respondent Michigan Department of Natural Resources (MDNR) examined the site for environmental damage, it found the land littered with thousands of leaking and even exploding drums of waste, and the soil and water saturated with noxious chemicals. . . .

By 1981, the federal Environmental Protection Agency had undertaken to see the site cleaned up, and its long-term remedial plan called for expenditures well into the tens of millions of dollars. To recover some of that money, the United States filed this action under §107 in 1989, naming [CPC and Arnold Ott as two of the defendants]. . . . Because the parties stipulated that the Muskegon plant was a "facility" within the meaning of §101(9), that hazardous substances had been released at the facility, and that the United States had incurred reimbursable response costs to clean up the site, the trial focused on the issues of whether CPC . . . as the parent corporation[] of Ott II . . . , had "owned or operated" the facility within the meaning of §107(a)(2).

It is a general principle of corporate law deeply "ingrained in our economic and legal systems" that a parent corporation (so-called because of control through ownership of another corporation's stock) is not liable for the acts of its subsidiaries. Thus it is hornbook law that "the exercise of the 'control' which stock ownership gives to the stock-holders . . . will not create liability beyond the assets of the subsidiary. That 'control' includes the election of directors, the making of by-laws . . . and the doing of all other acts incident to the legal status of stock-holders. Nor will a duplication of some or all of the directors or executive officers be fatal." William O. Douglas & Carrol M. Shanks, Insulation from Liability through Subsidiary Corporations, 39 Yale L.J. 193 (1929) (hereinafter Douglas) 196. Although this respect for corporate distinctions when the subsidiary is a polluter has been severely criticized in the literature, . . . nothing in CERCLA purports to reject this bedrock principle, and against this venerable common-law backdrop, the congressional silence is audible. The Government has indeed made no claim that a corporate parent is liable as an owner or an operator under §107 simply because its subsidiary is subject to liability for owing or operating a polluting facility.

But there is an equally fundamental principle of corporate law, applicable to the parent-subsidiary relationship as well as generally, that the corporate veil may be pierced and the shareholder held liable for the corporation's conduct when, inter alia, the corporate form would otherwise be misused to accomplish certain wrongful purposes, most notably fraud, on the shareholder's behalf. Nothing in CERCLA purports to rewrite this well-settled rule, either. CERCLA is thus like many another congressional enactments in giving no indication "that the entire corpus of state corporation law is to be replaced simply because a plaintiff's cause of action is based upon a federal statute," . . . and the failure of the statute to speak to a matter as fundamental as the liability implications of corporate ownership demands application of the rule that "[i]n order to abrogate a common-law principle, the statute must speak directly to the question addressed by the common law." . . . The Court of Appeals was accordingly correct in holding that when (but only when) the corporate veil may be pierced may a parent corporation be charged with derivative CERCLA liability for its subsidiary's actions. . . .

If the act rested liability entirely on ownership of a polluting facility, this opinion might end here; but CERCLA liability may turn on operation as well as ownership, and nothing in the statute's terms bars a parent corporation from direct liability for its own actions in operating a facility owned by its subsidiary. As Justice (then-Professor) Douglas noted almost 70 years ago, derivative liability cases are to be distinguished from those in which "the alleged wrong can seemingly be traced to the parent through the conduit of its own personnel and management" and "the parent is directly a participant in the wrong complained of." Douglas 207, 208. In such instances, the parent is directly liable for its own actions. The fact that a corporate subsidiary happens to own a polluting facility operated by its parent does nothing, then, to displace the rule that the parent "corporation is [itself] responsible for the wrongs committed by its agents in the course of its business,". . . and whereas the rules of veil-piercing limit derivative liability for the actions of another corporation, CERCLA's "operator" provision is concerned primarily with direct liability for one's own actions. . . . It is this direct liability that is properly seen as being at issue here.

Under the plain language of the statute, any person who operates a polluting facility is directly liable for the costs of cleaning up the pollution. See §107(a)(2). This is so regardless of whether that person is the facility's owner, the owner's parent corporation or business partner, or even a saboteur who sneaks into the facility at night to discharge its poisons out of malice. If any such act of operating a corporate subsidiary's facility is done on behalf of a parent corporation, the existence of the parent-subsidiary relationship under state corporate law is simply irrelevant to the issue of direct liability. . . .

This much is easy to say; the difficulty comes in defining actions sufficient to constitute direct parental "operation." Here of course we may again rue the uselessness of CERCLA's definition of a facility's "operator" as "any person . . . operating" the facility, §101(20)(A)(ii), which leaves us to do the best we can to give the term its "ordinary or natural meaning.". . . In a mechanical sense, to "operate" ordinarily means "[t]o control the functioning of; run: operate a sewing machine." American Heritage Dictionary 1268 (3d ed. 1992). . . . And in the organizational sense more obviously intended by CERCLA, the word ordinarily means "[t]o conduct the affairs of; manage: operate a business.". . . So, under CERCLA, an operator is simply someone who directs the workings of, manages, or conducts the affairs of a facility. To sharpen the definition for purposes of CERCLA's concern with environmental contamination, an operator must manage, direct, or conduct operations specifically related to pollution, that is, operations having to do with the leakage or disposal of hazardous waste, or decisions about compliance with environmental regulations.

By emphasizing that "CPC is directly liable under section 107(a)(2) as an operator because CPC actively participated in and exerted significant control over Ott II's business and decision-making," 777 F. Supp., at 574, the District Court applied the "actual control" test of whether the parent "actually operated the business of its subsidiary.". . .

The well-taken objection to the actual control test, however, is its fusion of direct and indirect liability; the test is administered by asking a question about the relationship between the two corporations (an issue going to indirect liability) instead of a question about the parent's interaction with the subsidiary's facility (the source of any direct liability). If, however, direct liability for the parent's operation of the facility is to be kept distinct from derivative liability for the subsidiary's own operation, the focus of the enquiry must necessarily be different under the two tests. "The question is not whether the parent operates the subsidiary, but rather whether it operates the facility, and that operation is evidenced by participation in the activities of the facility, not the subsidiary.". . . The analysis should . . . have rested on the relationship between CPC and the Muskegon facility itself. . . .

In imposing direct liability on [the basis of the actions of dual officers of CPC and Ott II], the District Court failed to recognize that "it is entirely appropriate for directors of a parent corporation to serve as directors of its subsidiary, and that fact alone may not serve to expose the parent corporation to liability for its subsidiary's acts.". . .

This recognition that the corporate personalities remain distinct has its corollary in the "well established principle [of corporate law] that directors and officers holding positions with a parent and its subsidiary can and do 'change hats' to represent the two corporations separately, despite their common ownership.". . . The Government would have to show that, despite the general presumption to the contrary, the officers and directors were acting in their capacities as CPC officers and directors, and not as Ott II officers and directors, when they committed those acts. The District Court made no such enquiry here, however, disregarding entirely this time-honored common law rule.

In sum, the District Court's focus on the relationship between parent and subsidiary (rather than parent and facility), combined with its automatic attribution of the actions of dual officers and directors to the corporate parent, erroneously, even if unintentionally, treated CERCLA as though it displaced or fundamentally altered common law standards of limited liability. Indeed, if the evidence of common corporate personnel acting at management and directorial levels were enough to support a finding of a parent corporation's direct operator liability under CERCLA, then the possibility of resort to veil piercing to establish indirect, derivative liability for the subsidiary's violations would be academic. There would in essence be a relaxed, CERCLA-specific rule of derivative liability that would banish traditional standards and expectations from the law of CERCLA liability. But, as we have said, such a rule does not arise from congressional silence, and CERCLA's silence is dispositive.

We accordingly agree with the Court of Appeals that a participation-and-control test looking to the parent's supervision over the subsidiary, especially one that assumes that dual officers always act on behalf of the parent, cannot be used to identify operation of a facility resulting in direct parental liability. Nonetheless, a return to the ordinary meaning of the word "operate" in the organizational sense will indicate why we think that the Sixth Circuit stopped short when it confined its examples of direct parental operation to exclusive or joint ventures and declined to find at least the possibility of direct operation by CPC in this case.

In our enquiry into the meaning Congress presumably had in mind when it used the verb "to operate," we recognized that the statute obviously meant something more than mere mechanical activation of pumps and valves, and must be read to contemplate "operation" as including the exercise of direction over the facility's activities. The Court of Appeals recognized this by indicating that a parent can be held directly liable when the parent operates the facility in the stead of its subsidiary or alongside the subsidiary in some sort of a joint venture. We anticipated a further possibility above, however, when we observed that a dual officer or director might depart so far from the norms of parental influence exercised through dual office-holding as to serve the parent, even when ostensibly acting on behalf of the subsidiary in operating the facility. Yet another possibility, suggested by the facts of this case, is that an agent of the parent with no hat to wear but the parent's hat might manage or direct activities at the facility.

Identifying such an occurrence calls for line drawing yet again, since the acts of direct operation that give rise to parental liability must necessarily be distinguished from the interference that stems from the normal relationship between parent and subsidiary. Again norms of corporate behavior (undisturbed by any CERCLA provisions) are crucial reference points. Just as we may look to such norms in identifying the limits of the presumption that a dual officeholder acts in his ostensible capacity, so here we may refer to them in distinguishing a parental officer's oversight of a subsidiary from such an officer's control over the operation of the subsidiary's facility. "[A]ctivities that involve the facility but which are consistent with the parent's investor status, such as monitoring of the subsidiary's performance, supervision of the subsidiary's finance and capital budget decisions, and articulation of general policies and procedures, should not give rise to direct liability." Oswald[, 72 Wash. U. L.Q. 223,] 282. The critical question is whether, in degree and detail, actions directed to the facility by an agent of the parent alone are eccentric under accepted norms of parental oversight of a subsidiary's facility.

[The Court then remanded the case for a determination of whether CPC might be an operator through the direct actions of its own employee.]

## NOTES AND QUESTIONS

1. **Federal or State Law?** In holding that a parent corporation could be held liable for the acts of its subsidiary under ordinary rules for piercing the corporate veil, the Supreme Court declined to decide whether the courts should look to state law standards for veil piercing, or to a uniform federal standard, because the issue had not been briefed and argued by the parties. 524 U.S. 63 n.9. The Court of Appeals below had split on this question. Compare United States v. Cordova Chemical Company, 113 F.3d 562, 580 (6th Cir. 1997) (veil piercing a state law issue), with 113 F.3d 584-586 (Merritt, J. dissenting) (veil piercing to be determined under a uniform federal standard, which was met in this case). See also United States v. General Battery Corp., Inc., 423 F.3d 294 (3d Cir. 2005) (veil piercing a matter of uniform federal law). Does the logic of the Supreme Court's decision suggest how that court would decide the issue?

2. **What Constitutes Operating a Facility?** On the issue of what acts of the parent with respect to the facility would subject it to operator liability, how illuminating is the Court's opinion? Suppose a parent corporation wants to continue monitoring a subsidiary's activities but wishes to avoid operator liability. Based on the Court's opinion, what advice would you provide?

3. **Perverse Incentives?** Does the opinion create perverse incentives for a parent corporation who becomes knowledgeable of a potential problem at a subsidiary's facility to back away from intervening, in order to avoid exposure to liability? If so, is that desirable and consistent with CERCLA's objectives?

4. **Secured Lenders.** Secured lenders are another class whose exposure to PRP liability as owner or operator has evolved over the life of CERCLA. Section 101(20)(A) of CERCLA exempts from owner or operator status lenders who "hold indicia of ownership primarily to protect a security interest" without "participating in management." So long as a loan is not in trouble, interpreting this exemption caused little difficulty. However, whenever a lender undertook negotiations with a borrower in distress in an effort to avoid an outright default by altering the terms of the loan, the lender risked crossing the line of participating in management. In United States v. Fleet Factors, 901 F.2d 1550 (11th Cir. 1990), the court adopted an "ability to control" approach to the question of participating in management, saying that a lender loses the protection of the secured lender exemption "by participating in the financial management of a facility to a degree indicating a capacity to influence the corporation's treatment of hazardous wastes." 901 F.2d at 1557. After *Fleet Factors*, EPA attempted to provide guidance to lenders by issuing a rule interpreting the "participating in management" language of CERCLA, but in Kelley v. EPA, 15 F.3d 1100 (D.C. Cir. 1994), in a rare ruling of its type, the court held that the Congress had not given EPA rulemaking authority over the liability provisions of CERCLA, instead leaving those to judicial supervision under "evolving principles of the common law."

Finally, in 1996, the Congress enacted the Asset Conservation, Lender Liability, and Deposit Insurance Protection Act of 1996 (ACLLDIPA), adding to the statute section 101(20)(F), which sets forth standards for participating in management. That section defines participation to mean "actually participating in the management or operational affairs . . . and does not include merely having the capacity to influence, or the unexercised right to control . . . facility operations."

5. **State and Municipal Liability.** State and municipal governments are among the entities potentially subject to liability as owners or operators. Courts have typically held that issuing regulations governing land use activities is insufficient to subject cities or counties to owner or operator liability. E.g., United States v. Dart Industries, 847 F.2d 144 (4th Cir. 1988). On the other hand, in United States v. Stringfellow, 31 E.R.C. 1315 (C.D. Cal. 1990), the state of California was found to be liable as a result of its actions in selecting a site for hazardous waste dumping and controlling all the actions at the site.

The constitutional issues raised by holding states liable were first broached in Pennsylvania v. Union Gas Co., 491 U.S. 1 (1989), which held that the Eleventh Amendment did not prohibit states from being held liable to private parties under CERCLA. However, in Seminole Tribe v. Florida, 517 U.S. 44 (1996), the Court reversed itself, holding that Congress has no power under the Commerce Clause to abrogate states' Eleventh Amendment immunity from private suit in federal court. Individuals may still obtain injunctive relief against ongoing violations by state officials under the theory of Ex parte Young, 209 U.S. 123 (1908), but private damage actions are only available if the state waives sovereign immunity. In Alden v. Maine, 527 U.S. 706 (1999), the Court amplified states' protections against imposition of monetary liability by federal statute, holding that under the Constitution the states retain a "residuary and inviolable sovereignty" that prohibits suits for money damages against them in state court as well, absent a waiver of sovereign immunity. While *Seminole Tribe* and *Alden* reshaped constitutional principles of federalism, their effect on CERCLA has been limited because counties and munic-ipalities, which enjoy no sovereign immunity protection, are sued for contribution most frequently.

6. **Transporters.** Section 107(a)(4) of CERCLA makes anyone who accepts "hazardous substances for transport to disposal or treatment facilities . . . or sites selected by such person" liable for their releases. Note that transporter liability is premised on transporters playing some role in the selection of the site where the hazardous substances are to be taken. In Tippins, Inc. v. USX Corp., 37 F.3d 87 (3d Cir. 1994), the Third Circuit held that even if a transporter did not make the final decision concerning site selection, section 107(a)(4) "applies if the trans-porter's advice was a substantial contributing factor in the decision" to dispose of the waste at a particular facility. 37 F.3d at 90. The court determined that "a transporter selects the disposal facility when it actively and substantially partici-pates in the decision-making process which ultimately identifies a facility for dis-posal." Id. The transporter held liable in *Tippins* was a company that specialized in the transport and disposal of hazardous substances. The transporter surveyed alternative disposal sites, identified two candidate landfills that would accept the waste, and provided the generator with information concerning disposal costs at each. Although the generator made the ultimate choice between the two sites, the court held the transporter liable because of its substantial participation in the site selection process.

In Kaiser Aluminum & Chemical Corp. v. Catellus Development Corp., 976 F.2d 1338 (9th Cir. 1992), a contractor who excavated contaminated soil and spread it over uncontaminated portions of a site was held liable as a transporter of hazardous substances under section 107(a)(4) of CERCLA. The court rejected arguments that transporter liability could not attach unless the substances were taken to another site. "Whether a transporter moves hazardous material from one parcel of land to another, or whether he simply takes the material from a contaminated area of the same parcel, he has spread the contamination." 976 F.2d at 1343. The court found "no logical basis" for transporter liability "to hinge solely on whether he moves hazardous substances across a recognized property boundary."

## C.  Arrangers

Perhaps CERCLA's most substantial modification of common law liability is the imposition of liability on the nonnegligent owners or possessors of hazardous substances who arranged for its disposal or treatment. By imposing liability on those who arrange for disposal, CERCLA created powerful new incentives to ensure that wastes are managed carefully. Those who formerly let the cheapest waste hauler relieve them of their hazardous substances now must select treatment and disposal options, and monitor their implementation, with care. For if the generator's haz-ardous substances are sent to a site where a release occurs or is threatened, the arranger can be held strictly, jointly, and severally liable for response costs and nat-ural resource damages.

Generator liability is covered in section 107(a)(3) of CERCLA, which imposes liability on

> any person who by contract, agreement, or otherwise arranged for dis-
> posal or treatment, or arranged with a transporter for transport for dis-
> posal or treatment, of hazardous substances owned or possessed by such
> person, by any other party or entity, at any facility or incineration vessel
> owned or operated by another party or entity and containing such hazard-
> ous substances. [CERCLA §107(a)(3), 42 U.S.C. §9607(a)(3).]

By targeting persons who "arrange for" disposal, the Act seeks to put responsibility on persons who are in a position to take care regarding the disposal. Many
"arrangers" will be the companies who produced hazardous wastes as a by-product
to their production processes and then arranged for the disposal of that waste. However, the statutory term extends more broadly—or at least it appears to do so. For
instance, an early influential case was United States v. Aceto Agricultural Chemical
Corp., 872 F.2d 1373 (8th Cir. 1989). In that case, companies that manufactured pesticides had shipped raw materials to a company, Aidex, which mixed the materials
together to produce particular pesticide formulations. Aidex then shipped the formulated products either back to the manufacturers or on to their customers. After
the government spent $10 million to clean up the Aidex facility, the United States
sued the pesticide manufacturers as arrangers. The district court found that spills
of hazardous raw materials were an "inherent part" of the formulation process, and
that the manufacturers were aware that they were occurring. The Eighth Circuit concluded that CERCLA was broadly designed to hold those responsible for hazardous
substances also to be liable for cleaning up releases of them. It sustained the district
court's finding that the manufacturers were liable as arrangers.

The statutory language provides little guidance concerning what the government must prove to tie any particular arranger to a particular release of hazardous
substances. Many waste sites end up containing a "chemical soup" which may make
it impossible to prove that an arranger's waste is actually part of the contamination.
Because the language of section 107(a)(3) refers to "any facility . . . containing *such*
hazardous substances" (emphasis supplied), the statute suggests that the government has some obligation to prove that the generator's waste is at a facility where
releases occur, but it initially was unclear if this obligation required the government
to prove that the generator's wastes were part of the release in question.

Recognizing the difficulty the government would face if required to prove
whose wastes are physically present in a given release, courts have interpreted section 107(a)(3) broadly to promote the remedial purposes of Congress. One circuit court opinion that has been widely cited held that the government's case was
satisfied once it had proved that "(1) [a generator] shipped hazardous substances
to the . . . facility; (2) hazardous substances 'like' those present in the generator's
waste . . . were found at the facility; and (3) there had been a release of hazardous
substances at the site." United States v. Monsanto, 858 F.2d 160, 166 (4th Cir. 1988).

Not all circuit courts followed the approach of *Aceto* in developing "arranger"
liability. Amcast Industrial Corp. v. Detrex Corp., 2 F.3d 746 (7th Cir. 1993), took a
different course. The case involved a facility run by Elkhart Products Corp., a subsidiary of Amcast, for the manufacture of copper fittings. The manufacturing process involved the use of trichloroethylene (TCE), which Elkhart purchased from
Detrex. Some 800 gallons of TCE were discovered in the groundwater adjacent to
Elkhart's plant, and investigation revealed that the truck drivers accidentally spilled

TCE on Elkhart's premises while filling Elkhart's tanks. Holding that the words "arranged for" "imply intentional action," the court held that Detrex was not liable because it did not hire the trucker for the purpose of spilling TCE. 3 F.3d at 751.

South Florida Water Management Dist. v. Montalvo, 84 F.3d 402 (11th Cir. 1996) adopted a "totality of the circumstances" approach to arranger liability. It stated that "while factors such as a party's knowledge (or lack thereof) of the disposal, ownership of the hazardous substances, and intent are relevant to determining whether there has been an 'arrangement' for disposal, they are not necessarily determinative of liability in every case." 84 F.3d at 407. The Third Circuit canvassed the cases on arranger liability and noted that there was wide agreement that the liability determination was fact-sensitive and not dependent upon the defendant's characterization of the arrangement or transaction—but little agreement beyond these two points. In the end, the Third Circuit concluded: "After carefully examining the language of the statute and considering the standards adopted by other courts, we conclude that the most important factors in determining 'arranger liability' are: (1) ownership or possession; and (2) knowledge; or (3) control. Ownership or possession of the hazardous substance must be demonstrated, but this factor alone will not suffice to establish liability. A plaintiff must also demonstrate either control over the process that results in a release of hazardous waste *or* knowledge that such a release will occur during the process." Morton Int'l, Inc. v. A.E. Staley Mfg. Co. 343 F.3d 669, 677-678 (3d Cir. 2003).

A number of courts, including *Aceto* and *Montalvo*, recognized that the seller of a "useful product" is not subject to arranger liability, although they will look through "sham" transactions. In some cases, courts have held that even bona fide sales of spent materials can subject the seller to liability. Noting that "all that is necessary is that the [disposal or] treatment be inherent in the particular arrangement, even though the arranger does not retain control over its details," the Ninth Circuit held liable a seller of spent automotive batteries to a lead reclamation plant. Catellus Development Corp. v. United States, 34 F.3d 748, 753 (9th Cir. 1994).

In 2009, the United States Supreme Court took up the issue of arranger liability for the very first time.

## Burlington Northern & Santa Fe Railway Co. v. United States

556 U.S. 599 (2009)

Justice Stevens delivered the opinion of the Court.

### I

In 1960, Brown & Bryant, Inc. (B&B), began operating an agricultural chemical distribution business, purchasing pesticides and other chemical products from suppliers such as Shell Oil Company (Shell). Using its own equipment, B&B applied its products to customers' farms. B&B opened its business on a 3.8 acre parcel of former farmland in Arvin, California, and in 1975, expanded operations onto an adjacent .9 acre parcel of land owned jointly by the Atchison, Topeka & Santa Fe Railway Company, and the Southern Pacific Transportation Company (now known respectively as the Burlington Northern and Santa Fe Railway Company and Union Pacific Railroad Company) (Railroads). Both parcels of the Arvin facility were graded toward a sump and drainage pond located on the southeast corner of the primary parcel. Neither the sump nor the drainage pond was lined until 1979, allowing waste water and chemical runoff from the facility to seep into the ground water below.

During its years of operation, B&B stored and distributed various hazardous chemicals on its property. Among these were the herbicide dinoseb, sold by Dow Chemicals, and the pesticides D-D and Nemagon, both sold by Shell. Dinoseb was stored in 55-gallon drums and 5-gallon containers on a concrete slab outside B&B's warehouse. Nemagon was stored in 30-gallon drums and 5-gallon containers inside the warehouse. Originally, B&B purchased D-D in 55-gallon drums; beginning in the mid-1960's, however, Shell began requiring its distributors to maintain bulk storage facilities for D-D. From that time onward, B&B purchased D-D in bulk.

When B&B purchased D-D, Shell would arrange for delivery by common carrier, f.o.b. destination.[2] When the product arrived, it was transferred from tanker trucks to a bulk storage tank located on B&B's primary parcel. From there, the chemical was transferred to bobtail trucks, nurse tanks, and pull rigs. During each of these transfers leaks and spills could—and often did—occur. Although the common carrier and B&B used buckets to catch spills from hoses and gaskets connecting the tanker trucks to its bulk storage tank, the buckets sometimes overflowed or were knocked over, causing D-D to spill onto the ground during the transfer process.

Aware that spills of D-D were commonplace among its distributors, in the late 1970's Shell took several steps to encourage the safe handling of its products. Shell provided distributors with detailed safety manuals and instituted a voluntary discount program for distributors that made improvements in their bulk handling and safety facilities. Later, Shell revised its program to require distributors to obtain an inspection by a qualified engineer and provide self-certification of compliance with applicable laws and regulations. B&B's Arvin facility was inspected twice, and in 1981, B&B certified to Shell that it had made a number of recommended improvements to its facilities.

Despite these improvements, B&B remained a "'[s]loppy' [o]perator." Over the course of B&B's 28 years of operation, delivery spills, equipment failures, and the rinsing of tanks and trucks allowed Nemagon, D-D and dinoseb to seep into the soil and upper levels of ground water of the Arvin facility. In 1983, the California Department of Toxic Substances Control (DTSC) began investigating B&B's violation of hazardous waste laws, and the United States Environmental Protection Agency (EPA) soon followed suit, discovering significant contamination of soil and ground water. Of particular concern was a plume of contaminated ground water located under the facility that threatened to leach into an adjacent supply of potential drinking water.

---

2. F.o.b. destination means "the seller must at his own expense and risk transport the goods to [the destination] and there tender delivery of them. . . ." U.C.C. §2-319(1)(b) (2001). The District Court found that B&B assumed "stewardship" over the D-D as soon as the common carrier entered the Arvin facility.

Although B&B undertook some efforts at remediation, by 1989 it had become insolvent and ceased all operations. That same year, the Arvin facility was added to the National Priorities List and subsequently, DTSC and EPA (Governments) exercised their authority under §104 to undertake cleanup efforts at the site. By 1998, the Governments had spent more than $8 million responding to the site contamination; their costs have continued to accrue.

In 1991, EPA issued an administrative order to the Railroads directing them, as owners of a portion of the property on which the Arvin facility was located, to perform certain remedial tasks in connection with the site. The Railroads did so, incurring expenses of more than $3 million in the process. Seeking to recover at least a portion of their response costs, in 1992 the Railroads brought suit against B&B in the United States District Court for the Eastern District of California. In 1996, that lawsuit was consolidated with two recovery actions brought by DTSC and EPA against Shell and the Railroads.

The District Court conducted a 6-week bench trial in 1999 and four years later entered a judgment in favor of the Governments. In a lengthy order supported by 507 separate findings of fact and conclusions of law, the court held that both the Railroads and Shell were potentially responsible parties (PRPs) under CERCLA — the Railroads because they were owners of a portion of the facility, see §§107(a)(1)-(2), and Shell because it had "arranged for" the disposal of hazardous substances through its sale and delivery of D-D, see §107(a)(3). . . .

The Court of Appeals acknowledged that Shell did not qualify as a "traditional" arranger under §107(a)(3), insofar as it had not contracted with B&B to directly dispose of a hazardous waste product. Nevertheless, the court stated that Shell could still be held liable under a "'broader' category of arranger liability" if the "disposal of hazardous wastes [wa]s a foreseeable byproduct of, but not the purpose of, the transaction giving rise to" arranger liability. Ibid. Relying on CERCLA's definition of "disposal," which covers acts such as "leaking" and "spilling," §103(3), the Ninth Circuit concluded that an entity could arrange for "disposal . . . even if it did not intend to dispose" of a hazardous substance.

Applying that theory of arranger liability to the District Court's findings of fact, the Ninth Circuit held that Shell arranged for the disposal of a hazardous substance through its sale and delivery of D-D:

> "Shell arranged for delivery of the substances to the site by its subcontractors; was aware of, and to some degree dictated, the transfer arrangements; knew that some leakage was likely in the transfer process; and provided advice and supervision concerning safe transfer and storage. Disposal of a hazardous substance was thus a necessary part of the sale and delivery process." Id., at 950.

Under such circumstances, the court concluded, arranger liability was not precluded by the fact that the purpose of Shell's action had been to transport a useful and previously unused product to B&B for sale.

## II

. . . In these cases, it is undisputed that the Railroads qualify as PRPs under both §§107(a)(1) and 107(a)(2) because they owned the land leased by B&B at the time of the contamination and continue to own it now. The more difficult question is whether Shell also qualifies as a PRP under §107(a)(3) by virtue of the circumstances surrounding its sales to B&B.

To determine whether Shell may be held liable as an arranger, we begin with the language of the statute. As relevant here, §107(a)(3) applies to an entity that "arrange[s] for disposal . . . of hazardous substances." It is plain from the language of the statute that CERCLA liability would attach under §107(a)(3) if an entity were to enter into a transaction for the sole purpose of discarding a used and no longer useful hazardous substance. It is similarly clear that an entity could not be held liable as an arranger merely for selling a new and useful product if the purchaser of that product later, and unbeknownst to the seller, disposed of the product in a way that led to contamination. Less clear is the liability attaching to the many permutations of "arrangements" that fall between these two extremes—cases in which the seller has some knowledge of the buyers' planned disposal or whose motives for the "sale" of a hazardous substance are less than clear. In such cases, courts have concluded that the determination whether an entity is an arranger requires a fact-intensive inquiry that looks beyond the parties' characterization of the transaction as a "disposal" or a "sale" and seeks to discern whether the arrangement was one Congress intended to fall within the scope of CERCLA's strict-liability provisions.

Although we agree that the question whether §107(a)(3) liability attaches is fact intensive and case specific, such liability may not extend beyond the limits of the statute itself. Because CERCLA does not specifically define what it means to "arrang[e] for" disposal of a hazardous substance, we give the phrase its ordinary meaning. In common parlance, the word "arrange" implies action directed to a specific purpose. See Merriam-Webster's Collegiate Dictionary 64 (10th ed. 1993) (defining "arrange" as "to make preparations for: plan[;] . . . to bring about an agreement or understanding concerning"). Consequently, under the plain language of the statute, an entity may qualify as an arranger under §107(a)(3) when it takes intentional steps to dispose of a hazardous substance.

The Governments do not deny that the statute requires an entity to "arrang[e] for" disposal; however, they interpret that phrase by reference to the statutory term "disposal," which the Act broadly defines as "the discharge, deposit, injection, dumping, spilling, leaking, or placing of any solid waste or hazardous waste into or on any land or water." §103(3); see also §101(29) (adopting the definition of "disposal" contained in the Solid Waste Disposal Act). The Governments assert that by including unintentional acts such as "spilling" and "leaking" in the definition of disposal, Congress intended to impose liability on entities not only when they directly dispose of waste products but also when they engage in legitimate sales of hazardous substances knowing that some disposal may occur as a collateral consequence of the sale itself. Applying that reading of the statute, the Governments contend that Shell arranged for the disposal of D-D within the meaning of §107(a)(3) by shipping D-D to B&B under conditions it knew would result in the spilling of a portion of the hazardous substance by the purchaser or common carrier. See Brief for United States 24 ("Although the delivery of a useful product was the ultimate purpose of the arrangement, Shell's continued participation in the delivery, with knowledge that spills and leaks would result, was sufficient to establish Shell's intent to dispose of hazardous substances"). Because these spills resulted in wasted D-D, a result Shell anticipated, the Governments insist that Shell was properly found to have arranged for the disposal of D-D.

While it is true that in some instances an entity's knowledge that its product will be leaked, spilled, dumped, or otherwise discarded may provide evidence of the entity's intent to dispose of its hazardous wastes, knowledge alone is insufficient to prove that an entity "planned for" the disposal, particularly when the disposal occurs as a peripheral result of the legitimate sale of an unused, useful product. In order to qualify as an arranger, Shell must have entered into the sale of D-D with the intention that at least a portion of the product be disposed of during the transfer process by one or more of the methods described in §103(3). Here, the facts found by the District Court do not support such a conclusion.

Although the evidence adduced at trial showed that Shell was aware that minor, accidental spills occurred during the transfer of D-D from the common carrier to B&B's bulk storage tanks after the product had arrived at the Arvin facility and had come under B&B's stewardship, the evidence does not support an inference that Shell intended such spills to occur. To the contrary, the evidence revealed that Shell took numerous steps to encourage its distributors to reduce the likelihood of such spills, providing them with detailed safety manuals, requiring them to maintain adequate storage facilities, and providing discounts for those that took safety precautions. Although Shell's efforts were less than wholly successful, given these facts, Shell's mere knowledge that spills and leaks continued to occur is insufficient grounds for concluding that Shell "arranged for" the disposal of D-D within the meaning of §107(a)(3). Accordingly, we conclude that Shell was not liable as an arranger for the contamination that occurred at B&B's Arvin facility.

JUSTICE GINSBURG, dissenting.

Although the question is close, I would uphold the determinations of the courts below that Shell qualifies as an arranger within the compass of the Comprehensive Environmental Response, Compensation and Liability Act (CERCLA). §107(a)(3). As the facts found by the District Court bear out, Shell "arranged for disposal . . . of hazardous substances" owned by Shell when the arrangements were made.

In the 1950's and early 1960's, Shell shipped most of its products to Brown and Bryant (B&B) in 55-gallon drums, thereby ensuring against spillage or leakage during delivery and transfer. Later, Shell found it economically advantageous, in lieu of shipping in drums, to require B&B to maintain bulk storage facilities for receipt of the chemicals B&B purchased from Shell. By the mid-1960's, Shell was delivering its chemical to B&B in bulk tank truckloads. As the Court recognizes, "bulk storage of the chemical led to numerous tank failures and spills as the chemical rusted tanks and eroded valves."

Shell furthermore specified the equipment to be used in transferring the chemicals from the delivery truck to B&B's storage tanks.[2] In the process, spills and leaks were inevitable, indeed spills occurred every time deliveries were made.

---

2. Shell shipped the chemicals to B&B "F.O.B. Destination." At oral argument, the Court asked Shell's counsel: Suppose there had been "no transfer of ownership until the delivery [was] complete?" In that event, counsel responded, "Shell would have been the owner of the waste." The Court credits the fact that at the time of the spills, the chemicals, having been shipped "F.O.B. Destination, . . . had come under B&B's stewardship." In my view, CERCLA liability, or the absence thereof, should not turn, in any part, on such an eminently shipper-fixable specification as "F.O.B. Destination."

That Shell sold B&B useful products, the Ninth Circuit observed, did not exonerate Shell from CERCLA liability, for the sales "necessarily and immediately result[ed] in the leakage of hazardous substances." The deliveries, Shell was well aware, directly and routinely resulted in disposals of hazardous substances (through spills and leaks) for more than 20 years. "[M]ere knowledge" may not be enough, but Shell did not simply know of the spills and leaks without contributing to them. Given the control rein held by Shell over the mode of delivery and transfer, the lower courts held and I agree, Shell was properly ranked an arranger. Relieving Shell of any obligation to pay for the cleanup undertaken by the United States and California is hardly commanded by CERCLA's text and is surely at odds with CER-CLA's objective—to place the cost of remediation on persons whose activities contributed to the contamination rather than on the taxpaying public.

## NOTES AND QUESTIONS

1. The Court holds that to be considered an arranger for disposal of a hazardous substance, it is not enough simply to know that spills of a hazardous substance are occurring. The decision suggests that there must be more evidence of an intent to dispose. The Court states that knowledge of spills may be probative of an intent to dispose, but it does not articulate what else must be shown. What else would need to be shown before an entity could be deemed an "arranger" under CERCLA §107(a)(3)?

2. Is the *Aceto* approach to arranger liability still good law in light of *Burlington Northern*? In *Aceto*, the companies supplying the chemicals to the reformulator retained ownership of them throughout the entire process, but in *Burlington Northern*, Shell simply sold the chemicals to B&B. The simple sale of a useful product was long held not to give rise to arranger liability. District courts in several cases have continued to treat *Aceto* as good law, see, e.g., Duke Energy Progress, Inc. v. Alcan Aluminum Corp., 2013 U.S. Dist. LEXIS 65165 (E.D.N.C. May 6, 2013) (sending transformers for repair that necessarily required extracting and disposing PCBs can support finding of arranger liability).

3. In United States v. Dico, Inc., 920 F.3d 1174 (8th Cir. 2019), the Eighth Circuit held that the sale of a building that contained PCB insulation could give rise to arranger liability based on the following factors: (1) the defendants knew the buyer was going to dismantle the buildings and sold the buildings with the intent that they be dismantled; (2) the "removal, disposal, and sampling costs Dico avoided from the sale exceeded by ten times the value received" from the buyer, supporting the finding that defendants tried to avoid environmental liability by selling the buildings; (3) the buildings no longer were commercially useful and required costly repairs and upkeep to comply with an EPA order; (4) defendants "did not have the buildings appraised, advertise their sale, or seek another buyer"; (5) they did not tell the buyer that the buildings were contaminated or subject to an EPA order; and (6) they had reason to believe the buyer "would not discover the contamination before purchasing the buildings." Id. at 1178-1180.

4. In Consolidation Coal Co. v. Georgia Power Co., 781 F.3d 129 (4th Cir. 2015), a split panel of the Fourth Circuit held that a company that sold used transformers containing PCBs to a reconditioning company did not incur CERCLA

liability as an arranger for disposal. The court concluded that "the intent to sell a product that happens to contain a hazardous substance is not equivalent to intent to dispose of a hazardous substance under CERCLA. For arranger liability to attach, there must be something more." Id. at 149. The court noted that there was no evidence that the transformers were sold "with the intention that at least a portion of the product be disposed of during the transfer process by one or more of the methods within the statutory definition of disposal." Id. at 155. In NCR Corp. v. George A. Whiting Paper Co., 768 F.3d 682 (7th Cir. 2014), the court held that a company's sale of copy paper trimming and waste containing PCBs to recycling mills was not an arrangement for disposal of the PCBs. In Vine Street LLC v. Borg Warner Corp., the Fifth Circuit reversed a district court decision holding a company liable as an arranger due to leaks of PCE from equipment the company had sold to a dry-cleaning business decades before. Citing *Burlington Northern*, the court concluded that "knowledge alone is insufficient to prove that an entity 'planned for' the disposal, particularly when the disposal occurs as a peripheral result of the legitimate sale of an unused, useful product." Id. at 317-318.

5. Consider the following hypothetical: A private individual took his car to a service station to have the brakes checked. The mechanic examined the brakes and decided that, in connection with brake repairs, the brake fluid needed to be replaced. The old fluid was removed and placed into a leaky tank at the service station, along with hazardous substances from other sources, eventually resulting in federal cleanup expenditures. Under the approach of *Aceto*, would the automobile owner be liable under section 107(a)(3)? Under *Burlington Northern*? See Garrett, The *Aceto* Case: CERCLA Liability for Products?, 21 Envtl. Rep. 704 (1989).

6. In General Electric Co. v. AAMCO Transmissions, Inc., 962 F.2d 281 (2d Cir. 1992), the Second Circuit refused to hold major oil companies liable under section 107(a)(3) as "arrangers" for the disposal of waste oil collected by the lessees of their service stations. The court rejected the argument that "arranger" liability should turn on whether a company has the ability or authority to control the waste disposal practices of another even if this authority has not been exercised. While noting that arranger liability can attach even to parties who do not have active involvement in "the timing, manner or location of disposal," the court stated that "there must be some nexus between the potentially responsible party and the disposal of the hazardous substance" that "is premised upon the potentially liable party's conduct with respect to the disposal or transport of hazardous wastes." Finding that "Congress employed traditional notions of duty and obligation in deciding which entities would be liable under CERCLA as arrangers for the disposal of hazardous substances," the court concluded that "it is the *obligation* to exercise control over hazardous waste disposal, and not the mere ability or opportunity to control the disposal of hazardous substances that makes an entity an arranger under CERCLA's liability provision." 962 F.2d at 286. Is this approach to arranger liability still sound after *Burlington Northern*? The Second Circuit distinguished other arranger cases by noting that "the oil companies did not own the hazardous substance, nor did they control the process by which waste motor oil was generated." While noting that the oil companies may have encouraged dealers to buy virgin motor oil from them, the court found it significant that they did not require dealers to perform oil changes. A federal district court has held that even an oil company that did require

its dealers to perform oil changes is not liable as an "arranger" under CERCLA so long as it did not attempt to control their disposal practices. United States v. Arrowhead Refining Co., 35 E.R.C. 2065 (D. Minn. 1992).

7.  In Team Enterprises, LLC v. Western Investment Real Estate Trust, 647 F.3d 901 (9th Cir. 2011), the Ninth Circuit rejected an attempt to apply "arranger" liability to the manufacturer of a "filter-and-still" machine for recycling water containing perchloroethylene used in dry cleaning. Applying *Burlington Northern*, the court held that the manufacturer was the seller of a useful product who did not have the requisite intent to qualify as an "arranger." The court explained: "The useful product doctrine serves as a convenient proxy for the intent element because of the general presumption that persons selling useful products do so for legitimate business purposes." Id. at 908. Thus, the court explained, the seller of motor oil to car owners would not be considered an arranger, but "persons selling or otherwise arranging for the transfer of hazardous waste (which no longer serves any useful purpose)" probably are "entering into such a transaction . . . to dispose of hazardous waste." Id. In United States v. General Electric Co., 670 F.3d 377 (1st Cir. 2012), the First Circuit rejected GE's effort to invoke the "useful product" defense. The court held that GE's sale to a paint manufacturer of scrap pyranol containing PCBs did not constitute the sale of a useful product that would preclude arranger liability. The court emphasized that, unlike the chemicals involved in *Burlington Northern*, the material was not a new product, it was not marketed to anyone else, and it was of uneven quality. The court also cited other evidence indicating that GE's predominant motivation for the sale was disposal.

### Shrinking the Net of CERCLA Liability

In recent years, Congress has amended CERCLA to include several statutory exemptions from arranger liability, often modeling these statutory provisions on settlement policies established earlier by EPA to deal with certain special circumstances. The Superfund Recycling Equity Act, 42 U.S.C. §127, exempts from CERCLA liability arrangers (and transporters) who arrange for "recycling of recyclable materials." Recyclable materials include "scrap paper, scrap plastic, scrap glass, scrap textiles, scrap rubber (other than whole tires), scrap metal, or spent lead-acid, spent nickel-cadmium, and other spent batteries. . . ." §127(b). Qualifying for the exemption requires proving a number of conditions have been met and is denied anyone who had an objectively reasonable basis to believe that the materials would not be recycled. It is only an arranger exemption and does not affect liability as an owner or operator, past or present.

The Small Business Liability Relief and Brownfields Revitalization Act (SBLRBRA) added an exemption for "*de micromis*" generators or transporters, persons who contributed or transported less than 110 gallons of liquid materials or 200 pounds of solid materials to a facility, at least part of which had to occur before April 1, 2001. §107(o). Section 107(o)(2) does not apply if the president determines that the hazardous substances contributed significantly to response costs or if the person seeking to qualify for the exemption impeded the response action or committed a crime by generating or transporting the substance. Liability as owner or operator is once again unaffected. The SBLRBRA also added section 107(p), which exempts homeowners, certain small businesses, and certain nonprofit organizations from liability for their generation of municipal solid waste (MSW).

Over the years, EPA has responded to some objections to the fairness of CER-CLA administratively, by establishing settlement policies or interpretations of the statute that removed or mitigated the full effects of liability for particular persons who would otherwise be PRPs. Groups benefited in this way have included residential property owners, *de micromis* contributors, lending institutions that do not actively participate in their debtor's waste management decisions, persons offering to buy brownfield sites, and generators of municipal solid waste.

Congress has enacted several targeted amendments aimed at scope-of-coverage questions, many times building on prior administrative decisions by EPA. Thus, in SARA in 1986, Congress enacted the innocent purchaser provisions, discussed above; in ACLLDIPA in 1996, the lending institutions provisions, discussed above; in SREA in 1999, the recycling provisions; and in SBLRBRA in 2002, the bona fide prospective purchaser provisions, the *de micromis* provisions §107(o), the municipal solid waste exemption §107(p), discussed below, and provisions for owners of properties contiguous to a CERCLA facility (see §107(q)).

The municipal solid waste exemption applies to the generators of MSW—including you, us, and all households throughout the United States. MSW is present at 25 percent of the sites on the NPL, and while EPA estimates that only 1 percent by weight is hazardous, its volume is so great that this 1 percent can generate significant problems (which is one reason RCRA addresses MSW as well as hazardous waste disposal). Besides, under the strict, joint and several liability scheme, MSW would not itself have to be very hazardous in order to provide a basis for private parties to seek contribution from generators of MSW.

Although EPA announced a municipal settlement policy in 1989, stating that EPA would generally not identify generators and transporters of MSW as PRPs, private parties are not so constrained. Not only have they sought to sue the municipalities who ultimately dispose of MSW, some also have sought to bring in homeowners and small private businesses whose wastes were among those picked up by municipal garbage services. In B.F. Goodrich v. Murtha, 840 F. Supp. 180 (D. Conn. 1993), the court refused to permit inclusion of some 1,100 homeowners and small business operators, because the allegation that each of them arranged for the disposal of hazardous substances was based solely on generic statistical studies showing the likely presence of hazardous substances in the homeowners' waste, rather than individualized proof. The 24 small Connecticut cities named as PRPs could be sued, however. B.F. Goodrich v. Murtha, 958 F.2d 1192 (2d Cir. 1992). See also B.F. Goodrich v. Betkoski, 99 F.3d 505 (2d Cir. 1996) (holding that generators of even minuscule or nominal amounts of CERCLA hazardous substances can be held liable).

When it adopted the SBLRBRA in 2002, Congress restricted such actions by adding sections 107(o) & (p) to CERCLA. As noted above, section 107(o) adds a *de micromis* exemption that exempts generators of less than 110 gallons of liquid materials or 200 pounds of solid materials whose waste was disposed before April 1, 2001. Nongovernmental plaintiffs bringing contribution actions have the burden of proving that defendants do not qualify for this exemption. For wastes disposed after April 1, 2001, section 107(p) provides a blanket exemption for MSW generators who are residential property owners or small businesses or nonprofit organizations with no more than 100 full-time employees. This exemption includes protection from private party actions and entitles exempt entities to recover attorneys' fees and other costs of defense should they be sued and the plaintiff be unable to prove the exemption does not apply. As with the *de micromis* exemption, the exemption does not apply if the president determines that the waste could contribute significantly to the cost of response actions or if the defendant impeded performance of a response action. These various amendments to CERCLA are designed to improve the fairness of the statute's liability scheme by narrowing the types of parties that may be held responsible for the costs of remediating releases of hazardous substances.

Consider the impact of SBLRBRA's exemption for *de micromis* generators or transporters on the automobile repair hypothetical discussed in Note 5 on page 378. Suppose that a private individual takes his automobile to a service station to have the vehicle's brakes repaired. If an automobile repair mechanic examines the brakes and decides that, in connection with brake repairs, the brake fluid needs to be replaced. If the old brake fluid is removed and placed into a leaky storage tank at the service station, along with hazardous substances from other sources, and the leaking tank releases hazardous substances that eventually trigger a CERCLA response action, does the *de micromis* exemption contained in § 107(o) absolve the automobile owner of arranger liability?

Brownfields have become important as cities, developers, and the EPA search for ways to facilitate the acquisition of less severely contaminated properties that are in locations suitable for redevelopment or in-filling. Use of previously contaminated urban sites has the potential for slowing urban sprawl, placing fewer demands on construction of new infrastructure, and accruing tax revenues to financially strapped cities. Acquisition and development of these brownfields sites can be deterred by worries of potential purchasers that they face an uncertain cleanup liability. EPA initially responded administratively to try to reduce these uncertainties. In 1995, it announced that it would encourage greater use of "comfort letters," assuring owners that their properties would not be targets of further CERCLA actions. Noah, EPA Plans Rules to Limit Liability of Superfund Sites, Wall St. J., Jan. 26, 1995, at A5. The agency also expressed willingness to enter into "prospective purchaser agreements," which provide similar assurances to potential buyers, contingent on performing specific cleanup tasks.

In 2002, Congress codified a bona fide purchaser exemption from CERCLA liability in section107(r). Under it, purchasers who undertake appropriate inquiry to discover the extent of contamination, who take steps to stop any continuing release and prevent future releases, and who cooperate fully with government and others undertaking response actions are exempted from PRP liability. If as a result of cleanup the property increases in value above the purchase price, the statute provides the government with a windfall profits lien in the amount of unrecouped cleanup costs, so that the bona fide purchaser does not profit at the expense of the taxpayers. The SBLRBRA also sets up a program of federal grants for brownfields development and provides other incentives for states, localities, and Indian tribes to revitalize brownfields.

# PROBLEM EXERCISE: CERCLA LIABILITY

Chemspray is a pesticide formulator. Its wholly owned subsidiary is Chemairspray, an aerial spraying company. Both are controlled by Chemspray's sole stockholder, Jones. Fruitgrowers (Growers) contract with Chemairspray for aerial application of various pesticides, which Chemspray supplies. Chemspray buys its raw materials from large chemical companies, including Bayer. Under the terms of their contracts, the Growers become owners of the pesticides to be applied to their farmland as soon as they contract for Chemairspray's services.

The airstrip used by Chemairspray and the adjoining land become a Superfund site because employees of Chemairspray sometimes spill pesticides on the runway and surrounding land while mixing and loading them onto the planes. They also rinse out the airplanes' tanks after each flight to prepare for different pesticide runs. Hosing down the runways, or rain, then washes the pesticides onto the land and eventually into the groundwater near the airstrip.

**Question One.** The United States incurs response costs for cleaning up the contamination at the Superfund site. It brings an action under section 107 of CERCLA to recover its response costs against Chemairspray, Chemspray, and Jones. Discuss the liability of each of these defendants.

**Question Two.** After paying response costs, Chemairspray brings a contribution action against Growers and Monsanto. (On contribution actions, see the discussion of section 113(f) below.) Chemairspray asserts that (a) Growers owned the pesticides that were spilled; and (b) Growers, some of whom visited the airstrip prior to planes taking off to spray their properties, were aware of Chemairspray's mixing, loading, and rinsing practices. Growers and Bayer both move to dismiss the suit on the ground that they are not liable under section 107. What result?

**Question Three.** In order to hold Monsanto liable, what additional facts must Chemairspray prove as a result of the addition of section 107(o) to CERCLA?

**Question Four.** Suppose that a public water supply system located adjacent to the airstrip is found to be contaminated with polyfluoroalkyl substances (PFAS) found in aqueous film-forming foam (AFFF) used by a contractor to contain fires at the airstrip. If the particular PFAS found in the drinking water were to become listed as CERCLA hazardous substances, who may be held liable for the costs of removing them from the drinking water: the water supply system, the company that manufactured the AFFF, the company that used the AFFF to fight fires, and/or the owner of the airstrip who hired the contractor to fight fires at the airstrip?

## 4. Strict, Joint, and Several Liability

References to "strict, joint, and several liability" are nowhere to be found in CERCLA. Yet courts almost uniformly have found that CERCLA imposes strict, joint, and several liability on responsible parties. This result seems odd to some, particularly since express references to strict, joint, and several liability were deleted from the Senate bill that became CERCLA shortly before the Senate floor vote.

The only reference to a standard of liability is in the definitional section of CERCLA. Section 101(32) states that the "term 'liable' or 'liability' under this subchapter shall be construed to be the standard of liability which obtains under section 1321 of Title 33 [section 311 of the federal Clean Water Act]." Philip C. Cummings, who was then chief counsel of the Senate Environment and Public Works Committee, explains that this was the final compromise prior to Senate passage of CERCLA. He tells the following story:

> The committee staff had argued that strict, joint, and several liability, explicitly referred to in S. 1480 and the November 18 substitute, was not radical but was the standard of liability under §311 of the CWA. Alan Simpson (R-Wyoming) was skeptical; if that were so, he countered, why not just say that. The committee staff agreed to put in the reference to the standard of liability under §311 that is now §101(32) of CERCLA. [Cummings, Completing the Circle, Envtl. Forum 11, 15 (Nov.-Dec. 1990).]

Strict liability relieves the government of the obligation to prove that hazardous substances were released as the result of negligence or that the defendant's conduct was intentional and unreasonable. As experience with oil spill liability had demonstrated, strict liability was necessary if the government was to have a realistic chance of recovering response costs. Section 311's oil spill liability program provided for strict liability, premised on the notion that the burden of environmental injuries of this sort should be placed on the industry that created the risk.

While oil spills typically come from a single source, hazardous substances released at dump sites can be a complex mixture of wastes from many sources, so it was something of an open question how extending section 311 liability to the typical multi-party CERCLA actions would translate. All of the early decisions interpreting section 101(32) found that it authorized imposition of strict, joint, and several liability unless a defendant could demonstrate that the harm caused by its wastes is divisible. United States v. Chem-Dyne Corp., 572 F. Supp. 802 (S.D. Ohio 1983); United States v. Bliss, 667 F. Supp. 1298 (E.D. Mo. 1987). This approach is firmly grounded in common law principles reflected in the Second Restatement of Torts. At common law, a finding of joint and several liability still leaves any tortfeasor who believes he has paid more than his fair share the option of filing a contribution action against the other tortfeasors to recover from them. When all PRPs are solvent, the net effect of this system is to facilitate more expeditious payment of cleanup costs at the front end, leaving the sorting out of relative liability to the backend contribution action. When PRPs who would otherwise shoulder significant liability are bankrupt or insolvent, however, the effect can be to leave tortfeasors who were relatively minor contributors—but solvent—bearing a far greater share of financial responsibility. In those cases, a contribution action against an insolvent joint tortfeasor is essentially useless. The prospect of being responsible for these "orphan shares" of liability has been one of the spurs to litigation over when the liability is properly apportionable, rather than joint and several. Despite a number of district court and court of appeals decisions on apportionment over the years, the Supreme Court had never weighed in on the issue until the 2009 *Burlington Northern* decision, below.

## Burlington Northern & Santa Fe Railway Co. v. United States

556 U.S. 599 (2009)

[Most of the background facts of this case are described in the excerpt addressing arranger liability, which is reproduced above.]

Although the court found the parties liable, it did not impose joint and several liability on . . . the Railroads for the entire response cost incurred by the Governments. The court found that the site contamination created a single harm but concluded that the harm was divisible and therefore capable of apportionment. Based on three figures—the percentage of the total area of the facility that was owned by the Railroads, the duration of B&B's business divided by the term of the Railroads' lease, and the Court's determination that only two of three polluting chemicals spilled on the leased parcel required remediation and that those two chemicals were responsible for roughly two-thirds of the overall site contamination requiring remediation—the court apportioned the Railroads' liability as 9% of the Governments' total response cost.[4] . . .

The Governments appealed the District Court's apportionment. . . .

On the subject of apportionment, the Court of Appeals found "no dispute" on the question whether the harm caused [by] . . . the Railroads was capable of apportionment. Id., at 942. The court observed that a portion of the site contamination occurred before the Railroad parcel became part of the facility, only some of the hazardous substances were stored on the Railroad parcel, and "only some of the water on the facility washed over the Railroads' site." Ibid. Given those facts, the court readily concluded that "the contamination traceable to the Railroads . . . , with adequate information, would be allocable, as would be the cost of cleaning up that contamination." Ibid. Nevertheless, the Court of Appeals held that the District Court erred in finding that the record established a reasonable basis for apportionment. Because the burden of proof on the question of apportionment rested with . . . the Railroads, the Court of Appeals reversed the District Court's apportionment of liability and held . . . the Railroads jointly and severally liable for the Governments' cost of responding to the contamination of the Arvin facility.

The seminal opinion on the subject of apportionment in CERCLA actions was written in 1983 by Chief Judge Carl Rubin of the United States District Court for the Southern District of Ohio. United States v. Chem-Dyne Corp., 572 F. Supp. 802. After reviewing CERCLA's history, Chief Judge Rubin concluded that although the Act imposed a "strict liability standard," it did not mandate

---

4. Although the Railroads did not produce precise figures regarding the exact quantity of chemical spills on each parcel in each year of the facility's operation, the District Court found it "indisputable that the overwhelming majority of hazardous substances were released from the B&B parcel." The court explained that "the predominant activities conducted on the Railroad parcel through the years were storage and some washing and rinsing of tanks, other receptacles, and chemical application vehicles. Mixing, formulating, loading, and unloading of ag-chemical hazardous substances, which contributed most of the liability causing releases, were predominantly carried out by B&B on the B&B parcel."

"joint and several" liability in every case. Rather, Congress intended the scope of liability to "be determined from traditional and evolving principles of common law[.]" The *Chem-Dyne* approach has been fully embraced by the Courts of Appeals.

Following *Chem-Dyne*, the courts of appeals have acknowledged that "[t]he universal starting point for divisibility of harm analyses in CERCLA cases" is §433A of the Restatement (Second) of Torts. Under the Restatement,

> "when two or more persons acting independently caus[e] a distinct or single harm for which there is a reasonable basis for division according to the contribution of each, each is subject to liability only for the portion of the total harm that he has himself caused. Restatement (Second) of Torts, §§433A, 881 (1976); Prosser, Law of Torts, pp. 313-314 (4th ed. 1971). . . . But where two or more persons cause a single and indivisible harm, each is subject to liability for the entire harm. Restatement (Second) of Torts, §875; Prosser, at 315-316." *Chem-Dyne Corp.*, 572 F. Supp., at 810.

In other words, apportionment is proper when "there is a reasonable basis for determining the contribution of each cause to a single harm." Restatement (Second) of Torts §433A(1)(b), p. 434 (1963-1964).

Not all harms are capable of apportionment, however, and CERCLA defendants seeking to avoid joint and several liability bear the burden of proving that a reasonable basis for apportionment exists. See *Chem-Dyne Corp.*, 572 F. Supp., at 810 (citing Restatement (Second) of Torts §433B (1976)) (placing burden of proof on party seeking apportionment). When two or more causes produce a single, indivisible harm, "courts have refused to make an arbitrary apportionment for its own sake, and each of the causes is charged with responsibility for the entire harm." Restatement (Second) of Torts §433A, Comment i, p. 440 (1963-1964).

Neither the parties nor the lower courts dispute the principles that govern apportionment in CERCLA cases, and both the District Court and Court of Appeals agreed that the harm created by the contamination of the Arvin site, although singular, was theoretically capable of apportionment. The question then is whether the record provided a reasonable basis for the District Court's conclusion that the Railroads were liable for only 9% of the harm caused by contamination at the Arvin facility.

The District Court criticized the Railroads for taking a "'scorched earth,' all-or-nothing approach to liability," failing to acknowledge any responsibility for the release of hazardous substances that occurred on their parcel throughout the 13-year period of B&B's lease. According to the District Court, the Railroads' position on liability, combined with the Governments' refusal to acknowledge the potential divisibility of the harm, complicated the apportioning of liability. See App. to Pet. for Cert. in No. 07-1601, at 236a-237a ("All parties . . . effectively abdicated providing any helpful arguments to the court and have left the court to independently perform the equitable apportionment analysis demanded by the circumstances of the case").[9] Yet despite the parties' failure to assist the court in linking the evidence supporting apportionment to the proper allocation of liability, the District Court ultimately concluded that this was "a classic 'divisible in terms of degree' case, both as to the time period in which defendants' conduct occurred, and ownership existed, and as to the estimated maximum contribution of each party's activities that released hazardous substances that caused Site contamination." Consequently, the District Court apportioned liability, assigning the Railroads 9% of the total remediation costs.

The District Court calculated the Railroads' liability based on three figures. First, the court noted that the Railroad parcel constituted only 19% of the surface area of the Arvin site. Second, the court observed that the Railroads had leased their parcel to B&B for 13 years, which was only 45% of the time B&B operated the Arvin facility. Finally, the court found that the volume of hazardous-substance-releasing activities on the B&B property was at least 10 times greater than the releases that occurred on the Railroad parcel, and it concluded that only spills of two chemicals, Nemagon and dinoseb (not D-D), substantially contributed to the contamination that had originated on the Railroad parcel and that those two chemicals had contributed to two-thirds of the overall site contamination requiring remediation. The court then multiplied .19 by .45 by .66 (two-thirds) and rounded up to determine that the Railroads were responsible for approximately 6% of the remediation costs. "Allowing for calculation errors up to 50%," the court concluded that the Railroads could be held responsible for 9% of the total CERCLA response cost for the Arvin site. Id., at 252a.

The Court of Appeals criticized the evidence on which the District Court's conclusions rested, finding a lack of sufficient data to establish the precise proportion of contamination that occurred on the relative portions of the Arvin facility and the rate of contamination in the years prior to B&B's addition of the Railroad parcel. The court noted that neither the duration of the lease nor the size of the leased area alone was a reliable measure of the harm caused by activities on the property owned by the Railroads, and—as the court's upward adjustment confirmed—the court had relied on estimates rather than specific and detailed records as a basis for its conclusions.

Despite these criticisms, we conclude that the facts contained in the record reasonably supported the apportionment of liability. The District Court's detailed

---

9. As the Governments point out, insofar as the District Court made reference to equitable considerations favoring apportionment, it erred. Equitable considerations play no role in the apportionment analysis; rather, apportionment is proper only when the evidence supports the divisibility of the damages jointly caused by the PRPs. As the Court of Appeals explained, "[a]pportionment . . . looks to whether defendants may avoid joint and several liability by establishing a fixed amount of damage for which they are liable," while contribution actions allow jointly and severally liable PRPs to recover from each other on the basis of equitable considerations. See also §113(f)(1) (providing that, "[i]n resolving contribution claims, the court may allocate response costs among liable parties using such equitable factors as the court determines are appropriate"). The error is of no consequence, however, because despite the District Court's reference to equity, its actual apportionment decision was properly rooted in evidence that provided a reasonable basis for identifying the portion of the harm attributable to the Railroads.

findings make it abundantly clear that the primary pollution at the Arvin facility was contained in an unlined sump and an unlined pond in the southeastern portion of the facility most distant from the Railroads' parcel and that the spills of hazardous chemicals that occurred on the Railroad parcel contributed to no more than 10% of the total site contamination, some of which did not require remediation. With those background facts in mind, we are persuaded that it was reasonable for the court to use the size of the leased parcel and the duration of the lease as the starting point for its analysis. Although the Court of Appeals faulted the District Court for relying on the "simplest of considerations: percentages of land area, time of ownership, and types of hazardous products," these were the same factors the court had earlier acknowledged were relevant to the apportionment analysis.

The Court of Appeals also criticized the District Court's assumption that spills of Nemagon and dinoseb were responsible for only two-thirds of the chemical spills requiring remediation, observing that each PRP's share of the total harm was not necessarily equal to the quantity of pollutants that were deposited on its portion of the total facility. Although the evidence adduced by the parties did not allow the court to calculate precisely the amount of hazardous chemicals contributed by the Railroad parcel to the total site contamination or the exact percentage of harm caused by each chemical, the evidence did show that fewer spills occurred on the Railroad parcel and that of those spills that occurred, not all were carried across the Railroad parcel to the B&B sump and pond from which most of the contamination originated. The fact that no D-D spills on the Railroad parcel required remediation lends strength to the District Court's conclusion that the Railroad parcel contributed only Nemagon and dinoseb in quantities requiring remediation.

The District Court's conclusion that those two chemicals accounted for only two-thirds of the contamination requiring remediation finds less support in the record; however, any miscalculation on that point is harmless in light of the District Court's ultimate allocation of liability, which included a 50% margin of error equal to the 3% reduction in liability the District Court provided based on its assessment of the effect of the Nemagon and dinoseb spills. Had the District Court limited its apportionment calculations to the amount of time the Railroad parcel was in use and the percentage of the facility located on that parcel, it would have assigned the Railroads 9% of the response cost. By including a two-thirds reduction in liability for the Nemagon and dinoseb with a 50% "margin of error," the District Court reached the same result. Because the District Court's ultimate allocation of liability is supported by the evidence and comports with the apportionment principles outlined above, we reverse the Court of Appeals' conclusion that the Railroads are subject to joint and several liability for all response costs arising out of the contamination of the Arvin facility.

JUSTICE GINSBURG, dissenting.

As to apportioning costs, the District Court undertook an heroic labor. The Railroads and Shell, the court noted, had pursued a "'scorched earth,' all-or-nothing approach to liability. Neither acknowledged an iota of responsibility. . . .

Appendix to opinion of the Court

## APPENDIX

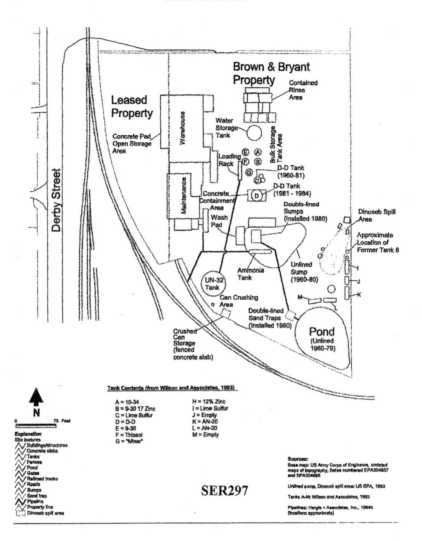

SER297

Neither party offered helpful arguments to apportion liability." Consequently, the court strived "independently [to] perform [an] equitable apportionment analysis." Given the party presentation principle basic to our procedural system, it is questionable whether the court should have pursued the matter *sua sponte.*

The trial court's mode of procedure, the United States urged before this Court, "deprived the government of a fair opportunity to respond to the court's theories of apportionment and to rebut their factual underpinnings—an opportunity the governmen[t] would have had if those theories had been advanced by petitioners themselves." Brief for United States 41.[3] I would return these cases to the District Court to give all parties a fair opportunity to address that court's endeavor to allocate costs. Because the Court's disposition precludes that opportunity, I dissent from the Court's judgment.

## NOTES AND QUESTIONS

1. What impact is joint and several liability likely to have on the willingness of defendants to settle? Will it make them more disposed to settlement for fear of being held liable for all the costs and damages or will it make them fight harder to avoid any liability? On the other hand, what effect does the belief that liability may be apportioned by the trial court have on a PRP's inclination to settle for amounts greater than what the PRP considers her fair share?

2. As the operator of the site and the entity responsible for the actual improper disposal of wastes there, B&B would be expected to bear the greatest share of the cleanup costs. After *Burlington Northern*, who will bear those costs? If joint and several liability had been sustained, who would bear them?

3. In *Burlington Northern*, the Railroads were being held liable as landowners who played no active role in creating the contamination. In such cases, does the Supreme Court's opinion suggest that apportionment will become the rule rather than the exception?

4. Apportionment cases frequently involve arrangers. How does *Burlington Northern* apply to them? Consider, for instance, a case in which a PRP argued that its waste had been dumped into a distinct area of the site and that a division based on volume of wastes at that location was appropriate. The district court, however, found the PRP had not sustained its burden on proving the first claim, because there just was not sufficient affirmative evidence to confirm it. It failed to sustain its burden on division by volume being appropriate because it had introduced no evidence of the "relative toxicity, migratory potential, degree of migration, and synergistic capacity" of the wastes at the site. New York v. Panex, 2004 WL 3008733 (W.D.N.Y. 2004). After *Burlington Northern*, what facts would an arranger need to prove in order to apportion its liability?

5. Is it fair to hold a defendant responsible for all response costs in circumstances where it is not possible to demonstrate that the harm is divisible? Would it be reasonable to require the government to bear the burden of showing that the harm is not divisible? What impact would this have on the government's ability to recover CERCLA response costs and damages? If joint and several liability were abolished in CERCLA cases, what would the government have to demonstrate in order to recover response costs?

---

3. For example, on brief, the United States observed: "[P]etitioners identify no record support for the district court's assumption that each party's contribution to the overall harm is proportional to the relative volume of hazardous substances attributable to it." And at oral argument, counsel for the United States stressed that the District Court "framed the relevant inquiry as what percentage of the contamination was attributable to the railroad parcel, to the Shell-controlled deliveries, and to the B&B parcel. But it made no finding . . . as to what the cost of [remediation] would have been . . . if the only source of contamination had been the railroad parcel."

6. During the debates over CERCLA reauthorization that culminated in 1986 with the enactment of SARA, the insurance industry and others lobbied for repeal of strict, joint, and several liability. Citing studies indicating that a great deal of money was being spent on CERCLA litigation, these companies argued that administrative costs would be lower and more funds would be available for actual cleanup if strict, joint, and several liability were abolished. How would you respond to these arguments? What additional information, if any, would you like to have to evaluate them? Although the Reagan administration was not sympathetic to environmental regulation, its Justice Department successfully opposed efforts to repeal CERCLA's liability standard.

7. Richard Epstein argues that joint and several liability actually dilutes the incentives for those handling toxic waste to take precautions to prevent releases because they know that ultimately liability may be broadly shared. Epstein, The Principles of Environmental Protection: The Case of Superfund, 2 Cato J. 9 (1982). Epstein notes that efforts by any one party to take greater precautions reduce the ultimate liability of all parties, while careless actions that result in additional releases only increase the damage that ultimately may be shared by all. Epstein, Two Fallacies in the Law of Joint Torts 73 Geo. L.J. 1377 (1985). How would you respond to these concerns?

8. In theory, joint and several liability should reduce the transaction costs of CERCLA cleanups by reducing the importance of arguments over the relative degree of fault among PRPs. Some have argued, however, that by making any PRP potentially liable for the total costs of cleanup, joint and several liability actually increases transaction costs by making PRPs more resistant to settlement. During the reauthorization process that culminated in the enactment of SARA, a number of industry lobbyists cited the transaction costs of early CERCLA litigation and the potential unfairness of joint and several liability in support of proposals to abolish it. What impact would abolition of joint and several liability have on EPA's ability to recover response costs from PRPs?

### 5.   The CERCLA Remediation Process and State Law Remedies

CERCLA and the National Contingency Plan (NCP) recognize two kinds of responses to releases of hazardous substances: (1) short-term removal actions designed to alleviate immediate dangers to public health or the environment; and (2) longer-term remedial actions designed to provide a permanent remedy to the maximum extent practicable. §104. The government can order cleanups under section 106, or it can conduct the cleanup and then recover costs "not inconsistent with the NCP" from PRPs under section 107. Private parties also can clean up facilities and then recover costs "consistent with the NCP." §107(a)(4)(B).

By October 2019 EPA had taken 14,000 removal actions at 10,424 sites. It had proposed, listed, or deleted 1,810 National Priorities List (NPL) sites where it can take or compel the more expensive remedial actions. Citizens or state authorities can notify EPA of a site, which then receives a preliminary assessment to see if the site warrants further investigation and eventual placement on the NPL. A total of 45,567 sites have been assessed, and the most serious ones are then scored on EPA's

Hazard Ranking System (HRS), an omnibus risk scale that EPA constructed for this purpose. Sites above the HRS cut-off level of 28.5 are placed on the NPL. EPA has completed construction of remediation measures at more than 1,211 NPL sites.

Since the 1986 SARA Amendments, section 121(b) instructs EPA to "select a remedial action that is protective of human health and the environment, that is cost-effective, and that utilizes permanent solutions and alternative treatment technologies to the maximum extent practicable." §121(b). Section 121(d) specifies that the degree of cleanup to be required should be partially based on consideration of other environmental standards. It provides that remedial actions under CERCLA must assure "protection of human health and the environment" and "be relevant and appropriate under the circumstances." Remedial actions must also provide a level of cleanup that attains that required by any "legally applicable or relevant and appropriate . . . standard, requirement, criteri[on], or limitation under any Federal environmental law" and "any promulgated standard, requirement, criteri[on], or limitation under a State environmental or facility siting law that is more stringent than any Federal" provisions when identified by the state in a timely manner. §121(d)(2). Collectively, these standards are commonly referred to as ARARs.

Section 121(d) provides a number of exceptions to cleanup according to ARARs, but it also gives states the opportunity to challenge in federal court EPA decisions to deviate from them. In any event, if the state agrees to pay the incremental costs, it has the right to insist on cleanup that is more extensive than the option chosen by EPA. §121(f).

Remediation of an NPL site is determined after an extensive analysis known as a Remedial Investigation/Feasibility Study (RI/FS) conducted by a government agency or a PRP. Section 122(e)(6) of CERCLA provides that once a remedial investigation/feasibility study begins "no potentially responsible party may undertake any remedial action" at the site without EPA approval. Once the RI/FS is complete, EPA conducts a hearing that produces a Record of Decision (ROD), embodying the data collected concerning the site, the evaluation of remedial options, submissions by PRPs, as well as the public, and the final remediation design. Section 113(b) of CERCLA provides that once the remediation plan is finalized, federal district courts have "exclusive original jurisdiction over all controversies arising under" the Act, and section 113(h) strips those courts of jurisdiction "to review any challenges to removal and remediation actions" except in limited circumstances.

One of the first and largest NPL sites in the country covers 300 square miles contaminated by the now-closed Anaconda Copper smelter in Butte, Montana. For 35 years EPA has worked to remediate lead and arsenic contamination at the site. It estimates that the cleanup will continue through 2025. Frustrated with the slow pace of the cleanup, 98 owners of property within the NPL site sued Atlantic Richfield (ARCO), current owner of the closed smelter, in Montana state court, asserting claims for trespass and nuisance under state common law and seeking restoration damages that must be used to restore the property. The landowners propose a more extensive cleanup that would reduce arsenic contamination to no more than 155 parts per million instead of the 250 ppm level set by EPA. They wish to dig up contaminated soil to a depth of two feet instead of EPA's chosen depth of one foot. It is estimated that the landowners' plan would cost ARCO an extra $50-58 million. After the Montana Supreme Court rejected ARCO's claim that the actions were barred by CERCLA, the U.S. Supreme Court granted review. After rejecting ARCO's claim that CERCLA sections 113(b) and (h) strip the Montana courts of jurisdiction, the Court considered whether section 122(e)(6) required the landowners to get EPA permission before undertaking their own cleanup actions.

## Atlantic Richfield Company v. Christian

140 S.Ct. 1335 (2020)

CHIEF JUSTICE ROBERTS delivered the opinion of the Court.

Although the Montana Supreme Court answered the jurisdictional question correctly, the Court erred by holding that the landowners were not potentially responsible parties under the Act and therefore did not need EPA approval to take remedial action. Section 122(e)(6), titled "Inconsistent response action," provides that "[w]hen either the President, or a potentially responsible party . . . has initiated a remedial investigation and feasibility study for a particular facility under this chapter, no potentially responsible party may undertake any remedial action at the facility unless such remedial action has been authorized by the President." 122(e)(6). Both parties agree that this provision would require the landowners to obtain EPA approval for their restoration plan if the landowners qualify as potentially responsible parties.

To determine who is a potentially responsible party, we look to the list of "covered persons" in §107, the liability section of the Act. §107(a). "Section 107(a) lists four classes of potentially responsible persons (PRPs) and provides that they 'shall be liable' for, among other things, 'all costs of removal or remedial action incurred by the United States Government.'" The first category under §107(a) includes any "owner" of "a facility." "Facility" is defined to include "any site or area where a hazardous substance has been deposited, stored, disposed of, or placed, or otherwise come to be located." §101(9)(B). Arsenic and lead are hazardous substances. Because those pollutants have "come to be located" on the landowners' properties, the landowners are potentially responsible parties. . . .

Interpreting "potentially responsible parties" to include owners of polluted property reflects the Act's objective to develop, as its name suggests, a "Comprehensive Environmental Response" to hazardous waste pollution. Section 122(e)(6) is one of several tools in the Act that ensure the careful development of a single EPA-led cleanup effort rather than tens of thousands of competing individual ones.

Yet under the landowners' interpretation, property owners would be free to dig up arsenic-infected soil and build trenches to redirect lead-contaminated groundwater without even notifying EPA, so long as they have not been sued within six years of commencement of the cleanup. We doubt Congress provided such a fragile remedy for such a serious problem. And we suspect most other landowners would not be too pleased if Congress required EPA to sue each and every one of them just to ensure an orderly cleanup of toxic waste in their neighborhood. A straightforward reading of the text avoids such anomalies. . . .

Turning from text to consequences, the landowners warn that our interpretation of §122(e)(6) creates a permanent easement on their land, forever requiring them "to get permission from EPA in Washington if they want to dig out part of their backyard to put in a sandbox for their grandchildren." The grandchildren of Montana can rest easy: The Act does nothing of the sort.

Section 122(e)(6) refers only to "remedial action," a defined term in the Act encompassing technical actions like "storage, confinement, perimeter protection using dikes, trenches, or ditches, clay cover, neutralization, cleanup of released hazardous substances and associated contaminated materials," and so forth. §101(24). While broad, the Act's definition of remedial action does not reach so far as to cover planting a garden, installing a lawn sprinkler, or digging a sandbox. In addition, §122(e)(6) applies only to sites on the Superfund list. The Act requires EPA to annually review and reissue that list. §105(a)(8)(B). EPA delists Superfund sites once responsible parties have taken all appropriate remedial action and the pollutant no longer poses a significant threat to public health or the environment.

The landowners and JUSTICE GORSUCH alternatively argue that the landowners are not potentially responsible parties because they did not receive the notice of settlement negotiations required by §122(e)(1). Under a policy dating back to 1991, EPA does not seek to recover costs from residential landowners who are not responsible for contamination and do not interfere with the agency's remedy. EPA, Policy Towards Owners of Residential Property at Superfund Sites, OSWER Directive #9834.6 (July 3, 1991), https://www.epa.gov/sites/production/files/documents/policy-owner-rpt.pdf. EPA views this policy as an exercise of its "enforcement discretion in pursuing potentially responsible parties." Because EPA has a policy of not suing innocent homeowners for pollution they did not cause, it did not include the landowners in settlement negotiations.

But EPA's nonenforcement policy does not alter the landowners' status as potentially responsible parties. Section 107(a) unambiguously defines potentially responsible parties and EPA does not have authority to alter that definition. Section 122(e)(1) requires notification of settlement negotiations to all potentially responsible parties. To say that provision determines who is a potentially responsible party in the first instance would render the Act circular. Even the Government does not claim that its decisions whether to send notices of settlement negotiations carry such authority.

In short, even if EPA ran afoul of §122(e)(1) by not providing the landowners notice of settlement negotiations, that does not change the landowners' status as potentially responsible parties. . . .

JUSTICE GORSUCH also contends that our interpretation violates the Act's "saving clauses," which provide that the Act does not preempt liability or requirements under state law. But we have long rejected interpretations of sweeping saving clauses that prove "absolutely inconsistent with the provisions of the act" in which they are found. Interpreting the Act's saving clauses to erase the clear mandate of §122(e)(6) would allow the Act "to destroy itself."

What is more, Atlantic Richfield remains potentially liable under state law for compensatory damages, including loss of use and enjoyment of property, diminution of value, incidental and consequential damages, and annoyance and discomfort. The damages issue before the Court is whether Atlantic Richfield is also liable for the landowners' own remediation beyond that required under the Act. Even then, the answer is yes – so long as the landowners first obtain EPA approval for the remedial work they seek to carry out.

## NOTES AND QUESTIONS

1. The Court's decision was viewed as a victory by environmentalists because it preserved state common law remedies for environmental contamination, while preventing interference with EPA's ability to direct site remediation. The solicitor general, representing EPA, had sided with ARCO and argued that restoration damages were entirely preempted, as did the Washington Legal Foundation. However, the Pacific Legal Foundation in its amicus brief argued that preemption of state common law remedies would be tantamount to taking private property.

2. Will the Court's decision reduce the incentive for PRPs to settle with EPA because such settlements will not bar state claims for restoration damages against the PRP? Will it promote more extensive remediation at Superfund sites?

3. Writing in dissent, Justice Gorsuch, joined by Justice Thomas, argued that the majority's decision "strips away ancient common law rights from innocent landowners and forces them to suffer toxic waste in their backyards, playgrounds and farms." Writing for the majority, Chief Justice Roberts replies by noting that "the Act's definition of remedial action does not reach so far as to cover planting a garden" or "digging a sandbox." Who is correct? Why has EPA long followed a policy that it will not seek to hold individual homeowners liable for CERCLA remediation costs?

4. CERCLA was adopted in large part because of the perceived inadequacy of common law remedies for hazardous substance contamination. When provisions for victim compensation were dropped from the legislation that eventually became CERCLA, Congress added section 301(e) that directed that a study be made of the adequacy of existing common law and statutory remedies. This study, known not surprisingly as the "section 301(e) study," identified three major barriers to recovery of personal injuries for exposure to hazardous substances: (1) the difficulty of proving causation, (2) statutes of limitations that may operate to bar suits before damage is discovered, and (3) the difficulty of apportioning damages among multiple tortfeasors. Senate Committee on Environment and Public Works, Injuries and Damages from Hazardous Wastes—Analysis and Improvement of Legal Remedies, Serial No. 97-12, 97th Cong., 2d Sess. (Sept. 1982). Congress was concerned that application of CERCLA's liability standard to recovery of damages for personal injury would open up the floodgates to enormous numbers of claims, many of which would be meritless. Thus, when it enacted SARA in 1986, Congress narrowly rejected a proposal for a pilot program to provide administrative compensation to victims of exposure to hazardous substances.

5. To overcome one of the significant obstacles to state common law remedies for hazardous substance contamination Congress added § 309 to CERCLA in 1986. Section 309 tolls the commencement of state statutes of limitations in cases involving exposures to hazardous substances until injury is or should have been discovered. In 2014, the U.S. Supreme Court reversed a Fourth Circuit decision holding that section 309 also preempts state statutes of repose. In CTS Corp. v. Waldburger, 573 U.S. 1 (2014), a North Carolina statute of repose barred claims for damage to real property brought more than ten years after the last act giving rise to the claim while the statute of limitations barred lawsuits more than three years after discovery of the claim. Property owners whose well water had been contaminated

by a hazardous chemical sued less than three years after discovery of the contamination, but more than ten years after the defendant manufacturer had sold the contaminated property. By a vote of 7-2 the Court held that section 309's federally required commencement date for state statutes of limitations does not also apply to state statutes of repose. The Court majority noted that the text of section 309 only refers to statutes of limitations even though the section 301(e) study had separately referred to statutes of repose.

Less than two weeks after the *Waldburger* decision the North Carolina General Assembly passed legislation lifting the state's statute of repose for claims of groundwater contamination from hazardous substances. The legislation, which was promptly signed into law by Governor Pat McCrory, is accompanied by a legislative finding "that the Supreme Court's decision is inconsistent with the legislature's intentions and the legislature's understanding of federal law at the time that certain actions were filed." The legislation provides that the ten-year bar in the state's statute of repose "shall not be construed to bar an action for personal injury or property damages caused or contributed to by the consumption, exposure, or use of water supplied from groundwater contaminated by a hazardous substance, pollutant or contaminant" that exceeds state groundwater quality standards. N.C. Session Law 2014-17, S.B. 574.

## 6. *Allocation of Liability and Contribution Actions*

Even when CERCLA imposes joint and several liability on PRPs falling within one of its four classes, there are a variety of means through which PRPs with certain characteristics can avoid being held liable for the entire costs of cleanup. An important one for many small contributors is the de minimis settlement provision in section 122(g). Section 122(g) seeks to encourage prompt settlements between the government and PRPs that contributed small amounts of substances whose toxic or other hazardous effects are minimal in comparison with the contributions of others. EPA's settlement policy presumes that de minimis contributors should pay some premium over and above what their proportionate contribution to the site would dictate in return for receiving an early settlement that absolves them of liability for cost overruns or potential future response costs. In United States v. Cannons Engineering Corporation, 899 F.2d 79 (1st Cir. 1990), the First Circuit approved a de minimis settlement reached between EPA and 300 generators who agreed to pay 160 percent of their projected share of all past and future response costs based on calculations of the amount of waste by volume each had contributed to a site. The court rejected the argument of nonsettling PRPs that EPA should have based its apportionment of liability on the relative toxicity of the wastes rather than on each party's volumetric share. The court also approved EPA's policy of encouraging prompt settlements by seeking greater contributions from parties who refuse initial settlement offers.

Following the enactment of section 122(g), EPA did not move quickly to pursue settlements with de minimis contributors. See Kornhauser & Revesz, De Minimis Settlements Under Superfund: An Empirical Study, in Analyzing Superfund: Economics, Science, and Law 187 (Revesz & Stewart eds., 1995) (study finding that EPA had underutilized de minimis settlements prior to 1992). More recently, EPA has taken steps to settle more quickly with de minimis PRPs. During the first 13 years of CERCLA administration, EPA had settled with approximately 6,000 de minimis PRPs. In 1994, EPA announced it would expand its efforts to reach de minimis settlements. Through the end of 1998, it had settled an additional 12,000 de minimis shares. EPA, Superfund Reforms Annual Report 20 (1999). In the 2002 SBLRBRA legislation, Congress authorized expedited and reduced settlements to people who lack the ability to pay or who have limited ability to pay.

In addition, EPA has announced new policies to pick up part of the so-called orphan shares, the liabilities of entities who are insolvent or unidentifiable. Through the end of FY 2003, EPA had made 160 offers of orphan share contribution totaling approximately $235 million. EPA, Superfund Reforms Round 3-11: Orphan Share Compensation. EPA has also been trying to speed up the cost allocation process by experimenting with neutral parties establishing nonbinding allocations of responsibility among PRPs. EPA then offers settlements to PRPs according to the terms of the neutral allocation. These are all measures designed to reduce the transaction costs of making final determinations of liability shares.

Another mechanism available to PRPs to reduce their liability is the statutory contribution provision in section 113(f). This section bars contribution from parties who have settled with the government for matters addressed in the settlement. This not only provides a degree of liability certainty for settling PRPs, but it also further enhances EPA's leverage in negotiating settlements by diminishing the number of PRPs subject to later contribution actions by the nonsettlers. The section 113(f) action was added to CERCLA in 1986. It supplements the action that "any person" has always had under section 107(B) against PRPs for "costs of response incurred . . . consistent with the national contingency plan."

For those PRPs who have incurred liability and who are not protected from contribution actions, the contribution action under section 113(f) constitutes the last act of the CERCLA drama, as a PRP who believes it has paid a greater than fair share of the cleanup costs brings suit to shift some of those costs to others. A court hearing such a contribution suit is authorized to "allocate response costs among liable parties using such equitable factors as the court determines are appropriate." Consequently, contribution actions are as much about what equitable formula will be used to distribute costs as they are about the facts.

As the Superfund program has matured, the nature of the litigation it has spawned has matured as well. Early on, litigation concentrated on the front-end issues—the program's constitutionality, the nature of joint and several liability, the scope of defenses to PRP status, and the consistency of the costs incurred with the national contingency plan. While these front-end issues still are being litigated, many have been resolved and the parties have moved onto the back end of the process—the allocation of responsibility among the numerous PRPs associated with many of the complicated Superfund sites. As we have seen, the Superfund statute throws a broad joint and several liability net over PRPs, but after cleanup costs have been incurred, section 113(f) does provide the PRPs the opportunity to allocate responsibility among themselves. Unresolved issues concerning these actions for contribution among the jointly liable PRPs produced the next wave of Superfund litigation.

With the addition of section 113(f), the choice of action—section 113(f) or section 107—has significant ramifications. First, liability is to be "equitably allocated" among PRPs under section 113(f) in contrast to the joint and several liability of section 107. Second, the statute of limitations for section 107 actions is three to six years from completion of removal work or initiation of remediation work, compared to three years from the date of judgment or settlement under section 113(f). §§113(g)(2) and (g)(3). Third, "contribution protection" exists only for section 113(f) actions. §113(f)(2). See Jeffrey M. Gaba, United States v. Atlantic Research: The Supreme Court Almost Gets It Right, 37 Envtl. L. Rep. 10810, 10811-10812 (2007).

As litigation resolved more and more of the front-end responsibilities of PRPs, an increasing number of site cleanups have been performed on a voluntary basis. Typically, a coalition of the willing PRPs—understanding that they would not escape liability—band together to remediate the site in compliance with EPA guidelines, sometimes after EPA or a state agency has issued an administrative order finding the site to be in violation, but prior to any lawsuit having been commenced, and prior to EPA or the state having incurred any cleanup costs themselves. Once significant costs have been incurred by the "volunteer" PRPs, these coalitions then institute a section 113(f) action against nonparticipating PRPs to allocate final cost responsibility according to a loose set of equitable principles the courts have been articulating and applying on a case-by-case basis. (For more on the allocation process, see the *Vertac* decision and notes following, pages 404-412.) Appeals courts allowed PRPs' contribution claims under section 113(f) for costs incurred from settlements, government orders, or voluntary action until 2004, when the Supreme Court caught many Superfund observers by surprise when it issued its decision in Cooper Industries, Inc. v. Aviall Services, Inc., 543 U.S. 157.

Cooper Industries sold four aircraft maintenance sites to Aviall Services, who eventually discovered that the ground and groundwater had been contaminated by leaks of petroleum and other hazardous chemicals. The Texas Natural Resource Conservation Commission instructed Aviall to remediate the site, and threatened, but did not pursue, judicial action if Aviall refused. After spending at least $5 million in remediation costs, Aviall sued Cooper to recover remediation costs, initially filing claims under both section 107(a) and section 113(f)(1). It later dropped the section 107 claim. Ultimately, on motion for summary judgment, the district court dismissed Aviall's section 113(f)(1) claim, holding that the statutory contribution action was only available to persons who had been sued for cost recovery under section 107. The Fifth Circuit, sitting en banc, reversed, finding that section 113(f)(1) allowed contribution claims even when the PRP had not been sued.

The Supreme Court then reversed the Fifth Circuit, holding that PRPs could utilize section 113 to seek contribution only after they had been sued for cost recovery. Speaking for seven Justices, Justice Thomas explained:

> . . . §113 provides two express avenues for contribution: §113(f)(1) ("during or following" specified civil actions) and §113(f)(3)(B) (after an administrative or judicially approved settlement that resolves liability to the United States or a State). . . . Notably absent from §113(g)(3) is any provision for starting the limitations period if a judgment or settlement never occurs, as is the case with a purely voluntary cleanup.

The Supreme Court declined to decide whether a person in Aviall's situation could sue for cost recovery under section 107. In dissent, Justice Ginsburg argued that such a cost recovery suit should be available to persons who engage in voluntary cleanups. Justice Ginsburg pointed to Key Tronic Corp. v. United States, 511 U.S. 809, 818 (1994) in support of her claim that section 107(a)(4)(B) "allows *any* person who has incurred costs for cleaning up a hazardous waste site to recover all or a portion of those costs from any other person liable under CERCLA."

In declining to reach the section 107 issue, Justice Thomas did note that the First, Second, Third, Fourth, Sixth, Seventh, Tenth, and Eleventh Circuit Courts of Appeals' decisions have held that a private party that is itself a PRP may not pursue a section 107(a) action against other PRPs for joint and several liability. One reason for these results is that section 107(a)(4)(B) apparently authorizes a PRP who has incurred costs to recover all of them from the other PRPs, rather than being expressly limited to some appropriate share of those costs. At the same time, however, the circuit decisions that ruled against a section 107 action for a potentially responsible party did so pre-*Aviall*, when it was widely thought that the section 113 contribution action was available to PRPs who cleaned up on a voluntary basis.

After *Aviall*, commentators worried that the decision would hamper voluntary cleanups and settlements. In addition, it spawned renewed interest in the use of section 107 as a means of providing equitable sharing of costs. Three years after the decision, the following case reached the Supreme Court.

## United States v. Atlantic Research Corp.

551 U.S. 128 (2007)

JUSTICE THOMAS delivered the opinion of the Court.

Two provisions of the CERCLA—§§107(a) and 113(f)—allow private parties to recover expenses associated with cleaning up contaminated sites. In this case, we must decide a question left open in *Cooper Industries, Inc. v. Aviall Services, Inc.*: whether §107(a) provides so-called potentially responsible parties (PRPs), §§107(a) (1)-(4), with a cause of action to recover costs from other PRPs. We hold that it does.

### I

### A

Courts have frequently grappled with whether and how PRPs may recoup CERCLA-related costs from other PRPs. The questions lie at the intersection of two statutory provisions—CERCLA §§107(a) and 113(f). Section 107(a) defines four categories of PRPs and makes them liable for, among other things:

(A) all costs of removal or remedial action incurred by the United States Government or a State or an Indian tribe not inconsistent with the national contingency plan; [and]

(B) any other necessary costs of response incurred by any other person consistent with the national contingency plan. §9607(a)(4)(A)-(B).

§113(f) authorizes one PRP to sue another for contribution in certain circumstances. Prior to the advent of §113(f)'s express contribution right, some courts held that §107(a)(4)(B) provided a cause of action for a private party to recover voluntarily incurred response costs and to seek contribution after having been sued. . . .

In *Cooper Industries*, we held that a private party could seek contribution from other liable parties only after having been sued under §106 or §107(a). This narrower interpretation of §113(f) caused several Courts of Appeals to reconsider whether PRPs have rights under §107(a)(4)(B), an issue we declined to address in *Cooper Industries*. . . . Today, we resolve this issue.

### B

In this case, respondent Atlantic Research leased property at the Shumaker Naval Ammunition Depot, a facility operated by the Department of Defense. At the site, Atlantic Research retrofitted rocket motors for petitioner United States. Using a high-pressure water spray, Atlantic Research removed pieces of propellant from the motors. It then burned the propellant pieces. Some of the resultant wastewater and burned fuel contaminated soil and groundwater at the site.

Atlantic Research cleaned the site at its own expense and then sought to recover some of its costs by suing the United States under both §107(a) and §113(f). After our decision in *Cooper Industries* foreclosed relief under §113(f). . .[t]he United States moved to dismiss, arguing that §107(a) does not allow PRPs (such as Atlantic Research) to recover costs. The District Court granted the motion to dismiss. . . .

The Court of Appeals for the Eighth Circuit reversed. . . . [I]t held that §107(a) (4)(B) provides a cause of action to Atlantic Research. To prevent perceived conflict between §107(a)(4)(B) and §113(f)(1), the Court of Appeals reasoned that PRPs that "have been subject to §§106 or 107 enforcement actions are still required to use §113, thereby ensuring its continued vitality." We . . . affirm.

### II

### A

The parties' dispute centers on what "other person[s]" may sue under §107(a) (4)(B). The Government argues that "any other person" refers to any person not identified as a PRP in §§107(a)(1)-(4). . . . In accord with the Court of Appeals, Atlantic Research believes that subparagraph (B) provides a cause of action to anyone except the United States, a State, or an Indian tribe—the persons listed in subparagraph (A). We agree with Atlantic Research.

Statutes must "be read as a whole." Applying that maxim, the language of subparagraph (B) can be understood only with reference to subparagraph (A). The provisions are adjacent and have remarkably similar structures. . . . Bolstering the structural link, the text also denotes a relationship between the two provisions. By using the phrase "other necessary costs," subparagraph (B) refers to and differentiates the relevant costs from those listed in subparagraph (A).

In light of the relationship between the subparagraph, it is natural to read the phrase "any other person" by referring to the immediately preceding subparagraph (A), which permits suit only by the United States, a State, or an Indian tribe.

The phrase "any other person" therefore means any person other than those three. See 42 U.S.C. §9601(21) (defining "person" to include the United States and the various States). Consequently, the plain language of subparagraph (B) authorizes cost-recovery actions by any private party, including PRPs. . . .

Moreover, the statute defines PRPs so broadly as to sweep in virtually all persons likely to incur cleanup costs. Hence, if PRPs do not qualify as "any other person" for purposes of §107(a)(4)(B), it is unclear what private party would. . . .

### B

The Government also argues that our interpretation will create friction between §107(a) and §113(f), the very harm courts of appeals have previously tried to avoid. In particular, the Government maintains that our interpretation, by offering PRPs a choice between §107(a) and §113(f), effectively allows PRPs to circumvent §113(f)'s shorter statute of limitations. Furthermore, the Government argues, PRPs will eschew equitable apportionment under §113(f) in favor of joint and several liability under §107(a). Finally, the Government contends that our interpretation eviscerates the settlement bar set forth in §113(f)(2).

We have previously recognized that §§107(a) and 113(f) provide two "clearly distinct" remedies. *Cooper Industries.* "CERCLA provide[s] for a *right to cost recovery* in certain circumstances, §107(a), and *separate rights to contribution* in other circumstances, §§113(f)(1), 113(f)(3)(B)." (emphases added). The Government, however, uses the word "contribution" as if it were synonymous with any apportionment of expenses among PRPs. This imprecise usage confuses the complementary yet distinct nature of the rights established in §§107(a) and 113(f).

Section 113(f) explicitly grants PRPs a right to contribution. Contribution is defined as the "tortfeasor's right to collect from others responsible for the same tort after the tortfeasor has paid more than his or her proportionate share, the shares being determined as a percentage of fault." Nothing in §113(f) suggests that Congress used the term "contribution" in anything other than this traditional sense. The statute authorizes a PRP to seek contribution "during or following" a suit under §106 or §107(a). 42 U.S.C. §9613(f)(1). Thus, §113(f)(1) permits suit before or after the establishment of common liability. In either case, a PRP's right to contribution under §113(f)(1) is contingent upon an inequitable distribution of common liability among liable parties.

By contrast, §107(a) permits recovery of cleanup costs but does not create a right to contribution. A private party may recover under §107(a) without any establishment of liability to a third party. Moreover, §107(a) permits a PRP to recover only the costs it has "incurred" in cleaning up a site. When a party pays to satisfy a settlement agreement or a court judgment, it does not incur its own costs of response. Rather, it reimburses other parties for costs that those parties incurred.

Accordingly, the remedies available in §§107(a) and 113(f) complement each other by providing causes of action "to persons in different procedural circumstances." Section 113(f)(1) authorizes a contribution action to PRPs with common liability stemming from an action instituted under §106 or §107(a). And §107(a) permits cost recovery (as distinct from contribution) by a private party that has itself incurred cleanup costs. Hence, a PRP that pays money to satisfy a settlement agreement or a court judgment may pursue §113(f) contribution. But by reimbursing response costs paid by other parties, the PRP has not incurred its own costs of response and therefore cannot recover under §107(a). As a result, though eligible to seek contribution under §113(f)(1), the PRP cannot simultaneously seek to recover the same expenses under §107(a). Thus, at least in the case of reimbursement, the PRP cannot choose the 6-year statute of limitations for cost-recovery actions over the shorter limitations period for §113(f) contribution claims.

For similar reasons, a PRP could not avoid §113(f)'s equitable distribution of reimbursement costs among PRPs by instead choosing to impose joint and several liability on another PRP in an action under §107(a). The choice of remedies simply does not exist. In any event, a defendant PRP in such a §107(a) suit could blunt any inequitable distribution of costs by filing a §113(f) counterclaim. Resolution of a §113(f) counter-claim would necessitate the equitable apportionment of costs among the liable parties, including the PRP that filed the §107(a) action. 42 U.S.C. §9613(f)(a) ("In resolving contribution claims, the court may allocate response costs among liable parties using such equitable factors as the court determines are appropriate").

Finally, permitting PRPs to seek recovery under §107(a) will not eviscerate the settlement bar set forth in §113(f)(2). That provision prohibits §113(f) contribution claims against "[a] person who has resolved its liability to the United States or a State in an administrative or judicially approved settlement. . . ." 42 U.S.C. §9613(f)(2). The settlement bar does not by its terms protect against cost-recovery liability under §107(a). For several reasons, we doubt this supposed loophole would discourage settlement. First, as stated above, a defendant PRP may trigger equitable apportionment by filing a §113(f) counterclaim. A district court applying traditional rules of equity would undoubtedly consider any prior settlement as part of the liability calculus. Second, the settlement bar continues to provide significant protection from contribution suits by PRPs that have inequitably reimbursed the costs incurred by another party. Third, settlement carries the inherent benefit of finally resolving liability as to the United States or a State.

## III

Because the plain terms of §107(a)(4)(B) allow a PRP to recover costs from other PRPs, the statute provides Atlantic Research with a cause of action. We therefore affirm the judgment of the Court of Appeals.

## NOTES AND QUESTIONS

1. Does *Atlantic Research* discourage settlement? The settlement bar under section 113(f) prevents non-settling PRPs from filing section 113 claims against settling PRPs. However, section 107 claims are not similarly barred, so PRPs who settle with EPA may still find themselves a target for liability claims following *Atlantic Research*. See Mark Yeboah, United States v. Atlantic Research: Of Settlement and Voluntary Incurred Costs, 32 Harv. Envtl. L. Rev. 279 (2008); Jeffrey M. Gaba, United States v. Atlantic Research: The Supreme Court Almost Gets It Right, 37 Envtl. L. Rep. 10810, 10815-10816 (2007). In the *Atlantic Research* opinion, Justice Thomas discounted this possibility, arguing "we doubt this supposed loophole

would discourage settlement [because] . . . [a] district court applying traditional rules of equity would undoubtedly consider any prior settlement as part of the liability calculus."

2. After this decision, can PRPs recover costs in response to an administrative order or a settlement agreement? In *Aviall*, the Court explicitly chose not to consider whether PRPs subject to an administrative order could make a contribution claim under section 113(f)(1). Lower courts are split on whether cost recovery claims may be brought by PRPs who perform cleanup work pursuant to a settlement with the government. Compare Bernstein v. Bankert, 702 F.3d 964 (7th Cir. 2012), with Solutia, Inc. v. McWane, Inc., 672 F.3d 1230 (11th Cir. 2012). In *Atlantic Research*, Justice Thomas presumed settlement agreements would not fall under section 107:

> §107(a) permits a PRP to recover only the costs it has "incurred" in cleaning up a site. When a party pays to satisfy a settlement agreement or a court judgment, it does not incur its own costs of response. Rather, it reimburses other parties for costs that those parties incurred.

It may be that the settling PRP would have to file two claims: a section 113(f)(3)(B) contribution claim for costs reimbursed to the government and a section 107 claim for costs directly incurred.

3. Three years passed between the Court's 2004 decision in *Aviall*, eliminating a cause of action in contribution under section 113(f) for PRPs who voluntarily clean up property and the Court's 2007 decision in *Atlantic Research*, finding a direct right of cost recovery for those same PRPs under section 107(a)(4)(B). PRPs whose voluntary action cases were decided within that time frame may have some interesting procedural hurdles to overcome. For example, in 1991, Beazer East, Inc., after voluntarily starting a remediation process pursuant to an EPA Administrative Order to clean up hazardous waste on its property, sued the Mead Corporation, the former owner, in contribution for investigation and remediation costs. In 1996, a Pennsylvania District Court found Beazer's sections 107 and 113(f) claims duplicative and dismissed the section 107 claim. The Third Circuit heard oral argument on the case in fall 2004 and in June 2005 rejected the liability allocation by the magistrate judge and remanded for a new allocation proceeding before the District Judge. However, in December 2004, the *Aviall* decision came down, which at least implicitly precluded section 113(f) suits based on Administrative Orders. Mead failed to raise this defense in its appeal, waiting until January 2006 to raise its objection to the section 113(f) claim. After filing an interlocutory appeal on the question of the section 113(f) claim, the Supreme Court decided *Atlantic Research*. Unfortunately for Mead, its appeal came too late: The Third Circuit found that Mead waived its defense when it failed to raise the issue on its 2005 appeal. Beazer East, Inc. v. The Mead Corp. (*Beazer III*), 525 F.3d 255, 258 (3d Cir. 2008). The legal result could be described as paradoxical: The section 107 claim, under which Mead may have been liable after *Atlantic Research*, was dismissed, but the section 113(f) claim, under which Mead was not liable after *Aviall*, was upheld. The question remains: For cases where a court has (erroneously) dismissed a section 107 claim as duplicative with a section 113(f) claim, what is the correct outcome when it is

later determined that the PRP may only be legally liable under section 107? Should procedure take precedence over equity and fairness? Other courts have suggested that allowing an amended complaint is the correct recourse. See E.I. DuPont de Nemours & Co. v. United States, 508 F.3d 126, 136 n.6 (3d Cir. 2007); Montville Township v. Woodmont Builders, LLC, 244 Fed. Appx. 514, 518-519 (3d Cir. 2007); ITT Industries, Inc. v. BorgWarner, Inc., 506 F.3d 452, 458 (6th Cir. 2007).

4. Champion Laboratories, Inc. v. Metex Corp., Civ. No. 02-5284 (WHW), slip op., 2008 WL 1808309 (D.N.J. Apr. 21, 2008), is another case affected by the *Atlantic Research* decision. Champion and Metex own neighboring sites in New Jersey. Both sites are contaminated, and the Champion site groundwater contamination was caused by contamination migration from the Metex site. Champion filed suit against Metex in 2002, but amended pleadings were filed after the *Atlantic Research* decision in 2007. Champion seeks contribution under section 113(f)(1) and section 113(f)(3)(B). In its 2008 opinion, the district court dismissed Champion's section 113(f)(1) claim because Champion had not been sued under section 106 or section 107. Champion's section 113(f)(3)(B) claim was upheld because Champion has entered into a settlement with New Jersey DEP. Metex filed a section 113(f)(1) counterclaim, seeking contribution from Champion. Interestingly, the district court upheld Metex's counterclaim because Champion's 107(a) claim against Metex provides the basis for Metex's section 113(f)(1) counterclaim (section 113 claims are allowed during or following a section 106 or section 107(a) civil action).

5. Both the Sixth Circuit and the Seventh Circuit have held that parties who resolve their liability in a settlement with EPA and thus have rights of contribution under section 113 cannot seek contribution under section 107. Hobart Corp. v. Waste Management of Ohio, Inc., 758 F.3d 757 (6th Cir. 2014); NCR Corp. v. George A. Whiting Paper Co., 768 F.3d 682 (7th Cir. 2014). This holding is consistent with decisions by five other circuit courts of appeal. For an argument that cost recovery claims by potentially responsible parties should be treated as CERCLA contribution claims, see Justin R. Pidot & Dale Ratliff, The Common Law of Liable Party CERCLA Claims, 70 Stan. L. Rev. 191 (2018).

6. In Territory of Guam v. United States, 141 S.Ct. 1608 (2021), the Supreme Court held unanimously that a settlement not made pursuant to CERCLA cannot trigger the statute of limitations for bringing a section 113 contribution action. The Ordot Dump, the largest dumpsite in the U.S. Territory of Guam, was created by the U.S. Navy when it governed the island after World War II. The dump later was used for decades as a municipal dumpsite prior to its closing in 2011. In 2002, EPA sued Guam for violating the Clean Water Act due to discharges from the Ordot Dump leaching into the Lonfit River that flows into the ocean. The litigation was settled by consent decree between the Navy and Guam in 2004. In 2017, Guam sued the Navy seeking to recover for part of its costs of cleaning up the dump under section 107 of CERCLA or as a contribution action under section 113(f)(3)(B) of CERCLA. In February 2020, the U.S. Court of Appeals for the D.C. Circuit ruled that the 2004 settlement between the Navy and Guam meant that the territory could only recover from the Navy through a contribution action under section 113(f)(3)(B) of CERCLA. Because Guam's action had been filed after expiration of the three-year statute of limitations for CERCLA contribution claims, the court dismissed the action. Guam v. United States, 950 F.3d 104 (D.C. Cir. 2020). The Supreme Court reversed.

The Court held that only a CERCLA-specific settlement, and not one made under the Clean Water Act, triggers §113.

7. In cases where contribution actions do go forward, the court faces the task of determining an appropriate allocation of response costs among the numerous PRPs, some of whom are generators, some past landowners or operators, some transporters, and some present owners and operators, each with very different equitable considerations arguably appropriate. In the case that follows, the district court was trying to bring down the curtain on one of the oldest pieces of Superfund litigation, a case which had actually been begun by the government under RCRA and the CWA prior to CERCLA's enactment. The CERCLA counts were added soon after the bill became law. There are now roughly a dozen reported decisions in the district court and the Eighth Circuit Court of Appeals involving *Vertac.* Together, they trace the trajectory of CERCLA litigation as the statute and practice under it have matured over the years. *Vertac's* reaching the allocation of liability stage provides a good signal that the part of the CERCLA cleanup and liability scheme under the most intense litigation pressure has moved from initial questions of constitutionality, retroactivity, and definitions of PRPs to the final allocation-of-liability issues.

Although the decision below was vacated, United States v. Hercules, Inc., 247 F.3d 706 (8th Cir. 2001), because the court of appeals ruled the district court judge had misapplied the law regarding divisibility of harm, an issue for the liability phase of the case, its discussion of contribution remains an excellent example of this last phase of CERCLA litigation. In reading the following excerpt, note the many different considerations each party uses to urge adoption of an allocation favorable to it.

## United States v. Vertac Chemical Corp.

79 F. Supp. 2d 1034 (E.D. Ark. 1999)

GEORGE HOWARD, JR., District Judge.

. . . As can be expected, Hercules and Uniroyal each advance different arguments. On the one hand, Uniroyal relies primarily on the relative involvement of the liable parties. It contends that its role as an arranger was minimal. It asserts that the Court should use a volumetric calculation, which can be calculated based on the evidence presented at the hearing. Based on Uniroyal's calculations, a volumetric calculation would result in an initial allocation of 1.58% to Uniroyal and 98.42% to Hercules. In addition to its volumetric calculation, Uniroyal argues that it is then entitled to a "downward departure." Hercules, on the other hand, attempts to divvy up the site, so that it ends up with an allocation in which Uniroyal would be about 70 percent liable. In particular, Hercules advances a division in which it has no connection with the drummed waste, the EPA's single largest expenditure.

Hercules' attempt to limit its responsibility for response costs to about 30 percent is, on its face, absurd. Hercules operated or owned the plant from 1961 to 1976. It had the greatest presence, by far, of any of the responsible parties. The problem is that Uniroyal and Hercules are left "holding the bag" for Vertac, who at least arguably caused the greatest amount of harm.

Resolution of contribution claims under CERCLA is governed by 42 U.S.C. §9613(f). It provides: "In resolving contribution claims, the court may allocate response costs among liable parties using such equitable factors as the court determines are appropriate." 42 U.S.C. §9613(f)(1). The statute does not limit the courts to any particular factors, but grants the court "broad discretion to balance the equities in the interest of justice." Bedford Affiliates v. Sills, 156 F.3d 416, 429 (2d Cir. 1998). In an attempt to find an equitable resolution to what is at times a complex problem, the courts have employed a number of approaches. See David G. Mandelbaum, Toward a Superfund Cost Allocation Principle, 3 Envtl. Law. 117, 124 (1996) (noting the difficulty in allocating costs). Most have looked to what are referred to as the "Gore factors," proposed by then Senator Albert Gore as a method to apportion joint and several liability. These factors are:

(1) the ability of the parties to demonstrate that their contribution to a discharge, release, or disposal of a hazardous waste can be distinguished;

(2) the amount of hazardous waste involved;

(3) the degree of toxicity of the hazardous waste;

(4) the degree of involvement of the parties in the generation, transportation, treatment, storage, or disposal of the hazardous waste;

(5) the degree of care exercised by the parties with respect to the hazardous waste concerned, taking into account the characteristics of such hazardous waste; and

(6) the degree of cooperation by the parties with Federal, State, or local officials to prevent any harm to the public health or the environment.

The factors are neither an exhaustive nor exclusive list. . . . The primary emphasis is placed on the harm each party causes the environment and care on the part of the parties. . . .

Divisibility of harm is not a defense to a contribution action under §113(f), although the Court may consider separate harms caused by different parties in allocating costs. . . . But see Acushnet Co. v. Mohasco Corp., 191 F.3d 69, 77 (1st Cir. 1999) (party may avoid liability for response costs in contribution action "if it demonstrates that its share of hazardous waste deposited at the site constitutes no more than background amounts of such substances in the environment and cannot concentrate with other wastes to produce higher amounts.")

Hercules seeks to divide the Site into various areas, or "harms." The Court has previously rejected Hercules' attempt to divide the Site into "mini-sites." The Court, however, is not persuaded that the "mini-sites" represent "distinct" harms on which the Court can allocate costs. The history of this site reveals a commingling of the wastes. Furthermore, Hercules' proposed division is, at best, arbitrary, and couched in terms to reduce Hercules' liability. As the First Circuit recently noted in rejecting a quantitative minimum at which a party could be held responsible, the task of tracing chemical waste to particular sources in particular amounts "is often technologically infeasible due to the fluctuating quantity and varied nature of the pollution at a site over the course of many years." Acushnet Co. v. Mohasco Corp., 191 F.3d at 77.

The problem noted in Acushnet is illustrated by Hercules' argument regarding the costs associated with the incineration of the drummed wastes. When the

State ordered Vertac to shut down in the summer of 1979, there were approximately 2700 drums of 2,4,5-T still bottoms stored on-site. Workers spent much of the summer placing those 55-gallon drums into larger drums, shoveling up contaminated soil, and placing that soil into the larger overpack drums. When Vertac resumed production in the fall of 1979, it produced only 2,4-D and eventually accumulated about 26,000 drums of 2,4-D waste. This waste was accumulated between 1979 and 1986, when Hercules had no involvement or presence at the Site.

Hercules argues that no dioxin is produced in the 2,4-D manufacturing process. Thus, according to Hercules, none of the 2,4-D waste drums should have contained dioxin. Furthermore, Hercules presented expert testimony to demonstrate that there should not have been cross contamination of the 2,4-D waste with the 2,4,5-T wastes. According to Hercules, none of the 2,4-D wastes should have had any detectable concentration of dioxin from the fall of 1979 onward, when Vertac ceased manufacturing 2,4,5-T.

Hercules states that it had no involvement in management of the drummed wastes and should not be responsible for the costs of incineration of the drummed waste. Of course, Uniroyal, as an arranger, also did not have any involvement.

The Court has previously found that there was cross-contamination and commingling of the wastes at the entire Site. During the years Hercules operated the plant, Hercules generated hazardous substances which were disposed of at the Site through "leaks, spills, drum burial, and other releases into the environment. . . . The Hercules operation resulted in contamination of soil, ground-water, equipment, tanks, sewer lines, the sewage treatment plants, and sediments and flood plains in Rocky Branch Creek and Bayou Meto." United States v. Vertac Chemical Corp., 966 F. Supp. 1491, 1494-95 (E.D. Ark. 1997).

Furthermore, as noted in previous decisions, dioxin was found in the 2,4-D wastes. See United States v. Vertac Chemical Corp., 33 F. Supp. 2d at 780. The Court will not second guess the studies and find that they are incorrect or unreliable, as requested by Hercules. Additionally, Hercules admitted that some degree of dioxin contamination found in the 2,4-D drums could have come from contaminated soil being placed in the drums. That soil was contaminated by years of production.

Thus, the Court is not persuaded that Hercules has established "separate harms" on which to allocate responsibility.

The Court has considered carefully the arguments of the parties, the voluminous record and reviewed a large number of decisions and articles in an attempt to reach an equitable resolution to the problem. Allocation of costs between the two remaining parties is difficult, given the particular circumstances of this case where one of the major polluters is insolvent, a number of parties have settled, and the remaining parties' involvement at the site are quite different. See Browning-Ferris Industries of Ill. v. Ter Maat, 13 F. Supp. 2d 756, 777-78 (N.D. Ill. 1998), *rev'd on other grounds*, 195 F.3d 953 (7th Cir. 1999) (discussing difficulty in allocating response costs and stating that allocation in the case would be a "best guess" proposition).

At first glance, Uniroyal's argument that it is responsible for about 1 percent of the costs seems inequitable. It would amount to less than $1 million dollars, when the overall cleanup effort for which Uniroyal was held jointly and severally liable was almost $90 million. Nevertheless, it is clear that Hercules' "responsibility as an owner and operator, who was deeply involved in the daily operations of the waste-producing enterprise," should far exceed that of Uniroyal, whose involvement with the Vertac Site was indirect and for a limited time. See Bedford Affiliates, 156 F.3d at 430. The question, of course, is how much responsibility to assign in light of the circumstances.

As discussed above, Uniroyal argues for strictly a volumetric approach. In this instance, the Court is persuaded that volumetrics is the most significant factor and should be the starting point at which to assess each party's contribution. However, the Court is not persuaded that volume alone should be the measure of allocation.

Uniroyal presented evidence of the volumes of product produced at the plant during the various ownership periods. The rates of production were based on production records and other documents. Hercules does not dispute the production rates presented by Uniroyal's expert, Steven Michael Quigley. Reasor-Hill was estimated to have produced 6,240,000 pounds of 2,4-D and 2,4,5-T. Hercules produced about 33,231,400 pounds of 2,4-D, 2,4,5-T and 2,4,5-TP during the time it owned and operated the site. During the time Transvaal leased the Site from Hercules (1971-1976), it produced approximately 43,004,255 pounds of 2,4,-D, 2,4,5-T and 2,4,5-TP. Vertac produced 71,183,140 pounds of 2,4-D, 2,4,5-T, and 2,4,5-TP between 1976 and 1987. Of that, Vertac produced 1,344,000 pounds of 2,4,5-T for sale to Uniroyal. In all, about 153,658,795 pounds of 2,4-D, 2,4,5-T and 2,4,5-TP were produced at the plant site during its years of operation.

If Uniroyal's share of the total production was considered, it would amount to 0.87 percent. The more equitable approach, however, is to calculate the amount of Uniroyal's share in comparison to that of Hercules. Production during the years Hercules owned or operated the plant was 76,235,655 pounds of 2,4-D, 2,4,5-T and 2,4,5-TP. Uniroyal's production is 1.76 percent of that of Hercules.

Hercules argues that the volumes of the parties cannot be compared because Hercules produced the majority of its 2,4-D and 2,4,5-T to fulfill Agent Orange contracts during the 1960's. According to Hercules, only 2 million pounds of 2,4-D and 1 million pounds of 2,4,5-T or 2,4,5-TP were produced for "commercial customers." Uniroyal, by comparison, produced 1.34 million pounds of 2,4,5-T for commercial customers through its tolling arrangement with Vertac.

The Court has already discussed the Agent Orange contracts in United States v. Vertac Chemical Corp., 841 F. Supp. 884 (E.D. Ark. 1993), aff'd, 46 F.3d 803 (8th Cir. 1995), cert. denied, 515 U.S. 1158 (1995). In that decision, the Court noted that Hercules bid on the contracts, and profited from them. 841 F. Supp. at 890. The Court cannot find that Hercules' production of Agent Orange which was used as part of the country's military effort in Vietnam should be given any consideration.

Hercules also argues that Uniroyal's predecessor developed a process that led to the creation of the 2,4,5-T still bottoms which should be considered in determining each party's contribution. This argument requires the Court to find causation based on a tenuous thread. The Court refuses to impose greater costs on Uniroyal based on a process developed in the 1960's which Hercules purchased and used.

As stated above, production volume is the most significant factor in allocating the costs in this case. The volumetric approach takes into account the relative involvement of the parties at the Site and their contribution to the harm created. Uniroyal argues that it is entitled to a "downward departure" because of its limited involvement. Uniroyal was neither an operator nor owner. Hercules was an operator of the Site for nine years, an owner of the plant for fourteen years and a lessor for five years, during which it had the authority to control the lessee's operations. The Court is not persuaded, however, that Uniroyal's "lack of involvement" warrants a downward departure. The Court has already considered Uniroyal's relatively minor degree of involvement in looking at volumetrics. The Court is also not persuaded that Uniroyal is completely uninvolved, as it would have the Court find. It arranged for production of hazardous materials through a tolling arrangement, and it was aware of the production of hazardous wastes that would be produced as a result of the product. It benefitted from the production of hazardous materials at the Site.

It is, therefore, not inequitable to place a larger percentage of costs on Uniroyal than just what the difference in volume would support. In Browning-Ferris Industries of Illinois, Inc. v. Ter Maat, 195 F.3d 953 (7th Cir. 1999), the Court found that allocating a larger share of responsibility to one responsible party who had operated the landfill for fewer years and dumped less waste in it than other parties was equitable. The Court found that the polluter's conduct was a sufficient though not necessary condition of the clean up. Similarly, here, the production of 2,4,5-T for Uniroyal which resulted in the production of hazardous wastes was a sufficient condition for the clean up. The Court previously found that some of the drums and tanks contained dioxin contaminated waste from the production of Uniroyal's 2,4,5-T. That is, but for the production of 2,4,5-T for Uniroyal, there would not be a certain amount of wastes left and ultimately stored in the drums that had to be incinerated.

The Court finds that an "upward departure" is warranted in this instance. The percentage will be small given Uniroyal's limited involvement with the Site, but takes into account Uniroyal's role in the generation of hazardous material.

The Court has also given consideration to the parties' cooperation with government officials. Hercules responded to EPA's Orders under Section 106 of CERCLA and undertook extensive remediation. Hercules' efforts arguably had some effect on reducing the costs of remediation, and therefore Uniroyal's liability. Uniroyal did not respond, taking the position that it had cause to disregard Section 106 Orders because the Court did not find it liable until 1997. The Court notes, however, that the case on which it relied for finding Uniroyal liable as an arranger, United States v. Aceto Agricultural Chemicals Corp., 872 F.2d 1373 (8th Cir. 1989), had been decided several years before the first 106 Order. Thus, the Court finds that the sixth Gore factor also justifies finding Uniroyal to be responsible for more than the 1.76 percent and that Uniroyal and Hercules should share, pro rata, the orphan shares of Reasor-Hill and Vertac.

Hercules points to a number of other factors that the Court should consider in allocating the costs to reduce its costs. For example, Hercules introduced evidence that Vertac was not as concerned about safety and cleanliness as Hercules and that the plant went downhill under Vertac.

There is no doubt that Hercules' safety and environmental programs are to be commended. However, the degree of care used in Hercules in handling the waste does not have any weight in allocating the costs between Uniroyal and Hercules. Hercules owned and operated the plant, and therefore was in a position to oversee the care used at plant site. As discussed above, Hercules' safety and maintenance programs are laudatory; however, that being so does not mean that Uniroyal should assume more of the costs. Uniroyal was in no position to manage the disposal of any hazardous materials.

Hercules also introduced evidence regarding the knowledge the scientific community had of the problems with dioxin at the time Hercules manufactured the herbicides and pesticides. Although Hercules learned of the presence of dioxin by the mid-1960s, the technology did not exist at that time to adequately analyze the presence of dioxin in the soil or water during the years that Hercules operated the plant. Furthermore, the possibility of a link of dioxin to cancer did not surface until the mid to late 1970s.

The evidence regarding the state of knowledge of dioxin is interesting but irrelevant to this proceeding. It does not negate that the Court has found hazardous materials at the Site. . . .

In sum, after consideration of all the evidence, the Court finds that Uniroyal should be responsible for 2.6 percent of the costs for which it is jointly and severally liable. This includes the orphan shares. Thus, the parties are entitled to contribution from one another consistent with the allocation findings expressed herein.

The parties are directed to consult with each other, and the EPA regarding the offsets from other PRPs, the interest calculations, and the allocations as set forth in this Order. If the parties can agree on the amount, they should submit a proposed precedent for judgment within twenty days of the date of this Order. If not, each party should submit a proposed precedent setting forth its position.

## NOTES AND QUESTIONS

1. **On Remand.** The Eighth Circuit did not disturb the district court's allocation, but did remand for an evidentiary hearing on claims of divisibility advanced by Hercules. The district court then found against Hercules on all of its divisibility claims, except for one dealing with a discrete part of the site that accounted for a small share of the over $100 million in cleanup costs incurred so far. The district court reaffirmed its original allocation of liability after making this minor adjustment in total costs. United States v. Vertac Chemical Corp. 364 F. Supp. 2d 94 (E.D. Ark. 2005).

2. **Who Can Blame Them?** PRPs raise diverse considerations in a contribution action, limited only by their anticipation of what might be a plausible appeal to the equitable discretion of the trial judge. In a case such as *Vertac*, where each percentage point of liability is worth nearly $1 million, PRPs are perhaps not be criticized for the diversity of considerations that they bring to the court's attention.

3. **The Gore Factors.** Do the Gore factors make more sense when the court is trying to allocate liability among generators of wastes than they do when trying to allocate liability between a group of generators and an owner? Consider a group of generators representing 70 percent of the total wastes shipped to the site, none of whom played any active role in disposing or monitoring the waste once it reached the site. The previous site owner generated no waste, but it failed to dispose of other parties' waste properly. Once the current owner found out about the waste, she took immediate measures to contain the contamination and cooperated fully with government authorities. How do the Gore factors apply?

4. **Equitable Factors.** Courts have refused to limit the equitable factors that they are able to consider, treating this as a matter of case-by-case judgment. They can consider several factors or only one (e.g., volumetric allocation with equal weighting of all wastes; duration of ownership when allocating among owners). One court recently identified a list of (sometimes overlapping) factors relevant to other courts' holdings: "(1) the parties' relative fault or culpability, (2) the ability of the parties to demonstrate that their contribution to a discharge, release or disposal of a hazardous waste can be distinguished, (3) the amount of hazardous waste involved, (4) the degree of toxicity, (5) the degree of involvement of the parties in the generation, transportation, treatment, storage or disposal of the hazardous waste, (6) the degree of care exercised by the parties with respect to the hazardous waste, (7) the degree of cooperation by the parties with government agencies to prevent harm to the public health or the environment, (8) financial resources or economic status, (9) economic benefits received by the parties from contaminating activities or remediation, (10) knowledge and/or acquiescence of the parties in the contaminating activities, and (11) contracts between the parties." Waste Management of Alameda Cty. v. East Bay Regional Park Dist., 135 F. Supp. 2d 1071 (N.D. Cal. 2001).

5. **Zero Allocation for De Minimis Contributors.** The amount of cleanup attributable to Uniroyal's arranging was calculated by it to be 1.58 percent by volume. Is there a level of contribution so minor that a PRP ought to bear none of the costs of cleanup? In Acushnet Co. v. Mohasco Corp., 191 F.3d 69, 77 (1st Cir. 1999), cited by the *Vertac* district court, the First Circuit upheld grants of summary judgment and judgments as a matter of law to three small contributors to a site prior to a full allocation trial. One PRP had offered uncontradicted testimony that the creosote-soaked telephone poles that it had disposed of at the site could not leach polycyclic aromatic hydrocarbons (PAHs) into the groundwater at concentrations greater than the background level. Three others had deposited wastes that were minuscule in quantity compared to the entire site—in one case the court speculated that the PRPs' contribution would equate to a 1 in 500,000th share. Acushnet v. Coaters, 948 F. Supp. 128 (D. Mass. 1996). The district court acknowledged the fact that the linchpin of a contribution action is a holistic consideration of all the relevant equitable factors, so that it was impossible to identify any single bright-line criterion for granting summary dismissal to de minimis PRPs. Nonetheless, the court concluded that in a contribution action, the plaintiff bore a burden of proving a "minimum standard of significance of [a] defendant's responsibility as a source of one or more hazardous substances at the site." One determinant of that threshold-of-significance was a showing of "reasons for court intervention that outweigh the public interest against recognizing causes of action the enforcement of which exceed the added resources that would be tapped for waste-site remediation." Id. at 136. The court seems to say, in other words, plaintiffs needed to show that they are reasonably likely to recover more from a PRP than the public and private resources required to adjudicate that liability.

The First Circuit affirmed the district court decision, although it concluded that insofar as any element of the district court's decision turned on a conclusion that a PRP's contribution to the site had not caused the plaintiff to incur any response costs was inappropriate and out of place in a section 113(f) contribution action. 191 F.3d at 72. There is no "minimum quantity of hazardous waste before liability may be imposed [under CERCLA]. . . . [A]ny reasonable danger of release, however insignificant, would seem to give rise to liability." Id. at 76. However, while de minimis PRPs are to be held joint and severally liable at the liability stage of the trial, unless they can show divisibility, "[t]his does not mean . . . that the de minimis polluter must necessarily be held liable for all response costs. . . . [A] defendant may avoid . . . liability for response costs in a contribution action under §113(f) if it demonstrates that its share of hazardous waste deposited at the site constitutes no more than background amounts of such substances in the environment and cannot concentrate with other wastes to produce higher amounts. This rule is not based on CERCLA's causation requirement, but it is logically derived from §113(f)'s express authorization that a court take equity into account when fixing each defendant's fair share of response costs. We caution, however, that not every de minimis polluter will elude liability in this way. As always, an equitable determination must be justified by the record. . . . On the whole, the costs and inherent unfairness in saddling a party who has contributed only trace amounts of hazardous waste with joint and several liability for all costs incurred outweigh the public interest in requiring full contribution from de minimis polluters." Id. at 77-79.

6. **Allocating Orphan Shares.** PRPs who have gone out of business, been declared insolvent, or cannot be located leave behind "orphan shares" of liability. Superfund liability is joint and several, so that any or all of the remaining PRPs can be held liable for 100 percent of response costs, including the orphan shares. How should those orphan shares be dealt with in a contribution action, where the ruling concept is equitable allocation? Consider a site in which the site owner (O) has paid 100 percent of the cleanup expenses, totaling $1 million. O then brings a contribution action against another PRP, G. The contribution court allocates responsibility 20 percent to O, 20 percent to G, and 60 percent to D, a defunct corporation with no remaining assets. O can argue that it ought to bear only its 20 percent share of responsibility, in which case G is assigned the remaining 80 percent. G can make the identical argument, which would leave O with the remaining 80 percent. Both of these inequitable results are avoided if the contribution court divides up all the liability among the solvent plaintiff and defendant only. In that case, each end up bearing 50 percent of the cleanup costs, including the orphan shares. The burden of the orphan shares is shared among them in proportion to their comparative degrees of responsibility. This result is consistent with the Restatement of Torts section 886A(2), and followed in a number of CERCLA decisions. E.g., Pinal Creek Group v. Newmont Mining Corp., 118 F.3d 1298, 1301-1306 (9th Cir. 1997).

7. **Settlements.** Does this same principle work in cases where the plaintiff has settled with some of the PRPs, or simply has not sued all of them for contribution? Suppose that D was not solvent, but it had settled with O for $100,000. How should the court allocate liability? Should the court continue to limit its allocation just to the parties before the court according to their comparative degrees of responsibility? Is G liable to O for 50 percent of total cleanup costs ($500,000) or only 50 percent of the remaining costs ($450,000)? If the amount of G's settlement is to be subtracted prior to allocation, should O bear responsibility for allowing D to make a "sweetheart" settlement? After all, if O had settled with D for the whole amount

of D's liability, G would only pay $200,000. Would it matter if comparative responsibility had been completely unclear at the time of the settlement? The following decision bears on these questions.

## Akzo Nobel Coatings, Inc. v. Aigner Corp.

197 F.3d 302 (7th Cir. 1999)

EASTERBROOK, Circuit Judge.

[This is an appeal from a contribution action brought by Akzo against a consortium of other PRPs, including Aigner and about 50 others, all generators of hazardous wastes. After hearing arguments on other equitable allocation formulas, the district court settled on dividing liability among the plaintiff and defendants on the basis of the volume of hazardous waste disposed at the site, named Fisher-Calo, with all wastes being weighted equally.]

Having decided that all gallons of solvents shipped to Fisher-Calo count equally, the court then ordered Akzo to pay approximately one third more than equal-weighting implies. Akzo generated approximately 9% by volume of all solvents that Fisher-Calo processed, but the court ordered Akzo to reimburse Aigner for approximately 13% of the costs that Aigner has incurred or will expend in completing the cleanup. Aigner and the other firms in its consortium sent about 71% of the total volume of solvents to the Fisher-Calo site, so Akzo's shipments are approximately 13% of the Akzo + Aigner total; other shipments and shippers were ignored because they are not parties to this suit.

According to the district court, this outcome is required by the Uniform Comparative Fault Act. The district court read §2 and §6 of the UCFA to provide that the responsibility of non-parties must be disregarded, even if they are financially able to pay (indeed, even if they already *have paid*) their share of the cleanup. To take a simple example, suppose Firm A is responsible for 40% of the pollutants, Firm B for 10%, and Firm C for 50%. Firm A agrees with the EPA to perform the cleanup and sues B for contribution. On the district court's reading of the UCFA, B must pay 20% of the total cleanup costs, because B sent 20% of the pollutants that A and B generated jointly. That C is able to pay its 50% share — indeed, that C has *already* paid 50%, and that the outcome of the suit between A and B will leave A bearing only 30% of the total costs — is irrelevant on the district court's (and Aigner's) understanding of the UCFA. A polluter that agreed to clean up a Superfund site could turn a tidy profit if this were so. Suppose that ten firms, A through J, sent 10% each, and that A, having agreed to do the cleanup work, sues B for contribution. Firms A and B are responsible for equal volumes of wastes, so the court would order B to pay 50% of the total cleanup costs. Next A sues C and recovers another 50%. If all of Firms B through J were good for the judgments, then A would recover 450% of its total outlay for pollution control. Even if the court set a cap of 100%, to prevent A from making a profit, the upshot would be that of ten equally responsible polluters, B and C would pay 50% each, and the other eight would pay nothing. That is not a sensible outcome of a process that is supposed to yield an "equitable" allocation of expenses.

Akzo contends that the UCFA requires the district court to undertake a global assessment of responsibility, so that Akzo cannot be required to pay anything until every shipper's share has been determined. That might take years of trial time. Akzo would be happy to skip the trial and chip in 9%, but that would leave Aigner holding the bag if the other shippers were unable to pay their shares. Aigner, for its part, contends that the UCFA requires courts to ignore non-parties just as the district court concluded. None of these approaches is sound. Akzo's would either complicate an already difficult allocation process or saddle firms such as Aigner with excess costs. The Supreme Court has cautioned against the adoption of any contribution rule that would complicate litigation. . . . Aigner's approach would lead to disproportionate liability, with contribution shares turning not on actual responsibility (or on the actual collections of the party performing the cleanup) but on litigation strategy. It is of course possible that both sides are wrong, and that the UCFA requires the inclusion of either pollution shares of, or the actual recoveries from, the additional parties with which Aigner has reached settlements. But we resist all temptation to give the UCFA a close reading—and this despite the fact that Akzo and Aigner agreed in the district court that it supplies the rule of decision. Section 113(f)(1) provides otherwise: "Such claims [for contribution] shall be brought in accordance with this section and the Federal Rules of Civil Procedure, and shall be governed by Federal law." The UCFA is not a federal law, and we are not bound by the parties' agreement to an inapplicable body of legal rules. . . .

Although federal law governs, it is possible and often desirable to borrow a rule from state law, when the alternative is judicial invention. . . . The reference to "Federal law" in §113(f)(1) implies that the law should be nationally uniform, rather than varying according to each state's idea of appropriate contribution. Yet the UCFA would not be an attractive national rule. Unlike the Uniform Commercial Code [upon which the Supreme Court has looked for guidance in other contexts], the UCFA has not been adopted throughout the United States. Only two states (Iowa and Washington) have enacted the UCFA; eleven have adopted the Uniform Contribution Among Tortfeasors Act, which supplies a different approach to contribution; the rest resolve contribution issues through the common law or non-uniform statutes. When one of the litigants has settled with a third party, the UCFA reduces other shares by the percentage of total fault of the person released in the settlement (UCFA §2); this is the source of Akzo's contention that the district court must hold a comprehensive trial to determine every shipper's share of liability. The UCATA, by contrast, reduces liability only by the dollar amount of third-party settlements (UCATA §4). These competing approaches can produce substantial differences in incentives to settle and in the complexity of litigation. . . . To the extent language in §113 speaks to the issue, it prefers the approach of the UCATA: A settlement with the United States or a state "does not discharge any of the other potentially liable persons unless its terms so provide, but it reduces the potential liability of the others by the amount of the settlement." Section 113(f)(2), 42 U.S.C. §9613(f)(2). Adopting the UCFA as a federal rule would undermine that decision.

As a proposition of federal law, the district court's approach has nothing to recommend it, for it produces disparities in liability when third parties have settled. We assume, with the district court, that the proportionate share of the parties is a good starting point. Suppose that Akzo and Aigner were the only two financially sound parties responsible for the pollution. Then the final contribution shares properly would reflect only their relative responsibility, and the 13% share for Akzo would stand. But they are not. Aigner has settled with some other firms that sent solvents to Fisher-Calo and with some past owner-operators of portions of the site. It has claims pending against still more potentially responsible parties. It is very unlikely that 13% is an accurate estimate of Akzo's share among the financially sound firms that will eventually chip in.

[McDermott v. AmClyde, 511 U.S. 202 (1994),] considered at length the proper treatment of settling parties under a body of federal law that includes contribution — the law of admiralty. The Court deemed two approaches "closely matched" (511 U.S. at 217): claim reduction (also known as "proportionate share"), see Restatement (2d) of Torts §886A Comment m(3), and reduction *pro tanto* by the actual amounts recovered in settlements, see *Restatement* §886A Comment m(2). The claim-reduction approach requires the court to determine the responsibility of all firms that have settled, as well as those still involved in the litigation, and to ignore any firms that have not settled. To return to the ten-firm hypothetical above, if Firm A had settled with C and D, then their shares of responsibility (and the corresponding cleanup costs) would be excluded from the calculation. In a contribution suit between A and B, Firm B would be ordered to pay 50% of the costs after excluding C and D, or 40% of the total costs of restoring the site. It would not matter how much A actually had recovered from C and D. By contrast, under the *pro tanto* approach, anything A recovered from C and D in settlement would be deducted from the total cleanup costs, and the court would order A and B to bear the remaining costs equally. In *McDermott* the Court adopted claim reduction, deeming it most compatible with the way related issues in admiralty have been handled.

If as *McDermott* explained the choice between the *pro tanto* approach and claim reduction is a tossup, 511 U.S. at 217, then it is best to match the handling of settlements with the way intersecting principles of law work. For admiralty that meant claim reduction. For CERCLA the most closely related rule of law is §113(f)(2), which reduces third-party claims by the actual cash value of settlements reached with governmental bodies. Extending the *pro tanto* approach of §113(f)(2) to claims under §113(f)(1) enables the district court to avoid what could be a complex and unproductive inquiry into the responsibility of missing parties. The extended litigation between Akzo and Aigner well illustrates the difficulties of fixing responsibility for wastes sent years (if not decades) ago to a firm that did not keep good records and contaminated a wide area. Excluding only actual collections from third parties enables the court to conserve its resources.

On remand, the district court should determine how much Aigner has collected from third parties in settlement, then require Akzo to pay 12.56% of the costs net of those recoveries, rather than of Aigner's total outlay. The total must be reduced not only by collections Aigner has realized to date, but also by future third-party payments. Phrasing Akzo's liability as "12.56% of the cleanup cost net of third-party collections" or some similar formula will avoid any need to reopen the judgment under Fed. R. Civ. P. 60(b)(5) to account for the outcome of litigation now pending or to be filed in the future.

If some of Aigner's settlements provide for percentage-of-cost payments rather than cash payments, then the district court should exclude that percentage from the pool. (To this extent the *pro tanto* approach works like claim reduction, but without the need for the court to determine the responsibility of the settling parties.) Even if, as Akzo believes, Aigner settled for too little with any of these third parties, it is not free to bring its own contribution actions against them. *McDermott* labeled "clearly inferior" the possibility of collecting more from parties who reached private settlements in good faith. 511 U.S. at 211. A potentially responsible party (PRP in CERCLA jargon) that wants to guard against inadequate collections from third parties must either intervene in the suits against them or challenge the bona fides of the settlements immediately after they are reached. Id. at 212-14. . . .

The judgment is vacated to the extent it quantifies Akzo's contribution liability, and the case is remanded for further proceedings consistent with this opinion.

---

## PROBLEM EXERCISE: CERCLA COST ALLOCATION, SETTLEMENTS, AND CONTRIBUTION

Suppose that Scientific Disposal Services owns and operates a dumpsite that has been listed on the National Priorities List for cleanup under the Superfund program. Scientific ceases operations and EPA excavates and removes some drums buried at the site. After performing a remedial investigation/feasibility study (RI/FS), EPA issues a record of decision (ROD) calling for removal of hot spots of soil contaminated with metals, a pump-and-treat system to remediate groundwater contaminated with metals and organic wastes, construction of a slurry wall to prevent further off-site migration of contaminants, and installation of a clay cap over the entire site, including the municipal landfill. EPA estimates that the total cost of remedial action will be $60 million.

**Question One.** If the PRPs believe that EPA has selected a remedy that is too expensive, what legal action can they take to challenge it? See CERCLA §121.

**Question Two.** Assume that you are the attorney for Toxicology Lab, which shipped only a small quantity of arsenic in a metal drum to the site. What would you advise your client concerning potential liability? What should Toxicology do to try to minimize its liability?

**Question Three.** Amalgamated Pesticide has disposed liquid wastes containing dioxin, among other hazardous substances. True Value shipped metallic waste to Scientific with the understanding that they will be recycled, which Scientific did not do. And Toxicology shipped one metal drum. Prior to Scientific, an industrial firm owned the site and disposed of small amounts of their own waste at the site. The PRPs would like to reach agreement among themselves concerning how to allocate the costs of the remedial action. What arguments would each of the PRPs make in an effort to minimize their share of the costs? How should they proceed in an effort to reach agreement on cost allocation? If they fail to agree, what legal options are open to EPA and the PRPs to resolve the cost allocation issues?

**Question Four.** Suppose that a wealthy developer expresses interest in purchasing the site in order to build a baseball stadium on the property after its environmental problems have been remediated. The developer is willing to contribute $2 million toward the cost of remedial action, in return for ironclad assurances that she will incur no further liability. What options are available to the developer?

## E.  DUMPSITE REGULATION, THE DORMANT COMMERCE CLAUSE, AND ENVIRONMENTAL JUSTICE CONCERNS

As federal policy has regulated land disposal with increasing stringency, this option has become much more costly. RCRA's minimum technology standards for subtitle C facilities and the new subtitle D standards for municipal dumps have reduced the supply, and increased the cost, of land disposal facilities. The RCRA land ban has created explicit technology-based standards for treatment of hazardous wastes. By restricting the use of land disposal facilities, the land ban and regulations that raise the costs of land disposal, along with the fear of CERCLA liability, have substantially increased incentives for waste reduction, and recycling. While significant progress is being made in waste reduction, controversies over whose waste is being disposed of where continue to create tensions among states.

As awareness of the environmental hazards of waste disposal has increased, the siting of new waste disposal capacity has become a particularly controversial issue. Low-income and minority communities that often hosted such facilities are now resisting them on environmental justice grounds. States that have become dumping grounds for waste generated in other states have tried a variety of measures to restrict waste imports. These measures frequently have been struck down on constitutional grounds. The sections that follow examine controversies spawned by the search for disposal alternatives and the controversies they have spawned, including Commerce Clause restrictions. These include the impact of environmental justice concerns on facility siting.

### 1.  Commerce Clause Limitations

The production of growing quantities of solid waste, the increasingly stringent regulation of sanitary and hazardous landfills, and the enormous unpopularity of such facilities to the local communities in which they are located have combined to make new land-based waste disposal capacity a scarce commodity. When a particular state receives more out-of-state waste bound for disposal inside the state than it exports, placing limits on the importation of waste presents one possible strategy for that state to mitigate the problems associated with dwindling capacity.

Consider the situation Alabama faced with the hazardous waste facility owned and operated by Chemical Waste Management in Sumter County, near Emelle, Alabama. With a population approximately 70 percent Black, more than one-third of Sumter's residents live below the poverty line, making it one of Alabama's poorest counties. Emelle itself is a small community of fewer than 1,000 residents, 90 percent of whom are Black. Robert D. Bullard, Dumping in Dixie 59-60 (2d ed. 1994). In 1989, 17 percent of the landfilled hazardous waste in the country was shipped to

Emelle, totalling some 488,000 tons, up from 341,000 tons in 1985. These amounts are vastly in excess of the amount of hazardous waste shipped out of the state by Alabama generators.

When Alabama sought to reduce the volume of wastes being received at Chem-Waste's site, it thought first of reducing the flow of out-of-state wastes, thus preserving the facility's capacity to deal with waste generated in Alabama. One of the chief obstacles such a strategy faces is the Commerce Clause, which vests in the Congress the power "to regulate commerce . . . among the several states." In 1978, the Supreme Court decided the following case, dealing with an early New Jersey attempt to limit the importation of municipal solid waste ("garbage") to its landfills.

## Philadelphia v. New Jersey

437 U.S. 617 (1978)

Mr. Justice Stewart delivered the opinion of the Court.

A New Jersey law prohibits the importation of most "solid or liquid waste which originated or was collected outside the territorial limits of the State. . . ." In this case we are required to decide whether this statutory prohibition violates the Commerce Clause of the United States Constitution.

The statutory provision in question is ch. 363 of 1973 N.J. Laws, which took effect in early 1974. In pertinent part it provides:

> No person shall bring into this State any solid or liquid waste which originated or was collected outside the territorial limits of the State, except garbage to be fed to swine in the State of New Jersey, until the commissioner [of the State Department of Environmental Protection] shall determine that such action can be permitted without endangering the public health, safety, and welfare and has promulgated regulations permitting and regulating the treatment and disposal of such waste in this State.

N.J. Stat. Ann. §13:11-10 (West Supp. 1978).

[Private landfill owners in New Jersey, as well as several out-of-state cities, including Philadelphia, all of whom had disposal contracts with New Jersey landfills, sued in state court. The New Jersey Supreme Court upheld the statute as a legitimate health and safety statute that did not economically discriminate against interstate commerce and only slightly burdened it. The United States Supreme Court first remanded the case to the New Jersey court, instructing it to consider whether the New Jersey statute had been preempted by the newly enacted Resources Conservation and Recovery Act of 1976. The New Jersey court found no preemption. The plaintiffs appealed once again. After agreeing that no preemption had occurred, the Supreme Court proceeded to the Commerce Clause issues.]

### II

[First, the Court held that out-of-state wastes are "commerce" within the meaning of the Commerce Clause. Cases upholding quarantine laws that prohibited the importation of, for example, disease-carrying animal carcasses, sometimes state that these items were "not legitimate subjects of trade and commerce." The Court explained that in so stating, such cases were "stating [a] conclusion, not the starting point of [their] reasoning."]

## III

### A

Although the Constitution gives Congress the power to regulate commerce among the States, many subjects of potential federal regulation under that power inevitably escape congressional attention "because of their local character and their number and diversity." South Carolina State Highway Dept. v. Barnwell Bros., Inc., 303 U.S. 177, 185. In the absence of federal legislation, these subjects are open to control by the States so long as they act within the restraints imposed by the Commerce Clause itself. The bounds of these restraints appear nowhere in the words of the Commerce Clause, but have emerged gradually in the decisions of this Court giving effect to its basic purpose. That broad purpose was well expressed by Mr. Justice Jackson in his opinion for the Court in H.P. Hood & Sons, Inc. v. Du Mond, 336 U.S. 525, 537-538:

> This principle that our economic unit is the Nation, which alone has the gamut of powers necessary to control the economy, including the vital power of erecting customs barriers against foreign competition, has as its corollary that the states are not separable economic units. As the Court said in Baldwin v. Seelig, 294 U.S. [511], 527, "what is ultimate is the principle that one state in its dealings with another may not place itself in a position of economic isolation."

The opinions of the Court through the years have reflected an alertness to the evils of "economic isolation" and protectionism, while at the same time recognizing that incidental burdens on interstate commerce may be unavoidable when a State legislates to safeguard the health and safety of its people. Thus, where simple economic protectionism is effected by state legislation, a virtually per se rule of invalidity has been erected. The clearest example of such legislation is a law that overtly blocks the flow of interstate commerce at a State's borders. Cf. Welton v. Missouri, 91 U.S. 275. But where other legislative objectives are credibly advanced and there is no patent discrimination against interstate trade, the Court has adopted a much more flexible approach, the general contours of which were outlined in Pike v. Bruce Church, Inc., 397 U.S. 137, 142:

> Where the statute regulates evenhandedly to effectuate a legitimate local public interest, and its effects on interstate commerce are only incidental, it will be upheld unless the burden imposed on such commerce is clearly excessive in relation to the putative local benefits. . . . If a legitimate local purpose is found, then the question becomes one of degree. And the extent of the burden that will be tolerated will of course depend on the nature of the local interest involved, and on whether it could be promoted as well with a lesser impact on interstate activities.

The crucial inquiry, therefore, must be directed to determining whether ch. 363 is basically a protectionist measure, or whether it can fairly be viewed as a law directed to legitimate local concerns, with effects upon interstate commerce that are only incidental.

### B

The purpose of ch. 363 is set out in the statute itself as follows:

> The Legislature finds and determines that . . . the volume of solid and liquid waste continues to rapidly increase, that the treatment and disposal of these wastes continues to pose an even greater threat to the quality of the environment of New Jersey, that the available and appropriate landfill sites within the State are being diminished, that the environment continues to be threatened by the treatment and disposal of waste which originated or was collected outside the State, and that the public health, safety, and welfare require that the treatment and disposal within this State of all wastes generated outside of the State be prohibited.

The New Jersey Supreme Court accepted this statement of the state legislature's purpose. The state court additionally found that New Jersey's existing landfill sites will be exhausted within a few years; that to go on using these sites or to develop new ones will take a heavy environmental toll, both from pollution and from loss of scarce open lands; that new techniques to divert waste from landfills to other methods of disposal and resource recovery processes are under development, but that these changes will require time; and finally, that "the extension of the lifespan of existing landfills, resulting from the exclusion of out-of-state waste, may be of crucial importance in preventing further virgin wetlands or other undeveloped lands from being devoted to landfill purposes." Based on these findings, the court concluded that ch. 363 was designed to protect, not the State's economy, but its environment, and that its substantial benefits outweigh its "slight" burden on interstate commerce.

The appellants strenuously contend that ch. 363, "while outwardly cloaked 'in the currently fashionable garb of environmental protection,' . . . is actually no more than a legislative effort to suppress competition and stabilize the cost of solid waste disposal for New Jersey residents. . . ." They cite passages of legislative history suggesting that the problem addressed by ch. 363 is primarily financial: Stemming the flow of out-of-state waste into certain landfill sites will extend their lives, thus delaying the day when New Jersey cities must transport their waste to more distant and expensive sites.

The appellees, on the other hand, deny that ch. 363 was motivated by financial concerns or economic protectionism. In the words of their brief, "[no] New Jersey commercial interests stand to gain advantage over competitors from outside the state as a result of the ban on dumping out-of-state waste." Noting that New Jersey landfill operators are among the plaintiffs, the appellee's brief argues that "[the] complaint is not that New Jersey has forged an economic preference for its own commercial interests, but rather that it has denied a small group of its entrepreneurs an economic opportunity to traffic in waste in order to protect the health, safety, and welfare of the citizenry at large."

This dispute about ultimate legislative purpose need not be resolved, because its resolution would not be relevant to the constitutional issue to be decided in this case. Contrary to the evident assumption of the state court and the parties, the evil of protectionism can reside in legislative means as well as legislative ends. Thus, it does not matter whether the ultimate aim of ch. 363 is to reduce the waste disposal costs of New Jersey residents or to save remaining open lands from pollution, for we assume New Jersey has every right to protect its residents' pocketbooks as well as their environment. And it may be assumed as well that New Jersey may pursue those ends by slowing the flow of all waste into the State's remaining landfills, even though interstate commerce may incidentally be affected. But whatever New Jersey's ultimate purpose, it may not be accomplished by discriminating against articles of commerce coming from outside the State unless there is some reason, apart from their origin, to treat them differently. Both on its face and in its plain effect, ch. 363 violates this principle of nondiscrimination.

The Court has consistently found parochial legislation of this kind to be constitutionally invalid, whether the ultimate aim of the legislation was to assure a steady supply of milk by erecting barriers to allegedly ruinous outside competition, Baldwin v. G.A.F. Seelig, Inc., 294 U.S., at 522-524; to create jobs by keeping industry within the State, Foster-Fountain Packing Co. v. Haydel, 278 U.S. 1, 10; or to preserve the State's financial resources from depletion by fencing out indigent immigrants, Edwards v. California, 314 U.S. 160, 173-174. In each of these cases, a presumably legitimate goal was sought to be achieved by the illegitimate means of isolating the State from the national economy.

Also relevant here are the Court's decisions holding that a State may not accord its own inhabitants a preferred right of access over consumers in other States to natural resources located within its borders. West v. Kansas Natural Gas Co., 221 U.S. 229; Pennsylvania v. West Virginia, 262 U.S. 553. These cases stand for the basic principle that a "State is without power to prevent privately owned articles of trade from being shipped and sold in interstate commerce on the ground that they are required to satisfy local demands or because they are needed by the people of the State." Foster-Fountain Packing Co. v. Haydel, supra, at 10.

The New Jersey law at issue in this case falls squarely within the area that the Commerce Clause puts off limits to state regulation. On its face, it imposes on out-of-state commercial interests the full burden of conserving the State's remaining landfill space. It is true that in our previous cases the scarce natural resource was itself the article of commerce, whereas here the scarce resource and the article of commerce are distinct. But that difference is without consequence. In both instances, the State has overtly moved to slow or freeze the flow of commerce for protectionist reasons. It does not matter that the State has shut the article of commerce inside the State in one case and outside the State in the other. What is crucial is the attempt by one State to isolate itself from a problem common to many by erecting a barrier against the movement of interstate trade. The appellees argue that not all laws which facially discriminate against out-of-state commerce are forbidden protectionist regulations. In particular, they point to quarantine laws, which this Court has repeatedly upheld even though they appear to single out interstate commerce for special treatment. In the appellees' view, ch. 363 is analogous to such health-protective measures, since it reduces the exposure of New Jersey residents to the allegedly harmful effects of landfill sites.

It is true that certain quarantine laws have not been considered forbidden protectionist measures, even though they were directed against out-of-state commerce. But those quarantine laws banned the importation of articles such as diseased livestock that required destruction as soon as possible because their very movement risked contagion and other evils. Those laws thus did not discriminate against interstate commerce as such, but simply prevented traffic in noxious articles, whatever their origin.

The New Jersey statute is not such a quarantine law. There has been no claim here that the very movement of waste into or through New Jersey endangers health, or that waste must be disposed of as soon and as close to its point of generation as possible. The harms caused by waste are said to arise after its disposal in landfill sites, and at that point, as New Jersey concedes, there is no basis to distinguish out-of-state waste from domestic waste. If one is inherently harmful, so is the other. Yet New Jersey has banned the former while leaving its landfill sites open to the latter. The New Jersey law blocks the importation of waste in an obvious effort to saddle those outside the State with the entire burden of slowing the flow of refuse into New Jersey's remaining landfill sites. That legislative effort is clearly impermissible under the Commerce Clause of the Constitution.

Today, cities in Pennsylvania and New York find it expedient or necessary to send their waste into New Jersey for disposal, and New Jersey claims the right to close its borders to such traffic. Tomorrow, cities in New Jersey may find it expedient or necessary to send their waste into Pennsylvania or New York for disposal, and those States might then claim the right to close their borders. The Commerce Clause will protect New Jersey in the future, just as it protects her neighbors now, from efforts by one State to isolate itself in the stream of interstate commerce from a problem shared by all. The judgment is Reversed.

MR. JUSTICE REHNQUIST, with whom THE CHIEF JUSTICE joins, dissenting.

The question presented in this case is whether New Jersey must . . . continue to receive and dispose of solid waste from neighboring States, even though these will inexorably increase the health problems discussed above. The Court answers this question in the affirmative. New Jersey must either prohibit *all* landfill operations, leaving itself to cast about for a presently nonexistent solution to the serious problem of disposing of the waste generated within its own borders, or it must accept waste from every portion of the United States, thereby multiplying the health and safety problems which would result if it dealt only with such wastes generated within the State. Because past precedents establish that the Commerce Clause does not present appellees with such a Hobson's choice, I dissent.

The Court recognizes that States can prohibit the importation of items "which, on account of their existing condition, would bring in and spread disease, pestilence, and death, such as rags or other substances infected with the germs of yellow fever or the virus of small-pox, or cattle or meat or other provisions that are diseased or decayed, or otherwise, from their condition and quality, unfit for human use or consumption." Bowman v. Chicago & Northwestern R. Co., 125 U.S. 465, 489 (1888). As the Court points out, such "quarantine laws have not been considered forbidden protectionist measures, *even though they were directed against out-of-state commerce.*"

In my opinion, these cases are dispositive of the present one. Under them, New Jersey may require germ-infected rags or diseased meat to be disposed of as best as possible within the State, but at the same time prohibit the *importation* of such items for disposal at the facilities that are set up within New Jersey for disposal of such material generated within the State. The physical fact of life that New Jersey must somehow dispose of its own noxious items does not mean that it must serve as a depository for those of every other State. Similarly, New Jersey should be free under our past precedents to prohibit the importation of solid waste because of the health and safety problems that such waste poses to its citizens. The fact that New Jersey continues to, and indeed must continue to, dispose of its own solid waste does not mean that New Jersey may not prohibit the importation of even more solid waste into the State. I simply see no way to distinguish solid waste, on the record of this case, from germ-infected rags, diseased meat, and other noxious items.

The Court's effort to distinguish these prior cases is unconvincing. It first asserts that the quarantine laws which have previously been upheld "banned the importation of articles such as diseased livestock that required destruction as soon as possible because their very movement risked contagion and other evils." According to the Court, the New Jersey law is distinguishable from these other laws, and invalid, because the concern of New Jersey is not with the *movement* of solid waste but with the present inability to safely *dispose* of it once it reaches its destination. But I think it far from clear that the State's law has as limited a focus as the Court imputes to it: Solid waste which is a health hazard when it reaches its destination may in all likelihood be an equally great health hazard in transit.

Even if the Court is correct in its characterization of New Jersey's concerns, I do not see why a State may ban the importation of items whose movement risks contagion, but cannot ban the importation of items which, although they may be transported into the State without undue hazard, will then simply pile up in an ever increasing danger to the public's health and safety. The Commerce Clause was not drawn with a view to having the validity of state laws turn on such pointless distinctions.

Second, the Court implies that the challenged laws must be invalidated because New Jersey has left its landfills open to domestic waste. But, as the Court notes, this Court has repeatedly upheld quarantine laws "even though they appear to single out interstate commerce for special treatment." The fact that New Jersey has left its landfill sites open for domestic waste does not, of course, mean that solid waste is not innately harmful. Nor does it mean that New Jersey prohibits importation of solid waste for reasons other than the health and safety of its population. New Jersey must out of sheer necessity treat and dispose of its solid waste in some fashion, just as it must treat New Jersey cattle suffering from hoof-and-mouth disease. It does not follow that New Jersey must, under the Commerce Clause, accept solid waste or diseased cattle from outside its borders and thereby exacerbate its problems.

## NOTES AND QUESTIONS

1. **Some Commerce Clause Background.** Efforts to preserve local access to natural resources have faced constitutional obstacles in the past. In Pennsylvania v. West Virginia, 262 U.S. 553 (1923), the Supreme Court struck down a West

Virginia statute requiring producers of natural gas to give West Virginia residents preference over nonresident consumers in the purchase of natural gas. The West Virginia legislature had wanted to insulate state residents in the case of gas shortages and believed this was permissible because the gas originated in West Virginia. However, the Court stated that "[n]atural gas is a lawful article of commerce, and its transmission from one state to another for sale and consumption in the latter is interstate commerce." Id. at 596. West Virginia's stated interest in conserving natural resources could not justify the measure because "the purpose of its conservation is in a sense commercial — the business welfare of the State, as coal might be, or timber. . . . If the States have such power a singular situation might result. Pennsylvania might keep its coal, the Northwest its timber, the mining states their minerals. . . . Commerce will be halted at state lines." Id. at 599. In *West Virginia* and similar cases, the states' ostensible purpose was the conservation of a scarce resource. Should landfill capacity be viewed as a resource analogous to natural gas reserves?

In a case that some have thought hard to square with the recent Commerce Clause decisions, the Supreme Court has held that Montana could charge an out-of-state license fee for hunting Montana elk that was 25 times larger than the fee charged in-staters. Baldwin v. Fish & Game Comm'n, 436 U.S. 371 (1978). *Baldwin* was decided under the Privileges and Immunities Clause, not the Commerce Clause. The Court recognized that states were not "obliged to share those things they held in trust for their own people." Id. at 384. Moreover, such policies "manifest the State's special interest in regulating and preserving wildlife for the benefit of its citizens." Id. at 392. However, in a concurring opinion, Chief Justice Burger limited the majority holding by stating that if the wildlife became involved in interstate commerce, then access cannot be restricted in a manner that violates the Commerce Clause. Professor Tribe has the following to say about *Baldwin*:

> There . . . appear to be some goods and services that a state's citizens, having created or preserved for themselves, are entitled to keep for themselves. Thus Montana's carefully-tended elk herds are akin to public libraries, public schools, state universities, state-supported hospitals, and public welfare programs — things that the Court has suggested that a state may reserve for the use or enjoyment of its citizens. The Court implied in *Baldwin* that it would approve even a total exclusion of nonresident hunters upon a showing by the state that any additional hunting opportunities beyond those Montana chose to reserve to its citizens would endanger the elk population to the point of extinction. [L. Tribe, American Constitutional Law 539 (2d ed. 1988).]

A year after *Baldwin*, the Court decided Hughes v. Oklahoma, 441 U.S. 322 (1979). At issue was an Oklahoma statute banning the export of minnows caught in state waters. The state defended the ban as a conservation measure. The Court struck down the statute in a 7-2 decision. Once wild animals or other natural resources became objects in interstate commerce, said the Court, state laws concerning them had to be judged by the same Commerce Clause standards that are applicable to other items of commerce. While recognizing that conservation was a legitimate state interest, the majority held that the state had not shown its ban to be the least discriminatory means of furthering that interest. "Far from choosing the least discriminatory alternative, Oklahoma has chosen to 'conserve' its minnows in the way that most overtly discriminates against interstate commerce." 441 U.S. at 337-338.

In another line of decisions, the Supreme Court has taken a considerably more permissive view of efforts by states to ensure that state-created resources be reserved for use by their citizens. For example, in Reeves v. Stake, 447 U.S. 429 (1980), the Supreme Court upheld a South Dakota statute reserving all cement produced by a state-owned cement plant for use by state residents, in the event orders exceeded supply. According to the Court, "[c]ement is not a natural resource, like coal, timber, wild game, or minerals. . . . It is the end product of a complex process whereby a costly physical plant and human labor act on raw materials. South Dakota has not sought to limit access to the State's limestone or other materials used to make cement." Id. at 443-444. The Court acknowledged that South Dakota's policies "reflect the essential and patently unobjectionable purpose of state government—to serve the citizens of the State." Id. at 442.

2. **Back to Alabama.** In 1989, Alabama enacted a ban on the importation of hazardous wastes from any state that did not itself have a commercial hazardous waste facility. It attempted to distinguish its hazardous waste ban from New Jersey's garbage ban on the ground that hazardous waste posed greater health hazards. The Eleventh Circuit found this no basis for permitting a facially discriminatory state statute, and it declared Alabama's ban unconstitutional. National Solid Waste Management Association v. Alabama, 910 F.2d 713 (11th Cir. 1990).

In April 1990, the Alabama legislature adopted a different strategy. It enacted a law that (a) imposed a "base fee" of $25.60 per ton on all hazardous wastes disposed of in the state, (b) imposed an "additional fee" of $72.00 per ton on all out-of-state hazardous waste disposed of in the state, and (c) placed a cap on the amount of hazardous waste that could be disposed of in any Alabama facility during any one-year period.

ChemWaste challenged this new statute, which was struck down by the Supreme Court. Chemical Waste Management, Inc. v. Hunt, 504 U.S. 334 (1992). Holding that a facially discriminatory statute faces "the strictest scrutiny of any purported legitimate local purpose and of the absence of discriminatory alternatives," the Court found that "ultimately, the State's concern focuses on the volume of the waste entering the Emelle facility," and that there were other, less discriminatory means of reducing that volume. 504 U.S. at 344-345. As he did in *Philadelphia v. New Jersey*, Chief Justice Rehnquist dissented. Emphasizing the strength of Alabama's legitimate interest in a "safe and attractive environment," the Chief Justice saw the case as one in which the state was using its taxing authority to prevent the export of a valuable commodity—the "safe environment that attends appropriate disposal of hazardous wastes"—out of state. Especially when this commodity is a "public good that the state has helped to produce," the Chief Justice concluded that the Alabama statute was constitutionally permissible. 504 U.S. at 349.

3. **Oregon.** The *Chemical Waste* majority suggested that a differential fee or tax structure might be permissible under the Commerce Clause if the state had a basis for concluding that out-of-state waste imposed differential burdens on the state receiving the waste. The Court suggested "a generally applicable per-ton additional

fee on all hazardous waste disposed of within Alabama, or a per-mile tax on all vehicles transporting hazardous waste across Alabama roads, or an evenhanded cap on the total tonnage landfilled at Emelle, which would curtail volume from all sources." 504 U.S. at 345.

Even as the *Chemical Waste* litigation was proceeding, Oregon was pursuing this avenue. In 1989, it enacted legislation instructing its Environmental Quality Commission to set a surcharge "based on the costs to the State of Oregon and its political subdivisions of disposing of solid waste generated out-of-state which are not otherwise paid for" under specified statutes. After rulemaking the Commission set this figure at $2.25 per ton, compared to the $0.85 per ton fee the legislation charged to in-state waste haulers. Out-of-state haulers challenged this arrangement on Commerce Clause grounds. The Supreme Court analyzed the case using the "virtually per se rule of invalidity" of *Philadelphia v. New Jersey*, because the statute by its express terms treated in- and out-of-state waste differently.

Oregon did not claim that its costs of disposal differed between the two kinds of waste, nor that there were any health concerns unique to out-of-state waste. They justified the surcharge as means of recouping from out-of-state haulers an amount approximately equal to the costs of disposal that Oregon and its citizens pay, through income taxes and other means, that are not reflected in the $0.85 per ton fee. The Court, per Justice Thomas, held that such a "compensating tax" could only be justified if Oregon could point to other charges assessed against in-state haulers for which the surcharge was compensating, which it could not. It rejected the notion that Oregon could recoup the subsidies it was in effect providing to waste disposal, because income taxes and the disposal surcharge were taxing events that were not equivalent, and the Court refused to enter the "morass" of weighing comparative tax burdens. Chief Justice Rehnquist, joined by Justice Blackmun, dissented. He argued that because Oregon was imposing restrictions on its own citizens' generation of solid waste (through various state and local programs), thereby trying to preserve a scarce state recourse—landfill capacity—"it is not discriminating against interstate commerce by preventing the uncontrolled transfer of out-of-state solid waste into the State." Oregon Waste Systems, Inc. v. Department of Envtl. Quality, 511 U.S. 93 (1994).

4. **Michigan.** Michigan adopted a state law requiring each county to formulate a waste management plan that demonstrated that it had adequately arranged for disposal of solid wastes generated in the county over the next 20 years. The law also authorized a county to refuse to dispose of wastes from outside the county, ostensibly as a means for the county to preserve its own capacity to demonstrate adequate arrangements for its own wastes. The Supreme Court held that the fact that such a county ban would discriminate against wastes from elsewhere in Michigan as well as from outside the state did not save the law from invalidity under the Commerce Clause. Chief Justice Rehnquist dissented, this time joined by Justice Blackmun. Fort Gratiot Sanitary Landfill, Inc. v. Michigan Dep't of Natural Resources, 504 U.S. 353 (1992).

5. **Are There Other State Options?** In light of *Fort Gratiot, Chemical Waste Management,* and *Oregon Waste Systems,* what, if anything, can a state do to discourage importation of hazardous or solid waste that will not violate the dormant Commerce Clause? See, e.g., Government Suppliers Consolidating Servs. v. Bayh, 753 F. Supp. 769 (D.

Ind. 1990) (striking down a two-tier fee system, on a rationale similar to *Chemical Waste Management's*); BFI Medical Waste Sys. v. Whatcom County, 983 F.2d 911 (9th Cir. 1993) (citing *Fort Gratiot* in striking down a law authorizing a county option system similar to that at issue in *Fort Gratiot*). See also In re Southeast Arkansas Landfill, Inc. v. Arkansas, 981 F.2d 372 (8th Cir. 1992) (an Arkansas law limiting the amount of solid waste generated outside regional planning districts that landfills within the district could accept violates the Commerce Clause); Chemical Waste Management v. Templet, 967 F.2d 1058 (5th Cir. 1992) (prohibition of import or disposal of hazardous waste originating in foreign nations violates dormant Commerce Clause). But see Medical Waste Assocs. Ltd. v. Mayor and City Council of Baltimore, 966 F.2d 148 (4th Cir. 1992) (city ordinance requiring medical waste incinerator to burn only wastes generated within city does not violate Commerce Clause).

     6. **Recycling Programs.** Wisconsin sought to promote recycling by enacting a statute prohibiting the land disposal of 11 specific materials that the state deemed to be recyclable. The only such waste excepted from the law's prohibition was waste generated in communities with "an effective recycling program" as defined by the statute. While a federal district court upheld the law as facially nondiscriminatory, the Seventh Circuit reversed. The court concluded that the law discriminated against interstate commerce by attempting to "control[] the conduct of those engaged in commerce occurring wholly outside the State of Wisconsin. . . ." National Solid Wastes Mgmt. Ass'n v. Meyer, 63 F.3d 652, 658 (7th Cir. 1995). The court explained that the law's basic infirmity was that it required all persons in out-of-state communities to adhere to "effective recycling programs" whether or not they shipped their waste to Wisconsin in order for any members of their community to have access to Wisconsin landfills. The court indicated that Wisconsin could have pursued less discriminatory alternatives by applying the law only to persons who dispose of waste in Wisconsin or by requiring that all waste disposed in the state be processed first in a materials recovery facility that separates the 11 listed materials. Id. at 662.

     7. **Nondiscriminatory Measures.** Could a state avoid the problem of facially discriminatory legislation by simply banning all waste disposal within the boundaries of the state regardless of where the waste was generated? How would such a measure differ from the legislation struck down in Fort Gratiot Sanitary Landfill, Inc. v. Michigan Dep't of Natural Resources, 504 U.S. 353 (1992), discussed in note 4 above? Such a law effectively would require that all waste generated in the state be exported. Could it survive constitutional scrutiny under the Commerce Clause?

     8. **Other Nondiscriminatory Measures.** Measures that the Court determines regulate "even-handedly" are still subject to review, but under the more lenient *Pike v. Bruce Church* test. Avoiding the "virtually per se rule of invalidity" requires more than a statute that is nondiscriminatory on its face. For example, the *Fort Gratiot* statute did not expressly single out out-of-state waste and still was held to be discriminatory and subject to the tougher standard. As states continue to pursue ways of addressing their dwindling landfill problems, they can enact statutes that require intensive factual review to determine which test applies and whether the provisions are constitutional.

     9. **Discriminatory Purpose.** Even facially nondiscriminatory measures regulating waste disposal may be constitutionally suspect under the dormant Commerce Clause if there is evidence that they were enacted expressly to disadvantage waste

originating out of state. In March and April 1999, the Virginia General Assembly enacted legislation to cap the amount of municipal solid waste (MSW) that Virginia landfills can accept and to restrict the use of barges and trucks to transport such waste. The legislation was adopted after then-Governor James Gilmore declared that "the home state of Washington, Jefferson, and Madison has no intention o[f] becoming New York's dumping ground." In Waste Management Holdings, Inc. v. Gilmore, 252 F.3d 316 (4th Cir. 2001), the Fourth Circuit found unmistakable evidence that the purpose of the legislation was "to reduce the flow of MSW generated outside Virginia into Virginia for disposal." While the court found that "MSW generated outside Virginia poses health and safety risks not posed by MSW generated inside Virginia," it concluded that most of the Virginia regulations could not be justified as the least discriminatory means for achieving the state's health and safety goals.

10. **Flow Control Laws.** Some states have sought to address the dwindling supply of landfill capacity, as well as the environmental degradation caused by such landfills, through strategies that seek to minimize the amount of waste that needs to be landfilled. Recyclable materials can be separated from the waste stream through curbside recycling, separation at a centralized facility, or a combination of these approaches. Much waste can also be incinerated. Incineration brings its own environmental concerns, but some localities have used it as a least-worst approach to waste disposal. Central waste sorting facilities and waste-to-energy facilities represent costly capital investments. To ensure their viability local governments have sought ways to ensure that the facilities will receive a reliable flow of waste material once they have been constructed. This has led to the development of a number of "flow control" laws and regulations throughout the United States.

New Jersey, for example, has been one of the leaders in flow control waste management systems. In something of a reversal from its efforts initially to restrict the importation of out-of-state waste, which led to the decision in *Philadelphia v. New Jersey*, in the 1990s New Jersey built a statewide system of waste-to-energy incinerators, associated landfills, and recycling centers that it underwrote with some $1.7 billion in government bonds. It also enacted a set of rules to assure the operators of these facilities that they would have minimum flows of waste material—in effect, adopting a strategy of keeping much of its waste in the state. Nationwide, it has been estimated that there is some $20 billion in bond debt for similar waste facilities, as well as a number of accompanying flow control ordinances or laws to provide raw materials to those facilities.

The constitutionality of these strategies was addressed by the Supreme Court in the following decision.

## C & A Carbone, Inc. v. Town of Clarkstown

511 U.S. 383 (1994)

JUSTICE KENNEDY delivered the opinion of the Court.

. . . The town of Clarkstown, New York, lies in the lower Hudson River valley, just upstream from the Tappan Zee Bridge and by highway minutes from New Jersey. Within the town limits are the village of Nyack and the hamlet of West Nyack.

In August 1989, Clarkstown entered into a consent decree with the New York State Department of Environmental Conservation. The town agreed to close its landfill located on Route 303 in West Nyack and build a new solid waste transfer station on the same site. The station would receive bulk solid waste and separate recyclable from nonrecyclable items. Recyclable waste would be baled for shipment to a recycling facility; nonrecyclable waste, to a suitable landfill or incinerator.

The cost of building the transfer station was estimated at $1.4 million. A local private contractor agreed to construct the facility and operate it for five years, after which the town would buy it for one dollar. During those five years, the town guaranteed a minimum waste flow of 120,000 tons per year, for which the contractor could charge the hauler a so-called tipping fee of $81 per ton. If the station received less than 120,000 tons in a year, the town promised to make up the tipping fee deficit. The object of this arrangement was to amortize the cost of the transfer station: The town would finance its new facility with the income generated by the tipping fees.

The problem, of course, was how to meet the yearly guarantee. This difficulty was compounded by the fact that the tipping fee of $81 per ton exceeded the disposal cost of unsorted solid waste on the private market. The solution the town adopted was the flow control ordinance here in question, Local Laws 1990, No. 9 of the Town of Clarkstown. The ordinance requires all nonhazardous solid waste within the town to be deposited at the Route 303 transfer station. Id. §3.C (waste generated within the town), §5.A (waste generated outside and brought in). Noncompliance is punishable by as much as a $1,000 fine and up to 15 days in jail. §7.

The petitioners in this case are C & A Carbone, Inc., a company engaged in the processing of solid waste, and various related companies or persons, all of whom we designate Carbone. Carbone operates a recycling center in Clarkstown, where it receives bulk solid waste, sorts and bales it, and then ships it to other processing facilities—much as occurs at the town's new transfer station. While the flow control ordinance permits recyclers like Carbone to continue receiving solid waste, §3.C, it requires them to bring the nonrecyclable residue from that waste to the Route 303 station. It thus forbids Carbone to ship the nonrecyclable waste itself, and it requires Carbone to pay a tipping fee on trash that Carbone has already sorted. . . .

At the outset we confirm that the flow control ordinance does regulate interstate commerce, despite the town's position to the contrary. The town says that its ordinance reaches only waste within its jurisdiction and is in practical effect a quarantine: It prevents garbage from entering the stream of interstate commerce until it is made safe. This reasoning is premised, however, on an outdated and mistaken concept of what constitutes interstate commerce.

While the immediate effect of the ordinance is to direct local transport of solid waste to a designated site within the local jurisdiction, its economic effects are interstate in reach. The Carbone facility in Clarkstown receives and processes waste from places other than Clarkstown, including from out of State. By requiring Carbone to send the nonrecyclable portion of this waste to the Route 303 transfer station at an additional cost, the flow control ordinance drives up the cost for out-of-state interests to dispose of their solid waste. Furthermore, even as to waste originating in Clarkstown, the ordinance prevents everyone except the favored local operator from performing the initial processing step. The ordinance thus deprives out-of-state businesses of access to a local market. These economic effects are more than enough to bring the Clarkstown ordinance within the purview of the Commerce Clause. It is well settled that actions are within the domain of the Commerce Clause if they burden interstate commerce or impede its free flow.

The real question is whether the flow control ordinance is valid despite its undoubted effect on interstate commerce. For this inquiry, our case law yields two lines of analysis: first, whether the ordinance discriminates against interstate commerce, *Philadelphia*, 437 U.S. at 624; and second, whether the ordinance imposes a burden on interstate commerce that is "clearly excessive in relation to the putative local benefits," Pike v. Bruce Church, Inc., 397 U.S. 137, 142 (1970). As we find that the ordinance discriminates against interstate commerce, we need not resort to the *Pike* test. . . .

The central rationale for the rule against discrimination is to prohibit state or municipal laws whose object is local economic protectionism, laws that would excite those jealousies and retaliatory measures the Constitution was designed to prevent. We have interpreted the Commerce Clause to invalidate local laws that impose commercial barriers or discriminate against an article of commerce by reason of its origin or destination out of State. See, e.g., *Philadelphia*, supra (striking down New Jersey statute that prohibited the import of solid waste); Hughes v. Oklahoma, 441 U.S. 322 (1979) (striking down Oklahoma law that prohibited the export of natural minnows).

Clarkstown protests that its ordinance does not discriminate because it does not differentiate solid waste on the basis of its geographic origin. All solid waste, regardless of origin, must be processed at the designated transfer station before it leaves the town. Unlike the statute in *Philadelphia*, says the town, the ordinance erects no barrier to the import or export of any solid waste but requires only that the waste be channeled through the designated facility.

Our initial discussion of the effects of the ordinance on interstate commerce goes far toward refuting the town's contention that there is no discrimination in its regulatory scheme. The town's own arguments go the rest of the way. As the town itself points out, what makes garbage a profitable business is not its own worth but the fact that its possessor must pay to get rid of it. In other words, the article of commerce is not so much the solid waste itself, but rather the service of processing and disposing of it.

With respect to this stream of commerce, the flow control ordinance discriminates, for it allows only the favored operator to process waste that is within the limits of the town. The ordinance is no less discriminatory because in-state or in-town processors are also covered by the prohibition. In Dean Milk Co. v. Madison, 340 U.S. 349 (1951), we struck down a city ordinance that required all milk sold in the city to be pasteurized within five miles of the city lines. We found it "immaterial that Wisconsin milk from outside the Madison area is subjected to the same proscription as that moving in interstate commerce." Id., at 354, n.4. . . .

In this light, the flow control ordinance is just one more instance of local processing requirements that we long have held invalid. . . . The essential vice in laws of this sort is that they bar the import of the processing service. Out-of-state meat inspectors, or shrimp hullers, or milk pasteurizers, are deprived of access to local demand for their services. Put another way, the offending local laws hoard a local resource — be it meat, shrimp, or milk — for the benefit of local businesses that treat it.

The flow control ordinance has the same design and effect. It hoards solid waste, and the demand to get rid of it, for the benefit of the preferred processing facility. The only conceivable distinction from the cases cited above is that the flow control ordinance favors a single local proprietor. But this difference just makes the protectionist effect of the ordinance more acute. In *Dean Milk*, the local processing requirement at least permitted pasteurizers within five miles of the city to compete. An out-of-state pasteurizer who wanted access to that market might have built a pasteurizing facility within the radius. The flow control ordinance at issue here squelches competition in the waste-processing service altogether, leaving no room for investment from outside.

Discrimination against interstate commerce in favor of local business or investment is *per se* invalid, save in a narrow class of cases in which the municipality can demonstrate, under rigorous scrutiny, that it has no other means to advance a legitimate local interest. Maine v. Taylor, 477 U.S. 131 (1986) (upholding Maine's ban on the import of baitfish because Maine had no other way to prevent the spread of parasites and the adulteration of its native fish species). A number of *amici* contend that the flow control ordinance fits into this narrow class. They suggest that as landfill space diminishes and environmental cleanup costs escalate, measures like flow control become necessary to ensure the safe handling and proper treatment of solid waste.

The teaching of our cases is that these arguments must be rejected absent the clearest showing that the unobstructed flow of interstate commerce itself is unable to solve the local problem. The Commerce Clause presumes a national market free from local legislation that discriminates in favor of local interests. Here Clarkstown has any number of nondiscriminatory alternatives for addressing the health and environmental problems alleged to justify the ordinance in question. The most obvious would be uniform safety regulations enacted without the object to discriminate. These regulations would ensure that competitors like Carbone do not underprice the market by cutting corners on environmental safety.

Nor may Clarkstown justify the flow control ordinance as a way to steer solid waste away from out-of-town disposal sites that it might deem harmful to the environment. To do so would extend the town's police power beyond its jurisdictional bounds. States and localities may not attach restrictions to exports or imports in order to control commerce in other states. Baldwin v. G.A.F. Seelig, Inc., 294 U.S. 511 (1935) (striking down New York law that prohibited the sale of milk unless the price paid to the original milk producer equalled the minimum required by New York).

The flow control ordinance does serve a central purpose that a nonprotectionist regulation would not: It ensures that the town-sponsored facility will be profitable, so that the local contractor can build it and Clarkstown can buy it back at nominal cost in five years. In other words, as the most candid of *amici* and even Clarkstown admit, the flow control ordinance is a financing measure. By itself, of course, revenue generation is not a local interest that can justify discrimination against interstate commerce. Otherwise States could impose discriminatory taxes against solid waste originating outside the State. . . .

Clarkstown maintains that special financing is necessary to ensure the long-term survival of the designated facility. If so, the town may subsidize the facility through general taxes or municipal bonds. But having elected to use the open market to earn revenues for its project, the town may not employ discriminatory regulation to give that project an advantage over rival businesses from out of State. . . .

State and local governments may not use their regulatory power to favor local enterprise by prohibiting patronage of out-of-state competitors or their facilities. We reverse the judgment and remand the case for proceedings not inconsistent with this decision.

It is so ordered.

[In an opinion concurring in the judgment, Justice O'Connor expressed the view that the town's ordinance was "unconstitutional not because of facial or effective discrimination against interstate commerce, but rather because it imposes an excessive burden on interstate commerce."]

JUSTICE SOUTER, with whom THE CHIEF JUSTICE and JUSTICE BLACKMUN join, dissenting.

The majority may invoke "well-settled principles of our Commerce Clause jurisprudence," but it does so to strike down an ordinance unlike anything this Court has ever invalidated. Previous cases have held that the "negative" or "dormant" aspect of the Commerce Clause renders state or local legislation unconstitutional when it discriminates against out-of-state or out-of-town businesses such as those that pasteurize milk, hull shrimp, or mill lumber, and the majority relies on these cases because of what they have in common with this one: out-of-state processors are excluded from the local market (here, from the market for trash processing services). What the majority ignores, however, are the differences between our local processing cases and this one: the exclusion worked by Clarkstown's Local Law 9 bestows no benefit on a class of local private actors, but instead directly aids the government in satisfying a traditional governmental responsibility. The law does not differentiate between all local and all out-of-town providers of a service, but instead between the one entity responsible for ensuring that the job gets done and all other enterprises, regardless of their location. The ordinance thus falls outside that class of tariff or protectionist measures that the Commerce Clause has traditionally been thought to bar States from enacting against each other, and when the majority subsumes the ordinance within the class of laws this Court has struck down as facially discriminatory (and so avails itself of our "virtually *per se* rule" against such statutes, see Philadelphia v. New Jersey, 437 U.S. 617, 624 (1978)), the majority is in fact greatly extending the Clause's dormant reach.

There are, however, good and sufficient reasons against expanding the Commerce Clause's inherent capacity to trump exercises of state authority such as the ordinance at issue here. There is no indication in the record that any out-of-state trash processor has been harmed, or that the interstate movement or disposition of trash will be affected one whit. To the degree Local Law 9 affects the market for trash processing services, it does so only by subjecting Clarkstown residents and businesses to burdens far different from the burdens of local favoritism that dormant Commerce Clause jurisprudence seeks to root out. The town has found a way to finance a public improvement, not by transferring its cost to out-of-state economic interests, but by spreading it among the local generators of trash, an equitable result with tendencies that should not disturb the Commerce Clause and should not be disturbed by us.

There are . . . both analytical and practical differences between this and the earlier processing cases, differences the majority underestimates or overlooks but which, if given their due, should prevent this case from being decided the same way. First, the terms of Clarkstown's ordinance favor a single processor, not the class of all such businesses located in Clarkstown. Second, the one proprietor so favored is essentially an agent of the municipal government, which (unlike Carbone or other private trash processors) must ensure the removal of waste according to acceptable standards of public health. Any discrimination worked by Local Law 9 thus fails to produce the sort of entrepreneurial favoritism we have previously defined and condemned as protectionist.

. . . While our previous local processing cases have barred discrimination in markets served by private companies, Clarkstown's transfer station is essentially a municipal facility, built and operated under a contract with the municipality and soon to revert entirely to municipal ownership. This, of course, is no mere coincidence, since the facility performs a municipal function that tradition as well as state and federal law recognize as the domain of local government. Throughout the history of this country, municipalities have taken responsibility for disposing of local garbage to prevent noisome smells, obstruction of the streets, and threats to public health, and today 78 percent of landfills receiving municipal solid waste are owned by local governments. . . . The majority ignores this distinction between public and private enterprise, equating Local Law 9's "hoard[ing]" of solid waste for the municipal transfer station with the design and effect of ordinances that restrict access to local markets for the benefit of local private firms. But private businesses, whether local or out of State, first serve the private interests of their owners, and there is therefore only rarely a reason other than economic protectionism for favoring local businesses over their out-of-town competitors. The local government itself occupies a very different market position, however, being the one entity that enters the market to serve the public interest of local citizens quite apart from private interest in private gain. Reasons other than economic protectionism are accordingly more likely to explain the design and effect of an ordinance that favors a public facility.

[The concurring opinion of Justice O'Connor is omitted.]

## NOTES AND QUESTIONS

1. In the early aftermath of *Carbone*, it appeared that federal legislation authorizing flow control restrictions might be forthcoming, as municipalities with bonded indebtedness for facility construction pressed their case on the Congress, and as about 10 percent of those bonds were downgraded in quality ratings or placed on a credit watch because of facilities' need to reduce tipping fees in the face of increased competition. BNA State Environment Daily, Mar. 20, 1997. In order to reduce industry opposition, flow control proponents agreed to seek such authority only for those governments that had enacted flow control measures before *Carbone* was decided, and only until their bond financing was retired.

2. Flow control relief, however, became joined with the interstate waste transport issue, which pits net importing states, who favor Congress authorizing states to restrict importation of waste, against net exporting states, who oppose it. That opposition is joined by others who espouse free market principles, as well as by some environmental groups. Thus far, the impasse has deadlocked action on both flow control and interstate transport legislation.

3. Some environmentalists oppose federal legislation that would authorize states to ban waste imports on the ground that such laws discourage the development of better technologies for waste disposal. See, e.g., Congress Should Not Allow States to Ban Interstate Transport of Waste, Industry Says, 22 Envtl. Rep. 107 (1991). Do you agree? Grassroots environmental organizations look more favorably on proposals to authorize waste import bans. Environmentalists Release RCRA Wish List: Interstate Transport, Medical Waste Left Out, 22 Envtl. Rep. 334 (1991). Why do you think the views of the national groups diverge from those of the local groups on this subject?

4. Spurred in part by the NIMBY syndrome, local governments may be inclined to use their land use authorities to ban *all* land disposal of certain kinds of wastes, especially hazardous wastes, regardless of point of origin. These efforts face no Commerce Clause obstacles. Interestingly, however, federal legislation—which some states are hoping will *authorize* certain waste disposal bans (bans on out-of-state wastes)—may now operate to *prohibit* other kinds of waste disposal bans. See Rollins Environmental Services, Inc. v. Parish of St. James, 775 F.2d 627 (5th Cir. 1985) (effort to prohibit siting of PCB transfer facility preempted by section 18(a) (2) of the Toxic Substances Control Act).

5. Unlike the surcharges in *Chemical Waste Management* and *Oregon Waste Systems*, the Clarkstown ordinance applied to all solid waste brought within the town's jurisdiction without regard to its point of origin. Why did the Court majority find that the Clarkstown ordinance discriminated against interstate commerce?

6. A private contractor had agreed to build Clarkstown's $1.4 million transfer station and to sell it to the town for $1 after operating it for five years. Would it have made any difference to the outcome of the case if the city owned the facility instead, having built it with municipal funds? See Atlantic Coast Demolition & Recycling v. Board of Chosen Freeholders of Atlantic County, 112 F.3d 652 (3d Cir. 1997) (striking down New Jersey's statewide flow control scheme, which included many municipally owned and financed facilities).

7. Local governments have always been permitted to monopolize local garbage collection simply by doing it themselves. Justice Souter's dissent emphasizes that Clarkstown was attempting to discharge a traditional local governmental function by creating what was "essentially" a municipal facility. How does the majority respond to Justice Souter's argument?

8. Some municipalities had responded to the local garbage crisis by creating municipal entities to process and dispose of solid waste. Two counties in New York followed this route. After the *Carbone* decision, New York state legislation created the Oneida-Herkimer Solid Waste Management Authority to manage all solid waste within the two counties, pursuant to a management agreement entered into between the counties and the Authority. Private haulers could still pick up solid waste, but the waste had to be delivered to the Authority, which undertook to build

disposal, processing, and recycling facilities to handle the waste. The tipping fees ranged from $86/ton to $172/ton. Private haulers challenged the arrangement, arguing that it was prohibited by *Carbone*. The district court agreed, but the Second Circuit reversed. The case then reached the Supreme Court in United Haulers Ass'n, Inc. v. Oneida-Herkimer Solid Waste Management Authority, 550 U.S. 330 (2007). The Court held that the case was not controlled by *Carbone* because "[t]he flow control ordinances in this case benefit a clearly public facility, while treating all private companies exactly the same." The Court then concluded "that such flow control ordinances do not discriminate against interstate commerce for purposes of the dormant Commerce Clause." The Court noted that there were good reasons to treat government entities differently because "unlike private enterprise, government is vested with the responsibility of protecting the health, safety, and welfare of its citizens. . . . The dormant Commerce Clause is not a roving license for federal courts to decide what activities are appropriate for state and local government to undertake, and what activities must be the province of private market competition."

9. In Lebanon Farms Disposal, Inc. v. County of Lebanon, 538 F.3d 241 (3d Cir. 2008), the Third Circuit relied on *United Haulers* in refusing to invalidate a flow control ordinance requiring waste to be disposed at a landfill owned by a municipal waste authority. Pursuant to *United Haulers*, the court noted that a flow control ordinance that benefits a "clearly public facility" and that treats "private business interests exactly the same as out-of-state ones," does not discriminate against interstate commerce. The court remanded the case to the district court to apply the *Pike v. Bruce Church* balancing test comparing the local benefits to the burdens on interstate commerce.

## 2.  *Siting Controversies and the Environmental Justice Movement*

One of the major focal points of the environmental justice movement has been on the siting of locally undesirable land uses (LULUs), such as hazardous waste treatment and disposal facilities, sanitary landfills, and nuclear reactors. As noted in Chapter 1, some controversy attends the question of whether the pattern of LULUs presently located in largely poor, minority communities—such as the ChemWaste facility in Emelle, Alabama, discussed earlier in this chapter—is more attributable to decisions made to site in such locations or to the subsequent movement of populations to communities neighboring such facilities, which often offer low-cost housing because of the property value–depressing effects of the LULU. However that historical question is resolved, there can be little doubt that the concerns raised by the environmental justice movement have produced much more sensitivity to the distributional justice issues posed by such siting decisions now and in the future.

The Nuclear Regulatory Commission responded to President Clinton's environmental justice Executive Order 12,898 by adjusting its procedures for evaluating licensing applications. For more on EO 12,898, see Chapter 1, Section B. The following excerpt is from an opinion of its Atomic Safety and Licensing Board, which found insufficient attention had been paid to compliance with 12,898 in the NRC staff evaluation of a uranium enrichment plant proposed to be sited near predominantly minority communities in Louisiana.

## In the Matter of Louisiana Energy Services, L.P.

Decision of the Nuclear Regulatory Commission Atomic Safety and Licensing Board, May 1, 1997

Before Administrative Judges MOORE, COLE, and SHON.

This Final Initial Decision addresses the remaining contention—environmental justice contention J.9—filed by the Intervenor, Citizens Against Nuclear Trash ("CANT"), in this combined construction permit-operating license proceeding. The Applicant, Louisiana Energy Services, L.P. ("LES"), seeks a 30-year materials license to possess and use byproduct, source, and special nuclear material in order to enrich uranium using a gas centrifuge process at the Claiborne Enrichment Center ("CEC"). The Applicant plans to build the CEC on a 442-acre site in Claiborne Parish, Louisiana, that is immediately adjacent to and between the unincorporated African-American communities of Center Springs and Forest Grove, some five miles from the town of Homer, Louisiana. . . .

The community of Forest Grove was founded by freed slaves at the close of the Civil War and has a population of about 150. Center Springs was founded around the turn of the century and has a population of about 100. The populations of Forest Grove and Center Springs are about 97 percent African American. Many of the residents are descendants of the original settlers and a large portion of the landholdings remain with the same families that founded the communities. Aside from Parish Road 39 and State Road 9, the roads in Center Springs or Forest Grove are either unpaved or poorly maintained. There are no stores, schools, medical clinics, or businesses in Center Springs or Forest Grove. The Intervenor's evidence was undisputed that from kindergarten through high school the children of Center Springs and Forest Grove attend schools that are largely racially segregated. Many of the residents of the communities are not connected to the public water supply. Some of these residents rely on groundwater wells while others must actually carry their water because they have no potable water supply.

Although none of the parties put in any specific statistical evidence on the income and educational level of the residents of Forest Grove and Center Springs, the 1990 United States Bureau of the Census statistics in the record show they are part of a population that is among the poorest and most disadvantaged in the United States. Claiborne Parish is one of the poorest regions of the United States with a total population in 1990 of 17,405 and a racial makeup of 53.43 percent white and 46.09 percent African American. Over 30 percent of the parish population lives below the poverty level with over 58 percent of the black population and 11 percent of the white population living below the poverty line. Per capita income of the black population of Claiborne Parish is only 36 percent of that of the white population, compared to a national average of 55 percent. Over 69 percent of the black population of Claiborne Parish earns less than $15,000 annually, 50 percent earns less than $10,000, and 30 percent earns less than $5,000. In contrast, among whites in the parish, 33 percent earn less than $15,000 annually, 21.5 percent earn less than $10,000, and 6.5 percent earn less than $5,000. In Claiborne Parish, over 31 percent of blacks live in households in which there are no motor vehicles and over 10 percent live in households that lack complete plumbing. Over 50 percent of the African-American households in the parish have only one parent, 58 percent of the black population has less than a high school education, including almost 33 percent of the parish black population over 24 years old that has not attained a ninth grade education. . . .

The CEC site selection process began with a coarse screening of the 48 contiguous states to identify a region of the United States for the facility. This Coarse Screening Phase applied various selection criteria involving the service area of sponsoring electric utilities, transportation distances, and seismic and severe storm factors. In October 1987, the siting consultants recommended northern Louisiana to the Steering Committee as the regional location for the facility and the Steering Committee adopted this recommendation.

Because of a hold on the project, it was not until the spring of 1988 that the site selection consultants conducted what the ER labels a two-phase intermediate screening process to select the most suitable host community. In Intermediate Phase I, communities across northern Louisiana within 45 miles of Interstate 40 were solicited with the assistance of the Louisiana Department of Economic Development. The candidate communities were asked to nominate potential sites based on a set of criteria that, inter alia, indicated the proposed facility was a chemical plant. In answer to the solicitation, 21 communities in 19 parishes with over 100 sites responded and expressed an interest in hosting the project.

According to the ER, during Intermediate Phase I, the site selection personnel then visited each of the communities and, applying a second set of criteria, reduced to nine the number of candidate communities. . . .

The purpose of the second phase of intermediate screening was to select a host community from the nine communities still under consideration. . . .

During this phase, Mr. Engwall scored the remaining nine candidate communities against another set of criteria that had been refined and expanded from those used in the first intermediate phase. . . .

Mr. Engwall visited a number of the communities previously visited by his predecessor to learn more about Mr. Schaperkotter's evaluative process. His visits included several communities that had been eliminated in Intermediate Phase I because they had expressed a renewed interest or proposed additional sites. Mr. Engwall also visited each of the nine remaining candidate communities, including Homer, which he visited for the first time on May 22, 1989. . . . Based on Mr. Engwall's scoring, Homer was the highest rated community, with Winnsboro the runner up. The Steering Committee then selected Homer as the host community. On June 9, 1989, the then Senator of Louisiana, Bennett Johnson, came to Homer and announced that it had been selected as the CEC host community.

After selecting Homer as the host community, the ER states that a fine screening process, in two phases, was employed to obtain the three most preferred sites from the six sites nominated by Homer community leaders. In what the ER describes as Fine Screening Phase I, Mr. Engwall scored each of the six sites using the K-T decisional analysis against another set of criteria developed in conjunction with the Steering Committee. Although 11 sites in Claiborne Parish were initially nominated by community leaders, five sites were immediately dropped by Mr. Engwall for failing to meet the selection criteria and only six sites were seriously considered and scored. On the basis of the K-T analysis, the LeSage site was top rated and recommended for selection, pending confirmatory on-site studies. . . .

Intervenor witness Dr. Bullard in his prefiled direct testimony stated that, in his opinion, the process for selecting the CEC site was, among other things, biased and that racial considerations were a factor in the site selection process. Dr. Bullard based his conclusion that the CEC siting process was racially discriminatory on four major points. According to Dr. Bullard, the first factor and the most significant indication that institutionalized racism played a part in the site selection, was the fact that, at each progressively narrower stage of the site selection process, the level of poverty and African Americans in the local population rose dramatically, until it culminated in the selection of a site with a local population that is extremely poor and 97 percent African American. Specifically, Dr. Bullard stated:

> . . . [T]he aggregate average percentage of black population for a one mile radius around all of the 78 sites [that LES claims it seriously considered as candidate sites] (in 16 parishes) is 28.35 percent. When LES completed its initial site cuts, and reduced the list to 37 sites within nine communities (parishes), including Homer, the aggregate percentage of black population rose to 36.78 percent. When LES then further limited its focus to six sites in Claiborne Parish, the aggregate average percent black population rose again, to 64.74 percent. The final site selected, the "LeSage" site, has a 97.1 percent black population within a one-mile radius. . . .

Next, Dr. Bullard asserted, Mr. Engwall compounded the problem by using invalid and biased considerations in comparing the population level of the LeSage site to that of the Emerson site. The Emerson site, which was the overall second highest rated site in Fine Screening Phase I, was given a "low population" score of 7, yielding a significantly lower weighted score of 56. . . . [W]hen asked what he saw that caused him to score the site a seven, Mr. Engwall answered "[p]robably the proximity to the lake." Mr. Engwall went on to explain that "[w]e just felt opinion-wise people would probably not want this plant to be close to their pride and joy of their lake where they go fishing." The significance of the lake, Dr. Bullard asserted, also was emphasized a few pages earlier in his deposition when Mr. Engwall testified that the Emerson site was rated neutral to slightly negative because

> [i]t was right on the edge of this lake. This lake is a very nice lake. This lake is the pride and joy of this part of Louisiana, nice boating, nice homes along the lake. It was felt that an industrial facility real close to that lake would not be in keeping with the existing usage, which was nice homes, vacation and fishing, hunting.

Based on Mr. Engwall's deposition testimony, Dr. Bullard concluded it was clear that quality of life considerations improperly affected Mr. Engwall's scoring of the low population criterion for the Emerson site given that, at this stage of the evaluation process, there were no site specific criterion related to quality of life. He further maintained that Mr. Engwall's biased judgment on the quality of life concern regarding the desirability of avoiding the lakeside site where white, middle class people lived was directly related to the relative scoring of the low population criterion. Dr. Bullard asserted that the total effect of Mr. Engwall's actions was to discriminate against the Forest Grove and Center Springs communities because their residents' lifestyle and socioeconomic status were on a much lower plane.

The third factor Dr. Bullard testified about was racial discrimination inherent in the Fine Screening Phase I criterion of not siting the facility within at least 5 miles of institutions such as schools, hospitals, and nursing homes. He asserted that by its own terms, this criteria is inherently biased toward the selection of sites in minority and poor areas because these areas generally lack institutions such as schools, hospitals, and nursing homes that are the focus of this criteria. Dr. Bullard stated that even though Forest Grove and Center Springs are five miles from the nearest town, there are no schools, hospitals, or medical facilities of any kind or, for that matter, any other service institution in either community. He stated that, while it is not necessarily inappropriate to attempt to site a hazardous facility in an area that is far from these institutions, this criterion cannot be applied equitably unless the process is enlightened by consideration of the demographics of the affected population. Otherwise, he stated, disadvantaged populations will invariably be favored as hosts for more hazardous facilities as is evidenced by the fact that minority communities already host a disproportionate share of prisons, half-way houses, and mental institutions.

The fourth and final point, according to Dr. Bullard, was the use of various community support criteria in the selection process that had the effect of discriminating against the people of Forest Grove and Center Springs. He testified that during the siting process LES relied upon the opinions of Homer, a community five miles from the actual host community. This was inappropriate, he concluded, because Homer stood to minimize the risks and maximize the benefit to itself by placing the facility a good distance from its own residents. In contrast, the actual host communities of Forest Grove and Center Springs were never informed of the siting decision until it was too late for the residents to affect the selection process.

This was particularly significant, Dr. Bullard testified, because the principal criteria for site selection were support from the community and opinion leaders in the community. Indeed, LES considered it of primary importance that the facility should be located in a locale where it would be considered a community asset . . . . According to Dr. Bullard, the groups of community leaders with whom LES met and with whom it consulted to form its opinion of "community support," "active and cohesive community leadership," and "community leader preferences," were dominated by the Claiborne Parish Industrial Development Foundation — on which Forest Grove and Center Springs have no representatives — and elected officials from the towns of Homer and Haynesville, rather than Forest Grove and Center Springs. Thus, Dr. Bullard concluded that a racially neutral site selection process was perverted to give certain communities the discretion to decide who should accept the adverse impacts of the proposed facility. . . .

## C.  LICENSING BOARD DETERMINATION

The nondiscrimination component of Executive Order 12,898 requires that the NRC conduct its licensing activities in a manner that "ensures" those activities do not have the effect of subjecting any persons or populations to discrimination because of their race or color. 3 C.F.R. at 861. In the FEIS and in its prefiled direct testimony, the Staff stated that it sought to determine whether race played a role in the CEC site selection process by reviewing the information in the Applicant's ER. In taking this action, the Staff necessarily recognized the agency's obligation under the nondiscrimination component of the President's environmental justice directive to make sure the site selection process conducted by the original venturers in what subsequently became the LES project was free from racial discrimination.

In the circumstances presented in this licensing action, however, by limiting its consideration to a facial review of the information in the Applicant's ER, the Staff has failed to comply with the President's directive. As we discuss more fully below, a thorough and in-depth investigation of the Applicant's siting process by the Staff is essential to insure compliance with the President's nondiscrimination directive if that directive is to have any real meaning. Moreover, such a thorough Staff investigation is needed not only to comply with Executive Order 12,898, but to avoid the constitutional ramifications of the agency becoming a participant in any discriminatory conduct through its grant of a license.

Racial discrimination in the facility site selection process cannot be uncovered with only a cursory review of the description of that process appearing in an applicant's environmental report. If it were so easily detected, racial discrimination would not be such a persistent and enduring problem in American society. Racial discrimination is rarely, if ever, admitted. Instead, it is often rationalized under some other seemingly racially neutral guise, making it difficult to ferret out. Moreover, direct evidence of racial discrimination is seldom found. Therefore, under the circumstances presented by this licensing action, if the President's nondiscrimination directive is to have any meaning a much more thorough investigation must be conducted by the Staff to determine whether racial discrimination played a role in the CEC site selection process. . . .

Because this agency's primary responsibilities historically have dealt with technical concerns, investigating whether racial discrimination played a part in a facility siting decision is far afield from the Staff's past activities. Indeed, because racial discrimination questions have not previously been involved in agency licensing activities, this is an area in which the Staff has little experience or expertise. Nevertheless, if the President's directive is to have any meaning in this particular licensing action, the Staff must conduct an objective, thorough, and professional investigation that looks beneath the surface of the description of the site selection process in the ER. In other words, the Staff must lift some rocks and look under them.

Substantial evidence presented by the Intervenor in this proceeding demonstrates why it is imperative that the Staff conduct such a thorough investigation. As we have noted, direct evidence of racial discrimination is rare. Nonetheless, the Intervenor's evidence, the most significant portions of which are largely unrebutted or ineffectively rebutted, is more than sufficient to raise a reasonable inference that racial considerations played some part in the site selection process such that additional inquiry is warranted. In so stating, we do not make specific findings on the current record that racial discrimination did or did not influence the site selection process. When stripped of its abundant irrelevant chaff, the record is simply inadequate, objectively viewed, to reach any conclusion with the requisite degree of confidence. A finding that the selection process was tainted by racial bias is far too serious a determination, with potentially long-lasting consequences, to render without the benefit of a thorough and professional Staff investigation aided by whatever outside experts as may be necessary. Additionally, the Applicant, because of the allocation of the burden of proof in the adjudicatory process and the nature of this particular subject matter, is, to some extent, in the position of proving a negative.

Thus, in this instance any finding that racial considerations either did or did not play a part in the site selection process should be made only after the Staff has undertaken a complete and systematic examination of the entire process. . . .

Looking to the record of this proceeding, the Intervenor's statistical evidence . . . shows that as the site selection process progressed and the focus of the search narrowed, the level of minority representation in the population rose dramatically. The Intervenor's analysis did not include one of the 79 seriously considered proposed CEC sites because it was not clearly identified on the large map on which the siting consultants had marked the proposed sites. Of the remaining 78 proposed sites, however, the Intervenor's analysis reveals that the aggregate average percentage of black population within a one-mile radius of each of the sites across 16 parishes is 28.35 percent. After the initial site cuts reduced the list to 37 sites in nine parishes, including the sites in Claiborne Parish, the aggregate percentage of black population rose to 36.78 percent. Then, when the search narrowed to the six sites in Claiborne Parish, the aggregate average percent of black population increased to 64.74 percent. Ultimately, the process culminated in a chosen site with a black population of 97.1 percent within a one-mile radius of the LeSage site, which is the site with the highest percent black population of all 78 examined sites. This statistical evidence very strongly suggests that racial considerations played a part in the site selection process. It does not, of course, rule out all possibility that race played no part in the selection process. Nonetheless, the Intervenor's statistical evidence clearly indicates that the probability of this being the case is unlikely. Certainly, the possibility that racial considerations played a part in the site selection cannot be passed off as mere coincidence. . . .

To summarize, the Intervenor's statistical evidence and its evidence concerning the application of the low population criterion stand as significant probative evidence in the current record that racial considerations played a part in the site selection process. This evidence demonstrates that a thorough Staff investigation of the site selection process is needed in order to comply with the President's non-discrimination directive in Executive Order 12,898. The Intervenor did provide other evidence concerning the inherent racial bias in the fine screening criterion of siting the facility five miles from institutions such as schools, hospitals, and nursing homes and evidence on the manner in which various community opinion and support criteria in the selection process discriminated against the minority communities of Forest Grove and Center Springs. This evidence is, at most, only indirectly indicative that racial considerations played a part in the site selection process. Nevertheless, when coupled with the Intervenor's statistical evidence and its evidence concerning the application of the low population criterion, this further Intervenor evidence raises concerns that deserve attention and should be further carefully analyzed as part of the Staff investigation. . . .

## NOTES AND QUESTIONS

1. There can be difficult methodological problems in assessing whether siting decisions have disproportionate impacts on minorities and the poor. As noted in Chapter 1, different conclusions can be reached depending upon whether siting decisions are analyzed by census block, postal zip code, or county. What methodology was used in the Louisiana siting controversy?

2. Does the Licensing Board's decision mean that whenever a site is selected near communities that have the highest minority population of all candidate sites, a license must be denied to comply with Executive Order 12,898? What other factors were present in this case that convinced the Board to deny the license?

3. What should the NRC staff do in response to the Board's decision? Is there any way in which they could continue to support licensing at the site selected by Louisiana Energy Services and still comply with Executive Order 12,898?

4. Examining environmental justice claims continues to be a part of NRC's environmental impact assessment process under NEPA. In making these assessments, the NRC says its approach to "environmental justice [is] to look at disparate environmental harms, not disparate economic benefits." NRC, In the Matter of Private Fuel Storage LLC (Independent Spent Fuel Storage Installation), CLI 04-04 (Feb. 4, 2004). In the Matter of Private Fuel Storage licensing proceeding, it found that the members of a particular band of the Goshute Indians in Utah would receive economic benefits greater than the environmental harms to which they would be exposed, and thus that environmental justice concerns had been adequately addressed. Id. Is this approach to environmental justice consistent with the executive order?

5. Arguing "that environmental justice is not cost-free," a report published by Resources for the Future observes:

> At least in theory, to the extent that priority is given to addressing the environmental needs of minorities and the poor, it may not be given to actions that may protect a larger number of people. The overarching strategy of environmental protection in this country has been based not on a standard of justice that assumes government regulation should be directed to improving the conditions of some particular members of society but on utilitarian principles—the greatest good for the greatest number of people. These utilitarian principles are incorporated into environmental policies through such tools as benefit-cost analysis and, more recently, comparative risk. The potential conflict between environmental justice and utilitarianism will not be easy to reconcile. [J. Clarence Davies & Jan Mazurek, Regulating Pollution: Does the U.S. System Work? 37 (1997).]

Do you agree? How would you respond in the context of the siting dispute addressed by the Licensing Board?

6. Efforts to challenge siting decisions on equal protection grounds generally have been unsuccessful because it is extremely difficult to prove intentional discrimination, as required to establish that state action violates the Fourteenth Amendment. In Bean v. Southwestern Waste Management Corp., 482 F. Supp. 673 (S.D. Tex. 1979), aff'd without opinion, 782 F.2d 1038 (5th Cir. 1986), a court held that statistical evidence of disparate impact was insufficient to establish intentional discrimination in the selection of a solid waste disposal site despite the fact that the community originally was told that a shopping mall or steel mill was being constructed. In R.I.S.E., Inc. v. Kay, 768 F. Supp. 1144 (E.D. Va. 1991), a court rejected a claim that a county's decision to site a landfill in a predominantly Black community violated the Equal Protection Clause despite statistical evidence of racially disproportionate impact. The court concluded that "the Equal Protection Clause

does not impose an affirmative duty to equalize the impact of official decisions on different racial groups." Id. at 1150.

7. The NRC licensing decision was challenged on the basis of environmental justice concerns raised by the process of siting one particular facility. Environmental justice is also concerned about the location of multiple facilities because of their cumulative impacts. Cumulative impacts were a major issue in the South Camden litigation.

8. The cleanup of problem sites also raises environmental justice issues. An analysis of Superfund sites concludes that "marginalized and poor populations are less likely to benefit from a cleanup program such as Superfund despite their over-representation in proximity to environmental hazards," because poor areas "have less chance of making the official Superfund list." Sandra O'Neil, Superfund: Evaluating the Impact of E.O. 12,898, 115 Envtl. Health Persps. 1087, 1091 (2007).

### 3. Factors Affecting Siting Decisions: The Yucca Mountain Case Study

Apart from the legal difficulties that surround the search for land-based disposal locations, weighing the pros and cons of locating large deposits of potentially harmful waste materials introduces complex problems and uncertainties. No single siting decision highlights these complexities and uncertainties better than the federal government's decades-long search to create a disposal facility for spent nuclear fuel and high-level radioactive waste. In recent years, that effort has focused on Yucca Mountain, Nevada, a site 90 miles northwest of Las Vegas. On February 14, 2002, U.S. Secretary of Energy Spencer Abraham, acting under section 114(a) of the Nuclear Waste Policy Act, 42 U.S.C. §10101ff, formally recommended that President Bush approve Yucca Mountain as the site for the geologic repository for nuclear waste. President Bush approved the siting recommendation and forwarded it to Congress, which endorsed the project in July 2002. This action permitted the Department of Energy to take the next step in the project, which is to make application to the Nuclear Regulatory Commission for an operating permit for the site, which DOE is currently preparing. While campaigning in Nevada during the 2000 presidential campaign, Bush had criticized the Clinton-Gore administration for proceeding with the Yucca Mountain project. Citing the risks of groundwater contamination from waste that will remain radioactive for tens of thousands of years and the risks of transporting 70,000 tons of such waste from all over the country, opponents of the project are pursuing every legal avenue they can to oppose the siting decision.

---

## PROBLEM EXERCISE: SHOULD THE NATION'S HIGH-LEVEL RADIOACTIVE WASTE BE DEPOSITED IN YUCCA MOUNTAIN?

For many years civilian and defense-related activities have produced spent nuclear fuel and high-level radioactive waste. More than 7,000 tons of spent nuclear fuel has accumulated and is stored at 75 operating and shutdown reactor sites in the

United States. More than 2,000 tons of additional nuclear waste is being generated each year. DOE also is storing another 2,500 tons of nuclear waste, mostly from past weapons programs, at a handful of government-owned facilities. Disposal of all this waste poses an unprecedented challenge because it will remain highly radioactive for thousands of years. DOE initially sought to build a repository for the waste inside Yucca Mountain in Nevada. The repository was to be located at least 1,000 feet below the surface and at least 1,000 feet above the present-day water table. See *https://www.epa.gov/radiation/what-yucca-mountain-repository*. DOE applied for a final construction license with the Nuclear Regulatory Commission in June 2008, while admitting that it could not meet its original 2017 projected date for project completion.

**Arguments in Favor of the Yucca Mountain Repository.**  Proponents of building the repository at Yucca Mountain argued that it was critical to national security, nuclear nonproliferation, and the ongoing environmental cleanup at former nuclear weapons production sites. More than 161 million Americans live within 75 miles of temporary nuclear waste storage sites. These sites were not designed to contain the waste for extended periods of time or to withstand terrorist attacks. Nuclear materials would be far better secured in a deep underground repository at Yucca Mountain. While Nevada has not generated any waste from nuclear power plants, the state will be adequately compensated for accepting the nation's radioactive waste.

DOE argued that experts throughout the world support its view that the safest and most feasible method for disposing of highly radioactive material is to store it deep underground. The physical characteristics that render Yucca Mountain a suitable site for waste disposal include: (1) its remote location and long distance from a large population center—100 miles from Las Vegas, Nevada; (2) its very dry climate—less than 6 inches of rainfall a year (water is the primary means by which radio-nuclides disposed of at Yucca Mountain could reach the accessible environment); and (3) its extremely deep water table—1,000 feet below the level of the potential repository.

**Arguments in Opposition to the Yucca Mountain Repository.**  Opponents of the Yucca Mountain repository argue that it is riskier to ship highly radioactive material from all over the country to Yucca Mountain than it would be to leave it dispersed at current sites. They note the risks of accidents during transport and that highly radioactive waste could be an attractive target for terrorist attacks, particularly when shipments pass through populated areas. Las Vegas Sun, Nevada to Emphasize Terrorist Threats to Shipping Nuclear Waste, Jan. 10, 2002. (Then-Governor Kenny Guinn and then-Senator John Ensign of Nevada argued that radioactive waste shipments would be a potential target for terrorist attacks since the waste would be carried on the nation's highways via trucks or on our nation's railways.) Supporters of the dump pointed to over 3,000 shipments of nuclear contaminants in the past 40 years, none of them resulting in any contamination incidents. The waste would be transported in special canisters strong enough to withstand any crash or attack.

Opponents of the project argue that the Yucca Mountain site should be disqualified because subsurface fracturing would allow contaminated groundwater to reach the environment in less than the 1,000 years required by DOE's original 1984 site suitability guidelines (10 C.F.R. pt. 960). DOE responds that these guidelines have been superseded by Yucca Mountain–specific guidelines it promulgated in 2001. (10 C.F.R. pt. 963.) Project opponents also argue that earthquakes and volcanoes will cause releases of radioactive waste. The DOE maintains that its EIS has adequately taken these concerns into account.

**Question One.** Should the nation's high-level radioactive waste be deposited in a repository at Yucca Mountain, Nevada? What should be the principal considerations on which this decision should be based? Can any present-day policy protect adequately against risks extending thousands of years into the future?

**Question Two.** Nevada residents and officials strongly opposed siting a high-level nuclear waste repository in their state. They maintained that it would be grossly unfair to their state since it has no nuclear power plants that generated the waste and that state residents already have suffered unfairly by being exposed to nuclear fallout from the federal government's Nevada nuclear test range. Would it be fair to make Nevada accept this facility despite its vigorous opposition?

**Question Three.** Section 801 of the Energy Policy Act of 1992 provides that the EPA "shall, based upon and consistent with the findings and recommendations of the National Academy of Sciences, promulgate, by rule, public health and safety standards for protection of the public from releases from radioactive materials stored or disposed of in the repository at the Mountain site." Pursuant to this provision, EPA promulgated standards requiring the DOE to "demonstrate, using performance assessment, that there is a reasonable expectation that, for 10,000 years following disposal, the reasonably maximally exposed individual receives no more than an annual committed effective dose equivalent of 150 microsieverts (15 millirems) from releases from the undisturbed Yucca Mountain disposal system." The National Academy of Sciences, however, had issued a report indicating that there was no scientific basis for limiting a performance standard for Yucca to 10,000 years and that peak radiation exposures could occur tens of thousands and even hundreds of thousands of years in the future. Comm. on Technical Bases for Yucca Mountain Standards, Nat'l Research Council, Technical Bases for Yucca Mountain Standards (1995). The inconsistency between EPA's regulation and the NAS study led a U.S. Court of Appeals to overturn the EPA regulation because it violated section 801 of the Energy Policy Act. Nuclear Energy Institute, Inc. v. Environmental Protection Agency, 373 F.3d 1251, 1262 (D.C. Cir. 2004). In 2008, EPA issued a new two-tiered radioactivity standard: 15 millirems per year for the first 10,000 years and 100 millirems for the next million years. 73 Fed. Reg. 61,256-01 (Oct. 15, 2008). How realistic is it to expect that any standards promulgated today can ensure the control of risks tens of thousands of years in the future?

**Question Four.** Consistent with his campaign promise, President Obama sharply scaled back funding for the Yucca Mountain project in his first budget. This action sounded the death knell for a project on which almost $8 billion had been spent by the federal government. Yet all agreed that it is urgent to develop an alternative plan for safely disposing of the nation's high-level radioactive waste. The growing pools of spent nuclear fuel that are building up at nuclear power plants operating in the United States may be even more dangerous than some of the pools at Japanese nuclear power plants that have contributed to the seriousness of the Fukushima Daiichi nuclear accident. What should be done with the volumes of high-level radioactive waste accumulating at nuclear power plants? In the absence of a permanent repository, should any new nuclear power plants be licensed?

**Stalemate and Policy Paralysis.**   In March 2010, the U.S. Department of Energy filed a motion to withdraw its application to the Nuclear Regulatory Commission (NRC) for a license for Yucca Mountain. Several states quickly filed lawsuits challenging the license application withdrawal, but the U.S. Court of Appeals for the D.C. Circuit concluded that these lawsuits were premature because the NRC had not taken any final action on the withdrawal. In January 2010, President Obama directed Energy Secretary Steven Chu to establish a 15-member Blue Ribbon Commission on America's Nuclear Future. Chartered pursuant to the Federal Advisory Committee Act, the Commission was asked to conduct a comprehensive review of policies for managing nuclear waste disposal and to recommend a new plan that will replace Yucca Mountain. On January 26, 2012, the Blue Ribbon Commission, chaired by former Congressman Lee H. Hamilton and former National Security Adviser Brent Scowcroft, released its final report. The report concluded that the "need for a new strategy is urgent." It recommended a consent-based approach to siting future storage and disposal facilities and the creation of a new organization independent of DOE to oversee development of at least one geologic disposal facility and at least one consolidated storage facility.

On August 13, 2013, a divided panel of the U.S. Court of Appeals for the D.C. Circuit ruled that the Nuclear Regulatory Commission must decide on whether or not to issue a permit for the Yucca Mountain nuclear waste disposal facility. The court majority held that the NRC "is simply defying a law enacted by Congress" and "doing so without any legal basis." The court took the extraordinary step of issuing a writ of mandamus directing the NRC to act. In dissent, Judge Merrick Garland argued that mandamus was not appropriate and that the court was ordering the NRC to do a useless act because there were insufficient funds appropriated to complete the licensing process. The court majority noted that $11.1 million had been appropriated by Congress for processing the licensing application and deemed this to be a mandate to proceed. It recognized, however, that Congress was under no obligation to appropriate additional funds for the licensing process. In re Aiken County, 725 F.3d 255 (D.C. Cir. 2013).

In response to this decision, the NRC resumed work on its technical and environmental reviews of the Yucca Mountain application using available funds. The staff completed and published the final volumes of the safety evaluation report in January 2015. The staff completed and issued an Environmental Impact Statement supplement in May 2016. The adjudicatory hearing, which must be completed before a licensing decision can be made, remains suspended. *https://www.nrc.gov/waste/hlw-disposal.html.* For a comparison of how various countries are dealing with the political challenge of siting a facility for disposal of high-level radioactive waste, see Kerri Morrison, National and Multinational Strategies for Radioactive Waste Disposal, 47 Envtl. L. Rep. 10300 (2017).

President Trump's first three budgets sought funding to complete the licensing process for Yucca Mountain. However, in an effort to attract support in the swing state of Nevada during a presidential election year, President Trump changed his position and announced on February 6, 2020, that he would not seek funding in the 2021 budget. Jennifer Granholm, Secretary of Energy in the Biden administration, opposes restarting the licensing process to build a nuclear waste repository at Yucca Mountain. Gary Martin, Granholm, Yucca Mountain opponent, confirmed as energy secretary, Las Vegas Review-Journal, Feb. 25, 2021.

# CHAPTER 5

# AIR POLLUTION CONTROL

The reasons we have been so much more successful than China in pursuing clean air can be understood by examining the history of a truly remarkable federal law—the Clean Air Act. . . . As we look back over the history of that law and prior efforts to protect air quality in the United States, there have been several critical junctures when we made bold decisions to prioritize clean air. These decisions were made despite claims that it was impossible and the technology did not exist. But a series of what now seem like political miracles have maintained our commitment to healthy air quality. . . .

The U.S. Clean Air Act is a model of comprehensiveness and adaptability. It has been able to respond to both new and old problems in a flexible fashion. We should never forget the doomsday forecasts that were made every time the United States made a bold move in favor of protecting air quality. Time and time again, we were told that if we strengthened controls on air pollution, it would [seriously damage] the economy and put people out of work. Yet because we defied the naysayers, our air is much cleaner and our economy remains strong. As our economy has adapted to air-pollution controls, . . . we have been able to have both clean air and a healthy economy. Clean air has now become a global imperative, and [the Clean Air Act] has made the United States the envy of the world.

*— Robert V. Percival**

The Administrator concludes that . . . the case for finding that greenhouse gases in the atmosphere endanger public health and welfare is compelling and, indeed, overwhelming. . . . The evidence points ineluctably to the conclusion that climate change is upon us as a result of greenhouse gas emissions, that climate changes already are occurring that harm our health and welfare, and that the effects will only worsen over time in the absence of regulatory action. . . . In both magnitude and probability, climate change is an enormous problem. The greenhouse gases that are responsible for it endanger public health and welfare within the meaning of the Clean Air Act.

*— The U.S. Environmental Protection Agency***

---

* Robert V. Percival, Against All Odds: How America's Century-Old Quest for Clean Air May Spur a New Era of Global Environmental Cooperation (2016).

** 74 Fed. Reg. 18,886, 18,904 (2009).

## A.  *AIR POLLUTION PROBLEMS*

Air pollution has been a persistent problem of the Industrial Age, much of it traceable to the combustion of fossil fuels for energy in electrical generating units, in automobiles, and in industry. Even when they are not combusted for fuels, hydrocarbons contribute to air pollution through the release of vapors from chemical solvents, paints, and at gasoline filling stations, as well as by virtue of being the feedstock for the petrochemical industry, which has given us some of our most serious toxic substances problems, some of them airborne. Although the ultimate source of our air pollution problems are heavily rooted in a common cause—fossil fuels—the immediate sources of air pollution are diverse, including most major industries, automobiles, trucks, buses, trains, planes and motorboats, hazardous waste sites and sanitary landfills, dry cleaners, construction sites, gas stations, lawnmowers, fireplaces, and woodstoves. The diversity of sources has strongly influenced the regulatory strategies employed to improve air quality.

Certain conventional air pollutants have become nearly ubiquitous, originating from many diverse sources and posing risks to human health and welfare. These include carbon monoxide, sulfur dioxide, oxides of nitrogen, volatile organic compounds, particulates, and lead. For these pollutants, the Clean Air Act establishes a regulatory regime in which EPA sets national ambient air quality standards for each of them, after first establishing criteria that relate exposure to these air pollutants to adverse effects on human health and welfare. Each of the pollutants just named is regulated in this way, either as a so-called criteria pollutant or as a precursor to such pollutants. The coverage of the Clean Air Act is broader than the criteria pollutants, however. Distinct provisions of the Act cover toxic pollutants, for example, while others extend to "any air pollutant . . . which in [the EPA administrator's] judgment cause, or contribute to, air pollution which may reasonably be anticipated to endanger public health or welfare." E.g., 42 U.S.C. §7521(a)(1) (auto emissions).

Today, more than half a century after the Clean Air Act Amendments of 1970 established the framework for today's federal air quality regime, pollutants that can cause serious health problems or exacerbate existing problems remain in the atmosphere at unhealthy levels. Ozone has proven the most difficult air pollution problem to resolve if measured by the number of Americans who continue to live in areas of the country that exceed the national air quality standards. Figure 5.1 presents an EPA description of the health problems associated with ozone. Other air pollutants can cause even more serious adverse effects, including birth defects, heart attacks, cancer, cognitive impairment, and other forms of morbidity and mortality.

Emissions of particulate matter have proven to be the most deadly conventional pollutants, especially those 2.5 micrometers and smaller (PM 2.5), because they can penetrate deep into the lungs. Particulates can be emitted directly from sources, or they can be produced when precursor chemicals react in the air. Sulfur dioxides and nitrogen oxides are significant precursors. Figure 5.2 describes the health and environmental effects of particulate matter.

**Figure 5.1    Adverse Health and Environmental Effects Associated with Ozone**

**Health Effects**

Ozone exposure reduces lung function and causes respiratory symptoms, such as coughing and shortness of breath. Ozone exposure also aggravates asthma and lung diseases such as emphysema, leading to increased medication use, hospital admissions, and emergency department visits. Exposure to ozone may also increase the risk of premature mortality from respiratory causes. Short-term exposure to ozone is also associated with increased total non-accidental mortality, which includes deaths from respiratory causes.

**Environmental Effects**

Ozone damages vegetation by injuring leaves, reducing photosynthesis, impairing reproduction and growth, and decreasing crop yields. Ozone damage to plants may alter ecosystem structure, reduce biodiversity, and decrease plant uptake of $CO_2$. Ozone is also a greenhouse gas that contributes to the warming of the atmosphere.

*Source:* EPA, Air Pollution Can Affect Our Health and Environment in Many Ways, *https://gispub.epa. gov/air/trendsreport/2019/#effects*

On October 26, 1948, residents of Donora, Pennsylvania, awoke to find that a blanket of warm air above a cool air mass had trapped the pollutants emitted from the town's factories. The deadly inversion lasted for four days. Within two days, visibility had been sharply reduced and the town's doctors were flooded with people with breathing difficulties. Twenty people and numerous animals died; more than half of the town's 12,000 residents became ill. Devra Davis, When Smoke Ran Like Water: Tales of Environmental Deception and the Battle Against Pollution 5-30 (2002). Such acute episodes no longer occur in the United States, except occasionally in the immediate vicinity of a chemical fire, but acute exposures are still a serious problem in a growing number of developing countries. More than two-thirds of the global urban population, mostly in low-income countries, breathes air that has unhealthy levels of particulate matter at least part of the year, and major cities outside the United States experience very high average concentrations, with peak levels higher still. The World Health Organization estimates that air pollution causes the premature death of 7 million people worldwide every year. *https://www.who.int/ news/item/02-05-2018-9-out-of-10-people-worldwide-breathe-polluted-air-but-more-countries- are-taking-action.* This number includes 1.6 million people in China alone. Robert A. Rohde & Richard A. Muller, Air Pollution in China: Mapping of Concentrations and Sources, *http://journals.plos.org/plosone/article?id=10.1371/journal.pone.0135749.*

As we move further into the twenty-first century, the entire planet is united in concern about yet another air pollution problem: climate change caused by emissions of carbon dioxide, methane, and other greenhouse gases (GHGs). The major cause of climate change is one familiar to the Clean Air Act—the combustion of fossil fuels. Climate change has exacerbated other air pollution problems by increasing the scale and intensity of wildfires that increase particulate pollution. Although the Clean Air Act initially was not designed to address the unique problems of GHGs, in the absence of comprehensive legislation to address climate change, it has been pressed into service to focus on this problem.

**Figure 5.2   Adverse Health and Environmental Effects Associated with Particulate Matter**

**Health Effects**

Exposures to PM, particularly fine particles referred to as PM2.5, can cause harmful effects on the cardiovascular system including heart attacks and strokes. These effects can result in emergency department visits, hospitalizations and, in some cases, premature death. PM exposures are also linked to harmful respiratory effects, including asthma attacks.

**Environmental Effects**

Fine particles ($PM_{2.5}$) are the main cause of reduced visibility (haze) in parts of the United States, including many national parks and wilderness areas. PM can also be carried over long distances by wind and settle on soils or surface waters. The effects of settling include making lakes and streams acidic; changing the nutrient balance in coastal waters and large river basins; depleting the nutrients in soil; damaging sensitive forests and farm crops; and affecting the diversity of ecosystems. PM can stain and damage stone and other materials, including culturally important objects such as statues and monuments.

*Source:* EPA, Air Pollution Can Affect Our Health and Environment in Many Ways, *https://gispub.epa.gov/air/trendsreport/2019/#effectsE.*

## B.   THE CLEAN AIR ACT: BASIC PRINCIPLES

The principal statutory authorities for controlling air pollution are contained in the Clean Air Act. While other federal environmental laws can be used to address some aspects of air pollution (e.g., air emissions from hazardous waste disposal facilities are regulated under RCRA, air contaminants in the workplace are regulated under the OSH Act, and the Emergency Planning and Community Right to Know Act requires reporting of toxic air emissions), the Clean Air Act establishes comprehensive sets of measures to control air pollution throughout the nation.

The Clean Air Act Amendments of 1970 were the first in a series of comprehensive, federal regulatory statutes to protect the environment. Because most of these laws emerged from the same congressional committees, the concepts and language adopted in the Clean Air Act provided important precedents for much of the environmental legislation that followed. These modern statutory authorities were preceded by a history of litigation sounding in private and public nuisance, which was reviewed in Chapter 2.

Like other pollution problems now regulated at the federal level, air pollution initially was considered a local responsibility. Municipal smoke abatement ordinances were among the first environmental regulations adopted in the United States, with ordinances in Chicago, Cincinnati, New York, and Pittsburgh, among others, dating back to the 1880s and 1890s. By 1920 there were 175 municipalities with smoke abatement ordinances. Arthur C. Stern, History of Air Pollution

Legislation in the United States, 32 J. Air Poll. Control Ass'n, 44, 45 (1982). Oregon created the first state agency to regulate air pollution in 1951. Faced with horrendous smog problems, California in 1959 became the first state to establish air quality standards and to focus on what controls on vehicle emissions would be necessary to meet them.

Through a series of legislative enactments—the 1955 Air Pollution Control Act, the Clean Air Act of 1963, the Motor Vehicle Air Pollution Control Act of 1965, and the Air Quality Act of 1967—Congress expanded the federal role to encompass research and monitoring of air pollution while laying the groundwork for a comprehensive, national regulatory program. Such a program was mandated for the first time when President Nixon signed the Clean Air Act Amendments of 1970 into law on December 31, 1970. This legislation, which we now call the Clean Air Act, marked a significant departure from prior approaches and stamped federal regulatory policy with major features that it retains today. The 1970 Act was comprehensively amended in 1977, and again in 1990 to expand and strengthen its reach.

The diversity of air pollution problems, sources of air pollution, available regulatory strategies, and governments empowered to regulate different aspects of those problems have produced a very complex national regulatory strategy. Here is a highly simplified overview of the national regulatory programs established by the Clean Air Act.

Controlling the six criteria air pollutants (carbon monoxide, lead, nitrogen dioxide, ozone, particulates (PM2.5 and PM10), and sulfur dioxide) has proven to be very difficult, despite the attention it has received from EPA and the states. The Act sets up a system of shared responsibility for addressing them. On the federal side, EPA establishes national ambient air quality standards (NAAQSs) for these pollutants (§109) based on what air quality criteria say about their effects on public health and welfare (§108). State governments then decide how the numerous existing sources within their jurisdictions whose emissions contribute to the ambient levels of these pollutants ought to be controlled in order to meet those NAAQSs for their jurisdictions. Each state's set of regulations to meet the NAAQSs is called its state implementation plan (SIP) (§110). The SIPs must be submitted to EPA, which approves their adequacy to accomplish the statutory requirements. If a state does not prepare a SIP that meets the requirements of the Act, EPA must prepare a federal implementation plan (FIP) that ensures the NAAQSs will be met. Among other requirements, each SIP must avoid interfering with the efforts of other states to achieve compliance with the NAAQSs (§110(a)(2)(D) and §126).

As a further elaboration on the basic NAAQS/SIP structure, federal law now classifies parts of the country that continue to exceed the NAAQSs as nonattainment areas (NAs). It also classifies areas that have air quality better than the NAAQSs as attainment areas; these are regulated by a prevention of significant deterioration (PSD) program (§§160-169) designed to maintain clean and healthy air. The law also contains visibility protections for national parks and other areas where visibility is found to have special value (§169A), and these must be taken into account before new pollution sources can be approved.

The federal government also establishes new source performance standards for stationary sources of air pollution (§111). Beginning with the 1990 Amendments, the Act created a permitting program for new sources, through which the various new source standards are implemented and enforced (Title V).

In addition to stationary sources, mobile sources — autos, trucks, buses, trains, planes — are significant sources of pollution. The federal government takes the lead in regulating mobile sources. Responding to the argument that the producers of autos, trucks, and so forth were serving a nationally integrated national market and as such were most appropriately regulated by a single set of federal standards, the Clean Air Act invests the EPA with the authority to regulate both the content of fuels burned by mobile sources of air pollution as well as the emissions standards for new vehicles (§§202-234). For the components of mobile source emissions that contribute to the criteria pollutants, Congress has established many of the numerical emissions standards by statute. For other pollutants associated with mobile source emissions "which in [the EPA administrator's] judgment cause, or contribute to, air pollution which may reasonably be anticipated to endanger public health or welfare," EPA has authority to regulate both mobile source emissions (§202) and the fuel that goes into them (§211).

All state authority to regulate mobile source emissions is preempted by the federal statute (§209), except California's and any other state that adopts standards identical to California's. Although they cannot regulate tailpipe emissions directly, states retain substantial authority to affect the use of motor vehicles within their jurisdiction through transportation control plans (TCPs), by increasing the use of mass transit, and in other ways. See Section D, below, for discussion of federal regulation of mobile sources and fuel content. Occasionally, the federal government has developed TCPs itself or has enacted laws requiring specific transportation control measures, such as the employee trip reduction program included in the 1990 Amendments, but attempts to federalize TCPs have failed. What do you believe explains the different elements of the allocation of authority over the motor vehicle segment of the air pollution problem?

In addition to the responsibilities already noted, EPA establishes national emissions standards for existing sources of hazardous air pollutants, pollutants thought to pose a particularly acute danger to public health (§112). Hazardous air pollutant controls are discussed in Chapter 3. EPA also administers a national program for the reduction of acid rain (Title IV), see Section F below, as well as for the elimination of pollutants that destroy the ozone layer, such as chlorofluorocarbons (Title VI), see Chapter 11B1.

This overview of the Clean Air Act shows that it assigns responsibilities for addressing different aspects of our country's air pollution problems to federal and state governments. Figure 5.3 summarizes the major responsibilities. In addition, the Act establishes some regional entities to deal with problems that are inevitably multistate in nature, notably the Ozone Transport Commission, composed of the District of Columbia and the 12 states in the Northeast from Maryland to Maine, to assist in developing coordinated measures to respond to the interstate ozone problems in that region (§184).

The Clean Air Act has been an unqualified success. As indicated in Figure 5.4, between 1970 and 2018, combined emissions of the six criteria air pollutants dropped by 74 percent. This occurred at the same time Gross Domestic Product increased by more than 160 percent and vehicle miles traveled increased by nearly 150 percent. At the same time, many realize that end-of-the-pipe controls, whether they be at the end of an automobile tailpipe or at the end of a factory's smokestack, are inadequate to achieve the NAAQSs. Thus, the 1990 Clean Air Act Amendments responded to calls for reform through expanded deployment of incentive-based regulatory instruments, most notably the acid rain reduction program. They also require some nonattainment areas to participate in a clean fuels program, use market incentives to encourage utilities to switch to low-polluting fuels, and institute programs to promote the development of low emissions vehicles.

**Figure 5.3   Clean Air Act—Major Programs**

| Regulatory Targets | Federal | | | States |
|---|---|---|---|---|
| | General | NA | PSD | |
| EXISTING SOURCES | | ✓ | | ✓ |
| EXISTING HAP SOURCES | ✓ | | | |
| NEW SOURCES | ✓ | ✓ | ✓ | |
| ACID RAIN SOURCES | ✓ | | | |
| OZONE DEPLETING SOURCES | ✓ | | | |
| SMALL SOURCES | | | | ✓ |
| VEHICLE EXHAUST | ✓ | | | |
| FUEL CONTENT | ✓ | ✓ | ✓ | |
| I/M PROGRAMS | | ✓ | | |
| USE (TCPs) | | | | ✓ |

Check mark (✓) for federal gov't indicates it sets the standards, even if state administers them in its SIP.  NA refers to programs that apply only in nonattainment areas. PSD refers to programs that apply only in clean air areas subject to nondeterioration rules.

As you study the Clean Air Act, reflect on whether or not the country's air pollution strategy needs another major overhaul, either with respect to its goals, its methods for achieving those goals, or both.

**Figure 5.4    Comparison of Growth Areas and Declining Emissions 1970-2018**

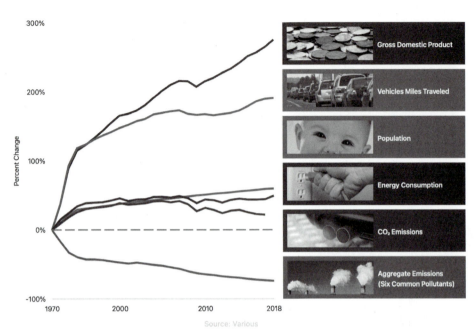

*Source:* EPA, Air Quality Improves as America Grows,  *https://gispub.epa.gov/air/trendsreport/2019/#growth.*

---

## Air Pollution Control: A Pathfinder

The federal Clean Air Act is the principal source of statutory authority for controlling air pollution. The 1970 Amendments established a comprehensive, national regulatory program for controlling air pollution that remains in effect today. The Clean Air Act was amended in comprehensive fashion in 1977, and, after a long legislative struggle, again in 1990. Although they are the product of more than a decade of legislative debate, the massive Clean Air Act Amendments of 1990 generated remarkably little formal legislative history. While the Amendments occupy nearly 100 pages of tiny print in the October 26, 1990, Congressional Record (pp. H13101-13197), the Joint Explanatory Statement of the Committee of Conference occupies less than 7 pages (H13197-13203). A more detailed explanation of the legislation was inserted into the October 27, 1990 Congressional Record by Senator Baucus, the floor manager of the legislation (S16969-16983).

The Congressional Research Service has prepared a highly readable, brief summary of the Clean Air Act, updated in 2020: CRS, Clean Air Act: A Summary of the Act and Its Major Requirements (2020). A detailed guide to the Act, published in the wake of the 1990 Amendments, is a three-part series of articles that appeared in the Environmental Law Reporter from April through June 1992.

Garrett & Winner, A Clean Air Act Primer: Part I, 22 Envtl. L. Rep. 10159 (1992) (history and structure of the Act, NAAQSs, SIPs, and nonattainment); Part II, 22 Envtl. L. Rep. 10235 (PSD, new and modified sources, acid deposition control, NESHAPs, mobile sources); Part III, 22 Envtl. L. Rep. 10301 (permit program, enforcement, judicial review, protection of the stratospheric ozone layer, legislative history). The ABA publishes a useful handbook, Julie R. Domike & Alec Chatham Zacaroli eds., The Clean Air Handbook (4th ed. 2016).

EPA regulations implementing the Clean Air Act are found at 40 C.F.R. pts. 50-97. EPA's Office of Air and Radiation maintains a website at *www.epa. gov/oar*. Current sources of air pollution data are available on an EPA webpage at *https://www.epa.gov/outdoor-air-quality-data*. EPA also has a site devoted to the growing number of market-based systems of pollution control, *www. epa.gov/airmarkets/*.

An early history of air pollution control efforts in the United States and Britain is Noga Morag-Levine, Chasing the Wind (2005). A useful survey of how the federal role in air pollution control evolved is contained in J. Krier & E. Ursin, Pollution and Policy (1977). An early history of the Act that emphasizes the many institutional actors that influenced its implementation is R. Shep Melnick, Regulation and the Courts: The Case of the Clean Air Act (1983). William Pederson's classic article, Why the Clean Air Act Works Badly, 199 U. Pa. L. Rev. 1059 (1981), spurred interest in the development of the kind of permit program now incorporated in the 1990 Amendments. Craig Oren and John-Mark Stensvaag have written a series of articles describing the complex PSD provisions of the Act. They are cited in Stensvaag, Preventing Significant Deterioration Under the Clean Air Act: New Facility Permit Triggers, 38 Envtl. L. Rep. 10003 (January 2008).

A valuable critique of the Clean Air Act, and in particular its New Source Review provisions, is Richard L. Revesz & Jack Lienke, Struggling for Air: Power Plants and the "War on Coal" (2016). Robert V. Percival, Against All Odds: Why America's Century-Old Quest for Clean Air May Usher in a New Era of Global Environmental Cooperation (2016) reviews the history of air pollution control and argues that the United States was enormously successful because at several crucial junctures Congress or the courts made bold decisions in favor of clean air.

## Major Provisions of the Clean Air Act

***TITLE I Section 108*** requires EPA to identify "air pollutants" anticipated to endanger public health or welfare and to publish air quality criteria.

***Section 109*** requires EPA to adopt nationally uniform ambient air quality standards (NAAQSs) for criteria air pollutants.

***Section 110*** requires states to develop and submit to EPA for approval state implementation plans (SIPs) specifying measures to assure that air quality within each state meets the NAAQSs.

*Section 111* requires EPA to establish nationally uniform, technology-based standards for major new stationary sources of air pollution — New Source Performance Standards (NSPSs).

*Section 112* mandates technology-based standards to reduce listed hazardous air emissions from major sources in designated industrial categories, with additional regulation possible if necessary to protect public health with an "ample margin of safety."

*Part C (Sections 160-169A)* specifies requirements to prevent significant deterioration of air quality (PSD) for areas with air quality that exceeds the NAAQSs.

*Part D (Sections 171-178)* specifies requirements for areas that fail to meet the NAAQSs (nonattainment areas).

*TITLE II (Sections 202-216)* requires EPA to establish nationally uniform emissions standards for automobiles and light trucks that manufacturers must meet by strict deadlines.

*TITLE III Section 304* authorizes citizen suits against violators of emissions standards and against the EPA administrator for failure to perform nondiscretionary duties.

*Section 307* authorizes judicial review of nationally applicable EPA actions exclusively in the U.S. Court of Appeals for the District of Columbia Circuit.

*TITLE IV (Sections 401-416)* creates a system of marketable allowances for sulfur dioxide emissions from power plants and major industrial sources to reduce acid precipitation.

*TITLE V (Sections 501-507)* requires permits for all major industrial sources with state administration and federal oversight.

*TITLE VI (Sections 601-617)* establishes a program for controlling substances that contribute to depletion of stratospheric ozone.

## C.   WHAT IS AN AIR POLLUTANT? GREENHOUSE GASES AND THE CLEAN AIR ACT

The meaning of the term "air pollutant" as used in the Clean Air Act has not, until recently, been the source of controversy. An "air pollutant" includes "any physical, chemical, biological, radioactive . . . substance or material which is emitted into or otherwise enters the ambient air," as well as any precursors to the formation of any air pollutant. §302(g). If any such air pollutant is then determined by the EPA administrator to endanger either public health or welfare, different provisions of the Act authorize the agency to regulate that pollutant, depending on whether the pollutant satisfies the definition of criteria pollutant, or toxic pollutant, or is emitted from mobile sources or from stationary sources. This latter determination — the endangerment determination — has occasionally been disputed, as it was in the case of EPA's early assertion of regulatory authority over lead emissions from automobiles. See *Ethyl Corp.*, discussed in Chapter 3.

After *Ethyl Corp.*, a second dispute arose concerning what implications an endangerment finding for an additive to gasoline, under section 211 of the Act, has for similar endangerment findings under other provisions of the Act. After EPA regulated lead in fuel, it was initially reluctant also to assert authority over lead as a criteria pollutant. Environmentalists eventually sued EPA to force its hand, and the D.C. Circuit ruled that because EPA had already made a determination that lead endangered public health in order to regulate lead in fuel, and because it was indisputable that lead satisfied the criteria pollutant standard of being emitted from "numerous or diverse mobile or stationary sources," EPA had a nondiscretionary duty to declare lead a criteria pollutant and regulate it under the provisions of the Act governing those pollutants as well. NRDC v. Train, 545 F.2d 320 (2d Cir. 1976). In neither lead dispute, however, did anyone question whether lead satisfied the statutory definition of "air pollutant."

### 1.  What Is an "Air Pollutant" Under the Clean Air Act?

Just this question was raised with respect to carbon dioxide, the major greenhouse gas. The history of EPA's efforts to define its responsibilities under the Act for greenhouse gases began shortly after Vice President Al Gore signed the 1997 Kyoto Protocol on greenhouse gases (GHGs) on President Clinton's behalf. Congress, highly skeptical of the treaty, never ratified it. (The story of Kyoto is told in Chapter 11.) Some members of Congress also became concerned that President Clinton might begin to implement Kyoto anyway, even without Senate ratification of the treaty. To prevent that, Congress enacted a series of appropriations riders prohibiting the use of any federal monies to implement Kyoto. Members of Congress further worried about the possibility that EPA might begin to regulate GHGs, particularly carbon dioxide, under its existing Clean Air Act authorities. While then-EPA Administrator Carol Browner was testifying in 1998 in defense of her agency's budget, she was asked directly by then-Representative Tom DeLay (R-TX) whether EPA already had the authority to regulate carbon dioxide. Several weeks after that hearing, EPA General Counsel issued a legal opinion that concluded carbon dioxide did satisfy the statutory definition of "air pollutant," but that regulation of any air pollutant also required a finding that carbon dioxide was "reasonably . . . anticipated to endanger public health or welfare"—an endangerment finding—which the EPA had never issued. Memorandum from Jonathan Z. Cannon, EPA General Counsel, to Carol M. Browner, EPA Administrator, EPA's Authority to Regulate Pollutants Emitted by Electric Power Generation Sources (Apr. 10, 1998).

In 1999, 19 organizations filed a petition with the EPA asserting that in light of this legal interpretation and the mounting evidence of climate change, EPA had a duty to issue the necessary endangerment finding and to regulate the emissions of GHGs from new motor vehicles. EPA did not respond to the petition during the remainder of the Clinton administration. After the George W. Bush administration took office, it was determined to dispel any notion that the Clean Air Act could be used to regulate GHG emissions. Thus, rather than ignore the petition, it made a huge strategic blunder that opened the door to judicial review of the question. In 2003, EPA formally denied the petition and issued a new General Counsel's opinion, reversing the conclusion reached in the Cannon memorandum. Memorandum from Robert E. Fabricant, EPA General Counsel to Marianne L. Horinko,

EPA Acting Administrator, EPA's Authority to Impose Mandatory Controls to Address Global Climate Change Under the Clean Air Act (Aug. 28, 2003). Because the denial of the petition constituted final agency action reviewable in court, the petitioners were able to challenge the EPA denial in the D.C. Circuit. Each of the judges thought the case was controlled by a different legal standard, but two agreed that EPA's denial should be upheld.

The petitioners then sought review in the Supreme Court, which granted a writ of certiorari and rendered the decision excerpted below, one of the most significant decisions in the history of environmental law. A superb analysis of the careful planning and strategic decisions made by the major participants in this litigation is provided in a book by Richard Lazarus called *The Rule of Five*, published by Harvard University Press in 2020.

## Massachusetts v. EPA

549 U.S. 497 (2007)

STEVENS, J., delivered the opinion of the Court, in which KENNEDY, SOUTER, GINSBURG, and BREYER, JJ., joined. ROBERTS, C.J., filed a dissenting opinion, in which SCALIA, THOMAS, and ALITO, JJ., joined. SCALIA, J., filed a dissenting opinion, in which ROBERTS, C.J., and THOMAS and ALITO, JJ., joined.

### I

Section 202(a)(1) of the Clean Air Act provides:

The [EPA] Administrator shall by regulation prescribe (and from time to time revise) in accordance with the provisions of this section, standards applicable to the emission of any air pollutant from any class or classes of new motor vehicles or new motor vehicle engines, which in his judgment cause, or contribute to, air pollution which may reasonably be anticipated to endanger public health or welfare. . . .

The Act defines "air pollutant" to include "any air pollution agent or combination of such agents, including any physical, chemical, biological, radioactive . . . substance or matter which is emitted into or otherwise enters the ambient air." §302(g). "Welfare" is also defined broadly: among other things, it includes "effects on . . . weather . . . and climate." §302(h).

When Congress enacted these provisions, the study of climate change was in its infancy.[8] In 1959, shortly after the U.S. Weather Bureau began monitoring atmospheric carbon dioxide levels, an observatory in Mauna Loa, Hawaii, recorded a

---

8. The Council on Environmental Quality had issued a report in 1970 concluding that "[m]an may be changing his weather." Environmental Quality: The First Annual Report 93. Considerable uncertainty remained in those early years, and the issue went largely unmentioned in the congressional debate over the enactment of the Clean Air Act. But see 116 Cong. Rec. 32914 (1970) (statement of Sen. Boggs referring to Council's conclusion that "[a]ir pollution alters the climate and may produce global changes in temperature").

mean level of 316 parts per million. This was well above the highest carbon dioxide concentration—no more than 300 parts per million—revealed in the 420,000-year-old ice-core record. By the time Congress drafted §202(a)(1) in 1970, carbon dioxide levels had reached 325 parts per million.

## II

Petitioners maintained that 1998 was the "warmest year on record"; that carbon dioxide, methane, nitrous oxide, and hydrofluorocarbons are "heat trapping greenhouse gases"; that greenhouse gas emissions have significantly accelerated climate change; and that the [Intergovernmental Panel on Climate Change's] 1995 report warned that "carbon dioxide remains the most important contributor to [man-made] forcing of climate change." The petition further alleged that climate change will have serious adverse effects on human health and the environment. As to EPA's statutory authority, the petition observed that the agency itself had already confirmed that it had the power to regulate carbon dioxide. In 1998, Jonathan Z. Cannon, then EPA's General Counsel, prepared a legal opinion concluding that "$CO_2$ emissions are within the scope of EPA's authority to regulate," even as he recognized that EPA had so far declined to exercise that authority.

Before the close of the comment period [on EPA's review of the petition], the White House sought "assistance in identifying the areas in the science of climate change where there are the greatest certainties and uncertainties" from the National Research Council, asking for a response "as soon as possible." The result was a 2001 report titled Climate Change: An Analysis of Some Key Questions (NRC Report), which, drawing heavily on the 1995 IPCC report, concluded that "[g]reenhouse gases are accumulating in Earth's atmosphere as a result of human activities, causing surface air temperatures and subsurface ocean temperatures to rise. Temperatures are, in fact, rising." NRC Report 1.

On September 8, 2003, EPA entered an order denying the rulemaking petition. The agency gave two reasons for its decision: (1) that contrary to the opinions of its former general counsels, the Clean Air Act does not authorize EPA to issue mandatory regulations to address global climate change; and (2) that even if the agency had the authority to set greenhouse gas emission standards, it would be unwise to do so at this time.

In concluding that it lacked statutory authority over greenhouse gases, EPA observed that Congress "was well aware of the global climate change issue when it last comprehensively amended the [Clean Air Act] in 1990," yet it declined to adopt a proposed amendment establishing binding emissions limitations." Congress instead chose to authorize further investigation into climate change. EPA further reasoned that Congress' "specially tailored solutions to global atmospheric issues,"—in particular, its 1990 enactment of a comprehensive scheme to regulate pollutants that depleted the ozone layer—counseled against reading the general authorization of §202(a)(1) to confer regulatory authority over greenhouse gases.

EPA stated that it was "urged on in this view" by this Court's decision in FDA v. Brown & Williamson Tobacco Corp., 529 U.S. 120 (2000). In that case, relying on "tobacco['s] unique political history," we invalidated the Food and Drug Administration's reliance on its general authority to regulate drugs as a basis for asserting jurisdiction over an "industry constituting a significant portion of the American economy."

EPA reasoned that climate change had its own "'political history': Congress designed the original Clean Air Act to address *local* air pollutants rather than a substance that "is fairly consistent in its concentration throughout the *world's* atmosphere," (emphasis added); declined in 1990 to enact proposed amendments to force EPA to set carbon dioxide emission standards for motor vehicles; and addressed global climate change in other legislation. Because of this political history, and because imposing emission limitations on greenhouse gases would have even greater economic and political repercussions than regulating tobacco, EPA was persuaded that it lacked the power to do so. In essence, EPA concluded that climate change was so important that unless Congress spoke with exacting specificity, it could not have meant the agency to address it.

Having reached that conclusion, EPA believed it followed that greenhouse gases cannot be "air pollutants" within the meaning of the Act. The agency bolstered this conclusion by explaining that if carbon dioxide were an air pollutant, the only feasible method of reducing tailpipe emissions would be to improve fuel economy. But because Congress has already created detailed mandatory fuel economy standards subject to Department of Transportation (DOT) administration, the agency concluded that EPA regulation would either conflict with those standards or be superfluous.

Even assuming that it had authority over greenhouse gases, EPA explained in detail why it would refuse to exercise that authority. The agency began by recognizing that the concentration of greenhouse gases has dramatically increased as a result of human activities, and acknowledged the attendant increase in global surface air temperatures. EPA nevertheless gave controlling importance to the NRC Report's statement that a causal link between the two "'cannot be unequivocally established.'" Given that residual uncertainty, EPA concluded that regulating greenhouse gas emissions would be unwise.

The agency furthermore characterized any EPA regulation of motor-vehicle emissions as a "piecemeal approach" to climate change, and stated that such regulation would conflict with the President's "comprehensive approach" to the problem. That approach involves additional support for technological innovation, the creation of non regulatory programs to encourage voluntary private-sector reductions in greenhouse gas emissions, and further research on climate change—not actual regulation. According to EPA, unilateral EPA regulation of motor-vehicle greenhouse gas emissions might also hamper the President's ability to persuade key developing countries to reduce greenhouse gas emissions.

## IV

[EPA and its supporters initially argued that none of the petitioners had standing to bring this case. In a lengthy analysis, Justice Stevens concluded that Massachusetts does have the required standing. This portion of the case is excerpted and discussed in Chapter 2.]

## VI

On the merits, the first question is whether §202(a)(1) of the Clean Air Act authorizes EPA to regulate greenhouse gas emissions from new motor vehicles in the event that it forms a "judgment" that such emissions contribute to climate change. We have little trouble concluding that it does. In relevant part, §202(a)(1) provides that EPA "shall by regulation prescribe . . . standards applicable to the emission of any air pollutant from any class or classes of new motor vehicles or new motor vehicle engines, which in [the administrator's] judgment cause, or contribute to, air pollution which may reasonably be anticipated to endanger public health or welfare." Because EPA believes that Congress did not intend it to regulate substances that contribute to climate change, the agency maintains that carbon dioxide is not an "air pollutant" within the meaning of the provision.

The statutory text forecloses EPA's reading. The Clean Air Act's sweeping definition of "air pollutant" includes "*any* air pollution agent or combination of such agents, including *any* physical, chemical . . . substance or matter which is emitted into or otherwise enters the ambient air. . . ," §7602(g) (emphasis added). On its face, the definition embraces all airborne compounds of whatever stripe, and underscores that intent through the repeated use of the word "any." Carbon dioxide, methane, nitrous oxide, and hydrofluorocarbons are without a doubt "physical [and] chemical . . . substance[s] which [are] emitted into . . . the ambient air." The statute is unambiguous.

Rather than relying on statutory text, EPA invokes post enactment congressional actions and deliberations it views as tantamount to a congressional command to refrain from regulating greenhouse gas emissions. Even if such post enactment legislative history could shed light on the meaning of an otherwise-unambiguous statute, EPA never identifies any action remotely suggesting that Congress meant to curtail its power to treat greenhouse gases as air pollutants. That subsequent Congresses have eschewed enacting binding emissions limitations to combat global warming tells us nothing about what Congress meant when it amended §202(a)(1) in 1970 and 1977. And unlike EPA, we have no difficulty reconciling Congress' various efforts to promote interagency collaboration and research to better understand climate change with the agency's pre-existing mandate to regulate "any air pollutant" that may endanger the public welfare. Collaboration and research do not conflict with any thoughtful regulatory effort; they complement it.

EPA's reliance on *Brown & Williamson Tobacco Corp.* is similarly misplaced. In holding that tobacco products are not "drugs" or "devices" subject to Food and Drug Administration (FDA) regulation pursuant to the Food, Drug and Cosmetic Act (FDCA) we found critical at least two considerations that have no counterpart in this case.

First, we thought it unlikely that Congress meant to ban tobacco products, which the FDCA would have required had such products been classified as "drugs" or "devices." Here, in contrast, EPA jurisdiction would lead to no such extreme measures. EPA would only *regulate* emissions, and even then, it would have to delay any action "to permit the development and application of the requisite technology, giving appropriate consideration to the cost of compliance," §7521(a)(2). However much a ban on tobacco products clashed with the "common sense" intuition that Congress never meant to remove those products from circulation, Brown & Williamson, 529 U.S., at 133, there is nothing counterintuitive to the notion that EPA can curtail the emission of substances that are putting the global climate out of kilter.

Second, in *Brown & Williamson* we pointed to an unbroken series of congressional enactments that made sense only if adopted "against the backdrop of the FDA's consistent and repeated statements that it lacked authority under the FDCA

to regulate tobacco." We can point to no such enactments here: EPA has not identified any congressional action that conflicts in any way with the regulation of greenhouse gases from new motor vehicles. Even if it had, Congress could not have acted
against a regulatory "backdrop" of disclaimers of regulatory authority. Prior to the
order that provoked this litigation, EPA had never disavowed the authority to regulate greenhouse gases, and in 1998 it in fact affirmed that it *had* such authority.
There is no reason, much less a compelling reason, to accept EPA's invitation to
read ambiguity into a clear statute.

EPA finally argues that it cannot regulate carbon dioxide emissions from
motor vehicles because doing so would require it to tighten mileage standards,
a job (according to EPA) that Congress has assigned to DOT. But that DOT sets
mileage standards in no way licenses EPA to shirk its environmental responsibilities. EPA has been charged with protecting the public's "health" and "welfare,"
a statutory obligation wholly independent of DOT's mandate to promote energy
efficiency. The two obligations may overlap, but there is no reason to think the two
agencies cannot both administer their obligations and yet avoid inconsistency.

While the Congresses that drafted §202(a)(1) might not have appreciated the
possibility that burning fossil fuels could lead to global warming, they did understand that without regulatory flexibility, changing circumstances and scientific
developments would soon render the Clean Air Act obsolete. The broad language
of §202(a)(1) reflects an intentional effort to confer the flexibility necessary to
forestall such obsolescence. . . . Because greenhouse gases fit well within the Clean
Air Act's capacious definition of "air pollutant," we hold that EPA has the statutory
authority to regulate the emission of such gases from new motor vehicles.

## VII

The alternative basis for EPA's decision—that even if it does have statutory
authority to regulate greenhouse gases, it would be unwise to do so at this time—rests
on reasoning divorced from the statutory text. While the statute does condition the
exercise of EPA's authority on its formation of a "judgment," that judgment must
relate to whether an air pollutant "cause[s], or contribute[s] to, air pollution which
may reasonably be anticipated to endanger public health or welfare." Put another
way, the use of the word "judgment" is not a roving license to ignore the statutory
text. It is but a direction to exercise discretion within defined statutory limits.

If EPA makes a finding of endangerment, the Clean Air Act requires the
agency to regulate emissions of the deleterious pollutant from new motor vehicles.
EPA no doubt has significant latitude as to the manner, timing, content, and coordination of its regulations with those of other agencies. But once EPA has responded
to a petition for rulemaking, its reasons for action or inaction must conform to the
authorizing statute. Under the clear terms of the Clean Air Act, EPA can avoid taking further action only if it determines that greenhouse gases do not contribute to
climate change or if it provides some reasonable explanation as to why it cannot or
will not exercise its discretion to determine whether they do. To the extent that this
constrains agency discretion to pursue other priorities of the Administrator or the
President, this is the congressional design.

EPA has refused to comply with this clear statutory command. Instead, it
has offered a laundry list of reasons not to regulate. For example, EPA said that

a number of voluntary executive branch programs already provide an effective response to the threat of global warming, that regulating greenhouse gases might impair the President's ability to negotiate with "key developing nations" to reduce emissions, and that curtailing motor-vehicle emissions would reflect "an inefficient, piecemeal approach to address the climate change issue." Although we have neither the expertise nor the authority to evaluate these policy judgments, it is evident they have nothing to do with whether greenhouse gas emissions contribute to climate change. Still less do they amount to a reasoned justification for declining to form a scientific judgment. In particular, while the President has broad authority in foreign affairs, that authority does not extend to the refusal to execute domestic laws. In the Global Climate Protection Act of 1987, Congress authorized the State Department—not EPA—to formulate United States foreign policy with reference to environmental matters relating to climate. EPA has made no showing that it issued the ruling in question here after consultation with the State Department. Congress did direct EPA to consult with other agencies in the formulation of its policies and rules, but the State Department is absent from that list.

Nor can EPA avoid its statutory obligation by noting the uncertainty surrounding various features of climate change and concluding that it would therefore be better not to regulate at this time. If the scientific uncertainty is so profound that it precludes EPA from making a reasoned judgment as to whether greenhouse gases contribute to global warming, EPA must say so. That EPA would prefer not to regulate greenhouse gases because of some residual uncertainty is irrelevant. The statutory question is whether sufficient information exists to make an endangerment finding.

In short, EPA has offered no reasoned explanation for its refusal to decide whether greenhouse gases cause or contribute to climate change. Its action was therefore "arbitrary, capricious, . . . or otherwise not in accordance with law." We need not and do not reach the question whether on remand EPA must make an endangerment finding, or whether policy concerns can inform EPA's actions in the event that it makes such a finding. We hold only that EPA must ground its reasons for action or inaction in the statute.

The judgment of the Court of Appeals is reversed, and the case is remanded for further proceedings consistent with this opinion.

## NOTES AND QUESTIONS

1. Both Chief Justice Roberts and Justice Scalia wrote dissents in the case; the Chief Justice disagreeing with the majority on the standing issue and Justice Scalia disagreeing with them on the merits. Justice Scalia agreed with the majority that when the EPA makes an endangerment judgment it must do so based on scientific facts and reasoning. But, he continued, "the statute says nothing at all about the reasons for which the Administrator may defer making a judgment—the permissible reasons for deciding not to grapple with the issue at the present time. . . . The reasons the EPA gave are surely considerations executive agencies regularly take into account (and ought to take into account) when deciding whether to consider entering a new field: the impact such entry would have on other Executive Branch

programs and on foreign policy. There is no basis in law for the Court's imposed limitation." Does Justice Scalia have a point?

2. Reread the following sentence that comes toward the end of the opinion: "We need not and do not reach the question whether on remand EPA must make an endangerment finding, or whether policy concerns can inform EPA's actions in the event that it makes such a finding." Does the latter half of this sentence suggest that EPA could determine that $CO_2$ from mobile sources does cause or contribute to endangering public health or welfare, and yet decline to regulate those emissions for the same or similar policy reasons that prompted it to refuse to issue an endangerment finding in the first place? Read section 202(a).

3. In his dissent Justice Scalia essentially argued that greenhouse gases should not be considered air pollutants because the mechanism by which they cause harm — buildup in the upper atmosphere contributing to the greenhouse effect — is radically different from the means by which air pollutants cause harm when humans inhale them. "In other words, regulating the buildup of $CO_2$ and other greenhouse gases in the upper reaches of the atmosphere, which is alleged to be causing global climate change, is not akin to regulating the concentration of some substance that is *polluting* the *air*."

4. EPA Administrator Steven Johnson sought to respond to the Supreme Court's decision by proposing to make a finding that GHG emissions endanger public health and welfare. However, he was blocked by the Office of Management and Budget, which refused even to open his email submitting the proposal for review. On January 31, 2008, Johnson wrote directly to President Bush proposing that EPA make an endangerment finding by the end of 2008 because "[t]he state of the latest climate change science does not permit a negative finding, nor does it permit a credible finding that we need to wait for more research." His proposal was rejected. On July 30, 2008, EPA issued an advance notice of proposed rulemaking that simply asked the public to comment generally on what EPA should do.

## 2.  *EPA's Endangerment Finding for Greenhouse Gases*

After President Obama assumed office in January 2009, his administration moved quickly to address the climate change problem that the George W. Bush administration had largely ignored. Within a week of taking office, President Obama directed federal agencies to consider dramatically increasing federal fuel economy standards and to reconsider the Bush administration's disapproval of California's program to control GHG emissions.

The Obama administration realized that the Clean Air Act is not ideally suited for regulation of GHG emissions. The Act's national ambient air quality standards (NAAQSs) are designed to achieve desired minimum levels of air quality in every state in the nation. Yet because GHG emissions contribute to climate change regardless of where they are emitted, all that matters is total emissions and not ambient levels in the various air quality control regions. The Obama administration proposed legislation to create a national cap-and-trade program to control GHG emissions. President Obama vowed that if Congress failed to adopt such legislation, EPA would use its Clean Air Act authority, confirmed in *Massachusetts v. EPA*, to regulate GHGs.

On June 26, 2009, the U.S. House of Representatives by a vote of 219-212 passed the American Clean Energy and Security Act of 2009, a bill that would have established a complex cap-and-trade program to reduce total U.S. emissions of GHGs by 15 percent below 2005 levels by 2020 and by 75 percent below 2005 levels by 2050. However, the legislation never came to a vote in the U.S. Senate. After Congress failed to adopt legislation to control GHG emissions, EPA used its existing regulatory power under the Clean Air Act to do so. On December 7, 2009, EPA issued an "endangerment finding," 74 Fed. Reg. 44,420 (2009), concluding that carbon dioxide and five other GHGs may "reasonably be anticipated to endanger public health and welfare" for current and future generations by contributing to global warming and climate change.

Under section 202, an endangerment finding triggers an obligation to regulate. That is not always the case in the Clean Air Act. See, e.g., §213(a)(4) (after an endangerment finding, the administrator "may" regulate). Most of the time, however, once the administrator makes an endangerment finding, he or she is under an obligation to act in response. And, as suggested by the chronology of lead regulation under the Clean Air Act, discussed above, once EPA has made an endangerment finding under one provision of the Act, it is likely that this endangerment decision will be applicable to other provisions as well.

Based on its endangerment finding for GHGs, EPA on April 1, 2010, promulgated GHG emission standards for new cars and light trucks ("the Tailpipe Rule"). 75 Fed. Reg. 25,324 (2010). Compliance with these standards essentially required significant improvements in average fuel economy as mandated by new corporate average fuel economy (CAFE) standards promulgated jointly by EPA and the Department of Transportation's National Highway Traffic Safety Administration. EPA also concluded that its Tailpipe Rule triggered provisions of the Clean Air Act that require construction and operating permits for stationary sources whose emissions of GHGs exceed statutory thresholds for any regulated pollutant. Rather than regulating the tens of thousands of sources that otherwise meet the Act's statutory permitting thresholds of 100 or 250 tons per year, on May 13, 2010, EPA issued a "Tailoring Rule." 75 Fed. Reg. 31,514 (2010). This rule applied the new permit requirements only to the very largest stationary sources of GHGs—those that meet or exceed a threshold of 75,000 or 100,000 tons per year. This subjected to regulation facilities responsible for nearly 70 percent of national GHG emissions from stationary sources.

Many members of the regulated community brought legal challenges to EPA's Endangerment Finding, Tailpipe Rule, and Tailoring Rule. The U.S. Court of Appeals for the D.C. Circuit, which has exclusive venue to hear cases challenging nationally applicable Clean Air Act regulations unanimously upheld the regulations on June 26, 2012. Coalition for Responsible Regulation v. EPA, 684 F.3d 102 (D.C. Cir. 2012), rev'd in part Utility Air Regulatory Group v. EPA, 573 U.S. 302 (2014). Upholding the Endangerment Finding, the panel found EPA's assessment of climate science to be rational. It also upheld the Tailpipe Rule and then held that states and regulated industries lacked standing to challenge the Tailoring Rule because they were not injured by EPA's failure to expand significantly the number of sources regulated.

Numerous parties then petitioned the Supreme Court to review the D.C. Circuit's decision. In their petitions for certiorari, many parties asked the Court to strike down EPA's endangerment finding, and a few states even asked the Court to reverse *Massachusetts v. EPA* and hold that the Clean Air Act cannot be used to regulate GHG emissions. But the Court refused to review the endangerment finding and Tailpipe Rule, granting review limited only to the question "whether regulation of GHG emissions from new mobile sources triggered permitting requirements for stationary sources that emit greenhouse gases." The Court's decision in that case (*Utility Air Regulatory Group v. EPA*) is covered in Section F2c below in connection with the discussion of permitting and the PSD program.

By electing not to review EPA's finding that GHGs endanger public health and welfare, that finding is now part of the law of the land. The D.C. Circuit panel that upheld it in *Coalition for Responsible Regulation* stated that "[w]hen EPA evaluates scientific evidence in its bailiwick, we ask only that it take the scientific record into account 'in a rational manner.'" 684 F.3d at 122. The court concluded that the petitioners had not shown that EPA failed to do so. So long as that finding remains intact, EPA has a legal obligation to regulate GHG emissions to mitigate climate change. Could a subsequent administration that questions climate science legally rescind the endangerment finding? What would it have to find to rescind it? Would a reviewing court be as deferential to such a finding as it was to the Obama administration's finding?

The cases and issues explored in the rest of this chapter review the major provisions of the Clean Air Act as they have been interpreted and applied throughout the years. We start our review with the provisions governing the regulation of mobile sources.

# D.   MOBILE SOURCE CONTROLS: A TECHNOLOGY-FORCING VENTURE

Emissions from automobiles and other mobile sources were the first forms of air pollution subjected to national regulation, although even before the 1970 Clean Air Act Amendments mandated federal standards, California had begun to do so in 1965. Emissions regulations have been successful in achieving a dramatic reduction in the amount of conventional pollution mobile sources produce per vehicle mile traveled. Nonetheless, emissions from automobiles and other mobile sources have also become an increasing fraction of the national air pollution load for carbon monoxide, oxides of nitrogen, and volatile organic compounds, due to the simultaneous reduction in the contribution of stationary sources to these pollutants as well as the increase in total vehicle miles traveled. In 2014, for instance, the transportation sector contributed more than half of the total national emissions of CO and $NO_x$, and approximately one-quarter of the emissions of VOCs. How can we reduce ambient levels of the pollutants associated with mobile sources once end-of-the-pipe emissions control technology for such sources has taken us as far as it can?

One answer is to transition from fossil-fuel-driven forms of transportation to other kinds. The options range from hydrogen fuel cell vehicles to battery powered. California's Zero Emissions Vehicle (ZEV) auto emissions program, has for years led the country in stimulating the development of alternative fuel vehicles. The California program is possible because California was given a statutory privilege to obtain a waiver from the federal preemption of any state regulation of auto emissions. In both 2009 and 2011, President Obama announced agreements with major U.S. automakers, federal and California officials to establish dramatically faster and more stringent increases in corporate average fuel economy (CAFE) standards for motor vehicles and trucks. The 2009 Agreement increased average fuel economy to 35.5 miles per gallon (mpg) by 2016. The 2011 Agreements, as promulgated in August 2012, require automakers to meet a 54.5 miles per gallon standard by 2025 and heavy trucks to increase fuel economy by 20 percent by model year 2018.

In addition to direct regulation of automobiles, trucks, and buses, the EPA has authority to develop fuel standards that can reap significant air quality dividends. The 1990 Amendments direct EPA to develop standards for "clean alternative fuel," §§241 et seq., and requires serious, severe, and extreme NA areas for ozone to adopt clean fuel programs for vehicle fleets. In the same EISA that raised the CAFE standards, Congress also augmented a renewable fuels program, designed to reach a goal of supplying 36 billion gallons of renewable fuel by the year 2022. While the interest in renewables stems largely from concern about climate change, some renewables can result in appreciable conventional air quality benefits with respect to the conventional pollutants, while the benefit of others is negligible. The environmental benefits of renewables depend critically on both the chemical composition of the fuels as well as on how much non-renewable energy is required to produce the renewables. The EISA adds to the Clean Air Act for the first time an explicit regulatory provision aimed at greenhouse gases. Section 211(o) requires that renewable fuels have "greenhouse gas lifecycle emissions" that are 20-60 percent less than conventional gasoline, depending on the type of renewable fuel. Lifecycle emissions, or well-to-wheel emissions, are the total emissions generated by the entire process of producing, delivering, and then consuming a fuel.

Absent fuel switching, reducing the air pollution impacts of the fossil-fuel-powered internal combustion vehicle must depend upon one of three strategies. One is to install equipment on each vehicle to capture pollutants before they become ambient. Historically, this was the first strategy employed, and such improvement as we have achieved in the mobile source sector is primarily attributable to this technique. Second, adjustments can be made in the additives to the fuel burned by mobile sources, including the complete elimination of hazardous additives. The amazing success we have had in reducing the adverse health effects of lead on children has come directly from the phasedown and then the phaseout of lead additives in gasoline. The 1990 Amendments emphasized fuel content strategies more than any previous version of the CAA. It established detailed statutory requirements for the content of reformulated gasoline to reduce emissions of volatile chemicals and toxic air pollutants. (Section 211(k), which states the requirements, contains more words than the entire fuels-related provisions of the CAA had contained up until then.) Third, we can reduce the rate at which we use mobile sources. This section reviews the contributions of each of these approaches to solving the problem of mobile source pollution.

**Figure 5.5    Percent Change in Fuel Economy, Horsepower and Weight Since 1975**

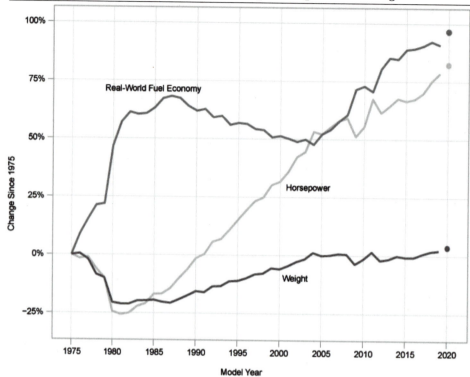

*Source:* EPA, Auto Trends Report, *https://www.epa.gov/automotive-trends/ highlights-automotive-trends-report.*

## 1.    Emissions Standards

The initial federal entry into the problem of mobile source emissions was the Schenck Act, which directed the Surgeon General to study the impact of motor vehicle emissions on human health. At the time, little was known either about the composition of auto emissions or about their environmental consequences. The automobile manufacturers, as chronicled in Ralph Nader's *Unsafe at Any Speed* (1965), downplayed the issue and resisted calls for research.

California was out in front of the federal effort. In 1960, the state established an emissions control board to oversee the development of emissions control equipment, establishing deadlines for the installation of emissions controls starting from the date the board certified that two satisfactory devices had been developed. Installation was required on new and used cars, and the law was enforced by refusals to register vehicles that lacked control devices. The California board certified seven devices by November 1962, and the registration requirements went into effect in 1965, over the vigorous opposition of the automobile manufacturers.

Congress took modest steps in 1965 and 1967, authorizing the Secretary of the Department of Health, Education and Welfare (HEW, now the Department of Health and Human Services) to establish auto emissions standards after considering costs and "technological feasibility," but the start of significant federal efforts can be traced to President Nixon's 1970 special message to Congress on the environment. In it, he endorsed even tighter controls on vehicle emissions based on estimates of the lowest emissions levels attainable with developing technology. Yet he recognized that even such stringent controls eventually would be insufficient because growth of the vehicle fleet could cancel out progress from emissions controls. Thus, he proposed the development of a clean alternative to the internal combustion engine. R. Nixon, Public Papers of the President 101 (1970). President Nixon ordered federal agencies to begin research and development for unconventional vehicles. As an incentive to the private sector to develop such vehicles, he pledged that federal agencies would purchase them even if they cost more than conventional vehicles.

In the 1970 Clean Air Act, Congress imposed "strong medicine" on automobile manufacturers to force the development of greatly improved emissions control technology. In what one senator described as perhaps the "biggest industrial judgment that has been made in the U.S. in this century," 116 Cong. Rec. 33085 (1970) (remarks of Sen. Baker), Congress directed automotive manufacturers to curtail emissions of hydrocarbons (VOCs) and carbon monoxide from new vehicles by 90 percent within five years, and a similar reduction in $NO_x$ by one year later. Congress decided on a 90 percent reduction by relying on the simple notion that since air pollution levels in major cities were approximately five times the expected levels of the NAAQSs, emissions would need to be reduced by at least 80 percent, with an additional 10 percent necessary to provide a cushion for growing vehicle use. S. Rep. No. 91-1196, 91st Cong., 2d Sess. at 25 (1970). A committee staff member involved in the legislative drafting process described the 90 percent rollback requirements as "a back of the envelope calculation. . . . We didn't have any particular methodology. We just picked what sounded like a good goal." Easterbrook, Cleaning Up, Newsweek, July 24, 1989, at 29. An earlier report from HEW's National Air Pollution Control Administration (which was absorbed into EPA when that agency was created in 1970) had estimated that reductions of 92.7 percent for CO, 99 percent for hydrocarbons, and 93.6 for $NO_x$ would be required to achieve healthy air levels, so there was some support for the general range of reductions being demanded. NACPA, Federal Motor Vehicle Emissions Goals for Carbon Monoxide, Hydrocarbons, and Nitrogen Oxides, Based on Desired Air Quality Levels, J. Air Pollution Control Ass'n, Aug. 1970, 20(8): 519-524. President Nixon had proposed a 1980 deadline for these standards to be met, but after Senator Nelson proposed banning the internal combustion engine by 1975, Senator Muskie fashioned a "compromise" appending the even tougher 1975 deadline to the administration's bill.

The mobile source regulations present a classic example of technology-forcing regulation. Congress adopted the rollback requirements with full knowledge that the technology to meet them did not yet exist, might not be available by the deadline, and had an unknown cost. The legislation gave EPA the power, at least in theory, to shut down the entire automobile industry if it failed to comply. The "statute was, indeed, deliberately designed as 'shock treatment' to the industry." International Harvester v. Ruckelshaus, 478 F.2d 615, 648 (D.C. Cir. 1973). In response, the auto companies began a battle in the courts, the Congress, and the media that continued for several decades.

To guard against the possibility that the auto manufacturers might not be able to meet the deadline, Congress provided the EPA administrator with limited discretion to grant the automobile companies a one-year extension, if the administrator determined that (i) such an extension was essential to the public interest or the public health and welfare, (ii) the auto companies had made all good-faith efforts to comply, (iii) the company petitioning for the extension had established that effective control technology was not available to meet the standards, and (iv) a study conducted by the National Academy of Sciences was consistent with the company's claim. §205(b)(5)(D).

After several auto manufacturers used this provision to petition for an extension, Administrator Ruckelshaus denied it on the ground that the companies had not met their burden with respect to requirement (iii). The administrator's conclusions depended heavily on EPA's own extrapolations from limited laboratory experiments with one design of the catalytic converter. The agency reasoned that, although the technology had not yet been demonstrated (in 1972, when the petition was filed) to be able to meet the standards over a 50,000-mile vehicle life as required under the Act, anticipated continued development of the technology would result in 1975 model year cars being able to meet the standards. Hence, in EPA's judgment, the technology was "available."

In *International Harvester v. Ruckelshaus,* the D.C. Circuit overturned EPA's decision not to extend the deadline. Reasoning that the risks associated with an erroneous denial of the extension were much greater than those associated with an erroneous grant, the court placed the burden of rebutting the companies' initial showing of non-availability on EPA and found that the agency had not met that burden.

This was not the last extension the auto industry received. EPA also granted a one-year extension of the 1976 deadline for nitrogen oxide controls. Congress amended the Clean Air Act in 1977 to grant the auto industry further extensions. As a result of these extensions, the original hydrocarbon and carbon monoxide standards did not take effect until 1980 and 1981, respectively, the very dates the industry originally had forecast that it could meet them. The final nitrogen oxide standard was relaxed and the deadline extended to 1981.

In the 1990 Amendments, Congress lowered some of the exhaust standards once again, to 3.4 grams per mile for carbon monoxide, 0.4 for $NO_x$, and 0.41 for hydrocarbons. It also instructed EPA to study whether further reductions were necessary and feasible. After issuing a "Tier II" report to Congress in 1998, EPA proposed stricter new Tier II standards in May 1999. 64 Fed. Reg. 26,004 (1999).

In December 1999, EPA adopted far-reaching exhaust and fuel content regulations. The standards require a 77 percent reduction in emissions from automobiles beginning in the 2004 model year; for the first time they extend the same strict automobile standards to sport utility vehicles (SUVs), pick-up trucks, and minivans beginning in the 2007 model year; and they require a 90 percent reduction in the sulfur content of gasoline by 2004 (lowering the standard to 30 ppm from a current average of 300 ppm). The standards were estimated to cost oil refiners and automobile manufacturers $5.3 billion in increased compliance costs, raising the price of new vehicles by $100 to $200 and adding a cent or two to the price of gasoline. However, the emissions reductions projected under the rules are designed to prevent 4,300 premature deaths annually and 173,000 cases of asthma and other respiratory illnesses among children, generating health-related benefits with an estimated value of $25.2 billion. K. Bradsher, Clinton Allays Criticism on New Pollution Rules, N.Y. Times, Dec. 22, 1999, at A20.

Assessments of the mobile source experience are mixed. Some believe it confirms the notion that "there is a certain comfort in being asked for the impossible: you know you will not actually have to do it." Margolis, The Politics of Auto Emissions, 49 Pub. Interest 3, 13 (1977). Others liken it to the fairy tale Rumpelstiltskin, wherein a maiden is ordered to weave straw into gold, a seemingly impossible task that she miraculously accomplishes. D. Currie, Air Pollution: Federal Law and Analysis (1981). It seems clear that emissions control technology would not have developed as quickly as it did without the regulations. Only a few months after the *International Harvester* remand, General Motors announced that it would install catalytic converters in all its 1975 model year cars that would last the life of the car while permitting improved fuel economy. See Ditlow, Federal Regulation of Motor Vehicle Emissions Under the Clean Air Amendments of 1970, 4 Ecology L.Q. 495, 514-516 (1975). Most vehicles failed to comply with even the revised standards, however, due to differences between test results for prototypes and actual performance on the road. Nevertheless, emissions controls ultimately produced dramatic reductions in vehicle emissions. As Currie notes, even though the industry knew EPA would not shut it down, perhaps "the cosmetic efforts industry felt compelled to make in order to establish its good faith could not, given the resourcefulness of its engineers, but have produced some improvement." D. Currie, supra at 2-114. Others argue that emissions controls were not a good investment, particularly since they encouraged consumers to keep older cars longer. R. Crandall, H. Gruenspecht, T. Keeler & L. Lave, Regulating the Automobile 115-116 (1986).

Technology forcing and technology forecasting may be to some extent inherently at odds. If the nature of the solution were evident, "forcing" would not be necessary. NRDC attorney David Doniger argued that "before a regulation exists, industry has little incentive to invent effective controls. Invariably industry later finds better and cheaper ways to cut emissions, so actual costs are nowhere near the dire predictions." Easterbrook, supra at 32. In an editorial in 1998, the New York Times observed: "Before Congress passed the 1970 Clean Air Act, Detroit argued that significant pollution reductions would be utterly impractical or prohibitively expensive. Then along came the catalytic converter that, at modest cost, eventually cut harmful tailpipe emissions by 95 percent. Likewise, the oil companies predicted economic doom when Congress mandated cleaner fuels in 1990. Their chemists, however, have since managed to produce such fuels without disturbing profits." Detroit Turns a Corner, N.Y. Times, Jan. 11, 1998, at 18.

## NOTES AND QUESTIONS

1.  Who should be responsible for developing improved emissions control technology—the auto manufacturers, the government, or independent entrepreneurs? California's ZEV program was premised on the notion that technology-forcing regulation would encourage entrepreneurs to develop technology, although auto manufacturers were reluctant to use devices developed by others. In 1969, the

federal government sued the four largest auto manufacturers, alleging that they had conspired to delay the development of emissions control devices. The suit was settled by consent decree. United States v. Automobile Manufacturers Ass'n, 307 F. Supp. 617 (C.D. Cal. 1969), aff'd sub nom. City of New York v. United States, 397 U.S. 248 (1970). Why would California's initial program premise the deadline for installing emissions control devices on certification that at least two such devices existed?

2. Professor Currie notes that it was never likely that EPA would seek to shut down the automobile industry. Why, then, was the law effective at all? Why didn't the manufacturers simply ignore the law and call EPA's bluff? See §§203(a)(1) and 205. Do these sections provide an adequate answer?

3. A major challenge faced by technology-forcing regulation is the question of what combination of carrots and sticks to use to provide an incentive for the development of new technology. The Clean Air Act's imposition of a deadline, coupled with the escape hatch of an extension, provided the auto industry with considerable incentives to maintain that the deadline could not be met and to lobby for extensions. In effect, the auto industry and EPA were engaged in a high-stakes game of chicken. Can you think of any alternative approaches to technology forcing that would avoid the all-or-nothing character of an absolute deadline while providing incentives for companies to develop control technology? Could a scheme of escalating taxes imposed on manufacturers of nonconforming vehicles guarantee the attainment of emissions control goals? Could tradeable emissions rights work for auto manufacturers?

4. Crandall notes the problem created by giving people an incentive to retain older cars longer and thereby avoid the expense of emissions controls and energy efficiency standards. In 1969, 12 percent of cars in the United States were 10 years old or older. By 1987, the figure had increased to 29 percent. States could regulate pre–Clean Air Act vehicles if they chose to do so. See T. Jorling, The Federal Law of Air Pollution Control, in Federal Environmental Law 1128-1130 (E. Dolgin & T. Guilbert eds., 1974).

Understanding that the emissions control approach to the mobile source problem would in the future be less and less able to achieve significant gains, governments have been exploring other approaches to the problem as well.

## 2. Fuel Content

The Act authorizes the EPA to restrict or prohibit the use of any fuel additive that "causes, or contributes, to air pollution which may reasonably be anticipated to endanger the public health or welfare." §211(c). The administrator used this authority to restrict the lead content of gasoline, see *Ethyl Corp.* in Chapter 3, to dramatic effect, as the correlation between lead content in children's blood to controls on lead in gasoline later demonstrated. Unfortunately, the approach taken with lead has little direct applicability to the contributions that fuel content makes to the other criteria pollutants because carbon monoxide, volatile organic compounds, and oxides of nitrogen are not produced as a result of additives to gasoline, but rather are inevitable by-products from burning fossil fuels.

Still, some gains with respect to these emissions can be obtained by adjusting fuel content because gasoline is a complex mixture of a variety of hydrocarbons and other chemicals, and the mix of the pollutants it produces can be varied somewhat through changes at the refinery. In 1990, Congress added fuel content provisions, establishing two different clean fuels programs. One operates in regions of the country that are nonattainment for ozone, and requires the use of reformulated gasoline, which results in lower hydrocarbon emissions, one of the principal ozone precursors. The second requires the use of oxygenated gasoline, which reduces carbon monoxide emissions, in regions of the country that are nonattainment for carbon monoxide.

The oxygenated gasoline program requires gasoline to contain a minimum oxygen content to ensure more complete combustion and hence lower carbon monoxide emissions. Additives, such as ethanol and methyl tertiary butyl ether (MTBE), were used to achieve the required oxygen content. After the 1990 Amendments, MTBE was the preferred option of most refineries in achieving the statutory requirement. It has since proven to be an outstanding example of unintended adverse environmental consequences, perhaps rivaling in scope the ill-advised authorization of tall chimney stacks to comply with early local air pollution demands. Tall stacks greatly exacerbated the acid deposition problem. MTBE leaked from underground storage tanks and contaminated groundwater systems. Because MTBE is soluble in water it travels much greater distances than other gasoline components once it has leaked into the groundwater. We now know it is a likely human carcinogen, as well. MTBE use was initially stimulated by EPA decisions prior to the 1990 Amendments, namely the decisions to remove lead additives from gasoline. MTBE is one of the substitutes used to enhance octane levels. Subsequently, the fuel content provisions of the 1990 Amendments greatly stimulated its use. See McGarity, MTBE: A Precautionary Tale, 28 Harv. Envtl. L. Rev. 281 (2004).

Numerous lawsuits were filed against oil companies by government entities and water suppliers for MTBE contamination of water supplies. In 2003, New Hampshire sued several gasoline suppliers, refiners, and chemical manufacturers seeking damages for groundwater contamination by MTBE. All defendants but ExxonMobil reached a settlement with the state. Ten years after the litigation was filed, the case against Exxon went to trial. The jury found that the state had suffered $816 million in damages and that Exxon's share of the gasoline market during the applicable time period was 28.9 percent. The court then entered a judgment of $236 million against Exxon. In New Hampshire v. ExxonMobil Corp., 126 A.3d 266 (N.H. 2015), the New Hampshire Supreme Court upheld the verdict and the damages awarded against ExxonMobil. The court rejected claims that the Clean Air Act's oxygenated fuels mandate preempted the lawsuit, and it upheld the trial court's use of a market share liability formula (akin to that used in the *Sindell* DES litigation) to determine Exxon's share of damages. Many MTBE lawsuits were consolidated before the U.S. District Court for the Southern District of New York, which also rejected the Clean Air Act preemption claim. In re Methyl Tertiary Butyl Ether (MTBE) Products, 457 F. Supp. 2d 324 (S.D.N.Y. 2006), aff'd, 725 F.3d 65 (2d Cir. 2013).

Even prior to Congress's enactment of CAA reformulated gasoline standards, a version of reformulated gasoline had been developed by ARCO in the 1960s as a substitute for leaded gasoline. Congress thus built on existing industry expertise in writing the clean fuels provisions, although not without some interesting twists. The original legislative proposal of President George H.W. Bush in 1989 contained provisions that would have led to the introduction of alternative fuels. The oil companies and oxygenate additive manufacturers opposed these measures and were eventually successful in substituting the current reformulated gasoline provisions for them, although they were also arguing that these provisions were too tough for them to meet. William Rosenberg, then EPA Assistant Administrator for Air, described what happened when Congress called their bluff: "Three days before the conference committee finished its work, representatives of the oil industry said they couldn't make reformulated gasoline to meet the standard. Three days after they finished, Amoco started selling it on Pennsylvania Avenue." Bush Signs Clean Air Act Amendment, Predicts Benefits for All U.S. Citizens, 21 Envtl. Rep. 1387 (1990).

The reformulated gasoline program applies to metropolitan regions with severe ozone problems—Los Angeles, San Diego, Hartford, New York, Philadelphia, Chicago, Baltimore, Houston, Milwaukee, and Sacramento—although other areas can and have opted in to the program if they wish to employ reformulated gasoline as a means for improving air quality. This program has had beneficial effects, because reformulated gasoline reduces hydrocarbon emissions by 15 percent and, as an added bonus, reduces toxic emissions by roughly the same amount. Mobil Oil, which had opposed the program as too costly, now declares: "In retrospect, we were wrong. Air quality is improving, at a cost acceptable to the motoring public." Mobil Corporation advertisement, Oct. 27, 1994.

In the Energy Policy Act of 2005 Congress added section 211(o) to the Clean Air Act, which imposed a renewable fuels standard requiring refiners to add increasing amounts of biofuels to gasoline sold in the United States. Recognizing that it may be more difficult for small refiners to comply with this mandate, Congress in section 211(o)(9) authorized the EPA administrator to grant them a "temporary exemption" and to extend the exemption for refiners demonstrating "disproportionate economic hardship." In Renewable Fuels Ass'n v. EPA, 948 F.3d 1206 (10th Cir. 2020), the Tenth Circuit held that extension of the exemption was only available to small refiners who continuously had been able to demonstrate disproportionate hardship and not to ones whose exemption had lapsed. The U.S. Supreme Court has agreed to review this decision at the behest of small refiners and it is likely to issue its decision by the end of June 2021. HollyFrontier Cheyenne Refining, LLC v. Renewable Fuels Ass'n, No. 20-472.

### 3.  Alternative Vehicles

Shortly before the 1990 Amendments were enacted, California exercised its unique ability to promulgate its own emissions standards to institute a program that took technology forcing a step beyond anything the federal government had attempted. California's initial Zero Emissions Vehicle (ZEV) standards required each manufacturer's vehicle fleet sold in California to meet an overall fleet average for emissions, which declined each year to the year 2003, with a certain percentage of the fleet required to be zero emissions vehicles, an objective that could be met only by non-fossil-fuel-driven vehicles (e.g., battery-electric cars or hydrogen fuel cell vehicles). Part of the ZEV mandate could be met by sale of autos that were close to zero emissions; the standards established various categories of automobiles that come close to being ZEV, such as low emission vehicles, ultra low emission vehicles, and partial zero emission vehicles (LEV, ULEV, and PZEV, respectively).

As the initial deadlines for producing marketable ZEVs approached, California's Air Resources Board (CARB) extended them several times. One significant change came in 2003, partially as the result of litigation filed by the auto manufacturers. They argued that because the only way to comply with California's standards for near ZEV vehicles was to market cars with very high fuel efficiency, these emissions standards amounted to fuel efficiency standards and as such were preempted by the Energy Policy and Conservation Act of 1975, which authorizes the National Highway Traffic Safety Administration to set fuel efficiency standards (the CAFE standards) and preempts state standards. The manufacturers prevailed in district court, and before the Ninth Circuit could decide the case, the CARB and the manufacturers reached a settlement that produced the 2003 regulations. The 2003 regulations once again set ZEV goals, but also established an "alternative compliance path" that manufacturers can meet by selling hybrid electric vehicles (HEVs) if they meet certain technological requirements.

In March 2008, the CARB voted to modify the program further, marking the fifth change since its initial adoption in 1990. It lowered the requirement for true ZEV vehicles (hydrogen fuel cell or battery) to 7,500 to be sold between 2012 and 2014, down from 25,000 called for by the 2003 program. It also created an additional category of enhanced advanced technology partial zero emissions vehicles (Enhanced AT PZEVs) that can satisfy part of this requirement. Enhanced AT PZEVs include plug-in hybrids like the Chevy Volt or internal combustion engines that run on hydrogen, like the BMW Hydrogen 7. CARB also introduced a 66,000 vehicles-sold requirement for plug-in hybrids for the same 2012-2014 period.

The California ZEV standards have been technology-forcing. In 2004, CARB claimed that the ZEV regulations had "spurred advances in natural gas and other alternative fueled vehicles, super-clean gasoline vehicles, fuel efficient hybrids that are powered by a combination of electric motors and internal combustion engines, and fuel cell vehicles powered by electricity created from pollution-free hydrogen." CARB, 2003 Zero Emission Vehicle Program Changes Fact Sheet (Mar. 18, 2004).

In January 2012, CARB adopted the California Advanced Clean Car rules that combine the state's rules to control vehicle emissions and the state's measures to promote alternative vehicles into a single coordinated package of measures covering vehicle model years 2017 through 2025. The rules require large volume and intermediate vehicle manufacturers to bring to and operate in California a certain percentage of ZEVs, clean plug-in hybrids, and clean gasoline vehicles with near-zero tailpipe emissions. Manufacturers who exceed their required quotas of such vehicles receive credits that can be transferred between manufacturers and third parties to comply with the regulations. In May 2013, Tesla Motors, which was producing more than 20,000 luxury, all-electric cars per year, reported its first-ever profit, fueled in large part by the sale of $85 million in such credits. CARB forecast that the number of advanced clean cars sold annually in California will grow from 65,000 in 2018 to 230,000 in 2025. Under the regulations, cars will emit 75 percent fewer smog-forming emissions by 2025 and greenhouse gas emissions from motor vehicles will decline by 34 percent.

California's program has had repercussions well beyond the state's borders. As the remaining options available to other states to meet the ozone NAAQS began to dwindle, other states that continue to have significant ozone problems had adopted California's standards. In 1990, Congress amended the Clean Air Act's preemption provisions to give states other than California the option to adopt California's auto emission standards if they so choose. That election has withstood judicial challenges by manufacturers, but only when the standards adopted by other states have been identical to current California standards. This means that each time California revises its standards, other states have only two choices—revise their standards to match California's or revert to the federal standards. Association of International Automobile Mfrs. v. Massachusetts Dep't of Envtl. Protection, 208 F.3d 1 (1st Cir. 2000). As of 2020 a total of 14 other states have adopted the California ZEV program.

As discussed below, the Trump administration tried to preempt California's more ambitious standards to control GHG emissions from motor vehicles. Undeterred, California in September 2020 announced that it plans to phase out the sale of new gasoline-powered cars and passenger trucks by the year 2035. All commercial trucks and vans in the state will be required to be zero emission vehicles by 2045. Countries including Japan, Norway, France, and the United Kingdom have announced similar plans to phase out the sale of new gasoline-powered vehicles.

## NOTES AND QUESTIONS

1. In response to the first technology-forcing directive, the 1970 Clean Air Act's call for a 90 percent reduction in emissions per vehicle, auto executives publicly warned that it "could prevent continued production of automobiles" and "do irreparable damage to the American economy." Weisskopf, Auto Pollution Debate Has Ring of the Past, Wash. Post, Mar. 26, 1990, at A1. The industry reacted similarly to the 1975 legislation mandating Corporate Average Fuel Economy standards. Both standards were then successfully met, although not without added costs to consumers. Miller, Cleaning the Air While Filling Corporate Coffers, 1990 Annual Survey of American Law 69 (1990). Given the examples of successful innovation in response to regulation, why isn't this approach used more often? Will agencies have more difficulty defending standards based on technology not already widely in use? See Stewart, Regulation, Innovation, and Administrative Law: A Conceptual Framework, 69 Cal. L. Rev. 1259, 1300 (1981). Would more precise legislative language help? See NRDC v. Herrington, 768 F.2d 1355, 1391-1400 (1985) (standards based on "maximum technologically feasible" levels).

2. Does technology forcing make economic sense? Isn't it possible that technology may be developed that isn't worth the cost? See Harrington, Walls &

McConnell, Using Economic Incentives to Reduce Auto Pollution, Issues in Science and Technology, Winter 1994-1995, pp. 26-32; R. Crandall et al., Regulating the Automobile (1986) (arguing that the marginal costs of meeting air quality goals greatly exceed the marginal benefits).

3. President George W. Bush advocated the development of new car technologies, including hydrogen vehicles, in his 2003 State of the Union Address. President Bush extolled the virtues of hydrogen-powered vehicles and proposed a $1.2 billion multi-year program to develop them. At that time he said, "A simple chemical reaction between hydrogen and oxygen generates energy, which can be used to power a car—producing only water, not exhaust fumes. With a new national commitment, our scientists and engineers will overcome obstacles to taking these cars from laboratory to showroom—so that the first car driven by a child born today could be powered by hydrogen, and pollution-free." In 2005, Congress passed energy legislation that provided up to $3,400 per vehicle in tax credits to consumers for purchase of fuel efficient, low emissions cars, based on their fuel savings potential.

4. The ZEV program is not the only air quality innovation to come from California. Another way to stimulate the introduction of alternative fuel vehicles into the market is to impose purchasing requirements on different entities that purchase quantities of vehicles, such as school districts, police departments, or private companies. In an effort to improve the air quality situation in the Los Angeles air basin, the regional air quality agency instituted a set of requirements for the owners of such vehicle fleets to purchase "clean fuel" vehicles, meaning vehicles that ran on fuels other than gasoline or diesel (the rules were aimed primarily at reducing the number of diesel-powered vehicles in the air basin, as diesel exhausts contribute significant amounts of toxic as well as criteria pollution), such as natural gas or electricity. In Engine Manufacturers Ass'n v. South Coast Air Quality Management District, 541 U.S. 246 (2004), the Supreme Court struck down these "Fleet Rules" as requiring federal approval, which California had not sought, to avoid preemption under section 209 of the Clean Air Act.

5. In March 2013, the Alliance of Automobile Manufacturers and the Association of Global Automakers petitioned EPA to block California's mandates for advanced clean cars. Mary Nichols, chair of CARB, argued that these trade associations were undermining the very progress their members have made in creating a market for electric cars: "Rather than rehashing the same, tired, legal battles of our past, why not work together to collectively support and develop this market?" In response to Nichols's statement, a spokesperson for one of the automaker trade associations stated: "Automakers hope that consumers will buy zero-emission vehicles in large volumes, but so far, sales have been lower than necessary to meet California's aspirational goals. It serves no one, not the state economy or consumers or automakers, to have these vehicles sit unsold on dealer lots." Seven years later the market for electric vehicles had dramatically changed. In 2020 General Motors announced that it had adopted a corporate strategy to pursue an all-electric future and Ford Motors announced in February 2021 that it too would go all electric. By January 2021, Tesla was selling more than 500,000 all-electric vehicles per year, and the company's market value had soared to more than $800 billion, more than three times the market value of its largest competitor.

## 4. *Greenhouse Gases and Mobile Sources: California's Special Role*

After President Trump announced his intention on June 1, 2017 to withdraw the United States from the Paris climate agreement, California officials announced that they would redouble their efforts to reduce GHG emissions. This continued the state's leadership on efforts to combat climate change. As noted above, California's leadership on clean air issues is reflected in the Clean Air Act's waiver process allowing California and other states that adopt California's regulations to regulate mobile sources more stringently than the federally required minimum. In 2002, California passed a law, AB 1493, requiring the CARB to issue regulations controlling the emissions of greenhouse gases from mobile sources. In order for these regulations to be lawful California had to obtain a waiver under section 209 from the Clean Air Act's preemption of all state regulations of auto emissions. Section 209 provides that if California "determines that the State standards will be in the aggregate, at least as protective of public health and welfare as applicable Federal standards," it can apply to EPA for a waiver. Section 209 then provides that "no such waiver shall be granted if the Administrator finds that:

> (A) the determination of the State is arbitrary and capricious;
> (B) [California] does not need such . . . standards to meet compelling and extraordinary conditions. . . .

Over the years, California successfully applied for approximately 50 past waivers and had never been turned down completely by EPA, although there had been several partial denials. In December 2007, under pressure from senior officials in the George W. Bush administration, EPA Administrator Steve Johnson announced the denial of California's section 209 waiver application. 73 Fed. Reg. 12,156 (2008). EPA acknowledged that global climate change will have substantial effects on California, but declined to find that these effects were "sufficiently different from conditions in the nation as a whole to justify separate state standards." It also concluded that while California's unique topography, weather conditions, and concentrations of automobiles had justified past waivers because these contributed to the severity of auto emissions impacts in the state, none of these factors had any relationship to the severity of the impact of greenhouse gas emissions, because a ton of $CO_2$ emitted in California contributed the same amount to the global problem—and hence to its impact on California—as a ton emitted anywhere else.

California and its supporters objected that EPA was applying a different standard to this waiver application than to any of the approximately 50 past waiver applications, all of which EPA had approved. In deciding those applications, EPA had taken the position that so long as local conditions justified having a set of separate standards in California, California did not have to demonstrate that this was the case for each and every standard it wished to establish. In other words, so long as there were going to be two standards—federal and California—auto manufacturers would not be further disadvantaged if California included in its standards further elements that could not be correlated to California's unique topography, weather conditions, and concentrations of automobiles.

California promptly challenged the waiver denial in federal court. Before the case could be decided, President Barack Obama took office in January 2009. In one of his first actions, President Obama instructed new EPA Administrator Lisa Jackson to reconsider the waiver decision. The waiver was granted on June 30, 2009. In May 2009, President Obama announced an agreement between the automobile manufacturers, EPA, and the state of California on new and more stringent national fuel economy standards that are consistent with AB 1493.

On July 29, 2011, the Obama administration announced an agreement with automakers to support further substantial increases in federal fuel economy standards for new motor vehicles. Thirteen automakers supported the proposal gradually to increase the standards to 54.5 miles per gallon (mpg) by 2025. At the time, the fleet average standard was 27.3 mpg, rising to 35.5 mpg by 2016. Significantly, the plan was supported not only by U.S. automakers, but also by many foreign companies, although Volkswagen and Daimler AG declined to support the plan. The deal was sealed when the Obama administration agreed at the last minute to abandon a more ambitious 56.2 mpg target and to revisit the standards mid-way through their implementation to determine if they are too strict or too lenient in light of fuel prices, consumer behavior, and the state of technology. Toyota, General Motors, Ford, Chrysler, Honda, Hyundai, Mazda, Nissan, BMW, Jaguar, Kia, Mitsubishi, and Volvo supported the plan. It was estimated that over the life of the program the stronger standards would save 12 billion barrels of oil, reduce $CO_2$ emissions by 6 billion tons, and save consumers an average of $8,200 in fuel purchases over the life of vehicles purchased in 2025.

On August 9, 2011, President Obama announced that heavy trucks also would be required to improve their fuel economy by up to 20 percent by the 2018 model year. It was estimated that the rules will save 530 million barrels of oil over the lifetime of trucks built from the 2014 to 2018 model years. Remarkably, the announcement was made with the support of truck manufacturers and trucking firms who reportedly agreed not to fight the initiative in part out of fear that California otherwise might adopt even more stringent rules. On August 28, 2012, the new fuel economy standards were promulgated in final form. The EPA published a final rule on October 25, 2016 establishing Phase II greenhouse gas emissions and fuel economy standards for new on-road, medium- and heavy-duty engines and vehicles, including combination tractors, buses, recreational vehicles, commercial trailers, and three-quarter-ton and one-ton pickup trucks and vans not covered by the Phase I standards.

After taking office in 2017 the Trump administration made aggressive efforts to roll back national fuel economy standards and to deprive California of the right to enforce more stringent standards for motor vehicles. In 2020 EPA and the National Highway Traffic Safety Administration (NHTSA) promulgated what they called the Safer Affordable Fuel Efficient (SAFE) Vehicles Rules. The rules first rescinded California's waiver to set its own emissions standards and preempted them, 84 Fed. Reg. 51,310 (Sept. 27, 2019); they then set less-stringent national fuel economy standards. 85 Fed. Reg. 24,174 (April 30, 2020). Led by the Union of Concerned Scientists, a host of environmental groups and state governments are challenging the rules in the D.C. Circuit. Because Trump political appointees at EPA sidelined the agency's technical staff, the analysis supporting the final rule is widely believed to be riddled with errors, including basic mathematical ones. Robinson Meyer, "We Knew They Had Cooked the Books," The Atlantic, Feb. 12, 2020. BMW, Ford, Volkswagen, and Honda have supported California's stricter emission and fuel economy standards. In November 2020 General Motors changed sides and dropped its support of the Trump rules and now supports California. On his first day in office, President Biden signed Executive Order 13,990, 86 Fed. Reg. 7037 (2021), directing EPA and NHTSA to consider "whether to propose suspending, revising or rescinding" the California waiver denial and preemption by April 2021, and the national fuel economy standards by July 2021. The agencies have indicated that they are likely to propose reversing the waiver and preemption and it is widely believed that more stringent fuel economy standards will be proposed.

## E.   NATIONAL AMBIENT AIR QUALITY STANDARDS

From the beginning, the goal of achieving air quality levels throughout the country that protect the public health and welfare has constituted the heart of the Clean Air Act. In this section we examine how the Act establishes national ambient air quality standards for the most common pollutants. The subsequent section then explores some problems in implementing practical programs that will achieve those standards, as well as how those programs have evolved over time as we have attempted to solve those problems.

The basic idea behind the Clean Air Act is deceptively simple: For the most common pollutants, the federal government will determine national ambient air quality standards (NAAQSs) and then the states will decide how to control local pollution sources so as to meet those standards. As you study the following materials, try to appreciate how complicated each step in this process actually is. Should Congress have anticipated the difficulties and written legislation that would have coped with them better? Do the difficulties suggest that these simple ideas are conceptually flawed and should be abandoned? If so, what principles should guide the nation's air pollution policies? Keep your eye on these questions as you are introduced to the intricacies of the Clean Air Act.

### 1.   Establishing NAAQSs

Section 109 of the Clean Air Act requires the EPA administrator to set primary NAAQSs at the level "which in the judgment of the Administrator, based on [the ambient air quality] criteria and allowing an adequate margin of safety, are requisite to protect the public health." The air quality criteria are supposed to "accurately reflect the latest scientific knowledge useful in indicating the kind and extent of all identifiable effects on public health or welfare which may be expected from the presence of such pollutant in the ambient air," CAA §108(a)(2).

Each step in this process is difficult and controversial. In the early stages of development of the NAAQS, scientific data was often lacking or inconsistent, especially at the relatively low levels of concentrations that are the focus of possible regulatory action. As the years have passed, studies of the criteria pollutants have accumulated (for example, in preparing for EPA's May 2008 proposal to revise the lead NAAQS downward, EPA staff reviewed approximately 6,000 health studies published since 1990), but there still remains considerable room for expert disagreement within the small range of potential adjustment that EPA now considers whenever it reviews any NAAQS, as it is required to do every five years. For instance, in April 2008, EPA announced it was lowering the 8-hour standard for ozone from .08 ppm to .075 ppm. EPA had available many health effects studies to aid its decision making, but its science advisory board as well as outside medical and science experts are disputing whether the reduction of .005 ppm is sufficient. Even if everyone agreed on the implications of the scientific evidence, however, setting the NAAQS would still be controversial.

In Chapter 3, we saw that the process of defining a concept like "acceptable risk" involves elements of both science and policy. The process of determining what level of ambient air quality is adequately protective of human health, as the Clean Air Act requires, is no less a mix of science and policy. The EPA has interpreted the requirement as protecting the public from adverse health effects. But the very idea of a health effect is also not fixed. Is a "health effect" any detectable change in blood chemistry, or only changes proved to have an adverse effect on bodily functions? When does it become "adverse"? What populations should be used as the measure of effects, given that small children and the elderly may be more susceptible to effects of air pollution? Should it matter that most human exposure to a particular air pollutant is from nonair sources? What constitutes an adequate margin of safety?

The answer to each of these questions is crucial, because the ambient air quality standards serve as the basis for both short-term and longer-term exposure limits applicable to the entire nation, with potentially billions of dollars in industry control costs dependent on the outcome.

The regulatory burden involved in establishing a NAAQS is so demanding that EPA has strong incentives to avoid making frequent changes in such standards, much less to promulgate new ones. Whenever EPA promulgates or revises an ambient standard, every SIP must be amended and reviewed. At the time of enactment of the Act in 1970, air quality criteria already had been promulgated by the Department of Health, Education and Welfare for five major pollutants: sulfur oxides, particulates, carbon monoxide, hydrocarbons, and photochemical oxidants (ozone). A sixth, nitrogen oxides, was added by EPA in 1971. Only one other pollutant, lead, has been added since then, as a result of a citizen suit. NRDC v. Train, 545 F.2d 320 (2d Cir. 1976). Lead was a unique case because EPA had formally recognized the health risk of airborne lead when it promulgated regulations under section 211 to limit lead in gasoline. In this situation, the court concluded that EPA had a nondiscretionary duty to set national ambient standards. More recent litigation suggests some uncertainty as to the specific actions necessary to trigger nondiscretionary duties. See, e.g., Thomas v. New York, 802 F.2d 1443 (D.C. Cir. 1986).

**Figure 5.6    National Ambient Air Quality Standards (NAAQSs)**

| Pollutant [final rule cite] | Primary/ Secondary | Averaging Time | Level | Form |
|---|---|---|---|---|
| Carbon Monoxide [76 FR 54294, Aug 31, 2011] | primary | 8 hours 1 hour | 9 ppm 35 ppm | Not to be exceeded more than once per year |
| Lead [73 FR 66964, Nov 12, 2008] | primary and secondary | Rolling 3-month average | 0.15 µg/m$^3$ | Not to be exceeded |
| Nitrogen Dioxide [75 FR 6474, Feb 9, 2010] [61 FR 52852, Oct 8, 1996] | primary | 1 hour | 100 ppb | 98th percentile of 1-hr daily maximum concentration, averaged over 3 years |
| | primary and secondary | 1 year | 53 ppb | Annual mean |
| Ozone [73 FR 16436, Mar 27, 2008] | primary and secondary | 8 hours | 0.070 ppm | Annual fourth-highest daily maximum 8-hr concentration, averaged over 3 years |
| Particle Pollution PM$_{2.5}$ Dec 14, 2012 | primary | 1 year | 12 µg/m$^3$ | Annual mean, averaged over 3 years |
| | secondary | | 15 µg/m$^3$ 1 year | Annual mean, averaged over 3 years |
| | primary and secondary | 24 hours | 35 µg/m$^3$ | 98th percentile averaged over 3 years |
| PM$_{10}$ | primary and secondary | 24 hours | 150 µg/m$^3$ | Not to be exceeded more than once per year on average over 3 years |
| Sulfur Dioxide [75 FR 35520, Jun 22, 2010] [38 FR 25678, Sept 14, 1973] | primary | 1 hour | 75 ppb | 99th percentile of 1-hr daily maximum concentrations, averaged over 3 years |
| | secondary | 3 hours | 0.5 ppm | Not to be exceeded more than once per year |

*Source:* EPA, NAAQS Table, *https://www.epa.gov/criteria-air-pollutants/naaqs-table.*

The current NAAQSs are listed in Figure 5.6. Primary standards are to protect the public health "allowing an adequate margin of safety," while secondary standards are "to protect the public welfare from any known or anticipated adverse effects" of air pollution. Notice that the concentrations of pollutants specified by the standards are expressed in terms of averages over different periods of time. Why would the standards be based on averages over different periods of time?

The first major case interpreting sections 108 and 109 involved the national ambient air quality standard for lead. It established several important principles concerning EPA's authority to set NAAQSs. One of those principles is that the Clean Air Act requires NAAQS to be set based on public health considerations alone, without balancing those considerations against the costs of meeting them. Costs play a substantial role in other steps of multi-step statutory processes for achieving air quality, but they play no role in setting the NAAQS. This principle, articulated in the following excerpt from *Lead Industries*, was definitely confirmed by the Supreme Court in its 2001 decision in *Whitman v. American Trucking Ass'ns*, discussed below.

The excerpt from *Lead Industries* also addresses the findings that EPA must make in order to justify setting a NAAQS on the basis of adverse health effects. Lead is a potent neurotoxin that damages the brain and nervous system in ways that are not outwardly obvious. In setting the standard for airborne lead, the administrator was concerned about lowering the levels of lead in the blood of the sensitive population, namely children in urban areas. EPA made the decision that "the maximum safe individual blood lead level should be no higher than the blood lead level used by the Centers for Disease Control in screening children for lead poisoning," 647 F.2d at 1144, which at the time was 30 µg/dl.

EPA's reasoning relied heavily upon evidence of the concentration at which lead in the blood begins to produce an elevation in the levels of the enzyme erythrocyte protoporphyrin (EP) in the blood. Early EP elevation is a "sub clinical" effect, meaning it does not cause any symptoms that can be detected in normal clinical examinations and requires blood to be drawn and analyzed to reveal it. In order to achieve its goal of lowering 99.5 percent of the target population to blood lead levels below 30 µg/dl, EPA calculated that the average total blood lead level in that population would have to be 15 µg/dl. This was based on an assumption that the ratio of airborne lead to blood lead levels was 1:2. While this was consistent with some existing studies, the EPA conceded that the relationship between airborne lead and blood lead was only imperfectly understood. EPA also employed a combination of partial studies and some assumptions to conclude that nonair sources of lead (e.g., lead-based paint, lead from canned foods and pipes) contributed 12 µg/dl to blood lead levels of children, on average. In accordance with these conclusions, the EPA set the primary air standard at 1.5 µg/m³.

## Lead Industries Association v. EPA

647 F.2d 1130 (D.C. Cir. 1980)

J. SKELLY WRIGHT, Chief Judge:

### III.  THE LEAD STANDARD RULEMAKING PROCEEDINGS

[The] Administrator examined the various health effects of lead exposure and proposed that EP elevation should be considered the first adverse health effect of lead exposure because it indicates an impairment of cellular functions, and should be the pivotal health effect on which the lead standards are based. Accordingly, he proposed that the air lead standards be designed to prevent the occurrence of EP elevation in children. . . .

None of the comments seriously questioned the selection of children between the ages of 1 and 5 years as the target population group. . . . The major areas of controversy were the Administrator's choice of EP elevation as the pivotal adverse health effect and his conclusion that the threshold blood lead level for EP elevation in children is 15 μg Pb/dl. . . .

A number of comments challenged the selection of EP elevation as the pivotal adverse health effect, insisting that EP elevation merely indicates a biological change or response which is in no way harmful to health, and in addition they criticized the Administrator's determination that the blood lead threshold for EP elevation in children is 15 μg Pb/dl. These comments suggested that a decrease in hemoglobin levels, which begins at blood lead levels no lower than 40 μg Pb/dl, should be the pivotal adverse health effect on which the standards are based. . . .

## V.  STATUTORY AUTHORITY

. . . St. Joe contends that EPA erred by refusing to consider the issues of economic and technological feasibility in setting the air quality standards for lead. St. Joe's claim that the Administrator should have considered these issues is based on the statutory provision directing him to allow an "adequate margin of safety" in setting primary air quality standards. In St. Joe's view, the Administrator must consider the economic impact of the proposed standard on industry and the technological feasibility of compliance by emission sources in determining the appropriate allowance for a margin of safety. St. Joe argues that the Administrator abused his discretion by refusing to consider these factors in determining the appropriate margin of safety for the lead standards, and maintains that the lead air quality standards will have a disastrous economic impact on industrial sources of lead emissions.

This argument is totally without merit. St. Joe is unable to point to anything in either the language of the Act or its legislative history that offers any support for its claim that Congress, by specifying that the Administrator is to allow an "adequate margin of safety" in setting primary air quality standards, thereby required the Administrator to consider economic or technological feasibility. To the contrary, the statute and its legislative history make clear that economic considerations play no part in the promulgation of ambient air quality standards under Section 109. . . .

. . . LIA argues that the legislative history of the Act indicates that Congress only intended to protect the public against effects which are known to be *clearly harmful* to health, maintaining that this limitation on the Administrator's statutory authority is necessary to ensure that the standards are not set at a level which is more stringent than Congress contemplated. The Administrator, on the other hand, agrees that primary air quality standards must be based on protecting the public from "adverse health effects," but argues that the meaning LIA assigns to that phrase is too limited. In particular, the Administrator contends that LIA's interpretation is inconsistent with the precautionary nature of the statute, and will frustrate Congress' intent in requiring promulgation of air quality standards. . . .

The Administrator begins by pointing out that the Act's stated goal is "to protect and enhance the quality of the Nation's air resources so as to promote the public health and welfare and the productive capacity of its population(.)" Section 101(b)(1). This goal was reaffirmed in the 1977 Amendments. For example, the House Report accompanying the Amendments states that one of its purposes is "(t)o emphasize the preventive or precautionary nature of the act, i.e., to assure that regulatory action can effectively prevent harm before it occurs; to emphasize the predominant value of protection of public health(.)" H.R. Rep. No. 95-294, 95th Cong., 1st Sess. 49 (1977). . . .

We agree that LIA's interpretation of the statute is at odds with Congress' directive to the Administrator. . . . The Senate Report explains that the Administrator is to set standards which ensure that there is "an absence of adverse effects." But LIA would require a further showing—that the effects on which the standards were based are *clearly* harmful or *clearly* adverse. We cannot, however, find the source of this further restriction that LIA would impose on the Administrator's authority. It may be that it reflects LIA's view that the Administrator must show that there is a "medical consensus that [the effects on which the standards were based] are harmful. . . ." If so, LIA is seriously mistaken. This court has previously noted that some uncertainty about the health effects of air pollution is inevitable. And we pointed out that "[a]waiting certainty will often allow for only reactive, not preventive regulat[ory action]." Ethyl Corp. v. EPA, 541 F.2d 1, 25 (D.C. Cir 1976) (*en banc*). Congress apparently shares this view; it specifically directed the Administrator to allow an adequate margin of safety to protect against effects which have not yet been uncovered by research and effects whose medical significance is a matter of disagreement. . . . Moreover, it is significant that Congress has recently acknowledged that more often than not the "margins of safety" that are incorporated into air quality standards turn out to be very modest or nonexistent, as new information reveals adverse health effects at pollution levels once thought to be harmless. Congress' directive to the Administrator to allow an "adequate margin of safety" alone plainly refutes any suggestion that the Administrator is only authorized to set primary air quality standards which are designed to protect against health effects that are known to be clearly harmful. . . .

Furthermore, we agree with the Administrator that requiring EPA to wait until it can conclusively demonstrate that a particular effect is adverse to health before it acts is inconsistent with both the Act's precautionary and preventive orientation and the nature of the Administrator's statutory responsibilities. Congress provided that the Administrator is to use his judgment in setting air quality standards precisely to permit him to act in the face of uncertainty. And as we read the statutory provisions and the legislative history, Congress directed the Administrator to err on the side of caution in making the necessary decisions. We see no reason why this court should put a gloss on Congress' scheme by requiring the Administrator to show that there is a medical consensus that the effects on which the lead standards were based are "clearly harmful to health." All that is required by the statutory scheme is evidence in the record which substantiates his conclusions about the health effects on which the standards were based.

## NOTES AND QUESTIONS

1. Subsequent to this decision, CDC lowered the screening level to 25 µg/dl, and in 1991 it lowered the level again, to 10 µg/dl. What impact, if any, should this have on the level of the NAAQS? What if it were impossible to get 99.5 percent of the children's blood lead levels below the CDC level, due to their exposure to other sources of lead?

2. In May 2008, EPA proposed its first revision of the lead standard since the 1978 standard was upheld in *Lead Industries*. EPA proposed a new NAAQS in the .10 µg/m³ to .30 µg/m³ range—80 percent to 93 percent lower than the 1978 standard—and solicited comments on standards outside that range as well. 73 Fed. Reg. 29,005 (May 20, 2008). In this proposal, EPA shifted away from EP elevation as the adverse health effect upon which the standard should be based, instead using interference with neurological and neurocognitive function in children. The Scientific Advisory Committee that by statute advises EPA on its NAAQS standards reported a unanimous consensus that a loss of 1 to 2 IQ points "could be significant from a public health perspective," and that this concern justified a new NAAQS of .2 µg/m³. In announcing the NAAQS proposal, the agency stated that "the Administrator first notes that ideally air-related (as well as other) exposures to environmental [lead] would be reduced to the point that no IQ impact in children would occur. The Administrator recognizes, however, that . . . he is required to make a judgment as to what degree of protection is requisite to protect public health with an adequate margin of safety. . . . [The] Administrator proposes to conclude that an air-related population mean IQ loss within the range of 1 to 2 points could be significant from a public health perspective, and that a standard level should be selected to provide protection from air-related population mean IQ loss in excess of this range." Id. In October 2008, EPA lowered the lead NAAQS to .15 µg/m³. 73 Fed. Reg. 66,964 (2008). Had EPA instead set a standard *above* .2 µg/m³ would the decision have been legally vulnerable under *Lead Industries*?

3. Only two areas of the country exceeded the old lead NAAQS, with an exposed population total of less than 5,000. Both of these, East Helena Montana and Herculaneum, Missouri, are the sites of lead smelters (East Helena's closed in 2001). Only 3 percent of the nation's counties have lead monitors; 24 states have none at all. It was estimated that the 2008 NAAQS for lead placed 18 additional counties in nonattainment. Overwhelmingly, the new counties also were sites of lead emitting facilities. The new standards expanded lead monitoring requirements for these counties and for metropolitan areas. EPA also lowered the secondary NAAQS for lead to the same .15 µg/m³ level in 2008. On October 18, 2016, the EPA finalized a rule retaining the current NAAQS for lead. The EPA concluded the existing primary and secondary standards were "requisite to protect public health with an adequate margin of safety" and "requisite to protect public welfare from known or anticipated adverse effects." 81 Fed. Reg. 71,906 (2016).

4. In Chapter 2, we introduced the tradeoff between regulatory strategies that are inflexible but relatively easy to administer and more complex but more flexible strategies. There, the contrast was between nationally uniform technology-based standards and cost-benefit balancing standards. Proponents of greater flexibility

have criticized the nationally uniform ambient standards of the Clean Air Act as well. In an early article, Professor Krier argued that uniform standards are a "fundamentally mistaken end":

> To justify uniform standards as efficient in cost-minimization terms one would have to assume that the costs of a given level of pollution and a given level of control are the same across the nation. This assumption, however, is manifestly not valid. For example, aesthetic costs and materials losses will be functions of the varying resource endowments, degree of development, and human attitudes that exist in different regions. Even health costs—which were of the greatest concern to Congress in passing the 1970 legislation—vary from place to place. Since such costs represent the aggregate of individual health effects, and since population varies significantly by region, so too will total health costs. If one believes that per capita and not aggregate health costs should be the relevant factor, efficiency considerations would still suggest some variation in air quality levels. This is because the costs of pollution control will also vary, depending upon population, density and nature of development, and meteorological and topographical conditions in any particular region. In short, since the costs of pollution and the costs of control vary across the country, it is difficult to see how a uniform standard can begin to take the varying costs into account. The standard that minimizes total costs for a region in Iowa is hardly likely to do so for all the regions of California or New York or Colorado as well. To require adherence to the same stringent standard everywhere will in many areas result in the imposition of control costs which are much larger than the pollution costs avoided. [Krier, The Irrational National Air Quality Standards: Macro- and Micro-Mistakes, 22 UCLA L. Rev. 323, 336-337 (1974).]

Krier contends that the only defensible rationale for nationally uniform standards is that it is simply too costly to set regional standards, but that this is a not very convincing rationale, because setting regional standards is not difficult. Does the information about the incidence of the lead NAAQS inform your assessment of Krier's arguments? In light of his criticisms, why do you suppose that Congress chose the nationally uniform approach?

The *Lead Industries* opinion describes the 1970 Clean Air Act Amendments as Congress's effort at "'taking a stick to the States.'. . . Congress was well aware that, together with Section 108 and 110, Section 109 imposes requirements of a 'technology-forcing' character." 647 F.2d at 1145. Does this characterization affect your answer?

Greater flexibility in standard setting, and especially the ability to balance costs of compliance against benefits on a localized level, is one of the centerpieces of reform proposals. For more on the arguments in favor of cost-benefit analysis in setting the NAAQS, see the notes after *American Trucking*, below.

5. At the time Professor Krier wrote the quoted article, states had just barely begun to implement their SIPs. Subsequently, it has become apparent that the SIP-writing process provides an occasion for states to take into account variations in pollution abatement costs in allocating emission controls among industries.

For instance, a study of the paper industry has found that the stringency of pollution controls in SIPs tends to vary with differences in costs and benefits. R. Luken, Efficiency in Environmental Regulation: A Benefit-Cost Analysis of Alternative Approaches (1990). As we will see below, states also have varied considerably in their progress toward attainment of the standards. Indeed, Krier later argued that national uniformity has been a chimerical goal of the Clean Air Act in light of the variable compliance history of different parts of the country. J. Krier, On the Topology of Uniform Environmental Standards in a Federal System—And Why It Matters, 54 Md. L. Rev. 1226 (1995). He maintains that it would be wiser and more efficient to abandon the fiction of uniformity in light of the "enormous costs, laughable delays, and extraordinary burdens" being incurred "for the sake of some-day achieving standards that are, in the extreme cases, probably impossible and in many instances not worthwhile." Id. at 1241.

6. Section 108(a) requires EPA to publish air quality criteria for any pollutant that contributes to air pollution that may endanger public health or welfare if its presence "in the ambient air results from numerous or diverse mobile or stationary sources." Lead is the only new criteria air pollutant that has been added to EPA's initial list and, as explained above, this occurred only because of a successful citizen suit. NRDC v. Train, 545 F.2d 320 (2d Cir. 1976). Similar litigation has been initiated by the states of Connecticut, Maine, and Massachusetts to compel EPA to establish a NAAQS for carbon dioxide, due to its contribution to global warming and climate change.

---

## PROBLEM EXERCISE: A NAAQS FOR $CO_2$?

Should a national ambient air quality standard (NAAQS) be established for carbon dioxide ($CO_2$) in light of evidence that it is the most significant greenhouse gas that contributes to global warming? In December 2009 two environmental organizations, the Center for Biological Diversity and 350.org, filed a Petition to Establish National Pollution Limits for Greenhouse Gases Pursuant to the Clean Air Act (Dec. 2, 2009). EPA denied the petition on Jan. 19, 2021, Trump's final day as president, *https://www.biologicaldiversity.org/programs/climate_law_institute/pdfs/21-01-19-GHG-NAAQS-Petition-Denial-2021-01-19.pdf*. It called for EPA to establish a NAAQS for $CO_2$ with the ultimate goal of reducing global $CO_2$ concentrations from 387 parts per million (ppm) to 350 ppm.

**Question One.** Should $CO_2$ be considered a criteria pollutant under section 108 of the CAA? This section applies to pollutants emitted from numerous or diverse sources whose emissions "cause or contribute to air pollution which may reasonably be anticipated to endanger public health or welfare." Proponents of including $CO_2$ on the list of criteria pollutants insist that: (1) $CO_2$ is emitted by numerous and diverse sources, (2) it contributes to the buildup of atmospheric concentrations of greenhouse gases, (3) these gases already are adversely affecting the earth's climate, and (4) changes in climate are known or may reasonably be anticipated to be causing a wide range of adverse effects on human health or welfare including heat stress, extreme storms, increased formation of ground-level ozone, and changes in the distribution and severity of diseases. How does the decision in *Massachusetts v.*

*EPA* influence your answer? Now that EPA has made an endangerment finding for GHGs (including $CO_2$) under section 202, how does that influence your answer?

**Question Two.** To justify its rejection of a petition to regulate emissions of greenhouse gases from automobiles, EPA concluded that it should not commence rulemaking "[u]ntil more is understood about the causes, extent and significance of climate change and the potential options for addressing it." 68 Fed. Reg. 52,822, 52,931 (Sept. 8, 2003). If EPA considers whether to classify $CO_2$ as a criteria pollutant, could it invoke scientific uncertainty as a reason to decline to do so, or is this possibility precluded by *Massachusetts v. EPA*? Even if the possibility is still available to EPA, is it consistent with *Ethyl Corp. v. EPA*, discussed in Chapter 3? Petitioners in *Massachusetts v. EPA* thought not, but in the Court of Appeals, Judge Randolph argued that "*Ethyl* supports EPA, not petitioners" because it "gives the Administrator considerable discretion" to act not solely on the basis of scientific assessments, but also to make "policy judgments" concerning whether regulation was appropriate. 415 F.3d at 57-58. Do you agree with Judge Randolph's interpretation of *Ethyl Corp.?*

**Question Three.** EPA denied the petition on Jan.19, 2021. It determined that "a NAAQS for GHG would be inconsistent with the text and structure of the Clean Air Act" because the "NAAQS regime is designed for local pollutants that state-level regulation can meaningfully control." EPA explained that because "GHG is a global pollutant that is dispersed evenly throughout the global atmosphere," no "state implementation plan could possibly have any measurable effect on the concentration of GHG within its own borders." Do you agree? EPA also denied petitions to use section 115 and  section 112 of the CAA to regulate GHG emissions.

## 2.  Revising NAAQSs

EPA is required to review and revise its air quality criteria and the NAAQSs at five-year intervals. Section 109(d) of the Clean Air Act directs EPA to "complete a thorough review" of the criteria and the NAAQSs and to make such revisions to them "as may be appropriate." To assist the agency in performing these tasks, EPA is required to appoint an independent scientific review committee, the Clean Air Scientific Advisory Committee (CASAC), which reviews the scientific data relied upon by the agency and recommends revisions in the criteria and the NAAQSs. While CASAC helps EPA to improve the quality of its analysis, its composition sometimes is controversial because it can include experts who work for industries EPA regulates. See S. Jasanoff, The Fifth Branch: Science Advisors as Policymakers 101-122 (1990).

Pursuant to these requirements, EPA in 1982 published new air quality criteria for particulate matter and sulfur oxide. The new criteria discussed in some detail how emissions of sulfur oxides contributed to the acid deposition problem. Despite issuing a three-volume "Critical Assessment" of the effects of sulfur oxides on acid deposition in 1984, EPA took no action with respect to revisions of the NAAQS.

In Environmental Defense Fund v. Thomas, 870 F.2d 892 (2d Cir. 1989), several environmental groups and six states sued EPA for failing to revise the NAAQS for sulfur oxides. The plaintiffs argued that EPA was required to revise the NAAQS to prevent acid deposition because the agency had published new criteria documents finding that sulfur oxide contributed to the acid deposition problem. EPA argued that the "as may be appropriate" language of section 109(d) made any decision concerning revision of the NAAQS wholly discretionary. The Second Circuit rejected the arguments made by both EPA and the plaintiffs. The court concluded that although it could not dictate to EPA whether or how the NAAQS should be revised, "the Administrator must make *some* decision regarding the revision of the NAAQS" that itself would be subject to judicial review. By publishing revised criteria documents, EPA "triggered a duty" on its part "to address and decide whether and what kind of revision is necessary."

As noted above, EPA has been reluctant to revise its NAAQSs in part because of the enormous administrative burden such revisions would generate. Whenever EPA changes a NAAQS, each state must prepare a revised state implementation plan (SIP) that must then undergo a cumbersome process of EPA review and approval. Lengthy delays have occurred in the revision of air quality criteria as members of CASAC struggle to reach consensus on the significance of new data. Scientific uncertainty has been the principal rationale used by EPA when it has declined to revise NAAQSs.

### Sensitive Populations and Short-Term Exposures to Spikes in $SO_2$ Emissions

The question of how much protection the NAAQSs should afford sensitive populations is an important one. In the *Lead Industries Association* decision, the D.C. Circuit stated that "air quality standards must also protect individuals who are particularly sensitive to the effects of pollution." The court noted that the Senate Report on the 1970 Clean Air Amendments was "particularly careful to note that especially sensitive persons such as asthmatics and emphysematics are included within the group that must be protected." Concern about the effect of air pollution on asthmatics has increased as the health problems of asthmatics have become more apparent.

$SO_2$ has been associated with asthma. Notwithstanding this, in 1988, EPA proposed not to revise its primary and secondary NAAQSs for $SO_2$. It did express concern over the effects of short-term $SO_2$ peaks on asthmatics and solicited public comment on the possibility of adding a new one-hour primary standard for $SO_2$ of 0.4 ppm. 53 Fed. Reg. 14,926 (1988). The agency subsequently estimated that 68,000 to 166,000 asthmatics could be exposed to at least one peak $SO_2$ concentration while exercising outdoors and that total exposure events could range from 180,000 to 395,000. 59 Fed. Reg. 58,967 (1994). One reason EPA was reluctant to revise the NAAQS was that short-term peaks of $SO_2$ are concentrated in the vicinity of several hundred large emissions sources, including power plants and petroleum refineries, and hence national standards may be inappropriate.

The main beneficiaries of a short-term standard would be asthmatics who suffer temporary and reversible bronchoconstriction while exercising. What significance should be attached to the temporary nature of these effects and the fact that they also can be induced by other stimuli? In *Lead Industries Association*, the D.C. Circuit rejected the notion that a primary NAAQS can only be used to protect against health effects known to be "clearly harmful." 647 F.2d at 1148. Can it be used to protect against bronchoconstriction experienced by asthmatics? One type of asthma medication can be effective in preventing bronchoconstriction if taken shortly before exposure to $SO_2$. But $SO_2$ exposures are unpredictable and the medication is not widely used. Should the fact that asthmatics can avoid adverse reactions to $SO_2$ by taking medication prior to exercising influence EPA's decision in any way? More generally, when EPA establishes NAAQSs, can it discount the adverse health effects of air pollutants that can be avoided by staying indoors or by not exercising?

In May 1996, EPA decided not to adopt a new short-term exposure NAAQS for $SO_2$. 61 Fed. Reg. 25,566 (1996). EPA conceded that exposure to short-term peak $SO_2$ concentrations causes bronchoconstrictive responses in exercising asthmatics, but it noted a divergence of opinion in the medical community concerning the significance of these effects. Although it acknowledged that "repeated occurrences of such effects should be regarded as significant from a public health standpoint," it concluded that this problem was more appropriately addressed at the state level.

Public health and environmental organizations sued EPA for its failure to adopt a short-term standard. In 1998, the D.C. Circuit Court of Appeals remanded the decision to EPA for further explanation, saying that EPA had failed to explain why exposure to peak $SO_2$ concentrations does not amount to a "public health" problem within the meaning of the Act. American Lung Association v. EPA, 134 F.3d 388 (D.C. Cir. 1998). "The link," the court wrote, "between this conclusion and the factual record as interpreted by EPA—that 'repeated' exposure is 'significant' and that thousands of asthmatics are exposed more than once a year—is missing. Why is the fact that thousands of asthmatics can be expected to suffer atypical physical effects from repeated five-minute bursts of high-level sulfur dioxide not a public health problem? Why are from 180,000 to 395,000 annual 'exposure events'. . . so 'infrequent' as to warrant no regulatory action? Why are disruptions of ongoing activities, use of medication, and hospitalization not 'adverse health effects' for asthmatics? . . . Without answers to these questions, the Administrator cannot fulfill her responsibility under the Clean Air Act to establish NAAQS's 'requisite to protect the public health.'. . . Given the gaps in the Final Decision's reasoning, we must remand this case to permit the Administrator to explain her conclusions more fully."

Twelve years after the *American Lung Ass'n* decision, EPA adopted a new one-hour, 75 parts per billion (ppb) primary NAAQS for sulfur dioxide. The standard replaced both the previous primary standards of 140 ppb over 24 hours and 30 ppb over an entire year. 75 Fed. Reg. 35,520 (2010).

### Revising the Ozone and Particulate NAAQSs

The Clean Air Act requires periodic review of the scientific evidence, and some of these reviews have resulted in revisions. In March 2008, EPA reduced the existing ozone standard; in October 2008, it drastically reduced the lead standard. The particulate matter standards were revised in 2006. Many revisions were conducted only after environmental organizations sued EPA for failure to discharge its statutory duty to review the NAAQS periodically.

When EPA promulgates revised NAAQSs, it invariably is sued by groups unhappy with the new standards. One set of such challenges produced a significant Supreme Court decision interpreting the Clean Air Act. In 1997, EPA lowered the ozone NAAQS from 0.12 ppm over a one-hour average to 0.08 ppm over an eight-hour average, and it added a NAAQS for fine particles of 2.5 microns or less, setting it at 15 µg per cubic meter on average annually, and at 65 µg per cubic meter over a 24-hour average. 62 Fed. Reg. 38,652 (1997), 62 Fed. Reg. 38,762 (1997).

Using models that projected costs to the year 2010, EPA estimated the new ozone standards would impose costs of $1.1 billion annually. While unable to quantify all health benefits, EPA estimated quantifiable benefits in a range from $0.4 billion to $2.1 billion per year. For particulate matter (PM), the comparable figures were $8.6 billion in costs, and a range of $19 to $104 billion in benefits. EPA Regulatory Impact Analysis for the Particulate Matter and Ozone Rule, Tables ES-3 and ES-4 (July 17, 1997). The PM benefits were largely attributed to new research linking specific components of concern such as acid aerosols, sulfates, nitrates, some metals, and diesel particulates, all of which are found predominantly on the fine particles, to adverse health effects. The existing PM standard had permitted compliance through the use of technologies not designed to reduce the fine particles.

The new NAAQSs were immediately challenged by many parties. In 1999, a three-judge panel of the D.C. Circuit voted 2-1 to invalidate both the ozone and the PM NAAQS. American Trucking Ass'ns v. EPA, 175 F.3d 1027 (D.C. Cir. 1999). Industry groups had argued in their petitions that *Lead Industries* was not controlling, and that EPA had erred in failing to consider the costs of compliance in setting the standards. One industry petition also briefly argued that if the Clean Air Act really did compel the administrator of EPA to set NAAQS without taking costs into account, then the delegation of authority was in effect standardless, because it did not identify how any point above zero could be chosen as a NAAQS, at least when EPA was considering a pollutant where there was no clear evidence of a level above zero where the pollutant had no adverse effects. Industry petitions also raised a number of other challenges to the evidence and to details in EPA's interpretation of the 1990 Amendments.

When the panel decision was announced, it rested on a much more breathtaking legal theory than anyone had anticipated. The panel acknowledged that EPA had provided information on criteria that it took into account in setting the NAAQS, such as the severity of adverse health effects at different levels of exposure, the number of people affected, the quality of the scientific evidence, and so on. Nonetheless, it concluded that EPA had violated the constitutional doctrine against delegating legislative authority to the executive branch because the agency had failed to identify how these criteria would all be combined to reach a judgment as to why a specific level would be chosen. Without identifying such a "determinate standard," the panel wrote, "it is as though Congress commanded EPA to select 'big guys,' and EPA announced that it would evaluate candidates based on height and weight, but revealed no cut-off point. The announcement, though sensible in what it does say, is fatally incomplete. The reasonable person responds, 'How tall? How heavy?'" Id. at 1034.

The panel's decision was both novel and potentially far-reaching. Previously, the non-delegation doctrine had only been invoked by the Supreme Court as a check on Congress's authority. Here, however, the panel did not find the Clean Air Act to be irretrievably flawed on non-delegation grounds. Instead, it held that EPA had failed to cure any non-delegation problem by not announcing a determinate standard or formula for combining all the relevant criteria. The theory was potentially far-reaching because its logic could be applied to many other areas of administrative rulemaking, both at EPA and in other agencies. Few were surprised when the Supreme Court accepted the case for review, thereby providing the Court with its first opportunity to review the proper interpretation of the standard-setting provisions of the Clean Air Act for NAAQSs.

## Whitman v. American Trucking Ass'ns

531 U.S. 457 (2001)

JUSTICE SCALIA delivered the opinion of the Court.

These cases present the following questions: (1) Whether §109(b)(1) of the Clean Air Act (CAA) delegates legislative power to the Administrator of the Environmental Protection Agency (EPA). (2) Whether the Administrator may consider the costs of implementation in setting national ambient air quality standards (NAAQS) under §109(b)(1). . . .

### II

In *Lead Industries Assn., Inc. v. EPA* the District of Columbia Circuit held that "economic considerations [may] play no part in the promulgation of ambient air quality standards under Section 109" of the CAA. In the present cases, the court adhered to that holding, as it had done on many other occasions. Respondents argue that these decisions are incorrect. We disagree; and since the first step in assessing whether a statute delegates legislative power is to determine what authority the statute confers, we address that issue of interpretation first and reach respondents' constitutional arguments in Part III, *infra*.

Section 109(b)(1) instructs the EPA to set primary ambient air quality standards "the attainment and maintenance of which . . . are requisite to protect the public health" with "an adequate margin of safety." Were it not for the hundreds of pages of briefing respondents have submitted on the issue, one would have thought it fairly clear that this text does not permit the EPA to consider costs in setting the standards. The language, as one scholar has noted, "is absolute." D. Currie, Air Pollution: Federal Law and Analysis 4-15 (1981). The EPA, "based on" the information about health effects contained in the technical "criteria" documents compiled under §108(a)(2), is to identify the maximum airborne concentration of a pollutant that the public health can tolerate, decrease the concentration to provide an "adequate" margin of safety, and set the standard at that level. Nowhere are the costs of achieving such a standard made part of that initial calculation.

Against this most natural of readings, respondents make a lengthy, spirited, but ultimately unsuccessful attack. They begin with the object of §109(b)(1)'s focus, the "public health." When the term first appeared in federal clean air legislation — in the Act of July 14, 1955 (1955 Act), 69 Stat. 322, which expressed "recognition of the dangers to the public health" from air pollution — its ordinary meaning was "[t]he health of the community." Webster's New International Dictionary 2005 (2d ed. 1950). Respondents argue, however, that §109(b)(1), as added by the Clean Air Amendments of 1970 (1970 Act), 84 Stat. 1676, meant to use the term's secondary meaning: "[t]he ways and means of conserving the health of the members of a community, as by preventive medicine, organized care of the sick, etc." Ibid. Words that can have more than one meaning are given content, however, by their surroundings, and in the context of §109(b)(1) this second definition makes no sense. Congress could not have meant to instruct the Administrator to set NAAQS at a level "requisite to protect" . . . "the art and science dealing with the protection and improvement of community health." Webster's Third New International Dictionary 1836 (1981). We therefore revert to the primary definition of the term: the health of the public.

Even so, respondents argue, many more factors than air pollution affect public health. In particular, the economic cost of implementing a very stringent standard might produce health losses sufficient to offset the health gains achieved in cleaning the air—for example, by closing down whole industries and thereby impoverishing the workers and consumers dependent upon those industries. That is unquestionably true, and Congress was unquestionably aware of it. . . . Other provisions explicitly permitted or required economic costs to be taken into account in implementing the air quality standards. Section 111(b)(1)(B), for example, commanded the Administrator to set "standards of performance" for certain new sources of emissions that as specified in §111(a)(1) were to "reflec[t]the degree of emission limitation achievable through the application of the best system of emission reduction which (taking into account the cost of achieving such reduction) the Administrator determines has been adequately demonstrated." Section 202(a)(2) prescribed that emissions standards for automobiles could take effect only "after such period as the Administrator finds necessary to permit the development and application of the requisite technology, giving appropriate consideration to the cost of compliance within such period." 84 Stat. 1690. We have therefore refused to find implicit in ambiguous sections of the CAA an authorization to consider costs that has elsewhere, and so often, been expressly granted.

Accordingly, to prevail in their present challenge, respondents must show a textual commitment of authority to the EPA to consider costs in setting NAAQS under §109(b)(1). And because §109(b)(1) and the NAAQS for which it provides are the engine that drives nearly all of Title I of the CAA, 42 U.S.C. §7401-7515, that textual commitment must be a clear one. Congress, we have held, does not alter the fundamental details of a regulatory scheme in vague terms or ancillary provisions—it does not, one might say, hide elephants in mouseholes. Respondents' textual arguments ultimately founder upon this principle.

Their first claim is that §109(b)(1)'s terms "adequate margin" and "requisite" leave room to pad health effects with cost concerns. Just as we found it "highly unlikely that Congress would leave the determination of whether an industry will be entirely, or even substantially, rate-regulated to agency discretion—and even more unlikely that it would achieve that through such a subtle device as permission to 'modify' rate-filing requirements," so also we find it implausible that Congress would give to the EPA through these modest words the power to determine whether implementation costs should moderate national air quality standards.

The same defect inheres in respondents' next two arguments: that while the Administrator's judgment about what is requisite to protect the public health must be "based on [the] criteria" documents developed under §108(a)(2), see §109(b)

(1), it need not be based solely on those criteria; and that those criteria themselves, while they must include "effects on public health or welfare which may be expected from the presence of such pollutant in the ambient air," are not necessarily limited to those effects. Even if we were to concede those premises, we still would not conclude that one of the unenumerated factors that the agency can consider in developing and applying the criteria is cost of implementation. That factor is both so indirectly related to public health and so full of potential for canceling the conclusions drawn from direct health effects that it would surely have been expressly mentioned in §§108 and 109 had Congress meant it to be considered. Yet while those provisions describe in detail how the health effects of pollutants in the ambient air are to be calculated and given effect, see §108(a)(2), they say not a word about costs.

Respondents point, finally, to a number of provisions in the CAA that *do* require attainment cost data to be generated. Section 108(b)(1), for example, instructs the Administrator to "issue to the States," simultaneously with the criteria documents, "information on air pollution control techniques, which information shall include data relating to the cost of installation and operation." And §109(d)(2)(C)(iv) requires the Clean Air Scientific Advisory Committee to "advise the Administrator of any adverse public health, welfare, social, economic, or energy effects which may result from various strategies for attainment and maintenance" of NAAQS. Respondents argue that these provisions make no sense unless costs are to be considered in setting the NAAQS. That is not so. These provisions enable the Administrator to assist the States in carrying out their statutory role as primary *implementers* of the NAAQS. It is to the States that the Act assigns initial and primary responsibility for deciding what emissions reductions will be required from which sources. It would be impossible to perform that task intelligently without considering which abatement technologies are most efficient, and most economically feasible—which is why we have said that "the most important forum for consideration of claims of economic and technological infeasibility is before the state agency formulating the implementation plan," *Union Elec. Co. v. EPA.* Thus, federal clean air legislation has, from the very beginning, directed federal agencies to develop and transmit implementation data, including cost data, to the States. That Congress chose to carry forward this research program to assist States in choosing the means through which they would implement the standards is perfectly sensible, and has no bearing upon whether cost considerations are to be taken into account in formulating the standards.

It should be clear from what we have said that the canon requiring texts to be so construed as to avoid serious constitutional problems has no application here. No matter how severe the constitutional doubt, courts may choose only between reasonably available interpretations of a text. The text of §109(b), interpreted in its statutory and historical context and with appreciation for its importance to the CAA as a whole, unambiguously bars cost considerations from the NAAQS-setting process, and thus ends the matter for us as well as the EPA.[4] We therefore affirm the judgment of the Court of Appeals on this point.

---

4. Respondents' speculation that the EPA is secretly considering the costs of attainment without telling anyone is irrelevant to our interpretive inquiry. If such an allegation could be proved, it would be grounds for vacating the NAAQS, because the Administrator had not followed the law. It would not, however, be grounds for this Court's changing the law.

## III

Section 109(b)(1) of the CAA instructs the EPA to set "ambient air quality standards the attainment and maintenance of which in the judgment of the Administrator, based on [the] criteria [documents of section 108] and allowing an adequate margin of safety, are requisite to protect the public health." The Court of Appeals held that this section as interpreted by the Administrator did not provide an "intelligible principle" to guide the EPA's exercise of authority in setting NAAQS. "[The] EPA," it said, "lack[ed] any determinate criteria for drawing lines. It has failed to state intelligibly how much is too much." 175 F.3d, at 1034. The court hence found that the EPA's interpretation (but not the statute itself) violated the nondelegation doctrine. We disagree.

In a delegation challenge, the constitutional question is whether the statute has delegated legislative power to the agency. Article I, §1, of the Constitution vests "[a]ll legislative Powers herein granted . . . in a Congress of the United States." This text permits no delegation of those powers, Loving v. United States, 517 U.S. 748, 771 (1996), and so we repeatedly have said that when Congress confers decision making authority upon agencies *Congress* must "lay down by legislative act an intelligible principle to which the person or body authorized to [act] is directed to conform." We have never suggested that an agency can cure an unlawful delegation of legislative power by adopting in its discretion a limiting construction of the statute. . . . The idea that an agency can cure an unconstitutionally standardless delegation of power by declining to exercise some of that power seems to us internally contradictory. The very choice of which portion of the power to exercise — that is to say, the prescription of the standard that Congress had omitted — would *itself* be an exercise of the forbidden legislative authority. Whether the statute delegates legislative power is a question for the courts, and an agency's voluntary self-denial has no bearing upon the answer.

We agree with the Solicitor General that the text of §109(b)(1) of the CAA at a minimum requires that "[f]or a discrete set of pollutants and based on published air quality criteria that reflect the latest scientific knowledge, [the] EPA must establish uniform national standards at a level that is requisite to protect public health from the adverse effects of the pollutant in the ambient air." Requisite, in turn, "mean[s] sufficient, but not more than necessary." These limits on the EPA's discretion are strikingly similar to the ones we approved in Touby v. United States, 500 U.S. 160 (1991), which permitted the Attorney General to designate a drug as a controlled substance for purposes of criminal drug enforcement if doing so was "'necessary to avoid an imminent hazard to the public safety.'" They also resemble the Occupational Safety and Health Act provision requiring the agency to "'set the standard which most adequately assures, to the extent feasible, on the basis of the best available evidence, that no employee will suffer any impairment of health'" — which the Court upheld in *Industrial Union Dept., AFL-CIO v. American Petroleum Institute*, and which even then-Justice Rehnquist, who alone in that case thought the statute violated the nondelegation doctrine, would have upheld if, like the statute here, it did not permit economic costs to be considered.

The scope of discretion §109(b)(1) allows is in fact well within the outer limits of our nondelegation precedents. In the history of the Court we have found the requisite "intelligible principle" lacking in only two statutes, one of which provided literally no guidance for the exercise of discretion, and the other of which conferred authority to regulate the entire economy on the basis of no more precise a standard than stimulating the economy by assuring "fair competition." See Panama Refining Go. v. Ryan, 293 U.S. 388 (1935); A.L.A. Schechter Poultry Corp. v. United States, 295 U.S. 495 (1935). We have, on the other hand, upheld the validity of §11(b)(2) of the Public Utility Holding Company Act of 1935, 49 Stat. 821, which gave the Securities and Exchange Commission authority to modify the structure of holding company systems so as to ensure that they are not "unduly or unnecessarily complicate[d]" and do not "unfairly or inequitably distribute voting power among security holders." We have approved the wartime conferral of agency power to fix the prices of commodities at a level that "'will be generally fair and equitable and will effectuate the [in some respects conflicting] purposes of th[e] Act.'" And we have found an "intelligible principle" in various statutes authorizing regulation in the "public interest." In short, we have "almost never felt qualified to second-guess Congress regarding the permissible degree of policy judgment that can be left to those executing or applying the law."

It is true enough that the degree of agency discretion that is acceptable varies according to the scope of the power congressionally conferred. While Congress need not provide any direction to the EPA regarding the manner in which it is to define "country elevators," which are to be exempt from new-stationary-source regulations governing grain elevators, it must provide substantial guidance on setting air standards that affect the entire national economy. But even in sweeping regulatory schemes we have never demanded, as the Court of Appeals did here, that statutes provide a "determinate criterion" for saying "how much [of the regulated harm] is too much." . . . Section 109(b)(1) of the CAA, which to repeat we interpret as requiring the EPA to set air quality standards at the level that is "requisite"—that is, not lower or higher than is necessary—to protect the public health with an adequate margin of safety, fits comfortably within the scope of discretion permitted by our precedent.

We therefore reverse the judgment of the Court of Appeals remanding for reinterpretation that would avoid a supposed delegation of legislative power. It will remain for the Court of Appeals—on the remand that we direct for other reasons—to dispose of any other preserved challenge to the NAAQS under the judicial-review provisions contained in 42 U.S.C. §7607(d)(9).

## NOTES AND QUESTIONS

1. The Court unanimously rejected the D.C. Circuit's holding that an agency could cure an unconstitutional delegation of legislative power by developing an "intelligible principle" to confine its exercise of its discretion. In his opinion for the Court, Justice Scalia argues that "the prescription of the standard that Congress had omitted would itself be an exercise of the forbidden legislative authority." Noting that the Court has only twice struck down statutes on non-delegation grounds, Justice Scalia found that the scope of discretion afforded EPA by section 109(b)(1) is "well within the outer limits of [the Court's] nondelegation precedents." He did so even though he concludes that to avoid non-delegation problems Congress must provide more substantial guidance when it authorizes regulations that can

affect the entire nation's economy. Where did the Court find adequate guidance in section 109(b)(1)? In light of this decision, what must EPA do in the future when deciding at what level to set the NAAQSs?

2. How does the Court compare the non-delegation issue in this case with the non-delegation challenge raised against OSHA's Benzene standard in *Industrial Union Dep't, AFL-CIO v. American Petroleum Institute*, discussed Chapter 3.

3. While the Court was unanimous in rejecting the notion that the Clean Air Act violated the non-delegation doctrine, some Justices had different views of how the doctrine should be interpreted. In a concurring opinion, Justice Stevens, joined by Justice Souter, argued that the Court should simply acknowledge that the power delegated to EPA is "legislative," but uphold the delegation as constitutional because it is adequately limited by the terms of the authorizing statute. Stevens and Souter maintained that neither Article I, §1, which vests "All legislative Powers" in the Congress, nor Article II, §1, which vests the "executive Power" in the president, purports to limit the authority of either to delegate authority to others. Thus, in their view, executive agency rulemaking "pursuant to a valid delegation from Congress is 'legislative,' but constitutional so long as the delegation provides a sufficiently intelligible principle" for exercising that authority. By contrast, Justice Thomas argued in another concurrence that even delegations accompanied by intelligible principles may be struck down as unconstitutional if the significance of the decision is simply too great to enable it to be delegated constitutionally.

4. The Court apparently did not think that the question of whether costs may be considered in setting NAAQSs was even a close one. As Justice Scalia wryly noted, "Were it not for the hundreds of pages of briefing respondents have submitted on the issue, one would have thought it fairly clear that this text does not permit the EPA to consider costs in setting the standards." In a concurring opinion not joined by any other Justice, Justice Breyer stressed that the Act does not require the elimination of all risk simply because it mandates a cost-blind standard-setting process. Citing the observation in Justice Stevens's plurality opinion in *Benzene* that "the word 'safe' is not the equivalent of 'risk-free,'" Justice Breyer argues that what is "requisite" to protect public health will "vary with background circumstances, such as the public's ordinary tolerance of the particular health risk in the particular context at issue." He maintains that the EPA administrator has considerable discretion in standard-setting under the statute because she can consider estimates of comparative health risks, the severity of adverse effects, the number and distribution of people affected by a pollutant, and the uncertainties surrounding each estimate. Additional background information on the *American Trucking* litigation may be found in Schroeder, The Story of *American Trucking*: The Blockbuster that Misfired, in Environmental Law Stories 321 (R.J. Lazarus & O.A. Houck eds., 2005).

5. The *American Trucking* decision indicates that the Court is loath to extend its revival of dormant constitutional limits on regulatory authority to dismantle basic elements of the federal regulatory infrastructure. As the oldest, most established and arguably most successful federal environmental statute, the Clean Air Act was a particularly ill-chosen target for a non-delegation claim. The Court also was unimpressed with the tired old tactic of pitting the environment against the

economy. Opponents of the Act argued that massive overregulation is inevitable if benefit-cost analysis is not used. However, when industry counsel told the Court at oral argument that "we can't live with" such a law, Chief Justice Rehnquist replied that we seem to have done pretty well with it for decades. The Court seems to have appreciated the notion that Congress intended for clean air standards to help stimulate the development of new pollution control technology when needed to protect public health.

6. Although the *American Trucking* decision in 2001 and the *Benzene* decision in 1980 definitively rejected arguments that regulatory statutes violate the non-delegation doctrine, many members of the U.S. Supreme Court have expressed interest in reviving the non-delegation doctrine. In *Gundy v. United States*, 139 S.Ct. 2116 (2019), Chief Justice Roberts and Justices Gorsuch and Thomas voted to revive the non-delegation doctrine, and Justice Alito said he would join them in an appropriate case. In an unusual "statement" accompanying a denial of cert in *Paul v. United States* on November 25, 2019, Justice Kavanaugh stated that "Justice Gorsuch's scholarly analysis of the Constitution's non-delegation doctrine in his *Gundy* dissent may warrant further consideration in future cases." He noted that this view would not allow "congressional delegations to agencies of authority to decide major policy questions—even if Congress expressly and specifically delegates that authority." The newest member of the Court, Justice Amy Coney Barrett, also appears to be an enthusiastic proponent of reviving the non-delegation doctrine. In a law review article written before she became a Justice, Judge Barrett refers to the current "intelligible principle" test for determining whether a delegation of legislative authority to an executive agency is constitutional as "notoriously lax." Barrett, Suspension and Delegation, 99 Cornell L. Rev. 251, 318 (2014).

### Revising the Ozone and Particulate NAAQS after *American Trucking*

A month after the *American Trucking* case was argued, a study provided powerful evidence linking particulate levels to substantial increases in mortality rates. The study by researchers at Johns Hopkins and Yale examined mortality rates in 20 U.S. cities following spikes in particulate pollution during the period from 1987 to 1994. It found that mortality rates increased immediately during the 24 hours following increases in particulate pollution. Unlike previous research, the study was able to isolate the effects of changes in particulate pollution from the effects of other pollutants.

Subsequent work strengthened these findings in a study examining the relationship between ozone and death rates in 95 large urban areas between 1987 and 2000. It was the first conclusive evidence that higher smog levels—in addition to fine particulate matter—contribute to death and that a reduction of 10 ppm in ozone levels could save 4,000 lives a year. Michelle L. Bell et al., Ozone and Short-term Mortality in 95 U.S. Urban Communities, 1987-2000, 2004 JAMA 372-378 (2004). Had mortality been recognized as an adverse health effect in 1997, EPA's calculation of monetized benefits from the revised ozone standard would have increased dramatically. EPA has now lowered the ozone standard further, in light of these and other health studies.

Despite fierce lobbying from industry groups, in 2001, the incoming Bush administration decided to retain the new NAAQS for ozone and particulates that initially had been promulgated by EPA in 1997 during the Clinton administration. In 2002, the U.S. Court of Appeals for the D.C. Circuit upheld the standards after they were challenged by various industry groups. American Trucking Ass'ns v. EPA, 283 F.3d 355 (D.C. Cir. 2002). During its next review of the adequacy of the ozone NAAQS, EPA's Clean Air Scientific Advisory Committee (CASAC) reviewed 1,700 scientific studies on the health effects of ground level ozone. However, the Bush administration rejected CASAC's advice that the standard should be lowered to a level within the range of 0.060 to 0.070 ppm to protect against a range of ozone-related health effects. In July 2007, EPA proposed "to revise the level of the 8-hour standard to a level within the range of 0.070 to 0.075 parts per million (ppm)." 72 Fed. Reg. 37,818 (2007). In March 2008, EPA promulgated a final rule that revised the primary ozone NAAQS to an 8-hour level of 0.075 ppm and that made the secondary NAAQS identical to the primary. 73 Fed. Reg. 16,436 (2008). This rule was controversial because EPA had rejected CASAC's advice that an even lower primary standard was required to protect children and other "at risk" populations against adverse health effects and that a new, seasonally adjusted secondary standard should be adopted. In April 2008, CASAC took the unusual step of sending EPA a letter expressing strong, unanimous disagreement with EPA's decision because it was not sufficiently protective of public health to provide the adequate margin of safety required by section 109 of the Clean Air Act. Various groups filed suit to challenge the standard.

While the lawsuits were pending, in September 2009, new EPA Administrator Lisa Jackson announced that the agency would reconsider the ozone standard in light of complaints that it was not as protective as recommended by CASAC. In January 2010, EPA proposed to revise the 8-hour ozone standard to a level within the range of 0.060 to 0.070 ppm. 75 Fed. Reg. 2,938 (2010). On July 11, 2011, EPA sent the Office of Management and Budget's Office of Information and Regulatory Affairs (OIRA) a draft final rule that would have lowered the primary ozone standard to 0.070 ppm. After fierce lobbying from industry groups, President Obama announced on September 2, 2011, that he had directed EPA Administrator Jackson to withdraw the draft final rule and to defer further consideration of changing the ozone standard until the next required five-year review in 2013. In his statement explaining the decision, President Obama cited "the importance of reducing regulatory burdens and regulatory uncertainty, particularly as our economy continues to recover." The president also argued that he "did not support asking state and local governments to begin implementing a new standard that will soon be reconsidered." The decision was condemned by environmental groups and praised by industry groups, who noted that they hoped that other forthcoming regulatory actions by EPA also would be blocked.

Simultaneous with the White House release of President Obama's statement, OIRA Administrator Cass Sunstein sent Administrator Jackson a "return letter" pursuant to Executive Order 12,866 directing her to reconsider the draft ozone rule. In his "return letter," Sunstein cited three factors: (1) "finalizing a new standard now is not mandatory and could produce needless uncertainty"; (2) the CASAC recommendation was based on a review of studies completed by 2006, while newer studies will be reviewed for the 2013 assessment; and (3) other recent rules, such as the heavy-duty truck fuel economy standards and the Cross-State Interstate Rule, also will reduce ozone pollution. In a statement released on September 2, 2011, Jackson appeared to accept the president's directive without endorsing it. After citing EPA's other actions to control air pollution during the Obama administration, she concluded: "We will revisit the ozone standard, in compliance with the Clean Air Act." On October 26, 2015, EPA issued a final NAAQS for ozone, lowering it to .070 ppm. EPA, Ozone Pollution: 2015 Revision to 2008 NAAQS Supporting Documents, *https://www.epa.gov/ground-level-ozone-pollution/2015-revision-2008-ozone-national-ambient-air-quality-standards-naaqs.*

### CASAC and the Trump Administration's "Secret Science" Rule

On April 12, 2018, President Trump directed EPA to speed up permitting of air pollution sources and to grant states more flexibility in meeting national ambient air quality standards. In a memorandum to EPA staff on May 9, 2018, EPA administrator Scott Pruitt ordered significant changes in the process for setting air quality standards under the Clean Air Act. Citing "cooperative federalism and the rule of law," Pruitt changed who advises the EPA, restricted the data they can use, and required them to shift their focus away from protecting public health. The memo expanded the Clean Air Scientific Advisory Committee's charge to include advice on any adverse "economic" or "energy effects" of emission control measures—even though the *American Trucking* decision does not allow costs to be considered during the standard-setting process. While paying lip service to the notion that compliance costs are not relevant to standard-setting, Pruitt's memo requested "robust feedback" on adverse effects of implementing air quality standards and directed CASAC to emphasize scientific uncertainty and research on naturally occurring air pollution. Pruitt's memo also emphasized that new members of CASAC review panels must be selected in accordance with his October 31, 2017 directive disqualifying experts who receive research funding from EPA—but not experts employed or funded by industry groups, a directive later overturned in court.

The Clean Air Scientific Advisory Committee (CASAC) provides counsel to EPA for its reviews of pollutants' health and environmental effects. To assist CASAC in this process, for decades, the seven-member CASAC has relied on panels of experts from universities and research institutions to support the body's deliberations on new pollution limits. For an excellent discussion of the innovations EPA has used throughout the years to insulate agency scientists and technical staff from political pressure while considering NAAQS revisions, see Wendy Wagner, It Isn't Easy Being a Bureaucratic Expert: Celebrating the EPA's Innovations, 70 Case Western Reserve L. Rev. 1093 (2020).

During the Trump administration, EPA Administrator Wheeler in October 2018 fired the CASAC panel that was assisting with the evaluation of limits on PM2.5. At the same time, he stopped plans to create a new panel that would assist in reviewing the ozone standards. In April 2019, CASAC members insisted that they still needed help in epidemiology and other specialized scientific areas, so in September of that year, Wheeler relented and named experts to a new panel of researchers to assist with the standards for PM2.5 and ozone. The new panelists were roundly criticized as biased and inexperienced; for example, two of the panelists work for industry consulting firms that have a stake in PM2.5 limits, and another two were endorsed by the National Cattlemen's Association, which had lobbied against tightening the PM2.5 limits in 2012. Another was on the advisory board for the American Council on Science and Health, which Greenpeace calls a "Koch Industries Climate Denial Front Group."

The changes to CASAC and its turn away from reputable science came to the fore because of EPA's decision not to strengthen the NAAQS for PM2.5. The 19 members of the auxiliary panel who were fired in 2018 wrote in *The New England Journal of Medicine* that they "unequivocally and unanimously concluded that the current PM2.5 standards do not adequately protect public health." Regardless, EPA made the decision in 2019 to keep the current PM2.5 standards. This contradicts the findings of EPA's career staff, too, who concluded that the existing annual limit for PM2.5 was too weak. However, CASAC, guided by the panel installed by Wheeler in April 2019, concluded in December 2019 that the evidence for strengthening the NAAQS for PM2.5 was too unsettled, and it recommended keeping the existing standards from 2012.

Among the studies supporting a stronger PM standard was a comprehensive epidemiological study of the medical records of more than 550,000 people in 151 cities, which found death rates 15 to 17 percent greater in cities with high levels of particulates, after controlling for other factors. Heath et al., Particulates Air Pollution as a Predictor of Mortality in a Prospective Study of U.S. Adults, 151 Am. J. Respiratory & Critical Care 669 (1995). Even in cities that were in compliance with the NAAQS for particulates, death rates were 3 to 8 percent higher than in complying cities with lower levels of exposure.

In an audacious effort to undermine epidemiological studies supporting stronger regulation of air pollution, the Trump EPA in January 2021 finalized what it called the "secret science" rule. The rule bars EPA from relying on any scientific study that does not reveal the identities of each of the participants, even if the participants have been promised confidentiality for reasons of medical privacy. The only authority EPA could cite for this regulation is the Federal Housekeeping Act, 5 U.S.C. §301 that states: "The head of an Executive department or military department may prescribe regulations for the government of his department, the conduct of its employees, the distribution and performance of its business, and the custody, use, and preservation of its records, papers, and property." The regulation could prevent EPA from relying on some of the most important epidemiological studies of the impact of air pollution, including the famous Harvard Six Cities Study. The Trump EPA argues that the rule promotes transparency, but the idea for the rule originated many years ago with tobacco industry lawyers seeking to obstruct federal agencies from regulating secondhand smoke. Lisa Friedman, A Plan Made to Shield Big Tobacco from Facts Is Now EPA Policy, N.Y. Times, Jan. 4, 2021.

On February 1, 2021, Chief Judge Brian Morris of the District Court of Montana struck down the rule as improperly issued under the Federal Housekeeping Statute, ruling that the statute only allows for procedural and not substantive rules. At the request of the Biden administration, Judge Morris vacated the rule and remanded it to the EPA, which will not reinstate the secret science rule under the Biden administration. See Juliet Eilperin, Judge Throws Out Trump Rule Limiting What Science EPA Can Use, Wash. Post, Feb. 1, 2021.

## F.   ATTAINING AND MAINTAINING THE NAAQS

### 1.   Implementation and Compliance—The Basic Structure

Writing national ambient air quality standards starts the process of bringing air quality to levels that protect human health, but it is only the beginning. NAAQSs have no real-world effect until they have been implemented—until actual sources of pollution have reduced emissions. The Clean Air Act rests primary responsibility for directing specific sources to reduce their emissions, and by what amount, to the states. Section 110 of the Act gives each state the responsibility for developing a state implementation plan (SIP) that details how compliance with the NAAQSs will be achieved in each air quality control region (AQCR). SIPs are at the heart of what has been described as the Clean Air Act's "bold experiment in cooperative federalism." Bethlehem Steel Corp. v. Gorsuch, 742 F.2d 1028, 1036 (7th Cir. 1984). After emissions limits have been established, they then must be enforced and air quality monitored. The Clean Air Act sets forth the basic statutory mechanisms for each of these steps in the process, while at the same time leaving substantial discretion in both EPA and the states to determine exactly how their respective statutory obligations will be met.

To develop an acceptable SIP, each state first has to determine existing and projected levels of the criteria air pollutant in each AQCR within the state's boundaries. These data are used to determine what emissions reductions are necessary to comply with the NAAQS for the pollutant. The state must inventory sources of emissions and project their expected future growth. It then must confront the politically sensitive task of deciding what control strategies to employ and how to allocate the burden of emission reductions among sources. Finally, the state must demonstrate to EPA that the measures adopted in its SIP are adequate to attain and maintain compliance with the NAAQS.

Section 110 specifies in detail the types of provisions states must include in their SIPs to obtain EPA approval. EPA's more than 1,700 pages of regulations are even more particular. 40 C.F.R. pts. 51-52 (1999). SIPs must provide for quantified emission limits, compliance timetables, monitoring and enforcement programs, limits on interstate pollution, measures that ensure compliance with nonattainment and PSD requirements, and assurances that the state has adequate resources and the legal authority to implement its plan. §110(a)(2). States have the most discretion in deciding how to regulate existing stationary sources, as other parts of the Clean Air Act impose federal emissions controls on mobile sources and new sources (section 111's new source performance standards). Most states have adopted some form of categorical emissions limits for existing stationary sources, usually based on judgments about what was technologically achievable and economically affordable. Among the emissions control strategies that the Clean Air Act now specifically endorses, but does not require states to adopt, are "economic incentives such as fees, marketable permits, and auctions of emissions rights." §110(a)(2).

The 1970 Clean Air Amendments directed each state to develop SIPs that would achieve compliance with the primary NAAQSs "as expeditiously as practicable," but no later than three years from the date the SIP is approved. Secondary standards were to be achieved within "a reasonable time." Section 116 of the Act expressly preserves the authority of states to adopt emissions standards that are stricter than the national standards.

The 1970 Amendments also required states to submit their initial SIPs to EPA for review within nine months after a NAAQS was promulgated. (The 1990 Amendments now give states three years to submit a SIP after a NAAQS is promulgated or revised unless EPA specifies a shorter time period. §110(a)(1).) The 1970 Amendments gave EPA a scant four months to approve or disapprove a state's submission; the 1990 Amendments expand this to 12 months. §110(k)(2). Upon EPA approval, the SIP becomes federally enforceable. A state that fails to submit a SIP or that submits an inadequate one whose deficiencies are not cured within a specified time period becomes subject to certain sanctions under section 179, including a loss of federal highway funds. If such a state fails to win EPA approval for a new SIP within two years after its SIP submission is disapproved, section 110(c) requires EPA to promulgate a federal implementation plan (FIP) for the state.

The Supreme Court fleshed out some of the contours of the federal-state partnership embodied in the Clean Air Act in two decisions involving the initial generation of SIPs submitted in response to the 1970 Amendments. In Train v. Natural Resources Defense Council, 421 U.S. 60 (1975), the Court upheld EPA's decision to approve a SIP that included a variance procedure for sources that found it difficult to comply with the state's immediately effective categorical emissions limits. So long as overall the SIP provided for timely attainment and maintenance of the NAAQS and met the Act's other requirements, the Court held that EPA must approve it. The Court explained that:

> The Act gives the Agency no authority to question the wisdom of a State's choices of emissions limitations if they are part of a plan which satisfies the standards of §110(a)(2), and the Agency may devise and promulgate a specific plan of its own only if a State fails to submit an implementation plan which satisfies those standards. §110(c). Thus, so long as the ultimate effect of a State's choice of emission limitations is compliance with the national standards for ambient air, the State is at liberty to adopt whatever mix of emission limitations it deems best suited to its particular situation. [421 U.S. at 179.]

This decision indicated that states had considerable freedom to choose what regulatory strategies to employ to meet the NAAQSs. During its very next term, the Court was asked to decide whether a state had gone too far in exercising that freedom.

In the case below, Missouri had adopted a SIP that required substantial reductions in emissions of $SO_2$ in the St. Louis metropolitan area, where $SO_2$ levels exceeded the NAAQS. Union Electric Company, the electric utility servicing St. Louis, challenged EPA's approval of Missouri's SIP. The utility argued that EPA should not have approved the SIP because it required the utility to do what was economically and technologically impossible.

## Union Electric Company v. EPA

427 U.S. 246 (1976)

JUSTICE MARSHALL delivered the opinion of the Court.

. . . The Administrator's position is that he has no power whatsoever to reject a state implementation plan on the ground that it is economically and technologically infeasible. . . . After surveying the relevant provisions of the Clean Air Amendments of 1970 and their legislative history, we agree that Congress intended claims of economic and technological infeasibility to be wholly foreign to the Administrator's consideration of a state implementation plan.

. . . [T]he 1970 Amendments to the Clean Air Act were a drastic remedy to what was perceived as a serious and otherwise unchecked problem of air pollution. The Amendments place the primary responsibility for formulating pollution control strategies on the States, but nonetheless subject the States to strict minimum compliance requirements. These requirements are of a "technology-forcing character," *Train v. NRDC,* and are expressly designed to force regulated sources to develop pollution control devices that might at the time appear to be economically or technologically infeasible.

This approach is apparent on the face of §110(a)(2). The provision sets out eight criteria that an implementation plan must satisfy, and provides that if these criteria are met and if the plan was adopted after reasonable notice and hearing, the Administrator "shall approve" the proposed state plan. The mandatory "shall" makes it quite clear that the Administrator is not to be concerned with factors other than those specified, and none of the eight factors appears to permit consideration of technological or economic infeasibility. . . .

Amici Appalachian Power Co. et al. . . . claim that the States are precluded from submitting implementation plans more stringent than federal law demands by §110(a)(2)'s second criterion—that the plan contain such control devices "as may be necessary" to achieve the primary and secondary air quality standards. §110(a)(2)(B). The contention is that an overly restrictive plan is not "necessary" for attainment of the national standards and so must be rejected by the Administrator. . . .

We read the "as may be necessary" requirement of §110(a)(2)(B) to demand only that the implementation plan submitted by the State meet the "minimum conditions" of the Amendments. Beyond that, if a State makes the legislative determination that it desires a particular air quality by a certain date and that it is willing to force technology to attain it—or lose a certain industry if attainment is not possible—such a determination is fully consistent with the structure and purpose of the Amendments, and §110(a)(2)(B) provides no basis for the EPA Administrator to object to the determination on the grounds of infeasibility. . . .

Our conclusion is bolstered by the recognition that the Amendments do allow claims of technological and economic infeasibility to be raised in situations where consideration of such claims will not substantially interfere with the primary congressional purpose of prompt attainment of the national air quality standards. Thus, we do not hold that claims of infeasibility are never of relevance in the formulation of an implementation plan or that sources unable to comply with emissions limitations must inevitably be shut down.

Perhaps the most important forum for consideration of claims of economic and technological infeasibility is before the state agency formulating the implementation plan. So long as the national standards are met, the State may select whatever mix of control devices it desires, and industries with particular economic or technological problems may seek special treatment in the plan itself. Moreover, if the industry is not exempted from, or accommodated by, the original plan, it may obtain a variance, as petitioner did in this case; and the variance, if granted after notice and a hearing, may be submitted to the EPA as a revision of the plan. Lastly, an industry denied an exemption from the implementation plan, or denied a subsequent variance, may be able to take its claims of economic or technological infeasibility to the state courts. . . .

. . . [T]he State has virtually absolute power in allocating emissions limitations so long as the national standards are met. . . . Congress plainly left with the States, so long as the national standards were met, the power to determine which sources would be burdened by regulation and to what extent. Technology forcing is a concept somewhat new to our national experience and it necessarily entails certain risks. But Congress considered those risks in passing the 1970 Amendments and decided that the dangers posed by uncontrolled air pollution made them worth taking. Petitioner's theory would render that considered legislative judgment a nullity, and that is a result we refuse to reach.

## NOTES AND QUESTIONS

1. The Court's decision confirmed the important role states were to play in deciding how to achieve compliance with the NAAQSs. While it established that states were free to "force" technology, few chose to do so in practice. Indeed, Missouri's SIP provided for temporary variances to sources that could not comply immediately. Pursuant to these provisions, Union Electric subsequently obtained a variance from the state and did not have to shut down.

2. In a concurring opinion joined by Chief Justice Burger, Justice Powell decried the "Draconian possibility" that the Clean Air Act could precipitate "the shutdown of an urban area's electrical service" that would "sacrifice the well-being of a large metropolitan area" to "technologically impossible" demands. 427 U.S. at 272 (Powell, J., concurring). The papers of the late Justice Thurgood Marshall reveal that during the Court's deliberations on the case Justice Rehnquist also expressed the view that the Act is a "harsh and draconian statute." Chief Justice Burger expressed the view that "the problems in this case are a consequence of letting a lot of little boys on Congressional staffs write legislation in noble prose that often takes little account of realities." Percival, Environmental Law in the Supreme Court: Highlights from the Marshall Papers, 23 Envtl. L. Rep. 10606, 10617 (1993). Do you agree that the Clean Air Act is so draconian that Congress did not appreciate the "realities" to which Chief Justice Burger refers? Is there anything in section 110(a)(2) that precludes states from taking such considerations into account when developing their SIPs? In a footnote not reproduced above, the Court noted that other portions of the Act expressly permit consideration of compliance costs and the state of existing technology, such as section 111's new source performance standards (NSPSs). Why would Congress require that such factors be taken into consideration for NSPSs, but not for achieving compliance with the NAAQSs?

3. Many states developed SIPs that sought to minimize the burden on local industry while appearing on paper to promise attainment of the NAAQSs. EPA's crucial role in reviewing SIPs is to ensure that they include measures that will in fact result in attainment and maintenance of the NAAQSs. Yet this requires EPA to have a crystal ball whose accuracy is heavily dependent on air quality modeling, which some view as "more sorcery than science." Reed, State Implementation Plans, in Law of Environmental Protection 11-28 (S. Novick ed., 1988). Does the Court's decision imply that EPA cannot disapprove a SIP that relies primarily on measures so draconian that there is no reasonable prospect that they would be implemented in practice?

4. Air quality dispersion models are subject to tremendous uncertainties, particularly as the number of sources increases and as pollutants travel longer distances. Courts generally have supported EPA's use of computer models, recognizing that they inevitably are subject to considerable uncertainty. See, e.g., Cleveland Elec. Illuminating Co. v. EPA, 572 F.2d 1150 (6th Cir. 1978). But there have been exceptions. In Ohio v. EPA, 784 F.2d 226 (6th Cir. 1986), the Sixth Circuit rejected EPA's use of a model, citing the absence of empirical validation of the model's results and studies at other sites that had produced "unimpressive" results. Cf. Connecticut v. EPA, 696 F.2d 147 (2d Cir. 1982) (burden on petitioners to demonstrate availability of better model).

5. While states have considerable freedom in choosing how to comply with the NAAQSs, the Clean Air Act does impose some limitations on the kind of controls states can employ. Section 123 bars states from relying on intermittent controls that try to vary the timing of emissions to coincide with times of favorable atmospheric conditions. As long as the end result complies with the NAAQS, why should states be prohibited from demonstrating compliance by "cutting emissions only when meteorological conditions likely will . . . concentrate [pollution] under a temperature inversion"? Section 123 also bars states from relying on tall stacks to disperse air pollutants, the strategy initially used by the copper smelters in *Georgia v. Tennessee Copper Company*, discussed in Chapter 2. Why should the use of tall stacks be barred as a SIP compliance strategy?

6. States seeking approval for SIP revisions have sometimes encountered lengthy delays. In General Motors v. United States, 496 U.S. 530 (1990), the Supreme Court held that EPA's failure to act for more than 32 months on a proposed SIP revision did not bar enforcement against a source whose violation of an existing SIP would be cured by the proposed SIP revision. The Court held that EPA can enforce the existing SIP even if the agency had delayed unreasonably action on the proposed SIP revision. Is this result fair? The 1990 Amendments now mandate that EPA take action on proposed SIP revisions within 12 months of their submission. §110(k).

7. The CAA contemplates an evolving program of air quality controls, in which Congress or EPA will from time to time revise or add to air quality requirements, thereby triggering downstream adjustments by the implementing agencies and ultimately compliance and enforcement officials. Congress, for example, revised the Act in 1977 to add requirements related to the prevention of significant deterioration and nonattainment issues, as well as visibility-related requirements. In 1990, it adopted a program to address the process of acid deposition. The EPA

not only issues original NAAQSs; it is also under a statutory obligation to revisit them every five years in light of new scientific information. EPA can also discover after a SIP has been approved that in fact it will be inadequate to meet the requirements of the Act. When one of these developments occurs, section 110(k)(5) gives EPA express authority to "call[] for plan revisions."

8. As it is preparing to issue a SIP call, EPA frequently has an opinion as to the best way to respond to the deficiency that it has discovered in existing SIPs (either because the requirements for them have been revised by the agency or the Congress or because one or more have been found to be inadequate to meet the requirements of the Act). In recent years, for instance, EPA has had a strong preference for emissions trading systems for addressing a variety of ambient problems. See pages 548-549 for discussion of such systems. The general design of the statute, however, pursuant to its system of cooperative federalism, leaves the selection of the best way to respond to the national requirements up to the states in the first instance. Can EPA decide that a SIP is "inadequate" unless it adopts the preferred approach of EPA? The following decision confronts an instance in which this question arose.

9. As background to the following decision, the 1990 Amendments enacted a variety of new provisions to address the ozone problem, especially the interstate and regional nature of the problem. One of these created the Northeast Ozone Transport Commission (OTC), composed of representatives of 12 northeastern states plus the District of Columbia. §184. The Act authorized the Commission to recommend control measures for the region "necessary to bring any area in such region into attainment" with the ozone NAAQS. §184(c)(1). Pursuant to that authorization, the Commission petitioned EPA to recognize that adoption of the California Low Emission Vehicle (LEV) program—which imposes stricter ozone controls than the federal auto emissions standards—was such a "necessary" control measure. Uncertain as to the constitutional soundness of the OTC provisions, EPA ultimately responded to the OTC petition by issuing an order both under the OTC provisions of the Act and under its section 110(k)(5) SIP call authority. EPA found the California LEV program to be necessary for the 13 member-jurisdictions; it also found that the SIPs of these jurisdictions were "substantially inadequate" unless they either adopted the California LEV program or else instituted alternative measures that were highly infeasible and more draconian than adopting the LEV program.

EPA's action was challenged. The portion of the court of appeals decision addressing EPA's SIP call authority is reproduced below.

## Virginia v. EPA

108 F.3d 1397 (D.C. Cir. 1997)

RANDOLPH, Circuit Judge.

[The court determined that EPA's SIP call effectively ordered the adoption of the California standards, because the measures required of a state choosing not to adopt it were so "unreasonable and impracticable" as to amount to no "real alternative" at all.]

Does section 110 give EPA the authority to condition approval of a state's plan on the state's adoption of control measures EPA has chosen? . . . [W]e are aware of no case (EPA has cited none) supporting the proposition EPA now urges upon us, namely, that under section 110 EPA may condition approval of a state's implementation plan on the state's adopting a particular control measure, here the California Low Emission Vehicle program. . . .

Section 110 governs the interplay between the states and EPA with respect to the formulation and approval of such State Plans. The basic procedure is that "each state determines an emission reduction program for its nonattainment areas, subject to EPA approval, within deadlines imposed by Congress." Natural Resources Defense Council v. Browner, 57 F.3d 1122, 1123 (D.C. Cir. 1995).

Should a state fail to submit an implementation plan, or should its plan fail to provide the required reductions in air pollution, certain penalties — some mandatory, others at EPA's discretion — may follow. . . . The noncomplying state may, for instance, be prevented from spending federal highway money in nonattainment areas. . . . This sanction becomes mandatory if the state fails to implement an adequate State Plan within 24 months of EPA's finding that the state's proposed plan is deficient. . . . At that same point, EPA must impose a "federal implementation plan" ("Federal Plan") on those areas of the state in nonattainment. . . . The Federal Plan "provides an additional incentive for state compliance because it rescinds state authority to make the many sensitive technical and political choices that a pollution control regime demands." Natural Resources Defense Council, 57 F.3d at 1124.

In 1975, the Supreme Court analyzed section 110's "division of responsibilities" between the states and the federal government. Train v. Natural Resources Defense Council. . . .

[A]"broader issue," the Court thought, was at stake in the case — namely, "whether Congress intended the States to retain any significant degree of control over the manner in which they attain and maintain national standards.". . . The Act expressly gave the states initial responsibility for determining the manner in which air quality standards were to be achieved. . . . Section 107(a) of the Act read then, as it does now: "Each State shall have the primary responsibility for assuring air quality within the entire geographic area comprising such State by submitting an implementation plan which will specify *the manner* in which national primary and secondary ambient air quality standards will be achieved and maintained within each air quality control region in such State" (emphasis added). In light of section 107(a), the Court construed section 110:. . .

> [So] long as the ultimate effect of a State's choice of emission limitations is compliance with the national standards for ambient air, the State is at liberty to adopt whatever mix of emission limitations it deems best suited to its particular situation. . . .

The Supreme Court repeated this interpretation in Union Electric Co. v. EPA: section 110 left to the states "the power to determine which sources would be burdened by regulations and to what extent."

[Bethlehem Steel Corp. v. Gorsuch, 742 F.2d 1028 (7th Cir. 1984) similarly stated:]

[T]he Clean Air Act creates a partnership between the states and the federal government. The state proposes, the EPA disposes. The federal government through the EPA determines the ends — the standards of air quality — but Congress has given the states the initiative and a broad responsibility regarding the means to achieve those ends through state implementation plans and timetables of compliance. . . . The Clean Air Act is an experiment in federalism, and the EPA may not run roughshod over the procedural prerogatives that the Act has reserved to the states, . . . especially when, as in this case, the agency is overriding state policy. . . .

[T]he 1990 amendments did not alter the division of responsibilities between EPA and the states in the section 110 process. It was with this understanding that we recently summarized the statutory system: "The states are responsible in the first instance for meeting the" national ambient standards "through state-designed plans that provide for attainment, maintenance, and enforcement of the" national standards "in each air quality control region. Thus, each state determines an emission reduction program for its nonattainment areas, subject to EPA approval, within deadlines imposed by Congress.". . .

Because section 110 does not enable EPA to force particular control measures on the states, EPA's authority to promulgate the rule under review must be derived from section 184 alone. [The court then held that section 184 provides EPA general authority to order adoption of specific control measures recommended by OTC, but that other provisions of the Act — section 177 read together with section 202 — specifically prohibit EPA from compelling any state to adopt auto emissions standards different from the national standards. The court concluded that this specific prohibition prevailed over the general grant of authority.]

In sum, we hold that EPA may not, under section 110, condition approval of a state's implementation plan on the state's adoption of a particular control measure. We also hold that EPA may not, under section 184, circumvent section 177, as we interpret it in light of section 202. For the reasons given, we hold that the SIP call EPA issued with respect to each state and the District of Columbia cannot stand.

The petitions for review are granted and the rule is vacated in its entirety.

## NOTES AND QUESTIONS

1. Why did EPA choose to include in its SIP call the instruction that states adopt a specific control measure, namely, the California LEV standards? Why did EPA think it would not be sufficient to base its SIP call simply upon a determination that the current ozone controls contained in the SIPs of the 13 jurisdictions within the OTC were substantially inadequate and interfered with the ability of neighboring states to meet the NAAQS?

2. Should a state choose not to submit a SIP that the EPA can determine to be adequate, the Act does provide a mechanism for the federal government to step in and make all the choices that would normally be reserved to the states. As indicated in *Virginia v. EPA*, above, EPA must promulgate a federal implementation

plan (FIP) 24 months after finding deficient a state implementation plan. EPA has been very reluctant to exercise this authority, however.

Sometimes EPA has been able to avoid writing FIPs by exercising its "conditional approval" authority for SIPs. Section 110(k)(4), added in 1990, authorizes EPA to condition its approval of a SIP on the state promulgating revisions that will bring the SIP into complete compliance so long as the SIP's deficiencies are minor and corrected within one year. EPA attempted to use section 110(k)(4) to approve conditionally SIPs that promised to adopt adequate measures within a year. In Natural Resources Defense Council v. EPA, 22 F.3d 1125, 1134-1136 (D.C. Cir. 1994), the D.C. Circuit held that this was illegal because "the conditional approval mechanism was intended to provide the EPA with an alternative to disapproving substantive, but not entirely satisfactory, SIPs submitted by the statutory deadlines and not, as EPA has used it, as a means of circumventing those deadlines." (Section 110(k)(4) superseded a more loosely phrased provision, under which EPA had adopted "partial" and "conditional" approvals of plans in situations where it otherwise might have had to impose bans on new construction in order to ensure NAAQS compliance. See City of Seabrook v. EPA, 659 F.2d 1349 (5th Cir. 1981) (upholding EPA's practice); but see Connecticut Fund for the Environment v. EPA, 696 F.2d 147 (2d Cir. 1982) (allowing conditional approvals but finding them insufficient to allow the state to avoid a construction ban).)

As an even more drastic way to avoid the FIP requirement, sometimes it has appeared the EPA has approved SIPs that had no realistic chance of attaining the NAAQSs. Occasionally, environmental organizations sued EPA to force it to write a FIP. After Abramowitz v. EPA, 832 F.2d 1071 (9th Cir. 1987), which held that for the South Coast Air Basin EPA's duty to do so was clear and mandatory, EPA was faced with developing a FIP that would cause massive economic and social dislocation or a FIP that would authorize decades of noncompliance. It opted not to pursue the option of adopting "a plan that provides for attainment in the South Coast immediately or even within five years," because such a plan "would have to prohibit most traffic, shut down major business activity, curtail the use of important consumer goods, and . . . destroy the economy of the South Coast, so that most of the population would be forced to resettle elsewhere." 53 Fed. Reg. 49,494, 49,495 (1988).

The Act also provides a series of sanctions EPA can apply against states that fail to submit satisfactory SIPs, including suspension of federal highway funds and increasing the ratio of pollution offsets required before new pollution sources can be located within nonattainment areas. In the past, EPA sometimes withheld sanctioning noncompliant states, but in 1990, Congress added section 179, which requires EPA to impose sanctions on states that fail to rectify deficiencies in the SIP submissions within 18 months.

3. Conflicts over the division of authority between state and federal governments can arise at other places in the implementation process as well. For example, section 113 gives EPA the authority to order SIP compliance by a pollution source if EPA determines it is not complying. That section also permits EPA to become the primary enforcer of SIPs if EPA detects "widespread" failure of the state to enforce its own regulations.

## 2.   *The Evolution of the Programs to Achieve and Maintain the NAAQS*

### A.   Nonattainment and Prevention of Significant Deterioration

As the country gained experience with how difficult achieving and maintaining the NAAQS has proven to be, the basic implementation structure reviewed in the previous section has evolved considerably. The first substantial evolutionary step came as a result of a 1972 district court decision, which held that the statutory purpose to "protect and enhance" air quality created an obligation not only to attain the NAAQS, but also to prevent the deterioration of air quality that was presently better than the NAAQS. After the district court decision was affirmed in an unpublished per curiam opinion by the D.C. Circuit it was then sustained when the Supreme Court split 4-4 on the merits. Sierra Club v. Ruckelshaus, 344 F. Supp. 253 (D.D.C. 1972), aff'd per curiam, 2 Envtl. L. Rep. 20656 (D.C. Cir. 1972), *aff'd by an equally divided court mem. sub nom.* Fri v. Sierra Club, 412 U.S. 541 (1973). The Supreme Court split resulted from Justice Powell's policy of recusing himself whenever Hunton and Williams, his former law firm, represented a party. (In the years after *Fri,* Justice Powell abandoned this policy.) Thus, it was that the decision of a single judge, Judge Pratt, created an entirely new and powerful component of the nation's air policy. In response to the decision, EPA wrote regulatory requirements that states must include in their SIPs a program for the preconstruction review of stationary sources, designed to prevent significant deterioration of so-called clean air areas. The PSD program had been born.

By 1976, it was clear that even the core function of the CAA—to attain the NAAQS—faced significant difficulties. Notwithstanding *Union Electric's* endorsement of the idea that the CAA was meant to apply strong medicine to the air quality problem, solving the air quality problems of dirty air areas was viewed as nearly intractable. When the states realized that only draconian measures such as severe restrictions on automobile movement, expensive and perhaps unachievable controls on existing sources, and moratoria on new stationary source construction would be adequate to meet the attainment deadlines, they simply declined to submit SIPs that contained such unpopular measures. The CAA provides EPA with backup authority to issue federal implementation plans (FIPs) if state plans prove inadequate, but the EPA was equally reluctant to exercise that authority. EPA had some disastrous early experiences with FIPs, including several instances in which it wrote FIPs that included significant land use and transportation controls, such as vehicle inspection and maintenance programs, bus and carpool lanes, parking fees, and, in the case of a FIP covering the South Coast Air Basin in California (which includes Los Angeles), severe gas rationing. State and public reaction to these plans was intensely hostile, and in 1974 Congress stripped EPA of any authority to include land use and transportation controls in a FIP. To avoid its own statutory obligation to write FIPs, EPA gave generous interpretations to the adequacy of state submissions and approved some SIPs that subsequently proved to be inadequate.

One of the major problems EPA faced was how to avoid imposing a moratorium on new sources of air pollution in parts of the country that were still "nonattainment" for one or more of the NAAQS. In response, the agency established an "offset policy," aimed at permitting continued economic expansion in the nonattainment areas. The policy provided that new sources could continue to be built if they (a) used even more stringent control technologies than the NSPS, (b) certified that any other facilities owned by the owner of the new construction were complying with their SIP obligations, and (c) offset the additional pollutants from the new source with reductions of similar pollutants coming from existing sources. These offsets had to be greater than 1 to 1, so that in principle the placement of a new facility would be making "reasonable further progress" toward attainment.

Whether the offset program would have survived judicial challenge will never be known, because Congress revisited the CAA for its first major revisions in 1976, and the next year enacted the 1977 Clean Air Act Amendments. These Amendments superseded the agency-created programs for the prevention of significant deterioration (PSD) and nonattainment (NA), by creating statutory programs that built on these early agency efforts. See Title I, Part C, 42 U.S.C. §§7470-7492 (PSD program); Part D, 42 U.S.C. §§7501-7515 (NA program). The basic NA and PSD statutory structures were subsequently refined once again in 1990. These provisions supply the statutory backdrop for the ongoing efforts of the states and the EPA to bring NA areas of the country into compliance and for maintaining air quality in clean air areas. (For good histories of the PSD program over the 1977-1990 time period, see Oren, Prevention of Significant Deterioration: Control-Compelling Versus Site-Shifting, 74 Iowa L. Rev. 1 (1988); Oren, Detail and Delegation: A Study in Statutory Specificity, 15 Colum. J. Envtl. L. 143 (1990). On both PSD and NA, see Theodore L. Garrett & Sonya D. Winner, A Clean Air Act Primer, Clean Air Deskbook, Environmental Law Institute (1992).)

When Congress revised these programs in 1990, they still faced the reality that the existing regulatory structure, even as modified in 1977, was not moving the country toward compliance very fast, and that large numbers of Americans continued to live in areas that were nonattainment for one or more of the criteria pollutants. Urban areas presented the most difficult problems, with ozone nonattainment being particularly hard, due to the fact that automobiles are major contributors to the problem, as are emissions from remote sources that are transported by wind circulation to urban and other areas. Particulate matter also has been a persistent problem, whose incidence overlaps considerably with the ozone problem. Figure 5.7 shows the nonattainment areas in 2015 for the 8-hour ozone NAAQS.

Besides making other refinements in the NA program, the 1990 Amendments added sections 181-185B, creating an elaborate regulatory system to address the ozone problem, 42 U.S.C. §§7511ff, and less elaborate ones for carbon monoxide and PM in sections 186-187 and 188-190. The ozone program creates different gradations of nonattainment, varying from moderate to extreme, and then imposes increasingly stringent regulatory requirements on them.

States must require reasonably available control technology (RACT) on existing stationary sources, while major new stationary sources in NA areas must install emissions control technology that will meet a "lowest achievable emissions reduction" (LAER) standard for that source. The definition of major source varies by nonattainment region; the worse the air quality problem, the lower the threshold for being considered a major source. Major sources must also meet offset requirements similar to those first instituted through EPA regulations in 1976, but once again these now vary according to the severity of the air quality problem at their location. Offset requirements range from 1.5 to 1 in the most extreme ozone nonattainment area down to 1.1 to 1 for marginal areas.

**Figure 5.7    Counties Designated Nonattainment for 8-Hour Ozone Standard**

8-Hour Ozone Nonattainment Areas (2015 Standard)

04/30/2021

8-hour Ozone Classification
- Extreme
- Severe-17
- Severe-15
- Serious
- Moderate
- Marginal
- Marginal (Rural Transport)

Nonattainment areas are indicated by color.
When only a portion of a county is shown in color,
it indicates that only that part of the county is within
a nonattainment area boundary.

*Source:* EPA, *https://www3.epa.gov/airquality/greenbook/map8hr_2015.html*

With respect to the PSD program, Congress established a schedule of allowable emissions increases, or "increments." An area whose air quality was better than the NAAQS is able to increase air pollution so long as the full increment is not consumed. Clean areas are assigned to one of three classes, each with different increments. Class I areas, the most stringent, include national parks, forests, wilderness areas, and other areas of special air quality concern. Separate visibility protections also apply to these areas. Class II and Class III areas permit successively more incremental air pollution, but in no case can the NAAQS be exceeded.

## B.  New Source Review

From the beginning, the Clean Air Act has required new sources to install advanced pollution control technology, 42 U.S.C. §7411, thereby establishing different regulatory regimes for new and existing sources. New sources that fall into categories that EPA has found generate air pollution "which may reasonably be anticipated to endanger public health or welfare" are required to install federally established new source performance standards (NSPS). These standards, which are called "best demonstrated technology" or BDT, have in large part been superseded by the tougher requirements of the PSD and NA programs, but they still serve as a technology floor for all new sources. Notice, too, that 42 U.S.C. §7411 extends to pollutants beyond the criteria pollutants and the pollutants covered by the hazardous air pollutants provision, 42 U.S.C. §7412. If EPA establishes new source performance standards for any category of new sources based on such otherwise unregulated pollutants, 42 U.S.C. §7411(d) then enables EPA also to establish procedures whereby states are required to regulate existing facilities in the same category. In contrast, existing sources of criteria pollutants are regulated through the SIP process, where states retain wide discretion in determining the mix of air pollution controls to be applied to the different existing stationary sources within each air quality control region. The nonattainment program impinges somewhat on that discretion by requiring existing sources in nonattainment areas to install reasonable available control technology, RACT, a less stringent requirement than NSPS. The NSPS defines "new source" to include existing sources that are modified, with a modification being defined as "any physical change in, or change in the method of operation of, a stationary source which increases the amount of any air pollutant emitted by such source or which results in the emission of any air pollutant not previously emitted." 42 U.S.C. §7411(a)(4).

The statutory PSD and NA programs carry forward this differential treatment of existing sources on the one hand and new (and modified) sources on the other, and they add even more onerous requirements on new sources. Each program

**Figure 5.8 Ozone Nonattainment SIP Requirements**

Marginal Areas:

- Must inventory emissions sources
- Apply RACT to existing sources
- Improve Auto Inspection & Maintenance Program
- Emissions offsets of 1.1 to 1

Moderate Areas—All Marginal requirements plus:

- 15% progress required in 5 years
- Emissions offsets of 1.15 to 1

Serious Areas—All Moderate requirements plus:

- Enhanced air quality monitoring program
- Enhanced I/M program
- Clean Fuel vehicle program
- Transportation control measures
- Major source threshold for VOCs = 50 tpy
- Emissions offsets of 1.2 to 1

Severe Areas (I and II)—All Serious requirements plus:

- Major source threshold for VOCs = 25 tpy
- Stricter transportation control measures
- Emissions offsets of 1.3 to 1
- Use of regulated gasoline

Extreme Areas—All Severe requirements plus:

- Major source threshold for VOCs = 10 tpy
- Emissions offsets of 1.5 to 1

requires any "major" new source (including any modified existing source) that will or has the potential to emit "significant" amounts of any of the criteria pollutants to install state-of-the-art pollution control technology. 42 U.S.C. §7475. The definitions of "major" and "significant" vary between the two programs and also according to the pollutants that are involved. See 42 U.S.C. §§7475(a), 7479(2) (C) (PSD program applies to any "major emitting facility on which construction is commenced" after the effective date of the program; "construction" defined as "includ[ing] the modification (as defined in section 7411(a)(4) of this title) of any source or facility"); sections 7501(4), 7502(5), 7503(a)(2) (NA program applies to any "new or modified major stationary source" and "'modified' means the same as the term 'modification' as used in section 7411(a)(4). . ."). The exact technology requirements also differ between the programs—lowest achievable emissions rate (LAER) for NA and best available control technology (BACT) for PSD. BACT must be met "for each pollutant subject to regulation under [the Clean Air Act]," not just the pollutant for which a statutory PSD increment applies. The NA program's LAER requirement, on the other hand, applies only to the pollutant whose NAAQS is being exceeded, and which thus triggers the NA review. The statutory NA program also carries over the offset and compliance certification requirements from EPA's regulatory offset policy, while under the statutory PSD program facility owners must perform computer modeling to determine the available increment, as well as to determine the effect of the new source on visibility.

The process for ensuring that these various new source requirements are met has become known as New Source Review (NSR). NSR is a critical component of efforts to maintain air quality in PSD areas and of efforts to improve air quality in NA areas. It has also been a source of friction between owners of existing facilities, EPA, and state air quality agencies, as the *ADEC* decision illustrates. For facility owners the process itself can be time-consuming and expensive, denying them desired flexibility in making capital improvements in response to market changes. If the preconstruction review determines that BACT or LAER is called for, these control requirements then add to the capital expense of the planned modification. Consequently, existing facility owners are extremely interested in finding ways to accomplish their expansion or modification without triggering full NSR requirements. One way to avoid NSR takes advantage of EPA's treatment of an entire facility, which may contain a number of different sources of pollution, as a single source. This approach has the effect of placing a facility's multiple emissions points under a single "bubble." That, in turn, creates the possibility that a facility owner could reduce emissions elsewhere in the facility in an amount larger than the additional pollution from the modification, so that the change that occurs under the bubble will not be one that "increases the amount of any air pollutant emitted by such source." For example, a coal-fired power plant currently emitting $SO_2$, and consisting of three separate generating units might propose to build a fourth generating unit at the facility. It might install additional emissions control devices on one or more of the existing units in order to reduce these emissions sufficiently so that the net emissions of the new unit plus the existing units is kept below the major source threshold. In this way, the net emissions of the facility—new pollution minus contemporaneous reductions in existing emissions—would not trigger review.

This technique, called "netting out," is one way to avoid NSR. (Sources can also net out by agreeing to enforceable restrictions on emissions within their plant, for instance by agreeing to limitations on hours of operations.) Netting out is not always available or attractive to the source. The Red Dog Mine had considered netting out as a way to avoid having to install BACT, but it dropped the idea. See the last full paragraph of the *ADEC* decision. Why do you suppose it chose not to net out?

Besides netting out, sources look for other ways to avoid NSR. Facts disclosed in recent litigation demonstrate that one group of facilities that was very creative in finding ways to avoid NSR was coal-fired power plants already in existence in 1977. Consider this description from litigation brought by the EPA, charging Duke Energy with having engaged in a number of modifications of its power plants without complying with NSR:

> Duke Energy's eight plants in the Carolinas include thirty coal-fired generating units that were placed in service between 1940 and 1975. Each unit contains, as one of its three major components, a boiler, which is a large structure from six to twenty stories tall containing thousands of steel tubes. The tubes are arranged into sets of tube assemblies, including economizer tubes, in which water is initially heated; furnace waterwall tubes, in which water evaporates to steam; superheater tubes, in which the temperature of the steam is raised before being released into a turbine; and reheater tubes, in which steam released from the turbine is reheated and returned to the turbine.
>
> Between 1988 and 2000, as part of a plant modernization program, Duke Energy engaged in twenty-nine projects on the coal-fired generating units, most of which consisted of replacing and/or redesigning one or more of the boiler tube assemblies. These projects would both extend the life of the generating units and allow the units to increase their daily hours of operation. Duke Energy did not apply for or acquire new permits from the EPA for these projects, some of which, according to the Government, cost "more than seven times the original cost of the unit."
>
> The EPA and the Intervenors maintain that these life-extension projects constitute "major modifications" of Duke Energy's furnaces as defined in the PSD statutory and regulatory provisions — that is, physical changes leading to a significant net emissions increase — and thus Duke Energy was required to obtain permits for them. [United States v. Duke Energy, 411 F.3d 539, 544 (4th Cir. 2005), rev'd, 549 U.S. 561 (2007).]

Duke Energy's activities as well as similar ones by other utility companies came to light when the EPA conducted an extensive investigation to ascertain why so few utility companies had applied for NSR permits in the 1980s and 1990s. The relatively small number of applications ran contrary to expectations. EPA had anticipated that as the years went by under the NA and PSD programs, owners of existing sources would face a choice of either shutting down those sources because they had become outmoded and uneconomical, or else upgrading them through capital improvements triggering the NSR requirements. Instead, quite old existing plants were continuing to operate longer than anticipated. A GAO estimate, for example, concluded that in 2002 coal-fired power plants built prior to 1972 (with some decades older than that) still comprised nearly 60 percent of the nation's fossil-fuel-fired capacity. Government Accountability Office, Air Pollution: Emissions from Older Electricity Generating Units at 2 (June 2002).

Once EPA investigated, the agency concluded that a number of utility companies had violated the Clean Air Act by modifying their power plants without complying with the NSR. In November 1999, EPA filed lawsuits against seven electric utilities and a total of 51 power plants. John Fiakla, EPA Sues 7 Utilities, Tells TVA to Stop Practices, Wall St. J., Nov. 4, 1999, at A1. The lawsuits alleged that the utility companies had in fact invested in major life-extending capital improvements at the power plants without going through new source review. Wald, Old Plants with New Parts Present a Problem to EPA, N.Y. Times, Dec. 26, 1999, at A17. All told, in 1999 and 2000, EPA commenced litigation against ten utility companies. Jeanhee Hong, A New Deal for New Source Review, Trends, Vol. 37, no. 3, at 1 (Jan./Feb. 2006).

The utilities strenuously denied EPA's enforcement allegations, claiming that EPA was contradicting long-standing understandings by advancing "regulatory interpretations . . . best described as 'lawmaking by litigation.'" Peter E. Seley, Lawmaking Through Litigation: EPA's Gamble on New Source Review, 15 Nat. Resources & Env't 260, 260 (2001). Notwithstanding industry outcry, some utilities chose to settle rather than litigate. Virginia Electric Power Company (VEPCO) agreed to reduce significantly emissions of $NO_x$ and sulfur dioxide at a capital cost of $1.2 billion in addition to paying fines and underwriting supplemental environmental projects. Air Pollution: Virginia Utility Agrees to Major Reductions in $NO_x$ and Sulfur Dioxide at Eight Plants to Cut Transport, BNA Daily Envtl. Rep. (Nov. 17, 2000). Under a phased-in, ten-year schedule, VEPCO said it would reduce its $NO_x$ emissions from 105,000 tons per year (tpy) to 30,000 tpy. Installation of modern scrubbers will also reduce sulfur dioxide emissions from a current level of 263,000 tpy to 82,000 tpy. Cinergy Corporation, a Cincinnati-based utility, subsequently reached a similar settlement agreement. In addition to paying fines and underwriting supplemental environmental agreements, Cinergy said it would spend $1.4 billion installing up-to-date pollution reduction equipment. BNA Daily Envtl. Rep. (Dec. 27, 2000). More recently, American Electric Power agreed to settle an NSR enforcement action on terms requiring installation of $4.6 billion in pollution control equipment, plus payment of a $15 million fine and $60 million in environmental mitigation projects. EPA's Multi-Billion NSR Settlement May Blunt Enforcement Criticism, Inside EPA Clean Air Act Report, Oct. 18, 2007.

Some utilities did decide to litigate, however. As the litigation unfolded, it became clear that the disagreement between the EPA and the utility companies over when modifications triggered NSR implicated both parts of the definition of modification: under the statute, a modification requires a "physical change" that "increases emissions." The disputes over the first part of the definition focused on whether the capital improvements made by the utilities were exempt from NSR because they came within an exemption for routine maintenance, repair, or replacement (RMRR). From very early on, EPA had always exempted certain alterations from being considered "physical changes" if those modifications constituted "maintenance, repair, and replacement which the Administrator determines to be routine for a source category. . . ." 40 C.F.R. §52.21(b)(2). This exemption, the RMRR exemption, was intended to permit maintenance of existing facilities if the maintenance was the sort of activity that was normally expected to occur during the economic life of a facility, without thereby extending that economic life significantly.

Up until this litigation, the meaning of the RMRR exemption had rarely been tested in litigation, although EPA had been victorious in a significant case in the late 1980s. In that case, Wisconsin Power (WEPCO) contested an EPA determination that renovations planned for some of the company's coal-fired generating units could not qualify for an RMRR exception. "WEPCO proposes to replace rear steam drums on units 2, 3, 4 and 5; each of these steam drums measures 60 feet in length, 50.5 inches in diameter and 5.25 inches in thickness. In addition, WEPCO plans to replace another major component, the air heaters, in units 1-4. To implement this four-year program, WEPCO will need to make the replacements by taking the units successively out of service for nine-month periods." Wisconsin Elec. Power Co. v. Reilly, 893 F.2d 901, 907-908 (7th Cir. 1990). Employing an analysis that it termed "case-by-case," and that weighed "the nature, extent, purpose, frequency, and cost of the work, as well as other relevant factors, to arrive at a common-sense finding," EPA found these changes to be non-routine and the court upheld the determination. (Perhaps internal company memoranda referring to these renovations as "life-extension projects" had something to do with the result.)

In the enforcement actions filed in 1999, EPA claimed that it was applying the RMRR exemption as it had in *WEPCO*, but the utilities argued the agency's interpretation was a significant change from prior practice, and that because they lacked fair notice of EPA's changed approach they could not be charged with violations. The fair notice defense has been unsuccessful so far, with United States v. Southern Indiana Gas and Electric Co., 245 F. Supp. 2d 994 (S.D. Ind. 2003), United States v. Cinergy Corp, 495 F. Supp. 2d 892 (S.D. Ind. 2007), and United States v. Ohio Edison, 276 F. Supp. 2d 829 (S.D. Ohio 2003), all rejecting it, on the ground that after *WEPCO*, EPA had been sufficiently consistent in reiterating the "case-by-case, fact intensive" nature of the RMRR review, as well as the major considerations that go into that review, to satisfy the fair notice requirement.

In addition to this threshold fair notice defense, the utilities focused on one particular aspect of EPA's interpretation of the RMRR exemption. EPA based part of its determination of RMRR on whether the capital improvements at issue were routine, prevalent, or commonplace for the specific unit being evaluated. Industry claimed this was the wrong standard, and that their improvements were routine because they were routine for the industry.

The significance of the dispute over the proper frame of reference for determining whether a project was routine, prevalent, or commonplace was summarized by a district court in one of the enforcement actions:

> [The utility companies focus] the inquiry on one factor, and interpret[] that factor in a way that could lead to exempting numerous projects as routine maintenance. If the "prevalent or commonplace in the industry" standard [is used], then a regulated party would only have to point to other similar projects in industry to show that they take place elsewhere to avoid the strictures of NSR. The end result could be many industry projects qualifying for routine maintenance just because others in the industry have taken on similar projects, projects that may or may not have been subject to NSR for various reasons. The comparisons could be misleading for a simple reason: perhaps many companies have made "major modifications" at their facilities. It is the frequency of the activity at other individual units within the industry that seems to us most relevant in this context. The mere fact that a number of different facilities within an industry may

have undertaken these projects strikes us as less instructive with respect to whether a project under review should be considered 'routine,' than the observation that this kind of replacement is, for an individual unit, an unusual or once or twice-in-a-lifetime occurrence. In sum, this focus on whether or not projects are prevalent throughout industry could lead to exempting numerous expensive and complex projects, a result that strains the meaning of the word "routine," and clashes with the guidance gleaned from the regulatory context. [United States v. Southern Indiana Gas and Electric Co., 245 F. Supp. 2d 994, 1014 (S.D. Ind. 2003).]

Industry countered EPA's position first by drawing attention to the language of the RMRR exemption, which speaks of activities that are routine "for a source category." They also observed that precisely because the kinds of projects at issue *were* undertaken numerous times within the industry throughout the 1990s, even though they might be once in a lifetime projects for any single unit, EPA had ample opportunity to challenge them if the agency really had adopted a "routine for the unit" interpretation of the exemption. As another district court put the matter, "Using a plant specific test for activities that occurred as far back as 1985, when it was patently obvious what [the utility] was doing, and the EPA said and did nothing by way of enforcement to require any of the work to be permitted, strikes the court as a 'gotcha' test."

The utilities also defended based on the second part of the statutory definition of modification, which requires that the modification increase emissions. EPA took the position that the question of an emissions increase was to be answered by whether or not the facility's emissions over an annual time period after the improvements exceeded its actual emissions over an annual time period prior to the improvements. The utilities countered that a physical change did not increase emissions unless it increased the facility's emissions rate, calculated on an hourly basis. Which method was chosen could have great consequences. If, for example, an improvement made operating the unit more efficient or economical without changing its hourly emissions rate—or even decreasing it due to operating efficiencies—a utility might then elect to run it for more hours during the year after the improvements. In that case, its annual emissions would go up even though its hourly emissions rate had not. Under EPA's approach, the improvements would constitute modifications; under the utility companies' approach they would not. Because most of the changes the utilities had made did not increase the unit's hourly emissions rate, winning on this point alone would secure them a meaningful victory regardless of how the RMRR issues were decided.

By July 2008, four decisions in EPA enforcement actions against utilities had been issued in four different district court actions. One of these cases reached the Supreme Court. In United States v. Duke Energy Corp., 278 F. Supp. 2d 619 (M.D.N.C. 2003), the court ruled on cross summary judgment motions, finding for the utility on both the routine in the industry versus routine at the unit issue and the total emissions versus emissions rate question. The United States appealed from the portion of the ruling holding that as a matter of law the EPA had to interpret "increases emissions" for purposes of NSR to mean increases the hourly emissions rate. The Fourth Circuit affirmed. The United States chose not to seek Supreme Court review, but Environmental Defense, who had intervened in the case, did appeal. In a rare move, the Supreme Court decided to hear the case notwithstanding the refusal of the United States to appeal.

## Environmental Defense v. Duke Energy Corp.

549 U.S. 561 (2007)

JUSTICE SOUTER delivered the opinion of the Court.

### I

EPA's 1975 regulations implementing NSPS provided generally that "any physical or operational change to an existing facility which results in an increase in the emission rate to the atmosphere of any pollutant to which a standard applies shall be considered a modification within the meaning of [S]ection 111." [42 U.S.C. §7411.] Especially significant here is the identification of an NSPS "modification" as a change that "increase[s] . . . the emission rate," which "shall be expressed as kg/hr of any pollutant discharged into the atmosphere." §60.14(b).

NSPS, however, did too little to "achiev[e] the ambitious goals of the 1970 Amendments," and the Clean Air Act Amendments of 1977, included the PSD provisions, which aimed at giving added protection to air quality in certain parts of the country "notwithstanding attainment and maintenance of" the NAAQS. The 1977 amendments required a PSD permit before a "major emitting facility" could be "constructed" in an area covered by the scheme. §165(a). As originally enacted, PSD applied only to newly constructed sources, but soon a technical amendment added the following subparagraph: "The term 'construction' when used in connection with any source or facility, includes the modification (as defined in [S]ection 111(a)) of any source or facility." In other words, the "construction" requiring a PSD permit under the statute was made to include (though it was not limited to) a "modification" as defined in the statutory NSPS provisions.

In 1980, EPA issued PSD regulations, which "limited the application of [PSD] review" of modified sources to instances of "'major' modificatio[n]," defined as "any physical change in or change in the method of operation of a major stationary source that would result in a significant net emissions increase of any pollutant subject to regulation under the Act." 40 CFR §51.166(b)(2)(i) (1987). Further regulations in turn addressed various elements of this definition, three of which are to the point here. First, the regulations specified that an operational change consisting merely of "[a]n increase in the hours of operation or in the production rate" would not generally constitute a "physical change or change in the method of operation." §51.166(b)(2)(iii). For purposes of a PSD permit, that is, such an operational change would not amount to a "modification" as the Act defines it. Second, the PSD regulations defined a "net emissions increase" as "[a]ny increase in actual emissions from a particular physical change or change in the method of operation," net of other contemporaneous "increases and decreases in actual emissions at the source." §51.166(b)(3). "Actual emissions" were defined to "equal the average rate, in tons per year, at which the unit actually emitted the pollutant during a two-year period which precedes the particular date and which is representative of normal source operation." §51.166(b)(21)(ii). "[A]ctual emissions" were to be "calculated using the unit's actual operating hours [and] production rates." Third, the term "significant" was defined as "a rate of emissions that would equal or exceed" one or another enumerated threshold, each expressed in "tons per year." §51.166(b)(23)(i).

The Court of Appeals held that Congress's provision defining a PSD modification by reference to an NSPS modification caught not only the statutory NSPS definition, but also whatever regulatory gloss EPA puts on that definition at any given time (for the purposes of the best technology requirement). When, therefore, EPA's PSD regulations specify the "change" that amounts to a "major modification" requiring a PSD permit, they must measure an increase in "the amount of any air pollutant emitted," 42 U.S.C. §7411(a)(4), in terms of the hourly rate of discharge, just the way NSPS regulations do. Petitioners and the United States say, on the contrary, that when EPA addresses the object of the PSD scheme it is free to put a different regulatory interpretation on the common statutory core of "modification," by measuring increased emission not in terms of hourly rate but by the actual, annual discharge of a pollutant that will follow the modification, regardless of rate per hour. This disagreement is the nub of the case.

## II

Respondent Duke Energy Corporation runs 30 coal-fired electric generating units at eight plants in North and South Carolina. The units were placed in service between 1940 and 1975, and each includes a boiler containing thousands of steel tubes arranged in sets. Between 1988 and 2000, Duke replaced or redesigned 29 tube assemblies in order to extend the life of the units and allow them to run longer each day.

The United States and intervenor-plaintiffs (collectively, plaintiffs) subsequently stipulated "that they do not contend that the projects at issue in this case caused an increase in the maximum hourly rate of emissions at any of Duke Energy's units." Rather, their claim "is based solely on their contention that the projects would have been projected to result in an increased utilization of the units at issue." Duke, for its part, stipulated to plaintiffs' right to appeal the District Court's determination that projects resulting in greater operating hours are not "major modifications" triggering the PSD permit requirement, absent an increase in the hourly rate of emissions. The District Court then entered summary judgment for Duke on all PSD claims.

The Court of Appeals for the Fourth Circuit affirmed. . . .

We granted the petition for certiorari brought by intervenor-plaintiffs and now vacate.

### III

#### A

In applying the 1980 PSD regulations to Duke's conduct, the Court of Appeals thought that, by defining the term "modification" identically in its NSPS and PSD provisions, the Act required EPA to conform its PSD interpretation of that definition to any such interpretation it reasonably adhered to under NSPS. But principles of statutory construction are not so rigid. Although we presume that the same term has the same meaning when it occurs here and there in a single statute, the Court of Appeals mischaracterized that presumption as "effectively irrebuttable." We also understand that "[m]ost words have different shades of meaning and consequently may be variously construed, not only when they occur in different statutes, but when used more than once in the same statute or even in the same section." Thus, the "natural presumption that identical words used in different parts of the same act are intended to have the same meaning . . . is not rigid and readily yields whenever there is such variation in the connection in which the words are used as reasonably to warrant the conclusion that they were employed in different parts of the act with different intent." A given term in the same statute may take on distinct characters from association with distinct statutory objects calling for different implementation strategies. . . .

In fact . . . we recently declined to require uniformity when resolving ambiguities in identical statutory terms. In United States v. Cleveland Indians Baseball Co., 532 U.S. 200 (2001), we rejected the notion that using the phrase "wages paid" in both "the discrete taxation and benefits eligibility contexts" can, standing alone, "compel symmetrical construction;" we gave "substantial judicial deference" to the "longstanding," "reasonable," and differing interpretations adopted by the Internal Revenue Service in its regulations and Revenue Rulings. There is, then, no "effectively irrebuttable" presumption that the same defined term in different provisions of the same statute must "be interpreted identically." Context counts.

It is true that the Clean Air Act did not merely repeat the term "modification" or the same definition of that word in its NSPS and PSD sections; the PSD language referred back to the section defining "modification" for NSPS purposes. §169(2)(C). But that did not matter in [other cases], and we do not see the distinction as making any difference here. Nothing in the text or the legislative history of the technical amendments that added the cross-reference to NSPS suggests that Congress had details of regulatory implementation in mind when it imposed PSD requirements on modified sources; the cross-reference alone is certainly no unambiguous congressional code for eliminating the customary agency discretion to resolve questions about a statutory definition by looking to the surroundings of the defined term, where it occurs. . . . Absent any iron rule to ignore the reasons for regulating PSD and NSPS "modifications" differently, EPA's construction need do no more than fall within the limits of what is reasonable, as set by the Act's common definition.

**B**

The Court of Appeals's reasoning that the PSD regulations must conform to their NSPS counterparts led the court to read those PSD regulations in a way that seems to us too far a stretch for the language used. The 1980 PSD regulations on "modification" simply cannot be taken to track the agency's regulatory definition under the NSPS.

True, the 1980 PSD regulations may be no seamless narrative, but they clearly do not define a "major modification" in terms of an increase in the "hourly emissions rate." On its face, the definition in the PSD regulations specifies no rate at all, hourly or annual, merely requiring a physical or operational change "that would result in a significant net emissions increase of any" regulated pollutant. 40 CFR §51.166(b)(2)(i). But even when a rate is mentioned, as in the regulatory definitions of the two terms, "significant" and "net emissions increase," the rate is annual, not hourly. Each of the thresholds that quantify "significant" is described in "tons per year," §51.166(b)(23)(i), and a "net emissions increase" is an "increase in actual emissions" measured against an "average" prior emissions rate of so many "tons per year." §§51.166(b)(3) and (21)(ii). And what is further at odds with the idea that hourly rate is relevant is the mandate that "[a]ctual emissions shall be calculated using the unit's actual operating hours," §51.166(b)(21)(ii), since "actual emissions" must be measured in a manner that looks to the number of hours the unit is or probably will be actually running. What these provisions are getting at is a measure of actual operations averaged over time, and the regulatory language simply cannot be squared with a regime under which "hourly rate of emissions," is dispositive.

[The lower court's] understanding of the 1980 PSD regulations makes the mistake of overlooking the difference between the two separate components of the regulatory definition of "major modification": "[1] any physical change in or change in the method of operation of a major stationary source that [2] would result in a significant net emissions increase of any pollutant subject to regulation under the Act." §51.166(b)(2)(i). The exclusion of "increase in . . . hours . . . or . . . production rate," §51.166(b)(2)(iii)(*f*), speaks to the first of these components ("physical change . . . or change in . . . method," §51.166(b)(2)(i)), but not to the second ("significant net emissions increase," *ibid.*). As the preamble to the 1980 PSD regulations explains, forcing companies to obtain a PSD permit before they could simply adjust operating hours "would severely and unduly hamper the ability of any company to take advantage of favorable market conditions." 45 Fed. Reg. 52704. In other words, a mere increase in the hours of operation, standing alone, is not a "physical change or change in the method of operation." 40 CFR §51.166(b)(2)(iii).

The judgment of the Court of Appeals is vacated, and the case is remanded for further proceedings consistent with this opinion.

## NOTES AND QUESTIONS

1. Notice that the court refers to Duke Energy's capital investments as ones that would extend the life of the generating units. Which of the two possible definitions of "increases emissions" is more consistent with the original idea of providing then-existing facilities a limited grace period to continue operating?

2. In the October 2003 regulations, EPA adopted a bright-line test for determining whether or not a capital project qualified for the RMRR exemption. Under the new Equipment Replacement Rule (ERP), a capital project at an existing facility was exempt from NSR if: (1) the project replaces existing equipment with identical ones, or ones that serve the same purpose; (2) project costs do not exceed 20 percent of the current replacement value of the entire unit; (3) the project does not alter the basic design of the unit or cause it to exceed any applicable emissions limitations that apply to the unit. 68 Fed. Reg. 61,248, 62,252. In December 2003, a panel of the D.C. Circuit stayed implementation of the ERP based on its belief that challengers had shown a reasonable likelihood of success on the merits, New York v. EPA, 03-1380, Dec. 24, 2003, and in March 2006, the Court vacated the rule, finding such a large exemption to be "contrary to the plain language" of the Act. New York v. EPA, 443 F.3d 880 (D.C. Cir. 2006), cert. denied, 550 U.S. 928 (2007).

3. Notwithstanding having its annual emissions interpretation of "increases emissions" sustained in *New York v. EPA*, EPA proposed to switch to an hourly emissions rate approach. 70 Fed. Reg. 61,081 (Oct. 20, 2005). Is this action consistent with *Duke Energy*? At about the same time, EPA issued guidance to its regional offices that although it would continue to pursue the pending enforcement actions, the agency would only initiate future actions against improvements that violated current NSR standards, even if the improvements had occurred years ago while the old standards were in effect.

4. All of EPA's changes to its NSR regulations were attempts to make it easier for facilities, some of them over 50 years old, to avoid new source review. Does this reflect a basic problem with a strategy of regulating new sources of pollution more stringently than existing sources—that it encourages prolonging the life of old sources to take advantage of more relaxed emissions standards? Compare this approach with that of the Oil Pollution Act, Chapter 2, which phased in its double-hull requirement for oil tankers on a schedule based on the age of existing tankers. Which one is a better approach?

5. In their 2016 book *Struggling for Air: Power Plants and the "War on Coal,"* Richard Revesz and Jack Lienke are strongly critical of the 1970 Clean Air Act Amendments for "grandfathering" old power plants. Compare the CAA's new source review program with the way the Oil Pollution Act of 1990, discussed in Chapter 2, phased in the double-hull regulation over a 20-year period based on the age of the vessel. In response to the book, Leon Billings, who was staff director for Senator Edmund Muskie (chair of the Senate Environment Committee in 1970), and Thomas Jorling, who was minority counsel for Senator John Sherman Cooper in 1970, claim that it is "simply false" that existing power plants were intended to be grandfathered in the Clean Air Act. They write that Revesz and Lienke "give short shrift to the requirement that 'modifications' of existing sources would be required to achieve national emission standards. The fact that EPA, under both Democrat[ic] and Republican Administrators, ignored or failed to implement this provision was not a failure of the law." They question "why you would exonerate EPA for its . . . failure to implement this critical provision of the 1970 amendments and then indict Senator Muskie and his colleagues for 'missing the mark.'" Billings and Jorling continue, "EPA's nearly 30-year failure to implement the law's requirement to install best available technology on modified plants of all kinds missed huge opportunities to reduce emissions from existing sources. Whether that failure was the result of special interest intervention or just agency delinquency is a case for someone else to make." Letter from Leon Billings & Thomas Jorling to Richard Revesz & Jack Lienke, Sept. 8, 2016. On November 15, 2016, Leon Billings passed away at the age of 78.

6. When EPA responded to challengers' complaints in *New York v. EPA* that the changes in NSR procedures would have deleterious effects on the environment, one of the agency's responses was that NSR was only one of several federal air quality programs that served to reduce pollution from stationary sources. As air quality programs under the CAA now are well into their fourth decade, it is indeed true that the country's most persistent air quality problems are being addressed by an overlapping complex of approaches, each based on different regulatory authorities contained in the statute.

## C.   PSD Permitting and Regulation of Greenhouse Gas Emissions

As noted above, when EPA in December 2009 made its endangerment finding for emissions of greenhouse gases and adopted its Tailpipe Rule, the agency concluded that this finding triggered provisions of the Clean Air Act that require construction and operating permits for stationary sources whose emissions of GHGs exceed statutory thresholds for any regulated pollutant. After this was upheld by the D.C. Circuit, the U.S. Supreme Court granted review limited to the question "whether regulation of GHG emissions from new mobile sources triggered permitting requirements for stationary sources that emit greenhouse gases." That issue was decided by the Supreme Court in the case below. As you read the decision, note that because there is no NAAQS for greenhouse gas emissions, the Clean Air Act's PSD provisions, not its nonattainment provisions, apply to sources of GHG emissions throughout the country. The decision explains how the PSD permitting provisions apply to such sources.

## Utility Air Regulatory Group v. EPA

573 U.S. 302 (2014)

JUSTICE SCALIA announced the judgment of the Court and delivered the opinion of the Court with respect to Parts I and II.

Acting pursuant to the Clean Air Act the Environmental Protection Agency recently set standards for emissions of "greenhouse gases" (substances it believes contribute to "global climate change") from new motor vehicles. We must decide whether it was permissible for EPA to determine that its motor-vehicle greenhouse-gas regulations automatically triggered permitting requirements under the Act for stationary sources that emit greenhouse gases.

### I. BACKGROUND

#### A. Stationary-Source Permitting

The Clean Air Act regulates pollution-generating emissions from both stationary sources, such as factories and power plants, and moving sources, such as cars, trucks, and aircraft. This litigation concerns permitting obligations imposed on stationary sources under Titles I and V of the Act. Title I charges EPA with formulating national ambient air quality standards (NAAQS) for air pollutants. To date, EPA has issued NAAQS for six pollutants: sulfur dioxide, particulate matter, nitrogen dioxide, carbon monoxide, ozone, and lead. States have primary responsibility for implementing the NAAQS by developing "State implementation plans." A State must designate every area within its borders as "attainment," "nonattainment," or "unclassifiable" with respect to each NAAQS and the State's implementation plan must include permitting programs for stationary sources that vary according to the classification of the area where the source is or is proposed to be located.

Stationary sources in areas designated attainment or unclassifiable are subject to the Act's provisions relating to "Prevention of Significant Deterioration" (PSD). §§160-169. EPA interprets the PSD provisions to apply to sources located in areas that are designated attainment or unclassifiable for *any* NAAQS pollutant, regardless of whether the source emits that specific pollutant. Since the inception of the PSD program, every area of the country has been designated attainment or unclassifiable for at least one NAAQS pollutant; thus, on EPA's view, all stationary sources are potentially subject to PSD review.

It is unlawful to construct or modify a "major emitting facility" in "any area to which [the PSD program] applies" without first obtaining a permit. §§165(a)(1), 169(2)(C). To qualify for a permit, the facility must not cause or contribute to the violation of any applicable air-quality standard, §165(a)(3), and it must comply with emissions limitations that reflect the "best available control technology" (or BACT) for "each pollutant subject to regulation under" the Act. §165(a)(4). The Act defines a "major emitting facility" as any stationary source with the potential to emit 250 tons per year of "any air pollutant" (or 100 tons per year for certain types of sources). §169(1). It defines "modification" as a physical or operational change that causes the facility to emit more of "any air pollutant." §161(a)(4).[1]

In addition to the PSD permitting requirements for construction and modification, Title V of the Act makes it unlawful to *operate* any "major source," wherever located, without a comprehensive operating permit. §502(a). Unlike the PSD program, Title V generally does not impose any substantive pollution-control requirements. Instead, it is designed to facilitate compliance and enforcement by consolidating into a single document all of a facility's obligations under the Act. The permit must include all "emissions limitations and standards" that apply to the source, as well as associated inspection, monitoring, and reporting requirements. §504(a)-(c). Title V defines a "major source" by reference to the Act-wide definition of "major stationary source," which in turn means any stationary source with the potential to emit 100 tons per year of "any air pollutant." §§501(2)(B), 302(j).

### B. EPA's Greenhouse-Gas Regulations

In 2007, the Court held that Title II of the Act "authorize[d] EPA to regulate greenhouse gas emissions from new motor vehicles" if the Agency "form[ed] a 'judgment' that such emissions contribute to climate change." Massachusetts v. EPA, 549 U.S. 497, 528. In response to that decision, EPA embarked on a course of regulation resulting in "the single largest expansion in the scope of the [Act] in its history."

EPA first asked the public, in a notice of proposed rulemaking, to comment on how the Agency should respond to *Massachusetts*. In doing so, it explained that regulating greenhouse-gas emissions from motor vehicles could have far-reaching consequences for stationary sources. Under EPA's view, once greenhouse gases became

---

1. Although the statute sets numerical thresholds (100 or 250 tons per year) for emissions that will make a facility "major," it does not specify by how much a physical or operational change must increase emissions to constitute a permit-requiring "modification." Nor does it say how much of a given regulated pollutant a "major emitting facility" must emit before it is subject to BACT for that pollutant. EPA, however, has established pollutant-specific numerical thresholds below which a facility's emissions of a pollutant, and increases therein, are considered *de minimis* for those purposes.

regulated under any part of the Act, the PSD and Title V permitting requirements would apply to all stationary sources with the potential to emit greenhouse gases in excess of the statutory thresholds: 100 tons per year under Title V, and 100 or 250 tons per year under the PSD program depending on the type of source. Because greenhouse-gas emissions tend to be "orders of magnitude greater" than emissions of conventional pollutants, EPA projected that numerous small sources not previously regulated under the Act would be swept into the PSD program and Title V, including "smaller industrial sources," "large office and residential buildings, hotels, large retail establishments, and similar facilities." The Agency warned that this would constitute an "unprecedented expansion of EPA authority that would have a profound effect on virtually every sector of the economy and touch every household in the land," yet still be "relatively ineffective at reducing greenhouse gas concentrations."

In 2009, EPA announced its determination regarding the danger posed by motor-vehicle greenhouse-gas emissions. EPA found that greenhouse-gas emissions from new motor vehicles contribute to elevated atmospheric concentrations of greenhouse gases, which endanger public health and welfare by fostering global "climate change." 74 Fed. Reg. 66523, 66537 (hereinafter Endangerment Finding). . . .

Next, EPA issued its "final decision" regarding the prospect that motor-vehicle greenhouse-gas standards would trigger stationary-source permitting requirements. 75 Fed. Reg. 17004 (2010) (hereinafter Triggering Rule). EPA announced that beginning on the effective date of its greenhouse-gas standards for motor vehicles, stationary sources would be subject to the PSD program and Title V on the basis of their potential to emit greenhouse gases. As expected, EPA in short order promulgated greenhouse gas emission standards for passenger cars, light-duty trucks, and medium-duty passenger vehicles to take effect on January 2, 2011. 75 Fed. Reg. 25324 (hereinafter Tailpipe Rule).

EPA then announced steps it was taking to "tailor" the PSD program and Title V to greenhouse gases. 75 Fed. Reg. 31514 (hereinafter Tailoring Rule). Those steps were necessary, it said, because the PSD program and Title V were designed to regulate "a relatively small number of large industrial sources," and requiring permits for all sources with greenhouse-gas emissions above the statutory thresholds would radically expand those programs, making them both unadministrable and "unrecognizable to the Congress that designed" them. EPA nonetheless rejected calls to exclude greenhouse gases entirely from those programs, asserting that the Act is not "ambiguous with respect to the need to cover [greenhouse-gas] sources under either the PSD or title V program." Instead, EPA adopted a "phase-in approach" that it said would "appl[y] PSD and title V at threshold levels that are as close to the statutory levels as possible, and do so as quickly as possible, at least to a certain point."

The phase-in, EPA said, would consist of at least three steps. During Step 1, from January 2 through June 30, 2011, no source would become newly subject to the PSD program or Title V solely on the basis of its greenhouse gas emissions; however, sources required to obtain permits anyway because of their emission of conventional pollutants (so-called "anyway" sources) would need to comply with BACT for greenhouse gases if they emitted those gases in significant amounts, defined as at least 75,000 tons per year $CO_2e$. During Step 2, from July 1, 2011, through

June 30, 2012, sources with the potential to emit at least 100,000 tons per year $CO_2e$ of greenhouse gases would be subject to PSD and Title V permitting for their construction and operation and to PSD permitting for modifications that would increase their greenhouse-gas emissions by at least 75,000 tons per year $CO_2e$. At Step 3, beginning on July 1, 2013, EPA said it might (or might not) further reduce the permitting thresholds (though not below 50,000 tons per year $CO_2e$), and it might (or might not) establish permanent exemptions for some sources. Beyond Step 3, EPA promised to complete another round of rulemaking by April 30, 2016, in which it would "take further action to address small sources," which might (or might not) include establishing permanent exemptions. . . .

## II. ANALYSIS

This litigation presents two distinct challenges to EPA's stance on greenhouse-gas permitting for stationary sources. First, we must decide whether EPA permissibly determined that a source may be subject to the PSD and Title V permitting requirements on the sole basis of the source's potential to emit greenhouse gases. Second, we must decide whether EPA permissibly determined that a source already subject to the PSD program because of its emission of conventional pollutants (an "anyway" source) may be required to limit its greenhouse-gas emissions by employing the "best available control technology" for greenhouse gases. The Solicitor General joins issue on both points but evidently regards the second as more important; he informs us that "anyway" sources account for roughly 83% of American stationary-source greenhouse gas emissions, compared to just 3% for the additional, non "anyway" sources EPA sought to regulate at Steps 2 and 3 of the Tailoring Rule. . . .

### A. The PSD and Title V Triggers

We first decide whether EPA permissibly interpreted the statute to provide that a source may be required to obtain a PSD or Title V permit on the sole basis of its potential greenhouse-gas emissions.

### 1

EPA thought its conclusion that a source's greenhouse gas emissions may necessitate a PSD or Title V permit followed from the Act's unambiguous language. The Court of Appeals agreed and held that the statute "compelled" EPA's interpretation. We disagree. The statute compelled EPA's greenhouse-gas-inclusive interpretation with respect to neither the PSD program nor Title V. . . .

*Massachusetts* does not strip EPA of authority to exclude greenhouse gases from the class of regulable air pollutants under other parts of the Act where their inclusion would be inconsistent with the statutory scheme. The Act-wide definition to which the Court gave a "sweeping" and "capacious" interpretation is not a command to regulate, but a description of the universe of substances EPA may *consider* regulating under the Act's operative provisions. *Massachusetts* does not foreclose the Agency's use of statutory context to infer that certain of the Act's provisions use "air pollutant" to denote not every conceivable airborne substance, but only those that may sensibly be encompassed within the particular regulatory program. As certain *amici* felicitously put it, while *Massachusetts* "rejected EPA's categorical contention that greenhouse gases *could not* be 'air pollutants' for any purposes of the Act," it did not "embrace EPA's current, equally categorical position that greenhouse gases *must* be air pollutants for all purposes" regardless of the statutory context. . . .

In sum, there is no insuperable textual barrier to EPA's interpreting "any air pollutant" in the permitting triggers of PSD and Title V to encompass only pollutants emitted in quantities that enable them to be sensibly regulated at the statutory thresholds, and to exclude those atypical pollutants that, like greenhouse gases, are emitted in such vast quantities that their inclusion would radically transform those programs and render them unworkable as written.

## 2

Having determined that EPA was mistaken in thinking the Act *compelled* a greenhouse-gas-inclusive interpretation of the PSD and Title V triggers, we next consider the Agency's alternative position that its interpretation was justified as an exercise of its "discretion" to adopt "a reasonable construction of the statute." We conclude that EPA's interpretation is not permissible. . . .

EPA itself has repeatedly acknowledged that applying the PSD and Title V permitting requirements to greenhouse gases would be inconsistent with—in fact, would overthrow—the Act's structure and design. In the Tailoring Rule, EPA described the calamitous consequences of interpreting the Act in that way. Under the PSD program, annual permit applications would jump from about 800 to nearly 82,000; annual administrative costs would swell from $12 million to over $1.5 billion; and decade-long delays in issuing permits would become common, causing construction projects to grind to a halt nationwide. The picture under Title V was equally bleak: The number of sources required to have permits would jump from fewer than 15,000 to about 6.1 million; annual administrative costs would balloon from $62 million to $21 billion; and collectively the newly covered sources would face permitting costs of $147 billion. Moreover, "the great majority of additional sources brought into the PSD and title V programs would be small sources that Congress did not expect would need to undergo permitting." EPA stated that these results would be so "contrary to congressional intent," and would so "severely undermine what Congress sought to accomplish," that they necessitated as much as a 1,000-fold increase in the permitting thresholds set forth in the statute.

Like EPA, we think it beyond reasonable debate that requiring permits for sources based solely on their emission of greenhouse gases at the 100- and 250-tons-per-year levels set forth in the statute would be "incompatible" with "the substance of Congress' regulatory scheme." . . .

The fact that EPA's greenhouse-gas-inclusive interpretation of the PSD and Title V triggers would place plainly excessive demands on limited governmental resources is alone a good reason for rejecting it; but that is not the only reason. EPA's interpretation is also unreasonable because it would bring about an enormous and transformative expansion in EPA's regulatory authority without clear congressional authorization. When an agency claims to discover in a long-extant statute an unheralded power to regulate "a significant portion of the American economy," we typically greet its announcement with a measure of skepticism. We expect Congress to speak clearly if it wishes to assign to an agency decisions of vast "economic and political significance." The power to require permits for the construction and modification of tens of thousands, and the operation of millions, of small sources nationwide falls comfortably within the class of authorizations that we have been reluctant to read into ambiguous statutory text. Moreover, in EPA's assertion of that authority, we confront a singular situation: an agency laying claim to extravagant statutory power over the national economy while at the same time strenuously asserting that the authority claimed would render the statute "unrecognizable to the Congress that designed" it. Since, as we hold above, the statute does not compel EPA's interpretation, it would be patently unreasonable—not to say outrageous—for EPA to insist on seizing expansive power that it admits the statute is not designed to grant.

### 3

EPA thought that despite the foregoing problems, it could make its interpretation reasonable by adjusting the levels at which a source's greenhouse-gas emissions would oblige it to undergo PSD and Title V permitting. Although the Act, in no uncertain terms, requires permits for sources with the potential to emit more than 100 or 250 tons per year of a relevant pollutant, EPA in its Tailoring Rule wrote a new threshold of *100,000* tons per year for greenhouse gases. Since the Court of Appeals thought the statute unambiguously made greenhouse gases capable of triggering PSD and Title V, it held that petitioners lacked Article III standing to challenge the Tailoring Rule because that rule did not injure petitioners but merely relaxed the pre-existing statutory requirements. Because we, however, hold that EPA's greenhouse-gas-inclusive interpretation of the triggers was *not* compelled, and because EPA has essentially admitted that its interpretation would be unreasonable without "tailoring," we consider the validity of the Tailoring Rule.

We conclude that EPA's rewriting of the statutory thresholds was impermissible and therefore could not validate the Agency's interpretation of the triggering provisions. An agency has no power to "tailor" legislation to bureaucratic policy goals by rewriting unambiguous statutory terms. Agencies exercise discretion only in the interstices created by statutory silence or ambiguity; they must always "'give effect to the unambiguously expressed intent of Congress.'" It is hard to imagine a statutory term less ambiguous than the precise numerical thresholds at which the Act requires PSD and Title V permitting. When EPA replaced those numbers with others of its own choosing, it went well beyond the "bounds of its statutory authority.". . .

Were we to recognize the authority claimed by EPA in the Tailoring Rule, we would deal a severe blow to the Constitution's separation of powers. Under our system of government, Congress makes laws and the President, acting at times through agencies like EPA, "faithfully execute[s]" them. U.S. Const., Art. II, §3. The power of executing the laws necessarily includes both authority and responsibility to resolve some questions left open by Congress that arise during the law's administration. But it does not include a power to revise clear statutory terms that turn out not to work in practice.

In the Tailoring Rule, EPA asserts newfound authority to regulate millions of small sources—including retail stores, offices, apartment buildings, shopping centers, schools, and churches—and to decide, on an ongoing basis and without regard for the thresholds prescribed by Congress, how many of those sources to regulate. We are not willing to stand on the dock and wave goodbye as EPA embarks on this multiyear voyage of discovery. We reaffirm the core administrative-law principle that an agency may not rewrite clear statutory terms to suit its own sense of how the statute should operate. EPA therefore lacked authority to "tailor" the Act's unambiguous numerical thresholds to accommodate its greenhouse-gas-inclusive interpretation of the permitting triggers. Instead, the need to rewrite clear provisions of the statute should have alerted EPA that it had taken a wrong interpretive turn. Agencies are not free to "adopt. . . unreasonable interpretations of statutory provisions and then edit other statutory provisions to mitigate the unreasonableness." Because the Tailoring Rule cannot save EPA's interpretation of the triggers, that interpretation was impermissible under *Chevron*.

### B. BACT for "Anyway" Sources

For the reasons we have given, EPA overstepped its statutory authority when it decided that a source could become subject to PSD or Title V permitting by reason of its greenhouse-gas emissions.

But what about "anyway" sources, those that would need permits based on their emissions of more conventional pollutants (such as particulate matter)? We now consider whether EPA reasonably interpreted the Act to require those sources to comply with "best available control technology" emission standards for greenhouse gases. . . .

#### 2

The question before us is whether EPA's decision to require BACT for greenhouse gases emitted by sources otherwise subject to PSD review is, as a general matter, a permissible interpretation of the statute under *Chevron*. We conclude that it is. The text of the BACT provision is far less open-ended than the text of the PSD and Title V permitting triggers. It states that BACT is required "for each pollutant subject to regulation under this chapter" (*i.e.*, the entire Act), §165(a)(4), a phrase that—as the D.C. Circuit wrote 35 years ago—"would not seem readily susceptible [of] misinterpretation." Alabama Power Co. v. Costle, 636 F.2d 323, 404 (1979). Whereas the dubious breadth of "any air pollutant" in the permitting triggers suggests a role for agency judgment in identifying the subset of pollutants covered by the particular regulatory program at issue, the more specific phrasing of the BACT provision suggests that the necessary judgment has already been made by Congress. The wider statutory context likewise does not suggest that the BACT provision can bear a narrowing construction: There is no indication that the Act elsewhere uses, or that EPA has interpreted, "each pollutant subject to regulation under this chapter" to mean anything other than what it says.

Even if the text were not clear, applying BACT to greenhouse gases is not so disastrously unworkable, and need not result in such a dramatic expansion of agency authority, as to convince us that EPA's interpretation is unreasonable. We are not talking about extending EPA jurisdiction over millions of previously unregulated entities, but about moderately increasing the demands EPA (or a state permitting authority) can make of entities already subject to its regulation. And it is not yet clear that EPA's demands will be of a significantly different character from those traditionally associated with PSD review. In short, the record before us does not establish that the BACT provision as written is incapable of being sensibly applied to greenhouse gases.

We acknowledge the potential for greenhouse-gas BACT to lead to an unreasonable and unanticipated degree of regulation, and our decision should not be taken as an endorsement of all aspects of EPA's current approach, nor as a free rein for any future regulatory application of BACT in this distinct context. Our narrow holding is that nothing in the statute categorically prohibits EPA from interpreting the BACT provision to apply to greenhouse gases emitted by "anyway" sources.

However, EPA may require an "anyway" source to comply with greenhouse-gas BACT only if the source emits more than a *de minimis* amount of greenhouse gases. As noted above, the Tailoring Rule applies BACT only if a source emits greenhouse gases in excess of 75,000 tons per year $CO_2e$, but the Rule makes clear that EPA did not arrive at that number by identifying the *de minimis* level. EPA may establish an appropriate *de minimis* threshold below which BACT is not required for a source's greenhouse-gas emissions. We do not hold that 75,000 tons per year $CO_2e$ necessarily exceeds a true *de minimis* level, only that EPA must justify its selection on proper grounds.

\* \* \*

To sum up: We hold that EPA exceeded its statutory authority when it interpreted the Clean Air Act to require PSD and Title V permitting for stationary sources based on their greenhouse-gas emissions. Specifically, the Agency may not treat greenhouse gases as a pollutant for purposes of defining a "major emitting facility" (or a "modification" thereof) in the PSD context or a "major source" in the Title V context. To the extent its regulations purport to do so, they are invalid. EPA may, however, continue to treat greenhouse gases as a "pollutant subject to regulation under this chapter" for purposes of requiring BACT for "anyway" sources. The judgment of the Court of Appeals is affirmed in part and reversed in part.

JUSTICE BREYER, with whom JUSTICE GINSBURG, JUSTICE SOTOMAYOR, and JUSTICE KAGAN join, concurring in part and dissenting in part.

These cases take as a given our decision in *Massachusetts* that the Act's *general definition* of "air pollutant" includes greenhouse gases. One of the questions posed by these cases is whether those gases fall within the scope of the phrase "any air pollutant" as that phrase is used in the more specific provisions of the Act here at issue. The Court's answer is "no." I disagree. . . .

I agree with the Court that the word "any," when used in a statute, does not normally mean "any in the universe.". . .

The law has long recognized that terms such as "any" admit of unwritten limitations and exceptions. . . .

I also agree with the Court's point that "a generic reference to air pollutants" in the Clean Air Act need not "encompass every substance falling within the Act-wide definition" that we construed in *Massachusetts*. . . .

But I do not agree with the Court that the only way to avoid an absurd or otherwise impermissible result in these cases is to create an atextual greenhouse gas exception to the phrase "any air pollutant." After all, the word "any" makes an earlier appearance in the definitional provision, which defines "major emitting facility" to mean "*any* . . . source with the potential to emit two hundred and fifty tons per year or more of any air pollutant." §169(1) (emphasis added). As a linguistic matter, one can just as easily read an implicit exception for small-scale greenhouse gas emissions into the phrase "any source" as into the phrase "any air pollutant." And given the purposes of the PSD program and the Act as a whole, as well as the specific roles of the different parts of the statutory definition, finding flexibility in "any source" is far more sensible than the Court's route of finding it in "any air pollutant."

The implicit exception I propose reads almost word for word the same as the Court's, except that the location of the exception has shifted. To repeat, the Court reads the definition of "major emitting facility" as if it referred to "any source with the potential to emit two hundred fifty tons per year or more of any air pollutant *except for those air pollutants, such as carbon dioxide, with respect to which regulation at that threshold would be impractical or absurd or would sweep in smaller sources that Congress did not mean to cover.*" I would simply move the implicit exception, which I've italicized, so that it applies to "source" rather than "air pollutant": "any Source with the potential to emit two hundred fifty tons per year or more of any air pollutant *except for those sources, such as those emitting unmanageably small amounts of greenhouse gases, with respect to which regulation at that threshold would be impractical or absurd or would sweep in smaller sources that Congress did not mean to cover.*"

From a legal, administrative, and functional perspective — that is, from a perspective that assumes that Congress was not merely trying to arrange words on paper but was seeking to achieve a real-world *purpose* — my way of reading the statute is the more sensible one. For one thing, my reading is consistent with the specific purpose underlying the 250 tpy threshold specified by the statute. The purpose of that number was not to prevent the regulation of dangerous air pollutants that cannot be sensibly regulated at that particular threshold, though that is the effect that the Court's reading gives the threshold. Rather, the purpose was to limit the PSD program's obligations to larger sources while exempting the many small sources whose emissions are low enough that imposing burdensome regulatory requirements on them would be senseless. . . .

The Court's decision to read greenhouse gases out of the PSD program drains the Act of its flexibility and chips away at our decision in *Massachusetts.* What sense does it make to read the Act as generally granting the EPA the authority to regulate greenhouse gas emissions and then to read it as denying that power with respect to the programs for large stationary sources at issue here? It is anomalous to read the Act to require the EPA to regulate air pollutants that pose previously unforeseen threats to human health and welfare where "250 tons per year" is a sensible regulatory line but not where, by chemical or regulatory happenstance, a higher line must be drawn. And it is anomalous to read an unwritten exception into the more important phrase of the statutory definition ("any air pollutant") when a similar unwritten exception to less important language (the particular number used by the statute) will do just as well. The implicit exception preferred by the Court produces all of these anomalies, while the source-related exception I propose creates none of them. . . .

* * *

I agree with the Court's holding that stationary sources that are subject to the PSD program because they emit other (non-greenhouse-gas) pollutants in quantities above the statutory threshold—those facilities that the Court refers to as "anyway" sources—must meet the "best available control technology" requirement of §165(a)(4) with respect to greenhouse gas emissions. I therefore join Part II-B-2 of the Court's opinion. But as for the Court's holding that the EPA cannot interpret the language at issue here to cover facilities that emit more than 100,000 tpy of greenhouse gases by virtue of those emissions, I respectfully dissent.

JUSTICE ALITO, with whom JUSTICE THOMAS joins, concurring in part and dissenting in part.

In Massachusetts v. EPA, 549 U.S. 497 (2007), this Court considered whether greenhouse gases fall within the Clean Air Act's general definition of an air "pollutant." The Environmental Protection Agency cautioned us that "key provisions of the [Act] cannot cogently be applied to [greenhouse gas] emissions," but the Court brushed the warning aside and had "little trouble" concluding that the Act's "sweeping definition" of a pollutant encompasses greenhouse gases. I believed *Massachusetts v. EPA* was wrongly decided at the time, and these cases further expose the flaws with that decision.

## I

As the present cases now show, trying to fit greenhouse gases into "key provisions" of the Clean Air Act involves more than a "little trouble." These cases concern the provisions of the Act relating to the "Prevention of Significant Deterioration" (PSD), as well as Title V of the Act. And in order to make those provisions apply to greenhouse gases in a way that does not produce absurd results, the EPA effectively amended the Act. The Act contains specific emissions thresholds that trigger PSD and Title V coverage, but the EPA crossed out the figures enacted by Congress and substituted figures of its own. I agree with the Court that the EPA is neither required nor permitted to take this extraordinary step, and I therefore join Parts I and II-A of the Court's opinion.

## II

I do not agree, however, with the Court's conclusion that what it terms "anyway sources," *i.e.*, sources that are subject to PSD and Title V permitting as the result of the emission of conventional pollutants, must install "best available control technology" (BACT) for greenhouse gases. As is the case with the PSD and Title V thresholds, trying to fit greenhouse gases into the BACT analysis badly distorts the scheme that Congress adopted. . . .

## A

With respect to the text, it is curious that the Court, having departed from a literal interpretation of the term "pollutant" in Part II-A, turns on its heels and adopts a literal interpretation in Part II-B. The coverage thresholds at issue in Part

II-A apply to any "pollutant." The Act's general definition of this term is broad, and in *Massachusetts v. EPA* the Court held that this definition covers greenhouse gases. The Court does not disturb that holding, but it nevertheless concludes that, as used in the provision triggering PSD coverage, the term "pollutant" actually means "pollutant, other than a greenhouse gas." In Part II-B, the relevant statutory provision says that BACT must be installed for any "pollutant subject to regulation under [the Act]." §7475(a)(4). If the term "pollutant" means "pollutant, other than a greenhouse gas," as the Court effectively concludes in Part II-A, the term "pollutant subject to regulation under [the Act]" in §7475(a)(4) should mean "pollutant, other than a greenhouse gas, subject to regulation under [the Act], and that is subject to regulation under [the Act]." The Court's literalism is selective, and it results in a strange and disjointed regulatory scheme.

Under the Court's interpretation, a source can emit an unlimited quantity of greenhouse gases without triggering the need for a PSD permit. Why might Congress have wanted to allow this? The most likely explanation is that the PSD permitting process is simply not suited for use in regulating this particular pollutant. And if that is so, it makes little sense to require the installation of BACT for greenhouse gases in those instances in which a source happens to be required to obtain a permit due to the emission of a qualifying quantity of some other pollutant that is regulated under the Act.

## NOTES AND QUESTIONS

1. The *UARG* Court by a vote of 5-4 rejected EPA's conclusion that regulation of greenhouse gases automatically triggers permitting requirements for stationary sources that emit GHGs. However, by a vote of 7-2 the Court also held that stationary sources that already are subject to PSD permitting requirements because they emit other (non-greenhouse-gas) pollutants in quantities above the statutory threshold ("anyway" sources) must comply with the "best available control technology" requirement of the PSD program with respect to greenhouse gas emissions. As a result, the decision was not considered to be a significant blow to EPA's efforts to control GHG emissions.

2. In *UARG*, only two of the four Justices who dissented in *Massachusetts v. EPA* (Justices Thomas and Alito) continued to reject *Massachusetts*'s holding that the Clean Air Act gives EPA the authority to regulate GHG emissions. Chief Justice Roberts and Justice Scalia accepted the holding that the Clean Air Act gives EPA the authority to regulate greenhouse gas emissions.

3. Compare the differing interpretations of the meaning of "any air pollutant" in the statute adopted by Justice Scalia and Justice Breyer. Scalia's interpretation effectively holds that this does not include GHGs and thus emissions of such pollutants cannot in themselves subject a stationary source to PSD permitting requirements. However, he believes that stationary sources that already need a PSD permit due to their emissions of other pollutants can be required to control their GHG emissions. Justice Breyer would interpret "any air pollutant" to include GHG emissions and thus uphold EPA's position that all large emitters of GHGs are subject to these permitting requirements. Justice Alito in dissent accuses them both of rewriting the statute.

4. In footnote 6 to his majority opinion, Justice Scalia notes another interpretation of "any air pollutant" that appeared in D.C. Circuit Judge Brett Kavanaugh's dissent from the denial of the petition for rehearing en banc. Judge Kavanaugh argued that the PSD provisions should be read to apply only to pollutants subject to national ambient air quality standards (NAAQS), which would not include GHGs. The Court did not express an opinion on the merits of this construction, though it upheld EPA's inclusion of "anyway" sources.

5. Note that Justice Scalia's majority opinion in *UARG* holds that EPA may require sources that otherwise are required to obtain a PSD or Title V permit to install best available control technology (BACT) for GHGs "if the source emits more than a *de minimis* amount" of them. EPA on October 3, 2016, proposed to amend its PSD and Title V regulations to formally establish a 75,000 tons per year $CO_2e$ (carbon dioxide equivalent) as the significant emission rate for greenhouse gases. Revisions to the Prevention of Significant Deterioration (PSD) and Title V Greenhouse Gas (GHG) Permitting Regulations and Establishment of a Significant Emissions Rate (SER) for GHG Emissions Under the PSD Program, 81 Fed. Reg. 68,110 (2016).

6. In another portion of his majority opinion, Justice Scalia delivered what many observers interpreted as a warning to EPA with respect to the development of its Clean Power Plan to regulate GHG emissions from existing power plants under section 111(d) of the Act. EPA was considering requiring existing power plants to take "beyond the fence" measures to improve energy efficiency, such as offering customers more energy efficient light bulbs. Scalia suggested that requiring such measures would exceed EPA's authority. Noting that BACT is based on "control technology" for a "facility," Scalia observed that "EPA has long interpreted BACT as required only for pollutants that the source itself emits; accordingly, EPA acknowledges that BACT may not be used to require 'reductions in a facility's demand for energy from the electric grid.'" This portion of Justice Scalia's opinion may have helped persuade EPA to drop demand-side measures from the final version of the Clean Power Plan (CPP) it adopted in 2015. Nevertheless, as noted below, in February 2016 Justice Scalia provided the decisive vote in the Court's unprecedented 5-4 order preventing the CPP from taking effect, the last vote Justice Scalia cast before he died unexpectedly.

### The Obama EPA's Clean Power Plan and the Trump EPA's Affordable Clean Energy Rule

On September 20, 2013, EPA proposed new source performance standards (NSPSs) for new fossil-fueled power plants that were widely viewed as precluding the construction of new coal-fired power plants unless they employed expensive carbon capture and storage technology. In June 2014, EPA proposed regulations to limit GHG emissions from existing power plants, which came to be known as the "Clean Power Plan" (CPP). Under the CPP, EPA assigned each state an individual goal for reducing emissions from power plants, but it left up to each state how to meet its goal. States were required to submit plans for reducing emissions beginning in 2022 and by 2030 achieving a 32 percent reduction in emissions below 2005 levels. The plans could include measures such as switching from coal to natural gas, expanding the use of renewable energy sources, putting a price on carbon emissions and creating a cap-and-trade program, and/or increasing energy efficiency. If a state refused to submit a plan, EPA would impose its own federal program.

The rarely used section 111(d) of the Act allows the agency to require states to regulate a pollutant for which it has established an NSPS if it is not already regulated as a criteria air pollutant with a national ambient air quality standard (NAAQS) or as a hazardous air pollutant subject to a national emissions standard for hazardous air pollutants (NESHAP).

The CPP regulations were published in the Federal Register on October 23, 2015, "Carbon Pollution Emission Guidelines for Existing Stationary Sources: Electric Utility Generating Units," 80 Fed. Reg. 64,662 (2015). The rule established (1) "final emission guidelines for states to follow in developing plans to reduce [GHG] emissions from existing fossil fuel-fired" electric generating units (EGUs), including $CO_2$ "emission performance rates representing the best system of emission reduction (BSER) for two subcategories of existing fossil fuel-fired EGUs—fossil fuel-fired electric utility steam generating units and stationary combustion turbines"; (2) "state-specific $CO_2$ goals reflecting the $CO_2$ emission performance rates"; and (3) "guidelines for the development, submittal and implementation of state plans that establish emission standards or other measures to implement the $CO_2$ emission performance rates." EPA adopted the Clean Power Plan only after considering 4.3 million comments, the most the agency has ever received in any rulemaking action during its then 45-year history.

The final regulations included some significant changes from the agency's initial proposal. EPA increased the flexibility afforded states in designing plans to determine the most efficient way to reduce emissions. It also delayed for two years the initial compliance date for power plants, while providing incentives for early action to invest in renewable energy sources. EPA also eliminated the fourth of the four "building blocks" it initially had proposed—one that focused on utilities getting their customers to use energy more efficiently. This was widely viewed as a response to Justice Scalia's questioning in *UARG* of EPA's authority to require demand-side reduction programs under the Clean Air Act, as discussed in Note 6 above.

Opponents of the new source performance standard for GHG emissions and the Clean Power Plan tried to use the Congressional Review Act (see Chapter 2) to veto the EPA regulations through a special fast-track procedure permitting an up-or-down vote in each house of Congress. On November 17, 2015, the U.S. Senate passed a joint resolution of disapproval of the NSPS by a vote of 52-46 with three Democrats supporting the resolution and three Republicans voting against it. The NSPS disapproval resolution was adopted by the House by a vote of 235-188 on December 1, 2015, even as the Paris climate negotiations were taking place. A resolution disapproving the CPP regulations for existing power plants passed the Senate on November 17, 2015, by a vote of 52-46. The resolution passed the House by a vote of 242-180 on December 1, 2015. As promised, President Obama vetoed both joint resolutions of disapproval on December 18, 2015. As a result, the regulations remained in effect.

Coal companies and attorneys general from red states then sought judicial review of the Clean Power Plan. Environmental groups and officials from blue states supported EPA. On January 21, 2016, the D.C. Circuit panel scheduled to hear challenges to the CPP denied the petitioners' request for a stay of the regulations pending completion of the litigation. The parties challenging the regulations then took the nearly unprecedented step of filing a stay request with the U.S. Supreme Court. In their motion requesting a stay, the petitioners cited the case of *Michigan v. EPA* (see Chapter 3), where because EPA's NESHAP for mercury was not stayed, more than 90 percent of power plants had complied with it by the time it was belatedly struck down by the Supreme Court. Although no legal observers expected the Court to intervene, on February 9, 2016, the Supreme Court, in an unprecedented action, granted the stay request by a vote of 5-4. The Court decreed that the CPP regulations were stayed until the completion of all legal challenges to them. Although the order was not a judgment on the merits, some observers saw it as a signal that the Court would likely strike down the CPP regardless of how the D.C. Circuit ruled on its legality. Four days after the stay was issued, Justice Antonin Scalia, one of the five Justices who voted for the stay, died suddenly.

The legal challenges to the Clean Power Plan, consolidated in the case of *West Virginia v. EPA*, were argued before the D.C. Circuit sitting *en banc* on September 27, 2016. The court took the case *en banc* on its own motion. Ten of the court's eleven judges in regular service (all but then-Supreme Court nominee Merrick Garland) heard the arguments that focused in large part on interpretation of section 111(d). Section 111(d) directs EPA to require states to establish "standards of performance" for existing stationary sources of air pollution. "Standards of performance" are defined as requiring "the best system of emissions reduction" that "has been adequately demonstrated." Opponents of the Clean Power Plan argued that section 111(d) cannot legally be used "to mandate emission reductions that cannot be implemented at individual regulated 'stationary sources.'" They noted that section 111(d) provides that "standards apply to the 'source,' not to owners and operators" and they argued that setting emissions rates based on "generation shifting" is "inconsistent with the statutory definition of 'standard of performance.'"

Opponents of the CPP argued that EPA was foreclosed from regulating existing power plants under section 111(d) because their emissions of mercury were already regulated as hazardous air pollutants under section 112. When the Clean Air Act was amended in 1990, Congress passed two different versions of section 111(d) as part of an amendment to delete an obsolete cross reference in section 111(d). Such mistakes often happen when enormously complex legislation is adopted under extreme time pressure. Neither version was discussed in committee hearings, floor debates, or the House/Senate conference, but they both were included in the final bill approved by both houses of Congress. The version of the amendment originating in the Senate provides that section 111(d) cannot be used to regulate *pollutants* that already are regulated as hazardous air pollutants under a different section of the Act, which GHGs are not. Opponents of the Clean Power Plan argued instead that the version originating in the House that appears to bar regulation of any *source category* (such as power plants) that emits hazardous pollutants regulated under a different section of the Act should prevail. EPA argued that the conflicting versions of section 111(d) create a statutory ambiguity that entitles the agency to receive deference for its interpretation of the Act—that the Senate version controls. EPA maintained that it makes policy sense to avoid duplicative regulation of particular *pollutants*, but not to exempt significant *sources* of a different pollutant from regulation.

Many who observed the day-long oral argument believed that the D.C. Circuit judges were leaning 7-3 in favor of upholding the CPP, but the D.C. Circuit never issued a decision in *West Virginia v. EPA*. On March 28, 2017, President Donald Trump issued Executive Order 13,783, directing EPA Administrator Scott Pruitt to reconsider the Clean Power Plan. EPA simultaneously asked the D.C. Circuit to hold the litigation in abeyance. On April 28, 2017, the D.C. Circuit agreed to EPA's request.

On October 10, 2017, EPA issued a Federal Register notice proposing to repeal the Clean Power Plan without proposing any rule to replace it. EPA argued that the CPP exceeded EPA's statutory authority and embraced a new interpretation of section 111. On December 18, 2017, EPA issued an advance notice of proposed rulemaking seeking comment on an alternative regulatory approach to the Clean Power Plan that would be consistent with the agency's new legal interpretation of section 111. In August 2018, EPA issued a proposed rule to replace the CPP that would largely leave it up to states to determine permissible emissions.

On June 19, 2019, the EPA issued the Affordable Clean Energy (ACE) rule, replacing the CPP. On September 17, 2019, the D.C. Circuit Court of Appeals dismissed *West Virginia v. EPA* as moot in light of the Trump administration's replacement regulation. ACE reversed EPA's position on the meaning of section 111(d), concluding that it could not be used to regulate power plants. It established guidelines for the states to set performance standards for affected electric generating units. States had three years to develop plans that set performance standards and associated emissions reduction targets for existing coal-fired power plants. While the CPP established carbon reduction targets on the federal level, under ACE the federal government only provided a list of "heat rate improvement measures" that would improve the operating efficiency of coal plants, and then the states were left to decide whether to implement any of them. The EPA projected that the ACE rule would only reduce carbon pollution 0.7 percent by 2030 compared to business-as-usual.

Several groups, states, and municipalities challenged the ACE rule in the D.C. Circuit. The challenges were consolidated in *American Lung Ass'n v. EPA* and argued before the D.C. Circuit on October 8, 2020. On January 19, 2021, the D.C. Circuit issued the following decision.


## American Lung Ass'n v. Environmental Protection Agency

985 F.3d 914 (D.C. Cir. 2021)

Before MILLETT, PILLARD, and WALKER, *Circuit Judges*

PER CURIAM

. . . The question in this case is whether the Environmental Protection Agency (EPA) acted lawfully in adopting the 2019 Affordable Clean Energy Rule (ACE Rule), 84 Fed. Reg. 32,520 (2019), as a means of regulating power plants' emissions of greenhouse gases. It did not. Although the EPA has the legal authority to adopt rules regulating those emissions, the central operative terms of the ACE

Rule and the repeal of its predecessor rule, the Clean Power Plan, 80 Fed. Reg. 64,662 (2015), hinged on a fundamental misconstruction of [§111(d), 42 U.S.C.] §7411(d) of the Clean Air Act. In addition, the ACE Rule's amendment of the regulatory framework to slow the process for reduction of emissions is arbitrary and capricious. For those reasons, the ACE Rule is vacated, and the record is remanded to the EPA for further proceedings consistent with this opinion.

## D. The ACE Rule

In 2019, the EPA issued a new rule that repealed and replaced the Clean Power Plan: The Affordable Clean Energy (ACE) Rule. 84 Fed. Reg. 32,520 (2019).

### 1. Repeal of the Clean Power Plan

At the outset, the ACE Rule repealed the Clean Power Plan. The EPA explained that it felt itself statutorily compelled to do so because, in its view, "the plain meaning" of Section 7411(d) "unambiguously" limits the best system of emission reduction to only those measures "that can be put into operation *at* a building, structure, facility, or installation." Because the Clean Power Plan's best system was determined by using some emission control measures that the EPA characterized as physically operating off the site of coal-fired power plants—such as some forms of generation shifting and emissions trading—the EPA concluded that it had no choice but to repeal the Plan. The EPA emphasized "that [its] action is based on the only permissible reading of the statute and [it] would reach that conclusion even without consideration of the major question doctrine," while adding that application of that latter doctrine "confirms the unambiguously expressed intent" of Section 7411.

### 2. Best System of Emission Reduction

Considering its authority under Section 7411 to be confined to physical changes to the power plants themselves, the EPA's ACE Rule determined a new best system of emission reduction for coal-fired power plants only. The EPA left unaddressed in this rulemaking (or elsewhere) greenhouse gas emissions from other types of fossil-fuel-fired power plants, such as those fired by natural gas or oil.

The EPA's proposed system relied solely on heat-rate improvement technologies and practices that could be applied at and to existing coal-fired power plants. The EPA selected only seven heat-rate improvement techniques as components of its best system. Six of those measures were new-to-the-plant technologies or "equipment upgrades." The seventh measure was the use of "best operating and maintenance practices" implementing heat-rate improvement techniques. The EPA limited itself to techniques that could be "applied broadly" to the Nation's coal-fired plants, which primarily amounted to upgrades to existing equipment.

The EPA predicted that its ACE Rule would reduce carbon dioxide emissions by less than 1% from baseline emission projections by 2035. That calculation did not reflect emission *increases* that could result from the rebound effect [of increasing the use of sources whose operations had been made more efficient].

### E.  Petitions For Review

Twelve petitions for review of the ACE Rule were timely filed in this court and consolidated in this case. The petitioners fall into three groups.

The first grouping consists of petitioners who seek review of the ACE Rule's conclusion that Section 7411 only permits emission reduction measures that can be implemented at and applied to the source. Those petitioners include (i) a coalition of State and municipal governments; (ii) power utilities; (iii) trade associations from the renewable energy industry; and (iv) several public health and environmental advocacy groups.

The second grouping is petitioners who challenge the ACE Rule's imposition of any emission limits as unlawful because, in their view, (i) the EPA failed to make a specific endangerment finding for carbon dioxide emitted from existing power plants; (ii) the EPA's regulation of mercury emissions from coal-fired power plants under Section 7412 precludes the regulation of greenhouse gas emissions under Section 7411; and (iii) the EPA should have regulated carbon dioxide from stationary sources, including power plants, under the NAAQS program, 42 U.S.C. §§7408–7410. . . .

The process for regulating existing sources — which raise distinct concerns about sunk costs and the health and environmental effects of older processes — involves more actors and steps. . . .

Two provisions of Section 7411 shape the existing-source framework. Subsection (a)(1) defines a standard of performance, by reference to the "degree of emission limitation" that the EPA determines is "achievable," as:

> a standard for emissions of air pollutants which reflects the degree of
> emission limitation achievable through the application of the best system
> of emission reduction which (taking into account the cost of achieving
> such reduction and any nonair quality health and environmental impact
> and energy requirements) the Administrator determines has been ade-
> quately demonstrated.

Subsection (d)(1), in turn, requires the Administrator to set up a system by which willing States can submit to the EPA "a plan which [ ] establishes standards of performance for any existing source." 42 U.S.C. §7411(d)(1). Only "where [a] State fails to submit a satisfactory plan" may the EPA step in and directly promulgate standards of performance for existing sources.

The issue before us arises at the first step — the EPA's determination of the best system of emission reduction. . . .

Based on what it now perceives to be an express and unambiguous textual limitation in Section 7411 that it says the Clean Power Plan overlooked, the EPA repealed that Plan and replaced it with the ACE Rule. The EPA's new reading of the statute requires the Agency, in modeling its "best system of emission reduction," to consider only emission-reduction measures that "can be applied at and to a stationary source."

The question here is a relatively discrete one. We are not called upon to decide whether the approach of the ACE Rule is a permissible reading of the statute as a matter of agency discretion. Instead, the sole ground on which the EPA defends its abandonment of the Clean Power Plan in favor of the ACE Rule is that the text of Section 7411 is clear and unambiguous in constraining the EPA to use only improvements at and to existing sources in its best system of emission reduction.

The EPA contends that its current interpretation is "the only permissible interpretation of the scope of the EPA's authority." Our task is to assess whether Section 7411 in fact compels the EPA's new interpretation. . . .

For the reasons explained below, Section 7411 does not, as the EPA claims, constrain the Agency to identifying a best system of emission reduction consisting only of controls "that can be applied at and to a stationary source." The EPA here "failed to rely on its own judgment and expertise, and instead based its decision on an erroneous view of the law." We accordingly must vacate and remand to the Agency "to interpret the statutory language anew."

It is the EPA's current position that is wrong. Nothing in Section 7411(a)(1) itself dictates the "at and to the source" constraint on permissible ingredients of a "best system" that the Agency now endorses. For the EPA to prevail, its reading must be required by the statutory text. It fails for at least three reasons, any of which is alone fatal.

*First,* the plain language of Section 7411(a)(1), the root of the EPA's authority to determine the best system, announces its own limitations. Those limitations simply do not include the source-specific caveat that the EPA now interposes and casts as unambiguous.

*Second,* there is no basis — grammatical, contextual, or otherwise — for the EPA's assertion that the source-specific language of subsection (d)(1) must be read upstream into subsection (a)(1) to equate the EPA's "application of the best system" with the controls States eventually will apply "at and to" an individual source. . . .

*Third,* even if subsections (a)(1) and (d)(1) were read together in the way the EPA proposes, they would not confine the EPA to designating a best system consisting of at-the-source controls. . . .

\* \* \*

In sum, traditional tools of statutory interpretation reveal nothing in the text, structure, history, or purpose of Section 7411 that compels the reading the EPA adopted in the ACE Rule. . . .

### B. The Major Questions Doctrine

The EPA also references the so-called "major questions" doctrine in defense of its statutory interpretation and the ACE Rule. But that doctrine does not confine the EPA to adopting solely emission standards that can be implemented physically to and at the individual plant.

The Supreme Court has said in a few cases that sometimes an agency's exercise of regulatory authority can be of such "extraordinary" significance that a court should hesitate before concluding that Congress intended to house such sweeping authority in an ambiguous statutory provision. *See King v. Burwell,* 576 U.S. 473, 485–486 (2015); *accord Utility Air Regulatory Group v. EPA (UARG),* 573 U.S. 302, 324 (2014). Where there are special reasons for doubt, the doctrine asks whether it is implausible in light of the statute and subject matter in question that Congress authorized such unusual agency action.

In the ACE Rule, the EPA stated that, while its interpretation of Section 7411 did not depend on the "major question[s] doctrine[,]" the Agency believed that "that doctrine should apply here[.]" 84 Fed. Reg. at 32,529. The Agency reasoned that the Clean Power Plan would have had "billions of dollars of impact on regulated parties and the economy," would have "affected every electricity customer[,]" was "subject to litigation involving almost every State," and would have upset the balance of regulatory authority between federal agencies and the States. For those reasons, the Agency concluded that the "interpretive question raised" — whether the "best system of emission reduction" can include measures other than improvements to and at the physical source — "must be supported by a clear[ ]statement from Congress." That was incorrect.

### 1. The EPA's Regulatory Mandate

Unlike cases that have triggered the major questions doctrine, each critical element of the Agency's regulatory authority on this very subject has long been recognized by Congress and judicial precedent.

Most importantly, there is no question that the regulation of greenhouse gas emissions by power plants across the Nation falls squarely within the EPA's wheelhouse. The Supreme Court has ruled specifically that greenhouse gases are "air pollutants" covered by the Clean Air Act. *Massachusetts v. EPA*, 549 U.S. at 532. More to the point, the Court has told the EPA directly that it is the Agency's job to regulate power plants' emissions of greenhouse gases under Section 7411. "Congress delegated to EPA the decision whether and how to regulate carbon-dioxide emissions from powerplants" through a "§7411 rulemaking[.]" *AEP*, 564 U.S. at 426–427. . . .

On top of that, the issuance of regulations addressing greenhouse gas pollution is mandatory under the statute because of longstanding endangerment findings. In *Massachusetts v. EPA*, the Supreme Court directed the EPA either to make an endangerment finding under the statute for greenhouse gas pollution, or to explain why it would not do so. The EPA complied. For now more than a decade — from 2009 to the present day in the ACE Rule itself — the EPA has consistently and repeatedly recognized the serious danger that greenhouse gas pollution poses to human health and welfare. By statute, that finding triggers a *mandatory* duty on the EPA to regulate greenhouse gas pollution.

So the EPA has not just the authority, but a statutory duty, to regulate greenhouse gas pollution, including specifically from power plants. . . .

In sum, the Clean Air Act expressly confers regulatory authority on the EPA to set standards for reducing greenhouse gas emissions from fossil-fuel-fired power plants nationwide. Congress knew both the scope and importance of what it was doing. And it cabined the EPA's authority with concrete and judicially enforceable statutory limitations. The major questions doctrine is meant to discern, not override, such statutory judgments. Doubly so when the regulatory authority and its reach have been affirmed and enforced by the Supreme Court.

## III. THE EPA'S AUTHORITY TO REGULATE CARBON DIOXIDE EMISSIONS UNDER SECTION 7411

### A. The Coal Petitioners' Challenges

The North American Coal Corporation and Westmoreland Mining Holdings LLC, both coal mine operators (the Coal Petitioners), bring two challenges to the ACE Rule. Both question the EPA's legal authority to enact the rule. First, the Coal

Petitioners argue that the EPA failed to make the required endangerment finding—that carbon dioxide emissions from power plants cause or contribute significantly to air pollution that may reasonably be anticipated to endanger public health or welfare—before regulating those emissions. Second, they claim that the EPA's previous regulation of a different air pollutant (mercury) from power plants under the Hazardous Air Pollutants provision, 42 U.S.C. § 7412, precludes the EPA from now regulating power plants' emission of greenhouse gases under Section 7411(d).

Both arguments fail. The EPA made the requisite endangerment finding in 2015, and the ACE Rule expressly retained that finding. As for the Section 7412 challenge, the EPA has correctly and consistently read the statute to allow the regulation both of a source's emission of hazardous substances under Section 7412 and of other pollutants emitted by the same source under Section 7411(d). The Coal Petitioners' argument rests not on the enacted statutory language, but instead on their own favored reading of one statutory amendment inserted by codifiers. Reading the statutory text as a whole—that is, all of the relevant language enacted by Congress, including two duly enacted amendments—the Clean Air Act authorizes the EPA to regulate both power plants' emissions of greenhouse gases under Section 7411(d) and hazardous air pollutants under Section 7412. That reading is reinforced by the statutory structure, purpose, and history. . . .

### 2. Section 7411 and Section 7412's Parallel Operation

#### a. *Background on the 1990 Amendments*

The Coal Petitioners next argue that the Clean Air Act expressly and unambiguously prohibits the EPA from regulating coal-fired power plants' carbon dioxide emissions under Section 7411(d) because those same power plants' mercury emissions are regulated under Section 7412's Hazardous Air Pollutants provision. The relevant statutory text says otherwise.

For the Coal Petitioners' challenge to succeed, we would have to agree with their ambitious reading of the House Amendment as *precluding* regulation under Section 7411 of even those pollutants that are not covered by Section 7412. We also would have to ignore the duly enacted Senate Amendment entirely. And we would have to reject out of hand the EPA's three-decade-old harmonizing reading of the statutory amendments, the text of Section 7411(d), and the statutory structure. We decline the invitation because that is not how statutory interpretation works. . . .

#### i. *The Consistent Meaning of Both Amendments*

In reconciling the Senate and House Amendments, we start with what the mission of the amendments was. The plain purpose of each amendment was to update Section 7411(d)'s outdated cross-reference to a list created by the EPA under Section 7412*(b)(1)(A)*, in light of Congress' publication of its new statutory list under Section 7412*(b)*. That is why the Senate labeled its provision a "[c]onforming [a]mendment," and the House called its version "[m]iscellaneous [g]uidance." Neither amendment was meant to work a major substantive change in the law.

At bottom, when confronted with two competing and duly enacted statutory provisions, a court's job is not to pick a winner and a loser. The judicial duty is to read statutory text as a harmonized whole, not to foment irreconcilability. Reading both amendments consistently "pursue[s] a middle course" that "vitiates neither provision but implements to the fullest extent possible the directives of each[.]" Said another way, the better and quite natural reading of all of the relevant enacted statutory text, structure, context, purpose, and history is one that harmonizes the House and Senate Amendments, avoids determining that one chamber of Congress smuggled dramatic and unlikely changes to the Agency's regulatory authority into the Act through miscellaneous "guidance," and instead faithfully accomplishes the legislative adjustment needed to respond to the changes to Section 7412.

### iii. *The Harmonized Reading Stands the Test of Time*

Reading the two provisions consistently as successfully performing their "conforming" and "miscellaneous" task of updating Section 7411(d)'s cross-reference to continue to exclude air pollutants already regulated under Section 7412 also maps onto the EPA's consistent interpretation of the statute. And that reading has stood the test of time, without congressional correction.

* * *

For all of those reasons, we hold that Section 7411(d) allows the EPA to regulate carbon dioxide emissions from power plants, even though mercury emitted from those same power plants is regulated as a hazardous air pollutant under Section 7412. . . .

## IV. AMENDMENTS TO THE IMPLEMENTING REGULATIONS

When the EPA repealed the Clean Power Plan and finalized the ACE Rule, it also changed the longstanding implementing regulations generally applicable to emission guidelines promulgated under Section 7411(d) of the Clean Air Act. The Public Health and Environmental Organization Petitioners (the Public Health Petitioners) challenge the implementing regulations insofar as they adopt new timing requirements that substantially extend the preexisting schedules for state and federal actions and sources' compliance under Section 7411(d). Because the challenged regulations lack reasoned support, they cannot stand.

The new implementing regulations extend the time allowed for States to submit their plans, for the EPA to review those plans, for the Agency to promulgate federal plans where state plans fall short, and for legally enforceable consequences to attach to sources that are slow to comply. Those extended timeframes apply unless the EPA otherwise specifies with respect to particular emission guidelines. The Public Health Petitioners argue that the amendments are arbitrary and capricious because the Agency altogether failed to address the urgency of controlling harmful emissions—especially the greenhouse gas emissions accelerating climate change. . . .

The EPA's weak grounds for routinizing additional compliance delays in the amended implementing regulations are overwhelmed by its total disregard of the added environmental and public health damage likely to result from slowing down the entire Section 7411(d) regulatory process. "Normally, an agency rule would be arbitrary and capricious if the agency entirely failed to consider an important aspect of the problem[.]" The extensions of implementation deadlines here give no consideration to the need for speed. Control of emissions from existing sources before they harm people and the environment is the central purpose of Section 7411(d) of the Clean Air Act. Yet when it deferred the compliance deadlines, the EPA did not even mention the need for prompt reduction of those emissions or the human and environmental costs of its substantial new delay. . . .

The EPA offered what is at best a radically incomplete explanation for extending the compliance timeline. It offered undeveloped reasons of administrative convenience and regulatory symmetry, even as it ignored the environmental and public health effects of the Rule's compliance slowdown. The EPA thus "failed to consider an important aspect of the problem,"—indeed, arguably the most important aspect. We accordingly vacate the implementing regulations' extensions of the Section 7411(d) compliance periods.

## VI.  CONCLUSION

Because promulgation of the ACE Rule and its embedded repeal of the Clean Power Plan rested critically on a mistaken reading of the Clean Air Act, we vacate the ACE Rule and remand to the Agency. We also vacate the amendments to the implementing regulations that extend the compliance timeline. Because the objections of the Coal Petitioners are without merit, we deny their petitions.

*So Ordered.*

WALKER, Circuit Judge, concurring in part, concurring in the judgment in part, and dissenting in part:

This case concerns two rules related to climate change. The EPA promulgated both rules under §111 of the Clean Air Act.

A major milestone in climate regulation, the first rule set caps for carbon emissions. Those caps would have likely forced shifts in power generation from higher-polluting energy sources (such as coal-fired power plants) to lower-emitting sources (such as natural gas or renewable energy sources). That policy is called generation shifting.

Hardly any party in this case makes a serious and sustained argument that §111 includes a clear statement unambiguously authorizing the EPA to consider off-site solutions like generation shifting. And because the rule implicates "decisions of vast economic and political significance," Congress's failure to clearly authorize the rule means the EPA lacked the authority to promulgate it.

The second rule repealed the first and partially replaced it with different regulations of coal-fired power plants. Dozens of parties have challenged both the repeal and the provisions replacing it.

In my view, the EPA was required to repeal the first rule and wrong to replace it with provisions promulgated under §111. That's because coal-fired power plants are already regulated under §112, and §111 excludes from its scope any power plants regulated under §112. Thus, the EPA has no authority to regulate coal-fired power plants under §111 . . .

Those conclusions lead to this respectful concurrence in part, concurrence in the judgment in part, and dissent in part.

## NOTES AND QUESTIONS

1. Notice that the court's decision was issued the day before the Trump administration left office. Why do you think the court issued its opinion instead of waiting for the new administration to determine whether or not to repeal the ACE rule?

2. During his confirmation hearings on February 3, 2021, Michael Regan, President Biden's nominee to be EPA administrator, indicated that the court's decision gave EPA a "significant opportunity" to write new rules governing GHG emissions from power plants. The administration has indicated that it does not intend to try to revive the Obama administration's Clean Power Plan. How should the Biden administration regulate GHG emissions from existing power plants? Should it designate GHG emissions as criteria air pollutants and promulgate an NAAQS for them? What advantages and disadvantages would this approach have?

3. The major questions doctrine has become a canon of statutory interpretation that is increasingly favored by conservative judges like Judge Justin Walker, who was 38 years old at the time of the decision and who had served as a federal district judge in Kentucky for only eight months before being confirmed to the D.C. Circuit on a party-line vote in June 2020. Compare the major questions doctrine with the non-delegation doctrine rejected in *Whitman v. American Trucking*. The former is a doctrine of statutory interpretation, while the latter is a constitutional law doctrine. Could Congress rescue a regulation invalidated for violating the major questions doctrine? Could it rescue a regulation struck down for violating the non-delegation doctrine?

4. One very noticeable evolution in air quality programming has been federal action aimed at addressing persistent air quality problems that involve multistate regions. Another has been the use of programs permitting affected sources to trade allowable emissions among themselves in order to seek the most cost-effective combination of controls possible. These two developments frequently go hand in hand. The next sections examine both of these developments.

### D.   Cap-and-Trade and Other Economic Incentive Programs

Many of the Clean Air Act's compliance programs employ different mechanisms that provide owners of air pollution sources incentives to find cost-effective means to lower air pollution. Treating multiple emissions sources located at the same facility as existing under a "bubble" for purposes of the NSR program is one such method. EPA calls this and other such mechanisms economic incentive programs or EIPs. Netting out similarly allows sources to look for lower cost alternatives within the facility in order to avoid more costly regulation. In phasing out lead in gasoline, EPA permitted refineries to average lead content across all its product lines so that the refiner could choose the most cost-effective mix of reductions. Cap-and-trade programs first establish caps on aggregate emissions and then let regulated parties trade emissions allowances among themselves to find the most cost-effective way to meet the cap limitations. (More on cap-and-trade in subsequent sections.)

In 1994, EPA issued policy guidance for states interested in implementing cap-and-trade programs as compliance mechanisms for various elements of the Clean Air Act. EPA, Economic Incentive Program Rules, 59 Fed. Reg. 16,609 (1994). In developing these rules, EPA drew on the experience of the South Coast Air Quality Management District (SCAQMD) in California, whose jurisdiction includes the Los Angeles Air Basin, which has the most significant air quality problems in the United States. Since the early 1990s, SCAQMD has been developing and implementing a number of trading mechanisms to assist in the reduction of emissions. See Drury et al., Pollution Trading and Environmental Injustice: Los Angeles' Failed Experiment in Air Quality Policy, 9 Duke Envtl. L. & Pol'y F. 231 (1999). Instead of writing specific regulations for existing sources, SCAQMD is relying largely upon a declining cap-and-trade approach to emissions reduction.

One component of SCAQMD's efforts is its Rule 1610 program, pursuant to which "licensed car scrappers" can acquire and then destroy old cars (which disproportionately contribute to car-related pollution), thereby obtaining from SCAQMD emissions credits representing the emissions eliminated by removing the car from service. A second central component is the Regional Clean Air Incentives Market (RECLAIM), which allocates an annually declining number of emissions credits to each covered source. Sources cannot emit more pollution than the credits that they own, so their choices are (1) to match their emissions to their assigned credits; (2) to emit less than their assigned credits and sell excess credits; or (3) to emit more than their assigned credits after they have purchased additional credits. Credits can be purchased from other stationary sources or from licensed car scrappers. RECLAIM currently applies to $SO_2$ and $NO_x$ emissions. Efforts to add VOCs to RECLAIM have been stalled due to concerns over the inability to monitor those emissions, as well as concerns about exacerbating hot spots of toxic VOC emissions.

The following problem exercise explores some of the issues raised by programs such as those being implemented by SCAQMD.

---

## PROBLEM EXERCISE: ECONOMIC INCENTIVE PROGRAMS

Rule 1610 permits scrapped cars to come from anywhere within the four-county South Coast Air Basin. To date, most of the emissions credits produced from the Rule 1610 program have been purchased by four oil refineries and marine terminals, three of which are located close together in the communities of Wilmington and San Pedro.

**Question One.** What concerns might arise from a program that permits widely dispersed automobile-related emissions reductions to substitute for pollution control at three concentrated pollution facilities? How might those concerns be mitigated?

**Question Two.** The populations living near the three marine terminals are approximately 80 percent minority (largely Latino), compared with a South Coast Air Basin minority population of 36 percent. Does this raise an environmental justice issue? If so, can EPA permit the California implementation plan to include the Rule 1610 trading program, consistent with the president's Executive Order on environmental justice and EPA's own policies, discussed in Chapter 2?

**Figure 5.9    How a Cap-and-Trade Program Works**

1. The regulating authority sets a cap on total mass emissions for a group of sources for a fixed compliance period (e.g., one year).
2. The regulating authority divides the cap into allowances, each representing an authorization to emit a specific quantity of pollutant (e.g., 1 ton of $SO_2$).
3. The regulating authority distributes allowances.
4. For the compliance period, each source measures and reports all of its emissions.
5. At the end of the period, each source must surrender allowances to cover the quantity of the pollutant it emitted.
6. If a source does not hold sufficient allowances to cover its emissions, the regulating authority imposes penalties.

**Question Three.** SCAQMD's Rule 1610 emissions credits are based on the assumption that scrapped automobiles would have been driven an average of 5,000 miles per year for an additional three years. Recent estimates suggest that between 100,000 and 200,000 automobiles would be scrapped or abandoned annually within the South Coast Air Basin without the intervention of the Rule 1610 program. Approximately 25,000 cars have been scrapped under that program. What issues do these facts raise about the legitimacy of permitting credits under the 1610 program to offset pollution from the marine terminals?

**Question Four.** A source must own emissions credits equal to its emissions. SCAQMD permits sources to calculate emissions based on formulas—emissions factors—developed by EPA. These are necessarily averages, meaning that within any source category half of the sources will have higher actual emissions, even if the emissions factors are accurate, which they sometimes are not. In fact, documents obtained through the Freedom of Information Act indicate that the marine terminals measured their actual emissions, and that those emissions ranged from 10 to 1,000 times higher than the amounts calculated using emissions factors. How does this discrepancy affect the RECLAIM program?

The Title IV acid rain program requires power plants to install continuous emissions monitors (CEMs) to provide accurate dates on actual emissions. §§402, 412. Should SCAQMD require CEMs?

**Question Five.** The baseline of SCAQMD's declining cap-and-trade program—the amount of credits initially allocated to each source—was set based on the highest annual level of source emissions for the five years prior to the program's initiation. Industry resisted basing credits on the immediate past year because the South Coast Air Basin was in recession. In the first three years of RECLAIM, actual industrial emissions of $NO_x$ declined by approximately 3 percent, while the amount of the RECLAIM cap declined 30 percent. In 2001, an EPA official observed that "for seven years, the program did absolutely nothing." Should SCAQMD have chosen a different baseline?

SCAQMD's record with RECLAIM provides a number of cautionary lessons concerning possible pitfalls that need to be taken into account in deciding whether cap-and-trade is a desirable regulatory instrument in particular circumstances. The problems with Rule 1610 and with an inflated baseline are illustrative. The inflated baseline concern was brought home vividly when California experienced electrical shortages in 2000. Supply shortages prompted Los Angeles area utilities to run gas turbine facilities (normally used only at times of peak consumption) much more often than usual. As a result, RECLAIM faced a sudden demand for $NO_x$ credits to cover the emissions from the turbines. Prices fluctuated wildly, sometimes topping $50,000 a ton, because there was an inadequate supply of credits. The tight market revealed that many facilities were still relying on purchasing readily available RECLAIM credits rather than installing pollution controls. In subsequent investigative reporting, the Los Angeles Times reported that "local air quality officials acknowledge that, from its inception, [RECLAIM] was embedded with powerful disincentives to cut smog. This is because they seeded it with too many credits, about 40 percent more than real-world emissions. Credits were so plentiful and cheap for so long that companies grew addicted to buying them instead of spending more for pollution controls." Gary Polakovic, Innovative Smog Plan Makes Little Progress, L.A. Times, Apr. 17, 2001, at B1. The SCAQMD estimated that the air emission targets it had set for that year would be exceeded by 14 percent.

Some analysts believe that another reason RECLAIM stumbled in 2001 was because the program did not permit the "banking" of emissions credits. Banking, or saving allowances by "overcomplying" today so that the unused credits can be used in future years, is a feature of cap-and-trade programs under EPA's EIP guidance. In EPA's view, "banking provides direct incentives for continual reductions by giving credit for over compliance; these credits can be used toward future compliance obligations and, as such, allow manufacturers to put technology improvements in place when they are ready for market, rather than being forced to adhere to a strict regulatory schedule that may or may not conform to industry developments." EPA, Advance Notice of Proposed Rulemaking, Regulating Greenhouse Gas Emissions under the Clean Air Act, 73 Fed. Reg. 44,354, 44,412 (2008). Lacking a banking provision, "RECLAIM is the exception that proves the rule with respect to allowance banking. One way to help avoid the spike in prices would have been to allow allowance banking (in a simple form) all along. Had banking been allowed, sources with low-cost abatement options would have had an incentive to adopt them early and retain the allowances for future periods, even in the case where allocations were higher than the current demand for emissions. . . ." Burtraw et al., Economics of Pollution Trading for $SO_2$ and $NO_x$, Resources for the Future Discussion Paper 05-05 (March 2005), at 37.

The SCAQMD relieved the market pressure in May 2001 by removing electric generating facilities from $NO_x$ market, and adopting for them a technology-based compliance plan, requiring existing facilities to install Best Available Retrofit Control Technology. This and other changes returned the RECLAIM market prices to more customary trading levels. By 2005, SCAQMD could report that "in Calendar Year 2004, the price trend for $NO_x$ [credits] valid for the same period returned to the pattern seen prior to the energy crisis in 2000, in that prices for [credits] started out high at the beginning of the compliance year and gradually declined over the course of the year. $NO_x$ [credits] that expired in December 2003 and June 2004 were traded at prices less than $1 per pound in the 60-day period following their expiration date during which facilities are allowed to trade to reconcile their emissions." SCAQMD, Annual RECLAIM Audit Report for the 2003 Compliance Year, pp. 2-12 (March 2005).

## E.   Acid Deposition

Cap-and-trade programs are by far the most prominent EIP mechanisms. Building from experience in Los Angeles with its local cap-and-trade program, EPA has become a strong advocate for using this approach to air quality control whenever it can. (Nor are such programs limited to air quality. Cap-and-trade has many potential applications.) This is especially true with respect to EPA's efforts to address transboundary or multistate air pollution problems. This section examines the use of cap-and-trade to manage the problem of acid deposition, or acid rain, a phenomenon that is particularly serious in the Northeast, where sulfur dioxide and nitrogen dioxide emissions from power plants and other sources in the Midwest contribute to acidification. The following section turns to other applications of cap-and-trade in the multistate context.

In 1990, Congress amended the CAA to add Title IV to address the problem of acid deposition. Contributors to the problem include local emissions sources, trucks, and autos. They also include distant sources that send their emissions high enough into the atmosphere to be carried long distances before they are acidified and deposited. Many of these long-range sources exist because the federal program failed sufficiently to understand and address multistate pollution problems soon enough. In the 1970s, utility companies had responded to increasingly stringent control of local air pollution by building tall stacks that could project pollution plumes into the upper atmosphere, sending the pollution long distances. More than 175 stacks higher than 500 feet were constructed after enactment of the 1970 Act. This practice was terminated by section 123 of the 1977 Amendments, but not before utility companies had constructed the 111 "big dirties" that are the primary sources of acid rain in the eastern United States. In the 1990 Amendments, Congress finally created an extensive program to control interstate pollution in response to the acid rain problem.

The issue of acid deposition is intensely regional: Midwestern power plants contribute a major share of the pollution that causes acid deposition in the eastern part of the country. EPA dodged the divisive issue for years, abetted for a portion of that time by uncertainty over the causes and effects of the problem. Environmental organizations and eastern states pursued litigation strategies under existing Air Act provisions, but the courts, taking notice of Congress's and EPA's silence on the issue, refused to order EPA to act. See, e.g., New York v. EPA, 852 F.2d 574 (D.C. Cir. 1988).

In its 1981 Report, To Breathe Clean Air, the National Commission on Air Quality (created by the 1977 Amendments) recommended significant reductions in sulfur oxide emissions affecting the eastern states, despite the uncertainties and the potential of multiple factors contributing to forest dieback. Action on that report came nine years later, with the 1990 Amendments.

When Congress enacted Title IV in 1990 it relied exclusively on a cap-and-trade program.

The acid rain program begins with a nationwide cap on emissions. By the year 2000, sulfur dioxide emissions from fossil fuel–fired electric power plants had to be reduced by 10 million tons per year from 1980 levels. Nitrogen oxide emissions also had to be reduced, by approximately 2 million tons per year below 1980 levels.

Reductions are to be achieved in two phases. "Phase I applied primarily to the largest coal-fired electric generation sources from 1995 through 1999 for $SO_2$ and from 1996 through 1999 for $NO_x$. Phase II for both pollutants began in 2000. For $SO_2$, it applies to thousands of combustion units generating electricity nationwide; for $NO_x$ it generally applies to affected units that burned coal during 1990-1995." EPA, Acid Rain Program 2003 Progress Report 3 (2004). More specifically, Phase I applied to the 111 big dirties; the second phase applies to all power plants within the 48 contiguous states and the District of Columbia, plus additional sources. Compliance with the program is enhanced by continuous monitoring requirements and stiff penalties for violations.

The potential for trading is created by allocating pollution allowances to sources based on their past emissions and fuel consumption. In making these initial allocations to power plants, the government had good historical data, and Congress incorporated numerical allocations for the Phase I power plants directly into the text of the Act. §404(e), Table A. An allowance permits the holder to emit one ton of sulfur dioxide during or after the calendar year of issuance. Allowances may be reallocated within a company to cover multiple units, transferred to another owner, or even transferred to a later year.

In order to satisfy additional political objectives and operational concerns, the statute includes a number of provisions for "bonus" allowances. For instance, bonus allowances could have been obtained in Phase I by:

- units that install scrubbers and need an additional two years' delay;
- units that emit less than a specified amount of sulfur dioxide per unit of energy prior to 1995 receive two-for-one allowances, not to exceed 3.5 million allocated on a first-come, first-served basis;
- units that reduce emissions through the use of conservation or renewable energy and meet other related conditions can obtain bonuses from a pool of 300,000 allowances; and
- a pool of 200,000 allowances for each year of Phase I was available to utilities in Indiana, Ohio, and Illinois.

A different set of extensions and bonus opportunities is provided in Phase II to reward utilities that invest in "clean coal" technology, conservation, and renewable energy, to ease the transition for utilities in ten midwestern states, and to compensate utilities in "clean states" — states that had achieved low emission levels by 1985. To further complicate matters, industrial units can be brought into the Phase I and II programs. This can occur by voluntary "opt in" (why would an industry want to do this?) or by regulation, should EPA determine that industrial emissions are expected to exceed 5.6 million tons per year on the basis of a 20-year forecast. Finally, in order to promote the creation of a market and the availability of allowances, EPA withholds 2.8 percent of each unit's allowance allocation for auction each year.

The structure of the Title IV program and the nature of the environmental problem it addresses provide it with some advantages compared with more localized trading programs, such as RECLAIM. One difficulty with allowing trading for most conventional air pollutants is that the location and timing of emissions determine the severity of pollution; trading must be confined to identical pollutants within a single airshed or additional adjustments must be made to account for concentration and other measures of impact. T. Tietenberg, Emissions Trading: An Exercise in Reforming Pollution Policy (1985); Levin & Elman, The Case for Environmental Incentives, Envtl. Forum 7-11 (Jan.-Feb. 1990). In contrast, acid rain offers a problem well suited to a trading approach, since emissions reductions are of relatively constant value over time and space. Dudek & Palmisano, Emissions Trading: Why Is This Thoroughbred Hobbled?, 13 Colum. J. Envtl. L. 217 (1988).

A closely related problem is the need for sufficient trades to assure permits are available on competitive terms. This may not occur if the relevant market is small; for example, a pollutant emitted by only a few sources in an airshed. The large size of the national market for $SO_2$ trades lessens these concerns, and several provisions were included in the program specifically to promote the evolution of a competitive market, such as the restoration of some allowances for annual auction.

The Title IV program has been successful by many measures. Trading in allowances has been active. One of the surprises has been the price at which allowances trade—much lower than was initially projected. At the time of enactment of the 1990 Amendments, projections had the allowances selling at between $1,000 and $1,500 each, based on the assumption that most utilities would need to install scrubbers to achieve the required emissions reductions. Prices, however, fluctuated between $50 and slightly more than $200 during the first decade of the program, reflecting the fact that companies employed less expensive compliance techniques, even though the cost of scrubbers also fell significantly after 1990. Most utilities instead switched to low-sulfur coal or to blended fuel, which became a much more economical alternative due to plunging transportation costs following railroad deregulation. Ellerman, Schmalenese, Joskow, Montero & Bailey, Emissions Trading Under the U.S. Acid Rain Program: Evaluation of Compliance Costs and Allowance Market Performance 66 (1997).

Utility companies also "overcomplied" in the early years of the program, often with the purpose of banking allowances for use in Phase II, when their initial allocations were further reduced. The amount of allowances banked by Phase I units grew steadily until Phase II began. Now firms are apparently drawing down from banked allowances to help meet the more stringent requirements of Phase II, as banked allowance accounts shrunk by a total of 1.1 million in 2003. In 2003, current allowances under the Title IV program amounted to 9.54 million. In 2003, 8.6 million had been banked, meaning that 18.2 million allowances were available for use that year. However, sources emitted only 10.6 million tons in 2003, 1.1 million over the allowances granted in 2003, but still a 32 percent reduction from 1990 levels. Acid Rain Program 2003 Progress Report at 4. In 2006, sulfur dioxide emissions were 9.4 million tons, about a 40 percent reduction from 1990. These emissions were just below the 2006 emissions cap of 9.5 million tons, and substantially below the total 2006 allowance (including previously banked allowances) of 15.7 million tons of emissions. EPA, Acid Rain Program 2006 3-4 (2007). Banked allowances had declined to 6.1 million tons, indicating that those who had taken advantage of early compliance opportunities were beginning to draw down their saved allowances.

Title IV also allows companies that were not initially covered by the Phase I program to opt in to it. A number of companies have elected to do so, in order to build up emissions allowances for sale later on. (Opt-in firms are able to wait until the first week in December to see if they have had a good emission year, compared with their historical average. If their actual emissions are low, they can opt in and collect last-minute excess allowances for the year.) The same study that documented more fuel switching than expected also reported that the program's opt-in provisions may actually have resulted in a net increase in emissions due to overly generous allowance allocations to facilities that would have opted in anyway. Ellerman et al.

A 2005 EPA study estimated the program's benefits at $122 billion annually in 2010, while cost estimates are around $3 billion annually (in 2000 dollars). These reductions also were estimated to produce between $290 million and $1.87 billion in annual health benefits in Canada. EPA, Human Health Benefits from Sulfate Reduction Under Title IV of the 1990 Clean Air Act Amendments 8 (1995). Most of these benefits are calculated to result from reductions in premature deaths (more than 9,600 per year) and reduced cases of chronic bronchitis (more than 14,500 per year). These estimates do not even include the environmental benefits of reduced damage to forests, lakes, streams, and buildings, or of improved visibility—benefits that played a central role in the debate over enactment. Because the costs of complying with Title IV were then expected to be only $2 to $3 billion per year, the program looked like a terrific bargain. Mathews, Clean Sweeps: Two Success Stories for the Environment, Wash. Post, Dec. 18, 1995, at A23. Title IV looks like an even better bargain now because projected compliance costs have continued to fall. A cost estimate is $1.1 billion per year in the year 2010. Carlson, Burtraw, Cropper & Palmer, $SO_2$ Control by Electric Utilities: What Are the Gains from Trade?, 108 J. Pol. Econ. 1292-1326 (2000). OMB estimated that the acid rain program has a benefits-to-cost ratio of 40:1, and the largest quantified human health benefits of any program instituted in the past 10 years. OMB, Office of Information and Regulatory Affairs, Informing Regulatory Decisions: 2003 Report to Congress on the Costs and Benefits of Federal Regulations and Unfunded Mandates on State, Local, and Tribal Entities (2003).

## NOTES AND QUESTIONS

1. How was the objective of reducing sulfur dioxide emissions by 10 million tons per year chosen? One factor may have been a study of the costs per ton of emissions reduction by the Congressional Budget Office (CBO). The CBO estimated that costs would be $270 per ton for an 8-million-ton-per-year program, $360 per ton in a 10-million-ton-per-year program, and $720 per ton in a 12-million-ton-per-year program. CBO, Curbing Acid Rain: Cost, Budget, and Coal-Market Effects xix (1986).

2. What is the legal status of allowances? The Act states they are not "property" rights but rather "limited authorizations." EPA can, for example, reduce their value by ratcheting down Phase II allowances pro rata if necessary to stay within the 8.95-million-ton annual cap.

3. What is the relationship between the allowances and other regulatory requirements, including the ambient air quality standards for sulfur dioxide and the new source standards for power plants? If trading stimulates technological

innovation (as economists predict), will this trigger more stringent technology-based requirements for new sources, and if so, will this undermine the value of allowances?

4. Since utility investments are subject to state regulation, utilities may have incentives quite different from those of other businesses. For example, because they have long planning horizons they may prefer to hold on to allowances in order to ensure an adequate supply in the future, unless an effective options market develops. They may also question the value of selling allowances if state regulators demand that most of the earnings obtained be passed on to the customers who paid for the pollution control measures earlier through higher rates. Utilities that share power regionally through power pools also will have to establish rules governing whether allowances can be pooled.

5. Why should existing sources be given allowances? Doesn't this policy discriminate against new sources and reward utilities for their past pollution? Consider other ways in which emission rights might have been distributed. What explains the distribution chosen by Congress?

6. If trading offers such large opportunities for cost reductions, where does resistance to it originate? One study suggests that the only constituency for efficiency has been economists. See S. Kelman, What Price Incentives? Economists and the Environment (1981). Others suggest a variety of factors. Some environmentalists express moral outrage at the notion of "rights to pollute"; they also may resent industry profits from trades. Many fear that trading systems will be difficult to police effectively, resulting in higher levels of emissions than otherwise would be the case. See the discussion of economic incentive programs, pages 548-551. If this last reason is valid, then the use of cap-and-trade may snowball as its use increases and people become more familiar with it. Regulators and industry may prefer the system they know, and the latter also may be concerned by the prospects of additional costs for the acquisition of permits. See generally Hahn & Stavins, supra; Hanley, Hallet & Moffatt, Why Is More Notice Not Taken of Economists' Prescriptions for the Control of Pollution?, 22 Env't & Planning 1241 (1990).

7. Can trading schemes, even if they are policed rigorously, result in increased pollution? One result of the use of trading mechanisms may be that companies whose emissions otherwise would be below legal limits will acquire pollution rights to sell to other companies. By ensuring that companies in the aggregate discharge the maximum levels of pollution permitted by law, allowance trading may increase emissions. Of course, the overall levels of allowable pollution permitted could be ratcheted downward to counteract this tendency.

8. Recall the offset provisions of the Clean Air Act that govern new sources in nonattainment areas. The Minnesota Mining and Manufacturing Company (3M), a pioneer in source reduction, has a corporate policy that it will neither use nor sell offset allowances it acquires by voluntarily reducing emissions of chemicals. "Top management felt if we sold credits all we would have done is transfer emissions, not reduce them," explains a company spokesperson. 3M has returned credits (reportedly worth more than $1 million) that otherwise would have allowed emissions of more than 1,000 pounds of organic solvents per day in the Los Angeles area. Holusha, Hutchinson No Longer Holds Its Nose, N.Y. Times, Feb. 3, 1991, at C1. Is such a decision economically rational? (The company does take a tax deduction

for the value of the credits.) Should such voluntary emissions reductions be taken into account in determining the amount by which other sources must reduce emissions? According to a company spokesperson, 3M later made an exception to its policy to sell some emissions credits to a Procter & Gamble facility in Camarillo, California in order to prevent job losses. 3M donated the proceeds of the sale to an environmental group.

9. In January 1993, the Long Island Lighting Company (LILCO) announced plans to sell emissions allowances to an undisclosed company believed to be located in the Midwest. Some environmentalists expressed concern that such a transaction would increase emissions from sources in the Midwest that contribute to acid deposition in New York, while reducing emissions from LILCO's stacks, which usually drift over the Atlantic Ocean. Should utilities be required to disclose the details of allowance sales and purchases including the location of the parties involved in the transactions? Are there circumstances in which it might make sense to impose geographical restrictions on sales of allowances? EPA maintains that even if individual trades arguably aggravate the distribution of pollution, the overall emissions reductions mandated by Title IV will require midwestern utilities to reduce emissions substantially. Dao, A New, Unregulated Market: Selling the Right to Pollute, N.Y. Times, Feb. 6, 1993, at A1. Should allowance trades be subject to environmental impact statement requirements? Overall, $NO_x$ reductions seem to be occurring where they should. The states with the highest emissions prior to 1990 are also the states where the largest reductions have occurred, with the midwestern states of Ohio, Indiana, Illinois, and Missouri leading the way.

10. A trade between utilities at opposite ends of the country that did not raise environmental concerns was announced in November 1994. An Arizona utility, Arizona Public Service, traded 25,000 allowances to the Niagara Mohawk Power Corporation in upstate New York. Niagara Mohawk agreed to donate the allowances to an environmental group that would retire them unused, enabling the utility to take a $3.75 million tax deduction. Niagara Mohawk promised to use the money saved from the tax deduction to reduce greenhouse gas emissions by 1.75 million tons. The credit for the reductions in greenhouse gases was then transferred to Arizona Public Service to help it satisfy its voluntary commitment to reduce greenhouse emissions as part of the Climate Change Accord, which several utilities signed in April 1994. Passell, For Utilities, New Clean-Air Plan, N.Y. Times, Nov. 18, 1994, at D1.

11. Some environmental and public health groups acquired allowances and then let them expire unused in order to *reduce* permissible levels of pollution. In March 1994, the Maryland Environmental Law Society (MELS) became the first law student group to purchase allowances. Five other law schools followed suit in 1995. Students Buy and Hold Pollution Rights, N.Y. Times, Mar. 31, 1995, at A28. A nonprofit group formed expressly for the purpose of retiring allowances, the National Healthy Air License Exchange (INHALE), purchased 150 allowances in 1995 and more than 300 at the CBOT's 1996 auction.

12. In his encyclical *Laudato Si*, discussed in Chapter 1, Pope Francis is strongly critical of emissions trading. He criticizes carbon trading as a possible "ploy which permits maintaining the excessive consumption of some countries." This view was criticized by Robert N. Stavins, director of the environmental economics program at Harvard University, who has been a champion of emissions trading. "I

respect what the pope says about the need for action, but this is out of step with the thinking and the work of informed policy analysts around the world, who recognize that we can do more, faster, and better with the use of market-based policy instruments—carbon taxes and/or cap-and-trade systems." The Pope's approach, according to Stavins, is similar to that of "a small set of socialist Latin American countries that are opposed to the world economic order, fearful of free markets, and . . . utterly dismissive and uncooperative in the international climate negotiations." Coral Davenport, Championing Environment, Francis Takes Aim at Global Capitalism, N.Y. Times, June 18, 2015. Is emissions trading a kind of religious article of faith for environmental economists? The Pope argues that market forces cannot adequately protect the environment. He argues for "redefining our notion of progress," noting that "technological and economic development which does not leave in its wake a better world and an integrally higher quality of life cannot be considered progress."

13. By encouraging utilities to switch to low-sulfur coal, Title IV has had a profound impact on the domestic coal industry. Demand for low-sulfur coal has soared, while many mines with high-sulfur lodes have been forced to close. This has caused significant dislocations in many communities. Some states have attempted to require their local utilities to continue using high-sulfur local coal. Such a law was challenged in the case below by an alliance of western coal companies.

## Alliance for Clean Coal v. Bayh

72 F.3d 556 (7th Cir. 1995)

CUMMINGS, Circuit Judge:

Because of the sulfur contained in the coal they burn, coal-fired generating plants are a principal source of atmospheric sulfur dioxide emissions. The sulfur content of coal burned by utilities depends upon the geological origin of the coal: whereas coal mined in the western United States has the lowest sulfur content, almost all of the coal mined in the "Illinois Basin," including most of Illinois and parts of Indiana and western Kentucky, has a relatively high sulfur content.

Congressional enactment of the Clean Air Act Amendments of 1970 required newly constructed generating units to use systems of emissions control approved by the Environmental Protection Agency ("EPA"). The EPA initially provided two methods for controlling sulfur dioxide emissions: (1) the use of low-sulfur coal; and (2) the installation of a device to scrub high-sulfur coal emissions before they reach the atmosphere. Because scrubbing was costlier than using low-sulfur western coal, states producing high-sulfur coal suffered competitively. In 1990 the Clean Air Act was amended again to require drastic reductions in industrial sulfur dioxide emissions by the year 2000. 42 U.S.C. §§7401-7671q. The 1990 Act implemented an innovative market-driven approach to emissions regulation, allowing for the free transfer of emissions "allowances." The Act is aimed at reducing emissions efficiently and allows utilities to meet the standards in the cheapest manner possible. To comply with the new emissions limitations, utilities now have a choice of the following strategies: (1) installing pollution control devices; (2) using low-sulfur coal;

(3) purchasing allowances to emit sulfur dioxide; (4) switching to another fuel; (5) closing down certain units; (6) offsetting emissions at one plant by over-complying at another; or (7) adopting some combination. According to [appellant] Alliance [for Clean Coal], because of the high costs associated with installing pollution devices, the 1990 amendments should result in a decline in demand for the Illinois Basin's high-sulfur coal.

High-sulfur coal-mining states like Indiana considered legislation responsive to the foregoing federal acts. Thus in 1991 Indiana adopted its [Environmental Compliance Plans Act] ECPA. This statute permits electric utilities to avail themselves of early prudency review by submitting plans for complying with the federal legislation to the Commission. In order to approve a utility's plan, the Commission must find that the plan (A) meets the Clean Air Act Amendments of 1990; (B) constitutes a reasonable and least cost strategy over the life of the investment consistent with providing reliable, efficient, and economical electrical service; (C) is in the public interest; and (D) either:

> (i) provides for continued or increased use of Indiana coal in the coal-consuming electric generating units owned or operated by the public utility and affected by the Clean Air Act Amendments of 1990; or
>  (ii) if the plan does not provide for continued or increased use of Indiana coal, such nonprovision is justified by economic considerations including the effects in the regions of Indiana in which the mining of coal provides employment and in the service territory of the public utility. 1C §8-1-27-8(1).

A plan that has a negative impact on Indiana coal is subject to continuing annual surveillance. . . .

In the court below Alliance moved for summary judgment on the ground that the ECPA unjustifiably discriminated against interstate commerce. The district court concluded that the ECPA was intended to promote high-sulfur coal at the expense of western coal and unconstitutionally burdens interstate commerce. . . .

The threshold inquiry we must make in deciding whether the ECPA violates the Commerce Clause is whether it "is basically a protectionist measure, or if it can fairly be viewed as a law directed to legitimate local concerns with effects upon interstate commerce that are only incidental." Oregon Waste Systems, Inc. v. Dept. of Environmental Quality, 114 S. Ct. 1345, 1350 (1994).

As the district judge recognized, the outcome of this case is controlled by Alliance for Clean Coal v. Miller, 44 F.3d 591 (7th Cir. 1995). There we invalidated the Illinois Coal Act, also enacted on the heels of the Clean Air Act Amendments of 1990, on the ground that it was repugnant to the Commerce Clause of the United States Constitution. The Illinois Coal Act provided that in preparing and approving compliance plans, the Illinois Commerce Commission and utilities were required to "take into account . . . the need to maintain and preserve as a valuable State resource the mining of coal in Illinois." The Act also encouraged implementing scrubbers to allow the continued use of high-sulfur coal by guaranteeing utilities the ability to recover the installation costs of scrubbers by including such costs in their rate base. Id. We stated "the Illinois Coal Act is a none-too-subtle attempt to prevent Illinois electric utilities from switching to low-sulphur western coal as a Clean Air Act compliance option." Id. at 595. Therefore, we concluded that the Act was "repugnant to the Commerce Clause and the principle of a unitary national economy which that clause was intended to establish." Id.

The ECPA contains provisions that are virtually identical to the sections of the Illinois Coal Act discussed above. First, in determining whether to approve a plan that includes a compliance option calling for a decrease in the use of Indiana coal, the ECPA requires the Commission to take into account "the effects in the regions of Indiana in which the mining of coal provides employment and in the service territory of the public utility." The ECPA also provides incentives for utilities to install scrubbers to continue to use high-sulfur fuel by guaranteeing a recoupment of the implementation costs.

We agree with the district court that, just as in *Miller,* the ECPA discriminates against interstate commerce based solely upon geographic origin, and thus violates the Commerce Clause. The clear intent of the statute is to benefit Indiana coal at the expense of western coal. The fact that the ECPA does not explicitly forbid the use of out-of-state coal or require the use of Indiana coal, but "merely encourages" utilities to use high-sulfur coal by providing economic incentives does not make the ECPA any less discriminatory. . . .

Because the ECPA discriminates against interstate commerce, the burden lies with the defendants to prove that this discrimination is justified by a legitimate and compelling governmental interest. [Wyoming v. Oklahoma, 502 U.S. 437, 456 (1992).] Defendants provide the following justification. They argue that a viable competitive Midwest high-sulfur coal market is a major component of low-cost electrical service by Indiana utilities and that the ECPA seeks only to ensure that market. . . . However, ensuring such a regional market is not a proper justification for discriminating against interstate commerce. . . .

While we do not doubt that a healthy Indiana mining industry and a fully employed workforce may aid Indiana in achieving a low cost electrical service, that is not a legitimate justification for discrimination against interstate commerce. Protection of local, or even regional, industry is simply not a legislative action that is consistent with the Commerce Clause.

## NOTES AND QUESTIONS

1. PSI Energy, Inc. intervened on the side of the plaintiff in this case, while the United Mine Workers intervened on the side of the state. Shortly after the 1990 Amendments were signed into law, James E. Rogers Jr., the chairman of PSI, had stated in an interview that switching to low-sulfur coal was an option that he had ruled out. He noted that half of the coal burned by the utility came from Indiana mines and that "[s]ome of the coal companies are our largest customers. . . ." He continued, "Because of the politics of the state, because of who we serve, we have to comply with clean air [regulations] and continue to use high-sulfur coal." Lippman, Clean Air Law Forces Choices, Wash. Post, Nov. 27, 1990, at D1, D4. In light of its prior support for continued use of local, high-sulfur coal, why would PSI now support a legal challenge to the Indiana law?

2. Coal mines in the West and in eastern Kentucky and southern West Virginia, where low-sulfur coal is found, benefited due to the shift in demand toward low-sulfur coal. However, in other places in the East that are heavily dependent

on the mining of high-sulfur coal, the economic impact of this shift in demand was severe, as many high-sulfur coal mines closed and many miners lost their jobs. Kilborn, East's Coal Towns Wither in the Name of Cleaner Air, N.Y. Times, Feb. 15, 1996, at A1. Between 1990 and 1995, coal production in the eastern United States fell 14 percent, while in the West it has increased by 26 percent. Id. at A16. Altogether nearly 1,000 coal mines in the United States closed between 1990 and 1995, leaving 2,000; yet coal production in 1995 was at a record 1.05 billion tons annually. Should the environmental justice movement be concerned about the impact of regulation on miners' jobs?

3. Should the environmental laws attempt to compensate those who are adversely affected when regulation alters demand for particular products? One of the most hotly debated provisions in the 1990 Amendments was the creation of a program to provide financial assistance to displaced miners. The program pays for miners who lose their jobs due to the shift away from high-sulfur coal to go to school for two years to learn new skills and it generally keeps unemployment benefits, that normally would expire after six months, running for the duration. Id.

4. Instead of requiring utilities to purchase local coal, could a state choose to subsidize the coal industry directly? For example, in 1996 the Virginia General Assembly adopted legislation to subsidize the price of local coal by two dollars per ton through a complicated tax-credit formula for coal mining companies in the state. Relief for Coal Industry, Wash. Post, Mar. 2, 1996, at B3. Would this $188 million subsidy program violate the dormant Commerce Clause? Recall the *Carbone* and *United Haulers* decisions in Chapter 4. Could a state purchase local coal and provide it to utilities at a reduced price without violating the dormant Commerce Clause?

## F.  Multistate Air Quality Problems

Acid deposition is not the only air quality problem that does not respect state boundaries. The interstate nature of many air quality problems was often raised during the 1970 legislative debates over the Clean Air Act Amendments as a principal justification of the need for federal legislation. From the beginning, all state implementation plans were supposed to take into account the impact of upwind state emissions on the air quality problems of downwind states. The original form of this "good neighbor" provision, §110(a)(2)(E), provided that each SIP had to contain measures to ensure that in-state emissions will not "prevent attainment or maintenance by any other State or any such [NAAQS]." EPA did not interpret this provision to impose tough requirements on states, however, see Connecticut v. EPA, 696 F.2d 147 (2d Cir. 1982), and in 1990 Congress amended the statute to require SIP provisions preventing emissions that "contribute significantly to nonattainment in, or interfere with maintenance by, any other State with respect to any such national primary or secondary ambient air quality standard." §110(a)(2)(D) (i). The CAA has also long contained a provision permitting a downwind state to petition the EPA for a finding that a major stationary source or group of sources was interfering with the downwind state's air quality efforts in violation of their section 110(a)(2)(D)(i) obligations. §126. (Section 126 as currently drafted refers to a state's section 110(a)(2)(D)(ii) obligations, but EPA determined that this reference was a scrivener's error which arose when the provisions of section 110 were renumbered after elimination of one of its subparts, and the D.C. Circuit agreed in *Appalachian Power Co. v. EPA*, 249 F.3d 1032 (D.C. Cir. 2001).)

Perhaps the most obvious of the interstate NAAQS problems has been the ozone problem in the Northeast and along the eastern seaboard of the United States. See Figure 5.7 on page 514.

Ozone is the product of chemical interaction of volatile organic compounds and oxides of nitrogen in the presence of sunlight. Major sources of these precursor pollutants include vehicles, electric utilities, industrial facilities, gasoline vapors (at filling stations and petroleum plants, for example), chemical solvents, as well as natural sources. Because sunlight accelerates the chemical reactions that produce ozone, the problem is worse in the summer months; May through September is considered "ozone season." The problem is worse in urban areas, due to the concentration of local sources of the precursors, but as EPA explains, "even rural areas with relatively low amounts of local emissions may experience high ozone levels because the wind transports ozone and the pollutants that form it hundreds of miles away from their original sources." EPA, The Ozone Report: Measuring Progress through 2003 (EPA 454/K-04-001, April 2004), p. 1.

In 1990, the Congress added section 184 to the CAA as one method for addressing the northeastern regional ozone problem. That section created the Ozone Transport Commission (OTC), composed of representatives of the 12 eastern seaboard states from Virginia to Maine, plus the District of Columbia. The EPA and the OTC are charged with jointly studying the ozone problem. By majority vote, the OTC can develop recommendations for additional control measures that it determines are "necessary to bring [any region within the OTC] into attainment. . . ." §184((c). The dispute over EPA's authority to order specific compliance measures that culminated in *Virginia v. EPA*, pages 508-510, began as a recommendation from the OTC under this section. In addition to authority under section 184, EPA has authority under the general SIP provisions to call for a revision of any SIP whenever EPA determines that the current plan is "substantially inadequate to attain or maintain the relevant NAAQS, to mitigate adequately the interstate pollutant transport described in §176A or §184, or to otherwise comply with any requirement of this Act. . . ." §110(k)(5). Among the requirements covered by the last phrase of section 110(k)(5) are those relating to the prohibition on sources significantly contributing to NA, PSD, or visibility problems of other states. Section 176 also authorizes EPA to create additional interstate ozone commissions.

In 1995, at the request of the Environmental Council of the States, EPA convened a work group, named the Ozone Transport Assessment Group (OTAG), consisting of the 37 easternmost states and the District of Columbia, together with industry and environmental representatives, to examine the interstate transport effects on ozone of a larger geographical region than represented by the OTC. Eventually, 32 of the 37 states voted in favor of a set of recommendations that included regulating $NO_x$ emissions from utilities in 26 states within the region. (In order to achieve as broad a consensus as possible, OTAG only recommended a range of possible regulatory standards, ranging from existing controls to the lesser of an 85 percent reduction from 1990 rates or .15 lb/mmBtu. CRS, Air Quality: EPA's Proposed Ozone Transport Rule, OTAG, and Section 126 Petitions—A Hazy Solution? Issue Brief 98-326 (May 14, 1998).)

**Figure 5.10    About Ground-Level Ozone**

---

### About Ground-Level Ozone

**Location & Formation:** Beneficial ozone occurs naturally in Earth's upper atmosphere (the stratosphere), where it shields the planet from the sun's harmful ultraviolet rays. At ground level, harmful ozone pollution forms when emissions of $NO_x$ and VOCs react in sunlight. Because ground-level ozone is highest when sunlight is most intense, the warm summer months (May 1 to September 30) are generally referred to as the "ozone season."

**Health Effects:** Ozone can aggravate respiratory diseases, such as asthma, emphysema, and bronchitis, and can reduce the respiratory system's ability to fight off bacterial infections. Even healthy people can have symptoms related to ozone exposure. Over time, ozone reduces lung function. And recent research suggests that acute exposure to ozone likely contributes to premature death.

**Transport:** Wind can affect both the location and concentration of ozone pollution. $NO_x$ and VOC emissions can travel hundreds of miles on air currents, forming ozone far from the original emission sources. Ozone also can travel long distances, affecting areas far downwind. High winds tend to disperse pollutants and can dilute ozone concentrations. Light winds, on the other hand, allow pollution levels to build up and become more concentrated.

**Ecological Impacts:** Ground-level ozone damages vegetation and ecosystems, leading to reduced agricultural crop and commercial forest yields, and increased plant susceptibility to diseases, pests, and other stresses, such as harsh weather. Ozone also damages the foliage of trees and other plants, adversely affecting the landscape of cities and national parks, forests, and recreation areas.

To learn more about ozone and its health impacts, please visit the AIRNow Web site at <www.airnow.gov>. For information on the health and ecological effects of ozone, go to <http://cfpub.epa.gov/ncea/cfm/recordisplay.cfm?deid=114523>. For more about the relationship between emissions and ozone formation, visit <www.epa.gov/airtrends>.

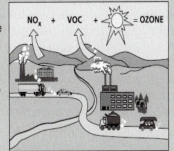

---

In 1998, building on OTAG's work, EPA made the tough decisions concerning the stringency and mechanism for further $NO_x$ reductions that OTAG had avoided, and invoked this section 110(k)(5) authority to address the regional transport of $NO_x$. The SIP Call implicated 22 states and the District of Columbia. In an innovative approach to determining an upwind state's "significant contribution" to downwind attainment or maintenance problems, EPA pegged significant contribution at the amount of $NO_x$ that could be eliminated through the use of "highly cost-effective controls," which it defined as control that removed $NO_x$ at a cost of less than $2,000 per ton. The rule also set out procedures for each state covered by the SIP Call to participate in a cap-and-trade program whereby $NO_x$ sources within each state could trade with other sources throughout the SIP Call region. For each jurisdiction, EPA identified a $NO_x$ budget, which essentially was an EPA mandate prohibiting $NO_x$ emissions in the 23 jurisdictions from exceeding a tonnage specific to that jurisdiction. EPA then gave each jurisdiction the option of adopting an interstate trading program that allows it to purchase $NO_x$ allowances from sources that have elected to over-control.

The rule and the litigation following it were complicated by the fact that EPA's 1997 revision of the ozone NAAQS was being challenged in litigation that was finally resolved by the Supreme Court in the *American Trucking* decision, above. Prior to the Supreme Court's ruling, the D.C. Circuit had stayed implementation of the new 8-hour ozone standard. Eventually, however, challenges by midwestern states, electric utilities, and industry groups were resolved in Michigan v. EPA, 213 F.3d 663 (D.C. Cir. 2000). The D.C. Circuit largely upheld EPA's NO$_x$ SIP Call. The court concluded that "EPA's NO$_x$ budget program reasonably establishes reduction levels and leaves the control measure selection decision to the states." Judge Sentelle dissented on the question of whether the statute permitted EPA to consider costs. In Judge Sentelle's view:

> The majority makes a fundamental mistake by divorcing the adverb "significantly" from the verb it modifies, "contribute." The majority compounds its error by divorcing significantly from the rest of the statutory provision in issue. Id. at 674-79. By focusing on "significance" or what it means to be "significant," the majority ignores the fact that the statute permits EPA to address that which is "*contribut[ed]* significantly." (emphasis added). And what should EPA look for as being contributed significantly? Congress clearly answered that question for the agency as being an "amount" of an "air pollutant." *Id.* Considering that Congress expressly gave EPA authority with regard to "any *air pollutant* in *amounts* which will . . . *contribute* significantly to nonattainment. . . ," *id.* (emphasis added), I marvel at an interpretation that permits cost effectiveness to find a place in a statutory provision addressing amounts of air pollutant contribution. While the contribution must affect nonattainment significantly, no reasonable reading of the statutory provision in its entirety allows the term significantly to springboard costs of alleviation into EPA's statutorily-defined authority. Given §7410(a)(2)(D)(i)(I)'s mandate as a whole, it becomes clear that EPA and the majority have to contort the statute's language by isolating the term significantly and ignoring the terms air pollutant, amounts, and contribute in order to work cost considerations into the statute. I just cannot agree with such an unusual exercise in statutory construction.

Phase I of the EPA NO$_x$ budget program went into effect in 2003. All states that were covered by the final rule decided to participate in the cap-and-trade program. For 2004 EPA reported nearly 100 percent compliance from the approximately 2,500 units covered by the cap-and-trade program. EPA, Evaluating Ozone Control Programs in the Eastern United States: Focus on the NO$_x$ Budget Trading Program, p. 6, Figure 4, EPA-454-K-05-001 (2005). EPA reports that electrical power industry NO$_x$ emissions during ozone season were "about 30 percent lower than in 2003, when a limited number of states were subject to NO$_x$ SIP Call requirements; 50 percent lower than in 2000, before the NO$_x$ SIP Call was implemented; and 70 percent lower than in 1990, before implementation of the Clean Air Act Amendments." Id. By 2006, NO$_x$ emissions were 60 percent lower than in 2000. EPA, NO$_x$ Budget Program 2006 Progress Report Executive Summary, p. ii, EPA-430-R-07-009 (Sept. 2007). As for overall ozone air quality, EPA estimated that ozone concentrations in the region declined 5-8 percent since the implementation of the program. Overall, EPA reported that "in most of the eastern United States, reductions in ozone concentrations (adjusted for weather) more than doubled after the $NO_x$ SIP Call was implemented. Ozone concentrations declined where EPA expected they would. Areas with the greatest decline in ozone concentrations are near, and downwind of, areas with greatest reductions in $NO_x$ emissions." Id. In 2004, EPA designated 104 areas in the eastern United States as 8-hour ozone nonattainment areas; based on 2004 to 2006 data, ozone concentrations have improved in all of these areas, and in 2006, 80 percent (83 areas) had attained the 8-hour NAAQS. EPA found the $NO_x$ trading program to be "the most significant contributor to these improvements."

A number of the northeastern-most states in the OTC were not content to wait upon EPA's SIP Call approach. They filed section 126 petitions, claiming that stationary sources upwind of them, including in some states outside the OTC, were interfering with their ability to comply with the ozone NAAQS. On April 30, 1999, EPA found these petitions to be largely meritorious. 64 Fed. Reg. 28,250 (1999). See also 64 Fed. Reg. 33,956 (1999) (staying effective date of April 30 final rule until Nov. 30, 1999). EPA did not immediately trigger the requirements that upwind sources cease their interference with downwind state compliance, however, because it preferred to address the problem through its SIP Call approach.

In December 1999, EPA did grant section 126 petitions filed by New York, Connecticut, Massachusetts, and Pennsylvania. It then issued a rule mandating a cap-and-trade program for affected sources that was premised on the same analysis that EPA had used as the basis for the $NO_x$ SIP Call, assigning $NO_x$ allowances to major sources, based upon application of the same "highly effective controls" which EPA had included in the SIP Call. The order affected nearly 400 plants, mostly utility power plants, in 12 states as far south as North Carolina and as far west as Indiana. EPA estimates compliance costs at $950 million per year. However, EPA's ruling provided that the finding of a section 126 violation was to be withdrawn upon approval of a SIP that complied with the $NO_x$ SIP Call that was sustained in *Michigan v. EPA*. In effect, EPA determined that compliance with the SIP Call would result in emissions reductions that satisfied section 126. The D.C. Circuit upheld the vast bulk of EPA's section 126 rule in Appalachian Power Co. v. EPA, 249 F.3d 1032 (D.C. Cir. 2001). The obligations imposed on facilities via the section 126 petition essentially duplicate those resulting from the $NO_x$ SIP Call, because all the states affected by the Call have elected to adopt the EPA's $NO_x$ trading program. The section 126 obligations affect pollution sources in only 12 states plus the District of Columbia, while the $NO_x$ SIP Call affects 22 states.

EPA continued strongly to prefer trading programs in its multistate initiatives to reduce levels of the criteria pollutants. On May 12, 2005, it finalized its Clean Air Interstate Rule (CAIR) aimed at further reductions in sulfur dioxide and nitrogen oxides in order to help achieve the lowered NAAQS for ozone and PM2.5. 70 Fed. Reg. 25,162 (May 12, 2005). (Sulfur dioxide and $NO_x$ are precursors of fine particles, many of which are formed through chemical reactions in the atmosphere. Nitrogen oxides, as already discussed, are ozone precursors.) The CAIR was a SIP Call directed at 28 states in the eastern and midwestern parts of the country. It was based on air quality analyses similar to those that formed the basis for EPA's $NO_x$ SIP Call and its response to the section 126 petitions. Likewise, the CAIR gave these states the option of participating in a cap-and-trade program for fossil-fuel-fired electrical generating units or else selecting other options for achieving the required $SO_2$ and $NO_x$ reductions.

Both the CAIR and the $NO_x$ SIP Call imposed $NO_x$ budgets on states and facilities, with the budget assignments being slightly more stringent under the CAIR, where they overlapped. Describing the relationship between the CAIR and the $NO_x$ SIP Call, however, is complicated. Six states covered by CAIR were not in the $NO_x$ SIP Call. One state, Rhode Island, was subject to the $NO_x$ SIP Call, but not to the CAIR. It also was complicated by the fact that the CAIR's concern over $NO_x$ was based on both PM and ozone concerns and addressed both PM2.5 precursors and ozone precursors, whereas the $NO_x$ SIP Call was aimed exclusively at ozone. The seasonal variations for ozone mean that particular attention must be given to emissions during the ozone season, May through September, whereas the PM2.5 concerns are constant year-round. For the states subject to both CAIR and the $NO_x$ SIP Call, EPA says:

> States subject to the CAIR for PM2.5 [will] be subject to an annual limitation and . . . States subject to the CAIR for ozone [will] be subject to an ozone season limitation. This means that States subject to the CAIR for both PM2.5 and ozone are subject to both an annual and an ozone season $NO_x$ limitation. . . . States subject to the CAIR for ozone only are only subject to an ozone season $NO_x$ limitation. To implement these $NO_x$ limitations, EPA will establish and operate two $NO_x$ trading programs, i.e., a CAIR annual $NO_x$ trading program and a CAIR ozone season $NO_x$ trading program. The CAIR ozone season $NO_x$ trading program will replace the current $NO_x$ SIP Call as discussed in more detail later in this section. [70 Fed. Reg. at 25,289-25,290.]

The CAIR sought to accomplish some of the programming President Bush had put forth in his Clear Skies proposal, which would have introduced an expanded cap-and-trade program for $NO_x$, replacing the SIP Call program. However, Clear Skies stalled in the 109th Congress when a 9-9 vote in the Senate Environment and Public works Committee prevented the bill from moving to the floor of the Senate. CRS, Clean Air Act Issues in the 109th Congress, p. 6, RL33552 (Nov. 2, 2006). After that vote, EPA moved forward with CAIR.

A variety of petitioners challenged CAIR in the D.C. Circuit, which struck it down in North Carolina v. EPA, 531 F.3d 896 (D.C. Cir. 2008). While finding "more than several fatal flaws" in CAIR, the court emphasized that EPA had failed to measure each state's "significant contribution" to downwind nonattainment. Instead, EPA apportioned regional emissions on the basis of what could be controlled in a "cost effective" manner, establishing state $NO_x$ and $SO_2$ budgets that were arbitrary and capricious. "Because EPA evaluated whether its proposed emissions reductions were 'highly cost effective,' at the regionwide level assuming a trading program, it never measured the 'significant contribution' from sources within an individual state to downwind nonattainment areas." "Thus," the court concluded, "EPA's apportionment decisions have nothing to do with each state's 'significant contribution' because under EPA's method of analysis, state budgets do not matter for significant contribution purposes." In an effort to reconcile its decision with *Michigan v. EPA*, the court stated: "In *Michigan* we never passed on the lawfulness of the NO$_x$ SIP Call's trading program. It is unclear how EPA can assure that the trading programs it has designed in CAIR will achieve section 110(a)(2)(D)(i)(I)'s goals if we do not know what each upwind state's 'significant contribution' is to another state. Despite *Michigan*'s approval of emissions controls that do not correlate directly with each state's relative contribution to a specific downwind nonattainment area, CAIR must include some assurance that it achieves something measurable towards the goal of prohibiting sources 'within the State' from contributing to nonattainment or interfering with maintenance in 'any other State.'"

The court stated that to satisfy the "good neighbor" provision, EPA must promulgate "a rule that achieves something measurable toward the goal of prohibiting sources 'within the State' from contributing to nonattainment or interfering with maintenance in any other State." The Court suggested that EPA could satisfy the statute by capping each state's emissions. A cap could be established by first calculating each state's significant contribution, then subtracting that amount from current emissions to produce the cap. Instead of capping each state's emissions, however, EPA designated a NO$_x$ budget for each state. The state budgets as a whole sum up to a regional cap, but for any individual state, its budget does not equal a cap. Instead, the budget represents how many allowances that state will receive. Its actual emissions can go over that amount if sources in the state buy allowances from sources in other states.

The CAIR had been widely acknowledged to be the Bush administration's most meritorious and potentially successful program for reducing ozone and particulate matter air quality problems in the northeast. If these problems truly are regional in nature, as the evidence clearly suggests, it should not matter whether a particular amount of pollution is not being reduced by a Michigan source, for example — because it bought an allowance from an Indiana source — if a like amount of pollution is being reduced by that Indiana source, so long as the overall regional reductions are substantial and significantly reduce the out-of-state effects on downwind states.

On December 23, 2008, the U.S. Court of Appeals for the D.C. Circuit, acting on a petition for rehearing in *North Carolina v. EPA*, stayed its decision to vacate the CAIR rule in order to give EPA time to develop a new rule. North Carolina v. EPA, 550 F.3d 1176 (D.C. Cir. 2008). EPA responded on July 6, 2011 by promulgating what came to be known as the "Transport Rule" or "Cross-State Air Pollution Rule" as a replacement for CAIR. 76 Fed. Reg. 40,662 (2011). The Transport Rule required 26 states to reduce emissions of sulfur dioxide and nitrogen oxide from power plants, cutting emissions of SO$_2$ by 73 percent and NO$_x$ emissions by 54 percent from 2005 levels. EPA estimated that the rule would save between 13,000 and 34,000 lives annually by 2014.

After the rule was challenged in court, the D.C. Circuit stayed its January 1, 2012 effective date. The court then struck down the rule by a 2-1 vote in EME Homer City Generation, L.P. v. EPA, 696 F.3d 7 (D.C. Cir. 2012), reversed 572 U.S. 489. In a majority opinion by Judge Kavanaugh, the panel found that EPA's Transport Rule exceeded the agency's authority because "upwind States may be required to reduce emissions by more than their own significant contributions to a downwind State's nonattainment." The court majority faulted EPA for not calculating more precisely exactly how much each upwind state contributes to nonattainment in downwind states. EPA had calculated emissions floors that would avoid transboundary interference, but the court majority feared this could require some upwind states to control pollution more than absolutely necessary to avoid interference with attainment downwind. Writing in dissent, Judge Rogers accused the majority of trying to redesign "Congress's vision of cooperative federalism based on the court's own notions of absurdity and logic that are unsupported by a factual record" and "blindsid[ing EPA] by arguments raised for the first time in this court."

The court's decision was the second time in four years that EPA's effort to tighten standards on transboundary air pollution was rejected in the D.C. Circuit. It blocked regulations that EPA had estimated would prevent between 13,000 and 34,000 premature deaths each year, generating annual benefits of between $120 billion to $280 billion at a projected annual cost of only $2.4 billion. The court's decision was sharply criticized by a prominent business journalist as the product of "a new breed of activist judges [who] are waging a determined and largely successful war on federal regulatory agencies" through the use of "legal sophistry, procedural hair-splitting and scientific conjecture." Steven Pearlstein, The Judicial Jihad Against the Regulatory State, Wash. Post, Oct. 13, 2012. EPA sought review in the U.S. Supreme Court, which reversed the D.C. Circuit by a vote of 6-2.

## EPA v. EME Homer City Generation, L.P.

572 U.S. 489 (2014)

JUSTICE GINSBURG delivered the opinion of the Court.

### I

### B

Over the past 50 years, Congress has addressed interstate air pollution several times and with increasing rigor. In 1963, Congress directed federal authorities to "encourage cooperative activities by the States and local governments for the prevention and control of air pollution." 77 Stat. 393, 42 U.S.C. §1857a (1964 ed.). In 1970, Congress made this instruction more concrete, introducing features still key to the Act. For the first time, Congress directed EPA to establish national ambient air quality standards (NAAQS) for pollutants at levels that will protect public health. See 84 Stat. 1679-1680, as amended, 42 U.S.C. §§7408, 7409 (2006 ed.). Once EPA settles on a NAAQS, the Act requires the Agency to designate "nonattainment" areas, i.e., locations where the concentration of a regulated pollutant exceeds the NAAQS. §7407(d).

The Act then shifts the burden to States to propose plans adequate for compliance with the NAAQS. Each State must submit a State Implementation Plan, or SIP, to EPA within three years of any new or revised NAAQS. §7410(a)(1). If EPA determines that a State has failed to submit an adequate SIP, either in whole or in part, the Act requires the Agency to promulgate a Federal Implementation Plan, or FIP, within two years of EPA's determination, "unless the State corrects the deficiency" before a FIP is issued. §7410(c)(1).

The Act lists the matters a SIP must cover. Among SIP components, the 1970 version of the Act required SIPs to include "adequate provisions for intergovernmental cooperation" concerning interstate air pollution. This statutory requirement, with its text altered over time, has come to be called the Good Neighbor Provision.

In 1977, Congress amended the Good Neighbor Provision to require more than "cooperation." It directed States to submit SIPs that included provisions "adequate" to "prohibi[t] any stationary source within the State from emitting any air pollutant in amounts which will . . . prevent attainment or maintenance [of air quality standards] by any other State." §108(a)(4), 42 U.S.C. §7410(a)(2)(E). The amended provision thus explicitly instructed upwind States to reduce emissions to account for pollution exported beyond their borders. As then written, however, the provision regulated only individual sources that, considered alone, emitted enough pollution to cause nonattainment in a downwind State. Because it is often "impossible to say that any single source or group of sources is the one which actually prevents attainment" downwind, S. Rep. No. 101-228, p. 21 (1989), the 1977 version of the Good Neighbor Provision proved ineffective, see ibid. (noting the provision's inability to curb the collective "emissions [of] multiple sources").

Congress most recently amended the Good Neighbor Provision in 1990. The statute, in its current form, requires SIPs to "contain adequate provisions . . . prohibiting . . . any source or other type of emissions activity within the State from emitting any air pollutant in amounts which will . . . contribute significantly to nonattainment in, or interfere with maintenance by, any other State with respect to any . . . [NAAQS]." 42 U.S.C. §7410(a)(2)(D)(i) (2006 ed.). The controversy before us centers on EPA's most recent attempt to construe this provision.

### C

Three times over the past two decades, EPA has attempted to delineate the Good Neighbor Provision's scope by identifying when upwind States "contribute significantly" to nonattainment downwind. In 1998, EPA issued a rule known as the "$NO_X$ SIP Call." That regulation limited $NO_X$ emissions in 23 upwind States to the extent such emissions contributed to nonattainment of ozone standards in downwind States. See 63 Fed. Reg. 57356, 57358. In Michigan v. EPA, 213 F.3d 663 (D.C. Cir. 2000), the D.C. Circuit upheld the $NO_X$ SIP Call, specifically affirming EPA's use of costs to determine when an upwind State's contribution was "significan[t]" within the meaning of the statute.

In 2005, EPA issued the Clean Air Interstate Rule, or CAIR. CAIR regulated both $NO_X$ and $SO_2$ emissions, insofar as such emissions contributed to downwind nonattainment of two NAAQS, both set in 1997, one concerning the permissible annual measure of $PM_{2.5}$, and another capping the average ozone level gauged over an 8-hour period. The D.C. Circuit initially vacated CAIR as arbitrary and capricious. On rehearing, the court decided to leave the rule in place, while encouraging EPA to act with dispatch in dealing with problems the court had identified.

The rule challenged here—the Transport Rule—is EPA's response to the D.C. Circuit's North Carolina decision. Finalized in August 2011, the Transport Rule curtails $NO_X$ and $SO_2$ emissions of 27 upwind States to achieve downwind attainment of three different NAAQS: the two 1997 NAAQS previously addressed by CAIR, and the 2006 NAAQS for $PM_{2.5}$ levels measured on a daily basis.

Under the Transport Rule, EPA employed a "two-step approach" to determine when upwind States "contribute[d] significantly to nonattainment," and therefore in "amounts" that had to be eliminated. At step one, called the "screening" analysis, the Agency excluded as de minimis any upwind State that contributed less than one percent of the three NAAQS to any downwind State "receptor," a location at which EPA measures air quality. If all of an upwind State's contributions fell below the one-percent threshold, that State would be considered not to have "contribute[d] significantly" to the nonattainment of any downwind State. States in that category were screened out and exempted from regulation under the rule.

The remaining States were subjected to a second inquiry, which EPA called the "control" analysis. At this stage, the Agency sought to generate a cost-effective allocation of emission reductions among those upwind States "screened in" at step one.

The control analysis proceeded this way. EPA first calculated, for each upwind State, the quantity of emissions the State could eliminate at each of several cost thresholds. Cost for these purposes is measured as cost per ton of emissions prevented, for instance, by installing scrubbers on powerplant smokestacks. EPA estimated, for example, the amount each upwind State's $NO_x$ emissions would fall if all pollution sources within each State employed every control measure available at a cost of $500 per ton or less. The Agency then repeated that analysis at ascending cost thresholds.

Armed with this information, EPA conducted complex modeling to establish the combined effect the upwind reductions projected at each cost threshold would have on air quality in downwind States. Agency then identified "significant cost threshold[s]," points in its model where a "noticeable change occurred in downwind air quality, such as . . . where large upwind emission reductions become available because a certain type of emissions control strategy becomes cost-effective." For example, reductions of $NO_x$ sufficient to resolve or significantly curb downwind air quality problems could be achieved, EPA determined, at a cost threshold of $500 per ton (applied uniformly to all regulated upwind States). "Moving beyond the $500 cost threshold," EPA concluded, "would result in only minimal additional . . . reductions [in emissions]."

Finally, EPA translated the cost thresholds it had selected into amounts of emissions upwind States would be required to eliminate. For each regulated upwind State, EPA created an annual emissions "budget." These budgets represented the quantity of pollution an upwind State would produce in a given year if its in-state sources implemented all pollution controls available at the chosen cost thresholds. If EPA's projected improvements to downwind air quality were to be realized, an upwind State's emissions could not exceed the level this budget allocated to it, subject to certain adjustments not relevant here.

Taken together, the screening and control inquiries defined EPA's understanding of which upwind emissions were within the Good Neighbor Provision's ambit. In short, under the Transport Rule, an upwind State "contribute[d] significantly" to downwind nonattainment to the extent its exported pollution both (1) produced one percent or more of a NAAQS in at least one downwind State (step one) and (2) could be eliminated cost-effectively, as determined by EPA (step two). Upwind States would be obliged to eliminate all and only emissions meeting both of these criteria.

For each State regulated by the Transport Rule, EPA contemporaneously promulgated a FIP allocating that State's emission budget among its in-state sources. For each of these States, EPA had determined that the State had failed to submit a

SIP adequate for compliance with the Good Neighbor Provision. These determinations regarding SIPs became final after 60 days and many went unchallenged. EPA views the SIP determinations as having triggered its statutory obligation to promulgate a FIP within two years, a view contested by respondents. . . .

## II

### B

. . . Turning to the merits, we hold that the text of the statute supports EPA's position. As earlier noted, the CAA sets a series of precise deadlines to which the States and EPA must adhere. Once EPA issues any new or revised NAAQS, a State has three years to adopt a SIP adequate for compliance with the Act's requirements. Among those requirements is the Act's mandate that SIPs "shall" include provisions sufficient to satisfy the Good Neighbor Provision. §110(a)(2).

If EPA determines a SIP to be inadequate, the Agency's mandate to replace it with a FIP is no less absolute:

"[EPA] shall promulgate a [FIP] at any time within 2 years after the [Agency]

"(A) finds that a State has failed to make a required submission or finds that the plan or plan revision submitted by the State does not satisfy the minimum [relevant] criteria . . . , or

"(B) disapproves a [SIP] in whole or in part,

"unless the State corrects the deficiency, and [EPA] approves the plan or plan revision, before the [Agency] promulgates such [FIP]." §110(c)(1).

In other words, once EPA has found a SIP inadequate, the Agency has a statutory duty to issue a FIP "at any time" within two years (unless the State first "corrects the deficiency," which no one contends occurred here).

The D.C. Circuit, however, found an unwritten exception to this strict time prescription for SIPs aimed at implementing the Good Neighbor Provision. Expecting any one State to develop a "comprehensive solution" to the "collective problem" of interstate air pollution without first receiving EPA's guidance was, in the Court of Appeals' assessment, "set[ting] the States up to fail." The D.C. Circuit therefore required EPA, after promulgating each State's emission budget, to give the State a "reasonable" period of time to propose SIPs implementing its budget.

However sensible (or not) the Court of Appeals' position, a reviewing court's "task is to apply the text [of the statute], not to improve upon it." Nothing in the Act differentiates the Good Neighbor Provision from the several other matters a State must address in its SIP. Rather, the statute speaks without reservation: Once a NAAQS has been issued, a State "shall" propose a SIP within three years, §110(a)(1), and that SIP "shall" include, among other components, provisions adequate to satisfy the Good Neighbor Provision, §110(a)(2).

Nor does the Act condition the duty to promulgate a FIP on EPA's having first quantified an upwind State's good neighbor obligations. As Judge Rogers observed in her dissent from the D.C. Circuit's decision, the Act does not require EPA to furnish upwind States with information of any kind about their good neighbor obligations before a FIP issues. Instead, a SIP's failure to satisfy the Good Neighbor Provision, without more, triggers EPA's obligation to issue a federal plan within two years. §110(c). After EPA has disapproved a SIP, the Agency can wait up to two years to issue a FIP, during which time the State can "correc[t] the deficiency" on its own. Ibid. But EPA is not obliged to wait two years or postpone its action even a single day: The Act empowers the Agency to promulgate a FIP "at any time" within the two-year limit. Carving out an exception to the Act's precise deadlines, as the D.C. Circuit did, "rewrites a decades-old statute whose plain text and structure establish a clear chronology of federal and State responsibilities."

The practical difficulties cited by the Court of Appeals do not justify departure from the Act's plain text. When Congress elected to make EPA's input a prerequisite to state action under the Act, it did so expressly. States developing vehicle inspection and maintenance programs under the CAA, for example, must await EPA guidance before issuing SIPs. A State's obligation to adopt a SIP, moreover, arises only after EPA has first set the NAAQS the State must meet. §110(a)(1). Had Congress intended similarly to defer States' discharge of their obligations under the Good Neighbor Provision, Congress, we take it, would have included a similar direction in that section.

In short, nothing in the statute places EPA under an obligation to provide specific metrics to States before they undertake to fulfill their good neighbor obligations. By altering the schedule Congress provided for SIPs and FIPs, the D.C. Circuit stretched out the process. It allowed a delay Congress did not order and placed an information submission obligation on EPA Congress did not impose. The D.C. Circuit, we hold, had no warrant thus to revise the CAA's action-ordering prescriptions. . . .

## III

### A

The D.C. Circuit also held that the Transport Rule's two-step interpretation of the Good Neighbor Provision conflicts with the Act. . . .

### B

We routinely accord dispositive effect to an agency's reasonable interpretation of ambiguous statutory language. Chevron U.S.A. Inc. v. Natural Resources Defense Council, Inc., 467 U.S. 837 (1984), is the pathmarking decision, and it bears a notable resemblance to the cases before us. . . .

We conclude that the Good Neighbor Provision delegates authority to EPA at least as certainly as the CAA provisions involved in *Chevron*. The statute requires States to eliminate those "amounts" of pollution that "contribute significantly to *nonattainment*" in downwind States. §110(a)(2)(D)(i) (emphasis added). Thus, EPA's task is to reduce upwind pollution, but only in "amounts" that push a downwind State's pollution concentrations above the relevant NAAQS. As noted earlier, however, the nonattainment of downwind States results from the collective and interwoven contributions of multiple upwind States. The statute therefore calls upon the Agency to address a thorny causation problem: How should EPA allocate among multiple contributing upwind States responsibility for a downwind State's excess pollution? . . .

Persuaded that the Good Neighbor Provision does not dictate the particular allocation of emissions among contributing States advanced by the D.C. Circuit, we must next decide whether the allocation method chosen by EPA is a "permissible construction of the statute." As EPA interprets the statute, upwind emissions rank as "amounts [that] . . . contribute significantly to nonattainment" if they (1) constitute one percent or more of a relevant NAAQS in a nonattaining downwind State and (2) can be eliminated under the cost threshold set by the Agency. In other words, to identify which emissions were to be eliminated, EPA considered both the magnitude of upwind States' contributions and the cost associated with eliminating them.

The Industry respondents argue that, however EPA ultimately divides responsibility among upwind States, the final calculation cannot rely on costs. The Good Neighbor Provision, respondents and the dissent emphasize, "requires each State to prohibit only those 'amounts' of air pollution emitted within the State that 'contribute significantly' to another State's nonattainment." The cost of preventing emissions, they urge, is wholly unrelated to the actual "amoun[t]" of air pollution an upwind State contributes. Because the Transport Rule considers costs, respondents argue, "States that contribute identical 'amounts' . . . may be deemed [by EPA] to have [made] substantially different" contributions.

But, as just explained, the Agency cannot avoid the task of choosing which among equal "amounts" to eliminate. The Agency has chosen, sensibly in our view, to reduce the amount easier, i.e., less costly, to eradicate, and nothing in the text of the Good Neighbor Provision precludes that choice.

Using costs in the Transport Rule calculus, we agree with EPA, also makes good sense. Eliminating those amounts that can cost-effectively be reduced is an efficient and equitable solution to the allocation problem the Good Neighbor Provision requires the Agency to address. Efficient because EPA can achieve the levels of attainment, i.e., of emission reductions, the proportional approach aims to achieve, but at a much lower overall cost. Equitable because, by imposing uniform cost thresholds on regulated States, EPA's rule subjects to stricter regulation those States that have done relatively less in the past to control their pollution. Upwind States that have not yet implemented pollution controls of the same stringency as their neighbors will be stopped from free riding on their neighbors' efforts to reduce pollution. They will have to bring down their emissions by installing devices of the kind in which neighboring States have already invested. . . .

Obligated to require the elimination of only those "amounts" of pollutants that contribute to the nonattainment of NAAQS in downwind States, EPA must decide how to differentiate among the otherwise like contributions of multiple upwind States. EPA found decisive the difficulty of eliminating each "amount," i.e., the cost incurred in doing so. Lacking a dispositive statutory instruction to guide it, EPA's decision, we conclude, is a "reasonable" way of filling the "gap left open by Congress."

### C

. . . If any upwind State concludes it has been forced to regulate emissions below the one-percent threshold or beyond the point necessary to bring all downwind States into attainment, that State may bring a particularized, as-applied challenge to the Transport Rule, along with any other as-applied challenges it may have. Satisfied that EPA's cost-based methodology, on its face, is not "arbitrary, capricious, or manifestly contrary to the statute," we uphold the Transport Rule. The possibility that the rule, in uncommon particular applications, might exceed EPA's statutory authority does not warrant judicial condemnation of the rule in its entirety.

In sum, we hold that the CAA does not command that States be given a second opportunity to file a SIP after EPA has quantified the State's interstate pollution obligations. We further conclude that the Good Neighbor Provision does not require EPA to disregard costs and consider exclusively each upwind State's physically proportionate responsibility for each downwind air quality problem. EPA's cost-effective allocation of emission reductions among upwind States, we hold, is a permissible, workable, and equitable interpretation of the Good Neighbor Provision.

JUSTICE ALITO took no part in the consideration or decision of these cases.

JUSTICE SCALIA, with whom JUSTICE THOMAS joins, dissenting.

Too many important decisions of the Federal Government are made nowadays by unelected agency officials exercising broad lawmaking authority, rather than by the people's representatives in Congress. With the statute involved in the present cases, however, Congress did it right. It specified quite precisely the responsibility of an upwind State under the Good Neighbor Provision: to eliminate those amounts of pollutants that it contributes to downwind problem areas. But the Environmental Protection Agency was unsatisfied with this system. Agency personnel, perhaps correctly, thought it more efficient to require reductions not in proportion to the amounts of pollutants for which each upwind State is responsible, but on the basis of how cost-effectively each can decrease emissions.

Today, the majority approves that undemocratic revision of the Clean Air Act. The Agency came forward with a textual justification for its action, relying on a far-fetched meaning of the word "significantly" in the statutory text. That justification is so feeble that today's majority does not even recite it, much less defend it. The majority reaches its result ("Look Ma, no hands!") without benefit of text, claiming to have identified a remarkable "gap" in the statute, which it proceeds to fill (contrary to the plain logic of the statute) with cost-benefit analysis—and then, with no pretended textual justification at all, simply extends cost-benefit analysis beyond the scope of the alleged gap.

Additionally, the majority relieves EPA of any obligation to announce novel interpretations of the Good Neighbor Provision before the States must submit plans that are required to comply with those interpretations. By according the States primacy in deciding how to attain the governing air-quality standards, the Clean Air Act is pregnant with an obligation for the Agency to set those standards before the States can be expected to achieve them. The majority nonetheless approves EPA's promulgation of federal plans implementing good-neighbor benchmarks before the States could conceivably have met those benchmarks on their own.

I would affirm the judgment of the D.C. Circuit that EPA violated the law both in crafting the Transport Rule and in implementing it. . . .

## I. THE TRANSPORT RULE. . .

### D. Our Precedent

The majority agrees with EPA's assessment that "[u]sing costs in the Transport Rule calculus . . . makes good sense." Its opinion declares that "[e]liminating those amounts that can cost-effectively be reduced is an efficient and equitable solution to the allocation problem the Good Neighbor Provision requires the Agency to address." Efficient, probably. Equitable? Perhaps so, but perhaps not. But the point is that whether efficiency should have a dominant or subordinate role is not for EPA or this Court to determine.

This is not the first time parties have sought to convert the Clean Air Act into a mandate for cost-effective regulation. Whitman v. American Trucking Assns., Inc., 531 U.S. 457 (2001) confronted the contention that EPA should consider costs in setting NAAQS. The provision at issue there, like this one, did not expressly bar cost-based decisionmaking — and unlike this one, it even contained words that were arguably ambiguous in the relevant respect. Specifically, §109(b)(1) instructed EPA to set primary NAAQS "the attainment and maintenance of which . . . are requisite to protect the public health" with "an adequate margin of safety." One could hardly overstate the capaciousness of the word "adequate," and the phrase "public health" was at least equally susceptible (indeed, much more susceptible) of permitting cost-benefit analysis as the word "significantly" is here. As the respondents in *American Trucking* argued, setting NAAQS without considering costs may bring about failing industries and fewer jobs, which in turn may produce poorer and less healthy citizens. But we concluded that "in the context of" the entire provision, that interpretation "ma[de] no sense." As quoted earlier, we said that Congress "does not alter the fundamental details of a regulatory scheme in vague terms or ancillary provisions — it does not . . . hide elephants in mouseholes."

In *American Trucking*, the Court "refused to find implicit in ambiguous sections of the [Clear Air Act] an authorization to consider costs that has elsewhere, and so often, been expressly granted," citing a tradition dating back to Union Elec. Co. v. EPA, 427 U.S. 246, 257, and n.5 (1976). There are, indeed, numerous Clean Air Act provisions explicitly permitting costs to be taken into account. *American Trucking* thus demanded "a textual commitment of authority to the EPA to consider costs," 531 U.S., at 468 — a hurdle that the Good Neighbor Provision comes nowhere close to clearing. Today's opinion turns its back upon that case and is incompatible with that opinion.

## NOTES AND QUESTIONS

1. The Supreme Court's *EME Homer* decision represented a considerable victory for EPA by putting to rest the D.C. Circuit's repeated invalidation of EPA's efforts to craft a program to control transboundary pollution. Both Chief Justice Roberts and Justice Kennedy joined in the majority opinion, leaving only Justices Scalia and Thomas in dissent (with Justice Alito recusing himself).

2. When the Supreme Court released the initial *EME Homer* slip opinion, Justice Scalia's dissent contained an embarrassing mistake. Part I-D of the dissent was entitled "Plus Ça Change: EPA's Continuing Quest for Cost-Benefit Authority." The first two sentences of this part read as follows: "This is not the first time EPA has sought to convert the Clean Air Act into a mandate for cost-effective regulation. Whitman v. American Trucking Assns., Inc., 531 U.S. 457 (2001) confronted EPA's contention that it could consider costs in setting NAAQS." As you may recall, EPA's position in *American Trucking*, a unanimous decision written by Justice Scalia, was just the opposite — that it could *not* consider costs when setting NAAQS. To some

observers this mistake suggested an unseemly eagerness on Justice Scalia's part to lend support to the political campaign then underway to demonize EPA. After an alert law professor pointed out the mistake to the Court, it was corrected electronically on the Court's website in less than 24 hours by changing the language of subheading I-D to "Our Precedent" and altering a few words in the first two sentences of the second paragraph of this subsection. After a law review article was published criticizing the Court's failure to notify litigants of such corrections, Richard J. Lazarus, The (Non)Finality of Supreme Court Opinions, 128 Harv. L. Rev. 540 (2014), the Court announced in 2015 new procedures for providing public notice of all changes in the text of its decisions after the release of the initial slip opinion.

3.  In the July 13, 2015 Federal Register, EPA published a final rule "finding that [24] states have failed to submit infrastructure [SIPs] to satisfy certain interstate transport requirements of the [CAA] with respect to the 2008 [8]-hour ozone [NAAQS]" and establishing "a [two]-year deadline for the EPA to promulgate a [FIP] to address the interstate transport SIP requirements" in these states, unless the state submits, and EPA approves, a SIP meeting the requirements. 80 Fed. Reg. 39,961 (2015). In the October 26, 2016 Federal Register, the EPA published a final rule updating the Cross-State Air Pollution Rule for the 2008 Ozone NAAQS to reduce ozone season emissions of $NO_x$ in 22 eastern states. 81 Fed. Reg. 74,504 (2016).

4.  In 2018 the Trump administration EPA determined that no further emissions reductions were necessary for all but two of 22 states covered by the 2016 Update. However, that decision was immediately challenged by downwind states who argued that the mandated emissions reductions didn't satisfy upwind states' Good Neighbor obligations under the 2008 Ozone NAAQS. In 2019, the D.C. Circuit vacated and remanded both the 2016 CSAPR Update (*Wisconsin v. EPA*, 938 F.3d 303 (D.C. Cir. 2019)) and the 2018 Closeout Rule (*New York v. EPA*), finding that those rulemakings unlawfully allowed upwind states to continue significantly contributing to downwind air quality problems beyond the 2021 attainment deadline for the 2008 ozone standard. In response, EPA developed a revised Cross-State Air Pollution Rule.

EPA's revised CSAPR reinstates ozone season $NO_x$ reductions for 12 states and proposes new FIPs for those states. For all of the remaining states except Kentucky, EPA concluded that the existing CSAPR FIPs sufficiently address interstate ozone obligations under the 2008 Ozone NAAQS. For Kentucky, EPA plans to reverse its 2018 approval of the state's Good Neighbor SIP and require additional emission reductions. EPA's proposed rule followed the four-step analytical framework used in the original CSAPR and the CSAPR Update: (1) reviewing ozone modeling projections and identifying downwind nonattainment and maintenance receptors, (2) estimating each of the upwind states' largest modeled ozone contribution, (3) identifying uniform $NO_x$ emission control level, and (4) addressing features of the emissions allowance trading program designed to implement ozone-season $NO_x$ emission budgets. On March 15, 2021, EPA adopted a final rule that tracked the changes in its proposal. Starting in the 2021 ozone season, the rule requires additional reductions of 17,000 tons of $NO_x$ emissions annually from power plants in 12 states. EPA estimates that this will yield public health and climate benefits valued, on average, at up to $2.8 billion each year from 2021 to 2040.

# CHAPTER 6

# WATER POLLUTION
# CONTROL

The federal Clean Water Act (CWA) could lay claim to being the most successful environmental program in America. Since its enactment in 1972, industrial discharges to the nation's waters are precipitously down, rates of wetlands loss have slowed and in some regions even reversed, and municipal loadings . . . have dropped by nearly 50 percent while their populations served have doubled. . . .

Yet, we do not have clean water. . . . What has gone wrong, of course, is that unregulated sources have blossomed like algae to consume the gains. . . . Individually small, it is their cumulative impacts that are the problem. . . . Most importantly, they are by nature diffuse, not outfalls from pipes, and therefore long considered to be beyond those regulatory requirements of the Clean Water Act that have led to its success.

Which would end the story, but for the remarkable resurrection of a long-dormant provision of the Clean Water Act, Sec. 303(d), now taking the field and forcing a showdown on the last water quality frontier, nonpoint source pollution.

— *Oliver A. Houck**

Water is nature's most precious resource. Most of the water on Earth today was on this planet shortly after its formation several billion years ago, "and it may be about all the planet will ever have." William K. Stevens, Water: Pushing the Limits of an Irreplaceable Resource, 14 Nat. Resources & Env't 3 (Summer 1999). The vast majority of this water—97.5 percent—is salt water found in the oceans. The 2.5 percent that constitutes the world's freshwater supply is primarily locked in glaciers. Only eight-thousandths of the water on Earth is part of the renewable freshwater supply found on land, and it is this resource that, except for oxygen, "is the most vital substance on the planet" for human existence. Id.

Water has been a source of enormous conflict throughout history as humans have competed to trap it, "tap it, rechannel it, transfer it, pollute it, consume it, feed it to livestock, ladle it onto farm fields (by far the biggest single use) and flush it through factories, power plants and toilets." Id. This human activity has significantly altered the planet's water cycle, disrupting freshwater ecosystems. After discussing the changing nature and scope of water pollution problems, this chapter reviews legal authorities for protecting water resources. It then examines controls on discharges from point sources, water-quality-based controls, and wetland

---

\* TMDLs IV: The Final Frontier, 29 Envtl. L. Rep. 10469 (Aug. 1999).

protection programs. The chapter concludes by exploring efforts to redirect policy toward a watershed protection approach that seeks to address serious problems caused by pollution from nonpoint sources.


## A.   WATER POLLUTION PROBLEMS

Although our understanding of water pollution problems is improving significantly, it is surprising how much we still do not know. Despite decades of research and regulation, it is still not possible to make a comprehensive assessment of the quality of the nation's waters. When EPA in 2016 reported to Congress on the state of the nation's waters, it found that water quality data were available for only about 31 percent of the nation's river and stream miles, 44 percent of its acres of lakes and ponds, and 64 percent of the area of its bays and estuaries. The agency found that 53 percent of assessed river and stream miles, 71 percent of assessed lake acres, and 79 percent of assessed estuarine areas did not meet applicable water quality standards. EPA, Watershed Assessment, Tracking & Environmental Results (2016) (*http://iaspub.epa.gov/waters10/attains_nation_cy.control*). It has long been recognized that these data were inadequate to permit an objective, overall assessment of whether the quality of the nation's waters is getting better or worse. While efforts are being made to improve water quality monitoring, some conclusions are possible. Clearly there have been some dramatic improvements in water quality in certain rivers and lakes, though coastal and estuarine waters have been under severe stress. In the following excerpt, Professor William Andreen summarizes the successes and challenges facing efforts to protect water quality in the United States.


William L. Andreen

### Success and Backlash: The Remarkable (Continuing) Story of the Clean Water Act

4 J. Energy & Envtl. L. 25 (Winter 2013)

Our nation recently celebrated the fortieth anniversary of a truly transformative statute: the Clean Water Act of 1972 ("Act"). The Act instituted a fundamental shift in the nation's approach to water pollution control. Prior to its enactment, the primary responsibility for regulating water pollution resided with the states, although the federal government had aided state efforts for years by providing technical and financial support. In addition, Congress created a program in 1965 that called upon the states to set and implement water quality standards for their interstate waters. Although some state programs made progress, this regulatory paradigm largely failed. As late as 1968 seventy percent of industrial discharges remained untreated, while the rest often received only rudimentary treatment. At the same time, pollutant discharges from municipal waste systems were growing ever larger, and fish kills had reached record proportions.

By 1972, Congress had grown weary of rivers that resembled "little more than sewers to the seas" (quoting Sen. Edmund Muskie) and the many states that were unable, or unwilling, to submit acceptable water quality standards and implementation plans. Even if every state had submitted fully acceptable water quality standards, federal enforcement would have been difficult because the government would have had to prove which particular polluter was responsible for a violation of the relevant stream standards. This was a nearly insurmountable challenge because the government possessed virtually no data about the location, volume, or composition of industrial discharges, and the challenge was even greater when there were more than a few likely suspects. So, instead of continuing to rely primarily upon state water quality standards, Congress adopted a wholly new approach and, in doing so, vastly expanded the federal role in water pollution control.

Congress based its new approach upon the federal establishment of uniform, technology-based effluent limitations that set performance standards for new and existing facilities in hundreds of industrial categories and subcategories. These limitations, in turn, were applied to thousands of point source dischargers through a new permit system—the National Pollutant Discharge Elimination System ("NPDES") permit program—that specifically defines the enforceable obligations of the individual discharger. Congress retained and expanded the state water quality standard program, however, to ensure that water quality objectives were met. Accordingly, in cases where compliance with effluent limitations alone was not enough to meet water quality standards, Congress directed permit writers to issue NPDES permits with even tougher permit conditions designed to bring about compliance with water quality standards. The Act thereby combined technology-based limitations with ambient-based quality standards in a creative attempt to combat rising levels of water pollution. . . .

The Act and the regulatory programs it created have proven remarkably successful. Both municipal and industrial discharges have declined sharply, the loss of wetlands has been cut decisively, and water quality has broadly improved across the country. All of this was achieved without causing any significant harm to the economy in terms of employment, growth, or investment. It is, in short, a real success story. . . .

The Act is showing its age, however. Twenty-five years have passed since it was last amended in comprehensive fashion, and more than a little fine-tuning is necessary to finish the task that began in 1972. The most significant problem involves nonpoint source pollution—the indirect discharge of polluted runoff from fields and roads, clear cuts, and parking lots. . . . [N]onpoint source pollution has evolved into the largest single source of water quality impairment in the country. These diffuse sources of water pollution are, furthermore, much more diverse than we once thought. In addition to obvious sources such as polluted runoff from agriculture, urban areas, logging operations, and mines, nonpoint source pollution also includes cross-media transfers, including the deposition of air pollutants such as mercury and nitrogen, into our waters. . . .

The nation's existing infrastructure for collecting and treating municipal wastewater is aging while the population is growing, and sanitary sewer overflows persist as problems in hundreds of cities. EPA's efforts to update the technology-based effluent limitations are seriously lagging due to inadequate funding, while permit compliance and state enforcement efforts remain too inconsistent.

## NOTES AND QUESTIONS

1. In what respects do water pollution problems differ from air pollution problems? Which should be easier to control—water pollution or air pollution? Which is more naturally variable in quality—water or air? How should regulatory policy take these differences into account?

2. Figure 6.2 lists some of the principal point and nonpoint sources of water pollution and the types of pollutants they generate. Biochemical oxygen demand (BOD) measures the oxygen-depleting capacity of substances such as organic wastes and chemicals that consume oxygen as they decompose. Human and animal wastes contribute bacteria to water, such as fecal coliform and fecal streptococcus. Nitrogen and phosphorus discharges cause nutrient overenrichment and algae blooms. Siltation and soil erosion block sunlight necessary for the growth of submerged aquatic vegetation. Figure 6.2 is not a comprehensive list of the sources of water quality problems. As Professor Andreen notes, atmospheric deposition of pollutants can be a major factor degrading water quality; altered stream flows also affect the health of aquatic ecosystems.

3. Nonpoint sources now are generating the most serious problems affecting nearly every major watershed, although the precise sources vary from state to state. Nutrient runoff from commercial fertilizers is widely credited with causing a huge "dead zone" in the Gulf of Mexico. "The waters of northern Wisconsin are polluted by dairy farms, in North Carolina by hogs, in Maryland by chickens, in south Florida by sugar, in Wyoming by beef cattle, in Oregon by clearcuts, in Maine by logging roads." Houck, TMDLs IV: The Final Frontier, 29 Envtl. L. Rep. 10469, 10470 (1999).

**Figure 6.1    National Summary Water Quality Attainment in Assessed Rivers and Streams**

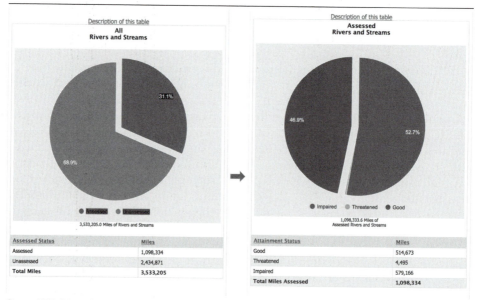

*Source:* EPA, Watershed Assessment, Tracking & Environmental Results (2016) (*http://iaspub.epa.gov/waters10/attains_nation_cy.control*).

### Figure 6.2   Pollutants and Their Sources

| | BOD | Bacteria | Nutrients | Ammonia | Turbidity | TDS | Acids | Toxics |
|---|---|---|---|---|---|---|---|---|
| **Point Sources** | | | | | | | | |
| Municipal Sewage Treatment Plants | • | • | • | • | | | | • |
| Industrial Facilities | • | | | | | | | • |
| Combined Sewer Overflows | • | • | • | • | • | • | | • |
| **Nonpoint Sources** | | | | | | | | |
| Agricultural Runoff | • | • | • | | • | • | | • |
| Urban Runoff | • | • | • | | • | • | | • |
| Construction Runoff | | | • | | • | | | • |
| Mining Runoff | | | | | • | • | • | • |
| Septic Systems | • | • | • | | | | | • |
| Landfills/Spills | • | | | | | | | • |
| Silviculture Runoff | • | | • | | • | | | • |

*Source:* Modified from 1986 305(b) National Report.
Abbreviations: Biological Oxygen Demand, BOD; Total Dissolved Solids, TDS.

4. Despite improvements in sewage treatment technology, many cities still use combined sewer overflow (CSO) systems that channel stormwater through sewers. In major storms these systems discharge untreated sewage directly into surface waters. In a report to Congress in 2002, EPA estimated that CSOs result in the untreated discharge of 850 billion gallons of untreated waste annually and that the cost of fully controlling these discharges over the next 20 years would be $140 billion. EPA, Report to Congress on Impacts and Control of Combined Sewer Overflows and Sanitary Sewer Overflows (2002).

5. In June 2003, the Pew Oceans Commission issued a report, America's Living Oceans: Charting a Course for Sea Change, which concluded that "America's oceans are in crisis and the stakes could not be higher." Among the problems highlighted by the report are coastal development and sprawl destroying wetlands and estuaries, overfishing, nutrient runoff in coastal rivers and bays, and the introduction of invasive species. The Commission, which included a diverse group of American leaders with backgrounds in science, fishing, conservation, government, education, business, and philanthropy, recommended significant legal and policy reforms to protect ocean and coastal ecosystems. In September 2004, the U.S. Commission on Ocean Policy submitted to the president and Congress a report entitled An Ocean Blueprint for the 21st Century. The report reached conclusions similar to those of the Pew Commission, finding that nearly 80 percent of assessed coastal waters were impaired or threatened for aquatic life or human use. It made

more than 200 recommendations for improving oceans policy. Many of these recommendations were implemented by Executive Order 13,547 issued by President
Obama in July 2010. It created a National Ocean Council chaired by the chair of
the Council on Environmental Quality and the director of the Office of Science
and Technology Policy. This order was repealed by President Trump in Executive
Order 13,480, issued in June 2018, that placed more emphasis on extraction and
use of ocean resources and protection of national security.


## B.  THE SCOPE OF FEDERAL AUTHORITY TO REGULATE WATER

### 1.  Water Pollution Control: A Historical Perspective

The shift to waterborne methods of human waste disposal made water pollution a major concern of large cities in the nineteenth century. Typhoid outbreaks
were not uncommon in areas where raw sewage was dumped into sources of drinking water. The discovery that disease was transmitted by germs exacerbated public concern over sewage disposal practices. As noted in Chapter 2, these practices
spawned early common law nuisance actions between states. Missouri v. Illinois, 200
U.S. 496 (1906); New York v. New Jersey, 256 U.S. 296 (1921).

Even though states asked the Supreme Court to umpire interstate sewage disposal disputes, water pollution control was considered largely a local responsibility.
When Congress enacted the Rivers and Harbors Act of 1899, which barred unpermitted discharges of refuse into navigable waters, its aim was not to protect water
quality but to prevent interferences with navigation, the lifeblood of American
commerce then. After major U.S. cities began chlorinating their drinking water,
typhoid outbreaks were virtually eliminated by 1930. V. Tschinkel, The Rise and Fall
of Environmental Expertise, in Technology and the Environment 160 (J. Ausabel &
H. Sladovich eds., 1989). Public concern over water pollution shifted to its impact
on recreation and aquatic life. See, e.g., New Jersey v. City of New York, 284 U.S.
585 (1931).

After World War II water pollution problems intensified as industrial activity
accelerated. Congress initially responded by funding research and by providing
federal grants for state water pollution control programs in the Water Quality Act
of 1948. Federal funding was expanded in the Federal Water Pollution Control Act
of 1956, enacted despite President Eisenhower's opposition to direct federal aid for
the construction of municipal sewage treatment facilities.

Like the legislation that preceded enactment of the 1970 Clean Air Act, the
Federal Water Pollution Control Act in theory authorized the federal government
to act against interstate pollution through a cumbersome procedure of abatement
conferences. In the Water Quality Act of 1965, Congress strengthened these provisions by requiring states to adopt water quality standards for interstate waters subject
to the approval of a new agency, the Federal Water Pollution Control Administration. If a state did not adopt water quality standards within two years the federal
government in theory could intervene and adopt its own standards, after a lengthy

and difficult process. States also were required to promulgate state implementation plans, though federal officials could not impose an implementation plan if a state failed to act. As a result, even when water quality standards were adopted, there was no effective mechanism to translate them into workable requirements on individual dischargers, and the federal government had no meaningful enforcement authority. Thus, it is not surprising that the 1965 Act produced only slow progress. By 1972 only about one-half of the states had water quality standards, and the Senate Committee on Public Works (chaired by Senator Muskie) issued a report concluding that "the Federal water pollution program . . . has been inadequate in every vital aspect."

Despite amendments gradually expanding and strengthening federal authorities, the modern era of comprehensive federal regulation of water pollution was not born until enactment of the Federal Water Pollution Control Act of 1972. An unlikely catalyst for this legislation was the revival of the long-dormant Rivers and Harbors Act of 1899, or, as it came to be known, the Refuse Act. To protect navigation, section 13 of the Act prohibited discharges into navigable waters of the United States of "any refuse matter of any kind or description whatever other than that flowing from streets and sewers and passing therefrom in a liquid state." Exceptions were to be made only with the permission of the Secretary of the Army. The Act had not been considered a pollution control law until two Supreme Court decisions in the 1960s construed the Act to encompass discharges of industrial wastes, whether or not they threatened navigation. United States v. Republic Steel Corp., 362 U.S. 482 (1960); United States v. Standard Oil Co., 384 U.S. 224 (1966).

The discharges at issue in those cases could have been found in virtually any waterway around the country. In 1970 Congressman Henry Reuss of Wisconsin, chairman of the House Subcommittee on Conservation and Natural Resources, saw the Refuse Act's promise as a tool for dramatic action against the growing water pollution problem. His subcommittee issued a report publicizing the Act's *qui tam* provisions, a common law remedy allowing citizens to prosecute crimes and keep half of the fines paid. Reuss cleverly decided to test these provisions by compiling a list of 270 Wisconsin companies discharging wastes without a permit. Suits were brought against four companies, and Congressman Reuss sent his share of the resulting fines back to the state Department of Natural Resources to help fund construction of sewage treatment plants. Several hundred suits ultimately were filed under the Refuse Act, though the average fine collected was only about $2,000.

The Refuse Act experience illustrates the capacity of different institutional actors to influence the evolution of environmental policy as issues move between the courts, the executive branch, and the Congress. Congressman Reuss's role illustrates one of the unique features of American environmental law — the fact that one person can make an enormous difference by looking for laws applicable to new problems and by using the courts to demand that they be enforced. His actions helped change the political dynamic by creating an immediate demand among dischargers for some form of permit program to protect them from lawsuits. In December 1970, while legislation was being debated in Congress, President Nixon by executive order created a permit program to be administered by the Army Corps of Engineers and EPA. After the administration announced that it would not take enforcement action against any discharger that had applied for a permit, more than 23,000 permit applications were filed. Ironically, the permit program faltered when a court enjoined its operation for failure to comply with the environmental impact statement requirement of the new National Environmental Policy Act (NEPA). Kalur v. Resor, 335 F. Supp. 1 (D.D.C. 1971). Before that decision could be appealed, Congress acted.

## 2.   Statutory Authorities

Spurred by the Refuse Act experience and growing concern over the demonstrated inadequacies of state water pollution controls, Congress in October 1972 adopted the Federal Water Pollution Control Act Amendments (FWPCA), or, as it is now called, the Clean Water Act. Pub. L. No. 92-500, 33 U.S.C. §§1251 et seq. The FWPCA was enacted when Congress overrode a veto by President Nixon, who opposed its massive increase in federal funds for sewage treatment. (Nixon's subsequent effort to impound half of the funds authorized led to the Congressional Budget and Impoundment Act of 1974.)

In order "to restore and maintain the chemical, physical, and biological integrity of the Nation's waters," the FWPCA broke new ground in three important areas. First, it mandated the imposition of technology-based discharge limits that "facilitate enforcement by making it unnecessary to work backward from an overpolluted body of water to determine which point sources are responsible and which must be abated." EPA v. California ex rel. State Water Resources Control Board, 426 U.S. 200, 204 (1976). Second, as a result of experience with the Refuse Act, Congress imposed a nationwide permit system on point source dischargers while retaining the previously required water quality standards. This served "to transform generally applicable effluent limitations and other standards—including those based on water quality—into the obligations (including a timetable for compliance) of the individual discharger." 426 U.S. at 204-205. Finally, Congress substantially expanded the federal role in financing construction of municipal treatment facilities.

The FWPCA, which was renamed the Clean Water Act when amended in 1977, remains the principal federal statute regulating water pollution. However, the Clean Water Act is not the only federal statute that seeks to protect water quality. In 1972, Congress also enacted the Marine Protection, Research, and Sanctuaries Act, known as the Ocean Dumping Act, and the Coastal Zone Management Act.

The Ocean Dumping Act prohibits all dumping of wastes in the ocean except where permits are issued by EPA (for nondredged materials) or by the U.S. Army Corps of Engineers (for dredged materials). Permits are conditioned on a showing that the dumping will not "unreasonably degrade" the environment. A major motivation for the Act was to prevent dischargers from evading the Clean Water Act's permit requirements by simply dumping wastes into the ocean. While EPA's stated policy since 1973 has been to phase out all ocean dumping, Congress eventually had to amend the Ocean Dumping Act to establish deadlines for phasing out dumping of industrial waste and municipal sewage sludge. After New York City won an extension of the deadline for ending ocean dumping of sewage sludge in City of New York v. EPA, 543 F. Supp. 1084 (S.D.N.Y. 1981), the Act was amended in 1988 to impose escalating disposal fees (increasing over time from $100 to $200 per ton), culminating in a ban on such dumping in 1992.

The Coastal Zone Management Act provides financial assistance to encourage states to adopt federally approved coastal management plans. The Act requires certification that activities affecting land or water use in a coastal zone conform to such plans before federal permits can be issued. Legislation to require *all* states to develop land use control plans had passed the Senate in 1972 but ultimately failed to win adoption despite President Nixon's support for establishing a national land use policy. In 1990, Congress adopted the Oil Pollution Act, discussed in Chapter 2, and strengthened the Coastal Zone Management Act to require states with approved plans to adopt measures to control nonpoint source pollution. By 1991, coastal management programs had been developed for 29 states and territories, covering nearly 95 percent of the U.S. coastline and the shores of the Great Lakes. CEQ, Environmental Quality—22d Annual Report 38 (1992).

In addition to the statutes, discussed above, the Safe Drinking Water Act regulates the quality of drinking water supplied by public water systems. RCRA and CERCLA have considerable relevance for groundwater protection and remediation, as discussed in Chapter 4. Many states also have adopted their own groundwater protection legislation. This chapter focuses primarily on the regulatory programs established under the federal Clean Water Act to control pollution of surface waters and to encourage states to develop programs to address nonpoint sources.

---

# Principal Federal Laws Addressing Water Pollution

*The Clean Water Act* prohibits all unpermitted discharges into the waters of the United States (including the territorial sea) of pollutants from point sources, imposes effluent limitations on dischargers, and requires statewide planning for control of pollution from nonpoint sources.

*The Ocean Dumping Act* prohibits the transportation of wastes for dumping and the dumping of wastes in the area seaward of the inner boundary of the U.S. territorial sea unless a permit has been obtained. EPA is responsible for issuing permits for all materials except for dredged materials, for which permits must be obtained from the U.S. Army Corps of Engineers.

*The Oil Pollution Act* makes owners of vessels discharging oil liable for costs of cleanup; establishes an Oil Spill Liability Trust Fund to pay response costs; and imposes minimum design standards to prevent spills by vessels operating in U.S. waters.

*The Coastal Zone Management Act* offers federal financial assistance to states that adopt federally approved coastal management plans and requires federal actions in coastal areas to be consistent with state programs. Amended in 1990 to require states to adopt programs to control nonpoint sources of coastal water pollution.

*The Safe Drinking Water Act* regulates contaminants in drinking water supplied by public water systems, establishes a permit program regulating the underground injection of hazardous waste, and restricts activities that threaten sole-source aquifers.

## 3.   The Structure of the Clean Water Act

The Clean Water Act is the most comprehensive source of federal regulatory authority to control water pollution. To assist you in developing an understanding of the structure of the Clean Water Act, the major provisions of the Act are outlined below. Following a brief description of these provisions, their operation and implementation are discussed in more detail in the sections that follow.

---

# Major Provisions of the Clean Water Act

*§101 Goals:* declares national goals of fishable/swimmable waters by 1983 and the elimination of pollutant discharges into navigable waters by 1985.

*§301 Effluent Limitations:* prohibits "the discharge of any pollutant" (defined in §502(12) as the addition of any pollutant to navigable waters from any point source or to the waters of the ocean or contiguous zone from any point source other than a vessel) except those made in compliance with the terms of the Act, including the permit requirements of section 402. Imposes multi-tiered effluent limitations on existing sources whose stringency and timing depends on the nature of the pollutant discharged and whether the outfall is directed to a water body or a publicly owned treatment works (POTW).

*§302 Water Quality Related Effluent Limitations:* authorizes the imposition of more stringent effluent limitations when necessary to prevent interference with the attainment or maintenance of desired water quality.

*§303 Water Quality Standards & TMDLs:* requires states and tribes to adopt and to review triennially water quality criteria and standards subject to EPA approval, to identify waters where effluent limits are insufficient to achieve such standards, and to establish total maximum daily loads (TMDLs) of pollutants for such waters.

*§304 Federal Water Quality Criteria and Guidelines:* requires EPA to adopt water quality criteria and guidelines for effluent limitations, pretreatment programs, and administration of the NPDES permit program.

*§306 New Source Performance Standards:* requires EPA to promulgate new source performance standards reflecting best demonstrated control technology.

*§307 Toxic and Pretreatment Effluent Standards:* requires dischargers of toxic pollutants to meet effluent limits reflecting the best available technology economically achievable. Requires EPA to establish pretreatment standards to prevent discharges from interfering with POTWs.

*§309 Enforcement Authorities:* authorizes compliance orders and administrative, civil, and criminal penalties for violations of the Act.

*§319 Nonpoint Source Management Programs:* requires states and tribes to identify waters that cannot meet water quality standards due to nonpoint sources, identify the activities responsible for the problem, and prepare management plans identifying controls and programs for specific sources.

§401 State Water Quality Certification: requires applicants for federal licenses or permits that may result in a discharge into navigable water to obtain a certification from the state in which the discharge will occur that it will comply with various provisions of the Act.

§402 NPDES Permit Program: establishes a national permit program, the national pollution discharge elimination system (NPDES), that may be administered by EPA or by states or Indian tribes under delegated authority from EPA.

§404 Dredge and Fill Operations: requires a permit from the Army Corps of Engineers for the disposal of dredged or fill material into navigable waters with the concurrence of EPA unless associated with "normal" farming.

§505 Citizen Suits: authorizes citizen suits against any person who violates an effluent standard or order, or against EPA for failure to perform a nondiscretionary duty.

§509 Judicial Review: authorizes judicial review of certain EPA rulemaking actions in the U.S. Courts of Appeals.

§518 Indian Tribes: authorizes EPA to treat Indian tribes as states for purposes of the Act for tribes that have governing bodies carrying out substantial governmental duties and powers.

The Clean Water Act adopts breathtakingly ambitious goals in section 101(a) ("that the discharge of pollutants into the navigable waters be eliminated by 1985," section 101(a)(1), and that fishable/swimmable waters be achieved "wherever attainable" by July 1, 1983, section 101(a)(2)) that suggest a virtually cost-blind determination to control water pollution. While the Act concentrates its regulatory firepower on pollution from point sources, in 1987, Congress added section 101(a)(7), which articulates a new goal of developing and implementing "programs for the control of nonpoint sources of pollution." §101(a)(7).

The construction grants program of the Act, which provided $54 billion in federal funds to build sewage treatment plants between 1972 and 1990, played an important role in federal-state interactions until it was replaced by a revolving loan fund. The program often had produced a tug-of-war between federal and local officials, with the latter seeking to use federal funds to encourage development by extending their sewer systems and the former bent on ensuring that treatment works were constructed at the end of the sewer line.

The heart of the Clean Water Act is section 301's requirement for nationally uniform, technology-based limits on point source discharges administered through a national permit program required by section 402. CEQ explained the rationale for this approach as follows:

> Perhaps the predominant influence on the law was the universal recognition that basing compliance and enforcement efforts on a case-by-case judgment of a particular facility's impacts on ambient water quality is both scientifically and administratively difficult. To minimize the difficulties in relating discharges to ambient water quality, the law requires minimum effluent limitations for each category of discharger, based on technological and economic feasibility, regardless of receiving water requirements. [CEQ, Environmental Quality—1973, at 171 (1973).]

Congress mandated that standards be uniform by industrial category, recognizing that industries varied in their capabilities for reducing pollution. Existing discharg- ers were to employ "best practicable" control technology (BPT) by 1977 and "best available" technology (BAT) by 1983. New dischargers were required by section 306 to meet BAT-based requirements.

Implementation of these requirements, like implementation of the Clean Air Act, has featured missed deadlines, lawsuits, court orders, and, ultimately, statu- tory extensions. Congress in 1977 adopted major amendments to the Clean Water Act that extended the deadlines for compliance with the technology-based effluent limitations and that adjusted the requirements for certain dischargers. The BAT deadline was extended to July 1, 1984, for dischargers of toxic pollutants. For dis- chargers of "conventional pollutants"—BOD, fecal coliform, suspended solids, and pH—BAT requirements were relaxed. Instead of BAT, they were required to achieve "best conventional" technology (BCT) by July 1, 1984, if the incremental benefit of such upgrading exceeded the costs. §304(b)(4). In 1987, these deadlines again were extended because it had taken EPA far longer to establish effluent lim- itations than anticipated.

The 1972 Act required POTWs to provide secondary treatment by 1977 and advanced treatment by 1983. Congress later extended the secondary treatment deadline to July 1988 and eliminated the advanced treatment requirement. POTWs also were required to obtain permits for sludge disposal. Industrial dischargers into POTWs were required by section 307(b) to obtain pretreatment permits to assure that their waste discharges do not interfere with the treatment process. In 1987, Congress allowed POTWs discharging into "marine waters" to receive a waiver from second- ary treatment requirements if there was no interference with water quality standards. §301(h). Effluent limits on point source discharges are discussed in Section C, below. A summary of how they have changed over time is presented in Figure 6.3.

**Figure 6.3   Technology-Based Effluent Limits and Deadlines for Compliance**

| Source | 1972 Act | 1977 Amendments | 1987 Amendments |
|---|---|---|---|
| INDUSTRIAL FACILITIES | BPT by 1977 | For toxics BAT by 1984 or within 3 years | For toxics BAT and for conventional pollutants BCT as soon as possible or within 3 years and no later than 3/31/89 |
| | BAT by 1983 | For conventional pollutants BCT by 1984 | |
| | | *1981 Amendments* | |
| | Secondary treatment by 1977 | Secondary treatment by 1988 | |
| POTWs | Advanced treatment by 1983 | Advanced treatment requirement eliminated | |

The system of ambient water quality standards that Congress had initiated in the 1965 Act was retained primarily to be used as a backup when effluent limitations proved insufficient to protect water quality. States must designate uses for which the water bodies within their jurisdiction are to be protected subject to EPA review of their adequacy to "protect the public health or welfare, enhance the quality of water, and serve the purposes of this Act." §303(c)(2). Permits for point sources must incorporate any more stringent conditions necessary to meet water quality standards, which may be modified for conventional pollutants only if EPA finds the added costs bear no reasonable relationship to the benefits. §302(a). Section 303(d) requires states and tribes to identify waters that do not meet water quality standards and to establish total maximum daily loads (TMDLs) for pollutants that cause violations of such standards. In 1987, Congress in section 304(l) required states to identify waters impaired by toxic pollutants and to establish individual control strategies for sources of such pollutants. Water quality-based controls are discussed in Section D, below.

Nonpoint sources of water pollution are not subject to permit requirements. While section 208 of the Act has long required states to engage in area-wide planning that can encompass measures to control nonpoint source pollution, this program has been ineffective. In 1987, Congress added section 319, which requires states to identify waters impaired by nonpoint source pollution and the sources of such pollution and to prepare management plans for controlling it, subject to EPA approval. See Section F, below.

Section 404 establishes a permit requirement for disposal of dredged and fill material into navigable waters. As discussed in Section E, this permit program, which is administered jointly by the Army Corps of Engineers and EPA, plays an important role in efforts to protect wetlands.

The National Pollutant Discharge Elimination System (NPDES), created in section 402, is the administrative system for issuance of permits to the thousands of individual point source dischargers. States meeting minimum federal requirements may assume primary responsibility for issuance of permits. In states that decline to do so, EPA is required to administer the permit program. EPA retains oversight authority over state permit decisions as well as independent enforcement authority. The Act provides several enforcement options, including administrative compliance orders, administrative penalties, and civil and criminal fines in government actions taken under section 309. Citizen enforcement suits are authorized by section 505(a). Enforcement problems are discussed in Chapter 10, which compares the Clean Water Act's enforcement authorities with those contained in other federal environmental laws.

## NOTES AND QUESTIONS

1. The "zero discharge" and "fishable/swimmable" goals contained in section 101(a) have been widely condemned by economists, who question the logic of even articulating an aspirational standard that appears so expensive and infeasible. Why would Congress adopt such a seemingly unrealistic goal? One clue may be found in Senator Muskie's statement during the debates prior to enactment that "[w]hat we need to produce the technology required by the bill is a national commitment to what we want to achieve — come up with modern technology, new and changed . . ."

2. Consider the principal types of pollution control regulations mandated by the Clean Water Act: (1) a general prohibition on point source discharges except as authorized by permits requiring (a) compliance with technology-based effluent limitations or (b) more stringent effluent limitations when necessary to protect the quality of receiving waters, (2) pretreatment requirements for dischargers to POTWs, and (3) permit requirements for dredge and fill operations. Is the range of controls available under the Clean Water Act more extensive or less extensive than that available under the Clean Air Act? Which Act is most likely to force the development of new technology?

3. Economists have been extremely critical of the Clean Water Act's use of nationally uniform effluent standards for classes and categories of industries. They note that a discharge may be insignificant in one water body (e.g., the Mississippi) but catastrophic in another (a small trout stream or a lake that supplies a town's water supply). Consequently, the benefits of control will vary geographically. Moreover, a focus on the technology available to each industry may result in inefficient allocation of costs *among* industries that may have different costs for controlling the same pollution. Pedersen, Turning the Tide on Water Quality, 15 Ecology L.Q. 69, 83 (1988). You may recall similar concerns in the context of the Clean Air Act. Is the case of uniformity any different in the context of water quality? Cf. Currie, Congress, the Court, and Water Pollution, 1977 Sup. Ct. Rev. 39 (uniformity can lead to overexpenditure but use-based regulation assumes greater knowledge than is practical, is inadequate to allow for growth, does not deal with high concentrations in mixing zones, and does not address aesthetic concerns).

4. A. Myrick Freeman III estimated that the costs of federal water pollution control policy in 1985 ranged from $25 to $30 billion, while the range of estimated benefits was only $6 to $28 billion. Freeman, Water Pollution Policy, in Public Policies for Environmental Protection 125-126 (P. Portney ed., 1990). While Freeman noted that these estimates probably understate benefits (by excluding the benefits of controls on toxic effluents) and overestimate costs (because engineering estimates fail to reflect cost-reducing technological innovation), he deemed it likely that costs outweigh benefits in the aggregate. Freeman argues that the Clean Water Act's current approach should be replaced with "the principle that pollution control policies should be designed to maximize the net benefits from pollution control activities." Id. at 127. Do you agree? Freeman would set water quality standards for each segment of a water body at the point where the "marginal benefits of raising water quality to that point would just equal the marginal cost of doing so," and effluent reduction requirements would vary across dischargers even within the same industrial category. Why do you think Congress eschewed Freeman's approach to pollution control?

5. The distinction between water quality standards and effluent limitations is critical. Water quality standards describe tolerable limits for particular uses (e.g., water suitable for swimming may be limited to no more than 200 fecal coliform bacteria per 100 milliliters). Effluent standards describe an amount of pollution discharged in a time period (e.g., 1 pound of *x* pollutant per day) or more typically a maximum amount per unit of production (e.g., 1 pound of *x* per ton of steel). Which type of system is more responsive to considerations of economic efficiency? Which is more responsive to equity concerns?

6. Water quality standards are roughly comparable to ambient air quality standards. Why was Congress willing to adopt a regulatory scheme for air quality based on ambient standards at almost the same time it was coming to the conclusion that such a system had been a failure in the context of water pollution? Some authorities advocate reconsideration of the water quality standards approach, e.g., Pedersen, above. Based on the Clean Air Act experience, how could such a system be employed effectively?

### 4. The Scope of Federal Authority to Regulate Water Pollution

The Clean Water Act prohibits unpermitted discharges of pollutants to "navigable waters." The term "navigable waters" is defined in section 502(7) to mean "the waters of the United States, including the territorial seas." Questions concerning how broadly to interpret "waters of the United States" and the extent of Congress's constitutional authority to regulate certain waters have generated considerable litigation.

The question of what constitutes the "waters of the United States" for purposes of defining the jurisdictional limits of federal authority under the Clean Water Act is enormously important even apart from the issue of controlling discharges to groundwater. It is estimated that approximately 98 to 99 percent of the nation's water bodies are not waters that would be considered traditionally navigable. The quality of navigable waters is significantly affected by the quality of both their non-navigable tributaries and of wetlands adjacent to both navigable waters and their non-navigable tributaries. In the case that follows the U.S. Supreme Court considered whether wetlands adjacent, but not physically connected to, navigable waters were part of the "waters of the United States," covered by the Clean Water Act's section 404 permit program. Both section 404 and section 402 of the Clean Water Act use "navigable waters" as their touchstone for federal jurisdiction.

## United States v. Riverside Bayview Homes, Inc.

474 U.S. 121 (1985)

WHITE, J., delivered the opinion for a unanimous Court.

This case presents the question whether the Clean Water Act, together with certain regulations promulgated under its authority by the Army Corps of Engineers, authorizes the Corps to require landowners to obtain permits from the Corps before discharging fill material into wetlands adjacent to navigable bodies of water and their tributaries.

The relevant provisions of the Clean Water Act originated in the Federal Water Pollution Control Act Amendments of 1972 and have remained essentially unchanged since that time. Under §§301 and 502 of the Act, any discharge of dredged or fill materials into "navigable waters"—defined as the "waters of the United States"—is forbidden unless authorized by a permit issued by the Corps of Engineers pursuant to §404. After initially construing the Act to cover only waters navigable in fact, in 1975 the Corps issued interim final regulations redefining "the waters of the United States" to include not only actually navigable waters but also tributaries of such waters, interstate waters and their tributaries, and nonnavigable intrastate waters whose use or misuse could affect interstate commerce. 40 Fed. Reg. 31320 (1975). More importantly for present purposes, the Corps construed the Act to cover all "freshwater wetlands" that were adjacent to other covered waters. A "freshwater wetland" was defined as an area that is "periodically inundated" and is "normally characterized by the prevalence of vegetation that requires saturated soil conditions for growth and reproduction." 33 C.F.R. §209.120(d)(2)(h) (1976). In 1977 the Corps refined its definition of wetlands by eliminating the reference to periodic inundation and making other minor changes. The 1977 definition reads as follows:

> The term "wetlands" means those areas that are inundated or saturated by surface or ground water at a frequency and duration sufficient to support, and that under normal circumstances do support, a prevalence of vegetation typically adapted for life in saturated soil conditions. Wetlands generally include swamps, marshes, bogs and similar areas. 33 CFR §323.2(c) (1978).

In 1982, the 1977 regulations were replaced by substantively identical regulations that remain in force today. See 33 C.F.R. §323.2 (1985).

Respondent Riverside Bayview Homes, Inc. (hereafter respondent), owns 80 acres of low-lying, marshy land near the shores of Lake St. Clair in Macomb County, Michigan. In 1976, respondent began to place fill materials on its property as part of its preparations for construction of a housing development. The Corps of Engineers, believing that the property was an "adjacent Wetland" under the 1975 regulation defining "waters of the United States," filed suit in the United States District Court for the Eastern District of Michigan, seeking to enjoin respondent from filling the property without the permission of the Corps.

The District Court held that the portion of respondent's property lying below 575.5 feet above sea level was a covered wetland and enjoined respondent from filling it without a permit. Respondent appealed, and the Court of Appeals remanded for consideration of the effect of the intervening 1977 amendments to the regulation. On remand, the District Court again held the property to be a wetland subject to the Corps' permit authority.

Respondent again appealed, and the Sixth Circuit reversed. 729 F.2d 391 (1984). The court construed the Corps' regulations to exclude from the category of adjacent wetlands—and hence from that of "waters of the United States"—wetlands that were not subject to flooding by adjacent navigable waters at a frequency sufficient to support the growth of aquatic vegetation. . . . Under the court's reading of the regulations, respondent's property was not within the Corps' jurisdiction, because its semi-aquatic characteristics were not the result of frequent flooding by the nearby navigable waters. Respondent was therefore free to fill the property without obtaining a permit.

We granted certiorari to consider the proper interpretation of the Corps' regulations defining "waters of the United States" and the scope of the Corps' jurisdiction under the Clean Water Act, both of which were called into question by the Sixth Circuit's ruling. We now reverse.

[The Court rejected the Sixth Circuit's interpretation of the Corps' regulations and held that they do not require frequent flooding by navigable waters. Rather, "saturation by either surface or ground water is sufficient to bring an area within the category of wetlands, provided that the saturation is sufficient to and does support wetland vegetation." This interpretation "plainly brings [respondent's] property within the category of wetlands as defined by the current regulations."] Hence, it is part of the "waters of the United States" as defined by 33 C.F.R. §323.2 (1985), and if the regulation itself is valid as a construction of the term "waters of the United States" as used in the Clean Water Act, a question which we now address, the property falls within the scope of the Corps' jurisdiction over "navigable waters" under §404 of the Act.

An agency's construction of a statute it is charged with enforcing is entitled to deference if it is reasonable and not in conflict with the expressed intent of Congress. Chevron U.S.A., Inc. v. Natural Resources Defense Council, Inc., 467 U.S. 837 (1984). Accordingly, our review is limited to the question whether it is reasonable, in light of the language, policies, and legislative history of the Act for the Corps to exercise jurisdiction over wetlands adjacent to but not regularly flooded by rivers, streams, and other hydrographic features more conventionally identifiable as "waters."

On a purely linguistic level, it may appear unreasonable to classify "lands," wet or otherwise, as "waters." Such a simplistic response, however, does justice neither to the problem faced by the Corps in defining the scope of its authority under §404(a) nor to the realities of the problem of water pollution that the Clean Water Act was intended to combat. In determining the limits of its power to regulate discharges under the Act, the Corps must necessarily choose some point at which water ends and land begins. Our common experience tells us that this is often no easy task: the transition from water to solid ground is not necessarily or even typically an abrupt one. Rather, between open waters and dry land may lie shallows, marshes, mudflats, swamps, bogs — in short, a huge array of areas that are not wholly aquatic but nevertheless fall far short of being dry land. Where on this continuum to find the limit of "waters" is far from obvious.

Faced with such a problem of defining the bounds of its regulatory authority, an agency may appropriately look to the legislative history and underlying policies of its statutory grants of authority. Neither of these sources provides unambiguous guidance for the Corps in this case, but together they do support the reasonableness of the Corps' approach of defining adjacent wetlands as "waters" within the meaning of §404(a). Section 404 originated as part of the Federal Water Pollution Control Act Amendments of 1972, which constituted a comprehensive legislative attempt "to restore and maintain the chemical, physical, and biological integrity of the Nation's waters." CWA §101. This objective incorporated a broad, systemic view of the goal of maintaining and improving water quality: as the House Report on the legislation put it, "the word 'integrity' . . . refers to a condition in which the natural structure and function of ecosystems is [*sic*] maintained." H.R. Rep. No. 92-911, p. 76 (1972). Protection of aquatic ecosystems, Congress recognized, demanded broad federal authority to control pollution, for "[w]ater moves in hydrologic cycles and it is essential that discharge of pollutants be controlled at the source." S. Rep. No. 92-414, p. 77 (1972).

In keeping with these views, Congress chose to define the waters covered by the Act broadly. Although the Act prohibits discharges into "navigable waters," the Act's definition of "navigable waters" as "the waters of the United States" makes it clear that the term "navigable" as used in the Act is of limited import. In adopting this definition of "navigable waters," Congress evidently intended to repudiate limits that had been placed on federal regulation by earlier water pollution control statutes and to exercise its powers under the Commerce Clause to regulate at least some waters that would not be deemed "navigable" under the classical understanding of that term.

Of course, it is one thing to recognize that Congress intended to allow regulation of waters that might not satisfy traditional tests of navigability; it is another to assert that Congress intended to abandon traditional notions of "waters" and include in that term "wetlands" as well. Nonetheless, the evident breadth of congressional concern for protection of water quality and aquatic ecosystems suggests that it is reasonable for the Corps to interpret the term "waters" to encompass wetlands adjacent to waters as more conventionally defined. Following the lead of the Environmental Protection Agency, the Corps has determined that wetlands adjacent to navigable waters do as a general matter play a key role in protecting and enhancing water quality:

> The regulation of activities that cause water pollution cannot rely on . . . artificial lines . . . but must focus on all waters that together form the entire aquatic system. Water moves in hydrologic cycles, and the pollution of this part of the aquatic system, regardless of whether it is above or below an ordinary high water mark, or mean high tide line, will affect the water quality of the other waters within that aquatic system.
>
> For this reason, the landward limit of Federal jurisdiction under Section 404 must include any adjacent wetlands that form the border of or are in reasonable proximity to other waters of the United States, as these wetlands are part of this aquatic system. 42 Fed. Reg. 37128 (1977).

We cannot say that the Corps' conclusion that adjacent wetlands are inseparably bound up with the "waters" of the United States—based as it is on the Corps' and EPA's technical expertise—is unreasonable. In view of the breadth of federal regulatory authority contemplated by the Act itself and the inherent difficulties of defining precise bounds to regulable waters, the Corps' ecological judgment about the relationship between waters and their adjacent wetlands provides an adequate basis for a legal judgment that adjacent wetlands may be defined as waters under the Act.

This holds true even for wetlands that are not the result of flooding or permeation by water having its source in adjacent bodies of open water. The Corps has concluded that wetlands may affect the water quality of adjacent lakes, rivers, and streams even when the waters of those bodies do not actually inundate the wetlands. . . . Again, we cannot say that the Corps' judgment in these matters is unreasonable, and we therefore conclude that a definition of "waters of the United States" encompassing all wetlands adjacent to other bodies of water over which the Corps has jurisdiction is a permissible interpretation of the Act. Because respondent's property is part of a wetland that actually abuts on a navigable waterway, respondent was required to have a permit in this case. . . .

## NOTES AND QUESTIONS

1. Acknowledging the difficulty of defining jurisdictional boundaries with precision, the Court in *Riverside Bayview* appeared to endorse a functional approach that interprets the jurisdictional reach of section 404 expansively to promote the goals of the Act. The decision reflects concern that a more restrictive interpretation of regulatory authority could undermine the congressional goal of providing comprehensive protection to water quality.

2. While the federal government has not sought to extend its jurisdiction to groundwater, EPA and the Corps broadly defined "waters of the United States" to include not only waters used in, or susceptible to use in interstate commerce, but also:

> (3) All other waters such as intrastate lakes, rivers, streams (including intermittent streams), mudflats, sandflats, wetlands, sloughs, prairie potholes, wet meadows, playa lakes, or natural ponds, the use, degradation or destruction of which could affect interstate or foreign commerce including any such waters:
>
> (i) Which are or could be used by interstate or foreign travelers for recreational or other purposes; or
>
> (ii) From which fish or shellfish are or could be taken and sold in interstate or foreign commerce; or
>
> (iii) Which are or could be used for industrial purposes by industries in interstate commerce. [33 C.F.R. §328.3(a) (Corps), 40 C.F.R. §230.3(s)(3) (EPA).]

3. In a preamble to its regulations, the Corps also suggested that "waters of the United States" include waters that could be used as habitat by migratory birds or endangered species or to irrigate crops sold in interstate commerce. In Hoffman Homes, Inc. v. Administrator, EPA, 999 F.2d 256 (7th Cir. 1993), the Seventh Circuit considered whether section 404's reach extended to an isolated, one-acre wetland. Unlike the wetland area in *Riverside Bayview*, the wetland in *Hoffman Homes* was not adjacent to another body of water, but rather was separated from a small creek by 750 feet. EPA argued that Clean Water Act jurisdiction could be premised on the notion that the wetland was a suitable or potential habitat for migratory birds. The Seventh Circuit agreed with EPA that federal jurisdiction could be premised on a potential effect on interstate commerce, but it found that the agency had failed to provide sufficient evidence to support the conclusion that the wetland was a suitable habitat for migratory birds. The court noted that there was no evidence that migratory birds actually used the wetland and that the area was not shown to have "characteristics whose use by and value to migratory birds is well established. . . ." 999 F.2d at 261. Thus, it found that the wetland was not subject to section 404.

4. The Supreme Court's decision in United States v. Lopez, 514 U.S. 549 (1995), raised new questions concerning the jurisdictional reach of the Clean Water Act. In *Lopez*, the Court held that the Commerce Clause did not give Congress the authority to prohibit the possession of firearms in the vicinity of schools because the statute at issue regulated an activity that did not "substantially affect" interstate commerce. Unlike the statute in *Lopez*, which contained "no jurisdictional element which would ensure, through case-by-case inquiry, that the firearm

possession in question affects interstate commerce," 514 U.S. at 561, the Clean Water Act extends only to "waters of the United States," 33 U.S.C. §1362(7). However, because *Lopez* now requires that regulated activities *substantially* affect interstate commerce, some activities previously deemed regulable because they had some potential effect on interstate commerce could escape federal jurisdiction if their impact is not considered substantial enough. In Solid Waste Agency of Northern Cook County v. U.S. Army Corps of Engineers (SWANCC) the Court was asked to consider whether Congress has the constitutional authority to regulate isolated wetlands used by migratory birds. The provision of the Army Corps of Engineers' definition of "waters of the United States" that extends section 404 jurisdiction on the basis of the use of waters by migratory birds was challenged in this case. Relying on *Lopez*, the petitioner in *SWANCC* argued that Congress could not require it to obtain a federal permit under section 404(a) of the Clean Water Act before it filled an abandoned sand and gravel pit to create a landfill. The Seventh Circuit had upheld application of section 404(a) to the isolated wetland, finding that because it served as habitat for migratory birds, substantial effects on interstate commerce could be inferred from the millions of hunters and bird watchers who travel interstate in pursuit of birds.

*SWANCC* involved land that had been used as a sand and gravel pit mine prior to 1960. Subsequently, the excavation trenches became permanent and seasonal ponds, and the entire area was overgrown. The county solid waste agency proposed to convert the site into a landfill. The Corps initially declined to assert section 404 jurisdiction over the site because it believed that the site contained no jurisdictional wetlands. Later, it reversed its position upon learning that the site was visited by over 100 species of migratory birds. After the Seventh Circuit found for the Corps in a challenge to the Corps' jurisdiction, the solid waste agency sought and was granted certiorari in the Supreme Court. In the following 5-4 decision, the Supreme Court reversed.

## Solid Waste Agency of Northern Cook County v. U.S. Army Corps of Engineers

531 U.S. 159 (2001)

CHIEF JUSTICE REHNQUIST delivered the opinion of the Court.

. . . Section 404(a) grants the Corps authority to issue permits "for the discharge of dredged or fill material into the navigable waters at specified disposal sites." The term "navigable waters" is defined under the Act as "the waters of the United States, including the territorial seas."§1362(7). The Corps has issued regulations defining the term "waters of the United States" to include "waters such as intrastate lakes, rivers, streams (including intermittent streams), mudflats, sandflats, wetlands, sloughs, prairie potholes, wet meadows, playa lakes, or natural ponds, the use, degradation or destruction of which could affect interstate or foreign commerce. . . ." 33 CFR §328.3(a)(3)(1999).

In 1986, in an attempt to "clarify" the reach of its jurisdiction, the Corps stated that §404(a) extends to intrastate waters:

a. Which are or would be used as habitat by birds protected by Migratory Bird Treaties; or

b. Which are or would be used as habitat by other migratory birds which cross state lines; or

c. Which are or would be used as habitat for endangered species; or

d. Used to irrigate crops sold in interstate commerce.

51 Fed. Reg. 41217. This last promulgation has been dubbed the "Migratory Bird Rule.". . .

This is not the first time we have been called upon to evaluate the meaning of §404(a). In United States v. Riverside Bayview Homes, Inc. we held that the Corps had §404(a) jurisdiction over wetlands that actually abutted on a navigable waterway. In so doing, we noted that the term "navigable" is of "limited import" and that Congress evidenced its intent to "regulate at least some waters that would not be deemed 'navigable' under the classical understanding of that term." But our holding was based in large measure upon Congress' unequivocal acquiescence to, and approval of, the Corps' regulations interpreting the CWA to cover wetlands adjacent to navigable waters. We found that Congress' concern for the protection of water quality and aquatic ecosystems indicated its intent to regulate wetlands "inseparably bound up with the 'waters' of the United States."

It was the significant nexus between the wetlands and "navigable waters" that informed our reading of the CWA in *Riverside Bayview Homes*. Indeed, we did not "express any opinion" on the "question of the authority of the Corps to regulate discharges of fill material into wetlands that are not adjacent to bodies of open water. . . ." In order to rule for respondents here we would have to hold that the jurisdiction of the Corps extends to ponds that are *not* adjacent to open water. But we conclude that the text of the statute will not allow this. . . .

Respondents next contend that whatever its original aim in 1972, Congress charted a new course five years later when it approved the more expansive definition of "navigable waters" found in the Corps' 1977 regulations. In July 1977, the Corps formally adopted 33 CFR §323.2(a)(5) (1978), which defined "waters of the United States" to include "isolated wetlands and lakes, intermittent streams, prairie potholes, and other waters that are not part of a tributary system to interstate waters or to navigable waters of the United States, the degradation or destruction of which could affect interstate commerce." Respondents argue that Congress was aware of this more expansive interpretation during its 1977 amendments to the CWA. Specifically, respondents point to a failed House bill, H.R. 3199, that would have defined "navigable waters" as "all waters which are presently used, or are susceptible to use in their natural condition or by reasonable improvement as a means to transport interstate or foreign commerce." The failure to pass legislation that would have overturned the Corps' 1977 regulations and the extension of jurisdiction in §404(g) to waters "other than" traditional "navigable waters," respondents submit, indicate that Congress recognized and accepted a broad definition of "navigable waters" that includes nonnavigable, isolated, intrastate waters.

Although we have recognized congressional acquiescence to administrative interpretations of a statute in some situations, we have done so with extreme care. . . . A bill can be proposed for any number of reasons, and it can be rejected for just as many others. The relationship between the actions and inactions of the

95th Congress and the intent of the 92d Congress in passing §404(a) is also considerably attenuated. Because "subsequent history is less illuminating than the contemporaneous evidence," respondents face a difficult task in overcoming the plain text and import of §404(a).

We conclude that respondents have failed to make the necessary showing that the failure of the 1977 House bill demonstrates Congress' acquiescence to the Corps' regulations or the "Migratory Bird Rule," which, of course, did not first appear until 1986. Although respondents cite some legislative history showing Congress' recognition of the Corps' assertion of jurisdiction over "isolated waters," as we explained in *Riverside Bayview Homes*, "[i]n both Chambers, debate on the proposals to narrow the definition of navigable waters centered largely on the issue of wetlands preservation." Beyond Congress' desire to regulate wetlands adjacent to "navigable waters," respondents point us to no persuasive evidence that the House bill was proposed in response to the Corps' claim of jurisdiction over non-navigable, isolated, intrastate waters or that its failure indicated congressional acquiescence to such jurisdiction. . . .

We thus decline respondents' invitation to take what they see as the next ineluctable step after *Riverside Bayview Homes*, holding that isolated ponds, some only seasonal, wholly located within two Illinois counties, fall under §404(a)'s definition of "navigable waters" because they serve as habitat for migratory birds. As counsel for respondents conceded at oral argument, such a ruling would assume that "the use of the word navigable in the statute . . . does not have any independent significance." We cannot agree that Congress' separate definitional use of the phrase "waters of the United States" constitutes a basis for reading the term "navigable waters" out of the statute. We said in *Riverside Bayview Homes* that the word "navigable" in the statute was of "limited effect" and went on to hold that §404(a) extended to nonnavigable wetlands adjacent to open waters. But it is one thing to give a word limited effect and quite another to give it no effect whatever. The term "navigable" has at least the import of showing us what Congress had in mind as its authority for enacting the CWA: its traditional jurisdiction over waters that were or had been navigable in fact or which could reasonably be so made.

Respondents — relying upon all of the arguments addressed above — contend that, at the very least, it must be said that Congress did not address the precise question of §404(a)'s scope with regard to nonnavigable, isolated, intra-state waters, and that, therefore, we should give deference to the "Migratory Bird Rule." See, e.g., Chevron U.S.A., Inc. v. Natural Resources Defense Council, Inc., 467 U.S. 837 (1984). We find §404(a) to be clear, but even were we to agree with respondents, we would not extend *Chevron* deference here.

Where an administrative interpretation of a statute invokes the outer limits of Congress' power, we expect a clear indication that Congress intended that result. . . . .

Twice in the past six years we have reaffirmed the proposition that the grant of authority to Congress under the Commerce Clause, though broad, is not unlimited. See United States v. Morrison, 529 U.S. 598 (2000); United States v. Lopez, 514 U.S. 549 (1995). . . .

These are significant constitutional questions raised by respondents' application of their regulations, and yet we find nothing approaching a clear statement from Congress that it intended §404(a) to reach an abandoned sand and gravel pit such as we have here. Permitting respondents to claim federal jurisdiction over ponds and mudflats falling within the "Migratory Bird Rule" would result in a significant impingement of the States' traditional and primary power over land and water use. Rather than expressing a desire to readjust the federal-state balance in this manner, Congress chose to "recognize, preserve, and protect the primary responsibilities and rights of States . . . to plan the development and use . . . of land and water resources. . . ." 33 U.S.C. §1251(b). We thus read the statute as written to avoid the significant constitutional and federalism questions raised by respondents' interpretation, and therefore reject the request for administrative deference.

We hold that 33 CFR §328.3(a)(3)(1999), as clarified and applied to petitioner's balefill site pursuant to the "Migratory Bird Rule," exceeds the authority granted to respondents under §404(a) of the CWA. The judgment of the Court of Appeals for the Seventh Circuit is therefore
*Reversed.*

## NOTES AND QUESTIONS

1.  In a sharp dissent, Justice Stevens, joined by Justices Souter, Ginsburg, and Breyer, argued that the Court had misapprehended the meaning of both the 1972 Act and Congress's 1977 acquiescence in the Corps' more expansive regulations.

2.  How did the Court distinguish *Riverside Bayview Homes*? Compare the approach to statutory construction used in *Riverside Bayview* with the approach used in *SWANCC*. Why does the Court find that wetlands adjacent to navigable waters are covered by section 404 in *Riverside Bayview*, but that the isolated wetlands in *SWANCC* are not? Does the statutory language make any distinction between these two? The U.S. Army Corps of Engineers argued in its brief that the term "isolated wetlands" is misleading because waters that are remote from and lack a direct connection to navigable waters may have other hydrologic connections to, and affect the quality of, traditional navigable waters, e.g., through groundwater connections and flood and erosion control.

3.  Why did the Court reject the Corps' argument for *Chevron* deference to its interpretation of the scope of its authority? Is the Court's use of *Chevron* in *SWANCC* consistent with its treatment in *Riverside Bayview*? See Michael P. Healy, Textualism's Limits on the Administrative State: Of Isolated Waters, Barking Dogs, and *Chevron*, 31 Envtl. L. Rep. 10928 (2001).

4.  *SWANCC* was decided by the same 5-4 lineup of Justices that prevailed in *Lopez*. While the Court declined to reach the *Lopez* question by refusing to decide whether Congress had the constitutional authority to regulate isolated wetlands, how did the constitutional question affect the Court's ultimate holding in *SWANCC*?

5.  In January 2003, EPA and the Army Corps of Engineers solicited comment on how they should redefine "waters of the United States" in response to *SWANCC*. 68 Fed. Reg. 1,991 (2003). The two agencies issued a joint memorandum stating that *SWANCC* "squarely eliminates CWA jurisdiction over isolated waters that are intrastate and non-navigable, where the sole basis for asserting federal jurisdiction is the actual or potential use of the waters as habitat for migratory birds that cross state lines in their migrations." Despite concern that EPA and the Corps would issue a more restrictive definition of "waters of the United States," the agencies abandoned this effort in December 2003 following a White House meeting where a

group of Republican sportsmen persuaded President Bush not to weaken wetlands protections.

6. Most lower courts interpreted *SWANCC* as restricting federal authority only where it turned solely on the potential presence of migratory birds. But the Fifth Circuit concluded that federal jurisdiction extended only to waters that are actually navigable or adjacent to an open body of navigable water. The U.S. Supreme Court agreed to review two Sixth Circuit decisions that upheld federal jurisdiction over wetlands adjacent to non-navigable tributaries of navigable waters. One of the cases involved review of a civil enforcement judgment, United States v. Rapanos, 376 F.3d 629 (6th Cir. 2004), against a man who had been convicted of criminal violations of section 404 for filling wetlands in open defiance of both a state cease-and-desist order and an EPA administrative compliance order. The *Rapanos* case was consolidated with review of Carabell v. U.S. Army Corps of Engineers, 391 F.3d 704 (6th Cir. 2004), which had upheld section 404 jurisdiction over wetlands separated by an earthen berm from a non-navigable tributary of navigable waters. A sharply divided Court issued the following decision.

## Rapanos v. United States

547 U.S. 715 (2006)

JUSTICE SCALIA announced the judgment of the Court, and delivered an opinion, in which THE CHIEF JUSTICE, JUSTICE THOMAS, and JUSTICE ALITO join.

In April 1989, petitioner John A. Rapanos backfilled wetlands on a parcel of land in Michigan that he owned and sought to develop. This parcel included 54 acres of land with sometimes-saturated soil conditions. The nearest body of navigable water was 11 to 20 miles away. Regulators had informed Mr. Rapanos that his saturated fields were "waters of the United States" that could not be filled without a permit. Twelve years of criminal and civil litigation ensued. . . .

We first addressed the proper interpretation of §502(7)'s phrase "the waters of the United States" in United States v. Riverside Bayview Homes, Inc. That case concerned a wetland that "was adjacent to a body of navigable water," because "the area characterized by saturated soil conditions and wetland vegetation extended beyond the boundary of respondent's property to . . . a navigable waterway." Noting that "the transition from water to solid ground is not necessarily or even typically an abrupt one," and that "the Corps must necessarily choose some point at which water ends and land begins," we upheld the Corps' interpretation of "the waters of the United States" to include wetlands that "actually abut[ted] on" traditional navigable waters. . . .

In *SWANCC*, we considered the application of the Corps' "Migratory Bird Rule" to "an abandoned sand and gravel pit in northern Illinois." 531 U.S., at 162. Observing that "[i]t was the *significant nexus* between the wetlands and 'navigable waters'" that informed our reading of the CWA in *Riverside Bayview*," *id.* at 167 (emphasis added), we held that *Riverside Bayview* did not establish "that the jurisdiction of the Corps extends to ponds that are not adjacent to open water." 531 U.S., at 168 (emphasis deleted). On the contrary, we held that "nonnavigable, isolated, intrastate waters,"—which, unlike the wetlands at issue in *Riverside Bayview*, did not "actually abu[t] on a navigable waterway,"—were not included as "waters of the United States." . . .

The *Rapanos* petitioners contend that the terms "navigable waters" and "waters of the United States" in the Act must be limited to the traditional definition of *The Daniel Ball*, which required that the "waters" be navigable in fact, or susceptible of being rendered so. See 10 Wall., at 563. But this definition cannot be applied wholesale to the CWA. The Act uses the phrase "navigable waters" as a *defined* term, and the definition is simply "the waters of the United States." §502(7). Moreover, the Act provides, in certain circumstances, for the substitution of state for federal jurisdiction over "navigable waters . . . *other than* those waters which are presently used, or are susceptible to use in their natural condition or by reasonable improvement as a means to transport interstate or foreign commerce . . . including wetlands adjacent thereto." §404(g)(1) (emphasis added). This provision shows that the Act's term "navigable waters" includes something more than traditional navigable waters. We have twice stated that the meaning of "navigable waters" in the Act is broader than the traditional understanding of that term, *SWANCC*, 531 U.S., at 167; *Riverside Bayview*, 474 U.S., at 133. We have also emphasized, however, that the qualifier "navigable" is not devoid of significance.

We need not decide the precise extent to which the qualifiers "navigable" and "of the United States" restrict the coverage of the Act. Whatever the scope of these qualifiers, the CWA authorizes federal jurisdiction only over "waters." §502(7). The only natural definition of the term "waters," our prior and subsequent judicial constructions of it, clear evidence from other provisions of the statute, and this Court's canons of construction all confirm that "the waters of the United States" in §502(7) cannot bear the expansive meaning that the Corps would give it.

The Corps' expansive approach might be arguable if the CWA defined "navigable waters" as "water of the United States." But "the waters of the United States" is something else. The use of the definite article ("the") and the plural number ("waters") show plainly that §502(7) does not refer to water in general. In this form, "the waters" refers more narrowly to water "[a]s found in streams and bodies forming geographical features such as oceans, rivers, [and] lakes," or "the flowing or moving masses, as of waves or floods, making up such streams or bodies." Webster's New International Dictionary 2882 (2d ed. 1954) (hereinafter Webster's Second). On this definition, "the waters of the United States" include only relatively permanent, standing or flowing bodies of water. The definition refers to water as found in "streams," "oceans," "rivers," "lakes," and "bodies" of water "forming geographical features." All of these terms connote continuously present, fixed bodies of water, as opposed to ordinarily dry channels through which water occasionally or intermittently flows. Even the least substantial of the definition's terms, namely "streams," connotes a continuous flow of water in a permanent channel—especially when used in company with other terms such as "rivers," "lakes," and "oceans." None of these terms encompasses transitory puddles or ephemeral flows of water.

The restriction of "the waters of the United States" to exclude channels containing merely intermittent or ephemeral flow also accords with the commonsense understanding of the term. In applying the definition to "ephemeral streams," "wet meadows," storm sewers and culverts, "directional sheet flow during storm events," drain tiles, man-made drainage ditches, and dry arroyos in the middle of the desert, the Corps has stretched the term "waters of the United States" beyond parody. The plain language of the statute simply does not authorize this "Land Is Waters" approach to federal jurisdiction.

In addition, the Act's use of the traditional phrase "navigable waters" (the defined term) further confirms that it confers jurisdiction only over relatively *permanent* bodies of water. The Act adopted that traditional term from its predecessor statutes. On the traditional understanding, "navigable waters" included only discrete *bodies* of water. For example, in *The Daniel Ball*, we used the terms "waters" and "rivers" interchangeably. 10 Wall., at 563. And in *Appalachian Electric*, we consistently referred to the "navigable waters" as "waterways." Plainly, because such "waters" had to be navigable in fact or susceptible of being rendered so, the term did not include ephemeral flows. As we noted in *SWANCC*, the traditional term "navigable waters"—even though defined as "the waters of the United States"—carries *some* of its original substance: "[I]t is one thing to give a word limited effect and quite another to give it no effect whatever." That limited effect includes, at bare minimum, the ordinary presence of water.

Our subsequent interpretation of the phrase "the waters of the United States" in the CWA likewise confirms this limitation of its scope. In *Riverside Bayview*, we stated that the phrase in the Act referred primarily to "rivers, streams, and other *hydrographic features more conventionally identifiable as 'waters'*" than the wetlands adjacent to such features. 474 U.S., at 131 (emphasis added). We thus echoed the dictionary definition of "waters" as referring to "streams and bodies *forming geographical features* such as oceans, rivers, [and] lakes." Webster's Second 2882 (emphasis added). Though we upheld in that case the inclusion of wetlands abutting such a "hydrographic featur[e]"—principally due to the difficulty of drawing any clear boundary between the two—nowhere did we suggest that "the waters of the United States" should be expanded to include, in their own right, entities other than "hydrographic features more conventionally identifiable as 'waters.'" Likewise, in both *Riverside Bayview* and *SWANCC*, we repeatedly described the "navigable waters" covered by the Act as "open water" and "open waters." Under no rational interpretation are typically dry channels described as "*open* waters."

Most significant of all, the CWA itself categorizes the channels and conduits that typically carry intermittent flows of water separately from "navigable waters," by including them in the definition of "'point source.'" The Act defines "'point source'" as "any discernible, confined and discrete conveyance, including but not limited to any pipe, ditch, channel, tunnel, conduit, well, discrete fissure, container, rolling stock, concentrated animal feeding operation, or vessel or other floating craft, from which pollutants are or may be discharged." 33 U.S.C. §1362(14). It also defines "'discharge of a pollutant'" as "any addition of any pollutant *to* navigable waters *from* any point source." §1362(12)(A) (emphases added). The definitions thus conceive of "point sources" and "navigable waters" as separate and distinct categories. The definition of "discharge" would make little sense if the two categories were significantly overlapping. The separate classification of "ditch[es], channel[s], and conduit[s]"—which are terms ordinarily used to describe the watercourses through which *intermittent* waters typically flow—shows that these are, by and large, *not* "waters of the United States."

Moreover, only the foregoing definition of "waters" is consistent with the CWA's stated "policy of Congress to recognize, preserve, and protect the primary responsibilities and rights of the States to prevent, reduce, and eliminate pollution, [and] to plan the development and use (including restoration, preservation, and enhancement) of land and water resources. . . ." §1251(b). . . .

Even if the phrase "the waters of the United States" were ambiguous as applied to intermittent flows, our own canons of construction would establish that the Corps' interpretation of the statute is impermissible. As we noted in *SWANCC*, the Government's expansive interpretation would "result in a significant impingement of the States' traditional and primary power over land and water use." . . .

Likewise, just as we noted in *SWANCC*, the Corps' interpretation stretches the outer limits of Congress's commerce power and raises difficult questions about the ultimate scope of that power. (In developing the current regulations, the Corps consciously sought to extend its authority to the farthest reaches of the commerce power. See 42 Fed. Reg. 37127 (1977).) Even if the term "the waters of the United States" were ambiguous as applied to channels that sometimes host ephemeral flows of water (which it is not), we would expect a clearer statement from Congress to authorize an agency theory of jurisdiction that presses the envelope of constitutional validity.

In sum, on its only plausible interpretation, the phrase "the waters of the United States" includes only those relatively permanent, standing or continuously flowing bodies of water "forming geographic features" that are described in ordinary parlance as "streams[,] . . . oceans, rivers, [and] lakes." See Webster's Second 2882. The phrase does not include channels through which water flows intermittently or ephemerally, or channels that periodically provide drainage for rainfall. The Corps' expansive interpretation of the "the waters of the United States" is thus not "based on a permissible construction of the statute." *Chevron*, 467 U.S., at 843. . . .

When we characterized the holding of *Riverside Bayview* in *SWANCC*, we referred to the close connection between waters and the wetlands that they gradually blend into: "It was the *significant nexus* between the wetlands and 'navigable waters' that informed our reading of the CWA in *Riverside Bayview Homes*." 531 U.S. at 167 (emphasis added). In particular, *SWANCC* rejected the notion that the ecological considerations upon which the Corps relied in *Riverside Bayview*—and upon which the dissent repeatedly relies today—provided an *independent* basis for including entities like "wetlands" (or "ephemeral streams") within the phrase "the waters of the United States." *SWANCC* found such ecological considerations irrelevant to the question whether physically isolated waters come within the Corps' jurisdiction. It thus confirmed that *Riverside Bayview* rested upon the inherent ambiguity in defining where water ends and abutting ("adjacent") wetlands begin, permitting the Corps' reliance on ecological considerations *only to resolve that ambiguity* in favor of treating all abutting wetlands as waters. Isolated ponds were not "waters of the United States" in their own right and presented no boundary-drawing problem that would have justified the invocation of ecological factors to treat them as such.

Therefore, *only* those wetlands with a continuous surface connection to bodies that are "waters of the United States" in their own right, so that there is no clear demarcation between "waters" and wetlands, are "adjacent to" such waters and covered by the Act. Wetlands with only an intermittent, physically remote hydrologic connection to "waters of the United States" do not implicate the boundary-drawing problem of *Riverside Bayview*, and thus lack the necessary connection to covered waters that we described as a "significant nexus" in *SWANCC*. Thus, establishing that wetlands such as those at the Rapanos and Carabell sites are covered by the Act requires two findings: First, that the adjacent channel contains a "wate[r] of the United States," (*i.e.*, a relatively permanent body of water connected to traditional interstate navigable waters); and second, that the wetland has a continuous surface connection with that water, making it difficult to determine where the "water" ends and the "wetland" begins. . . .

Because the Sixth Circuit applied the wrong standard to determine if these wetlands are covered "waters of the United States," and because of the paucity of the record in both of these cases, the lower courts should determine, in the first instance, whether the ditches or drains near each wetland are "waters" in the ordinary sense of containing a relatively permanent flow; and (if they are) whether the wetlands in question are "adjacent" to these "waters" in the sense of possessing a continuous surface connection that creates the boundary-drawing problem we addressed in *Riverside Bayview*.

JUSTICE KENNEDY, concurring in the judgment.

These consolidated cases require the Court to decide whether the term "navigable waters" in the Clean Water Act extends to wetlands that do not contain and are not adjacent to waters that are navigable in fact. In *SWANCC*, the Court held, under the circumstances presented there, that to constitute "'navigable waters'" under the Act, a water or wetland must possess a "significant nexus" to waters that are or were navigable in fact or that could reasonably be so made. In the instant cases neither the plurality opinion nor the dissent by Justice Stevens chooses to apply this test; and though the Court of Appeals recognized the test's applicability, it did not consider all the factors necessary to determine whether the lands in question had, or did not have, the requisite nexus. In my view the cases ought to be remanded to the Court of Appeals for proper consideration of the nexus requirement. . . .

*Riverside Bayview* and *SWANCC* establish the framework for the inquiry in the cases now before the Court: Do the Corps' regulations, as applied to the wetlands in *Carabell* and the three wetlands parcels in *Rapanos*, constitute a reasonable interpretation of "navigable waters" as in *Riverside Bayview* or an invalid construction as in *SWANCC*? Taken together these cases establish that in some instances, as exemplified by *Riverside Bayview*, the connection between a nonnavigable water or wetland and a navigable water may be so close, or potentially so close, that the Corps may deem the water or wetland a "navigable water" under the Act. In other instances, as exemplified by *SWANCC*, there may be little or no connection. Absent a significant nexus, jurisdiction under the Act is lacking. Because neither the plurality nor the dissent addresses the nexus requirement, this separate opinion, in my respectful view, is necessary. . . .

[Justice Kennedy then rejects the plurality's interpretation that only waters with a continuous surface connection to standing or continuously flowing waters are covered by section 404. He argues that this is contrary to the statutory text and congressional purpose.]

In sum the plurality's opinion is inconsistent with the Act's text, structure, and purpose. As a fallback the plurality suggests that avoidance canons would compel its reading even if the text were unclear. In *SWANCC*, as one reason for rejecting the Corps' assertion of jurisdiction over the isolated ponds at issue there, the Court observed that this "application of [the Corps'] regulations" would raise significant questions of Commerce Clause authority and encroach on traditional state land-use regulation. . . .

The concerns addressed in *SWANCC* do not support the plurality's interpretation of the Act. In *SWANCC*, by interpreting the Act to require a significant nexus with navigable waters, the Court avoided applications—those involving waters without a significant nexus—that appeared likely, as a category, to raise constitutional difficulties and federalism concerns. Here, in contrast, the plurality's interpretation does not fit the avoidance concerns it raises. On the one hand, when a surface-water connection is lacking, the plurality forecloses jurisdiction over wetlands that abut navigable-in-fact waters—even though such navigable waters were traditionally subject to federal authority. On the other hand, by saying the Act covers wetlands (however remote) possessing a surface-water connection with a continuously flowing stream (however small), the plurality's reading would permit applications of the statute as far from traditional federal authority as are the waters it deems beyond the statute's reach. Even assuming, then, that federal regulation of remote wetlands and nonnavigable waterways would raise a difficult Commerce Clause issue notwithstanding those waters' aggregate effects on national water quality, but cf. Wickard v. Filburn, 317 U.S. 111 (1942), the plurality's reading is not responsive to this concern. As for States' "responsibilities and rights," §101(b), it is noteworthy that 33 States plus the District of Columbia have filed an *amici* brief in this litigation asserting that the Clean Water Act is important to their own water policies. These *amici* note, among other things, that the Act protects downstream States from out-of-state pollution that they cannot themselves regulate. . . .

Consistent with *SWANCC* and *Riverside Bayview* and with the need to give the term "navigable" some meaning, the Corps' jurisdiction over wetlands depends upon the existence of a significant nexus between the wetlands in question and navigable waters in the traditional sense. The required nexus must be assessed in terms of the statute's goals and purposes. Congress enacted the law to "restore and maintain the chemical, physical, and biological integrity of the Nation's waters," §101(a), and it pursued that objective by restricting dumping and filling in "navigable waters," §§301(a), 502(12). With respect to wetlands, the rationale for Clean Water Act regulation is, as the Corps has recognized, that wetlands can perform critical functions related to the integrity of other waters—functions such as pollutant trapping, flood control, and runoff storage. 33 CFR §320.4(b)(2). Accordingly, wetlands possess the requisite nexus, and thus come within the statutory phrase "navigable waters," if the wetlands, either alone or in combination with similarly situated lands in the region, significantly affect the chemical, physical, and biological integrity of other covered waters more readily understood as "navigable." When, in contrast, wetlands' effects on water quality are speculative or insubstantial, they fall outside the zone fairly encompassed by the statutory term "navigable waters."

Although the dissent acknowledges that wetlands' ecological functions vis-à-vis other covered waters are the basis for the Corps' regulation of them, it concludes that the ambiguity in the phrase "navigable waters" allows the Corps to construe the statute as reaching all "non-isolated wetlands," just as it construed the Act to reach the wetlands adjacent to navigable-in-fact waters in *Riverside Bayview*. This, though, seems incorrect. The Corps' theory of jurisdiction in these consolidated cases — adjacency to tributaries, however remote and insubstantial — raises concerns that go beyond the holding of *Riverside Bayview*, and so the Corps' assertion of jurisdiction cannot rest on that case.

As applied to wetlands adjacent to navigable-in-fact waters, the Corps' conclusive standard for jurisdiction rests upon a reasonable inference of ecologic interconnection, and the assertion of jurisdiction for those wetlands is sustainable under the Act by showing adjacency alone. That is the holding of *Riverside Bayview*. Furthermore, although the *Riverside Bayview* Court reserved the question of the Corps' authority over "wetlands that are not adjacent to bodies of open water," and in any event addressed no factual situation other than wetlands adjacent to navigable-in-fact waters, it may well be the case that *Riverside Bayview*'s reasoning — supporting jurisdiction without any inquiry beyond adjacency — could apply equally to wetlands adjacent to certain major tributaries. Through regulations or adjudication, the Corps may choose to identify categories of tributaries that, due to their volume of flow (either annually or on average), their proximity to navigable waters, or other relevant considerations, are significant enough that wetlands adjacent to them are likely, in the majority of cases, to perform important functions for an aquatic system incorporating navigable waters.

The Corps' existing standard for tributaries, however, provides no such assurance. As noted earlier, the Corps deems a water a tributary if it feeds into a traditional navigable water (or a tributary thereof) and possesses an ordinary high-water mark, defined as a "line on the shore established by the fluctuations of water and indicated by [certain] physical characteristics," §328.3(e). This standard presumably provides a rough measure of the volume and regularity of flow. Assuming it is subject to reasonably consistent application, it may well provide a reasonable measure of whether specific minor tributaries bear a sufficient nexus with other regulated waters to constitute "navigable waters" under the Act. Yet the breadth of this standard — which seems to leave wide room for regulation of drains, ditches, and streams remote from any navigable-in-fact water and carrying only minor water-volumes towards it — precludes its adoption as the determinative measure of whether adjacent wetlands are likely to play an important role in the integrity of an aquatic system comprising navigable waters as traditionally understood. Indeed, in many cases wetlands adjacent to tributaries covered by this standard might appear little more related to navigable-in-fact waters than were the isolated ponds held to fall beyond the Act's scope in *SWANCC*.

When the Corps seeks to regulate wetlands adjacent to navigable-in-fact waters, it may rely on adjacency to establish its jurisdiction. Absent more specific regulations, however, the Corps must establish a significant nexus on a case-by-case basis when it seeks to regulate wetlands based on adjacency to nonnavigable tributaries. Given the potential overbreadth of the Corps' regulations, this showing is necessary to avoid unreasonable applications of the statute. Where an adequate nexus is established for a particular wetland, it may be permissible, as a matter of administrative convenience or necessity, to presume covered status for other comparable wetlands in the region. That issue, however, is neither raised by these facts nor addressed by any agency regulation that accommodates the nexus requirement outlined here.

This interpretation of the Act does not raise federalism or Commerce Clause concerns sufficient to support a presumption against its adoption. To be sure, the significant nexus requirement may not align perfectly with the traditional extent of federal authority. Yet in most cases regulation of wetlands that are adjacent to tributaries and possess a significant nexus with navigable waters will raise no serious constitutional or federalism difficulty. As explained earlier, moreover, and as exemplified by *SWANCC*, the significant-nexus test itself prevents problematic applications of the statute. The possibility of legitimate Commerce Clause and federalism concerns in some circumstances does not require the adoption of an interpretation that departs in all cases from the Act's text and structure. See Gonzalez v. Raich, 545 U.S. 1 (2005).

In both the consolidated cases before the Court the record contains evidence suggesting the possible existence of a significant nexus according to the principles outlined above. Thus the end result in these cases and many others to be considered by the Corps may be the same as that suggested by the dissent, namely, that the Corps' assertion of jurisdiction is valid. Given, however, that neither the agency nor the reviewing courts properly considered the issue, a remand is appropriate, in my view, for application of the controlling legal standard.

JUSTICE STEVENS, with whom JUSTICE SOUTER, JUSTICE GINSBURG, and JUSTICE BREYER join, dissenting.

. . . The narrow question presented . . . is whether wetlands adjacent to tributaries of traditionally navigable waters are "waters of the United States" subject to the jurisdiction of the Army Corps . . . . The broader question is whether regulations that have protected the quality of our waters for decades, that were implicitly approved by Congress, and that have been repeatedly enforced in case after case, must now be revised in light of the creative criticisms voiced by the plurality and Justice Kennedy today. Rejecting more than 30 years of practice by the Army Corps, the plurality disregards the nature of the congressional delegation to the agency and the technical and complex character of the issues at stake. Justice Kennedy similarly fails to defer sufficiently to the Corps, though his approach is far more faithful to our precedents and to principles of statutory interpretation than is the plurality's.

In my view, the proper analysis is straightforward. The Army Corps has determined that wetlands adjacent to tributaries of traditionally navigable waters preserve the quality of our Nation's waters by, among other things, providing habitat for aquatic animals, keeping excessive sediment and toxic pollutants out of adjacent waters, and reducing downstream flooding by absorbing water at times of high flow. The Corps' resulting decision to treat these wetlands as encompassed within the term "waters of the United States" is a quintessential example of the Executive's reasonable interpretation of a statutory provision.

Our unanimous decision in *Riverside Bayview* was faithful to our duty to respect the work product of the Legislative and Executive Branches of our Government. Today's judicial amendment of the Clean Water Act is not.

## NOTES AND QUESTIONS

1. Given the 4-1-4 split of the Justices, what is the Court's holding?

2. What would the government have to show to satisfy Justice Kennedy's "substantial nexus" test? How do the plurality, Justice Kennedy, and the dissenters each differ in their interpretation of what was decided by the Court in *Riverside Bayview* and *SWANCC?*

3. In a concurring opinion, Chief Justice Roberts expressed regret that because "no opinion commands a majority of the Court . . . [l]ower courts and regulated entities will now have to feel their way on a case-by-case basis." He suggested that this problem "could have been avoided" if the Corps had issued new regulations clarifying section 404's reach because such regulations would qualify for *Chevron* deference. Is the Chief Justice suggesting that *Chevron* deference would leave the Corps free to adopt a broader definition of "waters of the United States" than that articulated by Justice Scalia, whose opinion the Chief Justice joined?

4. In other portions of his opinion, Justice Scalia claimed that section 404 imposes high costs on landowners, and he dismissed ecological concerns about filling wetlands. Justice Kennedy called Scalia's opinion "unduly dismissive" of the "[i]mportant public interests . . . served by the Clean Water Act in general and by the protection of wetlands in particular." Justice Stevens decried the plurality's "antagonism to environmentalism." Responding to Scalia's claim that his dissent is "policy-laden" Stevens observed that "[t]he policy considerations that have influenced my thinking are Congress' rather than my own."

5. Could the plurality's interpretation of "waters of the United States" affect federal jurisdiction to require NPDES permits under section 402? While both section 404 and section 402 use the same jurisdictional terms, Justice Scalia emphatically rejected the government's argument that it could. He noted that "[t]he Act does not forbid the 'addition of any pollutant *directly* to navigable waters from any point source,' but rather the 'addition of any pollutant *to* navigable waters.'" §502(12)(A) (emphasis added); §301(a). Thus, he maintained that "the discharge into intermittent channels of any pollutant *that naturally washes downstream* likely violates §301(a), even if the pollutants discharged from a point source do not emit 'directly into' covered waters, but pass 'through conveyances' in between." As discussed below, this subsequently influenced Justice Kavanaugh's vote in County of Maui v. Hawaii Wildlife Fund, see page 618.

6. On remand, the government had little trouble satisfying Justice Kennedy's "substantial nexus" test. Thus, in December 2008, John Rapanos and his co-defendants agreed to settle with the federal government by paying a $150,000 civil penalty, restoring approximately 100 acres of wetlands at a cost of $750,000, and granting the state of Michigan a conservation easement over another 134 acres of wetlands. Associated Press, Deal Reached in Decades-Old Michigan Wetlands Dispute, Dec. 29, 2009.

7. Despite efforts by some members of Congress to reverse the *Rapanos* decision, no legislation has been adopted given political gridlock in Congress. If you were to draft a bill to reverse *Rapanos* and restore federal jurisdiction to what it was before the decision, how would you define "waters of the United States"? Would you remove the word "navigable" from the Clean Water Act's jurisdictional definition?

8. *Rapanos* understandably created enormous confusion concerning the scope of federal jurisdiction under the Clean Water Act. While Justice Kennedy cast the decisive vote in the case, his "substantial nexus" test was expressly rejected by the other eight Justices. The Supreme Court refused to hear cases that would provide an opportunity to clarify the *Rapanos* decision, despite the urging of the U.S. Department of Justice. Finally, EPA and the Army Corps of Engineers ("the agencies") tried to clarify the reach of federal jurisdiction by adopting what became known as the "Waters of the U.S." (WOTUS) Rule.

### The Waters of the U.S. (WOTUS) and Navigable Waters Protection Rules (NWPR)

In September 2013, EPA's Science Advisory Board (SAB) released for public comment a new draft scientific report on "Connectivity of Streams and Wetlands to Downstream Waters: A Review and Synthesis of the Scientific Evidence." The report, based on review of more than 1,000 scientific studies, served as the basis for a new EPA rulemaking to clarify the scope of federal jurisdiction under the Clean Water Act. The "waters of the U.S." or WOTUS rulemaking began in April 2014, 79 Fed. Reg. 28,188 (2014), and concluded in May 2015. A copy of the SAB report is archived online at *http://cfpub.epa.gov/ncea/cfm/recordisplay.cfm?deid=238345.*

Based on the conclusions of the SAB report, EPA proposed to clarify federal jurisdiction under the Clean Water Act by defining "waters of the U.S." with particular reference to what would satisfy the "substantial nexus" test articulated in *Rapanos* by Justice Kennedy. EPA's proposed rule retained the same general structure as the 1986 regulation and many of the same provisions. The agencies did not propose to change the status of primary waters (traditional navigable waters, interstate waters, and the territorial seas) or impoundments. Nor did the agencies propose any revisions to the existing exclusions for waste treatment systems, prior converted cropland, or any of the exemptions from CWA permitting requirements. The agencies did propose clarifying "bright line categories" of waters that would be covered, additional categories of waters that would not be covered, and waters that would be protected only after case-specific analyses. The agencies also proposed to define several terms relevant to the significant nexus standard.

EPA received more than one million comments on the proposed rule and conducted 400 meetings with stakeholders during the rulemaking process. The rulemaking record contained 20,400 documents running more than 350,000 pages. EPA and the Corps provided 17 volumes of responses to the comments they received in the rulemaking. On June 29, 2015, the final rule was published in the Federal Register, 80 Fed. Reg. 37,054 (2015). The final rule sought to provide "simpler, clearer, and more consistent approaches for identifying the geographic scope of the CWA" by defining "significant nexus." It grouped waters into three categories: (1) jurisdictional waters, (2) waters that will be found to be jurisdictional only upon a case-specific showing of a "significant nexus" with a primary water, and (3) waters and aquatic features expressly excluded from Clean Water Act jurisdiction. 80 Fed. Reg. at 37,057.

The rule explained that a water meets the "significant nexus" test if it is "a water, including wetlands, either alone or in combination with other similarly situated waters in the region" that "significantly affects the chemical, physical, or biological integrity" of a primary water. Under the rule, jurisdictional waters include:

(1) primary waters and impoundments, (2) tributaries of primary waters, and (3) adjacent waters. Other waters become jurisdictional only if a case-specific analysis reveals the requisite "significant nexus." These include (1) prairie potholes, (2) Carolina and Delmarva bays, (3) pocosins, (4) western vernal pools in California, and (5) Texas coastal prairie wetlands. With the exception of these five types of waters, the only others that will be evaluated on a case-specific basis are waters that are located within the 100-year floodplain of a primary water or within 4,000 feet of the high-tide line or ordinary high-water mark of a primary water, impoundment, or tributary.

Waters specifically excluded from federal jurisdiction under the final rule included prior converted cropland, water treatment systems, erosional features, ditches not located in tributaries or that do not drain wetlands, and groundwater. By for the first time specifically excluding by rule waters that are neither among the five categories listed above nor located within a 100-year floodplain or within 4,000 feet of the high-tide line or high-water mark, the agencies believed that the rule actually narrowed slightly the reach of federal jurisdiction. The rule no longer included all other waters the use, degradation, or destruction of which could affect interstate or foreign commerce. The agencies estimated that the rule would produce a small overall increase in positive jurisdictional determinations compared to those made under their post-*Rapanos* guidance, but that there would be fewer waters within the scope of federal jurisdiction compared with their previous regulation.

Numerous lawsuits challenging the rule were filed in both federal district courts and the courts of appeals. There was considerable confusion concerning which court had jurisdiction to hear initial challenges to the rule. The judicial review provision in section 509(b) of the Clean Water Act, 33 U.S.C. §3969, gives the courts of appeals original jurisdiction to hear challenges to "any effluent limitation or other limitation" promulgated under section 301 of the Act, §509(b)(1)(E), and an action issuing or denying a permit under §402, 509(b)(1)(F). After a series of conflicting decisions in the district courts and the U.S. Court of Appeals for the Sixth Circuit, the U.S. Supreme Court agreed to decide whether the rule first should be challenged in the courts of appeals or the federal district courts. In January 2018 the Court unanimously decided that the proper venue for filing challenges to the WOTUS rule was in the federal district courts because it was neither a §301 effluent limit nor an action issuing or denying a §402 permit. National Association of Manufacturers v. Department of Defense, 138 S.Ct. 617 (2018).

On February 28, 2017, President Donald Trump signed Executive Order 13,778 directing the EPA administrator and the Army Corps of Engineers to reconsider the WOTUS rule and to propose a new rule rescinding or revising it. The executive order also directed that the agencies "shall consider interpreting the term 'navigable waters,' as defined in §502(7), in a manner consistent with the opinion of Justice Antonin Scalia in Rapanos v. United States, 547 U.S. 715 (2006)." Thus, the executive order directed EPA to consider adopting Justice Scalia's "continuous surface connection" test that would sharply restrict federal jurisdiction.

The Obama administration's WOTUS rule was repealed on October 22, 2019. On January 23, 2020, the Trump administration announced the Navigable Waters Protection Rule (NWPR), which was published in the Federal Register on April

21, 2020. 85 Fed. Reg. 22250 (2020). The rule lists four categories of waters that may be federally regulated: (1) territorial seas and traditional navigable waters, (2) perennial and intermittent tributaries, (3) certain lakes, ponds, and impoundments, and (4) wetlands that are adjacent to jurisdictional waters. The NWPR also lists 12 categories of exclusions that will not be considered waters of the United States "such as features that only contain water in direct response to rainfall (e.g., ephemeral features); groundwater; many ditches; prior converted cropland; and waste treatment systems." Importantly, the NWPR defines "adjacent wetlands" as wetlands that are "meaningfully connected to other jurisdictional waters, for example, by directly abutting or having regular surface water communication with jurisdictional waters."

Although the originally proposed definition for "adjacent wetlands" aligned with Justice Scalia's plurality opinion in *Rapanos*, the final text of the rule provided a slightly broader definition. In the final rule, "adjacent" is not just "those that abut or otherwise have a direct hydrologic surface connection to other covered waters in a typical year" as originally proposed, but also "wetlands separated from other jurisdictional waters only by natural berms, banks, or dunes." The rule also allows for certain non-jurisdictional waters to "maintain jurisdictional connectivity between wetlands and other waters of the United States that are separated only by artificial dike and other barriers." Although the NWPR is not as narrow as originally proposed, opponents claim it will undermine national water quality. A coalition of 17 states and two cities challenged the NWPR's rollback of water standards in the United States District Court for the Northern District of California. On his first day in office, President Biden revoked Trump's Executive Order 13,778 that had directed EPA and the Army Corps of Engineers to reconsider the WOTUS rule. See Sec. 7 of Executive Order 13,990, 86 Fed. Reg. 7037. It is not clear what the Biden administration's plans will be concerning the NWPR.

## NOTES AND QUESTIONS

1. The states and industry groups challenging the WOTUS rule made the following arguments, among others. First, they maintained that it violated the Tenth Amendment principles of federalism and exceeded the federal government's constitutional authority under the Commerce Clause. Second, they argued that it is inconsistent with the Clean Water Act by interpreting "waters of the U.S." in a manner inconsistent with Supreme Court precedent in the *Rapanos* decision. Third, they argued that it violated the Administrative Procedure Act because changes were made in the final rule, such as the adoption of the 100-year floodplain and 4,000 feet of high-tide mark, that were not a "logical outgrowth" of what had been in the proposed rule.

2. On January 13, 2017, the U.S. Department of Justice filed a 284-page brief defending the WOTUS rule. Brief for Respondents, Murray Energy Corp. v. U.S. EPA, No. 15-3751 (Jan. 13, 2017), available online at *https://www.eenews.net/assets/2017/01/13/document_pm_02.pdf*.

3. Recall that Justice Scalia's test in *Rapanos* was rejected by a majority of the Court (Justice Kennedy and the four dissenters). Yet President Trump instructed EPA and the Corps to adopt a new rule (the NWPR) that embraces this test. Is the NWPR likely to survive judicial review? A review by the Corps of 55,519 waters

in the Corps' database found that 40,000 of them no longer would be subject to federal jurisdiction under the NWPR. Trump rule imperils more than 40,000 waterways, E&E News, Mar. 19, 2021.

4. Groundwater has not been considered part of the "waters of the U.S.," as both the WOTUS rule and the NWPR make clear. But, as discussed in the next section, that did not resolve questions concerning whether point source discharges that reach the waters of the United States after passing through groundwater require a §402 permit.

## C.   REGULATION OF DISCHARGES FROM POINT SOURCES

Building on the Refuse Act's simple strategy of requiring a permit for all discharges to navigable waters, section 301(a) of the Clean Water Act flatly declares that "the discharge of any pollutant by any person shall be unlawful," except in compliance with certain sections of the Act, including the permit requirements of section 402 (discharge of pollutants) and section 404 (discharge of dredged or fill material). Permits to discharge pollutants are governed by section 402's national pollution discharge elimination system (NPDES) program and must incorporate effluent limitations—restrictions on the quantities of pollutants that may be discharged—mandated by section 301. Section 404 establishes a separate permit program that allows discharges of dredged or fill material into wetlands at sites designated in the permit. Thus, on its face the Act appears to be both remarkably simple and comprehensive: It prohibits all discharges of water pollutants unless the discharger has a §402 permit that incorporates effluent limitations, and it requires a separate §404 permit for discharges of dredged or fill material in regulated wetlands.

### 1.   Do Discharges That Pass Through Groundwater Require a Permit?

Although groundwater is not part of the "waters of the U.S.," do point source discharges that reach navigable waters after passing through groundwater require a §402 permit? In Quivira Mining Co. v. United States, 765 F.2d 126 (10th Cir. 1985), the Tenth Circuit held that EPA has the power to require NPDES permits for discharges into a remote arroyo because they could reach surface waters through underground aquifers. But in Umatilla Water Quality Protective Ass'n v. Smith Frozen Foods, 962 F. Supp. 1312 (D. Or. 1997), a district court declined to apply the Clean Water Act to discharges to groundwater hydrologically connected to surface waters, noting that EPA had not asserted such authority and Oregon already had a separate permit program for groundwater discharges.

The Supreme Court weighed in on the question in the case below. A wastewater treatment plant in Hawaii disposed of its partially treated sewage by injecting it through wells into groundwater that eventually flowed to the Pacific Ocean. Under §402 of the Clean Water Act (CWA) a permit is required for pollutant discharges to "the waters of the United States, including the territorial seas." The County of Maui, owner of the treatment plant, maintained that it did not need to obtain a

§402 permit because its discharges first passed through groundwater. The U.S. Court of Appeals for the Ninth Circuit ruled in favor of a citizens' group that sued the County for an unpermitted discharge, holding that a pollutant discharge to the ocean that was "fairly traceable" to the county's point source discharge to groundwater requires a §402 permit. The Obama EPA supported the group before the Ninth Circuit, but before the Supreme Court the Trump administration changed sides and issued an Interpretive Statement stating that any pollutant discharge that passed through groundwater was exempt from §402 permit requirements. A majority of the Supreme Court disagreed in the following case.

## County of Maui v. Hawaii Wildlife Fund

140 S.Ct. 1462 (2020)

JUSTICE BREYER delivered the opinion of the Court.

The Clean Water Act forbids the "addition" of any pollutant from a "point source" to "navigable waters" without the appropriate permit from the Environmental Protection Agency (EPA). . . . The question here . . . is whether, or how, this statutory language applies to a pollutant that reaches navigable waters only after it leaves a "point source" and then travels through groundwater before reaching navigable waters. In such an instance, has there been a "discharge of a pollutant," that is, has there been "any addition of any pollutant to navigable waters from any point source?" . . .

### II

The linguistic question here concerns the statutory word "from." Is pollution that reaches navigable waters only through groundwater pollution that is "from" a point source, as the statute uses the word? The word "from" is broad in scope, but context often imposes limitations. "Finland," for example, is often not the right kind of answer to the question, "Where have you come from?" even if long ago you were born there. . . .

### III

Virtually all water, polluted or not, eventually makes its way to navigable water. This is just as true for groundwater. Given the power of modern science, the Ninth Circuit's limitation, "fairly traceable," may well allow EPA to assert permitting authority over the release of pollutants that reach navigable waters many years after their release (say, from a well or pipe or compost heap) and in highly diluted forms. . . .

Our view is that Congress did not intend the point source-permitting requirement to provide EPA with such broad authority as the Ninth Circuit's narrow focus on traceability would allow. First, to interpret the word "from" in this literal way would require a permit in surprising, even bizarre, circumstances, such as for pollutants carried to navigable waters on a bird's feathers, or, to mention more mundane instances, the 100-year migration of pollutants through 250 miles of groundwater to a river.

Second, and perhaps most important, the structure of the statute indicates that, as to groundwater pollution and nonpoint source pollution, Congress intended to leave substantial responsibility and autonomy to the States. . . .

The Act envisions EPA's role in managing nonpoint source pollution and groundwater pollution as limited to studying the issue, sharing information with and collecting information from the States, and issuing monetary grants. . . .

Finally, longstanding regulatory practice undermines the Ninth Circuit's broad interpretation of the statute. EPA itself for many years has applied the permitting provision to pollution discharges from point sources that reached navigable waters only after traveling through groundwater. But, in doing so, EPA followed a narrower interpretation than that of the Ninth Circuit. EPA has opposed applying the Act's permitting requirements to discharges that reach groundwater only after lengthy periods. Indeed, in this very case (prior to its recent Interpretive Statement), EPA asked the Ninth Circuit to apply a more limited "direct hydrological connection" test. The Ninth Circuit did not accept this suggestion.

### IV

### A

Maui and the Solicitor General argue that the statute's permitting requirement does not apply if a pollutant, having emerged from a "point source," must travel through any amount of groundwater before reaching navigable waters. That interpretation is too narrow, for it would risk serious interference with EPA's ability to regulate ordinary point source discharges.

Consider a pipe that spews pollution directly into coastal waters. There is an "addition of " a "pollutant to navigable waters from [a] point source." Hence, a permit is required. But Maui and the Government read the permitting requirement *not* to apply if there is *any* amount of groundwater between the end of the pipe and the edge of the navigable water. If that is the correct interpretation of the statute, then why could not the pipe's owner, seeking to avoid the permit requirement, simply move the pipe back, perhaps only a few yards, so that the pollution must travel through at least some groundwater before reaching the sea? We do not see how Congress could have intended to create such a large and obvious loophole in one of the key regulatory innovations of the Clean Water Act.

### B

Maui argues that the statute's language requires its reading. That language requires a permit for a "discharge." A "discharge" is "any addition" of a pollutant to navigable waters "*from any point source.*" And a "point source" is "any discernible, confined and discrete *conveyance*" (such as a pipe, ditch, well, etc.). Reading "from" and "conveyance" together, Maui argues that the statutory meaning of "from any point source" is not about *where* the pollution originated, but about *how* it got there. Under what Maui calls the means-of-delivery test, a permit is required only if a point source itself ultimately delivers the pollutant to navigable waters. Under this view, if the pollutant must travel through groundwater to reach navigable waters, then it is the groundwater, not the pipe, that is the conveyance.

Congress sometimes adopts less common meanings of common words, but this esoteric definition of "from," as connoting a means, does not remotely fit in this context. The statute couples the word "from" with the word "to"—strong evidence that Congress was referring to a destination ("navigable waters") and an origin ("any point source"). Further underscoring that Congress intended this every day meaning is that the object of "from" is a "point *source*"—a source, again, connoting an origin. That Maui's proffered interpretation would also create a serious loophole in the permitting regime also indicates it is an unreasonable one.

### C

The Solicitor General agrees that, as a general matter, the permitting requirement applies to at least some additions of pollutants to navigable waters that come indirectly from point sources. But the Solicitor General argues that the proper interpretation of the statute is the one reflected in EPA's recent Interpretive Statement. After receiving more than 50,000 comments from the public, and after the Ninth Circuit released its opinion in this case, EPA wrote that "the best, if not the only, reading" of the statutory provisions is that "*all* releases of pollutants to groundwater" are excluded from the scope of the permitting program, "even where pollutants are conveyed to jurisdictional surface waters via groundwater."

Neither the Solicitor General nor any party has asked us to give what the Court has referred to as *Chevron* deference to EPA's interpretation of the statute. Even so, we often pay particular attention to an agency's views in light of the agency's expertise in a given area, its knowledge gained through practical experience, and its familiarity with the interpretive demands of administrative need. But here, as we have explained, to follow EPA's reading would open a loophole allowing easy evasion of the statutory provision's basic purposes. Such an interpretation is neither persuasive nor reasonable. . . .

EPA's new interpretation is . . . difficult to reconcile with the statute's reference to " *any* addition" of a pollutant to navigable waters. It is difficult to reconcile EPA's interpretation with the statute's inclusion of "wells" in the definition of "point source," for wells most ordinarily would discharge pollutants through groundwater. And it is difficult to reconcile EPA's interpretation with the statutory provisions that allow EPA to delegate its permitting authority to a State *only if* the State (among other things) provides " 'adequate authority' " to " 'control the disposal of pollutants into wells.'" §402(b). What need would there be for such a proviso if the federal permitting program the State replaces did not include such discharges (from wells through groundwater) in the first place?

In short, EPA's oblique argument about the statute's references to groundwater cannot overcome the statute's structure, its purposes, or the text of the provisions that actually govern.

### D

Perhaps, as the two dissents suggest, the language could be narrowed to similar effect by reading the statute to refer only to the pollutant's immediate origin. But there is no linguistic basis here to so limit the statute in that way. Again, whether that is the correct reading turns on context. JUSTICE THOMAS insists that in the case of a discharge through groundwater, the pollutants are added "from the groundwater." Indeed, but that does not mean they are not also "from the point source." When John comes to the hotel, John might have come from the train station, from Baltimore, from Europe, from any two of those three places, or from all three. A sign that asks all persons who arrive *from* Baltimore to speak to the desk clerk includes those who took a taxi *from* the train station. There is nothing unnatural about such a construction. As the plurality correctly noted in *Rapanos v. United States*, the statute here does not say "directly" from or "immediately" from. Indeed, the expansive language of the provision — *any* addition from *any* point source — strongly suggests its scope is not so limited. . . .

And although JUSTICE THOMAS resists the inevitable implications of his reading of the statute that reading would create the same loopholes as those offered by the petitioner and the Government, and more. It would necessarily exclude a pipe that drains onto the beach next to navigable waters, even if the pollutants then flow to those waters. It also seems to exclude a pipe that hangs out over the water and adds pollutants to the air, through which the pollutants fall to navigable waters. The absurdity of such an interpretation is obvious enough.

We therefore reject this reading as well: Like Maui's and the Government's, it is inconsistent with the statutory text and simultaneously creates a massive loophole in the permitting scheme that Congress established.

### E

For the reasons set forth in Part III and in this Part, we conclude that, in light of the statute's language, structure, and purposes, the interpretations offered by the parties, the Government, and the dissents are too extreme.

### V

Over the years, courts and EPA have tried to find general language that will reflect a middle ground between these extremes. The statute's words reflect Congress' basic aim to provide federal regulation of identifiable sources of pollutants entering navigable waters without undermining the States' longstanding regulatory authority over land and groundwater. We hold that the statute requires a permit when there is a direct discharge from a point source into navigable waters or when there is the *functional equivalent of a direct discharge*. We think this phrase best captures, in broad terms, those circumstances in which Congress intended to require a federal permit. That is, an addition falls within the statutory requirement that it be "from any point source" when a point source directly deposits pollutants into navigable waters, or when the discharge reaches the same result through roughly similar means.

Time and distance are obviously important. Where a pipe ends a few feet from navigable waters and the pipe emits pollutants that travel those few feet through groundwater (or over the beach), the permitting requirement clearly applies. If the pipe ends 50 miles from navigable waters and the pipe emits pollutants that travel with groundwater, mix with much other material, and end up in navigable waters only many years later, the permitting requirements likely do not apply.

The object in a given scenario will be to advance, in a manner consistent with the statute's language, the statutory purposes that Congress sought to achieve. As we have said (repeatedly), the word "from" seeks a "point source" origin, and context imposes natural limits as to when a point source can properly be considered the origin of pollution that travels through groundwater. That context includes the need, reflected in the statute, to preserve state regulation of groundwater and other nonpoint sources of pollution. Whether pollutants that arrive at navigable waters after traveling through groundwater are "from" a point source depends upon how similar to (or different from) the particular discharge is to a direct discharge.

The difficulty with this approach, we recognize, is that it does not, on its own, clearly explain how to deal with middle instances. But there are too many potentially relevant factors applicable to factually different cases for this Court now to use more specific language. Consider, for example, just some of the factors that may prove relevant (depending upon the circumstances of a particular case): (1) transit time, (2) distance traveled, (3) the nature of the material through which the pollutant travels, (4) the extent to which the pollutant is diluted or chemically changed as it travels, (5) the amount of pollutant entering the navigable waters relative to the amount of the pollutant that leaves the point source, (6) the manner by or area in which the pollutant enters the navigable waters, (7) the degree to which the pollution (at that point) has maintained its specific identity. Time and distance will be the most important factors in most cases, but not necessarily every case.

At the same time, courts can provide guidance through decisions in individual cases. The Circuits have tried to do so, often using general language somewhat similar to the language we have used. And the traditional common-law method, making decisions that provide examples that in turn lead to ever more refined principles, is sometimes useful, even in an era of statutes.

The underlying statutory objectives also provide guidance. Decisions should not create serious risks either of undermining state regulation of groundwater or of creating loopholes that undermine the statute's basic federal regulatory objectives.

EPA, too, can provide administrative guidance (within statutory boundaries) in numerous ways, including through, for example, grants of individual permits, promulgation of general permits, or the development of general rules. Indeed, over the years, EPA and the States have often considered the Act's application to discharges through groundwater.

Both Maui and the Government object that to subject discharges to navigable waters through groundwater to the statute's permitting requirements, as our interpretation will sometimes do, would vastly expand the scope of the statute, perhaps requiring permits for each of the 650,000 wells like petitioner's or for each of the over 20 million septic systems used in many Americans' homes.

But EPA has applied the permitting provision to some (but not to all) discharges through groundwater for over 30 years. In that time we have seen no evidence of unmanageable expansion. EPA and the States also have tools to mitigate those harms, should they arise, by (for example) developing general permits for recurring situations or by issuing permits based on best practices where appropriate. Judges, too, can mitigate any hardship or injustice when they apply the statute's penalty provision. That provision vests courts with broad discretion to set a penalty that takes account of many factors, including "any good-faith efforts to comply" with the Act, the "seriousness of the violation," the "economic impact of the penalty on the violator," and "such other matters as justice may require." See §309(d). We expect that district judges will exercise their discretion mindful, as we are, of the complexities inherent to the context of indirect discharges through groundwater, so as to calibrate the Act's penalties when, for example, a party could reasonably have thought that a permit was not required.

In sum, we recognize that a more absolute position, such as the means-of-delivery test or that of the Government or that of the Ninth Circuit, may be easier to administer. But, as we have said, those positions have consequences that are inconsistent with major congressional objectives, as revealed by the statute's language, structure, and purposes. We consequently understand the permitting requirement, §301, as applicable to a discharge (from a point source) of pollutants that reach navigable waters after traveling through groundwater if that discharge is the functional equivalent of a direct discharge from the point source into navigable waters.

JUSTICE KAVANAUGH, concurring.

I join the Court's opinion in full. I write separately to emphasize three points.

*First,* the Court's interpretation of the Clean Water Act regarding pollution "from" point sources adheres to the interpretation set forth in Justice Scalia's plurality opinion in *Rapanos* v. *United States.* . . . In that case, Justice Scalia stated that polluters could not "evade the permitting requirement of §402(a) simply by discharging their pollutants into noncovered intermittent watercourses that lie upstream of covered waters." Justice Scalia reasoned that the Clean Water Act does not merely "forbid the 'addition of any pollutant *directly* to navigable waters from any point source,' but rather the 'addition of any pollutant *to* navigable waters.' Thus, from the time of the CWA's enactment, lower courts have held that the discharge into intermittent channels of any pollutant *that naturally washes downstream* likely violates §301(a), even if the pollutants discharged from a point source do not emit 'directly into' covered waters, but pass 'through conveyances' in between."

In other words, under Justice Scalia's interpretation in *Rapanos,* the fact that the pollutants from Maui's wastewater facility reach the ocean via an indirect route does not itself exempt Maui's facility from the Clean Water Act's permitting requirement for point sources. The Court today adheres to Justice Scalia's analysis in *Rapanos* on that issue.

*Second,* as Justice Scalia's opinion in *Rapanos* pointed out and as the Court's opinion today explains, the statute does not establish a bright-line test regarding when a pollutant may be considered to have come "from" a point source. The source of the vagueness is Congress' statutory text, not the Court's opinion. The Court's opinion seeks to translate the vague statutory text into more concrete guidance.

*Third,* JUSTICE THOMAS' dissent states that "the Court does not commit" to "which factors are the most important" in determining whether pollutants that enter navigable waters come "from" a point source. That critique is not accurate, as I read the Court's opinion. The Court identifies relevant factors to consider and emphasizes that "[t]ime and distance are obviously important." And the Court expressly adds that "[t]ime and distance will be the most important factors in most cases, but not necessarily every case." Although the statutory text does not supply a bright-line test, the Court's emphasis on time and distance will help guide application of the statutory standard going forward.

Justices THOMAS, ALITO and GORSUCH dissented.

## NOTES AND QUESTIONS

1. What reasons did the Court articulate for rejecting the Ninth Circuit's "fairly traceable" test for determining when pollutants initially discharged from point sources that reach jurisdictional waters require a §402 permit? Do you agree with them?

2. Why did the Court think that the positions taken by EPA and the County of Maui would have opened up a large loophole in the CWA's permitting scheme? Do you agree?

3. In his dissent, Justice Alito criticized the majority for not providing a bright-line test for determining when discharges that pass through groundwater require a permit. What test did the Court articulate, and what factors did it state should be considered in determining how to apply the test? Which of these factors should be given the greatest weight?

4. Although Justice Scalia's plurality opinion in *Rapanos* articulated a very narrow view of federal jurisdiction under the Clean Water Act, in this case it was cited in support of a more expansive view of CWA permit requirements. How did this happen?

5. The majority notes that the County of Maui did not ask for *Chevron* deference for EPA's Interpretative Statement even though it supported the county's position in this case. *Chevron* now is rarely cited before the Supreme Court because a majority of Justices on the current Court are known to be critics of the doctrine. Note that the Court went out of its way to state that *Chevron* deference would not have been appropriate in this case, even if the county and EPA had asked for it. Why?

6. During the waning days of the Trump administration, EPA issued guidance on how the *County of Maui* decision should be applied. The guidance emphasized "system design and performance" as a factor to consider in determining if a discharge was the "functional equivalent" of a direct discharge. It was widely viewed as an effort to undermine the *County of Maui* decision. King, *Maui* guidance may undermine Supreme Court ruling, E & E News, Dec. 8, 2020. Can EPA guidance undermine a Supreme Court decision?

### 2. Defining the "Addition of Any Pollutant"

As with so many other areas of environmental regulation, the definition of "regulatory targets" under the Clean Water Act becomes more complicated the closer one looks. Section 502(12) of the Act defines "discharge of a pollutant" to include "any addition of any pollutant to navigable waters from any point source" or "to the waters of the contiguous zone or the ocean from any point source other than a vessel or other floating craft." This language indicates that the Act's permit requirements do not cover *all* pollutant discharges, but rather only discharges from point sources that involve the addition of a pollutant. Thus, what is meant by the "addition of any pollutant . . . from any point source" will have important jurisdictional consequences.

As noted above, for a pollutant discharge to be regulated under either section 402 or 404, it must meet the statutory definition of "discharge" which requires that it involve the "addition of any pollutant." Just as some of the most important cases defining "navigable waters" arose in the context of section 404's permit program, so too have many of the cases defining what constitutes a "discharge" for purposes of the Act. Since the late 1970s, the U.S. Army Corps of Engineers had maintained that de minimis discharges associated with normal dredging activities were not covered by section 404. However, in 1993 the Corps adopted a final rule (known as the "Tulloch Rule" after the lawsuit that inspired it) to clarify that excavation activities producing any incidental redeposit of dredged materials, "however temporary or small," require section 404 permits when they would degrade or destroy wetlands. 58 Fed. Reg. 45,008 (1993). In the case that follows the Tulloch Rule was challenged by a trade association that argued that incidental redeposits of dredged materials could not be regulated as "discharges" because they did not result in the net addition of any pollutants to receiving waters.

## National Mining Association v. Army Corps of Engineers

145 F.3d 1399 (D.C. Cir. 1998)

WILLIAMS, Circuit Judge:

Section 404 of the Clean Water Act (the "Act") authorizes the United States Army Corps of Engineers (the "Corps") to issue permits "for the discharge of dredged or fill material into the navigable waters at specified disposal sites." 33 U.S.C. §1344. Section 301(a) of the Act provides that the "discharge of any pollutant by any person" is unlawful unless in compliance with Act's permit requirements, including those of §404(a). "Discharge," in turn, is defined as "any addition of any pollutant to navigable waters from any point source." §502(12).

In 1986 the Corps issued a regulation defining the term "discharge of dredged material," as used in §404, to mean "any addition of dredged material into the waters of the United States," but expressly excluding "de minimis, incidental soil movement occurring during normal dredging operations." 51 Fed. Reg. 41,206, 41,232 (Nov. 13, 1986). In 1993, responding to litigation, the Corps issued a new rule removing the de minimis exception and expanding the definition of discharge to cover "any addition of dredged material into, *including any redeposit of dredged material within*, the waters of the United States." 33 CFR §323.2(d)(1) (emphasis added). Redeposit occurs when material removed from the water is returned to it; when redeposit takes place in substantially the same spot as the initial removal, the parties refer to it as "fallback." In effect the new rule subjects to federal regulation virtually all excavation and dredging performed in wetlands.

The plaintiffs, various trade associations whose members engage in dredging and excavation, mounted a facial challenge to the 1993 regulation, claiming that it exceeded the scope of the Corps' regulatory authority under the Act by regulating fallback. . . .

The 1993 rulemaking under challenge here was prompted by a lawsuit, North Carolina Wildlife Federation v. Tulloch (E.D.N.C. 1992), concerning a developer who sought to drain and clear 700 acres of wetlands in North Carolina. Because the developer's efforts involved only minimal incidental releases of soil and other dredged material, the Corps' field office personnel determined that, under the terms of the 1986 regulation, §404's permit requirements did not apply.

Environmental groups, concerned by what they viewed as the adverse effects of the developer's activities on the wetland, filed an action seeking enforcement of the §404 permit requirement. As part of the settlement of the Tulloch case (a settlement to which the developer was not a party), the two administering agencies agreed to propose stiffer rules governing the permit requirements for landclearing and excavation activities. The result—the regulation at issue here—has come to be called the "Tulloch Rule."

As mentioned above, the Tulloch Rule alters the preexisting regulatory framework primarily by removing the de minimis exception and by adding coverage of incidental fallback. Specifically, the rule defines "discharge of dredged material" to include "any addition, *including any redeposit*, of dredged material, including excavated material, into waters of the United States which is incidental to any activity, including mechanized landclearing, ditching, channelization, or other excavation." 33 CFR §323.2(d)(1)(iii) (emphasis added).

The Tulloch Rule does have its own de minimis exception, but it is framed in terms of the Act's overall goals. A permit is not required for "any incidental addition, including redeposit, of dredged material associated with any activity that does not have or would not have the effect of destroying or degrading an area of waters of the United States." 33 CFR §323.2(d)(3)(i). Persons engaging in "mechanized landclearing, ditching, channelization and other excavation activity," however, bear the burden of proving to the Corps that their activities would not have destructive or degrading effects. Degradation is defined as any effect on the waters of the United States that is more than de minimis or inconsequential. Id. §323.2(d)(5). Thus, whereas the 1986 rule exempted de minimis soil movement, the Tulloch Rule covers all discharges, however minuscule, unless the Corps is convinced that the *activities with which they are associated* have only minimal adverse effects. In promulgating the new rule the Corps "emphasized that the threshold of adverse effects for the de minimis exception is a very low one." 56 Fed. Reg. at 45,020.

It is undisputed that by requiring a permit for "*any* redeposit," 33 CFR §323.2(d)(1)(iii) (emphasis added), the Tulloch Rule covers incidental fallback. According to the agencies, incidental fallback occurs, for example, during dredging, "when a bucket used to excavate material from the bottom of a river, stream, or wetland is raised and soils or sediments fall from the bucket back into the water." Agencies' Br. at 13. (There is no indication that the rule would not also reach soils or sediments falling out of the bucket even before it emerged from the water.) Fallback and other redeposits also occur during mechanized landclearing, when bulldozers and loaders scrape or displace wetland soil, as well as during ditching and channelization, when draglines or backhoes are dragged through soils and sediments. Indeed, fallback is a practically inescapable by-product of all these activities. In the preamble to the Tulloch Rule the Corps noted that "it is virtually impossible to conduct mechanized landclearing, ditching, channelization or excavation in waters of the United States without causing incidental redeposition of dredged material (however small or temporary) in the process." As a result, the Tulloch Rule effectively requires a permit for all those activities, subject to a limited exception for ones that the Corps in its discretion deems to produce no adverse effects on waters of the United States. . . .

The plaintiffs claim that the Tulloch Rule exceeds the Corps' statutory jurisdiction under §404, which, as we have noted, extends only to "discharge," defined as the "addition of any pollutant to navigable waters." §§404, 502(12). It argues that fallback, which returns dredged material virtually to the spot from which it came, cannot be said to constitute an addition of anything. Therefore, the plaintiffs contend, the Tulloch Rule conflicts with the statute's unambiguous terms and cannot survive even the deferential scrutiny called for by Chevron U.S.A., Inc. v. NRDC, 467 U.S. 837 (1984). The "jurisdictional" character of the issue has no effect on the level of deference, as the plaintiffs seem to acknowledge by their silence on the subject.

The agencies argue that the terms of the Act in fact demonstrate that fallback may be classified as a discharge. The Act defines a discharge as the addition of any pollutant to navigable waters, §502(12), and defines "pollutant" to include "dredged spoil," as well as "rock," "sand," and "cellar dirt." §502(6). The Corps in turn defines "dredged material" as "material that is excavated or dredged from waters of the United States," 33 CFR §323.2(c), a definition that is not challenged here. Thus, according to the agencies, wetland soil, sediment, debris, or other material in the waters of the United States undergoes a legal metamorphosis during the dredging process, becoming a "pollutant" for purposes of the Act. If a portion of the material being dredged then falls back into the water, there has been an addition of a pollutant to the waters of the United States. Indeed, according to appellants National Wildlife Federation et al. ("NWF"), who intervened as defendants below, this reasoning demonstrates that regulation of redeposit is actually *required* by the Act.

We agree with the plaintiffs, and with the district court, that the straightforward statutory term "addition" cannot reasonably be said to encompass the situation in which material is removed from the waters of the United States and a small portion of it happens to fall back. Because incidental fallback represents a net withdrawal, not an addition, of material, it cannot be a discharge. As we concluded recently in a related context, "the nearest evidence we have of definitional intent by Congress reflects, as might be expected, that the word 'discharge' contemplates the addition, not the withdrawal, of a substance or substances." North Carolina v. FERC, 112 F.3d 1175, 1187 (D.C. Cir. 1997). The agencies' primary counterargument—that fallback constitutes an "addition of any pollutant" because material becomes a pollutant only upon being dredged—is ingenious but unconvincing. Regardless of any legal metamorphosis that may occur at the moment of dredging, we fail to see how there can be an addition of *dredged material* when there is no addition of *material*. Although the Act includes "dredged spoil" in its list of pollutants, §502(6), Congress could not have contemplated that the attempted removal of 100 tons of that substance could constitute an addition simply because only 99 tons of it were actually taken away. In fact the removal of material from the waters of the United States, as opposed to the discharge of material into those waters, is governed by a completely independent statutory scheme. Section 10 of the Rivers and Harbors Act of 1899, 33 U.S.C. §403, makes it illegal "to excavate or fill" in the navigable waters of the United States without the Corps' approval. As the general counsel of the Army noted in a law review article published a few years after the passage of the Clean Water Act, Congress enacted "two separate statutory frameworks. Section 10 of the 1899 Act covers the act of dredging, while Section 404 [of the Clean Water Act] covers the disposal of the dredged material." Charles D.

Ablard and Brian B. O'Neill, Wetland Protection and Section 404 of the Federal Water Pollution Control Act Amendments of 1972: A Corps of Engineers Renaissance, 1 Vt. L. Rev. 51, 93 (1976).

The agencies, though acknowledging that the Tulloch Rule effectively requires a permit for all mechanized landclearing, ditching, channelization or excavation in waters of the United States, locate their permitting requirement under §404, not under the Rivers and Harbors Act's explicit coverage of "excavat[ion]." The explanation for this choice is apparently that the scope of the Corps' geographic jurisdiction is narrower under the Rivers and Harbors Act than under the Clean Water Act, extending only to waters subject to the ebb and flow of the tide, or waters that are used, have been used, or may be susceptible for use to transport interstate or foreign commerce.

There may be an incongruity in Congress' assignment of extraction activities to a statute (the Rivers and Harbors Act) with a narrower jurisdictional sweep than that of the statute covering discharges (the Clean Water Act). This incongruity, of course, could be cured either by narrowing the jurisdictional reach of the Clean Water Act or broadening that of the Rivers and Harbors Act. But we do not think the agencies can do it simply by declaring that incomplete removal constitutes addition.

The agencies also point to some specific exemptions set forth in §404(f) of the Act in support of their view that fallback can reasonably be said to constitute discharge. Congress added the subsection in 1977, apparently in response to the broad construction of "discharge" in the 1977 regulations. It provides that "the discharge of dredged or fill material . . . is not prohibited . . . or otherwise subject to regulation" under the Act's permitting requirements when the discharge results from any of a number of specifically exempted activities, including "normal farming, silviculture, and ranching activities such as plowing, seeding, cultivating, [or] minor drainage," 404(f)(1)(A), and "maintenance of drainage ditches," 404(f)(1)(C). After listing these exemptions, §404(f) provides that a permit shall nonetheless be required for any activity "having as its purpose bringing an area of the navigable waters into a use to which it was not previously subject, where the flow or circulation of navigable waters may be impaired or the reach of such waters be reduced." §404(f)(2).

The agencies claim these exemptions show that as a general matter Congress considered fallback to be covered by §404. They especially note that §404(f)(1) uses the term "*discharge* of dredged or fill material" to describe the consequences of the protected activities, supposedly reflecting a congressional belief that fallback is a form of discharge.

We find the exemptions far less telling. Some of the named activities — plowing, ditch maintenance, and the like — may produce fallback, but they may also produce actual discharges, i.e., additions of pollutants, so that §404(f) accomplishes a useful purpose simply by exempting them insofar as they produce the latter. Some others, such as seeding, seem to us just as unlikely to produce fallback as actual discharge, so we are reluctant to draw any inference other than that Congress emphatically did not want the law to impede these bucolic pursuits.

NWF complains that our understanding of "addition" reads the regulation of dredged material out of the statute. They correctly note that since dredged material comes from the waters of the United States, any discharge of such material into those waters could technically be described as a "redeposit," at least on a broad construction of that term. The Fifth Circuit made a similar observation fifteen years ago: "'[D]redged' material is by definition material that comes from the water itself. A requirement that all pollutants must come from outside sources would effectively remove the dredge-and-fill provision from the statute." Avoyelles Sportsmen's League v. Marsh, 715 F.2d 897, 924 n.43 (5th Cir. 1983). But we do not hold that the Corps may not legally regulate some forms of redeposit under its §404 permitting authority. We hold only that by asserting jurisdiction over "*any* redeposit," including incidental fallback, the Tulloch Rule outruns the Corps' statutory authority. Since the Act sets out no bright line between incidental fallback on the one hand and regulable redeposits on the other, a reasoned attempt by the agencies to draw such a line would merit considerable deference. But the Tulloch Rule makes no effort to draw such a line, and indeed its overriding purpose appears to be to expand the Corps' permitting authority to encompass incidental fallback and, as a result, a wide range of activities that cannot remotely be said to "add" anything to the waters of the United States. . . .

In a press release accompanying the adoption of the Tulloch Rule, the White House announced: "Congress should amend the Clean Water Act to make it consistent with the agencies' rulemaking." White House Office on Environmental Policy, Protecting America's Wetlands: A Fair, Flexible, and Effective Approach 23 (Aug. 24, 1993). While remarkable in its candor, the announcement contained a kernel of truth. If the agencies and NWF believe that the Clean Water Act inadequately protects wetlands and other natural resources by insisting upon the presence of an "addition" to trigger permit requirements, the appropriate body to turn to is Congress. Without such an amendment, the Act simply will not accommodate the Tulloch Rule. The judgment of the district court is Affirmed.

Silberman, Circuit Judge, concurring:

I join the opinion of the court and write separately only to make explicit what I think implicit in our opinion. We hold that the Corps' interpretation of the phrase "*addition* of any pollutant to navigable waters" to cover incidental fallback is "unreasonable," which is the formulation we use when we have first determined under *Chevron* that neither the statutory language nor legislative history reveals a precise intent with respect to the issue presented—in other words, we are at the second step of the now-familiar *Chevron* Step I and Step II analysis. As our opinion's discussion of prior cases indicates, the word addition carries both a temporal and geographic ambiguity. If the material that would otherwise fall back were moved some distance away and then dropped, it very well might constitute an "addition." Or if it were held for some time and then dropped back in the same spot, it might also constitute an "addition." But the structure of the relevant statutes indicates that it is unreasonable to call incidental fallback an addition. To do so perforce converts *all* dredging—which is regulated under the Rivers and Harbors Act—into discharge of dredged material which is regulated under the Clean Water Act.

Moreover, that Congress had in mind either a temporal or geographic separation between excavation and disposal is suggested by its requirement that dredged material be discharged at "specified disposal sites," §404, a term which simply does not fit incidental fallback.

The Corps attempts to avoid these difficulties by asserting that rock and sand are magically transformed into pollutants once dredged, so *all* dredging necessarily results in an addition of pollutants to navigable waters. But rock and sand only become pollutants, according to the statute, once they are "discharged into water." §502(6) (1994). The Corps' approach thus just leads right back to the definition of discharge.

## NOTES AND QUESTIONS

1. The Tulloch Rule was designed to prevent developers from simply draining wetlands as an end run around the section 404 permit process. As the court notes, those who can convince the Corps that their dredging activities would not destroy or degrade wetlands are exempt from the permit requirement. Why not permit the Corps to define the scope of activities covered by section 404's permit requirement by reference to the prospective environmental impact of the activity? What, in the court's view, was the critical defect in the Tulloch Rule?

2. The court notes that section 10 of the Rivers and Harbors Act explicitly regulates dredging activities by making it illegal "to excavate or fill" in navigable waters without the approval of the Corps. In light of this requirement, why does the Corps need to rely on section 404 to block the draining of wetlands?

3. As a result of the court's decision, what activities are now considered to involve the discharge of a pollutant and what activities are not? The National Wildlife Federation argued that invalidation of the Tulloch Rule could exempt all redeposits of dredged material from section 404 even when the material is redeposited in wetlands areas. Why does the court disagree? What redeposits would be regulable under section 404 in light of the court's decision? Where would Judge Silberman draw the line? In United States v. Deaton, 209 F.3d 331 (4th Cir. 2000), the Fourth Circuit rejected the argument that sidecasting of dredged material cannot be regulated under section 404 because it results in no net increase in the amount of material present in the wetland. The court concluded that "Congress determined that plain dirt, once excavated from the waters of the United States, could not be redeposited into those waters without causing harm to the environment." Id. at 336.

4. In the immediate aftermath of the *National Mining* decision, it was estimated that at least 20,000 acres of wetlands were degraded or destroyed and 150 miles of streams channelized without environmental review or mitigation. To close this loophole, EPA and the Corps issued new regulations in January 2001 that clarified the types of activities likely to result in a discharge of dredged material requiring a permit under section 404. 66 Fed. Reg. 4,549. The regulations modify the definition of "discharge of dredged materials" to create a rebuttable presumption that the use of mechanized earth-moving equipment to conduct land clearing, ditching, channelization, in-stream mining, or other earth-moving activity in waters of the United States results in a discharge of dredged material, unless project-specific evidence shows that the activity causes only "incidental fallback." The regulations also provide a definition of what constitutes nonregulable incidental fallback that is consistent with the court's decision.

5. In December 2002, the Court reviewed a decision by the Ninth Circuit upholding a judgment that a real estate developer, Angelo Tsakopoulos, had

violated section 404 by using "deep ripping" equipment to punch holes in a dense layer of soil (a clay pan) beneath a wetland to allow surface waters to penetrate and drain the wetlands. Borden Ranch Partnership v. U.S. Army Corps of Engineers, 261 F.3d 810 (9th Cir. 2001). The court majority held that "activities that destroy the ecology of a wetland are not immune from the Clean Water Act merely because they do not involve the introduction of material brought in from somewhere else." It concluded that deep ripping can constitute a discharge of a pollutant regulated under the Clean Water Act because it causes soil to be "wrenched up, moved around, and redeposited somewhere else." In a footnote the majority distinguished *National Mining Association* as a case involving only "incidental fallback." The court observed that the deep ripping does not involve mere incidental fallback, but constitutes environmental damage sufficient to constitute a regulable redeposit. A dissenting judge argued that *National Mining Association* should be extended to exempt deep ripping, because it involves the plowing of land and not the addition of dredged materials. In the U.S. Supreme Court, lawyers for Tsakopoulos challenged the Ninth Circuit's conclusion that deep ripping constitutes the discharge of a pollutant. Shortly after hearing oral argument, the Court announced that it had split 4-4, affirming the Ninth Circuit's decision by an equally divided Court. The split was the result of Justice Anthony Kennedy recusing himself from the case because he was an acquaintance of Tsakopoulos.

### Can a Water Transfer Qualify as the "Discharge of a Pollutant"?

In 2004, the Court reviewed a decision by the Eleventh Circuit that had held that a §402 NPDES permit was required for pumps that moved water polluted by stormwater runoff from a canal to a reservoir as part of the South Florida Flood Control Project because the pumping of the polluted water constituted the discharge of a pollutant. In South Florida Water Management District v. Miccosukee Tribe of Indians, 541 U.S. 95 (2004), the Court rejected the notion "that the NPDES program applies to a point source 'only when a pollutant originates from the point source,' and not when pollutants originating elsewhere merely pass through the point source." The Court stated that a "point source is, by definition, a 'discernible, confined, and discrete *conveyance*.' §502(14) (emphasis added)" which "makes plain that a point source need not be the original source of the pollutant; it need only convey the pollutant to 'navigable waters'." . . . Thus, the Court confirmed the §402 permit requirement can be applied to "point sources that do not themselves generate pollutants."

The Court concluded that merely moving water around within a unitary body of water did not constitute a discharge requiring a §402 permit. However, it declined to embrace EPA's broader argument that "permits are not required when water from one navigable water body is discharged, unaltered, into another navigable water body." The Court noted that "if one water body were polluted and the other pristine, and the two would not otherwise mix" the discharge would pollute the pristine water. On remand, the district court rejected the EPA's broader theory and held that diversion works such as pump stations required NPDES permits to the extent that they transfer water from "meaningfully distinct" water bodies. Friends of the Everglades Inc. v. South Florida Water Management District, 2006 WL 3635465 (S.D. Fla. 2006).

In June 2008, EPA adopted a final rule excluding water transfers from §402's NPDES permit requirements. 73 Fed. Reg. 33,697 (2008). EPA's rule defines an excluded water transfer as "an activity that conveys or connects waters of the United States without subjecting the transferred water to intervening industrial, municipal or commercial use." Under the rule, pollutants introduced to the water being transferred by the water transfer activity itself are still subject to NPDES permit requirements. Thus, if malfunctioning pumps contaminate the water being transferred with lubricants like oil and grease, they could be subject to NPDES permit requirements, but not if the pumping simply moved already polluted water to a new discharge site. In adopting the rule, EPA acknowledged that it was inconsistent with decisions like Catskill Mountains Chapter of Trout Unlimited, Inc. v. City of New York, 451 F.3d 77 (2d Cir. 2006), where the court held that New York City's interbasin water transfers constitute an "addition of a pollutant" to a navigable water and thus require an NPDES permit under §402. But the agency argued that the CWA is ambiguous on this issue and thus the agency's rule should be afforded deference under *Chevron*. Environmental groups filed suit to challenge the rule.

On January 18, 2017, a divided panel of the Second Circuit upheld EPA's water transfers rule. Catskill Mountain Chapter of Trout Unlimited, Inc. v. EPA (*Catskill III*), 846 F.3d 492 (2d Cir. 2017). In an opinion by Judge Sack, the court held that because the Clean Water Act does not directly address the question whether NPDES permits are required for water transfers, EPA's rule generally exempting them from permit requirements was entitled to *Chevron* deference. The court disagreed with the district court's decision that the rule was unreasonable and therefore did not warrant deference. "The EPA's interpretation need not be the 'only possible interpretation,' nor need it be 'the interpretation deemed *most* reasonable.' And even though . . . we might conclude that it is not the interpretation that would most effectively further the Clean Water Act's principal focus on water quality, it is reasonable nonetheless. Indeed, in light of the potentially serious and disruptive practical consequences of requiring NPDES permits for water transfers, the EPA's interpretation here involves the kind of 'difficult policy choices that agencies are better equipped to make than courts.'" In dissent, Judge Chin argued that "the plain language and structure of the Act is unambiguous and clearly expresses Congress's intent to prohibit the transfer of polluted water from one water body to another distinct water body without a permit." He maintained that "Congress did not intend to give a pass to interbasin transfers of dirty water, and excluding such transfers from permitting requirements is incompatible with the goal of the Act to protect our waters."

In January 2013, the U.S. Supreme Court again addressed whether the transfer of polluted water between two parts of the same water body could constitute a discharge of pollutants requiring a permit under the Clean Water Act. In the case below, the Natural Resources Defense Council sued a flood control district for allegedly violating an NPDES permit covering its operation of a municipal separate storm sewer system ("MS4"). In the 1987 Amendments to the Clean Water Act, Congress added section 402(p), which requires NPDES permits for stormwater discharges associated with industrial activity and those from MS4s serving a population of 100,000 or more. Congress confirmed that permits for industrial stormwater discharges must meet all applicable provisions of section 301 and section

402 including BAT/BCT, §402(p)(3)(A), and it required that municipal permits prohibit non-stormwater discharges into storm sewers while requiring controls to reduce pollutant discharges "to the maximum extent practicable." §402(p)(3)(B).

## Los Angeles County Flood Control District v. Natural Resources Defense Council, Inc.

568 U.S. 78 (2013)

JUSTICE GINSBURG delivered the opinion of the Court.

The Court granted review in this case limited to a single question: Under the Clean Water Act (CWA) does the flow of water out of a concrete channel within a river rank as a "discharge of a pollutant"? In this Court, the parties and the United States as amicus curiae agree that the answer to this question is "no." They base this accord on South Fla. Water Management Dist. v. Miccosukee Tribe, 541 U.S. 95 (2004), in which we accepted that pumping polluted water from one part of a water body into another part of the same body is not a discharge of pollutants under the CWA. Adhering to the view we took in *Miccosukee*, we hold that the parties correctly answered the sole question presented in the negative. The decision in this suit rendered by the Court of Appeals for the Ninth Circuit is inconsistent with our determination. We therefore reverse that court's judgment.

Petitioner Los Angeles County Flood Control District (District) operates a "municipal separate storm sewer system" (MS4) — a drainage system that collects, transports, and discharges storm water. See 40 CFR §122.26(b)(8) (2012). Because storm water is often heavily polluted, the CWA and its implementing regulations require the operator of an MS4 serving a population of at least 100,000 to obtain a National Pollutant Discharge Elimination System (NPDES) permit before discharging storm water into navigable waters. See 33 U.S.C. §§301(a), 402(p)(2)(C), and (D); 40 CFR §§122.26(a)(3), (b)(4), (b)(7). The District first obtained a NPDES permit for its MS4 in 1990; thereafter, the permit was several times renewed.

Respondents Natural Resources Defense Council, Inc. (NRDC) and Santa Monica Baykeeper (Baykeeper) filed a citizen suit against the District and several other defendants under §505 of the CWA, §505. They alleged, among other things, that water-quality measurements from monitoring stations located within the Los Angeles and San Gabriel Rivers demonstrated that the District was violating the terms of its permit.

The District Court granted summary judgment to the District on these claims. It was undisputed, the District Court acknowledged, that "data from the Los Angeles River and San Gabriel River [monitoring] stations indicate[d] that water quality standards ha[d] repeatedly been exceeded for a number of pollutants, including aluminum, copper, cyanide, fecal coliform bacteria, and zinc." But numerous entities other than the District, the court added, discharge into the rivers upstream of the monitoring stations. The record was insufficient, the District Court concluded, to warrant a finding that the District's MS4 had discharged storm water containing the standards-exceeding pollutants detected at the downstream monitoring stations.

The Ninth Circuit reversed in relevant part. The monitoring stations for the Los Angeles and San Gabriel Rivers, the Court of Appeals said, are located in "concrete channels" constructed for flood-control purposes. Based on this impression, the Court of Appeals held that a discharge of pollutants occurred under the CWA when the polluted water detected at the monitoring stations "flowed out of the concrete channels" and entered downstream portions of the waterways lacking concrete linings. Because the District exercises control over the concrete-lined portions of the rivers, the Court of Appeals held, the District is liable for the discharges that, in the appellate court's view, occur when water exits those concrete channels.

We granted certiorari on the following question: Under the CWA, does a "discharge of pollutants" occur when polluted water "flows from one portion of a river that is navigable water of the United States, through a concrete channel or other engineered improvement in the river," and then "into a lower portion of the same river"? As noted above, the parties, as well as the United States as amicus curiae, agree that the answer to this question is "no."

That agreement is hardly surprising, for we held in *Miccosukee* that the transfer of polluted water between "two parts of the same water body" does not constitute a discharge of pollutants under the CWA. We derived that determination from the CWA's text, which defines the term "discharge of a pollutant" to mean "any *addition* of any pollutant to navigable waters from any point source." §502(12) (emphasis added). Under a common understanding of the meaning of the word "add," no pollutants are "added" to a water body when water is merely transferred between different portions of that water body. See Webster's Third New International Dictionary 24 (2002) ("add" means "to join, annex, or unite (as one thing to another) so as to bring about an increase (as in number, size, or importance) or so as to form one aggregate"). "As the Second Circuit [aptly] put it. . . , '[i]f one takes a ladle of soup from a pot, lifts it above the pot, and pours it back into the pot, one has not "added" soup or anything else to the pot.'" *Miccosukee*, 541 U.S., at 109-110.

In *Miccosukee*, polluted water was removed from a canal, transported through a pump station, and then deposited into a nearby reservoir. We held that this water transfer would count as a discharge of pollutants under the CWA only if the canal and the reservoir were "meaningfully distinct water bodies." It follows, a fortiori, from *Miccosukee* that no discharge of pollutants occurs when water, rather than being removed and then returned to a water body, simply flows from one portion of the water body to another. We hold, therefore, that the flow of water from an improved portion of a navigable waterway into an unimproved portion of the very same waterway does not qualify as a discharge of pollutants under the CWA. Because the decision below cannot be squared with that holding, the Court of Appeals' judgment must be reversed.

The NRDC and Baykeeper urge that the Court of Appeals reached the right result, albeit for the wrong reason. The monitoring system proposed by the District and written into its permit showed numerous instances in which water-quality standards were exceeded. Under the permit's terms, the NRDC and Baykeeper maintain, the exceedances detected at the instream monitoring stations are by themselves sufficient to establish the District's liability under the CWA for its upstream discharges. This argument failed below. It is not embraced within, or even touched by, the narrow question on which we granted certiorari. We therefore do not address, and indicate no opinion on, the issue the NRDC and Baykeeper seek to substitute for the question we took up for review.

\* \* \*

For the reasons stated, the judgment of the Court of Appeals for the Ninth Circuit is reversed, and the case is remanded.

It is so ordered.

JUSTICE ALITO concurs in the judgment.

## NOTES AND QUESTIONS

1. How can violations of the L.A. County Flood Control District's NPDES permit be ascertained? At the time the case was decided by the Supreme Court, there was only one monitoring station in the Los Angeles River and none at the outfalls where water from the stormwater system flows into the river. While the monitoring showed that pollutant levels in the river were in excess of water quality standards, the district court had found that there was insufficient evidence to hold the Flood Control District liable for the exceedances. NRDC convinced the Ninth Circuit that the trial court had erred because there was sufficient evidence to connect the District to the pollution. It is possible that the Ninth Circuit erroneously believed that the monitor was located at the outfall where the stormwater system discharges into the river. Because the monitor instead is located in the river, the Flood Control District apparently convinced the Supreme Court that the Ninth Circuit actually had held that there was a "discharge" of pollutants within the river itself where the monitoring station is located.

2. Does the decision in any way suggest that municipal stormwater discharges do not need permits under Clean Water Act section 402(p)? Or that such permits do not need to ensure that such stormwater discharges do not cause or contribute to exceedances of water quality standards?

3. On remand, on August 8, 2013, the U.S. Court of Appeals for the Ninth Circuit issued a decision finding that the flood control district violated its NPDES stormwater discharge permits. Natural Resources Defense Council, Inc. v. County of Los Angeles, 725 F.3d 1194 (9th Cir. 2013). The court noted that regulating pollution from storm sewer systems is "substantially more complicated than regulating pollution from a few defined point sources." As a result, EPA's stormwater regulations provide "broad discretion to issue permits 'on a system-wide or jurisdiction-wide basis,' 40 C.F.R. §122.26(a)(1)(v), rather than requiring cities and counties to obtain separate permits for millions of individual stormwater discharge points." While such "permits need not require monitoring of each stormwater source at the precise point of discharge, they may instead establish a monitoring scheme 'sufficient to yield data which are *representative of the monitored activity.* . . .' 40 C.F.R. §122.48(b) (emphasis added)." Noting that the County agreed to the monitoring system established in the permit, the court concluded: "Because the results of County Defendants' pollution monitoring conclusively demonstrate that pollution levels in the Los Angeles and San Gabriel Rivers are in excess of those allowed under the Permit, the County Defendants are *liable* for permit violations as a matter of law." The decision indicates that the Supreme Court's *LA County Flood Control District* decision need not be an obstacle to enforcement of stormwater discharge permits.

4. While the Court in *Miccosukee* had no trouble finding that a pump consti-tuted a point source even though it did not generate the pollutants it conveyed, the question of what constitutes a point source remains alive in other circumstances. At oral argument in the Supreme Court in the *Borden Ranch* case, there was consider-able discussion of the meaning of "point source" and whether a deep ripper could qualify as one. Justice Scalia was skeptical of the notion that anything that moved dirt could be considered a conveyance that would make it a point source, arguing that under this view anyone who used a rake on a beach could be considered a point source. The government noted that a deep ripper is an enormous piece of specialized machinery that weighs over 100,000 pounds and whose very purpose is to move dirt. We now turn to the question of what constitutes a point source under the Clean Water Act.

### 3.   Defining "Point Sources" Subject to Permit Requirements

Why would Congress have chosen to focus federal water pollution control efforts almost exclusively on point source discharges? Congress was aware that non-point sources made a considerable contribution to water pollution, though it may not have fully appreciated their importance. But it recognized that point sources are easier to control, both politically and administratively, particularly when pollu-tion control technology emphasized end-of-the-pipe solutions. Control of nonpoint source pollution requires some form of land use control, which has been politically unpopular, even at the state level, as we will see in Chapter 7. Thus, it was not until the Clean Water Act was amended in 1987 that Congress explicitly identified con-trol of nonpoint source pollution as a goal of the Act.

Even limited to point source dischargers, implementation of a national per-mit program posed major administrative challenges for EPA. Recognizing the enor-mous task it faced, EPA announced that it would focus first on processing permit applications from major dischargers in areas where water pollution was the worst. Fearing that it would have to process millions of permit applications, the agency also issued regulations exempting certain categories of point sources from the Act's permit requirements on the ground of administrative infeasibility. An environmen-tal group challenged EPA's decision in the case that follows.

## NRDC v. Costle

568 F.2d 1369 (D.C. Cir. 1977)

LEVENTHAL, Circuit Judge:

In 1973 the EPA Administrator issued regulations that exempted certain cat-egories of "point sources" of pollution from the permit requirements of §402. The Administrator's purported authority to make such exemptions turns on the proper interpretation of §402.

A "point source" is defined in §502(14) as "any discernible, confined and discrete conveyance, including but not limited to any pipe, ditch, channel, tun-nel, conduit, well, discrete fissure, container, rolling stock, concentrated animal feeding operation, or vessel or other floating craft, from which pollutants are or may be discharged."

The 1973 regulations exempted discharges from a number of classes of point sources from the permit requirements of §402, including all silvicultural point sources; all confined animal feeding operations below a certain size; all irrigation return flows from areas of less than 3,000 contiguous acres or 3,000 noncontiguous acres that use the same drainage system; all nonfeedlot, nonirrigation agricultural point sources; and separate storm sewers containing only storm runoff uncontaminated by any industrial or commercial activity. The EPA's rationale for these exemptions is that in order to conserve the Agency's enforcement resources for more significant point sources of pollution, it is necessary to exclude these smaller sources of pollutant discharges from the permit program.

The National [*sic*] Resources Defense Council, Inc. (NRDC) sought a declaratory judgment that the regulations are unlawful under the FWPCA. Specifically, NRDC contended that the Administrator does not have authority to exempt any class of point source from the permit requirements of §402. It argued that Congress in enacting §§301, 402 of the FWPCA intended to prohibit the discharge of pollutants from *all* point sources unless a permit had been issued to the discharger under §402 or unless the point source was explicitly exempted from the permit requirements by statute. The District Court granted NRDC's motion for summary judgment. It held that the FWPCA does not authorize the Administrator to exclude any class of point sources from the permit program. NRDC v. Train, 396 F. Supp. 1393 (D.D.C. 1975). The EPA has appealed to this court. . . .

## I.  LEGISLATIVE HISTORY

The NPDES permit program established by I. §402 is central to the enforcement of the FWPCA. It translates general effluent limitations into the specific obligations of a discharger. . . .

The appellants argue that §402 not only gives the Administrator the discretion to grant or refuse a permit, but also gives him the authority to exempt classes of point sources from the permit requirements entirely. They argue that this interpretation is supported by the legislative history of §402 and the fact that the unavailability of this exemption power would place an unmanageable administrative burden on EPA. . . .

Under the EPA's interpretation the Administrator would have broad discretion to exempt large classes of point sources from any or all requirements of the FWPCA. This is a result that the legislators did not intend. Rather they stressed that the FWPCA was a tough law that relied on explicit mandates to a degree uncommon in legislation of this type. . . .

There are innumerable references in the legislative history to the effect that the Act is founded on the "basic premise that a discharge of pollutants without a permit is unlawful and that discharges not in compliance with the limitations and conditions for a permit are unlawful." Even when infeasibility arguments were squarely raised, the legislature declined to abandon the permit requirement. . . .

The wording of the statute, legislative history, and precedents are clear: the EPA Administrator does not have the authority to exempt categories of point sources from the permit requirements of §402. . . .

## II. ADMINISTRATIVE INFEASIBILITY

The appellants have stressed in briefs and at oral argument the extraordinary burden on the EPA that will be imposed by the above interpretation of the scope of the NPDES program. The spectre of millions of applications for permits is evoked both as part of appellants' legislative history argument—that Congress could not have intended to impose such burdens on the EPA—and as an invitation to this court to uphold the regulations as deviations from the literal terms of the FWPCA necessary to permit the agency to realize the general objectives of that act. . . .

### A. Uniform National Effluent Limitations

EPA argues that the regulatory scheme intended under Titles III and IV of the FWPCA requires, first, that the Administrator establish national effluent limitations and, second, that these limitations be incorporated in the individual permits of dischargers. EPA argues that the establishment of such limitations is simply not possible with the type of point sources involved in the 1973 regulations, which essentially involve the discharge of runoff—i.e., wastewaters generated by rainfall that drain over terrain into navigable waters, picking up pollutants along the way. . . . EPA contends that certain characteristics of runoff pollution make it difficult to promulgate effluent limitations for most of the point sources exempted by the 1973 regulations:

> The major characteristic of the pollution problem which is generated by runoff . . . is that the owner of the discharge point . . . has no control over the quantity of the flow or the nature and amounts of the pollutants picked up by the runoff. The amount of flow obviously is unpredictable because it results from the duration and intensity of the rainfall event, the topography, the type of ground cover and the saturation point of the land due to any previous rainfall. Similar factors affect the types of pollutants which will be picked up by that runoff, including the type of farming practices employed, the rate and type of pesticide and fertilizer application, and the conservation practices employed. . . .
>
> An effluent limitation must be a precise number in order for it to be an effective regulatory tool; both the discharger and the regulatory agency need to have an identifiable standard upon which to determine whether the facility is in compliance. That was the principle of the passage of the 1972 Amendments.

Implicit in EPA's contentions is the premise that there must be a uniform effluent limitation prior to issuing a permit. That is not our understanding of the law. . . .

As noted in NRDC v. Train[, 510 F.2d 692 (D.C. Cir. 1975)], the primary purpose of the effluent limitations and guidelines was to provide uniformity among the federal and state jurisdictions enforcing the NPDES program and prevent the "Tragedy of the Commons" that might result if jurisdictions can compete for industry and development by providing more liberal limitations than their neighboring states. 510 F.2d at 709. The effluent limitations were intended to create floors that had to be respected by state permit programs.

But in *NRDC v. Train* it was also recognized that permits could be issued before national effluent limitations were promulgated and that permits issued subsequent to promulgation of uniform effluent limitations could be modified to take account of special characteristics of subcategories of point sources. . . .

In [*Train*] this court fully appreciated that technological and administrative constraints might prevent the Administrator from developing guidelines and corresponding uniform numeric effluent limitations for certain point sources anytime in the near future. The Administrator was deemed to have the burden of demonstrating that the failure to develop the guidelines on schedule was due to administrative or technological infeasibility. 510 F.2d at 713. Yet the underlying teaching was that technological or administrative infeasibility was a reason for adjusting court mandates to the minimum extent necessary to realize the general objectives of the Act. It is a number of steps again to suggest that these problems afford the Administrator the authority to exempt categories of point sources from the NPDES program entirely.

With time, experience, and technological development, more point sources in the categories that EPA has now classed as exempt may be amenable to national effluent limitations achieved through end-of-pipe technology or other means of pollution control. . . .

In sum, we conclude that the existence of uniform national effluent limitations is not a necessary precondition for incorporating into the NPDES program pollution from agricultural, silvicultural, and storm water runoff point sources. The technological or administrative infeasibility of such limitations may result in adjustments in the permit programs, as will be seen, but it does not authorize the Administrator to exclude the relevant point source from the NPDES program.

### B. Alternative Permit Conditions Under §402(a)

EPA contends that even if it is possible to issue permits without national effluent limitations, the special characteristics of point sources of runoff pollution make it infeasible to develop restrictions on a case-by-case basis. EPA's implicit premise is that whether limitations are promulgated on a class or individual source basis, it is still necessary to articulate any limitation in terms of a numerical effluent standard. That is not our understanding.

Section 402 provides that a permit may be issued upon condition "that such discharge will meet either all applicable requirements under sections 301, 302, 306, 307, 308 and 403 of this Act, *or prior to taking of necessary implementing actions relating to all such requirements, such conditions as the Administrator determines are necessary to carry out the provisions of this Act*." 33 U.S.C. §1342(a) (Supp. V 1975) (emphasis added). This provision gives EPA considerable flexibility in framing the permit to achieve a desired reduction in pollutant discharges. The permit may proscribe industry practices that aggravate the problem of point source pollution. . . .

[W]hen numerical effluent limitations are infeasible, EPA may issue permits with conditions designed to reduce the level of effluent discharges to acceptable levels. This may well mean opting for a gross reduction in pollutant discharge rather than the fine-tuning suggested by numerical limitations. But this ambitious statute is not hospitable to the concept that the appropriate response to a difficult pollution problem is not to try at all.

It may be appropriate in certain circumstances for the EPA to require a permittee simply to monitor and report effluent levels; EPA manifestly has this authority.

Such permit conditions might be desirable where the full extent of the pollution problem is not known.

## C. General Permits

Finally, EPA argues that the number of permits involved in the absence of an exemption authority will simply overwhelm the Agency. Affidavits filed with the District Court indicate, for example, that the number of silviculture point sources may be over 300,000 and that there are approximately 100,000 separate storm sewer point sources. We are and must be sensitive to EPA's concerns of an intolerable permit load. But the District Court and the various parties have suggested devices to mitigate the burden — to accommodate within a practical regulatory scheme Congress' clear mandate that all point sources have permits. All that is required is that EPA make full use of its interpretational authority. The existence of a variety of options belies EPA's infeasibility arguments.

Section 402 does not explicitly describe the necessary scope of a NPDES permit. The most significant requirement is that the permit be in compliance with limitation sections of the Act described above. As a result NRDC and the District Court have suggested the use of area or general permits. The Act allows such techniques. Area-wide regulation is one well-established means of coping with administrative exigency. An instance is area pricing for natural gas producers, which the Supreme Court upheld in Permian Basin Area Rate Cases, 390 U.S. 747 (1968). A more dramatic example is the administrative search warrant which may be issued on an area basis despite the normal Fourth Amendment requirement of probable cause for searching specific premises. Camara v. Municipal Court, 387 U.S. 523 (1967).

In response to the District Court's order, EPA promulgated regulations that make use of the general permit device. 42 Fed. Reg. 6846-53 (Feb. 4, 1977). The general permit is addressed to a class of point source dischargers, subject to notice and opportunity for public hearing in the geographical area covered by the permit. Although we do not pass on the validity of the February 1977 regulations, they serve to dilute an objection of wholesale infeasibility.

Our approach is not fairly subject to the criticism that it elevates form over substance [such] that the end result will look very much like EPA's categorical exemption. It is the function of the courts to require agencies to comply with legislative intent when that intent is clear, and to leave it to the legislature to make adjustments when the result is counterproductive. At the same time, where intent on an issue is unclear, we are instructed to afford the administering agency the flexibility necessary to achieve the general objectives of the Act. . . . These lines of authority conjoin in our approach. We insist, as the Act insists, that a permit is necessary; the Administrator has no authority to exempt point sources from the NPDES program. But we concede necessary flexibility in the shaping of the permits that is not inconsistent with the clear terms of the Act.

There is also a very practical difference between a general permit and an exemption. An exemption tends to become indefinite: the problem drops out of sight, into a pool of inertia, unlikely to be recalled in the absence of crisis or a strong political protagonist. In contrast, the general or area permit approach forces the Agency to focus on the problems of specific regions and requires that the problems of the region be reconsidered at least every five years, the maximum duration of a permit. . . .

## NOTES AND QUESTIONS

1. In general, the more comprehensive a regulatory program is, the greater is the administrative burden on the agency that must implement it. At some point the universe of regulatory targets becomes so large that it simply is not feasible to apply the same standards to all. Rather than requiring that *all* point sources be regulated, would it make more sense to give EPA the authority to require permits for whatever sources (point or nonpoint) that it determines pose the greatest problems? If EPA had the authority to issue permits authorizing discharges, why did it not have the authority to exempt point sources from permit requirements?

2. The court offers several suggestions for easing the administrative burden of permitting the sources EPA sought to exempt, including the use of general permits and other alternatives to numerical effluent limitations. Is there any "very practical difference" between a general or area-wide permit and an exemption, and if so, how could a general permit contribute to achieving the objectives of the Act?

3. Under what circumstances should pollutant discharges that occur due to weather conditions be considered discharges from point sources? The American Iron and Steel Institute had argued that only "volitional flows" that add pollutants to navigable waters should be considered point source discharges. Would this interpretation be more sensible because it would exempt from permit requirements natural runoff that happens to flow through a discrete conveyance? Or should it depend on whether or not the conveyance usually collects pollution? Why not simply abandon the point-nonpoint source distinction in favor of one that turns on whether the discharge is caused by human activities or naturally occurring ones? Would this be an easy distinction to make? Should the determination of point source status depend instead on how amenable the discharge is to control?

4. Examine the current statutory definition of "point source," which is contained in section 502(14). Note that the definition is the same as that quoted in *NRDC v. Costle*, except that Congress has added a sentence exempting "agricultural stormwater discharges and return flows from irrigated agriculture." Return flows from irrigated agriculture were exempted in the 1977 Amendments in response to *NRDC v. Costle*. This exemption has generated considerable criticism because agricultural irrigation has created severe pollution problems in some areas. For example, at California's Kesterson National Wildlife Refuge, return flows produced a buildup of naturally occurring selenium in concentrations toxic to wildlife.

5. Is it clear that all of the sources EPA initially sought to exempt from permit requirements in *NRDC v. Costle* were indeed point sources? Industry intervenors argued that some of them were not. Does the court ever specify what a point source is? In response to the decision, EPA issued new regulations to define with greater precision which categories of discharges come from point sources. These regulations included what came to be known as the "Silvicultural Rule." This rule defined silvicultural point sources to include "any discernible, confined and discrete conveyance related to rock crushing, gravel washing, log sorting, or log storage facilities which are operated in connection with silvicultural activities and from which pollutants are discharged into the waters of the United States." 40 C.F.R. §122.27(b)(1). The rule specified that "non-point source silvicultural activities . . . from which there is natural runoff" are not silvicultural point sources.

6. As noted above, Congress in the 1987 Amendments to the Clean Water Act added section 402(p), which specifies requirements for NPDES permitting of

storm sewer systems. Faced with permit requirements applicable to 114,000 industrial facilities and 220 cities, 55 Fed. Reg. 47,990 (1990), EPA belatedly issued permit application regulations under court order in October 1990. In April 1992, EPA adopted a four-tiered approach to industrial stormwater permitting that relies on general permits for most dischargers. 57 Fed. Reg. 11,394 (1992). If stormwater discharges in particular watersheds, or from certain industries or specific facilities, are found to contribute to water quality problems, watershed-, industry-, or facility-specific permits may be required. In 1999, EPA issued Phase II of its stormwater regulations, which broadened their reach to include smaller municipalities and construction sites that disturb between one and five acres of land. In Environmental Defense Center v. EPA, 344 F.3d 832 (9th Cir. 2003), the Ninth Circuit upheld EPA's authority to issue the Phase II rules, and it rejected claims that they violated the Tenth Amendment. However, the court held that EPA must provide for public review of notices of intent to obtain coverage under the Phase II general permit because these notices indicate how dischargers plan to comply with the requirement to reduce discharges "to the maximum extent practicable."

7. Noting that Congress had not exempted stormwater discharges "associated with industrial activity," §402(p)(2)(B), an environmental group sued Oregon officials and timber companies, alleging that they violated the Clean Water Act by discharging stormwater from ditches alongside logging roads in a state forest without an NPDES permit. The plaintiff argued that logging constitutes "industrial activity" for which stormwater permits are required. EPA maintained instead that it intended "to regulate traditional industrial sources such as sawmills," but not temporary, outdoor logging operations. In Decker v. Northwest Environmental Defense Center, 568 U.S. 597 (2013), the Supreme Court deferred to EPA's interpretation and reversed a decision by the Ninth Circuit that had required NPDES permits to control stormwater runoff from logging operations. The Court noted that EPA's interpretation "is reinforced by the Industrial Stormwater Rule's definition of discharges associated with industrial activity as discharges 'from any conveyance that is used for collecting and conveying storm water and that is directly related to manufacturing, processing or raw materials storage areas at an industrial plant.' 40 C.F.R. §122.26(b)(14) (2006)." The Court noted that this "language lends support to the EPA's claim that the regulation does not cover temporary, outdoor logging installations."

In the case below, the U.S. Court of Appeals for the Second Circuit addressed the question whether a person can be a point source for purposes of the Clean Water Act.

## United States v. Plaza Health Laboratories, Inc.

3 F.3d 643 (2d Cir. 1993)

Before: OAKES, REARSE, and PRATT, Circuit Judges.

GEORGE C. PRATT, Circuit Judge:

Defendant Geronimo Villegas appeals from a judgment entered in the United States District Court for the Eastern District of New York, Edward R. Korman, Judge, convicting him of two counts of knowingly discharging pollutants into the Hudson River in violation of the Clean Water Act ("CWA"). See 33 U.S.C. §§301 and 309(c)(2). . . .

### FACTS AND BACKGROUND

Villegas was co-owner and vice president of Plaza Health Laboratories, Inc., a blood-testing laboratory in Brooklyn, New York. On at least two occasions between April and September 1988, Villegas loaded containers of numerous vials of human blood generated from his business into his personal car, and drove to his residence at the Admirals Walk Condominium in Edgewater, New Jersey. Once at his condominium complex, Villegas removed the containers from his car and carried them to the edge of the Hudson River. On one occasion he carried two containers of the vials to the bulkhead that separates his condominium complex from the river, and placed them at low tide within a crevice in the bulkhead that was below the high-water line.

On May 26, 1988, a group of eighth graders on a field trip at the Alice Austin House in Staten Island, New York, discovered numerous glass vials containing human blood along the shore. Some of the vials had washed up on the shore; many were still in the water. Some were cracked, although most remained sealed with stoppers in solid-plastic containers or ziplock bags. Fortunately, no one was injured. That afternoon, New York City workers recovered approximately 70 vials from the area.

On September 25, 1988, a maintenance worker employed by the Admirals Walk Condominium discovered a plastic container holding blood vials wedged between rocks in the bulkhead. New Jersey authorities retrieved numerous blood vials from the bulkhead later that day.

Ten of the retrieved vials contained blood infected with the hepatitis-B virus. All of the vials recovered were eventually traced to Plaza Health Laboratories. . . .

Villegas contends that one element of the CWA crime, knowingly discharging pollutants from a "point source," was not established in his case. He argues that the definition of "point source," 33 U.S.C. §502(14), does not include discharges that result from the individual acts of human beings. Raising primarily questions of legislative intent and statutory construction, Villegas argues that at best, the term "point source" is ambiguous as applied to him, and that the rule of lenity should result in reversal of his convictions. . . .

#### 1. Language and Structure of Act

Human beings are not among the enumerated items that may be a "point source." Although by its terms the definition of "point source" is nonexclusive, the words used to define the term and the examples given ("pipe, ditch, channel, tunnel, conduit, well, discrete fissure," etc.) evoke images of physical structures and instrumentalities that systematically act as a means of conveying pollutants from an industrial source to navigable waterways.

In addition, if every discharge involving humans were to be considered a "discharge from a point source," the statute's lengthy definition of "point source" would have been unnecessary. It is elemental that Congress does not add unnecessary words to statutes. Had Congress intended to punish any human being who polluted navigational waters, it could readily have said: "any person who places pollutants in navigable waters without a permit is guilty of a crime."

The Clean Water Act generally targets industrial and municipal sources of pollutants, as is evident from a perusal of its many sections. Consistent with this focus, the term "point source" is used throughout the statute, but invariably in sentences referencing industrial or municipal discharges. See, e.g., §301 (referring to "owner or operator" of point source); §301(e) (requiring that effluent limitations established under the Act "be applied to all point sources of discharge").  . . .

Finally on this point, we assume that Congress did not intend the awkward meaning that would result if we were to read "human being" into the definition of "point source." Section 1362(12)(A) defines "discharge of a pollutant" as "any addition of any pollutant to navigable waters from any point source." Enhanced by this definition, §1311(a) reads in effect "the addition of any pollutant to navigable waters *from any point source by any person* shall be unlawful" (emphasis added). But were a human being to be included within the definition of "point source," the prohibition would then read: "the addition of any pollutant to navigable waters *from any person by any person* shall be unlawful," and this simply makes no sense. As the statute stands today, the term "point source" is comprehensible only if it is held to the context of industrial and municipal discharges.

### 2. Legislative History and Context

. . . The legislative history of the CWA, while providing little insight into the meaning of "point source," confirms the act's focus on industrial polluters. Congress required NPDES permits of those who discharge from a "point source." The term "point source," introduced to the act in 1972, was intended to function as a means of identifying industrial polluters—generally a difficult task because pollutants quickly disperse throughout the subject waters. The Senate report for the 1972 amendments explains:

> In order to further clarify the scope of the regulatory procedures in the Act the Committee had added a definition of point source to distinguish between control requirements where there are *specific confined conveyances, such as pipes,* and control requirements which are imposed to control runoff. The control of pollutants from runoff is applied pursuant to section 209 and the authority resides in the State or other local agency.

S. Rep. No. 92-414, reprinted in 1972 U.S.C.C.A.N. 3668, 3744. . . .

We find no suggestion either in the act itself or in the history of its passage that Congress intended the CWA to impose criminal liability on an individual for the myriad, random acts of human waste disposal, for example, a passerby who flings a candy wrapper into the Hudson River, or a urinating swimmer. Discussions during the passage of the 1972 amendments indicate that Congress had bigger fish to fry. . . .

In sum, although Congress had the ability to so provide, §502(14) of the CWA does not expressly recognize a human being as a "point source"; nor does the act make structural sense when one incorporates a human being into that definition. The legislative history of the act adds no light to the muddy depths of this issue, and cases urging a broad interpretation of the definition in the civil-penalty context do not persuade us to do so here, where Congress has imposed heavy criminal sanctions. Adopting the government's suggested flexibility for the definition would effectively read the "point source" element of the crime out of the statute, and not even the EPA has extended the term "point source" as far as is urged here.

We accordingly conclude that the term "point source" as applied to a human being is at best ambiguous.

## B. Rule of Lenity

In criminal prosecutions the rule of lenity requires that ambiguities in the statute be resolved in the defendant's favor. . . .

Since the government's reading of the statute in this case founders on our inability to discern the "obvious intention of the legislature" to include a human being as a "point source," we conclude that the criminal provisions of the CWA did not clearly proscribe Villegas' conduct and did not accord him fair warning of the sanctions the law placed on that conduct. Under the rule of lenity, therefore, the prosecutions against him must be dismissed. . . .

OAKES, Circuit Judge, dissenting:

. . . [B]ecause I do not agree that a person can never be a point source, and because I believe that Mr. Villegas' actions, as the jury found them, fell well within the bounds of activity proscribed by the Clean Water Act's bar on discharge of pollutants into navigable waters, I am required to dissent. . . .

I begin with the obvious, in hopes that it will illuminate the less obvious: the classic point source is something like a pipe. This is, at least in part, because pipes and similar conduits are needed to carry large quantities of wastewater, which represents a large proportion of the point source pollution problem. Thus, devices designed to convey large quantities of wastewater from a factory or municipal sewage treatment facility are readily classified as point sources. Because not all pollutants are liquids, however, the statute and the cases make clear that means of conveying solid wastes to be dumped in navigable waters are also point sources. See, e.g., §502(14) ("rolling stock," or railroad cars, listed as an example of a point source); Avoyelles Sportsmen's League, Inc. v. Marsh, 715 F.2d 897, 922 (5th Cir. 1983) (backhoes and bulldozers used to gather fill and deposit it on wetlands are point sources).

What I take from this look at classic point sources is that, at the least, an organized means of channeling and conveying industrial waste in quantity to navigable waters is a "discernible, confined and discrete conveyance." The case-law is in accord: courts have deemed a broad range of means of depositing pollutants in the country's navigable waters to be point sources. See, e.g., Rybachek v. EPA, 904 F.2d 1276 (9th Cir. 1990) (placer mining; sluice box from which discharge water is redeposited in stream is point source, despite provisions protecting some mining activities); United States v. M.C.C. of Fla., Inc., 772 F.2d 1501, 1505-1506 (11th Cir. 1985) (tugs redepositing dirt from bottom of water body onto beds of water grass are point sources discharging the dirt), vacated on other grounds, 481 U.S. 1034 (1987) (defendants' right to jury trial); Sierra Club v. Abston Constr. Co., 620 F.2d 41, 45 (5th Cir. 1980) (spill of contaminated runoff from strip mine, if collected or channeled by the operator, is point source discharge); United States v. Earth Sciences, Inc., 599 F.2d 368, 374 (10th Cir. 1979) (same); Appalachian Power Co. v. Train, 545 F.2d 1351, 1372 (4th Cir. 1976) (same); O'Leary v. Moyer's Landfill, Inc., 523 F. Supp. 642, 655 (E.D. Pa. 1981) (same). Nor have courts been inclined to exclude mining or agricultural point sources, despite the fact that portions of the Clean Water Act protect these industries to some extent. . . .

Further, the legislative history indicates that the Act was meant to control periodic, as well as continuous, discharges. S. Rep. No. 92-414, 92d Cong., 1st Sess. (1971).

In short, the term "point source" has been broadly construed to apply to a wide range of polluting techniques, so long as the pollutants involved are not just humanmade, but reach the navigable waters by human effort or by leaking from a clear point at which wastewater was collected by human effort. From these cases, the writers of one respected treatise have concluded that such a "man-induced gathering mechanism plainly is the essential characteristic of a point source" and that a point source, "put simply, . . . is an identifiable conveyance of pollutants." 5 Robert E. Beck, Waters & Water Rights §53.01(b)(3) at 216-17 (1991). . . .

. . . [T]o further refine the definition of "point source," I consider what it is that the Act does not cover: nonpoint source discharges.

Nonpoint source pollution is, generally, runoff: salt from roads, agricultural chemicals from farmlands, oil from parking lots, and other substances washed by rain, in diffuse patterns, over the land and into navigable waters. The sources are many, difficult to identify and difficult to control. Indeed, an effort to greatly reduce nonpoint source pollution could require radical changes in land use patterns which Congress evidently was unwilling to mandate without further study. The structure of the statute — which regulates point source pollution closely, while leaving nonpoint source regulation to the states under the Section 208 program — indicates that the term "point source" was included in the definition of discharge so as to ensure that nonpoint source pollution would not be covered. Instead, Congress chose to regulate first that which could easily be regulated: direct discharges by identifiable parties, or point sources.

This rationale for regulating point and nonpoint sources differently — that point sources may readily be controlled and are easily attributable to a particular source, while nonpoint sources are more difficult to control without radical change, and less easily attributable, once they reach water, to any particular responsible party — helps define what fits within each category. Thus, Professor Rodgers has suggested, "the statutory discernible, confined and discrete conveyance . . . can be understood as singling out those candidates suitable for control-at-the-source." 2 William H. Rodgers, Jr., Environmental Law: Air and Water §4.10 at 150 (1986). And, as Professor Rodgers notes, "case law confirms the controllability theory, adding to it a responsibility component, so that 'point sources' are understood both as sources that can be cleaned up and as sources where fairness suggests the named parties should do the cleaning." Id. . . .

While Villegas' activities were not prototypical point source discharges — in part because he was disposing of waste that could have been disposed of on land, and so did not need a permit or a pipe — they much more closely resembled a point source discharge than a nonpoint source discharge. First, Villegas and his lab were perfectly capable of avoiding discharging their waste into water: they were, in Professor Rodgers' terms, a "controllable" source.

Furthermore, the discharge was directly into water, and came from an identifiable point, Villegas. Villegas did not dispose of the materials on land, where they could be washed into water as nonpoint source pollution. Rather, he carried them, from his firm's laboratory, in his car, to his apartment complex, where he placed them in a bulkhead below the high tide line. I do not think it is necessary to determine whether it was Mr. Villegas himself who was the point source, or whether it was his car, the vials, or the bulkhead: in a sense, the entire stream of Mr. Villegas' activity functioned as a "discrete conveyance" or point source. The point is that the source of the pollution was clear, and would have been easy to control. Indeed, Villegas was well aware that there were methods of controlling the discharge (and that the materials were too dangerous for casual disposal): his laboratory had hired a professional medical waste handler. He simply chose not to use an appropriate waste disposal mechanism.

Villegas' method may have been an unusual one for a corporate officer, but it would undermine the statute—which, after all, sets as its goal the elimination of discharges, §301(a)—to regard as "ambiguous" a Congressional failure to list an unusual method of disposing of waste. I doubt that Congress would have regarded an army of men and women throwing industrial waste from trucks into a stream as exempt from the statute. Since the Act contains no exemption for de minimus violations—since, indeed, many Clean Water Act prosecutions are for a series of small discharges, each of which is treated as a single violation—I cannot see that one man throwing one day's worth of medical waste into the ocean differs (and indeed, with this type of pollution, it might be that only a few days' violations could be proven even if the laboratory regularly relied on Villegas to dispose of its waste by throwing it into the ocean). A different reading would encourage corporations perfectly capable of abiding by the Clean Water Act's requirements to ask their employees to stand between the company trucks and the sea, thereby transforming point source pollution (dumping from trucks) into nonpoint source pollution (dumping by hand). Such a method is controllable, easily identifiable, and inexcusable. To call it nonpoint source pollution is to read a technical exception into a statute which attempts to define in broad terms an activity which may be conducted in many different ways. . . .

I do not think technical arguments about whether the toxic substances were in discrete containers are fruitful when the activity is discrete, conveys pollutants, and is confined to a clear, traceable single source. When a company chooses to use the nation's waters as a dumpsite for waste it has created and gathered in a manageable place, it should ask for a permit or face prosecution.

I am of course given pause, however, by the nature of the criminal sanctions attached to point source discharges under §1319. Given the broad statutory definitions of pollutant and point source, it would appear that a knowing violation would include intentionally throwing a candy wrapper into the ocean—and that this is an activity which could subject the thrower to a $25,000 fine and three years in jail. It seems improbable to me that this could have been Congress' intent. Consequently, I would with the majority read the statute as ambiguous as it pertains to individual litterers, as opposed to disposers of industrial and municipal waste. The latter were the principal targets of the authors of the CWA, and, as professional creators of waste, charged with knowledge that disposal of waste into navigable waters is a crime.

## NOTES AND QUESTIONS

1. The court majority says that the Clean Water Act was never designed to address the random, individual polluter. Why not? Is the court majority correct when they argue that interpreting "point source" to embrace humans could subject to criminal penalties a urinating swimmer or a passerby who flings a candy wrapper into surface waters?

2.  In a portion of the majority opinion not reproduced above, the court noted that the Rivers and Harbors Act makes it a misdemeanor "to throw, discharge, or deposit . . . any refuse matter" into surface waters. Why do you think the government chose not to prosecute Mr. Villegas under this statute, which would not have presented the "point source" problem?

3.  The court invokes the rule of lenity to resolve statutory ambiguities in favor of a defendant in a criminal case. The purpose of this rule is to ensure that individuals will have fair warning concerning what behavior is criminal. Do you think that most people would consider the dumping of contaminated vials of blood into water where they could wash onto beaches on which children play to be a criminal act?

4.  On what does Judge Oakes premise his dissenting view that persons are point sources? Is he right that under the majority's interpretation a company could avoid compliance with the Clean Water Act simply by having its employees hurl waste into water? How would Judge Oakes deal with the problem of criminalizing the urinating swimmer or the candy wrapper tosser? Concerned that this decision could undermine the Clean Water Act, the government appealed to the Supreme Court, but the Court declined to review the case. United States v. Villegas, cert. denied, 512 U.S. 1245 (1994).

5.  In a subsequent case, Judge Oakes, writing for a unanimous court, reversed a district court holding that a liquid manure spreading operation was not a point source for purposes of the Clean Water Act. In Concerned Area Residents for the Environment v. Southview Farm, 34 F.3d 114 (2d Cir. 1994), the Second Circuit held that because the liquid manure was collected by human effort and channeled through ditches that led to a stream, the operation was a point source. The court also held that manure spreading vehicles used by the operation were point sources because they collected liquid manure and discharged it on fields from which the manure directly flowed into navigable waters. It rejected arguments that the operation involved "agricultural storm-water discharges" exempted from the definition of "point source" in section 502(14), finding that it instead involved the kind of "concentrated animal feeding operation" (CAFO) specifically listed in the point source definition.

6.  Improperly managed animal feeding operations (AFOs) now are widely recognized as an important source of water pollution. EPA estimates that out of 1.3 million farms with livestock, approximately 238,000 maintain confined animal feeding operations (CAFOs). These CAFOs produce more than 500 million tons of animal manure each year, more than three times the amount of waste excreted by humans. In March 1999, EPA and USDA issued their "Unified National Strategy for Animal Feeding Operations." The strategy sought to accelerate the issuance of NPDES permits for large CAFOs (i.e., operations with greater than 1,000 animal units) and to require that comprehensive nutrient management plans be incorporated in these permits. In December 2002, EPA issued final CAFO regulations that require approximately 15,500 large CAFOs to apply for NDPES permits by 2006. The regulations require these entities to apply for a permit, submit an annual report, and develop and follow a plan for handling manure and wastewater. Large CAFOs are defined in the rule as operations raising more than 1,000 cattle, 700 dairy cows, 2,500 swine, 10,000 sheep, 125,000 chickens, 82,000 laying hens, or 55,000 turkeys in confinement. As revised in 2003, EPA's regulations require all CAFOs to apply for NPDES permits and to develop and implement nutrient management plans. 68 Fed. Reg. 7,176 (2003).

7. In November 2008, EPA revised its CAFO regulations to require CAFO owners and operators that discharge or propose to discharge to apply for an NPDES permit. 73 Fed. Reg. 70,418 (2008). The 2008 CAFO Rule also created a voluntary option for unpermitted CAFO owners and operators to certify that the CAFO does not discharge or propose to discharge. In March 2011, the United States Court of Appeals for the Fifth Circuit struck down the portion of the 2008 CAFO Rule that required CAFOs that propose to discharge to apply for an NPDES permit. National Pork Producers Council v. EPA, 635 F.3d 738, 756 (5th Cir. 2011). The court held that EPA did not have the authority to regulate CAFOs that *proposed* to discharge. EPA's regulatory authority extends only to *actual* discharges. In July 2012, EPA amended its CAFO regulations to comply with the *National Pork Producers Council* decision by removing the requirement that CAFOs that "propose to discharge" must apply for an NPDES permit. 77 Fed. Reg. 44,494 (2012).

8. Consider whether or not the following activities involve discharges from point sources that require an NPDES permit. Is a dam that discharges water whose oxygen content has been reduced due to the dam's presence a point source? See National Wildlife Fed. v. Gorsuch, 693 F.2d 156 (D.C. Cir. 1982) (EPA properly determined that Congress did not intend to require dams to obtain NPDES permits). Does the discharge of dead fish from a hydroelectric plant's penstocks require an NPDES permit? See National Wildlife Fed. v. Consumers Power Co., 862 F.2d 580 (6th Cir. 1988) (no permit required following holding in *Gorsuch*). Is a permit required if toxic materials are discharged into a stream when a settling pond used to process gold ore overflows during an unusually sudden snowmelt? See United States v. Earth Sciences, Inc., 599 F.2d 368 (10th Cir. 1979) (permit required because Congress defined "point source" to embrace "the broadest possible definition of any identifiable conveyance from which pollutants might enter the waters of the United States"); see also Sierra Club v. Abston Constr. Co., 620 F.2d 41 (5th Cir. 1980) (surface runoff from strip mine is a point source when spoil piles are designed so that it is reasonably likely pollutants will be discharged through ditches or other discrete conveyances); compare section 402(1) (1987 amendment exempting from permit requirements discharges of storm water runoff from oil, gas, and mining operations that do not come into contact with products or waste material). Are a series of surface impoundments designed to capture, contain, and evaporate toxic runoff from an abandoned mine a point source when their contents occasionally spill into a nearby river? See Committee to Save Mokelumne River v. East Bay Mun. Util. Dist., 13 F.3d 305 (9th Cir. 1993) (impoundments held to be a point source, although a concurring judge noted that because the facility was like a dam and had been constructed to help reduce pollution, he would have been willing to defer to EPA if it had determined that the facility was not a point source). Is the application of aquatic herbicides to irrigation canals a discharge from a point source that must be authorized by an NPDES permit? (In Headwaters Inc. v. Talent Irrigation District, 243 F.3d 526 (9th Cir. 2001), the court said that it was.)

9. In Upstate Forever v. Kinder Morgan Energy Partners, L.P., 887 F.3d 637 (4th Cir. 2018), the Fourth Circuit held that the rupture of an underground pipeline violated the Clean Water Act because the oil eventually reached surface waters. This decision was vacated by the Supreme Court, 140 S. Ct. 2736 (2020), to enable a lower court to apply the new Maui test. In two cases, the Fourth and Sixth Circuits have held that pollutants that leak from coal ash impoundments and travel to navigable waters through groundwater do not violate the Clean Water Act

because the impoundments are not point sources. In Sierra Club v. Virginia Electric & Power Co., 903 F.3d 403 (4th Cir. 2018), the Fourth Circuit held that arsenic leaking from coal ash piles and settling ponds through groundwater into navigable waters did not violate the Clean Water Act (CWA) because the pollutants did not come from a point source discharge. In Kentucky Waterways v. Kentucky Utilities Co., 905 F.3d 925 (6th Cir. 2018), the Sixth Circuit held that seepage of pollutants from coal ash ponds that migrated through groundwater into a lake were not covered by the CWA because the coal ash ponds are not point sources. In Tennessee Clean Water Network v. Tennessee Valley Authority, 905 F.3d 436 (6th Cir. 2018), another panel of the Sixth Circuit held that pollutants leaking from ponds of coal ash do not violate the Act because "[t]he CWA does not extend liability to pollution that reaches surface waters via groundwater."

10. In November 2007, EPA issued a final rule exempting from section 402 permit requirements pesticides applied to surface waters for the purpose of controlling pests and pesticides unavoidably deposited on such waters as a result of aerial spraying operations. 71 Fed. Reg. 68,483 (2007). EPA reasoned that pesticides generally are not "pollutants" except when they become wastes and that by the time they become wastes they no longer are present as a result of a "point source" discharge. EPA's rule was struck down in January 2009 by the U.S. Court of Appeals for the Sixth Circuit. The National Cotton Council of America v. U.S. EPA, 553 F.3d 927 (6th Cir. 2009). The court rejected EPA's claim that the rule was entitled to *Chevron* deference because it determined that there is no ambiguity under the Clean Water Act: pesticides are "pollutants" under the Act and, in light of the Supreme Court's *Miccosukee* decision, their deposit into surface waters is from "point sources." In response to the decision, EPA in October 2011 issued a Pesticides General Permit that applies to pesticide spraying activities. 76 Fed. Reg. 68,750 (2011).

## 4. Technology-Based Effluent Limitations

At the heart of the Clean Water Act are technology-based effluent limitations applicable to all point source dischargers and implemented through enforceable permits. Congress intended that the effluent limits be uniform throughout the nation for "similar point sources with similar characteristics," in part to prevent geographic competition for industry from undermining water pollution control standards. As noted above, this approach is criticized by economists who favor standards that would base controls on individualized assessments of costs and benefits. Consider whether more flexible standards realistically could be implemented by EPA as you learn about the agency's difficulties in implementing the existing technology-based approach.

### A. Application to Industrial Discharges

#### i. The Development of Effluent Limitations

The 1972 Act sought to force existing dischargers to employ progressively more stringent pollution control technology in two phases. Section 301(b)(1) originally required existing sources to employ the "best practicable control technology currently available" (BPT) by July 1, 1977, followed by the "best available technology economically achievable for each category or class" (BAT) by July 1, 1983. New sources were required by section 306 to meet a more stringent standard that would reduce their effluents to the greatest degree "achievable through application of the best available demonstrated control technology" (BADT), which could include process changes and a zero-discharge standard.

EPA faced a formidable task in determining how to translate technology-based standards into enforceable limits on industrial source categories. Section 304(b) of the FWPCA gave EPA one year to publish guidelines identifying the degree of effluent reduction attainable through the application of the levels of technology required by the Act. Swift action was crucial because Congress had given EPA and the states only two years to implement the new NPDES permit program. The Act specified that a discharger would not be considered in violation of the Act for the first two years after enactment if it had applied for a permit within six months of enactment. Congress had contemplated that the states would shoulder most of the actual burden of issuing permits (permits may be issued either by EPA or by states with programs approved by EPA), and it had required EPA to issue procedural guidelines to govern state operation of the NPDES permit program within two months after enactment of the Act.

Six months after enactment of the Clean Water Act, EPA had received nearly 33,000 applications for NPDES permits. By mid-1974 EPA had received 65,000 applications, but only 15 states had taken over responsibility for permit issuance. It soon became apparent that EPA would have to write more than 50,000 permits and define the range of technologically possible effluent limits for dozens of different industries, an enormous technical and administrative burden. The process of writing permits had already begun due to the Refuse Act experience, but without the detailed, industry-based assessment of technology dictated by section 304. Moreover, the section 304 process was supposed to be completed in only 12 months. Recall, too, that EPA was then a new agency with equally substantial tasks under the Clean Air Act.

EPA recognized that it would be unable to meet the one-year deadline in section 304(b)(1)(A) for promulgating effluent guidelines for classes and categories of point sources. The agency announced that instead it would publish the guidelines in three groups over a two-year period, concentrating first on the 27 industry categories identified by section 306(b)(1)(A) as targets for new source performance standards. NRDC then sued EPA for failure to meet the deadline for issuing the guidelines, and EPA was placed on a court-ordered schedule requiring issuance of guidelines for all point source effluent discharges by December 31, 1974. NRDC v. Train, 510 F.2d 692 (D.C. Cir. 1975).

To further complicate matters, it soon became apparent that the Act was ambiguous concerning a crucial point: Were effluent limits intended to be uniform by industry, or individually determined with reference to the industry effluent guidelines required by section 304? Section 304(b) required EPA to "publish regulations providing guidelines for effluent limitations," but EPA had not issued such guidelines when it adopted effluent limits for existing sources under section 301(b) and for new sources under section 306. EPA needed to issue regulations rapidly to give industries subject to them time to meet the 1977 deadline for installing certain levels of pollution control technology.

EPA determined that it would issue industry-wide effluent limitations under section 301 without waiting to promulgate guidelines under section 304(b). It proceeded to set numerical limits for various pollutants that were to be applied to different industries based on analyses of the capabilities of alternative pollution control technologies. Dischargers argued that effluent limits should be determined in individual permit proceedings and that issuance of the guidelines was a prerequisite to issuance of individual permits. Had this argument prevailed, final permit issuance would have been delayed for years, and industry would have been afforded many more opportunities to seek plant-specific adjustments in effluent limits during permit proceedings.

After six different United States Courts of Appeals reached varying opinions on this question, the Supreme Court finally resolved the issue in Du Pont v. Train, 430 U.S. 112 (1977). The Court agreed with EPA that section 301 limitations "are to be adopted by the Administrator, . . . they are to be based primarily on classes and categories, and . . . they are to take the form of regulations." The Court noted that the Act's BAT requirement provided expressly for regulation by "categories and classes" of dischargers, language difficult to reconcile with case-by-case permits. While the Act's BPT requirement did not contain similar language, the Court held that industry-wide BPT regulation was permissible "so long as some allowance is made for variations in individual plants as EPA has done by including a variance clause in its 1977 limitations." 430 U.S. at 128. The Court noted the "impossible burden" that would be imposed on EPA were it to be required to determine BPT in tens of thousands of individual permits proceedings sufficiently in advance of the 1977 compliance deadline.

The *Du Pont* decision established the validity of EPA's basic approach. What remained was the task of defining, implementing, and defending effluent limitations for every industrial category. Because the BPT effluent limitations had not been issued at the time most of the first round of discharge permits were issued, most permits did not contain categorical limits on discharges but rather incorporated individually negotiated limits based on the permit writer's "best professional judgment." Thus, the imposition of nationally uniform, categorical effluent limits was deferred long beyond the initial deadlines.

The task of implementing sections 301 and 304 required an enormous administrative effort. EPA discovered that it was even more complicated than expected. While only 27 industrial categories were identified in the Act, EPA identified 180 industrial subcategories and 45 other classifications for which it believed distinct effluent standards were needed. CEQ Environmental Quality—1974, at 141 (1974). Relying heavily on outside contractors for analysis of treatment technologies and industrial processes, EPA promulgated effluent guidelines for 30 industries by July 1974. The BPT guidelines, reflecting the performance of technology to be employed by 1977, relied largely on end-of-the-pipe treatment technologies for common pollutants and their parameters (e.g., biochemical oxygen demand, metals, pH, total suspended solids). The BAT guidelines, to be achieved by 1983, emphasized not only control technology but also process changes that for a few industries could result in attainment of the "no discharge" goal.

EPA's effluent standards were invariably challenged in court. By 1977, more than 200 lawsuits had been filed. While this litigation delayed implementation of the effluent limits, judicial decisions helped clarify the requirements of the Act.

Claims that the condition of receiving waters should be taken into account in establishing effluent limitations were rejected in Weyerhaeuser Co. v. Costle, 590 F.2d 101 (D.C. Cir. 1978). In EPA v. National Crushed Stone Association, 449 U.S. 64 (1980), the Supreme Court held that firms could be required to comply with technology-based effluent limits that would force some firms in an industry subcategory to go out of business. In many other cases courts reviewed industry claims that the technology was not available to comply with EPA's standards. By 1989, United States Courts of Appeals had decided at least 27 cases challenging the validity of effluent guidelines.

Section 308 of the Clean Water Act gives EPA data collection authority to assist in the development of effluent guidelines. This authority includes the right to impose record-keeping, sampling, and reporting requirements on point sources and a right of entry to inspect and gather data on the premises of such sources. A study of the guidelines development process found that this authority had not been of much help to EPA in developing BPT standards because legal challenges by industry delayed data gathering and "forced data collection through Section 308 authority created or worsened an adversarial relationship between EPA and an industry." W. Magat, A. Krupnick & W. Harrington, Rules in the Making 36 (1986). As a result, "[i]ndustry was capable of manipulating the rulemaking process by withholding data on costly, but effective, abatement technologies and by supplying excessive and confusing data."

The process used by EPA to develop effluent standards for industrial dischargers is illustrated in Figure 6.4. As EPA acquired more experience in promulgating effluent standards, the process improved somewhat, though it remains

**Figure 6.4   The Industrial Water Pollution Standard-Setting Process**

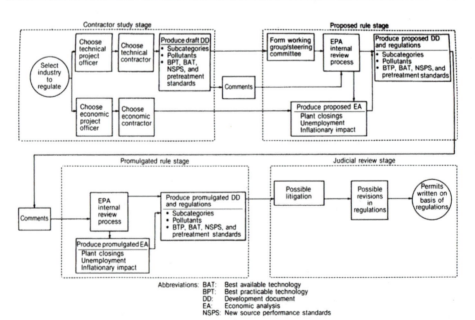

*Source:* W. Magat, A. Krupnick & W. Harrington, Rules in the Making 36 (1986).

extraordinarily cumbersome and data-intensive. EPA staff may take as many as 20 samples of wastewater at a plant and analyze each for 100 different pollutants in order to contribute to development of a database to support effluent guidelines. Settlement with NRDC Puts EPA on Schedule to Issue Effluent Guidelines for 20 Industries, 22 Envtl. Rep. 2323, 2324 (1992).

William Pedersen viewed the process of establishing effluent guidelines to be a wasteful exercise that produced standards that quickly become out of date:

> Each guideline has required a major and expensive rulemaking. Most of the effort was spent on exploring, for EPA's education, details of the costs and achievable reductions for various technologies in the industry under consideration at the time the guideline was being developed. That knowledge had only short-term value; it quickly became outdated with economic changes and the advance of technology. Moreover, the process demanded that EPA develop expertise in an impossibly wide variety of fields, duplicating knowledge already acquired by the industries involved. [Pedersen, Turning the Tide on Water Quality, 15 Ecology L.Q. 69, 85 (1988).]

Pedersen maintained that the fundamental flaw in the effluent standards is their technology-based approach, which "makes environmental performance irrelevant" while bringing costs to center stage. The result "has been a slight and variable willingness to cut back unduly strict requirements, coupled with a complete inability to strengthen unduly lenient standards."

### ii. Effluent Standards for Toxic Water Pollutants

Ironically, Congress turned to technology-based effluent standards because of wide agreement that water quality–based approaches were far more difficult to implement. In the one area where Congress initially sought to retain a water quality–based approach—control of toxic pollutants—EPA soon agreed to substitute a technology-based approach as well. Deficiencies in this approach resulted in yet another shift in regulatory emphasis when the 1987 Amendments placed renewed emphasis on a water quality–based approach for controlling toxics, as we will see in Section D.

The 1972 Act reflected congressional concern that discharges of toxic pollutants posed potentially serious health risks. Thus, Congress created a regulatory scheme for toxics very different from the technology-based program otherwise applicable to point sources. To implement section 101(a)(3)'s ambitious goal that there be no discharge of "toxic pollutants in toxic amounts," section 307(a) of the 1972 Act required EPA to establish a list of toxic water pollutants and to set health-based standards for controlling them within 90 days. Unlike the technology-based standards, in which cost considerations could play a limited role, these regulations were to be strictly health-based and were to be established without regard to cost, technological feasibility, or economic impact.

EPA found the task Congress had given it to be hopelessly difficult. After proposing standards for nine toxic water pollutants, the agency determined that defensible standards could not be promulgated given the dearth of available data on aquatic toxicology and the fate and transport of pollutants. Environmental groups brought several lawsuits against EPA after it missed the deadline for promulgating standards under section 307(a).

After lengthy negotiations between EPA and the environmental groups and several meetings with industry intervenors, a comprehensive settlement agreement was reached. Incorporated into a consent decree, called the "Flannery Decree" after the judge who approved it, the settlement committed EPA to a schedule for promulgating effluent guidelines, pretreatment standards, and new source performance standards for 65 toxic pollutants and 21 industries. The agreement shifted EPA's focus from health-based regulation to technology-based standards with tight deadlines for issuance.

The Flannery Decree was subsequently ratified, amended in some details, and incorporated in section 301 of the Act by the 1977 Amendments. A statement by the House conferees noted that the approach in section 307(a) had failed primarily due to "the formal, cumbersome rulemaking process."

Although the Flannery Decree originally required EPA to establish technology-based standards for 65 toxic pollutants discharged by 21 primary industries, it was subsequently broadened to cover 126 pollutants from 34 industrial categories. These 126 pollutants, which by no means include all significant toxic pollutants of concern today, became known as "priority pollutants."

### iii.   Variances

The tradeoff between flexibility and complexity is well illustrated by efforts to fine-tune national effluent standards. Standards established for industrial categories containing as many as 100 or more dischargers may be inappropriate for individual plants with special circumstances not easily taken into account in a national standard. For example, a plant may have a shortage of land on which to build additional waste treatment capacity, or air quality controls may prevent the use of certain treatment processes. How should EPA take such factors into account without either defeating the goal of nationally uniform standards or hopelessly complicating the standard-setting process?

The 1972 Act did not explicitly address this issue other than to allow EPA flexibility to define additional industry subcategories. In its early regulations, EPA devised an alternative approach allowing individual permit applicants an opportunity to request a variance for factors "fundamentally different" from those considered by EPA. As noted above, in the *Du Pont* decision the Supreme Court strongly endorsed this "FDF variance" for BPT, although it later held in EPA v. National Crushed Stone Association, 449 U.S. 64 (1980), that EPA need not consider an individual firm's ability to afford BPT requirements.

While Congress authorized some modifications of effluent standards in sections 301(c) and 301(g), the 1977 Amendments added section 301(*l*), which prohibited modification of any requirements applicable to toxic pollutants. In Chemical Manufacturers Association v. NRDC, 470 U.S. 116 (1985), the Supreme Court reviewed a Third Circuit decision holding that FDF variances could not be granted for discharges of toxics into sewage treatment systems, which are known as "indirect" discharges and governed by the pretreatment program. The Court had to decide whether an FDF variance was a "modification" in the sense used by section 301(*l*).

## Chemical Manufacturers Association v. NRDC

470 U.S. 116 (1985)

JUSTICE WHITE delivered the opinion of the Court.

Section 301(*l*) states that EPA may not "modify" any requirement of §301 inso-far as toxic materials are concerned. EPA insists that §301(*l*) prohibits only those modifications expressly permitted by other provisions of §301, namely, those that §301(c) and §301(g) would allow on economic or water-quality grounds. Section 301(*l*), it is urged, does not address the very different issue of FDF variances. . . .

### A

NRDC insists that the language of §301(*l*) is itself enough to require affir-mance of the Court of Appeals, since on its face it forbids any modifications of the effluent limitations that EPA must promulgate for toxic pollutants. If the word "modify" in §301(*l*) is read in its broadest sense, that is, to encompass any change or alteration in the standards, NRDC is correct. But it makes little sense to construe the section to forbid EPA to amend its own standards, even to correct an error or to impose stricter requirements. . . . As NRDC does and must concede, §301(*l*) cannot be read to forbid every change in the toxic waste standards. The word "modify" thus has no plain meaning as used in §301(*l*), and is the proper subject of construc-tion by EPA and the courts. . . . We should defer to [EPA's] view unless the legis-lative history or the purpose and structure of the statute clearly reveal a contrary intent on the part of Congress. NRDC submits that the legislative materials evince such a contrary intent. We disagree. . . .

[Based on an examination of the legislative history of section 301(*l*), the Court concludes that Congress intended for it to bar only waivers based on the economic capability of dischargers under section 301(c) or on water quality considerations under section 301(g).]

After examining the wording and legislative history of the statute, we agree with EPA and CMA that the legislative history itself does not evince an unambigu-ous congressional intention to forbid all FDF waivers with respect to toxic materi-als. . . .

### C

Neither are we convinced that FDF variances threaten to frustrate the goals and operation of the statutory scheme set up by Congress. The nature of FDF vari-ances has been spelled out both by this Court and by the Agency itself. The regu-lation explains that its purpose is to remedy categories which were not accurately drawn because information was either not available to or not considered by the Administrator in setting the original categories and limitations. An FDF variance does not excuse compliance with a correct requirement, but instead represents an acknowledgement that not all relevant factors were taken sufficiently into account in framing that requirement originally, and that those relevant factors, properly considered, would have justified — indeed, required — the creation of a subcategory for the discharger in question. As we have recognized, the FDF vari-ance is a laudable corrective mechanism, "an acknowledgment that the uniform . . .

limitation was set without reference to the full range of current practices, to which the Administrator was to refer." EPA v. National Crushed Stone Assn., 449 U.S. 64, 77-78 (1980). It is, essentially, not an exception to the standard-setting process, but rather a more fine-tuned application of it.

We are not persuaded by NRDC's argument that granting FDF variances is inconsistent with the goal of uniform effluent limitations under the Act. . . .

NRDC concedes that EPA could promulgate rules under §307 of the Act creating a subcategory for each source which is fundamentally different from the rest of the class under the factors the EPA must consider in drawing categories. The same result is produced by the issuance of an FDF variance for the same failure properly to subdivide a broad category. Since the dispute is therefore reduced to an argument over the means used by EPA to define subcategories of indirect dischargers in order to achieve the goals of the Act, these are particularly persuasive cases for deference to the Agency's interpretation.

NRDC argues, echoing the concern of the Court of Appeals below, that allowing FDF variances will render meaningless the §301(*l*) prohibition against modifications on the basis of economic and water quality factors. That argument ignores the clear difference between the purpose of FDF waivers and that of §301(c) and (g) modifications, a difference we explained in *National Crushed Stone*. A discharger that satisfies the requirements of §301(c) qualifies for a variance "simply because [it] could not afford a compliance cost that is not fundamentally different from those the Administrator has already considered" in creating a category and setting an effluent limitation. A §301(c) modification forces "a displacement of calculations already performed, not because those calculations were incomplete or had unexpected effects, but only because the costs happened to fall on one particular operator, rather than on another who might be economically better off." FDF variances are specifically unavailable for the grounds that would justify the statutory modifications. Both a source's inability to pay the foreseen costs, grounds for a §301(c) modification, and the lack of a significant impact on water quality, grounds for a §301(g) modification, are irrelevant under FDF variance procedures.

EPA and CMA point out that the availability of FDF variances makes bearable the enormous burden faced by EPA in promulgating categories of sources and setting effluent limitations. Acting under stringent timetables, EPA must collect and analyze large amounts of technical information concerning complex industrial categories. Understandably, EPA may not be apprised of and will fail to consider unique factors applicable to atypical plants during the categorical rulemaking process, and it is thus important that EPA's nationally binding categorical pretreatment standards for indirect dischargers be tempered with the flexibility that the FDF variance mechanism offers, a mechanism repugnant to neither the goals nor the operation of the Act.

### III

Viewed in its entirety, neither the language nor the legislative history of the Act demonstrates a clear congressional intent to forbid EPA's sensible variance mechanism for tailoring the categories it promulgates. In the absence of a congressional directive to the contrary, we accept EPA's conclusion that §301(*l*) does not prohibit FDF variances.

JUSTICE MARSHALL dissenting.

. . . EPA's argument that §301(*l*) proscribes only those modifications otherwise authorized by §§301(c) and (g) . . . is clearly inconsistent with congressional intent; the plain meaning of the statute and its legislative history show a clear congressional intent to ban all "modifications." . . .

If these two modifications are the only ones now prohibited, the result is wholly counterintuitive. EPA is in effect contending that economic and water-quality factors present the most compelling case for modification of the standard in the nontoxic context—as they are explicitly authorized by statute—but the least compelling case for modification in the toxic context—as they are the only modifications prohibited by §301(*l*). As might be expected, EPA does not present any theory, much less a logical argument, for evidence in the legislative history, to support this extremely inconsistent result. . . .

EPA's second construction of the statutory scheme is, on the surface, a more plausible one. EPA argues that FDF variances do not excuse compliance with the correct standards, but instead provide a means for setting more appropriate standards. It is clear that, pursuant to §307(b)(2), EPA can "revise" the pretreatment standards, as long as it does so "following the procedure established . . . for the promulgation of such standards." The statute contemplates that the standards will be set and revised through notice-and-comment rulemaking and will be applicable to categories of sources. EPA argues that such a "revision," which is clearly not proscribed by §301(*l*), would be substantively indistinguishable from an FDF variance. . . .

To support its argument, EPA points out that the factors that may justify an FDF variance are the same factors that may be taken into account in setting and revising the national pretreatment standards. . . . EPA acknowledges that the statute requires that the national pretreatment standards be established—and therefore revised—for "categories" of dischargers and not on a case-by-case basis. It argues, however, that nothing in the Clean Water Act precludes EPA from defining a subcategory that has only one discharger.

The logic of EPA's position is superficially powerful. If EPA can, through rulemaking, define a subcategory that includes only one discharger, why should it not be able to do so through a variance procedure? In fact, if rulemaking and the variance procedure were alternative means to the same end, I might have no quarrel with EPA's position, which the Court has accepted. . . .

However, the Agency's position does not withstand more than superficial analysis. An examination of the legislative history of the 1972 amendments to the Clean Water Act—the relevance of which both the Court and EPA ignore—reveals that Congress attached great *substantive* significance to the method used for establishing pollution control requirements.

The Conference Committee Report directed EPA to "make the determination of the economic impact of an effluent limitation on the basis of classes and categories of point sources, *as distinguished from a plant by plant determination.*" 1972 Leg. Hist. 304 (emphasis added). . . .

The legislative history also makes clear why Congress found it so important that the standards be set for "categories" of dischargers, and not for individual dischargers. Congress intended to use the standards as a means to "force" the introduction of more effective pollution control technology. . . . By requiring that the standards be set by reference to either the "average of the best" or very "best" technology, the Act seeks to foster technological innovation. . . .

Unlike the statutory revision mechanism of §307(b), FDF variances are set not by reference to a category of dischargers, but instead by reference to a single discharger. In evaluating an application for a variance, EPA does not look at the group of dischargers in the same position as the applicant, but instead focuses solely on the characteristics of the applicant itself. Under the FDF program, there is no mechanism for EPA to ascertain whether there are any other dischargers in that position. Moreover, there is no mechanism for EPA to group together similarly situated dischargers. Quite to the contrary, a scheme in which the initial screening may be done by the individual States, at times determined by when the variance application is filed, is unlikely to lead to the identification of new subcategories. . . .

In the aggregate, if EPA defines a new pretreatment subcategory through rulemaking, the BAT-level pollution control requirement of each discharger would be determined by reference to the capability of the "best" performer. In contrast, if EPA provides individual variances to each plant in this group, only one discharger would have a requirement based on the capability of the best performer—the best performer itself. The others would necessarily be subject to less stringent standards. . . .

It is true, of course, that even the statutory revision procedure might identify a subcategory with only one discharger. That procedure, however, will have established that this discharger is uniquely situated. In contrast, an FDF variance sets an individual requirement even where there may be similarly situated dischargers.

## NOTES AND QUESTIONS

1. How do the majority and the dissent differ in their characterizations of the purpose of FDF variances? To what extent do these differences reflect different conceptions of the role of the effluent standards in forcing the development of improved pollution control technology?

2. The Court split 5-4 in this case, with three other Justices joining Justice Marshall's dissent. Justice Marshall's papers reveal that the outcome was even closer than the vote suggests. When the Justices met to vote on the merits, following oral argument, they split 4-4, with Justice White finding the case too close to call. A week later, Justice White voted in favor of EPA, while still expressing some doubt about the outcome. He then was assigned to write the majority opinion and expressed some ambivalence about the result after seeing Justice Marshall's "very good dissent." Percival, Environmental Law in the Supreme Court: Highlights from the Marshall Papers, 23 Envtl. L. Rep. 10606, 10613 (1993).

3. At the time the Court decided this case, EPA headquarters had received 58 applications for FDF variances and granted only 4. Pedersen, Turning the Tide on Water Quality, 15 Ecology L.Q. 69, 86 n.81 (1988). By September 1995, EPA had granted only 8 FDF variances, while denying nearly 200. Given the small number of favorable applications for variances, why do you think there has been so much litigation concerning them? What impact is the availability of FDF variances likely to have on the administrative costs of implementing effluent limitations?

4. BAT regulations are now coming into effect for many industries, spurring more applications for FDF variances. Because these applications generally require EPA to assess plant-specific technical data on production processes and control technologies, EPA has been slow to rule on such applications, taking an average of

three years to process them. To expedite the FDF process, the 1987 Amendments required EPA to rule on FDF variance applications within 180 days of submission, a deadline that EPA has found to be difficult to meet. EPA's failure to meet this deadline has been held not to stay a discharger's obligation to comply with the effluent limits that are the subject of the application. See Chemical Mfrs. Ass'n v. EPA, 870 F.2d 177 (5th Cir. 1989) (citing §505(a)(2)).

5. The 1987 CWA Amendments specifically addressed the FDF variance for the first time. A new section 301(n) sets out permissible grounds for FDF variances for toxic pollutants. Could the FDF variance provision ever be used to justify more *stringent* conditions on a discharger? What circumstances might justify such action, and how might it come about? EPA's regulations allow for the possibility. Does section 301(n)?

### iv. Effluent Limitations: The State of the Art

The process of implementing the Clean Water Act's technology-based approach to water pollution control has been laborious, technically complex, and marked by repeated delays and missed deadlines. Having "shifted our faith from science to engineering," Houck, The Regulation of Toxic Pollutants Under the Clean Water Act, 21 Envtl. L. Rep. 10528, 10536 (1991), the Act and the Flannery Decree forced EPA to make engineering judgments based on detailed studies of production processes and pollution control technologies on an industry subcategory-by-subcategory basis. Many effluent guidelines have taken five or more years to develop. 55 Fed. Reg. 80, 81 (1990). When ultimately implemented, "BAT had lost its bite," though it "has probably been the most effective pollution control program in the world in terms of producing identifiable abatement—short of outright bans—if only because alternative programs have proven equally burdensome and so much less effective." Houck, supra at 10538, 10541.

The Flannery Decree ultimately produced numerous effluent guidelines, but it did not ensure comprehensive coverage of industrial dischargers. By 1990, EPA had promulgated effluent guidelines and standards covering 51 categories of dischargers and had completed all but one of the rulemakings required under the Flannery Decree. Despite this progress, EPA's effluent guidelines remained far from comprehensive. Nearly 80 percent of existing industrial dischargers of toxics (59,338 of 74,525) still were not covered by BAT standards. Natural Resources Defense Council v. Reilly, 32 ERC (BNA) 1969, 1972 n.25 (D.D.C. 1991). Moreover, the guidelines that had been issued by EPA often failed to cover significant substances or were based on data that were woefully outdated. As a result, even though all dischargers must have a permit, large quantities of toxics were being discharged because they were uncontrolled or poorly controlled in existing permits.

When it amended the Clean Water Act in 1987, Congress expressly required EPA to strengthen, expand, and revise existing technology-based controls to ensure that significant sources of discharges did not escape regulation. Congress added section 304(m), which required EPA to review and revise existing effluent guidelines by set deadlines, and to establish new effluent guidelines and new source performance standards for dischargers of toxics and unconventional pollutants not previously covered by such standards.

While the Clean Water Act's technology-based effluent limits have generated significant reductions in pollution from industrial sources, they have received considerable criticism from many quarters. Industry groups argue that the standards are inflexible and inefficient because they do not take into account the condition of receiving waters or differences among firms in the marginal costs of controlling pollution. Environmentalists decry the length of time it takes EPA to issue technology-based standards and the weakness of the ultimate standards EPA has set. Technology-based standards also provide little incentive for industries to develop better pollution control technology and they do not guarantee that health-based goals will be achieved.

Consider, for example, EPA's effluent guidelines for the organic chemical, plastics, and synthetic fiber (OCPSF) industries. When EPA issued the standards after 11 years of study and rulemaking proceedings, the agency had produced an administrative record more than 600,000 pages long. The standards then were challenged in court by a variety of industry groups and NRDC. Legal briefs in the litigation consumed more than 3,000 pages with a 9,000-page appendix. The court ultimately remanded standards for 20 pollutants to EPA on the ground that the agency had failed "to demonstrate a reasonable basis for its conclusion that in-plant treatment can eliminate pollutants as effectively as end-of-the-pipe systems" on which biological treatment is used. Chemical Mfrs. Ass'n v. EPA, 870 F.2d 177 (5th Cir. 1989). The court also agreed with NRDC that EPA had erred by failing to consider recycling technologies when establishing a new source performance standard (NSPS). The court concluded that when 36 plants—more than one-quarter of the industry—already had achieved zero discharges through recycling, it was arbitrary and capricious for EPA not to consider recycling technology when setting the NSPS. Six years after the court's decision, EPA still had not completed action on all of the issues remanded to it by the court.

Frustration with technology-based standards is inspiring proposals for more flexible and more efficient approaches for controlling water pollution. In March 1995, the Clinton administration supported proposals to allow companies that agree to adopt innovative treatment approaches to prevent pollution to take more time to comply with effluent standards. B. Clinton & A. Gore, Reinventing Environmental Regulations 43 (1995). It also endorsed effluent trading, which would allow sources that reduce pollution below the required minimum to acquire pollution allowances that could be sold to other firms. The administration estimated that trades between industrial point sources could save between $8.4 million and $1.9 billion in compliance costs for industry. To provide an incentive for pollutant reductions that exceed technology-based standards, others have proposed to impose effluent charges or to negotiate a "public contract" between regulators and industries that will require pollution to be phased out over a fixed period of time.

## NOTES AND QUESTIONS

1. Should effluent trading be permitted between industrial point sources? What advantages would it have? What disadvantages? Would it be possible to implement such a system without changing existing law?

2. Oliver Houck concludes that the stringency of EPA's technology-based standards often depends primarily on the industry's political clout:

> It is an astonishing but commonplace fact that when a BAT-limited industry is required to reduce $x$ further—due to water quality, health, public relations, or other considerations—it finds the ability to do so. In this regard, BAT appears to be more a problem of lead time and amortization of costs than a problem of engineering. BAT remains as driven by the most an industry will accept as by the most it can do.
>
>     This conclusion is reinforced by the equally disturbing fact that discharge standards have emerged unevenly, with a heavy "zero discharge" hand on such unfortunates as seafood canners and placer mine operators, and a remarkably blind eye to available closed-cycle systems for some of the nation's highest-volume dischargers of broad-spectrum toxins. The disparities in these standards reflect nothing more starkly than a disparity in clout. These disparities are amplified by the fact that, for the decade of the 1980s, EPA only worked with any intensity on that limited group of industries and that limited set of toxic compounds mandated by the 1976 decree. [Houck, The Regulation of Toxic Pollutants Under the Clean Water Act, 21 Envtl. L. Rep. 10528, 10539 (Sept. 1991).]

Does this experience suggest that a technology-*forcing* approach to regulation should be employed more extensively? Would industries with little political clout be any better off under alternative approaches to regulation?

    3. In April 2009, the U.S. Supreme Court reversed a decision by the U.S. Court of Appeals for the Second Circuit that had prohibited EPA from using cost-benefit analysis when setting effluent limitations for cooling water intake structures. Section 316(b) of the Clean Water Act provides that such standards "shall require that the location, design, construction, and capacity of cooling water intake structures reflect the best technology available for minimizing adverse environmental impact." 33 U.S.C. §1326(b). In an opinion by future Supreme Court Justice Sonia Sotomayor, the Second Circuit had interpreted this provision to require the technology that achieves the greatest reduction in adverse environmental impacts at a reasonable cost to industry. However, the Supreme Court, in an opinion by Justice Scalia, disagreed. The Court concluded that whether it is reasonable to bear a particular cost can very well depend on the resulting benefits. It noted that the environmental plaintiffs had conceded that the EPA need not require that industry spend billions to save one more fish and found that there is "no statutory basis for limiting" the comparison of costs and benefits "to situations where the benefits are *de minimis* rather than significantly disproportionate." Entergy Corp. v. Riverkeeper, Inc., 556 U.S. 208, 1510 (2009).

## B. POTWs and the Pretreatment Program

Sewage disposal became a water pollution problem in the late nineteenth century when urban areas turned to sewer systems for disposing of human waste. The percentage of the U.S. population served by sewer systems rose from 3 percent in 1860 to 33 percent in 1900 and 50 percent in 1930. Council on Environmental

Quality, Environmental Quality—1974, at 144 (1974). Sewer systems improved sanitary conditions in cities by collecting waste and transporting it downstream. While it was widely assumed that rivers and streams could easily assimilate wastes, growing volumes of raw sewage eventually created problems so severe that water pollution became a national concern. By 1910, 38 percent of the nation's population was served by sewer systems, but only 4 percent was served by sewage treatment plants. Id.

Municipalities were reluctant to invest in expensive treatment facilities that would primarily benefit downstream populations. Beginning in 1956, the federal government sought to overcome this resistance by providing federal funds for the construction of sewage treatment plants. Nearly $100 billion in federal, state, tribal, and local funds has been invested in the construction of thousands of sewage treatment plants, which now serve 173 million people with at least secondary treatment systems. However, the continued expansion of sewer systems has outpaced the expansion of treatment capacity in some areas, such as New York City. Gold, Despite Decades of Spending, Sewage Plants Are Full Up, N.Y. Times, Aug. 18, 1991, at E16.

Publicly owned wastewater treatment works (POTWs) are regulated separately from industrial point source dischargers under the Clean Water Act, which applies a separate set of effluent limits to them under section 301(b)(1)(B) of the Act. In 1972, Congress required POTWs to achieve at least secondary treatment levels by 1977 and an even more advanced level of treatment by 1983. The latter requirement was eliminated in 1981, though limits more stringent than secondary treatment limits may still be imposed if necessary to meet applicable water quality standards. §301(b)(1)(C). Congress also relaxed treatment requirements in 1977 when it added section 301(h), which authorizes POTWs discharging directly into marine waters to waive secondary treatment requirements in certain circumstances.

POTWs are substantial point source dischargers whose effluent contains by-products of municipal sewage and industrial discharges subject to the pretreatment program. Sludge is the potentially hazardous by-product of the treatment process, which POTWs must manage in large quantities. Most sludge is disposed on land; it no longer may legally be dumped into the ocean as New York City and some of its neighbors in New Jersey had done for years. The 1987 Amendments added section 405 to the Clean Water Act, which required EPA to develop standards for disposal of sewage sludge to be implemented through the NPDES permits issued to POTWs.

In 1993, EPA issued regulations governing the use and disposal of sewage sludge pursuant to section 405(d) of the Clean Water Act. 58 Fed. Reg. 9,248 (1993). The regulations impose numeric limits on concentrations of various heavy metals and pathogens in sewage sludge that apply except when sludge is taken to a municipal landfill. EPA's decision to exempt from the numeric limits sludge taken to municipal landfills was upheld in Sierra Club v. EPA, 992 F.2d 337 (D.C. Cir. 1993). The court found that EPA had insufficient information to establish scientifically defensible numeric limits on sludge taken to such landfills. In Leather Industries of America v. EPA, 40 F.3d 392 (D.C. Cir. 1994), EPA's numeric limits on selenium and chromium in sludge were struck down as insufficiently supported in the administrative record. However, the court upheld EPA's refusal to provide for site-specific variances and it confirmed that the agency has the authority to regulate sludge to protect against phytotoxicity, the reduction in crop yields that occurs when plants absorb toxic metals.

Section 405(e) of the Clean Water Act specifies that "the manner of disposal or use of sludge is a local determination" so long as federal regulations are not violated. In Welch v. Board of Supervisors of Rappahannock County, 860 F. Supp. 328 (W.D. Va. 1994), a county ordinance banning the application of sewage sludge to farmland was held not to be preempted by federal law because state and local governments may adopt more stringent limits on sludge disposal, so long as they at least meet federal minimum standards.

As controls on toxic discharges into surface waters have been strengthened, more pressure has been placed on a particularly weak link in the Clean Water Act's system of controls: the pretreatment program. Many industrial sources have chosen to avoid the NPDES permit process and to escape RCRA standards by discharging toxics and hazardous waste into sewers. These indirect dischargers are exempt from NPDES permit requirements. (Remember that the NPDES requirements apply only to point sources that discharge into surface waters and that domestic sewage is exempt from regulation as a hazardous waste under RCRA.) The Office of Technology Assessment reported in 1987 that more than 160,000 industrial facilities discharged more than one trillion gallons of wastewater containing RCRA hazardous wastes into municipal sewers each year. If not treated at industrial facilities, these "indirect" waste discharges would contain 160,000 metric tons of hazardous components, including 62,000 metric tons of metals that are priority pollutants, 40,000 tons of organic chemicals that are priority pollutants, and 64,000 tons of other hazardous organic chemicals. OTA, Wastes in Marine Environments 212 (1987).

The rationale for exempting indirect dischargers from the NPDES program was that it would be redundant to require controls on discharges that already would be subject to treatment in POTWs. To prevent indirect discharges from interfering with the operation of POTWs, section 307 of the Clean Water Act requires pretreatment of such discharges to control pollutants that are not susceptible to treatment by POTWs. EPA has promulgated general pretreatment regulations that prohibit the discharge of pollutants that might interfere with or pass through POTWs and that require the development of local pretreatment programs. In Arkansas Poultry Fed'n v. EPA, 852 F.2d 324 (8th Cir. 1988), the Eighth Circuit upheld EPA's definitions of "interference" and "pass through," which provide that indirect dischargers may only be penalized for discharges that actually cause permit violations at POTWs. EPA is promulgating technologically based pretreatment requirements on an industry-wide basis ("categorical pre-treatment requirements"). Individual POTWs also are authorized to impose local limits.

Plagued with problems of nonimplementation and lax enforcement, the pretreatment program had long been considered by many to be a failure, though belated efforts to beef up enforcement appear to be producing some results. Problems with the program are described in Houck, Ending the War: A Strategy to Save America's Coastal Zone, 47 Md. L. Rev. 358, 384-388 (1988). Professor Houck questions the basic premise of assigning responsibility for implementing a national program to local governments. He notes that "even if the purpose of a *national* discharge program were to offset the political pressures placed on states to relax their programs, those same pressures are even more formidable at the local level, producing a wide variety of standards and levels of compliance among the local municipal systems." Houck also questions the basic concept on which the nation's sewage disposal policy is founded: using waterways for sewage disposal, which he terms "a little barbaric." He notes that alternative technology exists that could avoid "the illogic of first putting human wastes into our water and then building ever more expensive plants to take them out." Id. at 381-383. But given the enormous investment society has made in waterborne sewage disposal systems, he recognizes the futility of his complaint.

## NOTES AND QUESTIONS

1. Is the delegation of program authority to hundreds of local entities subject to intense local political pressure from dischargers a basic flaw in the pretreatment program? Why doesn't support for a clean environment effectively counterbalance local political pressures? Many federal environmental programs delegated to the states are subject to EPA supervision. EPA must approve POTWs's pretreatment programs. Could the system of program delegation be improved, or is the concept fundamentally flawed? Is the basic problem that indirect dischargers are too numerous and mobile to be subject to effective enforcement action?

2. One reason why so many toxic materials are discharged into sewers is the domestic sewage exclusion to RCRA. RCRA's definition of "solid waste" expressly exempts "solid or dissolved materials in domestic sewage . . . or industrial discharges which are point sources subject to permits under section [402 of the Clean Water Act]." RCRA §1004(27). Thus, facilities can escape RCRA regulation by discharging hazardous waste into surface waters subject to NPDES permits, and they can escape the NPDES permit process by discharging such waste into sewers. Should the domestic sewage exclusion apply to hazardous waste mixed with sewage from an industrial plant rather than from residences? In Comite Pro Rescate de la Salud v. Puerto Rico Aqueduct and Sewer Authority, 888 F.2d 180 (1st Cir. 1989), the First Circuit said "No."

3. The pretreatment program was supposed to prevent the domestic sewage exclusion from causing harm. When Congress amended RCRA in 1984, it required EPA to undertake a comprehensive study of the impact of the domestic sewage exclusion. RCRA §3018. EPA completed the Domestic Sewage Study in February 1986. The study found that many significant hazardous waste discharges are not covered by existing pretreatment regulations because they involve chemicals that, while hazardous, are not among the 126 priority pollutants covered by the Flannery Decree. The study noted that pretreatment standards for certain industries "do not specifically regulate nonpriority organics, despite the fact that many of these pollutants are discharged in significant concentrations and/or loadings." More than 38.3 million pounds of toxic pollutants discharged annually were not covered by effluent limits under the Flannery Decree, and more than 7.2 million pounds of hazardous metals and between 81 and 132 million pounds of priority hazardous organic constituents were discharged to POTWs even after implementation of categorical pretreatment standards. EPA, Report to Congress on the Discharge of Hazardous Wastes to Publicly Owned Treatment Works 7-9 (Feb. 1986).

4. In response to its Domestic Sewage Study, EPA in 1990 revised its pretreatment regulations. 55 Fed. Reg. 30,082 (1990). While the new regulations place numerical limits on discharges of ignitable waste, restrictions on discharges of toxic

or corrosive waste are left largely to individual POTWs because of the variability of waste streams. The regulations require discharges of trucked or hauled waste to be made only at specific discharge points designated by POTWs. POTWs are required to use permits or an equivalent mechanism to control discharges by significant industrial users, who must file semiannual reports on their discharges. See Hogeland, EPA's Pretreatment Regulation Amendments: Forcing Enforcement, 20 Envtl. Rep. 889 (1990).

5. In a 1991 report to Congress, EPA reaffirmed its faith in the pretreatment program, which it found had reduced discharges of metals by 95 percent and discharges of toxic organics by 40 to 75 percent. The report noted that data from the Toxic Release Inventory indicated that at least 680 million pounds of toxics were discharged to 1,700 POTWs in 1988. While the report found that two-thirds of POTWs had not established local limits for dischargers, it maintained that the flexibility afforded to POTWs by the program was necessary because of wide variations in local circumstances. EPA, Report to Congress on the National Pretreatment Program (1991). The growth of new industries that generate new types of pollutants, such as the rapid rise of the semiconductor industry during the 1990s, poses a particular challenge for the pretreatment program. EPA, EPA's National Pretreatment Program, 1973-2003: Thirty Years of Protecting the Environment (2004). Yet many new contaminants passing through POTWs may be the product of waste generated by households. A study released in 2002 by the U.S. Geological Survey found that of 139 streams analyzed in 30 states 80 percent had some contamination from antibiotics, steroids, synthetic hormones, and other commonly used pharmaceutical drugs. Pharmaceuticals, Hormones, and Other Organic Wastewater Contaminants in U.S. Streams 1999-2000: A National Reconnaissance, 36 Envtl. Sci. & Tech. 1202 (2002).

6. POTWs discharging into marine waters may obtain waivers from treatment requirements under section 301(h) of the Clean Water Act. More than 50 POTWs have obtained such waivers, which EPA may approve only with the concurrence of the state in which the POTW is located. EPA issued regulations governing the section 301(h) waiver process in August 1994. 59 Fed. Reg. 40,642 (1994).

## Water Pollution Control: A Pathfinder

The U.S. Environmental Protection Agency's regulations implementing the Clean Water Act are codified at 40 C.F.R. pts. 100-140. Effluent guidelines and standards and general pretreatment regulations are located at 40 C.F.R. pts. 400-471. EPA's regulations governing the issuance of permits under §404 of the Act can be found at 40 C.F.R. pts. 230-233; the regulations governing the U.S. Army Corps of Engineers' section 404 permit program are found at 33 C.F.R. pts. 323-331. These CFR sections are available online through the National Archives and Records Administration's website, which includes a searchable version of the Code of Federal Regulations and an electronic version of the CFR ("e-CFR") updated continuously, which can be found at *http://www.ecfr.gov.*

EPA's Office of Water (OW) is responsible for implementing the Clean Water Act. See the EPA website at *https://www.epa.gov/environmental-topics/water-topics*. A webpage describing the laws and regulations pertinent to EPA's water programs is located at *https://www.epa.gov/regulatory-information-topic/regulatory-information-topic-water*. EPA's Strategic Plan and Guidance for the National Water Program is located at *https://www.epa.gov/sites/production/files/2019-06/documents/fy-20-21-ow-np-guidance.pdf*. EPA's efforts to encourage action to control nonpoint sources of pollution are described at *https://www.epa.gov/nps*. The activities of the agency's Office of Wastewater Management are explained at *https://www.epa.gov/aboutepa/office-wastewater-management-annual-reports*.

EPA's Office of Water allows the public to subscribe to a variety of water newsletters, including Water Headlines, a Climate and Water E-Newsletter, a Water Quality Standards News Listserv, a Fish Advisory Newsletter, NPDES News, and a Water Research Updates Newsletter. Information on how to subscribe is located at *https://www.epa.gov/aboutepa/about-office-water*.

To enable citizens to obtain more information about their watersheds and the groups working to preserve them, EPA maintains a "How's My Waterway" webpage that has a search function for locating watersheds by zip code, city, river, county, or state. The page is located at *https://www.epa.gov/waterdata/hows-my-waterway*.

EPA operates a toll-free Wetlands Helpline that provides information about wetlands issues and regulatory requirements concerning development in wetlands areas. The Army Corps of Engineers has a website with links to regulatory documents concerning its §404 permit program at *http://www.usace.army.mil/Missions/Civil-Works/Regulatory-Program-and-Permits/Obtain-a-Permit/*.

The Natural Resources Defense Council's webpage includes an extensive set of links to other nonprofit organizations working on various aspects of clean water issues. It can be accessed at *https://www.nrdc.org/issues/water*.

## D. WATER QUALITY–BASED CONTROLS: THE REGULATORY "SAFETY NET"

The enactment of the Clean Water Act in 1972 reflected a fundamental shift away from a water quality–based approach to pollution control toward an approach that emphasized technology-based effluent limitations. This shift was a result of a broad consensus that previous water quality–based control efforts had been a dismal failure. Congress recognized that ambient water quality standards were ineffective because of "the character of the standards themselves, which focused on the tolerable effects rather than the preventable causes of water pollution," EPA v. California ex rel. State Water Res. Control Bd. 426 U.S. 200, 202 (1976). To ensure that reductions were required in pollutant discharges, Congress required the use of certain technology-based levels of control regardless of the conditions of the receiving waters, as illustrated by Weyerhaeuser v. Costle, 590 F.2d 1011 (D.C. Cir. 1978).

Despite the Act's new emphasis on a technology-based approach, Congress did not entirely abandon water quality–based controls; rather, it retained them as a "safety net" to back up the technology-based controls on which the Act primarily relies. Section 301(b)(1)(C) requires that NPDES permits include any more stringent limits that are necessary to ensure compliance with water quality standards the states and qualifying tribes must adopt pursuant to section 303. To implement this requirement, section 303(d) directs states to identify waters with insufficient controls and to calculate limits on pollutant loadings necessary for such waters to achieve water quality standards with a margin of safety. As discussed below, these provisions are becoming quite important as gains from technology-based reductions diminish.

## 1. Water Quality Standards

Water quality standards have two components: (1) identification of the designated uses of a water body and (2) water quality criteria designed to protect the designated use. "Designated uses" represent the purposes for which each water segment is to be protected (e.g., public water supplies, propagation of fish and wildlife, recreational purposes, agriculture). "Water quality criteria" reflect judgments concerning the degree of protection from individual pollutants that is necessary to attain designated uses. When combined with designated uses, water quality criteria yield what are called "water quality standards," limits on ambient concentrations of pollutants in particular classes of waters. States and tribes must review and revise their water quality standards every three years (a "triennial review") and they must submit such standards to EPA for review and approval. §303(c). EPA can modify state or tribal standards that fail to meet the requirements of the Act. §303(c)(4).

### A. Designated Uses and Antidegradation

While states and tribes have some flexibility in establishing designated uses for water segments, section 303(c)(2)(A) directs them in vague terms to "protect the public health or welfare, enhance the quality of water and serve the purposes" of the Act. States and tribes are directed to consider the use and value of their waters "for public water supplies, propagation of fish and wildlife, recreational purposes, and agricultural, industrial, and other purposes," including navigation. This ambiguous language has been interpreted by EPA to require at a minimum that water quality standards meet the "fishable/swimmable" goal of section 101(a)(2) unless that would result in "substantial and widespread economic and social impact." EPA also has required states and tribes to establish antidegradation policies designed to protect existing uses of water segments and to prevent deterioration of waters that exceed the purity necessary to meet the fishable/swimmable goal unless "necessary to accommodate important economic or social development." 40 C.F.R. §131.12(a)(2).

### B. Water Quality Criteria

States and tribes must adopt water quality criteria that specify maximum ambient levels of pollutants that will ensure that waters can be used for their designated purposes. EPA is directed by section 304(a) of the Act to develop water quality criteria, which can be used as a point of reference for states promulgating their own criteria. EPA's regulations do not specify for what pollutants criteria must be adopted by the states and tribes. Rather, they simply require that sufficient criteria be adopted "to protect the designated use."

The section 304(a) criteria are scientific recommendations that EPA develops for states to consider in adopting regulatory criteria under section 303(c). EPA's initial approach to issuing criteria was to conduct reviews of the scientific literature, which resulted in a series of water quality criteria documents, known as the 1968 "Green Book," the 1973 "Blue Book," and the 1976 "Red Book." The agency subsequently adopted more formal procedures for developing water quality criteria, and it promulgated guidelines for developing criteria to protect aquatic life and human health when it published criteria for 64 toxic pollutants in November 1980. 45 Fed. Reg. 79,318. Additional criteria were adopted later, as summarized in the 1986 "Gold Book," called Quality Criteria for Water 1986. By 1999, EPA had established water quality criteria for more than 100 pollutants. Criteria to protect aquatic life have been published for 31 chemicals; criteria to protect human health have been published for 100 chemicals.

States were slow to promulgate water quality standards, despite issuance of EPA criteria. Most states failed to promulgate numerical standards for toxics or adopted standards far more lenient than those recommended by EPA's criteria. The Reagan administration contributed to the problem by expressing the view that EPA's criteria were scientifically flawed and should not be relied on by states.

In light of the uneven record of the states in adopting water quality criteria, the 1987 Amendments added a requirement that states adopt criteria for toxic pollutants "the discharge or presence of which in the affected waters could reasonably be expected to interfere with those designated uses adopted by the State." §303(c)(2)(B). Because of the difficulty in determining what levels of pollutants are safe for attaining designated uses, some states had adopted "narrative criteria" (e.g., "free from toxicity") that do not specify numerical limits on the ambient concentration of pollutants but that could form the basis for whole effluent toxicity testing. In the absence of numeric criteria for specific chemicals, however, it is difficult to employ water quality standards to impose additional limitations on discharges to a water body. The 1987 Amendments addressed this problem by requiring that numerical criteria be adopted for toxic pollutants, section 303(c)(2)(B), and they expressly endorsed the use of biological assessment criteria when numerical criteria are not available.

EPA has issued regulations requiring permit writers to translate state water quality standards that contain narrative criteria into chemical-specific effluent limits for permitees. The EPA regulations give permit writers three options: (1) use a calculated numeric water quality criterion derived from proposed state numeric criteria or other state policy interpreting the narrative criteria, (2) use EPA's recommended numeric criteria, or (3) rely on limits on the discharge of other pollutants found in the source's effluent ("indicator parameters"). These regulations were upheld in American Paper Institute, Inc. v. EPA, 996 F.2d 346 (D.C. Cir. 1993). The court stated that they "provide an eminently reasonable means of effectuating the intent of the previously adopted narrative criteria as well as Congress's own intent, made explicit in section 301 of the CWA, that *all* state water quality standards be enforced through meaningful limitations in individual NPDES permits."

Some states have adopted water quality standards that are far more lenient than recommended by EPA's criteria. For example, EPA's 1984 criteria document for dioxin recommends that the concentration of dioxin be no greater than .0013 parts per quadrillion (ppq) in water bodies used as sources of drinking water or edible fish. Yet Virginia and Maryland adopted water quality standards limiting dioxin concentrations to 1.2 ppq, a level nearly 1,000 times more lenient than recommended by EPA's criteria. After EPA approved the standards, environmental groups brought suit. In Natural Resources Defense Council v. EPA, 16 F.3d 1395 (4th Cir. 1993), the court held that EPA could approve such standards so long as they were scientifically defensible and protective of designated uses, even though they were based on assumptions different from those employed by EPA in assessing the toxicity of dioxin. The court emphasized that states have the primary role in establishing water quality standards and that EPA's decision to approve them should be upheld if there is a rational basis for it in the record. The court also held that the availability of new data does not obligate EPA to update its water quality criteria guidance documents, and that such documents are not subject to judicial review under the Administrative Procedure Act because they do not represent final agency action.

Thus, even though new data indicated that EPA had greatly underestimated dioxin's tendency to bioconcentrate in fish (by factors ranging from 4 to 30 times), the court held that EPA had not acted improperly in allowing Virginia and Maryland to use even lower estimates of dioxin's potency and risk. Citing the complexity and uncertainty of the science, the court concluded that it would not second-guess EPA's decision. The court acknowledged that the 1.2 ppq water quality standard adopted by Virginia and Maryland could tolerate cancer risks as high as 1 in 10,000, while EPA's criteria were designed to tolerate risks only as great as 1 in 10 million. The court held that EPA had acted properly in approving the Virginia and Maryland standards, even though section 303(c)(3) of the CWA requires the EPA administrator to determine whether a state water quality standard "meets the requirements" of the Act.

## NOTES AND QUESTIONS

1. The environmental groups in *NRDC v. EPA* argued that Virginia's water quality standard for dioxin was inadequate to protect groups of Native Americans living near a Virginia paper mill who consume large quantities of fish. If subsistence fishers tend to be from low-income and minority communities, does EPA's approach of basing its criteria on *average* fish consumption across the population raise environmental justice concerns? President Clinton's environmental justice executive order (Executive Order 12,898) directs all federal agencies, "whenever practicable and appropriate," to "collect, maintain, and analyze information on the consumption patterns of populations who principally rely on fish and/or wildlife for subsistence." The order directs agencies to "communicate to the public the risks of those consumption patterns." It also instructs agencies to incorporate consideration of "differential patterns of consumption of natural resources among minority populations and low-income populations" in their agency-wide environmental justice strategies. Could this require EPA to revise its water quality criteria for dioxin?

2.  The Fourth Circuit rejected the argument that the dioxin standards should be stricter in order to protect recreational and subsistence fishers who consume much higher quantities of fish than the national average used in calculating the dioxin criteria. One approach for protecting subsistence users of contaminated fish has been to post warnings advising against consumption of certain types of fish. However, such warnings often are ignored. See Steinberg, Anglers Ignore Hudson Warnings, N.Y. Times, Sept. 3, 1994, at 24 (survey of fishermen by a New York environmental group found that more than 35 percent ate more fish than recommended).

3.  EPA's review of the state dioxin water quality standards was based only on consideration of human health effects. Are there any regulations that could be used to restrict dioxin discharges more stringently in order to protect aquatic organisms and wildlife?

4.  In 2019 the Fourth Circuit upheld EPA's rejection of a West Virginia water quality standard for copper for the receiving water of a waste treatment facility. The court agreed that EPA had acted properly in finding that the standard was insufficient to protect the designated use of the river for fish and fisheries. Sanitary Board of City of Charleston v. Wheeler, 918 F.3d 324 (4th Cir. 2019).

5.  Tremendous uncertainty surrounds efforts to assess the effects on humans and aquatic organisms of a bewildering mix of toxic water pollutants. Can uncertainty be used to justify dramatically different water quality standards in different states?

### Water Quality Criteria: Sources of Scientific Uncertainty

Consider the following sources of uncertainty concerning the effects of water pollutants on humans and aquatic organisms. Only a small fraction of the tens of thousands of commonly used chemicals have been tested for toxicity to aquatic organisms. Most testing has focused on acute toxicity because it is faster and easier to perform such tests. Thus, our knowledge of chronic effects is quite limited even though they may be more serious than acute effects.

Pollutants have different impacts on different organisms. Scientists typically select surrogate species of aquatic organisms, usually a crustacean, a fish, and an alga, for use in testing. But some aquatic species, e.g., some species of freshwater mussels, are more sensitive to exposure to some chemicals than the surrogate species are. Aquatic toxicity testing traditionally has had gross lethality as one endpoint of concern with additional tests needed to assess effects on aquatic reproduction and development. Such testing may make scientists reasonably confident that they know what dose of a given chemical will kill half of the species within a given period of time (the LC50, or lethal concentration for 50 percent of the test organisms), but it does not necessarily reveal much about the full range of effects of chemicals on actual ecosystems. Moreover, tests of specific substances on isolated species do not reflect actual conditions in a water body where organisms encounter complex mixtures of chemical compounds and are affected by ecosystem processes as well as interactions with other organisms.

Water quality criteria are based on concern for protecting human health or aquatic life from concentrations of pollutants in the water. Yet scientists have discovered that concentrations of pollutants on a water body's surface, or microlayer, often are very different from concentrations below. As a result, compliance with water quality criteria in the water column may not be sufficient to protect the health of aquatic organisms, particularly those for whom the microlayer is unusually important. Also, many toxic pollutants accumulate in sediments in concentrations different from those in the water. They may become resuspended in the water column when sediments are disturbed, and they may have severe impacts on benthic organisms. While there is voluminous research on contamination of aquatic sediments, EPA has not promulgated any sediment quality criteria, though some states have begun to do so. See Marcus, Managing Contaminated Sediments in Aquatic Environments: Identification, Regulation, and Remediation, 21 Envtl. L. Rep. 10020 (1991). For more than a decade, EPA has been gathering data that will support the development of sediment quality criteria for some of the priority pollutants. See *http://www.epa.gov/waterscience/cs/library/guidelines.htm#epa/.*

There also are practical obstacles to implementing water quality–based approaches, including difficulties in detecting and measuring reliably the presence of certain substances in environmental media and the absence of low-cost screening techniques for scanning large numbers of samples. It can be difficult to measure with precision levels of individual pollutants in effluent discharges; it is even more difficult to determine how pollutant flows mix with receiving waters in order to assess the impact of individual discharges on overall water quality. Finally, all these sources of uncertainty are compounded when the potential effects of climate change are taken into account, including rising water temperatures and increased runoff pollution from storms.

All of these factors greatly complicate the task of implementing water quality–based approaches to regulation. While scientists are working to develop improved toxicity testing procedures (the development of biomarkers that focus on cellular and biological responses in aquatic organisms eventually may enable scientists to develop a better early warning system), they simply are unable, given current knowledge, to predict reliably the impact of specific contaminants on specific aquatic resources. Uncertainty seems destined to dominate debates over the significance of changes in water quality for years to come.

## 2. The Impact of Water Quality Standards on Permit Limits

For water quality standards to be effective in preventing pollution, they must be translated into effective discharge limits. Section 301(b)(1)(c) of the Clean Water Act provides that NPDES permits must include limits that will ensure that water quality standards are not violated. In the sections that follow we consider various means by which water quality standards can affect permit limits. These include: (1) the application of water quality standards to discharges that contribute to interstate water pollution, (2) individual control strategies for toxics under section 304(1), (3) section 401(a) certifications, and (4) the establishment of total maximum daily loadings (TMDLs) of pollutants under section 303(d).

### A.  Application of Water Quality Standards to Interstate Pollution

When water pollutants cross the boundaries of states or Indian reservations they may affect the ability of downstream states or tribes to meet their own water quality standards. In the case below, Oklahoma argued that discharges from an

Arkansas wastewater treatment plant should not be permitted because they would degrade water quality in the upper Illinois River in Oklahoma in violation of Oklahoma's water quality standards. Oklahoma had designated the upper Illinois River as a scenic river. The portion of the river downstream from the Arkansas border is used primarily for recreational boating and fishing. It is a particularly popular site for canoeing and rafting.

## Arkansas v. Oklahoma

503 U.S. 91 (1992)

JUSTICE STEVENS delivered the opinion for a unanimous Court.

### I

In 1985, the City of Fayetteville, Arkansas, applied to the EPA, seeking a permit for the City's new sewage treatment plant under the National Pollution Discharge Elimination System (NPDES). After the appropriate procedures, the EPA, pursuant to §402(a)(1) of the Act, 33 U.S.C. §1342(a)(1), issued a permit authorizing the plant to discharge up to half of its effluent (to a limit of 6.1 million gallons per day) into an unnamed stream in northwestern Arkansas. That flow passes through a series of three creeks for about 17 miles, and then enters the Illinois River at a point 22 miles upstream from the Arkansas-Oklahoma Border.

The permit imposed specific limitations on the quantity, content, and character of the discharge and also included a number of special conditions, including a provision that if a study then underway indicated that more stringent limitations were necessary to ensure compliance with Oklahoma's water quality standards, the permit would be modified to incorporate those limits.

Respondents challenged this permit before the EPA, alleging, inter alia, that the discharge violated the Oklahoma water quality standards. Those standards provide that "no degradation [of water quality] shall be allowed" in the upper Illinois River, including the portion of the River immediately downstream from the state line. . . .

Both the petitioners (collectively Arkansas) and the respondents in this litigation sought judicial review. Arkansas argued that the Clean Water Act did not require an Arkansas point source to comply with Oklahoma's water quality standards. Oklahoma challenged the EPA's determination that the Fayetteville discharge would not produce a detectable violation of the Oklahoma standards.

### IV

The parties have argued three analytically distinct questions concerning the interpretation of the Clean Water Act. First, does the Act require the EPA, in crafting and issuing a permit to a point source in one State, to apply the water quality standards of downstream States? Second, even if the Act does not *require* as much, does the Agency have the statutory authority to mandate such compliance? Third, does the Act provide, as the Court of Appeals held, that once a body of water fails to meet water quality standards no discharge that yields effluent that reach[es] the degraded waters will be permitted?

In this case, it is neither necessary nor prudent for us to resolve the first of these questions. In issuing the Fayetteville permit, the EPA assumed it was obligated by both the Act and its own regulations to ensure that the Fayetteville discharge would not violate Oklahoma's standards. As we discuss below, this assumption was permissible and reasonable and therefore there is no need for us to address whether the Act requires as much. Moreover, much of the analysis and argument in the briefs of the parties relies on statutory provisions that govern not only federal permits issued pursuant to §§401(a) and 402(a), but also state permits issued under §402(b). It seems unwise to evaluate those arguments in a case such as this one, which only involves a federal permit.

Our decision not to determine at this time the scope of the Agency's statutory *obligations* does not affect our resolution of the second question, which concerns the Agency's statutory *authority*. Even if the Clean Water Act itself does not require the Fayetteville discharge to comply with Oklahoma's water quality standards, the statute clearly does not limit the EPA's authority to mandate such compliance.

Since 1973, EPA regulations have provided that an NPDES permit shall not be issued "[w]hen the imposition of conditions cannot ensure compliance with the applicable water quality requirements of all affected States." 40 CFR §122.4(d) (1991); see also 38 Fed. Reg. 13533 (1973); 40 CFR §122.44(d)(1991). Those regulations—relied upon by the EPA in the issuance of the Fayetteville permit—constitute a reasonable exercise of the Agency's statutory authority.

Congress has vested in the Administrator broad discretion to establish conditions for NPDES permits. Section 402(a)(2) provides that for EPA-issued permits "[t]he Administrator shall prescribe conditions for such permits to assure compliance with the requirements of [§402(a)(1)] and *such other requirements as he deems appropriate*." 33 U.S.C. §1342(a)(2) (emphasis supplied). Similarly, Congress preserved for the Administrator broad authority to oversee state permit programs:

> No permit shall issue . . . if the Administrator . . . objects in writing to the issuance of such permit as being outside the guidelines and requirements of this chapter.

33 U.S.C. §1342(d)(2).

The regulations relied on by the EPA were a perfectly reasonable exercise of the Agency's statutory discretion. The application of state water quality standards in the interstate context is wholly consistent with the Act's broad purpose, "to restore and maintain the chemical, physical, and biological integrity of the Nation's waters." 33 U.S.C. §1251(a). Moreover, as noted above, §301(b)(1)(C) expressly identifies the achievement of state water quality standards as one of the Act's central objectives. The Agency's regulations conditioning NPDES permits are a well-tailored means of achieving this goal.

Notwithstanding this apparent reasonableness, Arkansas argues that our description in [International Paper Co. v.] Ouellette[, 479 U.S. 481 (1987),] of the role of affected States in the permit process and our characterization of the affected States' position as "subordinate," see 479 U.S., at 490-491, indicates that the EPA's application of the Oklahoma standards was error. We disagree. Our statement in *Ouellette* concerned only an affected State's input into the permit process; that input is clearly limited by the plain language of §402(b). Limits on an affected

State's direct participation in permitting decisions, however, do not in any way constrain the *EPA's* authority to require a point source to comply with downstream water quality standards.

Arkansas also argues that regulations requiring compliance with downstream standards are at odds with the legislative history of the Act and with the statutory scheme established by the Act. Although we agree with Arkansas that the Act's legislative history indicates that Congress intended to grant the Administrator discretion in his oversight of the issuance of NPDES permits, we find nothing in that history to indicate that Congress intended to preclude the EPA from establishing a general requirement that such permits be conditioned to ensure compliance with downstream water quality standards.

Similarly, we agree with Arkansas that in the Clean Water Act Congress struck a careful balance among competing policies and interests, but do not find the EPA regulations concerning the application of downstream water quality standards at all incompatible with that balance. Congress, in crafting the Act, protected certain sovereign interests of the States; for example, §510 allows States to adopt more demanding pollution-control standards than those established under the Act. Arkansas emphasizes that §510 preserves such state authority only as it is applied to the waters of the regulating State. Even assuming Arkansas' construction of §510 is correct, cf. id., at 493, that section only concerns *state* authority and does not constrain the *EPA's* authority to promulgate reasonable regulations requiring point sources in one State to comply with water quality standards in downstream States.

For these reasons, we find the EPA's requirement that the Fayetteville discharge comply with Oklahoma's water quality standards to be a reasonable exercise of the Agency's substantial statutory discretion.

## V

The Court of Appeals construed the Clean Water Act to prohibit any discharge of effluent that would reach waters already in violation of existing water quality standards. We find nothing in the Act to support this reading.

The interpretation of the statute adopted by the court had not been advanced by any party during the agency or court proceedings. Moreover, the Court of Appeals candidly acknowledged that its theory "has apparently never before been addressed by a federal court." The only statutory provision the court cited to support its legal analysis was §402(h), which merely authorizes the EPA (or a state permit program) to prohibit a publicly owned treatment plant that is violating a condition of its NPDES permit from accepting any additional pollutants for treatment until the ongoing violation has been corrected.

Although the Act contains several provisions directing compliance with state water quality standards, see, e.g., §301(b)(1)(C), the parties have pointed to nothing that mandates a complete ban on discharges into a waterway that is in violation of those standards. The statute does, however, contain provisions designed to remedy existing water quality violations and to allocate the burden of reducing undesirable discharges between existing sources and new sources. See, e.g., §303(d). Thus, rather than establishing the categorical ban announced by the Court of Appeals—which might frustrate the construction of new plants that would improve existing conditions—the Clean Water Act vests in the EPA and States broad authority to develop long-range, area-wide programs to alleviate and eliminate existing pollution. See, e.g., §208(b)(2).

To the extent that the Court of Appeals relied on its interpretation of the Act to reverse the EPA's permitting decision, that reliance was misplaced.

## VI

The Court of Appeals also concluded that the EPA's issuance of the Fayetteville permit was arbitrary and capricious because the Agency misinterpreted Oklahoma's water quality standards. The primary difference between the court's and the Agency's interpretation of the standards derives from the court's construction of the Act. Contrary to the EPA's interpretation of the Oklahoma standards, the Court of Appeals read those standards as containing the same categorical ban on new discharges that the court had found in the Clean Water Act itself. Although we do not believe the text of the Oklahoma standards supports the court's reading (indeed, we note that Oklahoma itself had not advanced that interpretation in its briefs in the Court of Appeals), we reject it for a more fundamental reason—namely, that the Court of Appeals exceeded the legitimate scope of judicial review of an agency adjudication. . . .

As discussed above, EPA regulations require an NPDES permit to comply "with the applicable water quality requirements of all affected States." 40 CFR §122.4(d) (1991). This regulation effectively incorporates into federal law those state law standards the Agency reasonably determines to be applicable. In such a situation, then, state water quality standards—promulgated by the States with substantial guidance from the EPA and approved by the Agency—are part of the federal law of water pollution control.

Two features of the body of law governing water pollution support this conclusion. First, as discussed more thoroughly above, we have long recognized that interstate water pollution is controlled by *federal* law. Recognizing that the system of federally approved state standards as applied in the interstate context constitutes federal law is wholly consistent with this principle. Second, treating state standards in interstate controversies as federal law accords with the Act's purpose of authorizing the EPA to create and manage a uniform system of interstate water pollution regulation.

Because we recognize that, at least insofar as they affect the issuance of a permit in another State, the Oklahoma standards have a federal character, the EPA's reasonable, consistently held interpretation of those standards is entitled to substantial deference. In this case, the Chief Judicial Officer ruled that the Oklahoma standards—which require that there be "no degradation" of the upper Illinois River—would only be violated if the discharge effected an "actually detectable or measurable" change in water quality.

This interpretation of the Oklahoma standards is certainly reasonable and consistent with the purposes and principles of the Clean Water Act. As the Chief Judicial Officer noted, "unless there is some method for measuring compliance, there is no way to ensure compliance." Moreover, this interpretation of the Oklahoma standards makes eminent sense in the interstate context: If every discharge that had some theoretical impact on a downstream State were interpreted as "degrading" the downstream waters, downstream States might wield an effective veto over upstream discharges.

The EPA's application of those standards in this case was also sound. On remand, the ALJ scrutinized the record and made explicit factual findings regarding four primary measures of water quality under the Oklahoma standards: eutrophication, aesthetics, dissolved oxygen, and metals. In each case, the ALJ found that the Fayetteville discharge would not lead to a detectable change in water quality. He therefore concluded that the Fayetteville discharge would not violate the Oklahoma water quality standards. Because we agree with the Agency's Chief Judicial Officer that these findings are supported by substantial evidence, we conclude that the Court of Appeals should have affirmed both the EPA's construction of the regulations and the issuance of the Fayetteville permit. . . .

In sum, the Court of Appeals made a policy choice that it was not authorized to make. Arguably, as that court suggested, it might be wise to prohibit any discharge into the Illinois River, even if that discharge would have no adverse impact on water quality. But it was surely not arbitrary for the EPA to conclude—given the benefits to the River from the increased flow of relatively clean water and the benefits achieved in Arkansas by allowing the new plant to operate as designed—that allowing the discharge would be even wiser. It is not our role, or that of the Court of Appeals, to decide which policy choice is the better one, for it is clear that Congress has entrusted such decisions to the Environmental Protection Agency.

## NOTES AND QUESTIONS

1. Does the Court's decision effectively make EPA the umpire of interstate water pollution disputes? EPA issued the permit challenged in this case only because Arkansas had not been delegated the authority to operate the NPDES program. If Arkansas had been delegated such authority and had issued the permit, how, if at all, would Oklahoma's ability to challenge the permit have been affected?

2. The Court declined to decide whether EPA was required to apply the water quality standards of the downstream state, holding only that it was permissible for EPA to do so. Suppose that in another case an upstream state's discharges did cause "an actually detectable or measurable change in water quality" in violation of a downstream state's standards. Could EPA legally issue a permit for such discharges?

3. How did Arkansas interpret *Ouellette*? How does the Court distinguish it from the instant case? Could Oklahoma file a common law nuisance action against the Arkansas plant? In light of *Ouellette*, what law would apply to such an action?

4. Arkansas argued that it would be chaotic to require dischargers to comply with the water quality standards of all downstream states because some rivers flow through numerous states (e.g., the Mississippi). Is this a valid concern? Could a downstream state effectively dictate the terms of NPDES permits in upstream states by adopting very stringent water quality standards? What checks exist to prevent downstream states from adopting unreasonably stringent water quality standards?

5. What would Oklahoma need to show in order to convince EPA to deny issuance of the permit? In light of the Court's decision, do the existing violations of Oklahoma's water quality standards have any significance for dischargers in upstream states?

6. As the Court notes, §510 of the Clean Water Act expressly preserves the right of states to adopt and enforce more stringent standards than those required

by federal law. While §518 of the Act provides that Indian tribes may be treated by EPA as states for the purposes of certain enumerated sections of the Act, §510 is not one of the sections expressly referenced by section 518. Nonetheless, in City of Albuquerque v. Browner, 97 F.3d 415 (10th Cir. 1996), the Tenth Circuit upheld EPA's decision to allow a tribe to impose a more stringent water quality standard on a portion of the Rio Grande River downstream from the city of Albuquerque.

The Isleta Pueblo had designated the use of the water segment as "Primary Contact Ceremonial" because it was used by tribal members for ceremonial immersions. The court held that this could be used to restrict discharges by the upstream city. The court explained that "Congress' failure to incorporate [§510] into §518 does not prevent Indian tribes from exercising their inherent sovereign power to impose standards or limits that are more stringent than those imposed by the federal government." 97 F.3d at 423. The court noted that, in *Arkansas v. Oklahoma*, the Supreme Court had explained that section 510 "only concerns *state* authority and does not constrain EPA's authority," 503 U.S. at 107 (emphasis in original). It concluded that section 510 did not implicitly constrain tribes' sovereign authority and that EPA's construction of the Act as permitting tribes to establish water quality standards more stringent than the federal minimum "is permissible because it is in accord with powers inherent in Indian tribal sovereignty." See also Flathead Reservation v. EPA, 137 F.3d 1135 (9th Cir. 1998) (upholding regulation allowing tribes to apply water quality standards to non-Indian irrigators owning land within tribal reservation).

## B. Individual Control Strategies for Toxic Pollutants

Having largely abandoned the water quality–based approach to pollution control in 1972, Congress in 1987 sought to resuscitate it as a supplementary mechanism for controlling toxic water pollutants. The 1987 Amendments added section 304(*l*) to the Clean Water Act, which directs EPA and the states to identify waters with toxic problems and to impose new controls on sources of discharges to them. Recognizing that eventual compliance with BAT standards would be insufficient to meet water quality standards for toxics in some waters, Congress required states to identify such waters and to develop "individual control strategies" for reducing toxic discharges to them.

Section 304(*l*)(1) required all states to submit three lists of waters to EPA: (A) waters that "cannot reasonably be anticipated to attain or maintain (i) water quality standards for such waters . . . due to toxic pollutants" (the A(i) list), "or (ii) that water quality which shall assure protection of public health, public water supplies, agricultural and industrial uses, and the protection and propagation of a balanced population of shellfish, fish and wildlife, and allow recreational activities in and on the water" (the A(ii) list), and (B) waters not expected to meet water quality standards even after application of BAT due entirely or substantially to toxic pollution from point sources (the B list). Note that the A(i) list is considerably broader than the B list because it apparently includes waters not expected to meet water quality standards due to toxic pollution from nonpoint sources. The A(ii) list is the broadest because it includes even some waters that comply with state water quality standards if they are not expected to meet the water quality goals of the Act.

For each water segment "included on such lists," states are required to determine "the specific point sources discharging any such toxic pollutant which is believed to be preventing or impairing such water quality and the amount of each such toxic pollutant discharged by each such source," §304($l$)(1)(C). Although EPA initially interpreted this requirement as applicable only to waters on the B list, in Natural Resources Defense Council v. EPA, 915 F.2d 1314, 1319 (9th Cir. 1990), the Ninth Circuit held that the reference to "lists" made it applicable to waters on any of the three lists. Thus, states must identify point sources contributing to waters whose impairment is not primarily a product of point source pollution. The court reserved judgment on the question of whether individual control strategies had to be applied to waters on each of these lists.

Section 304($l$)(1)(D) requires each state to develop "an individual control strategy which . . . will produce a reduction in the discharge of toxic pollutants from point sources identified by the State, . . . which reduction is sufficient, in combination with existing controls on point and nonpoint sources of pollution, to achieve the applicable water quality standard as soon as possible, but not later than 3 years after the date of the establishment of such strategy." §304($l$)(1)(D). "The effect of the individual control strategies is simply to expedite the imposition of water-quality-based limitations on polluters—limitations which otherwise would have had to be imposed when the polluters' NPDES permits expired." Natural Resources Defense Council v. EPA, 915 F.2d 1314, 1319 (9th Cir. 1990). Because the states were given until June 1989 to submit their lists to EPA, the control strategies were supposed to achieve water quality standards by June 1992.

Implementation of section 304($l$)'s water quality–based "regulatory safety net" has been hampered by the same informational and conceptual obstacles that traditionally have bedeviled such approaches to pollution control. Monitoring data are sparse, and few states have adopted comprehensive water quality criteria for toxics. Many state standards for toxics are expressed in narrative, rather than numerical, form and are difficult to translate into individual controls. Section 303(c)(2) requires states to adopt numerical water quality criteria for all priority pollutants that could reasonably be expected to interfere with the state's designated uses for which EPA has published water quality criteria under section 304(a). By February 1990, only six states had established criteria for toxic pollutants fully acceptable to EPA. By November 1991, EPA determined that 35 states had complied with §303(c)(2). The agency ultimately issued its own numeric criteria for 98 toxic pollutants in 14 states. 57 Fed. Reg. 60,848 (1992).

States varied considerably in the thoroughness of their section 304($l$) lists of affected waters and dischargers. In the initial lists submitted in February 1989 some states listed dozens of affected water segments while others listed none. (The number of dischargers included in the states' lists ranged from zero to 180.) Much of the variation in state responses stemmed from differences in the quantity and quality of toxics monitoring data as well as differences in the thoroughness with which existing data sources were reviewed. Few states have adequate toxics monitoring programs; some responded to perceived data inadequacies with a "what-you-don't-know-won't-hurt-you" approach, incorporating only a few waters or dischargers for which the data were clearest. Many failed to consult additional data sources including the Toxics Release Inventory established by the Emergency Planning and

Community Right-to-Know Act. Although EPA had encouraged states to include waters affected by any toxic pollutant, rather than just the 126 priority pollutants, few states did so. Yet Connecticut found that nearly one-half of the facilities causing toxic pollution problems in the state's waters were discharging nonpriority pollutants such as biocides, water conditioning agents, and oxidative treatment chemicals. Surface Water "Toxic Hot Spots" Program Criticized as Inadequate at Senate Hearing, 20 Envtl. Rep. 466 (1989).

In June 1989, EPA released a list of 595 water segments and 879 dischargers that the states, supplemented by EPA, had determined to be subject to the requirements of section 304($l$). Id. Several environmental and citizen groups petitioned EPA to add certain water segments and dischargers to the lists. Petitions by Environmental Groups Could Add Many Industries to 304($l$) List, 20 Envtl. Rep. 627 (1989). EPA advised the states that it interprets the section 304($l$) requirements to be part of a continuing process and that the section 304($l$) lists should be reviewed and updated periodically as additional data about toxic pollution become available. Some states disagree, arguing that the statutory language indicates that it should be a one-time process.

EPA's regulations provide that an individual control strategy (ICS) should be incorporated into a final NPDES permit and be supported by documentation indicating that the permit's effluent limits are sufficient to meet applicable water quality standards. 40 C.F.R. §123.46(c). EPA is required to approve or disapprove ICSs submitted by states. If EPA disapproves a state's control strategy, or if the state fails to submit one, EPA must develop and implement its own control strategy. While section 509(b)(1) makes EPA's promulgation of any individual control strategy reviewable in the United States Courts of Appeals, several circuits held that it does not authorize such review of EPA decisions to *approve* state ICSs. Borough of St. Marys v. EPA, 945 F.2d 67 (3d Cir. 1991); Roll Coater, Inc. v. Reilly, 932 F.2d 668 (7th Cir. 1991); Boise Cascade Corp. v. EPA, 942 F.2d 1427 (9th Cir. 1991); Lake Cumberland Trust, Inc. v. EPA, 954 F.2d 1218 (6th Cir. 1992); see also Hecla Mining Co. v. EPA, 12 F.3d 164 (9th Cir. 1993) (EPA's inclusion of additional waters on section 304($l$) list not subject to judicial review).

## C.   State Water Quality Certification under Section 401

As discussed in *Arkansas v. Oklahoma*, section 401(a)(1) of the Clean Water Act requires applicants for a federal license or permit to conduct any activity that "may result in any discharge into navigable waters" to provide the licensing or permitting authority with a certification from the state in which the discharge will occur that the discharge will comply with various provisions of the Act. Section 401(d) provides that such certifications "shall set forth any effluent limitations and other limitations, and monitoring requirements necessary to assure that" the applicant complies with the Act "and with any other appropriate requirement of State law set forth in" the certification, which then becomes a condition of the federal permit. Section 401 has been considered a "sleeping giant" of the Clean Water Act because of the potentially broad scope of the conditions it enables states to impose. In the case below, the Supreme Court considered whether a state could condition a section 401 certification for a Federal Energy Regulatory Commission (FERC) license to construct a hydroelectric dam on the imposition of minimum stream flow rates.

## PUD No. 1 of Jefferson County v. Washington Department of Ecology

511 U.S. 700 (1994)

JUSTICE O'CONNOR delivered the opinion of the Court. . . .

### II

Petitioners propose to build the Elkhorn Hydroelectric Project on the Dosewallips River. If constructed as presently planned, the facility would be located just outside the Olympic National Park on federally owned land within the Olympic National Forest. The project would divert water from a 1.2-mile reach of the River (the bypass reach), run the water through turbines to generate electricity and then return the water to the River below the bypass reach. Under the Federal Power Act (FPA), 16 U.S.C. §791 et seq., the Federal Energy Regulatory Commission has authority to license new hydroelectric facilities. As a result, the petitioners must get a FERC license to build or operate the Elkhorn Project. Because a federal license is required, and because the project may result in discharges into the Dosewallips River, petitioners are also required to obtain State certification of the project pursuant to §401 of the Clean Water Act, 33 U.S.C. §1341.

The water flow in the bypass reach, which is currently undiminished by appropriation, ranges seasonally between 149 and 738 cubic feet per second (cfs). The Dosewallips supports two species of salmon, Coho and Chinook, as well as Steelhead trout. As originally proposed, the project was to include a diversion dam which would completely block the river and channel approximately 75 percent of the River's water into a tunnel alongside the streambed. About 25 percent of the water would remain in the bypass reach, but would be returned to the original riverbed through sluice gates or a fish ladder. Depending on the season, this would leave a residual minimum flow of between 65 and 155 cfs in the River. Respondent undertook a study to determine the minimum stream flows necessary to protect the salmon and steelhead fisheries in the bypass reach. On June 11, 1986, respondent issued a §401 water quality certification imposing a variety of conditions on the project, including a minimum stream-flow requirement of between 100 and 200 cfs depending on the season.

A state administrative appeals board determined that the minimum flow requirement was intended to enhance, not merely maintain, the fishery, and that the certification condition therefore exceeded respondent's authority under state law. On appeal, the state Superior Court concluded that respondent could require compliance with the minimum flow conditions. The Superior Court also found that respondent had imposed the minimum flow requirement to protect and preserve the fishery, not to improve it, and that this requirement was authorized by state law.

The Washington Supreme Court held that the antidegradation provisions of the State's water quality standards require the imposition of minimum stream flows. 849 P.2d 646, 650 (1993). The court also found that §401(d), which allows States to impose conditions based upon several enumerated sections of the Clean Water Act and "any other appropriate requirement of State law," §401(d), authorized the stream flow condition. Relying on this language and the broad purposes of the Clean Water Act, the court concluded that §401(d) confers on States power to "consider all state action related to water quality in imposing conditions on section 401 certificates." We granted certiorari to resolve a conflict among the state courts of last resort.

## III

The principal dispute in this case concerns whether the minimum stream flow requirement that the State imposed on the Elkhorn project is a permissible condition of a §401 certification under the Clean Water Act. To resolve this dispute we must first determine the scope of the State's authority under §401. We must then determine whether the limitation at issue here, the requirement that petitioners maintain minimum stream flows, falls within the scope of that authority.

### A

There is no dispute that petitioners were required to obtain a certification from the State pursuant to §401. Petitioners concede that, at a minimum, the project will result in two possible discharges—the release of dredged and fill material during the construction of the project, and the discharge of water at the end of the tailrace after the water has been used to generate electricity. Petitioners contend, however, that the minimum stream flow requirement imposed by the State was unrelated to these specific discharges, and that as a consequence, the State lacked the authority under §401 to condition its certification on maintenance of stream flows sufficient to protect the Dosewallips fishery.

If §401 consisted solely of subsection (a), which refers to a state certification that a "discharge" will comply with certain provisions of the Act, petitioners' assessment of the scope of the State's certification authority would have considerable force. Section 401, however, also contains subsection (d), which expands the State's authority to impose conditions on the certification of a project. Section 401(d) provides that any certification shall set forth "any effluent limitations and other limitations . . . necessary to assure that *any applicant*" will comply with various provisions of the Act and appropriate state law requirements. §401(d) (emphasis added). The language of this subsection contradicts petitioners' claim that the State may only impose water quality limitations specifically tied to a "discharge." The text refers to the compliance of the applicant, not the discharge. Section 401(d) thus allows the State to impose "other limitations" on the project in general to assure compliance with various provisions of the Clean Water Act and with "any other appropriate requirement of State law." Although the dissent asserts that this interpretation of §401(d) renders §401(a)(1) superfluous, we see no such anomaly. Section 401(a)(1) identifies the category of activities subject to certification—namely those with discharges. And §401(d) is most reasonably read as authorizing additional conditions and limitations on the activity as a whole once the threshold condition, the existence of a discharge, is satisfied.

Our view of the statute is consistent with EPA's regulations implementing §401. The regulations expressly interpret §401 as requiring the State to find that "there is a reasonable assurance that the *activity* will be conducted in a manner which will not violate applicable water quality standards." 40 CFR §121.2(a)(3) (1992) (emphasis added). See also EPA, Wetlands and 401 Certification 23 (Apr.

1989) ("In 401(d), the Congress has given the States the authority to place any conditions on a water quality certification that are necessary to assure that the applicant will comply with effluent limitations, water quality standards, . . . and with 'any other appropriate requirement of State Law.'"). EPA's conclusion that *activities*—not merely discharges—must comply with state water quality standards is a reasonable interpretation of §401, and is entitled to deference.

Although §401(d) authorizes the State to place restrictions on the activity as a whole, that authority is not unbounded. The State can only ensure that the project complies with "any applicable effluent limitations and other limitations, under [§§301, 302]" or certain other provisions of the Act, "and with any other appropriate requirement of State law." §401(d). The State asserts that the minimum stream flow requirement was imposed to ensure compliance with the state water quality standards adopted pursuant to §303 of the Clean Water Act.

We agree with the State that ensuring compliance with §303 is a proper function of the §401 certification. Although §303 is not one of the statutory provisions listed in §401(d), the statute allows states to impose limitations to ensure compliance with §301 of the Act. Section 301 in turn incorporates §303 by reference. As a consequence, state water quality standards adopted pursuant to §303 are among the "other limitations" with which a State may ensure compliance through the §401 certification process. This interpretation is consistent with EPA's view of the statute. Moreover, limitations to assure compliance with state water quality standards are also permitted by §401(d)'s reference to "any other appropriate requirement of State law." We do not speculate on what additional state laws, if any, might be incorporated by this language. But at a minimum, limitations imposed pursuant to state water quality standards adopted pursuant to §303 are "appropriate" requirements of state law. Indeed, petitioners appear to agree that the State's authority under §401 includes limitations designed to ensure compliance with state water quality standards.

### B

Having concluded that, pursuant to §401, States may condition certification upon any limitations necessary to ensure compliance with state water quality standards or any other "appropriate requirement of State law," we consider whether the minimum flow condition is such a limitation. Under §303, state water quality standards must "consist of the designated uses of the navigable waters involved and the water quality criteria for such waters based upon such uses." In imposing the minimum stream flow requirement, the State determined that construction and operation of the project as planned would be inconsistent with one of the designated uses of Class AA water, namely "[s]almonid [and other fish] migration, rearing, spawning, and harvesting." The designated use of the River as a fish habitat directly reflects the Clean Water Act's goal of maintaining the "chemical, physical, and biological integrity of the Nation's waters." §101(a). Indeed, the Act defines pollution as "the man-made or man-induced alteration of the chemical, physical, biological, and radiological integrity of water." §502(19). Moreover, the Act expressly requires that, in adopting water quality standards, the State must take into consideration the use of waters for "propagation of fish and wildlife." §303(c)(2)(A).

Petitioners assert, however, that §303 requires the State to protect designated uses solely through implementation of specific "criteria." According to petitioners, the State may not require them to operate their dam in a manner consistent with a designated "use"; instead, say petitioners, under §303 the State may only require that the project comply with specific numerical "criteria."

We disagree with petitioners' interpretation of the language of §303(c)(2)(A). Under the statute, a water quality standard must "consist of the designated uses of the navigable waters involved *and* the water quality criteria for such waters based upon such uses." §303(c)(2)(A) (emphasis added). The text makes it plain that water quality standards contain two components. We think the language of §303 is most naturally read to require that a project be consistent with *both* components, namely the designated use *and* the water quality criteria. Accordingly, under the literal terms of the statute, a project that does not comply with a designated use of the water does not comply with the applicable water quality standards.

Consequently, pursuant to §401(d) the State may require that a permit applicant comply with both the designated uses and the water quality criteria of the state standards. In granting certification pursuant to §401(d), the State "shall set forth any . . . limitations . . . necessary to assure that [the applicant] will comply with any . . . limitations under [§303] . . . and with any other appropriate requirement of State law." A certification requirement that an applicant operate the project consistently with state water quality standards—i.e., consistently with the designated uses of the water body and the water quality criteria—is both a "limitation" to assure "compliance with . . . limitations" imposed under §303, and an "appropriate" requirement of State law.

EPA has not interpreted §303 to require the States to protect designated uses exclusively through enforcement of numerical criteria. In its regulations governing state water quality standards, EPA defines criteria as "*elements* of State water quality standards expressed as constituent concentrations, levels, or narrative statements, representing a quality of water that supports a particular use." §40 CFR 131.3(b) (1992) (emphasis added). The regulations further provide that "when criteria are met, water quality will *generally* protect the designated use." Ibid. (emphasis added). Thus, the EPA regulations implicitly recognize that in some circumstances, criteria alone are insufficient to protect a designated use.

Petitioners also appear to argue that use requirements are too open-ended, and that the Act only contemplates enforcement of the more specific and objective "criteria." But this argument is belied by the open-ended nature of the criteria themselves. As the Solicitor General points out, even "criteria" are often expressed in broad, narrative terms, such as "there shall be no discharge of toxic pollutants in toxic amounts." In fact, under the Clean Water Act, only one class of criteria, those governing "toxic pollutants listed pursuant to section 307(a)(1)," need be rendered in numerical form. See §303(c)(2)(B); 40 CFR §131.11(b)(2) (1992).

Washington's Class AA water quality standards are typical in that they contain several open-ended criteria which, like the use designation of the River as a fishery, must be translated into specific limitations for individual projects. For example, the standards state that "[t]oxic, radioactive, or deleterious material concentrations shall be less than those which may affect public health, the natural aquatic environment, or the desirability of the water for any use." WAC 173-201-045(c)(vii).

Similarly, the state standards specify that "aesthetic values shall not be impaired by the presence of materials or their effects, excluding those of natural origin, which offend the senses of sight, smell, touch, or taste." 173-201-045(c)(viii). We think petitioners' attempt to distinguish between uses and criteria loses much of its force in light of the fact that the Act permits enforcement of broad, narrative criteria based on, for example, "aesthetics."

Petitioners further argue that enforcement of water quality standards through use designations renders the water quality criteria component of the standards irrelevant. We see no anomaly, however, in the State's reliance on both use designations and criteria to protect water quality. The specific numerical limitations embodied in the criteria are a convenient enforcement mechanism for identifying minimum water conditions which will generally achieve the requisite water quality. And, in most circumstances, satisfying the criteria will, as EPA recognizes, be sufficient to maintain the designated use. See 40 CFR §131.3(b)(1992). Water quality standards, however, apply to an entire class of water, a class which contains numerous individual water bodies. For example, in the State of Washington, the Class AA water quality standard applies to 81 specified fresh surface waters, as well as to all "surface waters lying within the mountainous regions of the state assigned to national parks, national forests, and/or wilderness areas," all "lakes and their feeder streams within the state," and all "unclassified surface waters that are tributaries to Class AA waters." WAC 173-201-070. While enforcement of criteria will in general protect the uses of these diverse waters, a complementary requirement that activities also comport with designated uses enables the States to ensure that each activity—even if not foreseen by the criteria—will be consistent with the specific uses and attributes of a particular body of water.

Under petitioners' interpretation of the statute, however, if a particular criterion, such as turbidity, were missing from the list contained in an individual state water quality standard, or even if an existing turbidity criterion were insufficient to protect a particular species of fish in a particular river, the State would nonetheless be forced to allow activities inconsistent with the existing or designated uses. We think petitioners' reading leads to an unreasonable interpretation of the Act. The criteria components of state water quality standards attempt to identify, for all the water bodies in a given class, water quality requirements generally sufficient to protect designated uses. These criteria, however, cannot reasonably be expected to anticipate all the water quality issues arising from every activity which can affect the State's hundreds of individual water bodies. Requiring the States to enforce only the criteria component of their water quality standards would in essence require the States to study to a level of great specificity each individual surface water to ensure that the criteria applicable to that water are sufficiently detailed and individualized to fully protect the water's designated uses. Given that there is no textual support for imposing this requirement, we are loath to attribute to Congress an intent to impose this heavy regulatory burden on the States.

The State also justified its minimum stream flow as necessary to implement the "antidegradation policy" of §303(d)(4)(B). When the Clean Water Act was enacted in 1972, the water quality standards of all 50 States had antidegradation provisions. These provisions were required by federal law. By providing in 1972 that existing state water quality standards would remain in force until revised, the Clean Water

Act ensured that the States would continue their antidegradation programs. See §303(a). EPA has consistently required that revised state standards incorporate an antidegradation policy. And, in 1987, Congress explicitly recognized the existence of an "antidegradation policy established under [§303]." §303(d)(4)(B).

EPA has promulgated regulations implementing §303's antidegradation policy, a phrase that is not defined elsewhere in the Act. These regulations require States to "develop and adopt a statewide antidegradation policy and identify the methods for implementing such policy." 40 CFR §131.12 (1992). These "implementation methods shall, at a minimum, be consistent with the . . . existing instream water uses and the level of water quality necessary to protect the existing uses shall be maintained and protected." Ibid. EPA has explained that under its antidegradation regulation, "no activity is allowable . . . which could partially or completely eliminate any existing use." EPA, Questions and Answers re: Antidegradation 3 (1985). Thus, States must implement their antidegradation policy in a manner "consistent" with existing uses of the stream. The State of Washington's antidegradation policy in turn provides that "existing beneficial uses shall be maintained and protected and no further degradation which would interfere with or become injurious to existing beneficial uses will be allowed." WAC 173-201-035(8)(a). The State concluded that the reduced streamflows would have just the effect prohibited by this policy. The Solicitor General, representing EPA, asserts, and we agree, that the State's minimum stream flow condition is a proper application of the state and federal antidegradation regulations, as it ensures that an "existing instream water use" will be "maintained and protected." 40 CFR §131.12(a)(1) (1992).

Petitioners also assert more generally that the Clean Water Act is only concerned with water "quality," and does not allow the regulation of water "quantity." This is an artificial distinction. In many cases, water quantity is closely related to water quality; a sufficient lowering of the water quantity in a body of water could destroy all of its designated uses, be it for drinking water, recreation, navigation or, as here, as a fishery. In any event, there is recognition in the Clean Water Act itself that reduced stream flow, i.e., diminishment of water quantity, can constitute water pollution. First, the Act's definition of pollution as "the man-made or man-induced alteration of the chemical, physical, biological, and radiological integrity of water" encompasses the effects of reduced water quantity. §502(19). This broad conception of pollution—one which expressly evinces Congress' concern with the physical and biological integrity of water—refutes petitioners' assertion that the Act draws a sharp distinction between the regulation of water "quantity" and water "quality." Moreover, §304 of the Act expressly recognizes that water "pollution" may result from "changes in the movement, flow, or circulation of any navigable waters . . . including changes caused by the construction of dams." §304(f). This concern with the flowage effects of dams and other diversions is also embodied in the EPA regulations, which expressly require existing dams to be operated to attain designated uses. 40 CFR §131.10(g)(4). . . .

In summary, we hold that the State may include minimum stream flow requirements in a certification issued pursuant to §401 of the Clean Water Act insofar as necessary to enforce a designated use contained in a state water quality standard. The judgment of the Supreme Court of Washington, accordingly, is affirmed.

[In his concurring opinion, Justice Stevens emphasized that this was "an easy case" because the Clean Water Act "explicitly recognizes States' ability to impose stricter standards than federal law requires."]

JUSTICE THOMAS, with whom JUSTICE SCALIA joins, dissenting.

. . . The terms of §401(a)(1) make clear that the purpose of the certification process is to ensure that discharges from a project will meet the requirements of the CWA. . . .

The minimum stream flow condition imposed by respondents in this case has no relation to any possible "discharge" that might "result" from petitioners' proposed project. The term "discharge" is not defined in the CWA, but its plain and ordinary meaning suggests "a flowing or issuing out," or "something that is emitted." Webster's Ninth New Collegiate Dictionary 360 (1991). Cf. §502(16) ("The term 'discharge' when used without qualification includes a discharge of a pollutant, and a discharge of pollutants"). A minimum stream flow requirement, by contrast, is a limitation on the amount of water the project can take in or divert from the river. That is, a minimum stream flow requirement is a limitation on intake—the opposite of discharge. Imposition of such a requirement would thus appear to be beyond a State's authority as it is defined by §401(a)(1). . . .

If, as the Court asserts, §401(d) permits States to impose conditions unrelated to discharges in §401 certifications, Congress' careful focus on discharges in §401(a)(1)—the provision that describes the scope and function of the certification process—was wasted effort. The power to set conditions that are unrelated to discharges is, of course, nothing but a conditional power to deny certification for reasons unrelated to discharges. Permitting States to impose conditions unrelated to discharges, then, effectively eliminates the constraints of §401(a)(1).

Subsections 401(a)(1) and (d) can easily be reconciled to avoid this problem. To ascertain the nature of the conditions permissible under §401(d), §401 must be read as a whole. As noted above, §401(a)(1) limits a State's authority in the certification process to addressing concerns related to discharges and to ensuring that any discharge resulting from a project will comply with specified provisions of the Act. It is reasonable to infer that the conditions a State is permitted to impose on certification must relate to the very purpose the certification process is designed to serve. Thus, while §401(d) permits a State to place conditions on a certification to ensure compliance of the "applicant," those conditions must still be related to discharges. In my view, this interpretation best harmonizes the subsections of §401. Indeed, any broader interpretation of §401(d) would permit that subsection to swallow §401(a)(1). . . .

The Court states that, "at a minimum, limitations imposed pursuant to state water quality standards adopted pursuant to §303 are 'appropriate' requirements of state law" under §401(d). A water quality standard promulgated pursuant to §303 must "consist of the designated uses of the navigable waters involved and the water quality criteria for such waters based upon such uses." 33 U.S.C. §1313(c)(2)(A). The Court asserts that this language "is most naturally read to require that a project be consistent with both components, namely the designated use and the water quality criteria." In the Court's view, then, the "use" of a body of water is independently enforceable through §401(d) without reference to the corresponding criteria.

The Court's reading strikes me as contrary to common sense. It is difficult to see how compliance with a "use" of a body of water could be enforced without reference to the corresponding criteria. In this case, for example, the applicable "use" is contained in the following regulation: "Characteristic uses shall include, but not be limited to . . . [s]almonid migration, rearing, spawning, and harvesting." Wash. Admin. Code (WAC) 173-201-045(1)(b)(iii) (1990). The corresponding criteria, by contrast, include measurable factors such as quantities of fecal coliform organisms and dissolved gases in the water. WAC 173-201-045(1)(c)(i) and (ii). Although the Act does not further address (at least not expressly) the link between "uses" and "criteria," the regulations promulgated under §303 make clear that a "use" is an aspirational goal to be attained through compliance with corresponding "criteria." Those regulations suggest that "uses" are to be "achieved and protected," and that "water quality criteria" are to be adopted to "protect the designated uses." 40 CFR §§131.10(a), 131.11(a)(1) (1993).

The problematic consequences of decoupling "uses" and "criteria" become clear once the Court's interpretation of §303 is read in the context of §401. In the Court's view, a State may condition the §401 certification "upon *any limitations* necessary to ensure compliance" with the "uses of the water body" (emphasis added). Under the Court's interpretation, then, state environmental agencies may pursue, through §401, their water goals in any way they choose; the conditions imposed on certifications need not relate to discharges, nor to water quality criteria, nor to any objective or quantifiable standard, so long as they tend to make the water more suitable for the uses the State has chosen. In short, once a State is allowed to impose conditions on §401 certifications to protect "uses" in the abstract, §401(d) is limitless.

To illustrate, while respondents in this case focused only on the "use" of the Dosewallips River as a fish habitat, this particular river has a number of other "characteristic uses," including "recreation (primary contact recreation, sport fishing, boating, and aesthetic enjoyment)." WAC 173-201-045(1)(b)(v). Under the Court's interpretation, respondents could have imposed any number of conditions related to recreation, including conditions that have little relation to water quality. In Town of Summersville, 60 FERC 161,291, p. 61,990 (1992), for instance, the state agency required the applicant to "construct . . . access roads and paths, low water stepping stone bridges, . . . a boat launching facility . . . , and a residence and storage building." These conditions presumably would be sustained under the approach the Court adopts today. In the end, it is difficult to conceive of a condition that would fall outside a State's §401(d) authority under the Court's approach.

## NOTES AND QUESTIONS

1. In his dissent, Justice Thomas argues that section 401(d) should not be interpreted to allow states to impose conditions unrelated to discharges. Why does Justice Thomas think that a minimum stream flow requirement is unrelated to a pollutant discharge? Why does the Court majority deem the minimum stream flow requirement an appropriate requirement? Does the majority view this requirement as unrelated to pollutant discharges? How does the majority's view in this regard differ from that of Justice Thomas?

2. Justice O'Connor's opinion for the Court states that while "§401(d) authorizes the State to place restrictions on the activity as a whole, that authority is not unbounded." Yet, in his dissent, Justice Thomas argues that the majority's decision "places no meaningful limitations on a State's authority under §401 to impose

conditions on certification." What limits, if any, does the Court place on a state's ability to impose conditions on a section 401 certification? How meaningful are they?

3. As noted in the opinions above, Washington state had not established any specific stream flow water quality criteria. Yet the Court majority holds that section 401(d) can be used to protect designated uses (here the protection of fish habitat) independent of specific criteria. In the majority's view, what is the relationship between designated uses and water quality criteria? How does this view differ from that of Justice Thomas in his dissent?

4. The *PUD No. 1* decision was hailed as a victory for states that could enable them to rouse the "sleeping giant" of the Clean Water Act to impose broad environmental conditions on federally licensed activities. However, in North Carolina v. FERC, 112 F.3d 1175 (D.C. Cir. 1997), the D.C. Circuit limited section 401's reach by adopting a narrow interpretation of its applicability. At issue was an amendment to a federal hydropower license that would authorize construction of an intake structure to withdraw 60 million gallons of water a day from a lake on the North Carolina/Virginia border. FERC argued that section 401 did not apply because the project would *withdraw* water from the lake rather than *discharging* it into navigable waters. North Carolina, joined by EPA and 39 other states, argued that section 401 did apply because the withdrawal of water from the lake would alter the nature of the discharges from the hydropower project. However, the court sided with FERC, holding that a "decrease in the volume of water passing through the dam turbines cannot be considered a 'discharge' as that term is defined in the CWA." 112 F.3d at 1188. The court concluded that "the word 'discharge' contemplates the addition, not the withdrawal, of a substance or substances." 112 F.3d at 1187. In dissent, Judge Wald argued that "if a State must consent before a new discharge is introduced into its waters, then a change in that discharge must require a new consent." 112 F.3d at 1196. She maintained that the notion that a discharge required the addition of a substance was inconsistent with the Supreme Court's decision in *PUD No. 1*. The majority maintained that *PUD No. 1* did not "define a discharge and in no way indicated that an alteration of a discharge was sufficient to invoke the certification requirement of Section 401(a)(1)."

5. In Oregon Natural Desert Ass'n v. Dombeck, 172 F.3d 1092 (9th Cir. 1998), the Ninth Circuit reversed a district court decision that had required a section 401 certification as a condition to the grant of a grazing permit by the U.S. Forest Service. Rejecting the argument that the term "discharge" in section 401 could encompass pollution from nonpoint sources like runoff from grazing, the court held that section 401 applies only to activities that cause point source discharges. The court distinguished *PUD No. 1* by finding that it did not broaden the meaning of "discharge" because "[a]ll parties conceded that the construction of the dam would result in discharges from both the release of dredge and fill material and the release of water through the dam's tailrace," conveyances that involve point sources.

6. The Federal Energy Regulatory Commission issues long-term licenses for hydroelectric projects. Because the licenses for many large hydroelectric projects are expiring in coming years, the Court's decision in *PUD No. 1* offers states a significant tool for using section 401 to protect water quality. In S.D. Warren v. Maine

Board of Environmental Protection, 547 U.S. 370 (2006), the U.S. Supreme Court upheld the application of section 401 to a FERC hydropower relicensing proceeding. The Court held that the meaning of "discharge" in section 401 is somewhat broader than the meaning of discharge in section 301 (the section of the Act that triggers the sections 402 and 404 permitting requirements). The Court noted that, unlike section 301, section 401 does not refer to a discharge *of pollutants* and that section 502(16) provides that the "term 'discharge' when used without qualification *includes* a discharge of a pollutant, and a discharge of pollutants, indicating that it may cover more than just activities that add pollutants to navigable waters (emphasis supplied)."

7. In three decisions issued in 2016, the Federal Energy Regulatory Commission (FERC) ruled that it had the authority to conditionally approve a pipeline project subject to the requirement that the pipeline company obtain a section 401 certification prior to starting construction. FERC rejected the argument by opponents of the pipelines that it could not legally approve them until the section 401 certification was issued. Constitution Pipeline Co., Order Denying Rehearing and Approving Variance, 154 FERC ¶61,046 (Jan. 26, 2016); Northwest Pipeline, LLC, Order on Rehearing, 157 FERC ¶61,093 (Nov. 8, 2016); Transcontinental Gas Pipe Line Co., Order Denying Rehearing, 157 FERC ¶61,095 (Nov. 9, 2016).

8. In June 2020, EPA adopted the Clean Water Act Section 401 Certification Rule. The rule requires that a state or tribe act within one year on requests for §401 certification. It changes prior policy that had held that the one-year period does not start running until a "complete application" is received by providing that it runs from the receipt of a certification request. The rule emphasizes that the scope of the certification should be limited to assuring that a discharge from a federally licensed or federally permitted activity will comply with water quality requirements.

## D. Total Maximum Daily Loadings

Section 303(d)(1)(A) of the Clean Water Act requires states to identify those waters for which effluent limitations for nontoxic pollutants are not stringent enough to achieve water quality standards. States then are required by section 303(d)(1)(C) to establish the total maximum daily loadings (TMDLs) of these pollutants "at a level necessary to implement the applicable water quality standards" subject to EPA review and approval. TMDLs define the maximum amount of a pollutant that can be discharged into the water segment without violating the water quality standard. By including estimates of pollutant loadings from all sources, including nonpoint sources and natural background levels, TMDLs are supposed to permit a comprehensive assessment of what reductions are necessary to achieve water quality standards.

Interest in TMDLs grew rapidly as gains from technology-based effluent limits were being exhausted. EPA repeatedly has been held to have a duty to establish TMDLs for states that fail to meet their obligations under section 303(d). Scott v. City of Hammond, 741 F.2d 992 (7th Cir. 1984). In Alaska Center for the Environment v. Reilly, 762 F. Supp. 1422 (W.D. Wash. 1991), aff'd, 20 F.3d 981 (9th Cir. 1994), an environmental group sued to require EPA to issue federal TMDLs for Alaska. While Alaska's biennial section 305(b) reports had included several hundred water segments as "impaired" or "threatened" by pollution, in 11 years the state had not submitted a single TMDL to EPA for review and approval. Finding that the state's failure to act was the constructive equivalent of a submission that no TMDLs were necessary, the court held that EPA had a nondiscretionary duty to promulgate TMDLs in the face of state inaction. While EPA and the state subsequently agreed to assess eight water segments, the court ultimately ordered EPA to develop a long-term "schedule for the establishment of TMDLs for all waters designated as water quality limited." Alaska Center for the Environment v. Reilly, 796 F. Supp. 1374, 1381 (W.D. Wash. 1992). The court's decision was affirmed in Alaska Center for the Environment v. Browner, 20 F.3d 981 (9th Cir. 1994).

TMDLs have become the true "sleeping giant" of the Clean Water Act. As Oliver Houck notes, as a result of "the remarkable resurrection of a long-dormant provision of the Clean Water Act, Section 303(d)," TMDLs are "now taking the field and forcing a showdown on the last water quality frontier, non-point source pollution." Houck, TMDLs IV: The Final Frontier, 29 Envtl. L. Rep. 10469, 10471 (1999). By 2002, EPA was under court order to establish TMDLs in 22 states; litigation seeking similar orders was pending in 5 other states. This wave of TMDL litigation by citizen groups forced EPA to develop a draft TMDL Implementation Strategy, which it issued in November 1996. EPA then convened a federal advisory committee to "provide consensus recommendations" on the TMDL program. The advisory committee's final report was issued in July 1998. TMDLs are in place in every U.S. state and the District of Columbia. By mid-2013, EPA reported that 49,622 TMDLs were being used to address 52,650 causes of impairment of surface waters.

One of the most contentious issues involving TMDLs is the question whether section 303(d)'s TMDL requirements apply to nonpoint sources. Agricultural interests, joined by the U.S. Forest Service, have been vocal opponents of including nonpoint sources in load allocations within TMDLs. They argued that section 319 should be the exclusive remedy for nonpoint source pollution because Congress addressed nonpoint sources specifically in section 319 but remained silent about them in section 303(d). EPA long argued that section 303(d) covers nonpoint sources because its text does not exclude from its requirements waters impaired by nonpoint sources. In Pronsolino v. Nastri, 291 F.3d 1123 (9th Cir. 2002), the U.S. Court of Appeals for the Ninth Circuit addressed the question whether EPA has the authority under section 303(d) of the Clean Water Act to set total maximum daily loadings (TMDLs) for all navigable waters impaired by pollution, including those whose impairment is due to nonpoint sources. After EPA disapproved California's 303(d)(1) list because it omitted 16 water segments that were impaired only by nonpoint sources, EPA promulgated its own list including these segments. For one of them, the Garcia River, EPA subsequently established a TMDL requiring a 60 percent reduction in sediment loadings. After California sought to comply with the TMDL by regulating activities, such as logging, that generate sediment runoff, a number of farm organizations sued. In *Pronsolino*, the Ninth Circuit ruled that "the CWA is best read to include in the 303(d)(1) listing and TMDLs requirements waters impaired only by nonpoint sources of pollution." Thus, the court held "that the EPA did not exceed its statutory authority in identifying the Garcia River pursuant to 303(d)(1)(A) and establishing the Garcia River TMDL, even though the river is polluted only by nonpoint sources of pollution."

Another challenge to EPA's authority to promulgate TMDLs focused on the Chesapeake Bay. A coalition led by the American Farm Bureau Federation (AFBF) filed suit in federal district court in Pennsylvania, claiming that EPA had exceeded its authority in promulgating a TMDL for the Bay that included detailed allocations of pollution reduction levels for both point and nonpoint sources. The AFBF argued that EPA had exceeded its authority by determining how to allocate the pollution reductions between types of pollution. The Chesapeake Bay TMDL seeks to reduce nitrogen runoff by 25 percent, phosphorus by 24 percent, and sediment by 20 percent from 2010 levels by 2025. Sixty percent of these reductions were to be achieved by 2016. The AFBF argues that this meant that 20 percent of land adjoining the Bay that was used for agriculture production would have to be taken out of production. The federal district court rejected the challenge to the TMDL. The court ruled that EPA had acted reasonably in allocating pollution reductions among point and nonpoint sources, determined that the TMDL was not an unlawful federal implementation plan, and upheld the procedures and models used in establishing the TMDL. American Farm Bureau Federation v. U.S. EPA, 984 F. Supp. 2d 289 (M.D. Pa. 2013), aff'd, 792 F.3d 281 (3d Cir. 2015). This decision was affirmed on appeal by a unanimous panel of the Third Circuit in the decision below.

## American Farm Bureau Federation v. U.S. EPA

792 F.3d 281 (3d Cir. 2015)

Before AMBRO, SCIRICA and ROTH, Circuit Judges.

AMBRO, Circuit Judge:

## I. INTRODUCTION

The Environmental Protection Agency ("EPA") published in 2010 the "total maximum daily load" ("TMDL") of nitrogen, phosphorous, and sediment that can be released into the Chesapeake Bay (the "Bay") to comply with the Clean Water Act, 33 U.S.C. §1251 *et seq.* The TMDL is a comprehensive framework for pollution reduction designed to "restore and maintain the chemical, physical, and biological integrity" of the Bay, 33 U.S.C. §1251, the subject of much ecological concern over several decades.

Trade associations with members who will be affected by the TMDL's implementation — the American Farm Bureau Federation, the National Association of Home Builders, and other organizations for agricultural industries that include fertilizer, corn, pork, and poultry operations (collectively, "Farm Bureau") — sued. They allege that all aspects of the TMDL that go beyond an allowable sum of pollutants (*i.e.*, the most nitrogen, phosphorous, and sediment the Bay can safely absorb per day) exceeded the scope of the EPA's authority to regulate, largely because the agency may intrude on states' traditional role in regulating land use. . . .

## IV. MERITS

Farm Bureau interprets the words "total maximum daily load" in the Clean Water Act, codified at 33 U.S.C. §1313(d)(1)(C), as unambiguous: a TMDL can consist only of a number representing the amount of a pollutant that can be discharged into a particular segment of water and nothing more. Thus it argues that the EPA overstepped its statutory authority in drafting the Chesapeake Bay TMDL when the agency (1) included in the TMDL allocations of permissible levels of nitrogen, phosphorous, and sediment among different kinds of sources of these pollutants, (2) promulgated target dates for reducing discharges to the level the TMDL envisions, and (3) obtained assurance from the seven affected states that they would fulfill the TMDL's objectives. In Farm Bureau's view, even if allocations, target dates, and reasonable assurance are useful in calculating the number that is the TMDL, the final document may not specify a distribution of pollutants from point and nonpoint sources or deadlines for meeting the target reductions in pollutant discharge, nor may the EPA in drafting the document obtain any assurance from states that they will meet the targets. . . .

### 2. Statutory Text

Farm Bureau's strongest argument is that Congress specifically authorized the EPA to publish "*total* maximum daily *load*[s] . . . at a *level* necessary to implement the applicable water quality standards. . . ." 33 U.S.C. §1313(d)(1)(C) (emphases added). Under Farm Bureau's reading, a "total load" is just a number, like the "total" at the bottom of a restaurant receipt. This ordinary understanding of the word "total" is supported, the argument continues, because the load is to be established at a "level," which can be high or low (so long as it is necessary to implement the water quality standards); in any event it should not be expressed as a comprehensive framework, and in no event can a TMDL include allocations among point and nonpoint sources, deadlines, and the reasonable assurance requirement.

This argument has some intuitive appeal, but other readings are possible. Our most significant textual concern is that Farm Bureau's analysis makes the word "total" redundant. "Maximum daily load[s] . . . established at a level necessary to implement the applicable water standard" would mean the same thing that Farm Bureau argues "total maximum daily load" means: a number set at a level needed to alleviate water pollution. Applying the canon against surplusage, a plausible understanding of "total" is that it means the sum of the constituent parts of the load. The load is still set at the level necessary to fight pollutants, but it is expressed in terms of a total of the different relevant allocations. . . .

Additionally, although Congress explicitly required the EPA to establish "total maximum daily loads," it nowhere prescribed *how* the EPA is to do so. The agency has chosen to lay out in detail (1) how and why it arrived at the number it chose; (2) how it thinks it and affected jurisdictions will be able to achieve that number; (3) why that number is "necessary to implement the applicable water quality standard[ ]," *id.* §1313(d)(1)(C); (4) when it expects the TMDL to achieve the applicable water quality standard; and (5) what it will do if the water quality standard is not met. As the EPA has chosen to use notice-and-comment rulemaking to promulgate TMDLs, the APA likely requires the EPA to provide sufficient information in connection with the TMDL for the public adequately to comment on the agency's judgment and to make suggestions where appropriate. The EPA would fall afoul of this requirement if it published only a number with no supporting information, as the public would be unable to comment on the number without knowing whether or how the EPA thought such a level of discharged pollutant could be achieved.

The EPA's approach also fits the statute's requirement that the load be established in light of "seasonal variations and a margin of safety which takes into account any lack of knowledge concerning the relationship between effluent limitations and water quality." 33 U.S.C. §1313(d)(1)(C). Under Farm Bureau's approach, these factors that affect the EPA's calculation would need to remain absent from the TMDL. It would be strange to require the EPA to take into account these specific considerations but at the same time command the agency to excise them from its final product. If anything, the requirements that the TMDL (1) be established at a level necessary to implement water quality standards, with (2) seasonal variations, and (3) a margin of safety that takes into account (4) any lack of knowledge concerning the relationship between effluent limitations and water quality, taken together, tend to suggest that "total maximum daily load" is a term of art meant to be fleshed out by regulation, and certainly something more than a number. . . .

### 3.  Statutory Structure and Purpose

#### i.  *Allocations Between Point and Nonpoint Sources*

As noted, the Act assigns the primary responsibility for regulating point sources to the EPA and nonpoint sources to the states. The EPA sets limits on pollution that may come from point sources via a permitting process (which can be delegated to the states) known as the National Pollutant Discharge Elimination System. 33 U.S.C. §1342. Nonetheless, in drafting a TMDL the Clean Water Act unambiguously *requires* the author (here, the EPA) to take into account nonpoint sources (though whether those sources must be expressed is not obvious). This conclusion follows when we consider the steps that precede and culminate in a TMDL.

1.  Each state must designate a use for each body of water within its borders and set a target water quality based on that use. 33 U.S.C. §1313(c)(1) & (2). The state must then enact "water quality standards" pursuant to state law. *Id.* §1313(a) & (b).

2.  In order to meet water quality standards, the EPA (or the states to which the EPA has delegated this responsibility) sets "effluent limitations," which are pollution limits on point sources. *Id.* §§1311(b)(1)(A) & 1362(11).

3.  States must submit to the EPA a list of the waters within their boundaries for which effluent limitations (a.k.a. point-source pollution limits) are, by themselves, inadequate to attain the applicable water quality standard—*i.e.*, those waters for which *both* point source *and* nonpoint source limitations will be necessary. *Id.* §1313(d).

4.  It is only for these waters, for which point source effluent limitations alone are insufficient, that a state must establish a TMDL.

5.  TMDLs set the maximum amount of pollution a water body can absorb before violating applicable water quality standards. In the statutory context noted above, it is impossible to meet those standards by point-source reductions alone. Therefore, the Clean Water Act *requires* the drafter of a TMDL to consider nonpoint-source pollution.

"As should be apparent, TMDLs are central to the Clean Water Act's water-quality scheme because . . . they tie together point-source and nonpoint-source pollution issues in a manner that addresses the whole health of the water." [Sierra Club v.] Meiburg, 296 F.3d [1021,] 1025 [(11th Cir. 2002)]. As far as allocations are concerned, the EPA's construction of the TMDL requirement comports well with the Clean Water Act's structure and purpose. Specifically allocating the pollution load between point sources (primarily the EPA's responsibility) and nonpoint sources (the states' dominion) is a commonsense first step to achieve the target water quality.

Because TMDLs only relate to bodies of water for which point source limitations are insufficient, they must take into account pollution from both point and nonpoint sources. We believe the congressional silence on how to promulgate a TMDL and the congressional command that a TMDL be established only for waters that cannot be cleaned by point-source limitations alone (necessarily implying that, whatever form the TMDL takes, it must incorporate nonpoint source limitations) combine to authorize the EPA to express load and waste load allocations. To be sure, the statute does not command the EPA's final regulation to allocate explicitly parts of a load among different kinds of sources, but we agree with the EPA that it may do so.

### ii.  *"Deadlines" or "Target Dates"*

Similarly, it is common sense that a timeline complements the Clean Water Act's requirement that all impaired waters achieve applicable water quality standards. The amount of acceptable pollution in a body of water is necessarily tied to the date at which the EPA and the states believe the water should meet its quality standard; if the target date is 100 years from now, more pollution per day will be allowable than if the target date is five years from now. Additionally, any meaningful pollution-reduction plan needs to take into account the dynamic nature of watersheds, particularly the fact that they change over time. Robert W. Adler, *Addressing Barriers to Watershed Protection*, 25 Envtl. L. 973, 982 (1995) ("[R]iver systems are four-dimensional in nature: 1) longitudinal (upstream-downstream); 2) lateral (floodplain-uplands); 3) vertical (groundwater-surface water); and 4) temporal (all three spatial dimensions change over time)."). As promulgating an accurate TMDL — that is, one that states a pollutant load "necessary to implement the applicable water quality standards," 33 U.S.C. §1313(d)(1)(C) — requires consideration of a timeline and of changes over time, it is more consistent with the purpose of the Clean Water Act to express the deadline that the EPA relied on in calculating the TMDL than to make states and the public guess what it is.

### iii.  *Reasonable Assurance*

Farm Bureau's argument that the Act forbids the EPA from seeking reasonable assurance from the states that their Watershed Improvement Plans will meet their stated goals is also inconsistent with the purpose and structure of the Clean Water Act. The TMDL must be set "at a level necessary to implement the applicable water quality standards." 33 U.S.C. §1313(d)(1)(C). The EPA chose to set the TMDL with substantial input from the states but, in order to comply with the Clean Water Act and the APA, the EPA would not blindly accept states' submissions. Instead it decided to satisfy itself that the states' proposals would actually "implement the applicable water quality standards." *Id.* This requirement made sure that the EPA could exercise "reasoned judgment" in evaluating the states' proposed standards and was thus consistent with the Clean Water Act. . . .

### 4. Avoidance Canons

Farm Bureau [argues] that the Chesapeake Bay TMDL intrudes on land use, an area traditionally regulated by states. It contends that we should not accept the EPA's construction of the words "total maximum daily load" without a clear statement that Congress intended federal involvement in this realm of state policymaking. . . .

#### i. Federalism

. . . In [*SWANCC* and *Rapanos*], Congress's intent to alter the traditional federal-state balance was doubtful, as it was unclear whether the Corps even had jurisdiction over the areas at issue. The Court in *SWANCC* and a plurality in *Rapanos* were unwilling to accept the Corps' assertion of jurisdiction over what looked like places traditionally regulated by the states.

In our case, however, jurisdiction over the Chesapeake Bay is not at issue. The question is far finer grained: what is a "total maximum daily load"? Even if the consequences of defining the terms of the statute as the EPA has done intrudes more significantly on certain state prerogatives than Farm Bureau's proposal, we already know that the term "total maximum daily load" exists within a cooperative federalism framework and that the area being regulated is clearly within the agency's jurisdiction. In this context, requiring another "clear statement" of congressional intent for every ambiguous term in a highly technical statute, before accepting an interpretation that could affect our federal structure, would defeat one of the central virtues of the *Chevron* framework: Congress may leave interstitial details to expert agencies and need not think through at the drafting stage every possible permutation of agencies' plausible future interpretations. To use the Supreme Court's language disposing of a similar argument (in a different regulatory context), the TMDL provision "explicitly supplants state authority by *requiring*" states to participate in pollution-reduction programs by, in part, submitting a TMDL, "and the meaning of that phrase [here, total maximum daily load] is indisputably a question of federal law." Nor can we say that defining "loads" of pollution as allocated among different sources or expressed as a single number is a matter of regulation traditionally reserved to the states. Thus, to the extent the TMDL may affect land-use decisions, we do not see that as foreclosing the EPA's interpretation.

Perhaps we would reach a different result if the TMDL in fact made land-use decisions diminishing state authority in a significant way; we might then say that Congress delegated some authority over the definitions of technical terms in the Clean Water Act but not so much discretion as to usurp states' zoning powers. Indeed, the heart of Farm Bureau's federalism argument is that the TMDL impermissibly grants the EPA the authority to make land-use and zoning regulations. The challenge is long on swagger but short on specificity. That is likely because the TMDL's provisions that could be read to affect land use are either explicitly allowed by federal law or too generalized to supplant state zoning powers in any extraordinary way.

The TMDL comes closest to dictating a land-use regulation by allocating pollution limits to specific point sources. As each of these sources is regulated by the

National Pollutant Discharge Elimination System, *see* 33 U.S.C. §1342, and the TMDL's allocations are not alleged to be inconsistent with that scheme, these waste load allocations do not trespass onto an area of traditional state regulation to some greater degree than the Clean Water Act anticipates.

The next most intrusive aspect of the TMDL is its allocations of limits to non-point-source *sectors*, as opposed to specific *sources*. The TMDL prescribes daily Land Based [Load Allocation]s for specific nonpoint source *sectors:* agriculture, forest, nontidal atmospheric deposition, onsite septic, and urban. Land Based [Load Allocations] are presented as delivered load for each of the 92 impaired segments by jurisdiction and by nonpoint source *sector* for [total nitrogen, total phosphorous, and total suspended solids]. In presenting load allocations by sector, the TMDL gives the states flexibility in achieving the limits the EPA set—preserving state autonomy in land-use and zoning.

Further undermining the claim that the TMDL impermissibly takes over state power to regulate land is that the TMDL nowhere prescribes any particular *means* of pollution reduction to any individual point or nonpoint source. Instead, it contains pollution limits and allocations to be used as an informational tool used in connection with a *state's* efforts to regulate water pollution. This conclusion is confirmed by the Act, as it requires states to have a "continuing planning process," which must include (but is not limited to) "total maximum daily load[s]." 33 U.S.C. §1313(e) (1) & (3). It is further confirmed by the language of the TMDL, which provides that "[t]he cornerstone of the accountability framework is the jurisdictions' development of [Watershed Improvement Plans], which serve as roadmaps for how and when a jurisdiction plans to meet its pollutant allocations under the TMDL," and by the EPA's repeated concessions that it will not undertake any enforcement action under the TMDL. . . .

. . . [I]t is illogical to assert that the EPA usurps states' traditional land-use authority when it (1) makes no actual, identifiable, land-use rule and (2) proposes regulatory actions that are specifically allowed under federal law. Hence we fail to see how this case presents federalism concerns so significant as to require a "clear statement" from Congress called for in *SWANCC* before we prohibit the EPA's interpretation of the statute. When a statutory scheme clearly inserts the federal Government into an area of typical state authority, we may require a plain statement from Congress about the scope of the statute's applicability before upholding an agency's assertion of jurisdiction over an area (physical or legal) historically regulated by the states. But, as here, once an agency is operating in the weeds of a statute that obviously requires federal oversight of some state functions, we will not require subordinate clear statements of congressional intent every time an interpretation arguably varies the usual balance of responsibilities between federal and state sovereigns.

We add an important caveat: if an agency interprets a statute in a way that pushes a constitutional boundary (whether that boundary comes from the federal structure or a different constitutional principle), we may find that interpretation outside the scope of Congress's delegation if it does not clearly flow from the statutory text. That brings us to the next question. Does the EPA's interpretation of "total maximum daily load" push at the Constitution's outer bounds?

### ii. *Constitutional Avoidance*

When the TMDL is implemented, some land will need to be used differently from the way it is now, and it is true that land use law is an area typically within the states' police power. At the same time, federal power over interstate waterways, "from the commencement of the [federal] government, has been exercised with the consent of all, and has been understood by all to be a commercial regulation." Gibbons v. Ogden, 22 U.S. (9 Wheat) 1, 190 (1824). And for at least a century, federal common law has governed disputes over interstate water pollution.

Regulation of the channels of interstate commerce lies at the very core of Congress's commerce power. And there can be no serious question that the Chesapeake Bay is a channel of interstate commerce: it produces 500 million pounds of seafood per year, leads ships to many port towns (including Baltimore), and has an estimated economic value of more than one *trillion* dollars. Broadly speaking, then, the federal Government's traditional authority to regulate this part of the country is secure.

By contrast, in Clean Water Act cases where there were arguable Commerce Clause problems, the *SWANCC* Court would not interpret the Act to confer federal jurisdiction over an abandoned, man-made sand and gravel pit absent a "clear statement" from Congress to that effect because such an interpretation raised serious constitutional concerns (that the Government had failed to identify an activity that substantially affected interstate commerce, 531 U.S. at 173), and the *Rapanos* plurality rejected the Corps' interpretation of the "waters of the United States" to include wetlands near ditches that eventually drain into navigable waters because that understanding "presses the envelope of constitutional validity."

Moreover, in *Rapanos* it appears five justices had no constitutional concerns in any event. Justice Kennedy, who provided the fifth vote to vacate the Sixth Circuit's judgment, concluded only that the Court of Appeals had not faithfully applied *SWANCC.* He forcefully rejected the plurality's reasoning, ("[T]he plurality's opinion is inconsistent with the Act's text, structure, and purpose."), and asserted a broad theory of federal authority under the Commerce Clause.

Even assuming, then, that federal regulation of remote wetlands and nonnavigable waterways would raise a difficult Commerce Clause issue notwithstanding those waters' aggregate effects on national water quality, the plurality's reading is not responsive to this concern. As for States' "responsibilities and rights," [33 U.S.C.] §1251(b), it is noteworthy that 33 States plus the District of Columbia have filed an *amici* brief in this litigation asserting that the Clean Water Act is important to their own water policies. These *amici* note, among other things, that the Act protects downstream States from out-of-state pollution that they cannot themselves regulate. Justice Stevens and the three other dissenters who joined him would have held that it was reasonable and constitutional for the Corps to include within the definition of "waters of the United States" wetlands that drain into navigable waters.

Notwithstanding the constitutional concerns raised in those cases, *SWANCC* and *Rapanos* are easily distinguishable on the critical and obvious ground that we are not concerned here with a small intrastate area of wetland; we are dealing with North America's largest estuary. Indeed, the *Rapanos* plurality approvingly quoted a previous case for the proposition that "'[i]n view of the breadth of federal regulatory authority contemplated by the Act itself and *the inherent difficulties of defining precise bounds to regulable waters,* the Corps' ecological judgment about the relationship between waters and their adjacent wetlands provides an adequate basis for a legal judgment that adjacent wetlands may be defined as waters under the Act.'" (emphasis in *Rapanos*). It is beyond debate that navigable-in-fact waters are regulable and that the Chesapeake Bay is navigable-in-fact. *SWANCC* and *Rapanos* are also distinguishable because no one here is challenging the EPA's authority to set a total maximum daily load; rather, Farm Bureau challenges how the EPA is allowed to express the load and what it may consider in drafting the TMDL. And, although Justice Kennedy's concurrence is Delphic on this point, it appears that in *Rapanos* five Justices had no constitutional concerns. For us, the key point is that, in terms of the conflict between state and federal regulatory authority, we are far removed from *SWANCC* and *Rapanos*.

Because the TMDL forms part of a plan to clean up a channel of interstate commerce, we have no constitutional concerns with the EPA's interpretation of the statute.

### D.  Chevron *Step Two*

As noted above, "total" can mean "a sum of parts," and interpreting "total" that way gives greater guidance to states in cleaning their waters, provides greater transparency to the public who may comment on a TMDL, and furthers the Act's requirement that the TMDL account for both point and nonpoint sources. Moreover, expressing the allocation of pollution limits between the EPA-regulated point sources and state-regulated nonpoint sources furthers the Clean Water Act's goal of achieving water quality standards. Including deadlines in a TMDL furthers the Act's goal that the TMDL promptly achieve something beneficial (recall that the enacting Congress's goal was to have the Nation's waters clean by 1985), and the reasonable assurance requirement helps guide the EPA's discretion in determining whether to approve a TMDL or a state's mandatory "continuing planning process," which must include the TMDL, 33 U.S.C. §1313(e), as it would surely be arbitrary or capricious for the EPA to approve a plan that a state is incapable of following. . . .

Although the parties do not cite any pre-enactment legislative history that describes the meaning of "total maximum daily load," one committee report, by the House Public Works Committee, commented in discussing draft legislation that "[a] maximum daily load shall also be developed by a State for all waters within its boundaries which are not identified as requiring more stringent effluent limitations to meet water quality standards. The committee recognizes that this is a time-consuming and difficult task." H.R. Rep. No. 92-911, at 106 (1972). This is the only discussion in the pre-enactment legislative history of the TMDL requirement, and it provides no help beyond recognizing that developing a TMDL is "time consuming and difficult." If anything, this undercuts the idea that a TMDL is just a number, but it offers only weak support at best for the EPA.

Post-enactment developments are more informative. Specifically, in 1987, after the EPA had defined "total maximum daily load" as the sum of waste load allocations for point sources and load allocations for nonpoint sources, Congress added §1313(d)(4)(A) & (B) governing the revision of effluent limitations "based on a total maximum daily load or *otherwaste load allocation* established under this section." P.L. 100-4 §404(b) (Feb. 4, 1987) (emphasis added). The word "other" suggests that a TMDL contains a waste load allocation. Interestingly, §1313 makes no reference to a "waste load allocation"; that phrase occurs only in the EPA's regulations. The EPA therefore has a strong argument that Congress not only agreed to its definition of TMDL as the sum of load and waste load allocations, but also affirmatively incorporated the EPA's rule in an addition to the statute.

A second development in 1987 was that Congress ratified the Chesapeake Bay Program, a voluntary partnership among several watershed states and the EPA. *See* 33 U.S.C. §1267. The 1987 legislation supported cleanup efforts by a program of grants and study; in 2000 Congress added §1267(g), which directed the EPA to "ensure that management plans are developed and implementation is begun" to meet the goals of the Chesapeake Bay Agreement. Although §1267 does not add to the EPA's regulatory authority, it strongly suggests that cleaning up the Bay is a priority for Congress and that it did not have a problem with the EPA's role in developing goals for the watershed even though the EPA had promulgated its TMDL rules long before §1267 was added to the U.S. Code. . . .

. . . Although Farm Bureau claims that the Chesapeake Bay will be cleaned up without EPA intervention, the contention defies common sense and experience. The Clean Water Act sought to eliminate water pollution by 1985, but by 2010 62% of the Bay had insufficient oxygen to support aquatic life, and only 18% of the Bay had acceptable water clarity. . . . Our experience in state regulation of water pollution gave environmentalists poster material in the 1969 burning of the Cuyahoga River, the consequence of a classic "tragedy of the commons," which occurs when society fails to create incentives to use a common resource responsibly. Producers of industrial waste used the Cuyahoga River to diffuse oil and other chemicals—and thus the river "ooze[d] rather than flow[ed]" and a person who fell in would "not drown but decay"—until the waste caught fire. *Time*, America's Sewage System and the Price of Optimism (Aug. 1, 1969). In response to that fire and to the general degradation of American water that followed the post-war industrial boom, Congress determined that the EPA should have a leadership role in coordinating among states to restore the Nation's waters to something approaching their natural state. *See* 33 U.S.C. §1251. The EPA has carried out that duty by publishing approximately 61,000 TMDLs with a level of detail commensurate with the challenge of cleaning and maintaining our waters. The EPA's approach makes sense, as even Farm Bureau acknowledges, and therefore represents a reasonable policy choice at *Chevron*'s second step.

Farm Bureau's reading of the Act would stymie the EPA's ability to coordinate among all the competing possible uses of the resources that affect the Bay. At best, it would shift the burden of meeting water quality standards to point source polluters, but regulating them alone would not result in a clean Bay. As the Supreme Court has admonished in the water-pollution context, "We cannot, in these circumstances, conclude that Congress has given authority inadequate to achieve with reasonable effectiveness the purposes for which it has acted." Establishing a comprehensive, watershed-wide TMDL—complete with allocations among different kinds of sources, a timetable, and reasonable assurance that it will actually be implemented—is reasonable and reflects a legitimate policy choice by the agency in administering a less-than-clear statute. Therefore we uphold these decisions at *Chevron* Step Two.

## V.  CONCLUSION

Water pollution in the Chesapeake Bay is a complex problem currently affecting at least 17,000,000 people (with more to come). Any solution to it will result in winners and losers. To judge from the arguments and the *amici* briefs filed in this case, the winners are environmental groups, the states that border the Bay, tourists, fishermen, municipal waste water treatment works, and urban centers. The losers are rural counties with farming operations, nonpoint source polluters, the agricultural industry, and those states that would prefer a lighter touch from the EPA. Congress made a judgment in the Clean Water Act that the states and the EPA could, working together, best allocate the benefits and burdens of lowering pollution. The Chesapeake Bay TMDL will require sacrifice by many, but that is a consequence of the tremendous effort it will take to restore health to the Bay—to make it once again a part of our "land of living," Robert Frost, *The Gift Outright* line 10—a goal our elected representatives have repeatedly endorsed. Farm Bureau's arguments to the contrary are unpersuasive, and thus we affirm the careful and thorough opinion of the District Court.

## NOTES AND QUESTIONS

1. The petitioners sought review of the Third Circuit's decision in the U.S. Supreme Court. On February 29, 2016, the U.S. Supreme Court denied review of the Third Circuit's decision. 577 U.S. 1138 (2016).

2. If the court had ruled in favor of the petitioners in this case, what would the consequences have been for the prospects of cleaning up the Chesapeake Bay? How would such a decision have affected the Chesapeake Bay TMDL? The petitioners argued that the Bay would be cleaned up even without EPA's "intervention," but the Third Circuit was not persuaded.

3. As the court notes, several states filed amicus briefs in this case. Challenging the legality of EPA action became a significant cause for "red state" attorneys general promoting the narrative that under the Obama administration EPA was an out-of-control agency exceeding its legal authority, trampling on the Constitution and usurping state prerogatives. None of the states within the Chesapeake watershed sued EPA over the TMDL. Maryland, Virginia, Delaware, and the District of Columbia filed amicus briefs supporting EPA. Pennsylvania and New York did not take part in the litigation, but West Virginia joined an amicus brief opposing EPA. One of the 20 other states arguing that EPA had exceeded its authority in promulgating the Chesapeake Bay TMDL was Oklahoma, represented by then-Attorney General E. Scott Pruitt who later was appointed by President Trump to be administrator of EPA.

4. Even if EPA can require states to adopt TMDLs that include waters polluted only by nonpoint sources, what authority, if any, does the agency have under the CWA to require states to implement and enforce controls on nonpoint sources? In the absence of direct federal controls over nonpoint source pollution, how can the agency effectively ensure attainment of water quality standards in water segments impaired by nonpoint sources?

5. EPA failed entirely to implement the provisions of section 303(d) and the TMDL program until the 1990s. What do you think accounts for EPA's failure to do so?

6. Translating a TMDL into permit limits for individual dischargers is scientifically and politically difficult. To estimate the impact of specific discharges on water quality under varying flow conditions, states apply dilution factors and mixing zones that vary wildly, often reflecting political rather than scientific judgments. Houck, The Regulation of Toxic Pollutants Under the Clean Water Act, 21 Envtl. L. Rep. 10528, 10546 (1991). Moreover, while "EPA has unhelpfully offered several alternative methods for making TMDL allocations, ranging from even to uneven percentage reductions among sources," these do not "even begin to resolve the [political] difficulties of whether a state regulatory agency wishes to place its head into the jaws of a public utility, a chemical plant, or local farmer" in establishing permit limits. Id.

7. The political difficulties of allocating pollutant loads among dischargers are compounded when interstate pollution is involved. In some cases, EPA has worked with states to establish TMDLs for water bodies subject to interstate discharges. To ensure that uniform standards applied to pollutants in New York Harbor, EPA proposed TMDLs for copper, lead, mercury, and nickel that would affect dischargers in both New York and New Jersey. 59 Fed. Reg. 41,293 (1994). At the request of the states of Oregon, Washington, and Idaho, EPA issued a TMDL for dioxin discharges into the Columbia River. Despite challenges from both industry and environmental groups, EPA's action was upheld in Dioxin/Organochlorine Center v. Clarke, 57 F.3d 1517 (9th Cir. 1995).

8. Oliver Houck has written a series of articles providing a comprehensive review of the history of water quality–based standards under the Clean Water Act from 1972 to the present, Houck, TMDLs: The Resurrection of Water Quality Standards–Based Regulation Under the Clean Water Act, 27 Envtl. L. Rep. 10329 (July 1997), and their recent resurrection due to an explosion of litigation over TMDLs, Houck, TMDLs, Are We There Yet? The Long Road Toward Water Quality–Based Regulation Under the Clean Water Act. 27 Envtl. L. Rep. 10391, 10401 (1997); TMDLs IV: The Final Frontier, 29 Envtl. L. Rep. 10469 (1999). Houck notes that given the large number of water segments that may not meet applicable water quality standards, the difficulty of obtaining data necessary to support load calculations and the overall cost of developing and implementing TMDLs (perhaps as much as "$1 million per study and an order of magnitude times that amount more for implementation"), the TMDL process may again remind us of the virtues of the Act's technology-based effluent limits.

9. To be effective, TMDLs must be more than paper exercises—they must have an effect on permitting decisions. In Friends of Pinto Creek v. EPA, 504 F.3d 1007 (9th Cir. 2007), the Ninth Circuit held that EPA was prohibited from issuing a permit to allow the discharge of dissolved copper into an impaired creek covered by a TMDL unless there was a sufficient remaining load allocation to allow the discharge. However, the court rejected the claims by the plaintiff citizens group that no permit could be issued before the water body was restored. It held instead that it was sufficient if existing dischargers were on a compliance schedule that ultimately would achieve the applicable water quality standards.

## WATER POLLUTION CONTROL: A PROBLEM EXERCISE

For nearly 60 years a gun manufacturer has owned a skeet shooting club on a point overlooking a river. It is estimated that 4 million pounds of lead shot and 11 million pounds of clay targets have fallen into the river from the club's 12 shooting ranges. Neither the gun manufacturer nor the club (nor any of the club's patrons) has ever had an NPDES permit authorizing them to discharge lead shot or clay targets into the river. Sediment samples taken from the riverbed have found high levels (up to 640,000 parts per million) of lead, a priority toxic pollutant under the Clean Water Act, and tests on shellfish and waterfowl in the area have found elevated levels of lead in their tissues and blood that the U.S. Fish and Wildlife Service believes to be acutely toxic.

**Question One.** Has the club or any of its patrons violated the Clean Water Act by discharging pollutants into surface waters without an NPDES permit? See §§502(12), 502(14), and Romero-Barcelo v. Brown, 643 F.2d 835 (1st Cir. 1981), rev'd on other grounds sub nom. Weinberger v. Romero-Barcelo, 456 U.S. 305 (1982). What, if anything, would you advise the club to do to ensure that neither it nor its patrons violates the law?

**Question Two.** Suppose that an NPDES permit were required in these circumstances and that an existing, industry-wide effluent standard has been promulgated for the firearms manufacturing industry. Should this standard be incorporated into the club's permit? Could the club obtain a variance from this standard? How? What alternative limits could be incorporated into the club's permit to reduce lead contamination of the river?

**Question Three.** Suppose that the state has adopted water quality criteria for lead to protect aquatic life and human health based on measurements of the presence of lead in the water column. If levels of lead in the water column are higher than permissible under these criteria, how, if at all, could section 303(d) or section 304(*l*) of the Clean Water Act be used to place additional restrictions on the club's discharges?

**Question Four.** Suppose that, despite the high concentration of lead in the sediment, lead levels in the water column do not exceed the criteria, although benthic organisms have accumulated dangerous levels of lead, apparently due to feeding on material in the sediment. Could the state be required to adopt sediment quality criteria under section 303(c)(2)(B)?

**Question Five.** If lead levels in the river violate the existing water quality standard for lead, can a foundry in another state located upstream from the club obtain an NPDES permit to discharge lead into the same river?

## E.   *WETLANDS PROTECTION AND THE SECTION 404 PERMIT PROGRAM*

While they can be areas of great beauty, to the untrained eye wetlands often appear as undesirable swamps that could only be improved by development. They were long viewed as "wastelands, sources of mosquitos and impediments to development and travel," J. Kusler, Our National Wetland Heritage 1 (1983), the draining and filling of which was a sign of progress, often subsidized by government. See Leovy v. United States, 177 U.S. 621, 636 (1900) ("[T]he police power is never more legitimately exercised than in removing such nuisances."). Scientists now realize that wetlands are among the most vital and productive of all ecosystems. They provide enormously valuable "ecosystem services," including flood control, as was widely recognized in the wake of Hurricane Katrina, whose catastrophic effects in September 2005 were compounded due to the previous loss of vast areas of coastal wetlands in Louisiana and Mississippi. Wetlands also "are the primary pollution control systems of the nation's waters," removing "heavy metals at efficiencies ranging from twenty to one hundred percent" and "up to ninety-five percent of phosphorus, nutrients, and conventional pollutants." Houck & Rolland, Federalism in Wetlands Regulation: A Consideration of Delegation of Clean Water Act Section 404 and Related Programs to the States, 54 Md. L. Rev. 1242, 1245 (1995). Wetlands serve as feeding and breeding grounds for fish and waterfowl. They are a particularly critical link in the ecological chain, even though their environmental importance is not reflected in their market price.

Wetlands also can be attractive sites for development, due in part to humans' love for proximity to water. Development pressures have destroyed a precious part of the nation's ecological heritage. Scientists estimate that more than half (53 percent) of the wetlands in the original 48 states have been destroyed, with total wetland acreage there declining from an estimated 215 million acres to only about 100 million acres today. EPA, Wetlands Fact Sheet 11 (1995). Wetlands remain under relentless assault. Nearly 300,000 acres are disappearing each year, due largely to agricultural and urban development.

## 1. The Structure of the Section 404 Program

The most visible (and controversial) wetlands protection program is a product of section 404 of the Clean Water Act. When it adopted the FWPCA in 1972, Congress established a separate permit program, in addition to the NPDES, to govern discharges of dredge and fill material. Section 404 of the Act, whose importance was not immediately appreciated, requires all dischargers of dredge and fill to the waters of the United States to obtain a permit from the U.S. Army Corps of Engineers. The Corps administers the section 404 permit program in cooperation with EPA.

The scope of the waters subject to federal regulation under section 404 is discussed in this chapter on pages 582-612. The definition of dredge and fill material determines whether a permit must be obtained from the Corps under section 404 or from EPA under section 402 of the Clean Water Act, which covers all discharges of pollutants from point sources. The section 404 permit program covers discharges of dredge and fill materials. The former are defined by EPA and the Corps as "material that is excavated or dredged from the waters of the United States." 40 C.F.R. §232.2(g); 33 C.F.R. §323.2(c). Material not excavated from such waters is subject to the section 404 permit program if it is used as fill material. The Corps defines "fill material" as "material used for the primary purpose of replacing an aquatic area with dry land or of changing the bottom elevation of a water body,"

33 C.F.R. §323.2(k), while EPA considers any pollutant that has such an effect to be fill. 40 C.F.R. §232.2(i).

Note that the language of section 404 only refers to discharges of dredge and fill material. As a result, there has been considerable uncertainty concerning whether section 404 covers activities that destroy wetlands through ditching, channelization, or excavation. In Avoyelles Sportsmen's League v. Marsh, 715 F.2d 897 (5th Cir. 1983), the Fifth Circuit held that mechanized landclearing activities require a section 404 permit when they redeposit soil in wetland areas. But in Save Our Community v. EPA, 971 F.2d 1155 (5th Cir. 1992), the same court held that drainage of a wetland does not require a section 404 permit unless there is a discharge of some kind.

In 1977, Congress added section 404(e) to the Clean Water Act to authorize the Corps to "issue general permits on a state, regional or nationwide basis for categories of activities that are substantially similar in nature and cause only minimal adverse effects on the environment." These general permits have five-year terms. In 1982, the Corps established 26 nationwide permits. While many of these authorize routine and relatively noncontroversial activities (such as the placement of navigation aids and surveying activities), NWP 26 was the focus of great controversy. Promulgated by the Corps over EPA's objections, it authorized the filling of so-called isolated waters and "headwaters," which resulted in the destruction of large wetlands areas. In 1984, NWP 26 was revised to limit its application to projects of less than ten acres and in 1996 it was revised to limit its application to projects disturbing less than three acres of wetlands. In March 2000, NWP 26 was modified to reduce the acreage of wetlands that may be disturbed without obtaining an individual permit from three acres to one-half acre and to require predischarge notification to the Corps of any activity that will destroy more than one-tenth of an acre of wetlands. 65 Fed. Reg. 12,818 (2000).

The section 404 program has been controversial because it extends the reach of federal regulation more broadly and in a manner that potentially affects more individuals than virtually any other environmental law. However, the potentially expansive reach of section 404 has been tempered in significant ways. Section 404(f)(1) exempts discharges from normal farming, forestry, and ranching operations. Section 404(f)(2) qualifies this exemption by refusing to extend it to activities designed to convert a wetland "into a use to which it was not previously subject." Thus, discharges from the draining or filling of a wetland in order to convert it into additional farmland have been held not to be exempt from section 404's permit requirement even if undertaken by a farming operation. United States v. Bruce, 41 F.3d 117 (3d Cir. 1994). In the *Borden Ranch* case discussed on pages 626 and 631 of this book, the Ninth Circuit rejected the argument that deep ripping to drain a wetland qualified for the section 404(f) exemption for discharges from normal farming activities because the developer was trying to convert the wetlands to a use to which they were not previously subject. Borden Ranch Partnership v. U.S. Army Corps of Engineers, 261 F.3d 810 (9th Cir. 2001), affirmed by an equally divided Court, 537 U.S. 99 (2002). Wetlands that were drained and converted to cropland prior to enactment of the Swampbuster provisions of the Food Security Act in December 1985 have been exempted from section 404 by regulation. This removed 53 million acres of land from coverage under section 404 even in areas where wetlands vegetation would return to the land if cropping ceased.

In the case below, Coeur Alaska, an American mining company, sought to open a gold mine in southeast Alaska. Because EPA's new source performance standard for "froth-flotation" gold mines, promulgated under section 306, prohibited section 402 NPDES permits from authorizing tailings discharges, the company initially won approval for land disposal of the tailings. However, after the price of gold dropped below $400 an ounce, it sought a less expensive disposal method. It proposed using the tailings to fill a large portion of a lake, and it obtained a section 404 permit authorizing their discharge as "fill material." After the Ninth Circuit held that section 404 could not be used to authorize discharges forbidden by section 402, the U.S. Supreme Court granted review and issued the decision below.

## Coeur Alaska, Inc. v. Southeast Alaska Conservation Council

557 U.S. 261 (2009)

KENNEDY, J., delivered the opinion of the Court.

. . . At issue is Coeur Alaska's plan to dispose of the mixture of crushed rock and water left behind in the tanks. This mixture is called slurry. Some 30 percent of the slurry's volume is crushed rock, resembling wet sand, which is called tailings. . . .

Rather than build a tailings pond, Coeur Alaska proposes to use Lower Slate Lake, located some three miles from the mine in the Tongass National Forest. . . . The parties agree the lake is a navigable water of the United States and so is subject to the CWA. They also agree there can be no discharge into the lake except as the CWA and any lawful permit allow.

Over the life of the mine, Coeur Alaska intends to put 4.5 million tons of tailings in the lake. This will raise the lakebed 50 feet—to what is now the lake's surface—and will increase the lake's area from 23 to about 60 acres. To contain this wider, shallower body of water, Coeur Alaska will dam the lake's downstream shore. The transformed lake will be isolated from other surface water. Creeks and stormwater runoff will detour around it. Ultimately, lakewater will be cleaned by purification systems and will flow from the lake to a stream and thence onward. . . .

The CWA classifies crushed rock as a "pollutant." §502(6). On the one hand, the Act forbids Coeur Alaska's discharge of crushed rock "[e]xcept as in compliance" with the Act. CWA §301(a), 33 U.S.C. §1311(a). Section 404(a) of the CWA, on the other hand, empowers the Corps to authorize the discharge of "dredged or fill material." 33 U.S.C. §404(a). The Corps and the EPA have together defined "fill material" to mean any "material [that] has the effect of . . . [c]hanging the bottom elevation" of water. 40 CFR §232.2. The agencies have further defined the "discharge of fill material" to include "placement of . . . slurry, or tailings or similar mining-related materials." Ibid.

In these cases the Corps and the EPA agree that the slurry meets their regulatory definition of "fill material." On that premise the Corps evaluated the mine's plan for a §404 permit. After considering the environmental factors required by §404(b), the Corps issued Coeur Alaska a permit to pump the slurry into Lower Slate Lake. . . .

Section 402 gives the EPA authority to issue "permit[s] for the discharge of any pollutant," with one important exception: The EPA may not issue permits for fill material that fall under the Corps' §404 permitting authority. Section 402(a) states:

> "*Except as provided in . . . [CWA §404]*, the Administrator may . . . issue a permit for the discharge of any pollutant, . . . notwithstanding [CWA §301(a)], upon condition that such discharge will meet either (A) all applicable requirements under [CWA §301, CWA §302, CWA §306, CWA §307, CWA §308, CWA §403], or (B) prior to the taking of necessary implementing actions relating to all such requirements, such conditions as the Administrator determines are necessary to carry out the provisions of this chapter." §402(a)(1) (emphasis added).

Section 402 thus forbids the EPA from exercising permitting authority that is "provided [to the Corps] in" §404. . . .

The Act is best understood to provide that if the Corps has authority to issue a permit for a discharge under §404, then the EPA lacks authority to do so under §402.

Even if there were ambiguity on this point, the EPA's own regulations would resolve it. Those regulations provide that "[d]ischarges of dredged or fill material into waters of the United States which are regulated under section 404 of CWA" "do not require [§402] permits" from the EPA. 40 CFR §122.3.

[The Southeast Alaska Conservation Council (SEACC) argues that] this regulation implies that some "fill material" discharges are not regulated under §404—else, SEACC asks, why would the regulation lack a comma before the word "which," and thereby imply that only a subset of "discharges of . . . fill material" are "regulated under section 404."

The agencies, however, have interpreted this regulation otherwise. In the agencies' view the regulation essentially restates the text of §402, and forbids the EPA from issuing permits for discharges that "are regulated under section 404." 40 CFR §122.3(b); cf. CWA §402(a) ("[e]xcept as provided in . . . [§404], the Administrator may . . . issue a permit"). Before us, the EPA confirms this reading of the regulation. The agency's interpretation is not "plainly erroneous or inconsistent with the regulation"; and so we accept it as correct.

The question whether the EPA is the proper agency to regulate the slurry discharge thus depends on whether the Corps of Engineers has authority to do so. If the Corps has authority to issue a permit, then the EPA may not do so. We turn to the Corps' authority under §404.

Section 404(a) gives the Corps power to "issue permits . . . for the discharge of dredged or fill material." 33 U.S.C. §1344(a). As all parties concede, the slurry meets the definition of fill material agreed upon by the agencies in a joint regulation promulgated in 2002. That regulation defines "fill material" to mean any "material [that] has the effect of . . . [c]hanging the bottom elevation" of water—a definition that includes "slurry, or tailings or similar mining-related materials." 40 CFR §232.2. . . .

Rather than challenge the agencies' decision to define the slurry as fill, SEACC instead contends that §404 contains an implicit exception. According to SEACC, §404 does not authorize the Corps to permit a discharge of fill material if that material is subject to an EPA new source performance standard.

But §404's text does not limit its grant of power in this way. Instead, §404 refers to all "fill material" without qualification. Nor do the EPA regulations support SEACC's reading of §404. The EPA has enacted guidelines, pursuant to §404(b), to guide the Corps permitting decision. 40 CFR pt. 230. Those guidelines do not strip the Corps of power to issue permits for fill in cases where the fill is also subject to an EPA new source performance standard. . . .

The regulatory scheme discloses a defined, and workable, line for determining whether the Corps or the EPA has the permit authority. Under this framework, the Corps of Engineers, and not the EPA, has authority to permit Coeur Alaska's discharge of the slurry.

A second question remains: . . . Do EPA performance standards, and §306(e), apply to discharges of fill material? . . . SEACC claims the CWA §404 permit is unlawful because §306(e) forbids the slurry discharge. Petitioners and the federal agencies, in contrast, contend that §306(e) does not apply to the slurry discharge. . . .

When the performance standard applies to a point source, §306(e) makes it "unlawful" for that point source to violate it: "[I]t shall be unlawful for any owner or operator of any new source to operate such source in violation of any standard of performance applicable to such source." CWA §306(e).

SEACC argues that this provision, §306(e), forbids the mine from discharging slurry into Lower Slate Lake. SEACC contends the new source performance standard is, in the words of §306(e), "applicable to" the mine. Both the text of the performance standard and the EPA's application of it to the discharge of mining waste from Lower Slate Lake demonstrate that the performance standard is "applicable to" Coeur Alaska's mine in some circumstances. And so, SEACC reasons, it follows that because the new source performance standard forbids even minute discharges of solid waste, it also forbids the slurry discharge, 30% of which is solid waste.

For their part, the State of Alaska and the federal agencies claim that the Act is unambiguous in the opposite direction. They rely on §404 of the Act. . . . [T]hey note that nothing in §404 requires the Corps to consider the EPA's new source performance standard or the §306(e) prohibition. That silence advances the argument that §404's grant of authority to "issue permits" contradicts §306(e)'s declaration that discharges in violation of new source performance standards are "unlawful."

. . . The CWA is ambiguous on the question whether §306 applies to discharges of fill material regulated under §404. On the one hand, §306 provides that a discharge that violates an EPA new source performance standard is "unlawful"—without any exception for fill material. On the other hand, §404 grants the Corps blanket authority to permit the discharge of fill material—without any mention of §306. This tension indicates that Congress has not "directly spoken" to the "precise question" of whether §306 applies to discharges of fill material. *Chevron*, 467 U.S., at 842.

Before turning to how the agencies have resolved that question, we consider the formal regulations that bear on §§306 and 404. . . .

The regulations do not give a definitive answer to the question whether §306 applies to discharges regulated by the Corps under §404, but we do find that agency interpretation and agency application of the regulations are instructive and to the point. The question is addressed and resolved in a reasonable and coherent way by the practice and policy of the two agencies, all as recited in a memorandum written in May 2004 by Diane Regas, then the Director of the EPA's Office of Wetlands,

Oceans and Watersheds, to Randy Smith, the Director of the EPA's regional Office of Water with responsibility over the mine (Regas Memorandum). The Memorandum, though not subject to sufficiently formal procedures to merit *Chevron* deference, see *Mead* [page 197], is entitled to a measure of deference because it interprets the agencies' own regulatory scheme.

The Regas Memorandum explains:

> "As a result [of the fact that the discharge is regulated under §404], the regulatory regime applicable to discharges under section 402, including effluent limitations guidelines and standards, such as those applicable to gold ore mining. . .do not apply to the placement of tailings into the proposed impoundment [of Lower Slate Lake]. See 40 CFR §122.3(b)."

The regulation that the Memorandum cites—40 CFR §122.3—is one we considered above and found ambiguous. That regulation provides: "[d]ischarges of dredged or fill material into waters of the United States which are regulated under section 404 of CWA" "do not require [§402] permits." The Regas Memorandum takes an instructive interpretive step when it explains that because the discharge "do[es] not require" an EPA permit, the EPA's performance standard "do[es] not apply" to the discharge. The Memorandum presents a reasonable interpretation of the regulatory regime. We defer to the interpretation because it is not "plainly erroneous or inconsistent with the regulation[s]."

. . . The judgment of the Court of Appeals is reversed, and these cases are remanded for further proceedings consistent with this opinion.

JUSTICE BREYER, concurring.

As I understand the Court's opinion, it recognizes a legal zone within which the regulating agencies might reasonably classify material either as "dredged or fill material" subject to §404 of the Clean Water Act, or as a "pollutant," subject to §§402 and 306. Within this zone, the law authorizes the environmental agencies to classify material as the one or the other, so long as they act within the bounds of relevant regulations, and provided that the classification, considered in terms of the purposes of the statutes and relevant regulations, is reasonable. [He found the agency's position reasonable.]

JUSTICE SCALIA, concurring in part and concurring in the judgment.

I join the opinion of the Court, except for its protestation that it is not according *Chevron* deference to the reasonable interpretation set forth in the [Regas] memorandum. [He reiterated his long-standing position that United States v. Mead Corp., 533 U.S. 218 (2001), should be overruled and *Chevron* deference applied to authoritative agency positions.]

JUSTICE GINSBURG, with whom JUSTICE STEVENS and JUSTICE SOUTER join, dissenting.

. . . The litigation before the Court . . . presents a single question: Is a pollutant discharge prohibited under §306 of the Act eligible for a §404 permit as a discharge of fill material? In agreement with the Court of Appeals, I would answer no. The statute's text, structure, and purpose all mandate adherence to EPA pollution-control requirements. A discharge covered by a performance standard must be authorized, if at all, by EPA. . . .

No part of the statutory scheme, in my view, calls into question the governance of EPA's performance standard. The text of §306(e) states a clear proscription: "[I]t shall be unlawful for any owner or operator of any new source to operate such source in violation of any standard of performance applicable to such source." §306(e). Under the standard of performance relevant here, "there shall be no discharge of process wastewater to navigable waters from mills that use the froth-flotation process" for mining gold. 40 CFR §440.104(b)(1). The Act imposes these requirements without qualification.

Section 404, stating that the Corps "may issue permits" for the discharge of "dredged or fill material," does not create an exception to §306(e)'s plain command. Section 404 neither mentions §306 nor states a contrary requirement. The Act can be home to both provisions, with no words added or omitted, so long as the category of "dredged or fill material" eligible for a §404 permit is read in harmony with §306. Doing so yields a simple rule: Discharges governed by EPA performance standards are subject to EPA's administration and receive permits under the NPDES, not §404. . . .

The Court's reading, in contrast, strains credulity. A discharge of a pollutant, otherwise prohibited by firm statutory command, becomes lawful if it contains sufficient solid matter to raise the bottom of a water body, transformed into a waste disposal facility. Whole categories of regulated industries can thereby gain immunity from a variety of pollution-control standards. The loophole would swallow not only standards governing mining activities, but also standards for dozens of other categories of regulated point sources.

. . . Would a rational legislature order exacting pollution limits, yet call all bets off if the pollutant, discharged into a lake, will raise the water body's elevation? To say the least, I am persuaded, that is not how Congress intended the Clean Water Act to operate.

## NOTES AND QUESTIONS

1.  How realistic are Justice Ginsburg's fears that the decision could open a loophole allowing industries to escape section 402 effluent limits by categorizing their discharges as "fill" subject to permitting under section 404? Does it depend on the nature of the material discharged or the kind of water body into which the discharge occurs? Should it matter whether the "fill" serves no purpose other than to dispose of waste? See Kentuckians for Commonwealth, Inc. v. Rivenbaugh, 317 F.3d 425 (4th Cir. 2003) (Corps may issue section 404 permit for valley-fill from mountain-top coal mining even if it serves "no purpose other than to dispose of excess overburden," id. at 439).

2.  In the wake of this decision, could EPA legally change its position and require that sources of such tailings discharges obtain permits under section 402 instead of section 404? Compare Justice Breyer's concurrence with Justice Kennedy's majority opinion.

3.  In portions of the opinion not reproduced above, the majority sought to downplay the environmental consequences of its decision. Justice Kennedy

emphasized that the lake might eventually recover even if the tailings initially killed most of the fish. Both Justices Kennedy and Breyer noted that EPA could still exercise its authority under section 404(c) to veto any section 404 permit issued by the Corps, an argument Justice Ginsburg countered by noting that EPA had vetoed only 12 permits in 36 years. Justice Kennedy also noted that while the tailings discharges into the lake did not require a section 404 permit, EPA retains the authority to regulate under section 402 the discharge of suspended solids from the lake into downstream waters.

4. The plunge in gold prices below $400 an ounce that initially motivated Coeur Alaska to seek a cheaper disposal method has subsequently been reversed. When the Court decided the case on June 22, 2009, gold was selling for more than $920 an ounce. After averaging nearly $1,400 during 2019, it soared to $1,850/ounce by January 2021.

5. In June 2010, Coeur Alaska began mining ore from the Kensington Gold Mine. The mine was expected to provide approximately 180 direct jobs to the city of Juneau and to produce 2,000 tons of gold concentrate per day. The mine was projected to generate an estimated 7 million tons of tailings. Lower Slate Lake has now been redesignated as a "tailings treatment facility" and all life that once existed in it has been extinguished. With the increase in gold prices, Coeur Alaska in 2019 submitted an amended Plan of Operations to double the amount of tailings stored there and to allow another ten years of operational capacity for the mine.

### A Note on Wetlands Identification and Delineation

Identifying what areas are wetlands for purposes of section 404 has been difficult and controversial. In 1977, EPA and the Corps adopted identical regulatory definitions of wetlands: "Wetlands are those areas that are inundated or saturated by surface or groundwater at a frequency and duration sufficient to support, and that under normal circumstances do support, a prevalence of vegetation typically adapted for life in saturated soil conditions." 33 C.F.R. §328.3(b) (Corps) and 40 C.F.R. §230.3(t) (EPA).

Despite using the same regulatory definition, for years each agency followed different procedures for identifying and delineating wetlands. In 1987, the Corps issued its own Wetlands Delineation Manual which required that the presence of three conditions be demonstrated for an area to be considered a wetland—wetlands hydrology, wetlands vegetation, and wetlands soil conditions. To provide more uniform standards for wetlands delineation, an inter-agency task force from EPA, the Corps, the Soil Conservation Service, and the Fish and Wildlife Service jointly published the Federal Manual for Identifying and Delineating Jurisdictional Wetlands in 1989. While focusing on the same three conditions as the Corps' 1987 Manual, the 1989 Manual permitted the presence of the requisite hydrology or soil conditions to be inferred, in certain circumstances, from the presence of certain vegetation.

After agriculture and oil interests protested that the 1989 Manual would enlarge the scope of the section 404 program, in August 1991 the Bush administration proposed a new approach to delineation that would drastically reduce the wetlands acreage subject to protection. Scientists who field tested the proposed 1991 revisions denounced them as "without scientific basis" and reported that they would drastically reduce the coverage of the section 404 program. EPA ultimately announced that it would use the Corps' 1987 Manual, pending completion of a study of wetlands delineation by the National Academy of Sciences (NAS).

In May 1995, the NAS Committee on Characterization of Wetlands released its report. National Research Council, Wetlands: Characteristics and Boundaries (1995). While the report generally confirmed the scientific soundness of delineation practices in the 1987 and 1989 manuals, it recommended that a single delineation manual be adopted and that one federal agency be given lead responsibility for wetlands regulation. The report defines a wetland as "an ecosystem that depends on constant or recurrent, shallow inundation or saturation at or near the surface of the substrate." It recommends that wetlands delineation continue to be based on consideration of hydrology, soil characteristics, and the presence of hydrophytic vegetation.

To provide greater predictability to the section 404 permit process, EPA and the Corps have been working with states to conduct advance identification projects that render advisory determinations concerning what areas are wetlands and their suitability for the discharge of dredged or fill material.

On May 31, 2016, the U.S. Supreme Court ruled unanimously that jurisdictional determinations (JDs) by the U.S. Army Corps of Engineers that property contains wetlands subject to section 404 of the Clean Water Act (CWA) are judicially reviewable. The decision in U.S. Army Corps of Engineers v. Hawkes, Inc., 136 S. Ct. 1807 (2016), was not a surprise, even though most U.S. Courts of Appeals had ruled that the issuance of a JD did not trigger judicial review. In a majority opinion written by Chief Justice Roberts, the Court held that the issuance of a JD is "final agency action" that may be challenged in court under the Administrative Procedure Act because it is definitive in nature and has direct legal consequences. The Chief Justice noted that a memorandum of understanding between the Corps and EPA makes a JD binding on both agencies for five years. An extraordinary concurring opinion by Justice Kennedy, joined by Justices Thomas and Alito, harshly criticized the "ominous reach" of the CWA and stated that the CWA "continues to raise troubling questions regarding the Government's power to cast doubt on the full use and enjoyment of private property throughout the Nation."

## 2. The Section 404 Permit Process

The permit process established by section 404 has produced bitter confrontations between developers and environmental groups, each of whom has been highly critical of the process. Development interests argue that the process is too cumbersome and takes too long. Environmentalists argue that the Corps has been far too lenient in granting permits to development interests and that EPA has been too willing to defer to the Corps.

Under EPA guidelines for issuing section 404 permits, permit applicants must demonstrate that (1) there is no "practicable alternative to the proposed discharge" which would be less damaging to the aquatic environment, (2) the proposed activity will not "cause or contribute to significant degradation of the waters of the United States," (3) "appropriate and practicable steps have been taken which will minimize potential adverse impacts of the discharge on the aquatic ecosystem," and (4) the proposed discharge will not violate state water quality standards, toxic effluent standards, the Endangered Species Act or regulations to protect marine sanctuaries under the Marine Mammal Protection Act. 40 C.F.R. §230.10.

Decisions concerning permit applications under section 404 turn largely on an analysis of alternatives to a proposed project. Alternatives analysis is a central feature of several environmental laws, most notably section 102 of the National Environmental Policy Act (NEPA), which requires the preparation of environmental impact statements on major federal actions; section 4(f) of the Department of Transportation Act, which prohibits the construction of federal highways in parklands unless there is no "feasible and prudent alternative"; and section 7 of the Endangered Species Act, which prohibits federal actions that threaten endangered species unless a special committee finds that there are no alternatives, the benefits of the proposal outweigh the benefits from alternatives, and the action is of regional or national significance. NEPA is discussed in Chapter 8 and the Endangered Species Act is discussed in Chapter 9.

The section 404(b)(1) guidelines provide that "no discharge of dredged or fill material shall be permitted if there is a practicable alternative . . . which would have less adverse impact on the aquatic ecosystem. . . ." 40 C.F.R. §230.10(a). The guidelines define an alternative as "practicable" if it is "available" and "capable of being done after taking into consideration cost, existing technology, and logistics in light of overall project purposes." Thus, the guidelines employ a kind of feasibility-limited approach to regulation that is supposed to tolerate environmental damage only if no alternative is available. If alternatives are available, the permit is to be denied without further inquiry into the suitability of the site and the environmental impact of the discharge.

The guidelines are designed to place a heavy burden on developers who seek approval to locate in wetland areas projects that do not "require access or proximity" to the water. For such non-water-dependent projects, the guidelines presume that a less damaging alternative is available "unless clearly demonstrated otherwise." The developer bears the burden of proving that no alternative is available, which under the guidelines includes demonstrating that no other property could "reasonably" be obtained to fulfill the "basic purpose of the proposed activity." 40 C.F.R. §230.10(a)(2).

How the purposes of a project are defined has a major effect on analysis of the availability of alternatives under section 404. For example, in National Wildlife Federation v. Whistler, 27 F.3d 1341 (8th Cir. 1994), a developer sought a section 404 permit to open an old river channel to provide boat access for a planned housing development near the Missouri River. By defining the project's purpose to be the provision of boat access, the Corps found the project to be water-dependent and concluded that no other alternative was practicable to achieve the project's purpose. After the Corps granted the permit, an environmental group and an adjacent properly owner sued. While plaintiffs argued that the Corps failed to consider the alternative of having residents of the development use a nearby public boat ramp, the court deferred to the Corps' judgment and upheld issuance of the permit. The court distinguished several cases upholding denials of section 404 permits for riverside residential developments by noting that the development in the instant case was on upland property and would have been built even if the Corps denied the permit to provide boat access.

In Bersani v. Robichaud, 850 F.2d 36 (2d Cir. 1988), the Second Circuit addressed the question whether the "availability" of alternative property should be assessed at a project's inception or at the time of permit application. EPA had vetoed the issuance of a section 404 permit for a shopping mall because a non-wetland site subsequently purchased by another developer had been available when the permit applicant entered the market and purchased the wetlands property. A panel of the Second Circuit, by a 2-1 vote, upheld EPA's veto and the "market entry" theory on which it was premised. The court noted that the purpose of the practicable alternatives analysis required by the section 404(b)(1) guidelines is "to create an incentive for developers to avoid choosing wetlands when they could choose an alternative upland site." If this analysis were applied at the time of permit application, rather than at the time of site selection, "it would remove the incentive for a developer to search for an alternative site at the time such an incentive is needed, i.e., at the time it is making the decision to select a particular site." 850 F.2d at 44. In dissent, Judge Pratt argued that EPA's "market entry theory in effect taints a particular developer with respect to a particular site, while ignoring the crucial question of whether the site itself should be preserved." He explained that "developer A would be denied a permit on a specific site because when he entered the market alternatives were available, but latecomer developer B, who entered the market after those alternatives had become unavailable, would be entitled to a permit for developing the same site." 850 F.2d at 48 (Pratt, J., dissenting).

The developer who sought the section 404 permit in *Bersani* had rejected an alternative, upland site because of poor road access and strong community resistance to previous development efforts there. A consultant hired by the Corps' regional office had reported that it was feasible to develop either site but that "from a commercial standpoint only one mall could survive in the area." 850 F.2d at 42. The developer whose permit was vetoed subsequently entered into a joint venture with the owner of the other site and built a shopping mall there that opened in September 1989.

EPA rarely has exercised its authority under section 404(c) to veto the issuance of permits. In August 2008, EPA announced that it was vetoing its first section 404 permit in 16 years when it disapproved the Yazoo Backwater Area Pumps Project. 73 Fed. Reg. 54,398 (2008). The project, originally authorized by Congress in 1941, was designed to protect a sparsely populated area of soybean fields from flooding by the Yazoo River. However, EPA concluded that it "would significantly degrade the critical ecological functions provided by approximately 67,000 acres of wetlands." The veto was only the thirteenth time the agency had exercised its veto authority.

In January 2007, the U.S. Army Corps of Engineers issued a section 404 permit to a mountaintop coal mining operation operated by the Mingo Logan Coal Company. The permit authorized the dumping of residue from mountaintop coal mining into three streams. EPA criticized the draft environmental impact statement that had been prepared by the Corps, noting that "even with the best practices, mountaintop mining yields significant and unavoidable environmental impacts that had not been adequately described in the document." EPA initially did not exercise its veto authority under section 404(c). In January 2011, after the Obama administration had taken office, and four years after the permit was issued, EPA exercised its veto authority. Mingo Logan then sued EPA and won a district court judgment that EPA did not have the authority retroactively to revoke a section 404 permit. This decision was reversed by the U.S. Court of Appeals for the D.C. Circuit in April 2013. Mingo Logan Coal Co. v. EPA, 714 F.3d 608 (D.C. Cir. 2013). The court explained that "Section 404 imposes no temporal limit on the Administrator's authority to withdraw the Corps's specification but instead expressly empowers him to prohibit, restrict or withdraw the specification '*whenever*' he makes a determination that the statutory 'unacceptable adverse effect' will result. 33 U.S.C. §1344(c) (emphasis added)." The court concluded that because the statute used "the expansive conjunction 'whenever,' the Congress made plain its intent to grant the Administrator authority to prohibit/deny/restrict/withdraw a specification at *any* time." As a result, the court found that "subsection 404(c) affords EPA two distinct (if overlapping) powers to veto the Corps's specification: EPA may (1) 'prohibit the specification (including the withdrawal of specification) of any defined area as a disposal site' or (2) 'deny or restrict the use of any defined area for specification (including the withdrawal of specification).'" This convinced the court that "the unambiguous language of subsection 404(c) manifests the Congress's intent to confer on EPA a broad veto power extending beyond the permit issuance." Id. at 613 n.2. On remand, the district court held that EPA's section 404(c) veto was not arbitrary or capricious, a decision affirmed on appeal in Mingo Logan Coal Co. v. EPA, 829 F.3d 710 (D.C. Cir. 2016). The court noted that EPA had adequately explained the project's effect on the environment and its impact on downstream water quality.

## NOTES AND QUESTIONS

1. In National Wildlife Federation v. Whistler, 27 F.3d 1341 (8th Cir. 1994), why was the project for which a section 404 permit was sought deemed to be "water-dependent"? If the developer had sought to build the housing development in a wetlands area, would the project have been considered water-dependent? Should it make any difference whether the housing development would be built even without water access and, if so, what effect should this have on the permit decision?

2. Measures to mitigate wetlands losses by enhancing degraded areas or creating new wetlands have become an important aspect of the section 404 permit process. The developer seeking boat access for the planned housing development in *Whistler* had agreed to a mitigation plan that would enhance an existing 20-acre wetlands area by providing it with year-round water and saturated soil conditions. In upholding issuance of the permit, the Eighth Circuit emphasized the Corps' finding that, due to the mitigation measures, the project would result in little or no net loss of wetlands. Id. at 1346. In *Bersani*, the developer had promised to turn an abandoned gravel pit into new wetlands that would be larger than the wetlands destroyed by the project. While the Corps maintained that this mitigation measure meant that the non-wetlands site no longer was a less damaging alternative, EPA refused to accept this conclusion. In 1990, EPA and the Corps entered into a Memorandum of Agreement on Mitigation requiring that proposed discharges respond

to potential wetlands losses in the following sequence: (1) by avoiding them, (2) by minimizing them, and (3) by compensating for unavoidable adverse effects. Mitigation measures have been controversial. Environmentalists maintain that they have made it too easy to get a section 404 permit when practicable alternatives exist and that the destruction of natural wetlands almost always outweighs the gains from artificial enhancement measures that sometimes fail altogether.

3. What impact will *Bersani*'s "market theory" approach to determining availability have on developers' future choices of sites for non-water-dependent activities? How would you respond to Judge Pratt's criticism of the market entry theory? Is he right that another developer who had not previously entered the market subsequently could use the market entry theory to obtain a section 404 permit for developing the identical site? Or would EPA require an applicant to show that no practicable alternative existed both when it could have entered the market and when it applied for the permit?

4. The Corps has been criticized in the past for giving disproportionate weight to the interests of developers when performing alternatives analysis. For example, the Corps frequently found that alternatives that substantially reduce a developer's profit are not practicable (citing the section 404(b)(1) regulations' directive to consider "cost") without considering the magnitude of environmental losses. See Comment, *Bersani v. EPA*: Toward a Plausible Interpretation of the §404(b)(1) Guidelines for Evaluating Permit Applications for Wetland Development, 15 Colum. J. Envtl. L. 99, 104 (1990). The Corps initially subsumed its section 404(b)(1) review within the "public interest" review the Corps had performed under the old Rivers and Harbors Act, which emphasized nonenvironmental values. 33 C.F.R. §320.4(a)(1). However, after a lawsuit by environmentalists, National Wildlife Federation v. Marsh, 14 E.L.R. 20,262, 20,264 (D.D.C. 1984), the Corps agreed that EPA's section 404(b)(1) guidelines take precedence, and a permit may not be issued if it would not comply with the guidelines.

5. In April 1989, the Corps of Engineers issued interim guidance described by Professor Houck as "one of the most astonishing about-faces in the history of federal environmental law." Houck, supra at 795. The guidance, issued in the context of an application to develop a waterfront resort in Louisiana called Plantation Landing, acknowledges that section 404 is designed to discourage development in wetlands. It establishes that cost savings alone cannot justify a permit, because development in wetlands usually is less expensive, and that the relative size of adverse impacts also cannot justify a permit, since the Act is designed to avoid cumulative losses.

6. Professor Houck recommends abandoning the alternatives test and restricting permits in wetland areas to water-dependent activities—activities that must be located there, such as a pier. He would allow only two exceptions: the first for the rare circumstance in which a wetland location is less harmful than an upland alternative as provided in section 404(b)(1), the second for discharges demonstrating "fundamentally different factors" that justify a finding that the applicant is in effect water-dependent.

### "No Net Loss," Mitigation Banking, and the Future of Wetlands Protection

The goal of "no net loss" of wetlands, initially proposed in 1988 by the National Wetlands Policy Forum, has been endorsed as national policy by the past three administrations. Even if regulatory programs to prevent wetland losses are strengthened, no net loss can only be achieved if aggressive restoration efforts are pursued. A National Research Council panel recommended in 1991 an ambitious program to restore 10 million acres of wetlands by the year 2010. Noting that mitigation projects have often failed when undertaken by developers, the panel recommended that a National Aquatic Ecosystem Restoration Trust Fund be established to fund restoration efforts by federal and state agencies. The agencies would offer financial incentives to private landowners to restore wetlands in cooperation with volunteer efforts. The panel also recommended that restoration efforts be undertaken for 2 million acres of polluted lakes and 400,000 miles of rivers and streams. Stevens, Panel Urges Big Wetlands Restoration Project, N.Y. Times, Dec. 12, 1991, at B16.

In August 1993, the Clinton administration unveiled its program for protecting wetlands. White House Office of Environmental Policy, Protecting America's Wetlands: A Fair, Flexible and Effective Approach (1993). While endorsing the goal of no net loss of wetlands, the program emphasized measures to increase the flexibility and fairness of the section 404 permit process by including new deadlines for permit decisions and by creating a new administrative appeal process. The Clinton plan rejected the concept of categorizing wetlands based on assessment of their functional value, on the grounds that it would be unworkable, inordinately costly, and could lead to approval of wetland losses for projects that could easily be pursued elsewhere.

The Clinton wetlands program endorsed mitigation banking and emphasized giving state and local governments greater responsibility for wetlands protection. A wetlands mitigation bank is a wetland area that has been restored, created, or enhanced and then set aside to compensate for future losses of wetlands from development activities. Developers needing to mitigate wetlands losses can purchase credits from a mitigation bank rather than restoring or creating wetlands in the vicinity of the development site. Mitigation banking is now being tried in some states. In Florida, sales of credits generated by wetlands restoration totaled $8 million in the first six months of the program, with prices ranging as high as $42,000 an acre. Firms seeking to acquire credits by restoring wetlands were seeking approval for credits covering 125,000 acres. Binkley, Builders Snap Up Wetland Credits, but Concerns Rise over Regulation, Wall St. J. (Fla. ed.), Aug. 30, 1995, at F1.

Environmentalists criticize mitigation banking by arguing that it "encourages: (1) off site mitigation that cannot replace many wetlands values which are site specific; (2) an excess of certain kinds of wetlands, such as marshes and shrub wetlands, because they are easier and cheaper to create than other wetlands types; and (3) issuance of fill permits based on wetlands creation when avoidance and minimization alternatives exist." Blumm, The Clinton Wetlands Plan 9 J. Land Use & Envtl. L. 203, 227 (1994). Data indicating that only a small percentage of compensatory mitigation projects by developers have succeeded in creating functional wetlands have contributed to environmentalists' skepticism, while leading others to conclude that a bank run by governmental agencies would be a preferable alternative. Malakoff, Restored Wetlands Flunk Real-World Test, 280 Science 371 (1998).

Efforts to transfer greater responsibility for wetlands protection to state and local governments have also been met by skepticism from the environmental community. As Michael Blumm notes, because development benefits tend to be more localized than the benefits wetlands generate, federal regulation almost always will be more effective. Id. at 229. While agreeing that the federal interest in wetlands protection is stronger than variable state interests, Oliver Houck and Michael Rolland argue that with proper funding and clearer goals, states could be enlisted to improve wetlands protections. They note that the few states with delegated section 404 programs "exercise significantly more control over smaller permit applications than the federal system, activities that largely escape federal review and cause a continuing wetlands hemorrhage." Houck & Rolland, Federalism in Wetlands Regulation: A Consideration of Delegation of Clean Water Act Section 404 and Related Programs to the States, 54 Md. L. Rev. 1242 (1995).

In April 2004, President George W. Bush endorsed the goal of going beyond "no net loss" toward a policy goal of annually *increasing* the amount of wetlands acreage in the United States. Environmental groups were skeptical of this goal, which the Bush administration indicated could be accomplished through greater use of wetlands restoration programs administered by the U.S. Fish and Wildlife Service and through greater use of conservation incentives in the Farm Bill.

In April 2008, EPA and the U.S. Army Corps of Engineers issued new regulations on wetland mitigation. 73 Fed. Reg. 19,594 (2008). The regulations address situations where compensation is required because harm to wetlands cannot be avoided or minimized and require that conservation experts be involved in the mitigation process. The regulations establish a "watershed approach" for mitigation projects and create a preferred hierarchy of approaches. Mitigation banks are the preferred approach, followed by mitigation supported by "in-lieu" fees paid to nonprofit organizations, with permitee-conducted site mitigation being the least favored approach. With conservation experts more involved in the process, the market for mitigation banks grew quickly. As of May 2020, there were more than 1,900 approved mitigation banks.

## F. NONPOINT SOURCE CONTROLS, WATERSHED PROTECTION, AND EFFLUENT TRADING

Despite significant progress in controlling pollution from point sources, serious water quality problems remain due in large part to pollution from nonpoint sources. Nonpoint sources include urban and cropland runoff; animal wastes; discharges from storm sewers, construction sites, and mining and logging operations; and atmospheric deposition. Pollution from these sources causes severe water quality problems, accounting for nearly all the sediment and the vast majority of nitrogen and phosphorus reaching the nation's surface waters. Beginning in 1997, massive fish kills caused by outbreaks of *Pfiesteria piscidia* focused attention on runoff from chicken farms as a source of harmful nutrients. In 1999, Hurricane Floyd swept vast quantities of animal wastes into surface waters, causing serious public health problems in North Carolina.

With the impacts of climate change and little progress in nutrient pollution prevention, this problem has only become worse in subsequent decades. Nonpoint source pollution is the primary cause of massive dead zones in some of the country's most important waterways. The annual dead zone in the Gulf of Mexico is one of the largest in the world, recorded at 8,776 square miles in 2017. Nonpoint source pollution is also responsible for dangerous algae blooms, such as devastating "red tide" events off the coast of Florida that have killed ocean life, threatened local industries, and caused public health problems.

Wholly apart from these headline-grabbing incidents, EPA and most states have identified nonpoint sources as the primary reason that water quality is insufficient to support designated uses. By the end of the twentieth century, runoff of manure from animal feeding operations, which produce 130 times more waste than humans generate each year, was responsible for tens of thousands of "impaired river miles" in 22 states. Blount, Henderson & Cline, The New Nonpoint Source Battleground: Concentrated Animal Feeding Operations, 14 Nat. Resources & Env't 42 (Summer 1999). It is estimated that 54 percent of all nitrogen emitted by power plants and motor vehicles ends up in watersheds or coastal estuaries.

The importance of nonpoint sources to water pollution problems has been recognized for decades. Yet nonpoint sources have largely escaped federal regulation because of political, administrative, and technical difficulties. Recall that EPA initially deemed it infeasible to regulate pollution generated by runoff even when conveyed through a point source. The agency argued that it could not "instruct each individual farmer on his farming practices." Natural Resources Defense Council v. Costle, 568 F.2d 1369, 1380 (D.C. Cir. 1977). Considerable progress has been made since then in understanding how improved land use management practices can reduce nonpoint source pollution. But progress in controlling nonpoint sources has been slow in part because land use controls face fierce political resistance, as explored in more detail in Chapter 7.

## 1.  Federal Efforts to Control Nonpoint Source Pollution

When it created the Clean Water Act's NPDES permit program in 1972, Congress confined the program to point sources, though it included any "concentrated animal feeding operation . . . from which pollutants are or may be discharged" within the definition of "point source" in section 502(14). Permits issued to concentrated animal feeding operations (CAFOs), defined as those that contain more than 1,000 "animal units" and whose discharges are not limited to a 25-year, 24-hour storm event, were to have limits based on the permit writer's "best professional judgment" relating to manure management practices. Yet less than 10,000 of the nation's 1.1 million farms were subjected to the NPDES permit program. C.F. Runge, Environmental Protection from Farm to Market, in Thinking Ecologically 61 (M. Chertow & D. Esty eds., 1997).

Aside from treating CAFOs as point sources, the Clean Water Act did not directly regulate sources of runoff. Instead, it relied on a largely ineffective planning process established by section 208. This section requires states to develop "areawide waste treatment management plans" that were to include a process for identifying nonpoint sources and establishing feasible control measures. Plans prepared under section 208 were to be submitted to EPA in return for receiving federal financial assistance for the planning process. Decisions concerning NPDES permits and section 404 permits are supposed to be consistent with the section 208 plans. In 1977, Congress added section 208(j), which authorized the Department of Agriculture to share the costs of "best management practices" adopted by farmers to control nonpoint pollution. This program was not widely embraced by farmers.

The section 208 planning process is widely viewed as a failure. While more than 200 plans were prepared under section 208, they accomplished very little for reasons that included lack of incentives to link planning to implementation and "the basic resistance of local governments to federal efforts to dictate planning structures and results, however flexibly those programs are designed." Adler, Addressing Barriers to Watershed Protection, 25 Envtl. L. 973, 1044 (1995). Federal funding for the section 208 program, which had been at less than half of authorized levels, was discontinued in 1981.

When it amended the Clean Water Act in 1987, Congress expressly declared that in order to meet the goals of the Act "it is the national policy that programs for the control of nonpoint sources of pollution be developed and implemented in an expeditious manner." §101(a)(7). One such program addressed urban runoff from municipal and storm sewers. Congress required EPA to bring discharges from these storm sewers into the NPDES permit program pursuant to section 402(p). These permits prohibit non-stormwater discharges into storm sewers and aim to "reduce the discharge of pollutants to the maximum extent practicable."

Congress also added section 319 to the Clean Water Act in the 1987 Amendments. Section 319 requires states to prepare "state assessment reports" that identify waters that cannot reasonably be expected to meet water quality standards because of nonpoint pollution. These reports are to identify significant sources of nonpoint pollution for each affected water segment. §319(a)(1). States are to develop "management programs" that include identification and implementation of best management practices to control significant sources of nonpoint pollution. These programs are to contain schedules for implementation of best management practices, certification that sufficient state authority exists to implement the program, and identification of sources of financial support.

States were to submit their assessment reports and management programs to EPA for review and approval. States with approved programs are eligible for federal financial assistance to implement their programs. By 1992, EPA had approved assessment reports for all states and management programs for 44 states. EPA, Managing Nonpoint Pollution: Final Report to Congress on Section 319 (1992).

The 1987 Amendments generated early enthusiasm for the section 319 program by authorizing $400 million for grants to state programs. However, only a small portion of these funds actually were appropriated, and only $40 million in grants was distributed during the next three years. Noting that 47 states already had some kind of program for addressing nonpoint sources, Oliver Houck predicted that "[a]t best, the new federal funding will encourage more specificity in these plans. More likely, it will produce a second round of paperwork comparable to that generated in the early 1970s by the hauntingly similar section 208 program." Houck, Ending the War: A Strategy to Save America's Coastal Zone, 47 Md. L. Rev. 358, 377 (1988). This prediction may have been accurate as section 319 has not made great strides in controlling pollution from nonpoint sources. Professor

Robert Adler notes that EPA "elected not to play hardball" in approving state plans and did not insist that states adopt regulatory programs to control nonpoint sources. Adler, Addressing Barriers to Watershed Protection, 25 Envtl. L. 973, 1045 n.427 (1995).

In 1990, Congress continued to encourage states to adopt nonpoint source control programs when it added section 1455b to the Coastal Zone Management Act. 16 U.S.C. §1455b. This amendment requires states with federally approved coastal zone management programs to develop a Coastal Nonpoint Pollution Control Program subject to review and approval by EPA and NOAA. While the addition of yet another planning requirement to federal law is not in itself of any great significance, section 1455b of the CZMA requires far more specificity in nonpoint source management planning than ever before. States must identify land uses that contribute to degradation of threatened or impaired coastal waters and critical areas adjacent to them and provide for the implementation of additional management measures to achieve water quality standards. "Management measures" are defined in section 1455b(g)(5) as "economically achievable measures for the control of" nonpoint sources "which reflect the greatest degree of pollutant reduction achievable through the application of the best available nonpoint pollution control practices, technologies, processes, siting criteria, operating methods, or other alternatives."

The state programs must conform to guidance EPA and NOAA issued in 1993. Minimum requirements for the guidance are outlined in section 1455b(g)(2), which reflects an effort to require as much specificity as possible in the description of control measures, regulatory targets, pollutants to be controlled, costs, effects of controls, and monitoring. However, once again, Congress failed to put its money where its mouth was. While EPA estimated that the cost of adopting nonpoint source control measures as recommended in the guidance documents would range from $390 to $590 million, only $50 million in grant money was made available to the states through EPA, and less than $2 million was made available from NOAA.

## 2.   *Toward a Watershed Approach to Pollution Control*

Because today's most serious water pollution problems tend to be diffuse in origin and involve all the parts of an interconnected ecosystem, federal policy has shifted emphasis toward community- and watershed-based environmental protection and ecosystem management policies. These programs involve efforts to involve all levels of government and nongovernmental organizations in hydrologically defined drainage basins—watersheds—to develop coordinated strategies for addressing pollution problems that transcend political boundaries.

In February 1998, EPA and the USDA jointly announced a "Clean Water Action Plan" that sought to organize efforts to protect water quality around a "watershed approach." Declaring the watershed approach "the key to the future" of water pollution control, the plan proposed a new collaborative effort by federal, state, tribal, and local governments and the private sector to restore and protect watersheds. The plan proposed to involve these groups in preparing unified watershed assessments and restoration action strategies that will be eligible for special federal funding. It notes that a watershed focus would help "strike the best balance among efforts to control point source pollution and polluted runoff," as well as identifying "the most cost-effective pollution control strategies to meet clean water goals." C. Browner & D. Glickman, Clean Water Action Plan: Restoring and Protecting America's Waters iii (1998).

Although watershed management may sound like a new idea, the concept actually has a long history. See Adler, Addressing Barriers to Watershed Protection, 25 Envtl. L. 973, 1003 (1995). Robert Adler notes that after the outright rejection of early basinwide planning proposals, the watershed concept was abducted "to justify mission-oriented water development programs, as reflected in statutes such as the Reclamation Act, the Federal Power Act, and federal navigation and flood control laws." Id. at 1013. While the new generation of environmental statutes are not designed with a watershed approach in mind, several regional efforts have employed this concept, such as the Chesapeake Bay Program, the Great Lakes Program, and the National Estuary Program.

Whereas previous efforts to use federal financial assistance to encourage states to adopt controls on nonpoint source pollution have not been a notable success, the Clean Water Action Plan's watershed approach may facilitate emissions trading between point and nonpoint sources of water pollution. Emissions trading was part of the Bush administration's strategy for reducing the costs of pollution control. EPA developed a policy promoting effluent trading within watersheds. EPA, Effluent Trading in Watersheds Policy Statement, 61 Fed. Reg. 4,994 (1996). The policy endorses effluent trading as an innovative means for developing solutions to water quality problems that will yield economic, environmental, and social benefits. The program is being implemented on a voluntary basis under existing law, which may involve directing permit writers to allow effluent trades as part of the NPDES permit system. For example, POTWs discharging into North Carolina's Tar Pamlico Basin have engaged in point/nonpoint discharge trades through a program that permits them to pay into a state fund supporting implementation of best management practices on farmlands.

Under the administration of President George W. Bush, EPA continued to emphasize a watershed-based approach to controlling pollution and to encourage effluent trading schemes. In January 2003, EPA published its Water Quality Trading Policy, which encourages effluent trading to reduce nutrient and sediment loads. The agency published draft guidance on how watershed-based NPDES permitting can be implemented in August 2003. 68 Fed. Reg. 51,011 (2003). In November 2004, EPA issued detailed guidance on how effluent trading may be used to improve water quality more efficiently. EPA, Water Quality Trading Assessment Handbook (2004).

In October 2008, EPA reported that more than 100 facilities had participated in water quality trading programs, but that 80 percent of the trades had occurred within a single trading program. EPA, Water Quality Trading Evaluation (2008). The agency explained that both legal and practical obstacles hampered expansion of trading programs:

- The Clean Water Act does not mention water quality trading, and has several requirements that pose potential impediments to trading (e.g., anti-backsliding and anti-degradation requirements; permitting and public comment requirements). A significant amount of creativity and staff time is necessary to work around the complexities caused by statutory ambiguity. Overburdened permit writers and cautious legal counsel may be unwilling or unable to make such an investment.

- Water quality trading appears to be viable and sustainable only in locations where a narrow set of regulatory, economic, hydrologic, and geographic circumstances exist. Likewise, it may be limited to areas where program coordinators have both a high level of interest in trading and the talent needed to shepherd stakeholders through a challenging program development and implementation process.

Due in part to these challenges, growth of water quality trading programs has been limited. The GAO reported that by 2014, only 19 trading programs had been established in 11 states. Policy makers continue to work to bring more participants to water quality trading markets, and a February 6, 2019 memo from EPA Assistant Administrator David P. Ross reiterates EPA's "strong support for water quality trading" and encourages regional administrators to support these market-based approaches.

## NOTES AND QUESTIONS

1. Why have the various federal programs that address nonpoint pollution not been more successful in controlling the problem? Is it a product of their largely nonregulatory approach, which seeks to encourage states voluntarily to adopt control measures? Is the problem primarily one of inadequate state resources to invest in control measures, or is it a lack of technical information concerning what control measures actually work?

2. Are nonpoint sources so numerous and diverse that a regulatory program is simply infeasible? While there are hundreds of thousands of farmers, the Soil Conservation Service (SCS) has an army of 13,000 employees who are charged with providing technical advice and support to them. The SCS and others maintain that only a voluntary approach will induce change in agricultural practices because farmers resist any program that smacks of regulation. Note that the FSA's requirements apply to farmers who wish to continue to receive federal subsidies. Could this be a sufficient "carrot" to permit the SCS to implement an aggressive "best management practices" program?

3. The 1987 Amendments to the Clean Water Act were enacted over President Reagan's veto. In the message accompanying his unsuccessful veto, the president decried them as potentially "the ultimate whip hand for Federal regulators." Do you agree? Examine the provisions of section 402(p) for controlling urban nonpoint pollution and the provisions of section 319 for controlling nonpoint pollution generally. To what extent do these impose pollution control requirements enforceable by citizen suit? Past efforts to control nonpoint sources sought to create incentives for state action, without much effect. How do the provisions of section 319 differ from those of section 208?

4. The Environmental Law Institute has published comprehensive reviews of state controls on nonpoint sources of water pollution. ELI, Enforceable State Mechanisms for the Control of Nonpoint Source Water Pollution (1997), and ELI, Almanac of Enforceable State Laws to Control Nonpoint Source Water Pollution (1998).

The reports find that nearly all states have statutory authority to control discharges that can be shown to result in water pollution and that in about half the states this authority is not limited to point sources. While state erosion and sediment control laws could be significant vehicles for controlling nonpoint source pollution, most exempt agricultural activities. The reports review several ways in which states have contrived to make best management practices enforceable or to link them to other enforcement mechanisms. They conclude that there is a diverse array of tools that states can apply to fill in regulatory gaps left by federal programs.

5. In December 2012, EPA's National Water Program released a report entitled National Water Program 2012 Strategy: Response to Climate Change. The report found that climate change is leading to increased water pollution problems, more extreme water-related weather events, changes to the availability of drinking water supplies, waterbody boundary movement and displacement, changing aquatic biology, and collective impacts on coastal waters. Hurricane Sandy, which devastated the northeast coast of the United States in October 2012, demonstrated the more extreme water-related weather events that previously had been forecast. In addition to the loss of life and the enormous property damage Sandy caused, the coastal flooding it generated washed more than 10 billion gallons of raw and partly treated sewage into rivers, canals, and bays, primarily in New York and New Jersey. Climate Central, Sewage Overflows from Hurricane Sandy (2013). A report published in January 2021 found that climate change has caused an additional $2.5 billion per year of flood damage in the United States. Davenport, Burke & Diffenbaugh, Contribution of Historical Precipitation Change to U.S. Flood Damages, Proceedings of the National Academy of Sciences, Jan. 2021.

# CHAPTER 7

# LAND USE REGULATION AND REGULATORY TAKINGS

The regulation of private land use to achieve environmental protection objectives remains the weakest link in modern environmental law. Many of the major environmental challenges, such as the control of non-point source water pollution, the conservation of biodiversity, and the limitation of automobile emissions, including carbon dioxide, are at the core of land use regulation problems. Yet, in the main, we continue to develop and abuse land, regardless of environmental stresses that development causes.

—*A. Dan Tarlock**

Although federal law rarely regulates private real estate directly, federal policies have had dramatic effects on land use patterns. The nation's energy, transportation, and housing policies have reshaped the development of urban and rural areas, often with disastrous environmental consequences. We now realize that these policies have a significant impact not only on nonpoint source pollution, but also on the amount of greenhouse gases emitted in the United States, because they affect energy use in nearly every aspect of our economy. Yet regulation of land use generally remains the fiercely guarded province of local levels of government. As Professor Tarlock notes, at the local level there is a "mismatch between physical problem areas and the crazy-quilt and increasingly dysfunctional overlay of political jurisdictions" coupled with "a deep-seated resistance to land use regulation." While air and water "always have been common property resources," land use has been "another story," with law enshrining "the idea that land should be controlled at the lowest level of government, if at all." Despite the tempering forces of the common law of nuisance and the police power, "the bottom line is that it is still much harder to limit activities that degrade ecosystems than to limit air, soil and water as waste disposal sinks." Id.

As the environmental consequences of unplanned growth and urban sprawl become more evident, land use management has become a prominent part of the environmental agenda. Renewed concern for environmental justice has highlighted the environmental consequences of long-time racial disparities in lending and housing policies. During the 1930s, federal officials "redlined" many Black

---

* Land Use Regulation: The Weak Link in Environmental Protection, 82 Wash. L. Rev. 651, 652 (2007).

neighborhoods, declaring them too risky for investment. A study of 108 cities, published in 2020, found that these "redlined" neighborhoods today are 5 to 20 percent hotter during the summer because they have far fewer trees and parks and more paved surfaces. J.S. Hoffman, V. Shandas, and N. Pendleton, The Effects of Historical Housing Policies on Resident Exposure to Intra-Urban Heat: A Study of 108 U.S. Urban Areas. 8 Climate 12 (2020). Efforts to develop programs to improve land use management are now being pursued to protect the environment, reduce the carbon footprint of urban areas, and promote environmental justice.

After examining how land use development affects the environment, this chapter reviews federal and state programs to control land use. It discusses state growth management initiatives and the political obstacles they face. The chapter traces the history of regulatory takings doctrine, and it explores why takings claims now seem to be raised whenever land use is regulated more stringently. It concludes by examining how contemporary environmental problems are challenging traditional conceptions of property rights.

## A.   LAND USE AND THE ENVIRONMENT

The environmental consequences of how humans use land have been a public concern since 1864 when George Perkins Marsh published the first edition of his classic work *Man and Nature; or, Physical Geography as Modified by Human Action.* Popularized by the second edition of his book, renamed *The Earth as Modified by Human Action,* Marsh's warnings concerning the environmental effects of development were influential worldwide. Marsh helped inspire legislation to preserve forests in Italy and New Zealand, and he boosted the late-nineteenth-century campaign to establish national parks in the United States. Today 28 percent of the land area of the United States remains under federal ownership, much of it protected as national parks, national monuments, or wilderness areas.

How land is managed has an immense impact on environmental conditions in all media. Land use patterns influence the severity of water and air pollution problems, the health of wetlands and other ecosystems, and the overall quality and aesthetic flavor of human life. Dramatic changes have occurred in land use patterns in the United States, producing enormous environmental consequences. Residential development in rural areas now consumes much prime farmland, complicating watershed management strategies. As growing populations have fled central cities for suburban venues, the depressing consequences of urban sprawl, traffic congestion, and pollution problems have awakened many communities to the need for more intelligent planning and growth management policies. The following excerpt describes how public policies have influenced land use patterns and the environmental consequences of these changes.

Turner & Rylander

Land Use: The Forgotten Agenda, in Thinking Ecologically

(M. Chertow & D. Esty eds., 1997)

Our land use patterns affect the environment in many ways. Most notably, development pressures have significant impacts on habitat. Even where forests and wetlands are preserved, new housing and commercial developments pave over open spaces, alter water courses and runoff flows, and rearrange scenic vistas. Our land use choices also impact air quality. For example, vehicle miles traveled by California's sprawling population have increased more than 200 percent in the past two decades as a consequence of distant suburbanization, exacerbating an already well-known smog problem in the region. Mass transit, which is only viable at relatively high population densities, becomes increasingly impractical as people spread out across the land. . . .

. . . As a whole, the United States' land regulatory system is a failure. It is a policy of directed chaos—multiple programs and policies designed to address usually worthwhile goals but implemented in too small an area without regard to the health of the region and oblivious to their unintended consequences. As Aldo Leopold noted, "To build a better motor we tap the uttermost powers of the human brain; to build a better country-side we throw dice.". . .

Transportation and housing policies have been major contributors to America's wasteful land use patterns. Transportation policies, designed almost exclusively for the automobile, greatly exacerbated suburban sprawl. . . . The linkage between transportation and land use was rarely made, and national development patterns reflect that disconnect.

Federal housing policies also contributed to the growth of suburbia and the segregation of housing by class and race.

Although many people recoil from the thought of a federal land use policy, the reality is that the United States does have such a policy, albeit one that exists not by design but by default, arising from an uncoordinated collection of overlapping and often conflicting mandates and programs. Transportation policies, farm programs, disaster relief, water and sewer support, wetlands and endangered species laws, public housing and financial lending programs combine to create a de facto national land use plan.

## NOTES AND QUESTIONS

1. To what extent are the problems identified by Turner and Rylander the unintended consequences of policies adopted to pursue other laudable goals? Are they caused by inadequate planning or deliberate decisions to tolerate certain forms of environmental and aesthetic degradation in return for other benefits?

2. Because authority over land use decisions generally is concentrated in local levels of government, development decisions in one jurisdiction have a great potential to generate externalities that affect conditions in other jurisdictions. To what extent can this problem be solved by creating regional entities and making them responsible for coordinating land use planning?

3. More detailed analyses of racial and economic disparities in exposure to pollutants are documenting the damaging consequences of historic discrimination in housing patterns. A comprehensive study of exposure to small particulate pollution (PM2.5) sought to identify which emission sources explain racial disparities in exposure to pollutants and whether differences exist by emission sector, geography, or demographics. The researchers were surprised to discover that racial-ethnic exposure disparities were pervasive. "[N]early all major emission

categories—consistently across states, urban and rural areas, income levels and exposure levels—contribute to the systemic PM2.5 exposure disparity experienced by people of color." They noted that "[b]ecause of a legacy of racist housing policy and other factors, racial-ethnic exposure disparities have persisted even as overall exposure has decreased." Christopher W. Tessum et al., "PM2.5 polluters disproportionately and systemically affect people of color in the United States," 7 Science Advances (2021), *https://advances.sciencemag.org/content/7/18/eabf4491*.

4. A study by the Environmental Integrity Project found that in 2020 thirteen U.S. oil refineries exceeded action levels for exposure to benzene emissions at the fenceline. Of the 530,000 people who live within three miles of the refineries 57 percent were people of color and 43 percent were people with incomes below the poverty line. Environmental Integrity Project, Environmental Justice and Refinery Pollution (2021). The study noted that one of these refineries was the Pennsylvania Energy Systems refinery discussed in Chapter 1. "Although shut down after a fire and explosion in July of 2019, fenceline benzene concentrations" still averaged "more than three times EPA's action level . . . likely due to the ongoing removal of petrochemical products from the site." Id. at 4.

5. As concern grows over the impact of climate change, more attention is being focused on the impact of urban development policies on greenhouse gas (GHG) emissions. In 2008, California adopted S.B. 375, which requires the state transportation planning process to focus on achieving reductions in greenhouse gas emissions. The law promotes a "sustainable communities strategy" by providing incentives to developers and local communities to reduce the carbon footprint of local development. The legislation mandates the establishment of sustainable regional growth plans. In 2011, the San Diego region adopted a regional transportation plan that became the first to link GHG emissions reduction targets with land use, housing, and transportation planning. The plan seeks to achieve a 14 percent per capita reduction in GHG emissions by emphasizing walkable communities with 80 percent of new housing growth being multi-family.

6. The "green building" industry has made significant strides in recent years. Several states, counties, and municipalities are adopting green building ordinances. California's Green Building Standards Code requires commercial and residential construction to meet the equivalent of a "silver" rating under the U.S. Green Building Council's Leadership in Energy and Environmental Design (LEED) standards. Effective on January 1, 2020, California became the first state to require new homes to install solar photovoltaic systems. Title 24, Part 6 of California Building Standards Code.

## B.  FEDERAL REGULATION OF LAND USE

The federal government plays an important role in land use management in two areas. First, federal agencies are responsible for managing lands owned by the federal government, which comprise one-third of the land area of the United States. Under the Property Clause of Article IV, Section 3 of the Constitution, Congress has broad authority to control the management and disposition of federal property. The laws governing federal management of public lands and the resources they contain cover an immense field that is worthy of separate study. They are briefly introduced below in Section B1. While the federal government generally does not directly regulate lands held by private parties, federal policies have a profound effect on the management and use of private lands. These policies are outlined in Section B2.

## 1.   *Federal Management of Public Lands*

The role the federal government should play in managing public lands is a subject of continuing controversy. For the first century of the republic the dominant federal role was to transfer public lands to private parties to encourage settlement and development. The focus of public land management has now shifted. Most laws encouraging disposal of public lands have been repealed — one can no longer "homestead" on the public domain. The result is that one-third of the nation's land is now held permanently in federal ownership. Some of these public lands are protected for their natural, cultural, or scenic values — as parks, wilderness areas, or wildlife refuges. Most are entrusted to the stewardship of the Bureau of Land Management (BLM) and the Forest Service under broad mandates to manage for "multiple uses" that "will best meet the needs of the American public." Multiple Use, Sustained Yield Act, 16 U.S.C. §531(a). See the Federal Land Policy and Management Act of 1976 (FLPMA), 43 U.S.C. §§1701 et seq.; and the National Forest Management Act of 1976, 16 U.S.C. §§1600 et seq. See generally Wilkinson & Anderson, Land and Resource Planning in the National Forests, 64 Or. L. Rev. 1 (1985). That mandate has been a recipe for controversy. See Huffman, Public Lands Management in an Age of Deregulation and Privatization, 10 Pub. Land L. Rev. 29 (1989). The laws governing management of public lands are outlined in the following Pathfinder.

---

## Public Land and Natural Resources Law: A Pathfinder

The Congressional Research Service has published a useful overview of federal public lands, CRS, Federal Land Ownership: Overview and Data (updated Feb. 21, 2020), available online at *https://fas.org/sgp/crs/misc/ R42346.pdf.*

*Public Land Management Systems.* Public lands are managed in four systems: general public lands, managed by the Bureau of Land Management (BLM); National Forests, managed by the U.S. Forest Service; National Wildlife Refuges, managed by the U.S. Fish and Wildlife Service; and National Parks, managed by the National Park Service. Wilderness areas, governed by the Wilderness Act of 1964, and National Monuments, given permanent protection by Congress or by the president through use of the Antiquities Act, may be designated on lands in any of the four systems. The Antiquities Act allows the president to reserve "parcels of land as a part of the national monuments," but those parcels must "be confined to the smallest area compatible with the proper care and management of the objects to be protected." 54 U.S.C. §320301(b).

*Multiple Use.* Congress has mandated that most public lands, including the 248 million acres managed by BLM and the 193 million acres in the National Forests (except for wilderness areas), be managed for "multiple use" as defined in the Federal Land Policy and Management Act (FLPMA) for BLM lands and the National Forest Management Act (NFMA) for the National Forests. Despite elaborate planning and public participation requirements, "multiple-use" management has been vulnerable to local politics, with land managers often emphasizing economic uses—grazing, logging, and mineral development—over wildlife and wilderness values. Congress also has often undercut the FLPMA and NFMA by, for example, forbidding BLM from raising grazing fees or by specifying the "annual cut" that must be allowed in the National Forests.

*Dominant Use.* For one class of lands—the National Wildlife Refuges—Congress has placed a thumb on the balance, establishing as a dominant use the conservation of wildlife. Other uses, such as grazing or motorboating, are allowed on a refuge only if "compatible" with the purposes for which the refuge was established. The National Wildlife Refuge System now includes 562 units totaling 150 million acres. Sixteen of these refuges, accounting for 77 million acres, are in Alaska and were created or expanded in the Alaska National Interest Lands Conservation Act of 1980.

*Preservation.* Two classes of federal lands enjoy almost absolute protection—the National Parks and the National Wilderness Areas. Congress in 1916 created the National Park Service and charged it with management of what today are 417 natural, historic, and recreational preserves covering 80 million acres. "The Park Service's mission is to conserve the scenery and the natural and historic objects and wildlife therein and to provide for the enjoyment of the same in such manner and by such means as will leave them unimpaired for the enjoyment of future generations." 16 U.S.C. §1. Wilderness Areas must be managed under the Wilderness Act to preserve their "primeval character and influence" and "natural condition" with motorized equipment, permanent roads, and commercial activity generally prohibited. 16 U.S.C. §1131(c).

*Public Resources.* The Mining Law of 1872 guarantees citizens a right to discover, develop, and patent hardrock mineral deposits on any public lands, unless the lands have been expressly withdrawn from mineral entry. Other minerals are subject to lease by the government, principally under the Mineral Leasing Act of 1920 and, offshore, under the Outer Continental Shelf Lands Act of 1953. Congress has also acted to protect important wildlife resources through measures such as the Migratory Bird Treaty Act, the Marine Mammal Protection Act, and other laws.

Fierce conflicts over management of public resources are nothing new. In the early twentieth century a proposal to dam the Hetch Hetchy Valley, a wilderness preserve near Yosemite National Park, to provide water and power for the city of

San Francisco, spawned a bitter national battle that raged for more than six years, leaving John Muir and President Theodore Roosevelt, who once had camped together in Yosemite, on opposite sides of the dispute. This episode is described in Roderick Nash, Wilderness and the American Mind 161 (1982). More contemporary versions of these battles include the debate over oil drilling in the Arctic, described in Chapter 1, and controversies over protection of the spotted owl and endangered salmon species in the Pacific Northwest.

What has changed about today's controversies is the emergence of concern for ecosystem management and protection of biodiversity. As the inadequacies of an eleventh hour, species-by-species approach to conservation have become more apparent, efforts to reorient public policy toward more forward-looking and comprehensive approaches have gained momentum. These efforts have spawned new initiatives for managing public resources to promote environmental values and to preserve biodiversity.

Environmentalists argue that federal resource management policies have caused substantial environmental damage while subsidizing private mining, timber, and grazing interests. A particularly egregious example is the Mining Act of 1872, which gives private parties the right to develop and extract hardrock mineral deposits from public lands without payment of royalties. Twenty-acre tracts of public land on which such minerals are found may be acquired by private interests for $5, even if the land is worth millions. More than 3 million acres of public land were patented in this manner, including land later converted to ski resorts, condominiums, and golf courses.

In February 1995, the Bureau of Land Management (BLM) adopted new regulations governing grazing on public lands. 60 Fed. Reg. 9,894 (1995). These regulations, which allow the BLM to alter authorized uses of rangeland to adjust to environmental conditions when permits are renewed, were upheld in Public Lands Council v. Babbitt, 145 F.3d 154 (10th Cir. 1998).

A tug-of-war over public lands has occurred during different presidential administrations. During President Clinton's final year in office, the U.S. Forest Service adopted a far-reaching Roadless Area Conservation Rule that banned the construction of new roads in 58.5 million acres of inventoried roadless areas on public lands. 36 C.F.R. pt. 294 (2001). In 2005 the Bush administration adopted its own State Petitions for Inventoried Roadless Areas Management Rule, 36 C.F.R. pt. 294 (2005). That rule in turn was struck down by a federal district court in California, which reinstated the Roadless Rule. In Wyoming v. U.S. Dep't of Agriculture, 661 F.3d 1209 (10th Cir. 2011), the U.S. Court of Appeals for the Tenth Circuit upheld the legality of the Roadless Rule. The U.S. Supreme Court subsequently refused to review the Tenth Circuit's decision.

In February 2016, BLM proposed new rules to govern the planning process for the public lands it manages. The rules were part of BLM's Planning 2.0 initiative to "(1) Improve the BLM's ability to respond to social and environmental change in a timely manner; (2) provide meaningful opportunities for other Federal agencies, State and local governments, Indian tribes, and the public to be involved in the development of BLM resource management plans; and (3) improve the BLM's ability to address landscape-scale resource issues and to apply landscape-scale management approaches." The rules, which would have comprehensively revised regulations dating from 1983, were promulgated shortly before the end of the Obama administration. On March 27, 2017, President Trump signed H.J. Res. 44, using the Congressional Review Act to veto the regulations.

President Trump sought to reduce the size of National Monuments established by prior administrations and to expand dramatically leasing of public lands for development by extractive industries. He lifted restrictions on commercial fishing in 5,000 square miles of the northern Atlantic Ocean imposed by President Obama when he used the Antiquities Act to create the Northeast Canyons and Seamounts Marine National Monument. In *Massachusetts Lobstermen's Ass'n v. Ross*, 945 F.3d 535 (D.C. Cir. 2019), the U.S. Court of Appeals for the D.C. Circuit rejected the claim that President Obama's monument designation was overly broad and improperly interfered with commercial fishing operations. When the Supreme Court refused to review this decision on March 22, 2021, Chief Justice Roberts issued an unusual statement inviting challenges to future monument designations. He noted that the Court has "not explained how the [Antiquities] Act's corresponding 'smallest area compatible' limitation interacts with the protection of such an imprecisely demarcated concept as an ecosystem." The Chief Justice declared that the "scope of the objects that can be designated under the Act, and how to measure the area necessary for their proper care and management, may warrant consideration — especially given the myriad restrictions on public use this purely discretionary designation can serve to justify."

Upon taking office, the Biden administration halted, at least temporarily, leasing of public lands for oil and gas extraction. In Executive Order 13,990, 86 Fed. Reg. 7037 (2021), the president announced an "abiding commitment . . . to restore and expand our national treasures and monuments." On January 27, 2021, President Biden issued Executive Order 14,008, 86 Fed. Reg. 7619, which promises "to put a new generation of Americans to work conserving our public lands and waters" and commits the nation to the goal of conserving at least 30 percent of public lands and oceans by the year 2030. It also directs the secretary of interior to develop a plan for creating a Civilian Climate Corps, modeled on the Civilian Conservation Corps used during the Great Depression.

## 2. Federal Programs Affecting Private Land Use

In 1964 Stewart Udall, President Kennedy's secretary of interior, wrote a seminal book called *The Quiet Crisis* that popularized the land ethic first articulated in Aldo Leopold's *Sand County Almanac*. As public concern for the environment surged, Congress enacted the Wilderness Act of 1964. In the early 1970s, Congress came close to enacting the National Land Use Policy and Planning Act. Endorsed by President Nixon, the legislation would have required all states to establish land use control programs as a condition for receiving federal funds for highway, airport, and recreation projects. It passed the Senate, but failed to win enactment in the House due to strong opposition from local interests who opposed federal involvement in land use decisions. The resistance to federal involvement in land use issues was illustrated by the political backlash against EPA's efforts to mandate land use controls in federal implementation plans to combat air pollution. Responding to this fallout, Congress expressly prohibited EPA from imposing land use controls (such as parking surcharges, reductions in the number of parking spaces, and controls on the location of facilities that attract motor vehicles) when it amended the Clean Air Act in 1977.

Despite political resistance to a federal regulatory role, federal policies have an enormous influence over the nation's land use patterns. Federal programs with overlapping and often conflicting mandates, including programs for farm aid, highway construction, disaster relief, environmental protection, and public housing, help shape patterns of development and their attendant environmental consequences. As discussed in Chapter 8, the National Environmental Policy Act requires that environmental effects be considered before any major federal action likely to have significant environmental effects is taken. This legislation provides a vehicle for incorporating environmental concerns into the decision-making processes of federal agencies.

Few federal laws directly regulate land use. As discussed in Chapter 6, section 404 of the Clean Water Act has evolved into a major program for protecting wetlands, but its jurisdictional trigger requires the discharge of dredged or fill material into navigable waters. As a result of the Supreme Court's *SWANCC* and *Rapanos* decisions, the jurisdictional reach of section 404 has become a major political battleground.

A rare federal statute that directly regulates land use is the Surface Mining Control and Reclamation Act (SMCRA), 30 U.S.C. §§1201-1328. Enacted by Congress in 1977, this Act prohibits strip mining in areas where it is deemed to be too damaging to the environment. The Act is administered by the Office of Surface Mining in the Department of the Interior. It was upheld by the U.S. Supreme Court in Hodel v. Virginia Surface Mining & Reclamation Association, Inc., 452 U.S. 264 (1981), despite arguments that it violated states' Tenth Amendment rights by interfering with their traditional police power to regulate land use. The Act creates a fund financed by per-tonnage fees on coal producers, which funds efforts by states and tribes to reclaim abandoned mine land through federally approved reclamation projects.

Other federal environmental statutes influence land use patterns without directly regulating them. As discussed in Chapter 4, CERCLA's liability scheme for recovering the costs of remediating releases of hazardous substances has complicated efforts to redevelop contaminated industrial properties. This has spurred EPA to develop a program for encouraging development of brownfields by providing potential developers with assurances concerning future liability. As discussed in Chapter 6, the Clean Water Act has provided federal funds to states to encourage land use planning to prevent nonpoint source pollution. The Coastal Zone Management Act encourages states to adopt plans to preserve coastal areas, and it directs federal agencies to respect these plans by ensuring that they act in a manner consistent with them. The Coastal Barrier Resources Act denies federal financial aid for developments in sensitive coastal areas.

The federal Endangered Species Act (ESA) is affecting development decisions in certain parts of the country due to its prohibition on "taking" any member of a species on the endangered species list. As discussed in Chapter 9, this prohibition encompasses habitat modifications that may harm endangered species unless an incidental take permit has been issued pursuant to an approved habitat conservation plan. The development of habitat conservation plans has helped spawn considerable land use planning in areas where endangered species are found.

For example, in southern California, an unusual partnership of 5 counties, 59 local governments, federal and state officials, and private landowners launched the Natural Community Conservation Planning Program (NCCP) to preserve southern coastal sage scrub habitat, home for the California gnatcatcher and nearly 100 other potentially threatened or endangered species. The program has created a 37,000-acre nature reserve through a series of phased land dedications while creating clear ground rules to channel future development to areas that are less sensitive environmentally. The goal of the program is to enhance the long-term stability of multispecies wildlife and plant communities while accommodating development in rapidly growing urban areas. See *https://wildlife.ca.gov/Conservation/Planning/ NCCP.*

The U.S. Fish and Wildlife Service (FWS) has established a "Partners for Wildlife" program to encourage private landowners to preserve potential habitat for endangered species. In the past, the Endangered Species Act created perverse incentives for landowners to destroy such habitat for fear that the discovery of an endangered species could restrict future development prospects. FWS's program provides assurance to landowners that further development restrictions will not be imposed on their property if they preserve potential wildlife habitat.

The federal environmental laws also influence transportation and construction projects that have a major effect on future land use and development patterns. Section 176(c) of the Clean Air Act requires that local transportation planning conform to state implementation plans (SIPs) for meeting the national ambient air quality standards (NAAQSs). In the 1990 Clean Air Act Amendments, Congress substantially strengthened these conformity requirements by specifying in more detail what was required to satisfy them and by integrating Clean Air Act standards with the transportation planning process prescribed by the Urban Mass Transportation Act. The latter requires each urban area with more than 50,000 people to create a metropolitan planning organization (MPO) to develop regional transportation plans. The Clean Air Act's section 176(c) prohibits federal agencies from approving or funding any transportation plan, program, or project that has not been found to conform with the applicable SIP for meeting national air quality standards. These provisions have been taken seriously by the courts. In Environmental Defense Fund v. EPA, 167 F.3d 641 (D.C. Cir. 1999), the D.C. Circuit invalidated EPA's conformity regulations because they would have permitted federal funding of projects that had not been demonstrated to conform to currently approved SIPs.

In an effort to make federal highway programs more responsive to environmental concerns, Congress enacted the Intermodal Surface Transportation Efficiency Act (ISTEA), 49 U.S.C. §5501, in 1991. ISTEA requires transportation planners to give greater consideration to environmental concerns and to consider alternatives to highway construction, including mass transit projects. The law directs states to spend $1 billion of their annual $20 billion in federal highway funds on air pollution control projects, and it creates a $400 million environmental enhancement fund to be used for acquiring scenic easements, building bike paths, or for historic preservation. Reauthorized in 1998 as the Transportation Equity Act for the 21st Century (TEA-21), the legislation gives increased authority to regional planning bodies to determine how federal transportation funds are spent, and it increases states' flexibility to use highway funds for alternative projects to reduce traffic congestion. TEA-21's Congestion Mitigation and Air Quality program authorizes the Department of Transportation to spend $1.4 billion annually on alternative transit projects to improve air quality. The law also extends a federal tax break to employers who subsidize their employees' use of mass transit, a benefit previously available only to those who subsidized employee parking.

Many other federal programs affect private land use decisions. Federal disaster relief programs have been criticized for promoting excessive development in floodplain areas, which have been estimated to constitute nearly 180 million acres, or more than 7 percent of the land area of the United States. The Great Flood of 1993 in the upper Mississippi and Missouri River basins revived concerns that the establishment of an extensive system of levees and dikes along these rivers had exacerbated flooding by reducing natural floodplain areas. Efforts to protect some communities from flooding actually have worsened localized damage to others, although a report by the Interagency Floodplain Management Review Committee in 1994 found that federal flood control programs have worked overall by substantially reducing damages from flooding.

In the aftermath of the 1993 floods, the federal government provided funds to relocate or elevate more than 12,000 flood-damaged properties and incentives to restore as wetlands some lands that were enrolled in the Emergency Wetlands Reserve Program. Congress revised the National Flood Insurance Program in 1994 to make people who choose to live in floodplains bear a greater share of the risk. Congress prohibited post-disaster federal support to those who could purchase flood insurance but who fail to do so, and it incorporated protection of the natural functions of floodplains into the program's rating system, reducing insurance premiums in communities with good floodplain management programs.

Federal farm programs also have become more sensitive to the environmental consequences of land use management. The Food Security Act of 1985 (FSA), 16 U.S.C. §§3811-3813, required farmers on highly erodible lands to adopt conservation plans employing "best management practices" to control runoff and to implement those plans by 1995 on penalty of loss of federal farm subsidies. Another provision of the 1985 farm bill created a Conservation Reserve Program (CRP) that provides subsidies to farmers who remove land from agricultural production to restore it to a natural state. This program has been enormously valuable. For an excellent account of the development and implementation of the CRP, see James T. Hamilton, Conserving Data in the Conservation Reserve: How a Regulatory Program Runs on Imperfect Information (2010).

The 2008 farm bill included an important step to promote development of markets for ecosystem services, a concept discussed in Chapter 1. Section 2709 of the Food, Conservation and Energy Act of 2008 established the Office of Ecosystem Services and Markets within the U.S. Department of Agriculture. This office is responsible for assisting the secretary of agriculture in establishing science-based, technical guidelines for measuring the environmental services benefits from conservation and land management activities. These guidelines are designed to facilitate the participation of farmers, ranchers, and forest landowners in emerging environmental services markets. Three types of these markets are emerging: private deals negotiated between businesses or between businesses and communities, trading schemes allowing industries to trade credits below an established cap, and public payment mechanisms through which government agencies purchase services.

## NOTES AND QUESTIONS

1. When lobbying on behalf of the Nixon administration's proposal for national land use legislation, Russell Train, who then was the chairman of the Council on Environmental Quality, testified that land use is "the single most important element affecting the quality of our environment which remains substantially unaddressed as a matter of national policy." Diamond, Land Use: Environmental Orphan, Envtl. Forum, Jan./Feb. 1993, at 31, 32. Is Train's assessment still accurate today? In his memoirs Train observes that Nixon's proposed National Land Use Policy Act "was an idea that was probably ahead of its time, and in retrospect it is surprising that the legislation got as far as it did, including passage in the Senate twice." Train, Politics, Pollution and Pandas: An Environmental Memoir 109 (2003). He credits White House aide John Ehrlichman as a major champion of the legislation and concludes that his departure from the White House as a result of the Watergate scandal doomed its prospects for enactment. Train argues that the concept behind the legislation "badly needs revisiting" because local land use decisions have significant consequences for the environment and local governments lack both the broader perspective and financial resources necessary to deal with development pressures. Id.

2. Should Congress enact national land use legislation? What advantages and disadvantages would a federal regulatory program have? See Do We Need a Federal Land Act?, Envtl. Forum, Jan./Feb. 1993, at 28. In light of the welter of different federal laws and programs that influence land use decisions, it has been argued that "rationalization of current federal land-use controls may result in less regulation rather than more." Diamond, Land Use: Environmental Orphan, Envtl. Forum, Jan./Feb. 1993, at 31, 32. Do you agree?

3. Private initiatives to preserve land for environmental purposes have assumed greater importance in recent years. The Nature Conservancy, a private organization with more than 1 million members, purchases land for nature preservation throughout the world. The group manages private nature reserves that protect 125 million acres of habitat in the United States and 71 other countries. See *http://nature.org.*

---

# Land Use Regulation: A Pathfinder

Land use regulation in the United States traditionally has been the province of local governments using *zoning ordinances and building codes* as their principal regulatory tools. Several states have enacted comprehensive *growth management* or *critical area protection legislation* in recent years. States with some form of statewide growth management legislation include Connecticut, Florida, Georgia, Maine, Maryland, New Hampshire, New Jersey, Oregon, Rhode Island, Vermont, and Washington.

A broad array of *federal laws* affect land use patterns, including federal transportation policies, farm programs, flood insurance, disaster relief, lending, and public housing programs. Some federal laws directly encourage state and local land use planning. The **Coastal Zone Management Act (CZMA)** provides federal financial assistance to states that develop approved plans for managing coastal areas and it requires federal agencies to act in a manner consistent with the plans. The **Intermodal Surface Transportation Efficiency Act (ISTEA)** requires state and local governments to use metropolitan planning organizations to develop comprehensive transportation plans and it requires that transportation projects receiving federal funds conform to these plans. The **National Environmental Policy Act (NEPA)** requires federal agencies to prepare environmental impact statements (EISs) before undertaking actions likely to have significant environmental effects. The **Religious Freedom Restoration Act**, which prohibits the government from "substantially burdening" a person's "exercise of religion," has spawned challenges to land use management policies, see, e.g., Navajo Nation v. U.S. Forest Service, 535 F.3d 1058 (9th Cir. 2008) (en banc decision rejecting tribal claim that use of recycled wastewater for snowmaking on public land violated the Act by desecrating a sacred mountain). The **Energy Policy Act of 2005** authorizes FERC to designate national interest corridors for pipeline and transmission facilities to expedite their construction.

A few federal statutes directly regulate activities involving land use. The **Surface Mining Control and Reclamation Act (SMCRA)** requires owners of surface mining operations to restore land after mining operations and it creates a fund to assist states and tribes to reclaim abandoned mine land through federally approved reclamation projects. The **Endangered Species Act (ESA)** requires developers to have approved habitat conservation plans before they can undertake actions that may result in an incidental "take" of protected species. The **Clean Water Act**, which requires developers to have a permit before they discharge dredge or fill materials in the waters of the United States, restricts development in wetlands areas.

*Reports* on land use policy include the report of the Task Force on Land Use and Urban Growth, *The Use of Land: A Citizen's Policy Guide to Urban Growth*, published in 1973, and the report of the Sustainable Use of Land Project, *Land Use in America*, published in 1996. The Environmental Law Institute has published *Municipal Green Building Policies: Strategies for Transforming Building Practices in the Private Sector* (2008), which evaluates various municipal policies for promoting green building. The American Planning Association has published a guidebook for comprehensive planning law that incorporates smart growth and green building codes. Robert Freilich & S. White, *21st Century Land Development Code* (2008).

A broad coalition of groups, called the *Smart Growth Network*, maintains a website providing information on smart growth initiatives at *www.smartgrowth.org*. The U.S. Green Building Council maintains a website at *http://www.usgbc.org/*.

## C.   *LAND USE REGULATION BY STATE AND LOCAL GOVERNMENTS*

Land use regulation has evolved from the initial municipal zoning ordinances, first adopted by American cities early in the twentieth century, to ambitious state-wide programs that seek to manage growth to conform to long-range development plans. While zoning was designed to segregate incompatible land uses, a host of new growth management tools now seek to create economic incentives to improve land use management. These include clustered development or open space zoning, urban growth boundaries, conservation easements, land trusts, tax incentives, transferable development rights (TDRs), and state "smart growth" policies.

Given the high stakes involved in land use decisions, it is not surprising that virtually every one of the tools now used by government to regulate land use has been the subject of legal and political challenges. The materials that follow review state authority to regulate land use, some of the practical and political problems faced by state growth management initiatives, and the question whether land use regulation constitutes a taking of private property for public use for which just compensation must be paid by government.

### *1.   Zoning and State Authority to Regulate Land Use*

The first comprehensive municipal zoning ordinance was adopted by New York City in 1916. Six years later an Ohio municipality, the Village of Euclid, adopted a comprehensive zoning plan. A real estate company that owned 68 acres of vacant land that had been zoned residential challenged the constitutionality of the zoning ordinance. The company alleged that it had held the land for years in anticipation of selling and developing it for industrial uses for which it would have a market value of $10,000 per acre, but that the residential zoning would reduce the property's market value to less than $2,500 per acre. In the case that follows, the U.S. Supreme Court made a landmark ruling rejecting due process and equal protection challenges to the constitutionality of zoning.

## Village of Euclid v. Ambler Realty Co.

272 U.S. 365 (1926)

Mr. Justice Sutherland delivered the opinion of the Court.

Building zone laws are of modern origin. They began in this country about twenty-five years ago. Until recent years, urban life was comparatively simple; but with the great increase and concentration of population, problems have developed, and constantly are developing, which require, and will continue to require, additional restrictions in respect of the use and occupation of private lands in urban communities. Regulations, the wisdom, necessity, and validity of which, as applied to existing conditions, are so apparent that they are now uniformly sustained, a century ago, or even half a century ago, probably would have been rejected as arbitrary and oppressive. Such regulations are sustained, under the complex conditions of our day, for reasons analogous to those which justify traffic regulations, which, before the advent of automobiles and rapid transit street railways, would have been condemned as fatally arbitrary and unreasonable. And in this there is no inconsistency, for while the meaning of constitutional guarantees never varies, the scope of their application must expand or contract to meet the new and different conditions which are constantly coming within the field of their operation. In a changing world, it is impossible that it should be otherwise. But although a degree of elasticity is thus imparted, not to the *meaning*, but to the *application* of constitutional principles, statutes and ordinances, which, after giving due weight to the new conditions, are found clearly not to conform to the Constitution, of course, must fall.

The ordinance now under review, and all similar laws and regulations, must find their justification in some aspect of the police power, asserted for the public welfare. The line which in this field separates the legitimate from the illegitimate assumption of power is not capable of precise delimitation. It varies with circumstances and conditions. A regulatory zoning ordinance, which would be clearly valid as applied to the great cities, might be clearly invalid as applied to rural communities. In solving doubts, the maxim *sic utere tuo ut alienum non laedas*, which lies at the foundation of so much of the common law of nuisances, ordinarily will furnish a fairly helpful clue. And the law of nuisances, likewise, may be consulted, not for the purpose of controlling, but for the helpful aid of its analogies in the process of ascertaining the scope of, the power. Thus the question whether the power exists to forbid the erection of a building of a particular kind or for a particular use, like the question whether a particular thing is a nuisance, is to be determined, not by an abstract consideration of the building or of the thing considered apart, but by considering it in connection with the circumstances and the locality. Sturgis v. Bridgeman, L.R. 11 Ch. 852, 865. A nuisance may be merely a right thing in the wrong place—like a pig in the parlor instead of the barnyard. If the validity of the legislative classification for zoning purposes be fairly debatable, the legislative judgment must be allowed to control.

There is no serious difference of opinion in respect of the validity of laws and regulations fixing the heights of buildings within reasonable limits, the character of materials and methods of construction, and the adjoining area which must be left open, in order to minimize the danger of fire or collapse, the evils of over-crowding, and the like, and excluding from residential sections offensive trades, industries and structures likely to create nuisances. . . .

We find no difficulty in sustaining restriction of the kind thus far reviewed. The serious question in the case arises over the provisions of the ordinance excluding from residential districts, apartment houses, business houses, retail stores and shops, and other like establishments. This question involves the validity of what is really the crux of the more recent zoning legislation, namely, the creation and maintenance of residential districts, from which business and trade of every sort, including hotels and apartment houses, are excluded. Upon that question, this Court has not thus far spoken. . . .

The matter of zoning has received much attention at the hands of commissions and experts, and the results of their investigations have been set forth in comprehensive reports. These reports, which bear every evidence of painstaking consideration, concur in the view that the segregation of residential, business, and industrial buildings will make it easier to provide fire apparatus suitable for the character and intensity of the development in each section; that it will increase the safety and security of home life; greatly tend to prevent street accidents, especially to children, by reducing the traffic and resulting confusion in residential sections; decrease noise and other conditions which produce or intensify nervous disorders; preserve a more favorable environment in which to rear children, etc. With particular reference to apartment houses, it is pointed out that the development of detached house sections is greatly retarded by the coming of apartment houses, which has sometimes resulted in destroying the entire section for private house purposes; that in such sections very often the apartment house is a mere parasite, constructed in order to take advantage of the open spaces and attractive surroundings created by the residential character of the district. Moreover, the coming of one apartment house is followed by others, interfering by their height and bulk with the free circulation of air and monopolizing the rays of the sun which otherwise would fall upon the smaller homes, and bringing, as their necessary accompaniments, the disturbing noises incident to increased traffic and business, and the occupation, by means of moving and parked automobiles, of larger portions of the streets, thus detracting from their safety and depriving children of the privilege of quiet and open spaces for play, enjoyed by those in more favored localities—until, finally, the residential character of the neighborhood and its desirability as a place of detached residences are utterly destroyed. Under these circumstances, apartment houses, which in a different environment would be not only entirely unobjectionable but highly desirable, come very near to being nuisances.

If these reasons, thus summarized, do not demonstrate the wisdom or sound policy in all respects of those restrictions which we have indicated are pertinent to the inquiry, at least, the reasons are sufficiently cogent to preclude us from saying as it must be said before the ordinance can be declared unconstitutional, that such provisions are clearly arbitrary and unreasonable, having no substantial relation to the public health, safety, morals, or general welfare.

## NOTES AND QUESTIONS

1. Under the Court's approach, what must be demonstrated in order for a zoning ordinance to be held to have exceeded the state's police power authority? Who has the burden of proof: the party seeking to challenge the validity of a zoning ordinance or the municipality adopting it?

2. Following the *Euclid* decision, the use of zoning by municipalities spread rapidly. By 1930, nearly a thousand cities with more than two-thirds of the nation's urban population had adopted zoning ordinances. C. Haar & M. Wolf, Land-Use Planning 189 (1989).

3. The basic framework established by the *Euclid* decision has proven to be remarkably durable. Professor Michael Allan Wolf identifies three elements of the decision that "have remained inviolate, despite years of experimentation and variation" with land use regulation:

> First, the Court prescribed a flexible approach in the legislative implementation and judicial review of public land use planning devices. Second, the Court endorsed careful, expert-based planning, eschewing the haphazard vagaries of the market. Third, the Court approved the transfer,

from individual to collective ownership, of development rights above a level often labeled "reasonable return." [Wolf, *Euclid* at Threescore Years and Ten: Is This the Twilight of Environmental and Land-Use Regulation? 30 U. Rich. L. Rev. 961, 963-964 (1996).]

4. Are there limits to the kinds of land uses that the police power properly may be used to exclude? Justice Sutherland suggests that some of the land uses excluded by the zoning ordinance would "come very near to being nuisances" in residential areas. Can only nuisance-like land uses be excluded through zoning? What is the relationship between nuisance law and zoning? See Wolf, Fruits of the "Impenetrable Jungle": Navigating the Boundary Between Land-Use Planning and Environmental Law, 50 J. Urban & Contemp. L. 5 (1996).

5. Zoning has been used to exclude minorities and the poor from certain neighborhoods, as the New Jersey Supreme Court recognized when striking down zoning that prevented construction of low-income housing. Southern Burlington County NAACP v. Township of Mt. Laurel, 336 A.2d 713 (N.J. 1975). The zoning ordinance at issue in *Village of Euclid* initially was invalidated by the trial court because of its potentially discriminatory impacts on minorities and the poor. Village of Euclid v. Ambler Realty Co., 297 F. 307 (N.D. Ohio 1924), rev'd, 272 U.S. 365 (1926). At a time where outdoor parks are a refuge for people looking to get together while social distancing, the Trust for Public Land found that "parks serving mostly low-income households are, on average, four times smaller—and potentially four times more crowded—than parks that serve mostly high-income households." Laurel Wamsley, Parks in Nonwhite Areas Are Half the Size of Ones in Majority-White Areas, Study Says, npr.com (Aug. 5, 2020).

### "Public Use" and the *Kelo* Decision

In June 2005, the U.S. Supreme Court decided a case interpreting the Fifth Amendment Takings Clause's "public use" requirement. In Kelo v. City of New London, 545 U.S. 469 (2005), the Court considered whether the city of New London, Connecticut could use its powers of eminent domain to acquire private, residential property for an economic development area adjacent to the site of the Pfizer Corporation's new global research facility. The city sought to acquire the property to enable a nonprofit private economic development corporation to develop a project including parks, a marina support facility, and privately owned buildings. In the trial court plaintiffs obtained an injunction by arguing that their property was not being acquired for public use in violation of the Fifth Amendment's Takings Clause that requires the payment of compensation for private property acquired for public use. However, the Connecticut Supreme Court reversed, holding that economic development can be a public use and that the acquisition of the property was primarily intended to benefit the public interest, rather than private entities. Kelo v. City of New London, 843 A.2d 500 (2004).

The private landowners in the *Kelo* case hoped that the court would be influenced by the Michigan Supreme Court's July 2004 reversal of its famous *Poletown* decision (Poletown Neighborhood Council v. Detroit, 304 N.W.2d 455 (1981)), which had upheld condemnation of private land to build a plant for the General Motors Corporation. In County of Wayne v. Hathcock, 684 N.W.2d 765 (Mich.

2004), the Michigan Supreme Court held that a county's efforts to use its powers of eminent domain to take private property for a 1,300-acre business and technology park violated the Takings Clause of the Michigan Constitution because the transfer of condemned properties to private parties did not constitute a "public use." While finding ample evidence that the project would benefit the public by providing jobs and reinvigorating the local economy, the court ruled that the transfer of the condemned property to private parties violated the state constitution's Takings Clause because it was not in accordance with three principles governing "public use." The court held that transfer of condemned property to a private entity can satisfy the public use requirement only upon three conditions: "(1) Where 'public necessity of the extreme sort' requires collective action [citing private railroads, canals, or highways]; (2) where the property remains subject to public oversight after the transfer to a private entity; and (3) where the property is selected because of 'facts of independent public significance,' rather than the interests of the private entity to which the property is eventually transferred." 684 N.W.2d at 783. Because the language of the Michigan constitution's Takings Clause is nearly identical to that of the Fifth Amendment to the United States Constitution, this decision may be influential in takings cases outside of Michigan.

However, in *Kelo* the U.S. Supreme Court ruled 5-4 that economic development could be considered a "public purpose" for which states properly could exercise their powers of eminent domain. The Court majority concluded that while the state could not take private land simply to confer a private benefit on a particular private party, economic development projects could satisfy the Fifth Amendment's "public use" requirement if they had a "public purpose." The Court stated that the judiciary should defer to legislative judgments that economic development projects will provide appreciable benefits to a community. Noting that promotion of economic development is a traditional and long-accepted government function, the Court concluded that there is no principled way to distinguish it from other public purposes. Thus, it rejected the landowners' proposal to require the government to show that there is a reasonable certainty that the expected public benefits actually will accrue.

Because it pertains to physical takings for economic development projects, the *Kelo* decision itself is unlikely to have any direct effect on regulatory takings claims involving environmental regulations. However, it generated a strong outcry from the property rights movement, which used it to crusade for new legislative limits on state acquisition of private property. The U.S. House of Representatives adopted a resolution deploring the Court's decision by a vote of 365 to 33 and it voted 231 to 189 to prohibit the use of federal funds "to enforce the judgment of the Supreme Court" in the case. While *Kelo* did not change existing law, see Testimony of Thomas A. Merrill, U.S. Senate Committee on the Judiciary, Sept. 20, 2005, property rights groups effectively harnessed the negative public reaction to it to promote legislation to restrict the use of eminent domain. See Ilya Somin, The Limits of Backlash: Assessing the Political Response to *Kelo*, 93 Minn. L. Rev. 2100 (2009). Within five years of *Kelo* being decided, 43 states had adopted constitutional amendments or statutes to increase protection for property rights. For an argument that *Kelo* is best understood on federalism grounds, see Robert C. Ellickson, Federalism and *Kelo*: A Question for Richard Epstein, 44 Tulsa L. Rev. 751 (2009).

## 2. State Growth Management and Critical Area Protection Programs

Despite a strong tradition of local control over land use decisions, several states have created programs to manage development and to protect environmentally sensitive areas. These laws generally give state-level entities greater authority over land use decisions, premised on the notion that local interests may not have adequate incentives to take into account larger state interests when making development decisions. When the American Law Institute adopted a Model Land Development Code in 1976 that included critical area protection legislation, some states already had established programs to protect critical areas.

In 1972, California voters approved Proposition 20, the "Coastal Conservation Initiative," which created a state Coastal Commission and required it to adopt a coastal protection plan. The California Coastal Plan, adopted in 1975, served as the basis for the 1976 California Coastal Act, which created one of the nation's strictest critical area protection programs. The Act restricts development along the state's 1,100-mile coastline by requiring a permit for any development in the coastal zone. Permits may be approved only if a development conforms with state coastal policies and local coastal protection plans (LCPs) that the Act required all cities and counties in the coastal zone to prepare. The LCPs must be reviewed and approved by the Coastal Commission, which also has the authority to issue permits and to review permits issued by local authorities. The Commission also reviews federal projects for consistency with the state's Coastal Management Program pursuant to the federal Coastal Zone Management Act.

Maryland has a comprehensive critical area protection program, adopted in 1984 to protect the Chesapeake Bay. Maryland's Critical Areas Act created a state Critical Area Commission and required it to adopt strict criteria to control development in a 1,000-foot buffer zone around the Bay. Following the adoption of the criteria, Maryland counties in the critical area were required to develop comprehensive plans that had to be reviewed and approved by the Commission. These plans are to ensure that local land use decisions will conform with the statewide criteria.

When natural resources transcend state boundaries, efforts to protect them require coordination between neighboring states. Maryland's critical areas program was a product of the state's participation in the Chesapeake Bay Program, a collaborative effort to protect and restore the Chesapeake by EPA and the state governments in the Bay's watershed. To protect Lake Tahoe, which is located in the Sierra Nevada range on the border between California and Nevada, the two states formed an interstate compact. The compact, ratified by Congress in 1969, created the Tahoe Regional Planning Agency (TRPA), the first bi-state regional environmental planning agency in the nation. In 1980, the Compact was amended to require the TRPA to adopt a plan prohibiting any development that would exceed the "environmental threshold carrying capacity" of the area, defined by reference to "standards for air quality, water quality, soil conservation, vegetation preservation and noise."

The TRPA's initial long-range regional plan, adopted in April 1984, was challenged in court as inadequate to protect the environment. Faced with a court-ordered moratorium on new building in the area, the TRPA adopted a new Regional Plan in 1987. The plan includes a complex system for rating the suitability of undeveloped land for development. No additional development is permitted on property located in certain areas that carry runoff into the watershed (called "stream environment zones"). However, owners of such property automatically receive certain transferable development rights (TDRs) that can be sold or used to qualify to develop property in a more suitable location. The idea behind using TDRs, which were promoted initially by John Costonis, Development Rights Transfer: An Exploratory Essay, 83 Yale L.J. 75 (1973), is that owners of property located in areas where development is not desired will be compensated for the impact of the development restriction by acquiring valuable rights that can be transferred to owners of property in areas where development is permissible. More than 100 jurisdictions now incorporate TDRs in their land use control schemes.

Statewide land use planning legislation has been adopted in several states. These programs generally require that local land use decisions conform to statewide land use plans. The most far-reaching statewide growth management program was adopted by Oregon in 1973. Liberty, Oregon's Comprehensive Growth Management Program: An Implementation Review and Lessons for Other States, 22 Envtl. L. Rep. 10367 (1992). The Oregon program created a citizen commission, the Land Conservation and Development Commission (LCDC), and charged it with the task of adopting statewide planning goals. The LCDC adopted 14 statewide planning goals and 5 additional goals applicable to the Oregon coast and Willamette River. All Oregon cities and counties were required to adopt comprehensive land use plans to implement the statewide goals, and the LCDC could require revisions in these plans to ensure consistency with the goals. City, county, and regional land use decisions could be appealed to the Oregon Land Use Board of Appeals to ensure consistency with the plans and goals.

The Oregon program required every city to establish an Urban Growth Boundary (UGB) encompassing the city's urban core and sufficient land to accommodate development during the 20- or 50-year planning period. Future urban growth is to be directed inside the UGB, with urban uses generally prohibited outside it. Aside from a few areas where rural development occurred prior to adoption of the program, virtually all private land outside the UGBs is zoned for farming, ranching, or forestry. Land zoned for exclusive farm use (EFU) is strictly regulated to prohibit the construction of residences and other structures unrelated to farming activities.

One of the most thoughtful participants in the Oregon planning process has been Robert Liberty, executive director of 1000 Friends of Oregon, a nonprofit citizens group concerned with growth management. Writing in 1988, Liberty provided some interesting insights into the political difficulties of implementing state land use controls. Liberty, The Oregon Planning Experience: Repeating the Success and Avoiding the Mistakes, 1 Md. Policy Studies 45 (1988). After initial favorable publicity focusing on the benefits of land use controls, press coverage became less favorable as news stories focused on how the program restricted particular individuals' development plans. The initial enthusiasm many administrators had shown for the program diminished in the face of "endlessly repeated cries of outrage over the loss of purely local control over land use decisions," even though the failure of local control had widely been acknowledged as making the legislation necessary. Id.

In November 2004, Oregon voters dealt a potentially serious blow to the state's growth management program by approving a voter initiative called "Measure 37" by a margin of 60 to 40 percent. The measure provides that state or local governments must provide compensation to landowners or forgo enforcement of land use restrictions that reduce the fair market value of property owned by anyone whose family owned the property before the regulations were adopted. The measure does not apply to regulations that restrict activities that are a public nuisance or that protect public health and safety, though it specifies that the measure is to be construed narrowly in favor of providing compensation. Many supporters of the measure who own farmland that would be more valuable if residential development is permitted hoped that the state would simply forgo enforcement of its existing land use regulations. Oregon Governor Ted Kulongoski expressed the view that the state should provide compensation rather than waiving regulations. See John Pendergrass, Oregon Voters Strike at Land Use Regs, 22 Envtl. Forum 6 (Jan./Feb. 2005). A Circuit Court decision invalidating the ballot measure was reversed by the Supreme Court of Oregon in February 2006. MacPherson v. Dep't of Administrative Services, 340 Or. 117 (2006). In November 2007, Oregon voters approved Measure 49 that tightens the standards for receiving compensation under Measure 37 while further restricting development on agricultural, forest, and rural lands.

Florida relaxed its state growth management laws in 2011, giving local governments the ability to opt out of some state controls and revising the definition of urban sprawl to make it less restrictive.

# D. LAND USE CONTROLS AND REGULATORY TAKINGS

The Fifth Amendment of the U.S. Constitution provides that "private property [shall not] be taken for public use, without just compensation." Virtually every form of land use regulation that affects property values has been challenged as a "taking" of private property rights for which government is constitutionally required to provide compensation. While judicial interpretations of the Takings Clause have followed a tortuous and often confusing course, the U.S. Supreme Court and the Federal Court of Claims have been more sympathetic to regulatory takings claims in recent years.

## 1. The Evolution of Regulatory Takings Doctrine

The original understanding of the scope of the Takings Clause appears to have been more limited than subsequent judicial interpretations of it. There is evidence indicating that the framers of the Constitution envisioned the Takings Clause as applying only to actual physical invasions of property. Note, The Origins and Original Significance of the Just Compensation Clause, 94 Yale L.J. 694 (1985). In early cases, government actions that caused a physical invasion of property were considered takings, Pumpelly v. Green Bay Co., 80 U.S. 166 (1871) (construction of dam that flooded private property), while regulations that severely affected the value of property were not. Mugler v. Kansas, 123 U.S. 623 (1887) (compensation not required to brewery owners for ban on production and sale of alcoholic beverages), Hadacheck v. Sebastian, 239 U.S. 394 (1915) (upholding ordinance banning use of brick kilns in neighborhood where brick manufacturer operates).

The notion that regulation could constitute a taking if it destroyed the value of property even if it did not involve a direct physical invasion was endorsed by the Supreme Court in Pennsylvania Coal Co. v. Mahon, 260 U.S. 393 (1922). A statute prohibiting the mining of coal in a manner that could cause the subsidence of homes on the surface was held to be a taking because it effectively abolished the value of underlying mineral rights. Justice Holmes declared that "while property may be regulated to a certain extent, if regulation goes too far it will be recognized as a taking." 260 U.S. at 415. While noting that "[g]overnment hardly could go on if to some extent values incident to property could not be diminished without paying for every such change in general law," Holmes argued that this sort of damage to a private residence was not the kind of public nuisance that must yield to the state's police power. In dissent, Justice Brandeis argued that the regulation was not a taking, but rather "merely the prohibition of a noxious use."

Six years after deciding *Pennsylvania Coal*, the Supreme Court upheld a Virginia law that had been used to require that a tree on private land be destroyed in order to prevent the spread of infection to trees owned by others. In Miller v. Schoene, 276 U.S. 272 (1928), the Supreme Court stated that "[w]here the public interest is involved, preferment of that interest over the property interest of the individual, to the extent even of its destruction, is one of the distinguishing characteristics of every exercise of the police power which affects property." Id. at 279-280. This decision, which did not even cite *Pennsylvania Coal*, suggests that even regulations that result in the destruction of property will not be viewed as takings if they are designed to protect against at least some kinds of harm.

The growth of national regulatory programs to protect the environment in the early 1970s raised concerns that regulatory takings problems would occur with more frequency. In 1973, the Council on Environmental Quality (CEQ) devoted an entire chapter of its fourth annual report to the takings problem. CEQ argued that conceptions of property rights were changing in the wake of society's increased environmental consciousness. Council on Environmental Quality, Envtl. Quality 149-150 (1973). Land was now being viewed as a scarce resource that society had an interest in protecting for future generations.

This notion was reflected in a decision by the Wisconsin Supreme Court in Just v. Marinette County, 201 N.W.2d 761 (1972). In *Just*, property owners challenged a wetlands protection law that barred them from building on lakefront property. The court rejected the takings claim, holding that it was not reasonable for the property owners to expect to build in a wetland. Noting that the property could be used for harvesting wild crops, hunting, and fishing, the court observed that "[t]his is not a case where an owner is prevented from using his land for natural and indigenous uses. . . . The changing of wetlands and swamps to the damage of the general public by upsetting the natural environment and the natural relationship is not a reasonable use of that land which is protected from police power regulation." Id. at 768.

The Supreme Court has had a difficult time articulating a principled method for determining when regulation "goes too far" and constitutes a taking. In the case that follows, the Court conceded that it had been unable to develop any single formula for defining a regulatory taking. The case involved a challenge to New York City's historic landmark preservation law because it prohibited a railroad from building a 55-story office building above Grand Central Terminal, a landmark designated under the law. Under the legislation, owners of historic structures who were denied permission to build received transferable development rights (TDRs) that could be sold to permit development elsewhere.

## Penn Central Transportation Co. v. City of New York

438 U.S. 104 (1978)

Mr. Justice Brennan delivered the opinion of the Court.

Before considering appellants' specific contentions, it will be useful to review the factors that have shaped the jurisprudence of the Fifth Amendment injunction "nor shall private property be taken for public use, without just compensation." The question of what constitutes a "taking" for purposes of the Fifth Amendment has proved to be a problem of considerable difficulty. While this Court has recognized that the Fifth Amendment's guarantee . . . [is] designed to bar Government from forcing some people alone to bear public burdens which, in all fairness and justice, should be borne by the public as a whole, Armstrong v. United States, 364 U.S. 40, 49 (1960), this Court, quite simply, has been unable to develop any "set formula" for determining when "justice and fairness" require that economic injuries caused by public action be compensated by the government, rather than remain disproportionately concentrated on a few persons. Indeed, we have frequently observed that whether a particular restriction will be rendered invalid by the government's failure to pay for any losses proximately caused by it depends largely "upon the particular circumstances [in that] case."

In engaging in these essentially ad hoc, factual inquiries, the Court's decisions have identified several factors that have particular significance. The economic impact of the regulation on the claimant and, particularly, the extent to which the regulation has interfered with distinct investment-backed expectations are, of course, relevant considerations. So, too, is the character of the governmental action. A "taking" may more readily be found when the interference with property can be characterized as a physical invasion by government than when interference arises from some public program adjusting the benefits and burdens of economic life to promote the common good.

"Government hardly could go on if, to some extent, values incident to property could not be diminished without paying for every such change in the general law," Pennsylvania Coal Co. v. Mahon, 260 U.S. 393, 413 (1922), and this Court has accordingly recognized, in a wide variety of contexts, that government may execute laws or programs that adversely affect recognized economic values. Exercises of the taxing power are one obvious example. A second are the decisions in which this Court has dismissed "taking" challenges on the ground that, while the challenged government action caused economic harm, it did not interfere with interests that were sufficiently bound up with the reasonable expectations of the claimant to constitute "property" for Fifth Amendment purposes.

More importantly for the present case, in instances in which a state tribunal reasonably concluded that "the health, safety, morals, or general welfare" would be promoted by prohibiting particular contemplated uses of land, this Court has upheld land use regulations that destroyed or adversely affected recognized real property interests. Zoning laws are, of course, the classic example, which have been viewed as permissible governmental action even when prohibiting the most beneficial use of the property. . . .

In contending that the New York City law has "taken" their property in violation of the Fifth and Fourteenth Amendments, appellants make a series of arguments, which, while tailored to the facts of this case, essentially urge that any substantial restriction imposed pursuant to a landmark law must be accompanied by just compensation if it is to be constitutional. . . .

They first observe that the airspace above the Terminal is a valuable property interest. They urge that the Landmarks Law has deprived them of any gainful use of their "air rights" above the Terminal and that, irrespective of the value of the remainder of their parcel, the city has "taken" their right to this superjacent airspace, thus entitling them to "just compensation" measured by the fair market value of these air rights.

Apart from our own disagreement with appellants' characterization of the effect of the New York City law, the submission that appellants may establish a "taking" simply by showing that they have been denied the ability to exploit a property interest that they heretofore had believed was available for development is quite simply untenable. Were this the rule, this Court would have erred not only in upholding laws restricting the development of air rights, but also in approving those prohibiting both the subjacent, and the lateral development of particular parcels. "Taking" jurisprudence does not divide a single parcel into discrete segments and attempt to determine whether rights in a particular segment have been entirely abrogated. In deciding whether a particular governmental action has effected a taking, this Court focuses rather both on the character of the action and on the nature and extent of the interference with rights in the parcel as a whole—here, the city tax block designated as the "landmark site."

Secondly, appellants, focusing on the character and impact of the New York City law, argue that it effects a "taking" because its operation has significantly diminished the value of the Terminal site. Appellants concede that the decisions sustaining other land use regulations, which, like the New York City law, are reasonably related to the promotion of the general welfare, uniformly reject the proposition that diminution in property value, standing alone, can establish a "taking," see Euclid v. Ambler Realty Co., 272 U.S. 365 (1926) (75% diminution in value caused by zoning law); Hadacheck v. Sebastian, 239 U.S. 394 (1915) (87-1/2% diminution in value); and that the "taking" issue in these contexts is resolved by focusing on the uses the regulations permit. . . .

Stated baldly, appellants' position appears to be that the only means of ensuring that selected owners are not singled out to endure financial hardship for no reason is to hold that any restriction imposed on individual landmarks pursuant to the New York City scheme is a "taking" requiring the payment of "just compensation." Agreement with this argument would, of course, invalidate not just New York City's law, but all comparable landmark legislation in the Nation. We find no merit in it. . . .

Rejection of appellants' broad arguments is not, however, the end of our inquiry, for all we thus far have established is that the New York City law is not rendered invalid by its failure to provide "just compensation" whenever a landmark owner is restricted in the exploitation of property interests, such as air rights, to a greater extent than provided for under applicable zoning laws. We now must consider whether the interference with appellants' property is of such a magnitude that "there must be an exercise of eminent domain and compensation to sustain [it]." Pennsylvania Coal Co. v. Mahon, 260 U.S. at 413. That inquiry may be narrowed to the question of the severity of the impact of the law on appellants' parcel, and its resolution, in turn, requires a careful assessment of the impact of the regulation on the Terminal site.

Unlike the governmental acts in *Goldblatt, Miller, Causby, Griggs,* and *Hadacheck,* the New York City law does not interfere in any way with the present uses of the Terminal. Its designation as a landmark not only permits, but contemplates, that appellants may continue to use the property precisely as it has been used for the past 65 years: as a railroad terminal containing office space and concessions. So the law does not interfere with what must be regarded as Penn Central's primary expectation concerning the use of the parcel. More importantly, on this record, we must regard the New York City law as permitting Penn Central not only to profit from the Terminal but also to obtain a "reasonable return" on its investment.

Appellants, moreover, exaggerate the effect of the law on their ability to make use of the air rights above the Terminal in two respects. First, it simply cannot be maintained, on this record, that appellants have been prohibited from occupying any portion of the airspace above the Terminal. While the Commission's actions in denying applications to construct an office building in excess of 50 stories above the Terminal may indicate that it will refuse to issue a certificate of appropriateness for any comparably sized structure, nothing the Commission has said or done suggests an intention to prohibit any construction above the Terminal. The Commission's report emphasized that whether any construction would be allowed depended upon whether the proposed addition "would harmonize in scale, material, and character with [the Terminal]." Since appellants have not sought approval for the construction of a smaller structure, we do not know that appellants will be denied any use of any portion of the airspace above the Terminal.

Second, to the extent appellants have been denied the right to build above the Terminal, it is not literally accurate to say that they have been denied all use of even those preexisting air rights. Their ability to use these rights has not been abrogated; they are made transferable to at least eight parcels in the vicinity of the Terminal, one or two of which have been found suitable for the construction of new office buildings. Although appellants and others have argued that New York City's transferable development rights program is far from ideal, the New York courts here supportably found that, at least in the case of the Terminal, the rights afforded are valuable. While these rights may well not have constituted "just compensation" if a "taking" had occurred, the rights nevertheless undoubtedly mitigate whatever financial burdens the law has imposed on appellants and, for that reason, are to be taken into account in considering the impact of regulation.

On this record, we conclude that the application of New York City's Landmarks Law has not effected a "taking" of appellants' property. The restrictions imposed are substantially related to the promotion of the general welfare, and not only permit reasonable beneficial use of the landmark site, but also afford appellants opportunities further to enhance not only the Terminal site proper but also other properties.

Affirmed.

## NOTES AND QUESTIONS

1. Justice Rehnquist dissented in an opinion joined by Chief Justice Burger and Justice Stevens. Rehnquist argued that the historic landmark law unfairly singled out one-tenth of 1 percent of all buildings in New York City without providing them the "reciprocity of advantage" that zoning ordinances provide because zoning typically is applied to all property in a designated area. 438 U.S. at 138-140 (Rehnquist, J. dissenting). The Court majority rejected the notion that Penn Central had been singled out, noting that the law was part of "a comprehensive plan to preserve structures of historic or aesthetic interest wherever they might be found in the city," and that it had been applied to 400 structures and 31 historic districts. 438 U.S. at 132.

2. Penn Central had argued that historic landmark preservation "is inevitably arbitrary, or at least subjective, because it is basically a matter of taste," Reply Brief for Appellants 22, thus unavoidably singling out individual landowners for disparate and unfair treatment. The Court rejected this argument. Noting that Penn Central had failed to challenge the designation of Grand Central Terminal as a landmark, the Court stated that "there is no basis whatsoever for a conclusion that courts will have any greater difficulty identifying arbitrary or discriminatory action in the context of landmark regulation than in the context of classic zoning or indeed in any other context." 438 U.S. at 133.

3. What impact, if any, should the provision of TDRs have on takings claims? While the Court did not decide whether TDRs could constitute just compensation, it suggested that their existence was one factor to consider in weighing whether the regulation unreasonably burdened Penn Central. The company owned several nearby properties, at least eight of which were eligible to use the TDRs.

4. In the years following *Penn Central*, the Court continued to follow the categorical rule that permanent physical invasions of property constituted takings no matter how small the invasion. Loretto v. Teleprompter Manhattan CATV Corp., 458 U.S. 419 (1982) (requirement that landlord must permit installation of cable TV access facilities on roof of building is a taking). But the Court continued to be reluctant to define under what circumstances a land use regulation so diminished the value of property as to constitute a taking. In a series of decisions, the Court avoided directly confronting this question by holding that plaintiffs had to apply for variances and exhaust state remedies before a takings claim would be ripe for review. Agins v. City of Tiburon, 447 U.S. 255 (1980); McDonald, Sommer & Prates v. County of Yolo, 477 U.S. 340 (1986). In *Agins* the Court suggested that regulatory action "effects a taking" if it "does not substantially advance legitimate state interests," 447 U.S. at 260, implying a kind of means-ends test for takings apparently derived from due process precedents. When the Court again confronted the regulatory takings question more directly, it was sharply divided.

### 2.   *The Modern Revival of Regulatory Takings Jurisprudence*

Takings jurisprudence remained unsettled as courts acquiesced in states' efforts to subject plaintiffs raising takings claims to lengthy procedural gauntlets. California courts limited the remedy for a taking to invalidation of the regulation, refusing to allow monetary relief. A major shift in takings jurisprudence was signaled in 1987 when the Supreme Court finally confronted regulatory takings claims in three cases decided during the same term. A sharply divided Court rejected one takings claim, remanded another, and upheld a third.

In Keystone Bituminous Coal v. DeBenedictis, 480 U.S. 470 (1987), the Court held, by a 5-4 margin on facts virtually identical to those of *Pennsylvania Coal,* that a law restricting the exercise of mineral rights was not a taking because it was designed to protect public health and safety by preventing subsidence of surface areas. The Court noted that the law responded to what was perceived to be a significant threat to public welfare. It distinguished *Pennsylvania Coal* by noting that there was no basis for finding that the law made it impossible for the company to profitably engage in its business or that it had unduly interfered with investment-backed expectations.

In First English Evangelical Lutheran Church v. County of Los Angeles, 482 U.S. 304 (1987), the Court reviewed a decision that summarily dismissed an inverse condemnation case raising a takings claim on the ground that the only remedy available under California law for a taking was invalidation of the regulation effecting a taking. The plaintiff was a church prohibited from rebuilding a summer camp for handicapped children by a regulation barring rebuilding in a floodplain. The Court held that while invalidation of an ordinance could make any taking a temporary one, the Constitution "requires that the government pay the landowner for the value of the use of the land during this period." 482 U.S. at 319. The Court remanded the case to the state courts to consider whether the ordinance constituted a taking. On remand, the California Court of Appeal had little trouble finding that no taking was involved because the regulation prevented harm to public health and safety. First English Evangelical Lutheran Church v. County of Los Angeles, 210 Cal. App. 3d 1353 (1989).

The third takings case decided by the U.S. Supreme Court, Nollan v. California Coastal Commission, 483 U.S. 825 (1987), challenged a decision by the California Coastal Commission. James and Marilyn Nollan, who had agreed to purchase beachfront property located between two public beach areas, wanted to replace a small bungalow (used as a guest house until it had fallen into disrepair) with a three-bedroom house. They applied for a coastal development permit from the Coastal Commission. The Commission agreed to grant the permit conditioned on the Nollans' granting the public an easement to pass along a portion of their property between the two public beaches. Maintaining that this condition constituted a taking, the Nollans challenged it in court. In a decision authored by Justice Scalia, the Court agreed.

Justice Scalia noted that the easement was tantamount to the kind of permanent physical occupation of property that normally would be a categorical taking. However, he observed that if the permit condition "serves the same legitimate police-power purpose as a refusal to issue the permit," 483 U.S. at 836, it would not be a taking unless a refusal to issue the permit would be a taking. He then examined whether the permit condition "substantially advances legitimate state interests," noting that if the "essential nexus is eliminated" between the "condition substituted for the prohibition" and "the end advanced as the justification for the prohibition," it is no longer constitutionally proper. The Commission argued that the permit condition was reasonably related to the public burden created by the Nollans' new house because it would create a "psychological barrier" to beach access and interfere with "visual access" to the beach. However, the Court concluded that it was "quite impossible to understand how a requirement that people already on public beaches be able to walk across the Nollans' property reduces any obstacles to viewing the beach created by the new house." 483 U.S. at 838. While the Commission could have required the Nollans to provide a viewing platform to provide visual access to the beach, Justice Scalia stated that the physical access requirement "utterly fails to further the end" advanced by the Commission. Thus, the Court held that the permit condition was unconstitutional because it did not serve the same governmental purpose as the development ban.

The three takings cases decided by the Court in 1987 spawned considerably more litigation challenging land use regulations as takings. With encouragement from a more receptive Supreme Court, takings claims were asserted against a wide variety of regulations. Some courts found that certain land use regulations resulted in regulatory takings, basing their findings on a more liberal application of the diminution-in-value approach and a more restrictive view of the public nuisance exemption.

The Supreme Court later agreed to review a decision by South Carolina's highest court, which had rejected a takings challenge to regulations that prohibited a landowner from building a home on undeveloped beachfront property. The Court issued the following decision.

## Lucas v. South Carolina Coastal Council

505 U.S. 1003 (1992)

JUSTICE SCALIA delivered the opinion of the Court, in which REHNQUIST, C.J., and WHITE, O'CONNOR, and THOMAS, JJ., joined.

In 1986, petitioner David H. Lucas paid $975,000 for two residential lots on the Isle of Palms in Charleston County, South Carolina, on which he intended to build single-family homes. In 1988, however, the South Carolina Legislature enacted the Beachfront Management Act (Act), which had the direct effect of barring petitioner from erecting any permanent habitable structures on his two parcels. A state trial court found that this prohibition rendered Lucas' parcels "valueless." This case requires us to decide whether the Act's dramatic effect on the economic value of Lucas' lots accomplished a taking of private property under the Fifth and Fourteenth Amendments requiring the payment of "just compensation.". . .

### III

#### A

Prior to Justice Holmes' exposition in Pennsylvania Coal Co. v. Mahon, 260 U.S. 393 (1922), it was generally thought that the Takings Clause reached only a "direct appropriation" of property, or the functional equivalent of a "practical ouster of [the owner's] possession." Justice Holmes recognized in *Mahon*, however, that if the protection against physical appropriations of private property was to be meaningfully enforced, the government's power to redefine the range of interests included in the ownership of property was necessarily constrained by constitutional limits. If, instead, the uses of private property were subject to unbridled, uncompensated qualification under the police power, "the natural tendency of human nature [would be] to extend the qualification more and more until at last private property disappeared." These considerations gave birth in that case to the oft-cited maxim that, "while property may be regulated to a certain extent, if regulation goes too far it will be recognized as a taking." Nevertheless, our decision in *Mahon* offered little insight into when, and under what circumstances, a given regulation would be seen as going "too far" for purposes of the Fifth Amendment. In 70-odd years of succeeding "regulatory takings" jurisprudence, we have generally eschewed any "set formula" for determining how far is too far, preferring to "engag[e] in . . . essentially ad hoc, factual inquiries," Penn Central Transportation Co. v. New York City, 438 U.S. 104 (1978). We have, however, described at least two discrete categories of regulatory action as compensable without case-specific inquiry into the public interest advanced in support of the restraint. The first encompasses regulations that compel the property owner to suffer a physical "invasion" of his property. In general (at least with regard to permanent invasions), no matter how minute the intrusion, and no matter how weighty the public purpose behind it, we have required compensation. For example, in Loretto v. Teleprompter Manhattan CATV Corp., 458 U.S. 419 (1982), we determined that New York's law requiring landlords to allow television cable companies to emplace cable facilities in their apartment buildings constituted a taking, even though the facilities occupied at most only 1-1/2 cubic feet of the landlords' property.

The second situation in which we have held categorical treatment appropriate is where regulation denies all economically beneficial or productive use of land. See *Agins*, 447 U.S., at 260. As we have said on numerous occasions, the Fifth Amendment is violated when land-use regulation "does not substantially advance legitimate state interests *or denies an owner economically viable use of his land.*"[7]

We have never set forth the justification for this rule. Perhaps it is simply, as Justice Brennan suggested, that total deprivation of beneficial use is, from the landowner's point of view, the equivalent of a physical appropriation. See San Diego

---

7. Regrettably, the rhetorical force of our "deprivation of all economically feasible use" rule is greater than its precision, since the rule does not make clear the "property interest" against which the loss of value is to be measured. When, for example, a regulation requires a developer to leave 90% of a rural tract in its natural state, it is unclear whether we would analyze the situation as one in which the owner has been deprived of all economically beneficial use of the burdened portion of the tract, or as one in which the owner has suffered a mere diminution in value of the tract as a whole. Unsurprisingly, this uncertainty regarding the composition of the denominator in our "deprivation" fraction has produced inconsistent pronouncements by the Court. Compare Pennsylvania Coal Co. v. Mahon, 260 U.S. 393, 414 (1922) (law restricting subsurface extraction of coal held to effect a taking), with Keystone Bituminous Coal Assn. v. DeBenedictis, 480 U.S. 470, 497-502 (1987) (nearly identical law held not to effect a taking); see also id., at 515-520 (Rehnquist, C.J., dissenting). The answer to this difficult question may lie in how the owner's reasonable expectations have been shaped by the State's law of property—i.e., whether and to what degree the State's law has accorded legal recognition and protection to the particular interest in land with respect to which the takings claimant alleges a diminution in (or elimination of) value. In any event, we avoid this difficulty in the present case, since the "interest in land" that Lucas has pleaded (a fee simple interest) is an estate with a rich tradition of protection at common law, and since the South Carolina Court of Common Pleas found that the Beachfront Management Act left each of Lucas' beachfront lots without economic value.

Gas & Electric Co. v. San Diego, 450 U.S., at 652 (Brennan, J., dissenting). "For what is the land but the profits thereof?" 1 E. Coke, Institutes ch. 1, §1 (1st Am. ed. 1812). Surely, at least, in the extraordinary circumstance when *no* productive or economically beneficial use of land is permitted, it is less realistic to indulge our usual assumption that the legislature is simply "adjusting the benefits and burdens of economic life," in a manner that secures an "average reciprocity of advantage" to everyone concerned. And the functional basis for permitting the government, by regulation, to affect property values without compensation — that "Government hardly could go on if to some extent values incident to property could not be diminished without paying for every such change in the general law," — does not apply to the relatively rare situations where the government has deprived a landowner of all economically beneficial uses.

On the other side of the balance, affirmatively supporting a compensation requirement, is the fact that regulations that leave the owner of land without economically beneficial or productive options for its use — typically, as here, by requiring land to be left substantially in its natural state — carry with them a heightened risk that private property is being pressed into some form of public service under the guise of mitigating serious public harm. . . .

We think, in short, that there are good reasons for our frequently expressed belief that when the owner of real property has been called upon to sacrifice *all* economically beneficial uses in the name of the common good, that is, to leave his property economically idle, he has suffered a taking.[8]

### B

The trial court found Lucas' two beachfront lots to have been rendered valueless by respondent's enforcement of the coastal-zone construction ban. Under Lucas' theory of the case, which rested upon our "no economically viable use" statements, that finding entitled him to compensation. Lucas believed it unnecessary to take issue with either the purposes behind the Beachfront Management Act, or the means chosen by the South Carolina Legislature to effectuate those purposes. The South Carolina Supreme Court, however, thought otherwise. In its view, the Beachfront Management Act was no ordinary enactment, but involved an exercise

---

8. Justice Stevens criticizes the "deprivation of all economically beneficial use" rule as "wholly arbitrary," in that "[the] landowner whose property is diminished in value 95% recovers nothing," while the landowner who suffers a complete elimination of value "recovers the land's full value." Post, at 4. This analysis errs in its assumption that the landowner whose deprivation is one step short of complete is not entitled to compensation. Such an owner might not be able to claim the benefit of our categorical formulation, but, as we have acknowledged time and again, "the economic impact of the regulation on the claimant and . . . the extent to which the regulation has interfered with distinct investment-backed expectations" are keenly relevant to takings analysis generally. Penn Central Transportation Co. v. New York City, 438 U.S. 104, 124 (1978). It is true that in at least *some* cases the landowner with 95% loss will get nothing, while the landowner with total loss will recover in full. But that occasional result is no more strange than the gross disparity between the landowner whose premises are taken for a highway (who recovers in full) and the landowner whose property is reduced to 5% of its former value by the highway (who recovers nothing). Takings law is full of these "all-or-nothing" situations.

of South Carolina's "police powers" to mitigate the harm to the public interest that petitioner's use of his land might occasion. By neglecting to dispute the findings enumerated in the Act or otherwise to challenge the legislature's purposes, petitioner "conceded that the beach/dune area of South Carolina's shores is an extremely valuable public resource; that the erection of new construction, inter alia, contributes to the erosion and destruction of this public resource; and that discouraging new construction in close proximity to the beach/dune area is necessary to prevent a great public harm." In the court's view, these concessions brought petitioner's challenge within a long line of this Court's cases sustaining against Due Process and Takings Clause challenges the State's use of its "police powers" to enjoin a property owner from activities akin to public nuisances. See Mugler v. Kansas, 123 U.S. 623 (1887) (law prohibiting manufacture of alcoholic beverages); Hadacheck v. Sebastian, 239 U.S. 394 (1915) (law barring operation of brick mill in residential area); Miller v. Schoene, 276 U.S. 272 (1928) (order to destroy diseased cedar trees to prevent infection of nearby orchards); Goldblatt v. Hempstead, 369 U.S. 590 (1962) (law effectively preventing continued operation of quarry in residential area).

It is correct that many of our prior opinions have suggested that "harmful or noxious uses" of property may be proscribed by government regulation without the requirement of compensation. For a number of reasons, however, we think the South Carolina Supreme Court was too quick to conclude that that principle decides the present case. The "harmful or noxious uses" principle was the Court's early attempt to describe in theoretical terms why government may, consistent with the Takings Clause, affect property values by regulation without incurring an obligation to compensate — a reality we nowadays acknowledge explicitly with respect to the full scope of the State's police power. . . .

"Harmful or noxious use" analysis was, in other words, simply the progenitor of our more contemporary statements that "'land-use regulation does not effect a taking if it substantially advances legitimate state interests.'" *Nollan*, supra, at 834 (quoting *Agins*).

The transition from our early focus on control of "noxious" uses to our contemporary understanding of the broad realm within which government may regulate without compensation was an easy one, since the distinction between "harm-preventing" and "benefit-conferring" regulation is often in the eye of the beholder. It is quite possible, for example, to describe in *either* fashion the ecological, economic, and aesthetic concerns that inspired the South Carolina legislature in the present case. One could say that imposing a servitude on Lucas' land is necessary in order to prevent his use of it from "harming" South Carolina's ecological resources; or, instead, in order to achieve the "benefits" of an ecological preserve. . . . Whether one or the other of the competing characterizations will come to one's lips in a particular case depends primarily upon one's evaluation of the worth of competing uses of real estate. . . .[12]

---

12. In Justice Blackmun's view, even with respect to regulations that deprive an owner of all developmental or economically beneficial land uses, the test for required compensation is whether the legislature has recited a harm-preventing justification for its action. Since such a justification can be formulated in practically every case, this amounts to a test of whether the legislature has a stupid staff. We think the Takings Clause requires courts to do more than insist upon artful harm-preventing characterizations.

[N]oxious-use logic cannot serve as a touchstone to distinguish regulatory "takings"—which require compensation—from regulatory deprivations that do not require compensation. A fortiori, the legislature's recitation of a noxious-use justification cannot be the basis for departing from our categorical rule that total regulatory takings must be compensated. If it were, departure would virtually always be allowed. The South Carolina Supreme Court's approach would essentially nullify *Mahon*'s affirmation of limits to the noncompensable exercise of the police power. Our cases provide no support for this: None of them that employed the logic of "harmful use" prevention to sustain a regulation involved an allegation that the regulation wholly eliminated the value of the claimant's land.

Where the State seeks to sustain regulation that deprives land of all economically beneficial use, we think it may resist compensation only if the logically antecedent inquiry into the nature of the owner's estate shows that the proscribed use interests were not part of his title to begin with. This accords, we think, with our "takings" jurisprudence, which has traditionally been guided by the understandings of our citizens regarding the content of, and the State's power over, the "bundle of rights" that they acquire when they obtain title to property. It seems to us that the property owner necessarily expects the uses of his property to be restricted, from time to time, by various measures newly enacted by the State in legitimate exercise of its police powers; "as long recognized, some values are enjoyed under an implied limitation and must yield to the police power." Pennsylvania Coal Co. v. Mahon, 260 U.S., at 413. And in the case of personal property, by reason of the State's traditionally high degree of control over commercial dealings, he ought to be aware of the possibility that new regulation might even render his property economically worthless (at least if the property's only economically productive use is sale or manufacture for sale), see Andrus v. Allard, 444 U.S. 51, 66-67 (1979) (prohibition on sale of eagle feathers). In the case of land, however, we think the notion pressed by the Council that title is somehow held subject to the "implied limitation" that the State may subsequently eliminate all economically valuable use is inconsistent with the historical compact recorded in the Takings Clause that has become part of our constitutional culture. . . .

Where "permanent physical occupation" of land is concerned, we have refused to allow the government to decree it anew (without compensation), no matter how weighty the asserted "public interests" involved, Loretto v. Teleprompter Manhattan CATV Corp., 458 U.S., at 426—though we assuredly would permit the government to assert a permanent easement that was a preexisting limitation upon the landowner's title. We believe similar treatment must be accorded confiscatory regulation, i.e., regulations that prohibit all economically beneficial use of land: Any limitation so severe cannot be newly legislated or decreed (without compensation), but must inhere in the title itself, in the restrictions that background principles of the State's law of property and nuisance already place upon land ownership. A law or decree with such an effect must, in other words, do no more than duplicate the result that could have been achieved in the courts—by adjacent landowners (or other uniquely affected persons) under the State's law of private nuisance, or by the State under its complementary power to abate nuisances that affect the public generally, or otherwise.

On this analysis, the owner of a lake bed, for example, would not be entitled to compensation when he is denied the requisite permit to engage in a landfilling operation that would have the effect of flooding others' land. Nor the corporate owner of a nuclear generating plant, when it is directed to remove all improvements from its land upon discovery that the plant sits astride an earthquake fault. Such regulatory action may well have the effect of eliminating the land's only economically productive use, but it does not proscribe a proactive use that was previously permissible under relevant property and nuisance principles. The use of these properties for what are now expressly prohibited purposes was *always* unlawful, and (subject to other constitutional limitations) it was open to the State at any point to make the implication of those background principles of nuisance and property law explicit. . . . When, however, a regulation that declares "off-limits" all economically productive or beneficial uses of land goes beyond what the relevant background principles would dictate, compensation must be paid to sustain it.

The "total taking" inquiry we require today will ordinarily entail (as the application of state nuisance law ordinarily entails) analysis of, among other things, the degree of harm to public lands and resources, or adjacent private property, posed by the claimant's proposed activities, see, e.g., Restatement (Second) of Torts §§826, 827, the social value of the claimant's activities and their suitability to the locality in question, see, e.g., id., §§828(a) and (b), 831, and the relative ease with which the alleged harm can be avoided through measures taken by the claimant and the government (or adjacent private landowners) alike. The fact that a particular use has long been engaged in by similarly situated owners ordinarily imports a lack of any common-law prohibition (though changed circumstances or new knowledge may make what was previously permissible no longer so, see Restatement (Second) of Torts, supra, §827, comment g). So also does the fact that other landowners, similarly situated, are permitted to continue the use denied to the claimant.

It seems unlikely that common-law principles would have prevented the erection of any habitable or productive improvements on petitioner's land; they rarely support prohibition of the "essential use" of land. The question, however, is one of state law to be dealt with on remand. We emphasize that to win its case South Carolina must do more than proffer the legislature's declaration that the uses Lucas desires are inconsistent with the public interest, or the conclusory assertion that they violate a common-law maxim such as *sic utere tuo ut alienum non laedas.* As we have said, a "State, by *ipse dixit,* may not transform private property into public property without compensation. . . ." Webb's Fabulous Pharmacies, Inc. v. Beckwith. Instead, as it would be required to do if it sought to restrain Lucas in a common-law action for public nuisance, South Carolina must identify background principles of nuisance and property law that prohibit the uses he now intends in the circumstances in which the property is presently found. Only on this showing can the State fairly claim that, in proscribing all such beneficial uses, the Beachfront Management Act is taking nothing. . . .[18]

---

18. Justice Blackmun decries our reliance on background nuisance principles at least in part because he believes those principles to be as manipulable as we find the "harm prevention"/"benefit conferral" dichotomy. There is no doubt some leeway in a court's interpretation of what existing state law permits — but not remotely as much, we think, as in a legislative crafting of the reasons for its confiscatory regulation. We stress that an affirmative decree eliminating all economically beneficial uses may be defended only if an *objectively reasonable application* of relevant precedents would exclude those beneficial uses in the circumstances in which the land is presently found.

The judgment is reversed and the case remanded for proceedings not inconsistent with this opinion.

JUSTICE KENNEDY, concurring in the judgment.

. . .The South Carolina Court of Common Pleas found that petitioner's real property has been rendered valueless by the State's regulation. The finding appears to presume that the property has no significant market value or resale potential. This is a curious finding, and I share the reservations of some of my colleagues about a finding that a beachfront lot loses all value because of a development restriction. . . .While the Supreme Court of South Carolina on remand need not consider the case subject to this constraint; we must accept the finding as entered below. Accepting the finding as entered, it follows that petitioner is entitled to invoke the line of cases discussing regulations that deprive real property of all economic value. See *Agins.*

The finding of no value must be considered under the Takings Clause by reference to the owner's reasonable, investment-backed expectations. . . .

There is an inherent tendency towards circularity in this synthesis, of course; for if the owner's reasonable expectations are shaped by what courts allow as a proper exercise of governmental authority, property tends to become what courts say it is. Some circularity must be tolerated in these matters, however, as it is in other spheres. The definition, moreover, is not circular in its entirety. The expectations protected by the Constitution are based on objective rules and customs that can be understood as reasonable by all parties involved.

In my view, reasonable expectations must be understood in light of the whole of our legal tradition. The common law of nuisance is too narrow a confine for the exercise of regulatory power in a complex and interdependent society. The State should not be prevented from enacting new regulatory initiatives in response to changing conditions, and courts must consider all reasonable expectations whatever their source. The Takings Clause does not require a static body of state property law; it protects private expectations to ensure private investment. I agree with the Court that nuisance prevention accords with the most common expectations of property owners who face regulation, but I do not believe this can be the sole source of state authority to impose severe restrictions. Coastal property may present such unique concerns for a fragile land system that the State can go further in regulating its development and use than the common law of nuisance might otherwise permit.

The Supreme Court of South Carolina erred, in my view, by reciting the general purposes for which the state regulations were enacted without a determination that they were in accord with the owner's reasonable expectations and therefore sufficient to support a severe restriction on specific parcels of property. The promotion of tourism, for instance, ought not to suffice to deprive specific property of all value without a corresponding duty to compensate. Furthermore, the means as well as the ends of regulation must accord with the owner's reasonable expectations. Here, the State did not act until after the property had been zoned for individual lot development and most other parcels had been improved, throwing the whole burden of the regulation on the remaining lots. This too must be measured in the balance. See *Mahon.*

JUSTICE BLACKMUN, dissenting. . . .

. . . If the state legislature is correct that the prohibition on building in front of the setback line prevents serious harm, then, under this Court's prior cases, the Act is constitutional. "Long ago it was recognized that all property in this country is held under the implied obligation that the owner's use of it shall not be injurious to the community, and the Takings Clause did not transform that principle to one that requires compensation whenever the State asserts its power to enforce it." *Keystone*, 480 U.S. at 491-492 (1987). The Court consistently has upheld regulations imposed to arrest a significant threat to the common welfare, whatever their economic effect on the owner. . . .

This Court repeatedly has recognized the ability of government, in certain circumstances, to regulate property without compensation no matter how adverse the financial effect on the owner may be. More than a century ago, the Court explicitly upheld the right of States to prohibit uses of property injurious to public health, safety, or welfare without paying compensation: "A prohibition simply upon the use of property for purposes that are declared, by valid legislation, to be injurious to the health, morals, or safety of the community, cannot, in any just sense, be deemed a taking or an appropriation of property." *Mugler v. Kansas*. On this basis, the Court upheld an ordinance effectively prohibiting operation of a previously lawful brewery, although the "establishments will become of no value as property." Id.

*Mugler* was only the beginning in a long line of cases. . . .

Ultimately even the Court cannot embrace the full implications of its per se rule: It eventually agrees that there cannot be a categorical rule for a taking based on economic value that wholly disregards the public need asserted. Instead, the Court decides that it will permit a State to regulate all economic value only if the State prohibits uses that would not be permitted under "background principles of nuisance and property law." Until today, the Court explicitly had rejected the contention that the government's power to act without paying compensation turns on whether the prohibited activity is a common-law nuisance. The brewery closed in *Mugler* itself was not a common-law nuisance, and the Court specifically stated that it was the role of the legislature to determine what measures would be appropriate for the protection of public health and safety. In upholding the state action in *Miller [v. Schoene]*, the Court found it unnecessary to "weigh with nicety the question whether the infected cedars constitute a nuisance according to common law; or whether they may be so declared by statute." Instead the Court has relied in the past, as the South Carolina Court has done here, on legislative judgments of what constitutes a harm.

The Court rejects the notion that the State always can prohibit uses it deems a harm to the public without granting compensation because "the distinction between 'harm-preventing' and 'benefit-conferring' regulation is often in the eye of the beholder." Since the characterization will depend "primarily upon one's evaluation of the worth of competing uses of real estate," the Court decides a legislative judgment of this kind no longer can provide the desired "objective, value-free basis" for upholding a regulation. The Court, however, fails to explain how its proposed common law alternative escapes the same trap.

The threshold inquiry for imposition of the Court's new rule, "deprivation of all economically valuable use," itself cannot be determined objectively. As the Court admits, whether the owner has been deprived of all economic value of his property will depend on how "property" is defined. The "composition of the denominator in our 'deprivation' fraction," is the dispositive inquiry. Yet there is no "objective" way to define what that denominator should be. "We have long understood that any land-use regulation can be characterized as the 'total' deprivation of an aptly defined entitlement. . . . Alternatively, the same regulation can always be characterized as a mere partial withdrawal from full, unencumbered ownership of the landholding affected by the regulation. . . ." Michelman, Takings, 1987, 88 Colum. L. Rev. 1600, 1614 (1988).

The Court's decision in *Keystone Bituminous Coal* illustrates this principle perfectly. In *Keystone,* the Court determined that the "support estate" was "merely a part of the entire bundle of rights possessed by the owner." Thus, the Court concluded that the support estate's destruction merely eliminated one segment of the total property. Ibid. The dissent, however, characterized the support estate as a distinct property interest that was wholly destroyed. The Court could agree on no "value-free basis" to resolve this dispute.

Even more perplexing, however, is the Court's reliance on common-law principles of nuisance in its quest for a value-free takings jurisprudence. In determining what is a nuisance at common law, state courts make exactly the decision that the Court finds so troubling when made by the South Carolina General Assembly today: they determine whether the use is harmful. Common-law public and private nuisance law is simply a determination whether a particular use causes harm. See Prosser, Private Action for Public Nuisance, 52 Va. L. Rev. 997, 997 (1966) ("*Nuisance* is a French word which means nothing more than harm"). There is nothing magical in the reasoning of judges long dead. They determined a harm in the same way as state judges and legislatures do today. If judges in the 18th and 19th centuries can distinguish a harm from a benefit, why not judges in the 20th century, and if judges can, why not legislators? There simply is no reason to believe that new interpretations of the hoary common-law nuisance doctrine will be particularly "objective" or "value-free." Once one abandons the level of generality of *sic utere tuo ut alienum non laedas,* one searches in vain, I think, for anything resembling a principle in the common law of nuisance. . . .

I dissent.

[The separate dissent by Justice Stevens is omitted.]

[Justice Souter filed a statement stating that he would dismiss the writ of certiorari as improvidently granted on the ground that the trial court's conclusion that Lucas's land was totally deprived of value was extremely questionable viewing the record as a whole. In his view, this deprived the Court of the ability to clarify the meaning of "total taking," and thus so impaired the ability of the Court to proceed that it should dismiss.]

## NOTES AND QUESTIONS

1. **Total Takings.** Justice Blackmun chides the majority for, among other things, articulating a rule of law applicable only in "extraordinary circumstances." These circumstances, namely, a statute's totally depriving property of value, rendering it "valueless," had never arisen in a Supreme Court decision before. In

announcing a categorical approach to a certain class of takings cases, what precisely is the Court's definition of that category? Does Justice Scalia's reference to "beneficial or *productive* options" imply that complete destruction of the property's value may not be required for an action to fall within this category?

2. **Other-Than-Total Takings.** What formulation of takings doctrine does *Lucas* suggest is to be applied to regulatory situations that fall outside this category of severe limitations on property rights? Responding to an observation by Justice Stevens that it is anomalous that someone who loses 95 percent of a property's value is entitled to no compensation, Justice Scalia in footnote 8 states that it is erroneous to assume that a "landowner whose deprivation is one step short of complete is not entitled to compensation." He notes that "[s]uch an owner might not be able to claim the benefit of our categorical formulation," but he suggests that *Penn Central's* "interfere[nce] with distinct investment-backed expectations" analysis might be "keenly relevant."

Insofar as Justice Scalia's opinion provides any clues about the jurisprudence outside the total takings category, it is truly delphic. Indeed, it is possible to read part of it as *relaxing* takings doctrine in cases of total takings. After quoting a portion of Justice Brennan's opinion in *Penn Central*, in which the Court refused to subject New York City's landmark preservation law to more severe scrutiny because it confers a benefit on society instead of preventing a harm to society (a nuisance), Justice Scalia writes that "harmful or noxious use" analysis was simply a progenitor of the Court's contemporary statements that "land-use regulation does not effect a taking if it substantially advances legitimate state interests," quoting from his own opinion in *Nollan* (which quotes from *Agins*). If that remark is to be taken literally, it means that a substantial connection to a legitimate state interest *always* saves a regulation from the requirement of compensation regardless of the extent of private deprivation or interference with reasonable investment-backed expectations. It would thus seem to be at least a partial rejection of the three-factor formulation of takings doctrine enunciated in *Penn Central* itself, pursuant to which the takings question turned on the character of the governmental action, its interference with reasonable investment-backed expectations, and the economic impact of the action. Most analysts have interpreted this to mean that each of these factors is relevant in all takings analyses, save for those few areas where categorical analysis takes over (permanent physical occupations, *Teleprompter*, and total takings, *Lucas*). Note that the Court subsequently disavowed the "substantially advances legitimate state interests" test in Lingle v. Chevron U.S.A., Inc., 544 U.S. 528 (2005), as discussed later in this chapter.

3. **Deprivation of Value and the "Nuisance Exception."** Without saying so explicitly, Justice Scalia's opinion adopts major portions of Chief Justice Rehnquist's dissents in several important prior cases, especially *Penn Central* and *Keystone Bituminous Coal*, thus indicating that the majority coalition on the Court has indeed shifted to a new, more property-protecting, position. In each of these earlier decisions, the Chief Justice had urged that the so-called nuisance exception to the requirement to compensate for taking private property was narrower than that suggested by the Court majorities. In his view, the Court had become too lax in accepting government arguments that regulation was necessary to prevent a harm to the public, to the degree that the concept of harm prevention had become practically

coterminous with the police power, insofar as anything that the government did under the police power to promote the public health, welfare, and morals could be articulated as a regulation preventing harm to the public health, welfare, and morals. He suggested that common law nuisance principles were the appropriate delimiters of the "nuisance exception."

The second objection the Chief Justice made in these two cases was to disagree with the premise that successfully invoking the nuisance exception meant that compensation never had to be paid. "Though nuisance regulations have been sustained despite a substantial reduction in value," he said in *Keystone*, "we have not accepted the proposition that the State may completely extinguish a property interest or prohibit all use without providing compensation."

It was this second objection of the Chief Justice's, coupled with the changed composition of the Court, that supplied Lucas's litigation strategy: In his brief, Lucas insisted that a person who has been deprived of all economically viable use of land is *always* entitled to compensation, whether or not the state is regulating a common law nuisance. This explains why he did not challenge the state's purposes in enacting the coastal zone protection legislation—debating the validity or nature of those purposes was irrelevant to his theory of the case.

In a significant amicus brief in *support* of Lucas written by Richard Epstein, the Institute for Justice rejected Lucas's theory and stressed the first of Justice Rehnquist's arguments: The "nuisance exception" had to be limited to traditional common law nuisances. Professor Epstein's theory was that compensation must be paid whenever government takes *any* "private property," unless it can justify the regulation as an exercise of common law nuisance principles. The extent of diminution is irrelevant; partial takings are as unconstitutional as total takings.

Justice Scalia's opinion for the *Lucas* majority is an interesting variation on these arguments. He announces that regulations that deprive owners of "all economically beneficial use of land" are a special category as to which the government must pay compensation unless it shows a justification under background principles of nuisance and property law, a category slightly larger than that proposed by Professor Epstein. He also agrees with Epstein's position and Chief Justice Rehnquist's earlier opinions by taking the crucial issue of characterizing the government's purpose out of the hands of the legislature and placing it in the hands of the courts. In permitting a showing of consistency with background nuisance principles to obviate compensation, Justice Scalia's opinion appears to diverge from the Chief Justice's earlier views, which were that total deprivation always required compensation. However, it may be that the Chief Justice concluded that as a matter of actual application, nuisance principles will never, or almost never, justify total deprivations, and thus that he was not shifting ground too much in signing onto Justice Scalia's opinion.

4. **The Remand in *Lucas*.** Because the case had not been litigated on the theory adopted by the Supreme Court, it was remanded for further proceedings. On remand, the lawyers for South Carolina Coastal Council believed that they would not be precluded from litigating the issue of valuelessness and were confident that Lucas would not be owed compensation. They also hoped that the coastal zone construction restrictions could satisfy the nuisance test laid down by the Court. Justice Stevens's omitted opinion stressed his belief that such restrictions may satisfy

the majority's formulation, noting that the 29 deaths and more than $6 billion in property damage suffered in South Carolina from the effects of Hurricane Hugo in 1989 — effects the state argues would have been mitigated if fewer coastal properties were developed — provide a substantial harm-prevention justification, which may pass muster. However, a change in membership had occurred on the South Carolina Supreme Court since it first decided *Lucas,* and on remand the court brushed aside the arguments of the Coastal Council. Without discussing whether Lucas had been deprived of all the value of his property, the court stated in conclusory fashion:

> Coastal Council has not persuaded us that any common law basis exists by which it could restrain Lucas' desired use of his land; nor has our research uncovered any such common law principle. We hold that the sole issue on remand from this Court to the circuit level is a determination of the actual damages Lucas has sustained as the result of his being temporarily deprived of the use of his property. [Lucas v. South Carolina Coastal Council, 424 S.E.2d 484, 486 (S.C. 1992).]

In 1993, the South Carolina Coastal Council agreed to grant Lucas conditional approval to build on his property. Nevertheless, he pursued a temporary takings claim in state court. In July 1993, the Coastal Council settled the litigation by agreeing to purchase Lucas's land for $850,000 plus $725,000 for interest, attorneys' fees, and costs, for a total settlement of $1,575,000. In February 1994, the state resold Lucas's lots. In the fall of 1994, a house was built on the western lot. Two years later, severe coastal erosion undermined the house built on the Lucas lot and an adjacent home. Sandbags, sand scraping, and beach nourishment were used to protect the structures. After Hurricane Irma passed 100 miles west of the Isle of Palms in the fall of 2017, ocean waves were lapping near the foundations of the home built on the Lucas property that was surrounded by an emergency sand berm. Photos of the property at the time are on the casebook website at *www.erlsp.com* (click on "Photo Tour").

5. **Less-Than-Total Takings after *Lucas.*** While *Lucas* is, by its terms, limited to enunciating the doctrine applicable to total takings, lower courts may well combine Justice Scalia's general logic with Justice Stevens's mocking of the distinction between 100 percent and 95 percent deprivation as arbitrary, to apply the same analysis outside the category. If that occurs, takings doctrine will be creeping toward Professor Epstein's position. Epstein, however, is not so confident. He believes that *Lucas* "appears to have adopted a powerful 'hands off' attitude to all forms of partial restriction on land use — a subject that dwarfs the importance of the peculiar circumstances of *Lucas,* the total wipeout of all land uses." Epstein, Yee v. City of Escondido: The Supreme Court Strikes Out Again, 26 Loy. L.A. L. Rev. 3 (1992). Epstein despairs that "the inexorable flow of decided cases under the Takings Clause has been ever more supportive of big government and ever less respectful to the place of private property in our government regime." Id. at 22.

6. **Evolving Conceptions of Property Rights and Environmental Harm.** Recall from Chapter 2 that one of the motivations for legislation in the area of environmental degradation has been a dissatisfaction with the capacity of the common law to mediate between individual property rights and emerging environmental harm

in a manner that adequately respects modern concerns about environmental quality. The 1973 CEQ report emphasized the need for changing our understanding of what constitutes "reasonable use" of private property in light of environmental considerations. Does the majority opinion in *Lucas* inhibit the ability of legislatures legitimately to adjust private and public rights and responsibilities to accommodate changing conceptions of "reasonable use"?

Justice Scalia at least recognizes that common law notions of reasonable use must adjust to changed circumstances. He states that "[t]he fact that a particular use has long been engaged in by similarly situated owners ordinarily imports a lack of any common-law prohibition (though changed circumstances or new knowledge may make what was previously permissible no longer so, see Restatement (Second) of Torts, §827, comment g)." 505 U.S. at 1025. Comment g notes that changes in the character of a locality over time may make a particular land use "wholly unsuited to that locality twenty years later." It does not discuss the possibility that new scientific understanding (e.g., concerning the impact of development on nonpoint source pollution) might justify a finding that an activity long thought to be unobjectionable (e.g., building a home in a critical area) creates a nuisance.

Are only common law notions of harm worthy of the Court's respect? In his concurrence, Justice Kennedy states that "[t]he State should not be prevented from enacting new regulatory initiatives in response to changing conditions, and courts must consider all reasonable expectations whatever their source. The Takings Clause does not require a static body of state property law." 505 U.S. at 1035 (Kennedy, J., concurring). How does this view differ from Justice Scalia's? What regulatory initiatives would Justice Kennedy be more inclined to uphold?

7. **Burdens of Proof of Environmental Harm.** Justice Scalia's fondness for common law principles of nuisance seems to be founded on the notion that legislators are not to be trusted to make honest legislative findings of environmental harm. In footnote 12, he observes that since a "harm-preventing justification . . . can be formulated in practically every case, this amounts to a test of whether the legislature has a stupid staff." 505 U.S. at 1026 n.12. Justice Kennedy seems willing to give legislators more leeway, though he does not think they acted properly in *Lucas*. After *Lucas*, under what circumstances could legislative findings that development in a critical area would create a nuisance avoid takings problems like those encountered by South Carolina's Beachfront Management Act?

8. **Real Property, Personal Property, and Investor Expectations.** Real estate is not the only kind of property whose value may be profoundly altered by government policy decisions. Investors bold enough to place their entire investment portfolios in interest rate options could easily lose everything if they guess wrong about the Federal Reserve Board's future policies. Yet such investors clearly are not entitled to compensation even though government action adjusting interest rates effectively can destroy the value of their property. Why then is real property entitled to special constitutional protection not afforded personal property? Justice Scalia appears to rely on investor expectations as the justification for this distinction. He states that "in the case of personal property, by reason of the State's traditionally high degree of control over commercial dealings, [the investor] ought to be aware of the possibility that new regulation might even render his property economically worthless." 505 U.S. at 1027-1028. If investor expectations are the key

to takings analysis, is a state free to change its conception of property law to alter what expectations concerning the risk of future regulation are reasonable? Richard Epstein argues that a major problem with *Lucas* is the Court's "failure to explain the relationship between expectations and entitlements" and that society should seek to determine what set of entitlements maximizes social welfare. Epstein, Lucas v. South Carolina Coastal Council: A Tangled Web of Expectations, 45 Stan. L. Rev. 1369, 1371 (1993).

9. How would *Just v. Marinette County* be decided under the *Lucas* rationale? Joseph Sax argues that *Lucas* may "be viewed as the Court's long-delayed answer" to *Just*. In his view, Justice Scalia "recognizes the emerging view of land as part of an ecosystem, rather than as purely private property," but sought to send a "clear message" limiting its application: "States may not regulate land use solely by requiring landowners to maintain their property in its natural state as part of a functioning ecosystem, even though those natural functions may be important to the ecosystem." Sax, Property Rights and the Economy of Nature: Understanding *Lucas v. South Carolina Coastal Council*, 45 Stan. L. Rev. 1433, 1438 (1993). A study published on the twenty-fifth anniversary of the *Lucas* decision found that more than 1,700 takings claims had been made premised on *Lucas*, but that only 27 had been successful. Brown & Merriam, On the Twenty-Fifth Anniversary of *Lucas*: Making or Breaking the Takings Claim, 102 Iowa L. Rev. 1847, 1849-1850 (2017).

10. Considerable additional background information on the *Lucas* case is provided in Carol M. Rose, The Story of *Lucas*: Environmental Land Use Regulation Between Developers and the Deep Blue Sea, in Environmental Law Stories 237 (Lazarus & Houck eds., 2005). Information concerning what the papers of the late Justice Harry A. Blackmun reveal about the Court's deliberations in *Lucas* and the takings decisions that preceded it is provided in Robert V. Percival, Environmental Law in the Supreme Court: Highlights from the Blackmun Papers, 35 Envtl. L. Rep. 10637, 10651-10657 (2005).

### The Impact of Post-Regulation Acquisition of Property: The *Palazzolo* Case

While *Lucas* spawned a new wave of regulatory takings litigation, few property owners have been able to make successful takings claims because regulation usually cannot be shown to deprive real estate of all its economic value. Another frequent reason for dismissal of regulatory takings claims has been because the property was acquired after it already had become subject to regulation. For example, in Creppel v. United States, 41 F.3d 627 (Fed. Cir. 1994), the Federal Circuit declared that because claimants need to show interference with "investment-backed expectations," in its view takings doctrine "limits recovery to owners who can demonstrate that they bought their property in reliance on the nonexistence of the challenged regulation." As the court explained: "One who buys with knowledge of a restraint assumes the risk of economic loss. In such a case, the owner presumably paid a discounted price for the property. Compensating him for a 'taking' would confer a windfall." 41 F.3d at 632.

In June 2001, the U.S. Supreme Court rejected the notion that post-regulation acquisition of property serves as an automatic bar to regulatory takings claims. In the case below, the Court, by a 5 to 4 vote, reversed a decision by the Supreme Court of Rhode Island that had rejected a regulatory takings claim on this ground.

The petitioner in the case, Anthony Palazzolo, owned waterfront property, almost all of which had been designated by the state as coastal wetlands that could not be developed without a permit due to enactment of a state coastal protection law in 1971. Palazzolo, whose company had purchased the property in 1959, acquired individual title to the property in 1978 by operation of law after the company's corporate charter was revoked for nonpayment of taxes. After two of Palazzolo's development proposals for the property were rejected by state authorities, he filed an inverse condemnation action in state court, alleging a regulatory taking. The Rhode Island Supreme Court affirmed the trial court's rejection of Palazzolo's takings claims. The court held that the claims were not ripe, that they were barred by Palazzolo's post-regulation acquisition of the property, and that they failed to meet the *Lucas* test because the upland portion of the property retained $200,000 in development value. Palazzolo obtained review of this judgment by the U.S. Supreme Court, which rendered the decision below.

## Palazzolo v. Rhode Island

533 U.S. 606 (2001)

JUSTICE KENNEDY delivered the opinion of the Court.

## II

. . . Since [Pennsylvania Coal Co. v.] Mahon, [260 U.S. 393 (1922)], we have given some, but not too specific, guidance to courts confronted with deciding whether a particular government action goes too far and effects a regulatory taking. First, we have observed, with certain qualifications, that a regulation which "denies all economically beneficial or productive use of land" will require compensation under the Takings Clause. Where a regulation places limitations on land that fall short of eliminating all economically beneficial use, a taking nonetheless may have occurred, depending on a complex of factors including the regulation's economic effect on the landowner, the extent to which the regulation interferes with reasonable investment-backed expectations, and the character of the government action. These inquiries are informed by the purpose of the Takings Clause, which is to prevent the government from "forcing some people alone to bear public burdens which, in all fairness and justice, should be borne by the public as a whole." Armstrong v. United States, 364 U.S. 40, 49 (1960).

Petitioner seeks compensation under these principles. At the outset, however, we face the two threshold considerations invoked by the state court to bar the claim: ripeness, and acquisition which postdates the regulation.

### A

[The Court then rejected the Rhode Island Supreme Court's conclusion that Palazzolo's taking claim was not ripe for review. After reviewing its decision in Williamson County Regional Planning Comm'n v. Hamilton Bank of Johnson City, 473 U.S. 172 (1985), and Suitum v. Tahoe Regional Planning Agency, 520 U.S. 725 (1997), the Court explained:]

These cases stand for the important principle that a landowner may not establish a taking before a land-use authority has the opportunity, using its own reasonable procedures, to decide and explain the reach of a challenged regulation. Under our ripeness rules a takings claim based on a law or regulation which is alleged to go too far in burdening property depends upon the landowner's first having followed reasonable and necessary steps to allow regulatory agencies to exercise their full discretion in considering development plans for the property, including the opportunity to grant any variances or waivers allowed by law. As a general rule, until these ordinary processes have been followed the extent of the restriction on property is not known and a regulatory taking has not yet been established. See *Suitum*, supra, at 736, and n.10 (noting difficulty of demonstrating that "mere enactment" of regulations restricting land use effects a taking). Government authorities, of course, may not burden property by imposition of repetitive or unfair land-use procedures in order to avoid a final decision. Monterey v. Del Monte Dunes at Monterey, Ltd., 526 U.S. 687 (1999).

With respect to the wetlands on petitioner's property, the Council's decisions make plain that the agency interpreted its regulations to bar petitioner from engaging in any filling or development activity on the wetlands, a fact reinforced by the Attorney General's forthright responses to our questioning during oral argument in this case. The rulings of the Council interpreting the regulations at issue, and the briefs, arguments, and candid statements by counsel for both sides, leave no doubt on this point: On the wetlands there can be no fill for any ordinary land use. There can be no fill for its own sake; no fill for a beach club, either rustic or upscale; no fill for a subdivision; no fill for any likely or foreseeable use. And with no fill there can be no structures and no development on the wetlands. Further permit applications were not necessary to establish this point.

As noted above, however, not all of petitioner's parcel constitutes protected wetlands. The trial court accepted uncontested testimony that an upland site located at the eastern end of the property would have an estimated value of $200,000 if developed. While Council approval is required to develop upland property which lies within 200 feet of protected waters, see CRMP §100.1(A), the strict "compelling public purpose" test does not govern proposed land uses on property in this classification, see id., §110, Table 1A, §120. Council officials testified at trial, moreover, that they would have allowed petitioner to build a residence on the upland parcel. . . . So there is no genuine ambiguity in the record as to the extent of permitted development on petitioner's property, either on the wetlands or the uplands. . . .

**B**

We turn to the second asserted basis for declining to address petitioner's takings claim on the merits. When the Council promulgated its wetlands regulations, the disputed parcel was owned not by petitioner but by the corporation of which he was sole shareholder. When title was transferred to petitioner by operation of law, the wetlands regulations were in force. The state court held the postregulation acquisition of title was fatal to the claim for deprivation of all economic use, and to the *Penn Central* claim. While the first holding was couched in terms of background principles of state property law, and the second in terms of petitioner's reasonable investment-backed expectations, the two holdings together amount to a single, sweeping, rule: A purchaser or a successive title holder like petitioner is deemed to have notice of an earlier-enacted restriction and is barred from claiming that it effects a taking.

The theory underlying the argument that post-enactment purchasers cannot challenge a regulation under the Takings Clause seems to run on these lines: Property rights are created by the State. So, the argument goes, by prospective legislation the State can shape and define property rights and reasonable investment-backed expectations, and subsequent owners cannot claim any injury from lost value. After all, they purchased or took title with notice of the limitation.

The State may not put so potent a Hobbesian stick into the Lockean bundle. The right to improve property, of course, is subject to the reasonable exercise of state authority, including the enforcement of valid zoning and land-use restrictions. The Takings Clause, however, in certain circumstances allows a landowner to assert that a particular exercise of the State's regulatory power is so unreasonable or onerous as to compel compensation. Just as a prospective enactment, such as a new zoning ordinance, can limit the value of land without effecting a taking because it can be understood as reasonable by all concerned, other enactments are unreasonable and do not become less so through passage of time or title. Were we to accept the State's rule, the postenactment transfer of title would absolve the State of its obligation to defend any action restricting land use, no matter how extreme or unreasonable. A State would be allowed, in effect, to put an expiration date on the Takings Clause. This ought not to be the rule. Future generations, too, have a right to challenge unreasonable limitations on the use and value of land.

Nor does the justification of notice take into account the effect on owners at the time of enactment, who are prejudiced as well. Should an owner attempt to challenge a new regulation, but not survive the process of ripening his or her claim (which, as this case demonstrates, will often take years), under the proposed rule the right to compensation may not be asserted by an heir or successor, and so may not be asserted at all. The State's rule would work a critical alteration to the nature of property, as the newly regulated landowner is stripped of the ability to transfer the interest which was possessed prior to the regulation. The State may not by this means secure a windfall for itself. See Webb's Fabulous Pharmacies, Inc. v. Beckwith, 449 U.S. 155, 164 (1980) ("[A] State, by *ipse dixit*, may not transform private property into public property without compensation"); cf. Ellickson, Property in Land, 102 Yale L.J. 1315, 1368-1369 (1993) (right to transfer interest in land is a defining characteristic of the fee simple estate). The proposed rule is, furthermore, capricious in effect. The young owner contrasted with the older owner, the owner with the resources to hold contrasted with the owner with the need to sell, would be in different positions. The Takings Clause is not so quixotic. A blanket rule that purchasers with notice have no compensation right when a claim becomes ripe is too blunt an instrument to accord with the duty to compensate for what is taken.

Direct condemnation, by invocation of the State's power of eminent domain, presents different considerations than cases alleging a taking based on a burdensome regulation. In a direct condemnation action, or when a State has physically invaded the property without filing suit, the fact and extent of the taking are known. In such an instance, it is a general rule of the law of eminent domain that any award goes to the owner at the time of the taking, and that the right to compensation is not passed to a subsequent purchaser. See Danforth v. United States, 308 U.S. 271, 284 (1939); 2 Sackman, Eminent Domain, at §5.01[5][d][i] ("It is well settled that when there is a taking of property by eminent domain in compliance with the law, it is the owner of the property *at the time of the taking* who is entitled to compensation"). A challenge to the application of a land-use regulation, by contrast, does not mature until ripeness requirements have been satisfied, under principles we have discussed; until this point an inverse condemnation claim alleging a regulatory taking cannot be maintained. It would be illogical, and unfair, to bar a regulatory takings claim because of the post-enactment transfer of ownership where the steps necessary to make the claim ripe were not taken, or could not have been taken, by a previous owner.

There is controlling precedent for our conclusion. Nollan v. California Coastal Comm'n, 483 U.S. 825 (1987), presented the question whether it was consistent with the Takings Clause for a state regulatory agency to require oceanfront landowners to provide lateral beach access to the public as the condition for a development permit. The principal dissenting opinion observed it was a policy of the California Coastal Commission to require the condition, and that the Nollans, who purchased their home after the policy went into effect, were "on notice that new developments would be approved only if provisions were made for lateral beach access." Id., at 860 (Brennan, J., dissenting). A majority of the Court rejected the proposition. "So long as the Commission could not have deprived the prior owners of the easement without compensating them," the Court reasoned, "the prior owners must be understood to have transferred their full property rights in conveying the lot." Id., at 834, n.2.

It is argued that *Nollan*'s holding was limited by the later decision in Lucas v. South Carolina Coastal Council, 505 U.S. 1003 (1992). In *Lucas* the Court observed that a landowner's ability to recover for a government deprivation of all economically beneficial use of property is not absolute but instead is confined by limitations on the use of land which "inhere in the title itself." Id., at 1029. This is so, the Court reasoned, because the landowner is constrained by those "restrictions that background principles of the State's law of property and nuisance already place upon land ownership." Id., at 1029. It is asserted here that *Lucas* stands for the proposition that any new regulation, once enacted, becomes a background principle of property law which cannot be challenged by those who acquire title after the enactment.

We have no occasion to consider the precise circumstances when a legislative enactment can be deemed a background principle of state law or whether those circumstances are present here. It suffices to say that a regulation that otherwise would be unconstitutional absent compensation is not transformed into a background principle of the State's law by mere virtue of the passage of title. This relative standard would be incompatible with our description of the concept in *Lucas*, which is explained in terms of those common, shared understandings of permissible limitations derived from a State's legal tradition. A regulation or common-law rule cannot be a background principle for some owners but not for others. The determination whether an existing, general law can limit all economic use of property must turn on objective factors, such as the nature of the land use proscribed.

A law does not become a background principle for subsequent owners by enactment itself. *Lucas* did not overrule our holding in *Nollan*, which, as we have noted, is based on essential Takings Clause principles.

For reasons we discuss next, the state court will not find it necessary to explore these matters on remand in connection with the claim that all economic use was deprived; it must address, however, the merits of petitioner's claim under *Penn Central*. That claim is not barred by the mere fact that title was acquired after the effective date of the state-imposed restriction.

## III

As the case is ripe, and as the date of transfer of title does not bar petitioner's takings claim, we have before us the alternative ground relied upon by the Rhode Island Supreme Court in ruling upon the merits of the takings claims. It held that all economically beneficial use was not deprived because the uplands portion of the property can still be improved. On this point, we agree with the court's decision. Petitioner accepts the Council's contention and the state trial court's finding that his parcel retains $200,000 in development value under the State's wetlands regulations. He asserts, nonetheless, that he has suffered a total taking and contends the Council cannot sidestep the holding in *Lucas* "by the simple expedient of leaving a landowner a few crumbs of value."

Assuming a taking is otherwise established, a State may not evade the duty to compensate on the premise that the landowner is left with a token interest. This is not the situation of the landowner in this case, however. A regulation permitting a landowner to build a substantial residence on an 18-acre parcel does not leave the property "economically idle."

In his brief submitted to us petitioner attempts to revive this part of his claim by reframing it. He argues, for the first time, that the upland parcel is distinct from the wetlands portions, so he should be permitted to assert a deprivation limited to the latter. This contention asks us to examine the difficult, persisting question of what is the proper denominator in the takings fraction. Some of our cases indicate that the extent of deprivation effected by a regulatory action is measured against the value of the parcel as a whole, but we have at times expressed discomfort with the logic of this rule, a sentiment echoed by some commentators. Whatever the merits of these criticisms, we will not explore the point here. Petitioner did not press the argument in the state courts, and the issue was not presented in the petition for certiorari. The case comes to us on the premise that petitioner's entire parcel serves as the basis for his takings claim, and, so framed, the total deprivation argument fails. . . .

For the reasons we have discussed, the State Supreme Court erred in finding petitioner's claims were unripe and in ruling that acquisition of title after the effective date of the regulations barred the takings claims. The court did not err in finding that petitioner failed to establish a deprivation of all economic value, for it is undisputed that the parcel retains significant worth for construction of a residence. The claims under the *Penn Central* analysis were not examined, and for this purpose the case should be remanded.

The judgment of the Rhode Island Supreme Court is affirmed in part and reversed in part, and the case is remanded for further proceedings not inconsistent with this opinion.

Justice O'Connor, concurring.

I join the opinion of the Court but with my understanding of how the issues discussed in Part II-B of the opinion must be considered on remand.

Part II-B of the Court's opinion addresses the circumstance, present in this case, where a takings claimant has acquired title to the regulated property after the enactment of the regulation at issue. As the Court holds, the Rhode Island Supreme Court erred in effectively adopting the sweeping rule that the preacquisition enactment of the use restriction *ipso facto* defeats any takings claim based on that use restriction. Accordingly, the Court holds that petitioner's claim under Penn Central Transp. Co. v. City of New York, 438 U.S. 104 (1978), "is not barred by the mere fact that title was acquired after the effective date of the state-imposed restriction."

The more difficult question is what role the temporal relationship between regulatory enactment and title acquisition plays in a proper *Penn Central* analysis. Today's holding does not mean that the timing of the regulation's enactment relative to the acquisition of title is immaterial to the *Penn Central* analysis. Indeed, it would be just as much error to expunge this consideration from the takings inquiry as it would be to accord it exclusive significance. Our polestar instead remains the principles set forth in *Penn Central* itself and our other cases that govern partial regulatory takings. Under these cases, interference with investment-backed expectations is one of a number of factors that a court must examine. Further, the regulatory regime in place at the time the claimant acquires the property at issue helps to shape the reasonableness of those expectations. . . .

We have "identified several factors that have particular significance" in these "essentially ad hoc, factual inquiries." *Penn Central,* 438 U.S., at 124. Two such factors are "[t]he economic impact of the regulation on the claimant and, particularly, the extent to which the regulation has interfered with distinct investment-backed expectations." Another is "the character of the governmental action." Ibid. The purposes served, as well as the effects produced, by a particular regulation inform the takings analysis. *Penn Central* does not supply mathematically precise variables, but instead provides important guideposts that lead to the ultimate determination whether just compensation is required.

The Rhode Island Supreme Court concluded that, because the wetlands regulations predated petitioner's acquisition of the property at issue, petitioner lacked reasonable investment-backed expectations and hence lacked a viable takings claim. The court erred in elevating what it believed to be "[petitioner's] lack of reasonable investment-backed expectations" to "dispositive" status. Ibid. Investment-backed expectations, though important, are not talismanic under *Penn Central.* Evaluation of the degree of interference with investment-backed expectations instead is *one* factor that points toward the answer to the question whether the application of a particular regulation to particular property "goes too far."

Further, the state of regulatory affairs at the time of acquisition is not the only factor that may determine the extent of investment-backed expectations. For example, the nature and extent of permitted development under the regulatory regime vis-à-vis the development sought by the claimant may also shape legitimate expectations without vesting any kind of development right in the property owner. We also have never held that a takings claim is defeated simply on account of the lack of a personal financial investment by a postenactment acquirer of property, such as a donee, heir, or devisee. Courts instead must attend to those circumstances which are probative of what fairness requires in a given case.

If investment-backed expectations are given exclusive significance in the *Penn Central* analysis and existing regulations dictate the reasonableness of those expectations in every instance, then the State wields far too much power to redefine property rights upon passage of title. On the other hand, if existing regulations do nothing to inform the analysis, then some property owners may reap windfalls and an important indicium of fairness is lost. As I understand it, our decision today does not remove the regulatory backdrop against which an owner takes title to property from the purview of the *Penn Central* inquiry. It simply restores balance to that inquiry. Courts properly consider the effect of existing regulations under the rubric of investment-backed expectations in determining whether a compensable taking has occurred. As before, the salience of these facts cannot be reduced to any "set formula." The temptation to adopt what amount to *per se* rules in either direction must be resisted. The Takings Clause requires careful examination and weighing of all the relevant circumstances in this context. The court below therefore must consider on remand the array of relevant factors under *Penn Central* before deciding whether any compensation is due.

JUSTICE SCALIA, concurring.

I write separately to make clear that my understanding of how the issues discussed in Part II-B of the Court's opinion must be considered on remand is not Justice O'Connor's.

The principle that underlies her separate concurrence is that it may in some (unspecified) circumstances be "[un]fai[r]," and produce unacceptable "windfalls," to allow a subsequent purchaser to nullify an unconstitutional partial taking (though, inexplicably, not an unconstitutional total taking) by the government. The polar horrible, presumably, is the situation in which a sharp real estate developer, realizing (or indeed, simply gambling on) the unconstitutional excessiveness of a development restriction that a naive landowner assumes to be valid, purchases property at what it would be worth subject to the restriction, and then develops it to its full value (or resells it at its full value) after getting the unconstitutional restriction invalidated.

This can, I suppose, be called a windfall—though it is not much different from the windfalls that occur every day at stock exchanges or antique auctions, where the knowledgeable (or the venturesome) profit at the expense of the ignorant (or the risk averse). There is something to be said (though in my view not much) for pursuing abstract "fairness" by requiring part or all of that windfall to be returned to the naive original owner, who presumably is the "rightful" owner of it. But there is nothing to be said for giving it instead to the *government*— which not only did not lose something it owned, but is both the *cause* of the miscarriage of "fairness" and the only one of the three parties involved in the miscarriage (government, naive original owner, and sharp real estate developer) which *acted unlawfully*— indeed *unconstitutionally*. Justice O'Connor would eliminate the windfall by giving the malefactor the benefit of its malefaction. It is rather like eliminating the windfall that accrued to a purchaser who bought property at a bargain rate from a thief clothed with the indicia of title, by making him turn over the "unjust" profit *to the thief.*

In my view, the fact that a restriction existed at the time the purchaser took title (other than a restriction forming part of the "background principles of the

State's law of property and nuisance,") should have no bearing upon the determination of whether the restriction is so substantial as to constitute a taking. The "investment-backed expectations" that the law will take into account do not include the assumed validity of a restriction that in fact deprives property of so much of its value as to be unconstitutional. Which is to say that a *Penn Central* taking, no less than a total taking, is not absolved by the transfer of title.

## NOTES AND QUESTIONS

1. Justice Stevens, in an opinion concurring in part and dissenting in part, agreed with the majority only that the case was ripe for review. Stevens maintained that Palazzolo had no standing to make a takings claim because he was not the owner of the property at the time the regulations were adopted. "If the regulations are invalid, either because improper procedures were followed when they were adopted, or because they have somehow gone 'too far,' petitioner may seek to enjoin their enforcement, but he has no right to recover compensation for the value of property taken from someone else."

Justice Ginsburg, joined by Justice Souter and Justice Breyer, dissented. They argued that Palazzolo's takings claim was not ripe for review because the record was ambiguous concerning the extent of permissible development on Palazzolo's land.

Justice Breyer filed a separate dissent in which he agreed with Justice O'Connor "that the simple fact that a piece of property has changed hands (for example, by inheritance) does not always and *automatically* bar a takings claim." Justice Breyer stated that "without in any way suggesting that Palazzolo has any valid takings claim, I believe his postregulatory acquisition of the property (through automatic operation of law) by itself should not prove dispositive." However, he observed that reasonable investment-backed expectations ordinarily "will diminish in force and significance — rapidly and dramatically — as property changes hands over time," a factor that can be taken into account under *Penn Central* to prevent takings doctrine from rewarding strategic property transfers.

2. Although the Court in *Palazzolo* did not hold that Rhode Island's actions constituted a regulatory taking, its decision that post-regulation transfer of title does not automatically bar takings claims could spawn an avalanche of new takings litigation. Under what circumstances can property owners now premise takings claims on regulations that predate their acquisition of title? Will such claims be limited to owners like Palazzolo who acquired the property by operation of law from those who owned the property when the regulations were adopted? Will they be limited to owners who acquired the property from parties who were unable to litigate takings claims to final judgment? Or will all subsequent purchasers be able to assert takings claims?

3. What justifications does the Court offer for its holding? Isn't the Court right that if takings claims may only be asserted by those who own property at the time of regulatory transitions, these owners still are disadvantaged by their inability to transfer their full pre-regulation interests in land? Is Justice Kennedy right when he asserts that states effectively could "put an expiration date on the Takings Clause" if post-enactment transfer of title bars takings claims?

4. In his partial dissent, Justice Stevens argued that only owners of property at the time regulations were adopted had standing to challenge the regulations as

regulatory takings. He argued that "[i]f the existence of valid land-use regulations does not limit the title that the first postenactment purchaser of the property inherits, then there is no reason why such regulations should limit the rights of the second, the third, or the thirtieth purchaser." Is he right? Is there any temporal limit on the ability of subsequent purchasers to bring takings claims?

5. The Court remanded the case for reconsideration of Palazzolo's takings claim under the *Penn Central* test. *Penn Central* focuses on the economic effect of regulation on the landowner, the extent of interference with reasonable investment-backed expectations, and the character of the government action. What relevance, if any, should it have for this analysis that Palazzolo acquired the property in his individual capacity only after the state regulations limiting development in wetlands areas were adopted? Compare Justice O'Connor's concurrence with that of Justice Scalia. Justice O'Connor maintains that post-regulation acquisition of property is one factor to consider in assessing the reasonableness of investment-backed expectations under *Penn Central*. Justice Scalia vehemently disagrees. He argues that it would be better for litigious subsequent purchasers to reap "windfalls" from landowners who naively accept unreasonable regulations than to reward the government for acting as a "thief." Who is right?

6. Suppose that David Lucas, the plaintiff in *Lucas v. South Carolina Coastal Council*, had sold his undeveloped South Carolina property for a token sum rather than pursuing his takings claim. Could the purchaser have successfully challenged the Coastal Council's development restrictions as a regulatory taking prior to *Palazzolo*? Could he do so now if he was not allowed to build?

7. Has *Palazzolo* moved the focus of regulatory takings jurisprudence toward the reasonableness of land use regulation rather than the reasonableness of developer expectations? In his majority opinion Justice Kennedy notes that some regulations are simply "unreasonable and do not become less so through passage of time or title." He notes that it made no difference in *Nollan v. California Coastal Commission*, that the Nollans purchased their home after the Coastal Commission had adopted a requirement that oceanfront landowners provide lateral beach access to the public as a condition for obtaining development permits. How should the reasonableness of land use regulation be assessed when considering regulatory takings claims? *Nollan* involved a regulatory exaction of a physical easement. Could *Palazzolo* presage extension to regulatory takings claims of the kind of "rough proportionality" analysis used to assess the reasonableness of regulatory exactions?

8. Citing *Lucas*, Justice Kennedy suggests that what is reasonable "is explained in terms of those common, shared understandings of permissible limitations derived from a State's legal tradition." What factors should govern assessments of the reasonableness of regulations that respond to new information or changed circumstances? Recall Justice Kennedy's discussion of this issue in *Lucas*. Have Kennedy's views changed?

9. On remand, the Superior Court of Rhode Island, in an unpublished decision, rejected Palazzolo's regulatory takings claim in its entirety. The court concluded that Palazzolo's "proposed residential development of the site would constitute a public nuisance under Rhode Island law." Moreover, it found that because Palazzolo could still build a single home on part of his property and because his proposed larger development was not economically viable, the regulations had

not adversely affected him. The court concluded: "[D]espite wishful thinking on Palazzolo's part, he paid a modest sum to invest in a proposed subdivision that he must have known from the outset was problematic at best. Under the facts and circumstances unique to this case, Palazzolo could have had little or no reasonable expectation to develop the parcel as he has now proposed. Constitutional law does not require the state to guarantee a bad investment." Palazzolo v. State, 2005 WL 1645974 (R.I. Super. Ct. July 5, 2005). A home subsequently was built on the upland part of the property.

### Are Development Moratoria Temporary Takings?: The *Tahoe-Sierra* Decision

In May 1997, the U.S. Supreme Court reversed the Ninth Circuit's dismissal on ripeness grounds of a takings challenge to regulations issued by the Tahoe Regional Planning Agency (TRPA). Suitum v. Tahoe Regional Planning Agency, 520 U.S. 735 (1997). The Court concluded that a landowner's claim that regulations effected a regulatory taking by denying her the right to develop her own property in return for receiving transferable development rights (TDRs) that could be used elsewhere, was not rendered unripe because she had failed to try to sell the TDRs. In April 2002, the U.S. Supreme Court rejected a claim that a temporary moratorium on land development adopted by the TRPA constituted a *per se*, temporary taking under *Lucas*. As noted above, the Tahoe Regional Planning Compact sought to protect Lake Tahoe by creating the TRPA to regulate development around the lake. While formulating its initial land use regulations, the TRPA imposed a temporary moratorium on most residential and all commercial construction on environmentally sensitive land near streams and wetlands. The moratorium, which first became effective on August 24, 1981, was to last only until the new land use regulations became effective. However, their effective date ultimately was postponed from 1984 to 1987 as a result of lawsuits challenging the regulations. A group of 450 landowners ultimately brought suit, claiming that the moratorium constituted a *per se* temporary taking of their property rights.

The Ninth Circuit rejected the property owners' temporary takings claim, though five judges dissented from a denial of rehearing en banc, arguing that the decision conflicted with *First English Evangelical Lutheran Church v. County of Los Angeles*. The U.S. Supreme Court granted review. Before the Supreme Court the Tahoe Regional Planning Agency was represented by John Roberts, a lawyer then in private practice who later became a judge on the U.S. Court of Appeals for the District of Columbia Circuit and subsequently the Chief Justice of the United States. In Tahoe-Sierra Preservation Council, Inc. v. Tahoe Regional Planning Agency, 535 U.S. 302 (2002), the Court refused to adopt a categorical rule that even a lengthy moratorium constituted a *per se* temporary taking. The Court stated that "the answer to the abstract question whether a temporary moratorium effects a taking is neither 'yes, always' nor 'no, never'; the answer depends upon the particular circumstances of the case. Resisting '[t]he temptation to adopt what amount to per se rules in either direction,' Palazzolo v. Rhode Island, 533 U.S. 606, 636 (2001) (O'Connor, J., concurring), we conclude that the circumstances in this case are best analyzed within the *Penn Central* framework." The Court stated that a "rule that required compensation for every delay in the use of property would render routine government processes prohibitively expensive or encourage hasty decisionmaking." 535 U.S. at 321, 335.

Like its *Palazzolo* decision, the Court's *Tahoe-Sierra* decision appears to have diminished the importance of *Lucas* while reinforcing the importance of *Penn*

*Central.* While rejecting the notion that a lengthy moratorium on development can be a *per se* regulatory taking, the *Tahoe-Sierra* Court indicates that the landowners could have raised a takings claim under *Penn Central*'s ad hoc approach, a strategy that the landowners eschewed in the lower courts. While not ruling out the possibility that some moratoria could be deemed a regulatory taking under *Penn Central*, Justice Stevens's majority opinion in *Tahoe-Sierra* indicated that this determination would require careful examination of all relevant circumstances, including the length of the moratorium, its purpose, how broadly it was applied, the landowners' reasonable expectations, and the moratorium's actual impact on property values. After nearly two decades of litigation, challenges to land use controls adopted by the Tahoe Regional Planning Agency (TRPA) during the 1980s finally ended when the U.S. Court of Appeals for the Ninth Circuit on remand dismissed the remaining challenges to the TRPA's actions. Tahoe Sierra Preservation Council, Inc. v. Tahoe Regional Planning Agency, 322 F.3d 1064 (9th Cir. 2003). The court held that most of the claims were barred by the doctrine of res judicata. "After eighteen years of litigation, ten years of which has been devoted to adjudicating harm allegedly done by the 1987 Plan and its implementation, the final judgments of [the earlier litigation] should finally rest in peace." The plaintiffs declined to seek further Supreme Court review of the Ninth Circuit's decision.

### The "Relevant Parcel" Issue: *Murr v. Wisconsin*

In *Murr v. Wisconsin*, owners of riverfront property that consisted of two contiguous lots sought to sell the second lot in order to raise money to renovate a home on the first lot. However, a local zoning ordinance, enacted after the properties were purchased, prohibited building on the second lot on the ground that it was not large enough to develop on its own and the two lots had been "merged" into one that already had a home. The owners claimed that the ordinance constituted a regulatory taking as applied to them because it deprived them of the value of the second lot. The case provided an opportunity for the Supreme Court to address its longstanding doctrine that regulatory takings claims should be evaluated based on the effect of regulation on "the parcel as a whole" by presenting the question of what constitutes the relevant parcel.

## Murr v. Wisconsin

137 S. Ct. 1933 (2017)

Justice Kennedy delivered the opinion of the Court, in which Ginsburg, Breyer, Sotomayor, and Kagan, JJ., joined.

### I

#### A

. . . Petitioners are two sisters and two brothers in the Murr family. Petitioners' parents arranged for them to receive ownership of two lots the family used for recreation along the Lower St. Croix River in the town of Troy, Wisconsin. The lots are adjacent, but the parents purchased them separately, put the title of one in the name of the family business, and later arranged for transfer of the two lots, on different dates, to petitioners. The lots, which are referred to in this litigation as Lots E and F, are described in more detail below.

For the area where petitioners' property is located, the Wisconsin rules prevent the use of lots as separate building sites unless they have at least one acre of land suitable for development. A grandfather clause relaxes this restriction for substandard lots which were "in separate ownership from abutting lands" on January 1, 1976, the effective date of the regulation. The clause permits the use of qualifying lots as separate building sites. The rules also include a merger provision, however, which provides that adjacent lots under common ownership may not be "sold or developed as separate lots" if they do not meet the size requirement. The Wisconsin rules require localities to adopt parallel provisions, so the St. Croix County zoning ordinance contains identical restrictions. The Wisconsin rules also authorize the local zoning authority to grant variances from the regulations where enforcement would create "unnecessary hardship."

### B

Petitioners' parents purchased Lot F in 1960 and built a small recreational cabin on it. In 1961, they transferred title to Lot F to the family plumbing company. In 1963, they purchased neighboring Lot E, which they held in their own names.

The lots have the same topography. A steep bluff cuts through the middle of each, with level land suitable for development above the bluff and next to the water below it. The line dividing Lot E from Lot F runs from the riverfront to the far end of the property, crossing the blufftop along the way. Lot E has approximately 60 feet of river frontage, and Lot F has approximately 100 feet. Though each lot is approximately 1.25 acres in size, because of the waterline and the steep bank they each have less than one acre of land suitable for development. Even when combined, the lots' buildable land area is only 0.98 acres due to the steep terrain.

The lots remained under separate ownership, with Lot F owned by the plumbing company and Lot E owned by petitioners' parents, until transfers to petitioners. Lot F was conveyed to them in 1994, and Lot E was conveyed to them in 1995. . . .

A decade later, petitioners became interested in moving the cabin on Lot F to a different portion of the lot and selling Lot E to fund the project. The unification of the lots under common ownership, however, had implicated the state and local rules barring their separate sale or development. Petitioners then sought variances from the St. Croix County Board of Adjustment to enable their building and improvement plan, including a variance to allow the separate sale or use of the lots. The Board denied the requests, and the state courts affirmed in relevant part. In particular, the Wisconsin Court of Appeals agreed with the Board's interpretation that the local ordinance "effectively merged" Lots E and F, so petitioners "could only sell or build on the single larger lot.". . .

### II

### B

This case presents a question that is linked to the ultimate determination whether a regulatory taking has occurred: What is the proper unit of property against which to assess the effect of the challenged governmental action? Put another way, "[b]ecause our test for regulatory taking requires us to compare the value that has been taken from the property with the value that remains in the property, one of the critical questions is determining how to define the unit of property 'whose value is to furnish the denominator of the fraction.'" *Keystone.* . . .

While the Court has not set forth specific guidance on how to identify the relevant parcel for the regulatory taking inquiry, there are two concepts which the Court has indicated can be unduly narrow.

First, the Court has declined to limit the parcel in an artificial manner to the portion of property targeted by the challenged regulation. In *Penn Central*, for example, the Court rejected a challenge to the denial of a permit to build an office tower above Grand Central Terminal. The Court refused to measure the effect of the denial only against the "air rights" above the terminal, cautioning that "'[t]aking' jurisprudence does not divide a single parcel into discrete segments and attempt to determine whether rights in a particular segment have been entirely abrogated."

In a similar way, in *Tahoe-Sierra*, the Court refused to "effectively sever" the 32 months during which petitioners' property was restricted by temporary moratoria on development "and then ask whether that segment ha[d] been taken in its entirety." That was because "defining the property interest taken in terms of the very regulation being challenged is circular." That approach would overstate the effect of regulation on property, turning "every delay" into a "total ban."

The second concept about which the Court has expressed caution is the view that property rights under the Takings Clause should be coextensive with those under state law. Although property interests have their foundations in state law, the *Palazzolo* Court reversed a state-court decision that rejected a takings challenge to regulations that predated the landowner's acquisition of title. The Court explained that States do not have the unfettered authority to "shape and define property rights and reasonable investment-backed expectations," leaving landowners without recourse against unreasonable regulations.

By the same measure, defining the parcel by reference to state law could defeat a challenge even to a state enactment that alters permitted uses of property in ways inconsistent with reasonable investment-backed expectations. For example, a State might enact a law that consolidates nonadjacent property owned by a single person or entity in different parts of the State and then imposes development limits on the aggregate set. If a court defined the parcel according to the state law requiring consolidation, this improperly would fortify the state law against a takings claim, because the court would look to the retained value in the property as a whole rather than considering whether individual holdings had lost all value.

## III

### A

As the foregoing discussion makes clear, no single consideration can supply the exclusive test for determining the denominator. Instead, courts must consider a number of factors. These include the treatment of the land under state and local law; the physical characteristics of the land; and the prospective value of the regulated land. The endeavor should determine whether reasonable expectations about property ownership would lead a landowner to anticipate that his holdings would be treated as one parcel, or, instead, as separate tracts. The inquiry is objective, and the reasonable expectations at issue derive from background customs and the whole of our legal tradition.

First, courts should give substantial weight to the treatment of the land, in particular how it is bounded or divided, under state and local law. The reasonable expectations of an acquirer of land must acknowledge legitimate restrictions affecting his or her subsequent use and dispensation of the property. A valid takings claim will not evaporate just because a purchaser took title after the law was enacted. A reasonable restriction that predates a landowner's acquisition, however, can be one of the objective factors that most landowners would reasonably consider in forming fair expectations about their property. In a similar manner, a use restriction which is triggered only after, or because of, a change in ownership should also guide a court's assessment of reasonable private expectations.

Second, courts must look to the physical characteristics of the landowner's property. These include the physical relationship of any distinguishable tracts, the parcel's topography, and the surrounding human and ecological environment. In particular, it may be relevant that the property is located in an area that is subject to, or likely to become subject to, environmental or other regulation. Cf. *Lucas*, 505 U.S. at 1035 (Kennedy, J., concurring) ("Coastal property may present such unique concerns for a fragile land system that the State can go further in regulating its development and use than the common law of nuisance might otherwise permit").

Third, courts should assess the value of the property under the challenged regulation, with special attention to the effect of burdened land on the value of other holdings. Though a use restriction may decrease the market value of the property, the effect may be tempered if the regulated land adds value to the remaining property, such as by increasing privacy, expanding recreational space, or preserving surrounding natural beauty. A law that limits use of a landowner's small lot in one part of the city by reason of the landowner's nonadjacent holdings elsewhere may decrease the market value of the small lot in an unmitigated fashion. The absence of a special relationship between the holdings may counsel against consideration of all the holdings as a single parcel, making the restrictive law susceptible to a takings challenge. On the other hand, if the landowner's other property is adjacent to the small lot, the market value of the properties may well increase if their combination enables the expansion of a structure, or if development restraints for one part of the parcel protect the unobstructed skyline views of another part. That, in turn, may counsel in favor of treatment as a single parcel and may reveal the weakness of a regulatory takings challenge to the law.

State and federal courts have considerable experience in adjudicating regulatory takings claims that depart from these examples in various ways. The Court anticipates that in applying the test above they will continue to exercise care in this complex area.

### B

[The Court then rejects the state of Wisconsin's position that the definition of the parcel should be tied entirely to state law as well as the Murrs' argument that lot lines should be presumed to define the relevant parcel.]

## IV

Under the appropriate multifactor standard, it follows that for purposes of determining whether a regulatory taking has occurred here, petitioners' property should be evaluated as a single parcel consisting of Lots E and F together.

First, the treatment of the property under state and local law indicates petitioners' property should be treated as one when considering the effects of the restrictions. As the Wisconsin courts held, the state and local regulations merged Lots E and F. The decision to adopt the merger provision at issue here was for a specific and legitimate purpose, consistent with the widespread understanding that lot lines are not dominant or controlling in every case. Petitioners' land was subject to this regulatory burden, moreover, only because of voluntary conduct in bringing the lots under common ownership after the regulations were enacted. As a result, the valid merger of the lots under state law informs the reasonable expectation they will be treated as a single property.

Second, the physical characteristics of the property support its treatment as a unified parcel. The lots are contiguous along their longest edge. Their rough terrain and narrow shape make it reasonable to expect their range of potential uses might be limited. The land's location along the river is also significant. Petitioners could have anticipated public regulation might affect their enjoyment of their property, as the Lower St. Croix was a regulated area under federal, state, and local law long before petitioners possessed the land.

Third, the prospective value that Lot E brings to Lot F supports considering the two as one parcel for purposes of determining if there is a regulatory taking. Petitioners are prohibited from selling Lots E and F separately or from building separate residential structures on each. Yet this restriction is mitigated by the benefits of using the property as an integrated whole, allowing increased privacy and recreational space, plus the optimal location of any improvements.

The special relationship of the lots is further shown by their combined valuation. Were Lot E separately saleable but still subject to the development restriction, petitioners' appraiser would value the property at only $40,000. We express no opinion on the validity of this figure. We also note the number is not particularly helpful for understanding petitioners' retained value in the properties because Lot E, under the regulations, cannot be sold without Lot F. The point that is useful for these purposes is that the combined lots are valued at $698,300, which is far greater than the summed value of the separate regulated lots (Lot F with its cabin at $373,000, according to respondents' appraiser, and Lot E as an undevelopable plot at $40,000, according to petitioners' appraiser). The value added by the lots' combination shows their complementarity and supports their treatment as one parcel.

The State Court of Appeals was correct in analyzing petitioners' property as a single unit. Petitioners allege that in doing so, the state court applied a categorical rule that all contiguous, commonly owned holdings must be combined for Takings Clause analysis. This does not appear to be the case, however, for the precedent relied on by the Court of Appeals addressed multiple factors before treating contiguous properties as one parcel. The judgment below, furthermore, may be affirmed on any ground permitted by the law and record. To the extent the state court treated the two lots as one parcel based on a bright-line rule, nothing in this opinion approves that methodology, as distinct from the result.

Considering petitioners' property as a whole, the state court was correct to conclude that petitioners cannot establish a compensable taking in these circumstances. Petitioners have not suffered a taking under *Lucas*, as they have not been deprived of all economically beneficial use of their property. They can use the property for residential purposes, including an enhanced, larger residential improvement. The property has not lost all economic value, as its value has decreased by less than 10 percent.

Petitioners furthermore have not suffered a taking under the more general test of *Penn Central.* The expert appraisal relied upon by the state courts refutes any claim that the economic impact of the regulation is severe. Petitioners cannot claim that they reasonably expected to sell or develop their lots separately given the regulations which predated their acquisition of both lots. Finally, the governmental action was a reasonable land-use regulation, enacted as part of a coordinated federal, state, and local effort to preserve the river and surrounding land.

* * *

Like the ultimate question whether a regulation has gone too far, the question of the proper parcel in regulatory takings cases cannot be solved by any simple test. Courts must instead define the parcel in a manner that reflects reasonable expectations about the property. Courts must strive for consistency with the central purpose of the Takings Clause: to "bar Government from forcing some people alone to bear public burdens which, in all fairness and justice, should be borne by the public as a whole." Treating the lot in question as a single parcel is legitimate for purposes of this takings inquiry, and this supports the conclusion that no regulatory taking occurred here.

The judgment of the Wisconsin Court of Appeals is affirmed.

*It is so ordered.*

JUSTICE GORSUCH took no part in the consideration or decision of this case.

CHIEF JUSTICE ROBERTS, with whom JUSTICE THOMAS and JUSTICE ALITO join, dissenting.

The Murr family owns two adjacent lots along the Lower St. Croix River. Under a local regulation, those two properties may not be "sold or developed as separate lots" because neither contains a sufficiently large area of buildable land. The Court today holds that the regulation does not effect a taking that requires just compensation. This bottom-line conclusion does not trouble me; the majority presents a fair case that the Murrs can still make good use of both lots, and that the ordinance is a commonplace tool to preserve scenic areas, such as the Lower St. Croix River, for the benefit of landowners and the public alike.

Where the majority goes astray, however, is in concluding that the definition of the "private property" at issue in a case such as this turns on an elaborate test looking not only to state and local law, but also to (1) "the physical characteristics of the land," (2) "the prospective value of the regulated land," (3) the "reasonable expectations" of the owner, and (4) "background customs and the whole of our legal tradition." Our decisions have, time and again, declared that the Takings Clause protects private property rights as state law creates and defines them. By securing such *established* property rights, the Takings Clause protects individuals from being forced to bear the full weight of actions that should be borne by the public at large. The majority's new, malleable definition of "private property"—adopted solely "for purposes of th[e] takings inquiry,"—undermines that protection.

I would stick with our traditional approach: State law defines the boundaries of distinct parcels of land, and those boundaries should determine the "private property" at issue in regulatory takings cases. Whether a regulation effects a taking of that property is a separate question, one in which common ownership of adjacent property may be taken into account. Because the majority departs from these settled principles, I respectfully dissent. . . .

### B

. . . Because a regulation amounts to a taking if it completely destroys a property's productive use, there is an incentive for owners to define the relevant "private property" narrowly. This incentive threatens the careful balance between property rights and government authority that our regulatory takings doctrine strikes: Put in terms of the familiar "bundle" analogy, each "strand" in the bundle of rights that comes along with owning real property is a distinct property interest. If owners could define the relevant "private property" at issue as the specific "strand" that the challenged regulation affects, they could convert nearly all regulations into *per se* takings.

And so we do not allow it. In *Penn Central Transportation Co. v. New York City*, we held that property owners may not "establish a 'taking' simply by showing that they have been denied the ability to exploit a property interest." In that case, the owner of Grand Central Terminal in New York City argued that a restriction on the owner's ability to add an office building atop the station amounted to a taking of its air rights. We rejected that narrow definition of the "property" at issue, concluding that the correct unit of analysis was the owner's "rights in the parcel as a whole." "[W]here an owner possesses a full 'bundle' of property rights, the destruction of one strand of the bundle is not a taking, because the aggregate must be viewed in its entirety."

The question presented in today's case concerns the "parcel as a whole" language from *Penn Central.* This enigmatic phrase has created confusion about how to identify the relevant property in a regulatory takings case when the claimant owns more than one plot of land. Should the impact of the regulation be evaluated with respect to each individual plot, or with respect to adjacent plots grouped together as one unit? According to the majority, a court should answer this question by considering a number of facts about the land and the regulation at issue. The end result turns on whether those factors "would lead a landowner to anticipate that his holdings would be treated as one parcel, or, instead, as separate tracts."

I think the answer is far more straightforward: State laws define the boundaries of distinct units of land, and those boundaries should, in all but the most exceptional circumstances, determine the parcel at issue. Even in regulatory takings cases, the first step of the Takings Clause analysis is still to identify the relevant "private property." States create property rights with respect to particular "things." And in the context of real property, those "things" are horizontally bounded plots of land. States may define those plots differently—some using metes and bounds, others using government surveys, recorded plats, or subdivision maps. But the definition of property draws the basic line between, as P.G. Wodehouse would put it, *meum* and *tuum*. The question of who owns what is pretty important: The rules must provide a readily ascertainable definition of the land to which a particular bundle of rights attaches that does not vary depending upon the purpose at issue.

Following state property lines is also entirely consistent with *Penn Central.* Requiring consideration of the "parcel as a whole" is a response to the risk that owners will strategically pluck one strand from their bundle of property rights—such as the air rights at issue in *Penn Central*— and claim a complete taking based on that strand alone.

That risk of strategic unbundling is not present when a legally distinct parcel is the basis of the regulatory takings claim. State law defines all of the interests that come along with owning a particular parcel, and both property owners and the government must take those rights as they find them.

The majority envisions that relying on state law will create other opportunities for "gamesmanship" by land owners and States: The former, it contends, "might seek to alter [lot] lines in anticipation of regulation," while the latter might pass a law that "consolidates . . . property" to avoid a successful takings claim. But such obvious attempts to alter the legal landscape in anticipation of a lawsuit are unlikely and not particularly difficult to detect and disarm. We rejected the strategic splitting of property rights in *Penn Central,* and courts could do the same if faced with an attempt to create a takings-specific definition of "private property."

Once the relevant property is identified, the real work begins. To decide whether the regulation at issue amounts to a "taking," courts should focus on the effect of the regulation on the "private property" at issue. Adjacent land under common ownership may be relevant to that inquiry. The owner's possession of such a nearby lot could, for instance, shed light on how the owner reasonably expected to use the parcel at issue before the regulation. If the court concludes that the government's action amounts to a taking, principles of "just compensation" may also allow the owner to recover damages "with regard to a separate parcel" that is contiguous and used in conjunction with the parcel at issue.

In sum, the "parcel as a whole" requirement prevents a property owner from identifying a single "strand" in his bundle of property rights and claiming that interest has been taken. Allowing that strategic approach to defining "private property" would undermine the balance struck by our regulatory takings cases. Instead, state law creates distinct parcels of land and defines the rights that come along with owning those parcels. Those established bundles of rights should define the "private property" in regulatory takings cases. While ownership of contiguous properties may bear on whether a person's plot has been "taken," *Penn Central* provides no basis for disregarding state property lines when identifying the "parcel as a whole.". . .

I respectfully dissent.

[In a separate dissent, Justice Thomas advocates taking "a fresh look at our regulatory takings jurisprudence, to see whether it can be grounded in the original public meaning of the Takings Clause of the Fifth Amendment or the Privileges or Immunities Clause of the Fourteenth Amendment."]

## NOTES AND QUESTIONS

1. The Court majority rejects both alternative tests for determining the relevant parcel advocated by the Murrs and by the state of Wisconsin. Why? Justice

Kennedy, in a portion of his majority opinion not reproduced above, states that a "central dynamic of the Court's regulatory takings jurisprudence . . . is its flexibility." He adopts a multi-factor approach advocated by the county and the federal government as amicus. Which factors does Justice Kennedy state a court should consider in determining the relevant parcel issue?

2. Chief Justice Roberts states that the no taking conclusion "does not trouble" him, yet he rejects Justice Kennedy's multi-factor analysis. What test does he propose instead? Is it possible that the same conclusion concerning whether a taking had occurred could be reached under either the majority's approach or that of the Chief Justice?

3. In his dissent, Chief Justice Roberts acknowledges the potential problem of "strategic unbundling" — subdividing property to create a legally distinct parcel that is undevelopable and then claiming a taking. How would his approach prevent such behavior?

4. In his majority opinion, Justice Kennedy acknowledges that land use restrictions can add value to property "such as by increasing privacy, expanding recreational space, or preserving surrounding natural beauty." A major reason why the Murrs' property was valuable, despite its small size and steep topography, was that few other properties in the area could be developed, preserving the area's beauty. Could the challenged regulations actually represent a kind of "regulatory giving"? If so, how should this be factored into analysis of regulatory takings claims?

### 3.   Regulatory Exactions

Regulators sometimes condition approvals of development projects on the developer's agreement to do something to provide benefits to the public. As discussed earlier, in Nollan v. California Coastal Commission, 483 U.S. 825 (1987), a state coastal commission had sought to condition a permit to build in a coastal area on landowners granting the public an easement over a portion of their beachfront property. However, the Supreme Court held that because the permit condition was not reasonably related to the project's environmental effects (interference with visual access to the beach), the condition represented a taking. The Supreme Court revisited the question of when regulatory exactions become takings in the case below.

## Dolan v. City of Tigard

512 U.S. 374 (1994)

CHIEF JUSTICE REHNQUIST delivered the opinion of the Court.

. . . Petitioner Florence Dolan owns a plumbing and electric supply store located on Main Street in the Central Business District of the city. The store covers approximately 9,700 square feet on the eastern side of a 1.67-acre parcel, which includes a gravel parking lot. Fanno Creek flows through the southwestern corner of the lot and along its western boundary. The year-round flow of the creek renders the area within the creek's 100-year floodplain virtually unusable for commercial development. The city's comprehensive plan includes the Fanno Creek floodplain as part of the city's greenway system.

Petitioner applied to the city for a permit to redevelop the site. Her proposed plans called for nearly doubling the size of the store to 17,600 square feet, and paving a 39-space parking lot. The existing store, located on the opposite side of the parcel, would be razed in sections as construction progressed on the new building. In the second phase of the project, petitioner proposed to build an additional structure on the northeast side of the site for complementary businesses and to provide more parking. The proposed expansion and intensified use are consistent with the city's zoning scheme in the Central Business District. [Community Development Code] CDC §18.66.030.

The City Planning Commission granted petitioner's permit application subject to conditions imposed by the city's CDC. The CDC establishes the following standard for site development review approval:

> Where landfill and/or development is allowed within and adjacent to the 100-year floodplain, the city shall require the dedication of sufficient open land area for greenway adjoining and within the floodplain. This area shall include portions at a suitable elevation for the construction of a pedestrian/bicycle pathway within the floodplain in accordance with the adopted pedestrian/bicycle plan. [CDC §18.120-180.A.8.]

Thus, the Commission required that petitioner dedicate the portion of her property lying within the 100-year floodplain for improvement of a storm drainage system along Fanno Creek and that she dedicate an additional 15-foot strip of land adjacent to the floodplain as a pedestrian/bicycle pathway. The dedication required by that condition encompasses approximately 7,000 square feet, or roughly 10 percent of the property. In accordance with city practice, petitioner could rely on the dedicated property to meet the 15 percent open space and landscaping requirement mandated by the city's zoning scheme. The city would bear the cost of maintaining a landscaped buffer between the dedicated area and the new store. . . .

The Commission made a series of findings concerning the relationship between the dedicated conditions and the projected impacts of petitioner's project. First, the Commission noted that "[i]t is reasonable to assume that customers and employees of the future uses of this site could utilize a pedestrian/bicycle pathway adjacent to this development for their transportation and recreational needs." City of Tigard Planning Commission Final Order No. 91-09 PC. The Commission noted that the site plan has provided for bicycle parking in a rack in front of the proposed building and "[i]t is reasonable to expect that some of the users of the bicycle parking provided for by the site plan will use the pathway adjacent to Fanno Creek if it is constructed." Ibid. In addition, the Commission found that creation of a convenient, safe pedestrian/bicycle pathway system as an alternative means of transportation "could offset some of the traffic demand on [nearby] streets and lessen the increase in traffic congestion." Ibid.

The Commission went on to note that the required floodplain dedication would be reasonably related to petitioner's request to intensify the use of the site given the increase in the impervious surface. The Commission stated that the "anticipated increased storm water flow from the subject property to an already strained creek and drainage basin can only add to the public need to manage the stream channel and floodplain for drainage purposes." Based on this anticipated increased storm water flow, the Commission concluded that "the requirement of dedication of the floodplain area on the site is related to the applicant's plan to intensify development on the site." The Tigard City Council approved the Commission's final order, subject to one minor modification; the City Council reassigned the responsibility for surveying and marking the floodplain area from petitioner to the city's engineering department.

[Arguing that the city's dedication requirements constituted an uncompensated taking of private property, Dolan challenged the Commission's order in the state courts. Because it found that both the pedestrian/bicycle pathway and storm drainage dedication requirements were reasonably related to the impact of the development, the Oregon Supreme Court rejected Dolan's claim.]

## II

The Takings Clause of the Fifth Amendment of the United States Constitution, made applicable to the States through the Fourteenth Amendment, Chicago, B. & Q.R. Co. v. Chicago, 166 U.S. 226, 239 (1897), provides: "[N]or shall private property be taken for public use, without just compensation." One of the principal purposes of the Takings Clause is "to bar Government from forcing some people alone to bear public burdens which, in all fairness and justice, should be borne by the public as a whole." Armstrong v. United States, 364 U.S. 40, 49 (1960). Without question, had the city simply required petitioner to dedicate a strip of land along Fanno Creek for public use, rather than conditioning the grant of her permit to redevelop her property on such a dedication, a taking would have occurred. Nollan, supra, 483 U.S., at 831. Such public access would deprive petitioner of the right to exclude others, "one of the most essential sticks in the bundle of rights that are commonly characterized as property." Kaiser Aetna v. United States, 444 U.S. 164, 176 (1979).

On the other side of the ledger, the authority of state and local governments to engage in land use planning has been sustained against constitutional challenge as long ago as our decision in Euclid v. Ambler Realty Co., 272 U.S. 365 (1926). "Government hardly could go on if to some extent values incident to property could not be diminished without paying for every such change in the general law." Pennsylvania Coal Co. v. Mahon, 260 U.S. 393, 413 (1922). A land use regulation does not effect a taking if it "substantially advance[s] legitimate state interests" and does not "den[y] an owner economically viable use of his land." Agins v. City of Tiburon, 447 U.S. 225, 260 (1980).

The sort of land use regulations discussed in the cases just cited, however, differ in two relevant particulars from the present case. First, they involved essentially legislative determinations classifying entire areas of the city, whereas here the city made an adjudicative decision to condition petitioner's application for a building permit on an individual parcel. Second, the conditions imposed were not simply a limitation on the use petitioner might make of her own parcel, but a requirement that she deed portions of the property to the city. In *Nollan*, supra, we held that governmental authority to exact such a condition was circumscribed by the Fifth and Fourteenth Amendments. Under the well-settled doctrine of "unconstitutional conditions," the government may not require a person to give up a constitutional right — here the right to receive just compensation when property is taken for a public use — in exchange for a discretionary benefit conferred by the government where the property sought has little or no relationship to the benefit. See *Perry v. Sindermann*, 408 U.S. 593 (1972); *Pickering v. Board of Ed. of Township High School Dist.*, 391 U.S. 563, 568 (1968).

Petitioner contends that the city has forced her to choose between the building permit and her right under the Fifth Amendment to just compensation for the public easements. Petitioner does not quarrel with the city's authority to exact some forms of dedication as a condition for the grant of a building permit, but challenges the showing made by the city to justify these exactions. She argues that the city has identified "no special benefits" conferred on her, and has not identified any "special burdens" created by her new store that would justify the particular dedications required from her which are not required from the public at large.

## III

In evaluating petitioner's claim, we must first determine whether the "essential nexus" exists between the "legitimate state interest" and the permit condition exacted by the city. *Nollan*, 483 U.S., at 837. If we find that a nexus exists, we must then decide the required degree of connection between the exactions and the projected impact of the proposed development. We were not required to reach this question in *Nollan*, because we concluded that the connection did not meet even the loosest standard. 483 U.S., at 838. Here, however, we must decide this question.

### A

We addressed the essential nexus question in *Nollan*. The California Coastal Commission demanded a lateral public easement across the Nollan's beachfront lot in exchange for a permit to demolish an existing bungalow and replace it with a three-bedroom house. 483 U.S., at 828. The public easement was designed to connect two public beaches that were separated by the Nollan's property. The Coastal Commission had asserted that the public easement condition was imposed to promote the legitimate state interest of diminishing the "blockage of the view of the ocean" caused by construction of the larger house.

We agreed that the Coastal Commission's concern with protecting visual access to the ocean constituted a legitimate public interest. Id., at 835. We also agreed that the permit condition would have been constitutional "even if it consisted of the requirement that the Nollans provide a viewing spot on their property for passersby with whose sighting of the ocean their new house would interfere." Id., at 836. We resolved, however, that the Coastal Commission's regulatory authority was set completely adrift from its constitutional moorings when it claimed that a nexus existed between visual access to the ocean and a permit condition requiring lateral public access along the Nollan's beachfront lot. Id., at 837. How enhancing the public's ability to "traverse to and along the shorefront" served the same governmental purpose of "visual access to the ocean" from the roadway was beyond our ability to countenance. The absence of a nexus left the Coastal Commission in the position of simply trying to obtain an easement through gimmickry, which converted a valid regulation of land use into "an out-and-out plan of extortion." Ibid., quoting J.E.D. Associates, Inc. v. Atkinson, 432 A.2d 12, 14-15 (N.H. 1981).

No such gimmicks are associated with the permit conditions imposed by the city in this case. Undoubtedly, the prevention of flooding along Fanno Creek and the reduction of traffic congestion in the Central Business District qualify as the type of legitimate public purposes we have upheld. *Agins*, supra, at 260-262. It seems equally obvious that a nexus exists between preventing flooding along Fanno Creek and limiting development within the creek's 100-year floodplain. Petitioner proposes to double the size of her retail store and to pave her now-gravel parking lot, thereby expanding the impervious surface on the property and increasing the amount of storm water run-off into Fanno Creek.

The same may be said for the city's attempt to reduce traffic congestion by providing for alternative means of transportation. In theory, a pedestrian/bicycle pathway provides a useful alternative means of transportation for workers and shoppers: "Pedestrians and bicyclists occupying dedicated spaces for walking and/or bicycling . . . remove potential vehicles from streets, resulting in an overall improvement in total transportation system flow." A. Nelson, Public Provision of Pedestrian and Bicycle Access Ways: Public Policy Rationale and the Nature of Private Benefits 11, Center for Planning Development, Georgia Institute of Technology, Working Paper Series (Jan. 1994). See also Intermodal Surface Transportation Efficiency Act of 1991, Pub. L. 102-240, 105 Stat. 1914 (recognizing pedestrian and bicycle facilities as necessary components of any strategy to reduce traffic congestion).

## B

The second part of our analysis requires us to determine whether the degree of the exactions demanded by the city's permit conditions bear the required relationship to the projected impact of petitioner's proposed development. *Nollan*, supra, at 834, quoting *Penn Central*, 438 U.S. 104, 127 (1978) ("[A] use restriction may constitute a taking if not reasonably necessary to the effectuation of a substantial government purpose"). Here the Oregon Supreme Court deferred to what it termed the "city's unchallenged factual findings" supporting the dedication conditions and found them to be reasonably related to the impact of the expansion of petitioner's business. 854 P.2d, at 443.

The city required that petitioner dedicate "to the city as Greenway all portions of the site that fall within the existing 100-year flood plain [of Fanno Creek] and all property 15 feet above [the floodplain] boundary." In addition, the city demanded that the retail store be designed so as not to intrude into the greenway area. The city relies on the Commission's rather tentative findings that increased storm water flow from petitioner's property "can only add to the public need to manage the [floodplain] for drainage purposes" to support its conclusion that the "requirement of dedication of the floodplain area on the site is related to the applicant's plan to intensify development on the site." City of Tigard Planning Commission Final Order No. 91-09 PC.

The city made the following specific findings relevant to the pedestrian/bicycle pathway:

In addition, the proposed expanded use of this site is anticipated to generate additional vehicular traffic thereby increasing congestion on nearby collector and arterial streets. Creation of a convenient, safe pedestrian/bicycle pathway system as an alternative means of transportation could offset some of the traffic demand on these nearby streets and lessen the increase in traffic congestion. [Id.]

The question for us is whether these findings are constitutionally sufficient to justify the conditions imposed by the city on petitioner's building permit. Since state courts have been dealing with this question a good deal longer than we have, we turn to representative decisions made by them.

In some States, very generalized statements as to the necessary connection between the required dedication and the proposed development seem to suffice. See, e.g., Billings Properties, Inc. v. Yellowstone County, 394 P.2d 182 (Mont. 1964); Jenad, Inc. v. Scarsdale, 218 N.E.2d 673 (N.Y. 1966). We think this standard is too lax to adequately protect petitioner's right to just compensation if her property is taken for a public purpose.

Other state courts require a very exacting correspondence, described as the "specific and uniquely attributable" test. The Supreme Court of Illinois first developed this test in Pioneer Trust & Savings Bank v. Mount Prospect, 176 N.E.2d 799, 802 (Ill. 1961). Under this standard, if the local government cannot demonstrate that its exaction is directly proportional to the specifically created need, the exaction becomes "a veiled exercise of the power of eminent domain and a confiscation of private property behind the defense of police regulations." Id., at 802. We do not think the Federal Constitution requires such exacting scrutiny, given the nature of the interests involved.

A number of state courts have taken an intermediate position, requiring the municipality to show a "reasonable relationship" between the required dedication and the impact of the proposed development. Typical is the Supreme Court of Nebraska's opinion in Simpson v. North Platte, 292 N.W.2d 297, 301 (Neb. 1980), where that court stated:

> The distinction, therefore, which must be made between an appropriate exercise of the police power and an improper exercise of eminent domain is whether the requirement has some reasonable relationship or nexus to the use to which the property is being made or is merely being used as an excuse for taking property simply because at that particular moment the landowner is asking the city for some license or permit.

Thus, the court held that a city may not require a property owner to dedicate private property for some future public use as a condition of obtaining a building permit when such future use is not "occasioned by the construction sought to be permitted." Id., at 302.

Some form of the reasonable relationship test has been adopted in many other jurisdictions. . . .

We think the "reasonable relationship" test adopted by a majority of the state courts is closer to the federal constitutional norm than either of those previously discussed. But we do not adopt it as such, partly because the term "reasonable relationship" seems confusingly similar to the term "rational basis" which describes the minimal level of scrutiny under the Equal Protection Clause of the Fourteenth Amendment. We think a term such as "rough proportionality" best encapsulates what we hold to be the requirement of the Fifth Amendment. No precise mathematical calculation is required, but the city must make some sort of individualized determination that the required dedication is related both in nature and extent to the impact of the proposed development. . . .

It is axiomatic that increasing the amount of impervious surface will increase the quantity and rate of storm water flow from petitioner's property. Record, Doc. No. F, ch. 4, p. 4-29. Therefore, keeping the floodplain open and free from development would likely confine the pressures on Fanno Creek created by petitioner's development. In fact, because petitioner's property lies within the Central Business District, the Community Development Code already required that petitioner leave 15 percent of it as open space and the undeveloped floodplain would have nearly satisfied that requirement. But the city demanded more—it not only wanted petitioner not to build in the floodplain, but it also wanted petitioner's property along Fanno Creek for its Greenway system. The city has never said why a public greenway, as opposed to a private one, was required in the interest of flood control.

The difference to petitioner, of course, is the loss of her ability to exclude others. As we have noted, this right to exclude others is "one of the most essential sticks in the bundle of rights that are commonly characterized as property." *Kaiser Aetna*, 444 U.S., at 176. It is difficult to see why recreational visitors trampling along petitioner's floodplain easement are sufficiently related to the city's legitimate interest in reducing flooding problems along Fanno Creek, and the city has not attempted to make any individualized determination to support this part of its request.

The city contends that recreational easement along the Greenway is only ancillary to the city's chief purpose in controlling flood hazards. It further asserts that unlike the residential property at issue in *Nollan*, petitioner's property is commercial in character and, therefore, her right to exclude others is compromised. United States v. Orito, 413 U.S. 139, 142 (1973) ("The Constitution extends special safeguards to the privacy of the home"). The city maintains that "there is nothing to suggest that preventing [petitioner] from prohibiting [the easements] will unreasonably impair the value of [her] property as a [retail store]." PruneYard Shopping Center v. Robins, 447 U.S. 74, 83 (1980).

Admittedly, petitioner wants to build a bigger store to attract members of the public to her property. She also wants, however, to be able to control the time and manner in which they enter. The recreational easement on the Greenway is different in character from the exercise of state-protected rights of free expression and petition that we permitted in *PruneYard*. In *PruneYard*, we held that a major private shopping center that attracted more than 25,000 daily patrons had to provide access to persons exercising their state constitutional rights to distribute pamphlets and ask passersby to sign their petitions. Id., at 85. We based our decision, in part, on the fact that the shopping center "may restrict expressive activity by adopting time, place, and manner regulations that will minimize any interference with its commercial functions." Id., at 83. By contrast, the city wants to impose a permanent recreational easement upon petitioner's property that borders Fanno Creek. Petitioner would lose all rights to regulate the time in which the public entered onto the Greenway, regardless of any interference it might pose with her retail store. Her right to exclude would not be regulated, it would be eviscerated.

If petitioner's proposed development had somehow encroached on existing greenway space in the city, it would have been reasonable to require petitioner to provide some alternative greenway space for the public either on her property or elsewhere. See *Nollan*, 483 U.S., at 836 ("Although such a requirement, constituting a permanent grant of continuous access to the property, would have to be considered a taking if it were not attached to a development permit, the Commission's assumed power to forbid construction of the house in order to protect the public's view of the beach must surely include the power to condition construction upon some concession by the owner, even a concession of property rights, that serves the same end"). But that is not the case here. We conclude that the findings upon which the city relies do not show the required reasonable relationship between the floodplain easement and the petitioner's proposed new building.

With respect to the pedestrian/bicycle pathway, we have no doubt that the city was correct in finding that the larger retail sales facility proposed by petitioner will increase traffic on the streets of the Central Business District. The city estimates that the proposed development would generate roughly 435 additional trips per day. Dedications for streets, sidewalks, and other public ways are generally reasonable exactions to avoid excessive congestion from a proposed property use. But on the record before us, the city has not met its burden of demonstrating that the additional number of vehicle and bicycle trips generated by the petitioner's development reasonably relate to the city's requirement for a dedication of the pedestrian/bicycle pathway easement. The city simply found that the creation of the pathway "could offset some of the traffic demand . . . and lessen the increase in traffic congestion."

As Justice Peterson of the Supreme Court of Oregon explained in his dissenting opinion, however, "the findings of fact that the bicycle pathway system 'could offset some of the traffic demand' is a far cry from a finding that the bicycle pathway system *will*, or is *likely to*, offset some of the traffic demand." 854 P.2d, at 447 (emphasis in original). No precise mathematical calculation is required, but the city must make some effort to quantify its findings in support of the dedication for the pedestrian/bicycle pathway beyond the conclusory statement that it could offset some of the traffic demand generated. . . .

JUSTICE STEVENS, with whom JUSTICE BLACKMUN and JUSTICE GINSBURG join, dissenting. . . .

Certain propositions are not in dispute. The enlargement of the Tigard unit in Dolan's chain of hardware stores will have an adverse impact on the city's legitimate and substantial interests in controlling drainage in Fanno Creek and minimizing traffic congestion in Tigard's business district. That impact is sufficient to justify an outright denial of her application for approval of the expansion. The city has nevertheless agreed to grant Dolan's application if she will comply with two conditions, each of which admittedly will mitigate the adverse effects of her proposed development. The disputed question is whether the city has violated the Fourteenth Amendment to the Federal Constitution by refusing to allow Dolan's planned construction to proceed unless those conditions are met.

The Court is correct in concluding that the city may not attach arbitrary conditions to a building permit or to a variance even when it can rightfully deny the application outright. I also agree that state court decisions dealing with ordinances that govern municipal development plans provide useful guidance in a case of this kind. Yet the Court's description of the doctrinal underpinnings of its decision, the phrasing of its fledgling test of "rough proportionality," and the application of that test to this case run contrary to the traditional treatment of these cases and break considerable and unpropitious new ground. . . .

. . . The Court's assurances that its "rough proportionality" test leaves ample room for cities to pursue the "commendable task of land use planning"—even twice avowing that "no precise mathematical calculation is required"—are wanting given the result that test compels here. Under the Court's approach, a city must not only "quantify its findings," and make "individualized determinations" with respect to the nature and the extent of the relationship between the conditions and the impact, but also demonstrate "proportionality." The correct inquiry should instead concentrate on whether the required nexus is present and venture beyond considerations of a condition's nature or germaneness only if the developer establishes that a concededly germane condition is so grossly disproportionate to the proposed development's adverse effects that it manifests motives other than land use regulation on the part of the city. The heightened requirement the Court imposes on cities is even more unjustified when all the tools needed to resolve the questions presented by this case can be garnered from our existing case law.

Applying its new standard, the Court finds two defects in the city's case. First, while the record would adequately support a requirement that Dolan maintain the portion of the floodplain on her property as undeveloped open space, it does not support the additional requirement that the floodplain be dedicated to the city. Second, while the city adequately established the traffic increase that the proposed development would generate, it failed to quantify the offsetting decrease in automobile traffic that the bike path will produce. Even under the Court's new rule, both defects are, at most, nothing more than harmless error.

In her objections to the floodplain condition, Dolan made no effort to demonstrate that the dedication of that portion of her property would be any more onerous than a simple prohibition against any development on that portion of her property. Given the commercial character of both the existing and the proposed use of the property as a retail store, it seems likely that potential customers "trampling along petitioner's floodplain," are more valuable than a useless parcel of vacant land. Moreover, the duty to pay taxes and the responsibility for potential tort liability may well make ownership of the fee interest in useless land a liability rather than an asset. That may explain why Dolan never conceded that she could be prevented from building on the floodplain. The City Attorney also pointed out that absent a dedication, property owners would be required to "build on their own land" and "with their own money" a storage facility for the water runoff. Dolan apparently "did have that option," but chose not to seek it. If Dolan might have been entitled to a variance confining the city's condition in a manner this Court would accept, her failure to seek that narrower form of relief at any stage of the state administrative and judicial proceedings clearly should preclude that relief in this Court now.

The Court's rejection of the bike path condition amounts to nothing more than a play on words. Everyone agrees that the bike path "could" offset some of the increased traffic flow that the larger store will generate, but the findings do not unequivocally state that it *will* do so, or tell us just how many cyclists will replace motorists. Predictions on such matters are inherently nothing more than estimates. Certainly the assumption that there will be an offsetting benefit here is entirely reasonable and should suffice whether it amounts to 100 percent, 35 percent, or only 5 percent of the increase in automobile traffic that would otherwise occur. If the Court proposes to have the federal judiciary micromanage state decisions of this kind, it is indeed extending its welcome mat to a significant new class of litigants. Although there is no reason to believe that state courts have failed to rise to the task, property owners have surely found a new friend today.

. . . In our changing world one thing is certain: uncertainty will characterize predictions about the impact of new urban developments on the risks of floods, earthquakes, traffic congestion, or environmental harms. When there is doubt concerning the magnitude of those impacts, the public interest in averting them must outweigh the private interest of the commercial entrepreneur. If the government can demonstrate that the conditions it has imposed in a land-use permit are rational, impartial, and conducive to fulfilling the aims of a valid land-use plan, a strong presumption of validity should attach to those conditions. The burden of demonstrating that those conditions have unreasonably impaired the economic value of the proposed improvement belongs squarely on the shoulders of the party challenging the state action's constitutionality. That allocation of burdens has served us well in the past. The Court has stumbled badly today by reversing it.

I respectfully dissent.

JUSTICE SOUTER, dissenting.

I cannot agree that the application of *Nollan* is a sound one here, since it appears that the Court has placed the burden of producing evidence of relationship on the city, despite the usual rule in cases involving the police power that the government is presumed to have acted constitutionally. Having thus assigned the burden, the Court concludes that the City loses based on one word ("could" instead of "would"), and despite the fact that this record shows the connection the Court looks for. Dolan has put forward no evidence that the burden of granting a dedication for the bicycle path is unrelated in kind to the anticipated increase in traffic congestion, nor, if there exists a requirement that the relationship be related in degree, has Dolan shown that the exaction fails any such test. The city, by contrast, calculated the increased traffic flow that would result from Dolan's proposed development to be 435 trips per day, and its Comprehensive Plan, applied here, relied on studies showing the link between alternative modes of transportation, including bicycle paths, and reduced street traffic congestion. City of Tigard's Comprehensive Plan ("Bicycle and pedestrian pathway systems will result in some reduction of automobile trips within the community"). *Nollan*, therefore, is satisfied, and on that assumption the city's conditions should not be held to fail a further rough proportionality test or any other that might be devised to give meaning to the constitutional limits.

## NOTES AND QUESTIONS

1. Unlike the situation in *Nollan*, the Court majority has no difficulty finding that an "essential nexus" exists between the legitimate state interests in preventing flooding and alleviating traffic congestion and the state's attempt to exact

dedications of land for storm drainage and a bike pathway. Why then did the exactions fail to satisfy constitutional muster? What would the city have to do under the Court's decision to justify the exactions it sought? How detailed would the city's findings have to be in order to justify the exactions?

2. What test does the Court enunciate for determining whether the degree of exactions demanded bears the constitutionally required relationship to the projected impact of development? How does the Court derive this test? Who bears the burden of proof on this issue — the city or the developer? What test does Justice Stevens propose in dissent? How would it differ from the majority's test?

3. Suppose the city simply had denied the permit request without seeking any exaction. Would the permit denial give rise to any kind of takings claim? If instead of asking Dolan to dedicate her property to public use the city had simply imposed a zoning ordinance requiring that a certain percentage of a lot be maintained as a greenway buffer, would there have been any constitutional problem?

4. Does the Court's decision call into question the constitutionality of charging developers impact fees to help compensate for the increased demand for municipal services caused by development? After issuing the *Dolan* decision, the Court vacated and remanded a California decision requiring a developer to pay mitigation fees for the right to build condominiums on what formerly had been a tennis club. Ehrlich v. Culver City, 19 Cal. Rptr. 2d 468 (1993). The developer was required to pay a $280,000 fee for the loss of public recreational facilities, $30,000 as a park fee, and $33,220 for public art. On remand, the California Supreme Court held that *Dolan*'s "rough proportionality" requirement applied to nonpossessory exactions, including monetary fees. While it upheld the propriety of charging an impact fee for loss of recreational facilities, it found insufficient evidence to support the $280,000 fee. Ehrlich v. Culver City, 50 Cal. Rptr. 2d 242 (1996). The court upheld a requirement that the developer provide public art because it found that this was the type of aesthetic control well within the authority of the city to impose. How should a court determine whether an impact fee satisfies the "rough proportionality" test?

5. On June 25, 2013, the U.S. Supreme Court decided Koontz v. St. Johns River Water Management District, 570 U.S. 595 (2013). By a 5-4 vote the Court held that a government agency could not require the funding of off-site mitigation projects on public lands as a condition for obtaining a permit to develop wetlands unless the government's mitigation demand had an "essential nexus" to, and was "roughly proportional" in magnitude to, the expected impact of the development. This decision extended the "essential nexus" and "rough proportionality" requirements of regulatory takings law that previously had only applied to permit conditions requiring a dedication of a portion of real property to public use to monetary exactions. These decisions are based on the U.S. Constitution's requirement that private property cannot be "taken" by government for public use without the payment of just compensation, known as the Takings Clause. In his majority opinion Justice Alito dismissed arguments that the decision will jeopardize land use regulation, noting that many states already apply similar limits on monetary exactions sought from developers. In dissent Justice Kagan claimed that the decision will subject local government to a flood of litigation by extending the Takings Clause "into the very heart of local land-use regulation and service delivery." Justice Alito

emphasized that the decision "does not affect the ability of governments to impose property taxes, user fees, and similar laws and regulations that may impose financial burdens on property owners."

6. Following the Supreme Court's decision in *Dolan*, Mrs. Dolan again sought permission to expand her hardware store. After further litigation in the state courts, the city eventually agreed to pay Mrs. Dolan $1.5 million to compensate her for a "temporary taking" and to grant her a permit to expand the business. 28 Envtl. Rep. 1474 (1997). In return Mrs. Dolan agreed to give the city the easement it had sought for the bicycle path and the flood control project. Today a new and much larger hardware store occupies the property abutting a bike path crossing over Fanno Creek. (See photo on the casebook website at *www.erlsp.comphoto-tour/*.)

7. Can the Due Process Clause be used to challenge regulations? In Eastern Enterprises v. Apfel, 524 U.S. 498 (1998), the Court struck down a requirement in the Coal Industry Retiree Health Benefit Act of 1992, mandating that the former owner of a coal mine make large financial contributions to a pension fund for retired coal miners. Four Justices held that the requirement constituted a taking because it placed a severe, disproportionate, and retroactive burden on the company. Justice Kennedy joined the four in invalidating the requirement, but on due process grounds, while refusing to adopt the takings rationale. Kennedy argued that the requirement could not constitute a taking, even though it "imposes a staggering financial burden" on the company, because it "regulates the former mine owner without regard to property." He explained that the Act "does not operate upon or alter an identified property interest and it is not applicable to or measured by a property interest." 524 U.S. at 540 (Kennedy, J., concurring in the judgment). For an argument that *Eastern Enterprises* renders the retroactive application of CERCLA liability to generators unconstitutional, see L. Salibra II, *Eastern Enterprises v. Apfel* and the Retroactive Application of CERCLA, 29 Envtl. L. Rep. 10695 (1999).

8. How far does *Dolan*'s "rough proportionality" requirement extend? In another takings case that established the propriety of submitting to juries regulatory takings claims brought against cities in federal court, City of Monterey v. Del Monte Dunes at Monterey, Ltd., 526 U.S. 687 (1999), the Court did clarify that *Dolan*'s "rough proportionality test" applied only to decisions to condition the approval of development on the dedication of private property to public use. Thus, the Court has confined this requirement to cases involving regulatory exactions. See J. Echeverria, Revving the Engines in Neutral: *City of Monterey v. Del Monte Dunes at Monterey, Ltd.*, 29 Envtl. L. Rep. 10682 (1999).

9. Property rights groups have sought legislation to require the government to pay landowners compensation when regulations reduce the value of property in circumstances that would not satisfy the requirements of the Takings Clause. Although they have not succeeded in winning enactment of such legislation at the federal level, more than two dozen states have adopted some form of state "takings" legislation. These laws take three basic forms: (1) assessment ("look before you leap") laws that require some form of pre-regulation assessment of the prospective impact of regulation on private property rights, (2) compensation laws that require the government to pay property owners when regulation reduces the value of their property by a certain percentage, and (3) conflict resolution laws that establish some procedure that can be used by aggrieved property owners to

negotiate solutions to disputes. Assessment laws have been the most popular. For a review of experience with state takings legislation prepared for the Competitive Enterprise Institute, see K. Dodd, And Justice for All: The State Experience with Property Rights Legislation (Oct. 1998).

10. In May 2005, the U.S. Supreme Court repudiated the notion that government regulation of private property effects a taking if it "does not substantially advance legitimate state interests." The "substantially advance" test had worked its way into regulatory takings doctrine largely through repetition in several takings cases of a phrase that first appeared in the Court's decision in Agins v. City of Tiburon, 447 U.S. 255 (1980). The case that precipitated this change involved the question whether a Hawaii law effects a regulatory taking by limiting the rent that oil companies can charge dealers who lease company-owned service stations. After hearing evidence that the law would not have the economic effects intended by the state, a federal district court ruled that the law constituted a regulatory taking because it did not substantially advance the legitimate state purpose of lowering consumer gasoline prices. On appeal, the U.S. Court of Appeals for the Ninth Circuit affirmed. Chevron U.S.A., Inc. v. Bronster, 363 F.3d 846 (9th Cir. 2004). In the decision below, the U.S. Supreme Court unanimously reversed the Ninth Circuit's decision. Writing for the Court, Justice O'Connor acknowledged the strange provenance of the "substantially advance" test. ("On occasion, a would-be doctrinal rule or test finds its way into our case law through simple repetition of a phrase—however fortuitously coined.") Recognizing that this test was essentially a due process concept, the Court repudiated it as an element of takings doctrine. Although the *Lingle* decision did not involve a takings challenge to an environmental regulation, the following excerpt from Justice O'Connor's opinion for the Court provides an excellent summary of the current state of takings doctrine that may be very helpful to students seeking to understand its application in environmental contexts.

## Lingle v. Chevron U.S.A., Inc.

544 U.S. 528 (2005)

JUSTICE O'CONNOR delivered the opinion of the Court.

. . . Our precedents stake out two categories of regulatory action that generally will be deemed per se takings for Fifth Amendment purposes. First, where government requires an owner to suffer a permanent physical invasion of her property—however minor—it must provide just compensation. See Loretto v. Teleprompter Manhattan CATV Corp., 458 U.S. 419 (1982) (state law requiring landlords to permit cable companies to install cable facilities in apartment buildings effected a taking). A second categorical rule applies to regulations that completely deprive an owner of "*all* economically beneficial us[e]" of her property. *Lucas*, 505 U.S., at 1019 (emphasis in original). We held in *Lucas* that the government must pay just compensation for such "total regulatory takings," except to the extent that "background principles of nuisance and property law" independently restrict the owner's intended use of the property. Id., at 1026-1032.

Outside these two relatively narrow categories (and the special context of land-use exactions discussed below), regulatory takings challenges are governed by the standards set forth in Penn Central Transp. Co. v. New York City, 438 U.S. 104 (1978). The Court in *Penn Central* acknowledged that it had hitherto been "unable to develop any 'set formula'" for evaluating regulatory takings claims, but identified "several factors that have particular significance." Id., at 124. Primary among those factors are "[t]he economic impact of the regulation on the claimant and, particularly, the extent to which the regulation has interfered with distinct investment-backed expectations." Ibid. In addition, the "character of the governmental action"—for instance whether it amounts to a physical invasion or instead merely affects property interests through "some public program adjusting the benefits and burdens of economic life to promote the common good"—may be relevant in discerning whether a taking has occurred. Ibid. The Penn Central factors—though each has given rise to vexing subsidiary questions—have served as the principal guidelines for resolving regulatory takings claims that do not fall within the physical takings or *Lucas* rules. See, e.g., Palazzolo v. Rhode Island, 533 U.S. 606, 617-618 (2001); id., at 632-634 (O'Connor, J., concurring).

Although our regulatory takings jurisprudence cannot be characterized as unified, these three inquiries (reflected in *Loretto, Lucas*, and *Penn Central*) share a common touchstone. Each aims to identify regulatory actions that are functionally equivalent to the classic taking in which government directly appropriates private property or ousts the owner from his domain. Accordingly, each of these tests focuses directly upon the severity of the burden that government imposes upon private property rights. The Court has held that physical takings require compensation because of the unique burden they impose: A permanent physical invasion, however minimal the economic cost it entails, eviscerates the owner's right to exclude others from entering and using her property—perhaps the most fundamental of all property interests. In the *Lucas* context, of course, the complete elimination of a property's value is the determinative factor. See *Lucas*, supra, at 1017 (positing that "total deprivation of beneficial use is, from the landowner's point of view, the equivalent of a physical appropriation"). And the *Penn Central* inquiry turns in large part, albeit not exclusively, upon the magnitude of a regulation's economic impact and the degree to which it interferes with legitimate property interests. . . .

In stark contrast to the three regulatory takings tests discussed above, the "substantially advances" inquiry reveals nothing about the magnitude or character of the burden a particular regulation imposes upon private property rights. Nor does it provide any information about how any regulatory burden is distributed among property owners. In consequence, this test does not help to identify those regulations whose effects are functionally comparable to government appropriation or invasion of private property; it is tethered neither to the text of the Takings Clause nor to the basic justification for allowing regulatory actions to be challenged under the Clause. . . .

[Justice O'Connor then discusses the implications of the Court's jettisoning the "substantial advance test" for cases involving regulatory exactions.] It might be argued that this formula played a role in our decisions in Nollan v. California Coastal Comm'n, 483 U.S. 825 (1987), and Dolan v. City of Tigard, 512 U.S. 374 (1994). But while the Court drew upon the language of *Agins* in these cases, it did not apply the "substantially advances" test that is the subject of today's decision. Both *Nollan* and *Dolan* involved Fifth Amendment takings challenges to adjudicative land-use exactions—specifically, government demands that a landowner dedicate an easement allowing public access to her property as a condition of obtaining a development permit. See *Dolan*, supra, at 379-380 (permit to expand a store and parking lot conditioned on the dedication of a portion of the relevant property for a "greenway," including a bike/pedestrian path); *Nollan*, supra, at 828 (permit to build a larger residence on beachfront property conditioned on dedication of an easement allowing the public to traverse a strip of the property between the owner's seawall and the mean high-tide line).

In each case, the Court began with the premise that, had the government simply appropriated the easement in question, this would have been a per se physical taking. The question was whether the government could, without paying the compensation that would otherwise be required upon effecting such a taking, demand the easement as a condition for granting a development permit the government was entitled to deny. The Court in *Nollan* answered in the affirmative, provided that the exaction would substantially advance the same government interest that would furnish a valid ground for denial of the permit. The Court further refined this requirement in *Dolan*, holding that an adjudicative exaction requiring dedication of private property must also be "'rough[ly] proportiona[l]'. . . both in nature and extent to the impact of the proposed development."

Although *Nollan* and *Dolan* quoted *Agins*' language, the rule those decisions established is entirely distinct from the "substantially advances" test we address today. Whereas the "substantially advances" inquiry before us now is unconcerned with the degree or type of burden a regulation places upon property, *Nollan* and *Dolan* both involved dedications of property so onerous that, outside the exactions context, they would be deemed per se physical takings. In neither case did the Court question whether the exaction would substantially advance some legitimate state interest. Rather, the issue was whether the exactions substantially advanced the same interests that land-use authorities asserted would allow them to deny the permit altogether. As the Court explained in *Dolan*, these cases involve a special application of the "doctrine of 'unconstitutional conditions,'" which provides that "the government may not require a person to give up a constitutional right—here the right to receive just compensation when property is taken for a public use—in exchange for a discretionary benefit conferred by the government where the benefit has little or no relationship to the property." That is worlds apart from a rule that says a regulation affecting property constitutes a taking on its face solely because it does not substantially advance a legitimate government interest. In short, *Nollan* and *Dolan* cannot be characterized as applying the "substantially advances" test we address today, and our decision should not be read to disturb these precedents.

Twenty-five years ago, the Court posited that a regulation of private property "effects a taking if [it] does not substantially advance [a] legitimate state interes[t]." The lower courts in this case took that statement to its logical conclusion, and in so doing, revealed its imprecision. Today we correct course. We hold that the "substantially advances" formula is not a valid takings test, and indeed conclude that it has no proper place in our takings jurisprudence. In so doing, we reaffirm that a plaintiff seeking to challenge a government regulation as an uncompensated taking of private property may proceed under one of the other theories discussed above—by alleging a "physical" taking, a *Lucas*-type "total regulatory taking," a *Penn Central* taking, or a land-use exaction violating the standards set forth in *Nollan* and *Dolan*.

Because Chevron argued only a "substantially advances" theory in support of its takings claim, it was not entitled to summary judgment on that claim. Accordingly, we reverse the judgment of the Ninth Circuit and remand the case for further proceedings consistent with this opinion.

## NOTES AND QUESTIONS

1.  While repudiating the "substantially advances" test as an element of regulatory takings doctrine, Justice O'Connor's majority opinion attempts to distinguish it from the foundations of the "rough proportionality" requirement for regulatory exactions established in *Nollan* and *Dolan*. How successful is she in doing so? As she acknowledges, both *Nollan* and *Dolan* cited *Agins*'s now-repudiated "substantially advances" language in justifying their conclusion that the regulatory exaction sought was unconstitutional. What impact, if any, will the *Lingle* decision have on regulatory exactions?

2.  Justice O'Connor's summary of the state of regulatory takings doctrine describes *Lucas* as establishing a "relatively narrow" category of regulatory takings when a regulation completely deprives the property owner of all "economically beneficial use" of real estate. While many regulations have been challenged as creating a *Lucas*-type "total wipeout," courts have routinely rejected such claims by finding that the land subject to regulation retains some economic value. As a result, the *Penn Central* test appears to have become the primary touchstone for evaluating regulatory takings claims. Is it fair to conclude that the Rehnquist Court's revival of regulatory takings doctrine has not had much direct effect on environmental regulation? While few judgments have been rendered requiring compensation for regulatory takings, could the Court's revival of regulatory takings doctrine have helped deter regulators from overreaching for fear of incurring liability for a taking?

3.  Not all Justices are happy that regulatory takings doctrine has largely returned to the ad hoc approach reflected in the Court's 1978 *Penn Central* decision. Dissenting from a denial of certiorari in Bridge Aina Le'A, LLC v. Hawaii Land Use Commission, No. 20-54 (Feb. 22, 2021), Justice Thomas argued that the "current doctrine is 'so vague and indeterminate that it invites unprincipled, subjective decision making' dependent upon the decisionmaker," citing Echeverria, Is the *Penn Central* Three-Factor Test Ready for History's Dustbin? 52 Land Use L. & Zon. Dig. 3, 7 (2000). Justice Thomas complained that a "know-it-when-you-see-it test is no good if one court sees it and another does not."

---

## PROBLEM EXERCISE: ENVIRONMENTAL REMEDIATION AND THE TAKINGS CLAUSE

A developer owns a 100-acre tract of undeveloped land located near a licensed waste disposal site. After it is discovered that toxic wastes from the nearby disposal site are leaching into groundwater and heavily contaminating it, the site is placed on Superfund's National Priorities List for cleanup. Operating under authority granted by CERCLA, EPA seeks the developer's permission to install groundwater

monitoring wells on the developer's property. EPA claims it needs the wells to monitor the movement of a plume of toxic chemicals moving through the aquifer from
the waste disposal site. After the developer denies EPA permission, EPA issues an
access order mandating that it be allowed to install the wells. Over a three-year
period, EPA installs 20 groundwater-monitoring wells on a 50-foot by 50-foot square
portion of the developer's undeveloped land. To use the wells for monitoring purposes, government officials periodically enter the property through a 16-foot-wide
access corridor. Monitoring data show that a plume of toxic contaminants is flowing directly under the developer's property. After years of expensive remediation
efforts, the contamination is removed. The government closes the monitoring wells
and terminates its access order 12 years after it first was issued.

The developer then sues the federal government seeking compensation under
the Takings Clause. The developer argues that the government's actions constituted a physical taking of the portion of his property on which the wells were
installed and a regulatory taking of the balance of the property. The developer
argues that the government's actions constituted a total taking because the access
order authorized virtually unlimited governmental activity on the portions of the
property on which the wells were installed, and it made the balance of the property
unmarketable for nearly 12 years by creating a false impression that the property
was contaminated.

The government denies that it owes the developer any compensation for a taking. The government claims it was necessary to place the groundwater monitoring
wells on the developer's property in order to respond to a public nuisance and that
the developer ultimately benefited from its monitoring and cleanup efforts. The
government argues that its actions saved the developer the expense of investigating, characterizing, and remediating contamination beneath his property. If the
property was unmarketable, it was a result of the contamination and not the presence of the monitoring wells. The property is now available for development. The
government notes that the part used for the monitoring wells could easily become
part of a parking lot or landscaped area without reducing the size of any future
development. The developer denies that he received any benefits from the government's actions cleaning up the contaminated groundwater because he never
planned to use the groundwater when he ultimately developed the property.

**Question One.** Has the government taken the developer's property for purposes of the Takings Clause? If so, what kind of taking has occurred—total or partial, physical or regulatory, temporary or permanent?

**Question Two.** What difference, if any, does it make for purposes of taking
analysis that the government believes its actions were necessary to respond to a
public nuisance? Would it make any difference if the government itself had caused
the contamination?

**Question Three.** What difference, if any, does it make for purposes of takings
analysis that the government has now terminated its access order and closed the
monitoring wells?

**Question Four.** If a taking has occurred, should the developer receive any compensation and, if so, how should it be calculated? See Hendler v. United States, 175
F.3d 1374 (Fed. Cir. 1999).

### 4. *Evolving Conceptions of Property Rights: The Public Trust, Climate Change, Sea Level Rise, and Judicial Takings*

Takings disputes raise fundamental questions concerning the meaning of property and the relationship between individuals and the state in our constitutional system. With the rise of environmental concerns and the growth of the regulatory state, property scholars have engaged in a vigorous debate over the nature and origins of property rights. See C.M. Rose, What Government Can Do for Property (and Vice Versa), in The Fundamental Interrelationships Between Government and Property 209 (1999) (contrasting the Lockean "bottom-up" view that human beings invent property prior to government with Bentham's "top-down" vision that property is simply a basis for expectations that are secured by government). As national regulatory programs to protect the environment rose to prominence, Joseph Sax and others articulated a new vision of property rights that emphasized the subordination of private rights to public trusts in commonly held natural resources. Sax, The Public Trust Doctrine in Natural Resources Law: Effective Judicial Intervention, 68 Mich. L. Rev. 471 (1970). Importing notions from Roman law and English and American cases holding that the government held certain natural resources in trust for the public, see Illinois Central Railroad Co. v. Illinois, 146 U.S. 387 (1892), Professor Sax argued that the public trust doctrine should be used to vindicate the evolving public interest in environmental protection. See Rose, Joseph Sax and the Idea of the Public Trust, 25 Ecology L.Q. 351 (1998). In *Illinois Central Railroad* the Supreme Court invalidated the Illinois legislature's grant of the entire Chicago lakefront to a private railroad by holding that the lakefront was subject to a public trust that barred the state from selling it to private parties. For a detailed analysis of the history of this case and its implications for the public trust doctrine, see Joseph D. Kearney & Thomas A. Merrill, The Origins of the American Public Trust Doctrine: What Really Happened in *Illinois Central*, 71 U. Chi. L. Rev. 799 (2004).

The U.S. Supreme Court's most recent reference to the public trust doctrine came in a decision holding that Montana does not hold title to segments of a river that were non-navigable at the time Montana became a state. PPL Montana, LLC v. Montana, 132 S. Ct. 1215 (2012). The Court rejected Montana's argument that denying the state title to the riverbeds would undermine the public trust doctrine, noting that the latter "remains a matter of state law," subject to federal regulatory power. The Court noted that "[u]nder accepted principles of federalism, the States retain residual power to determine the scope of the public trust over waters within their borders. . . ." Id. at 1235.

While the public trust concept has remained vague, it challenges the notion that regulations preventing private parties from using their land in ways that harm important environmental resources constitute takings. Sax, Takings, Private Property and Public Rights, 81 Yale L.J. 149 (1971). Another challenge arises from what has been described as the "narrative of natural use." Freyfogle, Owning the Land: Four Contemporary Narratives, 13 J. Land Use & Envtl. L. 279 (1998). This was the concept articulated by the Wisconsin Supreme Court in Just v. Marinette County, 201 N.W.2d 761 (1972), when it stated that "[a]n owner of land has no absolute and unlimited right to change the essential natural character of his land so as to use it for a purpose for which it was unsuited in its natural state and which injures the rights of others." Professor Freyfogle argues that, while this narrative description of the meaning of ownership is perhaps the simplest of all, despite uncertainties concerning the meaning of what is truly natural, nature itself cannot practicably serve as the source of rules in a democratic society.

Richard Epstein takes sharp exception to *Just* and argues that compensation should be required for a broad array of government actions that reduce the economic value of private property. R. Epstein, Takings (1985). Yet, Epstein does not appear to be suggesting that government conversely should recoup *increases* in property values that are the products of its activities. Professor Epstein appears to reject the application of the nuisance exception in cases of nonpoint source pollution by arguing that land use controls do not redress a physical invasion of the property of another, but rather pollution of one's own property. Id. at 123.

These competing conceptions of property rights reflect evolving (and diverging) notions of fairness as well as changes in our understanding of how environmental harm is caused. Lord Holt's ancient maxim that "every man must so use his own as not to damnify another" acquires new meaning once it is understood that actions long recognized as core aspects of property rights (e.g., the building of a home) may contribute to severe environmental damage by exacerbating nonpoint source pollution. Yet environmentalists who decry the unfairness of involuntary exposure to risk also should be concerned about the fairness of visiting disproportionate economic losses on any individual in the name of environmental protection. The CEQ's observation four decades ago remains accurate today:

> [D]espite the criticisms that have been aimed at various judicial formulations, it may well be that no single formula is either possible or desirable. In the final analysis, all such formulae seem to be attempts to extrapolate from what is at base an ethical judgment about the fairness of alternative means of distributing the costs of protecting certain land-related values that yield positive net benefits to society. In most cases that judgment has traditionally suggested that the proper balance between the interests of private landowners and the public is maintained by requiring compensation when land use regulations do not leave the landowner with any "reasonable" use of his property. Increasingly, as new concepts of property have become more firmly established and recognition of the value of land as a scarce resource has mounted, the definition of reasonable use has changed. [CEQ, Environmental Quality 150 (1973).]

Reconciling notions of fairness to individuals with the need to prevent formerly commonplace activities from contributing to serious environmental problems remains an important challenge facing environmental law.

Takings issues invariably arise at times of regulatory transition: when new laws are adopted that regulate land uses, when new regulations are promulgated to implement previously enacted laws, or when new information becomes available, or circumstances change, that results in property not previously thought to be subject to regulation to be so encumbered. There are many options available for making regulatory transitions less burdensome, as outlined by Carol Rose, Property Rights and Responsibilities, in Thinking Ecologically: The Next Generation of

Environmental Policy 49 (M. Chertow & D. Esty eds., 1997). Some of these include: phasing in new regulations during specified transitional periods, offering partial or temporary variances in cases of special hardships, and phasing out or restructuring counterproductive subsidies instead of restricting private uses of land.

Sea level rise is occurring much faster than initially predicted, threatening coastal properties. Some owners of coastal property are constructing erosion barriers that protect their property while contributing to intensified erosion of nearby unprotected lands. James Titus, project manager for sea level rise at EPA's Office of Policy, wrote a prescient law review article in 1998 addressing how property law should respond to sea level rise. James G. Titus, Rising Seas, Coastal Erosion, and the Takings Clause: How to Save Wetlands and Beaches Without Hurting Property Owners, 57 Md. L. Rev. 1279 (1998). Titus noted that "[v]irtually every state has made the policy decision to keep its ocean beaches and not to privatize ocean shores that are currently open to the public." Yet, the "rising sea has placed riparian owners' rights to protect their homes on a collision course with the public's ownership of the intertidal wetlands and beaches. Some of the shore has been given away, and more will be given away as wetlands and beaches erode."

Titus concluded that there are "three ways to protect tidelands: (1) prevent development in vulnerable areas seaward of a 'setback line,' (2) defer action, and (3) create rolling easements, which allow development but prohibit property owners from holding back the sea." The setback line approach is what the South Carolina Coastal Council attempted to implement, which gave rise to the *Lucas* litigation. Titus mentions two problems with it — the difficulty of defining an appropriate setback line given the uncertainties of forecasting future erosion, and the fact that shoreline eventually will retreat to any setback unless it is set extremely far back. Developments on the Isle of Palms after the *Lucas* litigation illustrate these difficulties. The ocean shoreline along the Isle has continued to fluctuate dramatically as a result of inlet shoal migration and attachment. When South Carolina adopted its Beachfront Management Act in 1988, the shoreline at Beachwood East, where Lucas's lots were located, was at its most-seaward known location in the previous 47 years. Yet by 1997, nine years later, it had shifted 200 feet landward. At nearby Summer Dunes Lane, the shoreline went from 230 feet seaward of the setback line in 1993 to 60 feet *landward* of it in 1997, a shift of 290 feet in four years.

Titus proposes several alternatives for implementing the use of "rolling easements." One approach is simply to prohibit the construction of bulkheads or other structures that interfere with naturally migrating shorelines. 57 Md. L. Rev. at 1313. Another approach is to have the government purchase an easement that would allow it to take possession of privately owned coastal land whenever the sea rises by a certain amount. Titus estimated that the nationwide cost of protecting tidelands with rolling easements purchased by the government would range between $373 million and $1.17 billion. Id. at 1398. Other alternatives would be to require that deeds to coastal property specify that the boundary between publicly owned tidelands and privately owned dryland migrates inland to the natural high-water mark, regardless of any human activities that artificially prevent water from intruding, or to enact a statute providing that all coastal land is subject to a rolling easement. Id. at 1313.

Titus notes that "For over a thousand years, the 'law of erosion' has held that the boundary between public and private land migrates inland as the shore erodes, and there is no right to increase one's land at the expense of a neighbor." Although "it does not automatically follow that there is no right to prevent a reduction in one's land at the expense of a neighbor, . . . the theoretical justifications are the same." Also "[a]nother ancient principle of property law, the public trust doctrine, provides independent support for this view." Even though some portions of the public trust "doctrine are controversial, no one disputes the rule that a state does not lose ownership of the shore unless it intends to do so. It follows that the state is never required to allow bulkheads that privatize the shoreline. Thus, rolling easements are a codification of the expectations that generally prevailed under the common law."

South Carolina does not allow the use of new hard erosion control devices to protect coastal properties from erosion. In the fall of 1994, a house was constructed on one of the lots formerly owned by Lucas. Two years later beach erosion undermined a dozen homes on the Isle of Palms, including the home built on Lucas's lot and three other nearby homes on Summer Dunes Lane, which had been built behind the most landward shoreline of the past 40 years. The property owners sued the state of South Carolina, seeking to overturn a decision denying them permits to use 31-ton sandbags to protect their homes. While the state allows the use of 5-gallon sandbags in emergencies, the plaintiffs argued that even the placement of 20,000 of these bags on the beach had been insufficient to protect their properties from erosion. Ellison Smith, attorney for the landowners, argued that no possible societal interest could be served by allowing houses to fall into the ocean. Mary Shahid, attorney for the state Office of Ocean and Coastal Resources management, responded that the "societal interest is to protect the beaches for the public of South Carolina." Langley, Panel Sack Sandbag Request, Charleston Post & Courier, Sept. 12, 1998. The Coastal Zone Management Panel voted 9-1 to uphold a decision by an administrative law judge denying the permits on the ground that the Beachfront Management Act does not allow new hard erosion control devices.

In subsequent years, the Isle of Palms suffered severe erosion, and multimillion-dollar beach replenishment projects for it have been funded by the Federal Emergency Management Agency. As discussed above, in September 2017 Hurricane Irma passed more than 100 miles to the west, but the Isle of Palms suffered considerable damage, again bringing the ocean right up to the foundation of the home that had been built on the property formerly owned by David Lucas. (Photos of the property as of October 2017 are available on the casebook website at *www. erlsp.comphoto-tour/.*)

### "Judicial Takings" and Beach Replenishment: The *Stop the Beach* Decision

As courts confront challenging issues of property law posed by rising sea levels, is it possible that a judicial decision interpreting state law could itself constitute a "judicial taking"? In the case below, the U.S. Supreme Court reviewed a decision by the Supreme Court of Florida rejecting a constitutional challenge to the Florida Beach and Shore Preservation Act. Under the Act, prior to the state funding a beach replenishment project, an "erosion control line" is set at the mean high-water line, the existing boundary between state-owned and private property. The Act provides that any accretions of land seaward of the erosion control line (including those caused by the project pumping additional sand) then belong to the state, but beachfront property owners are guaranteed continued access to the water over the state-owned accretions.

While popular with most owners of beachfront land because it prevents erosion of their property, the program was challenged by a group from Destin, Florida who called themselves Stop the Beach Renourishment, Inc. ("Stop the Beach"). Stop the Beach argued that the program was a taking requiring payment of just compensation because it deprived beachfront property owners of a common law right to continued contact with the water and ownership of future accretions. After a state district court agreed with them, the Florida Supreme Court reversed. Interpreting state law, the court found that the plaintiffs were not deprived of any property rights. The court described the right to accretions as a future contingent interest, not a vested property right, and held that there is no littoral right to contact with the water independent of the littoral right of access, which the Act does not infringe.

Stop the Beach then claimed that the Florida Supreme Court's decision constituted a "judicial taking" of their property because it "constitutes a sudden change in state law, unpredictable in terms of relevant precedents." It sought review in the U.S. Supreme Court, which rendered the following decision.

## Stop the Beach Renourishment, Inc. v. Florida Dep't of Environmental Protection

560 U.S. 702 (2010)

JUSTICE SCALIA announced the judgment of the Court and delivered the opinion of the Court with respect to Parts I, IV, and V, and an opinion with respect to Parts II and III, in which THE CHIEF JUSTICE, JUSTICE THOMAS, and JUSTICE ALITO join.

We consider a claim that the decision of a State's court of last resort took property without just compensation in violation of the Takings Clause of the Fifth Amendment, as applied against the States through the Fourteenth.

### I

### A

Generally speaking, state law defines property interests including property rights in navigable waters and the lands underneath them. In Florida, the State owns in trust for the public the land permanently submerged beneath navigable waters and the foreshore (the land between the low-tide line and the mean high-water line). Thus, the mean high-water line (the average reach of high tide over the preceding 19 years) is the ordinary boundary between private beachfront, or littoral property, and state-owned land.

Littoral owners have, in addition to the rights of the public, certain "special rights" with regard to the water and the foreshore, rights which Florida considers to be property, generally akin to easements. These include the right of access to the water, the right to use the water for certain purposes, the right to an unobstructed view of the water, and the right to receive accretions and relictions to the littoral property. This is generally in accord with well-established common law, although the precise property rights vary among jurisdictions.

At the center of this case is the right to accretions and relictions. Accretions are additions of alluvion (sand, sediment, or other deposits) to waterfront land; relictions are lands once covered by water that become dry when the water recedes. (For simplicity's sake, we shall refer to accretions and relictions collectively as accretions, and the process whereby they occur as accretion.) In order for an addition to dry land to qualify as an accretion, it must have occurred gradually and imperceptibly—that is, so slowly that one could not see the change occurring, though over time the difference became apparent. When, on the other hand, there is a "sudden or perceptible loss of or addition to land by the action of the water or a sudden change in the bed of a lake or the course of a stream," the change is called an avulsion.

In Florida, as at common law, the littoral owner automatically takes title to dry land added to his property by accretion; but formerly submerged land that has become dry land by avulsion continues to belong to the owner of the seabed (usually the State). Thus, regardless of whether an avulsive event exposes land previously submerged or submerges land previously exposed, the boundary between littoral property and sovereign land does not change; it remains (ordinarily) what was the mean high-water line before the event. It follows from this that, when a new strip of land has been added to the shore by avulsion, the littoral owner has no right to subsequent accretions. Those accretions no longer add to his property, since the property abutting the water belongs not to him but to the State.

### B

In 1961, Florida's Legislature passed the Beach and Shore Preservation Act, Fla. Stat. §§161.011-161.45 (2007). The Act establishes procedures for "beach restoration and nourishment projects," §161.088, designed to deposit sand on eroded beaches (restoration) and to maintain the deposited sand (nourishment). §§161.021(3), (4). A local government may apply to the Department of Environmental Protection for the funds and the necessary permits to restore a beach, see §§161.101(1), 161.041(1). When the project involves placing fill on the State's submerged lands, authorization is required from the Board of Trustees of the Internal Improvement Trust Fund, which holds title to those lands, §253.12(1).

Once a beach restoration "is determined to be undertaken," the Board sets what is called "an erosion control line." §§161.161(3)-(5). It must be set by reference to the existing mean high-water line, though in theory it can be located seaward or landward of that. See §161.161(5). Much of the project work occurs seaward of the erosion-control line, as sand is dumped on what was once submerged land. The fixed erosion-control line replaces the fluctuating mean high-water line as the boundary between privately owned littoral property and state property. §161.191(1). Once the erosion-control line is recorded, the common law ceases to increase upland property by accretion (or decrease it by erosion). §161.191(2). Thus, when accretion to the shore moves the mean high-water line seaward, the property of beachfront landowners is not extended to that line (as the prior law provided), but remains bounded by the permanent erosion-control line. Those landowners "continue to be entitled," however, "to all common-law riparian rights" other than the right to accretions. §161.201. If the beach erodes back landward of the erosion-control line over a substantial portion of the shoreline covered by the project, the Board may, on its own initiative, or must, if asked by the owners or lessees of a majority of the property affected, direct the agency responsible for maintaining the beach to return the beach to the condition contemplated by the project. If that is not done within a year, the project is canceled and the erosion-control line is null and void. §161.211(2), (3). Finally, by regulation, if the use of submerged land would "unreasonably infringe on riparian rights," the project cannot proceed unless the local governments show that they own or have a property interest in the upland property adjacent to the project site. Fla. Admin. Code Rule 18-21.004(3) (b) (2009).

### C

In 2003, the city of Destin and Walton County applied for the necessary permits to restore 6.9 miles of beach within their jurisdictions that had been eroded by several hurricanes. The project envisioned depositing along that shore sand dredged from further out. It would add about 75 feet of dry sand seaward of the mean high-water line (to be denominated the erosion-control line). The Department issued a notice of intent to award the permits and the Board approved the erosion-control line.

The petitioner here, Stop the Beach Renourishment, Inc., is a nonprofit corporation formed by people who own beachfront property bordering the project area (we shall refer to them as the Members). It brought an administrative challenge to the proposed project, which was unsuccessful; the Department approved the permits. Petitioner then challenged that action in state court under the Florida Administrative Procedure Act, Fla. Stat. §120.68 (2007). The District Court of Appeal for the First District concluded that, contrary to the Act's preservation of "all common-law riparian rights," the order had eliminated two of the Members' littoral rights: (1) the right to receive accretions to their property; and (2) the right to have the contact of their property with the water remain intact. This, it believed, would be an unconstitutional taking, which would "unreasonably infringe on riparian rights," and therefore require the showing under Fla. Admin. Code Rule 18-21.004(3)(b) that the local governments owned or had a property interest in the upland property. It set aside the Department's final order approving the permits and remanded for that showing to be made. It also certified to the Florida Supreme Court the following question (as rephrased by the latter court):

"On its face, does the Beach and Shore Preservation Act unconstitutionally deprive upland owners of littoral rights without just compensation?"

The Florida Supreme Court answered the certified question in the negative, and quashed the First District's remand. It faulted the Court of Appeal for not considering the doctrine of avulsion, which it concluded permitted the State to reclaim the restored beach on behalf of the public. It described the right to accretions as a future contingent interest, not a vested property right, and held that there is no littoral right to contact with the water independent of the littoral right of access, which the Act does not infringe. Petitioner sought rehearing on the ground that the Florida Supreme Court's decision itself effected a taking of the Members' littoral rights contrary to the Fifth and Fourteenth Amendments to the Federal Constitution.

## II

### A

. . . [I]t is a taking when a state regulation forces a property owner to submit to a permanent physical occupation, Loretto v. Teleprompter Manhattan CATV Corp., 458 U.S. 419, 425-426 (1982), or deprives him of all economically beneficial use of his property, Lucas v. South Carolina Coastal Council, 505 U.S. 1003, 1019 (1992). Finally (and here we approach the situation before us), States effect a taking if they recharacterize as public property what was previously private property.

The Takings Clause (unlike, for instance, the Ex Post Facto Clauses, see Art. I, §9, cl. 3; §10, cl. 1) is not addressed to the action of a specific branch or branches. It is concerned simply with the act, and not with the governmental actor ("nor shall private property *be taken*" (emphasis added)). There is no textual justification for saying that the existence or the scope of a State's power to expropriate private property without just compensation varies according to the branch of government effecting the expropriation. Nor does common sense recommend such a principle. It would be absurd to allow a State to do by judicial decree what the Takings Clause forbids it to do by legislative fiat.

Our precedents provide no support for the proposition that takings effected by the judicial branch are entitled to special treatment, and in fact suggest the contrary. Pruneyard Shopping Center v. Robins, 447 U.S. 74 (1980), involved a decision of the California Supreme Court overruling one of its prior decisions which had held that the California Constitution's guarantees of freedom of speech and of the press, and of the right to petition the government, did not require the owner of private property to accord those rights on his premises. The appellants, owners of a shopping center, contended that their private property rights could not "be denied by invocation of a state constitutional provision *or by judicial reconstruction of a State's laws of private property*," id., at 79 (emphasis added). We held that there had been no taking, citing cases involving legislative and executive takings, and applying standard Takings Clause analysis. We treated the California Supreme Court's application of the constitutional provisions as a regulation of the use of private property, and evaluated whether that regulation violated the property owners' "right to exclude others." Our opinion addressed only the claimed taking by the constitutional provision. Its failure to speak separately to the claimed taking by "judicial reconstruction of a State's laws of private property" certainly does not suggest that a taking by judicial action cannot occur, and arguably suggests that the same analysis applicable to taking by constitutional provision would apply.

*Webb's Fabulous Pharmacies, supra,* is even closer in point. There the purchaser of an insolvent corporation had interpleaded the corporation's creditors, placing the purchase price in an interest-bearing account in the registry of the Circuit Court of Seminole County, to be distributed in satisfaction of claims approved by a receiver. The Florida Supreme Court construed an applicable statute to mean that the interest on the account belonged to the county, because the account was "considered 'public money.'" We held this to be a taking. We noted that "[t]he usual and general rule is that any interest on an interpleaded and deposited fund follows the principal and is to be allocated to those who are ultimately to be the owners of that principal." "Neither the Florida Legislature by statute, nor the Florida courts by judicial decree," we said, "may accomplish the result the county seeks simply by recharacterizing the principal as 'public money.'"

In sum, the Takings Clause bars the State from taking private property without paying for it, no matter which branch is the instrument of the taking. To be sure, the manner of state action may matter: Condemnation by eminent domain, for example, is always a taking, while a legislative, executive, or judicial restriction of property use may or may not be, depending on its nature and extent. But the particular state actor is irrelevant. If a legislature or a court declares that what was once an established right of private property no longer exists, it has taken that property, no less than if the State had physically appropriated it or destroyed its value by regulation. "[A] State, by *ipse dixit*, may not transform private property into public property without compensation."

## III

Respondents put forward a number of arguments which contradict, to a greater or lesser degree, the principle discussed above, that the existence of a taking does not depend upon the branch of government that effects it. First, in a case claiming a judicial taking they would add to our normal takings inquiry a requirement that the court's decision have no "fair and substantial basis." This is taken from our jurisprudence dealing with the question whether a state-court decision rests upon adequate and independent state grounds, placing it beyond our jurisdiction to review. To assure that there is no "evasion" of our authority to review federal questions, we insist that the nonfederal ground of decision have "fair support." A test designed to determine whether there has been an evasion is not obviously appropriate for determining whether there has been a taking of property. But if it is to be extended there it must mean (in the present context) that there is a "fair and substantial basis" for believing that petitioner's Members did not have a property right to future accretions which the Act would take away. This is no different, we think, from our requirement that petitioners' Members must prove the elimination of an established property right.

Next, respondents argue that federal courts lack the knowledge of state law required to decide whether a judicial decision that purports merely to clarify property rights has instead taken them. But federal courts must often decide what state property rights exist in nontakings contexts. And indeed they must decide it to resolve claims that legislative or executive action has effected a taking. For example, a regulation that deprives a property owner of all economically beneficial use of his property is not a taking if the restriction "inhere[s] in the title itself, in the restrictions that background principles of the State's law of property and nuisance already place upon land ownership." A constitutional provision that forbids the uncompensated taking of property is quite simply insusceptible of enforcement by federal courts unless they have the power to decide what property rights exist under state law.

Respondents also warn us against depriving common-law judging of needed flexibility. That argument has little appeal when directed against the enforcement of a constitutional guarantee adopted in an era when, as we said, courts had no power to "change" the common law. But in any case, courts have no peculiar need of flexibility. It is no more essential that judges be free to overrule prior cases that establish property entitlements than that state legislators be free to revise pre-existing statutes that confer property entitlements, or agency-heads pre-existing regulations that do so. And insofar as courts merely clarify and elaborate property entitlements that were previously unclear, they cannot be said to have taken an established property right.

Finally, the city and county argue that applying the Takings Clause to judicial decisions would force lower federal courts to review final state-court judgments, in violation of the so-called *Rooker-Feldman* doctrine. That does not necessarily follow. The finality principles that we regularly apply to takings claims would require the claimant to appeal a claimed taking by a lower court to the state supreme court, whence certiorari would come to this Court. If certiorari were denied, the claimant would no more be able to launch a lower-court federal suit against the taking effected by the state supreme-court opinion than he would be able to launch such a suit against a legislative or executive taking approved by the state supreme-court opinion; the matter would be res judicata. And where the claimant was not a party to the original suit, he would be able to challenge in federal court the taking effected by the state supreme-court opinion to the same extent that he would be able to challenge in federal court a legislative or executive taking previously approved by a state supreme-court opinion.

For its part, petitioner proposes an unpredictability test. Quoting Justice Stewart's concurrence in Hughes v. Washington, 389 U.S. 290, 296 (1967), petitioner argues that a judicial taking consists of a decision that "constitutes a sudden change in state law, unpredictable in terms of relevant precedents." The focus of petitioner's test is misdirected. What counts is not whether there is precedent for the allegedly confiscatory decision, but whether the property right allegedly taken was established. A "predictability of change" test would cover both too much and too little. Too much, because a judicial property decision need not be predictable, so long as it does not declare that what had been private property under established law no longer is. A decision that clarifies property entitlements (or the lack thereof) that were previously unclear might be difficult to predict, but it does not eliminate established property rights. And the predictability test covers too little, because a judicial elimination of established private-property rights that is foreshadowed by dicta or even by holdings years in advance is nonetheless a taking. If, for example, a state court held in one case, to which the complaining property owner was not a party, that it had the power to limit the acreage of privately owned real estate to 100 acres, and then, in a second case, applied that principle to declare the complainant's 101st acre to be public property, the State would have taken an acre from the complainant even though the decision was predictable.

## IV

. . . Petitioner argues that the Florida Supreme Court took two of the property rights of the Members by declaring that those rights did not exist: the right to accretions, and the right to have littoral property touch the water (which petitioner distinguishes from the mere right of access to the water). Under petitioner's theory, because no prior Florida decision had said that the State's filling of submerged tidal lands could have the effect of depriving a littoral owner of contact with the water and denying him future accretions, the Florida Supreme Court's judgment in the present case abolished those two easements to which littoral property owners had been entitled. This puts the burden on the wrong party. There is no taking unless petitioner can show that, before the Florida Supreme Court's decision, littoral-property owners had rights to future accretions and contact with the water superior to the State's right to fill in its submerged land. Though some may think the question close, in our view the showing cannot be made.

Two core principles of Florida property law intersect in this case. First, the State as owner of the submerged land adjacent to littoral property has the right to fill that land, so long as it does not interfere with the rights of the public and the rights of littoral landowners. Second, as we described supra, if an avulsion exposes land seaward of littoral property that had previously been submerged, that land belongs to the State even if it interrupts the littoral owner's contact with the water. The issue here is whether there is an exception to this rule when the State is the cause of the avulsion. Prior law suggests there is not. In Martin v. Busch, 93 Fla. 535, 112 So. 274 (1927), the Florida Supreme Court held that when the State drained water from a lakebed belonging to the State, causing land that was formerly below the mean high-water line to become dry land, that land continued to belong to the State. Id., at 574. "'The riparian rights doctrine of accretion and reliction,'" the Florida Supreme Court later explained, "'does not apply to such lands.'" *Bryant*, supra, at 839 (quoting *Martin*, supra, at 578 (Brown, J., concurring)). This is not surprising, as there can be no accretions to land that no longer abuts the water.

Thus, Florida law as it stood before the decision below allowed the State to fill in its own seabed, and the resulting sudden exposure of previously submerged land was treated like an avulsion for purposes of ownership. The right to accretions was therefore subordinate to the State's right to fill. *Thiesen v. Gulf, Florida & Alabama R. Co.* suggests the same result. That case involved a claim by a riparian landowner that a railroad's state-authorized filling of submerged land and construction of tracks upon it interfered with the riparian landowners' rights to access and to wharf out to a shipping channel. The Florida Supreme Court determined that the claimed right to wharf out did not exist in Florida, and that therefore only the right of access was compensable. Significantly, although the court recognized that the riparian-property owners had rights to accretion, the only rights it even suggested would be infringed by the railroad were the right of access (which the plaintiff had claimed) and the rights of view and use of the water (which it seems the plaintiff had not claimed).

The Florida Supreme Court decision before us is consistent with these background principles of state property law. It did not abolish the Members' right to future accretions, but merely held that the right was not implicated by the beach-restoration project, because the doctrine of avulsion applied. The Florida Supreme Court's opinion describes beach restoration as the reclamation by the State of the public's land, just as *Martin* had described the lake drainage in that case. Although the opinion does not cite *Martin* and is not always clear on this point, it suffices that its characterization of the littoral right to accretion is consistent with *Martin* and the other relevant principles of Florida law we have discussed. . . .

The result under Florida law may seem counter-intuitive. After all, the Members' property has been deprived of its character (and value) as oceanfront property by the State's artificial creation of an avulsion. Perhaps state-created avulsions ought to be treated differently from other avulsions insofar as the property right to accretion is concerned. But nothing in prior Florida law makes such a distinction, and *Martin* suggests, if it does not indeed hold, the contrary. Even if there might be different interpretations of *Martin* and other Florida property-law cases that would prevent this arguably odd result, we are not free to adopt them. The Takings Clause only protects property rights as they are established under state law, not as they might have been established or ought to have been established. We cannot say that the Florida Supreme Court's decision eliminated a right of accretion established under Florida law. . . .

## V

Because the Florida Supreme Court's decision did not contravene the established property rights of petitioner's Members, Florida has not violated the Fifth and Fourteenth Amendments. The judgment of the Florida Supreme Court is therefore affirmed.

JUSTICE STEVENS took no part in the decision of this case.

JUSTICE KENNEDY, with whom JUSTICE SOTOMAYOR joins, concurring in part and concurring in the judgment.

The Court's analysis of the principles that control ownership of the land in question, and of the rights of petitioner's members as adjacent owners, is correct in my view, leading to my joining Parts I, IV, and V of the Court's opinion. As Justice Breyer observes, however, this case does not require the Court to determine whether, or when, a judicial decision determining the rights of property owners can violate the Takings Clause of the Fifth Amendment of the United States Constitution. This separate opinion notes certain difficulties that should be considered before accepting the theory that a judicial decision that eliminates an "established property right" constitutes a violation of the Takings Clause. . . .

If a judicial decision, as opposed to an act of the executive or the legislature, eliminates an established property right, the judgment could be set aside as a deprivation of property without due process of law. The Due Process Clause, in both its substantive and procedural aspects, is a central limitation upon the exercise of judicial power. And this Court has long recognized that property regulations can be invalidated under the Due Process Clause. It is thus natural to read the Due Process Clause as limiting the power of courts to eliminate or change established property rights.

The Takings Clause also protects property rights, and it "operates as a conditional limitation, permitting the government to do what it wants so long as it pays the charge." Eastern Enterprises v. Apfel, 524 U.S. 498, 545 (1998) (Kennedy, J., concurring in judgment and dissenting in part). Unlike the Due Process Clause, therefore, the Takings Clause implicitly recognizes a governmental power while placing limits upon that power. Thus, if the Court were to hold that a judicial taking exists, it would presuppose that a judicial decision eliminating established property rights is "otherwise constitutional" so long as the State compensates the aggrieved property owners. Ibid. There is no clear authority for this proposition.

When courts act without direction from the executive or legislature, they may not have the power to eliminate established property rights by judicial decision. "Given that the constitutionality" of a judicial decision altering property rights "appears to turn on the legitimacy" of whether the court's judgment eliminates or changes established property rights "rather than on the availability of compensation,. . . the more appropriate constitutional analysis arises under general due process principles rather than under the Takings Clause." Ibid. Courts, unlike the executive or legislature, are not designed to make policy decisions about "the need for, and likely effectiveness of, regulatory actions." *Lingle*, supra, at 545. State courts generally operate under a common-law tradition that allows for incremental modifications to property law, but "this tradition cannot justify a *carte blanche* judicial authority to change property definitions wholly free of constitutional limitations."

The Court would be on strong footing in ruling that a judicial decision that eliminates or substantially changes established property rights, which are a legitimate expectation of the owner, is "arbitrary or irrational" under the Due Process Clause. Thus, without a judicial takings doctrine, the Due Process Clause would likely prevent a State from doing "by judicial decree what the Takings Clause forbids it to do by legislative fiat." The objection that a due process claim might involve close questions concerning whether a judicial decree extends beyond what owners might have expected is not a sound argument; for the same close questions would arise with respect to whether a judicial decision is a taking.

To announce that courts too can effect a taking when they decide cases involving property rights, would raise certain difficult questions. Since this case does not require those questions to be addressed, in my respectful view, the Court should not reach beyond the necessities of the case to announce a sweeping rule that court decisions can be takings, as that phrase is used in the Takings Clause. The evident reason for recognizing a judicial takings doctrine would be to constrain the power of the judicial branch. Of course, the judiciary must respect private ownership. But were this Court to say that judicial decisions become takings when they overreach, this might give more power to courts, not less. . . .

The idea, then, that a judicial takings doctrine would constrain judges might just well have the opposite effect. It would give judges new power and new assurance that changes in property rights that are beneficial, or thought to be so, are fair and proper because just compensation will be paid. The judiciary historically has not had the right or responsibility to say what property should or should not be taken.

Indeed, it is unclear whether the Takings Clause was understood, as a historical matter, to apply to judicial decisions. The Framers most likely viewed this Clause as applying only to physical appropriation pursuant to the power of eminent domain. And it appears these physical appropriations were traditionally made by legislatures. Courts, on the other hand, lacked the power of eminent domain. The Court's Takings Clause jurisprudence has expanded beyond the Framers' understanding, as it now applies to certain regulations that are not physical appropriations. But the Court should consider with care the decision to extend the Takings Clause in a manner that might be inconsistent with historical practice.

JUSTICE BREYER, with whom JUSTICE GINSBURG joins, concurring in part and concurring in the judgment.

I agree that no unconstitutional taking of property occurred in this case, and I therefore join Parts I, IV, and V of today's opinion. I cannot join Parts II and III, however, for in those Parts the plurality unnecessarily addresses questions of constitutional law that are better left for another day.

In Part II of its opinion the plurality concludes that courts, including federal courts, may review the private property law decisions of state courts to determine whether the decisions unconstitutionally take "private property" for "public use without just compensation." U.S. Const., Amdt. 5. And in doing so it finds "irrelevant" that the "particular state actor" that takes private property (or unconstitutionally redefines state property law) is the judicial branch, rather than the executive or legislative branch.

In Part III, the plurality determines that it is "not obviously appropriate" to apply this Court's "'fair and substantial basis'" test, familiar from our adequate and independent state ground jurisprudence, when evaluating whether a state-court property decision enacts an unconstitutional taking. The plurality further concludes that a state-court decision violates the Takings Clause not when the decision is "unpredictab[le]" on the basis of prior law, but rather when the decision takes private property rights that are "established." And finally, it concludes that all those affected by a state-court property law decision can raise a takings claim in federal court, but for the losing party in the initial state-court proceeding, who can only raise her claim (possibly for the first time) in a petition for a writ of certiorari here.

I do not claim that all of these conclusions are unsound. I do not know. But I do know that, if we were to express our views on these questions, we would invite a host of federal takings claims without the mature consideration of potential procedural or substantive legal principles that might limit federal interference in matters that are primarily the subject of state law. Property owners litigate many thousands of cases involving state property law in state courts each year. Each state-court property decision may further affect numerous nonparty property owners as well. Losing parties in many state-court cases may well believe that erroneous judicial decisions have deprived them of property rights they previously held and may consequently bring federal takings claims. And a glance at Part IV makes clear that such cases can involve state property law issues of considerable complexity. Hence, the approach the plurality would take today threatens to open the federal court doors to constitutional review of many, perhaps large numbers of, state-law cases in an area of law familiar to state, but not federal, judges. And the failure of that approach to set forth procedural limitations or canons of deference would create the distinct possibility that federal judges would play a major role in the shaping of a matter of significant state interest-state property law. . . .

In the past, Members of this Court have warned us that, when faced with difficult constitutional questions, we should "confine ourselves to deciding only what is necessary to the disposition of the immediate case." I heed this advice here. There is no need now to decide more than what the Court decides in Parts IV and V, namely, that the Florida Supreme Court's decision in this case did not amount to a "judicial taking."

## NOTES AND QUESTIONS

1. Justice Stevens recused himself from the case because he owned a beachfront apartment in Florida. The other eight Justices unanimously rejected the takings claim, but four of the eight Justices accept in principle the notion that judicial decisions can give rise to takings claims. The four other Justices find it unnecessary

to decide whether there can ever be a "judicial taking," but Justices Kennedy and Sotomayor believe that due process would be a better vehicle for assessing the fairness of judicial decisions affecting property rights. The decision provided the first significant indication of the views of the Roberts Court on regulatory takings issues, and the Court is as sharply split as ever.

2. In light of the fact that all eight Justices agreed that there had been no taking, why did Justice Scalia and the three other Justices who joined his opinion find it necessary to address the judicial takings issue? Is Justice Breyer correct in arguing that normal principles of judicial restraint would dictate that the Court not address difficult constitutional issues when it is not necessary to decide them to decide the case?

3. If the "judicial takings" concept were embraced by a majority of the Justices, what test should they use to determine whether or not a judicial taking has occurred? Justice Scalia rejects the plaintiff's proposed unpredictability test. The plaintiff proposes that a judicial taking should be found when the lower court's decision "constitutes a sudden change in state law, unpredictable in terms of relevant precedents." Why does Justice Scalia reject this test?

4. Does the concept of judicial takings raise serious federalism concerns? Isn't the essence of a judicial takings claim directed at a state court the notion that the court deliberately has misinterpreted state property law to deprive parties of their property rights? Is the U.S. Supreme Court in a better position to interpret state property law than the highest court of a state?

### *Knick v. Township of Scott* and the Future of Takings Jurisprudence

As discussed in the *Palazzolo* decision above, the Supreme Court in Williamson County Regional Planning Comm'n v. Hamilton Bank of Johnson City, 473 U.S. 172 (1985), held that a property owner could not bring a takings claim in federal court until a state court had denied his or her claim for just compensation under state law. By a vote of 5-4, the Supreme Court in Knick v. Township of Scott, 139 S.Ct. 2162 (2019), expressly overruled *Williamson County*. The Court held, in the context of a local ordinance requiring property owners to allow cemeteries on their land to be open to the public during daylight hours, that "a property owner has a claim for violation of the Takings Clause as soon as the government takes his property for public use without paying for it." Thus, the Court concluded that a property owner suffering a taking "may bring his claim in federal court under [42 U.S.C.] §1983" without first seeking compensation in state court.

Observers differ over the impact of the *Knick* decision. Some believe that there has been a significant increase in federal lawsuits alleging Fifth Amendment takings claims, citing cases where COVID-19 restrictions have been challenged as takings in federal court. However, in O'Neil v. California Coastal Commission, 2020 WL 2522026, the U.S. District Court for the Central District of California held that *Knick* did not carve out an exception to a state's Eleventh Amendment immunity just because the plaintiff could file in federal court. Thus a federal takings claim against the California Coastal Commission was still held to be barred by the Eleventh Amendment.

Professor Bethany Berger of University of Connecticut School of Law argues that "[r]ightly or wrongly decided, for three reasons *Knick* may not have as great an effect as its supporters hope and its critics fear. First, the Supreme Court has already resolved when damages are available for temporary takings, and *Knick* does not expand it. Second, many takings plaintiffs should still choose to file in state court, as they have a better chance of success there. Third, and most important, federalism will often require federal courts to refrain from deciding takings claims until unsettled state law issues have been decided in state court." Bethany Berger, *Knick v. Township of Scott, Pennsylvania*; Not the Revolution Some Hope for and Other Fear, ABA Probate and Property, May/June 2020. She concludes that "the decision makes sense as a matter of civil rights law, and likely will not prevent most takings cases from being first heard in the place where they belong: state courts."

Following the death of Justice Ruth Bader Ginsburg in September 2020 and her swift replacement with Justice Amy Coney Barrett, the Supreme Court now has a 6-3 conservative majority believed to be more sympathetic to takings claims. An early indication of the Court's willingness to expand takings doctrine may come in *Cedar Point Nursery v. Hassid*, a case argued in March 2021. In that case the Court is considering whether a state regulation that provides union organizers with limited physical access to an agricultural employer's property amounts to a *per se* physical taking under the Fifth Amendment.

# CHAPTER 8

# ENVIRONMENTAL IMPACT ASSESSMENT

NEPA requires that an agency must—to the *fullest* extent possible under its other statutory obligations—consider alternatives to its actions which would reduce environmental damage. That principle establishes that consideration of environmental matters must be more than a *pro forma* ritual. Clearly, it is pointless to "consider" environmental costs without also seriously considering action to avoid them. Such a full exercise of substantive discretion is required at every important, appropriate, and nonduplicative stage of an agency's proceedings.

—*Judge J. Skelly Wright*[*]

The National Environmental Policy Act (NEPA) of 1969, the statute that launched the "environmental decade" of the 1970s, has been hailed as one of the nation's most important environmental laws. It has also been condemned with equal vigor on grounds that it imposes costly, dilatory, and pointless paper-shuffling requirements on federal agencies and, indirectly, on private parties. NEPA famously requires federal agencies to produce environmental impact statements (EISs) prior to undertaking "major Federal actions significantly affecting the quality of the human environment." It requires little else, and therein lies both its singular genius and its fatal flaw.

—*Bradley C. Karkkainen*[**]

The National Environmental Policy Act (NEPA), which has been called "the Magna Carta of environmental law," Daniel R. Mandelker, *The National Environmental Policy Act: A Review of Its Experience and Problems*, 32 Wash. U.J.L. & Pol'y 293 (2010), launched what came to be known as "the environmental decade" of the 1970s. Passed unanimously by the U.S. Senate and by a vote of 372-15 in the House of Representatives, NEPA was signed into law with great fanfare by President Nixon on New Year's Day 1970.

NEPA's environmental impact assessment (EIA) requirements have become the most widely emulated elements of U.S. environmental regulation in the world today. A quarter century after the adoption of NEPA, more than 80 countries and 25 states had adopted some form of environmental assessment requirement. CEQ, The National Environmental Policy Act: A Study of Its Effectiveness After Twenty-five Years (1997). By 2017 a total of 187 nations required some form of EIA,

---

[*] Calvert Cliffs Coordinating Committee v. U.S. Atomic Energy Commission, 448 F.2d 1109 (D.C. Cir. 1971).

[**] Toward a Smarter NEPA: Monitoring and Managing Government's Environmental Performance, 102 Colum. L. Rev. 903, 904 (2002).

UNEP, Environmental Rule of Law 105 (2019); in some countries EIA requirements are the centerpiece of national environmental regulation. EIA requirements also have been adopted by multilateral development banks, such as the World Bank and International Monetary Fund, and most private financial institutions that fund global development projects. This chapter focuses on NEPA and the process of environmental impact assessment in the United States.

## A.   *THE NATIONAL ENVIRONMENTAL POLICY ACT: AN OVERVIEW*

The National Environmental Policy Act (Pub. L. No. 91-190, codified at 42 U.S.C. §§4321-4370a), sets forth broad principles and goals for the nation's environmental policy. It established as "the continuing policy of the Federal Government . . . to use all practicable means and measures . . . to create and maintain conditions under which man and nature can exist in productive harmony, and fulfill the social, economic and other requirements of present and future generations of Americans." §101(a), 42 U.S.C. §4331(a).

NEPA adopted an unusual strategy to pursue this ambitious goal. Rather than erecting an elaborate regulatory scheme applicable to business and industry, NEPA instead mandated a significant change in the decision-making procedures used by federal agencies. The Act requires all federal agencies to consider the likely environmental effects of their activities. Specifically, section 102 of NEPA requires that all federal agencies

> include in every recommendation or report on proposals for legislation and other major federal actions significantly affecting the quality of the human environment, a detailed statement by the responsible official on—
>
> (i) the environmental impact of the proposed action, (ii) any adverse environmental effects which cannot be avoided should the proposal be implemented, (iii) alternatives to the proposed action, (iv) the relationship between local short-term uses of man's environment and the maintenance and enhancement of long-term productivity, and (v) any irreversible and irretrievable commitments of resources which would be involved in the proposed action should it be implemented. [42 U.S.C. §4332(C).]

The remarkably simple structure of NEPA is outlined below.

---

## Structure of the National Environmental Policy Act

*§101* establishes as the continuing policy of the federal government the use of all practicable means to create and maintain conditions under which man and nature can exist in productive harmony.

*§102(2)(C)* requires all federal agencies to prepare an environmental impact statement (EIS) on major federal actions significantly affecting the quality of the environment. The EIS must include a detailed statement of environmental impacts, alternatives to the proposed action and any irretrievable commitments of resources involved.

*§102(2)(E)* requires all federal agencies to study alternatives to actions involving unresolved resource conflicts.

*§201* requires the President to submit to Congress an annual Environmental Quality Report. (The report for the year 1997 was the last report issued due to enactment of the Federal Reports Elimination and Sunset Act, Pub. L. No. 104-66.)

*§202* establishes a three-member Council on Environmental Quality (CEQ) in the Executive Office of the President.

*§204* outlines duties and functions of CEQ including annual reporting on the condition of the environment, information gathering, and review and appraisal of federal programs and activities.

Reviewing federal agency actions for compliance with NEPA, the courts quickly established that section 102's obligations were substantial. The "detailed statement" required (known as an "environmental impact statement," or EIS) has become, through judicial and administrative interpretations, an often massive undertaking. While federal regulations provide that an EIS generally should not exceed 150 pages in length, many are far longer. The EIS on an offshore oil lease sale is likely to be several hundred pages, while the EIS for licensing of a nuclear power plant may reach several thousand.

Each federal agency is made responsible for implementing NEPA, but Congress also created a central agency, the Council on Environmental Quality (CEQ), to coordinate agencies' compliance with NEPA. CEQ developed guidelines for NEPA implementation and, in 1978, armed with an executive order from President Carter, CEQ promulgated regulations on NEPA implementation that are binding on all federal agencies. 40 C.F.R. pt. 1500. These regulations, which reflect much of the caselaw that had developed under the statute, are the first recourse for analysis of any NEPA problem. They spell out many of the details of the NEPA process, and they have received considerable deference from the courts. In July 2020, the Trump administration's CEQ promulgated new regulations designed to streamline the NEPA process. The legality of these regulations is being tested in court, and they may be changed by the Biden administration (President Biden revoked President Trump's executive orders pertaining to NEPA hours after his inauguration in January 2021). Thus, this chapter discusses both the initial and the revised NEPA regulations.

The principal arbiters of NEPA's requirements have been the federal courts. Hundreds of judicial decisions have examined and elaborated on NEPA's requirements, creating a kind of common law of environmental impact assessment. The most influential early decision interpreting the duties NEPA imposes on federal agencies was the product of a challenge to the way the Atomic Energy Commission (AEC) had construed the Act.

During the late 1960s, the AEC aggressively encouraged electric utilities to build nuclear power plants. In 1968, the Baltimore Gas and Electric Company began construction of a nuclear power plant at Calvert Cliffs, Maryland, along the western shore of the Chesapeake Bay, just a year after announcing the project. Environmentalists opposing the plant formed a group called the Calvert Cliffs Coordinating Committee. The group was particularly concerned about the effect of thermal discharges and radiological emissions from the plant on the Chesapeake Bay.

After NEPA became law in 1970, the AEC issued regulations requiring permit applicants to prepare an environmental report to accompany their applications. However, the AEC took the position that it did not have to consider the report unless parties raised specific challenges to it during the licensing process. In the case below the Calvert Cliffs Coordinating Committee argued that the AEC's regulations violated NEPA because they did not require the agency independently to assess environmental impacts.

## Calvert Cliffs Coordinating Committee v. United States Atomic Energy Commission

449 F.2d 1109 (D.C. Cir. 1971)

J. SKELLY WRIGHT, Circuit Judge:

These cases are only the beginning of what promises to become a flood of new litigation—litigation seeking judicial assistance in protecting our natural environment. Several recently enacted statutes attest to the commitment of the Government to control, at long last, the destructive engine of material "progress." But it remains to be seen whether the promise of this legislation will become a reality. Therein lies the judicial role. In these cases, we must for the first time interpret the broadest and perhaps most important of the recent statutes: the National Environmental Policy Act . . . (NEPA). We must assess claims that one of the agencies charged with its administration has failed to live up to the congressional mandate. Our duty, in short, is to see that important legislative purposes, heralded in the halls of Congress, are not lost or misdirected in the vast hallways of the federal bureaucracy.

NEPA, like so much other reform legislation of the last 40 years, is cast in terms of a general mandate and broad delegation of authority to new and old administrative agencies. It takes the major step of requiring all federal agencies to consider values of environmental preservation in their spheres of activity, and it prescribes certain procedural measures to ensure that those values are in fact fully respected. Petitioners argue that rules recently adopted by the Atomic Energy Commission to govern consideration of environmental matters fail to satisfy the rigor demanded by NEPA. The Commission, on the other hand, contends that the vagueness of the NEPA mandate and delegation leaves much room for discretion and that the rules challenged by petitioners fall well within the broad scope of the Act. . . .

### I

We begin our analysis with an examination of NEPA's structure and approach and of the Atomic Energy Commission rules which are said to conflict with the requirements of the Act. The relevant portion of NEPA is Title I, consisting of five sections. Section 101 sets forth the Act's basic substantive policy: that the federal government "use all practicable means and measures" to protect environmental values. Congress did not establish environmental protection as an exclusive goal; rather, it desired a reordering of priorities, so that environmental costs and benefits will assume their proper place along with other considerations. In Section 101(b), imposing an explicit duty on federal officials, the Act provides that "it is the continuing responsibility of the Federal Government to use all practicable means, consistent with other essential considerations of national policy," to avoid environmental degradation, preserve "historic, cultural, and natural" resources, and promote "the widest range of beneficial uses of the environment without. . .undesirable and unintended consequences."

Thus the general substantive policy of the Act is a flexible one. It leaves room for a responsible exercise of discretion and may not require particular substantive results in particular problematic instances. However, the Act also contains very important "procedural" provisions—provisions which are designed to see that all federal agencies do in fact exercise the substantive discretion given them. These provisions are not highly flexible. Indeed, they establish a strict standard of compliance. . . .

. . . Section 102(2)(C) requires that responsible officials of all agencies prepare a "detailed statement" covering the impact of particular actions on the environment, the environmental costs which might be avoided, and alternative measures which might alter the cost-benefit equation. The apparent purpose of the "detailed statement" is to aid in the agencies' own decisionmaking process and to advise other interested agencies and the public of the environmental consequences of planned federal action. Beyond the "detailed statement," Section [102(2)(E)] requires all agencies specifically to "study, develop, and describe appropriate alternatives to recommended courses of action in any proposal which involves unresolved conflicts concerning alternative uses of available resources." This requirement, like the "detailed statement" requirement, seeks to ensure that each agency decisionmaker has before him and takes into proper account all possible approaches to a particular project (including total abandonment of the project) which would alter the environmental impact and the cost-benefit balance. Only in that fashion is it likely that the most intelligent, optimally beneficial decision will ultimately be made. Moreover, by compelling a formal "detailed statement" and a description of alternatives, NEPA provides evidence that the mandated decisionmaking process has in fact taken place and, most importantly, allows those removed from the initial process to evaluate and balance the factors on their own.

Of course, all of these Section 102 duties are qualified by the phrase "to the fullest extent possible." We must stress as forcefully as possible that this language does not provide an escape hatch for foot-dragging agencies; it does not make NEPA's procedural requirements somehow "discretionary." Congress did not intend the Act to be such a paper tiger. Indeed, the requirement of environmental consideration "to the fullest extent possible" sets a high standard for the agencies, a standard which must be rigorously enforced by the reviewing courts. . . .

. . . [T]he Section 102 duties are not inherently flexible. They must be complied with to the fullest extent, unless there is a clear conflict of *statutory* authority. Considerations of administrative difficulty, delay, or economic cost will not suffice to strip the section of its fundamental importance.

We conclude, then, that Section 102 of NEPA mandates a particular sort of careful and informed decisionmaking process and creates judicially enforceable duties. The reviewing courts probably cannot reverse a substantive decision on its merits, under Section 101, unless it be shown that the actual balance of costs and benefits that was struck was arbitrary or clearly gave insufficient weight to environmental values. But if the decision was reached procedurally without individualized consideration and balancing of environmental factors—conducted fully and in good faith—it is the responsibility of the courts to reverse. As one District Court has said of Section 102 requirements: "It is hard to imagine a clearer or stronger mandate to the Courts."

In the cases before us now, we do not have to review a particular decision by the Atomic Energy Commission granting a construction permit or an operating license. Rather, we must review the Commission's recently promulgated rules which govern consideration of environmental values in all such individual decisions. The rules were devised strictly in order to comply with the NEPA procedural requirements—but petitioners argue that they fall far short of the congressional mandate. [The rules provided that an applicant seeking permission to build and operate a nuclear power plant must prepare an "environmental report" assessing the likely impacts of the facility and possible alternatives. On the basis of the report, Commission staff would then prepare its own "detailed statement." The report and the detailed statement would accompany the application through the review process. However, they would not be considered by the licensing board (which decides the application), or received into evidence, unless environmental issues were raised by a party to the proceeding.] . . .

The question here is whether the Commission is correct in thinking that its NEPA responsibilities may "be carried out in toto outside the hearing process"—whether it is enough that environmental data and evaluations merely "accompany" an application through the review process, but receive no consideration whatever from the hearing board.

We believe that the Commission's crabbed interpretation of NEPA makes a mockery of the Act. What possible purpose could there be in the Section 102(2) (C) requirement (that the "detailed statement" accompany proposals through agency review processes) if "accompany" means no more than physical proximity—mandating no more than the physical act of passing certain folders and papers, unopened, to reviewing officials along with other folders and papers? What possible purpose could there be in requiring the "detailed statement" to be before hearing boards, if the boards are free to ignore entirely the contents of the statement? NEPA was meant to do more than regulate the flow of papers in the federal bureaucracy. The word "accompany" in Section 102(2)(C) must not be read so narrowly as to make the Act ludicrous. It must, rather, be read to indicate a congressional intent that environmental factors, as compiled in the "detailed statement," be *considered* through agency review processes.

Beyond Section 102(2)(C), NEPA requires that agencies consider the environmental impact of their actions "to the fullest extent possible." The Act is addressed to agencies as a whole, not only to their professional staffs. Compliance to the *"fullest"* possible extent would seem to demand that environmental issues be considered at every important stage in the decisionmaking process concerning a particular action—at every stage where an overall balancing of environmental and nonenvironmental factors is appropriate and where alterations might be made in the proposed action to minimize environmental costs. . . .

NEPA mandates a case-by-case balancing judgment on the part of federal agencies. In each individual case, the particular economic and technical benefits of planned action must be assessed and then weighed against the environmental costs; alternatives must be considered which would affect the balance of values. The magnitude of possible benefits and possible costs may lie anywhere on a broad spectrum. Much will depend on the particular magnitudes involved in particular cases. In some cases, the benefits will be great enough to justify a certain quantum of environmental costs; in other cases, they will not be so great and the proposed action may have to be abandoned or significantly altered so as to bring the benefits and costs into a proper balance. The point of the individualized balancing analysis is to ensure that, with possible alterations, the optimally beneficial action is finally taken.

Certification by another agency that its own environmental standards are satisfied involves an entirely different kind of judgment. Such agencies, without overall responsibility for the particular federal action in question, attend only to one aspect of the problem: the magnitude of certain environmental costs. They simply determine whether those costs exceed an allowable amount. Their certification does not mean that they found no environmental damage whatever. In fact, there may be significant environmental damage (e.g., water pollution), but not quite enough to violate applicable (e.g., water quality) standards. Certifying agencies do not attempt to weigh that damage against the opposing benefits. Thus, the balancing analysis remains to be done. It may be that the environmental costs, though passing prescribed standards, are nonetheless great enough to outweigh the particular economic and technical benefits involved in the planned action. The only agency in a position to make such a judgment is the agency with overall responsibility for the proposed federal action—the agency to which NEPA is specifically directed. . . .

NEPA requires that an agency must—to the *fullest* extent possible under its other statutory obligations—consider alternatives to its actions which would reduce environmental damage. That principle establishes that consideration of environmental matters must be more than a *pro forma* ritual. Clearly, it is pointless to "consider" environmental costs without also seriously considering action to avoid them. Such a full exercise of substantive discretion is required at every important, appropriate, and nonduplicative stage of an agency's proceedings.

## NOTES AND QUESTIONS

1. The AEC had argued that NEPA should be interpreted to create "flexible" duties. How did the court respond to this argument? What must the AEC do to comply with NEPA as a result of this decision?

2. The AEC argued that it need not consider air and water pollution caused by a proposed plant because those effects already are subject to EPA regulation. Is that position unreasonable? Is it supported by NEPA? Why does the court reject it? How would such a rule affect the review envisioned by the court? Does the court's formulation make NEPA review redundant of reviews under other environmental laws?

3. The *Calvert Cliffs* decision is important because it established that NEPA creates judicially enforceable duties. What standard of compliance does the court establish? How much consideration must agencies give to environmental impacts? At what stages of the decision-making process must they be considered?

4. Fascinating background information on the enactment of NEPA and the *Calvert Cliffs* litigation is provided by Dan Tarlock in The Story of *Calvert Cliffs*: A

Court Construes the National Environmental Policy Act to Create a Powerful Cause of Action, in Environmental Law Stories 77 (Lazarus & Houck eds., 2005). Tarlock notes that the decision halted licensing of all nuclear power plants for 18 months and forced fundamental changes in the AEC licensing process. It "cemented the principle that the potential adverse environmental impacts and available alternatives of a wide range of government sponsored and licensed activities should be rigorously assessed in advance of the activities." Id. at 102. The result has been the development of what Tarlock refers to as "a 'common law' of impact assessment." Id. This has "democratized NEPA and environmental protection generally" by forcing agencies to open up their decision-making processes to citizen involvement in an effort to forestall subsequent challenges to agency EISs.

5. Another important issue raised by Judge Wright in *Calvert Cliffs* is whether NEPA imposes enforceable *substantive* obligations on federal agencies. What does Judge Wright say about that in his opinion? The issue was addressed by the Supreme Court several years later in the following case, which it decided summarily without hearing oral argument.

## Strycker's Bay Neighborhood Council, Inc. v. Karlen

444 U.S. 223 (1980)

[Plaintiffs sought to enjoin construction of a low-income housing project on the Upper West Side of Manhattan. They challenged the approval of the project by the U.S. Department of Housing and Urban Development (HUD). After the district court upheld HUD's decision, the Second Circuit reversed, holding that NEPA required consideration of alternatives to the proposed project, even though NEPA did *not* require preparation of an EIS. Following the Second Circuit's decisions, the case was remanded to HUD.]

PER CURIAM.

On remand, HUD prepared a lengthy report entitled Special Environmental Clearance (1977). After marshaling the data, the report asserted that, "while the choice of Site 30 for development as a 100 percent low-income project has raised valid questions about the potential social environmental impacts involved, the problems associated with the impact on social fabric and community structures are not considered so serious as to require that this component be rated as unacceptable." Special Environmental Clearance Report 42. The last portion of the report incorporated a study wherein the [New York City Planning] Commission evaluated nine alternative locations for the project and found none of them acceptable. While HUD's report conceded that this study may not have considered all possible alternatives, it credited the Commission's conclusion that any relocation of the units would entail an unacceptable delay of two years or more. According to HUD, "[m]easured against the environmental costs associated with the minimum two-year delay, the benefits seem insufficient to justify a mandated substitution of sites." Id., at 54.

After soliciting the parties' comments on HUD's report, the District Court again entered judgment in favor of petitioners. The court was "impressed with [HUD's analysis] as being thorough and exhaustive" and found that "HUD's consideration of the alternatives was neither arbitrary nor capricious"; on the contrary, "[i]t was done in good faith and in full accordance with the law."

On appeal, the Second Circuit vacated and remanded again. The appellate court focused upon that part of HUD's report where the agency considered and rejected alternative sites, and in particular upon HUD's reliance on the delay such a relocation would entail. The Court of Appeals purported to recognize that its role in reviewing HUD's decision was defined by the Administrative Procedure Act (APA), 5 U.S.C. §706(2)(A), which provides that agency actions should be set aside if found to be "arbitrary, capricious, an abuse of discretion, or otherwise not in accordance with law. . . ." Additionally, however, the Court of Appeals looked to "[t]he provisions of NEPA" for "the substantive standards necessary to review the merits of agency decisions. . . ." The Court of Appeals conceded that HUD had "given 'consideration' to alternatives" to redesignating the site. Nevertheless, the court believed that "'consideration' is not an end in itself." Concentrating on HUD's finding that development of an alternative location would entail an unacceptable delay, the appellate court held that such delay could not be "an overriding factor" in HUD's decision to proceed with the development. Ibid. According to the court, when HUD considers such projects, "environmental factors, such as crowding low-income housing into a concentrated area, should be given determinative weight." The Court of Appeals therefore remanded the case to the District Court, instructing HUD to attack the shortage of low-income housing in a manner that would avoid the "concentration" of such housing on Site 30.

In Vermont Yankee Nuclear Power Corp. v. NRDC we stated that NEPA, while establishing "significant substantive goals for the Nation," imposes upon agencies duties that are "essentially procedural." As we stressed in that case, NEPA was designed "to insure a fully informed and well-considered decision," but not necessarily "a decision the judges of the Court of Appeals or of this Court would have reached had they been members of the decisionmaking unit of the agency." Vermont Yankee cuts sharply against the Court of Appeals' conclusion that an agency, in selecting a course of action, must elevate environmental concerns over other appropriate considerations. On the contrary, once an agency has made a decision subject to NEPA's procedural requirements, the only role for a court is to insure that the agency has considered the environmental consequences; it cannot "interject itself within the area of discretion of the executive as to the choice of the action to be taken."

In the present litigation there is no doubt that HUD considered the environmental consequences of its decision to redesignate the proposed site for low-income housing. NEPA requires no more. The petitions for certiorari are granted, and the judgment of the Court of Appeals is therefore reversed.

Mr. Justice Marshall, dissenting.

The issue raised by these cases is far more difficult than the *per curiam* opinion suggests. . . .

The issue before the Court of Appeals . . . was whether HUD was free under NEPA to reject an alternative acknowledged to be environmentally preferable solely on the ground that any change in sites would cause delay. This was hardly a "peripheral issue" in the case. Whether NEPA, which sets forth "significant substantive goals," Vermont Yankee Nuclear Power Corp. v. NRDC, supra, at 558, permits a projected 2-year time difference to be controlling over environmental superiority is by no means clear. Resolution of the issue, however, is certainly within the normal scope of review of agency action to determine if it is arbitrary, capricious, or an abuse of discretion. The question whether HUD can make delay the paramount concern over environmental superiority is essentially a restatement of the question whether HUD in considering the environmental consequences of its proposed action gave those consequences a "hard look," which is exactly the proper question for the reviewing court to ask.

The issue of whether the Secretary's decision was arbitrary or capricious is sufficiently difficult and important to merit plenary consideration in this Court. Further, I do not subscribe to the Court's apparent suggestion that *Vermont Yankee* limits the reviewing court to the essentially mindless task of determining whether an agency "considered" environmental factors even if that agency may have effectively decided to ignore those factors in reaching its conclusion. Indeed, I cannot believe that the Court would adhere to that position in a different factual setting. Our cases establish that the arbitrary-or-capricious standard prescribes a "searching and careful" judicial inquiry designed to ensure that the agency has not exercised its discretion in an unreasonable manner. Believing that today's summary reversal represents a departure from that principle, I respectfully dissent.

## NOTES AND QUESTIONS

1. In *Strycker's Bay*, the Supreme Court states that "once an agency has made a decision subject to NEPA's procedural requirements, the only role for a court is to insure that the agency has considered the environmental consequences." If an agency has "considered" environmental consequences in an EIS, can it then give *no* weight to those factors in its final decision? Consider Justice Marshall's argument in dissent. Consider also Judge Wright's suggestion in *Calvert Cliffs* that a court could "reverse a substantive decision on its merits, under Section 101, [if] the actual balance of costs and benefits that was struck was arbitrary or clearly gave insufficient weight to environmental values." Does the Supreme Court reject that interpretation in *Strycker's Bay*? What "weight" had the Second Circuit required HUD to give to environmental values?

2. *Strycker's Bay* confirms the triumph of process over substance in the NEPA context. As Dan Tarlock notes, "[T]he formulation of affirmative environmental policies—the original purpose for enacting the statute—has become increasingly divorced from the EIS process." Judge Wright in *Calvert Cliffs* had "assumed that the agency would assemble the relevant environmental information and then use this information to make a reasoned choice, balancing between environmental and non-environmental values." But "[i]nstead of forcing agencies to prefer more environmentally sustainable options, . . . an agency need only seriously consider environmental values by displaying adverse impacts and agonizing a bit over the consequences of the proposed decision." A. Dan Tarlock, The Story of *Calvert Cliffs*: A Court Construes the National Environmental Policy Act to Create a Powerful Cause of Action, in Environmental Law Stories 102 (Lazarus & Houck eds., 2005). As a result, Tarlock argues, the EIS has become like a corporate filing with the Securities and Exchange Commission.

3. The papers of the late Justice Thurgood Marshall reveal that then-Justice Rehnquist authored the per curiam opinion in *Strycker's Bay*, and that it was approved by the Court with remarkable speed and virtually no debate. Five Justices joined the draft per curiam opinion the day after it was first circulated; the other two joined the very next day. Percival, Environmental Law in the Supreme Court: Highlights from the Marshall Papers, 23 Envtl. L. Rep. 10606, 10611 (1993).

4. Two major sets of issues arise frequently in NEPA litigation: (1) questions concerning the circumstances under which agencies are required to prepare EISs, and (2) questions concerning the adequacy of the EIS. In cases where an agency has not prepared an EIS, courts must determine whether an EIS is required and, if not, whether the agency has complied with NEPA's other requirements. Where the agency has prepared an EIS, judicial review often focuses on the adequacy of that document. We consider these two fundamental sets of questions in turn.

## B.   UNDER WHAT CIRCUMSTANCES MUST AN ENVIRONMENTAL IMPACT STATEMENT BE PREPARED?

The threshold for the EIS requirement is set out in the statute: An EIS must be prepared for "proposals for legislation and other major Federal actions significantly affecting the quality of the human environment." To determine the scope and timing of NEPA's obligations, the courts have parsed these statutory words and looked to the congressional purposes that lie behind them. To define the boundaries of the inquiry, courts have focused on the first clause: There must be a "proposal" either for "legislation" or for "major Federal action." Within these boundaries the crucial question then becomes whether the action's effects on the "human environment" will be "significant."

### 1.   *"Proposals for Legislation and Other Major Federal Actions"*

By its terms, NEPA applies both to proposals for "legislation" and to proposals for "other major Federal actions." The lion's share of litigation has centered around the application of NEPA to the latter. Before examining what constitutes "major Federal action," we consider why the legislative EIS requirement has rarely been enforced.

### A.   "Proposals for Legislation"

Even though NEPA's EIS requirement applies to agency "proposals for legislation," legislative EISs rarely have been performed. Although CEQ initially took the position that section 102(2)(C)'s requirements applied to an appropriations request, the council reversed itself when it issued regulations implementing NEPA in 1978. Stating that CEQ's regulations are due "substantial deference," the Supreme Court held in Andrus v. Sierra Club, 442 U.S. 347 (1979), that agencies' requests to Congress for appropriations are not "proposals for legislation" within the meaning of NEPA's EIS requirement.

Legislative EIS issues resurfaced when the Bush administration refused to prepare an EIS for the North American Free Trade Agreement (NAFTA). In 1990, the United States, Mexico, and Canada initiated negotiations on NAFTA, which would significantly reduce trade barriers between the three countries. While it is widely believed that trade liberalization can have significant environmental consequences (see Chapter 11), the Office of the U.S. Trade Representative (USTR) announced that it would not prepare an EIS for any trade agreement that would be submitted to Congress for approval. Public Citizen then filed suit seeking to compel the USTR to prepare an EIS for NAFTA. Because NEPA does not have its own citizen suit provision, Public Citizen relied on the APA's judicial review provisions, 5 U.S.C. §702. After losing in the district court on the ground that it lacked standing, Public Citizen appealed to the D.C. Circuit, which held that it lacked jurisdiction to hear the suit because the negotiations had not yet been concluded, which meant that there was no final agency action for purposes of the Administrative Procedure Act (APA).

After two years of negotiations, agreement on NAFTA was reached and signed on December 17, 1992. Public Citizen again filed suit. This time the district court granted Public Citizen's motion for summary judgment and ordered the USTR to prepare an EIS. The government filed an emergency appeal to the D.C. Circuit, which reversed in Public Citizen v. U.S. Trade Representative, 5 F.3d 549 (D.C. Cir. 1993).

The D.C. Circuit held that the failure to prepare an EIS for NAFTA was not judicially reviewable because it is the *president* and not USTR, who ultimately is responsible for submitting NAFTA to Congress for approval. Thus, the only "final action" was that of the president, who, unlike USTR, is not an agency whose actions are subject to review under the APA. The court relied on Franklin v. Massachusetts, 505 U.S. 788 (1992), which held that the method used by the Secretary of Commerce in the 1990 census to determine apportionment of congressional representatives was not judicially reviewable because the only final action affecting plaintiffs under the statute was the president's transmittal of the apportionment to Congress. Public Citizen attempted to distinguish *Franklin* by arguing that the EIS requirement is an independent statutory obligation of the USTR, but the court found that unpersuasive because preparation of the census report also was an independent statutory obligation of the Secretary of Commerce. Responding to the argument that this would be the "death knell" for judicial review of compliance with legislative EIS requirements, the court stated that its decision was "limited to those cases in which the President has final constitutional or statutory responsibility for the final step necessary for the agency action directly to affect the parties." In a concurring opinion, Judge Randolph opined that *Franklin*'s "direct effects" requirement should be viewed as the "death knell" of judicial review for failure to prepare a legislative EIS because "it is difficult to see how the act of proposing legislation could generate direct effects on parties, or anyone else for that matter."

In 1994, after the Clinton administration completed participation in the Uruguay Round of negotiations on the General Agreement on Tariffs and Trade (GATT), Public Citizen again sued USTR for failing to prepare an EIS. The district court promptly dismissed the case, holding that it was controlled by the D.C. Circuit's decision in the NAFTA litigation. Public Citizen v. Kantor, 864 F. Supp. 208 (D.D.C. 1994).

Congress ultimately approved both NAFTA and U.S. entry into the World Trade Organization (WTO), which was created by the Uruguay Round of GATT negotiations. As discussed in Chapter 11, one condition for U.S. approval of NAFTA was the successful negotiation of side agreements governing environmental and labor concerns. The WTO, which is not subject to such side agreements, has been heavily criticized as insufficiently sympathetic to environmental concerns.

In November 1999, President Clinton announced that he was issuing an executive order requiring that "environmental reviews" be conducted for future trade agreements. Executive Order 13,141 directs the U.S. Trade Representative to prepare an "environmental review" for three types of trade agreements: comprehensive multilateral trade rounds, bilateral or plurilateral free trade agreements, and major new trade agreements in natural resource sectors. While it did not specify how extensive the review is to be, or how it compares with an EIS, the executive order states that the focus of environmental reviews generally "will be impacts in the United States," though "global and transboundary impacts" can be examined when "appropriate and prudent."

---

## Implementing NEPA: A Pathfinder

The National Environmental Policy Act (NEPA) is codified at 42 U.S.C. §§4321-4370e. The Council on Environmental Quality (CEQ), part of the Executive Office of the President, is responsible for coordinating agency compliance with NEPA and for preparing the annual Environmental Quality Report, which the president submits to Congress. CEQ regulations governing compliance with NEPA are the most helpful elaboration of NEPA's requirements; they can be found at 40 C.F.R. pts. 1500-1508. Each federal agency also has regulations specifying their procedures for complying with NEPA. CEQ also maintains a homepage located at *http://www.whitehouse.gov/ceq* that provides considerable information about NEPA. EPA's website contains information on how to obtain copies of EISs at *https://www.epa.gov/nepa/how-obtain-copy-environmental-impact-statement.*

CEQ's study, The National Environmental Policy Act: A Study of Its Effectiveness After Twenty-five Years (Jan. 1997), provided a detailed critique of how well NEPA has worked. The report contains a useful bibliography. For a report describing how NEPA's requirements have been eroded and attacked in recent years, see Robert G. Dreher, NEPA Under Siege: The Political Assault on the National Environmental Policy Act (2005). In 2005, the House Committee on Resources prepared its own critique of NEPA. Task Force on Improving the National Environmental Policy Act and Task Force on Updating the National Environmental Policy Act, Recommendations to Improve and Update the National Environmental Policy Act (July 31, 2006). The Task Force's recommendations are contained in the appendix of a 2007 CRS report, available online at *https://fas.org/sgp/crs/misc/RL33267.pdf.* Although CEQ stopped gathering comprehensive data concerning the environmental impact assessment process, a law review article analyzing 13 years of NEPA litigation is John C. Ruple & Kayla M. Race, Measuring the NEPA Litigation Burden: A Review of 1,499 Federal Court Cases, 50 Envt'l Law 479 (2020).

Columbia Law School's Climate Law Blog has been carefully monitoring how EISs are dealing with issues of climate change. Columbia's Climate Law Blog is available at *http://blogs.law.columbia.edu/climatechange/*. This caselaw is particularly important in light of the Trump administration's comprehensive amendments to NEPA regulations promulgated in July 2020. The regulations, which are being challenged in court, attempt to remove consideration of cumulative and indirect impacts, like those from climate change, and establish strict timelines for environmental reviews. An article on how environmental impact assessments should consider climate change is Michael Burger & Jessica Wentz, Downstream and Upstream Greenhouse Gas Emissions: The Proper Scope of NEPA Review, 41 Harv. Envtl. L. Rev. 109 (2016).

## B.   "Major Federal Action"

It is now well settled that the term "major Federal action" is not confined to projects that the federal government is funding or carrying out. The courts have found that the term also includes private projects that require federal approval as well as federal programs, policies, and rules. The caselaw is summarized in the CEQ Regulations contained in 40 C.F.R. §1508.18. These regulations defined "major Federal action" to include "actions with effects that may be major and which are potentially subject to Federal control and responsibility." Id. However, the Trump administration's CEQ implemented regulatory changes to NEPA in July 2020 that attempt to alter the statute's implementation. Promoted as an effort to streamline NEPA, the new regulations narrow the scope of "major Federal actions" that trigger NEPA by carving out an exception to NEPA review for actions that have "minimal Federal funding or minimal Federal involvement."

Under CEQ's interpretation, major federal actions include "projects and programs entirely or partly financed, assisted, conducted, regulated, or approved by federal agencies" as well as "new or revised agency rules, regulations, plans, policies, or procedures." Id. Enforcement actions taken by federal agencies are not included within CEQ's definition of major federal action. The 2020 CEQ regulations note that federal actions generally fall within one of the following categories:

1. Adoption of official policy, such as rules, regulations, and interpretations adopted pursuant to the Administrative Procedure Act, 5 U.S.C. §§551 et seq. or other statutes; implementation of treaties and international conventions or agreements, including those implemented pursuant to statute or regulation; formal documents establishing an agency's policies which will result in or substantially alter agency programs.
2. Adoption of formal plans, such as official documents prepared or approved by federal agencies that prescribe alternative uses of federal resources, upon which future agency actions will be based.
3. Adoption of programs, such as a group of concerted actions to implement a specific policy or plan; systematic and connected agency decisions allocating agency resources to implement a specific statutory program or executive directive.

4. Approval of specific projects, such as construction or management activities located in a defined geographic area. Projects include actions approved by permit or other regulatory decision as well as federal and federally assisted activities. (40 C.F.R. §1508(q)(3).)

The 2020 CEQ regulation narrow the scope of "major Federal actions" and give agencies more flexibility to satisfy NEPA requirements. Difficult questions about the extent of NEPA's application to a private project arise when only a small but integral part of the project requires federal approval. This occasionally occurs in cases involving "segmentation" of a highway project. In those cases, courts have held that, in approving a proposed highway project, the Federal Highway Administration must consider the effects of possible future highway construction that will be made possible by the instant proposal, unless the proposed segment has "logical termini" and "independent utility." See, e.g., Lange v. Brinegar, 625 F.2d 812 (9th Cir. 1980); Swain v. Brinegar, 542 F.2d 364 (7th Cir. 1976). A somewhat similar issue arose in Winnebago Tribe of Nebraska v. Ray, 621 F.2d 269 (8th Cir. 1980). In that case, an Indian tribe argued that because construction of a proposed power line required a permit from the Army Corps of Engineers to cross the Missouri River, the Corps was required to prepare an EIS covering the impact of the entire transmission line. The Eighth Circuit rejected this argument and held that the Corps could restrict its consideration to the impact on the area in and around the navigable waters in determining whether the action required an EIS.

In Ross v. Federal Highway Administration, 162 F.3d 1046 (10th Cir. 1998), the Tenth Circuit upheld a district court decision that a state could not avoid application of NEPA simply by deciding not to use federal funds when it commenced construction of a segment of a highway construction project that affected spiritual sites and property of a Native American tribe. Faced with a ruling that it needed to prepare a supplemental EIS for the project, the Kansas Department of Transportation had asked the Federal Highway Administration to segment the project into four parts. It then began construction of the eastern leg of the project without federal funds. Plaintiffs succeeded in stopping the project by convincing a federal district court that the entire project was a major federal action subject to NEPA because Congress had designated it a federal demonstration project for which $10 million in federal funds could not be segmented.

In 1992, the federal government agreed to settle litigation it had brought against the Southern Florida Water Management District and the Florida Department of Environmental Regulation for contaminating a national wildlife refuge and a national park in the Everglades. The agreement required the state to undertake remedial action to address the contamination and to restore the Everglades. In United States v. Southern Florida Water Management District, 28 F.3d 1563 (11th Cir. 1994), the Eleventh Circuit reversed a district court ruling that an EIS was required because of the federal government's participation in negotiating and implementing the settlement agreement. The Eleventh Circuit explained that a settlement "to compel a nonfederal party to undertake its legal responsibility does not convert the proposed state remedial measures into federal responsibilities for NEPA purposes." The court noted that NEPA obligations may arise in the future if federal agencies get involved in funding the restoration or issuing permits for activities undertaken to implement the settlement. But it concluded that the mere fact that the federal government was involved in reaching the settlement was insufficient to trigger NEPA's requirements.

In other cases, there is a question whether any *action* has been taken by the federal agency. Prior to 1990, the U.S. Forest Service used herbicides to control vegetation in the Lake States National Forests. In 1990, however, the Forest Service decided not to use herbicides. In Minnesota Pesticide Information and Education, Inc. v. Espy, 29 F.3d 442 (8th Cir. 1994), the Eighth Circuit held that the Forest Service was not required to prepare an EIS for deciding not to use herbicides. The court explained that "[t]his is not a decision to do something; rather it is a decision to *not* do something (namely, apply herbicides), which does not trigger NEPA's requirements that an EIS be prepared." 29 F.3d at 443 (emphasis in original). The court explained that until the Forest Service actually decides upon an alternative method for controlling vegetation, "it has effectively elected a course of temporary inaction" to which NEPA does not apply.

In New Jersey Department of Environmental Protection v. Long Island Power Authority, 30 F.3d 403 (3d Cir. 1994), New Jersey sought an injunction to prevent the shipment of partially irradiated nuclear fuel through New Jersey coastal waters until an EIS had been performed. The Third Circuit held that the fact that the Coast Guard had been informed of the shipment but failed to object to it did not constitute major federal action because the Coast Guard was not required to approve the shipment. However, in Citizens Awareness Network, Inc. v. Nuclear Regulatory Commission, 59 F.3d 284 (1st Cir. 1995), the First Circuit rejected the NRC's claim that it had not engaged in "major Federal action" because it was passively monitoring a utility's activities decommissioning a nuclear power plant. The court noted that although the NRC had not specifically approved the utility's decommissioning plan, it had authorized the release of funds set aside by licensees to finance decommissioning activities and it had advised the utility that it could proceed with decommissioning, which itself is an activity that requires preparation of an EIS. In Sancho v. Department of Energy, 578 F. Supp. 2d 1258 (D. Haw. 2008), plaintiffs who believed that operation of the Large Hadron Collider (LHC), a subatomic particle accelerator straddling the French-Swiss border, could create a black hole leading to the destruction of the Earth, sought to require DOE to prepare an EIS for the project. However, the court held that because DOE had contributed less than 10 percent of the cost of the project (only $531 million of the $5.84 billion construction cost) and had only minimal control over it, DOE's action did not constitute "major Federal action" triggering NEPA review.

### C.  Problems of Timing and Scope

The most difficult and persistent questions in determining whether there is a "proposal for . . . major Federal action" have been the appropriate timing and scope of the review that NEPA requires. As several cases have illustrated, these two questions are bound up together.

The interplay of timing and scope is perhaps most pronounced in federal resource management programs. Thorough review in an EIS may serve useful functions at several stages in the development and implementation of such a program. Choosing the proper time and scope for EIS review thus requires hard choices: Should the agency prepare an EIS for its formulation of national policy so that it may consider the environmental consequences of the fundamental policy choices made at that stage? Should it prepare an EIS for each region of the country before the national program is implemented, so that the particular characteristics, needs, and problems of the region can be considered? Should it prepare an EIS for each action taken in implementing the program in the field (each timber sale, grazing lease, or mining permit approved), so that it can evaluate environmental consequences on the basis of the concrete information that only becomes available when one has a proposal for specific action at a specific site? Should it prepare an EIS at every one of these stages, at the risk of drowning itself, and the public, in paper?

In the case that follows, the Sierra Club argued that the Department of the Interior could not allow further development of federal coal reserves in a four-state area of the Northern Great Plains without preparing a comprehensive EIS on the entire region. Interior had conducted three studies of potential coal development in the region and had prepared a national "Coal Programmatic EIS" for the Department's coal leasing program throughout the country. The D.C. Circuit held that four factors should govern when a programmatic EIS must be commenced: (1) the likelihood and imminence of a program's coming to fruition, (2) the extent of information available on the effects of a program, (3) the extent to which irretrievable resource commitments are being made, and (4) the potential severity of environmental effects. After finding that factors (2) and (4) already made an EIS ripe, the court remanded the case to Interior, which obtained Supreme Court review in the case that follows.

## Kleppe v. Sierra Club

427 U.S. 390 (1976)

Mr. Justice Powell delivered the opinion of the Court.

. . . The major issue remains the one with which the suit began: whether NEPA requires petitioners to prepare an environmental impact statement on the entire Northern Great Plains region. Petitioners, arguing the negative, rely squarely upon the facts of the case and the language of §102(2)(C) of NEPA. We find their reliance well placed.

. . . [Section] 102(2)(C) requires an impact statement "in every recommendation or report on proposals for legislation and other major Federal actions significantly affecting the quality of the human environment." Since no one has suggested that petitioners have proposed legislation on respondents' region, the controlling phrase in this section of the Act, for this case, is "major Federal actions." Respondents can prevail only if there has been a report or recommendation on a proposal for major federal action with respect to the Northern Great Plains region. . . . [T]he relevant facts show[] there has been none; instead, all proposals are for actions of either local or national scope.

The local actions are the decisions by the various petitioners to issue a lease, approve a mining plan, issue a right-of-way permit, or take other action to allow private activity at some point within the region identified by respondents. Several Courts of Appeals have held that an impact statement must be included in the report of recommendation on a proposal for such action if the private activity to be permitted is one "significantly affecting the quality of the human environment" within the meaning of §102(2)(C). The petitioners do not dispute this requirement in this case, and indeed have prepared impact statements on several proposed actions of this type in the Northern Great Plains during the course of this litigation. Similarly, the federal petitioners agreed at oral argument that §102(2) (C) required the Coal Programmatic EIS that was prepared in tandem with the new national coal-leasing program and included as part of the final report on the proposal for adoption of that program. Their admission is well made, for the new leasing program is a coherent plan of national scope, and its adoption surely has significant environmental consequences.

But there is no evidence in the record of an action or a proposal for an action of regional scope. The District Court, in fact, expressly found that there was no existing or proposed plan or program on the part of the Federal Government for the regional development of the area described in respondents' complaint. It found also that the three studies initiated by the Department in areas either included within or inclusive of respondents' region — that is, the Montana-Wyoming Aqueducts Study, the North Central Power Study, and the NGPRP [Northern Great Plains Resources Program] — were not parts of any plan or program to develop or encourage development of the Northern Great Plains. That court found no evidence that the individual coal development projects undertaken or proposed by private industry and public utilities in that part of the country are integrated into a plan or otherwise interrelated. These findings were not disturbed by the Court of Appeals, and they remain fully supported by the record in this Court. . . .

### IV

. . . Even had the record justified a finding that a regional program was contemplated by the petitioners, the legal conclusion drawn by the Court of Appeals cannot be squared with the Act. The court recognized that the mere "contemplation" of certain action is not sufficient to require an impact statement. But it believed the statute nevertheless empowers a court to require the preparation of an impact statement to begin at some point prior to the formal recommendation or report on a proposal. The Court of Appeals accordingly devised its own four-part "balancing" test for determining when, during the contemplation of a plan or other type of federal action, an agency must begin a statement.

. . . The Court's reasoning and action find no support in the language or legislative history of NEPA. The statute clearly states when an impact statement is required and mentions nothing about a balancing of factors. Rather, as we noted last Term, under the first sentence of §102(2)(C) the moment at which an agency must have a final statement ready "is the time at which it makes a recommendation or report on a *proposal* for federal action." The procedural duty imposed upon agencies by this section is quite precise, and the role of the courts in enforcing that duty is similarly precise. A court has no authority to depart from the statutory language and, by a balancing of court-devised factors, determines a point during the germination process of a potential proposal at which an impact statement *should be prepared*. Such an assertion of judicial authority would leave the agencies uncertain as to their procedural duties under NEPA, would invite judicial involvement in the day-to-day decisionmaking process of the agencies, and would invite litigation. As the contemplation of a project and the accompanying study thereof do not necessarily result in a proposal for major federal action, it may be assumed that the balancing process devised by the Court of Appeals also would result in the preparation of a good many unnecessary impact statements. . . .

## V

Our discussion thus far has been addressed primarily to the decision of the Court of Appeals. It remains, however, to consider the contention now urged by respondents. They have not attempted to support the Court of Appeals' decision. Instead, respondents renew an argument they appear to have made to the Court of Appeals, but which that court did not reach. Respondents insist that, even without a comprehensive federal plan for the development of the Northern Great Plains, a "regional" impact statement nevertheless is required on all coal-related projects in the region because they are intimately related. . . .

. . . [Section] 102(2)(C) may require a comprehensive impact statement in certain situations where several proposed actions are pending at the same time. NEPA announced a national policy of environmental protection and placed a responsibility upon the Federal Government to further specific environmental goals by "all practicable means, consistent with other essential considerations of national policy." §101(b), 42 U.S.C. §4331(b). Section 102(2)(C) is one of the "action-forcing" provisions intended as a directive to "all agencies to assure consideration of the environmental impact of their actions in decisionmaking." Conference Report on NEPA, 115 Cong. Rec. 40416 (1969). By requiring an impact statement Congress intended to assure such consideration during the development of a proposal or—as in this case—during the formulation of a position on a proposal submitted by private parties. A comprehensive impact statement may be necessary in some cases for an agency to meet this duty. Thus, when several proposals for coal-related actions that will have cumulative or synergistic environmental impact upon a region are pending concurrently before an agency, their environmental consequences must be considered together. Only through comprehensive consideration of pending proposals can the agency evaluate different courses of action.

Agreement to this extent with respondents' premise, however, does not require acceptance of their conclusion that all proposed coal-related actions in the Northern Great Plains region are so "related" as to require their analysis in a single comprehensive impact statement. . . .

. . . Cumulative environmental impacts are, indeed, what require a comprehensive impact statement. But determination of the extent and effect of these factors, and particularly identification of the geographic area within which they may occur, is a task assigned to the special competency of the appropriate agencies. Petitioners dispute respondents' contentions that the interrelationship of environmental impacts is regionwide and, as respondents own submissions indicate, petitioners appear to have determined that the appropriate scope of comprehensive statements should be based on basins, drainage areas, and other factors. We cannot say that petitioners' choices are arbitrary. Even if environmental interrelationships could be shown conclusively to extend across basins and drainage areas, practical considerations of feasibility might well necessitate restricting the scope of comprehensive statements.

In sum, respondents' contention as to the relationships between all proposed coal-related projects in the Northern Great Plains region does not require that petitioners prepare one comprehensive impact statement covering all before proceeding to approve specific pending applications. As we already determined that there exists no proposal for regionwide action that could require a regional impact statement, the judgment of the Court of Appeals must be reversed, and the judgment of the District Court reinstated and affirmed. . . .

Mr. Justice Marshall, with whom Mr. Justice Brennan joins, concurring in part and dissenting in part.

While I agree with much of the Court's opinion, I must dissent from Part IV, which holds that the federal courts may not remedy violations of the National Environmental Policy Act of 1969 (NEPA), 83 Stat. 852, 42 U.S.C. §4321 et seq.—no matter how blatant—until it is too late for an adequate remedy to be formulated. As the Court today recognizes, NEPA contemplates agency consideration of environmental factors throughout the decisionmaking process.

Since NEPA's enactment, however, litigation has been brought primarily at the end of that process—challenging agency decisions to act made without adequate environmental impact statements or without any statements at all. In such situations, the courts have had to content themselves with the largely unsatisfactory remedy of enjoining the proposed federal action and ordering the preparation of an adequate impact statement. This remedy is insufficient because, except by deterrence, it does nothing to further early consideration of environmental factors. And, as with all after-the-fact remedies, a remand for preparation of an impact statement after the basic decision to act has been made invites post hoc rationalizations, rather than the candid and balanced environmental assessments envisioned by NEPA. Moreover, the remedy is wasteful of resources and time, causing fully developed plans for action to be laid aside while an impact statement is prepared.

Nonetheless, until this lawsuit, such belated remedies were all the federal courts had had the opportunity to impose under NEPA. In this case, confronted with a situation in which, according to respondents' allegations, federal agencies were violating NEPA prior to their basic decision to act, the Court of Appeals for the District of Columbia Circuit seized the opportunity to devise a different and effective remedy. It recognized a narrow class of cases—essentially those where both the likelihood of eventual agency action and the danger posed by nonpreparation of an environmental impact statement were great—in which it would allow judicial intervention prior to the time at which an impact statement must be ready. The Court today loses sight of the inadequacy of other remedies and the narrowness of the category constructed by the Court of Appeals, and construes NEPA so as to preclude a court from ever intervening prior to a formal agency proposal. This decision, which unnecessarily limits the ability of the federal courts to effectuate the intent of NEPA, is mandated neither by the statute nor by the various equitable considerations upon which the Court relies.

## NOTES AND QUESTIONS

1. What environmental reviews had the Secretary undertaken or agreed to undertake? Why did the Sierra Club want more?

2. Consider the question of *timing*. The majority seem to agree that an EIS must be completed by the time of the agency's "recommendation or report on a proposal" for action. What is the debate? What earlier obligations has the court of appeals imposed on the agencies? Why does Justice Marshall believe the lower court's approach is necessary? Why did the Sierra Club abandon this approach on appeal?

3. The majority in *Kleppe* relied largely on the interpretation of the statutory term "proposal" in deciding the timing of NEPA's obligations. Two years after *Kleppe*,

CEQ defined "proposal" in its regulations as existing "at that stage in the development of an action when an agency subject to the Act has a goal and is actively preparing to make a decision on one or more alternative means of accomplishing that goal and the effects can be meaningfully evaluated." 40 C.F.R. §1508.23. The CEQ reaffirmed that preparation of an EIS should be completed in time for inclusion in any recommendation or report on the proposal. Does this CEQ regulation depart from the Supreme Court's decision in *Kleppe?* The CEQ also issued more general guidance on the issue of "timing," which is contained in 40 C.F.R. §1502.5.

4.  CEQ's regulations direct that when "emergency circumstances make it necessary to take an action with significant environmental impact without observing the provisions of these regulations, the Federal agency taking the action should consult with the Council about alternative arrangements." 40 C.F.R. §1506.11. Only "actions necessary to control the immediate impacts of the emergency" can be exempted from NEPA review. In October 1993, CEQ approved a proposal by the Department of Energy to permit an emergency shipment of 144 spent nuclear fuel rods to enter the United States from Belgium without preparing an EIS. Under the Reduced Enrichment for Research and Test Reactors program, the U.S. government has sought to promote nuclear nonproliferation by agreeing to reclaim used nuclear fuel provided by it to foreign countries if they agree to stop using weapons-grade uranium. Legal challenges to the emergency shipment were rejected in South Carolina ex rel. Campbell v. O'Leary, 64 F.3d 892 (4th Cir. 1995). Noting that an elaborate EIS was being prepared for the full program of shipping 24,000 spent fuel rods back to the United States, the Fourth Circuit concluded that it was not necessary to complete the EIS prior to receiving an urgent shipment of the first fuel rods. The court held that this "segmented" shipment in itself would not have a significant effect on the environment because the fuel rods would be stored in existing and approved facilities, unlike the massive shipments to follow which would require construction of a new storage facility. CEQ also used its emergency authority in 1998 to allow the Forest Service to sell dead and dying timber on 22,000 acres of national forests in Texas following a massive windstorm. The Forest Service sought approval to prevent an immediate fire hazard for adjacent private lands, while agreeing to analyze the cumulative effects of the sales in a subsequent environmental assessment concerning future sales.

5.  In Winter v. Natural Resources Defense Council, 555 U.S. 7 (2008), the U.S. Navy was sued by an environmental group who argued that an EIS needed to be prepared before the Navy used mid-frequency active sonar in training exercises that might harm marine mammals. After the district court granted a preliminary injunction restricting use of sonar, the Navy asked CEQ to approve "alternative arrangements" for NEPA compliance in light of "emergency circumstances." The Navy claimed that testing of the sonar in waters off the coast of Southern California was vital to national security and military preparedness. The CEQ approved as "alternative arrangements" the Navy's use of voluntary mitigation measures it previously had adopted. After the district court refused to lift its injunction, the Navy appealed to the Ninth Circuit, which affirmed. The Ninth Circuit held that there was a serious question whether the CEQ's interpretation of the "emergency circumstances" regulation was lawful, that plaintiffs had carried their burden of establishing a "possibility" of irreparable injury, and that the preliminary injunction was

appropriate because the balance of hardships and consideration of the public interest favored the plaintiffs. The U.S. Supreme Court then granted expedited review. Without reaching the merits of the underlying NEPA issue, the Court reversed. The Court held that the district court had erred in granting the preliminary injunction because it had only required a showing that irreparable harm to marine mammals was "possible" when it should have required a showing that it was "likely." The Court also concluded that the district court had not properly balanced the equities because the alleged irreparable injury to marine mammals was outweighed by the public interest and the Navy's interest in effective, realistic training of its sailors.

6. In Monsanto Co. v. Geertson Seed Farms, 561 U.S. 139 (2010), the Supreme Court again reversed an injunction that had been issued to remedy a failure to complete an environmental impact statement (EIS). A federal district court had issued an injunction prohibiting nearly all planting of genetically engineered alfalfa until an EIS was completed by the Animal and Plant Health Inspection Service (APHIS). After the injunction was affirmed by the U.S. Court of Appeals for the Ninth Circuit, intervenor Monsanto Company, which produces the seed, sought review in the U.S. Supreme Court. Writing for the Court, Justice Alito stated:

> An injunction should issue only if the traditional four-factor test [irreparable harm, inadequate remedies at law, balance of harm favors plaintiff, and injunction would not be contrary to the public interest] is satisfied. In contrast, the statements [by the courts below] appear to presume that an injunction is the proper remedy for a NEPA violation except in unusual circumstances. No such thumb on the scales is warranted. Nor, contrary to the reasoning of the Court of Appeals, could any such error be cured by a court's perfunctory recognition that "an injunction does not automatically issue" in NEPA cases. It is not enough for a court considering a request for injunctive relief to ask whether there is a good reason why an injunction should not issue; rather, a court must determine that an injunction should issue under the traditional four-factor test set out above. [561 U.S. at 157-158.]

The Court majority concluded that the district court had abused its discretion in issuing the injunction.

Justice Stevens, the sole dissenter in the case (Justice Breyer recused himself because his brother had been the district judge who issued the injunction), argued that

> Congress recognized in NEPA that complex environmental cases often require exceptionally sophisticated scientific determinations, and that agency decisions should not be made on the basis of "incomplete information." Congress also recognized that agencies cannot fully weigh the consequences of these decisions without obtaining public comments through an EIS. While a court may not presume that a NEPA violation requires an injunction, it may take into account the principles embodied in the statute in considering whether an injunction would be appropriate. This District Court had before it strong evidence that gene transmission was likely to occur and that limits on growing could not be enforced. It also had a large amount of highly detailed evidence about whether

growing restrictions, even if enforced, can prevent transmission. That evidence called into question the agency's own claims regarding the risks posed by partial deregulation. In enjoining partial deregulation until it had the benefit of an EIS to help parse the evidence, the court acted with exactly the sort of caution that Congress endorsed in NEPA. [561 U.S. at 183-184.]

7. In a few cases, Congress has acted to exempt certain projects from NEPA. In section 102 of the REAL ID Act of 2005, Congress gave the Secretary of Homeland Security "the authority to waive all legal requirements" that he determines "necessary to ensure expeditious construction" of a fence on the U.S./Mexican border. On October 26, 2007, DHS Secretary Michael Chertoff exercised this waiver authority to waive application of NEPA and other environmental statutes. Chertoff's action came after a federal district court had enjoined construction of the fence in the biologically rich San Pedro Riparian National Conservation Area because of the government's failure to prepare an EIS. A challenge alleging that the waiver authority unconstitutionally delegated legislative power to an executive official was rejected in Defenders of Wildlife v. Chertoff, 527 F. Supp. 2d 119 (D.D.C. 2007). The court concluded that the REAL ID legislation simply granted waiver authority, rather than the authority to amend or repeal statutes, and that it included an intelligible principle to confine the exercise of this discretion. The Supreme Court, the only Court allowed by Congress to review challenges to the REAL ID waiver authority, denied review of the district court's decision. An effort to exempt from NEPA review projects funded by the American Recovery and Reinvestment Act of 2009, President Obama's economic stimulus package, failed. Congress instead confirmed in section 1609 of this legislation that NEPA fully applies to such projects, and it directed the president to report to it every 90 days about the status of NEPA reviews for projects funded by the stimulus.

8. On January 24, 2017, President Trump issued Executive Order 13,766, entitled "Expediting Environmental Reviews and Approvals for High Priority Infrastructure Projects." 82 Fed. Reg. 8,657 (2017). The executive order declared that "it is the policy of the executive branch to streamline and expedite, in a manner consistent with law, environmental reviews and approvals for all infrastructure projects, especially projects that are a high priority for the Nation, such as improving the U.S. electric grid and telecommunications systems and repairing and upgrading critical port facilities, airports, pipelines, bridges, and highways." The order directed the chairman of the Council on Environmental Quality to decide within 30 days of a request by a governor or agency head whether to designate a project as a "high priority infrastructure project." For projects so designated, the chairman was instructed to "coordinate with the head of the relevant agency to establish, in a manner consistent with law, expedited procedures and deadlines for completion of environmental reviews and approvals for such projects." Agencies were directed to "give highest priority to completing such reviews and approvals . . . using all necessary and appropriate means." Hours after taking office on January 20, 2021, President Biden revoked Executive Order 13,766.

9. On August 15, 2017, President Trump issued Executive Order 13,807, entitled "Establishing Discipline and Accountability in the Environmental Review

and Permitting Process for Infrastructure." 82 Fed. Reg. 40,463 (2017). This order directed CEQ to "simplify and accelerate the NEPA review process." In response, CEQ promulgated new regulations in July 2020. These regulations seek to speed up environmental reviews and approvals for "major infrastructure projects" (defined to include those for which an agency has determined it will prepare an EIS) so that they will take no more than two years on average. They do so by subjecting such projects to the Cross-Agency Priority (CAP) process and by consolidating reviews in a single lead federal agency that will produce "One Federal Decision." The regulations also curtail evaluation of "cumulative" and "indirect" effects from proposed actions, implementing a single definition of "effects," the sufficiency of which will be evaluated by the courts. All agencies were directed to complete their authorization decisions within 90 days of the completion of record of decision (ROD) by the lead federal agency. Executive Order 13,807 also revoked an executive order issued by President Obama in January 2015 (E.O. 13,690) that required agencies to incorporate a new flood risk reduction standard in their decision making for federally funded projects. President Biden revoked Executive Order 13,807 the day he took office on January 20, 2021.

10.  Returning to *Kleppe*, consider also the question of *scope*. In *Kleppe*, the Sierra Club argued that an EIS must be prepared for actions that are "intimately related." Did the Supreme Court reject this interpretation? What would the Sierra Club have to show to persuade a court to compel preparation of a regional EIS? What difficulties does that showing pose for environmental plaintiffs? Might the Sierra Club fare better under the CEQ's post-*Kleppe* regulations contained in 40 C.F.R. §1508.25? These regulations direct agencies to determine the scope of EISs by considering three types of actions (connected actions, cumulative actions, and similar actions), three types of alternatives, and three types of impacts (direct, indirect, and cumulative). Consider the impact and application of these regulations in the following cases.

## Thomas v. Peterson

753 F.2d 754 (9th Cir. 1985)

[The Forest Service planned construction of a gravel road to service timber harvesting in an area known as "Jersey Jack." The Service concluded that the road would not have "significant" effects on the environment and therefore approved construction without preparing an EIS. The Service subsequently approved two timber sales in the area, also without preparing an EIS. Conservation groups brought this action to enjoin construction of the road, alleging violations of the National Forest Management Act, the Endangered Species Act, and NEPA.]

Before WRIGHT, SNEED, and ALARCON, Circuit Judges.

SNEED, Circuit Judge.

### THE NEPA CLAIM

The central question that plaintiff's NEPA claim presents is whether the road and the timber sales are sufficiently related so as to require combined treatment in a single EIS that covers the cumulative effects of the road and the sales. If so, the Forest Service has proceeded improperly. An EIS must be prepared and considered by the Forest Service before the road can be approved. If not, the Forest Service may go ahead with the road, and later consider the environmental impacts of the timber sales.

Section 102(2)(C) of NEPA requires an EIS for "major Federal actions significantly affecting the quality of the human environment." 42 U.S.C. §4332(2)(C) (1982). While it is true that administrative agencies must be given considerable discretion in defining the scope of environmental impact statements, there are situations in which an agency is required to consider several related actions in a single EIS. Not to require this would permit dividing a project into multiple "actions," each of which individually has an insignificant environmental impact, but which collectively have a substantial impact.

Since the Supreme Court decided the *Kleppe* case, the Council on Environmental Quality (CEQ) has issued regulations that define the circumstances under which multiple related actions must be covered by a single EIS. The regulations are made binding on federal administrative agencies by Executive Order. See Exec. Order No. 11991, 3 C.F.R. 1977 Comp. 123 (1978). The CEQ regulations and this court's precedents both require the Forest Service to prepare an EIS analyzing the combined environmental impacts of the road and the timber sales.

### A.  CEQ Regulations

#### 1.  Connected Actions

The CEQ regulations require "connected actions" to be considered together in a single EIS. See 40 C.F.R. §1508.25(a)(1) (1984). "Connected actions" are defined as actions that "(i) Automatically trigger other actions which may require environmental impact statements, (ii) Cannot or will not proceed unless other actions are taken previously or simultaneously, (iii) Are interdependent parts of a larger action and depend on the larger action for their justification." Id.

The construction of the road and the sale of the timber in the Jersey Jack area meet the second and third, as well as perhaps the first, of these criteria. It is clear that the timber sales cannot proceed without the road, and the road would not be built but for the contemplated timber sales. This much is revealed by the Forest Service's characterization of the road as a "logging road," and by the first page of the environmental assessment for the road, which states that "[t]he need for a transportation route in the assessment area is to access the timber lands to be developed over the next twenty years." Moreover, the environmental assessment for the road rejected a "no action" alternative because that alternative would not provide the needed timber access. The Forest Service's cost-benefit analysis of the road considered the timber to be the benefit of the road, and while the Service has stated that the road will yield other benefits, it does not claim that such other benefits would justify the road in the absence of the timber sales. Finally, the close interdependence of the road and the timber sales is indicated by an August 1981 letter in the record from the Regional Forester to the Forest Supervisor. It states, "We understand that sales in the immediate future will be dependent on the early completion of portions of the Jersey Jack Road. It would be advisable to divide the road into segments and establish separate completion dates for those portions to be used for those sales."

We conclude, therefore, that the road construction and the contemplated timber sales are inextricably intertwined, and that they are "connected actions" within the meaning of the CEQ regulations.

### 2. Cumulative Actions

The CEQ regulations also require that "cumulative actions" be considered together in a single EIS. 40 C.F.R. §1508.25(a)(2). "Cumulative actions" are defined as actions "which when viewed with other proposed actions have cumulatively significant impacts." Id. The record in this case contains considerable evidence to suggest that the road and the timber sales will have cumulatively significant impacts. The U.S. Fish & Wildlife Service, the Environmental Protection Agency, and the Idaho Department of Fish & Game have asserted that the road and the timber sales will have significant cumulative effects that should be considered in an EIS. The primary cumulative effects, according to these agencies, are the deposit of sediments in the Salmon River to the detriment of that river's population of salmon and steelhead trout, and the destruction of critical habitat for the endangered Rocky Mountain Gray Wolf. These agencies have criticized the Forest Service for not producing an EIS that considers the cumulative impacts of the Jersey Jack road and the timber sales. For example, the Fish & Wildlife Service has written, "Separate documentation of related and cumulative potential impacts may be leading to aquatic habitat degradation unaccounted for in individual EA's (i.e., undocumented cumulative effects). . . . Lack of an overall effort to document cumulative impacts could be having present and future detrimental effects on wolf recovery potential." These comments are sufficient to raise "substantial questions" as to whether the road and the timber sales will have significant cumulative environmental effects. Therefore, on this basis also, the Forest Service is required to prepare an EIS analyzing such effects. . . .

### B. Timing of the EIS

The Forest Service argues that the cumulative environmental effects of the road and the timber sales will be adequately analyzed and considered in the EA's and/or EIS's that it will prepare on the individual timber sales. The EA or EIS on each action, it contends, will document the cumulative impacts of that action and all previous actions.

We believe that consideration of cumulative impacts after the road has already been approved is insufficient to fulfill the mandate of NEPA. A central purpose of an EIS is to force the consideration of environmental impacts in the decision-making process. That purpose requires that the NEPA process be integrated with agency planning "at the earliest possible time," 40 C.F.R. §1501.2, and the purpose cannot be fully served if consideration of the cumulative effects of successive, interdependent steps is delayed until the first step has already been taken.

The location, the timing, or other aspects of the timber sales, or even the decision whether to sell any timber at all, affects the location, routing, construction techniques, and other aspects of the road, or even the need for its construction. But the consideration of cumulative impacts will serve little purpose if the road has already been built. Building the road swings the balance decidedly in favor of timber sales even if such sales would have been disfavored had road and sales been considered together before the road was built. Only by selling timber can the bulk of the expense of building the road be recovered. Not to sell timber after building the road constitutes the "irrational" result that *Trout Unlimited*'s standard is intended to avoid [Trout Unlimited v. Morton, 509 F.2d 1276 (9th Cir. 1974)]. Therefore, the cumulative environmental impacts of the road and the timber sales must be assessed before the road is approved. The Forest Service argues that the sales are too uncertain and too far in the future for their impacts to be analyzed along with that of the road. This comes close to saying that building the road now is itself irrational. We decline to accept that conclusion. Rather, we believe that if the sales are sufficiently certain to justify construction of the road, then they are sufficiently certain for their environmental impacts to be analyzed along with those of the road. Cf. City of Davis v. Coleman, 521 F.2d 661, 667-676 (9th Cir. 1975) (EIS for a road must analyze the impacts of industrial development that the road is designed to accommodate). Where agency actions are sufficiently related so as to be "connected" within the meaning of the CEQ regulations, the agency may not escape compliance with the regulations by proceeding with one action while characterizing the others as remote or speculative.

## NOTES AND QUESTIONS

1. Is the Ninth Circuit's decision in *Thomas* consistent with the Supreme Court's decision in *Kleppe?* How have the CEQ's post-*Kleppe* regulations changed the analysis of timing and scope?

2. Consideration of cumulative impacts played a major role in lengthy litigation over construction of one of three dams in southern Oregon's Rogue River basin. In Oregon Natural Resources Council v. Marsh, 832 F.2d 1489 (9th Cir. 1987), the court held that the Army Corps of Engineers had violated NEPA by failing to consider the cumulative impact of all three dams in an EIS for construction of the Elk Creek Dam. Although the court's decision eventually was reversed on other grounds by the Supreme Court, Marsh v. Oregon Natural Resources Council, 490 U.S. 360 (1989), the Ninth Circuit subsequently held that the Corps' supplemental EIS again had failed to consider adequately cumulative impacts. Oregon Natural Resources Council v. Marsh, 52 F.3d 1485 (9th Cir. 1995). The court stated that it was not sufficient for the EIS to discuss cumulative impacts only in the context of two specific water quality factors—temperature and turbidity—when they could be significant with respect to other environmental factors as well.

3. CEQ's 2020 regulations collapse cumulative, direct, and indirect effects into a single definition of "effects." This new definition would include effects that are reasonably foreseeable and have a reasonably close causal relationship to the proposed action. Critics of this change worry that the failure to consider cumulative and indirect impacts will hinder efforts to incorporate climate-change concerns into NEPA review. Previous regulations defined "cumulative impact" to be "the impact on the environment which results from the incremental impact of the action when added to other past, present, and reasonably foreseeable future actions regardless of what agency (Federal or non-Federal) or person undertakes such other actions." 40 C.F.R. §1508.7. In Resources Limited, Inc. v. Robertson,

35 F.3d 1300, 1306 (9th Cir. 1993), the court held that agencies must consider the impacts that private acts on private lands could have when analyzing cumulative impacts. In Sierra Club v. U.S. Forest Service, 46 F.3d 835 (8th Cir. 1995), the court rejected claims that an environmental assessment prepared by the Forest Service did not give sufficient consideration to cumulative impacts from private acts on nearby private lands and to the effect of previous timber sales on habitat fragmentation. In light of NEPA's statutory requirements, will the 2020 NEPA regulations substantially change what effects must be considered?

## Sierra Club v. Peterson

717 F.2d 1409 (D.C. Cir. 1983)

Before WRIGHT and SCALIA, Circuit Judges, and MacKINNON, Senior Circuit Judge.

MacKINNON, Senior Circuit Judge:

In proceedings in the district court, the Sierra Club challenged the decision by the United States Forest Service (Forest Service) and the Department of the Interior (Department) to issue oil and gas leases on lands within the Targhee and Bridger-Teton National Forests of Idaho and Wyoming. The plaintiff alleged that the leasing program violated the National Environmental Policy Act (NEPA), 42 U.S.C. §4321 et seq. (1976), because no Environmental Impact Statement (EIS) was prepared prior to the action. On cross-motion for summary judgment the district court upheld the decision to issue the leases without preparing an EIS. . . .

In 1980, the Forest Service received applications for oil and gas leases in the Palisades Further Planning Area. After conducting an Environmental Assessment (EA), the Forest Service recommended granting the lease applications, but with various stipulations attached to the leases. Because the Forest Service determined that issuance of the leases with the recommended stipulations would not result in significant adverse impacts to the environment, it decided that, with respect to the *entire* area, no Environmental Impact Statement was required at the leasing stage.

The leasing program approved by the Forest Service divides the land within the Palisades Further Planning Area into two categories—"highly environmentally sensitive" lands and non-highly environmentally sensitive lands. The stipulations attached to each lease are determined by the particular character of the land. All of the leases for the Palisades contain "standard" and "special" stipulations. These stipulations require the lessee to obtain approval from the Interior Department before undertaking any surface disturbing activity on the lease, but do not authorize the Department to *preclude* any activities which the lessee might propose. The Department can only impose conditions upon the lessee's use of the leased land.

In addition, a No Surface Occupancy Stipulation (NSO Stipulation) is attached to the leases for lands designated as "highly environmentally sensitive." This NSO Stipulation *precludes* surface occupancy unless and until such activity is specifically approved by the Forest Service.

For leases *without* a[n NSO] Stipulation, the lessee must file an application for a permit to drill prior to initiating exploratory drilling activities. The application must contain a surface use and operating plan which details the proposed operations including access roads, well site locations, and other planned facilities. On land leased without a[n NSO] Stipulation the Department *cannot* deny the permit to drill; it can only impose "reasonable" conditions which are designed to mitigate the environmental impacts of the drilling operations. [Eighty percent of the leases issued in the Palisades contained NSO stipulations. The Sierra Club appealed the district court's judgment only with respect to those lands leased without an NSO stipulation.]. . .

### III

The National Environmental Policy Act (NEPA) requires preparation of an Environmental Impact Statement whenever a proposed major federal action will significantly affect the quality of the human environment. 42 U.S.C. §4332(2)(C) (1976). To determine the nature of the environmental impact from a proposed action and whether an EIS will be required, federal agencies prepare an environmental assessment. 40 C.F.R. §1501.4(b) & (c) (1982). If on the basis of the Environmental Assessment the agency finds that the proposed action will produce "no significant impact" on the environment, then an EIS need not be prepared. Id. at §1501.4(e).

An agency's finding of "no significant impact" and consequent decision not to prepare an EIS can only be overturned if the decision was arbitrary, capricious, or an abuse of discretion. Judicial review of an agency's finding of "no significant impact" is not, however, merely perfunctory as the court must insure that the agency took a "hard look" at the environmental consequences of its decision.

Cases in this circuit have employed a four-part test to scrutinize an agency's finding of "no significant impact." The court ascertains

(1) whether the agency took a "hard look" at the problem;
(2) whether the agency identified the relevant areas of environmental concern;
(3) as to the problems studied and identified, whether the agency made a convincing case that the impact was insignificant; and
(4) if there was an impact of true significance, whether the agency convincingly established that changes in the project sufficiently reduced it to a minimum.

Applying the foregoing test to this agency decision, we are satisfied that the agency has taken the requisite "hard look" and has "identified the relevant areas of environmental concern." However, in our opinion, the finding that "no significant impact" will occur as a result of granting leases *without* an NSO Stipulation is not supportable on this record.

The finding of "no significant impact" is premised upon the conclusion that the lease stipulations will prevent any significant environmental impacts until a site-specific plan for exploration and development is submitted by the lessee. At that time, the federal appellees explain, an appropriate environmental analysis, either an Environmental Assessment or an EIS, will be prepared. In bifurcating its environmental analysis, however, the agency has taken a foreshortened view of the impacts which could result from the act of *leasing*. The agency has essentially assumed that leasing is a discrete transition which will not result in any "physical or biological impacts." The Environmental Assessment concludes

> that there will be no significant adverse effects on the human environment due to oil and gas lease issuance. Therefore, no environmental impact statement will be prepared. The determination was based upon consideration of the following factors . . . (a) few issued leases result in active exploration operations and still fewer result in discovery or production of oil or gas; (b) the act of issuing a lease involves no physical or biological impacts; (c) the cumulative environmental effect of lease issuance on an area-wide basis is very small; (d) effects of lease activities once permitted will be mitigated to protect areas of critical environmental concern by appropriate stipulations including no-surface occupancy; (e) if unacceptable environmental impacts cannot be corrected, activities will not be permitted; and (f) the action will not have a significant effect on the human environment.

The conclusion that no significant impact will occur is improperly based on a prophecy that exploration activity on these lands will be insignificant and generally fruitless.

While it may well be true that the majority of these leases will never reach the drilling stage and that the environmental impacts of exploration are dependent upon the nature of the activity, nevertheless NEPA requires that federal agencies determine at the outset whether their major actions can result in "significant" environmental impacts. Here, the Forest Service concluded that any impacts which might result from the act of leasing would either be insignificant or, if significant, could be mitigated by exercising the controls provided in the lease stipulations.

Even assuming, arguendo, that all lease stipulations are fully enforceable, once the land is leased the Department no longer has the authority to *preclude* surface disturbing activities even if the environmental impact of such activity is significant. The Department can only impose "mitigation" measures upon a lessee who pursues surface disturbing exploration and/or drilling activities. None of the stipulations expressly provides that the Department or the Forest Service can *prevent* a lessee from conducting surface disturbing activities. Thus, with respect to the smaller area with which we are here concerned, the decision to allow surface disturbing activities has been made at the *leasing stage* and, under NEPA, this is the point at which the environmental impacts of such activities must be evaluated.

NEPA requires an agency to evaluate the environmental effects of its action at the point of commitment. The purpose of an EIS is to insure that the agency considers all possible courses of action and assesses the environmental consequences of each proposed action. The EIS is a decisionmaking tool intended to "insure that . . . environmental amenities and values may be given appropriate consideration in decisionmaking. . . ." 42 U.S.C. §4332(2)(B). Therefore, the appropriate time for preparing an EIS is *prior* to a decision, when the decision-maker retains a maximum range of options. An EIS is required when the "critical agency decision" is made which results in "irreversible and irretrievable commitments of resources" to an action which will affect the environment. On the facts of this case, that "critical time," insofar as lands leased without a[n NSO] Stipulation are concerned, occurred at the point of leasing.

Notwithstanding the assurance that a later site-specific environmental analysis will be made, in issuing these leases the Department made an irrevocable commitment to allow *some* surface disturbing activities, including drilling and roadbuilding. While theoretically the proposed two-stage environmental analysis may be acceptable, in this situation the Department has not complied with NEPA because it has sanctioned activities which have the potential for disturbing the environment without fully assessing the possible environmental consequences.

The Department asserts that it cannot accurately evaluate the consequences of drilling and other surface disturbing activities until site-specific plans are submitted. If, however, the Department is in fact concerned that it cannot foresee and evaluate the environmental consequences of leasing without site-specific proposals, then it may delay preparation of an EIS provided that it reserves both the authority to *preclude* all activities pending submission of site-specific proposals and the authority to *prevent* proposed activities if the environmental consequences are unacceptable. If the Department chooses not to retain the authority to *preclude* all surface disturbing activities, then an EIS assessing the full environmental consequences of leasing must be prepared at the point of commitment—when the leases are issued. The Department can decide, in the first instance, by which route it will proceed.

## NOTES AND QUESTIONS

1. In *Sierra Club v. Peterson*, the court focuses its review on the Forest Service's determination that the effects of its action will not be "significant." We will discuss that question later. For now, consider the question of timing: Why must the Forest Service prepare an EIS at the leasing stage? The Forest Service had argued that preparation of an EIS should not be required at this stage because "any impacts which might result from the act of leasing would either be insignificant or, if significant, could be mitigated by exercising the controls provided in the lease stipulations." Why does that argument fail? What could the Forest Service do differently in future leasing decisions to avoid the EIS requirement?

2. In Conner v. Burford, 605 F. Supp. 107 (D. Mont. 1985), aff'd in part and rev'd in part, 848 F.2d 1441 (9th Cir. 1988), cert. denied, 489 U.S. 1012 (1989), the plaintiffs pressed the question whether the Forest Service could ignore the possible impacts of oil exploration, development, and production when deciding to issue leases with no surface occupancy (NSO) stipulations. At issue was a Forest Service decision to lease 1.3 million acres of the Gallatin and Flathead National Forests in Montana. Placing NSO stipulations in more than 500 of the 700 leases to be issued, the Forest Service issued a "finding of no significant impact" for the sale, arguing that "the sale of an NSO lease has *no* effect on the environment, let alone a significant one." 848 F.2d at 1447 (emphasis in original). The District Court held that the Forest Service had violated NEPA:

> To use the NSO stipulation as a mechanism to avoid an EIS when issuing numerous leases on potential wilderness areas circumvents the spirit of NEPA. Subsequent site-specific analysis, prompted by a proposal from a lessee of one tract, may result in a finding of no significant environmental impact. Obviously, a comprehensive analysis of cumulative impacts of

several oil and gas development activities must be done before any single activity can proceed. Otherwise, a piecemeal invasion of the forests would occur, followed by realization of a significant and irreversible impact. [605 F. Supp. at 108-109.]

On appeal, the Ninth Circuit reversed. The court held that NEPA would apply to subsequent decisions to remove an NSO stipulation and that "piecemeal invasion of the forests will be avoided because . . . government evaluation of surface-disturbing activity on NSO leases must include consideration of the potential for further connected development and cumulative impacts from all oil and gas development activities pursuant to the federal leases." 848 F.2d at 1448. Is that reasoning persuasive? Is lease-by-lease review a good substitute for comprehensive review of the entire 1.3-million-acre sale? If the Forest Service is reviewing one lease at a time, what is the likely form of its review—full environmental impact statement or environmental assessment? If the Service considers the potential cumulative impacts of related development in reviewing a single lease, what options does it have to address those impacts? How would its options be different if it were reviewing the entire sale?

3.  The Makah Indian Tribe in Washington state sought approval to hunt the California gray whale following its removal from the endangered species list. Supported by the National Oceanic and Atmospheric Administration (NOAA) and the National Marine Fisheries Service (NMFS), the Makah obtained approval to resume limited whale hunting from the International Whaling Commission (IWC) under the "aboriginal subsistence" exception to the IWC's global whaling ban. Opponents of the hunt filed a lawsuit alleging that NOAA and the NMFS had violated NEPA by failing to conduct an environmental assessment before agreeing with the Makah to seek approval for resumed whale hunting. Alerted to a possible NEPA lawsuit, NOAA and the NMFS had quickly prepared an environmental assessment (EA) making a "finding of no significant impact" (FONSI), which had been released the day before the IWC meeting. After a district court dismissed the lawsuit, the plaintiffs appealed to the U.S. Court of Appeals for the Ninth Circuit, which reversed. Metcalf v. Daley, 214 F.3d 1135 (2001). The court concluded that NOAA and the NMFS "did not engage the NEPA process 'at the earliest possible time.'" It observed that the agencies "should not have fully committed to support the Makah whaling proposal before preparing the EA because doing so probably influenced their evaluation of the environmental impact of the proposal." Writing in dissent, Judge Kleinfeld argued that EAs and EISs "are unlikely to persuade agency personnel, who initiated a project, to change their minds." He maintained that their value "comes mostly after the agency has settled on a policy choice" because "[t]he process of preparing them mobilizes groups that may generate political pressure sufficient to defeat the executive initiative."

4.  Following the *Metcalf v. Daley* decision, NOAA and the NMFS prepared a new EA. When the new EA was released in July 2001, it again found no significant environmental impact from the Makah hunt. After the agencies approved renewed whaling by the tribe, animal rights groups filed suit, alleging violations of NEPA and the Marine Mammal Protection Act. These claims were rejected by a trial court, but upheld on appeal in Anderson v. Evans, 314 F.3d 1006 (2002). Rejecting the FONSI, the court held that an EIS should be prepared not because the impact on the entire

California gray whale population will be significant, but because of the potential significance of the impact on the resident whale population in the local area.

## 2. *"Significantly Affecting the Quality of the Human Environment"*

The crucial threshold question for NEPA's EIS requirement is whether a proposed action is likely to significantly affect the quality of the human environment. It is this question that is typically the focus of an agency's analysis of its obligations under NEPA. And it is this question that is most troublesome for the courts in enforcing those obligations. This is illustrated by the following early case, which involved the question whether an EIS had to be prepared for the construction of a jail and related facilities as an annex to the federal courthouse in Manhattan. After residents and businesses in the surrounding area filed suit under NEPA, a federal district court held that no EIS was required because the project would not significantly affect the quality of the environment. The Second Circuit affirmed as to an office building that was part of the project but reversed with respect to the detention center. Hanly v. Mitchell, 460 F.2d 640 (2d Cir. 1972) (*Hanly I*). The court required the General Services Administration (GSA) to evaluate more fully the effects of the detention center (e.g., the possibility of disturbances that would cause noise, the impact of an outpatient treatment center on crime in the neighborhood, and possible traffic and parking problems) before determining that an EIS was unnecessary. On remand, GSA prepared a 25-page "Assessment of the Environmental Impact" that considered these factors in more detail. On the basis of this assessment GSA decided that the detention center would not have a significant effect on the environment. After the district court denied an injunction, the case was again appealed to the Second Circuit, which issued the decision that follows.

## Hanly v. Kleindienst

471 F.2d 823 (2d Cir. 1972)

Before FRIENDLY, Chief Judge, and MANSFIELD and TIMBERS, Circuit Judges.

MANSFIELD, Circuit Judge: . . .

. . . [W]e believe that the appropriate criterion in the present case is the "arbitrary, capricious" standard established by the Administrative Procedure Act, since the meaning of the term "significantly" as used in §102(2)(C) of NEPA can be isolated as a question of law. . . .

Upon attempting, according to the foregoing standard, to interpret the amorphous term "significantly," as it is used in §102(2)(C), we are faced with the fact that almost every major federal action, no matter how limited in scope, has *some* adverse effect on the human environment. It is equally clear that an action which is environmentally important to one neighbor may be of no consequence to another. Congress could have decided that every major federal action must therefore be the subject of a detailed impact statement prepared according to the procedure prescribed by §102(2)(C). By adding the word "significantly," however, it demonstrated that before the agency in charge triggered that procedure, it should conclude that a greater environmental impact would result than from "any major federal action." Yet the limits of the key term have not been adequately defined by Congress or by guidelines issued by the CEQ and other responsible federal agencies vested with broad discretionary powers under NEPA. Congress apparently was willing to depend principally upon the agency's good faith determination as to what conduct would be sufficiently serious from an ecological standpoint to require use of the full-scale procedure.

Guidelines issued by the CEQ, which are echoed in rules for implementation published by the Public Buildings Service, the branch of GSA concerned with the construction of the MCC, suggest that a formal impact statement should be prepared with respect to "proposed actions, the environmental impact of which is likely to be highly controversial." See Council on Environmental Quality, Statements on Proposed Federal Actions Affecting the Environment, Guidelines §5(b), 36 Fed. Reg. 7724 (April 23, 1971). However, the term "controversial" apparently refers to cases where a substantial dispute exists as to the size, nature, or effect of the major federal action rather than to the existence of opposition to a use, the effect of which is relatively undisputed. This court in *Hanly I*, for instance, did not require a formal impact statement with respect to the office building portion of the Annex despite the existence of neighborhood opposition to it. The suggestion that "controversial" must be equated with neighborhood opposition has also been rejected by others.

In the absence of any Congressional or administrative interpretation of the term, we are persuaded that in deciding whether a major federal action will "significantly" affect the quality of the human environment the agency in charge, although vested with broad discretion, should normally be required to review the proposed action in the light of at least two relevant factors: (1) the extent to which the action will cause adverse environmental effects in excess of those created by existing uses in the area affected by it, and (2) the absolute quantitative adverse environmental effects of the action itself, including the cumulative harm that results from its contribution to existing adverse conditions or uses in the affected area. Where conduct conforms to existing uses, its adverse consequences will usually be less significant than when it represents a radical change. Absent some showing that an entire neighborhood is in the process of redevelopment, its existing environment, though frequently below an ideal standard, represents a norm that cannot be ignored. For instance, one more highway in an area honeycombed with roads usually has less of an adverse impact than if it were constructed through a roadless public park.

Although the existing environment of the area which is the site of a major federal action constitutes one criterion to be considered, it must be recognized that even a slight increase in adverse conditions that form an existing environmental milieu may sometimes threaten harm that is significant. One more factory polluting air and water in an area zoned for industrial use may represent the straw that breaks the back of the environmental camel. Hence the absolute, as well as comparative, effects of a major federal action must be considered. . . .

. . . Rather than encourage agencies to dispense with impact statements, we believe that application of the foregoing objective standards, coupled with compliance with minimum procedural requirements (specified below), which are designed to assure consideration of relevant facts, will lead agencies in doubtful cases (so-called "grey" areas) to obtain impact statements rather than to risk the delay and expense of protracted litigation. . . .

Appellants further contend that they have never been given an opportunity to discuss the MCC with any governmental agency prior to GSA's submission of its Assessment, which raises the question whether the agency acted "without observance of procedure required by law." We do not share the Government's view that the procedural mandates of §102(A), (B), and (D) and 42 U.S.C. §4332(2)(A), (B), and (D), apply only to actions found by the agency itself to have a significant environmental effect. While these sections are somewhat opaque, they are not expressly limited to "major Federal actions significantly affecting the quality of the human environment." Indeed if they were so limited §102(D), which requires the agency to develop appropriate alternatives to the recommended course of action, would be duplicative since §102(C), which does apply to actions "significantly affecting" the environment, specifies that the detailed impact statement must deal with "alternatives to the proposed action." 42 U.S.C. §4332(2)(C)(iii). However, in our view the Assessment does, in fact, satisfy the requirement of §102(2)(A) that an interdisciplinary approach taking into account the "natural and social sciences and the environmental design arts" be used. The GSA has retained architects familiar with the design requirements of the Civic Center and consulted with the Office of Lower Manhattan Development in an effort to harmonize the MCC with the Civic Center. The Assessment scrupulously takes into account the aesthetics and the tangible factors involved in the designing and planning of the MCC. Furthermore, we find that §102(2)(D) was complied with insofar as the GSA specifically considered the alternatives to continuing operation at the present facility at West Street and evaluated the selected site as compared with other specified possibilities. Although the assessment of the alternative sites was not as intensive as we might hope, its failure to analyze them in further detail does not warrant reversal.

A more serious question is raised by the GSA's failure to comply with §102(2) (B), which requires the agency to "identify and develop methods and procedures . . . which will insure that presently unquantified environmental amenities and values may be given appropriate consideration in decisionmaking along with economic and technical considerations." 42 U.S.C. §4332(2)(B). Since an agency, in making a threshold determination as to the "significance" of an action, is called upon to review in a general fashion the same factors that would be studied in depth for preparation of a detailed environmental impact statement, §102(2)(B) requires that some rudimentary procedures be designed to assure a fair and informed preliminary decision. Otherwise the agency, lacking essential information, might frustrate the purpose of NEPA by a threshold determination that an impact statement is unnecessary. Furthermore, an adequate record serves to preclude later changes in use without consideration of their environmental significance as required by NEPA.

Where a proposed major federal action may affect the sensibilities of a neighborhood, the prudent course would be for the agency in charge, before making a threshold decision, to give notice to the community of the contemplated action and to accept all pertinent information proffered by concerned citizens with respect to it. Furthermore, in line with the procedure usually followed in zoning disputes, particularly where emotions are likely to be aroused by fears, or rumors of misinformation, a public hearing serves the dual purpose of enabling the agency to obtain all relevant data and to satisfy the community that its views are being considered. However, neither NEPA nor any other federal statute mandates the specific type of procedure to be followed by federal agencies. . . .

Notwithstanding the absence of statutory or administrative provisions on the subject, this court has already held in *Hanly I* that federal agencies must "affirmatively develop a reviewable environmental record . . . even for purposes of a threshold section 102(2)(C) determination." We now go further and hold that before a preliminary or threshold determination of significance is made the responsible agency must give notice to the public of the proposed major federal action and an opportunity to submit relevant facts which might bear upon the agency's threshold decision. We do not suggest that a full-fledged formal hearing must be provided before each such determination is made, although it should be apparent that in many cases such a hearing would be advisable for reasons already indicated. The necessity for a hearing will depend greatly upon the circumstances surrounding the particular proposed action and upon the likelihood that a hearing will be more effective than other methods in developing relevant information and an understanding of the proposed action. The precise procedural steps to be adopted are better left to the agency, which should be in a better position than the court to determine whether solution of the problems faced with respect to a specific major federal action can better be achieved through a hearing or by informal acceptance of relevant data. . . .

FRIENDLY, Chief Judge (dissenting):

The learned opinion of my brother Mansfield gives these plaintiffs . . . both too little and too much. It gives too little because it raises the floor of what constitutes "major Federal actions significantly affecting the quality of the human environment," 42 U.S.C. §4332(2)(C), higher than I believe Congress intended. It gives too much because it requires that before making a threshold determination that no impact statement is demanded, the agency must go through procedures which I think are needed only when an impact statement must be made. The upshot is that a threshold determination that a proposal does not constitute major Federal action significantly affecting the quality of the human environment becomes a kind of mini-impact statement. The preparation of such a statement under the conditions laid down by the majority is unduly burdensome when the action is truly minor or insignificant. On the other hand, there is a danger that if the threshold determination is this elaborate, it may come to replace the impact statement in the grey area between actions which, though "major" in a monetary sense, are obviously insignificant (such as the construction of the proposed office building) and actions that are obviously significant (such as the construction of an atomic power plant). We would better serve the purposes of Congress by keeping the threshold low enough to insure that impact statements are prepared for actions in this grey area and thus to permit the determination that no statement is required to be made quite informally in cases of true insignificance. . . .

It is not readily conceivable that Congress meant to allow agencies to avoid [the EIS] requirement by reading "significant" to mean only "important," "momentous," or the like. One of the purposes of the impact statement is to insure that the relevant environmental data are before the agency and considered by it prior to the decision to commit Federal resources to the project; the statute must not be construed so as to allow the agency to make its decision in a doubtful case without the relevant data or a detailed study of it. This is particularly clear because of the absence from the statute of any procedural requirement upon an agency in making the threshold determination that an impact statement is not demanded, although the majority has managed to contrive one. What Congress was trying to say was "You don't need to make an impact statement, with the consequent expense and delay, when there is no sensible reason for making one." I thus agree with Judge J. Skelly Wright's view that "a statement is required whenever the action *arguably* will have an adverse environmental impact," with the qualification, doubtless intended, that the matter must be *fairly* arguable. . . .

[The CEQ Guidelines] provide that "if there is *potential* that the environment may be significantly affected, the statement is to be prepared." Guidelines §5(b), 36 Fed. Reg. 7724 (1971) (emphasis added). And they state further, in a remark highly relevant to this case:

> Proposed actions, the environmental impact of which is likely to be highly controversial, should be covered in all cases.

This Guideline has been expressly adopted by the GSA in its own regulations. With respect, I see no basis for reading this as limited to cases where there is a dispute over what the environmental effects actually will be. Rather, I would think it clear that this includes action which the agency should know is likely to arouse intense opposition, even if the actual environmental impact is readily apparent. Apart from the former being the natural meaning of the words, the CEQ may well have had in mind that when action having some environmental impact "is likely to be highly controversial," an agency assessment that the action does not constitute major Federal action significantly affecting the environment is almost certain to evoke challenge in the courts. The CEQ could well have believed that rather than to incur the delay incident to such a suit, and the further delay if a court sustains the challenge — both vividly illustrated in this case where nearly two years have elapsed since the initial assessment that an impact statement was not required and a further remand is being directed — the agency would do better to prepare an impact statement in the first instance. In addition to possibly providing new information making reconsideration or modification of the project appropriate, such a policy has the added benefits of allowing opponents to blow off steam and giving them a sense that their objections have been considered — an important purpose of NEPA, as it is of the British statutory inquiry. . . .

. . . The energies my brothers would require GSA to devote to still a third assessment designed to show that an impact statement is not needed would better be devoted to making one.

I would reverse and direct the issuance of an injunction until a reasonable period after the making of an impact statement.

## NOTES AND QUESTIONS

1. As the court's debate in *Hanly* makes clear, the threshold determination required by NEPA presents difficult questions of both substance and procedure:

What does "significantly" mean and how should significance be determined? What answers does the majority provide to these questions? How helpful are its formulations? Does Judge Friendly offer a more workable approach?

2. In another portion of his dissent, Judge Friendly notes that the "action agencies" that are responsible for implementation of NEPA often have "missions" (such as highway or jail construction) that NEPA only serves to impede. Should this influence the degree of deference courts afford to these agencies' interpretation of NEPA?

3. The amorphous and subjective character of the "significance" test continues to plague the agencies and the courts, as discussed below. However, there is much stronger consensus today on the procedure by which this determination must be made.

## A.   Procedure for Determining Whether or Not to Prepare an EIS

In the *Hanly* litigation and other early cases, the courts demanded that agencies "affirmatively develop a reviewable environmental record" to support the determinations that their actions would not "significantly affect the quality of the human environment." This "reviewable environmental record" has become what is now called an "environmental assessment." The CEQ regulations reflect these decisions in setting out the process by which agencies determine whether an EIS is required. Section 1501.4 of the CEQ regulations directs agencies to determine whether the proposal is one that "(1) [n]ormally requires an environmental impact statement, or (2) [n]ormally does not require either an environmental impact statement or an environmental assessment (categorical exclusion)." Actions in the first category presumptively require preparation of an EIS; actions in the second category presumptively do not. If the proposed action falls in neither of these two categories, agencies are directed to prepare an environmental assessment and to make the determination of whether or not to prepare an EIS on the basis of the results of that assessment. If an agency determines on the basis of the environmental assessment not to prepare an EIS, the agency must make the finding of no significant impact available to the affected public as specified in section 1506.6 of the CEQ regulations. In cases where the proposed action is without precedent or is very similar to one that normally requires preparation of an EIS, the CEQ regulations direct the agency to make a proposed finding of no significant impact available for public review for 30 days before the agency makes its final determination whether or not to prepare an EIS.

The updated 2020 CEQ regulations specify that an environmental assessment should "briefly discuss the purpose and need for the proposed action, alternatives as required by section 102(2)(E) of NEPA, and the environmental impacts of the proposed action and alternatives, and include a listing of agencies and persons consulted," in short, a kind of mini-EIS. 40 C.F.R. §1501.5. Under the CEQ regulations the "environmental assessment" serves two purposes. First, it provides the basis for the agency's determination whether to prepare an EIS. Second, when the agency concludes that an EIS is not required, the environmental assessment is the vehicle for the agency's compliance with NEPA's other requirements. Most important, in many cases, under section 102(2)(E), an agency must study alternatives to the proposed action, whether or not it is required to prepare an EIS.

Thus, there are three levels of NEPA review: (1) Categorical Exclusions, (2) Environmental Assessments, and (3) Environmental Impact Statements. Here is how CEQ described each of these levels of review in a 2009 report:

- Categorical Exclusion (CE): A CE is a category of actions established in the department or agency procedures for implementing NEPA, or established in legislation, that are expected to not have individually or cumulatively significant environmental impacts. Typically, a CE is concluded with the determination that a proposed action is included in the category of actions and there are no extraordinary circumstances that indicate environmental concerns merit further environmental review.
- Environmental Assessment (EA): When a CE is not appropriate and the agency has not determined whether the proposed action will cause significant environmental effects, then an environmental assessment is prepared. If, as a result of the EA, a finding of no significant impact (FONSI) is appropriate, then the NEPA review process is completed with the FONSI, otherwise an EIS is prepared.
- Environmental Impact Statements (EIS): The most intensive level of analysis is the environmental impact statement which is typically reserved for the analysis of proposed actions that are expected to result in significant environmental impacts. When an EIS is prepared, the NEPA review process is concluded when a record of decision (ROD) is issued.

CEQ, Report on the National Environmental Policy Act Status and Progress for American Recovery and Reinvestment Act of 2009 Activities and Projects (May 18, 2009). In its report, CEQ noted that as of April 24, 2009, more than 40,000 NEPA reviews were conducted for stimulus projects using categorical exclusions (CEs), 500 environmental assessments (EAs) were prepared that led to findings of no significant impact (FONSIs), and 150 projects or activities had been analyzed in EISs completed with a record of decision (ROD). CEQ also reported that work was underway on 23 EISs, 396 EAs, and that 4,566 additional projects or activities were subject to CEs.

A study of 13 years of NEPA decisions (from 2001 to 2013) found that only one in 450 NEPA decisions was litigated. The authors concluded that the "vast majority of federal actions that are subject to NEPA review are evaluated through an expedited analysis contained in either a [categorical exclusion] CE (95%) or an [environmental assessment] EA (5%)." John C. Ruple & Kayla M. Race, Measuring the NEPA Litigation Burden: A Review of 1,499 Federal Court Cases, 59 Envt'l Law 479 (2020).

Even when a project or activity is subject to a categorical exclusion, a party can petition the agency to prepare an EA or EIS. CEQ's regulations provide that agencies implementing categorical exclusions "shall provide for extraordinary circumstances in which a normally excluded action may have a significant environmental effect." Id. §§1508.4, 1507.3(e)(2)(ii).

In American Bird Conservancy, Inc. v. F.C.C., 516 F.3d 1027 (D.C. Cir. 2008), the D.C. Circuit ruled that the Federal Communications Commission had improperly dismissed a petition seeking protection of migratory birds from collisions with communications towers. The FCC's NEPA regulations categorically exclude communications towers from NEPA review because they "are deemed individually and cumulatively to have no significant effect on the quality of the human environment." 47 C.F.R. §1.1306(a). However, the regulations also provide that a party still may allege that a "particular action, otherwise categorically excluded, will have a significant environmental effect" and can file a petition "setting forth in detail the reasons justifying or circumstances necessitating environmental consideration in the decision-making process." If the FCC determines that the proposed action "may have a significant environmental impact," then it is supposed to require the applicant for a tower license to prepare an EA.

The court held that the FCC had failed to apply the proper NEPA standard when it dismissed a petition filed by the American Bird Conservancy and the Forest Conservation Council. The two groups had petitioned the FCC to prepare a programmatic environmental impact statement under NEPA analyzing the effects of all past, present, and reasonably foreseeable tower registrations on migratory birds in the Gulf Coast region. The court rejected the FCC's two reasons for dismissing the request for a programmatic EIS: (1) "the lack of specific evidence . . . concerning the impact of towers on the human environment," and (2) "the lack of consensus among scientists regarding the impact of communications towers on migratory birds." It concluded that "[n]either reason is sufficient to sustain the Commission's refusal to take action pursuant to NEPA, and together they demonstrate an apparent misunderstanding of the nature of the obligation imposed by the statute."

The court stated that:

> The reasons stated in the Order cannot, in light of the petition under review, sustain the Commission's refusal to prepare an EIS without at least first requiring the preparation of an EA. The Commission acknowledges that §1.1307(c) applies to the petition and that the regulation requires an EA when an action "may" have a significant environmental effect. The Order's demand for definitive evidence of significant effects—noting Petitioners' failure to make a "scientific showing that the population of any specific bird species has decreased as a result of collisions"—plainly contravenes the "may" standard. Similarly, the Order's suggestion that scientific consensus is a precondition to NEPA action is inconsistent with both the Commission's regulation and with the statute. As the court has admonished, "[i]t must be remembered that the basic thrust of the agency's responsibilities under NEPA is to predict the environmental effects of a proposed action before the action is taken and those effects fully known." A precondition of certainty before initiating NEPA procedures would jeopardize NEPA's purpose to ensure that agencies consider environmental impacts before they act rather than wait until it is too late.
>
> Based on the record before the court, there is no real dispute that towers "may" have significant environmental impact, and thus that the §1.1307(c) threshold has been met. Indeed, the Order's emphasis on "conflicting studies" and "sharply divergent views" regarding the number of birds killed confirms, rather than refutes, that towers may have the requisite effect. Under such circumstances, the Commission's regulations mandate at least the completion of an EA before the Commission may

refuse to prepare a programmatic EIS. Although Petitioners seek a programmatic EIS, and not an EA, the Commission's regulations allow it to
pursue an EA as an interim step, and such an EA will determine what subsequent action NEPA requires. [516 F.3d at 1033-1034.]

The court also criticized the FCC for only providing public notice of individual
tower applications *after* approving them. It noted that this evaded the agency's duty
to comply with NEPA regulations (40 C.F.R. §1506.6(a)) by providing the public
with "a hollow opportunity to participate in NEPA procedures." Thus, it ordered
the Commission to adopt new procedures to provide public notice.

On April 20, 2010, the largest oil spill in U.S. history occurred in the Gulf of
Mexico with the blowout of the Deepwater Horizon oil platform that killed 11 people and spilled 4.9 million barrels of oil, contaminating 1,000 miles of shoreline.
Following the spill, questions were raised about the adequacy of NEPA's environmental impact assessment process for the drilling site. Investigations revealed that
no EIS had been prepared for the drilling site because it received a "categorical
exclusion" on April 9, 2009. The exclusion covered (1) "[a]pproval of an offshore
lease or unit exploration, development/production plan . . . in the central or western Gulf of Mexico[,]" or (2) "[a]pproval of an Application for Permit to Drill . . .
an offshore oil and gas exploration or development well[.]" Minerals Management
Service Dep't Manual, Part 516, Ch. 15.4(C)(10), (12). It also was revealed that
BP, the British company that leased the drilling site, had been lobbying to expand
categorical exclusions for its drilling activities even though they were occurring in
unusually deep waters in the Gulf. Juliet Eilperin, U.S. Exempted BP's Gulf of Mexico Drilling from Environmental Impact Study, Wash. Post, May 5, 2010. See also
Sandra Zellmer, Joel A. Mintz & Robert Glicksman, Throwing Precaution to the
Winds: NEPA and the Deepwater Horizon Blowout, J. Energy & Envtl. L. 62 (Summer 2011) (identifying failure to consider worst-case scenarios, improper tiering
and categorical exclusions, and agency capture as problems that contributed to the
failure adequately to consider the risks of a spill).

In response to the revelation that offshore oil drilling in the Gulf of Mexico
had been excluded from NEPA review by a categorical exclusion, CEQ developed
new guidance. On November 23, 2010, CEQ issued final guidance on how to establish, apply, and revise categorical exclusions under section 102 of NEPA. See *https://
ceq.doe.gov/docs/ceq-regulations-and-guidance/NEPA_CE_Guidance_Nov232010.pdf.*
CEQ described this guidance in the following terms:

> The guidance recommends best practices for appropriate use of cate-
> gorical exclusions and was developed as part of CEQ's effort to mod-
> ernize and reinvigorate Federal agency implementation of NEPA. It was
> designed to ensure that agencies establish and use categorical exclusions
> appropriately and transparently. It also calls on agencies to review their
> existing categorical exclusions periodically to avoid the use of outdated
> NEPA procedures.

CEQ's guidance clarifies the requirements of NEPA, and the CEQ regulations
implementing NEPA, regarding categorical exclusions. Specifically, it suggests that
Agencies should:

- utilize information technology to inform the public about new or revised categorical exclusions and their justifications;
- remain alert to new conditions and information that would cause an agency to reconsider a categorical exclusion;
- consider further public documentation and disclosure in applying established categorical exclusions, particularly where they may implicate extraordinary circumstances; and
- in general, review their existing categorical exclusions at least every seven years to avoid the use of outdated NEPA procedures.

On January 14, 2011, CEQ issued guidance designed to clarify the appropriateness of "Findings of No Significant Impact" (FONSI) and to specify when there is a need to monitor environmental mitigation commitments. *https://ceq.doe.gov/docs/ceq-regulations-and-guidance/Mitigation_and_Monitoring_Guidance_14Jan2011.pdf.* At that time, CEQ explained the FONSI in the following terms:

> The guidance clarifies that the environmental impacts of a proposed action may be mitigated to the point when the agency may make a FONSI determination. When the FONSI depends on successful mitigation, however, such mitigation requirements should be made public and be accompanied by monitoring and reporting.

The guidance emphasizes that when agencies base their environmental analysis on a commitment to mitigate the environmental impacts of a proposed action, they should adhere to those commitments, monitor how they are implemented, and monitor the effectiveness of the mitigation.

Specifically, the guidance affirms that agencies should:

- commit to mitigation in decision documents when they have based environmental analysis upon such mitigation (by including appropriate conditions on grants, permits, or other agency approvals, and making funding or approvals for implementing the proposed action contingent on implementation of the mitigation commitments);
- monitor the implementation and effectiveness of mitigation commitments;
- make information on mitigation monitoring available to the public, preferably through agency web sites; and
- remedy ineffective mitigation when the Federal action is not yet complete.

Nancy Sutley, Appropriate Use of Mitigation and Monitoring and Clarifying the Appropriate Use of Mitigated Findings of No Significant Action, Jan. 14, 2011.

## B.  Determining the "Significance" of Action

In its 1978 regulations, the CEQ made its own attempt to elaborate on how to interpret the term "significantly" in NEPA. 40 C.F.R. §1508.27. The CEQ advised that "significantly" as used in NEPA requires consideration of both context and intensity:

> (a) *Context.* This means that the significance of an action must be analyzed in several contexts such as society as a whole (human, national), the affected region, the affected interests, and the

locality. Significance varies with the setting of the proposed action. For instance, in the case of a site-specific action, significance would usually depend upon the effects in the locale rather than in the world as a whole. Both short- and long-term effects are relevant.

(b) *Intensity*. This refers to the severity of impact. Responsible officials must bear in mind that more than one agency may make decisions about partial aspects of a major action. The following should be considered in evaluating intensity:

(1) Impact that may be both beneficial and adverse. A significant effect may exist even if the Federal agency believes that on balance the effect will be beneficial.

(2) The degree to which the proposed action affects public health or safety.

(3) Unique characteristics of the geographic area such as proximity to historic or cultural resources, parklands, prime farmlands, wetlands, wild and scenic rivers, or ecologically critical areas.

(4) The degree to which the effects on the quality of the human environment are likely to be highly controversial.

(5) The degree to which the possible effects on the human environment are highly uncertain or involve unique or unknown risks.

(6) The degree to which the action may establish a precedent for future actions with significant effects or represents a decision in principle about a future consideration.

(7) Whether the action is related to other actions with individually insignificant but cumulatively significant impacts. Significance exists if it is reasonable to anticipate a cumulatively significant impact on the environment. Significance cannot be avoided by terming an action temporary or by breaking it down into small component parts.

(8) The degree to which the action may adversely affect districts, sites, highways, structures, or objects listed in or eligible for listing in the National Register of Historic Places or may cause loss or destruction of significant scientific, cultural, or historical resources.

(9) The degree to which the action may adversely affect an endangered or threatened species or its habitat that has been determined to be critical under the Endangered Species Act of 1973.

(10) Whether the action threatens a violation of Federal, State, or local law or requirements imposed for the protection of the environment. [43 Fed. Reg. 56,005 (1978); 44 Fed. Reg. 874 (1979).]

In Anderson v. Evans, 314 F.2d 1006 (9th Cir. 2002), the Ninth Circuit cited factors 4, 5, and 6 of the intensity regulations in holding that an EIS must be prepared before the Makah Tribe can be granted permission to whale. Although conceding that the Tribe's hunting will not have a significant impact on the overall California gray whale population, the court noted that the likely impact of the hunt on the resident "whale population in the local area where the Tribe wants to hunt" is a matter of "hot dispute" surrounded by considerable uncertainty. 314 F.2d at 1018. It also concluded that the EIS should consider the precedential effect of allowing the Tribe to hunt whales because it could undermine efforts to keep the International Whaling Commission's aboriginal subsistence exception narrowly confined.

Factors 3, 4, and 5 of the intensity regulations were cited by the Ninth Circuit when it required the National Park Service (NPS) to prepare an EIS for its plan to permit more cruise ships to operate in Glacier Bay National Park in Alaska. In National Parks & Conservation Association v. Babbitt, 241 F.3d 722 (9th Cir. 2001), the court emphasized the unique characteristics of Glacier Bay, the substantial controversy surrounding the potential effects of increased vessel traffic, and the great uncertainty surrounding those effects. It rejected the Park Service's argument that an EIS need not be prepared because future mitigation measures could prevent the additional vessel traffic from adversely affecting humpback whales, endangered Steller sea lions, and air and water quality in the park. The court noted that there was "a paucity of analytical data to support the Park Service's conclusion that the mitigation measures would be adequate in light of the potential environmental harms."

In its revised 2020 regulations, CEQ removed the preceding interpretation of "significantly" that focused on an action's context and intensity. Future litigation will determine whether the factors utilized in cases such as *Anderson* and *National Parks & Conservation Association* are essential elements of NEPA's significance requirement.

## NOTES AND QUESTIONS

1. The rise of the environmental justice movement has increased public attention to the disparate impact of environmental problems on poor and minority communities. As discussed in Chapter 1, President Clinton's Executive Order 12,898 directs each federal agency to identify and address disproportionate "adverse human health or environmental effects of its programs, policies, and activities on minority and low-income populations." In December 1997, CEQ issued guidance to agencies concerning how to comply with the executive order. CEQ Environmental Justice: Guidance Under the National Environmental Policy Act (1997). CEQ takes the position that the executive order does not change NEPA law, but that it should stimulate agencies to give greater consideration to human health or ecological impacts on minority populations, low-income populations, and Indian tribes and to alternatives that would accommodate environmental justice concerns. The Nuclear Regulatory Commission's Atomic Safety and Licensing Board has ruled that environmental justice concerns must be considered in environmental impact statements prepared for licensing proceedings. The Board required Nuclear Regulatory Commission staff to revise an EIS to give greater consideration to the effects of siting a uranium enrichment plant in a poor and minority community. In re Louisiana Energy Services, L.P. (May 1, 1997).

2. While the circuits initially split over the question of what standard of review should be applied to a decision not to prepare an EIS, the Supreme Court appears to have resolved the debate in *Marsh v. Oregon Natural Resources Council*, discussed below. The Court adopted the "arbitrary and capricious" standard of review for decisions not to prepare a supplemental EIS. The Court emphasized, however, that "courts should not automatically defer to the agency's express reliance on an interest in finality without carefully reviewing the record and satisfying themselves that the agency has made a reasoned decision based on its evaluation of the significance — or lack of significance — of the new information." 490 U.S. at 378. Based on this statement, the Ninth Circuit has held that when disputes over whether or not to prepare a supplemental EIS involve "predominately legal questions" rather than "factual or technical matters," the reasonableness standard of review should be applied instead of the arbitrary and capricious standard. Alaska Wilderness Recreation & Tourism Ass'n v. Morrison, 67 F.3d 723, 727 (9th Cir. 1995). The Supreme Court's decision in *Marsh v. Oregon Natural Resources Council* has been interpreted to extend to reviews of *all* agency decisions not to prepare an EIS. Greenpeace Action v. Franklin, 14 F.3d 1324 (9th Cir. 1992); Village of Los Ranchos de Albuquerque v. Marsh, 956 F.2d 970 (10th Cir. 1992) (en banc).

3. In Idaho v. ICC, 35 F.3d 585 (D.C. Cir. 1994), the D.C. Circuit held that the Interstate Commerce Commission had violated NEPA by failing to prepare an EIS before conditionally approving a proposal to abandon a portion of a railroad line. Even though it authorized salvage activities along a heavily contaminated track bed, the ICC had claimed that its decision would not significantly affect the environment because it required the railroad to consult with federal and state environmental agencies about the environmental effects of salvage operations. Citing its decision in *Calvert Cliffs*, the D.C. Circuit held that "[a]n agency cannot delegate its NEPA responsibilities in this manner." The court concluded that the agency must take its own "hard look" at the environmental effects of its action and cannot abdicate its NEPA responsibilities in favor of a regulated party.

4. Four days after taking office in January 2017, President Trump directed the U.S. Army Corps of Engineers to grant an easement to allow the Dakota Access Pipeline (DAPL) to be completed and to consider rescinding the Corps's previous decision to prepare an EIS for the pipeline. The Corps granted the easement on February 8, 2017, and the pipeline quickly was completed and started operating. Federal district judge James Boasberg later concluded that issuance of the easement was illegal because an EIS should have been prepared. He shocked Energy Transfer Partners by ordering that operation of the pipeline be halted and that the pipeline be drained until after the EIS was completed. This was viewed as a sharp rebuke to a "build it first" strategy by pipeline owners who sought to make environmental approval a foregone conclusion by first building all the portions of a pipeline that did not require federal approval. On January 26, 2021, the D.C. Circuit upheld the decision that an EIS was required, but it stayed the order to halt operation of the pipeline, finding that Judge Boasberg had not conducted the appropriate analysis for issuing such an injunction. Standing Rock Sioux Tribe v. U.S. Army Corps of Engineers, 985 F.3d 1032 (D.C. Cir. 2021). The court concluded that unresolved controversies over DAPL's leak detection system, operator safety record, effects of winter conditions, and worst-case discharge analysis made the Corps easement decision "highly controversial," which required preparation of an EIS.

## C.   What "Effects" Must Be Considered

In determining whether the effects of an action are "significant," one must, of course, make some judgments about what "effects" must be considered. NEPA demands consideration of effects "on the human environment." The 2020 CEQ regulation defining "effects," 40 C.F.R. §1508.1(g)(1), provides the following explanation:

> Effects include ecological (such as the effects on natural resources and on the components, structures, and functioning of affected ecosystems), aesthetic, historic, cultural, economic (such as the effects on employment), social, or health effects. Effects may also include those resulting from actions that may have both beneficial and detrimental effects, even if on balance the agency believes that the effect will be beneficial.

The 2020 regulations removed the previous reference to "direct, indirect, or cumulative" effects and specified that a "but-for" causal relationship between agency action and an outcome is not sufficient to establish "significant" effects. The updated regulations also say that remote effects should not be considered, nor effects that an agency has "no ability to prevent." These regulations were inspired by the decision excerpted below in *Department of Transportation v. Public Citizen*.

The question of what "effects" are cognizable under NEPA was directly addressed by the Supreme Court in Metropolitan Edison Co. v. People Against Nuclear Energy (*PANE*), 460 U.S. 766 (1983). In *PANE*, the Court held that NEPA did not require agencies to evaluate the risk that restart of a nuclear power plant that is a companion to the damaged Three Mile Island reactor would harm the psychological health of the surrounding community. The Court concluded that regardless of the gravity of the harm alleged, NEPA does not apply unless the harm has a sufficiently close connection to the physical environment. The question of how direct the causal connection must be between the action under consideration and the environmental effects to be assessed was addressed by the Court in the case that follows.

## Department of Transportation v. Public Citizen

541 U.S. 752 (2004)

JUSTICE THOMAS delivered the opinion of the Court.

In this case, we confront the question whether the National Environmental Policy Act of 1969 (NEPA) and the Clean Air Act (CAA) require the Federal Motor Carrier Safety Administration (FMCSA) to evaluate the environmental effects of cross-border operations of Mexican-domiciled motor carriers, where FMCSA's promulgation of certain regulations would allow such cross-border operations to occur. Because FMCSA lacks discretion to prevent these cross-border operations, we conclude that these statutes impose no such requirement on FMCSA.

### I

[The Court discusses NEPA and notes that] "NEPA itself does not mandate particular results" in order to accomplish [its] ends. Robertson v. Methow Valley

Citizens Council, 490 U.S. 332, 350 (1989). Rather, NEPA imposes only procedural requirements on federal agencies with a particular focus on requiring agencies to undertake analyses of the environmental impact of their proposals and actions. . . .

FMCSA, an agency within the Department of Transportation (DOT), is responsible for motor carrier safety and registration. See 49 U.S.C. §113(f). FMCSA has a variety of statutory mandates, including "ensur[ing]" safety, §31136, establishing minimum levels of financial responsibility for motor carriers, §31139, and prescribing federal standards for safety inspections of commercial motor vehicles, §31142. Importantly, FMCSA has only limited discretion regarding motor vehicle carrier registration: It must grant registration to all domestic or foreign motor carriers that are "willing and able to comply with" the applicable safety, fitness, and financial-responsibility requirements. §13902(a)(1). FMCSA has no statutory authority to impose or enforce emissions controls or to establish environmental requirements unrelated to motor carrier safety.

[The Court notes that in 1982 Congress authorized the president to extend a two-year moratorium it had imposed on new Mexican motor carriers operating in the interior of the United States, authority he exercised. After an international arbitration panel ruled in February 2001 that the moratorium violated the North American Free Trade Agreement (NAFTA), President Bush declared his intention to lift it as soon as the FMCSA promulgated new regulations for such carriers, which it proposed in May 2001. In December 2001, Congress enacted section 350 of the Department of Transportation and Related Agencies Appropriations Act that barred the processing of applications by Mexican motor carriers to operate in the United States until the FMCSA adopted specific application and safety-monitoring regulations for them.]

In January 2002, acting pursuant to NEPA's mandates, FMCSA issued a programmatic [environmental assessment] EA for the proposed Application and Safety Monitoring Rules. . . . Because FMCSA concluded that the entry of the Mexican trucks was not an "effect" of its regulations, it did not consider any environmental impact that might be caused by the increased presence of Mexican trucks within the United States.

The particular environmental effects on which the EA focused, then, were those likely to arise from the increase in the number of roadside inspections of Mexican trucks and buses due to the proposed regulations. The EA concluded that these effects (such as a slight increase in emissions, noise from the trucks, and possible danger to passing motorists) were minor and could be addressed and avoided in the inspections process itself. The EA also noted that the increase of inspection-related emissions would be at least partially offset by the fact that the safety requirements would reduce the number of Mexican trucks operating in the United States. Due to these calculations, the EA concluded that the issuance of the proposed regulations would have no significant impact on the environment, and hence FMCSA, on the same day as it released the EA, issued a [finding of no significant impact] FONSI [and thus declined to prepare an environmental impact statement].

[After the FMCSA issued its regulations in March 2002, respondents sued, arguing that the regulations were promulgated in violation of NEPA and the CAA.] The Court of Appeals agreed with respondents, granted the petitions, and set aside the rules. . . .

## II

. . . Under NEPA, an agency is required to provide an EIS only if it will be undertaking a "major Federal actio[n]," which "significantly affect[s] the quality of the human environment." 42 U.S.C. §4332(2)(C). Under applicable CEQ regulations, "[m]ajor Federal action" is defined to "includ[e] actions with effects that may be major and which are potentially subject to Federal control and responsibility." 40 CFR §1508.18 (2003). "Effects" is defined to "include: (a) Direct effects, which are caused by the action and occur at the same time and place," and "(b) Indirect effects, which are caused by the action and are later in time or farther removed in distance, but are still reasonably foreseeable." §1508.8. Thus, the relevant question is whether the increase in cross-border operations of Mexican motor carriers, with the correlative release of emissions by Mexican trucks, is an "effect" of FMCSA's issuance of the Application and Safety Monitoring Rules; if not, FMCSA's failure to address these effects in its EA did not violate NEPA, and so FMCSA's issuance of a FONSI cannot be arbitrary and capricious.

[The Court then determined that the respondents had waived any challenge to the EA premised on its failure to consider possible alternatives to the proposed rule because they had not raised such alternatives in their comments during the rulemaking.] . . . With this point aside, respondents have only one complaint with respect to the EA: It did not take into account the environmental effects of increased cross-border operations of Mexican motor carriers. Respondents' argument that FMCSA was required to consider these effects is simple. Under §350, FMCSA is barred from expending any funds to process or review any applications by Mexican motor carriers until FMCSA implemented a variety of specific application and safety-monitoring requirements for Mexican carriers. This expenditure bar makes it impossible for any Mexican motor carrier to receive authorization to operate within the United States until FMCSA issued the regulations challenged here. The promulgation of the regulations, the argument goes, would "caus[e]" the entry of Mexican trucks (and hence also cause any emissions such trucks would produce), and the entry of the trucks is "reasonably foreseeable." 40 CFR §1508.8 (2003). Thus, the argument concludes, under the relevant CEQ regulations, FMCSA must take these emissions into account in its EA when evaluating whether to produce an EIS.

Respondents' argument, however, overlooks a critical feature of this case: FMCSA has no ability to countermand the President's lifting of the moratorium or otherwise categorically to exclude Mexican motor carriers from operating within the United States. To be sure, §350 did restrict the ability of FMCSA to authorize cross-border operations of Mexican motor carriers, but Congress did not otherwise modify FMCSA's statutory mandates. In particular, FMCSA remains subject to the mandate of 49 U.S.C. §13902(a)(1), that FMCSA "*shall* register a person to provide transportation . . . as a motor carrier if [it] finds that the person is willing and able to comply with" the safety and financial responsibility requirements established by the Department of Transportation. (Emphasis added.) Under FMCSA's entirely reasonable reading of this provision, it must certify any motor carrier that can show that it is willing and able to comply with the various substantive requirements for safety and financial responsibility contained in DOT regulations; only the moratorium prevented it from doing so for Mexican motor carriers before 2001. Thus, upon the lifting of the moratorium, if FMCSA refused to authorize a Mexican motor carrier for cross-border services, where the Mexican motor carrier was willing and able to comply with the various substantive safety and financial responsibilities rules, it would violate §13902(a)(1).

If it were truly impossible for FMCSA to comply with both §350 and §13902(a)(1), then we would be presented with an irreconcilable conflict of laws. As the later enacted provision, §350 would quite possibly win out. But FMCSA can easily satisfy both mandates: It can issue the application and safety inspection rules required by §350, and start processing applications by Mexican motor carriers and authorize those that satisfy §13902(a)(1)'s conditions. Without a conflict, then, FMCSA must comply with all of its statutory mandates.

Respondents must rest, then, on a particularly unyielding variation of "but for" causation, where an agency's action is considered a cause of an environmental effect even when the agency has no authority to prevent the effect. However, a "but for" causal relationship is insufficient to make an agency responsible for a particular effect under NEPA and the relevant regulations. As this Court held in Metropolitan Edison Co. v. People Against Nuclear Energy, 460 U.S. 766, 774 (1983), NEPA requires "a reasonably close causal relationship" between the environmental effect and the alleged cause. The Court analogized this requirement to the "familiar doctrine of proximate cause from tort law." In particular, "courts must look to the underlying policies or legislative intent in order to draw a manageable line between those causal changes that may make an actor responsible for an effect and those that do not."

Also, inherent in NEPA and its implementing regulations is a "rule of reason," which ensures that agencies determine whether and to what extent to prepare an EIS based on the usefulness of any new potential information to the decisionmaking process. Where the preparation of an EIS would serve "no purpose" in light of NEPA's regulatory scheme as a whole, no rule of reason worthy of that title would require an agency to prepare an EIS.

In these circumstances, the underlying policies behind NEPA and Congress' intent, as informed by the "rule of reason," make clear that the causal connection between FMCSA's issuance of the proposed regulations and the entry of the Mexican trucks is insufficient to make FMCSA responsible under NEPA to consider the environmental effects of the entry. The NEPA EIS requirement serves two purposes. First, "[i]t ensures that the agency, in reaching its decision, will have available, and will carefully consider, detailed information concerning significant environmental impacts." Second, it "guarantees that the relevant information will be made available to the larger audience that may also play a role in both the decisionmaking process and the implementation of that decision." Requiring FMCSA to consider the environmental effects of the entry of Mexican trucks would fulfil neither of these statutory purposes. Since FMCSA has no ability categorically to prevent the cross-border operations of Mexican motor carriers, the environmental impact of the cross-border operations would have no effect on FMCSA's decision-making — FMCSA simply lacks the power to act on whatever information might be contained in the EIS.

Similarly, the informational purpose is not served. The "informational role" of an EIS is to "giv[e] the public the assurance that the agency 'has indeed considered environmental concerns in its decisionmaking process,' and, perhaps more significantly, provid[e] a springboard for public comment" in the agency decisionmaking process itself, ibid. The purpose here is to ensure that the "larger audience," can provide input as necessary to the agency making the relevant decisions. But here, the "larger audience" can have no impact on FMCSA's decisionmaking, since, as just noted, FMCSA simply could not act on whatever input this "larger audience" could provide.

It would not, therefore, satisfy NEPA's "rule of reason" to require an agency to prepare a full EIS due to the environmental impact of an action it could not refuse to perform. Put another way, the legally relevant cause of the entry of the Mexican trucks is not FMCSA's action, but instead the actions of the President in lifting the moratorium and those of Congress in granting the President this authority while simultaneously limiting FMCSA's discretion.

Consideration of the CEQ's "cumulative impact" regulation does not change this analysis. An agency is required to evaluate the "[c]umulative impact" of its action, which is defined as "the impact on the environment which results from the incremental impact of the action when added to other past, present, and reasonably foreseeable future actions regardless of what agency (Federal or non-Federal) or person undertakes such other actions." §1508.7. The "cumulative impact" regulation required FMCSA to consider the "incremental impact" of the safety rules themselves, in the context of the President's lifting of the moratorium and other relevant circumstances. But this is exactly what FMCSA did in its EA. FMCSA appropriately and reasonably examined the incremental impact of its safety rules assuming the President's modification of the moratorium (and, hence, assuming the increase in cross-border operations of Mexican motor carriers). The "cumulative impact" regulation does not require FMCSA to treat the lifting of the moratorium itself, or consequences from the lifting of the moratorium, as an effect of its promulgation of its Application and Safety Monitoring Rules.

We hold that where an agency has no ability to prevent a certain effect due to its limited statutory authority over the relevant actions, the agency cannot be considered a legally relevant "cause" of the effect. Hence, under NEPA and the implementing CEQ regulations, the agency need not consider these effects in its EA when determining whether its action is a "major Federal action." Because the President, not FMCSA, could authorize (or not authorize) cross-border operations from Mexican motor carriers, and because FMCSA has no discretion to prevent the entry of Mexican trucks, its EA did not need to consider the environmental effects arising from the entry.

## NOTES AND QUESTIONS

1. This decision is yet another in a long line of Supreme Court cases construing NEPA's requirements narrowly. As Professor Richard Lazarus has noted, environmental interests have lost all 17 cases in which a NEPA issue has been decided by the U.S. Supreme Court. In Natural Resources Defense Council, Inc. v. Morton,

458 F.2d 827 (D.C. Cir. 1972), the D.C. Circuit had held that NEPA requires an agency to consider even some alternatives that it did not have the power to adopt on its own. Does *DOT v. Public Citizen* overrule this decision?

2.  Does *DOT v. Public Citizen* provide any insight into how the Court views the purposes of NEPA? Is it fair to say that the Court does not consider one of NEPA's purposes to be informing other agencies who may be able to control adverse environmental effects identified in the EIS?

3.  The Court in *Public Citizen* also held that the FMCSA did not violate the Clean Air Act by failing to determine that emissions from the cross-border operation of Mexican trucks would be in conformity with existing air quality standards because the FMCSA was powerless to stop the emissions.

4.  During the Obama administration, the U.S. State Department considered whether to grant approval for the construction of the Keystone XL pipeline from Canada, which would carry carbon-intensive oil from Alberta's oil sands. The Draft Supplemental EIS (DEIS) for the project estimated that lifecycle GHG emissions from oil sands crude would be 81 percent greater on a well-to-tank basis and 17 percent greater on a wheels-to-wheels basis than average crude oil refined in the United States in 2005. Yet the DEIS for Keystone XL concluded that the impact of the pipeline on GHG emissions would be neutral because the oil sands crude would be extracted and shipped to market by rail if the pipeline is not approved. How would you respond to this argument?

5.  In *Hanly*, the majority was uncertain "whether psychological and sociological effects upon neighbors constitute the type of factors that may be considered in making a determination [whether or not to perform an EIS] since they do not lend themselves to measurement." 471 F.2d at 833. Judge Friendly disagreed in his dissent, noting that NEPA speaks of "the overall welfare and development of man," 42 U.S.C. §4331(a), and requires federal agencies to act to "assure for all Americans safe, healthful, productive and esthetically and culturally pleasing surroundings." Id. §4331(b)(2). Is his view consistent with the Supreme Court's decision in *PANE*?

6.  Is an EIS required for federal actions likely to have a significant *positive* effect on the environment? In Pacific Legal Foundation v. Andrus, 657 F.2d 829 (6th Cir. 1981), the Sixth Circuit held that decisions to list species as threatened or endangered under the Endangered Species Act (ESA) were exempt from NEPA. At the urging of CEQ, the Secretary of Interior announced in 1983 that the Department would no longer prepare EISs in connection with listing determinations made under section 4 of the ESA. In Douglas County v. Babbitt, 48 F.3d 1495 (9th Cir. 1995), the Ninth Circuit held that decisions to designate critical habitat for an endangered species were not subject to NEPA because neither an EA nor an EIS is "necessary for federal actions that conserve the environment." In October 2011, federal district Judge Emmett Sullivan refused to defer to the Interior Department's policy of not applying NEPA to decisions to list endangered species. Although he held that a special rule issued under section 4(d) of the ESA barring the application of section 9's "take" prohibition to greenhouse gas emissions that may harm polar bears did not violate the ESA, he held that the Interior Department

had violated NEPA by not performing at least an environmental assessment prior to issuing the rule. In re Polar Bear Endangered Species Act Listing and 4(d) Rule Litigation, 818 F. Supp. 2d 214 (D.D.C. 2011).

7. In Center for Biological Diversity v. National Highway Traffic Safety Administration, 538 F.3d 1172 (9th Cir. 2008), the court rejected a finding of no significant impact in an EA prepared by NHTSA prior to revising national fuel economy standards. The court held that NHTSA failed to consider sufficiently the impact of the standards on climate change, and failed to consider a sufficiently wide range of alternatives, including significant increases in the standards. In both 1988 and 1990, the D.C. Circuit had upheld previous fuel economy standards, rejecting claims that NHTSA first had to prepare an EIS. In 1988, a three-judge panel of the court unanimously accepted, with little discussion, NHTSA's finding of no significant impact. Public Citizen v. NHTSA, 848 F.3d 256 (D.C. Cir. 1988). In 1990, another panel of the court split 2-1 in rejecting a claim that NHTSA was required to prepare an EIS considering effects on climate change when the agency slightly rolled back CAFE standards for model years 1987-1989. City of Los Angeles v. NHTSA, 912 F.2d 478 (D.C. Cir. 1990). In a footnote, the Ninth Circuit panel distinguished this case. It noted that then-Judge Ruth Bader Ginsburg had joined the majority opinion only because the environmental petitioners had failed to allege that the rollback "would produce any marginal effect on the probability, the severity, or the imminence" of climate change. 912 F.2d at 504. The court noted that, unlike that case, the petitioners in Center for Biological Diversity "provided substantial evidence that even a small increase in greenhouse gases could cause abrupt and severe climate changes." 538 F.3d at 1224 n.76. The court also noted that Chief Judge Patricia Wald had argued in dissent that NHTSA acted arbitrarily in concluding that the agency's action would not have a significant impact on global warming and it described her dissent as "not only prescient but persuasive." In her dissent Judge Wald wrote:

> While NHTSA did the calculations necessary to determine how much extra carbon dioxide would be emitted, it failed completely to discuss in any detail the global warming phenomenon itself, or to explain the benchmark for its determination of insignificance in relation to that environmental danger. Had the emissions been slightly over one percent, would that have been significant? Without some articulated criteria for significance in terms of contribution to global warming that is grounded in the record and available scientific evidence, NHTSA's bald conclusion that the mere magnitude of the percentage increase is enough to alleviate its burden of conducting a more thorough investigation cannot carry the day. [912 F.2d at 500.]

8. The CEQ's 2020 NEPA regulations consolidate the evaluation of cumulative and indirect effects into a single definition of "effects." Detractors to the changes fear a reduction in consideration of the impacts from climate change if NEPA review does not require consideration of cumulative or indirect effects. However, changing NEPA's implementing regulations does not modify the requirements under law.

9. In the case below, the D.C. Circuit considered whether an environmental impact statement had adequately considered the environmental justice effects of a pipeline project as well as whether it should have quantified the pipelines' impact on greenhouse gas emissions.

## Sierra Club v. Federal Energy Regulation Commission

867 F.3d 1357 (D.C. Cir. 2017)

GRIFFITH, Circuit Judge:

Environmental groups and landowners have challenged the decision of the Federal Energy Regulatory Commission to approve the construction of three new interstate natural gas pipelines in the southeastern United States. Their primary argument is that the agency's assessment of the environmental impact of the pipelines was inadequate. We agree that FERC's environmental impact statement did not contain enough information on the greenhouse-gas emissions that will result from burning the gas the pipelines will carry. In all other respects, we conclude that FERC acted properly. We thus grant Sierra Club's petition for review and remand for preparation of a conforming environmental impact statement.

**I**

The Southeast Market Pipelines Project comprises three natural-gas pipelines now under construction in Alabama, Georgia, and Florida. . . . By its scheduled completion in 2021, the project will be able to carry over one billion cubic feet of natural gas per day.

The three segments of the project have different owners, but they share a common purpose: to serve Florida's growing demand for natural gas and the electric power that natural gas can generate. At present, only two major natural-gas pipelines serve the state, and both are almost at capacity. Two major utilities, Florida Power & Light and Duke Energy Florida, have already committed to buying nearly all the gas the project will be able to transport. Florida Power & Light claims that without this new project, its gas needs will begin to exceed its supply this year. But the project's developers also indicate that the increased transport of natural gas will make it possible for utilities to retire older, dirtier coal-fired power plants.

Section 7 of the Natural Gas Act places these disputes into the bailiwick of the Federal Energy Regulatory Commission (FERC), which has jurisdiction to approve or deny the construction of interstate natural-gas pipelines. Before any such pipeline can be built, FERC must grant the developer a "certificate of public convenience and necessity," also called a Section 7 certificate, upon a finding that the project will serve the public interest. FERC is also empowered to attach "reasonable terms and conditions" to the certificate, as necessary to protect the public. A certificate holder has the ability to acquire necessary rights-of-way from unwilling landowners by eminent domain proceedings.

FERC launched an environmental review of the proposed project in the fall of 2013. The agency understood that it would need to prepare an environmental impact statement (EIS) before approving the project, as the National Environmental Policy Act of 1969 (NEPA) requires for each "major Federal action[] significantly affecting the quality of the human environment." FERC solicited public comment and held thirteen public meetings on the project's environmental effects, and made limited modifications to the project plan in response to public concerns, before releasing a draft impact statement in September 2015 and a final impact statement in December 2015. In the meantime, the pipeline developers formally applied for their Section 7 certificates in September and November 2014.

In the Certificate Order, issued on February 2, 2016, FERC granted the requested Section 7 certificates and approved construction of all three project segments, subject to compliance with various conditions not at issue here. . . .

Sierra Club argues that FERC's environmental impact statement failed to adequately consider the project's contribution to greenhouse-gas emissions and its impact on low-income and minority communities. . . .

### III

#### A

The principle of environmental justice encourages agencies to consider whether the projects they sanction will have a "disproportionately high and adverse" impact on low-income and predominantly minority communities. Executive Order 12,898 required federal agencies to include environmental justice analysis in their NEPA reviews, and the Council on Environmental Quality, the independent agency that implements NEPA, has promulgated environmental justice guidelines for agencies.

Sierra Club argues that the EIS failed to adequately take this principle into account. Like the other components of an EIS, an environmental justice analysis is measured against the arbitrary and capricious standard. The analysis must be "reasonable and adequately explained," but the agency's "choice among reasonable analytical methodologies is entitled to deference." As always with NEPA, an agency is not required to select the course of action that best serves environmental justice, only to take a "hard look" at environmental justice issues. We conclude that FERC's discussion of environmental justice in the EIS satisfies this standard.

The EIS explained that 83.7% of the pipelines' proposed route would cross through, or within one mile of, environmental-justice communities (defined as census tracts where the population is disproportionately below the poverty line and/or disproportionately belongs to racial or ethnic minority groups). That percentage varied from 54 to 80 percent for the alternative routes proposed by stakeholders and commenters, albeit with only one option below 70 percent. . . . [The EIS] also discussed one additional proposed route, which would cross the Gulf of Mexico and avoid Georgia completely. This option would affect far fewer environmental-justice communities, but in FERC's assessment would be infeasible because it would cost an additional two billion dollars.

FERC concluded that the various feasible alternatives "would affect a relatively similar percentage of environmental justice populations," and that the preferred route thus would not have a disproportionate impact on those populations. The agency also independently concluded that the project would not have a "high and adverse" impact on *any* population, meaning, in the agency's view, that it could not have a "*disproportionately* high and adverse" impact on any population, marginalized or otherwise.

Sierra Club contends that FERC misread "disproportionately high and adverse," the standard for when a particular environmental effect raises an environmental justice concern. By Sierra Club's lights, any effect can fulfill the test, regardless of its intensity, extent, or duration, if it is not beneficial and falls disproportionately on environmental-justice communities. But even if we assume that understanding to be correct, we cannot see how this EIS was deficient. It discussed the intensity, extent, and duration of the pipelines' environmental effects, and also separately discussed the fact that those effects will disproportionately fall on environmental justice communities. Recall that the EIS informed readers and the agency's ultimate decisionmakers that 83.7% of the pipelines' length would be in or near environmental-justice communities. The EIS also evaluated route alternatives in part by looking at the number of environmental-justice communities each would cross, and the mileage of pipeline each would place in low-income and minority areas. FERC thus grappled with the disparate impacts of the various possible pipeline routes. Perhaps Sierra Club would have a stronger claim if the agency had refused entirely to discuss the demographics of the population that will feel the pipelines' effects, and had justified this refusal by pointing to the limited intensity, extent, and duration of those effects. However, as the EIS stands, we see no deficiencies serious enough to defeat the statute's goals of fostering well-informed decisionmaking and public comment. . . .

To sum up, the EIS acknowledged and considered the *substance* of all the concerns Sierra Club now raises: the fact that the Southeast Market Pipelines Project will travel primarily through low-income and minority communities, and the impact of the pipeline on the city of Albany and Dougherty County in particular. The EIS also laid out a variety of alternative approaches with potential to address those concerns, including those proposed by petitioners, and explained why, in FERC's view, they would do more harm than good. The EIS also gave the public and agency decisionmakers the qualitative and quantitative tools they needed to make an informed choice for themselves. NEPA requires nothing more.

### B

It's not just the journey, though, it's also the destination. All the natural gas that will travel through these pipelines will be going somewhere: specifically, to power plants in Florida, some of which already exist, others of which are in the planning stages. Those power plants will burn the gas, generating both electricity and carbon dioxide. And once in the atmosphere, that carbon dioxide will add to the greenhouse effect, which the EIS describes as "the primary contributing factor" in global climate change. The next question before us is whether, and to what extent, the EIS for this pipeline project needed to discuss these "downstream" effects of the pipelines and their cargo. We conclude that at a minimum, FERC should have estimated the amount of power-plant carbon emissions that the pipelines will make possible.

An agency conducting a NEPA review must consider not only the direct effects, but also the *indirect* environmental effects, of the project under consideration. *See* 40 C.F.R. §1502.16(b). "Indirect effects" are those that "are caused by the [project] and are later in time or farther removed in distance, but are still reasonably foreseeable." *Id.* §1508.8(b). The phrase "reasonably foreseeable" is the key here. Effects are reasonably foreseeable if they are "sufficiently likely to occur that a person of ordinary prudence would take [them] into account in reaching a decision." EarthReports, Inc. v. FERC, 828 F.3d 949, 955 (D.C. Cir. 2016).

What are the "reasonably foreseeable" effects of authorizing a pipeline that will transport natural gas to Florida power plants? First, that gas will be burned in those power plants. This is not just "reasonably foreseeable," it is the project's entire purpose, as the pipeline developers themselves explain. It is just as foreseeable, and FERC does not dispute, that burning natural gas will release into the atmosphere the sorts of carbon compounds that contribute to climate change. . . .

The pipeline developers deny that FERC would be the legally relevant cause of any power plant carbon emissions, and thus contend that FERC has no obligation to consider those emissions in its NEPA analysis. They rely on Department of Transportation v. Public Citizen, 541 U.S. 752 (2004), a case involving the Federal Motor Carrier Safety Administration's development of safety standards for Mexican trucks operating in the United States. The agency had proposed those standards because the President planned to lift a moratorium on Mexican motor carriers operating in this country. These standards would require roadside inspections, which had the potential to create adverse environmental effects. The agency's EIS discussed the effects of these roadside inspection, but Public Citizen contended that the EIS was also required to address the environmental effects of increased truck traffic between the two countries.

The Supreme Court sided with the agency. The Court noted that the agency would have no statutory authority to exclude Mexican trucks from the United States once the President lifted the moratorium; it would only have power to set safety rules for those trucks. And because the agency could not exclude Mexican trucks from the United States, it would have no reason to gather data about the environmental harms of admitting them. The purpose of NEPA is to help agencies and the public make informed decisions. But when the agency has no *legal* power to prevent a certain environmental effect, there is no decision to inform, and the agency need not analyze the effect in its NEPA review.

We recently applied the *Public Citizen* rule in three challenges to FERC decisions licensing liquefied natural gas (LNG) terminals. *See* Sierra Club v. FERC (*Freeport*), 827 F.3d 36 (D.C. Cir. 2016); Sierra Club v. FERC (*Sabine Pass*), 827 F.3d 59 (D.C. Cir. 2016); EarthReports, Inc. v. FERC, 828 F.3d 949 (D.C. Cir. 2016). Companies can export natural gas from the United States through an LNG terminal, but such natural gas exports require a license from the Department of Energy. They also require physical upgrades to a terminal's facilities. The Department of Energy has delegated to FERC the authority to license those upgrades. A question presented to us in all of these cases was whether FERC, in licensing physical upgrades for an LNG terminal, needed to evaluate the climate-change effects of exporting natural gas. Relying on *Public Citizen*, we answered no in each case. FERC had no legal authority to consider the environmental effects of those exports, and thus no NEPA obligation stemming from those effects.

An agency has no obligation to gather or consider environmental information if it has no statutory authority *to act on that information.* That rule was the touchstone of *Public Citizen* and it distinguishes this case from the LNG-terminal trilogy. Contrary to our dissenting colleague's view, our holding in the LNG cases was not based solely on the fact that a second agency's approval was necessary before the environmental effect at issue could occur. Rather, *Freeport* and its companion cases rested on the premise that FERC had *no legal authority to prevent* the adverse environmental effects of natural gas exports.

This raises the question: what did the *Freeport* court mean by its statement that FERC could not prevent the effects of exports? After all, FERC *did* have legal authority to deny an upgrade license for a natural gas export terminal. And without such an upgrade license, neither gas exports nor their environmental effects could have occurred.

The answer must be that FERC was forbidden to rely on the effects of gas exports *as a justification for* denying an upgrade license. The holding in *Freeport* then turned not on the question "What activities does FERC regulate?" but instead on the question "What factors can FERC consider when regulating in its proper sphere?" In the LNG cases, FERC was acting not on its own statutory authority but under a narrow delegation from the Department of Energy. Thus, the agency would have acted unlawfully had it refused an upgrade license on grounds that it did not have delegated authority to consider.

Here, FERC is not so limited. Congress broadly instructed the agency to consider "the public convenience and necessity" when evaluating applications to construct and operate interstate pipelines. FERC will balance "the public benefits against the adverse effects of the project," including adverse environmental effects. Because FERC could deny a pipeline certificate on the ground that the pipeline would be too harmful to the environment, the agency is a "legally relevant cause" of the direct and indirect environmental effects of pipelines it approves. *Public Citizen* thus did not excuse FERC from considering these indirect effects. . . .

We conclude that the EIS for the Southeast Market Pipelines Project should have either given a quantitative estimate of the downstream greenhouse emissions that will result from burning the natural gas that the pipelines will transport or explained more specifically why it could not have done so. As we have noted, greenhouse-gas emissions are an indirect effect of authorizing this project, which FERC could reasonably foresee, and which the agency has legal authority to mitigate. The EIS accordingly needed to include a discussion of the "significance" of this indirect effect, as well as "the incremental impact of the action when added to other past, present, and reasonably foreseeable future actions."

Quantification would permit the agency to compare the emissions from this project to emissions from other projects to total emissions from the state or the region, or to regional or national emissions-control goals. Without such comparisons, it is difficult to see how FERC could engage in "informed decision making" with respect to the greenhouse-gas effects of this project, or how "informed public comment" could be possible.

We do not hold that quantification of greenhouse-gas emissions is required *every* time those emissions are an indirect effect of any agency action. We understand that in some cases quantification may not be feasible. But FERC has not provided a satisfactory explanation for why this is such a case. We understand that "emission estimates would be largely influenced by assumptions rather than direct parameters about the project," but some educated assumptions are inevitable in the NEPA process. And the effects of assumptions on estimates can be checked by disclosing those assumptions so that readers can take the resulting estimates with the appropriate amount of salt.

Nor is FERC excused from making emissions estimates just because the emissions might be partially offset by reduction elsewhere. We thus do not agree that the EIS was absolved from estimating carbon emissions by the fact that some of the new pipelines' transport capacity will make it possible for utilities to retire dirtier, coal-fired plants. The effects an EIS is required to cover "include those resulting from actions which may have both beneficial and detrimental effects, even if on balance the agency believes that the effect will be beneficial." In other words, when an agency thinks that the good consequences of a project will outweigh the bad, the agency still needs to discuss both the good and the bad. . . .

BROWN, Circuit Judge, concurring in part and dissenting in part:

I join today's opinion on all issues save the Court's decision to vacate and remand the pipeline certificates on the issue of downstream greenhouse emissions. Case law is clear: When an agency "has no ability to prevent a certain effect due to [its] 'limited statutory authority over the relevant action[],'" then that action 'cannot be considered a legally relevant cause'" of an indirect environmental effect under the National Environmental Policy Act. Thus, when the occurrence of an indirect environmental effect is contingent upon the issuance of a license from a separate agency, the agency under review is not required to address those indirect effects in its NEPA analysis. Although this case seems indistinguishable from earlier precedent, the Court now insists the action taken by the Federal Energy Regulatory Commission is the cause of an environmental effect, even though the agency has no authority to prevent the effect. Because the Court's holding is legally incorrect and contravenes our duty to examine all arguments presented, I respectfully dissent. . . .

. . . [J]ust as FERC in the DOE cases and the Federal Motor Carrier Safety Administration in *Public Citizen* did not have the legal power to prevent certain environmental effects, the Commission here has no authority to prevent the emission of greenhouse gases through newly-constructed or expanded power plants approved by the [Florida Power Plant Siting] Board. To be sure, the Commission could make it extremely inconvenient to deliver the same amount of natural gas to the plants, but this is an issue of practicality, which, as conceded by the majority, is irrelevant under NEPA. Accordingly, the Commission was not obligated under NEPA to discuss downstream greenhouse gas emissions, and I would deny the entire petition for review.

## NOTES AND QUESTIONS

1. Following the court's decision, it did not take long for FERC to supplement the EIS for the Southeast Market Pipelines Project. On September 27, 2017, five weeks after the court's decision, FERC issued a draft supplemental EIS. After taking comments on the draft for 45 days, FERC issued a final supplemental EIS on

February 5, 2018, less than six months after the court's decision. The final supplemental EIS quantified greenhouse gas emissions associated with the downstream consumption of natural gas to be transported by the pipeline. On March 14, 2018, FERC reinstated its approval of the pipeline.

2. The D.C. Circuit previously had relied on *Department of Transportation v. Public Citizen* to reject claims that FERC EISs were deficient because they did not quantify the upstream or downstream effects on greenhouse gas emissions of approving liquid natural gas export terminals. Sierra Club v. FERC (*Freeport*), 827 F.3d 36 (D.C. Cir. 2016). How does Judge Griffith distinguish the *Freeport* decision in his majority opinion? Why does Judge Brown in her dissent disagree with him?

3. As the court notes, traditionally, agencies conducting NEPA reviews had to consider both direct and indirect environmental effects. In 1997, the Council on Environmental Quality (CEQ) issued a draft guidance document concluding that because climate change is "reasonably foreseeable" it should be considered in EAs and EISs. Michael B. Gerrard, Climate Change and the Environmental Impact Review Process, 22 Nat. Resources & Env't 20 (Winter 2008). Many early EISs that discussed climate change often stated only that the GHG emissions from the particular project under review are only a tiny portion of total global emissions and thus unlikely to have a significant effect on the overall problem. Subsequent CEQ guidance on this issue is discussed in the Problem Exercise below.

4. Some states went even further than the federal government in requiring analysis of climate change in environmental impact assessments. In 2008, Massachusetts amended its Environmental Policy Act to require agencies to consider reasonably foreseeable climate change effects. In April 2007, California Attorney General Jerry Brown sued the County of San Bernardino to require it to consider the effects of its county growth plan on GHG emissions under the California Environmental Quality Act (CEQA). The lawsuit was settled by the county agreeing to prepare a plan for GHG emissions reductions as part of its implementation of the growth plan. In 2008, the California Governor's Office of Planning and Research (OPR) issued interim guidance on climate change assessment under CEQA, OPR, CEQA & Climate Change: Addressing Climate Change Through CEQA Review (June 2008), and the California legislature adopted legislation encouraging denser development to reduce vehicle GHG emissions. New York's Department of Environmental Conservation also issued draft guidance on the assessment of climate change impacts under the State Environmental Quality Review Act (SEQRA). N.Y. State Department of Environmental Conservation, Guide for Assessing Energy Use and Greenhouse Gas Emissions in Environmental Impact Statements (2008).

---

### PROBLEM EXERCISE: TO WHAT EXTENT SHOULD A PROJECT'S IMPACT ON GREENHOUSE GAS EMISSIONS AND CLIMATE CHANGE BE CONSIDERED IN AN EIS?

Reviewing how climate change is being considered in environmental impact assessments, Professor Michael Gerrard wrote in 2008 that the various protocols that are being developed for conducting such assessments "generally call for consideration of five different kinds of impacts." Michael B. Gerrard, Climate Change and the

Environmental Impact Review Process, 22 Nat. Resources & Env't 20, 23 (Winter 2008). These include: (1) A project's *direct operational impacts* on GHG emissions ("smokestack emissions from the facility, fugitive emissions such as methane escaping from oil and gas wells; emissions of methane and nitrous oxide from agricultural operations; methane from landfills and wastewater treatment plants; and impacts on carbon 'sinks,' such as forests, agricultural soils, and wetlands"). (2) GHG emissions generated to produce the *electricity purchased* by the project. (3) GHG emissions associated with the *transportation* of goods, materials, employees, customers, and vendors to and from the facility. (4) GHG emissions from the extraction and fabrication of *construction materials* and from *construction equipment* at the site. (5) The *impact of climate change* and measures to adapt to it on the project itself.

Professor Gerrard then suggested that NEPA could be used to create incentives to minimize the greenhouse gas footprints of new projects by establishing a minimum threshold under which their emissions would not trigger full NEPA review. Jessica Leber, Can NEPA Pass Tests Posed by Climate-Related Projects?, N.Y. Times, Mar. 26, 2009. This is the approach that the CEQ initially followed in February 2010 when it released draft guidance on when and how federal agencies must consider GHG emissions when taking actions subject to NEPA. This draft guidance included "a presumptive threshold of 25,000 metric tons of carbon dioxide equivalent emissions from the proposed action to trigger a quantitative analysis." Memorandum for Heads of Federal Departments and Agencies from Nancy H. Sutley, Draft NEPA Guidance on Consideration of the Effects of Climate Change and Greenhouse Gas Emissions, Feb. 18, 2010.

On December 24, 2014, CEQ issued revised draft guidance for public comment that was significantly more detailed than the 2010 draft. CEQ, Revised Draft Guidance for Greenhouse Gas Emissions and Climate Change Impacts. Like the February 2010 guidance, it used 25,000 metric tons of carbon dioxide equivalent emissions annually as "a reference point below which a quantitative analysis of greenhouse gas is not recommended unless it is easily accomplished based on available tools and data." Unlike the 2010 draft guidance, the 2014 guidance applied to all federal agency actions, including those by land and resource management agencies.

On August 2, 2016, the CEQ issued final guidance, which declared that the effects of climate change "fall squarely" within the effects that must be considered in conducting environmental impact assessments under NEPA. CEQ, Final Guidance for Federal Departments and Agencies on Consideration of Greenhouse Gas Emissions and the Effects of Climate Change in National Environmental Policy Act Reviews, 81 Fed. Reg. 51,866 (2016). Consistent with the draft 2014 guidance, it advised agencies to quantify projected greenhouse gas emissions from proposed federal actions "whenever the necessary tools, methodologies, and data inputs are available." It also directed agencies to consider the effects of climate change on the proposed action itself and its environmental impacts. One very significant change, however, was the elimination of the 25,000 ton/year $CO_2e$ threshold. The final guidance did not include any specific threshold for quantifying GHG emissions. Instead, as noted above, it directed agencies to quantify emissions whenever the methodologies and data are available to do so. It encouraged agencies to "draw on their experience and expertise to determine the appropriate level (broad, programmatic or project- or site-specific) and the extent of quantitative or qualitative analysis required to comply with NEPA."

Instead of referring to "upstream" or "downstream" effects, the final guidance advised agencies to consider "indirect" climate effects, citing as an example the expected combustion of coal as a reasonably foreseeable indirect effect of a decision to sell coal from federal lands. When agencies do not quantify a project's direct GHG emissions, the guidance recommended that they include a qualitative analysis and explain their basis for determining that quantification is not reasonably available. Although the final guidance was rescinded during the Trump administration in March 2017 through Executive Order 13,783, it was reinstated by President Biden through Executive Order 13,990.

On March 28, 2017, President Donald Trump issued Executive Order 13,783, "Promoting Energy Independence and Economic Growth," directing that CEQ's guidance be rescinded. On April 5, 2017, CEQ rescinded the 2016 guidance. In June 2019, the Trump administration's CEQ issued Draft NEPA Guidance on Consideration of Greenhouse Gas Emissions, 84 Fed. Reg. 30097 (2019). Hours after taking office on January 20, 2021, President Biden issued Executive Order 13,990, which revoked Executive Order 13,783 and ordered CEQ to rescind the Trump administration's June 2019 draft guidance on climate change. The order also directed CEQ to "review, revise and update" the Obama administration's August 2016 final guidance on consideration of GHG emissions and the effects of climate change in NEPA reviews.

Consider the following important questions that Professor Gerrard notes may have to be addressed as federal and state agencies develop policies for incorporating climate change considerations in environmental impact assessments. The good news is that nearly all of them can be addressed without having to change NEPA or state "little NEPAs." An excellent article on how environmental impact assessments should consider climate change, initially posted as a working paper by Professor Gerrard's Sabin Center for Climate Change Law at Columbia Law School, is Michael Burger & Jessica Wentz, Downstream and Upstream Greenhouse Gas Emissions: The Proper Scope of NEPA Review, 41 Harv. Envtl. L. Rev. 109 (2016).

**Question One.** Should the environmental impact assessment be purely a disclosure document, or will agencies require that mitigation measures identified in it be adopted? If the latter, how will compliance be monitored and enforced?

**Question Two.** Will analysis of the impact on GHG emissions be required for all projects subject to federal or state review or only for those of a certain type or larger than a certain size? Can impacts on climate change alone trigger the need for an EIS or must some other criterion of significance be met?

**Question Three.** How far upstream must the analysis of impacts on GHG emissions go? Should it consider the extraction of raw materials and the fabrication of building materials? How can transportation impacts account for the reality that people driving to the project might be driving somewhere else instead?

**Question Four.** Will acceptable mitigation measures include the purchase or trading of emissions offsets? If so, must such offsets be purchased nearby the project?

**Question Five.** Should impacts on GHG emissions outside the United States be considered? If a U.S. agency funds a project outside the United States or if a domestic project involves the purchase of materials made or grown in another country, how should these impacts be assessed? For the former, see Environmental Defense Fund v. Massey, 986 F.2d 528 (D.C. Cir. 1993) (application of NEPA to construction of an incinerator by the National Science Foundation in Antarctica); Friends of the Earth v. Mosbacher, 488 F. Supp. 2d 889 (N.D. Cal. 2007) (application of NEPA to projects funded by the Overseas Private Investment Corporation and the Export-Import Bank).

---

## C.  IS THE EIS ADEQUATE?

When an agency has prepared an EIS for its proposed action, the focus of judicial review naturally shifts to the adequacy of that document. The CEQ regulations describe the basic structure and content of the EIS. 40 C.F.R. §1502.10-1502.18. Each EIS must include: a summary (to facilitate public review); an explanation of the purpose of and need for the proposed action; a description and comparative assessment of alternatives; a description of the environment that will be affected by the action; and an analysis of the environmental consequences of the proposal and alternatives. Id. Litigation centers on the adequacy of the agency's assessment of alternatives and the scope and detail of its analysis of environmental consequences.

### 1.  Alternatives

NEPA requires that agencies assess and consider alternatives to proposed actions. These requirements are contained both in section 102(2)(C)(iii)'s description of the elements of an environmental impact statement ("a detailed statement by the responsible official on . . . alternatives to the proposed action") and in what is now section 102(2)(E)'s independent requirement that agencies must "study, develop, and describe appropriate alternatives to recommended courses of action in any proposal which involves unresolved conflicts concerning alternative uses of available resources."

Analysis of alternatives is arguably the most important part of NEPA. The question of the adequacy of an agency's assessment of alternatives arose in the early stages of the litigation that culminated in the *Strycker's Bay v. Karlen* decision discussed on pages 820-822. In Trinity Episcopal School Corp. v. Romney, 523 F.2d 88 (2d Cir. 1975), plaintiffs challenged the decision by the Department of Housing and Urban Development (HUD) to fund construction of low-income public housing on a site in New York City. They argued that HUD was required by NEPA to do more than simply accept the New York City Housing Authority's unsupported conclusion that there were no alternative sites for the public housing project because of the scarcity of land. The Second Circuit agreed. It held that what is now section 102(2)(E) required HUD to study alternatives to the project even though HUD was not obliged to prepare an EIS subject to section 102(2)(C)(iii). On remand, HUD prepared a study of alternatives, but rejected them all. HUD's decision was challenged again, culminating in the *Strycker's Bay* decision by the Supreme Court.

The Supreme Court previously had an opportunity to interpret directly NEPA's requirement for analysis of alternatives in *Vermont Yankee Nuclear Power Corp.*

*v. NRDC*, a different portion of which is discussed in Chapter 2 on pages 178-179. Recall that the case involved an Atomic Energy Commission licensing proceeding (a function now performed by the Nuclear Regulatory Commission) for a nuclear power plant being built by Consumers Power. Under the Commission's licensing procedures, when a utility applied for a permit to construct a nuclear power plant, Commission staff were responsible for preparing draft and final environmental impact statements. A public adjudicatory hearing was then held by the Atomic Safety and Licensing Board. In *Vermont Yankee*, the Court considered whether NEPA required the Commission to reopen the proceeding to consider energy conservation measures as an alternative to construction of the plant. In the late 1960s and early 1970s, environmentalists had opposed the construction of nuclear power plants on the grounds that they were unsafe and unneeded. Following the energy crises of the early 1970s, environmentalists increasingly turned to arguments that energy conservation measures could supply the equivalent power more cheaply. After the D.C. Circuit held that the Commission was required to address the conservation alternative, the Supreme Court granted review.

## Vermont Yankee Nuclear Power Corp. v. NRDC

435 U.S. 519 (1978)

MR. JUSTICE REHNQUIST delivered the opinion of the Court. . . .

These cases arise from two separate decisions of the Court of Appeals for the District of Columbia Circuit. In the first, the court remanded a decision of the Commission to grant a license to petitioner Vermont Yankee Nuclear Power Corp. to operate a nuclear power plant. In the second, the court remanded a decision of that same agency to grant a permit to petitioner Consumers Power Co. to construct two pressurized water nuclear reactors to generate electricity and steam.

With respect to the permit to Consumers Power, the court first held that the environmental impact statement for construction of the Midland reactors was fatally defective for failure to examine energy conservation as an alternative to a plant of this size. . . .

[In 1973,] the Council on Environmental Quality revised its regulations governing the preparation of environmental impact statements. The regulations mentioned for the first time the necessity of considering in impact statements energy conservation as one of the alternatives to a proposed project. . . . [Environmental intervenors] then moved the Commission to clarify its ruling and reopen the Consumers Power proceedings.

In a lengthy opinion, the Commission declined to reopen the proceedings. The Commission first ruled it was required to consider only energy conservation alternatives which were "reasonably available," would in their aggregate effect curtail demand for electricity to a level at which the proposed facility would not be needed, and were susceptible of a reasonable degree of proof. It then determined, after a thorough examination of the record, that not all of Saginaw's contentions met these threshold tests. . . .

The Court of Appeals ruled that the Commission's "threshold test" for the presentation of energy conservation contentions was inconsistent with NEPA's basic mandate to the Commission. The Commission, the court reasoned, is something more than an umpire who sits back and resolves adversary contentions at the hearing stage. And when an intervenor's comments "bring 'sufficient attention to the issue to stimulate the Commission's consideration of it,'" the Commission must "undertake its own preliminary investigation of the proffered alternative sufficient to reach a rational judgment whether it is worthy of detailed consideration in the EIS. Moreover, the Commission must explain the basis for each conclusion that further consideration of a suggested alternative is unwarranted." 547 F.2d, at 628, quoting from Indiana & Michigan Electric Co. v. FPC, 502 F.2d 336, 339 (1974), cert. denied, 420 U.S. 946 (1975).

While the court's rationale is not entirely unappealing as an abstract proposition, as applied to this case we think it basically misconceives not only the scope of the agency's statutory responsibility, but also the nature of the administrative process, the thrust of the agency's decision, and the type of issues the intervenors were trying to raise.

There is little doubt that under the Atomic Energy Act of 1954, state public utility commissions or similar bodies are empowered to make the initial decision regarding the need for power. 42 U.S.C. §2021(k). The Commission's prime area of concern in the licensing context, on the other hand, is national security, public health, and safety. §§2132, 2133, 2201. And it is clear that the need, as that term is conventionally used, for the power was thoroughly explored in the hearings. Even the Federal Power Commission, which regulates sales in interstate commerce, 16 U.S.C. §824 et seq. (1976 ed.), agreed with Consumers Power's analysis of projected need.

NEPA, of course, has altered slightly the statutory balance, requiring "a detailed statement by the responsible official on . . . alternatives to the proposed action." 42 U.S.C. §4332(C). But, as should be obvious even upon a moment's reflection, the term "alternatives" is not self-defining. To make an impact statement something more than an exercise in frivolous boilerplate the concept of alternatives must be bounded by some notion of feasibility. As the Court of Appeals for the District of Columbia Circuit has itself recognized:

> There is reason for concluding that NEPA was not meant to require detailed discussion of the environmental effects of "alternatives" put forward in comments when these effects cannot be readily ascertained and the alternatives are deemed only remote and speculative possibilities, in view of basic changes required in statutes and policies of other agencies—making them available, if at all, only after protracted debate and litigation not meaningfully compatible with the time-frame of the needs to which the underlying proposal is addressed. National Resources Defense Council v. Morton, 458 F.2d 827, 837-838 (1972).

Common sense also teaches us that the "detailed statement of alternatives" cannot be found wanting simply because the agency failed to include every alternative device and thought conceivable by the mind of man. Time and resources are simply too limited to hold that an impact statement fails because the agency failed to ferret out every possible alternative, regardless of how uncommon or unknown that alternative may have been at the time the project was approved.

With these principles in mind we now turn to the notion of "energy conservation," an alternative the omission of which was thought by the Court of Appeals to have been "forcefully pointed out by [intervenor] Saginaw in its comments on the draft EIS." Again, as the Commission pointed out, "the phrase 'energy conservation' has a deceptively simple ring in this context. Taken literally, the phrase suggests a virtually limitless range of possible actions and developments that might, in one way or another, ultimately reduce projected demands for electricity from a particular proposed plant." Moreover, as a practical matter, it is hard to dispute the observation that it is largely the events of recent years that have emphasized not only the need but also a large variety of alternatives for energy conservation. Prior to the drastic oil shortages incurred by the United States in 1973, there was little serious thought in most government circles of energy conservation alternatives. Indeed, the Council on Environmental Quality did not promulgate regulations which even remotely suggested the need to consider energy conservation in impact statements until August 1, 1973. See 40 CFR §1500.8(a)(4) (1977); 38 Fed. Reg. 20554 (1973). And even then the guidelines were not made applicable to draft and final statements filed with the Council before January 28, 1974. Id., at 20557, 21265. The Federal Power Commission likewise did not require consideration of energy conservation in applications to build hydroelectric facilities until June 19, 1973. 18 CFR pt. 2, App. A., §8.2 (1977); 38 Fed. Reg. 15946, 15949 (1973). And these regulations were not made retroactive either. Id., at 15946. All this occurred over a year and a half after the draft environmental statement for Midland had been prepared, and over a year after the final environmental statement had been prepared and the hearings completed.

We think these facts amply demonstrate that the concept of "alternatives" is an evolving one, requiring the agency to explore more or fewer alternatives as they become better known and understood. This was well understood by the Commission, which, unlike the Court of Appeals, recognized that the Licensing Board's decision had to be judged by the information then available to it. And judged in that light we have little doubt the Board's actions were well within the proper bounds of its statutory authority. Not only did the record before the agency give every indication that the project was actually needed, but also there was nothing before the Board to indicate to the contrary.

We also think the court's criticism of the Commission's "threshold test" displays a lack of understanding of the historical setting within which the agency action took place and of the nature of the test itself. In the first place, while it is true that NEPA places upon an agency the obligation to consider every significant aspect of the environmental impact of a proposed action, it is still incumbent upon intervenors who wish to participate to structure their participation so that it is meaningful, so that it alerts the agency to the intervenors' position and contentions. This is especially true when the intervenors are requesting the agency to embark upon an exploration of uncharted territory, as was the question of energy conservation in the late 1960s and early 1970s.

> [C]omments must be significant enough to step over a threshold requirement of materiality before any lack of agency response or consideration becomes of concern. The comment cannot merely state that a particular mistake was made . . . ; it must show why the mistake was of possible significance in the results. . . . Portland Cement Assn. v. Ruckelshaus, 486 F.2d 375, 394 (1973), cert. denied sub nom. Portland Cement Corp. v. Administrator, EPA, 417 U.S. 921 (1974).

Indeed, administrative proceedings should not be a game or a forum to engage in unjustified obstructionism by making cryptic and obscure reference to matters that "ought to be" considered and then, after failing to do more to bring the matter to the agency's attention, seeking to have that agency determination vacated on the ground that the agency failed to consider matters "forcefully presented." In fact, here the agency continually invited further clarification of Saginaw's contentions. Even without such clarification it indicated a willingness to receive evidence on the matters. But not only did Saginaw decline to further focus its contentions, it virtually declined to participate, indicating that it had "no conventional findings of fact to set forth" and that it had not "chosen to search the record and respond to this proceeding by submitting citations of matter which we believe were proved or disproved."

We also think the court seriously mischaracterized the Commission's "threshold test" as placing "heavy substantive burdens . . . on intervenors, . . ." 547 F.2d, at 627, and n.11. On the contrary, the Commission explicitly stated:

> We do not equate this burden with the civil litigation concept of a prima facie case, an unduly heavy burden in this setting. But the showing should be sufficient to require reasonable minds to inquire further. App. 344 n.27.

We think this sort of agency procedure well within the agency's discretion.

. . . Nuclear energy may some day be a cheap, safe source of power or it may not. But Congress has made a choice to at least try nuclear energy, establishing a reasonable review process in which courts are to play only a limited role. The fundamental policy questions appropriately resolved in Congress and in the state legislatures are *not* subject to reexamination in the federal courts under the guise of judicial review of agency action. Time may prove wrong the decision to develop nuclear energy, but it is Congress or the States with their appropriate agencies which must eventually make that judgment. In the meantime courts should perform their appointed function. NEPA does set forth significant substantive goals for the Nation, but its mandate to the agencies is essentially procedural. See 42 U.S.C. §4332. It is to insure a fully informed and well-considered decision, not necessarily a decision the judges of the Court of Appeals or of this Court would have reached had they been members of the decisionmaking unit of the agency. Administrative decisions should be set aside in this context, as in every other, only for substantial procedural or substantive reasons as mandated by statute, not simply because the court is unhappy with the result reached. And a single alleged oversight on a peripheral issue, urged by parties who never fully cooperated or indeed raised the issue below, must not be made the basis for overturning a decision properly made after an otherwise exhaustive proceeding.

## NOTES AND QUESTIONS

1. What does *Vermont Yankee* tell us about the scope of the agency's duty to consider alternatives? What duty had the Commission conceded? Why does the Court refuse to require it to consider the alternatives suggested by intervenor Saginaw? What should Saginaw have done differently? Was their basic problem a failure

to present their arguments to the Commission in a timely fashion, a failure to present sufficiently extensive evidence to bolster their arguments, or both?

2.  The Court observes that "the concept of 'alternatives' is an evolving one, requiring the agency to explore more or fewer alternatives as they become better known and understood." What result do you think the Court would reach if the licensing proceeding occurred today and the Commission refused to consider energy conservation as an alternative to construction of the plant?

3.  How obvious must an alternative be before it must be considered in an EIS? Can an agency be required to consider alternatives that employ technology that, while not currently available, could be developed in the future?

4.  In some cases the number of possible alternatives is virtually infinite. In such situations, the courts have required that agencies consider an array of alternatives that represent the range of possibilities. The Ninth Circuit addressed this problem in California v. Block, 690 F.2d 735 (9th Cir. 1982). The U.S. Forest Service had prepared an EIS on a national management plan for 62 million acres of "roadless areas" in the National Forest System. The Forest Service project, called the "Roadless Area Review and Evaluation II" (RARE II), inventoried all roadless areas and allocated them among three planning categories: wilderness, nonwilderness, and further planning. For the final EIS, the Forest Service used an elaborate set of decision criteria to develop 11 alternative allocations. These included three extremes (all wilderness, no wilderness, and no action), which served only as points of reference and were not seriously considered. Of the eight alternatives given serious consideration *none* allocated more than 33 percent of the roadless area to wilderness. The state of California challenged the EIS, arguing that the Forest Service had violated NEPA by unreasonably restricting the range of alternatives considered. The Ninth Circuit agreed, holding that while the Service's "decision criteria" were diverse, the resulting alternatives were not. The Forest Service was required to consider an alternative that allocated more than a third of the acreage to wilderness.

5.  In Resources Limited, Inc. v. Robertson, 35 F.3d 1300 (9th Cir. 1993), the Ninth Circuit rejected a challenge to the adequacy of the analysis of alternatives in a forest-wide EIS prepared for a national forest land and resource management plan. While the plaintiffs argued that the Forest Service failed to consider timber harvest levels that were substantially lower than existing harvest levels, the court noted that 5 of the 17 alternatives considered included harvest levels more than 18 percent lower than existing levels. While no alternative in the plan allocated less than 75 percent of the harvest to cutting of even-aged trees, the court noted that there were relatively few stands of trees available that were suitable for uneven-aged cutting. "Alternatives that are unlikely to be implemented need not be considered," the court concluded. 35 F.3d at 1307. Is this decision consistent with *California v. Block* discussed in note 4?

6.  In its regulation on the "scope" of an EIS, CEQ requires agencies to consider three types of alternatives: (1) no action, (2) other reasonable courses of action, and (3) mitigation measures not already included in the proposed action. 40 C.F.R. §1508.25. The 1978 CEQ regulations referred to this analysis of alternatives as "the heart of the environmental impact statement," which is designed to define the issues sharply and to provide "a clear basis for choice among options by the decisionmaker and the public."

7. In *Vermont Yankee*, Justice Rehnquist eschews Judge Wright's suggestion in *Calvert Cliffs* that NEPA imposes substantive obligations enforceable in court. He notes that "NEPA does set forth significant substantive goals for the Nation, but its mandate to the agencies is essentially procedural." Lynton Caldwell criticizes this as a "crabbed interpretation of NEPA" because it views the substantive mandate of section 101(b) as "largely rhetorical, imposing no mandate upon the agencies cognizable by the courts." Caldwell, NEPA Revisited: A Call for a Constitutional Amendment, 6 Envtl. Forum 18 (Nov.-Dec. 1989). Yet the question whether an agency has adequately complied with NEPA's procedural requirements often requires courts to perform some assessment of the quality of an agency's analysis, as explored below.

8. Brenda Mallory, President Biden's nominee to chair the CEQ, was confirmed by the Senate on April 14, 2021. She previously had been highly critical of the Trump administration's attempts to change NEPA regulations and particularly its guidance on addressing GHG impacts. Mallory has argued that "NEPA was not intended to be a process for rubber-stamping government decisions." Under Mallory, the Biden administration's CEQ is expected to implement NEPA requirements more broadly, including consideration of GHG impacts. See Executive Order 13,990, "Protecting Public Health and the Environment and Restoring Science to Tackle the Climate Crisis."

## 2.  Analysis

Each EIS must include a detailed assessment of the environmental consequences of the proposed action and the alternatives. The 1978 CEQ regulations specified that this assessment must include discussions of:

> (a) Direct effects and their significance.
>
> (b) Indirect effects and their significance.
>
> (c) Possible conflicts between the proposed action and the objectives of Federal, regional, State, and local (and, in the case of a reservation, Indian tribe) land use plans, policies, and controls for the area concerned.
>
> (d) The environmental effects of alternatives, including the proposed action. . . .
>
> (e) Energy requirements and conservation potential of various alternatives and mitigation measures.
>
> (f) Natural or depletable resource requirements and conservation potential of various alternatives and mitigation measures.
>
> (g) Urban quality, historic and cultural resources, and the design of the built environment, including the reuse and conservation potential of various alternatives and mitigation measures.
>
> (h) Means to mitigate adverse environmental impacts. [43 Fed. Reg. 55,996 (1978); 44 Fed. Reg. 873 (1979)]

Plaintiffs have identified a nearly infinite variety of flaws in agencies' analyses of "environmental consequences." We consider here three of the most important areas of attack: the quality of the analysis, problems in scope and timing, and assessment of unknown or uncertain effects.

## A. Quality of the Analysis in an EIS

As one might expect, courts often are reluctant to judge the quality of analysis in an EIS. In a few cases, however, plaintiffs have been able to demonstrate shortcomings sufficient to persuade a court that an EIS is inadequate. For example, in Sierra Club v. United States Army Corps of Engineers, 701 F.2d 1011 (2d Cir. 1983), plaintiffs challenging plans to construct the Westway, a superhighway that would run along the west side of Manhattan, argued that the final EIS was deficient because it characterized an area of the Hudson River that the project would fill as a "biological wasteland," despite data indicating the presence of a juvenile striped bass population there. EPA, the National Marine Fisheries Service, and the Fish and Wildlife Service all had objected to the EIS and to the Corps' decision to issue a permit to fill the area. Despite a new study finding that fish populations were much richer than previously thought, no supplemental EIS was prepared. After holding a trial that heard extensive testimony concerning how the EIS was prepared, a federal district court enjoined the project pending preparation of a supplemental EIS. The court's decision was appealed to the Second Circuit, which rendered the following decision.

## Sierra Club v. United States Army Corps of Engineers

701 F.2d 1011 (2d Cir. 1983)

KEARSE, Circuit Judge:

### A. NEPA

. . . The primary function of an environmental impact statement under NEPA is "'to insure a fully informed and well-considered decision,' [although] not necessarily 'a decision the judges of the Court of Appeals or of this Court would have reached had they been members of the decisionmaking unit of the agency.'" Strycker's Bay Neighborhood Council, Inc. v. Karlen, supra, 444 U.S. at 227 (quoting *Vermont Yankee*, supra, 435 U.S. at 558). In order to fulfill its role, the EIS must set forth sufficient information for the general public to make an informed evaluation and for the decisionmaker to "consider fully the environmental factors involved and to make a reasoned decision after balancing the risks of harm to the environment against the benefits to be derived from the proposed action." In so doing, the EIS insures the integrity of the process of decision by giving assurance that stubborn problems or serious criticisms have not been "swept under the rug." The "'detailed statement'" required by §102(2)(C) of NEPA thus "is the outward sign that environmental values and consequences have been considered during the planning stage of agency actions." Andrus v. Sierra Club, 442 U.S. 347, 350 (1979).

Given the role of the EIS and the narrow scope of permissible judicial review, the court may not rule an EIS inadequate if the agency has made an adequate compilation of relevant information, has analyzed it reasonably, has not ignored pertinent data, and has made disclosures to the public. . . .

In the present case the district court's rulings on the merits of plaintiffs' NEPA claims were consonant with the proper scope of its review and the proper view of the obligations imposed on FHWA and the Corps. With respect to the fisheries issues, the court found, inter alia, that the FEIS contained false statements depicting the interpier region as "biologically impoverished" and as a "biological wasteland," when in fact the interpier area in winter harbored a concentration of juvenile striped bass. The court found that the FEIS statements regarding aquatic impact had not been compiled in "objective good faith." Notwithstanding NYSDOT's contention that "the FEIS set forth the relevant facts that were known about the interpier area and the surrounding Hudson estuary at the time it was prepared . . . ," the court's findings to the contrary are amply supported by the record.

For example, after the DEIS was issued, the Project received critical comments regarding fisheries impact from Fisheries Service, Wildlife Service, and EPA to the effect that the fish life had been underestimated and that the information provided was inadequate. Although the FEIS purported to respond to these comments, no new studies were performed, no additional information was collected, no further inquiry was made, and the FEIS essentially reiterated or adopted the statements in the DEIS. Employees of the Project and FHWA testified that they knew before getting any data from the Lawler study that the Project's 1973 sampling had been faulty in both timing and technique and that these flaws were the reason the earlier study had revealed virtually no fish in the interpier area. Yet the Water Report, prepared in the wake of comments to the DEIS and appended to the FEIS, simply relied on the 1973 data. Bridwell, who was responsible for the preparation of the FEIS's fisheries discussion, testified that he was aware that the Water Report had not attempted to make any thorough or investigative inquiry into the existence of fish in the interpier area. He stated that the Water Report had attempted to verify only the existing literature on fish life in that area. It is not clear that even this academic study was performed: the Water Report neither identified any existing literature on the subject nor stated that there was no such literature; Bridwell himself was unaware of whether any literature existed. The evidence at trial suggested that there was no literature upon which the Report could have based its conclusion that the interpier area was biologically impoverished. . . .

In short, we concur in the district court's view that the FEIS did not reasonably adequately compile relevant information with respect to fisheries impact. The evidence as to the cavalier manner in which the Project had reached its conclusion that the interpier area was a biological wasteland, and as to FHWA's failure to make an independent evaluation or to react in any way to sister agencies' pointed comments that the draft EIS did not provide adequate information for a reasoned assessment of impact on fisheries, easily supports the district court's findings (1) that the FEIS's fisheries conclusions lacked a "substantial basis in fact," and (2) that a decisionmaker relying on the January 1977 EIS could not have fully considered and balanced the environmental factors. In the circumstances, we agree that FHWA's issuance of the FEIS, and the Corps' reliance on the FEIS, violated NEPA. . . .

The principal relief ordered by the district court was an injunction against any further Westway activities affecting the bed or waters of the Hudson River unless and until a supplemental EIS has been prepared by the Corps containing adequate and accurate information with respect to the fisheries issues. . . . [W]e regard this relief as well within the proper scope of the district court's discretion in the circumstances of the present case.

. . . [T]he record revealed that the authors of the FEIS had not made an adequate compilation of fisheries data, had not compiled information in objective good faith, had paid no heed to the experts' warnings that they lacked needed information, and hence had reached the erroneous conclusion that the interpier area was a biological wasteland. This baseless and erroneous factual conclusion then became a false premise in the decisionmakers' evaluations of the overall environmental impact of Westway and their balancing of the expected benefits of the proposed action against the risks of harm to the environment. Thus, the January 1977 EIS provided no valid "outward sign that environmental values and consequences [had] been considered" with respect to fisheries issues and hence furnished no assurance that the Westway approvals had been given on a reasoned basis.

Enforcement of NEPA requires that the responsible agencies be compelled to prepare a new EIS on those issues, based on adequately compiled information, analyzed in a reasonable fashion. Only if such a document is forthcoming can the public be appropriately informed and have any confidence that the decisionmakers have in fact considered the relevant factors and not merely swept difficult problems under the rug. Accordingly, we uphold the district court's requirement that before Westway landfill may proceed, FHWA or the Corps must prepare a new EIS on fisheries issues. Whether the new statement be called an amended EIS or a supplemental EIS, as in the judgments below, NEPA requires no less.

Our ruling on this point is not, however, an expansive one. We do not intend to suggest that inaccuracies in an EIS will always, or even usually, warrant a court's ordering the preparation of a supplemental EIS. Had the January 1977 EIS contained a reasoned analysis of fisheries data reasonably adequately compiled, and merely drawn an erroneous factual conclusion, we would not believe it proper to order FHWA or the Corps to prepare a SEIS. Or had reasonable investigative efforts resulted in less accurate data than later became available, the determination as to whether the later data warranted preparation of a SEIS, would be a matter committed to the discretion of the responsible agencies, not to the judgment of the court.

Nor do we express any view as to whether the decisionmakers' overall evaluation of the benefits and detriments of Westway was "wrong." We hold simply that a decision made in reliance on false information, developed without an effort in objective good faith to obtain accurate information, cannot be accepted as a "reasoned" decision.

## NOTES AND QUESTIONS

1. Note the deferential standard of review the Second Circuit applies in assessing the adequacy of an EIS. It states that "the court may not rule an EIS inadequate if the agency has made an adequate compilation of relevant information, has analyzed it reasonably, has not ignored pertinent data, and has made disclosures to the public." The court also indicates that inaccuracies in an EIS or reliance on data less accurate than that which subsequently becomes available will not routinely be enough to require preparation of a supplemental EIS. What did the court find most persuasive in convincing it that the EIS in this case was inadequate and must be supplemented? Is there anything that FHWA or the Corps could have done differently to avoid having to prepare a supplemental EIS?

2. Despite NEPA's largely procedural thrust, this decision illustrates the substantial impact a successful NEPA challenge can have. As a result of the injunction obtained in this case, the massive Westway highway project was abandoned. A more modest plan to replace the West Side Highway with a new boulevard has now been completed. In addition, several hundred million dollars initially intended for the highway project were diverted to mass transit.

3. Disputes over the adequacy of an EIS often turn on the scope of environmental effects it addresses. President Clinton's Executive Order 12,898 requires federal agencies to identify and to address disproportionate effects of their actions on minority and low-income populations. Must such effects be considered in preparing EISs? In October 1994, EPA objected to an EIS prepared by the Nuclear Regulatory Commission (NRC) because it concluded that locating a uranium enrichment facility near a low-income, minority community in Louisiana would not raise environmental justice concerns. While the EIS incorporated demographic information about the parish where the facility would be located, EPA argued that it failed to analyze the demographic characteristics of the population in the immediate vicinity of the site and that it ignored the cumulative nature of the environmental burdens imposed on the community. The NRC's Atomic Safety and Licensing Board ultimately decided that the EIS was inadequate because it had not analyzed the impacts on two low-income and minority communities of closing the only road linking them together. While the EIS had calculated how much additional gasoline would be used driving between the two communities if the road were relocated, a large percentage of the communities' population is too poor to own motor vehicles. "Adding 0.38 miles to the distance between the Forest Grove and Center Springs communities may be a mere 'inconvenience' to those who drive," the Board observed. "Yet permanently adding that distance to the one- or two-mile walk between these communities for those who must regularly make the trip on foot may be more than a 'very small impact,' especially if they are old, ill, or otherwise infirm." In re Louisiana Energy Services, L.P (May 1, 1997).

4. In 1990, a group of Wisconsin environmentalists and botanists launched an effort to use NEPA to improve the quality of the scientific analysis used by the Forest Service (FS). They sued the FS in an effort to require it to employ an ecosystems approach incorporating advanced principles of conservation biology to provide for diversity of plant and animal communities when making forest management decisions. The plaintiffs argued that the FS should consider the relationships between differing landscape patterns and among various habitats rather than measuring vegetative diversity solely through analysis of the number of plants and animals and the variety of species in a given area. Because the size of a habitat tends to affect its chances of survival, the botanists argued that the FS should reserve larger, unfragmented tracts of forest rather than smaller, fragmented parcels. Despite presenting testimony from 13 highly distinguished scientists, the plaintiffs lost. Sierra Club v. Marita, 46 F.3d 606 (7th Cir. 1995). The court noted that CEQ's regulations require agencies to ensure the "scientific integrity" of their analyses, to use "high quality" science, and to integrate the natural and social sciences. However, the court found nothing in NEPA, the National Forest Management Act, or implementing regulations that dictates that the FS analyzed diversity using any particular approach. Noting that the FS had considered, but rejected, using principles of conservation

biology because of their uncertain application, the court found that the Forest Service had not acted arbitrarily or capriciously. The court concluded that "[t]he Service is entitled to use its own methodology, unless it is irrational," 46 F.3d at 621, and it upheld the agency's choice.

5. In The Lands Council v. McNair, 537 F.3d 981 (9th Cir. 2008), the Ninth Circuit, sitting en banc, overruled two of its prior decisions concerning the application of NEPA to Forest Service projects. Emphasizing that a court must act as a panel of judges and not scientists, the court stated that an EIS need not address all uncertainties concerning the environmental impact of a forest management project. The court stated that "none of NEPA's statutory provisions or regulations requires the Forest Service to affirmatively present every uncertainty in its EIS. Thus, we hold that to the extent our case law suggests that a NEPA violation occurs every time the Forest Service does not affirmatively address an uncertainty in the EIS, we have erred." 537 F.3d at 1001. Overruling Ecology Center, Inc. v. Austin, 430 F.3d 1057 (9th Cir. 2005), the court held that the National Forest Management Act (NFMA) does not require the Forest Service always to verify its methodology through on-the-ground analysis. The court also overruled Idaho Sporting Congress v. Thomas, 137 F.3d 1146 (9th Cir. 1998), and held that the fact a proposed project involves some disturbance to the forest does not prohibit the Forest Service from assuming that maintaining a sufficient amount of suitable habitat will maintain a species' viability.

6. When new information becomes available after an EIS is completed, questions inevitably are raised concerning the obligation of agencies to supplement their EISs. The Supreme Court, in the case that follows, addressed that question and the question of what standard of review should be applied by courts reviewing decisions not to supplement EISs.

## Marsh v. Oregon Natural Resources Council

490 U.S. 360 (1989)

JUSTICE STEVENS delivered the opinion for a unanimous Court.

[The Army Corps of Engineers had completed an environmental impact statement for a three-dam project in Oregon's Rogue River Basin in 1971. In 1980, the Corps released its Final Environmental Impact Statement Supplement No. 1, but it subsequently refused to prepare a second supplemental EIS to review information developed after 1980. Plaintiffs argued that the Corps was required to prepare a second supplemental EIS because two memoranda prepared after 1980 — one by biologists with Oregon's Department of Fish and Wildlife and another by the U.S. Soil Conservation Service — indicated that the project would have greater adverse impacts on the environment than previously thought. The district court rejected this claim, but the Ninth Circuit reversed, holding that the two documents revealed significant new information that the Corps had failed to evaluate with sufficient care.]

The subject of post-decision supplemental environmental impact statements is not expressly addressed in NEPA. Preparation of such statements, however, is at times necessary to satisfy the Act's "action-forcing" purpose. NEPA does not work by mandating that agencies achieve particular substantive environmental results. Rather, NEPA promotes its sweeping commitment to "prevent or eliminate damage to the environment and biosphere" by focusing government and public attention on the environmental effects of proposed agency action. 42 U.S.C. §4321. By so focusing agency attention, NEPA ensures that the agency will not act on incomplete information, only to regret its decision after it is too late to correct. Similarly, the broad dissemination of information mandated by NEPA permits the public and other government agencies to react to the effects of a proposed action at a meaningful time. It would be incongruous with this approach to environmental protection, and with the Act's manifest concern with preventing uninformed action, for the blinders to adverse environmental effects, once unequivocally removed, to be restored prior to the completion of agency action simply because the relevant proposal has received initial approval. As we explained in TVA v. Hill, 437 U.S. 153, 188, n.34 (1978), although "it would make sense to hold NEPA inapplicable at some point in the life of a project, because the agency would no longer have a meaningful opportunity to *weigh* the benefits of the project versus the detrimental effects on the environment," up to that point, "NEPA cases have generally required agencies to file environmental impact statements when the remaining governmental action would be environmentally 'significant.'"

This reading of the statute is supported by Council on Environmental Quality (CEQ) and Corps regulations, both of which make plain that at times supplementation is required. The CEQ regulations, which we have held are entitled to substantial deference, impose a duty on all federal agencies to prepare supplements to either draft or final EIS's if there "are significant new circumstances or information relevant to environmental concerns and bearing on the proposed action or its impacts." Similarly, the Corps' own NEPA implementing regulations require the preparation of a supplemental EIS if "new significant impact information, criteria or circumstances relevant to environmental considerations impact on the recommended plan or proposed action.". . .

. . . [A]n agency need not supplement an EIS every time new information comes to light after the EIS is finalized. To require otherwise would render agency decisionmaking intractable, always awaiting updated information only to find the new information outdated by the time a decision is made. On the other hand, and as [the Government] concede[s], NEPA does require that agencies take a "hard look" at the environmental effects of their planned action, even after a proposal has received initial approval. See Brief for Petitioners 36. Application of the "rule of reason" thus turns on the value of the new information to the still pending decisionmaking process. In this respect the decision whether to prepare a supplemental EIS is similar to the decision whether to prepare an EIS in the first instance: If there remains "major Federal actio[n]" to occur, and if the new information is sufficient to show that the remaining action will "affec[t] the quality of the human environment" in a significant manner or to a significant extent not already considered, a supplemental EIS must be prepared. Cf. 42 U.S.C. §4332(2)(C).

The parties disagree, however, on the standard that should be applied by a court that is asked to review the agency's decision. [The Government] argue[s] that the reviewing court need only decide whether the agency decision was "arbitrary and capricious," whereas respondents argue that the reviewing court must make its own determination of reasonableness to ascertain whether the agency action complied with the law. . . .

The question presented for review in this case is a classic example of a factual dispute the resolution of which implicates substantial agency expertise. Respondents' claim that the Corps' decision not to file a second supplemental EIS should be set aside, primarily rests on the contentions that the new information undermines conclusions contained in the FEISS [Final Environmental Impact Statement Supplement No. 1], that the conclusions contained in the ODFW memorandum and the SCS survey are accurate, and that the Corps' expert review of the new information was incomplete, inconclusive, or inaccurate. The dispute thus does not turn on the meaning of the term "significant" or on an application of this legal standard to settled facts. Rather, resolution of this dispute involves primarily issues of fact. Because analysis of the relevant documents "requires a high level of technical expertise," we must defer to "the informed discretion of the responsible federal agencies." Kleppe v. Sierra Club, 427 U.S. 390, 412 (1976). Under these circumstances, we cannot accept respondents' supposition that review is of a legal question and that the Corps' decision "deserves no deference." Accordingly, as long as the Corps' decision not to supplement the FEISS was not "arbitrary or capricious," it should not be set aside.

. . . When specialists express conflicting views, an agency must have discretion to rely on the reasonable opinions of its own qualified experts even if, as an original matter, a court might find contrary views more persuasive. On the other hand, in the context of reviewing a decision not to supplement an EIS, courts should not automatically defer to the agency's express reliance on an interest in finality without carefully reviewing the record and satisfying themselves that the agency has made a reasoned decision based on its evaluation of the significance—or lack of significance—of the new information. A contrary approach would not simply render judicial review generally meaningless, but would be contrary to the demand that courts ensure that agency decisions are founded on a reasoned evaluation "of the relevant factors."

[Applying the standard of review outlined above, the Supreme Court reversed the Ninth Circuit and held that the Corps was not required to prepare a supplemental EIS.]

## NOTES AND QUESTIONS

1.  In light of the Court's decision, at what point can an agency simply refuse to consider new information? When an EIS has been completed? When a project has been approved? When construction has begun? When construction is completed?

2.  In Alaska Wilderness Recreation and Tourism Association v. Morrison, 67 F.3d 723 (9th Cir. 1995), the Ninth Circuit required the Forest Service to prepare a supplemental EIS for timber sales in the Tongass National Forest as a result of Congress's enactment of the Tongass Timber Reform Act (TTRA). The TTRA repealed a requirement that 4.5 billion board feet of timber be supplied from the Tongass National Forest and restricted harvest of old-growth timber. Previous EISs for the Forest Plans that governed timber sales in the area had routinely rejected alternatives that did not supply enough timber to meet the terms of 50-year contracts between the Forest Service and two paper companies. After the Forest Service canceled one of the contracts, the Ninth Circuit held that the contract cancellation

required preparation of a supplemental EIS because it "opened for consideration alternatives which could not be freely reviewed when the . . . contract was in force." 67 F.3d at 730.

## B.   Timing and Scope Revisited

Courts hearing challenges to EISs are often asked to review the agency's judgments about the appropriate timing and scope of its analysis. They generally have responded by emphasizing that the proper scope of an EIS varies with the nature of the proposed action and that its timing depends on how close the agency is to reaching a critical stage of the decision-making process. For example, in California v. Block, 690 F.2d 753 (9th Cir. 1982), discussed on page 879, the State of California argued that the EIS prepared for the Forest Service's national management plan for roadless areas had failed to examine adequately site-specific impacts. The Forest Service argued that a programmatic EIS describing the first step in a multistage national project need not include detailed examination of the kinds of site-specific impacts normally considered in EISs for more narrowly focused projects. Noting that the "detail that NEPA requires in an EIS depends upon the nature and scope of the proposed action," the Ninth Circuit concluded that the "critical inquiry . . . is not whether the project's site-specific impact should be evaluated in detail, but when. . . ." 690 F.2d at 761. Thus, the court concluded that when preparing a programmatic EIS, "site-specific impacts need not be fully evaluated until a 'critical decision' has been made to act on site development." Id.

Applying this standard, the Ninth Circuit focused on the impact of the designation of areas as wilderness or non-wilderness. The Forest Service argued that a non-wilderness designation meant only that an area will not be considered now for inclusion in the wilderness system and that separate EISs would be prepared when specific development proposals are made concerning specific areas. The Ninth Circuit, however, found that the Forest Service had made a "critical decision" to commit these areas to non-wilderness use because the non-wilderness designation meant that the areas would not be managed as wilderness for at least the next 10 to 15 years. Thus, it held that the EIS must contain detailed site-specific analysis of the program's environmental consequences.

The Forest Service then argued that it had adequately assessed the site-specific impacts of its action by relying on two-page computer printouts for each area in the RARE II inventory. These contained information on the location and acreage of the area, its basic land-form type, its ecosystem type, the number of wilderness-associated wildlife species in the area, and a numerical rating of the area's wilderness attributes. The numerical ratings were obtained by using the Wilderness Attribute Rating System (WARS). This system employed worksheets containing a series of check boxes to indicate generic qualities of the site, and then a small space for comments, described as follows by the district court:

> The comments are of a brief and very general nature. For example, one comment under the "opportunity for solitude" attribute merely stated "good topographical variation." The type of land features or vegetation present in this area is undisclosed. Major features of an area are reduced to highly generalized descriptions such as "mountain" or "river." One can

hypothesize how the Grand Canyon might be rated: "Canyon with river, little vegetation." [California v. Bergland, 483 F. Supp. 465, 486 n. 22 (E.D. Cal. 1980).]

The Ninth Circuit rejected the Forest Service's argument that any deficiencies in the EIS could be remedied simply by considering the WARS worksheets to be part of the final EIS. The court recognized that preparation of site-specific analyses for the RARE II decision would be a mammoth undertaking. However, it concluded that "[h]aving decided to allocate simultaneously millions of acres of land to non-wilderness use, the Forest Service may not rely upon forecasting difficulties or the task's magnitude to excuse the absence of a reasonably thorough site-specific analysis of the decision's environmental consequences." 690 F.2d at 765.

## NOTES AND QUESTIONS

1. The court in *California v. Block* demanded that the programmatic EIS prepared by the Forest Service include detailed analysis of every one of the hundreds of areas affected. Is that a realistic demand? If you were advising the Forest Service, what strategy would you suggest for their NEPA compliance?

2. CEQ's 2020 regulations emphasize "tiering," the practice of using existing studies and environmental analyses in the NEPA process. Consider the explanation of tiering from the 1978 CEQ regulations:

### §1508.28 Tiering

"Tiering" refers to the coverage of general matters in broader environmental impact statements (such as national program or policy statements) with subsequent narrower statements or environmental analyses (such as regional or basinwide program statements or ultimately site-specific statements) incorporating by reference the general discussions and concentrating solely on the issues specific to the statement subsequently prepared. Tiering is appropriate when the sequence of statements or analyses is:

(a) From a program, plan, or policy environmental impact statement to a program, plan, or policy statement or analysis of lesser scope or to a site-specific statement or analysis.

(b) From an environmental impact statement on a specific action at an early stage (such as need and site selection) to a supplement (which is preferred) or a subsequent statement or analysis at a later stage (such as environmental mitigation). Tiering in such cases is appropriate when it helps the lead agency to focus on the issues which are ripe for decision and exclude from consideration issues already decided or not yet ripe.

3. The successful use of tiered analysis is illustrated by an important case that was decided by the Sixth Circuit. Because there is no federal repository available yet for the storage of spent nuclear fuel, most nuclear power plants have been storing their waste in liquid pools within their containment vessels. Many are running out of this on-site storage capacity and could be forced to shut down if no extra storage space becomes available. To respond to this problem, the Nuclear

Regulatory Commission (NRC) approved the use of a new cask for dry storage of high-level radioactive waste at nuclear power plants. Citing CEQ's tiering regulations, the Sixth Circuit held that the NRC had not violated NEPA by failing to prepare an EIS before approving the use of the cask. Kelley v. Selin, 42 F.3d 1501 (6th Cir. 1995). Even though use of the new casks will enable utilities to expand significantly their capacity to store radioactive waste on-site, the court held that an EIS was not required because the NRC had conducted tiered analysis before approving the cask. Prior to approving use of the new cask, the NRC had prepared an environmental assessment (EA) finding that the new technology would have no significant impact on the environment. This finding was based in large part on the fact that EISs already had been prepared for each power plant that would use the cask at the time the plant was licensed by the NRC. While plaintiffs argued that site-specific EAs should have been prepared, the court held that the NRC had properly relied on the prior site-specific EISs prepared for each plant as well as on the NRC's previous generic analyses of the safety of on-site storage of radioactive waste.

4. Many of the principles of timing and scope that are articulated in *Kleppe*, *Thomas*, and *Sierra Club v. Peterson* are relevant to assessment of the adequacy of an EIS.

5. The CEQ's 2020 NEPA regulations increase the use of tiering and "codify the agency practice of using EAs where the effects of a proposed agency action are not likely to be significant." 85 Fed. Reg. 1697. The new regulations further explain the meaning of "tiering," indicating that agencies could use EAs at the programmatic stage as well as at subsequent stages. 85 Fed. Reg. 1710.

## C.  Analysis in Uncertainty

One of the most heated controversies concerning NEPA in recent years has been the debate over what agencies must do to assess adequately effects that are highly uncertain. In Sierra Club v. Sigler, 695 F.2d 957 (5th Cir. 1983), the Fifth Circuit considered an EIS for an oil distribution center and deepwater port in Galveston Bay. The Sierra Club argued that the Army Corps of Engineers should consider the possible effect on the Bay of a total cargo loss by a supertanker using the new port. While all agreed a total cargo loss could occur, there was considerable uncertainty about its likelihood and consequences. The court therefore required the Corps to prepare a "worst-case analysis" to assess the effects of such an accident.

In Save Our Ecosystems v. Clark, 747 F.2d 1240 (9th Cir. 1984), the Ninth Circuit considered the application of NEPA to decisions by the Bureau of Land Management (BLM) and the Forest Service to apply pesticides on lands subject to their jurisdiction. BLM and the Forest Service argued that they did not need to consider the risks associated with pesticide use as long as the pesticides had been approved for such use by the EPA. The court rejected this argument, emphasizing that the licensing of pesticides does not "reflect a conclusion that a pesticide is safe under *any* condition." Noting uncertainty about whether the pesticides were likely to cause cancer, the court held that the agencies must prepare a "worst-case analysis" to assess those risks—the agencies must estimate what the effects of pesticide use would be if the pesticides were in fact carcinogenic.

In response to *Save Our Ecosystems* and similar decisions from other courts, CEQ acted to curtail the worst-case-analysis requirement. The CEQ rescinded a "worst-case" regulation it had adopted in 1978 and replaced it with the following revised regulation in 1986:

### §1502.22 Incomplete or Unavailable Information

When an agency is evaluating reasonably foreseeable significant adverse effects on the human environment in an environmental impact statement and there is incomplete or unavailable information, the agency shall always make clear that such information is lacking.

(a) If the incomplete information relevant to reasonably foreseeable significant adverse impacts is essential to a reasoned choice among alternatives and the overall costs of obtaining it are not exorbitant, the agency shall include the information in the environmental impact statement.

(b) If the information relevant to reasonably foreseeable significant adverse impacts cannot be obtained because the overall costs of obtaining it are exorbitant or the means to obtain it are not known, the agency shall include within the environmental impact statement:

(1) a statement that such information is incomplete or unavailable;

(2) a statement of the relevance of the incomplete or unavailable information to evaluating reasonably foreseeable significant adverse impacts on the human environment;

(3) a summary of existing credible scientific evidence which is relevant to evaluating the reasonably foreseeable significant adverse impacts on the human environment; and

(4) the agency's evaluation of such impacts based upon theoretical approaches or research methods generally accepted in the scientific community. For the purposes of this section, "reasonably foreseeable" includes impacts which have catastrophic consequences, even if their probability of occurrence is low, provided that the analysis of the impacts is supported by credible scientific evidence, is not based on pure conjecture, and is within the rule of reason.

(c) The amended regulation will be applicable to all environmental impact statements for which a Notice of Intent (40 CFR 1508.22) is published in the Federal Register on or after May 27, 1986. For environmental impact statements in progress, agencies may choose to comply with the requirements of either the original or amended regulation. [51 Fed. Reg. 15,625 (1986).]

## NOTES AND QUESTIONS

1. Would this new regulation change the result in *Sigler* or in *Save Our Ecosystems*? Would the Corps still have to consider the effects of a total cargo loss by

a supertanker? Would BLM be required to assume the pesticide is carcinogenic? Should the NRC assess the environmental consequences of highly uncertain terrorist attacks when it licenses facilities handling nuclear material? See the Problem Exercise below.

2. In Robertson v. Methow Valley Citizens Council, 490 U.S. 332 (1989), a companion case to *Marsh v. Oregon Natural Resources Council*, the Supreme Court reversed a decision by the Ninth Circuit holding that NEPA requires the use of worst-case analysis despite the new CEQ regulations. The Supreme Court rejected the Ninth Circuit's conclusion that the rescinded CEQ regulations were "merely a codification of prior NEPA case law." Noting that the regulations had been amended only after "considerable criticism" of the worst-case-analysis requirement, the Court held that the new regulations were entitled to "substantial deference." 490 U.S. at 356.

---

## PROBLEM EXERCISE: SHOULD LIMITS BE IMPOSED ON THE LENGTH OF AND TIME FOR PREPARING ENVIRONMENTAL IMPACT ASSESSMENTS?

President Trump made it a top priority to speed up and simplify NEPA's environmental impact assessment process. For the first time since their adoption in 1978, CEQ's regulations governing the process were revised in a comprehensive fashion in July 2020.

On January 9, 2020, CEQ issued a notice of proposed rulemaking to issue revised NEPA regulations to "facilitate a more efficient, effective, and timely NEPA review process." CEQ received more than 1.1 million comments on its proposal. On June 15, 2020, CEQ promulgated its final rules. The rules change the definition of "major Federal actions" that can trigger NEPA review to exclude projects where "minimal federal funding" or "minimal federal involvement" limit the agency's control over "the outcome of the project." They allow agencies to forego environmental reviews by using categorical exclusions issued by other agencies for similar projects. The new regulations specify that most EAs should be completed within one year and be 75 pages or fewer and that most EISs should be completed within two years and be 150 pages or fewer (300 pages for unusually complex projects). They specify that agencies no longer have to consider "indirect" or "cumulative" environmental effects of their actions.

To buttress its case for speeding up the NEPA review process, CEQ released data on the length of environmental impact statements (EISs) prepared between 2013 and 2018. CEQ found that the average length of the 656 EISs it examined was 575 pages, while the median length was 397 pages. One-quarter were 279 pages or shorter, while one-quarter were 621 pages or longer. CEQ, Length of Environmental Impact Statements (2013-2018), June 12, 2020.

Based on a study of 1,276 EISs prepared between 2010 and 2018, CEQ determined that the average time to complete an EIS across all federal agencies was 4.5

years and the median time was 3.5 years. One-quarter took less than 2.2 years, while another one-quarter took more than 6.0 years to complete.

Based on their review of nearly 1,500 cases of NEPA litigation, Professors Ruple and Race found that "the amount of time spent on EIS preparation appears to be inversely related to the likelihood that an EIS will be challenged in court." They note that the U.S. "Forest Service spend[s] an average of 1.13 years less on EIS preparation and is sued at a much higher rate than its sister agencies." FERC "also proceeds faster than average and is sued at an above average rate," but the U.S. "Army Corps of Engineers and the Federal Highway Administration take considerably more time to prepare an EIS and are sued at much lower rates." John C. Ruple & Kayla M. Race, Measuring the NEPA Litigation Burden: A Review of 1,499 Federal Court Cases, 50 Envt'l Law 479, 498 (2020).

**Question One.** Should limits be imposed on the length of time agencies take to complete EAs and EISs? What are the likely consequences of such time limits?

**Question Two.** Should page limits be imposed on the length of EAs and EISs? What would be the likely consequences of such page limits?

---

## D. EPILOGUE: HOW WELL DOES NEPA WORK?

Critics of environmental regulation are arguing that NEPA is outdated and flawed and needs "reform," while environmentalists maintain that it is an essential bulwark in our regulatory infrastructure. How effective has NEPA been? NEPA clearly has provided environmental lawyers with a strategic tool that has been used at times to slow down and sometimes stop development projects. For a list of some natural areas, including Mineral King, that have been spared from development largely as a result of NEPA lawsuits, see Turner, The Legal Eagles, Amicus J. 25, 30 (Winter 1988). In the wake of Hurricane Katrina's devastation of New Orleans, NEPA litigation was blamed by some for having blocked construction of a massive hurricane barrier, David Schoenbrod, The Lawsuit That Sank New Orleans, Wall St. J., Sept. 27, 2005, a strange criticism of NEPA since *compliance* with the statute would not have stopped the project, which ultimately floundered for a variety of other reasons.

A more important question may be how frequently the requirement that agencies "consider" environmental effects has resulted in more environmentally responsible actions by agencies. Serge Taylor's classic study of NEPA, Making Bureaucracies Think: The Environmental Impact Statement Strategy of Administrative Reform (1984), found that when agencies allow environmental analysts to explore a wide range of alternatives, all projects tend to benefit from relatively inexpensive mitigation measures. When concerned outsiders with access to the courts also get involved, some of the worst projects—those with "the greatest environmental costs and little political support"—are eliminated. Id. at 251. Consider the following assessment of NEPA's impact from a former deputy general counsel of EPA.

Robert Dreher

## NEPA Under Siege

(2005)

In its thirty-five year history, the National Environmental Policy Act has been extraordinarily successful in accomplishing its goals.

First, NEPA has unquestionably improved the quality of federal agency decision-making in terms of its sensitivity to environmental concerns. Examples are legion in which proposed federal actions that would have had serious environmental consequences were dramatically improved, or even in some instances abandoned, as a result of the NEPA process.

To cite just a few instances:

- In the early 1990s, mounting problems with obsolete nuclear reactors at its Savannah River site put the Department of Energy under pressure to build enormously expensive new reactors to produce tritium, a key constituent of nuclear warheads. A programmatic EIS allowed DOE to evaluate alternative technologies, including using a particle accelerator or existing commercial reactors, leading ultimately to cancellation of the tritium production reactors. Admiral James Watkins, then Secretary of Energy, testified before the House Armed Services Committee: "Looking back on it, thank God for NEPA because there were so many pressures to make a selection for a technology that it might have been forced upon us and that would have been wrong for the country."
- The NEPA process led to improvements in a land management plan for the Los Alamos National Laboratory that averted a potentially serious release of radiation when the sensitive nuclear laboratory was swept by wildfire in May 2000. The laboratory's initial management plan did not address the risk of wildfire, but other federal agencies alerted the Los Alamos staff to that risk in comments on the draft EIS accompanying the plan. The laboratory prepared a fire contingency plan, cut back trees and underbrush around its buildings, and replaced wooden pallets holding drums of radioactive waste with aluminum. Those preparations turned out to be invaluable when a major wildfire swept Los Alamos the following year, damaging many buildings but not triggering a significant release of radiation.
- In 1997, the Federal Energy Regulatory Commission was considering issuance of a license for construction of a major new hydropower dam on the Penobscot River in Maine. The EIS disclosed that the proposed Basin Mills Dam would undermine long-standing federal, state and tribal efforts to restore wild Atlantic salmon populations to the Penobscot River. FERC received strong comments in opposition to the project from federal and state fishery managers and the Penobscot Indian Nation, among others, and concluded that the public interest was best served by denial of the license.
- The ivory-billed woodpecker, recently rediscovered, to great public celebration, in the swamplands of Arkansas, owes its survival in large part to NEPA. In 1971, shortly after NEPA's enactment, the Army Corps of Engineers advanced a proposal to dredge and channelize the Cache River for

flood control, threatening the vast tracts of bottomland hardwood wetlands in the river basin on which the woodpecker and many other species of wildlife depended. Environmentalists challenged the adequacy of the Corps's NEPA analysis in court, pointing out that the Corps had failed to evaluate alternatives to its massive dredging program that would cause less damage to wetland habitat. The court enjoined the Corps from proceeding until it fully considered alternatives, and public outcry subsequently led to the abandonment of the dredging project and the creation of the national wildlife refuge where the ivory-billed woodpecker was recently sighted.

- A massive timber sale proposed for the Gifford Pinchot National Forest in Oregon, stalled by controversy over impacts on sensitive forest habitat, was entirely rethought as a result of the NEPA process. A coalition of environmentalists, the timber industry, labor representatives and local citizens worked together to develop a plan to use timber harvesting to restore the forest's natural ecosystem. Instead of clearcuts, the new proposal focuses on thinning dense stands of Douglas fir (the result of previous clearcutting) to recreate a more natural, diverse forest structure, while still yielding 5.2 million board feet of commercial timber. The citizen alternative was adopted by the Forest Service and implemented without appeals or litigation. A local resident involved in the process says: "It's a win, win, win."

- In Michigan, communities concerned about the impacts of a proposed new four-lane freeway successfully used the NEPA process to force the state highway agency to consider alternatives for expanding and improving an existing highway, avoiding the largest wetland loss in Michigan's history and saving taxpayers $1.5 billion. Similarly, a proposed freeway in Kentucky's scenic bluegrass region was redesigned to protect historic, aesthetic and natural values thanks to public input and legal action during the NEPA planning process. The National Trust for Historic Preservation acclaimed the Paris Pike as a project that "celebrates the spirit of place instead of obliterating it."

These and other similar examples only begin to tell the story of NEPA's success, however. NEPA's most significant effect has been to deter federal agencies from bringing forward proposed projects that could not withstand public examination and debate. Prior to NEPA, federal agencies could embark on massive dam- or road-building projects, for example, without public consultation and with virtually no advance notice. As a result, family farms, valuable habitat, and sometimes whole communities were destroyed without the opportunity for full and fair debate. Today, many similar projects that could not survive such a debate simply never get off the drawing boards.

More broadly, NEPA has had pervasive effects on the conduct and thinking of federal administrative agencies. Congress's directive that federal agencies use an "interdisciplinary approach" in decision-making affecting the environment, together with the Act's requirement that agencies conduct detailed environmental analyses of major actions, has required federal agencies to add biologists, geologists, landscape architects, archeologists, and environmental planners to their staffs. These new employees brought new perspectives and sensitivities to agencies that formerly had relatively narrow, mission-oriented cultures. NEPA's requirement that agencies consult with federal and state agencies with special environmental expertise also has helped broaden agency awareness of environmental values.

Equally important, NEPA has succeeded in expanding public engagement in government decision-making, improving the quality of agency decisions and fulfilling principles of democratic governance that are central to our society. Today, citizens take it as a given that major governmental actions that could affect their lives and their communities will be subject to searching public examination and discussion. As CEQ concluded in a report commemorating NEPA's 25th anniversary, "NEPA's most enduring legacy is as a framework for collaboration between federal agencies and those who will bear the environmental, social, and economic impacts of their decisions." CEQ noted that "agencies today are more likely to consider the views of those who live and work in the surrounding community and others during the decision-making process." As a result, "Federal agencies today are better informed about and more responsible for the consequences of their actions than they were before NEPA was passed.". . .

In sum, NEPA functions as a critical tool for democratic government decision-making, establishing an orderly, clear framework for involving the public in major decisions affecting their lives and communities.

## NOTES AND QUESTIONS

1. As Dreher notes, on NEPA's twenty-fifth anniversary, CEQ conducted a study of the statute's effectiveness. CEQ, The National Environmental Policy Act: A Study of Its Effectiveness After Twenty-five Years (1997). The agency concluded that the statute had achieved considerable success, though falling far short of its goals. On the plus side, the study found that NEPA "has made agencies take a hard look at the potential environmental consequences of their actions, and it has brought the public into the agency decisionmaking process like no other statute." However, the study also found that some agencies "act as if the detailed statement called for in the statute is an end in itself, rather than a tool to enhance and improve decision-making." It also observed that "agencies sometimes engage in consultation only after a decision has—for all practical purposes—been made." This leads agencies to seek "litigation-proof" documents without adequately examining a full range of alternatives. The study also noted concerns about "the length of NEPA processes, the extensive detail of NEPA analyses, and the sometimes confusing overlay of other laws and regulations."

2. A more modest inquiry is whether NEPA assures a reliable assessment of a project's likely effects. Because NEPA entrusts the assessment of impacts to agencies that typically are project proponents, the quality of EISs often depends on the strength of outside pressures. Recall the controversy discussed in Chapter 1 concerning the report by the Fish and Wildlife Service that the environmental impact of oil development in Prudhoe Bay had been greatly underestimated. Some have suggested that projects approved under NEPA should be monitored so that unanticipated environmental consequences can be assessed and mitigated. Others have proposed that EISs be prepared by an independent agency without a vested interest in the results, as is done in some of the many countries that now require EISs.

Professor Bradley Karkkainen notes that agencies seeking to avoid NEPA litigation "often substitute quantity for quality, producing large, costly and uninformative documents" "while making findings of no significant impact that are premised on mitigation measures that NEPA cannot enforce." Bradley C. Karkkainen, Toward a Smarter NEPA: Monitoring and Managing Government's Environmental Performance, 102 Colum. L. Rev. 903 (2002). He argues that NEPA should be retooled to require "follow-up monitoring, adaptive mitigation, and an environmental management systems-oriented approach."

3. In April 2002, the Council on Environmental Quality announced the formation of a "NEPA Task Force" charged with focusing on "modernizing the NEPA process." In September 2003, the Task Force announced a series of recommendations concerning how agencies should interpret and implement NEPA. The report recommended that agencies take steps to streamline the process of obtaining approval for categorical exclusions. It also sought to make it easier to conduct environmental assessments by changing requirements for public involvement, consideration of alternatives, and mitigation to support findings of no significant impact. The Bush administration was highly critical of NEPA, and it pushed to exempt from NEPA many military activities and certain decisions concerning public forest management.

4. In 2006, the House Committee on Resources prepared a critique of NEPA. Task Force on Improving the National Environmental Policy Act and Task Force on Updating the National Environmental Policy Act, Recommendations to Improve and Update the National Environmental Policy Act (July 31, 2006). The Task Force's recommendations are contained in the appendix of a 2007 CRS report, available online at *https://fas.org/sgp/crs/misc/RL33267.pdf.* Among the recommendations in the report are establishing mandatory deadlines for completing NEPA documents and imposing page limits on them, allowing state environmental reviews to satisfy NEPA requirements, and adding a citizen suit provision to NEPA with time limits on when lawsuits may be filed.

5. NEPA's fortieth anniversary was celebrated in January 2010. On February 18, 2010, CEQ highlighted "steps to modernize and reinvigorate" NEPA. These steps included: (1) the formation of rapid response teams to help expedite the review process for transportation, transmission, and renewable energy projects; (2) a NEPA Pilot Projects Program that invites nominations of projects employing innovative approaches to completing environmental reviews more efficiently and effectively; (3) the release on March 5, 2013, of two handbooks that encourage more efficient environmental reviews by integrating the NEPA process with the review processes of the National Historic Preservation Act section 106 and the California Environmental Quality Act; and (4) Enhanced Public Tools for Reporting on NEPA Activities through the *www.nepa.gov* website.

6. As part of the celebration of NEPA's fortieth anniversary, the Environmental Law Institute published *NEPA Success Stories: Celebrating 40 Years of Transparency and Open Government* (August 2010), available online at *https://ceq.doe.gov/docs/get-involved/NEPA_Success_Stories.pdf.* In a foreword to the publication, Russell Train, first chair of CEQ and later the second EPA administrator, wrote: "It is fair to say that NEPA brought the environment front and center to federal agencies, and that this can be deemed a success brought about, in no small part, by the many federal

employees and citizens who have applied the law over these decades. It also opened up the federal decision-making process. No longer could federal agencies say 'we know best' and make decisions without taking environmental consequences into account. Nor could they simply pick one outcome or project and deem all others unworthy of consideration. NEPA democratized decisionmaking. It recognized that citizens, local and state governments, Indian tribes, corporations, and other federal agencies have a stake in government actions—and often unique knowledge of hazards, consequences, and alternatives that can produce better decisions."

### The Fixing America's Surface Transportation (FAST) Act

On December 4, 2015, President Obama signed the Fixing America's Surface Transportation (FAST) Act into law. Title 41 of the FAST Act (FAST-41) adopted measures to increase predictability, transparency, accountability, and inter-agency cooperation in federal environmental reviews and permitting decisions for significant infrastructure projects. 42 U.S.C. §4370m. FAST-41 is applicable to "covered projects" defined as infrastructure projects likely to require a total investment of more than $200 million or subject to environmental review involving more than two federal agencies. FAST-41 introduced the Permitting Dashboard, a searchable public web portal designed to track progress on multi-agency environmental reviews and authorizations in a single location. See *www.permits.performance.gov.* Once an entry for a new project is entered into the Permitting Dashboard, agencies with review or authorization responsibilities must keep the information up to date and provide information on the progress of agency procedures. FAST-41 also created a new interagency entity, the Federal Permitting Improvement Steering Council (FPISC). The FPISC is tasked with issuing guidance on implementation of FAST-41, adopting recommendations for best practices to enhance federal reviews and authorizations, and monitoring covered projects.

FAST-41 introduced several provisions to improve coordination between government agencies for covered projects. Much like CEQ's NEPA regulations, FAST-41 distinguishes between a lead agency, one with principal responsibility for an environmental review of a covered project; a facilitating agency, one that receives initial notice of a covered project from a project sponsor; a participating agency, any agency participating in a review or authorization for a covered project; and a cooperating agency, any agency with jurisdiction or special expertise that would affect a covered project. 42 U.S.C. §4370m. Under FAST-41 the lead agency has the authority to determine the methodologies to be used and the level of detail required in an environmental review. Additionally, the lead agency has the discretion to identify a preferred alternative for a project, which may be given a greater level of detail than nonpreferred alternatives. 42 U.S.C. §4370m-4(c).

When a project is considered a covered project for purposes of FAST-41, the lead agency must invite all participating or cooperating agencies to join a covered project no later than 45 days after the project is entered on the Permitting Dashboard. Agencies are then required to develop a concise Coordinated Project Plan that outlines the responsibilities of all entities; a timetable for milestones and completion; a discussion of potential avoidance, minimization, and mitigation strategies; and a schedule for public and tribal outreach. Once a permitting timetable is established, coordinating agencies are required to conform to the timetable.

Modifications to the completion date may not extend completion beyond a period of time greater than half the established timetable unless the reason for delay is outside of the government's control. 42 U.S.C. §4370m-2.

Where coordinated reviews by multiple agencies are required, FAST-41 instructs such agencies to carry out reviews concurrently to the maximum extent practicable. 42 U.S.C. §4370m-4(a). To reduce the burden on agencies performing a federal environmental review, agencies are authorized to adopt or incorporate state documents prepared for state level reviews so long as the documents were prepared under circumstances that allowed for public participation and consideration of alternatives. 42 U.S.C. §4370m-4(b). When a project is covered under FAST-41, the comment period has been shortened to no greater than 60 days for Draft Environmental Impact Statements (DEIS) and 45 days for all other environmental review processes. 42 U.S.C. §4370m-4(b)(1)(D).

President Trump sought to relax environmental impact assessment procedures, to truncate NEPA reviews, and to speed up permitting through a series of executive orders. These executive orders — including Executive Order 13,795 (issued on April 28, 2017), Executive Order 13,807 (issued on August 15, 2017), and Executive Order 13,868 (issued on April 10, 2019) — were all revoked by President Biden on the day he took office on January 20, 2021.

# CHAPTER 9

# PRESERVATION OF BIODIVERSITY

It may seem curious to some that the survival of a relatively small number of three-inch fish among all the countless millions of species extant would require the permanent halting of a virtually completed dam for which Congress has expended more than $100 million. . . . We conclude, however, that the explicit provisions of the Endangered Species Act require precisely that result.

*— Chief Justice Burger for the Court in* TVA v. Hill *(1978)*

Losing species means losing the potential to solve some of humanity's most intractable problems, including hunger and disease. The Endangered Species Act is more than just a law—it is the ultimate safety net in our life support system. As Earth has changed and as science has progressed since the Endangered Species Act was authorized in 1973, the ESA has served our nation well, largely because of its flexibility and its solid foundation in science. It is crucial to maintain these fundamental principles. The challenges of effective implementation of the Act should not be interpreted to require substantive rewriting of this valuable, well-functioning piece of legislation.

*—A Letter from 5,738 Biologists to the U.S. Senate Concerning Science in the Endangered Species Act (March 2006)*\*

For more than a century, Congress has been concerned about the need to protect certain species in danger of extinction. But it was only in the last 50 years that comprehensive regulatory programs to protect endangered species were developed. Beginning with modest legislation in 1966, Congress in 1973 adopted strict regulatory legislation, the Endangered Species Act. This law and an international convention (the Convention on International Trade in Endangered Species of Wild Fauna and Flora) created a comprehensive program that "restricts the taking of species in danger of extinction or likely to become so, regulates trade in them, provides authority to acquire habitat needed for their survival, and mandates that federal agencies consider the impacts of their activities on these species." M. Bean, The Evolution of National Wildlife Law 193 (3d ed. 1997).

More recently, protection of endangered species has come to be seen in its larger context—the conservation of biological diversity. The international Convention on Biological Diversity, signed at the Rio Earth Summit in 1992, defines biodiversity as "the variability among living organisms from all sources, including terrestrial, marine, and other aquatic ecosystems and the ecological complexes of

---

\* Available at *https://www.ucsusa.org/resources/letter-biologists-us-senate-concerning-science -endangered-species-act.*

which they are a part; this includes diversity within species, between species, and of ecosystems." As this definition indicates, "biological diversity" includes not only the diversity of species, but also genetic diversity—the variation among individuals of the same species—and the diversity of ecosystems, or natural communities. It also includes the ecological and evolutionary processes on which those systems depend, such as predation, mutation, and decay.

With this broader understanding, the conservation of biological diversity poses a fundamental challenge, implicating, for example, climate change, toxic chemicals, and land use. But the Endangered Species Act (ESA) is the cornerstone of U.S. efforts to conserve biological diversity. It is a mechanism for saving species, the diversity within them, and the natural systems on which they depend. It is, ultimately, the safety net when broader efforts fail. Before turning to that statute, however, it is worth considering the moral, economic, and political groundings of the conservation of species.

## A.   WHY SHOULD WE PRESERVE BIODIVERSITY?

In Chapter 1, we considered some of the intellectual and cultural roots of environmental protection. These issues come to the fore in debates about the extinction of species. Aesthetic concerns and moral principles are often invoked in support of conservation, but conservation may also be justified by narrower concerns for human health and economic well-being. Some of these arguments are set forth in the writings of Edward O. Wilson, prominent biologist and eloquent champion of biodiversity.

E.O. Wilson

Biophilia
_____

121 (1984)

The current rate [of species extinction] is still the greatest in recent geological history. It is also much higher than the rate of production of new species by ongoing evolution, so that the net result is a steep decline in the world's standing diversity. Whole categories of organisms that emerged over the past ten million years, among them the familiar condors, rhinoceros, manatees, and gorillas, are close to the end. For most of their species, the last individuals to exist in the wild state could well be those living there today. It is a grave error to dismiss the hemorrhaging as a "Darwinian" process, in which species autonomously come and go and man is just the latest burden on the environment. Human destructiveness is something new under the sun. Perhaps it is matched by the giant meteorites thought to smash into the Earth and darken the atmosphere every hundred million years or so (the last one apparently arrived 65 million years ago and contributed to the extinction of the dinosaurs). But even that interval is ten thousand times longer than the entire history of civilization. In our own brief lifetime, humanity will suffer an incomparable loss in aesthetic value, practical benefits from biological research, and worldwide biological stability. Deep mines of biological diversity will have been dug out and carelessly discarded in the course of environmental exploitation, without our even knowing fully what they contained.

By economic measure alone, the diversity of species is one of Earth's most important resources. It is also the least utilized. We have come to depend completely on less than 1 percent of living species for our existence, with the remainder waiting untested and fallow. In the course of history, according to estimates recently made by Norman Myers, people have utilized about 7,000 kinds of plants for food, with emphasis on wheat, rye, maize, and about a dozen other highly domesticated species. Yet at least 75,000 exist that are edible, and many of these are superior to the crop plants in use.

## NOTES AND QUESTIONS

1.  Why should we care about the extinction of species? What reasons does Wilson articulate? What other reasons are there? Recall the discussion in Chapter 1 of competing values and the different approaches economics and ecology employ in conceptualizing environmental problems. In what respects do arguments concerning the importance of biodiversity reflect an economic perspective? For an attempt to identify the various reasons why biodiversity is valuable to humans, even apart from purely utilitarian values, see S. Kellert, Biological Diversity and Human Society (1996).

2.  The Endangered Species Act (ESA) refers to the "esthetic, ecological, educational, historical, recreational, and scientific value" of species in danger of or threatened with extinction. §2(a)(3), 16 U.S.C. §1531(a)(3). Surely not all species have the same value to mankind, as the ESA implicitly recognizes by excluding from its protections insect pests determined to "present an overwhelming and overriding risk to man." Why then should all disappearing species be entitled to the same level of protection? From an economic perspective, wouldn't it make more sense to vary the level of protection on the basis of some assessment of the value of the species to mankind? How could such an assessment be done given our present knowledge?

3.  To what extent does uncertainty justify strict protection for endangered species? We have studied in detail less than one one-hundredth of 1 percent of all species. If we know so little about the characteristics of species that are fast disappearing, is it reasonable to assume that what we are losing includes some valuable resources? Is biodiversity inherently valuable because it is impossible to know what we are losing as species disappear?

4.  In its 1997 report, the Council on Environmental Quality (CEQ) noted that it was estimated that the world contained 13 to 14 million species, but only 1.75 million of them had even been described. Terrestrial vertebrates and higher plants were the best-known groups, though population trends data were available only for a few groups. CEQ, 1997 Report of the Council on Environmental Quality 70-71 (1999). Of the 20,439 species native to the United States for which sufficient data were available to make a status assessment, nearly one-third were in some danger of extinction. The Nature Conservancy, Priorities for Conservation, 1997 Annual Report Card for U.S. Plant and Animal Species (1997). A study in 2011 estimated that there were 8.7 million species, but that 86 percent of the land-based species and 91 percent of marine species had not yet been described. C. Mora et al., How Many Species Are There on Earth and in the Ocean?, PLoS Biol 9(8): e1001127. *https://doi.org/10.1371/journal.pbio.1001127.*

5. In his 1992 book *The Diversity of Life,* Wilson reported that his most conservative estimate of the current rate of species loss was 27,000 per year, the equivalent of 74 per day and 3 per hour. E.O. Wilson, The Diversity of Life 280 (1992). This estimate included only the loss of species that is caused by destruction of natural habitat and not loss produced by exotic species replacement or endangerment from pollution.

6. The World Wildlife Fund's 2020 Living Planet Index showed that there had been an average 68 percent decline in monitored vertebrate species populations between 1970 and 2016. The largest decline—94 percent—occurred in the tropical subregions of the Americas. The report found that the principal threats to biodiversity were habitat loss and degradation, species overexploitation, invasive species and disease, pollution, and climate change. WWF, Living Planet Report 2020 8, 21 (2020). To "bend the curve" of biodiversity decline, the report concluded, will require "an unprecedented and immediate focus on both conservation and a transformation of our modern food system," id. at 116.

7. An example of the pharmaceutical use of rare plants is the development of a drug called Taxol to treat breast cancer and ovarian cancer. The drug originally was made only from material found in the bark and needles of the rare Pacific yew tree. Environmentalists initially were concerned that this discovery threatened to decimate the yew population since it took six 100-year-old yews to make enough Taxol to treat a single patient. However, having developed an understanding of how Taxol production occurs within the yew tree, researchers were able to synthesize the drug using much smaller quantities of yew bark. Scientists also discovered that the drug could be extracted from the leaves of a tree found widely in the Himalayas, *Taxus baccata,* without killing the tree. In December 1994, the FDA approved a new, semi-synthetic version of Taxol that uses the Himalayan tree rather than the rare Pacific yew. New Version of Taxol Is Approved by FDA, N.Y. Times, Dec. 13, 1994, at C6.

8. Experiments conducted by conservation biologists have demonstrated that more biologically diverse communities have more productive ecosystem processes. This finding is a product of research conducted at a facility in England called the "Ecotron." The Ecotron has 16 environmental chambers that were used in an elaborate experiment to replicate terrestrial communities that differ only in their biodiversity. Naeem et al., Declining Biodiversity Can Alter the Performance of Ecosystems, 368 Nature 734 (1994). The study suggests that reduced biodiversity will indeed adversely affect the performance of ecosystems. Similar results were obtained in a large-scale field study of prairie plants, which found that the more species a plot of experimental prairie had, the more bio-mass it produced and the better it retained nitrogen. Yoon, Ecosystem's Productivity Rises with Diversity of Its Species, N.Y. Times, Mar. 5, 1996, at C4.

## B.   THE ENDANGERED SPECIES ACT: AN OVERVIEW

The most significant legislation for preserving biodiversity has been the Endangered Species Act (ESA) of 1973. The ESA was adopted in 1973 by overwhelming margins in Congress (92-0 in the U.S. Senate and 390-12 in the House). It was widely hailed by environmental philosophers as a significant breakthrough for recognizing that non-human species had a right to life.

The major provisions of the Endangered Species Act are outlined below. The Act protects species that are listed (under section 4) as either "endangered species" or "threatened species" by the secretary (of interior for terrestrial and freshwater species or of commerce for marine species).

---

# Major Provisions of the Endangered Species Act

### Section 3: Definitions

*§3(6)* defines "endangered species" as "any species which is in danger of extinction throughout all or a significant portion of its range."

*§3(20)* defines "threatened species" as "any species which is likely to become an endangered species within the foreseeable future throughout all or a significant portion of its range."

### Section 4: Listing Endangered and Threatened Species

*§4(a)* requires the secretary to determine whether any species is "endangered" or "threatened" and to designate critical habitat of such species.

*§4(b)* provides that the listing determination is to be based solely on "best scientific and commercial data available" and that the designation of critical habitat is to be based on the "best scientific data available . . . taking into consideration the economic impact, and any other relevant impact, of specifying any particular area as critical habitat."

*§4(b)(3)* provides that citizens may petition to force listing determination.

*§4(c)* requires the secretary to publish in the Federal Register a list of all endangered and threatened species and to review the list every five years to determine whether any species should be removed from the list or changed in status.

*§4(d)* requires the secretary to issue "such regulations as he deems necessary and advisable to provide for the conservation" of species listed as threatened, including prohibiting any acts prohibited under section 9 for endangered species of fish, wildlife, or plants.

*§4(f)* requires the secretary to develop and implement recovery plans for endangered and threatened species unless he finds they will not promote conservation of the species.

### Section 7: Review of Federal Actions

*§7(a)(1)* requires all federal agencies to carry out programs to conserve endangered and threatened species.

*§7(a)(2)* provides that all federal agencies must insure, in consultation with the secretary, that their actions are "not likely to jeopardize the continued existence of any endangered species or threatened species or result in the destruction or adverse modification" of such species' critical habitat.

*§7(c)* requires federal agencies to conduct a biological assessment of any endangered or threatened species likely to be affected by an agency action if the secretary advises the agency that such species may be present in the area of the proposed action.

*§§7(e)-(h)* provide that if action is barred by a "jeopardy" determination, its proponent may seek exemption from the Cabinet-level "Endangered Species Committee."

### Section 9: Prohibitions

*§9(a)* prohibits sale, import, export, or transport of any species listed as endangered.

*§§9(a)(1)(B) & (C)* make it unlawful to "take" (broadly defined by section 3(19) to cover harassing, harming, killing, capturing, or collecting) any endangered *animal* species.

*§9(a)(2)(B)* prohibits removal or damage of endangered *plants* on federal lands or anywhere else if in knowing violation of state law.

### Section 10: Habitat Conservation Plans

*§10(a)* authorizes the issuance of permits allowing the incidental taking of endangered species to parties with an approved habitat conservation plan to minimize and mitigate the impacts of such a taking where the taking will not appreciably reduce the likelihood of the survival and recovery of the species in the wild.

### Section 11: Enforcement and Citizen Suits

*§§11(a) & (b)* provide civil and criminal penalties for violations of the Act.

*§11(g)* authorizes citizen suits against any person alleged to be in violation of the Act and against the secretary for failure to perform any nondiscretionary duty.

---

Threatened species are not automatically subject to the same prohibition on "takes" that section 9 applies to endangered species. Section 4(d) provides that threatened species are to be protected by regulations "necessary and advisable to provide for the conservation of such species." In general, threatened species have been extended the same protections accorded species listed as endangered. Specific protections are provided in sections 7 and 9 of the Act. Section 7 of the Act requires all federal agencies to "insure that any action authorized, funded, or carried out" by them "is not likely to jeopardize the continued existence of any endangered species or threatened species or result in the destruction or adverse modification of [critical] habitat of such species," 16 U.S.C. §1536. Section 9 of the Act regulates private conduct by making it illegal for *any* person to sell, import, export, or transport any plant or animal species listed as endangered. Endangered fish or wildlife are given even greater protection by section 9(a)(1), which makes it illegal for anyone to "take" them. "Take" is broadly defined to mean "to harass, harm, pursue, hunt, shoot, wound, kill, trap, capture, or collect, or to attempt to engage in any such conduct."

Section 9(a)(2)(B) makes it illegal to remove or damage endangered plants from federal lands or from any other property if it is done in knowing violation of any state law or regulation including state criminal trespass law.

In the remaining sections of this chapter, we consider the three key sections of the statute: section 4, section 7, and section 9. Any study of the Endangered Species Act must begin, however, with one of the most celebrated cases in environmental law—TVA v. Hill, 437 U.S. 153 (1978)—in which the Supreme Court resoundingly affirmed the sweeping protections that this statute provides to species on the brink of extinction.

The Tennessee Valley Authority (TVA) is a federal agency established as part of New Deal efforts to promote economic development in a poor region of the southeastern United States. The TVA sought to bring cheap electric power to the region by constructing coal-fired power plants and building dams to generate hydroelectric power. By the 1960s, public support for the TVA had eroded as rising environmental concern confronted an agency relentlessly pursuing the construction of dams on virtually every major waterway in Tennessee. The Tellico Dam Project was launched in the early 1960s to dam the Little Tennessee River in order to create a reservoir that would slightly increase the hydropower capacity of the nearby Fort Loudon Dam. Using fanciful economic projections that "downplayed costs and inflated benefits in just about every way imaginable," the TVA obtained congressional approval for a project that would fail any objective cost-benefit scrutiny. Holly Doremus, The Story of *TVA v. Hill*: A Narrow Escape for a Broad Law, in Environmental Law Stories 109, 116 (Lazarus & Houck eds., 2005).

Construction of the Tellico Dam commenced in March 1967 on one of the last remaining stretches of free-flowing river in southeastern Tennessee, an area of great natural beauty rich in historical sites sacred to the Cherokee Indian Tribe. The project was halted temporarily in 1972 when the Environmental Defense Fund obtained an injunction requiring the TVA to prepare an environmental impact statement to comply with the newly enacted National Environmental Policy Act (NEPA). Environmental Defense Fund v. TVA, 468 F.2d 1164 (6th Cir. 1972). After the EIS was prepared, the injunction was dissolved in 1973. The litigation that resulted in the decision below involved a renewed effort to halt the project by using the newly enacted Endangered Species Act.

## TVA v. Hill

437 U.S. 153 (1978)

MR. CHIEF JUSTICE BURGER delivered the opinion of the Court.

The Little Tennessee River originates in the mountains of northern Georgia and flows through the national forest lands of North Carolina into Tennessee, where it converges with the Big Tennessee River near Knoxville. The lower 33 miles of the Little Tennessee takes the river's clear, free-flowing waters through an area of great natural beauty. . . .

In this area of the Little Tennessee River the Tennessee Valley Authority, a wholly owned public corporation of the United States, began constructing the Tellico Dam and Reservoir Project in 1967, shortly after Congress appropriated initial funds for its development. . . . When fully operational, the dam would impound water covering some 16,500 acres—much of which represents valuable and productive farmland—thereby converting the river's shallow, fast-flowing waters into a deep reservoir over 30 miles in length.

The Tellico Dam has never opened, however, despite the fact that construction has been virtually completed and the dam is essentially ready for operation. Although Congress has appropriated monies for Tellico every year since 1967, progress was delayed, and ultimately stopped, by a tangle of lawsuits and administrative proceedings. After unsuccessfully urging TVA to consider alternatives to damming the Little Tennessee, local citizens and national conservation groups brought suit in the District Court, claiming that the project did not conform to the requirements of the National Environmental Policy Act (NEPA). After finding TVA to be in violation of NEPA, the District Court enjoined the dam's completion pending the filing of an appropriate environmental impact statement. The injunction remained in effect until late 1973, when the District Court concluded that TVA's final environmental impact statement for Tellico was in compliance with the law.

A few months prior to the District Court's decision dissolving the NEPA injunction, a discovery was made in the waters of the Little Tennessee which would profoundly affect the Tellico Project. Exploring the area around Coytee Springs, which is about seven miles from the mouth of the river, a University of Tennessee ichthyologist, Dr. David A. Etnier, found a previously unknown species of perch, the snail darter, or *Percina (Imostoma) tanasi*. This three-inch, tannish-colored fish, whose numbers are estimated to be in the range of 10,000 to 15,000, would soon engage the attention of environmentalists, the TVA, the Department of the Interior, the Congress of the United States, and ultimately the federal courts, as a new and additional basis to halt construction of the dam.

Until recently the finding of a new species of animal life would hardly generate a cause celebre. This is particularly so in the case of darters, of which there are approximately 130 known species, 8 to 10 of these having been identified only in the last five years. The moving force behind the snail darter's sudden fame came some four months after its discovery, when the Congress passed the Endangered Species Act of 1973 ("Act"). This legislation, among other things, authorizes the Secretary of the Interior to declare species of animal life "endangered" and to identify the "critical habitat" of these creatures. . . .

In January 1975, the respondents in this case and others petitioned the Secretary of the Interior to list the snail darter as an endangered species. After receiving comments from various interested parties, including TVA and the State of Tennessee, the Secretary formally listed the snail darter as an endangered species on October 8, 1975. In so acting, it was noted that "the snail darter is a living entity which is genetically distinct and reproductively isolated from other fishes." More important for the purposes of this case, the Secretary determined that the snail darter apparently lives only in that portion of the Little Tennessee River which would be completely inundated by the reservoir created as a consequence of the Tellico Dam's completion. The Secretary went on to explain the significance of the dam to the habitat of the snail darter.

> [T]he snail darter occurs only in the swifter portions of shoals over clean gravel substrate in cool, low-turbidity water. Food of the snail darter is almost exclusively snails which require a clean gravel substrate for their

survival. *The proposed impoundment of water behind the proposed Tellico Dam would result in total destruction of the snail darter's habitat.* Ibid. (Emphasis added.)

Subsequent to this determination, the Secretary declared the area of the Little Tennessee which would be affected by the Tellico Dam to be the "critical habitat" of the snail darter. Using these determinations as a predicate, and notwithstanding the near completion of the dam, the Secretary declared that pursuant to §7 of the Act, "all Federal agencies must take such action as is necessary to insure that actions authorized, funded, or carried out by them do not result in the destruction or modification of this critical habitat area." This notice, of course, was pointedly directed at TVA and clearly aimed at halting completion or operation of the dam. . . .

In February 1976, pursuant to §11(g) of the Endangered Species Act, respondents filed the case now under review, seeking to enjoin completion of the dam and impoundment of the reservoir on the ground that those actions would violate the Act by directly causing the extinction of the species *Percina (Imostoma) tanasi.* The District Court denied respondents' request for a preliminary injunction and set the matter for trial. . . .

Trial was held in the District Court on April 29 and 30, 1976, and on May 25, 1976, the court entered its memorandum opinion and order denying respondents their requested relief and dismissing the complaint. The District Court found that closure of the dam and the consequent impoundment of the reservoir would "result in the adverse modification, if not complete destruction, of the snail darter's critical habitat," making it "highly probable" that "the continued existence of the snail darter" would be "jeopardize[d]." Despite these findings, the District Court declined to embrace the plaintiffs' position on the merits: that once a federal project was shown to jeopardize an endangered species, a court of equity is compelled to issue an injunction restraining violation of the Endangered Species Act. . . .

Thereafter, in the Court of Appeals, respondents argued that the District Court had abused its discretion by not issuing an injunction in the face of "a blatant statutory violation." The Court of Appeals agreed, and on January 31, 1977, it reversed, remanding "with instructions that a permanent injunction issue halting all activities incident to the Tellico Project which may destroy or modify the critical habitat of the snail darter." The Court of Appeals directed that the injunction "remain in effect until Congress, by appropriate legislation, exempts Tellico from compliance with the Act or the snail darter has been deleted from the list of endangered species or its critical habitat materially redefined." . . .

One would be hard pressed to find a statutory provision whose terms were any plainer than those in §7 of the Endangered Species Act. Its very words affirmatively command all federal agencies "to *insure* that actions *authorized, funded,* or *carried out* by them do not *jeopardize* the continued existence" of an endangered species or "*result* in the destruction or modification of habitat of such species. . . ." 16 U.S.C. §1536 (emphasis added.) This language admits of no exception. Nonetheless, petitioner urges, as do the dissenters, that the Act cannot reasonably be interpreted as applying to a federal project which was well under way when Congress passed the Endangered Species Act of 1973. To sustain that position, however, we would be forced to ignore the ordinary meaning of plain language. It has not been shown, for example, how TVA can close the gates of the Tellico Dam without "carrying out" an action that has been "authorized" and "funded" by a federal agency. Nor can we understand how such action will *"insure"* that the snail darter's habitat is not disrupted. Accepting the Secretary's determinations, as we must, it is clear that TVA's proposed operation of the dam will have precisely the opposite effect, namely the *eradication* of an endangered species.

Concededly, this view of the Act will produce results requiring the sacrifice of the anticipated benefits of the project and of many millions of dollars in public funds. But examination of the language, history, and structure of the legislation under review here indicates beyond doubt that Congress intended endangered species to be afforded the highest of priorities. . . .

The legislative proceedings in 1973 are, in fact, replete with expressions of concern over the risk that might lie in the loss of *any* endangered species.

. . . Congress was concerned about the *unknown* uses that endangered species might have and about the *unforeseeable* place such creatures may have in the chain of life on this planet. . . .

. . . The plain intent of Congress in enacting this statute was to halt and reverse the trend toward species extinction, whatever the cost. This is reflected not only in the stated policies of the Act, but in literally every section of the statute. All persons, including federal agencies, are specifically instructed not to "take" endangered species, meaning that no one is "to harass, harm,[30] pursue, hunt, shoot, wound, kill, trap, capture, or collect" such life forms. . . . The pointed omission of the type of qualifying language previously included in endangered species legislation reveals a conscious decision by Congress to give endangered species priority over the "primary missions" of federal agencies.

One might dispute the applicability of [this argument] to the Tellico Dam by saying that in this case the burden on the public through the loss of millions of unrecoverable dollars would greatly outweigh the loss of the snail darter. But neither the Endangered Species Act nor Art. III of the Constitution provides federal courts with authority to make such fine utilitarian calculations. On the contrary, the plain language of the Act, buttressed by its legislative history, shows clearly that Congress viewed the value of endangered species as "incalculable." Quite obviously, it would be difficult for a court to balance the loss of a sum certain — even $100 million — against a congressionally declared "incalculable" value, even assuming we had the power to engage in such a weighing process, which we emphatically do not. . . .

Having determined that there is an irreconcilable conflict between operation of the Tellico Dam and the explicit provisions of §7 of the Endangered Species Act, we must now consider what remedy, if any, is appropriate. It is correct, of course, that a federal judge sitting as a chancellor is not mechanically obligated to grant an injunction for every violation of law. This Court made plain in Hecht Co. v. Bowles,

---

30. We do not understand how TVA intends to operate Tellico Dam without "harming" the snail darter. The Secretary of the Interior has defined the term "harm" to mean "an act or omission which actually injures or kills wildlife, including acts which annoy it to such an extent as to significantly disrupt essential behavioral patterns, which include, but are not limited to, breeding, feeding or sheltering; *significant environmental modification or degradation which has such effects is included within the meaning of 'harm.'*" 50 CFR 17.3 (1976) (emphasis added).

321 U.S. 321, 329 (1944), that "[a] grant of *jurisdiction* to issue compliance orders hardly suggests an absolute duty to do so under any and all circumstances." As a general matter it may be said that "[s]ince all or almost all equitable remedies are discretionary, the balancing of equities and hardships is appropriate in almost any case as a guide to the chancellor's discretion." . . .

But these principles take a court only so far. Our system of government is, after all, a tripartite one, with each Branch having certain defined functions delegated to it by the Constitution. While "[i]t is emphatically the province and duty of the judicial department to say what the law is," Marbury v. Madison, 5 U.S. 137 (1803), it is equally—and emphatically—the exclusive province of the Congress not only to formulate legislative policies and mandate programs and projects, but also to establish their relative priority for the Nation. Once Congress, exercising its delegated powers, has decided the order of priorities in a given area, it is for the Executive to administer the laws and for the courts to enforce them when enforcement is sought.

Here we are urged to view the Endangered Species Act "reasonably," and hence shape a remedy "that accords with some modicum of common sense and the public weal." But is that our function? We have no expert knowledge on the subject of endangered species, much less do we have a mandate from the people to strike a balance of equities on the side of the Tellico Dam. Congress has spoken in the plainest of words, making it abundantly clear that the balance has been struck in favor of affording endangered species the highest of priorities, thereby adopting a policy which it described as "institutionalized caution." . . .

We agree with the Court of Appeals that in our constitutional system the commitment to the separation of powers is too fundamental for us to pre-empt congressional action by judicially decreeing what accords with "common sense and the public weal." Our Constitution vests such responsibilities in the political branches.

Affirmed.

## NOTES AND QUESTIONS

1. *TVA v. Hill* is one of the clearest instances of judicial repudiation of the kind of balancing approaches favored by the economics perspective. The majority opinion relies in part on committee reports expressing the view that biodiversity's genetic legacy is of "literally incalculable" value. Is the majority's rationale for refusing to balance the equities the notion that Congress already has done so? Or is the Court simply agreeing with Congress that such balancing cannot be done because it is impossible to calculate the value of genetic diversity?

2. Proponents of the project had argued that, even if completion of the dam would violate the Endangered Species Act, the judiciary should exercise its equitable discretion to decline to issue an injunction. Why did the Supreme Court instead order that an injunction be issued? Does the Court's decision imply that courts *must* enjoin all actions that violate the Act? If an injunction had not been issued in this case, would the finding of an ESA violation have any practical impact? Are courts required to enjoin violations of other environmental laws? See Weinberger v. Romero-Barcelo, 456 U.S. 305 (1982) (Clean Water Act does not foreclose the exercise of equitable discretion to decline to enjoin violation). What type of

judicial relief should be provided when agencies violate procedural requirements, for example, by failing to perform a study or to consult with a certain agency?

3. The papers of the late Justice Thurgood Marshall reveal that the Supreme Court came close to approving completion of the Tellico Dam without even hearing oral argument. When the Court first met to consider whether to review the case, five of the Court's nine Justices (Chief Justice Burger and Justices White, Powell, Blackmun, and Rehnquist) favored reversal while the other four Justices voted not to review the case. Justice Rehnquist circulated a per curiam opinion summarily reversing the court below, but the five Justices could not agree on the rationale for reversal. After vigorous draft dissents were circulated by Justices Stevens and Stewart (who were joined by Justices Brennan and Marshall), the Court agreed to hear oral argument. Chief Justice Burger, who initially had argued that continued appropriations for the dam had implicitly amended ESA, and Justice White ultimately changed their minds and voted with the four other Justices to uphold the lower court, transforming a prospective 5-4 defeat for the snail darter into a 6-3 victory. Percival, Environmental Law in the Supreme Court: Highlights from the Marshall Papers, 23 Envtl. L. Rep. 10606, 10610-10611 (1993). Justices Powell and Blackmun dissented on the ground that the Act should be interpreted to apply only prospectively and not to actions that are virtually complete when an endangered species is discovered. In a separate dissent, Justice Rehnquist, who had favored summary reversal, argued that the district court's refusal to issue an injunction should be upheld because it was not an abuse of discretion.

4. Following the Supreme Court's decision, Congress acted swiftly to amend the Endangered Species Act. Section 7 of the Act was extensively amended in 1978, 1979, and 1982. "From an original two sentences, the provision has been expanded to occupy nearly 10 pages of statutory text and now includes detailed procedures for its implementation, new federal duties, and a complex procedure for exempting qualified activities from its commands." M. Bean, The Evolution of National Wildlife Law 355 (2d ed. 1983). While these amendments qualified some of the duties imposed by section 7, "they remain stringent and highly protective" and section 7's "essential command remains intact." Id.

5. Section 7 requires all federal agencies to consult with the U.S. Fish and Wildlife Service (FWS) for freshwater species and wildlife and with the National Marine Fisheries Service (NMFS) for marine species if the agency is proposing an "action" that may affect endangered or threatened species. If the FWS or NMFS advise the agency that such species may be present in the area of the proposed action, section 7(c) requires the action agency to conduct a biological assessment. The biological assessment documents the agency's conclusions and rationale for determining what the impact of the action will be on the listed species. If the federal agency reviewing the biological assessment concludes that the project may adversely affect a listed species or their habitat, it prepares a "biological opinion." The biological opinion may recommend "reasonable and prudent alternatives" (RPAs) to the proposed action to avoid jeopardizing or adversely modifying habitat.

6. As amended, section 7 now includes a process for granting exemptions from its "no jeopardy" rule. Section 7 establishes a process for convening a committee of high-ranking government officials, known as the "God Squad" because of their power to decide the fate of species. The Committee is authorized to grant

any exemption if it determines that: (1) there are no reasonable and prudent alternatives to the federal action, (2) the action is in the public interest on a regional or national basis, and (3) the benefits of the action clearly outweigh the benefits of alternatives that do not jeopardize preservation of the species. In January 1979, a "God Squad" was convened for the first time to consider the Tellico Dam project. The Committee unanimously refused an exemption for the dam because it determined that there were reasonable alternatives to the project and that the project's benefits did not clearly outweigh the benefits of the alternatives. As the chairman of the President's Council of Economic Advisers explained: "The interesting phenomenon is that here is a project that is 95 percent complete, and if one takes just the cost of finishing it against the benefits and does it properly, it doesn't pay, which says something about the original design." Transcript of Meeting of Endangered Species Committee, Jan. 23, 1979, quoted in Holly Doremus, The Story of *TVA v. Hill*: A Narrow Escape for a Broad Law, in Environmental Law Stories 109, 133 (Lazarus & Houck eds., 2005). Since the Committee process was authorized, it has been used only four times, and the "God Squad" has never successfully granted a wholesale exemption from the Act.

7. In *TVA v. Hill*, the Supreme Court rejected the argument that continued congressional appropriations for the Tellico Dam reflected an intent to exempt it from ESA because courts disfavor "repeals by implication." Had the Court instead accepted this argument, what would the consequences have been for application of the ESA to federally funded projects? Congressional proponents of the dam, led by Senate Minority Leader Howard Baker from Tennessee, rammed through an appropriations rider in 1980 that expressly authorized completion of the dam notwithstanding the provisions of the ESA.

> [T]he pork barrel proponents, in forty-two seconds, in an empty House chamber, were able to slip a rider onto an appropriations bill, repealing all protective laws as they applied to Tellico and ordering the reservoir's completion. Despite a half-hearted veto threat by President Carter and a last-minute constitutionally-based lawsuit brought by the Cherokee Indians, the TVA was ultimately able to finish the dam, close the gates, and flood the valley on November 28, 1979. [Plater, In the Wake of the Snail Darter: An Environmental Law Paradigm and Its Consequences, 19 U. Mich. J.L. Reform 805, 813-814 (1986).]

While completion of the dam destroyed the last significant population of snail darters, small relict populations have been discovered elsewhere.

8. Zyg Plater, the University of Tennessee law school professor who argued *TVA v. Hill* on behalf of the snail darter, has written a terrific insider's account of the litigation. Zyg Plater, The Snail Darter and the Dam: How Pork-Barrel Politics Endangered a Little Fish and Killed a River (2013). Plater, now a professor at Boston College Law School, chronicles the extensive efforts supporters of the Endangered Species Act had to make to persuade the public and members of Congress of its importance.

9. The Tellico Dam is not the only project that Congress has exempted from compliance with ESA. In 1988, Congress specifically authorized the University of Arizona to construct three telescopes at a particular location on Arizona's Mt. Graham

even though it had been determined that the project, which was on national forest land, was likely to jeopardize the continued existence of the endangered Mt. Graham red squirrel. However, after the first two telescopes were built, the university sought to build the third telescope at a different location on a nearby peak. This plan was approved by the Forest Service without consultation with the Fish and Wildlife Service pursuant to section 7 of ESA. After opponents of the project brought suit, the Ninth Circuit found that Congress had not exempted construction at the new location from compliance with ESA. Mount Graham Coalition v. Thomas, 53 F.3d 970 (9th Cir. 1995). Thus, the court held that the Forest Service must comply with ESA section 7 prior to authorizing construction of the third telescope at another location.

## C.   *FEDERAL AUTHORITY TO PRESERVE BIODIVERSITY*

The Rehnquist Court's efforts to revive constitutional limitations on federal power have raised questions concerning the constitutional limits of federal authority under the Endangered Species Act. In the two cases that follow, plaintiffs, citing

**Figure 9.1    Delhi Sands Flower-Loving Fly**

United States v. Lopez, 514 U.S. 549 (1995), argued that Congress did not have the constitutional authority under its power to regulate interstate commerce to protect certain endangered species found only within a single state. In the first case the D.C. Circuit considered a challenge to Congress's constitutional authority to protect an endangered species of fly (the Delhi Sands Flower-Loving Fly, see Figure 9.1). The fly is located entirely within an eight-mile radius in two California counties. Plaintiffs argued on *Lopez* grounds that Congress did not have the power under the Commerce Clause to protect the fly's habitat because it did not bear a sufficient relationship to interstate commerce.

## National Association of Home Builders v. Babbitt

130 F.3d 1041 (D.C. Cir. 1997)

WALD, Circuit Judge:

. . . This dispute arose when the Fish and Wildlife Service ("FWS") placed the [Delhi Sands Flower-Loving] Fly, an insect that is native to the San Bernardino area of California, on the endangered species list. The listing of the Fly, the habitat of which is located entirely within an eight mile radius in southwestern San Bernardino County and northwestern Riverside County, California, forced San Bernardino County to alter plans to construct a new hospital on a recently purchased site that the FWS had determined contained Fly habitat. The FWS and San Bernardino County agreed on a plan that would allow the County to build the hospital and a power plant in the area designated as Fly habitat in return for modification of the construction plans and purchase and set aside of nearby land as Fly habitat. In November 1995, FWS issued a permit to allow construction of the power plant. During the same month, however, the County notified the FWS that it planned to redesign a nearby intersection to improve emergency vehicle access to the hospital. The FWS informed the County that expansion of the intersection as planned would likely lead to a "taking" of the Fly in violation of ESA section 9(a). After brief unsuccessful negotiations between the County and FWS, the County filed suit in district court challenging the application of section 9(a)(1) to the Fly. . . .

Appellants challenge the application of section 9(a)(1) of the ESA, which makes it unlawful for any person to "take any [endangered or threatened] species within the United States or the territorial sea of the United States," 16 U.S.C. §1538(a)(1), to the Delhi Sands Flower-Loving Fly. See also Babbitt v. Sweet Home Chapter of Communities for a Greater Oregon, 515 U.S. 687 (1995) (upholding agency's interpretation of the term "take" to include significant habitat degradation). Appellants argue that the federal government does not have the authority to regulate the use of non-federal lands in order to protect the Fly, which is found only within a single state. Indeed, they claim that "the Constitution of the United States does not grant the federal government the authority to regulate wildlife, nor does it authorize federal regulation of non-federal lands.". . .

Appellants' Commerce Clause challenge to the application of section 9(a)(1) of the ESA to the Fly rests on the Supreme Court's decision in United States v. Lopez, 514 U.S. 549 (1995). In *Lopez*, the Court held that the Gun-Free School

Zones Act of 1990, 18 U.S.C. §922(q), which made possession of a gun within a school zone a federal offense, exceeded Congress' Commerce Clause authority. Drawing on its earlier Commerce Clause jurisprudence, see especially Perez v. United States, 402 U.S. 146, 150 (1971), the *Lopez* Court explained that Congress could regulate three broad categories of activity: (1) "the use of the channels of interstate commerce," (2) "the instrumentalities of interstate commerce, or persons or things in interstate commerce, even though the threat may come only from intrastate activities," and (3) "those activities having a substantial relation to interstate commerce . . . i.e., those activities that substantially affect interstate commerce." *Lopez*, 514 U.S. at 558-59. . . .

It is clear that, in this instance, section 9(a)(1) of the ESA is not a regulation of the instrumentalities of interstate commerce or of persons or things in interstate commerce. As a result, only the first and the third categories of activity discussed in *Lopez* will be examined. . . .

## A. CHANNELS OF INTERSTATE COMMERCE

Application of section 9(a)(1) of the ESA to the Fly can be viewed as a proper exercise of Congress' Commerce Clause power over the first category of activity that the *Lopez* Court identified: the use of the "channels of interstate commerce." *Lopez*, 514 U.S. at 558. Although this category is commonly used to uphold regulations of interstate transport of persons or goods, it need not be so limited. Indeed, the power of Congress to regulate the channels of interstate commerce provides a justification for section 9(a)(1) of the ESA for two reasons. First, the prohibition against takings of an endangered species is necessary to enable the government to control the transport of the endangered species in interstate commerce. Second, the prohibition on takings of endangered animals falls under Congress' authority "to keep the channels of interstate commerce free from immoral and injurious uses." Id. (quoting Heart of Atlanta Motel Inc. v. United States, 379 U.S. 241, 256 (1964)). . . .

## B. SUBSTANTIALLY AFFECTS INTERSTATE COMMERCE

The takings clause in the ESA can also be viewed as a regulation of the third category of activity that Congress may regulate under its commerce power. According to *Lopez*, the test of whether section 9(a)(1) of the ESA is within this category of activity "requires an analysis of whether the regulated activity 'substantially affects' interstate commerce." 514 U.S. at 559. A class of activities can substantially affect interstate commerce regardless of whether the activity at issue—in this case the taking of endangered species—is commercial or noncommercial. As the *Lopez* Court, quoting Wickard v. Filburn, 317 U.S. 111 (1942), noted:

> "Even if appellee's activity be local and though it may not be regarded as commerce, it may still, whatever its nature, be reached by Congress if it exerts a substantial economic effect on interstate commerce, and this irrespective of whether such effect is what might at some earlier time have been defined as 'direct' or 'indirect'?"

*Lopez*, 514 U.S. at 556 (quoting *Wickard*, 317 U.S. at 125).[7]

The Committee Reports on the ESA reveal that one of the primary reasons that Congress sought to protect endangered species from "takings" was the importance of the continuing availability of a wide variety of species to interstate commerce. . . . This legislative history distinguishes the ESA from the statute at issue in *Lopez*. In *Lopez*, the Court noted that "as part of our independent evaluation of constitutionality under the Commerce Clause we of course consider legislative findings, and indeed even congressional committee findings regarding effect on interstate commerce." 514 U.S. at 562. The *Lopez* Court found, however, that there were no "congressional findings [that] would enable [it] to evaluate the legislative judgment that the activity in question substantially affected interstate commerce." Id. at 563. In this case, in contrast, the committee reports on the ESA discuss the value of preserving genetic diversity and the potential for future commerce related to that diversity. . . .

Congress could rationally conclude that the intrastate activity regulated by section 9 of the ESA substantially affects interstate commerce for two primary reasons. First, the provision prevents the destruction of biodiversity and thereby protects the current and future interstate commerce that relies upon it. Second, the provision controls adverse effects of interstate competition. . . .

### 1. Biodiversity

Approximately 521 of the 1,082 species in the United States currently designated as threatened or endangered are found in only one state. The elimination of all or even some of these endangered species would have a staggering effect on biodiversity — defined as the presence of a large number of species of animals and plants — in the United States and, thereby, on the current and future interstate commerce that relies on the availability of a diverse array of species. . . .

Each time a species becomes extinct, the pool of wild species diminishes. This, in turn, has a substantial effect on interstate commerce by diminishing a natural resource that could otherwise be used for present and future commercial purposes. Unlike most other natural resources, however, the full value of the variety of plant and animal life that currently exists is uncertain. Plants and animals that are lost through extinction undoubtedly have economic uses that are, in some cases, as yet unknown but which could prove vitally important in the future. A species whose worth is still unmeasured has what economists call an "option value" — the value of the possibility that a future discovery will make useful a species that is currently thought of as useless. To allow even a single species whose value is not currently apparent to become extinct therefore deprives the economy of the option value of that species. Because our current knowledge of each species and its possible uses is limited, it is impossible to calculate the exact impact that the loss of the option value of a single species might have on interstate

---

7. Indeed, the case at hand is in many ways directly analogous to *Wickard*. In both cases, the appellee's activity, growing wheat for personal consumption and taking endangered species, is local and is not "regarded as commerce." *Wickard*, 317 U.S. at 125. However, in both cases, the activity exerts a substantial economic effect on interstate commerce — by affecting the quantity of wheat in one case, and by affecting the quantity of species in the other.

commerce. In the aggregate, however, we can be certain that the extinction of species and the attendant decline in biodiversity will have a real and predictable effect on interstate commerce. . . .

### 2. Destructive Interstate Competition

The taking of the Fly and other endangered animals can also be regulated by Congress as an activity that substantially affects interstate commerce because it is the product of destructive interstate competition. It is a principle deeply rooted in Commerce Clause jurisprudence that Congress is empowered to act to prevent destructive interstate competition. As the Supreme Court explained in Hodel v. Virginia Surface Mining & Reclamation Ass'n, 452 U.S. 264 (1981) ("Hodel v. Virginia"), a case that the *Lopez* Court cited repeatedly, "prevention of . . . destructive interstate competition is a traditional role for congressional action under the Commerce Clause.". . .

The parallels between *Hodel v. Virginia* and the case at hand are obvious. The ESA and the Surface Mining Act both regulate activities—destruction of endangered species and destruction of the natural landscape—that are carried out entirely within a state and which are not themselves commercial in character. The activities, however, may be regulated because they have destructive effects, on environmental quality in one case and on the availability of a variety of species in the other, that are likely to affect more than one state. In each case, moreover, interstate competition provides incentives to states to adopt lower standards to gain an advantage vis-à-vis other states: In Hodel v. Virginia, 452 U.S. 264, the states were motivated to adopt lower environmental standards to improve the competitiveness of their coal production facilities, and in this case, the states are motivated to adopt lower standards of endangered species protection in order to attract development. . . .

KAREN LeCRAFT HENDERSON, Circuit Judge, concurring:

I agree with Judge Wald's conclusion that the "taking" prohibition in section 9(a)(1) of the Endangered Species Act (ESA) constitutes a valid exercise of the Congress' authority to regulate interstate commerce under the Commerce Clause. I cannot, however, agree entirely with either of her grounds for reaching the result and instead arrive by a different route.

. . . I do not see how we can say that the protection of an endangered species has any effect on interstate commerce (much less a substantial one) by virtue of an uncertain potential medical or economic value. Nevertheless, I believe that the loss of biodiversity itself has a substantial effect on our ecosystem and likewise on interstate commerce. In addition, I would uphold section 9(a)(1) as applied here because the Department's protection of the flies regulates and substantially affects commercial development activity which is plainly interstate.

. . . [A]t the time it passed ESA the Congress contemplated protecting endangered species through regulation of land and its development, which is precisely what the Department has attempted to do here. Such regulation, apart from the characteristics or range of the specific endangered species involved, has a plain and substantial effect on interstate commerce. In this case the regulation relates to both the proposed redesigned traffic intersection and the hospital it is intended to serve, each of which has an obvious connection with interstate commerce. Insofar as application of section 9(a)(1) of ESA here acts to regulate commercial development of the land inhabited by the endangered species, "it may . . . be reached by Congress" because "it asserts a substantial economic effect on interstate commerce."

SENTELLE, Circuit Judge, dissenting:

This case concerns the efforts of San Bernardino County, California ("the County"), to construct a hospital and supporting infrastructure for its citizens and other humans. Unfortunately, those efforts discomfit an insect—the Delhi Sands Flower-Loving Fly. According to the parties in this case, there are fewer than 300 breeding individuals of this species, all located within forty square miles in southern California. These flies live as larvae for nearly two years under Delhi Sands, a particular type of grit, apparently found only in those forty square miles of southern California, after which they emerge to feed and breed for two weeks before dying. . . .

The Department of Interior asserts that section 9(a)(1)(B) of the ESA, and specifically its use of that section to prohibit activities in southern California which might disturb a fly existing only in southern California, are constitutional under the Commerce Clause. U.S. Const. Art. I, §8, cl. 3. That clause empowers Congress to "regulate commerce with foreign nations, and among the several states, and with the Indian tribes." This brings the next question: Can Congress under the Interstate Commerce Clause regulate the killing of flies, which is not commerce, in southern California, which is not interstate? Because I think the answer is "no," I cannot join my colleagues' decision to affirm the district court's conclusion that it can. . . .

Judge Wald first asserts that the action taken by the Service under section 9(a)(1)(B) is a constitutional regulation of "the use of the 'channels of interstate commerce.'" (quoting *Lopez*, 514 U.S. at 558). The short disposition of this argument is to say it does not command a majority even without me. Judge Henderson rejects it out of hand, noting, correctly, that all authority offered by Judge Wald in support of the channels-of-commerce rationale upheld regulation "necessarily connected to movement of persons or things interstate. . . ." As Judge Henderson goes on to note, neither the whole of the endangered species, nor any of the individuals comprising it, travel interstate. The Delhi Sands Flower-Loving Fly is an inveterate stay-at-home, a purely intrastate creature. The Gun-Free School Zones Act, stricken as unconstitutional by the Supreme Court in *Lopez*, involved purely local possession of firearms, objects which do move in interstate commerce, presumably through its channels. The Supreme Court without difficulty determined that that section was "not a regulation of the use of the channels of interstate commerce." Neither is this. It does not purport to be.

. . . Judge Wald's supporting analysis of . . . *Heart of Atlanta* is far off the mark.

As Judge Wald notes, . . . *Heart of Atlanta* concerned congressional efforts to "rid the channels of interstate commerce of injurious uses." But . . . preventing habitat destruction contributes nothing to the goal of eliminating the fly, or any other endangered species, from the channels of commerce. The fact that activities like the construction of a hospital might involve articles that have traveled across state lines cannot justify federal regulation of the incidental local effects of every local activity in which those articles are employed. Judge Wald seems to be trying to extend Congress' power over the channels of commerce to allow direct federal regulation of any local effects caused by any activity using those channels of commerce. She focuses not on the fly in the channels of commerce, but everything else moving in the channels of commerce that may affect the fly. But this improperly inverts the third prong of *Lopez* and extends it without limit. Under Judge Wald's theory, instead of being limited to activities that *substantially affect* commerce, Congress may also regulate anything that is *affected* by commerce. . . .

None of the rationales offered by my colleagues pass . . . examination. Judge Wald offers two possible explanations as to why the challenged regulatory activity falls within category (3). First, she puts forth the "biodiversity" rationale. Under this rationale, she argues that the extinction of a species, and the concomitant diminution of the pool of wild species, "has a substantial effect on interstate commerce by diminishing a natural resource that could otherwise be used for present and future commercial purposes." As I understand her argument, because of some undetermined and indeed undeterminable possibility that the fly might produce something at some undefined and undetermined future time which might have some undefined and undeterminable medical value, which in turn might affect interstate commerce at that imagined future point, Congress can today regulate anything which might advance the pace at which the endangered species becomes extinct. Judge Henderson rejects this rationale, noting cogently that our colleague admits "that it is 'impossible to calculate the exact impact' of the economic loss of an endangered species." Judge Henderson further notes that "it is equally impossible to ascertain that there will be any such impact at all." She then reasons, and I agree, that we cannot then "say that the protection of an endangered species has any effect on interstate commerce (much less a substantial one) by virtue of an uncertain potential medical or economic value."

. . . [T]he rationale offered by Judge Wald to support this intrastate application of a statute unlimited by either of the other two subsidiary inquiries has no logical stopping point. As Judge Henderson suggests, the rationale dependent upon the purely speculative future impact of an action with no demonstrable impact at all cannot be said to "have any effect on interstate commerce (much less a substantial one). . . ." If it could, then I do not see how Congress could be prohibited from regulating any action that might conceivably affect the number or continued existence of any item whatsoever. A creative and imaginative court can certainly speculate on the possibility that any object cited in any locality no matter how intrastate or isolated might some day have a medical, scientific, or economic value which could then propel it into interstate commerce. There is no stopping point. If we uphold this statute under Judge Wald's first rationale, we have indeed not only ignored *Lopez* but made the Commerce Clause into what Judge Kozinski suggested: the "hey-you-can-do-whatever-you-feel-like clause."

Though Judge Henderson rejects Judge Wald's "biodiversity" rationale, she relies on a related justification of her own, which is to me indistinguishable in any meaningful way from that of Judge Wald. As I understand her rationale, it depends on "the interconnectedness of species and ecosystems," which she deems sufficient for us "to conclude that the extinction of one species affects others and their ecosystems and that the protection of a purely intrastate species [concededly including the Delhi Sands Flower-Loving Fly] will therefore substantially affect land and objects that are involved in interstate commerce." I see this as no less of a stretch than Judge Wald's rationale. First, the Commerce Clause empowers Congress "to regulate commerce" not "ecosystems." The Framers of the Constitution extended that power to Congress, concededly without knowing the word "ecosystems," but certainly knowing as much about the dependence of humans on other species and each of them on the land as any ecologist today. An ecosystem is an ecosystem, and commerce is commerce. . . .

In addition to their biodiversity/ecosystem justifications, each of my colleagues offers a second rationale for justifying Interior's actions under the third category of *Lopez* regulation. Judge Wald asserts that "the taking of the Fly and other endangered animals can also be regulated by Congress as an activity that substantially affects interstate commerce because it is the product of destructive interstate competition." I am not at all certain what that means in relation to the application of the ESA to the building of a hospital and supporting infrastructure in a single intrastate location. She relies on Hodel v. Virginia, 452 U.S. 264 (1981), Hodel v. Indiana, 452 U.S. 314 (1981), and United States v. Darby, 312 U.S. 100 (1940). Although she asserts "striking parallels" between those cases and the present one, I see no parallel at all. In each of those cases, Congress regulated arguably intrastate commercial activities, specifically mining and lumber production for interstate commerce.

Finally, Judge Henderson would justify the challenged section on the basis that "in enacting the ESA, the Congress expressed an intent to protect not only endangered species, but also the habitats that they, and we, occupy." I see no legally significant distinction between this justification and her "ecosystems" justification. The Commerce Clause empowers Congress to regulate "commerce," not habitat. People and animals lived in habitats at the time of the adoption of the Constitution, and we live in habitats now. Because the power to regulate habitats was "not delegated to the United States by the Constitution, nor prohibited by it to the states," that power is "reserved to the states respectively, or to the people." U.S. Const. Amend. X. For the reasons outlined with reference to the ecosystem justification, the habitat justification fails as well.

## NOTES AND QUESTIONS

1. Which of the rationales offered for finding that Congress has power under the Commerce Clause to protect endangered species is most persuasive? How do the various rationales for justifying federal regulatory authority compare with the reasons for conserving biodiversity offered in the excerpt from E.O. Wilson above? Emphasizing potential future commercial uses of endangered species has political appeal; in the aftermath of *Lopez*, is such a strategy now necessary to justify congressional authority to protect them?

2. Endangered species are less likely to have large populations that cross state lines than are healthy species. Does Congress therefore have greater authority to protect thriving species populations than endangered ones?

3. Not all endangered insects are entitled to protection under the ESA. Congress specifically excluded from the statutory definition of "endangered species" any "species of the Class Insecta determined by the Secretary to constitute a pest whose protection under the provisions of this chapter would present an

overwhelming and overriding risk to man." ESA §3(6), 16 U.S.C. §1532(6). Can you imagine any circumstances under which an insect that "is in danger of extinction throughout all or a significant portion of its range" ever could "present an overwhelming and overriding risk to man"?

4. In Gibbs v. Babbitt, 214 F.3d 483 (4th Cir. 2000), the Fourth Circuit rejected a constitutional challenge to the authority of Congress to prohibit private action that would harm an experimental population of endangered red wolves. In an effort to prevent extinction of the wolves, the government had captured surviving members of the species, pursuant to section 10(j) of the ESA, bred them in captivity, and then reintroduced them into wildlife refuges in North Carolina and Tennessee. Of the 75 wolves believed to be in the wild, it was estimated that approximately 41 wandered off the refuges onto private land. The lawsuit challenged the government's efforts to protect the wolves when found on private land. Writing for a 2-1 majority, Chief Judge J. Harvie Wilkinson stated: "Because the taking of red wolves can be seen as economic activity in the sense considered by *Lopez* and *Morrison*, the individual takings may be aggregated for the purpose of Commerce Clause analysis. While the taking of one red wolf on private land may not be 'substantial,' the takings of red wolves in the aggregate have a sufficient impact on interstate commerce to uphold this regulation. This is especially so where, as here, the regulation is but one part of the broader scheme of endangered species legislation." He went on to explain why protection of the red wolf "substantially affects interstate commerce through tourism, trade, scientific research, and other potential economic activities." Writing in dissent, Judge Luttig stated that regulation of the take of red wolves is an "activity that not only has no current economic character, but one that concededly has had no economic character for well over a century now."

5. The U.S. Supreme Court consistently has refused to review decisions rejecting constitutional challenges to federal authority to enforce the Endangered Species Act (ESA). GDF Realty Investments, Ltd. v. Norton, 326 F.3d 622, 640-641 (5th Cir. 2003); Rancho Viejo, LLC v. Norton, 323 F.3d 1062 (D.C. Cir. 2003). In June 2005, the Supreme Court decided Gonzales v. Raich, 545 U.S. 1 (2005). The Court upheld federal authority to prohibit the cultivation and use of marijuana for medical purposes. In an opinion by Justice Stevens that was joined by four other Justices, the Court held that Congress had a rational basis for concluding that the personal cultivation and use of marijuana would substantially affect interstate commerce because failure to regulate intrastate cultivation and use would leave a gaping hole in the comprehensive federal scheme for regulating illicit drugs. The Court majority emphasized that Congress clearly acted rationally in deciding that regulation of intrastate cultivation and use of marijuana was an essential part of the larger regulatory scheme. Justice Scalia, who did not join the majority opinion, filed a separate opinion concurring in the judgment. Scalia argued that Congress's authority to regulate intrastate activities that substantially affect interstate commerce derives from the Necessary and Proper Clause. "Where necessary to make a regulation of interstate commerce effective, Congress may regulate even those intrastate activities that do not themselves substantially affect interstate commerce," Scalia stated.

6. When it rejected a challenge to the constitutionality of applying the ESA to a purely intrastate species of fish, the Eleventh Circuit relied on *Gonzalez v. Raich*. In Alabama-Tombigbee Rivers Coalition v. Kempthorne, 477 F.3d 1250 (11th Cir. 2007), the court stated:

We are not convinced that the principle that Congress may regulate some intrastate activity as an essential part of a larger permissible regulation is limited to the facts of *Raich* and *Wickard*. The principle has a much richer history. . . . The discussion in *Raich* of the effect of intrastate marijuana use on national drug prices was not intended to limit to the sale of fungible goods a doctrine that had already been applied to discriminatory accommodations, *see* Katzenbach v. McClung, 379 U.S. 294, 302 (1964), to fair labor standards, *see Darby*, 312 U.S. at 115, to extortionate credit transactions, *see Perez*, 402 U.S. at 154, and to mining safety standards, *see Hodel*, 452 U.S. at 329. Instead, the Court's discussion of commodity pricing in *Raich* was part of its explanation of the rational basis Congress had for thinking that regulating home-consumed marijuana was an essential part of its comprehensive regulatory scheme aimed at controlling access to illegal drugs. . . . This case, like *Raich*, also turns on whether Congress had a rational basis for believing that regulation of an intrastate activity was an essential part of a larger regulation of economic activity. Unlike the statute involved in *Raich*, Congress did not rely on commodity pricing in justifying the Endangered Species Act. Instead, it made a determination that the most effective way to safeguard the commercial benefits of biodiversity was to protect all endangered species, regardless of their geographic range. That rational decision was within Congress' authority to make.

477 F.3d at 1277. *Raich* also was cited by the Ninth Circuit in rejecting a constitutional challenge to the ESA in San Luis & Delta-Mendota Water Authority v. Salazar, 638 F.3d 1163, 1174 (9th Cir. 2011) (rejecting challenges to ESA sections 7 and 9 because the Act "bears a substantial relation to commerce" (quoting Gonzales v. Raich, 545 U.S. 1, 17 (2005))).

7. As noted in Chapter 2, the U.S. Court of Appeals for the Tenth Circuit unanimously reversed a district court decision holding that Congress did not have the constitutional authority to protect the endangered Utah prairie dog when it is found on private land. Citing *Gonzales v. Raich*, the court held that even a purely intrastate species could be protected by Congress against non-commercial takes because it was necessary to preserve the integrity of a larger federal regulatory scheme. People for the Ethical Treatment of Property Owners (PETPO) v. U.S. Fish and Wildlife Service, 852 F.3d 990 (10th Cir. 2017). With this decision, all nine circuits of the U.S. Courts of Appeals that have considered the issue have upheld the constitutionality of the Endangered Species Act.

## D.  WHICH SPECIES ARE PROTECTED: SECTION 4

As *TVA v. Hill* makes clear, the Endangered Species Act provides potentially powerful protections. These protections, however, extend only to species that have been *listed* as "endangered" or "threatened" by the Secretary of the Interior (or, for certain marine species, the Secretary of Commerce). The determination to list a species, governed by section 4, is thus the key to the entire statute.

## 1. The Listing Process

*TVA v. Hill* also clearly illustrates that the determination to list a species also carries potentially enormous consequences. In the wake of the Supreme Court's decision, Congress amended the Act in 1978, imposing elaborate procedures and strict deadlines on the Secretary's listing determinations. See generally M. Bean, The Evolution of National Wildlife Law 334-341 (2d ed. 1983). These new requirements paralyzed the listing process. Published listing proposals for approximately 2,000 species were withdrawn because the Secretary could not meet the new deadlines. Id. at 335. Then, in 1981, OMB insisted that every listing proposal be subject to a "regulatory impact analysis" to assess its economic implications. Listings ceased almost entirely. In the first year of the Reagan administration, only two species made it through the process and onto the endangered species list: an orchid in Texas and the Hay Springs amphipod, a crustacean found only in the National Zoo in Washington, D.C.

In 1982, Congress moved to resurrect the listing process. It streamlined section 4, stripping away procedural requirements that it had added four years before and narrowing the Secretary's discretion. These new provisions were intended to ensure that listing decisions are based solely on scientific evidence concerning species' prospects for survival, to the exclusion of all other factors.

Listing decisions are enormously important because they trigger the requirement to designate critical habitat, and they are necessary to afford listed species the protections against federal actions that jeopardize them, and against private or public actions that "take" them. Fearful of the potential economic consequences of these protections, the Secretaries of Interior (responsible for listing terrestrial and freshwater species) and of Commerce (responsible for listing marine species) made listing decisions only with great reluctance. After enactment of the 1982 amendments, the pace of listings improved somewhat, but by 1988 nearly 1,000 species found to be eligible for listing were awaiting approval, more than 3,000 other species remained candidates for listing, while only about 50 species per year actually were being listed. Houck, The Endangered Species Act and Its Implementation by the U.S. Departments of Interior and Commerce, 64 U. Colo. L. Rev. 277, 284-285 (1993).

Two strategies for avoiding listings were to determine that listing is "warranted but precluded" by the press of other listing proposals or to conclude that other efforts to minimize harm to a species were likely to prevent extinction. For example, in 1988, the Fish and Wildlife Service denied petitions to list the northern spotted owl even though it found that "substantial data were available to indicate that the petitioned action may be warranted." Unlike the snail darter whose only habitat was thought to be in the vicinity of the Tellico Dam, the northern spotted owl roams over wide areas of old-growth forest. Scientists estimated that 1,000 acres of old-growth forest might be necessary to sustain one pair of such owls. Thus, the Fish and Wildlife Service was well aware that a listing decision could necessitate designating millions of acres of old-growth forest as critical habitat for the owl. Faced with potentially enormous economic consequences for the timber industry, the Service declined to add the owl to the endangered species list. This decision was overturned in Northern Spotted Owl v. Hodel, 716 F. Supp. 479 (W.D. Wash. 1988), which held that the decision not to list the northern spotted owl was arbitrary and capricious and contrary to law. The court noted that the Fish and Wildlife Service's documents did not contain any expert analysis supporting the decision not to list and that "the expert opinion is entirely to the contrary." This decision ultimately resulted in the owl being declared a threatened species, creating a major controversy in the Pacific Northwest.

To help protect species that are candidates for listing, but for which the government lacks resources to pursue a listing, the concept of Candidate Conservation Agreements with Assurances (CCAA) has been established. These are formal agreements between the Fish and Wildlife Service and those who make a voluntary commitment to actions that will remove or reduce the threats facing a candidate species. Most of these agreements have been reached with other federal agencies, state or local units of government, or conservation organizations. If they are successful in reducing the threat faced by the species, a listing decision may be avoided. The use of Candidate Conservation Agreements with Assurances is a means of providing nonfederal landowners with a commitment that the government will not impose additional restrictions on the development of their property over and above those the landowner voluntarily agrees to undertake as part of the CCAA.

In March 2003, the U.S. Fish and Wildlife Service (FWS) and National Marine Fisheries Service adopted a final Policy for Evaluating Conservation Efforts When Making Listing Decisions (PECE) under the ESA. 68 Fed. Reg. 15,100 (2003). The policy focuses on "(1) The certainty that the conservation efforts will be implemented and (2) the certainty that the efforts will be effective." To assess these criteria, PECE directs the agencies to consider whether the resources necessary to carry out the efforts are available, whether parties to the efforts have the authority to carry them out, and whether there is a schedule for completing and evaluating the efforts. In Defenders of Wildlife v. Jewell, 815 F.3d 1 (D.C. Cir. 2016), the D.C. Circuit upheld a decision not to list the dunes sagebrush lizard because a state plan to conserve the lizard's habitat was sufficiently certain to be implemented and effective.

In other cases, courts have found that the FWS overestimated the benefits of conservation efforts in deciding that particular listings were not warranted. In September 2015, a federal district court in Texas became the first to decide that FWS *underestimated* the benefits of conservation efforts when it listed the lesser prairie chicken as a threatened species. Permian Basin Petroleum Ass'n v. Dep't of Interior, 2015 WL 5192526 (W.D. Tex. 2015). The court rejected FWS's conclusion that a decision not to list the lesser prairie chicken would remove incentives for industry groups to participate in conservation efforts.

The *Northern Spotted Owl* case is only one of several holding that the Fish and Wildlife Service (FWS) or the National Marine Fisheries Service (NMFS) have improperly declined to list a species as threatened or endangered. In Oregon Natural Resources Council v. Daley, 6 F. Supp. 2d 1139 (D. Or. 1998), a court rejected a decision by the NMFS not to list the Oregon coast coho salmon as threatened. The court rejected the notion that the state's pledge of voluntary future conservation efforts should be considered in the listing decision as well as the rationale that a two-year time horizon was adequate for projecting the future fate of the fish. In Defenders of Wildlife v. Norton, 258 F.3d 1136 (9th Cir. 2001), the Ninth Circuit upheld a challenge to the Secretary of Interior's decision not to designate the flat-tailed horned lizard as a threatened species. The court rejected the government's argument that the threat of extinction of the species on private land did not warrant a listing because the species could survive on public land if protected through a voluntary conservation agreement. The court interpreted the statutory trigger for listing to mean that "a species can be extinct 'throughout . . . a significant portion of its range' if there are major geographical areas in which it is no longer viable but once was." Thus, it concluded that the Secretary of Interior "must at least explain her conclusion that the area in which the species can no longer live [on private land] is not a 'significant portion of its range.'" Quoting Aldo Leopold's *Sand County Almanac*, the court observed that "[t]he text of the ESA and its subsequent application seems to have been guided by the following maxim: 'There seems to be a tacit assumption that if grizzlies survive in Canada and Alaska, that is good enough. It is not good enough for me. . . . Relegating grizzlies to Alaska is about like relegating happiness to heaven; one may never get there.'" Aldo Leopold, A Sand County Almanac 277 (1966). 258 F.3d at 1145 n.10. The court also concluded that the Secretary had improperly relied upon a conservation agreement whose benefits were unclear in determining that the species was not threatened. Compare Selkirk Conservation Alliance v. Forsgren, 336 F.3d 944 (9th Cir. 2003) (holding that it was proper for the Fish and Wildlife Service to rely on an agreement with a private timber company as the grounds for making a finding of "no jeopardy" with respect to grizzly bears).

In March 2007, the Solicitor of the Department of the Interior issued a legal opinion concerning the meaning of the language in ESA section 3(6) "in danger of extinction throughout all or a significant portion of its range." Memorandum from Solicitor, DOI, to Director, FWS, on The Meaning of "In Danger of Extinction Throughout All or a Significant Portion of Its Range" (Mar. 16, 2007). This opinion subsequently was withdrawn in May 2011 following adverse court decisions. These decisions included Defenders of Wildlife v. Salazar, 729 F. Supp. 2d 1207 (D. Mont. 2010), concerning delisting of the Northern Rocky Mountain gray wolf, and Wild Earth Guardians v. Salazar, 2010 U.S. Dist. LEXIS 105253 (D. Ariz. Sept. 30, 2010), concerning a petition to list the Gunninson's prairie dog. The FWS had asserted in both of these determinations, based on the Solicitor's Opinion, that it had authority, in effect, to protect under the Act only some members of a species, as defined by the Act (i.e., taxonomic species, subspecies, or distinct population segment (DPS)). Both courts ruled that the determinations were arbitrary and capricious on the grounds that this approach violated the plain and unambiguous language of the Act. The courts concluded that reading the "significant portion of its range" (SPR) language to allow protecting only a portion of a species' range is inconsistent with the Act's definition of "species," which forecloses listing any population that does not qualify as a taxonomic species, subspecies, or DPS. These two decisions hold that the SPR language may not be used as a basis for listing less than all members of a species.

The *Defenders of Wildlife v. Salazar* decision, holding that the delisting of part of a DPS of gray wolf was illegal, prompted unprecedented action by Congress. In the Department of Defense and Continuing Appropriations Act of 2011, Congress ordered the FWS to reissue the rule the court had invalidated and provided that the rule "shall not be subject to judicial review." Pub. L. No. 112-10 (Apr. 15, 2011). The court then held that it was bound to uphold the new legislation, which represented the first time Congress had ever ordered the delisting of part of a species. Alliance for the Wild Rockies v. Salazar, 800 F. Supp. 2d 1123 (D. Mont. 2011), aff'd, 672 F.3d 1170 (9th Cir. 2012).

In December 2011, the FWS and the NMFS jointly proposed a new Policy on Interpretation of the Phrase "Significant Portion of Its Range." 76 Fed. Reg. 76,987 (2011). In July 2014, the agencies finalized the policy. 79 Fed. Reg. 37,578 (2014). The final policy states:

> The phrase "significant portion of its range" in the Act's definitions of "endangered species" and "threatened species" provides an independent basis for listing. Thus, there are two situations (or factual bases) under which a species would qualify for listing: a species may be endangered or threatened throughout all of its range or a species may be endangered or threatened throughout only a significant portion of its range.
>
> If a species is found to be endangered or threatened throughout only a significant portion of its range, the entire species is listed as endangered or threatened, respectively, and the Act's protections apply to all individuals of the species wherever found.
>
> Significant: A portion of the range of a species is "significant" if the species is not currently endangered or threatened throughout its range, but the portion's contribution to the viability of the species is so important that, without the members in that portion, the species would be in danger of extinction, or likely to become so in the foreseeable future, throughout all of its range.
>
> Range: The range of a species is considered to be the general geographical area within which that species can be found at the time FWS or NMFS makes any particular status determination. This range includes those areas used throughout all or part of the species' life cycle, even if they are not used regularly (e.g., seasonal habitats). Lost historical range is relevant to the analysis of the status of the species, but it cannot constitute a significant portion of a species' range.
>
> Reconciling SPR with DPS authority: If the species is endangered or threatened throughout a significant portion of its range, and the population in that significant portion is a valid DPS, we will list the DPS rather than the entire taxonomic species or subspecies.

During the Clinton administration (1993-2001), 522 new species listings were made, but only 59 species were listed during the George W. Bush administration (2001-2009). In September 2011, the FWS settled litigation brought by Wild Earth Guardians and the Center for Biological Diversity by agreeing to accelerate decisions on whether or not to list 800 candidate species by 2018. Under a schedule released in February 2013, decisions had to be made on 97 species by September 2013, including 70 species covered by the lawsuit. Preliminary work had been completed on more than 550 other species that would be the subject of future decisions. Michael Wines, Endangered or Not, but at Least No Longer Waiting, N.Y. Times, Mar. 6, 2013, at A12. During the Obama administration (2009-2017), a total of 340 new species listings were made and 29 listed species were delisted, a new record.

As of May 2021, there were 2,361 listed species. Of these, 1,415 were animal species (1,097 of these were listed as endangered and 318 as threatened) and 946 were plants (773 were listed as endangered and 173 as threatened). A total of 1,666 listed species were found in the United States (including 723 animals and 943 plants). States with the most listed species included Hawaii (501), California (287), Alabama (143), and Florida (134). *https://ecos.fws.gov/ecp/report/boxscore.*

## 2.   Critical Habitat Designations

Section 4 requires that when the Secretary lists a species as endangered or threatened, he or she must also designate the species' "critical habitat," to the extent that the critical habitat can be determined, and designation is prudent. These provisions were intended to ensure that listing decisions were not held up by uncertainty about critical habitat. They also provide enforceable standards. Indeed, when the FWS ultimately decided to list the northern spotted owl as "threatened," but declined to designate critical habitat, claiming inadequate information, the court held that critical habitat designation may be deferred only in "extraordinary circumstances," and ordered the Secretary to propose a designation within 60 days. Northern Spotted Owl v. Lujan, 758 F. Supp. 621 (W.D. Wash. 1991). In 1992, the Secretary designated nearly 7 million acres in 190 areas as critical habitat for the owl. Following that decision, for several years there was a virtual moratorium on designation of critical habitat with only a few marine animals having critical habitat designated.

As of 1999, critical habitat designations had not been made for nearly 90 percent of all listed species. Wiygul & Weiner, Critical Habitat Destruction, 16 Envtl. Forum, May/June 1999, at 13. In May 2003, Interior Secretary Gale Norton announced that the Bush administration was suspending designation of critical habitat for endangered species. The administration proposed that Congress remove the ESA's requirement for designating critical habitat and replace it with a new process. In the 2004 National Defense Authorization bill, Pub. L. No. 108-136, 117 Stat. 1392, Congress exempted land on military installations from designation as critical habitat if the Secretary of Interior determines that the military has prepared an integrated natural resources plan that benefits the species for which critical habitat otherwise would have been designated.

Decisions not to designate critical habitat came under fire in the courts. In Conservation Council for Hawaii v. Babbitt, 2 F. Supp. 2d 1280 (D. Haw. 1998), a court rejected the Fish and Wildlife Service's rationale for declining to designate critical habitat for 245 plant species. The FWS had argued that a critical habitat designation would increase threats posed to the plants by collectors and would have little benefit because the plants were found mostly on private, rather than federal, lands. After another court rejected the conclusion that critical habitat should not be designated for the endangered cactus ferruginous pygmy owl because it would increase threats from bird-watchers, more than 730,000 acres were designated as critical habitat for the species in Arizona. 63 Fed. Reg. 71,820 (1998).

The FWS announced in November 2000 that it was so overwhelmed by the need to make designations of critical habitat under court orders that it would cease listing new species, save for emergency situations, until the end of the 2001 fiscal year. At the time of the FWS announcement, 39 additional species were about to be listed and 236 others were considered candidates for listing. But the FWS was faced with the need to comply with court orders for designating critical habitat that were pending for more than 300 additional species. Michael Grunwald, Endangered List Faces New Peril, Wash. Post, Mar. 12, 2001, at A1. The agency stated that its budget for listing-related activities was being entirely consumed complying with court orders in existing litigation. Thus, it announced that it would not be able to respond to any more petitions for new listings.

Environmental groups charged that the FWS had created its own problem by intentionally budgeting only $6.3 million of its $1.3 billion budget for listings and designations of critical habitat. They noted that the agency had never requested a substantial increase in its budget for listing-related activities. In March 2001, the Bush administration created a furor by asking Congress to impose a moratorium on private lawsuits to force listings and designations of critical habitat. As of April 2001, there were nearly 80 lawsuits pending to force species listing, and notices of intent to sue had been served in 95 additional cases. The Species Litigation Act, Wall St. J., Apr. 20, 2001, at A14. While Congress rejected the proposed moratorium, former Secretary of Interior Bruce Babbitt supported the Bush administration's claim that the listing process had placed impossible demands on federal agencies.

On August 28, 2001, the FWS reached agreement with three environmental organizations to expedite the listing of 29 endangered species most in need of immediate protection in return for deferring by six months the designation of critical habitat for species already listed. By deferring the deadlines for critical habitat designations that were the products of prior lawsuits, the settlement freed up $600,000 that the FWS agreed to redirect to expedite the listing decisions. While this agreement was hailed as a breakthrough, see, e.g., A Victory for Endangered Species, N.Y. Times, Sept. 3, 2001, the basic problem of insufficient resources for species listing and critical habitat designation remained. FWS estimated that it would need at least $120 million simply to process the backlog that it then faced.

In Alabama-Tombigbee Rivers Coalition v. Kempthorne, 477 F.3d 1250 (11th Cir. 2007), the Eleventh Circuit stated that "it is clear that the [Fish and Wildlife] Service chronically fails to meet its statutory duty of designating critical habitat of endangered species within the time the Endangered Species Act requires. Noting the agency's funding limitations, the court observed that "the same legislature that has enacted standards for an executive agency's performance can through the appropriations process effectively prevent the agency from meeting those standards." But it rejected a business coalition's claim that the remedy for failure to make a timely designation of critical habitat should be delisting of the species. Such a remedy, concluded the court, would "make a bad situation worse, and defeat the Congressional intent behind the Endangered Species Act." 477 F.3d at 1269.

In February 2016, the FWS and NMFS revised their regulations governing designation of critical habitat. Listing Endangered and Threatened Species and Designating Critical Habitat; Implementing Changes to the Regulations for Designating Critical Habitat, 81 Fed. Reg. 7,414 (2016). The revisions provide that areas outside the geographical area occupied by the species at the time of listing should be designated as critical habitat if they are determined to be "essential for the conservation of the species." For example, the agencies note that if a butterfly depends on a particular host plant that is moving up a slope because of warming temperatures due to climate change, the agencies can rationally conclude that the butterfly's range will likely move up the slope. Thus, the agencies "would designate specific areas outside the geographical area occupied by the butterfly at the time it was listed if we concluded this area was essential based on this information." The revisions also clarified that a species need not be continuously present for an area to be considered "occupied by the species" if the area is periodically used by members of the species.

In Weyerhaeuser Co. v. U.S., 139 S.Ct. 361 (2018), a group of private landowners in Louisiana challenged the inclusion of their land in the designation of critical habitat for the dusky gopher frog. A divided panel of the Fifth Circuit rejected the challenge, granting *Chevron* deference to the FWS's determination that it was essential to include the private land because of the presence of rare ephemeral ponds on the property. The Supreme Court then granted review and reached the following decision.

## Weyerhaeuser Co. v. U.S. Fish and Wildlife Service

### 139 S.Ct. 361 (2018)

CHIEF JUSTICE ROBERTS delivered the opinion of the Court.

The Endangered Species Act directs the Secretary of the Interior, upon listing a species as endangered, to also designate the "critical habitat" of the species. A group of landowners whose property was designated as critical habitat for an endangered frog challenged the designation. The landowners urge that their land cannot be *critical* habitat because it is not *habitat*, which they contend refers only to areas where the frog could currently survive. The court below ruled that the Act imposed no such limitation on the scope of critical habitat. . . .

### I

### A

The amphibian *Rana sevosa* is popularly known as the "dusky gopher frog"—"dusky" because of its dark coloring and "gopher" because it lives underground. The dusky gopher frog is about three inches long, with a large head, plump body, and short legs. Warts dot its back, and dark spots cover its entire body. It is noted for covering its eyes with its front legs when it feels threatened, peeking out periodically until danger passes. Less endearingly, it also secretes a bitter, milky substance to deter would-be diners.

The frog spends most of its time in burrows and stump holes located in upland longleaf pine forests. In such forests, frequent fires help maintain an open canopy, which in turn allows vegetation to grow on the forest floor. The vegetation supports the small insects that the frog eats and provides a place for the frog's eggs to attach when it breeds. The frog breeds in "ephemeral" ponds that are dry for part of the year. Such ponds are safe for tadpoles because predatory fish cannot live in them.

The dusky gopher frog once lived throughout coastal Alabama, Louisiana, and Mississippi, in the longleaf pine forests that used to cover the southeast. But more than 98% of those forests have been removed to make way for urban development, agriculture, and timber plantations. The timber plantations consist of fast-growing loblolly pines planted as close together as possible, resulting in a closed-canopy forest inhospitable to the frog. The near eradication of the frog's habitat sent the species into severe decline. By 2001, the known wild population of the dusky gopher frog had dwindled to a group of 100 at a single pond in southern Mississippi. That year, the Fish and Wildlife Service, which administers the Endangered Species Act of 1973 on behalf of the Secretary of the Interior, listed the dusky gopher frog as an endangered species.

### B

When the Secretary lists a species as endangered, he must also designate the critical habitat of that species. The ESA defines "critical habitat" as:

"(i) the specific areas within the geographical area occupied by the species . . . on which are found those physical or biological features (I) essential to the conservation of the species and (II) which may require special management considerations or protection; and

"(ii) specific areas outside the geographical area occupied by the species . . . upon a determination by the Secretary that such areas are essential for the conservation of the species." [ESA §3(5)(A).]

Before the Secretary may designate an area as critical habitat, the ESA requires him to "tak[e] into consideration the economic impact" and other relevant impacts of the designation. [ESA §4(b)(2).] The statute goes on to authorize him to "exclude any area from critical habitat if he determines that the benefits of such exclusion outweigh the benefits of [designation]," unless exclusion would result in extinction of the species.

A critical-habitat designation does not directly limit the rights of private landowners. It instead places conditions on the Federal Government's authority to effect any physical changes to the designated area, whether through activities of its own or by facilitating private development. Section 7 of the ESA requires all federal agencies to consult with the Secretary to "[e]nsure that any action authorized, funded, or carried out by such agency" is not likely to adversely affect a listed species' critical habitat. If the Secretary determines that an agency action, such as issuing a permit, would harm critical habitat, then the agency must terminate the action, implement an alternative proposed by the Secretary, or seek an exemption from the Cabinet-level Endangered Species Committee.

Due to resource constraints, the Service did not designate the frog's critical habitat in 2001, when it listed the frog as endangered. In the following years, the Service discovered two additional naturally occurring populations and established another population through translocation. The first population nonetheless remains the only stable one and by far the largest.

In 2010, in response to litigation by the Center for Biological Diversity, the Service published a proposed critical-habitat designation. The Service proposed to designate as occupied critical habitat all four areas with existing dusky gopher frog populations. The Service found that each of those areas possessed the three features that the Service considered "essential to the conservation" of the frog and that required special protection: ephemeral ponds; upland open-canopy forest containing the holes and burrows in which the frog could live; and open-canopy forest connecting the two. But the Service also determined that designating only those four sites would not adequately ensure the frog's conservation. Because the existing dusky gopher frog populations were all located in two adjacent counties on the Gulf Coast of Mississippi, local events such as extreme weather or an outbreak of an infectious disease could jeopardize the entire species.

To protect against that risk, the Service proposed to designate as *unoccupied* critical habitat a 1,544-acre site in St. Tammany Parish, Louisiana. The site, dubbed "Unit 1" by the Service, had been home to the last known population of dusky gopher frogs outside of Mississippi. The frog had not been seen in Unit 1 since 1965, and a closed-canopy timber plantation occupied much of the site. But the Service found that the site retained five ephemeral ponds "of remarkable quality," and determined that an open-canopy forest could be restored on the surrounding uplands "with reasonable effort." Although the uplands in Unit 1 lacked the open-canopy forests (and, of course, the frogs) necessary for designation as occupied critical habitat, the Service concluded that the site met the statutory definition of unoccupied critical habitat because its rare, high-quality breeding ponds and its distance from existing frog populations made it essential for the conservation of the species.

After issuing its proposal, the Service commissioned a report on the probable economic impact of designating each area, including Unit 1, as critical habitat for the dusky gopher frog. Petitioner Weyerhaeuser Company, a timber company, owns part of Unit 1 and leases the remainder from a group of family landowners. While the critical-habitat designation has no direct effect on the timber operations, St. Tammany Parish is a fast-growing part of the New Orleans metropolitan area, and the landowners have already invested in plans to more profitably develop the site. The report recognized that anyone developing the area may need to obtain Clean Water Act permits from the Army Corps of Engineers before filling any wetlands on Unit 1. Because Unit 1 is designated as critical habitat, Section 7 of the ESA would require the Corps to consult with the Service before issuing any permits.

According to the report, that consultation process could result in one of three outcomes. First, it could turn out that the wetlands in Unit 1 are not subject to the Clean Water Act permitting requirements, in which case the landowners could proceed with their plans unimpeded. Second, the Service could ask the Corps not to issue permits to the landowners to fill some of the wetlands on the site, in effect prohibiting development on 60% of Unit 1. The report estimated that this would deprive the owners of $20.4 million in development value. Third, by asking the Corps to deny even more of the permit requests, the Service could bar all development of Unit 1, costing the owners $33.9 million. The Service concluded that those potential costs were not "disproportionate" to the conservation benefits of designation. "Consequently," the Service announced, it would not "exercis[e][its] discretion to exclude" Unit 1 from the dusky gopher frog's critical habitat.

## C

Weyerhaeuser and the family landowners sought to vacate the designation in Federal District Court. They contended that Unit 1 could not be critical habitat for the dusky gopher frog because the frog could not survive there: Survival would require replacing the closed-canopy timber plantation encircling the ponds with an open-canopy longleaf pine forest. The District Court nonetheless upheld the designation. The court determined that Unit 1 satisfied the statutory definition of unoccupied critical habitat, which requires only that the Service deem the land "essential for the conservation [of] the species."

Weyerhaeuser also challenged the Service's decision not to exclude Unit 1 from the dusky gopher frog's critical habitat, arguing that the Service had failed to adequately weigh the benefits of designating Unit 1 against the economic impact. In addition, Weyerhaeuser argued that the Service had used an unreasonable methodology for estimating economic impact and, regardless of methodology, had failed to consider several categories of costs. The court approved the Service's methodology and declined to consider Weyerhaeuser's challenge to the decision not to exclude.

The Fifth Circuit affirmed. The Court of Appeals rejected the suggestion that the definition of critical habitat contains any "habitability requirement." The court also concluded that the Service's decision not to exclude Unit 1 was committed to agency discretion by law and was therefore unreviewable. . . .

## II

## A

Our analysis starts with the phrase "critical habitat." According to the ordinary understanding of how adjectives work, "critical habitat" must also be "habitat." Adjectives modify nouns—they pick out a subset of a category that possesses a certain quality. It follows that "critical habitat" is the subset of "habitat" that is "critical" to the conservation of an endangered species.

. . . Section 4(a)(3)(A)(i), which the lower courts did not analyze, is the sole source of authority for critical-habitat designations. That provision states that when the Secretary lists a species as endangered he must also "designate any *habitat of such species* which is then considered to be critical habitat." §4(a)(3)(A)(1) (emphasis added). Only the "habitat" of the endangered species is eligible for designation as critical habitat. Even if an area otherwise meets the statutory definition of unoccupied critical habitat because the Secretary finds the area essential for the conservation of the species, Section 4(a)(3)(A)(i) does not authorize the Secretary to designate the area as *critical* habitat unless it is also *habitat* for the species.

The Center for Biological Diversity contends that the statutory definition of critical habitat is complete in itself and does not require any independent inquiry into the meaning of the term "habitat," which the statute leaves undefined. But the statutory definition of "critical habitat" tells us what makes habitat "critical," not what makes it "habitat." Under the statutory definition, critical habitat comprises areas occupied by the species "on which are found those physical or biological features (I) essential to the conservation of the species and (II) which may require special management considerations or protection," as well as unoccupied areas that the Secretary determines to be "essential for the conservation of the species." §3(5)(A). That is no baseline definition of habitat—it identifies only certain areas that are indispensable to the conservation of the endangered species. The definition allows the Secretary to identify the subset of habitat that is critical, but leaves the larger category of habitat undefined.

The Service does not now dispute that critical habitat must be habitat, although it made no such concession below. Instead, the Service argues that habitat includes areas that, like Unit 1, would require some degree of modification to support a sustainable population of a given species. Weyerhaeuser, for its part, urges that habitat cannot include areas where the species could not currently survive. (Habitat can, of course, include areas where the species does not currently *live*, given that the statute defines critical habitat to include unoccupied areas.) The Service in turn disputes Weyerhaeuser's premise that the administrative record shows that the frog could not survive in Unit 1.

The Court of Appeals concluded that "critical habitat" designations under the statute were not limited to areas that qualified as habitat. The court therefore had no occasion to interpret the term "habitat" in Section 4(a)(3)(A)(i) or to assess the Service's administrative findings regarding Unit 1. Accordingly, we vacate the judgment below and remand to the Court of Appeals to consider these questions in the first instance.

### B

Weyerhaeuser also contends that, even if Unit 1 could be properly classified as critical habitat for the dusky gopher frog, the Service should have excluded it from designation under Section 4(b)(2) of the ESA. That provision requires the Secretary to "tak[e] into consideration the economic impact . . . of specifying any particular area as critical habitat" and authorizes him to "exclude any area from critical habitat if he determines that the benefits of such exclusion outweigh the benefits of specifying such area as part of the critical habitat." §4(b)(2). To satisfy its obligation to consider economic impact, the Service commissioned a report estimating the costs of its proposed critical-habitat designation. The Service concluded that the costs of designating the proposed areas, including Unit 1, were not "disproportionate" to the conservation benefits and, "[c]onsequently," declined to make any exclusions.

Weyerhaeuser claims that the Service's conclusion rested on a faulty assessment of the costs and benefits of designation and that the resulting decision not to exclude should be set aside. Specifically, Weyerhaeuser contends that the Service improperly weighed the costs of designating Unit 1 against the benefits of designating *all* proposed critical habitat, rather than the benefits of designating Unit 1 in particular. Weyerhaeuser also argues that the Service did not fully account for the economic impact of designating Unit 1 because it ignored, among other things, the costs of replacing timber trees with longleaf pines, maintaining an open canopy through controlled burning, and the tax revenue that St. Tammany Parish would lose if Unit 1 were never developed. The Court of Appeals did not consider Weyerhaeuser's claim because it concluded that a decision not to exclude a certain area from critical habitat is unreviewable. . . .

Section 4(b)(2) states that the Secretary

"shall designate critical habitat . . . after taking into consideration the economic impact, the impact on national security, and any other relevant impact, of specifying any particular area as critical habitat. The Secretary may exclude any area from critical habitat if he determines that the benefits of such exclusion outweigh the benefits of specifying such area . . . unless he determines . . . that the failure to designate such area as critical habitat will result in the extinction of the species concerned." [ESA §4(b)(2).]

Although the text meanders a bit, we recognized in *Bennett v. Spear*, 520 U.S. 154 (1997), that the provision describes a unified process for weighing the impact of designating an area as critical habitat. The first sentence of Section 4(b)(2) imposes a "categorical requirement" that the Secretary "tak[e] into consideration" economic and other impacts before such a designation. The second sentence authorizes the Secretary to act on his consideration by providing that he may exclude an area from critical habitat if he determines that the benefits of exclusion outweigh the benefits of designation. The Service followed that procedure here (albeit in a flawed manner, according to Weyerhaeuser). It commissioned a report to estimate the costs of designating the proposed critical habitat, concluded that those costs were not "disproportionate" to the benefits of designation, and "[c]onsequently" declined to "exercis[e] [its] discretion to exclude any areas from [the] designation of critical habitat."

*Bennett* explained that the Secretary's "ultimate decision" to designate or exclude, which he "arriv[es] at" after considering economic and other impacts, is reviewable "for abuse of discretion." The Service dismisses that language as a "passing reference . . . not necessarily inconsistent with the Service's understanding," which is that the Secretary's decision not to exclude an area is wholly discretionary and therefore unreviewable. The Service bases its understanding on the second sentence of Section 4(b)(2), which states that the Secretary "*may* exclude [an] area from critical habitat if he determines that the benefits of such exclusion outweigh the benefits of [designation]."

The use of the word "may" certainly confers discretion on the Secretary. That does not, however, segregate his discretionary decision not to exclude from the procedure mandated by Section 4(b)(2), which directs the Secretary to consider the economic and other impacts of designation when making his exclusion decisions. Weyerhaeuser's claim is the familiar one in administrative law that the agency did not appropriately consider all of the relevant factors that the statute sets forth to guide the agency in the exercise of its discretion. Specifically, Weyerhaeuser contends that the Service ignored some costs and conflated the benefits of designating Unit 1 with the benefits of designating all of the proposed critical habitat. This is the sort of claim that federal courts routinely assess when determining whether to set aside an agency decision as an abuse of discretion under § 706(2)(A).

Section 4(b)(2) requires the Secretary to consider economic impact and relative benefits before deciding whether to exclude an area from critical habitat or to proceed with designation. The statute is, therefore, not "drawn so that a court would have no meaningful standard against which to judge the [Secretary's] exercise of [his] discretion" not to exclude.

Because it determined that the Service's decisions not to exclude were committed to agency discretion and therefore unreviewable, the Court of Appeals did not consider whether the Service's assessment of the costs and benefits of designation was flawed in a way that rendered the resulting decision not to exclude Unit 1 arbitrary, capricious, or an abuse of discretion. Accordingly, we remand to the Court of Appeals to consider that question, if necessary, in the first instance.

* * *

The judgment of the Court of Appeals for the Fifth Circuit is vacated, and the case is remanded for further proceedings consistent with this opinion.

*It is so ordered.*

## NOTES AND QUESTIONS

1. The Court's decision was unanimous, but Justice Kavanaugh, who joined the Court after the case was argued, did not take part in it. In light of the decision, under what circumstances, if any, can unoccupied habitat be designated as part of the critical habitat of a species? Can habitat include areas that require some modification before they can support a sustainable population of an endangered species?

2. In July 2019, the case was settled before the lower courts could rule on remand. In the settlement, the U.S. Fish and Wildlife Service agreed to remove Unit 1 (the unoccupied portion) from its designation of critical habitat.

3. In August 2019, the U.S. Fish & Wildlife Service and the National Marine Fisheries Service revised their regulations governing designation of critical habitat. 84 Fed. Reg. 45,020 (2019). The revised regulations provide that areas outside of the current range of a species should only be designated as critical habitat if it is first determined that the areas currently occupied by the species are insufficient to provide for the conservation of the species. This revision reinstates the regulatory standard that was in place from 1986 to 2016. Under the revised regulation, the Services will only consider an unoccupied area to be essential where a designation limited to the occupied areas would be inadequate to ensure the conservation of the species. The revisions also clarify that the unoccupied "area contains one or more of those physical or biological features" essential to the conservation of the species at the time of designation.

### 3. Threatened Species and Climate Change

Several species, including the polar bear and pikas, are threatened by climate change as global warming profoundly affects Arctic ecosystems. In response to a citizen petition, the FWS in January 2007 proposed listing the polar bear as a threatened species. After reviewing new research findings concerning the population of the Southern Bering Sea polar bear, the FWS reopened and later extended the comment period on its proposal. Faced with a court-ordered deadline to make a final determination, FWS in May 2008 listed the polar bear as a threatened species. 73 Fed. Reg. 28,212 (2008).

While the polar bear is threatened in large part because of the effects of climate change, the Interior Department concluded that its listing would not provide a basis for using the ESA to regulate emissions of greenhouse gases (GHG). The FWS issued section 4(d) rules for the polar bears that exempted from section 9's prohibition on "takes" any activity already authorized under the Marine Mammal Protection Act and, for any activity outside of Alaska, all "takes" incidental to a lawful purpose. 73 Fed. Reg. 28,306 (2008). The agency also issued a separate memorandum specifying that section 7(a)(2) consultations on federal agency actions need not analyze the effects of the actions' incremental GHG emissions on any listed species or their habitats because existing science and modeling are incapable of determining local, species- or habitat-specific impacts from these incremental emissions.

The decision by the Bush administration not to use the ESA to regulate emissions of GHG was controversial. However, it was embraced by the Obama administration, which did not believe the ESA is the proper vehicle for regulating GHG emissions. Andrew C. Revkin, U.S. Curbs Use of Species Act in Protecting Polar Bear, N.Y. Times, May 8, 2009. While some environmentalists believed that anything that forces action to control GHG emissions was desirable, others were concerned that an effort to use the ESA for such purposes could backfire. The already-overburdened agencies tasked with implementing the ESA easily could be overwhelmed if climate impacts had to be considered, and Congress might respond by creating new exemptions to the ESA. Some have suggested that the ESA's jeopardy and adverse modification standards could be used to require federally funded or permitted programs to be net carbon neutral in order to comply with section 7.

On October 17, 2011, federal district judge Emmett Sullivan upheld the section 4(d) rule for the threatened polar bear, which exempted emissions of greenhouse gases from liability for a "take" under section 9 of the ESA. Judge Sullivan held that section 4(d) gives the agency discretion to apply any or all of the section 9 take protections to a threatened species. In re Polar Bear Endangered Species Act Listing and 4(d) Rule Litigation, 818 F. Supp. 2d 214 (D.D.C. 2011). This judgment and the decision to list the bear as threatened were affirmed by the D.C. Circuit in March 2013. In re Polar Bear Endangered Species Act Listing and Section 4(d) Rule Litigation, 709 F.3d 1 (D.C. Cir. 2013). The court concluded: "The Listing Rule rests on a three-part thesis: the polar bear is dependent upon sea ice for its survival; sea ice is declining; and climatic changes have and will continue to dramatically reduce the extent and quality of Arctic sea ice to a degree sufficiently grave to jeopardize polar bear populations. No part of this thesis is disputed and we find that FWS's conclusion—that the polar bear is threatened within the meaning of the ESA—is reasonable and adequately supported by the record." 709 F.3d at 8. The court also upheld the use of a 45-year time frame for determining whether the polar bear is "likely to become an endangered species within the foreseeable future" to meet the definition of a threatened species. ESA §3(2), 16 U.S.C. §1532(20).

The designation of critical habitat for the polar bear in Alaska also was the subject of controversy. In October 2009, the FWS issued a proposed rule to designate more than 200,000 square miles as critical habitat. In May 2010, the FWS reopened the comment period on the proposed rule after releasing a draft economic analysis and making corrections to its proposed boundaries for sea-ice critical habitat to more accurately reflect the actual extent of U.S. territorial waters. 75 Fed. Reg. 24,545 (2010). After holding two public hearings on the new proposal in Alaska, the FWS in December 2010 issued a final rule designating critical habitat. 75 Fed. Reg. 76,086 (2010). The rule, which became effective on January 6, 2011, designated more than 187,000 square miles in Alaska and adjacent territorial and U.S. waters as critical habitat for the species. The state of Alaska sued the FWS to challenge what it called an "unprecedented, expansive designation of critical habitat for polar bears." In January 2013, federal district Judge Ralph Beistline rejected most of the state's challenges to the critical habitat designation, but found that the "current designation went too far and was too extensive." Thus, the court vacated the rule and remanded it to the FWS to correct "substantive and procedural deficiencies." Alaska Oil and Gas Ass'n v. Salazar, 916 F. Supp. 2d 974 (D. Alaska 2013). FWS and environmental intervenors appealed this decision, which was reversed by the Ninth Circuit in Alaska Oil and Gas Ass'n v. Jewell, 815 F.3d 544 (9th Cir. 2016). The court concluded that the FWS was not required to prove that polar bears currently used every part of the area designated as critical habitat.

In Alaska Oil & Gas Ass'n v. Pritzer, 840 F.3d 671 (9th Cir. 2016), the Ninth Circuit reversed another decision by Judge Beistline that had found the listing of the Pacific bearded seal subspecies as threatened to be arbitrary and capricious. The listing was based largely on the conclusion that due to climate change the seals would lose their habitat by the end of the century. The Ninth Circuit held that it was not arbitrary and capricious for the NMFS to extend the time horizon for its foreseeability analysis to the end of the century instead of 2050. The court concluded that a decision that a species is "more likely than not" to become endangered did not require quantification of species losses, an extension threshold, or extinction date.

In its August 2019 revision of ESA regulations, the FWS and NMFS define the term "foreseeable future" as extending "only so far into the future as the Services can reasonably determine that both the future threats and the species' response to those threats are likely." The determination of what is reasonably foreseeable is to be made on a case-by-case basis and the Services are not required to identify the foreseeable future in terms of a specific period of time. The regulatory revision would limit species listings predicated on long-term climate change projections, potentially reducing the number of new species listings in the future. With respect to critical habitat designations, the regulations now provide that it is not prudent to designate habitat as critical if threats to the species' habitat stem solely from causes that cannot be addressed through management actions resulting from consultations under Section 7(a)(2) of the Act. This provision was inserted in response to litigation seeking to have critical habitat designated to address impacts to habitat from climate change. The revised regulations also provide that species listed as threatened no longer automatically will receive the same protection against section 9 takes as species listed as endangered in the absence of an affirmative designation to that effect.

### 4.   Delisting Decisions and Species Recovery Plans

Species can be removed from the endangered species list through delisting determinations. By August 2017, 92 species had been delisted, 61 because the species had recovered, 11 because the species had become extinct, and 20 because the initial listing was determined to have been based on erroneous information. ECOS, Delisted Species, *https://ecos.fws.gov/ecp/report/species-delisted*. Perhaps the most dramatic recovery story is the recovery of the bald eagle in the lower 48 states, which led to its delisting in August 2007.

To promote the recovery of species, section 4(f) of the ESA requires the Secretary of Interior or the Secretary of Commerce to develop and implement "recovery plans" for the conservation and survival of species listed as endangered or threatened, unless the Secretary determines that "such a plan will not promote the conservation of the species." Of the 2,328 species listed as of August 2017, a total of 1,159 had active recovery plans. In Friends of Blackwater v. Salazar, 691 F.3d 428 (D.C. Cir. 2012), a divided panel of the D.C. Circuit held that the West Virginia Northern Flying Squirrel could be delisted even though it was uncertain whether several criteria in its recovery plan had been satisfied. The recovery plan specified that the squirrel could be delisted when "squirrel populations are stable or expanding" in at least 80 percent of certain designated areas. Yet the Fish and Wildlife Service did not have data that enabled it to estimate the actual population of the squirrels. Writing for the court majority, Judge Douglas Ginsburg noted that:

> Section 4(a)(1) of the Act provides the Secretary "shall" consider the five statutory factors when determining whether a species is endangered, and §4(c) makes clear that a decision to delist "shall be made in accordance" with the same five factors. 16 U.S.C. §1533(a), (c). Although §4(f) states the Secretary "shall develop and implement" a recovery plan and "shall . . . incorporate in [the recovery] plan . . . objective, measurable criteria," the Act does not similarly say the Secretary "shall" consult those criteria in making a delisting decision. Rather, §4(f)(1)(B)(ii) states simply that the criteria in the recovery plan should be those "which, when met, would result in a determination, in accordance with the provisions of this section, that the species be removed from the list."

The court majority rejected petitioner's argument "that interpreting the Recovery Plan as non-binding would render §4(f) of the Act a nullity." It noted that "with an exception not relevant here, §4(f) obliges the Secretary to 'develop and implement plans' for the recovery of any species designated as endangered. 16 U.S.C. §1533(f)(1). If the Secretary wants to change the plan, then he first must let the public comment. It does not follow, however, that with each criterion he includes in a recovery plan the Secretary places a further obligation upon the Service." The court then upheld the Secretary's interpretation that the ESA did not require the criteria in a species recovery plan to be satisfied before a species could be delisted "pursuant to the factors in the Act itself." In their 2019 revisions to ESA regulations the FWS and NMFS provided that a species can be delisted if it satisfies the factors to be considered for delisting, even if delisting conflicts with a recovery plan for the species. 84 Fed. Reg. 45020, at 45036.

## Protection of Biodiversity: A Pathfinder

The Endangered Species Act (ESA) is codified at 16 U.S.C. §§1531-1544. It is administered by the Secretaries of Interior, whose Fish and Wildlife Service (FWS) has responsibility for protecting endangered plants, fish and wildlife, and the Secretary of Commerce, whose National Marine Fisheries Service (NMFS) has the responsibility for protecting marine life. These two agencies have jointly promulgated regulations to govern implementation of the Act; they appear at 50 C.F.R. pt. 402. The official list of endangered and threatened species can be found in 50 C.F.R. pt. 17.

The U.S. Fish and Wildlife Service maintains an endangered species webpage, which is located at *http://endangered.fws.gov/index.html*. This page contains a list of species on the endangered species list, news concerning biodiversity protection, and information about the operation of the ESA and agencies' policies for promoting biodiversity. In 1996, the FWS and NMFS jointly published a Habitat Conservation Planning Handbook, which was revised and updated in 2016. Habitat Conservation Planning and Incidental Take Permit Process Handbook, *https://www.fws.gov/endangered/esa-library/pdf/HCP_Handbook.pdf*. The Handbook provides landowners with guidance concerning how to develop habitat conservation plans to qualify for incidental take permits under section 10 of the ESA. A useful factsheet on the process is FWS, Habitat Conservation Plans Under the Endangered Species Act, which is available at *https://www.fws.gov/endangered/esa-library/pdf/hcp.pdf*.

The most definitive treatise on the ESA and other wildlife protection statutes is Michael Bean's The Evolution of National Wildlife Law (3d ed. 1997), published by Praeger. Among the best scientific introductions to the biodiversity protection issues are E.O. Wilson's Biodiversity (1986), published by National Academy Press; The Diversity of Life (1992), published by Harvard University Press; and The Future of Life (2002). Endangered Species: A Documentary and Reference Guide (2016) by Edward P. Weber, published by ABC-CLIO, examines species conservation efforts in the United States and worldwide over the last 200 years. Current biodiversity scholarship is contained in the journals Conservation Biology, a bi-monthly, peer-reviewed scientific journal of the Society for Conservation Biology published by Wiley-Blackwell, and BioScience, a monthly, peer-reviewed scientific journal published by Oxford University Press for the American Institute of Biological Sciences.

The World Wildlife Fund's Living Planet Report provides a comprehensive overview of the state of biodiversity on the planet and reviews how to "bend the curve" to slow the rate of biodiversity loss. The 2020 report is available online at *https://www.worldwildlife.org/publications/living-planet-report-2020*. An independent review of the economics of biodiversity, released in February 2021, is The Economics of Biodiversity: The Dasgupta Report, available online at *https://assets.publishing.service.gov.uk/government/uploads/system/uploads/attachment_data/file/957291/Dasgupta_Review_-_Full_Report.pdf*.

## E.   REVIEW OF FEDERAL ACTIONS: SECTION 7

The most important protection accorded endangered and threatened species is contained in section 7, the provision made famous by *TVA v. Hill*. As that case explained, section 7 provides for review of all federal actions that may affect endangered species, and section 7(a)(2) prohibits those actions that are found to "jeopardize" the existence of any such species. These include not only activities undertaken directly by federal agencies, but also nonfederal actions that involve federal authorization or assistance, such as activities that require federal permits, are funded by federal agencies, or are undertaken by private parties on public lands. Section 7(a)(1) directs agencies to use their authorities to further the purposes of ESA by carrying out affirmative programs to conserve listed species. The following case explains the "consultation" process that section 7 establishes and the authorities that section provides.

## Thomas v. Peterson

753 F.2d 754 (9th Cir. 1985)

Before Wright, Sneed, and Alarcon, Circuit Judges.

Sneed, Circuit Judge:

Plaintiffs sought to enjoin construction of a timber road in a former National Forest roadless area. The District Court granted summary judgment in favor of defendant R. Max Peterson, Chief of the Forest Service, and plaintiffs appealed. We affirm in part, reverse in part, and remand for further proceedings consistent with this opinion. . . .

### THE ENDANGERED SPECIES ACT CLAIM

The plaintiffs' third claim concerns the Forest Service's alleged failure to comply with the Endangered Species Act (ESA) in considering the effects of the road and timber sales on the endangered Rocky Mountain Gray Wolf.

The ESA contains both substantive and procedural provisions. Substantively, the Act prohibits the taking or importation of endangered species, see 16 U.S.C. §1538, and requires federal agencies to ensure that their actions are not "likely to jeopardize the continued existence of any endangered species or threatened species or result in the destruction or adverse modification" of critical habitat of such species, see 16 U.S.C. §1536(a)(2).

The Act prescribes a three-step process to ensure compliance with its substantive provisions by federal agencies. Each of the first two steps serves a screening function to determine if the successive steps are required. The steps are:

> (1) An agency proposing to take an action must inquire of the Fish & Wildlife Service (F & WS) whether any threatened or endangered species "may be present" in the area of the proposed action. See 16 U.S.C. §1536(c)(1).
>
> (2) If the answer is affirmative, the agency must prepare a "biological assessment" to determine whether such species "is likely to be affected" by the action. Id. The biological assessment may be part of an environmental impact statement or environmental assessment. Id.
>
> (3) If the assessment determines that a threatened or endangered species "is likely to be affected," the agency must formally consult with the F & WS. Id. §1536(a)(2). The formal consultation results in a "biological opinion" issued by the F & WS. See id. §1536(b). If the biological opinion concludes that the proposed action would jeopardize the species or destroy or adversely modify critical habitat, see id. §1536(a)(2), then the action may not go forward

unless the F & WS can suggest an alternative that avoids such jeopardization, destruction, or adverse modification. Id. §1536(b)(3)(A). If the opinion concludes that the action will not violate the Act, the F & WS may still require measures to minimize its impact. Id. §1536(b)(4)(ii)-(iii).

Plaintiffs first allege that, with respect to the Jersey Jack road, the Forest Service did not undertake step (1), a formal request to the F & WS. The district court found that to be the case, but concluded that the procedural violation was insignificant because the Forest Service was already aware that wolves may be present in the area. The court therefore refused to enjoin the construction of the road. Plaintiffs insist, based on TVA v. Hill, 437 U.S. 153 (1978), that an injunction is mandatory once any ESA violation is found. Defendants respond, citing Village of False Pass v. Clark, 733 F.2d 605 (9th Cir. 1984), that *TVA* applies only to substantive violations of the ESA, and that a court has discretion to deny an injunction when it finds a procedural violation to be de minimis.

We need not reach this issue. The Forest Service's failure goes beyond the technical violation cited by the district court, and is not de minimis.

Once an agency is aware that an endangered species may be present in the area of its proposed action, the ESA requires it to prepare a biological assessment to determine whether the proposed action "is likely to affect" the species and therefore requires formal consultation with the F & WS. See supra. The Forest Service did not prepare such an assessment prior to its decision to build the Jersey Jack road. Without a biological assessment, it cannot be determined whether the proposed project will result in a violation of the ESA's substantive provisions. A failure to prepare a biological assessment for a project in an area in which it has been determined that an endangered species may be present cannot be considered a de minimis violation of the ESA.

The district court found that the Forest Service had "undertaken sufficient study and action to further the purposes of the ESA," Memorandum Decision at 1149, E.R. 103. Its finding was based on affidavits submitted by the Forest Service for the litigation. These do not constitute a substitute for the preparation of the biological assessment required by the ESA.

. . . The procedural requirements of the ESA are analogous to those of NEPA: under NEPA, agencies are required to evaluate the environmental impact of federal projects "significantly affecting the quality of the human environment," 42 U.S.C. §4332(2)(C); under the ESA, agencies are required to assess the effect on endangered species of projects in areas where such species may be present. 16 U.S.C. §1536(c). A failure to prepare a biological assessment is comparable to a failure to prepare an environmental impact statement. . . .

The Forest Service argues that the procedural requirements of the ESA should be enforced less stringently than those of NEPA because, unlike NEPA, the ESA also contains substantive provisions. We acknowledge that the ESA's substantive provisions distinguish it from NEPA, but the distinction acts the other way. If anything, the strict substantive provisions of the ESA justify *more* stringent enforcement of its procedural requirements, because the procedural requirements are designed to ensure compliance with the substantive provisions. The ESA's procedural requirements call for a systematic determination of the effects of a federal project on endangered species. If a project is allowed to proceed without substantial compliance with those procedural requirements, there can be no assurance that a violation of the ESA's substantive provisions will not result. The latter, of course, is impermissible. See TVA v. Hill, 437 U.S. 153.

The district court, citing Palila v. Hawaii Dept. of Land and Natural Resources, 639 F.2d 495 (9th Cir. 1981), held that "[a] party asserting a violation of the Endangered Species Act has the burden of showing the proposed action would have some prohibited effect on an endangered species or its critical habitat," and found that the plaintiffs in this case had not met that burden. This is a misapplication of *Palila*. That case concerned the ESA's prohibition of the "taking" of an endangered species, not the ESA's procedural requirements. Quite naturally, the court in *Palila* found that a plaintiff, in order to establish a violation of the "taking" provision, must show that such a "taking" has occurred. The holding does not apply to violations of the ESA's procedural requirements. A plaintiff's burden in establishing a procedural violation is to show that the circumstances triggering the procedural requirement exist, and that the required procedures have not been followed. The plaintiffs in this case have clearly met that burden.

. . . Congress has assigned to the agencies and to the Fish & Wildlife Service the responsibility for evaluation of the impact of agency actions on endangered species, and has prescribed procedures for such evaluation. Only by following the procedures can proper evaluation be made. It is not the responsibility of the plaintiffs to prove, nor the function of the courts to judge, the effect of a proposed action on an endangered species when proper procedures have not been followed.

We therefore hold that the district court erred in declining to enjoin construction of the Jersey Jack road pending compliance with the ESA.

Affirmed in part, reversed in part, and remanded.

## NOTES AND QUESTIONS

1. The ESA imposes a graduated review requirement somewhat reminiscent of NEPA's hierarchy of categorical exclusion, environmental assessment, and environmental impact statement. Recall that under NEPA, the proponent of an action makes each determination about what review NEPA requires. How is ESA different? How are the key determinations made? Who finally determines whether an action may go forward? The Secretary of Interior, who is responsible for protecting freshwater and terrestrial species, has delegated his responsibilities under ESA to FWS. The Secretary of Commerce, who is responsible for protecting most marine species, has delegated his responsibilities under ESA to the National Marine Fisheries Service (NMFS).

2. In Cottonwood Envtl. Law Ctr. v. U.S. Forest Serv., 789 F.3d 1075 (9th Cir. 2015), the Forest Service argued that the Supreme Court's decisions in *Winter v. Natural Resources Defense Council* and *Monsanto v. Geertson Seed Farms* effectively had overruled *Thomas*'s presumption of irreparable harm from a procedural violation of the ESA. Those decisions, which are discussed in Chapter 8, involved procedural violations of NEPA. But the Ninth Circuit found that "even though *Winter* and *Monsanto* address NEPA, not the ESA, they nonetheless undermine the theoretical foundation for our prior rulings on injunctive relief in *Thomas* and its progeny." The court therefore concluded "that there is no presumption of irreparable injury

where there has been a procedural violation in ESA cases. A plaintiff must show irreparable injury to justify injunctive relief." However, the court went on to note that "[i]n light of the stated purposes of the ESA in conserving endangered and threatened species and the ecosystems that support them, establishing irreparable injury should not be an onerous task for plaintiffs." 789 F.3d at 1091.

3. A study of the consultation process by the World Wildlife Fund found that nearly 100,000 section 7 consultations were undertaken between the FWS and other federal agencies during a five-year period. Approximately 95,000 of these were rapid, informal consultations, many of which occurred by telephone, and resulted in no delay or modification of a project. A total of 2,719 formal consultations occurred with 2,367 (87 percent) resulting in "no jeopardy" opinions. Only 352 "jeopardy" opinions were issued, and more than one-third of these involved only two proposed projects. Only 54 projects were terminated during the five-year period. Thus, only 0.3 percent of all consultations resulted in jeopardy opinions, and the vast majority of these projects were able to proceed after adopting "reasonable and prudent" alternatives identified by FWS in its opinion. World Wildlife Fund, Talk Is Cheaper Than We Think: The Consultation Process Under the Endangered Species Act (1994).

4. After reviewing many of the jeopardy findings, Oliver Houck concludes that "the great majority of them allowed projects to go forward with only minimal harm-avoiding conditions, such as 'don't dredge while the eagles are nesting,' speed limit signs in manatee waters, and a wider median strip in a federal highway routed through wolf habitat to enable wolves to pause safely while crossing." Houck, Reflections on the Endangered Species Act, 25 Envtl. L. Rep. 689, 692 (1995). Describing a variety of strategies employed by the Department of Interior to avoid jeopardy findings, Professor Houck concludes that the agency is "doing everything possible within law, and beyond, to limit the effect of protection under section 7(a)(2)." Houck, The Endangered Species Act and Its Implementation by the U.S. Departments of Interior and Commerce, 64 U. Colo. L. Rev. 277, 326 (1993).

5. A dramatic decline in the stocks of salmon in the Pacific Northwest resulted in the addition of several salmon species to the endangered species list. As a result, federal and state agencies in the area struggled to develop plans for protecting the salmon. In Pacific Rivers Council v. Thomas, 30 F.3d 1050 (9th Cir. 1994), the Ninth Circuit required a district court to enjoin all federal logging, grazing, and road construction projects in two national forests pending consultations between the Forest Service and NMFS concerning efforts to protect the Snake River Salmon. The intersection of section 7's consultation requirements and the high degree of federal involvement in resource management in the Pacific Northwest has had profound consequences because it has subjected many policies to systematic biological scrutiny for the first time, including fish hatchery practices, harvest management, and habitat management. This has created the "prospect of designing a restoration program that would address all major sources of salmon mortality, including public land and water use decisionmaking, not just hydropower." Michael C. Blumm & Greg D. Corbin, Salmon and the Endangered Species Act: Lessons from the Columbia Basin, 74 Wash. L. Rev. 519, 589 (1999). Based on their review of the consequences of the salmon listings in the Pacific Northwest, Blumm and Corbin

conclude that "contrary to some claims, the effect of ESA consultation is hardly draconian, and in fact is quite sensitive to economic considerations." Id. at 549. They note that the absence of a statutory definition of jeopardy has enabled the NMFS to accept "fairly modest probabilities for species recovery" and that key measures to protect salmon provided in NMFS's biological opinions (such as a reservoir drawdown) have not been implemented because of concern over their economic impact. Id. at 593-597. Federal officials are continuing to develop plans for protecting the endangered salmon.

6. In April 2001, a decision to stop the flow of federal irrigation water in California's Klamath River Basin to protect endangered salmon and suckerfish spawned harsh protests by farmers and ranchers who forcibly reopened the irrigation canal. After a new and highly controversial biological opinion was issued by the National Marine Fisheries Service, the Bush administration ordered the irrigation flows restored. In September 2002, 33,000 wild salmon suddenly died in a massive fish kill in the Klamath River. While federal officials deemed the cause of the fish kill a mystery, scientists from the California Department of Fish and Game released a report in January 2003 that attributed the fish kill to the federal diversions of water for irrigation.

7. The determination whether an action is likely to "jeopardize" a listed species must be based on "the best scientific and commercial data available." As several courts have indicated, the ESA's requirement that the agencies use the best available data does not require the agency to conduct new research, but rather only to seek out and consider existing scientific information. Heartwood, Inc. v. U.S. Forest Service, 380 F.3d 428, 436 (9th Cir. 2004).

8. The question of how to develop the best scientific data available has been a source of continuing controversy. Among the events triggering controversy over protection of endangered salmon in the Pacific Northwest was a court's rejection of a "no jeopardy" determination by the NMFS in its 1993 biological opinion on the effects of hydroelectric operations on salmon. The NMFS had premised its "no jeopardy" finding on the grounds that the salmon would experience improved survival over a base period of 1986-1990 and that salmon populations would stabilize within 15 years. The court found that the selection of a baseline period of 1986-1990 was not biologically sound because it involved years of drought and low salmon runs and that the NMFS had not employed the "best available" scientific information because it had ignored the views of scientists from states and tribes. Idaho Dep't of Fish & Game v. National Marine Fisheries Service, 850 F. Supp. 886 (D. Or. 1994). In September 1999, another NMFS "no jeopardy" determination was struck down because the agency had not assessed compliance at the project or site level and had failed to consider the short-term impacts of timber sales on endangered salmon. The court held that the agency's approach virtually guaranteed that no timber sale ever would be found to jeopardize salmon despite overwhelming evidence of ongoing degradation of their habitat. Pacific Coast Federation of Fishermen's Association v. National Marine Fisheries Service, 71 F. Supp. 2d 1063 (W.D. Wash. 1999).

9. Criticism of the science employed in connection with salmon recovery planning has led to the creation of an independent group of scientists to advise the agencies. Following the *Idaho Dep't of Fish & Game* decision, the NMFS's next

biological opinion on the effects of hydroelectric operations on salmon established a process called the Plan for Analyzing and Testing Hypotheses (PATH). PATH uses a working group of 25 scientists from federal and state agencies, Indian tribes, and academia who advise the agency on options for species recovery. Michael C. Blumm & Greg D. Corbin, Salmon and the Endangered Species Act: Lessons from the Columbia Basin, 74 Wash. L. Rev. 519, 558 (1999).

10. On March 4, 2021, the U.S. Supreme Court ruled 7-2 that a draft biological opinion shared by the U.S. Fish and Wildlife Service with EPA was protected from being disclosed under the federal Freedom of Information Act (FOIA) by the deliberative process privilege. The decision, the first written by Justice Amy Coney Barrett, reversed a Ninth Circuit decision (Sierra Club v. U.S. Fish & Wildlife Service, 925 F.3d 1000 (9th Cir. 2019)) that had required disclosure of the opinion. In her majority opinion Justice Barrett held that the deliberative process privilege protects from disclosure under FOIA in-house draft biological opinions that are both predecisional and deliberative, even if the drafts reflect the agencies' last views about a proposal. Dissenting Justice Breyer noted that the process of "determining whether an agency's position is final for purposes of the deliberative process privilege is a functional rather than formal inquiry" and that the privilege would not apply if "an agency has hidden a functionally final decision in draft form." U.S. Fish & Wildlife Service v. Sierra Club, Inc., 141 S.Ct. 777 (2021). Justice Breyer noted that it is "the Draft Biological Opinion, not the Final Biological Opinion" that informs agencies of the Services' conclusions about jeopardy and alternatives, noting that out of 6,829 formal consultations between 2008 and 2015, FWS issued a Final Biological Opinion finding jeopardy only twice. Thus he concluded that drafts of Draft Biological Opinions were protected from disclosure, but not the Draft Biological Opinions themselves.

### Section 7 Consultations and Delegation of Clean Water Act Permitting Authority

In American Forest and Paper Ass'n v. U.S. EPA, 137 F.3d 291 (5th Cir. 1998), the Fifth Circuit held that EPA could not require, as a condition for delegating operation of the Clean Water Act's NPDES permitting program to Louisiana, that the state consult with the U.S. Fish and Wildlife Service (FWS) and the National Marine Fisheries Service (NMFS) before issuing permits. Although Louisiana had consented to the arrangement, which allowed EPA to exercise its authority to veto permits if the federal agencies found that they threatened endangered species, a trade association of forest and paper products firms sued EPA to challenge it. The Fifth Circuit held that the arrangement exceeded EPA's authority because the Clean Water Act did not specifically enumerate protection of endangered species as a ground for denying delegation to a state. While acknowledging that ESA section 7(a)(2) requires EPA to consult with FWS or NMFS before undertaking action that may jeopardize species, the court held that the section confers no substantive powers on the agency to condition delegations of NPDES permitting authority.

In National Ass'n of Homebuilders v. Defenders of Wildlife, 551 U.S. 644 (2007), the Supreme Court, by a vote of 5-4, held that §7(a)(2)'s no-jeopardy duty covers only discretionary agency actions and does not attach to actions (like the NPDES permitting transfer authorization) that an agency is *required* by statute to undertake once certain specified triggering events have occurred. Writing for the majority, Justice Alito stated that this "reading not only is reasonable, inasmuch as it gives effect to the ESA's provision, but also comports with the canon against implied repeals because it stays §7(a)(2)'s mandate where it would effectively override otherwise mandatory statutory duties." The Court concluded that since "the transfer of NPDES permitting authority is not discretionary, but rather is mandated once a State has met the criteria set forth in §402(b) of the CWA, it follows that a transfer of NPDES permitting authority does not trigger §7(a)(2)'s consultation and no-jeopardy requirements."

If this decision only affects EPA delegations of permitting authority to states under the Clean Water Act, it is unlikely to have significant future consequences because EPA already has delegated such authority to nearly every state and several territories. However, the decision's true impact likely will turn on how broad is the class of other agency actions that courts will deem to be nondiscretionary. In dissent, Justice Stevens argued that the Court's decision was inconsistent with *TVA v. Hill.* Justice Alito suggested that the decision to continue with construction of the Tellico Dam was discretionary, which could indicate that the class of agency actions that will be deemed nondiscretionary may not be very large.

In his dissent, Justice Stevens cites the "God Squad" procedure established by section 7(e) of the ESA as embodying "the primacy of the ESA's mandate" and "the final mechanism for harmonizing that Act with other federal statutes." In Stevens's view, the "God Squad" process "reflects Congress' view that the ESA should not yield to another federal action except as a final resort and except when authorized by high level officials after serious consideration."

Justice Breyer filed a separate dissent where he indicated that he was reserving judgment concerning whether section 7(a)(2) "really covers every possible agency action even of totally unrelated agencies — such as, say, a discretionary determination by the Internal Revenue Service whether to prosecute or settle a particular tax liability." But he argued that "the majority cannot possibly be correct in concluding that the structure of §402(b) precludes application of §7(a)(2) to the EPA's discretionary action." He emphasized that statutes granting "discretionary authority always come with *some* implicit limits attached," but there "are likely numerous instances in which, prior to, but not after, the enactment of §7(a)(2), the statute might have implicitly placed 'species preservation' outside those limits," citing *TVA v. Hill.* He concluded that "the only meaningful difference" between section 402(b) of the Clean Water Act, and such other statutes is that "the very purpose of the former is to preserve the state of our natural environment — a purpose that the Endangered Species Act shares," which "shows that §7(a)(2) must apply to the Clean Water Act *a fortiori.*"

In Karuk Tribe of California v. U.S. Forest Service, 681 F.3d 1006 (9th Cir. 2012), the U.S. Court of Appeals for the Ninth Circuit, sitting en banc, addressed the discretionary acts principle of *NAHB v. Defenders of Wildlife.* An Indian tribe argued that the Forest Service had violated the ESA by approving four notices of intent to conduct mining activities in the critical habitat of the threatened coho salmon without conducting section 7 consultations with federal wildlife agencies. The court rejected the Forest Service's claim that consultation was not required under *NAHB v. Defenders.* The court stated that "to avoid the consultation obligation, an agency's competing statutory mandate must require that it perform specific nondiscretionary acts rather than achieve broad goals." The court concluded that "[t]o trigger the ESA consultation requirement, the discretionary control retained by the federal agency also must have the capacity to inure to the benefit of a protected species." The court held that the Forest Service's decision whether to approve a notice of intent to mine "is a discretionary determination through which the agency can influence private mining activities to benefit listed species." Thus, it found that consultation was required under section 7 of the ESA. In a bitter dissent, Judge Milan Smith, Jr., citing Jonathan Swift's classic novel *Gulliver's Travels*, blasted the Ninth Circuit's environmental decisions as "undermin[ing] the rule of law, and mak[ing] poor Gulliver's situation seem fortunate when compared to the plight of those entangled in the ligatures of new rules created out of thin air by such decisions." Id. at 1031 (Smith, J., dissenting).

In Alaska Wilderness League v. Jewell, 788 F.3d 1212 (9th Cir. 2015), the Ninth Circuit applied the *Home Builders* "discretionary control" principle to hold that the Bureau of Safety and Environmental Enforcement (BSEE) was not required to consult before approving oil spill response plans because BSEE has a mandatory duty to approve plans that meet the statutory criteria. But in Cottonwood Envtl. Law Ctr. v. U.S. Forest Serv., 789 F.3d 1075 (9th Cir. 2015), a Ninth Circuit panel held that the Forest Service was required to reinitiate consultation at a programmatic level when it expanded the critical habitat designation for the Canadian lynx to include land in national forests. The court noted that the Forest Service had ongoing discretion to take actions to protect the lynx, even though it had finalized its forest plan before revising the critical habitat designation.

When applying section 7, agencies and courts have focused on the "no jeopardy" proscription of section 7(a)(2). But section 7 proclaims a broader, more affirmative mandate, as outlined in the next case.

## Carson-Truckee Water Conservancy District v. Clark

741 F.2d 257 (9th Cir. 1984)

Before DUNIWAY, Senior Circuit Judge, PREGERSON, and NORRIS, Circuit Judges.

PREGERSON, Circuit Judge:

The Carson-Truckee Water Conservancy District and Sierra Pacific Power Company (appellants) sought a declaratory judgment that the Secretary of the Interior (Secretary) violated the Washoe Project Act, 43 U.S.C.A. §§614-614d (West 1964) and related reclamation laws in refusing to sell water from the Stampede Dam and Reservoir on the Little Truckee River for municipal and industrial (M & I) use in Reno and Sparks. In addition, Nevada sought a determination that the Secretary was required to obtain a permit from the Nevada State Engineer to operate the Stampede Dam in California. The Pyramid Lake Paiute Tribe of Indians (Tribe) intervened in support of the Secretary. We affirm in part and vacate in part.

### FACTUAL BACKGROUND AND DISTRICT COURT DECISIONS

. . . The Little Truckee River flows into the Truckee River, which then flows from California into Nevada and into Pyramid Lake. Stampede Dam is located on the Little Truckee in California. The Secretary now operates Stampede Dam in a way that conserves two species of fish, the cui-ui fish and Lahontan cutthroat trout, that are protected under the Endangered Species Act (ESA), 16 U.S.C. §§1531-1543 (1982). Appellants concede that the Secretary's obligations under ESA supersede his obligations under the Washoe Project Act and related federal reclamation laws. Appellants, however, challenge the extent of the Secretary's obligations under ESA. . . .

[The District Court held that the Secretary is required to sell water from Stampede Dam not needed to fulfill his trust obligations to the Tribe and his obligations under ESA, that ESA required the Secretary to give priority to conserving the cui-ui fish and Lahontan cutthroat trout as long as they were endangered and threatened, and that the Secretary's finding that there was no excess water to sell after fulfilling those statutory obligations was not arbitrary. The appellants challenged the court's interpretation of the ESA.]

Appellants urge a reading of ESA that would lead to a result at odds with the statute's clearly stated objectives. Appellants contend that the Secretary's authority is defined solely by ESA §7(a)(2), 16 U.S.C. §1536(a)(2). Thus, they argue that the Secretary is authorized only to take actions that avoid "jeopardizing" the continued existence of a species. Appellants contend that the Secretary may not do more than that.

In addition to its §7(a)(2) "jeopardy" provision, however, ESA also directs the Secretary to conserve threatened and endangered species to the extent that they are no longer threatened or endangered. Appellants, relying solely on §7(a)(2), would have us ignore the other sections of ESA directly applicable here and relied on by the district court. *Carson-Truckee II*, 549 F. Supp. At 708-710. ESA §2(b), (c), & §3(3), 16 U.S.C. §1531(b), (c), & §1532(3). ESA §7(a)(1), moreover, specifically directs that the Secretary "shall" use programs administered by him to further the conservation purposes of ESA. 16 U.S.C. §1536(a)(1). Those sections, as the district court found, direct that the Secretary actively pursue a species conservation policy. See also Tennessee Valley Authority v. Hill, 437 U.S. 153, 184 (1978) (ESA requires the Secretary to give highest priority to the preservation of endangered species; Congress intended to "halt *and reverse* the trend toward species extinction, whatever the cost." (emphasis added)).

The purpose of ESA §7(a)(2) is to ensure that the federal government does not undertake actions, such as building a dam or highway, that incidentally jeopardize the existence of endangered or threatened species. See TVA v. Hill, 437 U.S. 153 for an example of §7(a)(2)'s application. Contrary to appellants' contention, ESA §7(a)(2) is inapplicable here because the Secretary has not undertaken a project that threatens an endangered species. Instead, following the mandate of ESA §7(a)(1), §2(b), (c), & §3(3), 16 U.S.C. §1536(a)(1), §1531(c), (b), & §1532(3), the Secretary actively seeks to conserve endangered species. Thus, the district court properly applied ESA §2(b), (c), §3(3) rather than ESA §7(a)(2) to this case.

Applying the proper code sections to this case, the Secretary's decision is well justified. The Washoe Project Act anticipates but does not require the Secretary to sell water to recover project construction costs. See supra 741 F.2d at 260-261. ESA, on the other hand, directs the Secretary to use programs under his control for conservation purposes where threatened or endangered species are involved. Following this directive, the Secretary here decided to conserve the fish and not to sell the project's water. Given these circumstances, the ESA supports the Secretary's decision to give priority to the fish until such time as they no longer need ESA's protection.

## NOTES AND QUESTIONS

1. In September 1994, 12 federal agencies entered into a Memorandum of Understanding with the U.S. Fish and Wildlife Service (FWS) and the National Marine Fisheries Service (NMFS) to coordinate their species conservation efforts on the nearly 600 million acres of land and water resources they are responsible for managing. Professor J.B. Ruhl argues that this agreement provides a promising avenue for transforming section 7(a)(1)'s directive that agencies carry out programs to conserve endangered species into a powerful tool to promote species conservation. Ruhl, Section 7(a)(1) of the "New" Endangered Species Act: Rediscovering and Redefining the Untapped Power of Federal Agencies' Duty to Conserve Species, 25 Envtl. L. Rep. 1107 (1995).

2. Professor Ruhl describes the *Carson-Truckee* decision as an example of using section 7(a)(1) as a shield to defend prior agency action. He maintains that section 7(a)(1) also creates a duty to conserve that could be used "as a sword requiring a federal agency to maximize use of *significant* conservation measures in its action selection and [to] justify any departure from full attention to species conservation with relevant factors," such as countervailing statutory directives. Cf. Florida Key Deer v. Stickney, 864 F. Supp. 1222 (S.D. Fla. 1994) (agency failure to consider effects on endangered species of issuing new flood insurance policies in last remaining habitat of endangered deer violates section 7(a)(1)); Platte River Whooping Crane Critical Habitat Maintenance Trust v. FERC, 962 F.2d 27 (D.C. Cir. 1992) (section 7(a)(1) does not require FERC to evaluate the need for conditioning annual licensing of hydroelectric projects on measures to protect wildlife). Professor Ruhl also suggests that section 7(a)(1) could be used "as a prod" to require "each federal agency to implement all species conservation measures that are within the scope of the agency's authority, but which do not necessarily depend for their initiation or effect on the agency proposing or taking an action pursuant to the agency's primary mission authorities." Id. at 1137.

3. In Sierra Club v. Glickman, 156 F.3d 606 (5th Cir. 1998), the Fifth Circuit interpreted section 7(a)(1) as imposing "an affirmative duty on each federal agency to conserve each of the [species listed under section 4]." Id. at 616. Thus, it upheld a district court decision that the U.S. Department of Agriculture, which funded irrigation programs using the Edwards Aquifer in Texas, had violated section 7(a)(1) by failing to consult with the U.S. Fish and Wildlife Service and to develop programs to conserve endangered species dependent upon springs fed by the aquifer. The court rejected the notion that section 7(a)(1)'s obligations were too vague to be judicially reviewable.

4. In Florida Key Deer v. Paulison, 522 F.3d 1133 (11th Cir. 2008), the court held that a rating system developed by the Federal Emergency Management Agency (FEMA) for the National Flood Insurance Program was inconsistent with section 7(a)(1). The court noted that agencies have considerable discretion in establishing conservation programs under section 7(a)(1), but that they must actually be programs that will provide more than an insignificant conservation benefit. The program adopted by FEMA was voluntary and there was no evidence that it had produced any conservation benefits, according to the court.

### Clarifying the Section 7 Consultation Process: Defining Adverse Modification of Critical Habitat

While section 7(a)(2) is the "principal action-forcing mechanism in the ESA," Donald C. Baur, Michael J. Bean & William Robert Irvin, A Recovery Plan for the Endangered Species Act, 39 Envtl. L. Rep. 10006 (2009), it remains unclear precisely what actions it prohibits. The statutory language prohibits actions that are "likely to jeopardize the continued existence of any endangered species or threatened species or result in the destruction or adverse modification of habitat of such species which is determined . . . to be critical." For years the agencies implementing the ESA defined both "jeopardy" and "adverse modification of critical habitat" to mean the same thing—impacts that "appreciably diminish" prospects for "both the survival and recovery of a listed species." However, both the Fifth Circuit and the Ninth Circuit have invalidated this definition, Sierra Club v. Fish & Wildlife Service, 245 F.3d 434 (5th Cir. 2001); Gifford Pinchot Task Force v. Fish & Wildlife Service, 378 F.3d 1059 (9th Cir. 2004), reasoning that "adverse modification" must mean more than "mere survival."

In August 2008, the Bush administration proposed comprehensive changes in the section 7(a)(2) consultation process that were intended to remove most sources of GHG emissions from the process. As adopted on December 16, 2008, the Bush rules changed the definition of indirect effects of agency actions to include only effects that are an "essential cause" of the action and not just a "but for" cause, "reasonably certain to occur," and based on "clear and substantial information." They also specified that the section 7(a)(2) process would not apply to actions where no "take" is anticipated from the action and the effects of the action "are manifested through global processes" and "cannot be reliably predicted or measured at the scale of a listed species' current range" or "would result at most in extremely small, insignificant impact on a listed species or critical habitat" or "are such that the potential risk of harm to a listed species or critical habitat is remote," or the effects "are not capable of being measured or detected in a manner that permits meaningful evaluation." However, these regulations were rescinded by the Obama administration on April 28, 2009, pursuant to a specific appropriations rider authorizing this action. Effective March 2016 the Obama administration promulgated new regulations defining "destruction or adverse modification" to mean "a direct or indirect alteration that appreciably diminishes the value of critical habitat for the conservation of a listed species." The regulations clarify that such "alterations may include, but are not limited to, those that alter the physical or biological features essential to the conservation of a species or that preclude or significantly delay development of such features." 81 Fed. Reg. 7214.

## F.   PROTECTION AGAINST PRIVATE ACTION: SECTION 9

By its terms, section 7 applies only to federal actions. The Endangered Species Act also provides listed species some protection against private actions. Section 9 prohibits any "person" (including any corporation or other private entity, and any government agency) from taking, selling, importing, or exporting any protected species. 16 U.S.C. §1532(13). These provisions are designed to stop the trade in live animals, skins, and other parts that threatens the existence of many species, such as parrots, alligators, and elephants. But section 9 provides even broader restrictions on private action because of the prohibition on takings. As noted in *TVA v. Hill*, the term "take" is defined by section 3(19) of the Act to mean: "to harass, harm, pursue, hunt, shoot, wound, kill, trap, capture, or collect, or to attempt to engage in any such conduct."

In Palila v. Hawaii Department of Land and Natural Resources, 639 F.2d 495 (9th Cir. 1981), the Ninth Circuit affirmed a district court decision requiring Hawaiian officials to remove feral sheep and goats from the critical habitat of an endangered bird. These animals, which had been placed on the island by state officials to promote sport hunting, were found to be harming mamane trees. The endangered Palila, a bird found only in a small area on the upper slopes of Mauna Kea on the island of Hawaii, depends on mamane trees for food. Noting that "'[h]arm' is defined to include activity that results in significant environmental modification or degradation of the endangered animal's habitat," the Ninth Circuit held that the state violated section 9 of ESA by "maintaining feral sheep and goats in the critical habitat . . . since it was shown that the Palila was endangered by the activity."

Following the *Palila I* decision, the Secretary of Interior in 1981 sought to clarify the "take" prohibition in section 9 of the ESA by defining "harm" as:

> an act which actually kills or injures wildlife. Such act may include significant habitat modification or degradation where it actually kills or injures wildlife by significantly impairing essential behavioral patterns, including breeding, feeding, or sheltering. [50 C.F.R. §17.3 (1985).]

This definition became the focus of new litigation over the Palila bird in 1986. Having removed the feral sheep and goats, Hawaiian officials were still trying to maintain a mouflon (wild) sheep population for sport hunting on the island. Based on new research showing that the mouflon sheep also harmed the mamane trees, the Sierra Club filed suit to have the mouflon sheep removed.

When the district court decided *Palila I* in 1979, it was estimated that only 1,400 to 1,600 Palila remained. By 1986, approximately 2,200 Palila were on the island. Noting that the Palila population had grown since *Palila I*, state officials argued that there was no evidence that the mouflon sheep actually were harming the bird. However, the state's own experts conceded that the mouflon sheep, by eating the mamane, were degrading the mamane forest and suppressing its regeneration, and that continued degradation could drive the Palila into extinction because they depend on the mamane for food. The state argued that this indirect effect on the Palila was only a "potential" injury not encompassed within the Secretary's redefinition of "harm." The district court rejected this defense.

In *Palila II* (Palila v. Hawaii Department of Land and Natural Resources, 649 F. Supp. 1070 (D. Haw. 1986)), the court held that a finding of "harm" did not require a showing of death to individual members of a species, but rather only "an adverse impact on the protected species." Thus, the district court concluded that "harm" did not require a decline in population numbers. Instead, it held that "[i]f the habitat modification prevents the population from recovering, then this causes injury to the species and should be actionable under section 9." 649 F. Supp. at 1077. The court ordered the removal of the mouflon sheep on the grounds that their presence injured the Palila by decreasing its food and nesting sites.

State officials appealed the district court's decision to the Ninth Circuit. In affirming the district court, the Ninth Circuit stated: "We do not reach the issue of whether harm includes habitat degradation that merely retards recovery. The district court's (and the Secretary's) interpretation of harm as including habitat destruction that could result in extinction, and findings to that effect are enough to sustain an order for the removal of the mouflon sheep." Palila v. Hawaii Dep't of Land & Natural Resources, 852 F.2d 1106, 1110 (9th Cir. 1988).

## NOTES AND QUESTIONS

1. The *Palila* litigation was filed by the Sierra Club Legal Defense Fund and the Hawaii Audubon Society. When they filed their initial lawsuit in January 1978, they named as the lead plaintiff "Palila (*Psittirostra bailleui*), an endangered species." The opening sentence of the district court's initial opinion reads: "Palila (*Psittirostra bailleui*) seeks the protection of this Court from harm caused by feral sheep and goats." Environmental philosopher Rod Nash notes that "[f]or the first time in American legal history a non-human became a plaintiff in court. Moreover, the bird won!" Nash, The Rights of Nature 177 (1989).

2. What result would you expect if the *Palila* case arose on private land? On federal land? In Sierra Club v. Yeutter, 926 F.2d 429 (5th Cir. 1991), the Fifth Circuit held that the Forest Service had violated section 9 by authorizing clear-cutting in forests that were habitat for the endangered red-cockaded woodpecker, finding that the practice "resulted in significant habitat modification" that had "caused and accelerated the decline in the species." 926 F.2d at 438. In Defenders of Wildlife v. EPA, 882 F.2d 1294 (8th Cir. 1989), the Eighth Circuit held that EPA had violated section 9 when it registered pesticides containing strychnine. The court found that endangered species had been poisoned by the pesticides, which could not have been used without the EPA registration.

### PRIVATE ACTIONS, INCIDENTAL TAKINGS, AND HABITAT CONSERVATION PLANS

Section 9 of ESA is particularly significant because it applies to private as well as governmental action. The great majority of endangered species are found on private land or adjacent waterways and a substantial number of them occur entirely on such land. Bean, The Endangered Species Act and Private Land: Four Lessons Learned from the Past Quarter Century, 28 Envtl. L. Rep. 10701 (1998). Section 9's prohibition of "taking" applies broadly to proscribe even takings that are incidental to other activities. By contrast, section 7 has provided some flexibility for incidental takings. If an agency action and the resulting incidental taking are not likely to jeopardize the continued existence of the species and the impact of the taking will be minimized, section 7(b)(4) authorizes the Secretary to provide the agency with a written statement authorizing the taking. See Defenders of Wildlife v. EPA, 882 F.2d 1294, 1300 (8th Cir. 1989).

During its first decade, ESA provided no similar flexibility for private actions. Any private action that would incidentally harm a protected animal was subject to criminal sanctions. In 1982, Congress responded to this inconsistency by adding section 10(a) to ESA. This section authorizes the Secretary to permit "incidental" takings associated with private action if the actor prepares a habitat conservation plan (HCP) to minimize the impact of the taking and assures that it "will not appreciably reduce the likelihood of the survival and recovery of the species in the wild." §10(a)(2)(B)(iv). Congress intended for section 10 to apply the same basic standard that had been applied to permit incidental takings under section 7(a)(2).

When Congress adopted section 10 (a) it had a specific model in mind—an HCP being prepared for the development of San Bruno Mountain, the last bastion of the mission blue butterfly and San Bruno elfin butterfly. Approved in 1983, the San Bruno HCP was the product of lengthy negotiations among the landowner, developer, conservationists, and local governments. It produced a plan to permanently protect 87 percent of the butterfly habitat, while authorizing limited housing development on the remaining 13 percent. To provide continued funding to support habitat management and long-term enforcement of the plan, assessments were made on units within the development. By itself, construction of the housing development was estimated to reduce the species' chances of survival by 2 to 5 percent. However, this was more than offset by the effect of the HCP, which removed exotic vegetation, controlled recreational use, and provided for active habitat management, thus enhancing the butterflies' overall prospects for survival.

Because FWS had never enforced section 9 against incidental takings, there was little initial incentive for anyone to seek a permit. Thus, it was hardly surprising that before 1992 only 14 HCPs were put into place. But with the enthusiastic support of Interior Secretary Bruce Babbitt, who took office in 1993, by the end of the Clinton administration in 2001, a total of 330 HCPs had been approved and 200 more were being developed.

To obtain an incidental take permit, section 10(a)(2)(B) of the ESA specifies that the following criteria must be met: (1) the taking will be incidental; (2) the applicant will, to the maximum extent practicable, minimize and mitigate the impacts of the taking; (3) the applicant will ensure that adequate funding for the plan will be provided; (4) the taking will not appreciably reduce the likelihood of the survival and recovery of the species in the wild; and (5) other measures, as required by the Secretary, will be met. Habitat Conservation Plans are to include: (1) an assessment of impacts likely to result from the proposed taking; (2) measures that the permit applicant will undertake to monitor, minimize, and mitigate for such impacts; (3) funding available to implement such measures and procedures to deal with unforeseen or extraordinary circumstances; (4) alternative actions to the taking that the applicant analyzed, and the reasons why the applicant did not adopt such alternatives; and (5) additional measures that the Fish and Wildlife Service may require.

One example of an incidental take permit and HCP that was approved by FWS and later challenged in court involves a wind farm in Ohio. Because it realized that its wind turbines could harm the endangered Indiana bat, Buckeye Wind, LLC applied to FWS for an incidental take permit. Buckeye's HCP provided that it would site the turbines away from the known habitats of the bat, adjust the turbines' operating times and speeds, and protect additional bat habitat. After FWS issued the permit, opponents of the project sued, alleging violations of NEPA and the ESA. In Union Neighbors United, Inc. v. Jewell, 831 F.3d 564 (D.C. Cir. 2016), the D.C. Circuit upheld issuance of the incidental take permit, while finding that

FWS violated NEPA by failing to consider an economically feasible alternative that would take fewer bats than the company's proposal.

### Habitat Degradation and Section 9's "Take" Prohibition

A significant legal challenge to the Secretary of Interior's interpretation that section 9's "take" prohibition includes "significant habitat modification or degradation where it actually kills or injures wildlife" resulted in the following decision.

## Babbitt v. Sweet Home Chapter of Communities for a Great Oregon

515 U.S. 687 (1995)

JUSTICE STEVENS delivered the opinion of the Court.

. . . Respondents in this action are small landowners, logging companies, and families dependent on the forest products industries in the Pacific Northwest and in the Southeast, and organizations that represent their interests. They brought this declaratory judgment action against petitioners, the Secretary of the Interior and the Director of the Fish and Wildlife Service, in the United States District Court for the District of Columbia to challenge the statutory validity of the Secretary's regulation defining "harm," particularly the inclusion of habitat modification and degradation in the definition. Respondents challenged the regulation on its face. Their complaint alleged that application of the "harm" regulation to the red-cockaded woodpecker, an endangered species, and the northern spotted owl, a threatened species, had injured them economically. . . .

Because this case was decided on motions for summary judgment, we may appropriately make certain factual assumptions in order to frame the legal issue. First, we assume respondents have no desire to harm either the red-cockaded woodpecker or the spotted owl; they merely wish to continue logging activities that would be entirely proper if not prohibited by the ESA. On the other hand, we must assume *arguendo* that those activities will have the effect, even though unintended, of detrimentally changing the natural habitat of both listed species and that, as a consequence, members of those species will be killed or injured. Under respondents' view of the law, the Secretary's only means of forestalling that grave result—even when the actor knows it is certain to occur—is to use his §5 authority to purchase the lands on which the survival of the species depends. The Secretary, on the other hand, submits that the §9 prohibition on takings, which Congress defined to include "harm," places on respondents a duty to avoid harm that habitat alteration will cause the birds unless respondents first obtain a permit pursuant to §10.

The text of the Act provides three reasons for concluding that the Secretary's interpretation is reasonable. First, an ordinary understanding of the word "harm" supports it. The dictionary definition of the verb form of "harm" is "to cause hurt or damage to: injure." Webster's Third New International Dictionary 1034 (1966). In the context of the ESA, that definition naturally encompasses habitat modification that results in actual injury or death to members of an endangered or threatened species. Respondents argue that the Secretary should have limited the purview of "harm" to direct applications of force against protected species, but the dictionary definition does not include the word "directly" or suggest in any way that only direct or willful action that leads to injury constitutes "harm." Moreover, unless the statutory term "harm" encompasses indirect as well as direct injuries, the word has no meaning that does not duplicate the meaning of other words that §3 uses to define "take." A reluctance to treat statutory terms as surplusage supports the reasonableness of the Secretary's interpretation.

Second, the broad purpose of the ESA supports the Secretary's decision to extend protection against activities that cause the precise harms Congress enacted the statute to avoid. In TVA v. Hill, 437 U.S. 153 (1978), we described the Act as "the most comprehensive legislation for the preservation of endangered species ever enacted by any nation." Whereas predecessor statutes enacted in 1966 and 1969 had not contained any sweeping prohibition against the taking of endangered species except on federal lands, the 1973 Act applied to all land in the United States and to the Nation's territorial seas. As stated in §2 of the Act, among its central purposes is "to provide a means whereby the ecosystems upon which endangered species and threatened species depend may be conserved. . . ." 16 U.S.C. §1531(b).

In *Hill*, we construed §7 as precluding the completion of the Tellico Dam because of its predicted impact on the survival of the snail darter. Both our holding and the language in our opinion stressed the importance of the statutory policy. "The plain intent of Congress in enacting this statute," we recognized, "was to halt and reverse the trend toward species extinction, whatever the cost. This is reflected not only in the stated policies of the Act, but in literally every section of the statute." Although the §9 "take" prohibition was not at issue in *Hill*, we took note of that prohibition, placing particular emphasis on the Secretary's inclusion of habitat modification in his definition of "harm." In light of that provision for habitat protection, we could "not understand how TVA intends to operate Tellico Dam without 'harming' the snail darter." Congress' intent to provide comprehensive protection for endangered and threatened species supports the permissibility of the Secretary's "harm" regulation.

Respondents advance strong arguments that activities that cause minimal or unforeseeable harm will not violate the Act as construed in the "harm" regulation. Respondents, however, present a facial challenge to the regulation. Thus, they ask us to invalidate the Secretary's understanding of "harm" in every circumstance, even when an actor knows that an activity, such as draining a pond, would actually result in the extinction of a listed species by destroying its habitat. Given Congress' clear expression of the ESA's broad purpose to protect endangered and threatened wildlife, the Secretary's definition of "harm" is reasonable.

Third, the fact that Congress in 1982 authorized the Secretary to issue permits for takings that §9(a)(1)(B) would otherwise prohibit, "if such taking is incidental to, and not the purpose of, the carrying out of an otherwise lawful activity," strongly suggests that Congress understood §9(a)(1)(B) to prohibit indirect as well as deliberate takings. The permit process requires the applicant to prepare a "conservation plan" that specifies how he intends to "minimize and mitigate" the "impact" of his activity on endangered and threatened species, making clear that Congress had in mind foreseeable rather than merely accidental effects on listed species. No one could seriously request an "incidental" take permit to avert §9 liability for direct, deliberate action against a member of an endangered or threatened species, but respondents would read "harm" so narrowly that the permit procedure would have little more than that absurd purpose. "When Congress acts to amend a statute, we presume it intends its amendment to have real and substantial effect." Congress' addition of the §10 permit provision supports the Secretary's conclusion that activities not intended to harm an endangered species, such as habitat modification, may constitute unlawful takings under the ESA unless the Secretary permits them.

The Court of Appeals made three errors in asserting that "harm" must refer to a direct application of force because the words around it do.[15] First, the court's premise was flawed. Several of the words that accompany "harm" in the §3 definition of "take," especially "harrass," "pursue," "wound," and "kill," refer to actions or effects that do not require direct applications of force. Second, to the extent the court read a requirement of intent or purpose into the words used to define "take," it ignored §9's express provision that a "knowing" action is enough to violate the Act. Third, the court employed *noscitur a sociis* to give "harm" essentially the same function as other words in the definition, thereby denying it independent meaning. The canon, to the contrary, counsels that a word "gathers meaning from the words around it." The statutory context of "harm" suggests that Congress meant that term to serve a particular function in the ESA, consistent with but distinct from the functions of the other verbs used to define "take." The Secretary's interpretation of "harm" to include indirectly injuring endangered animals through habitat modification permissibly interprets "harm" to have "a character of its own not to be submerged by its association." . . .

We need not decide whether the statutory definition of "take" compels the Secretary's interpretation of "harm," because our conclusions that Congress did not unambiguously manifest its intent to adopt respondents' view and that the Secretary's interpretation is reasonable suffice to decide this case. The latitude the ESA gives the Secretary in enforcing the statute, together with the degree of regulatory expertise necessary to its enforcement, establishes that we owe some degree of deference to the Secretary's reasonable interpretation. . . .

JUSTICE O'CONNOR, concurring.

My agreement with the Court is founded on two understandings. First, the challenged regulation is limited to significant habitat modification that causes actual, as opposed to hypothetical or speculative, death or injury to identifiable protected animals. Second, even setting aside difficult questions of scienter, the regulation's application is limited by ordinary principles of proximate causation, which introduce notions of foreseeability. These limitations, in my view, call into

---

15. The dissent makes no effort to defend the Court of Appeals' reading of the statutory definition as requiring a direct application of force. Instead, it tries to impose on §9 a limitation of liability to "affirmative conduct intentionally directed against a particular animal or animals." Under the dissent's interpretation of the Act, a developer could drain a pond, knowing that the act would extinguish an endangered species of turtles, without even proposing a conservation plan or applying for a permit under §9(a)(1)(B); unless the developer was motivated by a desire "to get at a turtle," no statutory taking could occur. Because such conduct would not constitute a taking at common law, the dissent would shield it from §9 liability, even though the words "kill" and "harm" in the statutory definition could apply to such deliberate conduct. We cannot accept that limitation. In any event, our reasons for rejecting the Court of Appeals' interpretation apply as well to the dissent's novel construction.

question Palila v. Hawaii Dept. of Land and Natural Resources, 852 F.2d 1106 (9th Cir. 1988) (*Palila II*), and with it, many of the applications derided by the dissent. Because there is no need to strike a regulation on a facial challenge out of concern that it is susceptible of erroneous application, however, and because there are many habitat-related circumstances in which the regulation might validly apply, I join the opinion of the Court.

In my view, the regulation is limited by its terms to actions that actually kill or injure individual animals. Justice Scalia disagrees, arguing that the harm regulation "encompasses injury inflicted, not only upon individual animals, but upon populations of the protected species." At one level, I could not reasonably quarrel with this observation; death to an individual animal always reduces the size of the population in which it lives, and in that sense, "injures" that population. But by its insight, the dissent means something else. Building upon the regulation's use of the word "breeding," Justice Scalia suggests that the regulation facially bars significant habitat modification that actually kills or injures *hypothetical* animals (or, perhaps more aptly, causes potential additions to the population not to come into being). Because "impairment of breeding does not 'injure' living creatures," Justice Scalia reasons, the regulation *must* contemplate application to "a *population* of animals which would otherwise have maintained or increased its numbers."

I disagree. As an initial matter, I do not find it as easy as Justice Scalia does to dismiss the notion that significant impairment of breeding injures living creatures. To raze the last remaining ground on which the piping plover currently breeds, thereby making it impossible for any piping plovers to reproduce, would obviously injure the population (causing the species' extinction in a generation). But by completely preventing breeding, it would also injure the individual living bird, in the same way that sterilizing the creature injures the individual living bird. To "injure" is, among other things, "to impair." Webster's Ninth New Collegiate Dictionary 623 (1983). One need not subscribe to theories of "psychic harm" to recognize that to make it impossible for an animal to reproduce is to impair its most essential physical functions and to render that animal, and its genetic material, biologically obsolete. This, in my view, is actual injury. . . .

By the dissent's reckoning, the regulation at issue here, in conjunction with 16 U.S.C. §1540(1), imposes liability for any habitat-modifying conduct that ultimately results in the death of a protected animal, "regardless of whether that result is intended or even foreseeable, and no matter how long the chain of causality between modification and injury." Even if §1540(1) does create a strict liability regime (a question we need not decide at this juncture), I see no indication that Congress, in enacting that section, intended to dispense with ordinary principles of proximate causation. Strict liability means liability without regard to fault; it does not normally mean liability for every consequence, however remote, of one's conduct. See generally W. Keeton, D. Dobbs, R. Keeton, and D. Owen, Prosser and Keeton on Law of Torts 559-560 (5th ed. 1984) (describing "practical necessity for the restriction of liability within some reasonable bounds" in the strict liability context). I would not lightly assume that Congress, in enacting a strict liability statute that is silent on the causation question, has dispensed with this well-entrenched principle. In the absence of congressional abrogation of traditional principles of causation, then, private parties should be held liable under §1540(1) only if their habitat-modifying actions proximately cause death or injury to protected animals. The regulation, of course, does not contradict the presumption or notion that ordinary principles of causation apply here. Indeed, by use of the word "actually," the regulation clearly rejects speculative or conjectural effects, and thus itself invokes principles of proximate causation.

Proximate causation is not a concept susceptible of precise definition. It is easy enough, of course, to identify the extremes. The farmer whose fertilizer is lifted by a tornado from tilled fields and deposited miles away in a wildlife refuge cannot, by any stretch of the term, be considered the proximate cause of death or injury to protected species occasioned thereby. At the same time, the landowner who drains a pond on his property, killing endangered fish in the process, would likely satisfy any formulation of the principle. We have recently said that proximate causation "normally eliminates the bizarre," and have noted its "functionally equivalent" alternative characterizations in terms of foreseeability. Proximate causation depends to a great extent on considerations of the fairness of imposing liability for remote consequences. The task of determining whether proximate causation exists in the limitless fact patterns sure to arise is best left to lower courts. But I note, at the least, that proximate cause principles inject a foreseeability element into the statute, and hence, the regulation, that would appear to alleviate some of the problems noted by the dissent. See, e.g., infra (describing "a farmer who tills his field and causes erosion that makes silt run into a nearby river which depletes oxygen and thereby [injures] protected fish").

In my view, then, the "harm" regulation applies where significant habitat modification, by impairing essential behaviors, proximately (foreseeably) causes actual death or injury to identifiable animals that are protected under the Endangered Species Act. Pursuant to my interpretation, *Palila II*— under which the Court of Appeals held that a state agency committed a "taking" by permitting feral sheep to eat mamane-naio seedlings that, when full-grown, might have fed and sheltered endangered palila—was wrongly decided according to the regulation's own terms. Destruction of the seedlings did not proximately cause actual death or injury to identifiable birds; it merely prevented the regeneration of forest land not currently inhabited by actual birds. . . .

JUSTICE SCALIA, with whom THE CHIEF JUSTICE and JUSTICE THOMAS join, dissenting.

The Court's holding that the hunting and killing prohibition incidentally preserves habitat on private lands imposes unfairness to the point of financial ruin—not just upon the rich, but upon the simplest farmer who finds his land conscripted to national zoological use. I respectfully dissent. . . .

The regulation has three features which, for reasons I shall discuss at length below, do not comport with the statute. First, it interprets the statute to prohibit habitat modification that is no more than the cause-in-fact of death or injury to wildlife. Any "significant habitat modification" that in fact produces that result by "impairing essential behavioral patterns" is made unlawful, regardless of whether that result is intended or even foreseeable, and no matter how long the chain of causality between modification and injury. See, e.g., Palila v. Hawaii Dept. of Land and Natural Resources (*Palila II*), 852 F.2d 1106, 1108-1109 (9th Cir. 1988) (sheep grazing constituted "taking" of palila birds, since although sheep do not destroy full-grown mamane trees, they do destroy mamane seedlings, which will not grow to full-grown trees, on which the palila feeds and nests).

Second, the regulation does not require an "act": the Secretary's officially stated position is that an omission will do. The previous version of the regulation made this explicit. See 40 Fed. Reg. 44,412, 44,416 (1975) ("'Harm' in the definition of 'take' in the Act means an act or omission which actually kills or injures wildlife. . ."). When the regulation was modified in 1981 the phrase "or omission" was taken out, but only because (as the final publication of the rule advised) "the [Fish and Wildlife] Service feels that 'act' is inclusive of either commissions or omissions which would be prohibited by section [1538(a)(1)(B)]." 46 Fed. Reg. 54,748, 54,750 (1981). In its brief here the Government agrees that the regulation covers omissions (although it argues that "an 'omission' constitutes an 'act'. . . only if there is a legal duty to act").

The third and most important unlawful feature of the regulation is that it encompasses injury inflicted, not only upon individual animals, but upon populations of the protected species. "Injury" in the regulation includes "significantly impairing essential behavioral patterns, including *breeding*," 50 CFR §17.3 (1994) (emphasis added). Impairment of breeding does not "injure" living creatures; it prevents them from propagating, thus "injuring" a *population* of animals which would otherwise have maintained or increased its numbers. What the face of the regulation shows, the Secretary's official pronouncements confirm. The Final Redefinition of "Harm" accompanying publication of the regulation said that "harm" is not limited to "direct physical injury to an individual member of the wildlife species," 46 Fed. Reg. 54,748 (1981), and refers to "injury to a *population*," id., at 54,749 (emphasis added).

None of these three features of the regulation can be found in the statutory provisions supposed to authorize it. The term "harm" in §1532(19) has no legal force of its own. An indictment or civil complaint that charged the defendant with "harming" an animal protected under the Act would be dismissed as defective, for the only operative term in the statute is to "take." If "take" were not elsewhere defined in the Act, none could dispute what it means, for the term is as old as the law itself. To "take," when applied to wild animals, means to reduce those animals, by killing or capturing, to human control. See, e.g., 11 Oxford English Dictionary (1933) ("Take . . . To catch, capture (a wild beast, bird, fish, etc.)"); Webster's New International Dictionary of the English Language (2d ed. 1949) (take defined as "to catch or capture by trapping, snaring, etc., or as prey"); Geer v. Connecticut, 161 U.S. 519, 523 (1896) ("All the animals which can be taken upon the earth, in the sea, or in the air, that is to say, wild animals, belong to those who take them") (quoting the Digest of Justinian); 2 W. Blackstone, Commentaries 411 (1766) ("Every man . . . has an equal right of pursuing and taking to his own use all such creatures as are *ferae naturae*"). This is just the sense in which "take" is used elsewhere in federal legislation and treaty. See, e.g., Migratory Bird Treaty Act, 16 U.S.C. §703 (1988 ed., Supp. V) (no person may "pursue, hunt, take, capture, kill, [or] attempt to take, capture, or kill" any migratory bird); Agreement on the Conservation of Polar Bears, Nov. 15, 1973, Art. I, 27 U.S.T. 3918, 3921, T.I.A.S. No. 8409 (defining "taking" as "hunting, killing and capturing"). And that meaning fits neatly with the rest of §1538(a)(1), which makes it unlawful not only to take protected species, but also to import or export them (§1538(a)(1)(A)); to possess, sell, deliver, carry, transport, or ship any taken species (§1538(a)(1)(D)); and to transport, sell, or offer to sell them in interstate or foreign commerce (§§1538(a)(1)(E), (F)). The taking prohibition, in other words, is only part of the regulatory plan of §1538(a)(1), which covers all the stages of the process by which protected wildlife is reduced to man's dominion and made the object of profit. It is obvious that "take" in this sense — a term of art deeply embedded in the statutory and common law concerning wildlife — describes a class of acts (not omissions) done directly and intentionally (not indirectly and by accident) to particular animals (not populations of animals). . . .

[T]he Court's contention that "harm" in the narrow sense adds nothing to the other words underestimates the ingenuity of our own species in a way that Congress did not. To feed an animal poison, to spray it with mace, to chop down the very tree in which it is nesting, or even to destroy its entire habitat in order to take it (as by draining a pond to get at a turtle), might neither wound nor kill, but would directly and intentionally harm. . . .

[T]he Court and the concurrence suggest that the regulation should be read to contain a requirement of proximate causation or foreseeability, principally *because the statute does* — and "nothing in the regulation purports to weaken those requirements [of the statute]." I quite agree that the statute contains such a limitation, because the verbs of purpose in §1538(a)(1)(B) denote action directed at animals. *But the Court has rejected that reading.* The critical premise on which it has upheld the regulation is that, despite the weight of the other words in §1538(a)(1)(B), "the statutory term 'harm' encompasses indirect as well as direct injuries," ante. Consequently, unless there is some strange category of causation that is indirect and yet also proximate, the Court has already rejected its own basis for finding a proximate-cause limitation in the regulation. In fact "proximate" causation simply *means* "direct" causation. The only other reason given for finding a proximate-cause limitation in the regulation is that "by use of the word 'actually,' the regulation clearly rejects speculative or conjectural effects, and thus itself *invokes* principles of proximate causation." *Non sequitur*, of course. That the injury must be "actual" as opposed to "potential" simply says nothing at all about the length or foreseeability of the causal chain between the habitat modification and the "actual" injury. It is thus true and irrelevant that "the Secretary did not need to include 'actually' to connote 'but for' causation," ante, at 2414 n. 13; "actually" defines the requisite *injury*, not the requisite *causality*. The regulation says (it is worth repeating) that "harm" means (1) an act which (2) actually kills or injures wildlife. If that does not dispense with a proximate-cause requirement, I do not know what language would. And changing the regulation by judicial invention, even to achieve compliance with the statute, is not permissible. . . .

But since the Court is reading the regulation and the statute incorrectly in other respects, it may as well introduce this novelty as well — law a la carte. As I understand the regulation that the Court has created and held consistent with the statute that it has also created, habitat modification can constitute a "taking," but only if it results in the killing or harming of *individual animals*, and only if that consequence is the direct result of the modification. This means that the destruction of privately owned habitat that is essential, not for the feeding or nesting, but for the *breeding*, of butterflies, would not violate the Act, since it would not harm or kill any living butterfly. I, too, think it would not violate the Act—not for the utterly unsupported reason that habitat modifications fall outside the regulation if they happen not to kill or injure a living animal, but for the textual reason that only action directed at living animals constitutes a "take."

## NOTES AND QUESTIONS

1. In light of *Sweet Home*, what activities are prohibited by section 9? The Court upheld the Secretary of Interior's definition of "harm" prohibited by section 9 as including "significant habitat modification or degradation where it actually kills or injures wildlife. . . ." It rejected both the D.C. Circuit's interpretation that section 9 applies only to the direct application of force to endangered species and Justice Scalia's argument that it prohibits only "affirmative conduct intentionally directed against a particular animal or animals." In a portion of his dissent not reproduced above, Justice Scalia argued that any other interpretation could make many "routine private activities," such as farming, construction, and logging violations of section 9 "when they fortuitously injure protected wildlife, no matter how remote the chain of causation and no matter how difficult to foresee (or to disprove) the 'injury' may be (e.g., an 'impairment' of breeding)." 515 U.S. at 721-722 (Scalia, J., dissenting). Justice O'Connor took issue with this claim in her concurring opinion by arguing that normal principles of proximate cause would limit liability. While none of the other Justices in the majority joined Justice O'Connor's opinion, in a footnote to his majority opinion Justice Stevens indicated that he saw no reason why section 9 "should not be read to incorporate ordinary requirements of proximate causation and foreseeability." 515 U.S. at 701 n.15.

2. Citing *Sweet Home*, the Fifth Circuit in Aransas Project v. Shaw, 756 F.3d 801, 817 (5th Cir. 2014), concluded that "proximate cause and foreseeability are required to affix liability for ESA violations." Noting that these requirements "therefore mean that liability may be based neither on the 'butterfly effect' nor on remote actors in a vast and complex ecosystem," the court reversed a decision requiring the Texas Commission on Environmental Quality (TCEQ) to obtain an incidental take permit before issuing new permits to withdraw water from rivers feeding an estuary where endangered whooping cranes live. Although more than 20 whooping cranes had died as a result of rising salinity levels, the court found that withdrawals of water pursuant to the permits were not a proximate and foreseeable cause of the deaths.

3. How can landowners know what habitat modifications are prohibited by section 9? Should the government issue species-by-species guidelines or regulations that specify what habitat modifications are likely to harm which species? The U.S. Fish and Wildlife Service has established such guidelines for a few species. For example, they specify that a landowner located within a quarter mile of any active red-cockaded woodpecker colony may harvest timber without harming the bird so long as at least 60 acres of pine trees 10 inches or more in diameter with a total basal area of 3,000 square feet are left. U.S. Fish & Wildlife Service, Draft

Red-Cockaded Woodpecker Procedures Manual for Private Lands (Oct. 1992). If a landowner challenges the agency's judgment concerning whether certain actions will injure members of a particular species, should the guidelines be entitled to any deference?

4. In the wake of *Sweet Home*, what must the government prove to establish a violation of section 9? Does the government have to prove that a habitat modification actually caused death or injury to specific members of an endangered species? Can it still obtain an injunction to block activities that it fears will cause such harm even before the harm has become evident? In Marbeled Murrelet v. Babbitt, 83 F.3d 1060 (9th Cir. 1996), the Ninth Circuit rejected a timber company's argument that *Sweet Home* required proof of actual past injury to an endangered species before an injunction could be issued to prevent logging that would modify the habitat of an endangered bird. The court held that a "reasonably certain threat of imminent harm to a protected species is sufficient for issuance of an injunction under section 9 of the ESA," 83 F.3d at 1066, and that "habitat modification which significantly impairs the breeding and sheltering of a protected species amounts to 'harm' under the ESA." Id. at 1067. The court found that evidence that approximately 100 endangered birds had been detected in the area throughout their breeding season for three consecutive years, coupled with expert testimony that logging would impair breeding and increase attacks on the birds by predators, was sufficient evidence of future harm to sustain an injunction. In another case, the Ninth Circuit upheld a district court's rejection of an environmental group's request to enjoin construction of a high school complex on 60 acres of a 90-acre parcel of land used by endangered pygmy owls. The district judge found that the owls used only the 30 acres of the parcel that would remain undeveloped and fenced off. He noted that the Fish and Wildlife Service did not believe the school construction would harm the owls and that expert testimony offered by the parties on this issue was inconclusive. Defenders of Wildlife v. Bernal, 204 F.3d 920 (9th Cir. 2000).

When the federal government sought to enjoin logging of a 94-acre tract of old-growth forest because a pair of northern spotted owls nested a little more than a mile away, a district court required the government to produce radiotelemetry or other data showing that the owls actually used the tract in question. After giving the government a year to gather data to support its case, the court ultimately lifted its preliminary injunction after deciding that the government had failed to meet its burden of proving that the timber harvest would harm the endangered owls. The court concluded that evidence that the male owl of the pair had foraged on part of the 94-acre tract of old-growth forest was insufficient to prove a prospective take in light of the pair's home range of 3,600 acres and its high rate of reproduction. United States v. West Coast Forest Resources Ltd. P'ship, 2000 WL 298707 (D. Or. 2000). Evidence that a single endangered piping plover had been found dead in the tire tracks of an off-road vehicle (ORV) was deemed sufficient evidence of harm to grant federal authorities an order requiring a town to prohibit driving of ORVs on a beach where the endangered bird was nesting. United States v. Town of Plymouth, 6 F. Supp. 2d 81 (D. Mass. 1998). Compare Cold Mountain v. Garber, 375 F.3d 884 (9th Cir. 2004) (rejecting studies offered to prove that helicopter hazing harms buffalo).

5.  In Cascadia Wildlands v. Scott Timber Co., 190 F. Supp. 3d 1024 (D. Or. 2016), several environmental groups asked a court to enjoin a project to clear-cut 49 acres of old-growth and mature forest habitat allegedly occupied by the marbled murrelet, a threatened species. Despite a dispute over whether murrelets occupied the area to be cut, the court noted that if the project proceeded, "murrelets will not be able to nest in the clear-cut parcel for nearly a century while the forest regrows." Citing Cottonwood Environmental Law Center v. U.S. Forest Service, 789 F.3d 1075, 1091 (9th Cir. 2015), where the Ninth Circuit said that "when evaluating a request for injunctive relief to remedy an ESA procedural violation, the equities and public interest factors always tip in favor of the protected species," the court granted a preliminary injunction. But in Center for Environmental Science Accuracy & Reliability v. National Park Service, 2016 WL 4524758 (E.D. Cal. 2016), a court rejected claims that the National Park Service's operation of a dam had caused a take of listed fish species. The court concluded that while a "[t]ake can result from *direct* harm to a single, individual animal," for harm caused by habitat modification to be considered a take "a population level effect is necessary."

6.  Despite the government's victory in *Sweet Home*, section 9 has not had a sufficiently broad sweep to prevent many forms of habitat modification that are among the most significant causes of species endangerment. These include the decline of natural fires as a landscape shaping device (due to fire suppression efforts or roads that serve as barriers to the spread of fire), habitat fragmentation that causes "edge effects" by opening up formerly safe habitat to predation by other animals, and the introduction of non-native species that threaten naturally occurring ones. Michael J. Bean, The Endangered Species Act and Private Land: Four Lessons Learned from the Past Quarter Century, 28 Envtl. L. Rep. 10701, 10705 (1998). Invasive species encroachment is now considered one of the most significant threats to native ecosystems. To combat this threat, Congress passed the Nonindigenous Aquatic Nuisance Prevention and Control Act of 1990, Pub. L. No. 101-636, which creates a task force to develop and implement a program to control and prevent the introduction and dispersal of such species. In February 1999, President Clinton issued Executive Order 13,112 directing all federal agencies to prevent and control introductions of invasive species.

7.  The *Palila* case is still the only one to find a taking as a result of a failure to remove a non-native species. Ironically, as a result of the removal of the feral sheep and goats, highly flammable, non-native grasses have now proliferated in the palila's habitat, posing a new and different threat to the bird. Is *Palila II* still good law? In her concurring opinion, Justice O'Connor expressed the view that the case had been "wrongly decided." Do you agree? Noting that none of the other Justices had joined Justice O'Connor's opinion, the Ninth Circuit in Seattle Audubon Society v. Moseley, 80 F.3d 1401 (9th Cir. 1996) stated that "five Justices affirmed *Palila* in all respects." Id. at 1405. Do you agree with this assessment of *Sweet Home*'s impact on *Palila*?

8.  By the 1990s the number of grizzly bears in the Lower 48 states had declined from 50,000 to less than 1,000 living in isolated populations. Because researchers have found that "bears and roads don't mix," managers of national forests have been under pressure to close roads in areas of endangered bear habitat. Kenworthy, Wrestling with a Bear of a Problem in the Western Wilderness, Wash. Post, Nov. 21, 1994, at A3. In National Wildlife Federation v. Burlington Northern

Railroad, 23 F.3d 1508 (9th Cir. 1994), a railroad's accidental spillage of corn along tracks running through bear habitat that led to seven grizzlies being struck and killed by trains was held to be a taking in violation of section 9. However, the court refused to issue an injunction in light of the extensive efforts made by the railroad to avoid similar incidents that had helped ensure that no grizzlies had been hit by trains in more than three years.

### Incidental Takes and the Migratory Bird Treaty Act

The Migratory Bird Treaty Act of 1918 (MBTA) makes it "unlawful at any time, by any means or in any manner, to pursue, hunt, take, capture, kill, attempt to take, capture, or kill . . . any migratory bird." In United States v. CITGO Petroleum Corp., 801 F.3d 477, 488-489 (5th Cir. 2015), the Fifth Circuit held that a "taking" under the MBTA requires "deliberate acts done directly and intentionally to migratory birds." Thus, it reversed the misdemeanor conviction of an oil refiner for the deaths of birds that landed in uncovered tanks of oily waste. The court conceded that the Second and Tenth Circuits "hold that because the MBTA imposes strict liability, it must forbid acts that accidentally or indirectly kill birds." United States v. FMC Corp., 572 F.2d 902 (2d Cir. 1978); United States v. Apollo Energies, 611 F.3d 679 (10th Cir. 2010).

On January 10, 2017, ten days before the Obama administration left office, the outgoing Solicitor of the Interior issued an opinion siding with the courts holding that the MBTA prohibits incidental takes of migratory birds. *Incidental Take Prohibited Under the Migratory Bird Treaty Act* (Dep't of Interior, Solicitor's Opinion M-37041 Jan. 10, 2017). The opinion concluded that the United States, in enforcement proceedings against those charged with violating the Act, need not make a showing of willful or intentional taking of migratory birds to prove strict liability and demonstrate criminal violations of the Act.

Less than a year later, the Trump administration reversed this policy. On December 22, 2017, the Trump administration's Solicitor of the Interior withdrew the Obama Solicitor's Opinion and issued a new opinion concluding that the MBTA does not prohibit incidental takes. *The Migratory Bird Treaty Act Does Not Prohibit Incidental Take* (Dep't of Interior, Solicitor's Opinion M-37050 Dec. 22, 2017) (hereinafter "Trump Solicitor's Opinion"). The new Trump Solicitor's Opinion based this conclusion on the "text, history, and purpose of the MBTA, as well as relevant case law." The Trump Solicitor's Opinion found that "interpreting the MBTA to apply to incidental or accidental actions" by the oil, gas, and timber industries "hangs the sword of Damocles over a host of otherwise lawful and productive actions" and will deter investment and operation of the energy and timber industries. However, in August 2020 the Trump administration's interpretation was overturned in Natural Resources Defense Council v. U.S. Secretary of Interior, 478 F.Supp. 3d 469 (S.D.N.Y. 2020). Citing *Sweet Home* the court noted that there "is nothing in the text of the MBTA that suggests that in order to fall within its prohibition, activity must be directed specifically at birds. Nor does the statute prohibit only intentionally killing migratory birds. And it certainly does not say that only 'some' kills are prohibited."

Subsequently, the Trump administration initiated a rulemaking proceeding to codify the view that the MBTA only covered intentional killing of migratory birds. However, before the rule could go into effect, on February 8, 2021, the Biden administration delayed the rule and announced its plan to open the rule again to public comment. Matthew Brown, Biden Delays Trump Rule that Weakened Wild Bird Protections, Associated Press, Feb. 4, 2021. On February 26, 2021, the Biden administration told the Second Circuit that it was dropping the government's appeal of the district court decision striking down the Trump Solicitor's Opinion.

### The Impact of Section 9 on Incentives to Preserve Habitat on Private Property

Some have argued that section 9 of the ESA can be counterproductive by encouraging landowners to make their property inhospitable to endangered species in order to avoid restrictions on development. See Michael J. Bean, The Endangered Species Act and Private Land: Four Lessons Learned from the Past Quarter Century, 28 Envtl. L. Rep. 10701, 10706 (1998) (arguing that an exaggerated fear of land use restrictions has prompted preemptive land management practices), but cf. Jeffrey J. Rachlinski, Protecting Endangered Species Without Regulating Private Landowners: The Case of Endangered Plants, 8 Cornell J.L. & Pub. Pol'y 1, 7 (1998) (arguing that situations in which the ESA's land use restriction do more harm than good are probably rare).

Responding to these concerns, the federal government has pursued initiatives to encourage landowners to use land management practices that would benefit endangered species largely by making creative use of section 10's provisions for incidental take permits to landowners who implement approved habitat conservation plans (HCPs). Beginning in 1994, the Interior Department has followed a "no surprises" policy assuring participants in HCPs that if the measures in the plan to mitigate the impact of development proved inadequate, the government would bear the risk. This program was adopted as a rule in 1998, 63 Fed. Reg. 8,859 (1998). Since 1995, the government also has promoted a "safe harbors" program that allows landowners essentially to "freeze" their responsibilities to a species under the ESA at current levels in return for an agreement to create, enhance, or restore habitat for that species. The program seeks to ensure that landowners who successfully attract additional members of an endangered species to their land will not be "rewarded" with additional restrictions on development. It is implemented through section 10 habitat conservation plans approved by the Fish and Wildlife Service (FWS). For example, in Texas the coastal prairie habitat of the endangered Attwater's prairie chicken has been restored by ranchers under a safe harbor agreement, and in South Carolina owners of 84,000 acres of land have pledged to enroll in a program to protect the red-cockaded woodpecker. See Bean, supra at 10707.

The "no surprises" and "safe harbors" programs have been criticized by some environmentalists who argue that they weaken the protections of the ESA by limiting the options available to government authorities in the event that unforeseen circumstances arise. However, Michael Bean argues that while the addition of section 10 to the ESA in 1982 "appeared to weaken the Act by creating a new exception to its nearly absolute prohibition against taking," it actually did the opposite because it gave the FWS "its first practical means of influencing what private landowners did on their lands." Michael J. Bean, The Endangered Species Act and Private Land: Four Lessons Learned from the Past Quarter Century, 28 Envtl. L. Rep. 10701, 10708 (1998). He notes that HCPs "can be the vehicles for restoring former habitat, protecting existing but unoccupied habitat, reconnecting fragmented habitats, ensuring active management to replicate the effects of prior natural disturbances, controlling non-native species, and doing a host of other essential things that the taking prohibition has never been able to compel." Id.

### Protection for Endangered Plants

Section 9 provides lesser protection for endangered plants than for endangered species of fish and wildlife. Section 9(a)(2)(B) of the ESA makes it unlawful to "remove and reduce to possession any [listed] species [of plant] from areas under federal jurisdiction, maliciously damage or destroy any such species on any such area; or remove, cut, dig up, or damage or destroy any such species on any other area in knowing violation of any law or regulation of any State or in the course of any violation of a State criminal trespass law." Consider the following report.

## Ignoring Pleas of Environmentalists, Kansas Man Digs Up Virgin Prairie

N.Y. Times, Nov. 23, 1990, at B18

The largest remaining stretch of virgin prairie in northeast Kansas disappeared under the plow this week after futile attempts by the Nature Conservancy and local environmentalists to buy it. The plowing of the 80-acre Elkins Prairie was first noticed soon after sunrise on Sunday, and the news quickly spread to a community group that had worked for two years to preserve the land, one of the few remaining unspoiled pieces of the 200 million acres of tall grass prairie that once covered North America.

Environmentalists hurried to the site and pleaded with the landowner to stop his tractor. The Douglas County Commission called an emergency meeting and after negotiating half the night offered to pay the landowner $6,000 an acre within six months, the equivalent of what developers had recently paid for nearby land. But the owner, Jack Graham, rejected the offer and resumed plowing. By late Monday, only a small strip of virgin prairie remained.

"It's heart-wrenching," said Joyce Wolf, leader of a group that had hoped to buy the land for an environmental education area. "He has stolen a resource from a community." Mr. Graham, a 39-year-old businessman who bought the land five years ago, declined to comment on his action. His lawyer, Thomas Murray, said Mr. Graham and his family "simply wanted to make their property more productive," but he would not elaborate...

Last year the Nature Conservancy, a national land preservation organization, offered to buy the Elkins Prairie for $3,500 an acre within a year.

## NOTES AND QUESTIONS

1. Why does the Endangered Species Act provide less protection to plants than to other endangered species? Although it does not directly affect private landowners' use of their property, it can restrict their activities in certain situations, such as when federal permits (e.g., a Clean Water Act section 404 permit to develop wetlands) are needed for activities that may harm listed plants. In those circumstances section 7 of the ESA would prohibit issuance of a permit if it would jeopardize the continued existence of a listed plant or adversely affect land designated as critical habitat. See Jeffrey J. Rachlinski, Protecting Endangered Species Without Regulating Private Landowners: The Case of Endangered Plants, 8 Cornell J.L. & Pub. Pol'y 1, 9 (1998).

2. The Elkins Prairie was the home to 150 species of plants, including two threatened species, Mead's milkweed and the western prairie fringed orchid. If threatened plants are entitled to essentially the same protections under the Endangered Species Act as are endangered plants, did Mr. Graham act legally when he plowed up the virgin prairie? Why or why not?

3. Suppose that a local Earth First! group had gotten wind of Mr. Graham's plans to plow up the virgin prairie. They decide to sneak onto the Elkins Prairie in the middle of the night to dig up as many Mead's milkweeds and western prairie fringed orchids as possible and to transplant them elsewhere. Would such actions violate section 9 of the Endangered Species Act?

4. Does the local environmentalists' unwillingness to pay the price Mr. Graham wanted for the Elkins Prairie demonstrate that it was not worth preserving? A neighbor argued that because the land belonged to Mr. Graham it was his prerogative to plow it under. Do you agree or do individuals have a responsibility to preserve the environment even at the expense of their own profits?

## PROBLEM EXERCISE: THE ENDANGERED SPECIES ACT

The Four Seasons motel is located on private land in the center of the town of East Yellowstone, which is just outside Yellowstone National Park and in the heart of grizzly bear territory. The fine restaurant of this motel is surrounded by picture windows that overlook its grounds. On one edge of this panorama the motel has placed an open dumpster, where it disposes of all the waste from its kitchen. The dumpster is illuminated by a spotlight.

Garbage is an easy source of food for grizzly bears, and an open dumpster will quickly draw grizzlies away from their usual foraging. So it is no surprise that grizzly bears frequent the dumpster at the Four Seasons motel. Indeed, the bears have become a major attraction for the motel.

Garbage is not known to be harmful to grizzly bears. But the principal cause of grizzly bear mortality is confrontations with humans, and when bears are drawn into town on a regular basis it is likely that a human confrontation will eventually occur. For this reason, the Audubon Society has asked the Four Seasons motel to take the simple measures necessary to ensure that bears cannot get into its dumpster. The motel has refused.

The grizzly bear was listed as a threatened species in the Greater Yellowstone Ecosystem in 1975 when there were only 136 members of the species. Can Audubon establish that the Four Seasons motel is violating the Endangered Species Act? What should their theory be?

Due in large part to efforts to separate grizzlies from garbage, the species made a remarkable recovery. In 2019 it was estimated that there were 728 grizzlies in the Greater Yellowstone Ecosystem. In July 2017 the Trump administration delisted the Greater Yellowstone grizzly from the endangered species list, but this decision was overturned by a federal judge in September 2018. Crow Indian Tribe v. United States, 343 F.Supp.3d 999 (D. Mt. 2018), aff'd 965 F.3d 662 (9th Cir. 2020).

# G.   THE FUTURE OF BIODIVERSITY PROTECTION

As the inadequacies of an eleventh hour, species-by-species approach to conservation have become more apparent, efforts to reorient public policy toward more forward-looking and comprehensive approaches have gained momentum. These efforts have spawned various initiatives for managing public resources to promote environmental values and to preserve biodiversity.

Because the costs of species protection measures are far more visible and immediate than are the diffuse, long-term benefits of preserving biodiversity, efforts to relax the provisions of the ESA are likely to continue. Arguments by opponents of the ESA resemble those made by loggers protesting outside the "God Squad" hearings on the spotted owl, who carried signs reading "Loggers Pay Taxes, Owls Do Not" and "We Need Jobs, Not Birds." Egan, Politics Reign at Spotted Owl Hearing, N.Y. Times, Jan. 9, 1992, at A14. A BLM lawyer at the hearings argued that it is immoral to favor animals over humans and that current policy "is far more likely to result in homeless people rather than homeless owls." Id. Alaska Congressman Don Young argues that protection of the spotted owl is a product of "imperfect 'feel good' legislation [that causes] a comfortable urbanized population to be spared the costs of their compulsions" while imposing these costs on others. Young, The Survival of the Fittest, 1990 Envtl. Forum 34 (July-Aug. 1990).

Congressman Young and others argue that ESA should be amended to compensate private interests affected by the Act, to remove protections for certain species deemed not worth saving, and to require that listing decisions be based on a balancing of the costs and benefits of listing. Michael Bean, an attorney with the Environmental Defense Fund, replies that uncertainty makes it impossible to incorporate such approaches into the Endangered Species Act. Bean, We Don't Know the Benefits Side of the Equation, 7 Envtl. Forum 30 (July-Aug. 1990).

Public opinion polls show strong support for the Endangered Species Act even when the spotted owl controversy was in the news. A poll released in 1992 showed that voters supported the Act by 66 percent to 11 percent. When asked to choose between protecting species or saving jobs and businesses, species protection won out by a margin of 48 percent to 29 percent. Sawhill, Saving Endangered Species Doesn't Endanger Economy, Wall St. J., Feb. 20, 1992, at A15.

In an effort to win public support for proposals to relax the ESA, its critics argue that it has not been successful and thus needs "fixing." The National Research Council (NRC) has published a report evaluating experience under the ESA. NRC, Science and the Endangered Species Act (1995). The report, which had been commissioned by Congress, found that "the ESA is based on sound scientific principles." Id. at 4. Noting that the Earth is experiencing a major mass extinction of species, the report concluded that "[t]he major cause of the current extinction is human activity," unlike the other five mass extinctions of the past 500 million years. Id. at 5. While finding it "difficult to quantify the effectiveness of the act in preventing species extinction," the report concluded that "there is no doubt that it has prevented the extinction of some species and slowed the declines of others." Id. at 4. The NRC recommended that critical habitat for the survival of threatened or endangered species be designated immediately upon listing, rather than waiting for years after listing. It also endorsed the notion of protecting distinct subpopulations of species and it found no scientific reason for providing lesser protection for plants than for animals.

On September 29, 2005, the U.S. House of Representatives approved a bill that would make substantial changes in the ESA. Called the "Threatened and Endangered Species Recovery Act of 2006," the bill was championed by Congressman Richard Pombo, the Republican chairman of the House Resources Committee. It passed the House by a vote of 229-193 after an environmentally more sensitive substitute was defeated by a vote of 206-216. Under the bill, which died after failing to win approval in the Senate, private landowners could request a written determination of whether a proposed use of their property would violate section 9 of the ESA. If no such determination is issued within 180 days, the proposed use was to be deemed to comply with the ESA. If a determination is made that the proposed use would violate section 9, the legislation would have required the government to compensate the landowner based on the fair market value of the foregone use. One unusual provision in the bill was a requirement that customers of federal power projects receive a line-item on their bills for ESA compliance costs.

Supporters of the ESA deny that it has been a failure. They credit it with playing a substantial role in the dramatic recovery of many species, such as the bald eagle and the whooping crane, and they emphasize that programs like "SafeHarbors" and Candidate Conservation Agreements have helped reduce compliance burdens and provided private landowners with incentives to engage in voluntary actions to preserve biodiversity. For a list of 110 Success Stories for the Endangered Species Act, released in 2012, see *http://www.esasuccess.org.*

In March 2006, a group of 5,738 biologists signed a letter to the U.S. Senate "Concerning Science in the Endangered Species Act." The biologists praised the ESA and criticized proposals to weaken its protections. They observed that:

> [L]ess than one percent of listed species have gone extinct since 1973, while 10 percent of candidate species still waiting to be listed have suffered that fate. In addition to the hundreds of species that the Act has protected from extinction, listing has contributed to population increases or the stabilization of populations for at least 35 percent of listed species, and perhaps significantly more, as well as the recovery of such signature species as the peregrine falcon. While complete recovery has been realized for just two percent of species listed, given the precarious state of most species when listed, this represents significant progress. [Letter from 5,738 Biologists to the U.S. Senate Concerning Science in the Endangered Species Act, March 2006, available at *http://www.lawprofessors.typepad.com/ environmental_law/files/Biologists_Letter_full_list_whitecover.pdf.*]

The biologists stressed the importance of the ESA's emphasis on "best available science" and they criticized efforts to mandate the use of non-scientific factors to delay or block listing decisions, designations of critical habitat, or implementation of species recovery plans.

A working group convened by the Keystone Center in 2005 to consider how to improve the ESA's habitat protection provisions was unable to reach consensus on a recommendation for amending the Act. In April 2006, the Center released a useful report based on this process that focuses on how to make better use of incentives under the Act. Keystone Center, The Keystone Working Group on Endangered Species Act Habitat Issues (2006). A valuable article recommending how the Obama administration can improve implementation of the ESA without having to amend the statute is Donald C. Baur, Michael J. Bean & William Robert Irvin, A Recovery Plan for the Endangered Species Act, 39 Envtl. L. Rep. 10006 (2009). The article makes five sets of recommendations: (1) "Establish and Follow Science-Backed Priorities in the Listing Program," (2) "Reduce Regulatory Impediments to Clearly Beneficial Actions," (3) "Make Greater Use of Incentives to Encourage Nonfederal Landowners to Promote Species Conservation," (4) "Clarify the ESA §7(a)(2) Prohibitions and Procedures," and (5) "Improve Funding." For a summary of how the ESA was revitalized by administrative action during the Obama administration, see Michael J. Bean, A Statute Reborn, 34 Environmental Forum 30 (Sept./Oct. 2017).

Biologist Edward O. Wilson now estimates that there are roughly ten million species of plants, animals, fungi, and algae on Earth, give or take one million. About "two million species have been discovered, described and given a Latinized scientific name." But "except for the vertebrates (consisting of 63,000 described species of birds, mammals, reptiles, amphibians and fishes) and the flowering plants (with approximately 270,000 species), relatively little is collectively known about millions of kinds of fungi, algae and most diverse of all, the insects and other invertebrate animals." Edward O. Wilson, The Global Solution to Extinction, N.Y. Times, Mar. 12, 2016, *https://www.nytimes.com/2016/03/13/opinion/sunday/the -global-solution-to-extinction.html?_r=1.* Wilson notes that today "only 18,000 new species are being discovered and described each year," which would mean that "the task of mapping life on Earth, or what is left of it, will not be completed until the 23rd century." At the same time, species are "disappearing each year at upward of 1,000 times the rate that existed before the coming of humans."

Wilson argues that because "the disappearance of natural habitat is the primary cause of biological diversity loss at every level — ecosystems, species and genes," the only way to reduce extinction to a sustainable level is to preserve much more natural habitat. He concludes that the "only way to save upward of 90 percent of the rest of life is to vastly increase the area of refuges, from their current 15 percent of the land and 3 percent of the sea to half of the land and half of the sea." He maintains that this could be done without removing people or changing property rights.

# CHAPTER 10
# ENVIRONMENTAL ENFORCEMENT

Senior environmental officials at both the state and federal level often give the public the same reassurance about environmental compliance. *Almost all companies comply,* they say. *The large companies comply; it is mainly the small ones that have compliance issues.* Does the evidence agree? In a word: no.

The data reveal that for most rules the rate of serious noncompliance — the violations that pose the biggest risks to public health and the environment — is 25% or more. For many rules with big health consequences the serious noncompliance rates for large facilities are 50% to 70% or even higher. And those are just the ones we know about; for many rules the U.S. Environmental Protection Agency (EPA) has no idea what the rate of noncompliance is.

— Cynthia Giles, Assistant Administrator, EPA Office of Enforcement and Compliance Assurance 2009-2017[*]

If regulation is to achieve its goals, it must induce compliance. Thus, it is critical that the environmental laws include enforcement provisions that create incentives for compliance. While the environmental statutes provide broad enforcement authorities, compliance problems have been widespread. People were shocked in 1993 when a *National Law Journal* survey found that one-third of corporate counsel reported that their clients had recently violated the environmental laws. Lavelle, Environmental Vise: Law, Compliance, Nat'l L.J., Aug. 30, 1993, at S1. Most of the lawyers surveyed asserted that it was not possible to achieve full compliance with the environmental laws because of their cost, complexity, or the uncertainty that surrounds how they are interpreted. Yet virtually all believed that environmental regulation is becoming more stringent throughout the world, and nearly 70 percent agreed that greater attention to environmental concerns would enhance the long-term profitability of their companies.

More than 20 years after the *National Law Journal* survey, the world was stunned by revelations in September 2015 that for years Volkswagen (VW) had intentionally programmed its diesel engines to activate emissions controls only during laboratory testing. It had been widely thought that large, multinational corporations who have sophisticated environmental counsel would not deliberately violate pollution control regulations on such a massive scale. As the epigram above from Cynthia Giles notes, serious non-compliance rates can be shockingly high.

---

[*] Next Generation Compliance: Environmental Regulation for the Modern Era 3 (2021).

Many factors contribute to environmental enforcement problems. The vast number and diversity of regulatory targets make compliance monitoring difficult. Often, regulations are poorly designed from an enforcement perspective. Some judges still view regulatory violations as unimportant if they do not clearly cause substantial harm. Enforcement resources are limited, and the procedural protections afforded defendants increase with the stringency of potential penalties. When government agencies, which have included some of the most notorious polluters, break the environmental laws, they often do not face credible enforcement sanctions.

This chapter explores how environmental laws are enforced by governmental authorities and citizens. It begins by focusing on how compliance with environmental regulations is monitored and the controversy over policies providing incentives to encourage voluntary self-audits. The chapter then explores criminal enforcement of the environmental laws and the debate over what *mens rea* is required before criminal sanctions can be imposed on violators. Standing and citizen access to the courts is discussed next, followed by a discussion of the role of citizen suits in enforcing the laws. The chapter concludes by focusing on problems that arise when enforcement actions are brought against government agencies.

## A.   MONITORING AND DETECTING VIOLATIONS

Serious enforcement difficulties can be avoided if regulatory programs are designed to facilitate compliance. This is the central message of an important forthcoming book by former EPA enforcement chief Cynthia Giles. She writes that "the most important determinant of compliance results is the structure of the regulation and the extent to which it adopts—or ignores—strategies to make compliance the default." Giles, Next Generation Compliance: Environmental Rules for the Modern Era 3 (2021). Giles contrasts the compliance record under two important EPA regulations applying to coal-fired power plants: the program to reduce sulfur dioxide emissions from these plants, which has a nearly perfect compliance record, and the new source review program where more than 70 percent of large sources had serious violations. She notes:

> The Acid Rain Program is a master class in good design. It required continuous monitoring so that everyone knew exactly how much pollution there was. It contained incentives for making sure the monitors were operating properly. All results had to be electronically reported to a central database. It was easy for regulators to determine if a facility complied: just compare the number of tons emitted to the number of allowances the company held. Automatic penalties made compliance the cheaper option. Attempting to avoid the obligations was likely to be both more hassle and more expensive than complying. All these structural features combined to make compliance the path of least resistance: compliance was reported at over 99%.
>
> New Source Review for coal-fired power plants was the perfect storm of bad compliance design. Companies decided on their own whether the rules applied to their facilities and didn't have to inform regulators. Figuring out who was violating was both complicated and resource intensive. Almost all of the necessary evidence was held by the violators, and almost

none was available to regulators without a fight. Installing the required pollution controls was expensive, creating powerful incentives to make use of the many pathways to avoid, obscure, and evade. When they were caught, companies knew that even if they lost the enforcement case, they would still save money by delaying compliance. Violations became common, with serious consequences for people's health. [Id. at 8.]

Establishing objective means for measuring and monitoring compliance can be enormously difficult given the vast number, variety, and complexity of pollutants and dischargers subject to environmental regulation. The Clean Water Act regulates more than 350,000 point sources discharging hundreds of different pollutants. Yet the Act's permit provisions have become a model for other enforcement programs, including the Clean Air Act's national permit program. Permits embody a written record of the controls applicable to each source that can be compared with the results of monitoring to determine if violations have occurred.

Determining whether or not a discharger is in compliance with permit limits is not as easy as one might think. Inspectors cannot simply walk into any plant, insert "some perfectly accurate meter into the waste-water or smoke stack emission stream," and obtain "a constant rate-of-discharge result that could be expressed equally well in any time unit, from per second to per year." C. Russell, W. Harrington & W. Vaughan, Enforcing Pollution Control Laws 10 (1986). Inspectors first have to gain access to a plant, which usually involves announcing inspections in advance, giving the plant operator an opportunity to conceal violations. Sampling is costly and time-consuming and may yield results with large margins of error.

[E]ven when the source is trying to comply with the permit terms it will have fluctuating discharges. These fluctuations may have both periodic elements due to production patterns, boiler soot-blowing, or other routine causes as well as random components ultimately traceable to human or machine failure, fluctuations in ambient conditions such as temperature, or random startup and shutdown decisions. Thus, the stream being measured is not constant, and measurements at one time can be applied only to broader compliance questions through statistical inference with associated probabilities of errors of two types — that a violation will be found where none exists or that true violations will be missed. To further complicate matters, the measurement instruments have their own errors that must be accounted for in the inference procedure. The perfect instrument does not exist. [Id.]

Faced with these difficulties, environmental enforcement authorities rely heavily on self-monitoring and self-reporting requirements to detect violations. The pollution control statutes generally authorize EPA to impose monitoring, record-keeping, and reporting requirements (e.g., CWA §308(a)(A), CAA §114) on dischargers. Under the Clean Water Act, dischargers of water pollutants are required to monitor their discharges on a regular basis and to file discharge monitoring reports (DMRs) that are available to the public. When self-reported violations are included in DMRs, it is relatively easy for regulatory authorities or citizen groups to bring successful enforcement actions. Recognizing the danger that sources will not report adverse monitoring data truthfully, regulatory authorities prosecute reporting violations with vigor. When false reporting or tampering with monitoring data has been discovered, criminal prosecutions often follow. To make it possible to uncover false reports, the environmental laws generally give enforcement officials the right to conduct inspections. However, EPA needs a warrant before it can inspect a business without the consent of the owner. Marshall v. Barlow's, Inc., 436 U.S. 307 (1978).

Air pollution control monitors often miss major air quality problems caused by industrial accidents. On June 21, 2019, an explosion occurred at the Philadelphia Energy Solutions refinery whose impact on a poor, minority neighborhood of Philadelphia is discussed in Chapter 1. More than 600,000 pounds of hydrocarbons and 3,200 pounds of deadly hydrofluoric acid were released into the air by the explosion. Yet the impact on air quality was not measured because the nearest air quality monitor was programmed to record data only every sixth day. Data show that the "government network of 3,900 monitoring devices nationwide has routinely missed major toxic releases and day-to-day pollution dangers." Tim McLaughlin, Laila Kearney & Laura Sanicola, U.S. Air Monitors Routinely Miss Pollution — Even Refinery Explosions, Reuters, Dec. 1, 2020.

EPA encourages the reporting of environmental violations by maintaining a tip line at *www.epa.gov/tips*. Some of the most serious violations of the environmental laws are discovered as the result of whistle-blowers. A major exception was the Volkswagen diesel emissions scandal. Volkswagen deliberately programmed turbocharged direct injection diesel engines on 11 million model year 2009 through 2015 vehicles worldwide to only operate certain emissions control devices during emissions testing. The company believed that it was very unlikely that authorities could measure emissions while vehicles were operating on the road. However, John German, co-leader of the International Council on Clean Transportation (ICCT), was curious as to how diesel engines that produced high emissions in Europe were complying with more stringent U.S. standards for tailpipe emissions. Eschewing traditional emissions lab testing, the ICCT used a probe that could be placed in the vehicles' tailpipes connected to a machine in the cars' trunks that would measure actual emissions when the vehicles were on the road. Coupled with data from other portable emission measurement systems, it found emissions that were 5 to 35 times higher than permissible. The ICCT informed VW and turned its data over to EPA and the California Air Resources Board in May 2014. In December 2014, EPA announced that VW had agreed to fix its software, but further testing in May 2015 showed that the supposed fix had not corrected the problem. In September 2015, the company admitted the cheating. What is remarkable about this experience is the large number of VW employees who must have known about this intentional violation of the environmental laws without telling anyone.

Most of the major federal environmental statutes have provisions that protect employees who report violations by their employers. These provisions prohibit an employer from discharging or discriminating against any employee who reports environmental violations (e.g., CWA §507, CAA §322, OSHA §660(c), RCRA §7001, CERCLA §110, SDWA §1450(i), TSCA §23). These provisions are administered by the U.S. Department of Labor (DOL). Regulations implementing these statutes appear at 29 C.F.R. §§24.1 et seq. They generally provide that a worker must file a written complaint with the DOL within 30 days of the time that the employee learns that he or she will be, or has been, subjected to discrimination, harassment, or retaliation. Whistle-blowers may seek a hearing before a DOL administrative law judge who may award them back pay, reinstatement, or other relief, subject to judicial review and civil judicial enforcement.

These provisions have not been used extensively. Robert Devore of the Department of Labor reported that between 1983 and 1991, 490 whistle-blower complaints were heard by the Department; 92 employees won judgments, which totaled $822,900. Most cases involved the provisions of section 210 of the Energy Reorganization Act, which protects workers at nuclear power plants. The environmental laws are not the only federal statutes with whistle-blower protection provisions. The Sarbanes-Oxley Act also prohibits retaliation against employees who report corporate wrongdoing.

The DOL now maintains a website to inform employees of the whistle-blower protection laws and to report data on how the cases are handled. It is located at *www.whistleblowers.gov*. Data reported by DOL on the website indicate that a total of 326 whistle-blower complaints involving statutes administered by EPA were decided in the six years between 2014 and 2019. Only 8 of these (2.5%) were found to have merit, although 66 (22.2%) resulted in some form of settlement. A total of 193 (59.2%) were dismissed and 59 (18.1%) were withdrawn. See *https://www.osha.gov/sites/default/files/3D_Charts-Received_Closed.pdf*.

When it amended the Clean Air Act in 1990, Congress sought to help enforcement authorities acquire evidence of violations by adding a bounty provision in section 113(f) of the Act. This authorizes EPA to pay a reward of up to $10,000 to anyone who provides information that leads to a criminal conviction or civil penalty under the Act. Bounty provisions also are included in CERCLA section 109(d) and the Act to Prevent Pollution from Ships. The latter generated a $250,000 reward for tourists on a cruise ship who videotaped the ship's illegal waste disposal at sea, resulting in a $500,000 fine against the Princess Cruise Line.

In the 1990 Clean Air Act Amendments, Congress also sought to make it procedurally much easier to enforce the requirements of the Act. The original Clean Air Act had made it very difficult to prove violations. Prosecutors had to show that an individual source had acted in a manner that violated the applicable state implementation plan (SIP), which was very difficult, particularly since it was hard even to identify what SIP requirements were applicable to a specific source. To correct this problem, the 1990 Amendments established a federal operating permit system in Title V of the Clean Air Act, modeled in part on the Clean Water Act's NPDES permit program.

To make it easier to enforce Title V permits, Congress required major sources of air pollution to improve their emissions monitoring and reporting. To improve monitoring, utilities subject to Title IV of the Clean Air Act must install continuous emissions monitoring systems or their equivalent. CAA §412(a), 42 U.S.C. §7651k(a). Tampering with monitoring equipment may result in criminal prosecutions when detected. Congress directed EPA in section 412(d) of the Clean Air Act to issue regulations specifying the consequences of breakdowns in monitoring equipment. To provide an incentive for utilities to keep monitors operating properly (and to prevent them from turning off monitors to conceal high levels of emissions), EPA adopted a rule that assumes that emissions are at a higher level "the longer the gap in recorded data and/or the lower the annual monitor availability. . . ." 58 Fed. Reg. 3,590, 3,635 (1993). Maximum emissions levels are assumed for any outage from a continuous emissions monitor (CEM) that has not achieved at least 90 percent availability in the prior year, while average values are assumed for outages of less than 24 hours from CEMs that have been available more than 95 percent of the time.

Enforcement officials recognize that even effective emissions monitoring will not guarantee full compliance with all environmental regulations. Given the large number of entities subject to regulation, the diversity of the regulated community, and limited government enforcement resources, efforts to promote voluntary compliance are essential. Thus, enforcement officials are encouraging firms to perform voluntary self-audits to discover and correct environmental violations.

In response to concerns that self-audits could generate information that would make it easier to prosecute companies, several states have enacted laws making the results of such audits privileged information. In July 1993, Oregon became the first state to adopt a law creating a qualified "environmental self-audit privilege." The law provides that environmental audits will be protected from disclosure in criminal prosecutions if violations discovered in the audit are promptly corrected, unless the privilege is asserted for a fraudulent purpose or the prosecution can establish a compelling need for the information. By August 2017, 28 states had enacted some form of audit privilege and/or immunity statutes. EPA, State Audit Privilege and Immunity Laws and Self-Disclosure Laws and Policies, *https://www.epa.gov/compliance/state-audit-privilege-and -immunity-laws-self-disclosure-laws-and-policies.* The state laws have followed two principal models: (1) the "privilege-only" model, adopted in Oregon and five other states, which bars environmental audits and related documents from being used as evidence in civil or criminal proceedings, and (2) the "privilege and immunity" model, adopted in Colorado and 20 other states, which provides immunity from any type of penalty in addition to making the audit privileged. Van Cleve & Holman, Promise and Reality in the Enforcement of the Amended Clean Air Act—Part II: Federal Enforceability and Environmental Auditing, 27 Envtl. L. Rep. 10151, 10161 (1997). There are some variations on the privilege and immunity model. In Colorado, the legislation creates a presumption of immunity from all penalties for violations found during "self-evaluations" which are voluntarily disclosed and addressed within a reasonable time. The presumption of immunity can be rebutted only if an enforcement agency proves that the disclosure was not voluntary. The Texas law requires companies that wish to qualify for immunity to provide public notice of their intent to conduct a self-audit. During the first year of experience with the law, 239 companies in Texas gave notice of their intent to audit. Id.

While opposing legislation to create audit privileges, EPA and the Justice Department have sought to encourage voluntary self-auditing. In 1991, the Justice Department issued guidelines providing that self-auditing and voluntary disclosure of environmental violations would be considered important mitigating factors when prosecutorial discretion is exercised and at sentencing. Spurred in part by the proliferation of state privilege legislation, EPA began in 1994 to explore whether additional incentives were needed to encourage self-auditing. While developing its policy on self-auditing, EPA noted that a survey conducted by Price Waterhouse in 1995 found that half of corporate respondents would expand their environmental auditing efforts if penalties were reduced for violations voluntarily discovered and corrected. 60 Fed. Reg. 66,711 (1995).

After conducting several public meetings and receiving extensive public comment on an interim policy, EPA adopted a final policy statement in December 1995. The policy seeks to encourage firms voluntarily to discover, disclose, and correct environmental violations by reducing civil penalties for such violations and by agreeing not to pursue criminal prosecutions for them if certain conditions are met. In April 2000, EPA made minor revisions to its incentives for self-policing policy. An excerpt from EPA's policy, as revised, is reproduced below.

## EPA, Final Policy Statement on Incentives for Self-Policing of Violations

65 Fed. Reg. 19,618 (2000)

### C. Incentives for Self-Policing

#### 1. No Gravity-Based Penalties

If a regulated entity establishes that it satisfies all of the conditions of Section D of this Policy, EPA will not seek gravity-based penalties for violations of Federal environmental requirements discovered and disclosed by the entity.

#### 2. Reduction of Gravity-Based Penalties by 75%

If a regulated entity establishes that it satisfies all of the conditions of Section D of this Policy except for D(1) — systematic discovery — EPA will reduce by 75% gravity-based penalties for violations of Federal environmental requirements discovered and disclosed by the entity.

#### 3. No Recommendation for Criminal Prosecution

(a) If a regulated entity establishes that it satisfies at least conditions D(2) through D(9) of this Policy, EPA will not recommend to the U.S. Department of Justice or other prosecuting authority that criminal charges be brought against the disclosing entity, as long as EPA determines that the violation is not part of a pattern or practice that demonstrates or involves:

(i) A prevalent management philosophy or practice that conceals or condones environmental violations; or

(ii) High-level corporate officials' or managers' conscious involvement in, or willfull blindness to, violations of Federal environmental law;

(b) Whether or not EPA recommends the regulated entity for criminal prosecution under this section, the Agency may recommend for prosecution the criminal acts of individual managers or employees under existing policies guiding the exercise of enforcement discretion.

#### 4. No Routine Request for Environmental Audit Reports

EPA will neither request nor use an environmental audit report to initiate a civil or criminal investigation of an entity. For example, EPA will not request an environmental audit report in routine inspections. If the Agency has independent reason to believe that a violation has occurred, however, EPA may seek any information relevant to identifying violations or determining liability or extent of harm.

## D.  Conditions

### 1.  Systematic Discovery

The violation was discovered through:

(a) An environmental audit; or

(b) A compliance management system reflecting the regulated entity's due diligence in preventing, detecting, and correcting violations. The regulated entity must provide accurate and complete documentation to the Agency as to how its compliance management system meets the criteria for due diligence outlined in section B and how the regulated entity discovered the violation through its compliance management system. EPA may require the regulated entity to make publicly available a description of its compliance management system.

### 2.  Voluntary Discovery

The violation was discovered voluntarily and not through a legally mandated monitoring or sampling requirement prescribed by statute, regulation, permit, judicial or administrative order, or consent agreement. For example, the Policy does not apply to:

(a) Emissions violations detected through a continuous emissions monitor (or alternative monitor established in a permit) where any such monitoring is required;

(b) Violations of National Pollutant Discharge Elimination System (NPDES) discharge limits detected through required sampling or monitoring; or

(c) Violations discovered through a compliance audit required to be performed by the terms of a consent order or settlement agreement, unless the audit is a component of agreement terms to implement a comprehensive environmental management system.

### 3.  Prompt Disclosure

The regulated entity fully discloses the specific violation in writing to EPA within 21 days (or within such shorter time as may be required by law) after the entity discovered that the violation has, or may have, occurred. The time at which the entity discovers that a violation has, or may have, occurred begins when any officer, director, employee or agent of the facility has an objectively reasonable basis for believing that a violation has, or may have, occurred.

### 4.  Discovery and Disclosure Independent of Government or Third-Party Plaintiff

(a) The regulated entity discovers and discloses the potential violation to EPA prior to:

(i) The commencement of a Federal, State or local agency inspection or investigation, or the issuance by such agency of an information request to the regulated entity (where EPA determines that the facility did not know that it was under civil investigation, and EPA determines that the entity is otherwise acting in good faith, the Agency may exercise its discretion to reduce or waive civil penalties in accordance with this Policy);

(ii) Notice of a citizen suit;

(iii) The filing of a complaint by a third party;

(iv) The reporting of the violation to EPA (or other government agency) by a "whistleblower" employee, rather than by one authorized to speak on behalf of the regulated entity; or

(v) imminent discovery of the violation by a regulatory agency.

(b) For entities that own or operate multiple facilities, the fact that one facility is already the subject of an investigation, inspection, information request or third-party complaint does not preclude the Agency from exercising its discretion to make the Audit Policy available for violations self-discovered at other facilities owned or operated by the same regulated entity.

### 5. Correction and Remediation

The regulated entity corrects the violation within 60 calendar days from the date of discovery, certifies in writing that the violation has been corrected, and takes appropriate measures as determined by EPA to remedy any environmental or human harm due to the violation. EPA retains the authority to order an entity to correct a violation within a specific time period shorter than 60 days whenever correction in such shorter period of time is feasible and necessary to protect public health and the environment adequately. If more than 60 days will be needed to correct the violation, the regulated entity must so notify EPA in writing before the 60-day period has passed. Where appropriate, to satisfy conditions D(5) and D(6), EPA may require a regulated entity to enter into a publicly available written agreement, administrative consent order or judicial consent decree as a condition of obtaining relief under the Audit Policy, particularly where compliance or remedial measures are complex or a lengthy schedule for attaining and maintaining compliance or remediating harm is required.

### 6. Prevent Recurrence

The regulated entity agrees in writing to take steps to prevent a recurrence of the violation. Such steps may include improvements to its environmental auditing or compliance management system.

### 7. No Repeat Violations

The specific violation (or a closely related violation) has not occurred previously within the past three years at the same facility, and has not occurred within the past five years as part of a pattern at multiple facilities owned or operated by the same entity. For the purposes of this section, a violation is:

(a) Any violation of Federal, State or local environmental law identified in a judicial or administrative order, consent agreement or order, complaint, or notice of violation, conviction or plea agreement; or

(b) Any act or omission for which the regulated entity has previously received penalty mitigation from EPA or a State or local agency.

### 8. Other Violations Excluded

The violation is not one which (a) resulted in serious actual harm, or may have presented an imminent and substantial endangerment, to human health or the environment, or (b) violates the specific terms of any judicial or administrative order, or consent agreement.

### 9. Cooperation

The regulated entity cooperates as requested by EPA and provides such information as is necessary and requested by EPA to determine applicability of this Policy.

## E. Economic Benefit

EPA may forgive the entire penalty for violations that meet conditions D(1) through D(9) and, in the Agency's opinion, do not merit any penalty due to the insignificant amount of any economic benefit.

## F. Effect on State Law, Regulation or Policy

EPA will work closely with States to encourage their adoption and implementation of policies that reflect the incentives and conditions outlined in this Policy. EPA remains firmly opposed to statutory environmental audit privileges that shield evidence of environmental violations and undermine the public's right to know, as well as to blanket immunities, particularly immunities for violations that reflect criminal conduct, present serious threats or actual harm to health and the environment, allow noncomplying companies to gain an economic advantage over their competitors, or reflect a repeated failure to comply with Federal law. EPA will work with States to address any provisions of State audit privilege or immunity laws that are inconsistent with this Policy and that may prevent a timely and appropriate response to significant environmental violations. The Agency reserves its rights to take necessary actions to protect public health or the environment by enforcing against any violations of Federal law.

## NOTES AND QUESTIONS

1. Why does EPA's policy distinguish between violations discovered through an environmental audit or compliance management system that reflects due diligence and all other violations? What are the consequences of this distinction with respect to EPA's willingness to reduce penalties? If Volkswagen had voluntarily disclosed its years of using software to cheat on emissions testing prior to discovery by EPA, could it have taken advantage of EPA's policy to receive reduced penalties and no criminal prosecution?

2. Several environmental laws require regulated entities to self-report information that may include data indicating that a firm violated the law. EPA's initial interim self-audit policy statement did not allow disclosures of violations required to be reported by statute, regulation, or permit to qualify for penalty reductions. 60 Fed. Reg. 16,875, 16,877 (1995). However, after complaints that this would severely limit incentives for self-policing, EPA adopted a somewhat different approach. EPA concluded that the "final policy generally applies to any violation that is voluntarily discovered, regardless of whether the violation is required to be reported." 60 Fed. Reg. 66,706, 66,708 (1995). But the final policy states that violations identified through legally required monitoring will not be considered to have been voluntarily discovered. Would Exxon's notification to the Coast Guard that the *Exxon Valdez* was spilling enormous quantities of oil in Prince William Sound constitute "voluntary discovery" under EPA's policy? Could it qualify Exxon for a reduction of gravity-based penalties for the oil spill?

3. By August 1999, less than four years after EPA's self-audit policy was announced, a total of 430 companies had reported environmental violations at 1,788 facilities in order to qualify for reduced penalties. Relief was granted to 164 companies at 540 facilities where violations were disclosed and corrected. EPA, Enforcement and Compliance Assurance FY 1998 Accomplishments Report 4 (1999). Most of the companies were not required to pay penalties. Herman, It Takes a Partnership, 14 Envtl. Forum 26, 31 (May/June 1997). EPA reported in January 2002 that during fiscal year 2001 a total of 364 companies agreed to conduct self-audits and to correct environmental violations at 1,754 facilities in exchange for a waiver or significant reduction in penalties from EPA. While many industry groups have been critical of EPA's policy for not going far enough to create incentives for self-auditing, others have greeted it with cautious optimism. Banks, EPA's New Enforcement Policy: At Last, a Reliable Roadmap to Civil Penalty Mitigation for Self-Disclosed Violations, 26 Envtl. L. Rep. 10227 (1996). Through September 2013, EPA's policy had been used to resolve violations by more than 6,000 companies at more than 16,000 facilities. More than half of these were reporting and record-keeping violations.

4. EPA's policy offers to waive all or 75 percent of "gravity-based penalties," which the agency defines as "that portion of a penalty over and above the economic benefit," 60 Fed. Reg. 66,711 (1995). Why does EPA insist on retaining the discretion to recover a defendant's economic gain from non-compliance? Will this insistence tend to encourage or discourage prompt discovery and correction of violations? When it revised its initial incentives for self-policing policy in April 2000, EPA also adopted a Final Policy on Compliance Incentives for Small Business. 65 Fed. Reg. 19,630. The most significant aspect of EPA's policy for encouraging compliance by small businesses is that it provides that EPA will forgo all penalties—including recovery of the economic benefit of violations—for small businesses that make a "good faith" effort to comply with regulations either through conducting environmental audits or receiving on-site compliance assistance. Small businesses are defined as companies with 100 or fewer employees on a companywide basis. Why would EPA be willing to forgo recovery of the economic benefit of violations when small businesses are the violators?

5. During its 1996 session, a state legislature considered a bill that would grant immunity for environmental violations discovered during an environmental audit if they are voluntarily disclosed and corrected. The bill defined voluntary disclosure to mean a written disclosure that occurs prior to: (1) discovery or knowledge of the violation by the state environmental agency, (2) the initiation of an enforcement action by the state or EPA, or (3) the regulated entity's actual knowledge that the discovery of the violation by a regulatory agency or a third party is imminent. How is this legislation different from EPA's policy? Which would do more to encourage prompt disclosure and correction of violations, EPA's policy or the proposed state law?

6. On August 1, 2008, EPA issued a policy to encourage new owners of facilities to perform environmental audits and to voluntarily disclose and correct environmental violations. EPA, Interim Approach to Applying the Audit Policy to New Owners, 73 Fed. Reg. 44,991 (2008). The policy defines a new owner as someone who has owned a facility for less than nine months. The policy encourages auditing and reporting by promising reduced civil penalties for violations disclosed to EPA during the first nine months of ownership. In December 2015, EPA launched a new

eDisclosure web-based portal to make it easier for companies to self-report violations. Notice of eDisclosure Portal Launch: Modernizing Implementation of EPA's Self-Policing Incentive Policies, 80 Fed. Reg. 76,476 (2015). This portal centralizes self-reporting that previously had involved disclosures to individual EPA regional offices. Entities who disclose minor violations through the eDisclosure portal (including EPCRA violations) that meet all Audit Policy conditions and all Small Business Compliance conditions will automatically be issued an electronic Notice of Determination, confirming that the EPA considers the violation resolved and that no civil penalties will be assessed. Those that disclose more serious violations (Category 2 violations) will be issued a letter acknowledging that EPA received the disclosure and stating that EPA will determine the entity's eligibility for penalty mitigation if and when it decides to take any enforcement action. In the first years of the eDisclosure program, the EPA reported a 75 percent increase in the number of annual self-disclosures (increasing from 310 to approximately 545 annually) as well as an increase in the types of disclosures being reported.

7. On May 15, 2018, the EPA announced a "renewed emphasis on self-disclosed violation policies" to enhance the eDisclosure program. Under the new policy, all self-disclosed civil violations (with some exceptions) must be made through the eDisclosure Portal, and outreach efforts to its New Owner Audit and Small Business Compliance Programs were expanded. In FY2019, 635 entities with over 1,900 facilities voluntarily disclosed violations, representing a 20 percent increase in voluntary disclosures compared to the previous year.

8. In February 2021 the Biden administration reaffirmed EPA's emphasis on voluntary self-disclosure of violations. It reported that almost 28,000 facilities had disclosed violations under the Audit Policies between 1995 and 2020. Penalty mitigation was denied only 12 times because violations caused serious actual harm or imminent and substantial endangerment. Less than one percent of all disclosures were denied penalty mitigation due to repeat violations. EPA reconfirmed that regulated entities could report that they "may have" a violation without affirmatively admitting to one.

## B. ENFORCEMENT AUTHORITIES AND POLICIES

Even when violations of environmental regulations are discovered, enforcement can be time-consuming and expensive and its outcome uncertain. Defendants enjoy procedural protections that can make it costly for authorities to discharge their burden of proving violations. To facilitate enforcement, the environmental laws provide a wide menu of enforcement options — criminal, civil, and administrative — whose procedural requirements vary in stringency with the severity of potential sanctions. They also authorize citizens to sue violators when government authorities have failed to take enforcement action.

After the initial generation of federal environmental laws were enacted, officials seeking to enforce the new laws frequently encountered courts who were reluctant to impose substantial sanctions on those who violated environmental regulations. Some judges viewed regulatory violations as technical matters that should not be considered serious offenses, particularly if they were not clearly linked to substantial environmental damage. Over time, as public understanding of the purposes of environmental regulation has improved and as Congress has increased the potential penalties for regulatory violations, this attitude has diminished somewhat. However, considerable controversy remains concerning which of two competing approaches to environmental enforcement should be emphasized by government officials.

Deterrence-based enforcement seeks to ensure compliance by emphasizing the consequences of non-compliance. It seeks to ensure that those who violate environmental regulations will incur penalties substantial enough to deter future violations. Although this approach was emphasized by federal officials during the Clinton administration, many state officials and the Bush administration favored a more conciliatory, cooperation-oriented approach to enforcement. This approach is premised in part on the notion that companies will voluntarily comply with regulations if government officials help them understand what is necessary for compliance without threatening them with substantial penalties for violations. For a discussion of these two competing visions of environmental enforcement, see Clifford Rechtschaffen, Competing Visions: EPA and the States Battle for the Future of Environmental Enforcement, 30 Envtl. L. Rep. 10803 (2000).

## 1. Enforcement Authorities

The enforcement provisions of the Clean Water Act, which are typical of those found in the major federal environmental laws, are outlined below. As these provisions illustrate, the statutes provide a broad range of penalties for violators. Criminal violations can result in imprisonment and heavy fines. Civil suits can result in injunctive relief and substantial monetary penalties. Lesser monetary penalties may be imposed administratively. In addition, violators may be barred from receiving federal contracts or loans.

## Enforcement Provisions of the Clean Water Act

*§308* authorizes monitoring and reporting requirements and inspections by authorities.

*§309(a)* authorizes issuance of administrative compliance orders.

*§309(b)* authorizes civil enforcement actions for injunctive relief.

*§309(c)* provides criminal penalties for negligent violations (fines of $2,500 to $25,000 per day and up to 1 year in prison), knowing violations (fines of $5,000 to $50,000 per day of violation and up to 3 years in prison with doubled penalties for repeat violations), knowing endangerment of another (fines of up to $250,000 and 15 years in prison), and false statements (fines of up to $10,000 and 2 years in prison).

*§309(d)* provides civil penalties of up to $25,000 per day for each violation.

> *§§309(e) & (f)* require EPA to join states as defendants in suits against municipalities and authorizes suits against treatment works and dischargers for violations of pretreatment regulations.
>
> *§309(g)* authorizes administrative penalties (up to $10,000 per violation with a $25,000 maximum for violations heard without an adjudicatory hearing—"Class I penalties"—and up to $10,000 per day with a $125,000 maximum for violations subject to adjudicatory hearings—"Class II penalties") and gives citizens the right to comment on them.
>
> *§402(h)* authorizes a ban on new sewer hookups to publicly owned treatment works violating their discharge permits.
>
> *§504* authorizes EPA to sue to restrain any source contributing to pollution "presenting an imminent or substantial endangerment" to public health or welfare.
>
> *§505* authorizes citizen suits for injunctive relief and civil penalties against any person violating an effluent standard or order and provides for awards of attorneys' fees to prevailing parties.
>
> *§508* gives EPA authority to blacklist violators, barring them from all federal contracts and loans.

Virtually every time it has reauthorized the major environmental statutes, Congress has expanded and strengthened their enforcement authorities. For example, when the Clean Water Act was amended in 1987, Congress substantially increased the maximum civil and criminal penalties for violations and it gave EPA administrative enforcement authority under the Act for the first time. In 1990, Congress added even stronger enforcement provisions to the Clean Air Act. Penalties for the most serious criminal violations of the Clean Air Act (CAA) now can include imprisonment for up to 15 years and a fine of up to $1 million for each violation. CAA §113(c)(5). In October 2007, a subsidiary of British Petroleum agreed to pay a $50 million fine, the largest criminal fine ever under the CAA, for violations associated with a catastrophic refinery explosion in Texas that killed 15 employees.

Because judicial enforcement actions generally are more formal and more expensive, environmental authorities usually go to court only to prosecute the most egregious violations. A former assistant attorney general responsible for environmental enforcement has noted, "[t]he simple truth is that we cannot bring . . . even a significant number of these [enforcement] actions to court." Dinkins, Shall We Fight or Will We Finish: Environmental Dispute Resolution in a Litigious Society, 14 Envtl. L. Rep. 10398 (1984). While defendants do not have a constitutional right to a jury trial in suits that seek exclusively equitable relief, the Supreme Court has held that the Seventh Amendment's right to a jury trial applies in suits for civil penalties under the environmental laws. Tull v. United States, 481 U.S. 412 (1987). Trials are expensive and time-consuming; thus, more than 95 percent of environmental enforcement cases are resolved through settlements. Settlements often include negotiated penalties incorporated into consent decrees approved by a court.

Resources devoted to criminal enforcement efforts increased substantially during the 1990s. After enactment of the Pollution Prosecution Act of 1990, EPA expanded its criminal enforcement program. Under the administration of

President George W. Bush, the number of criminal prosecutions for environmental violations declined substantially, though certain industries, such as cruise ship lines, were targeted for criminal enforcement actions. During fiscal year 2008, EPA initiated 319 criminal cases and brought criminal charges against 176 defendants. A total of $63.5 million in criminal fines were imposed. Prison sentences totaling 57 years were imposed on persons convicted of environmental crimes. Most criminal prosecutions over the years have been for violations of the Clean Water Act and RCRA.

The vast majority of environmental enforcement actions never see the courthouse door. More than 95 percent are handled through administrative enforcement procedures, which are procedurally simpler but provide less stringent penalties. Administrative enforcement actions may involve the issuance of administrative orders and the assessment of civil penalties. Most environmental statutes authorize EPA to issue administrative orders (see, e.g., CAA §113(a), CWA §309(g), RCRA §3008(a)), which give officials flexibility to specify remedial action that must be taken by a certain date. If, after notice and an opportunity for a hearing, the action specified in the administrative order is not taken, environmental authorities can go to court to seek its enforcement. The environmental laws also authorize EPA to assess administrative civil penalties, which may be contested in hearings before an administrative law judge whose decisions are subject to judicial review based on the administrative record. Nearly all administrative cases ultimately are settled; fewer than 5 percent proceed to hearings before an administrative law judge. To hear appeals of administrative enforcement decisions, EPA has created a permanent, three-person Environmental Appeals Board.

Minor violations also can be handled by sending a notice of violation, which requires the recipient to correct a technical violation without assessing a penalty. Notices of violation may be used by federal enforcement officials to give state authorities operating delegated programs an opportunity to take enforcement action prior to the initiation of federal enforcement proceedings. The 1990 Clean Air Act Amendments also authorize EPA to issue field citations, akin to traffic tickets but with penalties of up to $5,000 per day of violation. CAA §113(d)(3).

The issuance of unilateral administrative orders (UAOs) has been an important but controversial tool in EPA's enforcement arsenal. CERCLA section 106 authorizes the president to issue "such orders as may be necessary to protect public health and welfare and the environment," authority he has delegated to the EPA administrator. Failure to comply can subject the recipient of such orders to damages of three times the cleanup costs and fines of $37,500 per day from the day the UAO was issued. EPA issued scores of UAOs to the General Electric Company (GE) to remediate environmental contamination, including extensive PCB contamination in the Hudson River. For more than a decade, GE fought a legal battle with EPA, claiming that it was a denial of due process not to be allowed to seek pre-enforcement review of such orders. In General Electric Co. v. Jackson, 610 F.3d 110 (D.C. Cir. 2010), the D.C. Circuit held that it was not a deprivation of due process for CERCLA to bar pre-enforcement judicial review of UAOs. The court stated that CERCLA "offers noncomplying PRPs several levels of protection: a PRP faces daily fines and treble damages only if a federal court finds (1) that the UAO was proper; (2) that the PRP 'willfully' failed to comply 'without sufficient cause'; and (3) that, in the court's discretion, fines and treble damages are appropriate. 42 U.S.C. §§9606(b) (1), 9607(c)(3)." 610 F.3d at 118. The court noted that although the recipient of the UAO must prove that it was not proper by a preponderance of evidence, EPA's determination is reviewed *de novo* and is not entitled to judicial deference. "CER-CLA's 'willfulness' and 'sufficient cause' requirements are quite similar to the good faith and reasonable grounds defenses the Supreme Court has found sufficient to satisfy due process," the court concluded. "Moreover, PRPs receive added protection from the fact that the district court has authority to decide not to impose fines even if it concludes that a recipient 'without sufficient cause, willfully violate[d], or fail[ed] or refuse[d] to comply with' a UAO." Id. at 119.

In 2012, the U.S. Supreme Court held that citizens who were the target of an administrative compliance order issued by EPA under section 309 of the Clean Water Act (CWA) could challenge it in court rather than being required first to violate it and wait for EPA to bring an enforcement action against them. Sackett v. EPA, 566 U.S. 120 (2012). The section 309 order directed property owners to restore a wetland area they had filled that the agency believed required a permit under section 404 of the CWA. The property owners sought to challenge the order in court, but EPA argued that judicial review was not available until the agency itself initiated action to enforce the compliance order. The Supreme Court unanimously held that citizens can obtain pre-enforcement judicial review of the compliance order. The Court concluded that the order is final agency action for which there is no adequate remedy other than APA review, and that the Clean Water Act does not preclude such review.

Prior to the *Sackett* decision, each of the five U.S. courts of appeal that had considered the issue had held that pre-enforcement judicial review of administrative compliance orders was not available under the Clean Water Act. Following the decision, commentators disagreed sharply on its likely impact. Professor Joel A. Mintz, author of *Enforcement at the EPA: High Stakes and Hard Choices* (2d ed. 2012) and a former EPA enforcement attorney, predicted that the decision will "create significant practical difficulties for EPA's enforcement staff." Mintz, After *Sackett*: What Next for Administrative Compliance Orders, Mar. 4, 2012, at *http://www .progressivereform.org/CPRBlog.cfm?idBlog=4530CE02-CDDC-F5B7-080BE0BBA3E97180.*

*Sackett*'s rationale is not applicable to CERCLA section 106 orders because, unlike the Clean Water Act, CERCLA expressly bars pre-enforcement review of administrative compliance orders issued by EPA. See 42 U.S.C. §9613(h) ("No Federal court shall have jurisdiction under Federal law . . . to review any order issued under §9606(a) of this title, in any action except . . . [a]n action to enforce an order issued under §9606(a) of this title or to recover a penalty for violation of such order [or] [a]n action under §9606 of this title in which the United States has moved to compel a remedial action.").

In Tennessee Valley Authority v. Whitman, 336 F.3d 1236 (11th Cir. 2003), the court had held unconstitutional EPA's effort to use an administrative compliance order to impose sanctions on the Tennessee Valley Authority (TVA) for alleged violations of the Clean Air Act. The EPA had issued an ACO against the TVA pursuant to CAA section 113(a), 42 U.S.C. §7413(a). After conferring with TVA and repeatedly modifying the ACO, EPA directed its Environmental Appeals Board (EAB) to informally adjudicate whether TVA had violated the CAA. After the EAB decided that the TVA had violated the Act, TVA sought review of this decision in the U.S.

Court of Appeals. In June 2003, the Eleventh Circuit determined that it had no jurisdiction to review the EAB's decision. The court held that ACOs did not constitute final agency action because it would be unconstitutional for EPA to be able to impose severe civil and criminal penalties for violating them without any adjudication or meaningful judicial review preceding their issuance. The court concluded that "EPA must prove the existence of a CAA violation in district court; until then, TVA is free to ignore the ACO without risking the imposition of penalties for noncompliance with its terms." 335 F.3d at 1239-1240. Due to the court's decision, EPA stopped issuing ACOs only in the states covered by the Eleventh Circuit. Christopher M. Wynn, Facing a Hobson's Choice? The Constitutionality of the EPA's Administrative Compliance Order Enforcement Scheme Under the Clean Air Act, 62 Wash. & Lee L. Rev. 1879, 1883 (2005). The court's decision did not call into question EPA's administrative penalty authority under section 113(d) because this requires the use of formal adjudicatory procedures to determine whether a violation has occurred.

### 2. Penalty Policies

Environmental officials have used their enforcement authorities to encourage companies to incorporate compliance concerns into management structures. Enforcement settlements now often feature agreements by violators to conduct environmental audits to help prevent future violations. Defendants also are agreeing to implement pollution prevention programs or to undertake supplemental environmental projects. Between FY 2006 and FY 2011, EPA concluded 20,705 enforcement cases that resulted in $606 million in administrative and judicial penalties, commitments of $228 million by companies to fund supplemental environmental projects, and injunctive relief expected to cost more than $62.5 billion to bring companies into compliance. EPA Office of Inspector General, Response to Congressional Request on EPA Enforcement, Feb. 28, 2013 (*http://www.epa.gov/oig/reports/2013/20130228 -13-P-0168.pdf*). In FY 2016, EPA initiated more than 2,400 civil enforcement actions, a slight increase from the 2,380 initiated in 2015, but a 30 percent decrease from the 3,436 filed in 2010. EPA also conducted 13,500 inspections in 2016, a 12 percent decrease from the 15,400 conducted in 2015 and a 36 percent decrease from the 21,000 in 2010. EPA's 2016 civil enforcement actions yielded penalties totaling approximately $5.79 billion and requirements for companies to invest $13.7 billion into programs for pollution control and environmental remediation. EPA and the Justice Department estimated that environmental enforcement actions concluded in 2016 reduced, treated, or eliminated 324 million pounds of pollution, and required 62 billion pounds of hazardous waste to be minimized, treated, or properly disposed.

In August 2017, the Environmental Integrity Project, founded by former federal environmental enforcement officials, reported that there had been a sharp decline in civil environmental enforcement during the Trump administration. Environmental Integrity Project, Environmental Enforcement Under Trump (Aug. 10, 2017). The report found that the Justice Department had collected 60 percent less in civil penalties than during the first six months of the administrations of the last three presidents. Only 26 civil enforcement actions were filed during the first six months of the Trump administration compared to 34 in the Obama administration and 31 during the George W. Bush administration. In a 2018 report, the Environmental Data and Governance Initiative concluded that the Trump EPA was no longer "capable of fulfilling its mission to ensure competent enforcement of federal environmental laws." A May 2019 update to the report showed that civil case conclusions were the lowest they had been since 1994 and that civil case initiations were the lowest they had been since 1982, with the most serious cases (those referred to the Department of Justice) at the lowest they had been since 1976. Data released in January 2021 showed that in federal fiscal year 2020 EPA had the lowest number of civil judicial environmental cases concluded and referred for prosecution in 20 years. Environmental Integrity Project, New EPA Enforcement Data Show Continued Downward Trend During Trump Administration (Jan. 14, 2021).

In response to the COVID-19 pandemic, the EPA issued a memo on March 26, 2020, saying the agency would use "enforcement discretion" to respond to compliance lapses during the pandemic. Further, the EPA stated it would not seek penalties for violations when it agrees COVID-19 was the cause of the non-compliance, and it did not plan to ask facilities to catch up on missed monitoring or reporting during these lapses. Environmental nonprofits argued this policy provided "blanket approval" of non-compliance and endangered millions.

Enforcement officials have acted to improve the deterrent effect of enforcement actions by publicizing enforcement actions. In 2009 OSHA adopted a policy of issuing a press release any time the agency levied a fine of $40,000 or more for serious violations of health or safety regulations. In response to complaints from industry groups that this constituted unfair "shaming," the Trump administration stopped the practice. However, a study published in June 2020 found that each press release OSHA issued had the deterrent effect of 210 compliance investigations of nearby companies in the same industry. Matthew S. Johnson, "Regulation by Shaming: Deterrent Effects of Publicizing Violations of Workplace Safety and Health Laws," 110 Amer. Econ. Rev. 1886 (2020). OSHA has only 200 inspectors and 8 million workplaces to inspect.

EPA's Policy on Civil Penalties is designed to ensure that penalties imposed on violators are sufficient to recoup the economic benefit of violations and to encourage future compliance. Under this policy, civil penalties are calculated based on the economic benefit of delayed compliance (as calculated by a computer program developed by EPA staff), the gravity of the offense (based on its actual and potential impact on public health and the environment, and its effect on EPA's ability to perform its regulatory functions), the willfulness of the offense, and the violator's past compliance and cooperation with enforcement authorities. Debarment of violators from government contracts also can be used as a sanction.

For many years, the Justice Department has insisted that defendants include funding for "supplemental environmental projects" (SEPs) in settlements of environmental enforcement actions. These SEPs usually are designed to help remediate the harm caused by the violations. Both the BP oil spill and Volkswagen settlements included payments of hundreds of millions of dollars to third parties for projects to mitigate environmental harm caused by the violations. On March 12, 2020, Jeffrey Bossert Clark, head of the Department of Justice's Environment and Natural Resources Divisions, issued a memorandum banning the use of SEPs in all future settlements of environmental violations. The ban would have precluded SEPs like the $4.7 billion Volkswagen agreed to invest in zero emissions vehicles and other clean transportation projects and the $8 million that Allied Chemical agreed to pay to the Virginia Environmental Endowment as part of a $13.2 million settlement for polluting the James River with kepone. Clark's memo declared that SEPs violate the Miscellaneous Receipts Act that requires federal officials receiving funds on behalf of the United States to deposit the funds with the U.S. Treasury. The memo was widely condemned because SEPs have proven to be a valuable means of encouraging settlements of environmental cases, see Seema Kakade, Remedial Payments in Agency Enforcement, 44 Harv. Envt'l L. Rev. 117 (2020), throughout the world (they are called "environmental undertakings" or EUs in Australia).

In July 2020, the Trump Department of Justice sought to extend the new policy prohibiting SEPs to bar a settlement of a lawsuit between the Sierra Club and an electric utility. In its settlement agreement with the Sierra Club DTE Energy had agreed to close three coal-fired powerplants and to spend $2 million on local environmental projects in poor and minority communities near its powerplants. The Trump Justice Department argued that any settlement money must be paid to the U.S. Treasury. It welcomed an amicus brief from Professor Richard Epstein (who had caught the eye of the White House four months earlier by forecasting that it was unlikely COVID-19 would cause more than 500 U.S. deaths (he later raised his estimate to 5,000)). Epstein argued that Clean Air Act citizen suits were unconstitutional because they "unconstitutionally vest the law enforcement power in private persons." In December 2020, Judge Bernard Friedman rejected the government's arguments "that DTE's separately negotiated agreement with Sierra Club 'conflict[s] with the statutory scheme,' is 'contrary to sound environmental enforcement policy,' and potentially interferes with constitutionally mandated separation of powers." He concluded that the "agreement in this case does none of these things, but accomplishes an enormous environmental benefit that is fully consistent with the goals of the CAA."

On February 4, 2021, Deputy Assistant Attorney General Jean E. Williams formally withdrew the Clark memorandum barring SEPs. Citing President Biden's Executive Order 13,990, Williams declared that the memorandum was "inconsistent with long-standing Division policy and practice" and "impede[d] the full exercise of enforcement discretion in the Division's cases."

An illustration of how courts have used EPA's civil penalties policy to determine the size of monetary penalties is provided by the following decision. This case involved a successful citizen suit against an oil company for discharging produced water (water generated during drilling operations that becomes contaminated with chemicals) into Galveston Bay without a permit. After finding that produced water was a "pollutant" whose discharge without a permit violated the Clean Water Act (CWA), the court considered how great a penalty to assess for the violation.

## Sierra Club v. Cedar Point Oil Co.

73 F.3d 546 (5th Cir. 1996)

The CWA directs district courts to assess civil penalties for violations of the CWA. 33 U.S.C. §1319(d). Specifically, the statute states that violators "shall be subject to a civil penalty not to exceed $25,000 per day for each violation." Id. Aside from this maximum amount, the statute guides the court's discretion in setting the penalty as follows:

In determining the amount of a civil penalty the court shall consider the seriousness of the violation or violations, the economic benefit (if any) resulting from the violation, any history of such violations, any good-faith efforts to comply with the applicable requirements, the economic impact of the penalty on the violator, and such other matters as justice may require.

Id. The Eleventh Circuit has taken these statutory directives and developed a procedural framework for calculating penalties under the CWA. [Atlantic States Legal Found., Inc. v.] Tyson Foods, [Inc.,] 897 F.2d [1128], 1142 [(11th Cir. 1990)]. First, the court is to calculate the maximum penalty that could be assessed against the violator. Id. Using that maximum as a starting point, the court should then determine if the penalty should be reduced from the maximum by reference to the statutory factors. Id.

The district court followed the *Tyson Foods* framework in this case. The parties had stipulated that there were 797 days of unpermitted discharge of produced water prior to trial. The judgment was entered twelve days later, during which time the discharge presumably continued. Accordingly, the court multiplied the statutory figure of $25,000 per day by 809 days of unpermitted discharge to arrive [at] a maximum penalty of $20,225,000.

The district court then made findings of fact with respect to the statutory factors. First, the court found that the violation was moderately serious because of the effect of the discharge on benthic organisms and the lack of monitoring and reporting with respect to the discharge. Second, the court found that the economic benefit to Cedar Point from the violation was $186,070, which the court determined was the amount that Cedar Point saved by not disposing of its produced water in a reinjection well. Third, the court found that Cedar Point had been violating the CWA since it began operating state well 1876. Fourth, the court found that Cedar Point had not demonstrated good faith in attempting to comply with the CWA. In this regard, the court noted that, although Cedar Point had attempted to obtain a NPDES permit for its discharge, it had not explored other ways to comply with the CWA. Finally, the court reviewed Cedar Point's financial position and expected future profits from the Cedar Point field and determined that Cedar Point could at least afford a penalty equal to the economic benefit attained from the violation.

In weighing these facts and calculating the penalty, the district court held that the maximum penalty of $20,225,000 was inappropriate. The court determined, however, that the penalty should at a minimum recapture the savings realized by Cedar Point because of the violation. Although the court's findings with respect to the other statutory factors were also not favorable to Cedar Point, the court apparently chose not to accord these factors any weight because it did not increase the penalty beyond what it found to be the economic benefit to Cedar Point. Accordingly, the court assessed a penalty of $186,070. . . .

. . . [W]e do not think that the district court abused its discretion in assessing a penalty in an amount that reflected only the economic benefit to Cedar Point. The Supreme Court has described the process of weighing the statutory factors in calculating civil penalties under the CWA as "highly discretionary" with the trial court. Tull v. United States, 481 U.S. 412, 427 (1987). It is clear from the district court's Memorandum Opinion that it considered all of the statutory factors before settling on an amount based only on economic benefit. Considering that the court could have imposed a penalty as high as $20,225,000, this appears to be a fair and just result. As such we perceive no abuse of discretion. Therefore, we affirm the district court's assessment of a penalty in the amount of $186,070 for Cedar Point's violation of the CWA.

## NOTES AND QUESTIONS

1. The civil penalty applied in this case was designed to recoup only the economic benefit of the violation. Should the district court have imposed a higher penalty in light of the other factors it considered? If civil penalties routinely were assessed in a manner that only recouped the economic gain enjoyed by the violator, what incentive would they provide for companies to comply on their own? If Cedar Point had discovered the violation, voluntarily disclosed it to EPA, and corrected it prior to receiving notice of the citizen's suit, would their penalty have been as great under EPA's self-audit policy?

2. Why should a violator's economic circumstances be taken into account when determining the size of civil penalties? Does this imply that firms that are marginally profitable need not fear substantial civil penalties for violating the Clean Water Act?

3. After receiving the Sierra Club's statutorily required notice of intent to file a citizen suit, Cedar Point filed suit against the Sierra Club and EPA, alleging that they were conspiring to deprive it of unspecified constitutional rights and seeking an injunction barring the citizen suit. Cedar Point's lawsuit was dismissed. A month later, Cedar Point filed a counterclaim against the Sierra Club's citizen suit alleging abuse of process and seeking compensatory damages for emotional distress allegedly suffered by its officers and directors and $10 million in punitive damages. This counterclaim also was dismissed.

4. As the court notes, section 309(d) of the Clean Water Act specifies five factors that courts should consider in determining the amount of a civil penalty, as well as "such other matters as justice may require." What other matters can you identify that would be relevant considerations for courts to use in determining the amount of civil penalties under this broad directive?

5. Should the maximum penalty for violations be based on the number of violations, the number of days of non-compliance, or some combination of both? The Clean Water Act provides for a civil penalty "not to exceed $25,000 per day for each violation." 33 U.S.C. §1319(d). The trial court in *Cedar Point* had computed the maximum penalty by multiplying the number of days on which violations occurred by the statutory figure of $25,000 per day. In Chesapeake Bay Foundation v. Gwaltney of Smithfield, Ltd., 791 F.2d 304 (4th Cir. 1986), rev'd on other grounds, 484 U.S. 49 (1987), the Fourth Circuit stated that "where a violation is defined in terms of a time period longer than a day, the maximum penalty assessable for that violation should be defined in terms of the number of days in that time period." Id. at 314. The court declined to reach the separate question of "whether multiple violations attributable to a single day may give rise to a maximum penalty in excess of [the penalty amount] for that day." Id. at 308. The latter issue was addressed in United States v. Smithfield Foods, Inc., 191 F.3d 516 (4th Cir. 1999), where the

court stated that "if the maximum penalty that could be levied against a violator on a single day was $25,000, no matter how many different Permit effluent limitations were violated, the permittee would have a strong disincentive to comply with the other permit limitations." Thus, the court treated each permit violation "as a separate and distinct infraction for purposes of penalty calculation." This approach also was followed in Borden Ranch Partnership v. U.S. Army Corps of Engineers, 261 F.3d 810 (9th Cir. 2001), aff'd by an equally divided Court, 537 U.S. 99 (2002), which upheld a penalty for violating section 404 of the Clean Water Act that had been calculated based on the number of unpermitted passes by a deep ripper through wetlands rather than the number of days on which the ripping occurred.

6. Should the amount of warning a company received prior to violating an environmental law be a factor taken into account in determining the size of a civil penalty? If a company mistakenly believes that it is in compliance, can it be fined when it later discovers that EPA interprets the regulations differently? In General Electric Co. v. EPA, 53 F.3d 1324 (D.C. Cir. 1995), the D.C. Circuit set aside a $25,000 fine against a company for violating TSCA regulations because EPA did not provide the company with fair warning of its interpretation of regulations that were unclear. The court upheld EPA's interpretation of regulations that required the immediate incineration of solvents used in extracting PCBs. However, the court found that it would violate due process for the company to be fined without fair warning that EPA interpreted the regulations to prohibit distillation and recycling of a portion of the solvents prior to their ultimate incineration. "In the absence of notice—for example, where the regulation is not sufficiently clear to warn a party about what is expected of it—an agency may not deprive a party of property by imposing civil or criminal liability." The court noted that "in many cases the agency's pre-enforcement efforts to bring about compliance will provide adequate notice," such as when a regulated entity is informed that it needs to obtain a permit. "If, by reviewing the regulations and other public statements issued by the agency, a regulated party acting in good faith would be able to identify with 'ascertainable certainty' the standard with which the agency expects parties to conform, then the agency has fairly notified a petitioner of the agency's interpretation."

7. In the more than two decades since *Cedar Point* was decided, the Fifth Circuit's tolerance for lower court decisions that impose lenient penalties on polluters may have diminished. In Environment Texas Citizen Lobby, Inc. v. ExxonMobil Corporation, 824 F.3d 507 (5th Cir. 2016), the Fifth Circuit vacated and remanded a decision by a district court that failed to impose any penalties on a major oil company for repeated violations of its Clean Air Act (CAA) permits. A citizens group in Texas alleged that air emissions from ExxonMobil's Baytown oil refinery and chemical plant complex violated the company's CAA permits thousands of times over an eight-year period. After a 13-day trial, a federal district judge found only 94 actionable violations of Exxon's permits, but declined to impose any penalty or grant injunctive relief to remediate the violations. On appeal, the Fifth Circuit held that the district judge had abused his discretion. It noted that the trial judge had concluded that even if all of the thousands of alleged violations had been established, he still would not have imposed any penalty on ExxonMobil.

On remand, the district judge found far more violations. He determined that the total maximum penalty ExxonMobil could incur for these violations was

$573,510,000. The environmental plaintiffs argued that the penalty should be 50 percent higher than the economic benefit of the violation. After finding that the economic benefit of non-compliance was $14,249,940, the court imposed a fine of $19,951,278 on ExxonMobil after deducting $1,423,632 that Exxon already had paid to the state of Texas. Environment Texas Citizen Lobby, Inc. v. ExxonMobil Corp., 2017 WL 2331679 (S.D. Tex. 2017). ExxonMobil then appealed this decision, claiming that plaintiffs were required to prove that they had standing for each violation among its 16,000 days of violations. While noting that "no court appears to have found standing for some Clean Air Act violations but not others," a panel of the Fifth Circuit reversed and remanded for determination of which violations were sufficiently serious to give rise to standing. The court stated that "because of the great variety of the challenged emissions—both in terms of type and scale—we cannot say that Plaintiffs' proving standing for some violations necessarily means they prove standing for the rest." Environment Texas Citizen Lobby, Inc. v. Exxon-Mobil Corp., 968 F.3d 357, 367 (5th Cir. 2020). On March 2, 2021 the district judge on remand reduced ExxonMobil's penalty to $14.25 million. The final penalty was calculated by imposing a fine 10 percent higher than the economic benefit of the violation and then reducing it by nearly $1.4 million to account for the amount ExxonMobil already had paid. Exxon is appealing this decision.

8. Federal law now requires EPA to update the maximum civil penalties it may levy in enforcement actions to keep up with inflation. In February 2004, EPA adopted a Civil Monetary Penalty Inflation Adjustment Rule, 69 Fed. Reg. 7,121 (Feb. 13, 2004). The rule, which was authorized by the Federal Civil Penalties Inflation Adjustment Act of 1990, as amended by the Debt Collection Improvement Act of 1996, increases the maximum amount of civil penalties that the Agency may collect from environmental violators to take inflation into account. For example, the statutory civil penalty of $25,000 under the Clean Water Act has been adjusted to $52,414 for violations occurring after November 2, 2015 that are assessed on or after January 15, 2017. The inflation-adjusted penalty amounts for civil penalties under each of the environmental statutes can be found at 82 Fed. Reg. 3,633, 3,636 (2017).

### 3.  *The Federal-State Enforcement Relationship*

The environmental laws authorize EPA to delegate to states responsibility for administering and enforcing the federal clean water, clean air, and hazardous waste programs. To qualify for program delegation, states must satisfy EPA that they can operate the programs in a manner that meets all federal requirements. EPA retains supervisory authority over the states' operation of the programs. If states operating delegated federal programs fail to meet minimum federal standards, EPA has the authority to withdraw the delegation, but this authority is virtually never exercised because the agency is loath to take over operation of state programs without receiving additional resources. The EPA also generally has the authority to take enforcement action on its own when it does not believe that states have adequately addressed certain violations. This "overfiling" authority was contested in Harmon Industries v. Browner, 191 F.3d 894 (8th Cir. 1999) where the Eighth Circuit held that EPA delegation of authority to a state to implement and enforce a RCRA program precluded federal overfiling. This decision has not been widely followed.

The Tenth Circuit explicitly rejected *Harmon* and upheld EPA's ability to overfile in United States v. Power Engineering Co., 303 F.3d 1232 (10th Cir. 2002). The Tenth Circuit systematically rejected every aspect of *Harmon*'s reasoning in holding that EPA could bring an RCRA enforcement action even when a state pursued its own action for the same violations. The EPA had filed suit against Power Engineering after the state of Colorado refused in its own enforcement action to demand that the company comply with financial assurance regulations to ensure coverage of the cost of remedying the violations. Although the state sought to impose penalties of $1.13 million for the violations, EPA won an order requiring the company to provide more than $2.11 million in financial assurances. The Tenth Circuit first rejected *Harmon*'s conclusion that "the administration and enforcement of the program are inexorably intertwined." The court stated:

> This interpretation fails to account for the placement of "enforcement" and "in lieu of" in separate clauses of section 6926(b), and it does not adequately consider the structure of the statute. Section 6926 addresses the administration and enforcement of state regulations by authorized states, while the federal enforcement of such regulations is addressed in a different part of the statute—section 6928. Given this statutory structure, the EPA's conclusion that administration and enforcement of RCRA are not inexorably intertwined—and that authorization of a state program therefore does not deprive the EPA of its enforcement powers—is not unreasonable. [303 F.3d at 1238.]

The Tenth Circuit noted that "the only explicit limitation" on EPA's enforcement authority "is that the EPA must provide prior notice to authorized states." Id. Noting that "[w]ithdrawal of authorization for a state program is an 'extreme' and 'drastic' step that requires the EPA to establish a federal program to replace the cancelled state program," the court concluded that "[n]othing in the text of the statute suggests that such a step is a prerequisite to EPA enforcement or that it is the only remedy for inadequate enforcement." Id. at 1238-1239. The court also rejected the notion that the "same force and effect" language in section 6926(d) indicated an intent to bar separate EPA enforcement. Noting that the provision is part of a section headed "Effect of a State permit," the court said this "suggests that this subsection only intends for state permits to have the 'same force and effect' as federal permits." Thus, "[i]t would be reasonable to conclude that Congress simply intended for section 6926(d) to clarify that recipients of state-issued permits need not obtain a permit from the EPA," preventing "the EPA from denying the effect of a state permit," but not preventing "the EPA from taking action when a violation occurs." Id. at 1239.

In United States v. Elias, 269 F.3d 1003 (9th Cir. 2001), the Ninth Circuit rejected an effort to use *Harmon* to challenge one of the largest criminal penalties ever imposed for an environmental violation—a 17-year prison term for a businessman convicted for knowingly endangering an employee while violating RCRA. The businessman, Allan Elias, had ordered an employee to clean out a storage tank containing cyanide without using safety equipment. Overcome by cyanide fumes, the employee suffered brain damage and nearly died. The court rejected the argument that the federal criminal prosecution for violating RCRA was barred by the fact that Idaho had delegated authority from EPA to operate the RCRA program. The Ninth Circuit concluded that nothing in *Harmon* foreclosed EPA's ability to bring criminal charges. The court explained that "under RCRA, the federal government retains both its criminal and its civil enforcement powers . . . even where a state law counterpart exists, for many of these 'counterparts' provide only misdemeanor punishments where federal law prescribes a felony." The court concluded that "RCRA only contemplates that the federal permitting scheme is supplanted by authorized state ones," meaning that "[w]hat changes, and what is supplanted by state law, is . . . the sovereign from whom generators must obtain the necessary permit originally—in this case, Idaho." 269 F.3d at 1012.

*Harmon*'s reasoning also has been found to be inapplicable in the context of the Clean Air Act. In United States v. LTV Steel Co., 118 F. Supp. 2d 827 (N.D. Ohio 2000), a steel company argued that a settlement it had reached with the city of Cleveland should bar EPA from overfiling and imposing penalties on it for violations involving fugitive dust emissions. Distinguishing *Harmon*, the court stated that: "Unlike RCRA, the Clean Air Act contains language in its enforcement section which seems to anticipate overfiling." The court noted that the Clean Air Act expressly provides for considering "payment by the violator of penalties previously assessed for the same violation" in computing penalties under the Act. 118 F. Supp. 2d at 833. The court also rejected the company's claim that res judicata barred the EPA action, noting that EPA and the city were not in privity and were enforcing separate bodies of law.

Cynthia Giles identifies another source of friction in federal-state cooperative enforcement. She argues that "States have a chokehold on environmental compliance information. States' failure to share that information with the feds—even when sharing is required by law—obscures violations, reduces protection, and prevents us from understanding how well our national laws are working." Giles finds fault in both sides of the federal/state relationship, noting that the "the federal government resists the states' important role as innovators and laboratories for new approaches." Claiming that "the model of federalism that made sense in the 1970s when most environmental laws were created is not working for us now," she calls for use of "today's monitoring and information technologies to build a federalism model for the modern era that strengthens protection and innovation at the same time." Giles, Next Generation Compliance: Environmental Regulation for the Modern Era 10 (2021).

## NOTES AND QUESTIONS

1. How credible is the threat that EPA would withdraw a state's delegated authority to operate a program? A rare example of EPA withdrawing state program authorization occurred in December 2001 when EPA withdrew Maryland's authority to operate the Clean Air Act's Title V permit program. After repeated extensions of deadlines for correcting deficiencies in state permit programs, EPA was sued by the Earthjustice Legal Defense Fund in June 2000. In settlement of the lawsuit, EPA agreed not to extend the deadline for any state to correct deficiencies in its

Title V permit program beyond December 1, 2001. Maryland missed the deadline because it failed to change state law to grant standing to challenge permit decisions to all parties who would have standing under federal law as required by section 502(b)(6) of the Clean Air Act. Thus, Maryland's Part 70 permit program was replaced by an EPA Part 71 federal operating permit program effective December 1, 2001. However, this change did not make much practical difference because EPA immediately delegated to Maryland the authority to implement and enforce the Part 71 federal permit program. 66 Fed. Reg. 63,236 (Dec. 5, 2001). While this program was to be implemented and enforced by Maryland, EPA retained final decision-making authority on all permit issues including the issuance or denial of permits and permit terms.

2. In 1998, EPA's inspector general issued a report finding widespread failures to enforce some of the basic requirements of the environmental laws. After auditing enforcement records in several states, the inspector general found that state officials frequently had failed to enforce the laws or to report violations to EPA and that EPA had been lax in supervising state enforcement. Cushman, EPA and State Found to Be Lax on Pollution Law, N.Y. Times, June 7, 1998, at A1. The report found that many major dischargers had expired NPDES permits that had not been reissued, often for periods as long as ten years, and that very few formal enforcement actions were taken against significant dischargers when they violated their permits.

3. Steven A. Herman, EPA's Assistant Administrator for Enforcement and Compliance Assurance at the time *Harmon* was decided, argues that it is important for EPA to have overfiling authority to prevent states from competing for industry through lax enforcement policies. He cites the case of Smithfield Foods as one where "EPA had to step in despite strong opposition both from the company and the state of Virginia." Herman, Environmental Enforcement at the Federal Level, Remarks to the Arizona Association of Industries Environmental Summit, Aug. 13, 1998.

> Smithfield Foods failed to install adequate pollution control equipment or to properly treat its wastewater, resulting in more than 5,000 violations involving pollutants such as phosphorous, ammonia, cyanide, oil, grease, and fecal coli-form. Company employees falsified documents and destroyed water quality records. Virginia only took perfunctory actions against the violations, which had major impacts on the Pagan River, the James River, and the Chesapeake Bay. Pursuant to EPA's enforcement action, a federal district court fined Smithfield Foods a record $12.6 million penalty. [Id.]

Could the *Harmon* decision affect EPA's ability to deal with situations like that which occurred at Smithfield Foods? A state legislative audit found "major deficiencies" in Virginia's enforcement policies—in FY 1996, the state collected *only $4,000* in civil penalties for Clean Water Act violations under a long-standing policy that the state *not* seek to recoup the economic benefit of violations. Joint Legislative Audit and Review Commission, Review of the DEQ, 119-120 (1996).

4. Surveying the response of other federal courts to *Harmon*, one observer reached the following conclusion: "The federal courts that have considered

overfiling after *Harmon* have uniformly distinguished, criticized, or flatly rejected its reasoning. The pattern that has emerged is not that of a hopeless morass of contradictory rulings, but of a single outlier renounced or distinguished by the weight of the federal judiciary. . . . *Harmon* has essentially been quarantined by the run of cases that followed it." Thomas A. Benson, Perfect *Harmony*: The Federal Courts Have Quarantined *Harmon* and Preserved EPA's Power to Overfile, 28 Wm. & Mary Envtl. L. & Pol'y Rev. 885, 886 (2005). A review in August 2017 of the case law since 2005 indicates that this conclusion remains accurate.

## C.   CRIMINAL ENFORCEMENT

While misdemeanor criminal penalties for environmental violations are found in the Refuse Act of 1899, criminal prosecutions only recently have played a significant role in environmental enforcement. Criminal penalties were included in the major federal environmental statutes enacted in the 1970s. As these acts have been reauthorized, Congress has expanded the range of violations for which criminal penalties apply while increasing substantially the size of the penalties. Federal and state authorities also have devoted increased resources to criminal enforcement of the environmental laws. The Pollution Prosecution Act of 1990 quadrupled the number of federal agents investigating environmental crimes. By 2009, EPA had 185 special agents who carried firearms, investigated environmental crimes, and made arrests. Thirty EPA lawyers then focused exclusively on criminal enforcement matters. Martin Harrell, Joseph J. Lisa & Catherine L. Votaw, Federal Environmental Crime: A Different Kind of "White Collar" Prosecution, 23 Nat. Resources & Env't 3 (Winter 2009). In large cities today, some U.S. attorneys' and district attorneys' offices have divisions that specialize in criminal enforcement of the environmental laws. To publicize its criminal enforcement efforts, in 2008 EPA established its own "Most Wanted" list of fugitives wanted for environmental crimes. The list is available online at *http://www.epa.gov/fugitives/*. In November 2010, the first woman on EPA's list was arrested. Albania Deleon, who had disappeared prior to sentencing for environmental crimes in connection with running a fraudulent asbestos training institute, was arrested in Santo Domingo, Dominican Republic. Leslie Kaufman, Woman Wanted by E.P.A. Is Arrested, N.Y. Times, Nov. 2, 2010.

EPA opened 170 environmental crimes cases in 2016, a 20 percent decrease from the 213 opened in 2015 and a 51 percent decrease from the 346 opened in 2010. EPA's 2016 criminal cases resulted in $207 million in fines and restitution, $775,000 in court-ordered environmental projects, and 93 total years of incarceration for convicted defendants. By 2017 Justice Department reports indicated that criminal prosecutions had fallen to the lowest they had been in a quarter of a century, with only 115 cases opened and 139 defendants charged. The EPA maintained that the decrease was because the agency was focusing on more "complex cases that involve a serious threat." However, 2017 was a record year in fines and restitution due to the Volkswagen prosecution, contributing to $2.98 billion in total criminal fines, restitution, and court-ordered projects. In its 2019 Annual Report on Enforcement and Compliance, the EPA reported 170 criminal cases opened and 137 criminal defendants charged in 2019.

Nearly all the federal environmental laws now provide criminal penalties for "knowing" or "wilful" violations of environmental regulations. See, e.g., Clean Air Act §113(c); Clean Water Act §309(c); CERCLA §§103(b), (c), and (d)(2); RCRA §§3008(d) and (e); TSCA §§15 and 16; FIFRA §14(b). The Clean Air Act Amendments of 1990 make virtually all knowing violations of any requirement of the Act a felony, including violations of record-keeping and reporting requirements.

Sometimes criminal intent is not difficult to infer. The officials who prosecuted Volkswagen described it as

> a classic example of intentional corporate noncompliance with known standards. Volkswagen knew that its diesel vehicles could not legally be sold or imported in the United States without the required EPA and CARB certifications. Volkswagen also knew that those vehicles could not be certified unless they met applicable emission standards, and that they were subject to testing for compliance with those standards. When Volkswagen could not technologically meet the standard in the desired timeframe, Volkswagen decided to cheat, engineering a complex system to deceive emissions testing. Because the illegal mechanisms were sophisticated and difficult to detect, involving computer code embedded in the ECM, Volkswagen ultimately calculated that cheating was worth the risk.

John Cruden, Bethany Engel, Nigel Cooney & Joshua Van Eaton, Dieselgate: How the Investigation, Prosecution and Settlement of Volkswagen's Emissions Cheating Scandal Illustrates the Need for Robust Environmental Enforcement, 36 Va. Envt'l L. J. 118, 181 (2018). Volkswagen ultimately was forced to pay $4.3 billion in fines and penalties, including a $2.8 billion criminal fine, to fund a $2.9 billion environmental mitigation trust, to invest $2 billion in zero emissions vehicle infrastructure, and to spend $11 billion buying back the offending vehicles. The company was placed on probation for three years during which time an independent corporate compliance monitor will monitor future compliance. Seven corporate executives were indicted and the two who were found in the United States served prison terms.

Both the Clean Water Act and Clean Air Act also impose criminal penalties for certain negligent acts that violate the statutes. CWA §309(c)(1); Apex Oil Co. v. United States, 530 F.2d 1291 (8th Cir.), cert. denied, 429 U.S. 827 (1976); United States v. Frezzo Brothers, Inc., 703 F.2d 62 (3d Cir.), cert. denied, 464 U.S. 829 (1983); CAA §113(c)(4). Courts have long drawn a distinction between regulatory statutes to protect public health or safety and common law crimes in addressing what needs to be proved to establish a criminal violation. In United States v. Dotterweich, 320 U.S. 277 (1943) and United States v. Park, 421 U.S. 658 (1975), the Supreme Court indicated that responsible corporate officials can be held criminally liable for violating health or safety regulations without requiring proof of evil intent. In *Park* the Court explained that a corporate officer can be held criminally liable if, "by reason of his position in the corporation, [he or she had] responsibility and authority either to prevent in the first instance, or promptly to correct, the violation complained of, and . . . failed to do so." 421 U.S. 673-674. As caselaw interpreting some of the criminal provisions of the environmental laws developed, courts have built on these decisions by allowing juries to infer that acts are "knowing" or "wilful" from evidence demonstrating that a defendant should have known that an act is a violation. See, e.g., United States v. Sellers, 926 F.2d 410 (5th Cir. 1991) ("knowingly" in RCRA does not require knowledge that materials were regulated as hazardous wastes, but rather only that the defendant knew that materials had potential to cause harm); United States v. McDonald & Watson Waste Oil Co., 933 F.2d 35 (1st Cir. 1991); United States v. Buckley, 934 F.2d 84 (6th Cir. 1991).

The environmental laws generally make both corporate officers and employees who make corporate decisions personally liable. United States v. Northeastern Pharmaceutical & Chemical Co., 810 F.2d 726, 745 (8th Cir. 1986). The Clean Water Act and Clean Air Act both expressly provide that "any responsible corporate officer" may be held liable for criminal acts. CWA §309(c)(6); CAA §113(c)(6). The Justice Department has taken the position that a corporation can be held criminally liable for the unlawful acts of its employees if the acts were done to benefit the corporation and related to the employees' duties, whether or not the acts violated the corporation's policies or instructions, and whether or not the offending employees had any managerial authority. Employees can be held criminally liable if they knew or should have known that their employer failed to comply with applicable regulations. United States v. Hong, 242 F.3d 528 (4th Cir. 2001) ("the pertinent question is whether the defendant bore such a relationship to the corporation that it is appropriate to hold him criminally liable for failing to prevent the charged violations of the CWA"). Even federal contractors have been found criminally liable. In United States v. Dee, 912 F.2d 741 (4th Cir. 1990), three civilian managers at the U.S. Army's Aberdeen Proving Ground were convicted of knowingly managing hazardous wastes without a permit in violation of RCRA.

Criminal penalties are particularly severe for knowing violations that endanger human life. The Clean Water Act provides penalties of up to 15 years in prison and fines of up to $250,000 for violations when a defendant knows "that he thereby places another person in imminent danger of death or serious bodily injury." §309(c)(3). However, in United States v. Borowski, 977 F.2d 27 (1st Cir. 1992), the First Circuit interpreted this "knowing endangerment" provision as applying only to endangerment that occurs *after* a violation has been committed. The court reversed the felony convictions of the owner of a nickel-plating company who violated pretreatment standards by having his employees ladle high quantities of nickel and nitric acid into plating-room sinks from which they flowed untreated into a sewer. This caused the employees to suffer daily nose bleeds, rashes, blisters, and difficulty breathing. Even though the defendant had placed his employees in danger, the court held that a conviction "cannot be premised upon danger that occurs before the pollutant reaches a publicly-owned sewer or treatment works," because the Act was not violated until then.

In October 1994, a plant manager and an employee of Durex Industries were sentenced to 27 months in prison for illegal disposal of hazardous waste in violation of RCRA. They placed waste chemicals into a dumpster, where their fumes killed two nine-year-old boys who climbed inside the dumpster. The defendants were acquitted of the more serious offense of knowing endangerment.

The Crime Victim's Rights Act (CVRA), 18 U.S.C. §3771, grants victims of crime the "reasonable right to confer with the attorney for the government" in order to inform the plea negotiation process by conferring with prosecutors before a plea agreement is reached. In the case of In re Dean, 527 F.3d 391 (5th Cir. 2008), the Fifth Circuit held that the government had violated the CVRA by not meeting with victims of a chemical explosion before negotiating a settlement of criminal charges under the Clean Air Act. In another Clean Air Act case involving Citgo Petroleum Corporation, a federal district court held a nine-day presentencing hearing to assess potential harm to the health of persons exposed to toxic vapors that had been illegally released. Judson W. Starr, Brian L. Flack & Allison D. Foley, A New Intersection: Environmental Crimes and Victims' Rights, 23 Nat. Resources & Env't 41 (Winter 2009).

Courts continue to wrestle with difficult issues that arise at the intersection between criminal law and environmental law. Conflicts over criminal enforcement of the environmental laws can be viewed in part as the latest battleground in a war between two fundamentally different views on environmental issues, which have been termed "moral outrage" and "cool analysis." The "morally outraged" view environmental standards as establishing a moral obligation, while "cool analysts" view sanctions as simply part of the cost of doing business. The two approaches differ over both the aims to be served by environmental standards and their attitudes toward compliance, as described in Schroeder, Cool Analysis Versus Moral Outrage in the Development of Federal Environmental Criminal Law, 35 Wm. & Mary L. Rev. 251 (1993). Professor Richard Lazarus argues that the sharply divergent characteristics of environmental law and criminal law make assimilation and integration of them an enormous challenge. Lazarus, Meeting the Demands of Integration in the Evolution of Environmental Law: Reforming Environmental Criminal Law, 83 Geo. L.J. 2407 (1995). He notes that: (1) environmental law deals with reducing risks of harm, while criminal laws are concerned with actual harm; (2) proof of causation is far more difficult in environmental cases than for traditional crimes; (3) pollution is inevitable and pervasive; and (4) environmental law is aspirational, dynamic, and inherently complex.

Two important works by environmental law scholars are highly critical of current policies for using criminal sanctions to enforce the law. In *Too Big to Jail: How Prosecutors Compromise with Corporations* (2016), Professor Brandon L. Garrett documents how federal prosecutors typically settle with corporations who violate the environmental laws, often with "deferred prosecution agreements," rather than sending corporate officials to prison. In *Why Not Jail? Industrial Catastrophes, Corporate Malfeasance, and Government Inaction* (2014), Professor Rena Steinzor reviews five case studies of industrial catastrophes that she argues should have resulted in more aggressive criminal prosecutions. In November 2016, the U.S. Department of Justice sponsored a symposium on the future of environmental law that included a panel on environmental enforcement. A transcript of "The Future of Environmental Enforcement" was published at 47 Envtl. L. Rep. 10206 (March 2017), *https://elr .info/news-analysis/47/10185/dojenrd-symposium-future-environmental-law.* Joel Mintz, a former EPA enforcement lawyer who was a panelist on that program, has written an important work on EPA enforcement: *Enforcement at the EPA: High Stakes and Hard Choices* (2012).

Consider the interface between environmental and criminal laws as you read the case below. It involves prosecution of two managers of a sewage treatment plant for illegal discharges of pollutants in violation of an NPDES permit. The government argued that it was not necessary to prove that the managers knew the discharges exceeded levels allowed in the permit in order to obtain criminal convictions. The panel's decision was so controversial that it generated five votes for a rehearing en banc accompanied by a vigorous dissent, also reproduced below, when that petition was denied.

## United States v. Weitzenhoff

35 F.3d 1275 (9th Cir. 1994)

FLETCHER, Circuit Judge:

Michael H. Weitzenhoff and Thomas W. Mariani, who managed the East Honolulu Community Services Sewage Treatment Plant, appeal their convictions for violations of the Clean Water Act ("CWA"), 33 U.S.C. §§1251 et seq., contending that the district court misconstrued the word "knowingly" under section 1319(c)(2) of the CWA. . . .

### FACTS AND PROCEDURAL HISTORY

In 1988 and 1989 Weitzenhoff was the manager and Mariani the assistant manager of the East Honolulu Community Services Sewage Treatment Plant ("the plant"), located not far from Sandy Beach, a popular swimming and surfing beach on Oahu. The plant is designed to treat some 4 million gallons of residential wastewater each day by removing the solids and other harmful pollutants from the sewage so that the resulting effluent can be safely discharged into the ocean. The plant operates under a permit issued pursuant to the National Pollution Discharge Elimination System ("NPDES"), which established the limits on the Total Suspended Solids ("TSS") and Biochemical Oxygen Demand ("BOD") — indicators of the solid and organic matter, respectively, in the effluent discharged at Sandy Beach. During the period in question, the permit limited the discharge of both the TSS and BOD to an average of 976 pounds per day over a 30-day period. It also imposed monitoring and sampling requirements on the plant's management.

The sewage treatment process that was overseen by Weitzenhoff and Mariani . . . [generates a substance] known as waste activated sludge ("WAS"), [that is] pumped to WAS holding tanks. From the holding tanks, the WAS could either be returned to other phases of the treatment process or hauled away to a different sewage treatment facility.

From March 1987 through March 1988, the excess WAS generated by the plant was hauled away to another treatment plant, the Sand Island Facility. In March 1988, certain improvements were made to the East Honolulu plant and the hauling was discontinued. Within a few weeks, however, the plant began experiencing a buildup of excess WAS. Rather than have the excess WAS hauled away as before, however, Weitzenhoff and Mariani instructed two employees at the plant to dispose of it on a regular basis by pumping it from the storage tanks directly into the outfall, that is, directly into the ocean. The WAS thereby bypassed the plant's effluent sampler so that the samples taken and reported to Hawaii's Department of Health ("DOH") and the EPA did not reflect its discharge.

The evidence produced by the government at trial showed that WAS was discharged directly into the ocean from the plant on about 40 separate occasions from April 1988 to June 1989, resulting in some 436,000 pounds of pollutant solids being discharged into the ocean, and that the discharges violated the plant's 30-day average effluent limit under the permit for most of the months during which they occurred. Most of the WAS discharges occurred during the night, and none was reported to the DOH or EPA. DOH inspectors contacted the plant on several occasions in 1988 in response to complaints by lifeguards at Sandy Beach that sewage was being emitted from the outfall, but Weitzenhoff and Mariani repeatedly denied that there was any problem at the plant. In one letter responding to a DOH inquiry in October 1988, Mariani stated that "the debris that was reported could not have been from the East Honolulu Wastewater Treatment facility, as our records of effluent quality up to this time will substantiate." One of the plant employees who participated in the dumping operation testified that Weitzenhoff instructed him not to say anything about the discharges, because if they all stuck together and did not reveal anything, "they [couldn't] do anything to us."

Following an FBI investigation, Weitzenhoff and Mariani were charged in a thirty-one-count indictment with conspiracy and substantive violations of the Clean Water Act ("CWA"), 33 U.S.C. §§1251 et seq. At trial, Weitzenhoff and Mariani admitted having authorized the discharges, but claimed that their actions were justified under their interpretation of the NPDES permit. The jury found them guilty of six of the thirty-one counts.

Weitzenhoff was sentenced to twenty-one months and Mariani thirty-three months imprisonment. Each filed a timely notice of appeal.

## DISCUSSION

### A. Intent Requirement

Section 1311(a) of the CWA prohibits the discharge of pollutants into navigable waters without an NPDES permit. 33 U.S.C. §1311(a). Section 1319(c)(2) makes it a felony offense to "knowingly violate[] section 1311, 1312, 1316, 1317, 1318, 1321(b)(3), 1328, or 1345, . . . or any permit condition or limitation implementing any of such sections in a permit issued under section 1342."

Prior to trial, the district court construed "knowingly" in section 1319(c)(2) as requiring only that Weitzenhoff and Mariani were aware that they were discharging the pollutants in question, not that they knew they were violating the terms of the statute or permit. According to appellants, the district court erred in its interpretation of the CWA and in instructing the jury that "the government is not required to prove that the defendant knew that his act or omissions were unlawful," as well as in rejecting their proposed instruction based on the defense that they mistakenly believed their conduct was authorized by the permit. Apparently, no court of appeals has confronted the issue raised by appellants.

We review a question of statutory construction de novo. . . .

As with certain other criminal statutes that employ the term "knowingly," it is not apparent from the face of the statute whether "knowingly" means a knowing violation of the law or simply knowing conduct that is violative of the law. We turn, then, to the legislative history of the provision at issue to ascertain what Congress intended.

In 1987, Congress substantially amended the CWA, elevating the penalties for violations of the Act. Increased penalties were considered necessary to deter would-be polluters. With the 1987 amendments, Congress substituted "knowingly" for the earlier intent requirement of "willfully" that appeared in the predecessor to section 1319(c)(2). The Senate report accompanying the legislation explains that the changes in the penalty provisions were to ensure that "criminal liability shall . . . attach to any person who is not in compliance with all applicable Federal, State and local requirements and permits *and causes* a POTW [publicly owned treatment works] to violate any effluent limitation or condition in any permit issued to the treatment works." Id. (emphasis added). Similarly, the report accompanying the House version of the bill, which contained parallel provisions for enhancement of penalties, states that the proposed amendments were to "provide penalties for dischargers or individuals who knowingly or negligently violate *or cause the violation of* certain of the Act's requirements." H.R. Rep. No. 189, 99th Cong., 1st Sess. 29-30 (1985) (emphasis added). Because they speak in terms of "causing" a violation, the congressional explanations of the new penalty provisions strongly suggest that criminal sanctions are to be imposed on an individual who knowingly engages in conduct that results in a permit violation, regardless of whether the polluter is cognizant of the requirements or even the existence of the permit. Our conclusion that "knowingly" does not refer to the legal violation is fortified by decisions interpreting analogous public welfare statutes. The leading case in this area is United States v. International Minerals & Chem. Corp., 402 U.S. 558 (1971). In *International Minerals*, the Supreme Court construed a statute which made it a crime to "knowingly violate[] any . . . regulation" promulgated by the [Interstate Commerce Commission] pursuant to 18 U.S.C. §834(a), a provision authorizing the agency to formulate regulations for the safe transport of corrosive liquids. The Court held that the term "knowingly" referred to the acts made criminal rather than a violation of the regulation, and that "regulation" was a shorthand designation for the specific acts or omissions contemplated by the act. "Where . . . dangerous or deleterious devices or products or obnoxious waste materials are involved, the probability of regulation is so great that anyone who is aware that he is in possession of them or dealing with them must be presumed to be aware of the regulation."

This court followed *International Minerals* in United States v. Hoflin, 880 F.2d 1033 (9th Cir. 1989), when it held that knowledge of the absence of a permit is not an element of the offense defined by 42 U.S.C. §6928(d)(2)(A), part of the Resource Conservation and Recovery Act ("RCRA"). "There can be little question that RCRA's purposes, like those of the Food and Drug Act, '. . . touch phases of the lives and health of people which, in the circumstances of modern industrialism, are largely beyond self-protection.'" Other courts have also followed *International Minerals* by similarly construing the knowledge requirement in statutes that regulate deleterious devices or obnoxious waste materials.

Appellants seek to rely on the Supreme Court's decision in Liparota v. United States, 471 U.S. 419 (1985), to support their alternative reading of the intent requirement. *Liparota* concerned 7 U.S.C. §2024(b)(1), which provides that anyone who "knowingly uses, transfers, acquires, alters, or possesses [food stamp] coupons or authorization cards in any manner not authorized by [the statute] or regulations" is subject to a fine or imprisonment. The Court, noting that the conduct at issue did not constitute a public welfare offense, distinguished the *International Minerals* line of cases and held that the government must prove the defendant knew that his acquisition or possession of food stamps was in a manner unauthorized by statute or regulations.

Subsequent to the filing of the original opinion in this case, the Supreme Court decided two cases which Weitzenhoff contends call our analysis into question. See Ratzlaf v. United States, 114 S. Ct. 655 (1994); Staples v. United States, 114 S. Ct. 1793 (1994). We disagree.

The statute in *Ratzlaf* does not deal with a public welfare offense, but rather with violations of the banking statutes. The Court construed the term "willfully" in the anti-structuring provisions of the Bank Secrecy Act to require both that the defendant knew he was structuring transactions to avoid reporting requirements and that he knew his acts were unlawful. The Court recognized that the money structuring provisions are not directed at conduct which a reasonable person necessarily should know is subject to strict public regulation and that the structuring offense applied to all persons with more than $10,000, many of whom could be engaged in structuring for innocent reasons. In contrast, parties such as Weitzenhoff are closely regulated and are discharging waste materials that affect public health. The *International Minerals* rationale requires that we impute to these parties knowledge of their operating permit. This was recognized by the Court in *Staples*.

The specific holding in *Staples* was that the government is required to prove that a defendant charged with possession of a machine gun knew that the weapon he possessed had the characteristics that brought it within the statutory definition of a machine gun. But the Court took pains to contrast the gun laws to other regulatory regimes, specifically those regulations that govern the handling of "obnoxious waste materials." It noted that the mere innocent ownership of guns is not a public welfare offense. The Court focused on the long tradition of widespread gun ownership in this country and, recognizing that approximately 50% of American homes contain a firearm, acknowledged that mere ownership of a gun is not sufficient to place people on notice that the act of owning an unregistered firearm is not innocent under the law.

*Staples* thus explicitly contrasted the mere possession of guns to public welfare offenses, which include statutes that regulate "dangerous or deleterious devices or products or obnoxious waste materials," and confirmed the continued vitality of statutes covering public welfare offenses, which "regulate potentially harmful or injurious items" and place a defendant on notice that he is dealing with a device or a substance "that places him in 'responsible relation to a public danger.'" Id. "In such cases Congress intended to place the burden on the defendant to ascertain at his peril whether [his conduct] comes within the inhibition of the statute."

Unlike "guns [which] in general are not 'deleterious devices or products or obnoxious waste materials,' *International Minerals*, supra, . . . that put their owners on notice that they stand 'in responsible relation to a public danger[,]' *Dotterweich*, 320 U.S. at 281," *Staples*, 114 S. Ct. at 1800, the dumping of sewage and other pollutants into our nation's waters is precisely the type of activity that puts the discharger on notice that his acts may pose a public danger. Like other public welfare offenses that regulate the discharge of pollutants into the air, the disposal of hazardous wastes, the undocumented shipping of acids, and the use of pesticides on our food, the improper and excessive discharge of sewage causes cholera, hepatitis, and other serious illnesses, and can have serious repercussions for public health and welfare.

The criminal provisions of the CWA are clearly designed to protect the public at large from the potentially dire consequences of water pollution and as such fall within the category of public welfare legislation. *International Minerals* rather than *Liparota* controls the case at hand. The government did not need to prove that Weitzenhoff and Mariani knew that their acts violated the permit or the CWA. . . .

KLEINFELD, Circuit Judge, with whom Circuit Judges REINHARDT, KOZINSKI, TROTT, and T.G. NELSON join, dissenting from the order rejecting the suggestion for rehearing en banc.

I respectfully dissent from our decision to reject the suggestion for rehearing en banc.

Most of us vote against most such petitions and suggestions even when we think the panel decision is mistaken. We do so because federal courts of appeals decide cases in three judge panels. En banc review is extraordinary, and is generally reserved for conflicting precedent within the circuit which makes application of the law by district courts unduly difficult, and egregious errors in important cases. In my view, this is a case of exceptional importance, for two reasons. First, it impairs a fundamental purpose of criminal justice, sorting out the innocent from the guilty before imposing punishment. Second, it does so in the context of the Clean Water Act. This statute has tremendous sweep. Most statutes permit anything except what is prohibited, but this one prohibits all regulated conduct involving waters and wetlands except what is permitted. Much more ordinary, innocent, productive activity is regulated by this law than people not versed in environmental law might imagine.

The harm our mistaken decision may do is not necessarily limited to Clean Water Act cases. Dilution of the traditional requirement of a criminal state of mind, and application of the criminal law to innocent conduct, reduces the moral authority of our system of criminal law. If we use prison to achieve social goals regardless of the moral innocence of those we incarcerate, then imprisonment loses its moral opprobrium and our criminal law becomes morally arbitrary.

We have now made felons of a large number of innocent people doing socially valuable work. They are innocent, because the one thing which makes their conduct felonious is something they do not know. It is we, and not Congress, who have made them felons. The statute, read in an ordinary way, does not. If we are fortunate, sewer plant workers around the circuit will continue to perform their vitally important work despite our decision. If they knew they risk three years in prison, some might decide that their pay, though sufficient inducement for processing the public's wastes, is not enough to risk prison for doing their jobs. We have decided that they should go to prison if, unbeknownst to them, their plant discharges exceed permit limits. Likewise for power plant operators who discharge warm water into rivers near their plants, and for all sorts of other dischargers in public and private life. If they know they are discharging into water, have a permit for the discharges, think they are conforming to their permits, but unknowingly violate their permit conditions, into prison they go with the violent criminals.

The statute does not say that. The statute at issue makes it a felony, subject to three years of imprisonment, to "knowingly violate[] . . . any permit condition or limitation." 33 U.S.C. §1319(c)(2)(A). . . . In this case, the defendants, sewage plant operators, had a permit to discharge sewage into the ocean, but exceeded the permit limitations. The legal issue for the panel was what knowledge would turn innocently or negligently violating a permit into "knowingly" violating a permit. Were the plant operators felons if they knew they were discharging sewage, but did not know that they were violating their permit? Or did they also have to know they were violating their permit? Ordinary English grammar, common sense, and precedent, all compel the latter construction.

As the panel opinion states the facts, these two defendants were literally "midnight dumpers." They managed a sewer plant and told their employees to dump 436,000 pounds of sewage into the ocean, mostly at night, fouling a nearby beach. Their conduct, as set out in the panel opinion, suggests that they must have known they were violating their National Pollution Discharge Elimination System (NPDES) permit. But we cannot decide the case on that basis, because the jury did not. The court instructed the jury that the government did not have to prove the defendants knew their conduct was unlawful, and refused to instruct the jury that a mistaken belief that the discharge was authorized by the permit would be a defense. Because of the way the jury was instructed, its verdict is consistent with the proposition that the defendants honestly and reasonably believed that their NPDES permit authorized the discharges.

This proposition could be true. NPDES permits are often difficult to understand and obey. The EPA had licensed the defendants' plant to discharge 976 pounds of waste per day, or about 409,920 pounds over the fourteen months covered by the indictment, into the ocean. The wrongful conduct was not discharging waste into the ocean. That was socially desirable conduct by which the defendants protected the people of their city from sewage-borne disease and earned their pay. The wrongful conduct was violating the NPDES permit by discharging 26,000 more pounds of waste than the permit authorized during the fourteen months. Whether these defendants were innocent or not, in the sense of knowing that they were exceeding their permit limitation, the panel's holding will make innocence irrelevant in other permit violation cases where the defendants had no idea that they were exceeding permit limits. The only thing they have to know to be guilty is that they were dumping sewage into the ocean, yet that was a lawful activity expressly authorized by their federal permit.

The statute says "knowingly violates . . . any permit condition or limitation." "Knowingly" is an adverb. It modifies the verb "violates." The object of the verb is "any permit condition or limitation." The word "knowingly" is placed before "violates" to "explain its meaning in the case at hand more clearly." George O. Curme, A Grammar of the English Language 72 (1935). Congress has distinguished those who knowingly violate permit conditions, and are thereby felons, from those who unknowingly violate permit conditions, so are not. The panel reads the statute as though it says "knowingly discharges pollutants." It does not. If we read the statute on the assumption that Congress used the English language in an ordinary way, the state of mind required is knowledge that one is violating a permit condition.

This approach has the virtue of attributing common sense and a rational purpose to Congress. It is one thing to defy a permit limitation, but quite another to violate it without realizing that one is violating it. Congress promulgated a parallel statute making it a misdemeanor "negligently" to violate a permit condition or limitation. 33 U.S.C. §1319(c)(1)(A). If negligent violation is a misdemeanor, why would Congress want to make it a felony to violate the permit without negligence and without even knowing that the discharge exceeded the permit limit? That does not make any sense. It would deter people from working in sewer plants, instead of deterring people from violating permits. All dischargers acting lawfully pursuant to a permit know that they are discharging pollutants. The presence or absence of that knowledge, which is the only mental element determining guilt under the panel's decision, has no bearing on any conduct Congress could have meant to turn into a felony. The only knowledge which could have mattered to Congress, the only knowledge which distinguishes good conduct from bad, is knowledge that the discharge violates the permit. That is what the statute says, "knowingly violates," not "knowingly discharges." There is no sensible reason to doubt that Congress meant what it said and said what it meant.

The panel reaches its surprising result in surprising ways. First, it says that the statute is ambiguous. "As with certain other criminal statutes that employ the term 'knowingly,' it is not apparent from the face of the statute whether 'knowingly' means a knowing violation of the law or simply knowing conduct that is violative of the law." As explained above, a grammatical and sensible reading of the statute leaves no room for ambiguity. But for the sake of discussion, suppose that the statute is ambiguous, as the panel says. Then the rule of lenity requires that the construction allowing the defendant more liberty rather than less be applied by the courts. . . .

The panel . . . tries to bolster its construction by categorizing the offense as a "public welfare offense," as though that justified more aggressive criminalization without a plain statutory command. This category is a modernized version of "*malum prohibitum*." Traditionally the criminal law distinguishes between *malum in se*, conduct wrong upon principles of natural moral law, and *malum prohibitum*, conduct not inherently immoral but wrong because prohibited by law. Black's Law Dictionary 1112 (4th ed. 1951). To put this in plain, modern terms, any normal person knows murder, rape, and robbery are wrong, and they would be wrong even in a place with no sovereign and no law. Discharging 6% more pollutants than one's permit allows is wrong only because the law says so. Substitution of the modern term "public welfare offense" for the traditional one, *malum prohibitum*, allows for confusion by rhetorical suggestion. The new term suggests that other offenses might merely be private in their impact, and therefore less serious. The older set of terms made it clear that murder was more vile than violating a federal regulation. The category of *malum prohibitum*, or public welfare offenses, makes the rule of lenity especially important, most particularly for felonies, because persons of good conscience may not recognize the wrongfulness of the conduct when they engage in it.

Staples v. United States, 114 S. Ct. 1793 (1994), reminds us that "offenses that require no *mens rea* generally are disfavored. . . ." *Mens rea* may be dispensed within public welfare offenses, but the penalty is a "significant consideration in determining whether the statute should be construed as dispensing with *mens rea*." . . . If Congress makes a crime a felony, the felony categorization alone is a "factor tending to suggest that Congress did not intend to eliminate a *mens rea* requirement. In such a case, the usual presumption that a defendant must know the facts that make his conduct illegal should apply." In the case at bar, "the facts that make his conduct illegal" are the permit violations, not the discharges of pollutants. Discharge of pollutants was licensed by the federal government in the NPDES permit. Under *Staples*, it would be presumed, even if the law did not plainly say so, that the defendant would have to know that he was violating the permit in order to be guilty of the felony. . . .

The panel cites United States v. International Minerals & Chem. Corp., 402 U.S. 558 (1971) . . . in support of its reading. *International Minerals* was a . . . misdemeanor case. Because of the syntactically similar statute at issue in that case, it is the strongest authority for the panel's decision and raises the most serious question for my own analysis. It held that a shipper of sulfuric acid could be convicted of violating a statute applying to those who "knowingly violate[]" regulations governing shipments of corrosive liquids, regardless of whether he had knowledge of the regulations. *International Minerals* expressly limits its holding to "dangerous or deleterious devices or products or obnoxious waste materials." The Court distinguished materials not obviously subject to regulation:

> Pencils, dental floss, paper clips may also be regulated. But they may be the type of products which might raise substantial due process questions if Congress did not require . . . "*mens rea*" as to each ingredient of the offense. But where, as here. . . , dangerous or deleterious devices or products or obnoxious waste materials are involved, the probability of regulation is so great that anyone who is aware that he is in possession of them or dealing with them must be presumed to be aware of the regulation.

*International Minerals* would have much persuasive force for Weitzenhoff, because of the grammatical similarity of the statute, if (1) the Clean Water Act limited pollutants to "dangerous or deleterious devices or products or obnoxious waste materials"; (2) the crime was only a misdemeanor; and (3) *Staples* had not come down this term. But all three of these conditions are contrary to fact. The pollutants to which the Clean Water Act felony statute applies include many in the "pencils, dental floss, paper clips" category. Hot water, rock, and sand are classified as "pollutants" by the Clean Water Act. Discharging silt from a stream back into the same stream may amount to discharge of a pollutant. For that matter, so may skipping a stone into a lake. So may a cafeteria worker's pouring hot, stale coffee down the drain. Making these acts a misdemeanor is one thing, but a felony is quite another as *Staples* teaches. . . .

The panel, finally, asserts that as a matter of policy, the Clean Water Act crimes "are clearly designed to protect the public at large from the dire consequences of water pollution." That is true, but the panel does not explain how the public is to be protected by making felons of sewer workers who unknowingly violate their plants' permits. Provision for sanitary sewage disposal is among the most ancient laws of civilization. Deuteronomy 23:12-13. Sewage workers perform essential work of great social value. Probably nothing has prevented more infant mortality, or freed more people from cholera, hepatitis, typhoid fever, and other disease, than the development in the last two centuries of municipal sewer systems. Sewage utility workers perform their difficult work in malodorous and dangerous environments. We have now imposed on these vitally important public servants a massive legal risk, unjustified by law or precedent, if they unknowingly violate their permit conditions.

Nor is the risk of prison limited to sewage plant workers. It applies to anyone who discharges pollutants pursuant to a permit, and unknowingly violates the permit. The panel suggests that criminalizing this innocent conduct will protect the public from water pollution. It is at least as likely that the increased criminal risk will raise the cost and reduce the availability of such lawful and essential public services as sewage disposal. We should not deprive individuals of justice, whether the judicial action would serve some desirable policy or not. It is by no means certain that the panel's construction will advance the underlying policy it attributes to Congress. We should apply the words Congress and the President promulgated as law, leaving the difficult policy choices to them.

We undermine the foundation of criminal law when we so vitiate the requirement of a criminal state of knowledge and intention as to make felons of the morally innocent.

## NOTES AND QUESTIONS

1. The defendants had argued at trial that their midnight dumping of toxic sludge actually was an effort to restore the treatment plant's biological balance to prevent a complete shutdown of the plant that would have caused far more environmental harm. While the plant's NPDES permit authorized bypasses for "essential maintenance to assure efficient operation" of the plant, the court found that the discharges were not permissible bypasses. The court found that the plant's permit was not unconstitutionally vague, noting that "appellants had adequate notice of the illegality of their dumping" as was indicated

> by the considerable pains they took to conceal their activities. The discharges were effected mainly at night; plant personnel were not to discuss them; and Weitzenhoff and Mariani consistently repeatedly denied the illicit operation when questioned by health authorities. These are not the ways of conscientious managers seeking to safeguard the environment.

Would the defendants have been more likely to prevail on appeal if they had made no effort whatsoever to conceal their activities?

2. Even the judges dissenting from the denial of a rehearing en banc agreed that the defendants' conduct "suggests that they must have known that they were violating their [NPDES] permit." Why then did the dissenting judges suggest the convictions should be reversed?

3. What is the rationale for not requiring a showing of specific intent to violate regulations when "public welfare" offenses are involved? What type of offenses should be considered public welfare offenses? Do the judges who dissented from denial of a rehearing en banc agree that violating the terms of an NPDES permit should be considered to be a public welfare offense? Do they differ from the majority in their views concerning the seriousness of the violations?

4. In United States v. Ahmad, 101 F.3d 386 (5th Cir. 1996), the Fifth Circuit reversed a criminal conviction under the Clean Water Act of a defendant who claimed at trial that he thought he was discharging water and not gasoline. The court held that the *mens rea* of knowledge applied to each element of the offense, thus requiring the government to prove that the defendant knew that what he was

discharging was a pollutant. The court distinguished *Weitzenhoff* as addressing only whether the language of the Clean Water Act creates a mistake-of-law defense, as opposed to the mistake-of-fact defense raised in *Ahmad*. In United States v. Wilson, 133 F.3d 251 (4th Cir. 1997), a panel of the Fourth Circuit followed the *Ahmad* interpretation of the *mens rea* required for a criminal conviction under the Clean Water Act. The *Wilson* court rejected the defendant's argument that it should construe the word "knowingly" as requiring that the defendant appreciate the illegality of his acts, finding that such an interpretation would obliterate the distinction between "knowingly" and "willfully." However, the court held that "Congress intended that the defendant have knowledge of each of the elements constituting the proscribed conduct even if he were unaware of their legal significance." Thus, it concluded that while a defendant's ignorance of his conduct's illegality does not provide a defense, a defendant can argue a mistake of fact as a defense. As a result, "to establish a felony violation of the Clean Water Act" the government

> must prove: (1) that the defendant knew that he was discharging a substance, eliminating a prosecution for accidental discharges; (2) that the defendant correctly identified the substance he was discharging, not mistaking it for a different, unprohibited substance; (3) that the defendant knew the method or instrumentality used to discharge the pollutants; (4) that the defendant knew the physical characteristics of the property into which the pollutant was discharged that identify it as a wetland, such as the presence of water and water-loving vegetation; (5) that the defendant was aware of the facts establishing the required link between the wetland and waters of the United States; and (6) that the defendant knew he did not have a permit. This last requirement does not require the government to show that the defendant knew that permits were available or required. Rather, it, like the other requirements, preserves the availability of a mistake of fact [defense] if the defendant has something he mistakenly believed to be a permit to make the discharges for which he is being prosecuted. [133 F.3d at 264.]

5. Some have proposed enacting legislation that would bar the imposition of civil or criminal penalties on defendants who "reasonably in good faith determined" that they were in compliance with an environmental regulation. What effect would such legislation have on enforcement efforts? In General Electric Company v. EPA, 53 F.3d 1324 (D.C. Cir. 1995), discussed on page 994, the D.C. Circuit barred the imposition of civil penalties on defendants who did not have "fair warning" of EPA's interpretation of regulations. The court held that "[w]here, as here, the regulations and other policy statements are unclear, where the petitioner's interpretation is reasonable, and where the agency itself struggles to provide a definitive reading of the regulatory requirements, a regulated party is not 'on notice' of the agency's ultimate interpretation of the regulations, and may not be punished." Does the availability of this defense make the use of a general intent standard for proving environmental felonies less troublesome?

6. Professor Richard Lazarus argues the public welfare rationale for dispensing with specific intent requirements, as represented by the *International Minerals* decision, should not be applied reflexively to environmental felonies. Lazarus, Meeting

the Demands of Integration in the Evolution of Environmental Law: Reforming Environmental Criminal Law, 83 Geo. L.J. 2407 (1995). He notes that *International Minerals,* which involved a misdemeanor, did not hold that persons dealing with hazardous materials *must* be presumed to be aware of the applicable regulations, but rather only that Congress could choose to assume such knowledge without violating due process. Lazarus observes that in many environmental law contexts it is not the case that regulations are readily discernible or that regulated entities are part of a specialized, highly regulated activity, factors that would make dispensing with specific intent requirements more palatable. Lazarus's arguments were challenged by then-Assistant and Deputy Assistant Attorneys General for the Environment and Natural Resources Division in Schiffer & Simon, The Reality of Prosecuting Environmental Criminals: A Response to Professor Lazarus, 83 Geo. L.J. 2531 (1995). They maintain that adopting a specific intent or "willfulness" requirement would make convictions impossible under the following circumstances:

    (1) A trucker dumps hundreds of drums of flammable, explosive, and toxic wastes in fields and vacant lots in a rural area. He knows that they are dangerous, but he has no knowledge of the laws that regulate the handling of such wastes.

    (2) A ship owner loads hazardous wastes as ballast and dumps those wastes at sea at a place unknown to authorities. He knows of the legal restrictions on dumping, but neither harm nor threat of harm can be determined reliably after the fact.

    (3) A laboratory that was paid to analyze environmental samples instead simply disposes of the samples and provides clients with fictitious results that always show that the clients are in compliance with their permits. Given those assurances, the clients take no steps to remove contaminants from their wastestreams. No one can reconstruct what contaminants were actually released to the environment or what harm was caused. [Id.]

Do you agree that requiring proof that the defendant knew the regulations were being violated would make prosecution impossible in these situations? Would this imply that environmental law needs to criminalize even some conduct that is nonculpable in order to make it possible to convict certain truly culpable individuals?

7. The debate over the proper intent standard for environmental felonies reflects concerns about how much discretion prosecutors have and how well they exercise that discretion. Then–Assistant Attorney General Lois Schiffer argues that there already are sufficient legal protections to prevent abuses of prosecutorial discretion, citing the rule of lenity and the doctrine that "an honest mistake regarding facts that would otherwise make . . . conduct criminal . . . negates the intent required for a felony conviction under the environmental laws." Id. at 2535. In addition, prosecutorial discretion is subject to policy guidance.

In January 1994, EPA issued a guidance document on criminal enforcement entitled The Exercise of Investigative Discretion. The publication directs agency investigators to focus on the "most significant and egregious violators" of the environmental laws based on the environmental consequences of the violations and the culpability of the conduct that generated them. Criteria for assessing the culpability of conduct include a history of repeat violations, evidence of deliberate misconduct, efforts to conceal violations, and operations conducted without permits or other regulatory documentation. For an argument that EPA has not done a good job of targeting only the most serious violations, see Gaynor & Bartman, Specific Intent Standard for Environmental Crimes: An Idea Whose Time Has Come, 25 Envtl. Rep. 2206 (1995). Citing potential abuses of prosecutorial discretion, Gaynor and Bartman maintain that the environmental laws should be amended to require that specific intent be proven before convictions can be obtained. EPA's guidance on criminal case selection suggests that cases involving neither culpable conduct nor significant harm ordinarily should not be prosecuted as criminal cases.

8. Staples v. United States, 511 U.S. 600 (1994), involved a statute which made it a felony to possess an unregistered "firearm." The statute defined "firearm" to include a fully automatic gun, which would fire more than one bullet on a single pull of the trigger, but not a semiautomatic. The defendant possessed a fully automatic gun but testified that he did not know it would fire more than one bullet with a single trigger pull. The trial judge had instructed the jury that his ignorance did not matter, so long as the government proved he possessed "a dangerous device of a type as would alert one to the likelihood of regulation." But the Supreme Court held this to be error, explaining that, unlike hand grenades, semiautomatics are innocently possessed by many people and that the mere knowledge that guns are dangerous and regulated is not enough to require their owners to ascertain regulatory compliance at the risk of a felony conviction.

> Congress might see fit to criminalize the violation of certain regulations concerning automobiles, and thus might make it a crime to operate a vehicle without a properly functioning emission control system. But we probably would hesitate to conclude on the basis of silence that Congress intended a prison term to apply to a car owner whose vehicle's emissions levels, wholly unbeknownst to him, began to exceed legal limits between regular inspection dates. [511 U.S. at 614.]

9. Despite the impassioned dissent of five judges from the denial of a rehearing en banc, the Supreme Court refused to review *Weitzenhoff*. The Second Circuit reached a similar result in United States v. Hopkins, 53 F.3d 533 (2d Cir. 1995), which the Supreme Court also declined to review. In *Hopkins*, the court held that deliberate and conscious avoidance of knowledge could satisfy the *mens rea* requirement of section 309(c)(2) of the Clean Water Act. The court upheld the conviction of a corporate official who had his employees manipulate samples of wastewater discharges to keep them within permit limits, while insisting that he not be told of the results. Hopkins was found guilty of tampering with a wastewater monitoring device and falsifying discharge monitoring reports in violation of the Clean Water Act. Testimony at trial showed that he routinely discarded monitoring samples that indicated permit violations and diluted others until they did not show violations. Citing *Weitzenhoff*, the Second Circuit held that the government was required to prove that the defendant "knew the nature of his acts and performed them intentionally, but was not required to prove that he knew that those acts violated the CWA, or any particular provision of that law, or the regulatory permit. . . ." 53 F.3d at 541.

10. In Yates v. United States, 574 U.S. 528 (2015), the Supreme Court held that the Sarbanes-Oxley Act of 2002, which makes it a crime for anyone to destroy any "tangible object" with the intent to impede or obstruct an investigation, could not be applied to a fisherman who threw undersized fish overboard after being told by a law enforcement officer to preserve them and to proceed to port. In a plurality opinion authored by Justice Ginsburg, four Justices concluded that the "tangible object" in Sarbanes-Oxley must be one used to record or preserve information.

---

## PROBLEM EXERCISE: WHO SHOULD BE PROSECUTED CRIMINALLY?

As discussed above, the exercise of prosecutorial discretion in deciding when to invoke the criminal sanctions in the environmental laws has been a topic of considerable controversy. Consider the following seven real-life scenarios posed by three EPA and Department of Justice enforcement attorneys in Martin Harrell, Joseph J. Lisa & Catherine L. Votaw, Federal Environmental Crime: A Different Kind of "White Collar" Prosecution, 23 Nat. Resources & Env't 3, 4 (Winter 2009).

1. A businessman with no criminal history stores hazardous waste for two years at a closed facility because he supposedly lacks funds to pay for disposal. He does not tell anyone about this storage while he deals with environmental regulators on other matters and operates a similar business nearby. The waste is discovered when a citizen reports smelling fumes, and the government spends $130,000 to clean up the location to protect neighbors. Should the businessman be prosecuted criminally?

2. A lazy or disinterested sewage treatment plant technician or private laboratory analyst does not perform effluent tests and then fabricates analytical results. It is impossible to determine if environmental violations occurred because the tests were not actually done. The individual did not obtain any monetary benefit from his conduct, has no criminal history, and loses his job. Should the technician be prosecuted criminally?

3. A supervisor fails to check the label on some containers of dangerous but unwanted material and dumps it into a sanitary sewer, disrupting the public sewage treatment plant and causing the death of 1,000 small fish in a creek. The company has a good environmental record. Should the supervisor be prosecuted criminally?

4. A company has five nonpermitted discharges from multiple mining operations into already heavily polluted streams over two years, all resulting from equipment failure or operator error. Three of the discharges discolor miles of stream and result in small fish kills. Should the company be prosecuted criminally?

5. A 50,000-person municipality receives several Notices of Violation over five years for storing hazardous waste longer than permitted and under poor conditions. After complying for a year, the city is caught again storing hazardous waste longer than permitted. It turns out that the city has no organized environmental compliance management system. Should the municipality be prosecuted criminally?

6. A 65-year-old businessman quietly empties wastewater down a sink connected to a publicly owned treatment works (POTW) designed to handle only domestic waste. He does not tell the POTW, but an employee informs a local regulator. A sampling device confirms metals are being discharged into the sewer system from his facility but not above categorical pretreatment limits. The businessman previously served a prison sentence for pretreatment violations at another facility. Should the businessman be prosecuted criminally?

7. An 81-year-old businessman with a long history of charitable works hires an asbestos abatement contractor to remove insulation prior to selling industrial property but pays his "handyman" to drain and dispose of 400 gallons of known polychlorinated biphenyl (PCB) fluid from two old transformers. The businessman had received two bids of more than $10,000 from reputable companies to dispose of the fluid. The fluid disappears, and PCB contamination is discovered in a nearby sanitary sewer. Should the businessman be prosecuted criminally?

## D.   CITIZEN SUITS

As noted above, the environmental laws do not leave enforcement entirely in the hands of government. Recognizing that federal agencies had a long history of unresponsiveness to environmental concerns, Congress sought to enlist citizens in the tasks of ensuring that the laws were implemented and enforced properly. It did so by authorizing citizen suits, a major innovation first incorporated in the Clean Air Act Amendments of 1970, 42 U.S.C. §7604, and included in virtually all the major environmental laws Congress subsequently adopted. See, e.g., CWA §505, ESA §11(g), RCRA §7002, TSCA §18, CERCLA §310.

### 1.   Citizen Suit Provisions in the APA and the Federal Environmental Laws

The federal environmental laws generally authorize private parties to bring three types of lawsuits. The first allows citizens to act as "private attorney generals" to supplement government enforcement against those who violate environmental regulations. We refer to these as citizen enforcement actions. These provisions generally authorize "any person" to commence an action against "any person" alleged to be in violation of the laws. They require citizens to notify the alleged violator and federal and state authorities prior to filing suit. Sixty days' notice usually is required, although the amount of notice can vary for certain violations (e.g., section 505(b) of the Clean Water Act authorizes suits alleging violations of NSPS requirements or toxic effluent standards to be brought immediately after notice, as does section 7002(b)(1)(A) of RCRA for violations of RCRA subtitle C). The citizen suit provisions usually specify that if federal or state authorities are diligently prosecuting an action to require compliance, filing of a citizen suit is barred, though citizens are authorized to intervene in federal enforcement actions as of right (e.g., CWA §505(b)(1)(B), CAA §304(b)(1)(B)).

While federal agencies and officials are among the "persons" who can be sued for violating environmental regulations, the statutes also generally authorize suits to force officials to perform their mandatory duties. For example, the Clean Water Act provides that the EPA administrator may be sued by citizens "where there is alleged a failure of the Administrator to perform any act or duty . . . which is not discretionary," 33 U.S.C. §1365(a)(1)(2). (The citizen suit provisions in the other statutes contain virtually identical language.) Suits such as these typically challenge an agency's failure to meet a statutory deadline to take some action. When they do, they generally are called "deadline suits." This type of litigation has been an important action-forcing device to ensure that regulations implementing the environmental statutes are issued.

As discussed in Chapter 2, the federal environmental laws also generally include judicial review provisions that authorize citizen suits to review the legality of agency actions. These provisions supplement the judicial review provisions of the Administrative Procedure Act, 5 U.S.C. §§701-706, by specifying additional procedural requirements, such as those contained in section 307(b) of the Clean Air Act (requiring that petitions for review of nationally applicable regulations must be filed in the U.S. Court of Appeals for the D.C. Circuit within 60 days of promulgation).

If an agency has failed to issue regulations by a deadline imposed by statute, a citizen suit generally may be brought to force the agency to issue the regulations. Cases seeking to force agencies to take other actions often turn on whether the courts view the agency as having a nondiscretionary duty to take such actions.

For example, in June 2004, the U.S. Supreme Court decided an important case challenging the failure of the Bureau of Land Management (BLM) to enforce laws governing management of public lands. The case arose when the Southern Utah Wilderness Alliance and other environmental groups sued the BLM in 1999, alleging that the agency had violated the Federal Land Policy Management Act (FLPMA) and the National Environmental Policy Act (NEPA) by failing to control off-road vehicle use on federal lands classified as wilderness study areas. The plaintiffs argued that BLM had failed to carry out its nondiscretionary duty to prevent impairment of wilderness study areas for suitability as wilderness and to undertake certain actions identified in its own land management plans as necessary to protect those areas, such as inventorying existing trails, closing areas to off-road vehicle (ORV) use, and monitoring such use. After the district court held that the claims were not reviewable under section 706(1) of the APA, the plaintiffs appealed to the Tenth Circuit, which reversed. The Tenth Circuit (Southern Utah Wilderness Alliance v. Norton, 301 F.3d 1217 (10th Cir. 2003)) held that the FLPMA imposed a mandatory, nondiscretionary duty upon the Secretary of Interior and that breach of that duty was subject to review under section 706(1) of the APA. The U.S. Supreme Court then reversed the Tenth Circuit in Norton v. Southern Utah Wilderness Alliance, 542 U.S. 55 (2004).

While acknowledging that the APA's definition of agency action includes "failure to act," the Court held "that the only agency action that can be compelled under the APA is action legally required." The Court concluded that this is limited to discrete actions that the agency is legally required to take. Thus, it held that SUWA could not seek judicial review to mandate that BLM manage wilderness study areas "in a manner so as not to impair the suitability of such areas for preservation as wilderness," 43 U.S.C. §1782(c), because this directive "leaves BLM a great deal of discretion in deciding how to achieve it. It assuredly does not mandate, with the clarity necessary to support judicial action under §706(1), the total exclusion of ORV use."

## 2.   *Citizen Enforcement Actions and the* **Gwaltney** *Problem*

While action-forcing litigation against EPA played a major role in the development of environmental law during the 1970s, citizen enforcement actions against private parties who violated environmental regulations were rarely filed during this period. This changed in 1982 due to concern over a dramatic decline in governmental enforcement efforts during the early years of the Reagan administration. The Natural Resources Defense Council (NRDC) initiated a national project to use citizen suits to fill the enforcement void.

The citizen suit project focused on enforcement of the Clean Water Act because it was easy to prove violations. Dischargers are required to file discharge monitoring reports (DMRs), which are available to the public and can serve as prima facie evidence of NPDES permit violations. Joined by local environmental groups, NRDC systematically scrutinized DMRs and sent 60-day notice letters to dischargers who reported violations of permit limits. Notice letters were then followed by citizen suits. As a result of this project, the total number of citizen suits brought under the Clean Water Act increased from 6 in 1981 to 62 in 1983, surpassing the 56 Clean Water Act cases referred by EPA to the Justice Department for prosecution that year. Miller, Private Enforcement of Federal Pollution Control Laws, 14 Envtl. L. Rep. 10407, 10424 (1984).

Based on self-reported violations contained in the DMRs, citizen suits became relatively easy to win, particularly after several courts rejected efforts to create new defenses to such suits (including claims that discharge monitoring reports prepared by defendants were too unreliable to serve as the basis for violations or that they violated the Fifth Amendment privilege against self-incrimination). After complaints from dischargers (the general counsel of the Chemical Manufacturers Association complained that his members would have contested permit provisions more aggressively if they had known that their permits were going to be enforced), EPA commissioned a comprehensive study of citizen suits in 1984. The study found that citizen suits generally had been operating in a manner consistent with the goals of the environmental statutes by both stimulating and supplementing government enforcement. Environmental Law Institute, Citizen Suits: An Analysis of Citizen Enforcement Actions Under EPA-Administered Statutes (1984). The study found no evidence that citizen suits had interfered with government enforcement efforts or that they had focused on trivial violations.

After courts rejected repeated efforts by dischargers in the early 1980s to create new defenses to citizen suits, defendants finally stumbled on a more successful strategy when they focused on the language of section 505 of the Clean Water Act, which authorizes suits against any person "alleged to be in violation" of the Act. Defendants argued that because this phrase used the present tense, it must mean that to prevail a citizen plaintiff had to prove that dischargers were in violation of the Act at the moment the suit was filed rather than simply relying on past monitoring reports. This argument received a mixed reception in the U.S. courts of appeals, culminating in the following Supreme Court decision.

## Gwaltney of Smithfield, Ltd. v. Chesapeake Bay Foundation

484 U.S. 49 (1987)

JUSTICE MARSHALL delivered the opinion of the Court.

In this case, we must decide whether §505(a) of the Clean Water Act, 33 U.S.C. §1365(a), confers federal jurisdiction over citizen suits for wholly past violations. . . .

The holder of a federal NPDES permit is subject to enforcement action by the Administrator for failure to comply with the conditions of the permit. The Administrator's enforcement arsenal includes administrative, civil, and criminal sanctions. §1319. The holder of a state NPDES permit is subject to both federal and state enforcement action for failure to comply. §§1319, 1342(b)(7). In the absence of federal or state enforcement, private citizens may commence civil actions against any person "alleged to be in violation of" the conditions of either a federal or state NPDES permit. §1365(a)(1). If the citizen prevails in such an action, the court may order injunctive relief and/or impose civil penalties payable to the United States Treasury. §1365(a).

The Commonwealth of Virginia established a federally approved state NPDES program administered by the Virginia State Water Control Board (Board). Va. Code §§62.1-44 et seq. (1950). In 1974, the Board issued a NPDES permit to ITT-Gwaltney authorizing the discharge of seven pollutants from the company's meat-packing plant on the Pagan River in Smithfield, Virginia. The permit, which was reissued in 1979 and modified in 1980, established effluent limitations, monitoring requirements, and other conditions of discharge. In 1981, petitioner Gwaltney of Smithfield acquired the assets of ITT-Gwaltney and assumed obligations under the permit.

Between 1981 and 1984, petitioner repeatedly violated the conditions of the permit by exceeding effluent limitations on five of the seven pollutants covered. These violations are chronicled in the Discharge Monitoring Reports (DMRs) that the permit required petitioner to maintain. The most substantial of the violations concerned the pollutants fecal coliform, chlorine, and total Kjeldahl nitrogen (TKN). Between October 27, 1981, and August 30, 1984, petitioner violated its TKN limitation 87 times, its chlorine limitation 34 times, and its fecal coliform limitation 31 times. Petitioner installed new equipment to improve its chlorination system in March 1982, and its last reported chlorine violation occurred in October 1982. The new chlorination system also helped to control the discharge of fecal coliform, and the last recorded fecal coliform violation occurred in February 1984. Petitioner installed an upgraded waste-water treatment system in October 1983, and its last reported TKN violation occurred on May 15, 1984.

Respondents Chesapeake Bay Foundation and Natural Resources Defense Council, two nonprofit corporations dedicated to the protection of natural resources, sent notice in February 1984, to Gwaltney, the Administrator of EPA, and the Virginia State Water Control Board, indicating respondents' intention to commence a citizen suit under the Act based on petitioner's violations of its permit conditions. Respondents proceeded to file this suit in June 1984, alleging that petitioner "has violated . . . [and] will continue to violate its NPDES permit." Respondents requested that the District Court provide declaratory and injunctive relief, impose civil penalties, and award attorney's fees and costs. The District Court granted partial summary judgment for respondents in August 1984, declaring Gwaltney "to have violated and to be in violation" of the Act. The District Court then held a trial to determine the appropriate remedy.

Before the District Court reached a decision, Gwaltney moved in May 1985 for dismissal of the action for want of subject-matter jurisdiction under the Act. Gwaltney argued that the language of §505(a), which permits private citizens to bring suit against any person "alleged to be in violation" of the Act, requires that a defendant be violating the Act at the time of suit. Gwaltney urged the District Court to adopt the analysis of the Fifth Circuit in Hamker v. Diamond Shamrock Chemical Co., 756 F.2d 392 (1985), which held that "a complaint brought under [§505] must allege a violation occurring at the time the complaint is filed." Id., at 395. Gwaltney contended that because its last recorded violation occurred several weeks before respondents filed their complaint, the District Court lacked subject-matter jurisdiction over respondents' action.

The District Court rejected Gwaltney's argument concluding that §505 authorizes citizens to bring enforcement actions on the basis of wholly past violations. . . .

The Court of Appeals affirmed, expressly rejecting the Fifth Circuit's approach in *Hamker* and holding that §505 "can be read to comprehend unlawful conduct that occurred only prior to the filing of a lawsuit as well as unlawful conduct that continues into the present." 791 F.2d 304, 309 (4th Cir. 1986). . . .

The Court of Appeals concluded that the "to be in violation" language of §505 is ambiguous, whereas petitioner asserts that it plainly precludes the construction adopted below. We must agree with the Court of Appeals that §505 is not a provision in which Congress' limpid prose puts an end to all dispute. But to acknowledge ambiguity is not to conclude that all interpretations are equally plausible. The most natural reading of "to be in violation" is a requirement that citizen-plaintiffs allege a state of either continuous or intermittent violation—that is, a reasonable likelihood that a past polluter will continue to pollute in the future. Congress could have phrased its requirement in language that looked to the past ("to have violated"), but it did not choose this readily available option.

Respondents urge that the choice of the phrase "to be in violation," rather than phrasing more clearly directed to the past, is a "careless accident," the result of a "debatable lapse of syntactical precision." But the prospective orientation of that phrase could not have escaped Congress' attention. Congress used identical language in the citizen suit provisions of several other environmental statutes that authorize only prospective relief. See, e.g., Clean Air Act, 42 U.S.C. §7604; Resource Conservation and Recovery Act of 1976, 42 U.S.C. §6972 (1982 ed. and Supp. III); Toxic Substances Control Act, 15 U.S.C. §2619 (1982 ed. and Supp. IV). Moreover,

Congress has demonstrated in yet other statutory provisions that it knows how to avoid this prospective implication by using language that explicitly targets wholly past violations. . . .

Our reading of the "to be in violation" language of §505(a) is bolstered by the language and structure of the rest of the citizen suit provisions in §505 of the Act. These provisions together make plain that the interest of the citizen-plaintiff is primarily forward-looking.

One of the most striking indicia of the prospective orientation of the citizen suit is the pervasive use of the present tense throughout §505. A citizen suit may be brought only for violation of a permit limitation "which is in effect" under the Act. 33 U.S.C. §1365(f). Citizen-plaintiffs must give notice to the alleged violator, the Administrator of EPA, and the State in which the alleged violation "occurs." §1365(b)(1)(A). A Governor of a State may sue as a citizen when the Administrator fails to enforce an effluent limitation "the violation of which is occurring in another State and is causing an adverse effect on the public health or welfare in his State." §1365(h). The most telling use of the present tense is in the definition of "citizen" as "a person . . . having an interest which is or may be adversely affected" by the defendant's violations of the Act. §1365(g). This definition makes plain what the undeviating use of the present tense strongly suggests: the harm sought to be addressed by the citizen suit lies in the present or the future, not in the past.

Any other conclusion would render incomprehensible §505's notice provision, which requires citizens to give 60 days notice of their intent to sue to the alleged violator as well as to the Administrator and the State. §1365(b)(1)(A). If the Administrator or the State commences enforcement action within that 60 day period, the citizen suit is barred, presumably because governmental action has rendered it unnecessary. §1365(b)(1)(B). It follows logically that the purpose of notice to the alleged violator is to give it an opportunity to bring itself into complete compliance with the Act and thus likewise render unnecessary a citizen suit. If we assume, as respondents urge, that citizen suits may target wholly past violations, the requirement of notice to the alleged violator becomes gratuitous. Indeed, respondents, in propounding their interpretation of the Act, can think of no reason for Congress to require such notice other than that "it seemed right" to inform an alleged violator that it was about to be sued.

Adopting respondents' interpretation of §505's jurisdictional grant would create a second and even more disturbing anomaly. The bar on citizen suits when governmental enforcement action is under way suggests that the citizen suit is meant to supplement rather than to supplant governmental action. The legislative history of the Act reinforces this view of the role of the citizen suit. The Senate Report noted that "[t]he Committee intends the great volume of enforcement actions [to] be brought by the State," and that citizen suits are proper only "if the Federal, State, and local agencies fail to exercise their enforcement responsibility." S. Rep. No. 92-414, p. 64 (1971), reprinted in 2 A Legislative History of the Water Pollution Control Act Amendments of 1972, p. 1482 (1973) (hereinafter Leg. Hist.). Permitting citizen suits for wholly past violations of the Act could undermine the supplementary role envisioned for the citizen suit. This danger is best illustrated by an example. Suppose that the Administrator identified a violator of the Act and issued a compliance order under §309(a). Suppose further that the Administrator agreed not to assess or otherwise seek civil penalties on the condition that the violator take some extreme corrective action, such as to install particularly effective but expensive machinery, that it otherwise would not be obliged to take. If citizens could file suit, months or years later, in order to seek the civil penalties that the Administrator chose to forgo, then the Administrator's discretion to enforce the Act in the public interest would be curtailed considerably. The same might be said of the discretion of state enforcement authorities. Respondents' interpretation of the scope of the citizen suit would change the nature of the citizens' role from interstitial to potentially intrusive. We cannot agree that Congress intended such a result. . . .

Our conclusion that §505 does not permit citizen suits for wholly past violations does not necessarily dispose of this lawsuit, as both lower courts recognized. The District Court found persuasive the fact that "[respondents'] allegation in the complaint, that Gwaltney was continuing to violate its NPDES permit when plaintiffs filed suits, appears to have been made fully in good faith." On this basis, the District Court explicitly held, albeit in a footnote, that "even if Gwaltney were correct that a district court has no jurisdiction over citizen suits based entirely on unlawful conduct that occurred entirely in the past, the Court would still have jurisdiction here." Ibid. The Court of Appeals acknowledged, also in a footnote, that "[a] very sound argument can be made that [respondents'] allegations of continuing violations were made in good faith," but expressly declined to rule on this alternative holding. Because we agree that §505 confers jurisdiction over citizen suits when the citizen-plaintiffs make a good-faith allegation of continuous or intermittent violation, we remand the case to the Court of Appeals for further consideration.

Petitioner argues that citizen-plaintiffs must prove their allegations of ongoing noncompliance before jurisdiction attaches under §505. We cannot agree. The statute does not require that a defendant "be in violation" of the Act at the commencement of suit; rather, the statute requires that a defendant be "*alleged* to be in violation." Petitioner's construction of the Act reads the word "alleged" out of §505. As petitioner itself is quick to note in other contexts, there is no reason to believe that Congress' drafting of §505 was sloppy or haphazard. We agree with the Solicitor General that "Congress's use of the phrase 'alleged to be in violation' reflects a conscious sensitivity to the practical difficulties of detecting and proving chronic episodic violations of environmental standards." Our acknowledgment that Congress intended a good-faith allegation to suffice for jurisdictional purposes, however, does not give litigants license to flood the courts with suits premised on baseless allegations. Rule 11 of the Federal Rules of Civil Procedure, which requires pleadings to be based on a good-faith belief, formed after reasonable inquiry, that they are "well grounded in fact," adequately protects defendants from frivolous allegations.

Petitioner contends that failure to require proof of allegations under §505 would permit plaintiffs whose allegations of ongoing violation are reasonable but untrue to maintain suit in federal court even though they lack constitutional standing. Petitioner reasons that if a defendant is in complete compliance with the Act at the time of suit, plaintiffs have suffered no injury remediable by the citizen suit provisions of the Act. Petitioner, however, fails to recognize that our standing cases uniformly recognize that allegations of injury are sufficient to invoke the jurisdiction of the court. In Warth v. Seldin, 422 U.S. 490, 501 (1975), for example, we made clear that a suit will not be dismissed for lack of standing if there are sufficient "allegations of fact"—not proof—in the complaint or supporting affidavits. This is not to say, however, that such allegations may not be challenged. In United States v. SCRAP, 412 U.S. 669, 689 (1973), we noted that if the plaintiffs' "allegations [of standing] were in fact untrue, then the [defendants] should have moved for summary judgment on the standing issue and demonstrated to the District Court that the allegations were sham and raised no genuine issue of fact." If the defendant fails to make such a showing after the plaintiff offers evidence to support the allegation, the case proceeds to trial on the merits, where the plaintiff must prove the allegations in order to prevail. But the Constitution does not require that the plaintiff offer this proof as a threshold matter in order to invoke the District Court's jurisdiction.

Petitioner also worries that our construction of §505 would permit citizen-plaintiffs, if their allegations of ongoing noncompliance become false at some later point in the litigation because the defendant begins to comply with the Act, to continue nonetheless to press their suit to conclusion. According to petitioner, such a result would contravene both the prospective purpose of the citizen suit provisions and the "case or controversy" requirement of Article III. Longstanding principles of mootness, however, prevent the maintenance of suit when "there is no reasonable expectation that the wrong will be repeated." In seeking to have a case dismissed as moot, however, the defendant's burden "is a heavy one." The defendant must demonstrate that it is "*absolutely clear* that the alleged wrongful behavior could not reasonably be expected to recur." United States v. Phosphate Export Assn., Inc., 393 U.S. 199, 203 (1968) (emphasis added). Mootness doctrine thus protects defendants from the maintenance of suit under the Clean Water Act based solely on violations wholly unconnected to any present or future wrongdoing, while it also protects plaintiffs from defendants who seek to evade sanction by predictable "protestations of repentance and reform."

Because the court below erroneously concluded that respondents could maintain an action based on wholly past violations of the Act, it declined to decide whether respondents' complaint contained a good-faith allegation of ongoing violation by petitioner. We therefore remand the case for consideration of this question. The judgment of the Court of Appeals is vacated, and the case is remanded for further proceedings consistent with this opinion.

## NOTES AND QUESTIONS

1. After *Gwaltney*, under what circumstances can a citizen suit be maintained in light of the "in violation" language of section 505? What must a plaintiff allege about the violation in order to be authorized to sue? Can a plaintiff be required to prove at trial that this allegation is true?

2. The Court's decision is premised on the notion that citizen suits can only be used to address present or future harms. Is Justice Marshall correct that "any other conclusion would render incomprehensible" the 60-day notice requirement? Could a notice requirement be useful even if citizen suits could be brought against wholly past violations?

3. As noted above, the Clean Water Act had been the most popular vehicle for citizen suits because it was easy to prove that a violation had occurred using defendants' own discharge monitoring reports (DMRs). After *Gwaltney*, citizens must be

prepared to prove the likelihood of ongoing violations. What constitutes an "ongoing" or "continuing" violation? Can a citizen prove an ongoing violation solely by reference to the DMRs? The Court did not accept Gwaltney's argument that the "in violation" language required plaintiffs to prove that the violation was occurring at the moment suit was filed. In a concurring opinion Justice Scalia noted that neither a "good or lucky day" nor "the dubious state in which a past effluent problem is not recurring at the moment but the cause of that problem has not been completely and clearly eradicated" was sufficient to place a discharger in a state of compliance. Can a one-shot discharge be considered an "ongoing" violation if its harmful effects still linger?

4. How did Justice Marshall answer the question of what happens if a good-faith allegation of a continuing violation proves to be untrue? In his concurrence Justice Scalia argued that if a violation had been corrected the plaintiff would not have standing because there would be "no remediable injury in fact that could support the suit." Is this correct? After a defendant has voluntarily corrected a violation is it really no longer possible to provide judicial redress? Wouldn't the possibility of a subsequent penalty provide some redress, by deterring future violations and reducing the likelihood that the past violation would ever be repeated? Has the Supreme Court construed the purpose of citizen suits too narrowly as abatement rather than deterrence, thus undermining efforts to use citizen suits to encourage pollution prevention?

5. Does *Gwaltney* make it possible for defendants to defeat any citizen suit for readily correctable violations? If so, will citizen suits only be able to deter violations that are the most difficult for defendants to avoid? The result in *Gwaltney* is a particularly ironic contrast to the Justice Department's 1970 policy for suits under the Refuse Act, which encouraged suits "to punish or prevent significant discharges which are either accidental or infrequent, but which are not of a continuing nature resulting from the ordinary operations of a manufacturing plant." United States Department of Justice, Guidelines for Litigation Under the Refuse Act §11 (1970). Can *Gwaltney* be reconciled with this policy?

6. The Court rejected the Chesapeake Bay Foundation's explanation that the phrase "to be in violation" was a "careless accident" by observing that Congress used identical language in the citizen suit provisions contained in other environmental laws. Yet isn't it reasonable to assume that Congress simply borrowed the same language whenever it wanted to include a citizen suit provision in subsequent legislation, thus buttressing CBF's argument?

### The Congressional Response to *Gwaltney*

*Gwaltney*'s impact was broad because the "to be in violation" language also appeared in the citizen suit provisions of other federal environmental statutes. However, Congress eventually was more careful in its choice of words. The citizen suit provision included in the Emergency Planning and Community Right-to-Know Act, EPCRA §326, 42 U.S.C. §11046, authorizes any person to sue an owner or operator of a facility "for *failure to do*" any of four enumerated requirements (e.g., submitting a toxic chemical release form required by section 313). When Congress amended the Clean Air Act in 1990 it replaced the language "alleged to be in violation" with the phrase "alleged to have violated (if there is evidence that the alleged violation has been repeated) or to be in violation." CAA §304(2)(1), 42 U.S.C. §7604(a)(1) (1993). Similar amendments have been proposed as Congress considers reauthorization of other statutes.

How should these provisions be interpreted? Do they authorize citizen suits for wholly past violations? See Atlantic States Legal Found. v. United Musical Instrument, Inc., 61 F.3d 473 (6th Cir. 1995) (EPCRA precludes citizen suits seeking civil penalties for violation cured after receipt of citizen-suit notice letter but before suit filed). Note that both section 326 of EPCRA and section 304 of the CAA retain the 60-day notice requirement that the Court found to be a striking sign of section 505's "prospective orientation." Do these amendments reflect a larger pattern of greater congressional specificity in response to narrow interpretations of public law by the Supreme Court? See Eskridge, Overriding Supreme Court Statutory Interpretation Decisions, 101 Yale L.J. 331 (1991).

### The *Gwaltney* Remand

On remand, the Fourth Circuit interpreted the *Gwaltney* decision to authorize citizens to file suit based on "a good faith allegation of ongoing violation" but to require proof of such a violation at trial. Chesapeake Bay Foundation v. Gwaltney of Smithfield, Ltd., 844 F.2d 170 (4th Cir. 1988). The court noted that this could be accomplished either "(1) by proving violations that continue on or after the date the complaint is filed, or (2) by adducing evidence from which a reasonable trier of fact could find a continuing likelihood of a recurrence in intermittent or sporadic violations." The district court then reinstated the entire judgment. The judge found that although the violations had not continued, when the suit was filed "there existed a very real danger and likelihood of further violation" because witnesses had expressed doubt that the upgraded wastewater treatment system would cure all nitrogen discharge violations. Chesapeake Bay Foundation v. Gwaltney of Smithfield, Ltd., 688 F. Supp. 1078, 1079 (E.D. Va. 1988). Gwaltney then appealed once again to the Fourth Circuit.

The Fourth Circuit affirmed the district court's conclusion that a penalty could be imposed even though the violations did not recur and rejected Gwaltney's claims of mootness and lack of standing. Chesapeake Bay Foundation v. Gwaltney of Smithfield, Ltd., 890 F.2d 690 (4th Cir. 1989). The court held that the plaintiffs did not lack standing because judicial redress could be provided to them through the deterrent effect of civil penalties. The court held that the case was not moot, regardless of subsequent events, because there was an ongoing violation when the suit was filed and "a suit seeking penalties is intrinsically incapable of being rendered moot by the polluter's corrective actions." However, the court held that "for purposes both of determining ongoing violations and of assessing penalties" it must consider separately each permit parameter alleged to have been violated. The court affirmed the $289,822 penalty for nitrogen (TKN) discharge violations by holding that even though the last violation occurred prior to filing of the lawsuit a "reasonable trier of fact could find a continuing likelihood of a recurrence in intermittent or sporadic violations" of the permit's TKN limits. But the court reversed the $995,500 penalty for chlorine violations.

### Citizen Suits in the Aftermath of *Gwaltney*

Questions raised by *Gwaltney* have been addressed by the lower federal courts in numerous subsequent cases as defendants have sought to block citizen suits. The post-*Gwaltney* cases generally indicate that: (1) determinations concerning whether or not a violation is ongoing are to be made as of the time the complaint is filed, Atlantic States Legal Found., Inc. v. Tyson Foods, Inc., 897 F.2d 1128 (11th Cir. 1990); (2) a violation is not ongoing if remedial measures ensure that there is no reasonable prospect for recurrence, Chesapeake Bay Found. v. Gwaltney of Smithfield, Ltd., 844 F.2d 170 (4th Cir. 1988) (*Gwaltney II*); (3) plaintiffs need only make a good-faith allegation of an ongoing violation in order to be able to file suit, Sierra Club v. Union Oil of California, 853 F.2d 667 (9th Cir. 1988), but they must be able to prove it to prevail at trial, *Gwaltney II*; Carr v. Alta Verde Indus., 924 F.2d 558 (5th Cir. 1991); and (4) courts are divided on whether a parameter-by-parameter assessment of violations must be made in determining whether a violation is ongoing, but ongoing violations can be established either by showing that violations continued on or after the filing of a complaint or by producing evidence from which a reasonable trier of fact could find a continuing likelihood that intermittent or sporadic violations would occur.

Another question that arose after *Gwaltney* is whether a violator may effectively escape liability by completing remedial action after the complaint is filed but before judgment is rendered. Discussions of mootness in *Gwaltney*, in the context of the jurisdictional issue, suggested to some courts that the main purpose of citizen suits was to abate existing violations and therefore subsequent compliance may "moot out" the pending action. For example, in Atlantic States Legal Found. v. Tyson Foods, Inc., 897 F.2d 1128 (11th Cir. 1990), a district court had stayed proceedings in a citizen suit to give a defendant time to come into compliance and then dismissed the suit as moot. Plaintiffs appealed and the Eleventh Circuit reversed, holding that claims for civil penalties were not mooted by post-complaint compliance. See also Atlantic States Legal Found. v. Stroh Die Casting Co., 116 F.3d 814 (7th Cir. 1997). In Steel Company v. Citizens for a Better Environment, 523 U.S. 83 (1998), the Supreme Court held that pre-complaint corrective action could defeat a citizen plaintiff's standing in an EPCRA enforcement action, see page 1040. Relying on this decision, the Fourth Circuit held that post-complaint corrective action rendered a citizen suit moot. Friends of the Earth v. Laidlaw Environmental Services, 149 F.3d 303 (4th Cir. 1998). However, as discussed below, the Supreme Court reversed the Fourth Circuit and held that post-complaint corrective action does not defeat standing because civil penalties can benefit plaintiffs by deterring future violations. Friends of the Earth v. Laidlaw Environmental Services, 528 U.S. 167 (2000).

### 3.   Standing in Citizen Enforcement Actions

The concept of standing to sue to enforce the environmental laws is introduced in Chapter 2, Section A. In recent years, the Supreme Court has articulated the requirements of standing as consisting of four parts. To have standing to sue, a plaintiff must allege:

1. that the challenged action will cause plaintiff some actual or threatened injury-in-fact;
2. that the injury is fairly traceable to the challenged action;
3. that the injury is redressable by judicial action; and
4. that the injury is to an interest arguably within the zone of interests to be protected by the statute alleged to have been violated.

It has also stated that the first three requirements are constitutional, based on Art. III, while the fourth is "prudential," and thus can be altered by Congress. (Congress could, for example, grant standing to everyone in the world who satisfied the first three requirements, thus eliminating the fourth part entirely.) See, e.g., Valley Forge Christian College v. Americans United for Separation of Church and State, 454 U.S. 464 (1982).

In several cases, the courts have used the "zone of interests" prong of standing doctrine to reject efforts by industry groups to use the environmental statutes to their benefit. For example, efforts by a group of ranchers to pursue alleged procedural violations of NEPA and the National Forest Management Act in order to block reductions in grazing levels were rejected in Nevada Land Action Association v. U.S. Forest Service, 8 F.3d 713 (9th Cir. 1993). The court found that the ranchers lacked standing because "[t]he purpose of NEPA is to protect the environment, not the economic interests of those adversely affected by agency decisions." 8 F.3d at 716. In Portland Audubon Society v. Hodel, 866 F.2d 302 (9th Cir. 1989), a timber industry group was held not to have standing to intervene in a NEPA lawsuit because the group's economic interests had no direct relation to the interests protected by the statute. In Competitive Enterprise Institute v. National Highway Safety Administration, 901 F.2d 107 (D.C. Cir. 1990), the D.C. Circuit held that a nonprofit group representing business interests fell within the zone of interests protected by the Energy Policy and Conservation Act by alleging that fuel-economy standards adversely affect the safety of vehicle occupants. However, the court held that the group did not fall within the zone of interests protected by NEPA. In Grocery Manufacturers Ass'n v. EPA, 693 F.3d 169 (D.C. Cir. 2012), the court held that food businesses did not have prudential standing to challenge the introduction of a new biofuel because their claimed injury—an increase in the price of corn—fell outside of the zone of interest protected by the Clean Air Act.

In Bennett v. Spear, 520 U.S. 154 (1997), ranch operators and irrigation districts who used water for commercial and recreational purposes challenged a decision to maintain a minimum water level in two public reservoirs to protect species of fish on the endangered species list. The Court held that because the ESA's citizen suit provision used the expansive language "any person may commence a civil suit," it expanded the zone of interests entitled to sue under the Act to embrace even business interests alleging "overenforcement" of environmental restrictions. The Court found that the irrigation districts could sue the director of the Fish and Wildlife Service and the Secretary of the Interior for failure to perform nondiscretionary duties under section 4 of the ESA to use "the best scientific data available" and to consider "the economic impact" when "specifying any particular area as critical habitat" for an endangered species. The Court emphasized that the zone of interests test was to be determined "not by reference to the overall purpose of the Act in question (here, species preservation), but by reference to the particular provision of law upon which the plaintiff relies." Thus, even though the irrigation districts obviously did not care about species preservation, the Court held them entitled to sue because it construed the "obvious purpose" of the "best data" requirement to be "to avoid needless economic dislocations produced by agency officials zealously but unintelligently pursuing their environmental objectives."

The Supreme Court has recognized that organizations have standing to assert the interests of their members if (1) at least one member would have standing to sue individually, (2) the interests the organization seeks to protect are "germane to the organization's purposes," and (3) neither the claims asserted nor the relief requested requires the participation in the lawsuit of individual members. Int'l Union, United Auto., Aerospace and Agr. Implement Workers v. Brock, 477 U.S. 274 (1986). Thus, so long as the subject of a lawsuit is environmental, an environmental group who has a member sufficiently affected by a decision to qualify for standing can sue in its organizational capacity. Non-governmental organizations that do not have members have a more difficult time establishing standing. Otsego 200 v. FERC, 767 Fed. Appx. (mem) (D.C. Cir. 2019); American Lung Ass'n v. EPA, 985 F.3d 914, at 988 (D.C. Cir. 2021).

In a 1983 law review article that was little noticed at the time, then–Circuit Judge Antonin Scalia argued that standing doctrine was a "critical and inseparable element" of separation of powers principles that should be more rigidly interpreted by the courts to reduce judicial intrusion into the operations of the other branches. Scalia, The Doctrine of Standing as an Essential Element of the Separation of Powers, 1983 Suffolk U. L. Rev. 881 (1983). What is remarkable about this article is not only how well it foreshadowed subsequent standing decisions Justice Scalia authored for the Supreme Court, but also its express hostility toward suits on behalf of environmental interests. Scalia argued that judges who enforce environmental laws are "likely (despite the best of intentions) to be enforcing the political prejudices of their own class." He explains that "[t]heir greatest success in such an enterprise—ensuring strict enforcement of the environmental laws . . . met with approval in the classrooms of Cambridge and New Haven, but not in the factories of Detroit and the mines of West Virginia." Quoting the language of Judge J. Skelly Wright in the *Calvert Cliffs* decision, he asks:

> Does what I have said mean that, so long as no minority interests are affected, "important legislative purposes, heralded in the halls of Congress, [can be] lost or misdirected in the vast hallways of the federal bureaucracy?" Of *course* it does—and a good thing, too. Where no peculiar harm to particular individuals or minorities is in question, lots of once-heralded programs ought to get lost or misdirected, in vast hallways or elsewhere. . . . The ability to lose or misdirect laws can be said to be one of the prime engines of social change, and the prohibition against such carelessness is (believe it or not) profoundly conservative. Sunday blue laws, for example, were widely unenforced long before they were widely repealed—and had the first not been possible the second might never have occurred. [Id. at 897 (emphasis in original).]

The first major standing decision authored by Justice Scalia addressed the question of how specific the allegations of a user of public lands have to be in order to establish standing. In Lujan v. National Wildlife Federation, 497 U.S. 871 (1990), the National Wildlife Federation (NWF) challenged decisions by the Bureau of Land Management (BLM) to lift protective restrictions on 180 million acres of public land. NWF alleged that BLM had violated both the Federal Land Policy and Management Act (FLPMA) and the National Environmental Policy Act (NEPA). After years of preliminary skirmishing that included entry of a preliminary injunction, the trial court ultimately dismissed the lawsuit on the ground that NWF lacked standing.

NWF had submitted affidavits from two of its members, one of whom stated that she used and enjoyed federal lands, "particularly those in the vicinity of South

Pass-Green Mountain, Wyoming," an area of some two million acres. Noting that only 4,500 acres of this land were affected by BLM's decisions, the district court determined the affidavits insufficiently specific to allege "use and enjoyment." After the D.C. Circuit reversed the trial court, the Supreme Court granted review.

In a majority opinion authored by Justice Scalia, the Court held that NWF had not made sufficient allegations to establish standing to challenge BLM's actions. He concluded that "averments which state only that one of respondent's members uses unspecified portions of an immense tract of territory, on some portions of which mining activity has occurred," were insufficiently specific. Justice Scalia also concluded that NWF could not challenge BLM's "land withdrawal review program" as a whole because it consisted of decisions about more than 1,200 discrete tracts of land that would not be ripe for judicial review until specific actions had been taken with respect to individual tracts.

The Supreme Court revisited environmental standing issues in the case below. The case involved a challenge to the Secretary of Interior's decision that the Endangered Species Act does not require other federal agencies to consult with the department when their activities may destroy critical habitat for endangered species outside the United States. Defenders of Wildlife sued the Secretary of Interior. The group tried to establish standing by offering affidavits from two of its members, as discussed in the following decision.

## Lujan v. Defenders of Wildlife

504 U.S. 555 (1992)

JUSTICE SCALIA delivered the opinion of the Court.

This case involves a challenge to a rule promulgated by the Secretary of the Interior interpreting §7 of the Endangered Species Act of 1973 (ESA) in such fashion as to render it applicable only to actions within the United States or on the high seas. [Section 7 of the ESA requires all federal agencies, in consultation with the Secretary of the Interior, to ensure that their actions do not jeopardize the continued existence of any endangered species.] The preliminary issue, and the only one we reach, is whether the respondents here, plaintiffs below, have standing to seek judicial review of the rule. . . .

### III . . .

Respondents had not made the requisite demonstration of (at least) injury and redressability.

### A

Respondents' claim to injury is that the lack of consultation with respect to certain funded activities abroad "increas[es] the rate of extinction of endangered and threatened species." Of course, the desire to use or observe an animal species, even for purely aesthetic purposes, is undeniably a cognizable interest for purpose of standing. "But the 'injury in fact' test requires more than an injury to a cognizable interest. It requires that the party seeking review be himself among the injured." To survive the Secretary's summary judgment motion, respondents had to submit affidavits or other evidence showing, through specific facts, not only that listed species were in fact being threatened by funded activities abroad, but also that one or more of respondents' members would thereby be "directly" affected apart from their "'special interest' in th[e] subject."

With respect to this aspect of the case, the Court of Appeals focused on the affidavits of two Defenders' members—Joyce Kelly and Amy Skilbred. Ms. Kelly stated that she traveled to Egypt in 1986 and "observed the traditional habitat of the endangered Nile crocodile there and intend[s] to do so again, and hope[s] to observe the crocodile directly," and that she "will suffer harm in fact as a result of [the] American . . . role . . . in overseeing the rehabilitation of the Aswan High Dam on the Nile . . . and [in] developing . . . Egypt's . . . Master Water Plan." Ms. Skilbred averred that she traveled to Sri Lanka in 1981 and "observed th[e] habitat" of "endangered species such as the Asian elephant and the leopard" at what is now the site of the Mahaweli Project funded by the Agency for International Development (AID), although she "was unable to see any of the endangered species"; "this development project," she continued, "will seriously reduce endangered, threatened, and endemic species habitat including areas that I visited . . . [, which] may severely shorten the future of these species"; that threat, she concluded, harmed her because she "intend[s] to return to Sri Lanka in the future and hope[s] to be more fortunate in spotting at least the endangered elephant and leopard." When Ms. Skilbred was asked at a subsequent deposition if and when she had any plans to return to Sri Lanka, she reiterated that "I intend to go back to Sri Lanka," but confessed that she had no current plans: "I don't know [when]. There is a civil war going on right now. I don't know. Not next year, I will say. In the future."

We shall assume for the sake of argument that these affidavits contain facts showing that certain agency-funded projects threaten listed species—though that is questionable. They plainly contain no facts, however, showing how damage to the species will produce "imminent" injury to Mss. Kelly and Skilbred. That the women "had visited" the areas of the projects before the projects commenced proves nothing. As we have said in a related context, "[p]ast exposure to illegal conduct does not in itself show a present case or controversy regarding injunctive relief . . . if unaccompanied by any continuing, present adverse effects." *Lyons*, 461 U.S., at 102. And the affiants' profession of an "inten[t]" to return to the places they had visited before—where they will presumably, this time, be deprived of the opportunity to observe animals of the endangered species—is simply not enough. Such "some day" intentions—without any description of concrete plans, or indeed even any specification of *when* the some day will be—do not support a finding of the "actual or imminent" injury that our cases require.[2]

---

2. . . . [T]here is certainly no reason in principle to demand evidence that third persons will take the action exposing the plaintiff to harm, while *presuming* that the plaintiff himself will do so. Our insistence upon these established requirements of standing does not mean that we would, as the dissent contends, "demand . . . detailed descriptions" of damages, such as a "nightly schedule of attempted activities" from plaintiffs alleging loss of consortium. That case and the others posited by the dissent all involve *actual* harm; the existence of standing is clear, though the precise extent of harm remains to be determined at trial. Where there is no actual harm, however, its imminence (though not its precise extent) must be established.

Besides relying upon the Kelly and Skilbred affidavits, respondents propose a series of novel standing theories. The first, inelegantly styled "ecosystem nexus," proposes that any person who uses *any part* of a "contiguous ecosystem" adversely affected by a funded activity has standing even if the activity is located a great distance away. This approach, as the Court of Appeals correctly observed, is inconsistent with our opinion in [*Lujan v.*] *National Wildlife Federation* which held that a plaintiff claiming injury from environmental damage must use the area affected by the challenged activity and not an area roughly "in the vicinity" of it. It makes no difference that the general-purpose section of the ESA states that the Act was intended in part "to provide a means whereby the ecosystems upon which endangered species and threatened species depend may be conserved," 16 U.S.C. §1531(b). To say that the Act protects ecosystems is not to say that the Act creates (if it were possible) rights of action in persons who have not been injured in fact, that is, persons who use portions of an ecosystem not perceptibly affected by the unlawful action in question.

Respondents' other theories are called, alas, the "animal nexus" approach, whereby anyone who has an interest in studying or seeing the endangered animals anywhere on the globe has standing; and the "vocational nexus" approach, under which anyone with a professional interest in such animals can sue. Under these theories, anyone who goes to see Asian elephants in the Bronx Zoo, and anyone who is a keeper of Asian elephants in the Bronx Zoo, has standing to sue because the Director of AID did not consult with the Secretary regarding the AID-funded project in Sri Lanka. This is beyond all reason. Standing is not "an ingenious academic exercise in the conceivable," United States v. Students Challenging Regulatory Agency Procedures (SCRAP), 412 U.S. 669, 688 (1973), but as we have said requires, at the summary judgment stage, a factual showing of perceptible harm. It is clear that the person who observes or works with a particular animal threatened by a federal decision is facing perceptible harm, since the very subject of his interest will no longer exist. It is even plausible — though it goes to the outermost limit of plausibility — to think that a person who observes or works with animals of a particular species in the very area of the world where that species is threatened by a federal decision is facing such harm, since some animals that might have been the subject of his interest will no longer exist. It goes beyond the limit, however, and into pure speculation and fantasy, to say that anyone who observes or works with an endangered species, anywhere in the world, is appreciably harmed by a single project affecting some portion of that species with which he has no more specific connection.[3] . . .

---

3. . . . It cannot be that a person with an interest in an animal automatically has standing to enjoin federal threats to that species of animal, anywhere in the world. Were that the case, the plaintiff in *Sierra Club*, for example, could have avoided the necessity of establishing anyone's use of Mineral King by merely identifying one of its members interested in an endangered species of flora or fauna at that location. Justice Blackmun's accusation that a special rule is being crafted for "environmental claims" is correct, but *he* is the craftsman. . . .

## IV

The Court of Appeals found that respondents had standing for an additional reason: because they had suffered a "procedural injury." The so-called "citizen-suit" provision of the ESA provides, in pertinent part, that "any person may commence a civil suit on his own behalf (A) to enjoin any person, including the United States and any other governmental instrumentality or agency . . . who is alleged to be in violation of any provision of this chapter." 16 U.S.C. §1540(g). The court held that, because §7(a)(2) requires interagency consultation, the citizen-suit provision creates a "procedural righ[t]" to consultation in all "persons"—so that *anyone* can file suit in federal court to challenge the Secretary's (or presumably any other official's) failure to follow the assertedly correct consultative procedure, notwithstanding their inability to allege any discrete injury flowing from that failure. To understand the remarkable nature of this holding one must be clear about what it does *not* rest upon: This is not a case where plaintiffs are seeking to enforce a procedural requirement the disregard of which could impair a separate concrete interest of theirs (e.g., the procedural requirement for a hearing prior to denial of their license application, or the procedural requirement for an environmental impact statement before a federal facility is constructed next door to them).[7] Nor is it simply a case where concrete injury has been suffered by many persons, as in mass fraud or mass tort situations. Nor, finally, is it the unusual case in which Congress has created a concrete private interest in the outcome of a suit against a private party for the government's benefit, by providing a cash bounty for the victorious plaintiff. Rather, the court held that the injury-in-fact requirement had been satisfied by congressional conferral upon *all* persons of an abstract, self-contained, noninstrumental "right" to have the Executive observe the procedures required by law. We reject this view.[8]

---

7. There is this much truth to the assertion that "procedural rights" are special: The person who has been accorded a procedural right to protect his concrete interests can assert that right without meeting all the normal standards for redressability and immediacy. Thus, under our case-law, one living adjacent to the site for proposed construction of a federally licensed dam has standing to challenge the licensing agency's failure to prepare an Environmental Impact Statement, even though he cannot establish with any certainty that the Statement will cause the license to be withheld or altered, and even though the dam will not be completed for many years. (That is why we do not rely, in the present case, upon the Government's argument that, *even if* the other agencies were obliged to consult with the Secretary, they might not have followed his advice.) What respondents' "procedural rights" argument seeks, however, is quite different from this: standing for persons who have no concrete interests affected—persons who live (and propose to live) at the other end of the country from the dam.

8. . . . We do *not* hold that an individual cannot enforce procedural rights; he assuredly can, so long as the procedures in question are designed to protect some threatened concrete interest of his that is the ultimate basis of his standing. . . . The dissent is unable to cite a single case in which we actually found standing solely on the basis of "procedural right" unconnected to the plaintiff's own concrete harm. Its suggestion that we did so in *Japan Whaling Association,* supra, and Robertson v. Methow Valley Citizens Council, 490 U.S. 332 (1989), is not supported by the facts. In the former case, we found that the environmental organizations had standing because the "whale watching and studying of their members would be adversely affected by continued whale harvesting," see 478 U.S., at 230-231, n.4; and in the latter we did not so much as mention standing, for the very good reason that the plaintiff was a citizen's council for the area in which the challenged construction was to occur, so that its members would obviously be concretely affected.

We have consistently held that a plaintiff raising only a generally available grievance about government—claiming only harm to his and every citizen's interest in proper application of the Constitution and laws, and seeking relief that no more directly and tangibly benefits him than it does the public at large—does not state an Article III case or controversy. . . .

JUSTICE KENNEDY, with whom JUSTICE SOUTER joins, concurring in part and concurring in the judgment.

Although I agree with the essential parts of the Court's analysis, I write separately to make several observations.

I agree with the Court's conclusion in Part III-A that, on the record before us, respondents have failed to demonstrate that they themselves are "among the injured." Sierra Club v. Morton, 405 U.S. 727, 735 (1972). . . .

While it may seem trivial to require that Mss. Kelly and Skilbred acquire airline tickets to the project sites or announce a date certain upon which they will return, this is not a case where it is reasonable to assume that the affiants will be using the sites on a regular basis, nor do the affiants claim to have visited the sites since the projects commenced. With respect to the Court's discussion of respondents' "ecosystem nexus," "animal nexus," and "vocational nexus" theories, I agree that on this record respondents' showing is insufficient to establish standing on any of these bases. I am not willing to foreclose the possibility, however, that in different circumstances a nexus theory similar to those proffered here might support a claim to standing. . . .

I also join Part IV of the Court's opinion with the following observations. As government programs and policies become more complex and far-reaching, we must be sensitive to the articulation of new rights of action that do not have clear analogs in our common-law tradition. Modern litigation has progressed far from the paradigm of Marbury suing Madison to get his commission, Marbury v. Madison, 1 Cranch 137 (1803), or Ogden seeking an injunction to halt Gibbons' steamboat operations. Gibbons v. Ogden, 9 Wheat. 1 (1824). In my view, Congress has the power to define injuries and articulate chains of causation that will give rise to a case or controversy where none existed before, and I do not read the Court's opinion to suggest a contrary view. In exercising this power, however, Congress must at the very least identify the injury it seeks to vindicate and relate the injury to the class of persons entitled to bring suit. The citizen-suit provision of the Endangered Species Act does not meet these minimal requirements, because while the statute purports to confer a right on "any person . . . to enjoin . . . the United States and any other governmental instrumentality or agency . . . who is alleged to be in violation of any provision of this chapter," it does not of its own force establish that there is an injury in "any person" by virtue of any "violation."

JUSTICE STEVENS, concurring in the judgment.

Because I am not persuaded that Congress intended the consultation requirement in §7(a)(2) of the Endangered Species Act of 1973 (ESA) to apply to activities in foreign countries, I concur in the judgment of reversal. I do not, however, agree with the Court's conclusion that respondents lack standing because the threatened injury to their interest in protecting the environment and studying endangered species is not "imminent." . . .

In my opinion a person who has visited the critical habitat of an endangered species, has a professional interest in preserving the species and its habitat, and intends to revisit them in the future has standing to challenge agency action that threatens their destruction. Congress has found that a wide variety of endangered species of fish, wildlife, and plants are of "aesthetic, ecological, educational, historical, recreational, and scientific value to the Nation and its people." 16 U.S.C. §1531(a)(3). Given that finding, we have no license to demean the importance of the interest that particular individuals may have in observing any species or its habitat, whether those individuals are motivated by aesthetic enjoyment, an interest in professional research, or an economic interest in preservation of the species. Indeed, this Court has often held that injuries to such interests are sufficient to confer standing, and the Court reiterates that holding today.

The Court nevertheless concludes that respondents have not suffered "injury in fact" because they have not shown that the harm to the endangered species will produce "imminent" injury to them. I disagree. An injury to an individual's interest in studying or enjoying a species and its natural habitat occurs when someone (whether it be the government or a private party) takes action that harms that species and habitat. In my judgment, therefore, the "imminence" of such an injury should be measured by the timing and likelihood of the threatened environmental harm, rather than—as the Court seems to suggest—by the time that might elapse between the present and the time when the individuals would visit the area if no such injury should occur. . . .

[W]e have denied standing to plaintiffs whose likelihood of suffering any concrete adverse effect from the challenged action was speculative. In this case, however, the likelihood that respondents will be injured by the destruction of the endangered species is not speculative. If respondents are genuinely interested in the preservation of the endangered species and intend to study or observe these animals in the future, their injury will occur as soon as the animals are destroyed. Thus the only potential source of "speculation" in this case is whether respondents' intent to study or observe the animals is genuine.[2] In my view, Joyce Kelly and Amy Skilbred have introduced sufficient evidence to negate petitioner's contention that their claims of injury are "speculative" or "conjectural." As Justice Blackmun explains, a reasonable finder of fact could conclude, from their past visits, their professional backgrounds, and their affidavits and deposition testimony, that Ms. Kelly and Ms. Skilbred will return to the project sites and, consequently, will be injured by the destruction of the endangered species and critical habitat. . . .

JUSTICE BLACKMUN, with whom JUSTICE O'CONNOR joins, dissenting.
. . . I think a reasonable finder of fact could conclude from the information in the affidavits and deposition testimony that either Kelly or Skilbred will soon

---

2. . . . [R]espondents would not be injured by the challenged projects if they had not visited the sites or studied the threatened species and habitat. But, as discussed above, respondents did visit the sites; moreover, they have expressed an intent to do so again. This intent to revisit the area is significant evidence tending to confirm the genuine character of respondents' interest, but I am not at all sure that an intent to revisit would be indispensable in every case. The interest that confers standing in a case of this kind is comparable, though by no means equivalent, to the interest in a relationship among family members that can be immediately harmed by the death of an absent member, regardless of when, if ever, a family reunion is planned to occur. Thus, if the facts of this case had shown repeated and regular visits by the respondents, proof of an intent to revisit might well be superfluous.

return to the project sites, thereby satisfying the "actual or imminent" injury standard. . . . Contrary to the Court's contention that Kelly's and Skilbred's past visits "prove[] nothing," the fact of their past visits could demonstrate to a reasonable factfinder that Kelly and Skilbred have the requisite resources and personal interest in the preservation of the species endangered by the Aswan and Mahaweli projects to make good on their intention to return again. . . . Similarly, Kelly's and Skilbred's professional backgrounds in wildlife preservation also make it likely—at least far more likely than for the average citizen—that they would choose to visit these areas of the world where species are vanishing.

By requiring a "description of concrete plans" or "specification of *when* the some day [for a return visit] will be," the Court, in my view, demands what is likely an empty formality. No substantial barriers prevent Kelly or Skilbred from simply purchasing plane tickets to return to the Aswan and Mahaweli projects. This case differs from other cases in which the imminence of harm turned largely on the affirmative actions of third parties beyond a plaintiff's control. To be sure, a plaintiff's unilateral control over his or her exposure to harm does not *necessarily* render the harm non-speculative. Nevertheless, it suggests that a finder of fact would be far more likely to conclude the harm is actual or imminent, especially if given an opportunity to hear testimony and determine credibility.

I fear the Court's demand for detailed descriptions of future conduct will do little to weed out those who are genuinely harmed from those who are not. More likely, it will resurrect a code-pleading formalism in federal court summary judgment practice, as federal courts, newly doubting their jurisdiction, will demand more and more particularized showings of future harm. Just to survive summary judgment, for example, a property owner claiming a decline in the value of his property from governmental action might have to specify the exact date he intends to sell his property and show that there is a market for the property, lest it be surmised he might not sell again. A nurse turned down for a job on grounds of her race had better be prepared to show on what date she was prepared to start work, that she had arranged daycare for her child, and that she would not have accepted work at another hospital instead. And a Federal Torts Claims Act plaintiff alleging loss of consortium should make sure to furnish this Court with a "description of concrete plans" for her nightly schedule of attempted activities.

The Court also concludes that injury is lacking, because respondents' allegations of "ecosystem nexus" failed to demonstrate sufficient proximity to the site of the environmental harm. To support that conclusion, the Court mis-characterizes our decision in Lujan v. National Wildlife Federation, 497 U.S. 871 (1990), as establishing a general rule that "a plaintiff claiming injury from environmental damage must use the area affected by the challenged activity." In *National Wildlife Federation,* the Court required specific geographical proximity because of the particular type of harm alleged in that case: harm to the plaintiff's visual enjoyment of nature from mining activities. One cannot suffer from the sight of a ruined landscape without being close enough to see the sites actually being mined. Many environmental injuries, however, cause harm distant from the area immediately affected by the challenged action. Environmental destruction may affect animals traveling over vast geographical ranges, see, e.g., Japan Whaling Assn. v. American Cetacean Soc., 478 U.S. 221 (1986) (harm to American whale watchers from Japanese whaling activities), or rivers running long geographical courses, see, e.g., Arkansas v. Oklahoma,

503 U.S. 91 (1992) (harm to Oklahoma residents from wastewater treatment plant 39 miles from border). It cannot seriously be contended that a litigant's failure to use the precise or exact site where animals are slaughtered or where toxic waste is dumped into a river means he or she cannot show injury.

The Court also rejects respondents' claim of vocational or professional injury. The Court says that it is "beyond all reason" that a zoo "keeper" of Asian elephants would have standing to contest his government's participation in the eradication of all the Asian elephants in another part of the world. I am unable to see how the distant location of the destruction necessarily (for purposes of ruling at summary judgment) mitigates the harm to the elephant keeper. If there is no more access to a future supply of the animal that sustains a keeper's livelihood, surely there is harm.

I have difficulty imagining this Court applying its rigid principles of geographic formalism anywhere outside the context of environmental claims. As I understand it, environmental plaintiffs are under no special constitutional standing disabilities. Like other plaintiffs, they need show only that the action they challenge has injured them, without necessarily showing they happened to be physically near the location of the alleged wrong. . . .

The Court concludes that any "procedural injury" suffered by respondents is insufficient to confer standing. It rejects the view that the "injury-in-fact requirement . . . [is] satisfied by congressional conferral upon *all* persons of an abstract, self-contained, noninstrumental 'right' to have the Executive observe the procedures required by law." Whatever the Court might mean with that very broad language, it cannot be saying that "procedural injuries" *as a class* are necessarily insufficient for purposes of Article III standing.

Most governmental conduct can be classified as "procedural." Many injuries caused by governmental conduct, therefore, are categorizable at some level of generality as "procedural" injuries. Yet, these injuries are not categorically beyond the pale of redress by the federal courts. When the Government, for example, "procedurally" issues a pollution permit, those affected by the permittee's pollutants are not without standing to sue. Only later cases will tell just what the Court means by its intimation that "procedural" injuries are not constitutionally cognizable injuries. In the meantime, I have the greatest of sympathy for the courts across the country that will struggle to understand the Court's standardless exposition of this concept today. . . .

It is to be hoped that over time the Court will acknowledge that some classes of procedural duties are so enmeshed with the prevention of a substantive, concrete harm that an individual plaintiff may be able to demonstrate a sufficient likelihood of injury just through the breach of that procedural duty. For example, in the context of the NEPA requirement of environmental-impact statements, this Court has acknowledged "it is now well settled that NEPA itself does not mandate particular results [and] simply prescribes the necessary process," but "*these procedures are almost certain to affect the agency's substantive decision.*" Robertson v. Methow Valley Citizens Council, 490 U.S., 332, 350 (1989) (emphasis added). This acknowledgement of an inextricable link between procedural and substantive harm does not reflect improper appellate factfinding. It reflects nothing more than the proper deference owed to the judgment of a coordinate branch—Congress—that certain procedures are directly tied to protection against a substantive harm. . . .

## NOTES AND QUESTIONS

1. In order for a plaintiff to qualify for standing, how close must the connection be in space and time between the action challenged in a lawsuit and the plaintiff's asserted injury? Does the closeness of the geographic nexus required for standing vary with the type of harm alleged? How do Justice Scalia and Justice Blackmun differ in their interpretation of *Lujan v. National Wildlife Federation?* Why does the majority reject the ecosystem, animal, and vocational nexus theories offered by *Defenders?* Note that two members of the majority, Justices Kennedy and Souter, indicate in their concurrence that they are more sympathetic to these theories than the majority and that it may be possible to establish standing using similar nexus claims in different circumstances. Eight years later, Justices Kennedy and Souter joined five other Justices in endorsing a more liberal view of standing in citizen enforcement suits in Friends of the Earth v. Laidlaw Environmental Services, Inc., 528 U.S. 167 (2000), a case discussed below.

2. Justice Kennedy states that "Congress has the power to define injuries and articulate chains of causation that will give rise to a case or controversy where none existed before. . . ." Does this mean that Congress can affect who has standing to sue by making legislative determinations of what constitutes injury and who is harmed by certain actions? Cass Sunstein argues that when Congress creates a right of action enabling people to sue over "destruction of environmental assets, it is really giving people a kind of property right in a certain state of affairs. Invasion of the property right is the relevant injury." Sunstein, What's Standing After *Lujan?* Of Citizen Suits, "Injuries," and Article III, 91 Mich. L. Rev. 163, 191 (1992). Can Congress create procedural rights whose injury can give rise to standing? Could it give anyone bringing a citizen enforcement action a financial stake in the outcome of the suit sufficient to confer standing simply by authorizing monetary rewards for successful plaintiffs?

3. What types of "procedural injury" does Justice Scalia recognize could give rise to standing? How does he attempt to distinguish the kind of procedural injury plaintiffs allege from the kind that he believes could give rise to standing? Why must Justice Scalia concede (in footnote 7 of his opinion) that in certain circumstances some "procedural rights" can be asserted "without meeting the normal standards for redressability and immediacy"?

4. The papers of the late Justice Harry Blackmun reveal that Justice Scalia's initial draft opinion sought to elevate the prudential bar on standing to redress generalized grievances to one of constitutional status. Scalia had argued that only particularized grievances were sufficiently concrete to meet the constitutional requirement of injury-in-fact. Justice Souter strenuously objected to this in a memo to Justice Scalia on May 28, 1992. "I doubt anyone would lack standing to sue on the basis of a concrete injury that everyone else has suffered; Congress might, for instance, grant everyone standing to challenge government action that would rip open the ozone layer and expose all Americans to unhealthy doses of radiation. Yet the repeated references to a particularity requirement, which might be taken as conceptually independent of a concreteness requirement, draw that conclusion into doubt." After Justice Kennedy endorsed Justice Souter's view, Justice Scalia removed the offending language from his draft opinion. Robert V. Percival, Environmental Law in the Supreme Court: Highlights from the Blackmun Papers, 35 Envtl. L. Rep. 10637, 10659 (2005).

5. In another portion of this opinion, Justice Scalia suggests that separation-of-powers principles limit the constitutional authority of Congress to open the courts to citizen enforcement suits. "To permit Congress to convert the undifferentiated public interest in executive officers' compliance with the law into an 'individual right' vindicable in the courts is to permit Congress to transfer from the President to the courts the Chief Executive's most important constitutional duty, to 'take Care that the Laws be faithfully executed.'" Does this call into question the constitutionality of the citizen suit provisions of the environmental laws? See Sunstein, supra at 165-166, 221. Professor Sunstein asks, "[I]f a court could set aside executive action at the behest of plaintiffs with a plane ticket, why does the Take Care Clause forbid it from doing so at the behest of plaintiffs without a ticket?" Id. at 213.

6. Justices Kennedy and Souter suggest that plaintiffs in *Defenders* could have established standing with relatively little extra effort by making specific travel plans. In his concurring opinion, Justice Kennedy concedes that "it may seem trivial to require that [the plaintiff's members] acquire airline tickets to the project site or announce a date certain upon which they will return." Because their votes were crucial to the majority in *Defenders*, does this statement suggest that the decision will have relatively little impact on environmental litigation, aside from encouraging environmentalists to get to know their travel agents better? What purpose is served by requiring plaintiffs to buy plane tickets? Is Justice Blackmun right that "the Court's demand for detailed descriptions of future conduct . . . will do little to weed out those who are genuinely harmed from those who are not"?

7. Could an animal welfare organization establish standing to challenge decisions affecting an endangered species of wildlife by having their members "adopt" particular members of the species by sending them a picture of the animal in return for a contribution? See Humane Society v. Babbitt, 46 F.3d 93 (D.C. Cir. 1995) (suggesting in dicta that even a deeply felt emotional attachment to Lota, an endangered Asian elephant, could not suffice to establish injury-in-fact).

### Standing in the Aftermath of *Defenders*

In the aftermath of *Defenders*, some courts rejected arguments that the decision (and *Lujan v. National Wildlife Federation*) wrought significant changes in standing doctrine by imposing greater burdens on plaintiffs to demonstrate injury-in-fact. In Seattle Audubon Society v. Espy, 998 F.2d 669 (9th Cir. 1993), the Ninth Circuit held that an Audubon Society chapter had standing to challenge the Forest Service's failure to prepare a management plan for critical habitat of the spotted owl. The court distinguished *Defenders* because the members of the local Audubon chapter lived near the affected forests and visited them regularly, 998 F.2d at 702-703, and it reaffirmed the validity of its pre-*Defenders* decision in Idaho Conservation League v. Mumma, 956 F.2d 1508 (9th Cir. 1992). In *Idaho Conservation League*, the court had upheld the standing of a conservation group to challenge a decision not to designate more than 100,000 acres of public land as wilderness. The court held that the group's allegation that it uses specific roadless areas which might be developed was sufficient to establish standing, noting that the plaintiffs in *National Wildlife Federation* had only alleged that they visited lands "in the vicinity of" those subject to the challenged action. 956 F.2d at 1515.

Other decisions distinguished *Defenders* because environmental plaintiffs alleged that they actually live near, visit, or study the animals they seek to protect. In Didrickson v. U.S. Dep't of Interior, 982 F.2d 1332 (9th Cir. 1992), a group called Friends of the Sea Otter (FSO) was found to have standing to challenge a regulation authorizing limited taking of sea otters because the group's Alaska members "have declared that they have observed, enjoyed and studied sea otters in specific areas in Alaska." In Idaho Farm Bureau v. Babbitt, 58 F.3d 1392 (9th Cir. 1995), two conservation groups were held to have standing to appeal a decision to delist the endangered Bruneau Hot Springs Snail because their members visit the area in which the snail is found and "maintain a factual and scientific understanding" of the snail and its habitat. Id. at 1399.

In a decision with echoes of the ripeness rationale invoked in Lujan v. National Wildlife Federation, the Supreme Court in 1998 held that a Sierra Club lawsuit challenging a land and resource management plan for Ohio's Wayne National Forest was not ripe for judicial review. The Court held that the Sierra Club had not suffered "practical harm" as a result of the Plan, which authorized logging on 126,000 acres of a national forest in Ohio, because site-specific environmental assessments still had to be performed before logging of any specific tracts could commence. However, the Court did note that "a person with standing who is impaired by a failure to comply with the NEPA procedure may complain of that failure at the time the failure takes place, for the claim can never get riper." Ohio Forestry Ass'n v. Sierra Club, 523 U.S. 726 (1998).

Some courts of appeals interpreted *Defenders* to make standing much harder for environmental plaintiffs to establish when they alleged a violation of law that had not caused clear environmental damage. See, e.g., Friends of the Earth v. Gaston Copper Recycling Corp., 179 F.3d 107 (4th Cir. 1999), reversed, 204 F.3d 149 (4th Cir. 2000) (en banc); Public Interest Research Group of New Jersey v. Magnesium Elektron, Inc., 123 F.3d 111 (3d Cir. 1997) (*MEI*). The plaintiffs in *MEI* had secured a judgment in the district court of $2.625 million in civil penalties plus attorneys' fees, after proving numerous discharges by MEI into the Wickecheoke Creek in excess of defendant's NPDES permit. At the penalty phase of the trial, defendant's limnologist had testified without rebuttal that MEI's discharges had caused no harm to the Creek's ecosystem. On appeal, the Third Circuit held that the plaintiff lacked standing. Plaintiffs' affidavits had stated that named individuals hiked, walked, studied nature, swam, and fished in the Delaware River and Raritan Canal, into which the Wickecheoke flows. They further stated that their enjoyment of these activities was lessened to the extent they knew of MEI's unlawful discharges, and one swore that she avoided eating fish caught in the Delaware River out of concern for contamination. By a 2-1 vote, the court majority, which included future Supreme Court Justice Samuel Alito, held that these allegations were insufficient to support standing. The majority wrote that "knowledge that MEI exceeded the effluent limits set by its NPDES permit does not, by itself demonstrate injury or threat of injury." In the court's view, plaintiffs constituted only "concerned bystanders," indistinguishable from environmentalists in Colorado or California who felt strongly about MEI's violations. Plaintiffs' reducing their recreational and other uses of the waterway "cannot support the injury prong of standing when a court also concludes that a polluter's violation of an effluent standard has not harmed the affected waterway and that it, in fact, poses no threat to that waterway."

In *Gaston Copper*, individuals also sued for NPDES violations, including the owner of a 67-acre lake in which he and his family fish and swim, located four miles downstream from defendant's plant. The lake owner swore that he fishes less frequently and lets his grandchildren swim in the lake only once each summer, out of concern over defendant's discharges. The panel majority, over a vigorous dissent by Judge J. Harvie Wilkinson, held this insufficient for standing because plaintiff had introduced no evidence that defendant's discharges had an "adverse effect" on the lake. Judge Wilkinson would have recognized that the plaintiff was within the acknowledged discharge area of the plant. "Whether we characterize the harm as the actual pollution to the waterway, [plaintiff's] reasonable fear or concern, or Gaston Copper's threat to the waterway is 'unimportant,'" he wrote.

*MEI* also addressed when plaintiffs could sue directly on the basis of reporting or monitoring violations. In a footnote, the court said that a plaintiff who had not suffered injury in fact as the court had defined it might sometimes still be able to sue a defendant solely for its failure to monitor and report if the plaintiff or some other individual had previously suffered injuries from some prior discharges. That history could give rise to reasonable decisions to forgo using the river when a defendant subsequently fails to report its discharges, which "might" constitute the type of injury necessary to support standing. Plaintiffs' bare desire for accurate reporting information from defendant, however, even when accompanied by decreased use of the river, was insufficient in the case itself, because plaintiff had failed to show the discharges had had any effect on the river, and the uncontradicted evidence was that defendant's discharges had not "caused the type of injury feared by [plaintiffs]."

One federal statute, the Emergency Planning and Community Right-to-Know Act (EPCRA), is unique in that the only duties it imposes on regulated parties are duties to report toxic emissions. One issue that courts have faced in EPCRA litigation is whether citizens can sue under its citizen suit provision for failures to report that companies cure after they receive the required notice from the citizen plaintiffs of an intent to sue. In part this is a question of whether specific wording of the EPCRA citizen suit provision is materially distinguishable from the citizen suit provision in the Clean Water Act, under which the Supreme Court has ruled suit cannot be brought for wholly past violations.

In Steel Company v. Citizens for a Better Environment, 523 U.S. 83 (1998), the Court held that plaintiffs lacked standing to sue for reporting violations that the defendant had cured between its receipt of the plaintiffs' notice of intention to sue and the date that the plaintiffs filed their case in federal court. The Court did not reach the statutory issue. The *Steel Company* plaintiffs had alleged an interest in having accurate discharge information so that they could react appropriately to it in various ways, such as working on emergency preparedness plans or working to achieve further reductions in neighborhood discharges. The Court expressly did not reach the question of whether the defendant's "failure to provide EPCRA information in a timely fashion and the lingering effects of that failure" gives rise to a concrete injury satisfying injury in fact, because it held in any event that the complaint failed the redressability prong of the standing requirement.

The plaintiffs had requested a number of remedies, including "any further relief as the court deems appropriate," but the Court concluded that none of them could redress the plaintiffs injury of failing to have access to timely EPCRA reports that had now been filed. Declaratory relief was "worthless to respondent [and] . . .

to all the world," in a case in which the defendant had conceded its wrongdoing. Civil penalties failed because they are payable to the United States Treasury, and consequently served to remediate not the plaintiffs' particular injury, but rather the "undifferentiated public interest" in faithful execution of EPCRA. In response to Justice Stevens's dissenting opinion stating that "it is enough that respondent will be gratified by seeing petitioner punished for its infractions and that the punishment will deter the risk of future harm," Justice Scalia wrote that "such a principle would make the redressability requirement vanish." The request for costs of investigating and prosecuting the case was insufficient because the plaintiff could not "achieve standing to litigate a substantive issue by bringing suit for the cost of bringing suit."

The last specific remedies sought were authority to inspect defendant's plant and records, and an order directing defendant to provide plaintiff copies of compliance reports filed with EPA in the future. Such forward-looking relief, the Court wrote, "cannot conceivably remedy any past wrong but is aimed at deterring petitioner from violating EPCRA in the future. The latter objective can of course be 'remedial' for Article III purposes, when threatened injury is one of the gravamens of the complaint. If respondent had alleged a continuing violation or the imminence of a future violation, the injunctive relief requested would remedy that alleged harm. But there is no such allegation here—and on the facts of the case, there seems to be no basis for it."

Shortly after *Steel Company*, the Supreme Court decided Federal Election Commission v. Akins, 524 U.S. 11 (1998), in which it upheld the standing of a group of voters to sue a federal agency for failing to require a lobbying group to register and disclose certain information. The Court held that the plaintiffs' inability to obtain information required to be disclosed by statute constituted sufficient injury-in-fact to give them standing. The Court distinguished this case from its traditional prudential ban on taxpayer standing by noting that a federal statute specifically gave the plaintiffs a right to receive the information they sought.

The next major standing controversy decided by the Court arose as a result of a decision by the U.S. Court of Appeals for the Fourth Circuit in Friends of the Earth v. Laidlaw Environmental Services, 149 F.3d 303 (4th Cir. 1998). Citing the doctrine that a plaintiff must satisfy all the elements of standing throughout the course of litigation, the Fourth Circuit dismissed a suit against a company whose wastewater treatment plant in Roebuck, South Carolina had nearly 900 violations of its NPDES discharge permit. Occasional violations continued after the complaint was filed in 1992, but the last recorded violation occurred two years prior to the entry of the district court judgment in 1997. Interpreting *Steel Company* to say that a plaintiff lacks standing to challenge wholly past violations when the only available remedies fail that opinion's redressability standard, the Fourth Circuit reversed an award by the district court of $405,880 in civil penalties plus attorneys' fees. On writ of certiorari, the Supreme Court reversed in the following decision.

## Friends of the Earth v. Laidlaw Environmental Services

528 U.S. 167 (2000)

JUSTICE GINSBURG delivered the opinion of the Court.

This case presents an important question concerning the operation of the citizen-suit provisions of the Clean Water Act. Congress authorized the federal district courts to entertain Clean Water Act suits initiated by "a person or persons having an interest which is or may be adversely affected." To impel future compliance with the Act, a district court may prescribe injunctive relief in such a suit; additionally or alternatively, the court may impose civil penalties payable to the United States Treasury. In the Clean Water Act citizen suit now before us, the District Court determined that injunctive relief was inappropriate because the defendant, after the institution of the litigation, achieved substantial compliance with the terms of its discharge permit. The court did, however, assess a civil penalty of $405,800. The "total deterrent effect" of the penalty would be adequate to forestall future violations, the court reasoned, taking into account that the defendant "will be required to reimburse plaintiffs for a significant amount of legal fees and has, itself, incurred significant legal expenses."

The Court of Appeals vacated the District Court's order. The case became moot, the appellate court declared, once the defendant fully complied with the terms of its permit and the plaintiff failed to appeal the denial of equitable relief. . . .

We reverse the judgment of the Court of Appeals. The appellate court erred in concluding that a citizen suitor's claim for civil penalties must be dismissed as moot when the defendant, albeit after commencement of the litigation, has come into compliance. In directing dismissal of the suit on grounds of mootness, the Court of Appeals incorrectly conflated our case law on initial standing to bring suit, see, e.g., Steel Co. v. Citizens for Better Environment, with our case law on post-commencement mootness, see, e.g., City of Mesquite v. Aladdin's Castle, Inc., 455 U.S. 283 (1982). A defendant's voluntary cessation of allegedly unlawful conduct ordinarily does not suffice to moot a case. The Court of Appeals also misperceived the remedial potential of civil penalties. Such penalties may serve, as an alternative to an injunction, to deter future violations and thereby redress the injuries that prompted a citizen suitor to commence litigation.

**I . . .**

**B**

[Between 1987 and 1995, Laidlaw violated its NPDES permit nearly 500 times by discharging greater than permitted quantities of mercury into the North Tyger River. After FOE filed suit in June 12, 1992, more exceedances occurred, the last reported one taking place on January, 1995, "long after the complaint was filed but about two years before judgment was rendered."]

On January 22, 1997, the District Court issued its judgment. It found that Laidlaw had gained a total economic benefit of $1,092,581 as a result of its extended period of noncompliance with the mercury discharge limit in its permit. The court concluded, however, that a civil penalty of $405,800 was adequate in light of the guiding factors listed in 33 U.S.C. §1319(d). In particular, the District Court stated that the lesser penalty was appropriate taking into account the judgment's "total deterrent effect." In reaching this determination, the court "considered that Laidlaw will be required to reimburse plaintiffs for a significant amount of legal fees." The court declined to grant FOE's request for injunctive relief, stating that an injunction was inappropriate because "Laidlaw has been in substantial compliance with all parameters in its NPDES permit since at least August 1992." FOE appealed the District Court's civil penalty judgment, arguing that the penalty was inadequate, but did not appeal the denial of declaratory or injunctive relief. Laidlaw cross-appealed, arguing, among other things, that FOE lacked standing to bring the suit. . . . The United States . . . participate[d] as amicus curiae in support of FOE.

[The Court of Appeals reversed.]

We granted certiorari, 525 U.S. 1176 (1999), to resolve the inconsistency between the Fourth Circuit's decision in this case and the decisions of several other Courts of Appeals, which have held that a defendant's compliance with its permit after the commencement of litigation does not moot claims for civil penalties under the Act.

## II

### A

. . . Laidlaw contends first that FOE lacked standing from the outset even to seek injunctive relief, because the plaintiff organizations failed to show that any of their members had sustained or faced the threat of any "injury in fact" from Laidlaw's activities. In support of this contention Laidlaw points to the District Court's finding, made in the course of setting the penalty amount, that there had been "no demonstrated proof of harm to the environment" from Laidlaw's mercury discharge violations. 956 F. Supp., at 602; see ibid. ("[T]he NPDES permit violations at issue in this citizen suit did not result in any health risk or environmental harm.").

The relevant showing for purposes of Article III standing, however, is not injury to the environment but injury to the plaintiff. To insist upon the former rather than the latter as part of the standing inquiry . . . is to raise the standing hurdle higher than the necessary showing for success on the merits in an action alleging noncompliance with an NPDES permit. Focusing properly on injury to the plaintiff, the District Court found that FOE had demonstrated sufficient injury to establish standing. For example, FOE member Kenneth Lee Curtis averred in affidavits that he lived a half-mile from Laidlaw's facility; that he occasionally drove over the North Tyger River, and that it looked and smelled polluted; and that he would like to fish, camp, swim, and picnic in and near the river between 3 and 15 miles downstream from the facility, as he did when he was a teenager, but would not do so because he was concerned that the water was polluted by Laidlaw's discharges. Curtis reaffirmed these statements in extensive deposition testimony. For example, he testified that he would like to fish in the river at a specific spot he used as a boy, but that he would not do so now because of his concerns about Laidlaw's discharges.

Other members presented evidence to similar effect. . . .

These sworn statements, as the District Court determined, adequately documented injury in fact. We have held that environmental plaintiffs adequately allege injury in fact when they aver that they use the affected area and are persons "for whom the aesthetic and recreational values of the area will be lessened" by the challenged activity. Sierra Club v. Morton. See also *Defenders of Wildlife* ("Of course, the desire to use or observe an animal species, even for purely aesthetic purposes, is undeniably a cognizable interest for purposes of standing."). . . .

In contrast [to *Lujan v. National Wildlife Federation*] the affidavits and testimony presented by FOE in this case assert that Laidlaw's discharges, and the affiant members' reasonable concerns about the effects of those discharges, directly affected those affiants' recreational, aesthetic, and economic interests. These submissions present dispositively more than the mere "general averments" and "conclusory allegations" found inadequate in *National Wildlife Federation*. Nor can the affiants' conditional statements—that they would use the nearby North Tyger River for recreation if Laidlaw were not discharging pollutants into it—be equated with the speculative "'some day' intentions" to visit endangered species halfway around the world that we held insufficient to show injury in fact in *Defenders of Wildlife*.

*Los Angeles v. Lyons* . . . does not weigh against standing in this case. In *Lyons*, we held that a plaintiff lacked standing to seek an injunction against the enforcement of a police chokehold policy because he could not credibly allege that he faced a realistic threat from the policy. In the footnote from *Lyons* cited by the dissent, we noted that "[t]he reasonableness of Lyons' fear is dependent upon the likelihood of a recurrence of the allegedly unlawful conduct," and that his "subjective apprehensions" that such a recurrence would even take place were not enough to support standing. Here, in contrast, it is undisputed that Laidlaw's unlawful conduct—discharging pollutants in excess of permit limits—was occurring at the time the complaint was filed. Under *Lyons*, then, the only "subjective" issue here is "[t]he reasonableness of [the] fear" that led the affiants to respond to the concededly ongoing conduct by refraining from use of the North Tyger River and surrounding areas. Unlike the dissent, we see nothing "improbable" about the proposition that a company's continuous and pervasive illegal discharges of pollutants into a river would cause nearby residents to curtail their recreational use of that waterway and would subject them to other economic and aesthetic harms. The proposition is entirely reasonable, the District Court found it was true in this case, and that is enough for injury in fact.

Laidlaw argues next that even if FOE has standing to seek injunctive relief, it lacked standing to seek civil penalties. Here the asserted defect is not injury but redressability. Civil penalties offer no redress to private plaintiffs, Laidlaw argues, because they are paid to the government, and therefore a citizen plaintiff can never have standing to seek them. . . .

[I]t is wrong to maintain that citizen plaintiffs facing ongoing violations never have standing to seek civil penalties.

We have recognized on numerous occasions that "all civil penalties have some deterrent effect." More specifically, Congress has found that civil penalties in Clean Water Act cases do more than promote immediate compliance by limiting the defendant's economic incentive to delay its attainment of permit limits; they also deter future violations. This congressional determination warrants judicial attention and respect. "The legislative history of the Act reveals that Congress wanted the district court to consider the need for retribution and deterrence, in addition to restitution, when it imposed civil penalties. . . . [The district court may] seek to deter future violations by basing the penalty on its economic impact." Tull v. United States, 481 U.S. 412 (1987).

It can scarcely be doubted that, for a plaintiff who is injured or faces the threat of future injury due to illegal conduct ongoing at the time of the suit, a sanction that effectively abates that conduct and prevents its recurrence provides a form of redress. Civil penalties can fit that description. To the extent that they encourage defendants to discontinue current violations and deter them from committing future ones, they afford redress to citizen plaintiffs who are injured or threatened with injury as a consequence of ongoing unlawful conduct. . . .

We recognize that there may be a point at which the deterrent effect of a claim for civil penalties becomes so insubstantial or so remote that it cannot support citizen standing. . . .

In this case we need not explore the outer limits of the principle that civil penalties provide sufficient deterrence to support redressability. Here, the civil penalties sought by FOE carried with them a deterrent effect that made it likely, as opposed to merely speculative, that the penalties would redress FOE's injuries by abating current violations and preventing future ones—as the District Court reasonably found when it assessed a penalty of $405,800.

Laidlaw contends that the reasoning of our decision in *Steel Co.* directs the conclusion that citizen plaintiffs have no standing to seek civil penalties under the Act. We disagree. *Steel Co.* established that citizen suitors lack standing to seek civil penalties for violations that have been abated by the time of the suit. We specifically noted in that case that there was no allegation in the complaint of any continuing or imminent violation, and that no basis for such an allegation appeared to exist. [S]ee also *Gwaltney* ("the harm sought to be addressed by the citizen suit lies in the present or the future, not in the past"). In short, *Steel Co.* held that private plaintiffs, unlike the Federal Government, may not sue to assess penalties for wholly past violations, but our decision in that case did not reach the issue of standing to seek penalties for violations that are ongoing at the time of the complaint and that could continue into the future if undeterred.

## B

Satisfied that FOE had standing under Article III to bring this action, we turn to the question of mootness.

The only conceivable basis for a finding of mootness in this case is Laidlaw's voluntary conduct—either its achievement by August 1992 of substantial compliance with its NPDES permit or its more recent shutdown of the Roebuck facility. It is well settled that "a defendant's voluntary cessation of a challenged practice does not deprive a federal court of its power to determine the legality of the practice." City of Mesquite, 455 U.S., at 289. "[I]f it did, the courts would be compelled to leave [t]he defendant . . . free to return to his old ways." In accordance with this principle, the standard we have announced for determining whether a case has been mooted by the defendant's voluntary conduct is stringent: "A case might become moot if subsequent events made it absolutely clear that the allegedly wrongful behavior could not reasonably be expected to recur." The "heavy burden of persua[ding]" the court that the challenged conduct cannot reasonably be expected to start up again lies with the party asserting mootness.

The Court of Appeals justified its mootness disposition by reference to *Steel Co.*, which held that citizen plaintiffs lack standing to seek civil penalties for wholly past violations. In relying on *Steel Co.*, the Court of Appeals confused mootness with standing. The confusion is understandable, given this Court's repeated statements that the doctrine of mootness can be described as "the doctrine of standing set in a time frame: The requisite personal interest that must exist at the commencement of the litigation (standing) must continue throughout its existence (mootness)." Arizonans for Official English, 520 U.S., at 68.

Careful reflection on the long-recognized exceptions to mootness, however, reveals that the description of mootness as "standing set in a time frame" is not comprehensive. As just noted, a defendant claiming that its voluntary compliance moots a case bears the formidable burden of showing that it is absolutely clear the allegedly wrongful behavior could not reasonably be expected to recur. By contrast, in a lawsuit brought to force compliance, it is the plaintiff's burden to establish standing by demonstrating that, if unchecked by the litigation, the defendant's allegedly wrongful behavior will likely occur or continue, and that the "threatened injury [is] certainly impending." Thus, in *Lyons,* as already noted, we held that a plaintiff lacked initial standing to seek an injunction against the enforcement of a police chokehold policy because he could not credibly allege that he faced a realistic threat arising from the policy. Elsewhere in the opinion, however, we noted that a citywide moratorium on police chokeholds—an action that surely diminished the already slim likelihood that any particular individual would be choked by police—would not have mooted an otherwise valid claim for injunctive relief, because the moratorium by its terms was not permanent. The plain lesson of these cases is that there are circumstances in which the prospect that a defendant will engage in (or resume) harmful conduct may be too speculative to support standing, but not too speculative to overcome mootness. . . .

Standing doctrine functions to ensure, among other things, that the scarce resources of the federal courts are devoted to those disputes in which the parties have a concrete stake. In contrast, by the time mootness is an issue, the case has been brought and litigated, often (as here) for years. To abandon the case at an advanced stage may prove more wasteful than frugal. This argument from sunk costs does not license courts to retain jurisdiction over cases in which one or both parties have settled or a plaintiff pursuing a nonsurviving claim has died. . . . But the argument surely highlights an important difference between the two doctrines. . . .

For the reasons stated, the judgment of the United States Court of Appeals for the Fourth Circuit is reversed, and the case is remanded for further proceedings consistent with this opinion.

## NOTES AND QUESTIONS

1. Laidlaw closed its facility after the Fourth Circuit rendered its decisions, and argued that this fact had rendered the case moot in any event. In another portion of the opinion, the Court noted that either this fact or "Laidlaw's earlier achievement of substantial compliance with its permit requirements, might moot the case, but—we once more reiterate—only if one or the other of these events made it absolutely clear that Laidlaw's permit violations could not reasonably be expected to recur." Because the effects of these events were disputed facts, the case was remanded for further consideration of them. In a concurring opinion Justice Stevens argued that post-judgment conduct could never invalidate an award of civil penalties.

2. Suppose Laidlaw had brought itself into substantial compliance prior to the filing of the suit. Would *Steel Company* then apply, with the result that FOE would have lacked standing?

3. What effect will the *Steel Company* and *Laidlaw* decisions have on incentives to comply? Will *Steel Company* give companies greater incentives not to comply until they receive 60-day notice letters? Will *Laidlaw* make the delivery of the 60-day notice letters a more powerful tool for stimulating compliance since putative defendants now know they can defeat citizen suits only by coming into compliance before lawsuits are filed? On the other hand, does the result in *Laidlaw* reduce the incentives for defendants to cure discharge situations once the suit has been filed, because they know that doing so will not provide them with a basis for having the case dismissed? Would amendments to environmental statutes such as EPCRA and CWA that allowed citizens to keep some portion of any monetary award levied, as a bounty for their vindicating the public interest, obviate the obstacle to standing created by *Steel Company*?

4. Justice Scalia, joined by Justice Thomas, decried the Court's decision as having "grave implications for democratic governance." Justice Kennedy concurred separately to note that the question whether a delegation of executive power to private parties to exact public fines is consistent with Article II had not been raised. In another standing case, the Supreme Court ruled that private plaintiffs had standing to seek *qui tam* recoveries on behalf of the federal government under the False Claims Act from defendants alleged to have defrauded the government. Vermont Agency of Natural Resources v. United States ex rel. Stevens, 529 U.S. 765 (2000). Writing for the Court, Justice Scalia concluded that injury in fact to the United States conferred standing on private relators to bring *qui tam* actions under the False Claims Act because relators stood in the shoes of the federal government. However, the Court also held that Congress had not intended to subject states to liability under the False Claims Act because states did not clearly fit within the definition of "person" for purposes of the Act. In a footnote, Justice Scalia sought to keep alive the question whether citizen suits violated principles of separation of powers by noting that the Court expressed "no view on the question whether *qui tam* suits violate Article II" on the ground that it had not been raised by the petitioner.

5. As a result of *Laidlaw*, the Fourth Circuit sitting en banc unanimously reversed the *Gaston Copper* panel decision, discussed above, that had dismissed a citizen suit for lack of standing. Friends of the Earth, Inc. v. Gaston Copper Recycling Corp., 204 F.3d 149 (4th Cir. 2000) (en banc). *Laidlaw* has made it easier for citizen groups to establish standing in environmental enforcement suits, although it has not guaranteed that their standing will be upheld. See, e.g., Central and South West Services v. EPA, 220 F.3d 683 (5th Cir. 2000) (dismissing Sierra Club's challenge to EPA regulations allowing disposal of PCB bulk product waste for failure of individual members who filed affidavits to demonstrate through objective evidence that PCBs from local landfill could leach into their town's water supply as they feared); Friends for Ferrell Parkway, LLC v. Stasko, 282 F.3d 315 (4th Cir. 2002); Puerto Rico Campers' Ass'n v. Puerto Rico Aqueduct & Sewer Authority, 219 F. Supp. 2d 201 (D.P.R. 2002) (association had standing to sue sewer authority for violations by one wastewater treatment plant, but not another because the affidavits by members reflect concern over the possible effects of contamination of beaches but not of the river into which the latter plant discharges, thus failing to meet the "mild burden" to establish standing under *Laidlaw*); American Bottom Conservancy v. U.S. Army Corps of Engineers, 650 F.3d 652, 656 (7th Cir. 2011) (claim that the destruction

of bird and butterfly habitat would diminish enjoyment of a state park is sufficient for standing because "it is enough to confer standing that [the Conservancy's members'] pleasure is diminished even if not to the point that they abandon the site").

6. Environmental groups now are bringing more complex citizen suits, some under the Clean Air Act (CAA). In one such suit a federal district court in Texas determined that ExxonMobil had 16,386 days of CAA permit violations for which it imposed a $19.95 million civil penalty. On appeal ExxonMobil argued, and the Fifth Circuit agreed, that the case should be remanded because the plaintiff citizens' group had to prove each element of standing for each separate violation. Environment Texas Citizen Lobby, Inc. v. ExxonMobil Corp., 968 F.3d 357 (5th Cir. 2020). To distinguish Laidlaw, the panel stated that "the Laidlaw plaintiffs . . . asserted injuries to their aesthetic and recreational interests because the defendant's discharges polluted a river that they otherwise would have enjoyed. Plaintiffs, by contrast, assert a variety of aesthetic and health-related injuries, allegedly traceable to 24 different pollutants emitted in a variety of ways (flaring, leaks, workplace accidents, etc.). The impact of those different violations varied greatly." The court found that the group clearly met the injury prong of standing because "throughout the claims period, at least one of Plaintiffs' members regularly saw flares, smoke, and haze coming from the complex; smelled chemical odors; suffered from allergy-like or respiratory problems; feared for their health; refrained from outdoor activities; or moved away." 968 F.3d at 368. The court found that causation/traceability had been satisfied because "Plaintiffs' members' observational injuries—seeing flares, smoke, and haze—were obviously traceable to Exxon because those visual blights originated from the Baytown complex. Chemical odors could likewise be traced to Exxon because they got stronger when Plaintiffs' members approached or happened to be downwind from the complex." But it required separate geographic nexus inquiries: "For violations that could not contribute to flaring, smoke, or haze, the district court should first consider whether the pollutant emitted could cause or contribute either to (a) chemical odors or (b) allergy-like or respiratory symptoms. If so, the district court will conduct the geographic nexus inquiry described above, finding it satisfied if the emission (i) violated a nonzero emissions standard, (ii) had to be reported under Texas regulations, or (iii) is otherwise proven to be of sufficient magnitude to reach Baytown neighborhoods outside the Exxon complex in quantities sufficient to cause chemical odors, allergy-like symptoms, or respiratory symptoms."

7. Following Washington Environmental Council v. Bellon, 732 F.3d 1131 (9th Cir. 2013), some courts have dismissed for lack of standing plaintiffs challenging emissions of greenhouse gases if the emissions are too small to make a "meaningful contribution" to the global problem. See, e.g., Amigo Bravos v. U.S. Bureau of Land Management, 816 F.Supp. 2d 1118, 1136 (D.N.M. 2011). But for air pollutants with localized impacts, even emissions that constitute a "small fraction" of local emissions can give rise to standing because "a causation standard that precludes citizens from suing for CAA violations directly contributing pollution to the air they breathe would seriously undermine the CAA's citizen enforcement provision." Utah Physicians for a Healthy Environment v. Diesel Power Gear, LLC, 374 F.Supp. 3d 1124 (D.Utah 2019).

8. Additional background information on the *Laidlaw* litigation can be found in William W. Buzbee, The Story of *Laidlaw*: Standing and Citizen Enforcement, in

Environmental Law Stories 201 (Lazarus & Houck eds., 2005). Professor Buzbee notes that despite the lengthy litigation and the Court's decision in their favor, the plaintiffs' law firm did not receive an attorneys' fee award due to the bankruptcy of the defendant.

9. As a tribute to the Court's *Laidlaw* decision, Professor Craig N. Johnston of Lewis & Clark has composed lyrics for a song to be sung to the tune of Eric Clapton's "Layla," the passionate anthem Clapton wrote about the woman who later became his wife (the song first appeared on the album "Layla and Other Assorted Love Songs" released December 1970 by Clapton's group Derek and the Dominos). As you read the lyrics below, reprinted by permission of Professor Johnston, recall that *Laidlaw* was decided by a 7-2 vote with only Justices Antonin Scalia and Clarence Thomas (C.T. in the lyrics) dissenting.

### *Laidlaw*

What do we do when we get sued now

if the Court's not on our side?

If we can't rely on standing constraints

do they expect us to comply?

Laidlaw!

What are these non-use injuries?

Laidlaw!

Based on subjectivity

Laidlaw!

Antonin, please ease our worried minds.

*Defenders* gave us consolation

and *Steel Co.* made us paint the town.

But like fools, we put our faith in you.

You and C.T. got voted down.

Laidlaw!

What about these penalties?

Laidlaw!

Where's the redressability?

Laidlaw!

Antonin, please ease our worried minds.

Let's make the best of the situation.

Article II's our last resort.

Please don't say we'll never find a way

to keep these plaintiffs out of court.

Laidlaw!

What was it Sandra didn't see?

Laidlaw!

Where were the Chief and Kennedy?

Laidlaw!

Antonin, please ease our worried minds.

Laidlaw!

We miss the old majority.

Laidlaw!

How can we pay these penalties?

Laidlaw!

Antonin, please ease our worried minds.

Lyrics by Professor Craig N. Johnston.

10. Even though Justice Scalia's narrow view of environmental standing was decisively rejected in *Laidlaw* and narrowly rejected in *Massachusetts v. EPA*, Justice Scalia was able to resurrect it in the case below after the Forest Service withdrew the project on which the environmental plaintiffs had premised their challenge to national forest management regulations.

## Summers v. Earth Island Institute

555 U.S. 488 (2009)

JUSTICE SCALIA delivered the opinion of the Court.

Respondents are a group of organizations dedicated to protecting the environment. (We will refer to them collectively as "Earth Island.") They seek to prevent the United States Forest Service from enforcing regulations that exempt small fire-rehabilitation and timber-salvage projects from the notice, comment, and appeal process used by the Forest Service for more significant land management decisions. We must determine whether respondents have standing to challenge the regulations in the absence of a live dispute over a concrete application of those regulations.

### I

In 1992, Congress enacted the Forest Service Decisionmaking and Appeals Reform Act. Among other things, this required the Forest Service to establish a notice, comment, and appeal process for "proposed actions of the Forest Service concerning projects and activities implementing land and resource management plans developed under the Forest and Rangeland Renewable Resources Planning Act of 1974."

The Forest Service's regulations implementing the Act provided that certain of its procedures would not be applied to projects that the Service considered categorically excluded from the requirement to file an environmental impact statement (EIS) or environmental assessment (EA). Later amendments to the Forest Service's manual of implementing procedures, adopted by rule after notice and comment, provided that fire-rehabilitation activities on areas of less than 4,200 acres, and salvage-timber sales of 250 acres or less, did not cause a significant environmental impact and thus would be categorically exempt from the requirement to file an EIS or EA. This had the effect of excluding these projects from the notice, comment, and appeal process.

In the summer of 2002, fire burned a significant area of the Sequoia National Forest. In September 2003, the Service issued a decision memo approving the Burnt Ridge Project, a salvage sale of timber on 238 acres damaged by that fire. Pursuant to its categorical exclusion of salvage sales of less than 250 acres, the Forest Service did not provide notice in a form consistent with the Appeals Reform Act, did not provide a period of public comment, and did not make an appeal process available.

In December 2003, respondents filed a complaint in the Eastern District of California, challenging the failure of the Forest Service to apply to the Burnt Ridge Project §215.4(a) of its regulations implementing the Appeals Reform Act (requiring prior notice and comment), and §215.12(f) of the regulations (setting forth an appeal procedure). The complaint also challenged six other Forest Service regulations implementing the Act that were not applied to the Burnt Ridge Project. They are irrelevant to this appeal.

The District Court granted a preliminary injunction against the Burnt Ridge salvage-timber sale. Soon thereafter, the parties settled their dispute over the Burnt Ridge Project and the District Court concluded that "the Burnt Ridge timber sale is not at issue in this case." Earth Island Inst. v. Pengilly, 376 F. Supp. 2d 994, 999 (E.D. Cal. 2005). The Government argued that, with the Burnt Ridge dispute settled, and with no other project before the court in which respondents were threatened with injury in fact, respondents lacked standing to challenge the regulations; and that absent a concrete dispute over a particular project a challenge to the regulations would not be ripe. The District Court proceeded, however, to adjudicate the merits of Earth Island's challenges. It invalidated five of the regulations (including §§215.4(a) and 215.12(f)), and entered a nationwide injunction against their application. . . .

The Government sought review of the question whether Earth Island could challenge the regulations at issue in the Burnt Ridge Project, and if so whether a nationwide injunction was appropriate relief.

## II

. . . The doctrine of standing . . . requires federal courts to satisfy themselves that "the plaintiff has 'alleged such a personal stake in the outcome of the controversy' as to warrant *his* invocation of federal-court jurisdiction." He bears the burden of showing that he has standing for each type of relief sought. To seek injunctive relief, a plaintiff must show that he is under threat of suffering "injury in fact" that is concrete and particularized; the threat must be actual and imminent, not conjectural or hypothetical; it must be fairly traceable to the challenged action of the defendant; and it must be likely that a favorable judicial decision will prevent or redress the injury. Friends of Earth, Inc. v. Laidlaw Environmental Services (TOC), Inc., 528 U.S. 167, 180-181 (2000). . . .

The regulations under challenge here neither require nor forbid any action on the part of respondents. The standards and procedures that they prescribe for Forest Service appeals govern only the conduct of Forest Service officials engaged in project planning. "[W]hen the plaintiff is not himself the object of the government action or inaction he challenges, standing is not precluded, but it is ordinarily 'substantially more difficult' to establish." *Defenders of Wildlife*, [504 U.S.] at 562. Here, respondents can demonstrate standing only if application of the regulations by the Government will affect *them* in the manner described above.

It is common ground that the respondent organizations can assert the standing of their members. To establish the concrete and particularized injury that standing requires, respondents point to their members' recreational interests in the National Forests. While generalized harm to the forest or the environment will not alone support standing, if that harm in fact affects the recreational or even the mere esthetic interests of the plaintiff, that will suffice. Sierra Club v. Morton, 405 U.S. 727, 734-736 (1972).

Affidavits submitted to the District Court alleged that organization member Ara Marderosian had repeatedly visited the Burnt Ridge site, that he had imminent plans to do so again, and that his interests in viewing the flora and fauna of the area would be harmed if the Burnt Ridge Project went forward without incorporation of the ideas he would have suggested if the Forest Service had provided him an opportunity to comment. The Government concedes this was sufficient to establish Article III standing with respect to Burnt Ridge. Marderosian's threatened injury with regard to that project was originally one of the bases for the present suit. After the District Court had issued a preliminary injunction, however, the parties settled their differences on that score. Marderosian's injury in fact with regard to that project has been remedied, and it is, as the District Court pronounced, "not at issue in this case." 376 F. Supp. 2d, at 999. We know of no precedent for the proposition that when a plaintiff has sued to challenge the lawfulness of certain action or threatened action but has settled that suit, he retains standing to challenge the basis for that action (here, the regulation in the abstract), apart from any concrete application that threatens imminent harm to his interests. Such a holding would fly in the face of Article III's injury-in-fact requirement.

Respondents have identified no other application of the invalidated regulations that threatens imminent and concrete harm to the interests of their members. The only other affidavit relied on was that of Jim Bensman. He asserted, first, that he had suffered injury in the past from development on Forest Service land. That does not suffice for several reasons: because it was not tied to application of the challenged regulations, because it does not identify any particular site, and because it relates to past injury rather than imminent future injury that is sought to be enjoined.

Bensman's affidavit further asserts that he has visited many National Forests and plans to visit several unnamed National Forests in the future. Respondents describe this as a mere failure to "provide the name of each timber sale that affected [Bensman's] interests." It is much more (or much less) than that. It is a failure to allege that *any* particular timber sale or other project claimed to be unlawfully subject to the regulations will impede a specific and concrete plan of Bensman's to enjoy the National Forests. The National Forests occupy more than 190 million acres, an area larger than Texas. There may be a chance, but is hardly a likelihood, that Bensman's wanderings will bring him to a parcel about to be affected by a project unlawfully subject to the regulations. Indeed, without further specification it is impossible to tell *which* projects are (in respondents' view) unlawfully subject to the regulations. The allegations here present a weaker likelihood of concrete harm than that which we found insufficient in *Lyons*, 461 U.S. 95, where a plaintiff who alleged that he had been injured by an improper police chokehold sought injunctive relief barring use of the hold in the future. We said it was "no more than conjecture" that Lyons would be subjected to that chokehold upon a later encounter. Here we are asked to assume not only that Bensman will stumble across a project tract unlawfully subject to the regulations, but also that the tract is about to be developed by the Forest Service in a way that harms his recreational interests, and that he would have commented on the project but for the regulation. Accepting an intention to visit the National Forests as adequate to confer standing to challenge any Government action affecting any portion of those forests would be tantamount to eliminating the requirement of concrete, particularized injury in fact.

The Bensman affidavit does refer specifically to a series of projects in the Allegheny National Forest that are subject to the challenged regulations. It does not assert, however, any firm intention to visit their locations, saying only that Bensman "'want[s] to'" go there. Vague desire to return is insufficient to satisfy the requirement of imminent injury: "Such 'some day' intentions—without any description of concrete plans, or indeed any specification of *when* the some day will be—do not support a finding of the 'actual or imminent' injury that our cases require." *Defenders of Wildlife*, 504 U.S., at 564.

Respondents argue that they have standing to bring their challenge because they have suffered procedural injury, namely that they have been denied the ability to file comments on some Forest Service actions and will continue to be so denied. But deprivation of a procedural right without some concrete interest that is affected by the deprivation—a procedural right *in vacuo*— is insufficient to create Article III standing. Only a "person who has been accorded a procedural right to protect *his concrete interests* can assert that right without meeting all the normal standards for redressability and immediacy." Id., at 572, n.7 (emphasis added). Respondents alleged such injury in their challenge to the Burnt Ridge Project, claiming that but for the allegedly unlawful abridged procedures they would have been able to oppose the project that threatened to impinge on their concrete plans to observe nature in that specific area. But Burnt Ridge is now off the table.

It makes no difference that the procedural right has been accorded by Congress. That can loosen the strictures of the redressability prong of our standing inquiry—so that standing existed with regard to the Burnt Ridge Project, for example, despite the possibility that Earth Island's allegedly guaranteed right to comment would not be successful in persuading the Forest Service to avoid impairment of Earth Island's concrete interests. Unlike redressability, however, the requirement of injury in fact is a hard floor of Article III jurisdiction that cannot be removed by statute. . . .

## III

The dissent proposes a hitherto unheard-of test for organizational standing: whether, accepting the organization's self-description of the activities of its members, there is a statistical probability that some of those members are threatened with concrete injury. Since, for example, the Sierra Club asserts in its pleadings that it has more than "'700,000 members nationwide, including thousands of members in California'" who "'use and enjoy the Sequoia National Forest,'" it is probable (according to the dissent) that some (unidentified) members have planned to visit some (unidentified) small parcels affected by the Forest Service's procedures and will suffer (unidentified) concrete harm as a result. This novel approach to the law of organizational standing would make a mockery of our prior cases, which have required plaintiff-organizations to make specific allegations establishing that at least one identified member had suffered or would suffer harm. In *Defenders of Wildlife* we held that the organization lacked standing because it failed to "submit affidavits . . . showing, through specific facts . . . that one or more of [its] members would . . . be 'directly' affected" by the allegedly illegal activity. *Morton* [Chapter 2, pages 116-119] involved the same Sierra Club that is a party in the present case, and a project in the Sequoia National Forest. The principal difference from the present case is that the challenged project was truly massive, involving the construction of motels, restaurants, swimming pools, parking lots, and other structures on 80 acres of the Forest, plus ski lifts, ski trails, and a 20-mile access highway. We did not engage in an assessment of statistical probabilities that one of the Sierra Club's members would be adversely affected, but held that the Sierra Club lacked standing. . . .

. . . The judgment of the Court of Appeals is reversed in part and affirmed in part.

JUSTICE KENNEDY, concurring.

I join in full the opinion of the Court. As the opinion explains, "deprivation of a procedural right without some concrete interest that is affected by the deprivation—a procedural right *in vacuo*—is insufficient to create Article III standing." The procedural injury must "impair a separate concrete interest." Lujan v. Defenders of Wildlife, 504 U.S. 555, 572 (1992).

This case would present different considerations if Congress had sought to provide redress for a concrete injury "giv[ing] rise to a case or controversy where none existed before." *Id.* at 580 (Kennedy, J., concurring in part and concurring in judgment). Nothing in the statute at issue here, however, indicates Congress intended to identify or confer some interest separate and apart from a procedural right.

JUSTICE BREYER, with whom JUSTICE STEVENS, JUSTICE SOUTER, and JUSTICE GINSBURG join, dissenting.

The Court holds that the Sierra Club and its members (along with other environmental organizations) do not suffer any "'concrete injury'" when the Forest Service sells timber for logging on "many thousands" of small (250-acre or less) woodland parcels without following legally required procedures—procedures which, if followed, could lead the Service to cancel or to modify the sales. Nothing in the record or the law justifies this counterintuitive conclusion.

## I

. . . The majority says that the plaintiffs lack *constitutional* standing to raise [their] claim. It holds that the dispute between the five environmental groups and the Forest Service consists simply of an abstract challenge; it does not amount to the concrete "Cas[e]" or "Controvers[y]" that the Constitution grants federal courts the power to resolve. Art. III, §2, cl. 1. I cannot agree that this is so.

To understand the *constitutional* issue that the majority decides, it may prove helpful to imagine that Congress enacted a *statutory* provision that expressly permitted environmental groups like the respondents here to bring cases just like the present one, provided (1) that the group has members who have used salvage-timber parcels in the past and are likely to do so in the future, and (2) that the group's members have opposed Forest Service timber sales in the past (using notice, comment, and appeal procedures to do so) and will likely use those procedures to oppose salvage-timber sales in the future. The majority cannot, and does not, claim that such a statute would be unconstitutional. See Massachusetts v. EPA, 549 U.S. 497, 516-518, Sierra Club v. Morton, 405 U.S. 727, 734-738 (1972). How then can it find the present case constitutionally unauthorized?

I believe the majority answers this question as follows: It recognizes, as this Court has held, that a plaintiff has constitutional standing if the plaintiff demonstrates (1) an "'injury in fact,'" (2) that is "fairly traceable" to the defendant's "challenged action," and which (3) a "favorable [judicial] decision" will likely prevent or redress. The majority does not deny that the plaintiffs meet the latter two requirements. It focuses only upon the first, the presence of "actual," as opposed to "conjectural or hypothetical," injury. In doing so, it properly agrees that the "organizations" here can "assert the standing of their members." It points out that injuries to the "members' recreational" or even "mere esthetic interests . . . will suffice." It does not claim that the *procedural* nature of the plaintiffs' claim makes the difference here, for it says only that "deprivation of a procedural right *without some concrete interest*" thereby affected, *i.e.*, "a procedural right *in vacuo*" would prove "insufficient to create Article III standing." The majority assumes, as do I, that these unlawful Forest Service procedures will lead to substantive actions, namely the sales of salvage timber on burned lands, that might not take place if the proper procedures were followed. But the majority then finds that the plaintiffs have not sufficiently demonstrated that these salvage-timber sales cause plaintiffs an actual injury, that is, harm to the recreational, aesthetic, or other environmental interests of organization members. To put the matter in terms of my hypothetical statute, the majority holds that the plaintiff organizations, while showing that they have members who have used salvage-timber sale parcels in the past (*i.e.*, parcels that the Service does not subject to the notice, comment, and appeal procedures required by law), have failed to show that they have members likely to use such parcels in the future.

## II

How can the majority credibly claim that salvage-timber sales, and similar projects, are unlikely to harm the asserted interests of the members of these environmental groups? The majority apparently does so in part by arguing that the Forest Service actions are not "imminent"—a requirement more appropriately considered in the context of ripeness or the necessity of injunctive relief. I concede that the Court has sometimes used the word "imminent" in the context of constitutional standing. But it has done so primarily to emphasize that the harm in question—the harm that was not "imminent"—was merely "conjectural" or "hypothetical" or otherwise speculative. Where the Court has directly focused upon the matter, *i.e.*, where, as here, a plaintiff has *already* been subject to the injury it wishes to challenge, the Court has asked whether there is a *realistic likelihood* that the challenged future conduct will, in fact, recur and harm the plaintiff. That is what the Court said in Los Angeles v. Lyons, 461 U.S. 95 (1983), a case involving a plaintiff's attempt to enjoin police use of chokeholds. The Court wrote that the plaintiff, who had been subject to the unlawful chokehold in the past, would have had standing had he shown "a *realistic* threat" that reoccurrence of the challenged activity would cause him harm "in the reasonably near future." Precedent nowhere suggests that the "realistic threat" standard contains identification requirements more stringent than the word "realistic" implies.

How could the Court impose a stricter criterion? Would courts deny *standing* to a holder of a future interest in property who complains that a life tenant's waste of the land will almost inevitably hurt the value of his interest—though he will have no personal interest for several years into the future? Would courts deny *standing* to a landowner who complains that a neighbor's upstream dam constitutes a nuisance—even if the harm to his downstream property (while bound to occur) will not occur for several years? Would courts deny *standing* to an injured person seeking a protection order from future realistic (but nongeographically specific) threats of further attacks?

To the contrary, a threat of future harm may be realistic even where the plaintiff cannot specify precise times, dates, and GPS coordinates. Thus, we recently held that Massachusetts has *standing* to complain of a procedural failing, namely, EPA's failure properly to determine whether to restrict carbon dioxide emissions, even though that failing would create Massachusetts-based harm which (though likely to occur) might not occur for several decades. *Massachusetts v. EPA.* The Forest Service admits that it intends to conduct thousands of further salvage-timber sales and other projects exempted under the challenged regulations "in the reasonably near future." How then can the Court deny that the plaintiffs have shown a "realistic" threat that the Forest Service will continue to authorize (without the procedures claimed necessary) salvage-timber sales, and other Forest Service projects, that adversely affect the recreational, aesthetic, and environmental interests of the plaintiffs' members?

Consider: Respondents allege, and the Government has conceded, that the Forest Service took wrongful actions (such as selling salvage timber) "thousands" of times in the two years prior to suit. The Complaint alleges, and no one denies, that the organizations, the Sierra Club for example, have hundreds of thousands of members who use forests regularly across the Nation for recreational, scientific, aesthetic, and environmental purposes. The Complaint further alleges, and no one denies, that these organizations (and their members), believing that actions such as salvage-timber sales harm those interests, regularly oppose salvage-timber sales (and similar actions) in proceedings before the agency. And the Complaint alleges, and no one denies, that the organizations intend to continue to express their opposition to such actions in those proceedings in the future.

Consider further: The affidavit of a member of Sequoia ForestKeeper, Ara Marderosian, attached to the Complaint, specifies that Marderosian had visited the Burnt Ridge Project site in the past and intended to return. The majority concedes that this is sufficient to show that Marderosian had standing to challenge the Burnt Ridge Project. The majority must therefore agree that "at least one identified member ha[s] suffered . . . harm." Why then does it find insufficient the affidavit, also attached to the Complaint, of Jim Bensman, a member of Heartwood, Inc.? That affidavit states, among other things, that Bensman has visited 70 National Forests, that he has visited some of those forests "hundreds of times," that he has often visited the Allegheny National Forest in the past, that he has "probably commented on a thousand" Forest Service projects including salvage-timber sale proposals, that he intends to continue to comment on similar Forest Service proposals, and that the Forest Service plans in the future to conduct salvage-timber sales on 20 parcels in the Allegheny National Forest—one of the forests he has visited in the past.

The Bensman affidavit does not say *which particular* sites will be affected by future Forest Service projects, but the Service itself has conceded that it will conduct thousands of exempted projects in the future. Why is more specificity needed to show a "realistic" threat that a project will impact land Bensman uses? To know, virtually for certain, that snow will fall in New England this winter is not to know the name of each particular town where it is bound to arrive. The law of standing does not require the latter kind of specificity. How could it? And *Sierra Club v. Morton*, on which the majority so heavily relies, involved plaintiffs who challenged (true, a "massive") development, but only on a single previously determined site, about 80 acres in size, in a portion of the forest with a "limited . . . number of visitors." The Court's unwillingness to infer harm to the Sierra Club's members there does not demand a similar unwillingness here, where the challenge is to procedures affecting "thousands" of sites, involving hundreds of times as much acreage, where the precise location of each may not yet be known. In *Sierra Club*, it may have been unreasonable simply to assume that members would suffer an "injury in fact." But here, given the very different factual circumstances, it is unreasonable to believe they would not. . . .

These allegations and affidavits more than adequately show a "realistic threat" of injury to plaintiffs brought about by reoccurrence of the challenged conduct—conduct that the Forest Service thinks lawful and *admits* will reoccur. Many years ago the Ninth Circuit warned that a court should not "be blind to what must be necessarily known to every intelligent person." In re Wo Lee, 26 F. 471, 475 (1886). Applying that standard, I would find standing here.

## NOTES AND QUESTIONS

1. Is the Court's decision consistent with its holding in *Massachusetts v. EPA*, discussed in Chapter 2, that the impact of climate change is sufficient injury to provide standing to the state of Massachusetts? In his majority opinion, Justice Scalia relies heavily on his opinion in *Lujan v. Defenders of Wildlife*, but he never once cites the Court's more recent standing decision in *Massachusetts v. EPA*. Justice Kennedy, who cast the crucial fifth vote to uphold standing in *Massachusetts v. EPA*, joins Justice Scalia as the deciding fifth vote to deny standing to the plaintiffs in *Summers*. In

his concurring opinion, Justice Kennedy describes the *Summers* plaintiffs as having suffered "deprivation of a procedural right without some concrete interest that is affected by the deprivation." Is Justice Kennedy correct? Is he being consistent with his vote for standing in *Massachusetts v. EPA*?

2. The Court's decision indicates that the Court was much more closely split on standing issues than it was when it decided *Laidlaw* by a 7-2 margin. Chief Justice Roberts and Justice Alito take a far more restrictive view of standing than Chief Justice Rehnquist and Justice O'Connor did in *Laidlaw*, as indicated by their opposition to standing in *Massachusetts v. EPA*. Justice Kennedy's vote thus becomes decisive in most controversies over standing.

3. One question left open by *Massachusetts v. EPA* was whether the Court had established a new, liberalized standing rule for states when it referred to their interests in protecting their citizens as worthy of "special solicitude in our standing analysis." When it rejected the standing of states to challenge EPA's regulation of greenhouse gases in Coalition for Responsible Regulation v. EPA, 684 F.3d 102 (D.C. Cir. 2012), see Chapter 5, the D.C. Circuit stated that "special solicitude" does not exempt states "from the burden of establishing a concrete and particularized injury in fact." 684 F.3d at 147-148. In Wyoming v. U.S. Dep't of Interior, 674 F.3d 1220 (10th Cir. 2012), the court denied standing to Wyoming to challenge regulations on snowmobile use in Yellowstone and Grand Teton National Parks. The court held that any effect of the regulations on tax revenues was too speculative to support standing and that allowing a generalized grievance to serve as a basis for standing could permit a flood of subsequent legislation.

4. Justice Scalia's approach to standing reflects the continuing influence of private common law models of injury that the Court had decisively rejected in *Laidlaw* and narrowly rejected in *Massachusetts v. EPA*. See Robert V. Percival, *Massachusetts v. EPA*: Escaping the Common Law's Growing Shadow, 2007 Sup. Ct. Rev. 111 (2008). Professor Jonathan Nash proposes that courts should recognize a new model of "precautionary-based standing" that would grant standing to plaintiffs based on allegations of harm that could be catastrophic and irreversible, but whose occurrence is subject to great uncertainty. Jonathan Nash, Standing and the Precautionary Principle, 108 Colum. L. Rev. 494 (2008).

5. The *Summers* decision indicates that it will continue to be difficult for environmental groups to establish standing to challenge forest management decisions because of the majority's demand that they use or visit specific parcels affected by the illegal activity they allege. In his dissent, Justice Breyer argues that this is unrealistic. "To know, virtually for certain, that snow will fall in New England this winter is not to know the name of each particular town where it is bound to arrive." In Pacific Rivers Council v. U.S. Forest Service, 689 F.3d 1012 (9th Cir. 2012), the court upheld the standing of a group challenging an amendment to Land and Resource Management Plans by the Forest Service even though the group did not identify any specific project that the amendment would authorize. The court stated that even without the identification of specific parcels of affected land "[t]here is little doubt that" implementation of the amendment will affect the group's "continued use and enjoyment of the forest." 689 F.3d at 1023. On March 18, 2013, the Supreme Court announced that it would review the Ninth Circuit's ruling. Fearing an adverse ruling from the Supreme Court, Pacific Rivers then agreed with the government to have the Ninth Circuit's judgment vacated and the Supreme Court dismissed the case in June 2013.

### 4. Government Preclusion of Citizen Suits

As noted above, citizen suits may be precluded if federal or state authorities have commenced and are "diligently prosecuting" their own civil or criminal enforcement action against the alleged violator. CWA §505(b)(1)(B), CAA §304(b)(1)(B). These provisions seek to prevent citizen suits from infringing on the exercise of enforcement discretion by federal and state authorities.

Courts have wrestled with the question whether a properly commenced citizen suit may continue after the defendant reaches a settlement agreement with government officials. In Atlantic States Legal Foundation v. Eastman Kodak Co., 933 F.2d 124 (2d Cir. 1991), the Second Circuit held that as long as the settlement reasonably assures that the violations alleged in the citizen suit have ceased and will not recur, then the citizen suit cannot proceed even though the state did not initiate enforcement proceedings during the 60-day statutory notice period. However, the court held that plaintiffs could seek an attorneys' fees recovery because they had motivated the settlement agreement. In EPA v. City of Green Forest, 921 F.2d 1394 (8th Cir. 1990), the Eighth Circuit reached a similar decision, holding that a consent decree filed by EPA after a properly commenced citizen suit could bar the citizen action. Even though the plaintiffs had been precluded from participating in the consent decree negotiations, the court noted that their role as private attorneys general was fully served by the EPA. While noting that "there may be some cases in which it would be appropriate to let a citizens' action go forward in the wake of a subsequently filed government enforcement action," the court emphasized that EPA must be afforded a preeminent role in enforcing CWA violations. 921 F.2d at 1404. Other courts have stressed that the government enforcement cannot bar a previously filed citizen suit unless it addresses the claims made in the citizen suit. See Hudson River Fishermen's Ass'n v. County of Westchester, 686 F. Supp. 1044 (S.D.N.Y. 1988).

Prior to the 1987 Amendments, the language of the Clean Water Act's citizen suit provision provided that the only government enforcement action that barred a citizen suit was "a civil or criminal action in a court of the United States," §505(b)(1)(B). Administrative enforcement actions were not held to bar citizen suits because they were limited to small penalties assessed in proceedings in which citizens could not intervene. Friends of the Earth v. Consolidated Rail Corp., 768 F.2d 57 (2d Cir. 1985). When it gave EPA administrative enforcement authority in the 1987 Amendments, Congress added a provision precluding citizens from obtaining civil penalties in citizen suits if EPA had filed an administrative enforcement action or if "a State has commenced and is diligently prosecuting an action under a State law comparable to [§309(g)]." §309(g)(6)(A)(ii). However, Congress required that citizens be given an opportunity to comment on proposed administrative penalties, §309(g)(4)(A), and to seek a hearing, §309(g)(4)(B), and judicial review to contest penalty assessments, §309(g)(8). In light of these provisions, courts have wrestled with how to determine the comparability of state administrative enforcement proceedings.

In North & South Rivers Watershed Association v. Town of Scituate, 949 F.2d 552 (1st Cir. 1992), the First Circuit held that a state administrative order which did not impose civil penalties barred a citizen suit even though the state did not have delegated authority to operate the NPDES program and even though state law provided no notice to citizens of agency orders or penalty proceedings. See also

Arkansas Wildlife Fed'n v. ICI Americas, Inc., 29 F.3d 376 (8th Cir. 1994) ("[T]he comparability requirement may be satisfied so long as the state law contains comparable penalty provisions which the state is authorized to enforce, has the same overall enforcement goals as the federal CWA, provides interested citizens a meaningful opportunity to participate at significant stages of the decision-making process, and adequately safeguards their interests."). The *Scituate* decision is criticized in Hodas, Enforcement of Environmental Law in a Triangular Federal System: Can Three Not Be a Crowd When Enforcement Authority Is Shared by the United States, the States, and Their Citizens?, 54 Md. L. Rev. 1552, 1633-1645 (1995). Professor Hodas maintains that this decision reflects "a compliance theory of enforcement" founded on the notion that "bringing an individual defendant into compliance is more important than sanctioning that violator with civil penalties sufficiently large to deter others." Id. at 1633. Other courts have held that citizen suits seeking civil penalties are not barred by administrative compliance orders that do not seek penalties. Washington Public Interest Research Group v. Pendleton Woolen Mills, 11 F.3d 883 (9th Cir. 1993).

Section 309(g)(6)(B) of the Clean Water Act provides that an administrative enforcement action does not bar a citizen suit if the 60-day notice of intent to sue is given prior to commencement of the administrative action and the citizen suit is filed before the 120th day after the notice is given. In Black Warrior Riverkeeper, Inc. v. Cherokee Mining, LLC, 548 F.3d 986 (11th Cir. 2008), the Eleventh Circuit held that this applies to both federal and state administrative enforcement actions. Thus, it rejected a claim that a citizen suit was barred when a state administrative enforcement action commenced 65 days after the notice of intent to sue and the citizen suit was filed 72 days after the notice. However, in Environmental Conservation Organization v. City of Dallas, 529 F.3d 519 (5th Cir. 2008), the Fifth Circuit concluded that even a properly filed citizen suit can be dismissed if it becomes moot due to subsequent enforcement action that adequately addressed the same violations.

Section 304(b)(1)(B) of the Clean Air Act bars citizen suits when EPA or a state is "diligently prosecuting a civil action in a court of the United States or a state." The Fifth Circuit has held that in light of this provision's clear reference to courts, state administrative enforcement actions do not bar citizen enforcement actions under the Clean Air Act. Texans United for a Safe Economy Education Fund v. Crown Central Petroleum Corp., 207 F.3d 789 (5th Cir. 2000).

While EPA's policy has been not to initiate preemptive enforcement actions in response to citizen-suit notice letters, several states have been aggressively preempting citizen suits at the behest of defendants. See Hodas, 54 Md. L. Rev. at 1648-1651. For example, in *Laidlaw* the defendant asked the state of South Carolina to file suit against it in order to bar the citizen suit by Friends of the Earth (FOE). The company drafted the complaint against itself and even paid the filing fee for the state. On the day before FOE's 60-day notice period was to expire, the company announced a settlement with the state in which it agreed to pay a $100,000 civil penalty and to make "every effort" to comply with its permit obligations. However, the district court found that the settlement did not bar FOE's citizen suit because it did not constitute the kind of "diligent prosecution" required by section 505(b)(1)(B). Friends of the Earth, Inc. v. Laidlaw Environmental Services, 528 U.S. 167, 176-177 (2000).

### 5. *Permit Shields*

An important issue that emerged in CWA enforcement actions was the question whether NPDES permits insulate dischargers from liability for discharges of pollutants not specifically regulated by their permits. In the case below, a public interest group filed a citizen suit after discovering that a company's TRI report included surface water discharges of pollutants not covered by the company's NPDES permit. The trial court agreed with the defendant that the CWA does not prohibit discharges of pollutants by a permittee that do not violate specific limits established in the permit. The court stated that although section 301(a) of the Act generally prohibits unpermitted discharges, "the statutory and regulatory scheme of the Act takes enforcement actions against permit holders *outside* that general prohibition." Atlantic States Legal Found. v. Eastman Kodak Co., 809 F. Supp. 1040, 1047 (W.D.N.Y. 1992). The decision was appealed to the Second Circuit, which reached the following decision.

## Atlantic States Legal Foundation, Inc. v. Eastman Kodak Co.

12 F.3d 353 (2d Cir. 1994)

Before: WINTER, McLAUGHLIN, and JACOBS, Circuit Judges.

WINTER, Circuit Judge:
This appeal raises the issue of whether private groups may bring a citizen suit pursuant to Section 505 of the Federal Water Pollution Control Act (commonly known as the Clean Water Act), 33 U.S.C. §1365, to stop the discharge of pollutants not listed in a valid permit issued pursuant to the Clean Water Act ("CWA" or "the Act"), 33 U.S.C. §1342 (1988). . . .

### BACKGROUND

Appellee Eastman Kodak Company ("Kodak") operates an industrial facility in Rochester, New York, that discharges wastewater into the Genesee River and Paddy Hill Creek under a State Pollutant Discharge Elimination System ("SPDES") permit issued pursuant to 33 U.S.C. §1342. Appellant Atlantic States Legal Foundation, Inc. ("Atlantic States") is a not-for-profit environmental group based in Syracuse, New York.

Kodak operates a wastewater treatment plant at its Rochester facility to purify waste produced in the manufacture of photographic supplies and other laboratory chemicals. The purification plant employs a variety of technical processes to filter harmful pollutants before discharge into the Genesee River at the King's Landing discharge point (designated Outfall 001) pursuant to its SPDES permit.

Kodak first received a federal permit in 1975. At that time, the pertinent regulatory scheme was the National Pollutant Discharge Elimination System ("NPDES") that was administered directly by the federal Environmental Protection Agency ("EPA"). Subsequently, 33 U.S.C. §1342(b), (c) delegated authority to the states to establish their own programs in place of the EPA's. As a result, Kodak applied in July 1979 to renew its permit to the New York State Department of Environmental

Conservation ("DEC"). The DEC declined to act on Kodak's renewal application, and Kodak's NPDES permit remained in effect. As part of the pending application for an SPDES permit, in April 1982 Kodak provided the DEC with a Form 2C describing estimated discharges of 164 substances from each of its outfalls. Kodak also submitted an Industrial Chemical Survey ("ICS") disclosing the amounts of certain chemicals used in Kodak's facility and whether they might appear in the plant's wastewater. Although the ICS originally requested information on 144 substances, including some broad classes such as "unspecified metals," the DEC restricted the inquiry to chemicals used in excess of specified minimum levels.

On the basis of these disclosures, DEC issued Kodak an SPDES permit, number 000-1643, effective November 1, 1984, establishing specific effluent limitations for approximately 25 pollutants. The permit also included "action levels" for five other pollutants as well as for three of the pollutants for which it had established effluent limits. DEC further required Kodak to conduct a semi-annual scan of "EPA Volatile, Acid and Base/Neutral Fractions and PCB's priority pollutants on a 24-hr, composite sample." In May 1989, Kodak applied to renew the SPDES permit submitting a new Form 2C and ICS, but the 1984 permit will continue to remain in effect until DEC issues a final determination. . . .

On November 14, 1991, Atlantic States filed the complaint in the instant matter. The complaint alleged that Kodak had violated Sections 301 and 402 of the Clean Water Act, 33 U.S.C. §§1311, 1342, by discharging large quantities of pollutants not listed in its SPDES permit. . . .

After discovery, Atlantic States moved for partial summary judgment as to Kodak's liability in relation to the post-April 1, 1990 discharge of one or more of 16 of the 27 pollutants listed in the complaint. The 16 pollutants are all listed as toxic chemicals under Section 313(c) of the Emergency Planning and Community Right-to-Know Act, 42 U.S.C. §11023(c). Atlantic States argued that General Provision 1(b) of the SPDES permit and Section 301 of the CWA, 33 U.S.C. §1311, prohibit absolutely the discharge of any pollutant not specifically authorized under Kodak's SPDES permit.

On December 28, 1992, the district court denied Atlantic States' motion for partial summary judgment, granted Kodak's cross-motion for summary judgment, and dismissed the case. Atlantic States Legal Found., Inc. v. Eastman Kodak Co., 809 F. Supp. 1040 (W.D.N.Y. 1992). Atlantic States appealed from the judgment entered on that order. . . .

## A.   "Standards and Limitations" of the Clean Water Act

Atlantic States argues first that the plain language of Section 301 of the CWA, 33 U.S.C. §1311, prohibits the discharge of any pollutants not expressly permitted. With regard to this claim, therefore, Atlantic States' standing to bring this action turns on the merits of the action itself.

Section 301(a) reads: "Except as in compliance with this section and sections 1312, 1316, 1317, 1328, 1342, and 1344 of this title, the discharge of any pollutant by any person shall be unlawful." This prohibition is tempered, however, by a self-referential host of exceptions that allow the discharge of many pollutants once a polluter has complied with the regulatory program of the CWA. The exception relevant to the instant matter is contained in Section 402, which outlines the NPDES, 33

U.S.C. §1342(a), and specifies the requirements for suspending the national system with the submission of an approved state program, 33 U.S.C. §1342(b), (c). Section 402(k) contains the so-called "shield provision," 33 U.S.C. §1342(k), which defines compliance with an NPDES or SPDES permit as compliance with Section 301 for the purposes of the CWA's enforcement provisions. The Supreme Court has noted that "The purpose of [Section 402(k)] seems to be . . . to relieve [permit holders] of having to litigate in an enforcement action the question whether their permits are sufficiently strict." E.I. du Pont de Nemours & Co. v. Train, 430 U.S. 112 (1977).

Atlantic States' view of the regulatory framework stands that scheme on its head. Atlantic States treats permits as establishing limited permission for the discharge of identified pollutants and a prohibition on the discharge of unidentified pollutants. Viewing the regulatory scheme as a whole, however, it is clear that the permit is intended to identify and limit the most harmful pollutants while leaving the control of the vast number of other pollutants to disclosure requirements. Once within the NPDES or SPDES scheme, therefore, polluters may discharge pollutants not specifically listed in their permits so long as they comply with the appropriate reporting requirements and abide by any new limitations when imposed on such pollutants.

The EPA lists tens of thousands of different chemical substances in the Toxic Substances Control Act Chemical Substance Inventory pursuant to 15 U.S.C. §2607(b) (1988). However, the EPA does not demand even information regarding each of the many thousand chemical substances potentially present in a manufacturer's wastewater because "it is impossible to identify and rationally limit every chemical or compound present in a discharge of pollutants." Memorandum from EPA Deputy Assistant Administrator for Water Enforcement Jeffrey G. Miller to Regional Enforcement Director, Region V, at 2 (Apr. 28, 1976). "Compliance with such a permit would be impossible and anybody seeking to harass a permittee need only analyze that permittee's discharge until determining the presence of a substance not identified in the permit." Id. Indeed, Atlantic States conceded at oral argument that even plain water might be considered a "pollutant" under its view of the Act.

The EPA has never acted in any way to suggest that Atlantic States' absolutist and wholly impractical view of the legal effect of a permit is valid. In fact, the EPA's actions and policy statements have frequently contemplated discharges of pollutants not listed under an NPDES or SPDES permit. It has addressed such discharges by amending the permit to list and limit a pollutant when necessary to safeguard the environment without considering pre-amendment discharges to be violations calling for enforcement under the CWA. 33 U.S.C. §§1319, 1365. The EPA thus stated in its comments on proposed 40 C.F.R. §122.68(a), which applied the "application-based" limits approach to implementation of the CWA reporting scheme,

> There is still some possibility . . . that a [NPDES or SPDES] permittee may discharge a large amount of a pollutant not limited in its permit, and EPA will not be able to take enforcement action against the permittee as long as the permittee complies with the notification requirements [pursuant to the CWA].

45 Fed. Reg. 33,516, 33,523 (1980). The EPA's statement went on to note that this possibility constituted a "regulatory gap," and that, "the final regulations

control discharges only of the pollutants listed in the [NPDES or SPDES] permit application, which consist primarily of the listed toxic pollutants and designated hazardous substances." Id. In a clarification of EPA policy on Section 304, 33 U.S.C. §1314, and water quality-based effluent limitations, an EPA official recently stated that:

> EPA did not intend to require water quality-based permit limitations on all pollutants contained in a discharge. . . . The proper interpretation of the regulations is that developing water quality-based limitations is a step-by-step process. . . . Water quality-based limits are established where the permitting authority reasonably anticipates the discharge of pollutants by the permittee at levels that have the reasonable potential to cause or contribute to an excursion above any state water quality criterion. . . .

Memorandum from Director, Office of Wastewater Enforcement and Compliance to Water Management Division Directors, Regions I-X, at 2-3 (Aug. 14, 1992).

The EPA is the federal agency entrusted with administration and enforcement of the CWA. 33 U.S.C. §1251(d). As such, EPA's reasonable interpretations of the Act are due deferential treatment in the courts. Chevron, U.S.A., Inc. v. Natural Resources Defense Council, 467 U.S. 837, 844 (1984). . . . Because the EPA's implementation of the CWA is entirely reasonable, we defer to it. . . .

## CONCLUSION

For the reasons stated above, we affirm the order of the district court granting summary judgment to Kodak.

## NOTES AND QUESTIONS

1. Does the court's decision mean that a discharger with an NPDES permit legally can discharge any material not specifically restricted in its permit? What, if anything, would prevent a discharger from dramatically changing the nature of its discharges once it has been granted an NPDES permit?

2. How did the court and Atlantic States differ in their interpretations of the effect of the language of section 301 providing that "the discharge of any pollutant by any person shall be unlawful" except as in compliance with other provisions of the Clean Water Act? The court's decision, its interpretation of the statutory language, and EPA's history of implementation of the permit provisions of the Clean Water Act are criticized in Axline and McGinley, Universal Statutes and Planetary Programs: How EPA Has Diluted the Clean Water Act, 8 J. Envtl. L. & Litig. 253 (1993).

3. The court suggests that its interpretation of the Clean Water Act is justified because it would be impossible for EPA to identify and to regulate every one of the thousands of chemicals that are discharged by industrial facilities. Is it true that compliance with the Act would be impossible if the court accepted Atlantic States's view that the discharge of unidentified pollutants is prohibited?

4. How realistic is the fear expressed by EPA that if Atlantic States's view was accepted, "anybody seeking to harass a permittee need only analyze that permittee's discharge until determining the presence of a substance not identified in the

permit"? How difficult would it be for citizen groups to sample and analyze discharges and to prove that pollutants are being discharged that are unauthorized in a permit? If citizens were successful in proving such discharges, wouldn't permittees seek to have these discharges specifically addressed in their permits?

5.  Does the court's decision preclude EPA from bringing an enforcement action against a permittee for discharges not addressed in an NPDES permit? In at least one other case a court has allowed the federal government to take enforcement action against discharges not regulated in an NPDES permit. United States v. Ketchikan Pulp Co., Civ. No. A92-587 (D. Alaska 1993).

6.  In October 1994, Kodak agreed to pay a $5 million fine and to spend more than $60 million as a result of violations of federal hazardous waste laws at the plant targeted in Atlantic States' citizen suit. McKinley, Kodak Fined $5 Million for Toxic Chemical Leaks, N.Y. Times, Oct. 8, 1994, at 29.

7.  In Southern Appalachian Mountain Stewards v. A & G Coal Corp., 758 F.3d 560 (4th Cir. 2014), the Fourth Circuit rejected an argument that *Atlantic States v. Eastman Kodak* shielded a mining company from a citizen suit for discharging selenium, which was not mentioned in the company's NPDES permit. The court concluded that the discharge of unlisted pollutants is permissible only when the pollutants have been disclosed to permitting authorities during the permit process. The court noted that selenium was one of 15 other toxic pollutants specifically listed by EPA as pollutants for which a permit applicant must disclose if it "knows or has reason to believe" that it may be discharging.

8.  Implementation of the permit provisions of the Clean Air Act Amendments of 1990 eventually may produce a new wave of citizen suits. Section 504 of the Clean Air Act mandates new monitoring and reporting requirements that will facilitate citizen suits for permit violations. The 1990 Amendments specifically authorize the imposition of "appropriate civil penalties" in citizen suits, §304(a), and they direct that such penalties either be deposited into a special fund "to finance air compliance and enforcement activities," §304(g)(1), or "be used in beneficial mitigation projects" (limited to $100,000 per action) consistent with the Act to "enhance the public health or the environment." §304(g)(2).

---

## PROBLEM EXERCISE: CITIZEN ENFORCEMENT OF THE CLEAN WATER ACT

On August 22, a volunteer for a local environmental group you represent informs you that a fish kill has been discovered in a nearby stream 500 yards downriver from an outfall pipe at a manufacturing plant. The plant has an NPDES permit issued by the state that limits the amount of phosphorus, nitrogen, and total suspended solids in discharges from its outfall. A friend who works at the plant subsequently informs you in confidence that an accident occurred at the plant on August 15 that caused a large quantity of toxic chemicals to spill into a holding tank. He tells you that similar accidents have occurred twice before during the five years he has worked at the plant. Although your friend does not know what happened to the chemicals, he notes that when he checked the holding tank on August 24, he discovered that it had been emptied.

On November 15, the environmental group checks with the state environmental agency to review the discharge monitoring report (DMR) the plant was required to file for August. After discovering that the plant failed to file a DMR for August, the environmental group asks you to file a citizen suit on their behalf. On November 25, you send a letter to the owner of the plant, the state environmental agency, and EPA informing them that you plan to file a citizen suit against the plant owner for failure to file a DMR for August and for discharging pollutants in violation of the plant's permit.

On March 25, you file a citizen suit against the owner of the plant, alleging that he has violated the Act by failing to file a DMR and by discharging pollutants in violation of the plant's NPDES permit. On April 7, the plant owner belatedly submits to the state environmental agency a DMR reporting no violations of the plant's permit during August.

**Question One.** Suppose that defense counsel, citing *Gwaltney*, files motions to dismiss and for summary judgment arguing that there is no ongoing violation because the missing DMR has now been filed, that the case is now moot, and that you lack standing since there is no relief available that would redress any injury to you. How would you respond? Is your case likely to survive the motion to dismiss? Would the result be different if the company had filed the missing DMR the day before you filed your citizen suit?

**Question Two.** Suppose that after your lawsuit is filed the state environmental agency assesses a $1,000 administrative penalty against the owner of the plant for failing to file a DMR in timely fashion. The owner agrees to pay the penalty in return for the state's agreement not to pursue further investigation into the fish kill. Although you are outraged by what you perceive to be a sweetheart settlement, state law does not permit you to challenge it in court. Defense counsel renews his motion to dismiss, arguing that the penalty should bar your citizen suit because it is now moot and that you lack standing since there is no relief available that would redress your alleged injury. How would you respond? Who is likely to prevail on this issue? Would it make any difference if the administrative settlement included a pledge by the company not to violate its permit terms in the future? Would it make any difference if the state had commenced its administrative enforcement action on March 20? See §309(g)(6). Is there any way to challenge the administrative settlement outside of state court? See §§309(g)(4) and (6).

**Question Three.** Your friend who works at the plant reports that the employee responsible for preparing DMRs was told by the plant manager that the plant would be closed and he would lose his job if the company lost the citizen suit. Your friend is reluctant to testify at trial because he is certain he would be fired. Without your friend's testimony it will be impossible to link the plant to the fish kill. What protection is available to your friend under section 507 of the Clean Water Act?

**Question Four.** Suppose that the court reserves judgment on the motion to dismiss and the case proceeds to trial. With Perry Mason as your co-counsel, you succeed in having the employee responsible for preparing the DMR break down on the stand and confess that he falsified it to cover up deliberate discharges of the toxics. Under section 309 of the Clean Water Act, what is the potential criminal liability of the following persons for the filing of the false DMR or the deliberate discharge of the toxics: (1) the employee who prepared the DMR, (2) the plant manager, and (3) the owner of the company?

**Question Five.** Citing its tough policy of not tolerating violations of the environmental laws by its employees, the company then fires the employee who broke down on the stand and blames him for any violations. Is he entitled to protection under section 507? See §507(d). If plant employees do not testify, what is the likely outcome of your citizen suit? If you win, what relief can the court grant and what penalties can be imposed on the company?

**Question Six.** Suppose the company is acquired by another firm pledging to "clean up" the plant in the wake of the adverse publicity concerning environmental violations. The acquiring firm had itself been in trouble with environmental officials for numerous violations of the Clean Water Act three years before. It hires an outside consultant to conduct an environmental audit at the plant. The audit discovers that for years plant employees routinely have been discarding vials containing toxic chemicals into a portion of the river upstream from the outfall pipe, which now has become a biological wasteland as a result of these discharges. This practice has saved the firm approximately $2 million in disposal costs. If the new firm promptly discloses these activities to the authorities and orders its employees to stop the practice, can it take advantage of EPA's self-auditing policy to seek a penalty reduction? Will the policy protect the workers against criminal liability? Should any penalty be imposed on the firm and, if so, how large should it be?

---

# E.   ENFORCEMENT AGAINST FEDERAL FACILITIES

Federal facilities have been some of the most notorious violators of the environmental laws. Although most federal environmental legislation is the product of concern over the inadequacy of decentralized regulatory approaches, federal environmental laws rely heavily on state authorities to administer and enforce the national programs. Enforcement against federal facilities has been particularly problematic.

Many of the environmental laws specify that their provisions are applicable to facilities owned or operated by federal agencies. For example, section 313(a) of the Clean Water Act provides that the federal government, its officers, agents, and employees "shall be subject to, and comply with, all Federal, State, interstate, and local requirements, administrative authority, and process and sanctions respecting the control and abatement of water pollution in the same manner, and to the same extent as any nongovernmental entity including the payment of reasonable service charges." Section 6001 of RCRA has virtually identical language. But federal agencies are not necessarily subject to the same sanctions as other violators of the environmental laws. Section 313(a) of the CWA provides that "the United States shall be liable only for those civil penalties arising under Federal law or imposed by a State or local court to enforce an order or the process of such court." RCRA section 6001 initially waived only federal immunity from sanctions for the enforcement of injunctive relief. EPA generally had been precluded from taking direct enforcement action against sister federal agencies, while states had been handicapped in recovering penalties from federal agencies due to narrow interpretations of waivers of sovereign immunity in the environmental laws. Congress amended RCRA in 1992 to make federal violators liable for civil penalties and to authorize EPA enforcement actions against them.

In 1990, the Congressional Budget Office found that the federal government was spending more money trying to bring its own facilities into compliance with the environmental laws than in administering the laws. CBO, Federal Liabilities Under Hazardous Waste Laws (May 1990). However, insufficient funding for environmental compliance and the absence of effective enforcement have contributed to serious compliance problems at some facilities owned or operated by federal agencies. In July 1988, the U.S. Department of Energy estimated that environmental cleanup at federal nuclear weapons facilities could cost between $66 to $100 billion. Department of Energy, Environmental, Safety, and Health Report for the Department of Energy Defense Complex (July 1, 1988). At the time, 32 federal land disposal facilities were on EPA's list of significant non-compliers with RCRA.

In United States v. Dee, 912 F.2d 741 (4th Cir. 1990), federal employees were convicted of criminal violations of RCRA for the first time. The defendants were engineers working for the United States Army who were convicted for knowing violations of RCRA's TSD standards. The Fourth Circuit rejected the argument that sovereign immunity barred the prosecution, stating that while "federal officers enjoy a degree of immunity for a particular sphere of official actions, there is no general immunity from criminal prosecution." Criminal prosecution of federal officials was one of the few effective sanctions for non-compliance when states were not permitted to impose civil penalties on federal facilities. However, there are substantial barriers to states' conducting criminal prosecutions for violators at federal facilities, including the fact that most crimes at such facilities occur on federal land. Smith, Shields for the King's Men: Official Immunity and Other Obstacles to Effective Prosecution of Federal Officials for Environmental Crimes, 16 Colum. J. Envtl. L. 1 (1991).

Justice Department officials argued that states should not be able to impose civil penalties for environmental violations by federal agencies because it would be a convenient means for states to line their coffers at federal expense while disrupting federal priorities for environmental compliance.

In Department of Energy v. Ohio, 503 U.S. 607 (1992), the Supreme Court held that federal agencies are immune from civil penalties for violations of the Clean Water Act and RCRA. Emphasizing that waivers of sovereign immunity must be unequivocal, the Court held that federal agencies are liable only for fines designed to induce them to comply with judicial orders to modify their behavior prospectively, and not for fines imposed as penalties for past violations. In dissent, Justice White complained that the Court's decision "deprives the States of a powerful weapon in combatting federal agencies that persist in despoiling the environment." 503 U.S. at 630.

The Supreme Court's decision was overridden in large part when Congress enacted the Federal Facility Compliance Act of 1992 (FFCA), Pub. L. No. 102-386 (1992), which President Bush signed into law on October 6, 1992. The FFCA expressly waives the federal government's immunity from civil penalties for violations of RCRA. The legislation that became the FFCA had actually passed both houses of Congress during the previous session in 1991, prior to the Supreme Court's *DOE v. Ohio* decision, which served as a catalyst for convening a conference committee and achieving final passage of the legislation.

The FFCA amended section 6001 of RCRA to waive federal sovereign immunity for civil or administrative penalties or fines, regardless of whether they are "punitive or coercive in nature or are imposed for isolated, intermittent, or continuing violations." This effectively overrode the Supreme Court's unanimous holding in *DOE v. Ohio* that the previous version of section 6001 did not waive federal sovereign immunity for punitive penalties. The FFCA also amended the definition of "person" in section 1004(15) of RCRA to "include each department, agency, and instrumentality of the United States," thus effectively overriding the Court's holding that federal facilities are immune from civil penalties under RCRA's citizen suit provision. However, the FFCA did not address the Court's holdings with respect to waivers of sovereign immunity in the Clean Water Act.

Opponents of the legislation had maintained that states could abuse their civil penalty authority to line their coffers at federal expense. In response to this concern, the legislation required that all funds collected by states for violations by federal agencies be used "only for projects designed to improve or protect the environment or to defray the costs of environmental protection or enforcement." While the term "environmental protection" is not defined in the FFCA, supporters of the Act maintained that it should be construed broadly to include wetlands protection and preservation of open space as well as pollution control. States with preexisting laws or constitutional provisions that bar earmarking of funds collected in enforcement actions are exempted from this limitation.

The Federal Facility Compliance Act also included provisions to force DOE to develop a plan for cleaning up the enormous quantities of mixed radioactive and hazardous waste it had generated. The Secretary of Energy was required to provide a comprehensive state-by-state inventory of the sources and amounts of such wastes to EPA and to the governor of each state where DOE stores or generates mixed wastes. This inventory had to include estimates of the amount of each type of mixed waste that DOE expected to generate at each of its facilities during the next five years and information concerning the technology available for treating such wastes. DOE was required to submit a detailed description of its plans for treating mixed wastes and for identifying and developing treatment technologies for wastes for which no treatment technology exists. EPA or states with delegated RCRA program authority had to review and approve the plans, which were then to be incorporated in administrative orders requiring compliance.

To improve EPA enforcement, the Act also amended section 3007(c) of RCRA to require EPA annually to inspect each federal facility used for the treatment, storage, or disposal of hazardous waste even in states authorized to administer the RCRA program. The 1984 Hazardous and Solid Waste Amendments had previously required such inspections only in states without delegated program authority. EPA was to be reimbursed for the costs of such inspections by the federal agency that owns or operates each facility. The initial EPA inspection had to include groundwater monitoring unless it had been performed during the year prior to enactment.

A particularly significant provision in FFCA authorized EPA to bring administrative enforcement actions against other federal agencies. While EPA had maintained that it had such authority under RCRA, the Justice Department maintained that it would violate constitutional principles of separation of powers for EPA to issue administrative orders against another executive agency, a position undermined by Morrison v. Olson, 487 U.S. 654, 695-696 (1988). The conference report describes the Act's express endorsement of EPA administrative enforcement actions against federal facilities as an effort "to reaffirm the original intent" of RCRA. 138 Cong. Rec. H8865 (Sept. 22, 1992 daily ed.). The report states that EPA should use its section 3008(a) administrative order authority against federal facilities for the same types of violations for which it is used against private parties. EPA had complained that other federal agencies were reluctant to negotiate compliance agreements with it because EPA had no credible threat of enforcement leverage to use against them in the absence of such an agreement. This authority allows EPA to move more rapidly to penalize recalcitrant agencies. FFCA requires that EPA give the defendant agency an opportunity to confer with the EPA administrator before any administrative order can become final.

While the FFCA effectively overruled the RCRA portion of the holding in *Department of Energy v. Ohio*, the scope of the congressional waiver of sovereign immunity is even broader than the penalties at issue in that decision. Because the federal government is now subject "to the full range of available enforcement tools . . . to penalize isolated, intermittent or continuing violations as well as to coerce future compliance," the legislation also effectively precludes assertion by federal defendants of a *Gwaltney* defense in citizen suits alleging violations of RCRA. As the conference report explains:

> By subjecting the federal government to penalties and fines for isolated, intermittent, or continuing violations, the waiver also makes it clear that the federal government may be penalized for any violation of federal, state, interstate or local law, whether a single or repeated occurrence, notwithstanding the holding of the Supreme Court in Gwaltney of Smithfield, Ltd. v. Chesapeake Bay Foundation, Inc., 484 U.S. 49 (1987). [Id.]

While the enactment of FFCA overruled the holding of *Department of Energy v. Ohio* with respect to RCRA, federal facilities may remain immune from civil penalties for violation of the Clean Water Act because the latter are not addressed by the FFCA. For a pessimistic assessment of the effectiveness of the FFCA, see Kassen, The Inadequacies of Congressional Attempts to Legislate Federal Facility Compliance with Environmental Requirements, 54 Md. L. Rev. 1475 (1995).

The Ninth Circuit has upheld the right of states to seek penalties in state court from a federal agency for violating the Clean Air Act. After a California state air quality management district sought penalties in state court for Clean Air Act violations at an Air Force base, the Air Force removed the case to federal court. While the federal district court found the Air Force to be immune from penalties under the Clean Air Act, the Ninth Circuit reversed and ordered the case returned to state court. The Ninth Circuit held that the Clean Air Act specifically preserves the right of state and local governments to seek penalties from federal agencies in state court for violations of state and local air quality regulations. California ex rel. Sacramento Metropolitan Air Quality Management District v. United States, 215 F.3d 1005 (9th Cir. 2000).

In December 2008, the U.S. Department of Justice's Office of Legal Counsel (OLC) issued an opinion upholding EPA's authority to issue cleanup orders to Department of Defense (DOD) facilities. Frustrated by DOD's failure to remediate contamination at DOD sites listed on the Superfund National Priorities List, EPA issued four facility-wide "imminent and substantial endangerment" cleanup orders under RCRA section 7003 and section 1431 of the Safe Drinking Water Act. The state of Maryland filed a RCRA section 7002(a)(1) notice of intent to sue to enforce one of these orders with respect to DOD's Fort Meade facility. DOD then sought an opinion from the Justice Department on the legality of EPA's actions. In an opinion issued on December 1, 2008, OLC concluded that EPA had acted properly and that it had the authority to issue the orders under RCRA and the SDWA even for sites covered by federal facility agreements (FFAs) under CERCLA section 120(e)(4). Steven G. Bradbury, Re: Issuance of Imminent and Substantial Endangerment Orders at Department of Defense Facilities, Dec. 1, 2008. The opinion concluded that the orders did not have to seek abatement of a specific threat, but instead could also seek implementation of facility-wide cleanups. It upheld EPA's ability to insist on inclusion of terms in a FFA that go beyond the requirements of CERCLA section 120(e)(4), but it noted that DOD is not necessarily required to agree to all extra-statutory terms demanded by EPA. OLC concluded that EPA may require DOD to adhere to the same terms applicable to non-federal facilities under CERCLA. The opinion also concluded that EPA may address in its cleanup orders releases beyond those identified in the initial NPL listing.

# CHAPTER 11

# PROTECTION OF THE GLOBAL ENVIRONMENT

The Paris Climate Accord is simply the latest example of Washington entering into an agreement that disadvantages the United States to the exclusive benefit of other countries, leaving American workers—who I love—and taxpayers to absorb the cost in terms of lost jobs, lower wages, shuttered factories, and vastly diminished economic production. Thus, as of today, the United States will cease all implementation of the non-binding Paris Accord and the draconian financial and economic burdens the agreement imposes on our country.

*—President Donald J. Trump, June 1, 2017*

I, Joseph R. Biden Jr., President of the United States of America, having seen and considered the Paris Agreement, done at Paris on December 12, 2015, do hereby accept the said Agreement and every article and clause thereof on behalf of the United States of America.

Done at Washington this 20th day of January, 2021.

The United States and the world face a profound climate crisis. We have a narrow moment to pursue action at home and abroad in order to avoid the most catastrophic impacts of that crisis and to seize the opportunity that tackling climate change presents. Domestic action must go hand in hand with United States international leadership, aimed at significantly enhancing global action. Together, we must listen to science and meet the moment.

*—President Joseph R. Biden, Jr.**

Perhaps the most stunning recent development in environmental policy has been the rapid rise of global concern for the environment. Environmental problems increasingly are viewed as transcending national borders and, in some cases, posing major risks to the health of the planet that could cause worldwide economic and social dislocation. The globalization of environmental concern is having a profound impact on international trade and diplomacy, stimulating the development of new international legal regimes that are assuming an increasingly important role in environmental policy.

The globalization of environmental problems is a product of many factors, including rapid worldwide population growth, the expanding scale of international

---

** Executive Order on Tackling the Climate Crisis at Home and Abroad, Jan. 27, 2021.

economic activity, and improvements in scientific understanding of humankind's impact on earth's ecosystems. As 2021 begins, the world's population is estimated to be 7.74 billion people, and it is projected to rise to 9.7 billion by the year 2050 with virtually all population growth occurring in less developed countries. The global pandemic of COVID-19 has demonstrated just how interconnected the nations of the world have become in matters of health, economics, and ecology. Global environmental problems are what the World Commission on Environment and Development has termed "interlocking crises," troubles spawned by the ecological impact of human activity and the scramble to meet the basic needs of a rapidly growing world population.

The link between poverty and environmental degradation is now widely recognized. It is estimated that 790 million people—more than one-tenth of the world's population—do not have access to safe drinking water and that 1.8 billion people lack proper toilets or sewage disposal systems. Millions of people die annually from water-borne diseases. Providing these people with basic human needs without taxing emerging limits on earth systems will require the creative application of technology, policy, and resources.

The number of treaties addressing environmental concerns has grown rapidly. In 1970, the UN listed 52 environment-related treaties. By 2020 there were more than 1,300 multilateral environmental agreements, with most having been adopted between 1975 and 2014. International Environmental Agreements Database Project, *https://iea.uoregon.edu.* While environmental treaty-making has slowed in recent years, environmental provisions continue to be routinely incorporated in trade agreements.

Globalization has affected environmental law in profound ways. As countries upgrade their environmental laws they often borrow law and regulatory innovations even from nations with very different legal traditions. Trade liberalization and the rise of global markets created new demands for harmonization of environmental standards. Non-governmental organizations (NGOs) and government officials increasingly collaborate in global networks to improve and coordinate environmental regulation. These forces are blurring traditional distinctions between domestic and international law, producing a kind of "global environmental law" reflected in the emergence of formal and informal norms for environmental regulation. See Robert V. Percival, The Globalization of Environmental Law, 26 Pace Envtl. L. Rev. 451 (2009); Tseming Yang & Robert V. Percival, The Emergence of Global Environmental Law, 36 Ecology L.Q. 101 (2009). Environmental activists have found that even multinational oil companies and seemingly intransigent governments sometimes can be forced to change plans in response to protests, media coverage, and consumer boycotts. Some industries now support voluntary initiatives to provide common baselines to apply even in countries with weak environmental laws.

After introducing international environmental law, this chapter explores international trade and the environment and protection of the global atmosphere from ozone depletion and climate change. It emphasizes that international law is developed, implemented, and enforced very differently than domestic law. The need to build consensus among states with vastly different cultures and resources presents great challenges to international law. However, there also are similarities as both international and domestic regimes need to overcome scientific uncertainty and to cope with short-term economic pressures while promoting long-term environmental values. The growing role of NGOs in a sphere traditionally dominated by states also offers interesting parallels to the importance of citizen participation in U.S. environmental law. The difficult problem of enforcing compliance with international agreements is addressed in Section E.

## A.　*INTRODUCTION TO INTERNATIONAL AND GLOBAL ENVIRONMENTAL LAW*

Unlike domestic law, where common law, legislation, and constitutional provisions provide a relatively clear framework for the operation of environmental regulation, international law depends largely on negotiations and political relationships to define the rights and responsibilities of sovereign states. For the most part, international law operates with "little procedural hierarchy" and does not give any court or agency an "accepted primacy over another." M. Janis, An Introduction to International Law 8 (4th ed. 2003). Litigation and adjudication are rare. International law is "soft law" that is largely the product of international diplomacy and custom and whose enforcement depends less on "legal" sanctions than on "moral" suasion or fear of diplomatic retribution. Id. at 3.

## International and Global Environmental Law: A Pathfinder

*Treaties* to which the United States is a party are published by the U.S. State Department in United States Treaties and Other International Agreements (UST). Prior to the appearance of the bound volumes of UST, slips of such treaties were published by the U.S. Government Printing Office (GPO) as Treaties and Other International Acts (TIAS). Treaties can be shepardized through Shepard's United States Citations: Statutes. The GPO also issues an annual publication, Treaties in Force: A List of Treaties and Other International Agreements of the United States. The American Society for International Law (ASIL) operates a webpage at *https://www.asil.org/topics/environment-health-science-and-technology*.

Valuable *periodicals* include Transnational Environmental Law, published by Cambridge University Press, the Bureau of National Affairs' International Environment Reporter, and the American Society of International Law's American Journal of International Law. A comprehensive, up-to-date compendium of documents relevant to public and private international law (including treaties to which the United States is not a party) can be found in the American Society of International Law's bimonthly publication, ILM: International Legal Materials, which is accessible through LEXIS. The Worldwatch Institute publishes an electronic newsletter as does the UN Environment Programme, and the OECD Observer.

The IUCN Academy of Environmental Law, founded in 2003, is a global consortium of environmental law professors from more than 200 institutions in 60 countries. Its website, which is at *http://www.iucnael.org*, includes an extensive bibliography of "essential readings" in various aspects of environmental law. Worldwatch Institute publishes an annual State of the World report that reviews environmental trends, as does the World Resources Institute. The World Wildlife Fund's International Atlas of the Environment also provides valuable data on international environmental conditions. Greenpeace and the World Wildlife Fund are among the largest *environmental groups* active in the international arena. The Center for International Environmental Law (*www.ciel.org*) in Washington and the Foundation for International Environmental Law and Development in London specialize in this area. Papers presented at the annual colloquia of the IUCN Academy of Environmental Law are published annually by Edward Elgar Publishing, see *The Impact of Environmental Law* (2020).

The leading casebook on international environmental law is D. Hunter, J. Salzman & D. Zaelke, International Environmental Law and Policy (5th ed. 2015). It also features a Treaty Supplement, ISBN 9781609303976. The first casebook on comparative and global environmental law is Yang, Telesetsky, Harmon-Walker & Percival, Comparative and Global Environmental Law and Policy (1st ed. 2020). In 2019 the UN Environment Programme (UNEP) published Environmental Rule of Law: First Global Report, which can be downloaded at *https://www.unep.org/resources/assessment/environmental-rule-law-first-global-report*. A detailed history of EPA's global activities is Percival, EPA as a Catalyst for the Development of Global Environmental Law, 70 Case Western L. Rev. 1151 (2020). An invaluable resource on climate litigation is Columbia Law School's Sabin Center for Climate Change Law's Climate Litigation Tracker, online at *https://climate.law.columbia.edu/content/climate-change-litigation*.

Many valuable online sources for international environmental documents and information have become available, and new sources appear regularly. The IUCN, FAO, and UNEP jointly operate the "Ecolex" website that provides an electronic portal to international environmental law resources at *http://www.ecolex.org/*. The Climate Convention secretariat has a website with access to the most recent documents and information on the status of national ratification (*http://unfccc.int*). The UN Environment Programme has a web page (*http://www.unep.org*) and it publishes an annual Emissions Gap Report reviewing the difference between where greenhouse gas emissions are predicted to be in 2030 and where they should be to avoid the worst impact of climate change (*https://www.unep.org/emissions-gap-report-2020*). The Earth Negotiations Bulletin (ENB) (*https://enb.iisd.org*), produced by the International Institute for Sustainable Development, provides updated summaries of important international environmental negotiations. The American Society for International Law (ASIL) provides an electronic resource guide on international environmental law, located online at *www.asil.org/resource/env1.htm*.

Agreements between sovereign states are the clearest and most significant sources of international environmental law. International treaties or conventions are akin to contracts in that they derive their legal force from the consent of the parties. Bilateral agreements to address cross-boundary environmental problems long have been popular. For example, the Boundary Waters Treaty of 1909 between the United States and Canada served as the basis for the *Trail Smelter* decision, and the Migratory Bird Treaty of 1916 between the same nations gave rise to the Supreme Court decision in Missouri v. Holland, 252 U.S. 416 (1920). While President Theodore Roosevelt's attempt to convene a world conference on conservation of natural resources failed in 1909, multilateral agreements, like the Montreal Protocol on Substances that Deplete the Ozone Layer, have now become an important means for addressing global environmental problems. The United States is a party to approximately one-third of these agreements, many of which have influenced the practices of nonsignatories. J. Sebenius, Grafting a Winning Coalition, in Greenhouse Warming: Negotiating a Global Regime 69, 70-71 (1991). For example, the United States has announced that it will abide by the provisions of the Biosafety Protocol to the Convention on Biological Diversity despite its failure to ratify the convention.

In the absence of express agreements between sovereigns, international law also can be derived from customary practices observed by nations in the course of their international relations, which give rise to reliance interests. The domestic practices of most or all states also can be a source for deriving general principles of international law. The assumption is that rules observed by nearly all sovereigns are sufficiently fundamental to be deemed a component of international law. M. Janis, An Introduction to International Law 5-6 (4th ed. 2003).

Like domestic common law, international law has rarely dealt effectively with transboundary pollution problems. The *Trail Smelter* arbitration in 1935 relied on common law nuisance principles, recognized in *Missouri v. Illinois* and *Georgia v. Tennessee Copper*, see Chapter 2, to hold a Canadian smelter liable for damage caused in the United States. The decision, however, is virtually the only case involving adjudication of a transboundary pollution dispute, and its precedential value is limited because it was founded on unusual stipulations and a bilateral agreement establishing procedures for resolving such disputes. Developments in the Law—International Environment Law, 104 Harv. L. Rev. 1484, 1500-1501 (1991). See also the International Court of Justice decision on the Gabcikovo dam controversy, discussed below. In addition to the problem of proving causal injury that has plagued the common law, there is no systematic set of legal procedures governing most international pollution disputes. See Liability for Environmental Harm and Emerging Global Environmental Law, 25 Md. J. Int'l L. 37 (2010).

## 1.  *The UN Conferences*

Efforts to develop general principles for resolving transboundary pollution disputes and for combating other international environmental problems have proceeded in both regional and global intergovernmental organizations (IGOs). In 1972, the United Nations convened the first Conference on the Human Environment in Stockholm. The 113 UN member states who were represented at the conference approved the Stockholm Declaration on Human Environment, which outlined international environmental rights and responsibilities in strong, but highly general, language. Principle I of the Stockholm Declaration provides that "Man has the fundamental right to freedom, equality and adequate conditions of life, in an environment of quality that permits a life of dignity and well-being." The Declaration states that governments have a responsibility to protect and improve the environment for both present and future generations. Echoing the ancient *sic utere* principle, it recognizes that nations have "the sovereign right to exploit their own resources pursuant to their own environmental policies" and it declares that they also have "the responsibility to ensure that activities within their jurisdiction or control do not cause damage to the environment of other States or of areas beyond the limits of national jurisdiction." Stockholm Declaration on the Human Environment, Principle 21.

Although it left the development of more specific principles of international environmental law to future negotiation, the Stockholm Conference was a landmark event. It spurred many countries to enact their first domestic environmental laws, and it launched a process of international collaboration on environmental policy that led to creation of the United Nations Environment Programme (UNEP). International cooperation intensified after a follow-up conference in Nairobi, UNEP's headquarters, in 1982. The Nairobi Conference led to the creation of the World Commission on Environment and Development. In 1987, the Commission issued a report, entitled Our Common Future, which proposed that the UN develop an international convention outlining new environmental rights and responsibilities for all nations based on principles of sustainable development, *http://www.un-documents.net/our-common-future.pdf.* Noting that no effective mechanism exists for settling international environmental disputes through binding procedures, the Commission proposed that new procedures be established to facilitate resolution of disputes parties are unable to resolve through negotiation.

UNEP's activities, and the Stockholm and Nairobi conferences, helped to promote international environmental agreements that address specific environmental problems, such as the Montreal Protocol on Substances that Deplete the Ozone Layer. Petsonk, The Role of the United Nations Environment Programme (UNEP) in the Development of International Environmental Law, 5 Am. U. J. Int'l L. 351 (1990). The process initiated with the 1972 Stockholm Conference continued with the 1992 United Nations Conference on Environment and Development in Rio de Janeiro. Known as the Rio "Earth Summit," the meeting was an event of unprecedented size and complexity, an Olympics of international environmental negotiation larger than any previous international summit.

The 178 nations that attended the 1992 Earth Summit approved a declaration of environmental principles called the Rio Declaration and adopted treaties that addressed global warming and the loss of biological diversity, as well as a nonbinding declaration of forest conservation principles. The most ambitious document, Agenda 21, which was also nonbinding, addressed in 800 pages almost every aspect of environment and development.

The Rio Declaration is comprised mainly of broadly worded principles, but the fact that it was endorsed unanimously by the nations of the world establishes it as a foundation for the development of global environmental law. For assessments of the Rio Declaration, see Wirth, The Rio Declaration on Environment and Development; Two Steps Forward and One Back, or Vice-Versa?, 30 Ga. L. Rev.

599 (1995); M. Grubb et al., Earth Summit Agreements: A Guide and Assessment (1993); J. Nanda, International Environmental Law and Policy 103-131 (1994). Excerpts from the Rio Declaration appear below.

## United Nations Conference on Environment and Development, Declaration of Principles

(1992)

The Conference on Environment and Development, . . .

Recognizing the integral and interdependent nature of the earth, our home, Proclaims that:

Principle 1. Human beings are at the center of concerns for sustainable development. They are entitled to a healthy and productive life in harmony with nature.

Principle 2. States have, in accordance with the Charter of the United Nations and the principles of international law, the sovereign right to exploit their own resources pursuant to their own environmental and developmental policies, and the responsibility to insure that activities within their jurisdiction or control do not cause damage to the environment of other states or of areas beyond the limits of national jurisdiction.

Principle 3. The right to development must be fulfilled so as to equitably meet developmental and environmental needs of present and future generations.

Principle 4. In order to achieve sustainable development, environmental protection shall constitute an integral part of the development process and cannot be considered in isolation from it. . . .

Principle 7. States shall cooperate in a spirit of global partnership to conserve, protect and restore the health and integrity of the Earth's ecosystem. In view of the different contributions to global environmental degradation, states have common but differentiated responsibilities. The developed countries acknowledge the responsibility that they bear in the international pursuit of sustainable development in view of the pressures their societies place on the global environment and of the technologies and financial resources they command.

Principle 8. To achieve sustainable development and a higher quality of life for all people, states should reduce and eliminate unsustainable patterns of production and consumption and promote appropriate demographic policies. . . .

Principle 10. Environmental issues are best handled with the participation of all concerned citizens, at the relevant level. At the national level, each individual shall have appropriate access to information concerning the environment that is held by public authorities, including information on hazardous materials and activities in their communities, and the opportunity to participate in decision-making processes. States shall facilitate and encourage public awareness and participation by making information widely available. Effective access to judicial and administrative proceedings, including redress and remedy, shall be provided. . . .

Principle 12. States should cooperate to promote a supportive and open international economic system that would lead to economic growth and sustainable development in all countries, to better address the problems of environmental degradation. Trade policy measures for environmental purposes should not constitute a means of arbitrary or unjustifiable discrimination or a disguised restriction on international trade. Unilateral actions to deal with environmental challenges out-side the jurisdiction of the importing country should be avoided. Environmental measures addressing transboundary or global environmental problems should, as far as possible, be based on international consensus.

Principle 13. States shall develop national law regarding liability and compensation for the victims of pollution and other environmental damage. States shall also cooperate in an expeditious and more determined manner to develop further international law regarding liability and compensation for adverse effects of environmental damage caused by activities within their jurisdiction or control to areas beyond their jurisdiction.

Principle 14. States should effectively cooperate to discourage or prevent the relocation and transfer to other states of any activities and substances that cause severe environmental degradation or are found to be harmful to human health.

Principle 15. In order to protect the environment, the precautionary approach shall be widely applied to states according to their capabilities. Where there are threats of serious or irreversible damage, lack of full scientific certainty shall not be used as a reason for postponing cost-effective measures to prevent environmental degradation.

Principle 16. National authorities should endeavor to promote the internalization of environmental costs and the use of economic instruments, taking into account the approach that the polluter should, in principle, bear the cost of pollution, with due regard to the public interest and without distorting international trade and investment.

## NOTES AND QUESTIONS

1. What is the value of the UNCED Declaration? Does it articulate any new substantive principles of international environmental law? Does it create any new rights or provide any new remedies for addressing international environmental problems?

2. Compare Principle 2 of the Rio Declaration with Principle 21 of the 1972 Stockholm Declaration, which reads: "States have, in accordance with the Charter of the United Nations and the principles of international law, the sovereign right to exploit their own resources pursuant to their own environmental policies, and the responsibility to ensure that activities within their jurisdiction or control do not cause damage to the environment of other States or of areas beyond the limits of national jurisdiction." The two are identical except for insertion of the adjective "developmental" in the Rio Declaration. Does this reflect the durability and importance of this *sic utere* principle, or is it a sign that the nations of the world have not been able to translate it into more specific requirements?

3. How much guidance does the Declaration provide concerning how to balance the competing values implicated by environmental protection? Compare Principle 13 of the Rio Declaration with Principle 22 of the 1972 Stockholm Declaration, which reads: "States shall cooperate to develop further the international law regarding liability and compensation for the victims of pollution and other environmental damage caused by activities within the jurisdiction or control of such States to areas beyond their jurisdiction." Does the reference to cooperation "in an expeditious and more determined manner" in the Rio Declaration reflect frustration with the failure of international environmental law to develop more specific principles of liability and compensation in the intervening two decades? The International Law Commission has

been working for more than two decades to develop principles of international liability for transboundary environmental harm, see *http://legal.un.org/ilc/guide/9_10.shtml*, but it has yet to achieve global consensus on the issue.

4.  Tensions between developing countries and the industrialized world are reflected throughout the UNCED Declaration and have continued to be a central theme of negotiations on biodiversity, climate change, trade, and other international environmental issues. Principle 7 states that because of their "different contributions to global environmental degradation, states have common but differentiated responsibilities." This language was repeated in Article 3 of the Framework Convention on Climate Change and Article 10 of the Kyoto Protocol. Other portions of the Rio Declaration declare eradication of poverty to be "an indispensible requirement for sustainable development" and state that the needs of developing countries "shall be given special priority." Noting that environmental "[s]tandards applied by some countries may be inappropriate and of unwarranted economic and social cost to other countries," it recommends that further measures to address "transboundary or global environmental problems should, as far as possible, be based on an international consensus." Why is a provision on consensus-based approaches included in a set of principles on environment and development?

### The 2002 World Summit on Sustainable Development

The World Summit on Sustainable Development (WSSD) met in Johannesburg, South Africa, in late August and early September 2002 to provide a ten-year review of progress since the Rio Conference. More than 21,000 participants from 191 countries attended the summit. However, there were no new treaties or major agreements and only 82 heads of state attended (compared with over 100 in 1992). The choice of South Africa was viewed as politically important in emphasizing the need for greater emphasis on African development and the linkages between poverty alleviation and sustainable development.

In contrast with 1992, the focus was primarily on more effective implementation of existing agreements rather than negotiation of new ones, an inherently more difficult task. There was much greater participation of non-state actors with more than 100 CEOs attending. Numerous companies had exhibits making the case for their environmental concern and accomplishments, generating praise in some quarters and worries in others about growing corporate influence on the UN.

### The 2012 Rio+20 Conference

Twenty years after the 1992 "Rio Earth Summit," leaders from around the world gathered in Rio de Janeiro, Brazil in June 2012 at the UN Conference on Sustainable Development. During the "Rio+20" Conference, the leaders sought to delineate an agenda for future global environmental policy. The Conference approved an outcome document titled The Future We Want, *https://sustainabledevelopment.un.org/futurewewant.html*, a largely aspirational document that lacks binding legal commitments. Rather than developing new treaties, emphasis was placed on obtaining voluntary commitments for environmental progress from a broad array of public and private entities.

As this edition of the casebook goes to press, planning is underway for the next global environmental summit in 2022, the 50th anniversary of the 1972 Stockholm Conference. It is widely expected that the conference will be held in Stockholm.

## NOTES AND QUESTIONS

1. Has the summit model been exhausted by overuse and the added cost and complexity associated with increasing security concerns? Such events seem generally to have become less newsworthy in and of themselves, and the availability of the Internet arguably reduces the need for bringing people together for information sharing. On the other hand, the periodic pressure to report on progress and debate emerging trends is difficult to replicate other than through an international summit.

2. Those concerned with developing more effective institutions of global environmental governance are debating several issues. These include: How and to what extent should existing institutions of environmental governance be restructured or replaced? How can coordination between them be improved? Should a World Environmental Organization, on a par with the WTO, be created, or would more decentralized approaches, built on emerging models of collaborative governance, offer more promise of success? Should new patterns of international governance and political authority be developed, and, if so, how can they be reconciled with traditional notions of state sovereignty? Can truly enforceable international environmental obligations be created? International human rights law has evolved to alter older concepts of state sovereignty; how should international environmental law evolve?

3. Gus Speth, a founder of the Natural Resources Defense Council, Administrator of the UN Development Programme, and former Dean of the Yale School of Forestry and Environmental Studies, argues that a legalistic approach to global environmental problems was understandable, but with few exceptions has proven to be woefully inadequate. He cites numerous deficiencies: The UN agencies charged with oversight of these issues "are among the weakest multilateral organizations"; the negotiation processes "give maximum leverage to any country with an interest in protecting the status quo"; the diplomats in international negotiations lack "a shared political culture" that might facilitate agreement; and discussions are typically unable to overcome perceptions of "environment versus economy" and "North versus South." The UN conferences were, in his view, part of this faulty paradigm, producing a global agenda that "emerged and moved forward thanks primarily to a relatively small international leadership community" and produced outcomes "forged top-down at the international level." Consequently, he concludes, these processes "underscore the weak political base on which our concern for the global environment has rested." Speth concludes that "[i]n light of these barriers to progress, it is a wonder that any progress was made." James Gustave Speth, Red Sky at Morning (2004). If a legal approach has lost its way, what is the alternative? We return to this question at the end of the chapter.

## 2.   *International Adjudication of Environmental Disputes*

Most international disputes that are adjudicated are decided by domestic, rather than international, courts. M. Janis, An Introduction to International Law 7 (2003). While some international tribunals have been established (e.g., the International Court of Justice, the European Court of Justice, and the European Court of Human Rights), sovereign states are reluctant to accede legal responsibility to a foreign tribunal. Proposals to create an international body with authority to enforce standards of environmental conduct have been opposed by nations fearful of encroachments on their sovereignty. Arrangements for adjudicating transboundary environmental disputes through new regional legal structures eventually may prove more effective, although progress toward a strong European environmental program has so far been mixed. See Visch, Implementation and Enforcement of EC Environmental Law, 7 Geo. Int'l Envtl. L. Rev. 377 (1995); Helfer & Slaughter, Toward a Theory of Effective Supranational Adjudication, 107 Yale L.J. 273 (1997).

In 1997, the International Court of Justice (ICJ) released a rare judgment on an environmental dispute. While under Soviet domination, Hungary and Czechoslovakia had been jointly building a dam across the Danube River, which marks the border between the two countries, pursuant to a 1977 treaty. Following the collapse of the Soviet Union and its satellite communist governments, Hungary withdrew from the massive project, citing the environmental damage it would cause. On January 1, 1993, Czechoslovakia split into the Czech Republic and Slovakia. After Slovakia continued to pursue the project, Hungary sought relief in the ICJ. The court's decision, which found fault with both parties and urged further negotiations to resolve the dispute, discussed the effect of new international environmental norms.

## International Court of Justice Case Concerning the Gabcíkovo-Nagymaros Project (Hungary/Slovakia)

25 September 1997

Finally, the Court will address Hungary's claim that it was entitled to terminate the 1977 Treaty because new requirements of international law for the protection of the environment precluded performance of the Treaty.

Neither of the Parties contended that new peremptory norms of environmental law had emerged since the conclusion of the 1977 Treaty, and the Court will consequently not be required to examine the scope of Article 64 of the Vienna Convention on the Law of Treaties. On the other hand, the Court wishes to point out that newly developed norms of environmental law are relevant for the implementation of the Treaty and that the parties could, by agreement, incorporate them through the application of Articles 15, 19 and 20 of the Treaty. These articles do not contain specific obligations of performance but require the parties, in carrying out their obligations to ensure that the quality of water in the Danube is not impaired and that nature is protected, to take new environmental norms into consideration when agreeing upon the means to be specified in the Joint Contractual Plan.

By inserting these evolving provisions in the Treaty, the parties recognized the potential necessity to adapt the Project. Consequently, the Treaty is not static, and is open to adapt to emerging norms of international law. By means of Articles 15 and 19, new environmental norms can be incorporated in the Joint Contractual Plan.

The responsibility to do this was a joint responsibility. The obligations contained in Articles 15, 19 and 20 are, by definition, general and have to be transformed into specific obligations of performance through a process of consultation and negotiation. Their implementation thus requires a mutual willingness to discuss in good faith actual and potential environmental risks.

It is all the more important to do this because as the Court recalled in its Advisory Opinion on the *Legality of the Threat or Use of Nuclear Weapons*, "the environment is not an abstraction but represents the living space, the quality of life and the very health of human beings, including generations unborn" (I.C.J. Reports 1996, para. 29).

The awareness of the vulnerability of the environment and the recognition that environmental risks have to be assessed on a continuous basis have become much stronger in the years since the Treaty's conclusion. These new concerns have enhanced the relevance of Articles 15, 19 and 20.

The Court recognizes that both Parties agree on the need to take environmental concerns seriously and to take the required precautionary measures, but they fundamentally disagree on the consequences this has for the joint Project. In such a case, third-party involvement may be helpful and instrumental in finding a solution, provided each of the Parties is flexible in its position. . . .

It is clear that the Project's impact upon, and its implications for, the environment are of necessity a key issue. The numerous scientific reports which have been presented to the Court by the Parties—even if their conclusions are often contradictory—provide abundant evidence that this impact and these implications are considerable.

In order to evaluate the environmental risks, current standards must be taken into consideration. This is not only allowed by the wording of Articles 15 and 19, but even prescribed, to the extent that these articles impose a continuing—and thus necessarily evolving—obligation on the parties to maintain the quality of the water of the Danube and to protect nature.

The Court is mindful that, in the field of environmental protection, vigilance and prevention are required on account of the often irreversible character of damage to the environment and of the limitations inherent in the very mechanism of reparation of this type of damage.

Throughout the ages, mankind has, for economic and other reasons, constantly interfered with nature. In the past, this was often done without consideration of the effects upon the environment. Owing to new scientific insights and to a growing awareness of the risks for mankind—for present and future generations—of pursuit of such interventions at an unconsidered and unabated pace, new norms and standards have been developed, set forth in a great number of instruments during the last two decades. Such new norms have to be taken into consideration, and such new standards given proper weight, not only when States contemplate new activities but also when continuing with activities begun in the past. This need to reconcile economic development with protection of the environment is aptly expressed in the concept of sustainable development.

For the purposes of the present case, this means that the Parties together should look afresh at the effects on the environment of the operation of the Gabcíkovo power plant. In particular they must find a satisfactory solution for the volume of water to be released into the old bed of the Danube and into the side-arms on both sides of the river.

## NOTES AND QUESTIONS

1. The International Court of Justice, created by the UN Charter in 1945, is the principal legal organ of the United Nations. The court, which is located at

the Peace Palace in The Hague, Netherlands, is composed of 15 judges elected for 9-year terms by the UN's General Assembly and the Security Council. Its purpose is to settle legal disputes submitted to it by states and to give advisory opinions on legal questions submitted to it by UN agencies. While its judgments are binding and cannot be appealed by the parties, its jurisdiction is dependent on both parties to a dispute agreeing to accept its jurisdiction. In 1993, the ICJ established a Chamber for Environmental Matters, but it was disbanded in 2006 because no state ever used it. The UN Convention on the Law of the Sea (UNCLOS) provides for mandatory dispute resolution through the appointment of an arbitral panel under Annex VII of UNCLOS.

2. The ICJ's judgment found that the 1977 Treaty between Slovakia and Hungary was still in force, and it called on both states to negotiate in good faith to ensure the achievement of the treaty's objectives. Because it found some fault on both sides while failing to direct specifically what must be done to resolve the dispute, the decision by the ICJ in this case was widely viewed as not resolving the controversy. A year after the decision, Slovakia asked the ICJ for an additional judgment in the case, alleging that Hungary was unwilling to implement the decision. The states later resumed negotiations, but the case was not settled until June 2017. Does this illustrate that international diplomacy remains more important than international "law" as a vehicle for resolving disputes between nations?

3. Notice that the court mentions the principle of "sustainable development" as a concept for reconciling "economic development with protection of the environment." A separate opinion by ICJ Vice-President Weeramantry reviewed the historical development of the concept of "sustainable development" and its endorsement in various international instruments including the Convention of Biological Diversity. Judge Weeramantry concluded that "sustainable development" had become part of customary international law with "normative value" crucial to the determination of the case. He noted that: "This case offers a unique opportunity for the application of [sustainable development], for it arises from a Treaty which had development as its objective, and has been brought to a standstill over arguments concerning environmental considerations." Yet Judge Weeramantry himself failed to give any indication of how application of the "sustainable development" principle to the facts of the dispute would resolve it.

4. In 2005, the government of Uruguay authorized Finnish and Spanish companies to build two of the world's largest paper mills along the banks of the Uruguay River, which forms the country's international border with Argentina. The mills together represented an investment of $1.75 billion, the largest in Uruguay's history. The Spanish company quickly canceled its project after non-governmental organizations filed lawsuits in both countries and complaints with the International Finance Corporation and the Inter-American Commission on Human Rights. After Botnia, the Finnish company, began construction of its paper mill, the government of Argentina asked the International Court of Justice to halt the project. While denying Argentina's request for provisional measures, the ICJ agreed to hear the merits of the dispute. In April 2010, the ICJ ruled that Uruguay had breached its procedural obligation under a 1975 treaty between the two countries by failing to consult with Argentina before issuing initial environmental approvals for construction of the paper mill. The treaty established a joint Administrative Commission

of the River that should have been used as the vehicle for consultation, according to the ICJ. Significantly, the court ruled that environmental impact assessment was now so widely accepted that it had become a requirement of international environmental law when a proposed activity may have a significant transboundary impact. But it found that Uruguay had not breached this obligation and that Argentina had failed to show that effluent from the mill had harmed the aquatic environment.

5. In 2014, the ICJ issued a judgment in a case brought by Australia against Japan for whaling in Antarctic waters, allegedly in violation of the International Convention for the Regulation of Whaling. ICJ, Whaling in the Antarctic (Mar. 31, 2014), *http://www.icj-cij.org/public/files/case-related/148/148-20140331-JUD-01-00-EN.pdf*. In 1982, the International Whaling Commission (IWC) imposed a moratorium on commercial whaling with exceptions for "aboriginal subsistence whaling" and whaling "for purposes of scientific research." Australia, supported by New Zealand as an intervenor, argued that Japan's whaling in Antarctic waters was so broad in scope that it did not qualify as whaling for research purposes. The ICJ found that while Japan conducted some activities that involved scientific research on whales, the special permits it issued for the taking of whales were not "for purposes of scientific research." After suspending its Antarctic whaling program for a year, Japan launched a new program of whaling in 2016 that it again claimed was "for purposes of scientific research." The Japanese government also announced that it no longer will agree to the ICJ adjudicating "any dispute arising out of, concerning, or relating to research on, or conservation, management or exploitation of, living resources of the sea." In January 2019 Japan announced that it was withdrawing from the IWC and resuming commercial whaling, but only within its coastal waters.

6. Many countries throughout the world are creating specialized environmental courts or tribunals (ECTs) to resolve environmental disputes. Rock and Kitty Pring, who conducted a comprehensive study of this phenomenon, found in 2009 that there were more than 350 ECTs in 41 countries. George (Rock) Pring and Catherine (Kitty) Pring, Greening Justice: Creating and Improving Environmental Courts and Tribunals (2009), *http://www.law.du.edu/ect-study*. In an update to their study published by the UN Environment Programme in 2016, the Prings reported that the number of ECTs had grown to more than 1,200 ECTs in 44 countries. George (Rock) Pring and Catherine (Kitty) Pring, Environmental Courts & Tribunals: A Guide for Policymakers (2016), *http://wedocs.unep.org/bitstream/handle/20.500.11822/10001/environmental-courts-tribunals.pdf?sequence=1&isAllowed=y*. The important role the judiciary has played in the development and implementation of environmental law around the world is reviewed in Robert V. Percival, The Greening of the Global Judiciary, 32 J. Land Use & Envtl. L. 333 (2017).

## B. PROTECTION OF THE GLOBAL ATMOSPHERE

The discovery that air pollutants are causing long-term, and potentially irreversible, damage to the global atmosphere has been a powerful catalyst for the development of international environmental law. Unlike transboundary pollution that primarily affects countries downwind or downriver, pollution of the Earth's atmosphere threatens serious damage to the entire planet. Mounting evidence of damage to this global commons has forced the countries of the world to join together in unprecedented efforts to develop international environmental controls.

Ozone depletion and climate change are the two most significant environmental problems caused on a global scale by atmospheric pollution. Many believed that the global community's highly successful response to the ozone depletion problem would serve as a model for dealing with climate change. Signed in 1985, the Vienna Convention for Protection of the Ozone Layer created a framework for negotiations that in 1987 produced the Montreal Protocol on Substances that Deplete the Ozone Layer. The Montreal Protocol's innovative approach for implementing global, technology-forcing regulation in the face of widely disparate national interests and considerable scientific and technological uncertainty made it a promising model for responding to other global problems, such as climate change.

At the Rio Earth Summit in 1992, the nations of the world launched the UN Framework Convention on Climate Change (UNFCC). This established a process that in 1997 generated the Kyoto Protocol to the convention, a global agreement for reducing greenhouse gas (GHG) emissions in developed countries. But the climate change problem has proved to be far more challenging than ozone depletion. It was not until December 2015 that the Paris Agreement established a new, global approach for coordinating national efforts to control GHG emissions.

## 1.  Ozone Depletion

High in the Earth's stratosphere is a layer of ozone, an unstable compound of three oxygen atoms, that is essential to the health of the planet. Because ozone absorbs certain wavelengths of ultraviolet radiation, it protects the Earth from excessive radiation that otherwise would cause millions of skin cancer deaths, widespread blindness, and other serious health problems, as well as severe damage to plants and animals.

### A.  Scientific Warnings

In 1974, two University of Michigan scientists, Richard S. Stolarsky and Ralph J. Cicerone, who were under contract with NASA to examine the agency's environmental impact statement for the space shuttle, concluded that a single chlorine atom released in the stratosphere could eliminate tens of thousands of ozone molecules. Stephen O. Andersen & K. Madhava Sarma, Protecting the Ozone Layer: The United Nations History 8 (2002). While space shuttle flights would be infrequent enough to be dismissed as a significant source of chlorine in the planet's stratosphere, two chemists from the University of California, Sherwood Rowland and Mario Molina, found a far more significant source of chlorine — chlorofluorocarbons (CFCs). In the June 24, 1974 issue of Nature, they published a paper hypothesizing that when CFCs reach the stratosphere, exposure to ultraviolet radiation would cause them to decompose and release chlorine atoms, setting off a chain reaction in which a single chlorine atom could destroy 100,000 molecules of ozone. At the time, more than 1 million tons of CFCs, once hailed as a miracle of modern science, were released into the atmosphere each year. CFCs were used in a wide variety of industrial applications, including aerosol propellants, foam blowing, air conditioning, and solvents. They were discovered in the 1920s by chemist Thomas Midgley, the inventor of tetraethyl lead, but only used widely beginning in the 1950s. Ironically, much of their attraction stemmed from their lack of other environmental risks—they are not toxic or flammable, and they have excellent insulating, cooling, and cleaning properties. Weisskopf, CFCs: Rise and Fall of Chemical "Miracle," Wash. Post, Apr. 10, 1988, at A1.

The remarkable stability of CFCs allows them to remain in the atmosphere for up to a century or more, unlike conventional air pollutants, which are broken down in a period of hours or days. Thus, Rowland and Molina hypothesized that CFCs would reach the upper atmosphere, where they would release chlorine. The chlorine would then act as a catalyst, converting ozone $(O_3)$ to oxygen, destroying the Earth's protective ozone shield.

In the mid-1970s, the United States accounted for almost one-half of global CFC use, the majority of it used as propellants for aerosol sprays. As publicity focused on potential harm to the ozone layer, American consumers stopped buying aerosol sprays (including those without CFCs); in less than two years the market for products with such sprays dropped by two-thirds without any government regulation. R. Benedick, Ozone Diplomacy: New Directions in Safeguarding the Planet 31 (1991). The United States banned most aerosol propellant uses of CFCs in 1978, but few other nations followed suit.

Pressure for companies in the United States to develop alternatives to CFCs continued to build following a further warning of the threat to the ozone layer from the National Academy of Sciences in 1979. But this pressure evaporated in the early 1980s after equivocal research results and the Reagan administration's deregulation campaign resulted in the announcement that the United States would no longer support international controls. Convinced that further regulation was unlikely, U.S. companies shelved research to develop CFC substitutes. For a discussion of whether the producers of CFCs should be held liable for their failure to swiftly reduce production, see Lisa Elges, Stratospheric Ozone Damage and Legal Liability (2017).

In 1983, after William Ruckelshaus had succeeded Anne Gorsuch Burford as EPA administrator, the United States reversed its position and supported international controls. Not surprisingly, the United States advocated a policy based on what it had already done, that is, a worldwide ban on aerosol propellant uses of CFCs. The European governments, in turn, advocated a ban on construction of new capacity—a policy in effect in the European Community and without adverse economic consequences due to substantial excess CFC production capacity there. Leaders of European industry and government "felt that the Americans had been panicked into 'over-hasty measures.'..." R. Benedick, Ozone Diplomacy 33 (1991). Finding agreement on regulation impossible, the parties in March 1985 approved the Vienna Convention to Protect the Ozone Layer, which established a framework to govern future scientific cooperation and negotiations.

While a major international research effort under the auspices of the World Meteorological Organization and UNEP was underway, scientists with the British Antarctic Survey published startling findings in May 1985. Based on measurements of springtime levels of ozone in the stratosphere over Halley Bay, Antarctica, they found that seasonal ozone loss had sharply accelerated to the point where a "hole" of greatly diminished ozone levels in the stratosphere had grown to cover an area the size of the United States. These findings were so astonishing that the scientists had delayed publication of them for three years while double-checking their accuracy. Because this discovery indicated that the ozone layer was in far greater jeopardy than previously thought, it spurred more detailed investigations and intensified international negotiations. In 1987, the Airborne Antarctic Ozone Experiment, using high-altitude airplanes, ground monitors, and satellites, launched studies that eventually found even greater ozone loss and linked it to the presence of human-made chemicals in the stratosphere. See CFCs and Stratospheric Ozone, 19 Ambio (Oct. 1990) (special issue).

## B.   The Montreal Protocol

Even before international research could confirm the role of CFCs in ozone depletion, the discovery of the ozone "hole" had demonstrated the vulnerability of the ozone layer. This contributed to a heightened sense of urgency that spurred international negotiations based on the framework established by the Vienna Convention. Four negotiating sessions, beginning in Geneva in December 1986, culminated in the signing of the Montreal Protocol on Substances that Deplete the Ozone Layer on September 16, 1987. The Protocol called for a freeze on production and consumption of CFCs and halons at 1986 levels, followed by a 50 percent reduction in CFC use by industrialized countries over a ten-year period. While developing countries were allowed to increase CFC consumption for ten years, trade restrictions were imposed on imports to, and exports from, nonparties to the Protocol.

On December 21, 1987, President Reagan transmitted the Montreal Protocol to the U.S. Senate for ratification. Calling it a "historic agreement," he noted that the United States "played a leading role in the negotiation of the Protocol" and he encouraged early ratification by the Senate to "encourage similar action by other nations whose participation is also essential." On March 14, 1988, the U.S. Senate ratified the Montreal Protocol by a vote of 83-0.

The Protocol represented a remarkable diplomatic achievement given the obstacles to agreement on international environmental controls. First, the science of ozone depletion was highly uncertain throughout the entire negotiation process. S. Roan, The Ozone Crisis (1989). Year-to-year measurements of global ozone had shown no statistically significant changes. Estimates of eventual ozone loss—anticipated to occur decades later—actually had *declined* from about 18 percent in 1979 to only 3 percent in 1983. Despite the discovery of the ozone "hole," scientists were unable to link it precisely to CFCs until after the Protocol was completed (some environmentalists even had sought to delay negotiations in hopes that better evidence would become available). R. Benedick, Ozone Diplomacy 9-20 (1991).

To further challenge negotiators, CFCs had high economic value and powerful advocates in industry who argued that reasonable substitutes were unavailable for many applications. Public concern was evident in the United States, but some Europeans were skeptical of U.S. motives. At the outset of the negotiations, the United States, which already had taken unilateral action against aerosols, was virtually the only major country actively seeking CFC reductions. Moreover, developing countries maintained that it would be unfair to restrict their access to a technology that had contributed to development of the industrialized world. Finally, the concept of damage to the ozone layer was not easily translated into identifiable risks except for skin cancer, a relatively manageable disease that afflicts only a subset of the population. Id.; Mathews, Introduction and Overview, in Greenhouse Warming: Negotiating a Global Regime (J. Mathews ed., 1991).

Gus Speth cites four factors arguably most responsible for the successful conclusion of the Montreal Protocol:

- The problem was successfully defined in the public mind in terms of cancer and other serious public health threats;
- the proponents succeeded in making the "precautionary principle" the decision rule, as opposed to waiting for certainty;
- the issue was given a major boost by the discovery of the ozone hole, which effectively focused media and public attention; and
- the NGOs and other advocates of regulation were more effectively organized and out-hustled the opposition.

Speth at 182, citing Grundmann, The Strange Success of the Montreal Protocol, 10 Int'l Envtl. Aff. 197 (1998).

Two issues in the evolution of the Protocol merit particular attention:

**1. The Role of Science.** Richard Benedick does not attribute the success of the negotiations to the discovery of the ozone hole because its cause had not been established when the Protocol was signed. Others disagree, arguing that the ozone hole led to media and public interest that in turn influenced political perceptions. Benedick notes that close collaboration and communication between scientists and government officials played an important role in overcoming obstacles to agreement at several stages of the negotiations. R. Benedick, Ozone Diplomacy 78-79 (1991). Scientists played an important role not only in the formulation of national policy but also as an informal transnational network outside government control.

**2. Technology Forcing and the Role of Industry.** The response of industry to the Protocol is remarkable as an example of technology forcing. As late as the spring of 1986, CFC producers were aggressively insisting that substitutes were not feasible and that regulation would be ruinous for many industries. Miller, Cleaning the Air While Filling Corporate Coffers: Technology Forcing and Economic Growth, 1990 N.Y.U. Ann. Survey Am. L. 69 (1991). After the Protocol was signed, substitutes for CFCs were announced at an astonishing rate, and their projected costs declined steadily. By mid-1989, industry accepted the feasibility of a complete phaseout of CFCs, and EPA estimated that a total phaseout would cost less than it had projected for a 50 percent reduction only two years earlier. While chemical companies produced substitutes, about half the market went to not-in-kind alternatives or process changes, rather than proprietary chemicals. Some CFC substitutes were found to offer superior performance. Pollack, Moving Fast to Protect the Ozone Layer, N.Y. Times, May 15, 1991, at D1. OTA, Environmental Policy Tools: A User's Guide (1995); Barrett, Montreal v. Kyoto: International Cooperation and the Global Environment, in Global Public Goods 192-219 (I. Kaul, I. Grunberg & M. Stern eds., 1999).

## C.   Accelerating the Phaseout

In March 1988, the Ozone Trends Panel, a team of more than 100 scientists from 10 countries, released the results of 16 months of research using newly developed methodology to analyze all previous measurements of the ozone layer. The Panel's alarming findings showed that significant ozone depletion already had occurred over heavily populated areas of the northern hemisphere, that a "large, sudden, and unexpected" decline in ozone levels had occurred over Antarctica, and that an ozone "hole" might soon be found over the Arctic and mid-latitudes of the northern hemisphere. The Panel was able to conclusively link CFCs and halons to ozone depletion for the first time. Kerr, Stratospheric Ozone Is Decreasing, 239 Science 1489 (1988).

In June 1990, under the Protocol review provisions described by Benedick, the parties met in London to consider measures to strengthen the Protocol. There were two priorities: agreement on faster, more comprehensive emission reductions, and participation from the major developing nations to avoid increased use by nonparties. The latter was problematic as the major developing nations, especially India and China, were quick to point out that roughly 90 percent of the world's CFCs had been used by nations with less than a quarter of the world's population.

Negotiating a phaseout of CFCs proved easier than working out an agreement with developing countries. The European Community, now fully converted, sought the most rapid timetable for emission reductions. The final agreement provided for the total elimination of CFC production and use by 2000, with scheduled interim reductions by 1993, 1995, and 1997. Separate reduction schedules were established for halons and other ozone-depleting chemicals. Developing countries were again extended an additional ten-year grace period and the possibility of continued use of halons if "necessary to satisfy essential uses for which no adequate alternatives are available." Restrictions on hydrochlorofluorocarbons (HCFCs), chemicals with about .02 of the ozone-depleting potential of CFCs due to shorter atmospheric lifetimes, were debated but left for future consideration. See generally Bryk, The Montreal Protocol and Recent Development to Protect the Ozone Layer, 15 Harv. Envtl. L. Rev. 275 (1991).

The participation of developing nations quickly became primarily a question of money. The parties agreed to establish a multilateral fund with an initial commitment of $240 million. The fund is managed by a secretariat and governed by a 14-nation council equally divided between donors and recipient nations. The processing of applications, design of projects, and distribution of funds is handled primarily by the World Bank and UN Development Programme. See the website of the Multilateral Fund for the Implementation of the Montreal Protocol at *www. multilateralfund.org.*

As evidence accumulated that ozone depletion had progressed much further than expected, concern grew that even the accelerated phaseout agreed to in London might be inadequate. The European Community responded by further accelerating its own phaseout of CFCs, shortening the deadline by three years to 1997. EPA bested the EC's new timetable by a year when it announced in February 1992 that it would require the phaseout to be completed in the United States by 1996. This continued acceleration of the phaseout was driven largely by two factors: scientific data revealing even greater damage to the ozone layer, and the discovery that the phaseout would be far less costly than initially anticipated.

U.S. production of ozone-depleting substances has varied over time—surging until environmental concerns were raised in the mid-1970s, falling sharply, and then increasing again until the Montreal Protocol's restrictions took effect. Their ultimate phasedown was accomplished through use of a market-based approach to regulation. Rather than attempting to determine what emissions reductions each of the five U.S. producers of CFCs were capable of achieving, EPA gave each company tradeable permits for CFC production based on its 1986 production level. As the annual supply of permits declined to comply with the Protocol, companies could ensure that reductions were achieved in the most efficient manner by buying and selling the diminishing pool of CFC production rights.

To create further incentives for finding substitutes for ozone-depleting compounds, Congress imposed an escalating tax on such substances that in 1990 more than doubled, and in 1995 more than tripled, the pre-regulation price of CFCs. The powerful price signal created by this tax helped reduce dramatically consumption of ozone-depleting compounds. Indeed, CFC production fell so much faster than anticipated that the tax raised only half of the $6 billion it had been expected to raise between 1990 and the end of 1995.

The Montreal Protocol is now widely recognized as the most effective international environmental treaty. It became the first international treaty to be ratified by all 197 UN members, and it quickly entered into force in 1989. It has reduced global production of CFCs and other ozone-depleting substances by 98 percent. The success of the Montreal Protocol in phasing out substances that deplete the ozone layer is reflected in Figure 11.1.

**Figure 11.1   Consumption of All Ozone-Depleting Substances (ODSs) and CFCs, 1986–2006 (Thousands of Metric Tons of Ozone-Depleting Potential)**

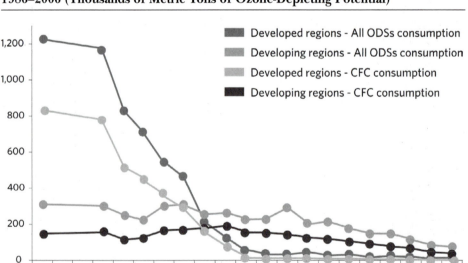

*Source:* United Nations, The Millennium Development Goals Report 24 (2008).

## NOTES AND QUESTIONS

1. What lessons can be learned from the acceleration of the Montreal Protocol's phaseout? A World Resources Institute review of the experience suggests some themes: (1) it is crucial to establish environmental goals in a manner that permits adjustments to reflect new scientific information; (2) market-based approaches to regulation can help government and industry implement regulatory policy with greater flexibility and at lower cost; (3) industries "can find ways to innovate and gain competitive advantages in response to environmental challenges." Cook, Marking a Milestone in Ozone Protection: Learning from the CFC Phase-Out 12-13 (1996). Jessica Mathews observes that "CFCs seemed irreplaceable only because there had never been a reason to look for substitutes." She notes that "[o]nce there was a need to replace them, a modest economic incentive (in this case a tax) and enough time to develop alternatives, innovation bloomed." Mathews, Clean Sweeps: Two Success Stories for the Environment, Wash. Post, Dec. 18, 1995, at A23.

2. Retail prices of CFCs skyrocketed with regulation and continuing demand, particularly for car air conditioners in all models prior to 1993. The federal tax created powerful incentives to develop substitutes, but it also made non-compliance more profitable. A large black market developed as CFCs purchased abroad, sometimes falsely labeled recycled, were smuggled into the United States to avoid the $5.35 per pound federal tax. Halpert, Freon Smugglers Find Big Market, N.Y Times, Apr. 30, 1995, at A1; "Focus Report," Global Envtl. Change Rep., Mar. 12, 1999, at 1. As production of CFCs in the developing countries has been gradually eliminated—a process well along by 2005—this problem has diminished.

3. The nineteenth meeting of the Parties in Montreal in September 2007 was a celebration of the unique success of the Montreal Protocol during its first 20 years. The Protocol not only has largely achieved its goals of eliminating the primary sources of ozone depletion, but in the process it also has done far more to reduce emissions of greenhouse gases than the Kyoto Protocol because CFCs and other ozone-depleting substances are mostly also GHGs. During its first 20 years, the Protocol had avoided emissions equivalent to 135 billion tons of $CO_2$ and delayed climate forcing by up to 12 years. UNEP, OzonAction, Special Issue Dedicated to HCFC Phaseout: Convenient Opportunity to Safeguard the Ozone Layer and Climate (Sept. 2008).

4. Subsequent meetings of the parties focused on linking the phaseout of ozone-depleting substances with the reduction of GHGs. Early substitutes for CFCs were sometimes greenhouse gases like hydrochlorofluorocarbons (HCFCs) and hydrofluorocarbons (HFCs). The parties to the Montreal Protocol then turned to ensuring that transition substitutes are climate friendly as well as non-ozone depleting—a sensible if unusual degree of coordination between two different legal agreements. On October 15, 2016, the 197 parties to the Montreal Protocol, meeting in Kigali, Rwanda at their twenty-eighth meeting, adopted far-reaching measures to phase out hydrofluorocarbons on a global basis. While HFCs do not survive in the atmosphere for as long as CFCs do, they are more than 11 times more potent a greenhouse gas than CFCs. Thus, it is estimated that the Kigali Amendment alone may slow global warming by as much as 0.5 degrees Celsius. Under the Kigali Amendment, rich and developed countries, like the United States and the UK, and the

EU, beginning in 2019, will phase down HFCs to 15 percent of 2012 levels by 2036. Emerging economies like China, Brazil, and some African countries will, beginning in 2024, phase down to 20 percent of 2021 levels by 2045. Developing countries and countries with some of the hottest climates, including Saudi Arabia, India, Pakistan, and Iran will, beginning in 2028, reduce HFC use to 15 percent of 2024-2026 levels by 2047. India obtained a more lenient phasedown schedule because it currently accounts for only 3 percent of global HFC consumption, compared to the United States with a 37 percent share and China with 25 percent. Major U.S. companies that manufacture air conditioners and refrigerators strongly supported the Kigali Amendment, noting that alternatives to HFCs are practical and affordable.

5. Congress had added Title VI to the Clean Air Act in the 1990 Amendments, which directs EPA to require the phaseout of ozone-depleting substances. Section 612 of the Act provides that ozone-depleting substances "[t]o the maximum extent practicable . . . shall be replaced by chemicals, product substitutes, or alternative manufacturing processes that reduce overall risks to human health and the environment." Although companies initially were permitted to replace CFCs and other ozone-depleting substances with HFCs, in 2015 EPA moved HFCs to the prohibited list. 80 Fed. Reg. 42,870 (2015). In Mexichem Fluor, Inc. v. EPA, 866 F.3d 451 (D.C. Cir. 2017), a divided panel of the D.C. Circuit held that, although EPA can move HFCs to the prohibited list because they are GHGs, EPA cannot require companies who previously replaced ozone-depleting chemicals with HFCs to discontinue their use under section 612 of the Clean Air Act. This problem was solved by legislation buried in the more than 5,000-page-long Consolidated Appropriations Act of 2021, P.L. 116-260, which President Trump signed into law on December 27, 2020. Section 103 of Division S of this legislation is known as the American Innovation and Manufacturing (AIM) Act. Approved as part of a bipartisan deal, the legislation authorizes EPA to require an 85 percent reduction in HFC production and use over the next 15 years consistent with the Kigali Amendment. On May 3, 2021, EPA announced a proposed rule to implement this new authority. The AIM legislation and the Kigali Amendment have such strong support from major U.S. companies that produce HFC-free refrigerant products that President Biden announced in January 2021 that he will submit the Kigali Amendment to the U.S. Senate for ratification.

### 2.   *Global Climate Change*

As a result of an unprecedented buildup of carbon dioxide and other greenhouse gases in the atmosphere, the Earth is experiencing severe global climate change. In the December 2015 Paris Climate Agreement the nations of the world established a goal of limiting global warming to well below 2 degrees Celsius (3.6 degrees Fahrenheit) above pre-industrial levels, with an ambition of limiting it to 1.5 degrees Celsius (2.7 degrees Fahrenheit). Despite a dip in GHG emissions due to the global pandemic, UNEP reports that the world is headed for a temperature rise in excess of 3 degrees Celsius (5.4 degrees Fahrenheit) this century. This already is causing widespread disruption of the Earth's ecosystems, significant sea level rise and coastal flooding, increased drought, and vast environmental and economic damage.

## A. Science and the "Greenhouse Effect"

The "greenhouse effect" at the root of global warming is not a new concept. It actually was hypothesized by chemists in the early nineteenth century. Now it has become a significant part of the evolution of climate and life on Earth. Carbon dioxide ($CO_2$) is known to have been present in the atmosphere at a concentration of about 280 ppm in the mid-eighteenth century prior to the Industrial Revolution. By 1997, its concentration had increased by about 30 percent to approximately 360 ppm. Roughly half of that increase occurred after 1970. Council on Environmental Quality, Environmental Quality—1997 Report 194 (1999). The atmospheric building of greenhouse gases (GHGs) has continued rapidly since then. On May 10, 2013, scientists discovered that concentrations of $CO_2$ in the atmosphere had passed 400 ppm for the first time in recorded history. This discovery was made by scientists at Hawaii's Mauna Loa observatory. The over 400 ppm level was a dramatic increase from the level of 316 ppm measured at Mauna Loa in 1958. At the dawn of the Industrial Revolution in the 1700s, it is estimated that global $CO_2$ levels were approximately 260 ppm. The last time levels of $CO_2$ were above 400 ppm is believed to have been in the Pliocene Epoch several million years ago, when the earth was 5 to 7 degrees warmer than today and sea levels tens of feet higher. The group 350.org long has campaigned for measures that would dramatically reduce GHG emissions to reduce $CO_2$ levels in the atmosphere to 350 ppm. But as of January 2021, atmospheric concentrations of $CO_2$ at Mauna Loa had risen to 415.5 ppm.

**Figure 11.2  $CO_2$ in the Atmosphere and Annual Emissions (1750-2019)**

CO$_2$ in the atmosphere and annual emissions (1750-2019)

NOAA Climate.gov
Data: NOAA, ETHZ, Our World in Data

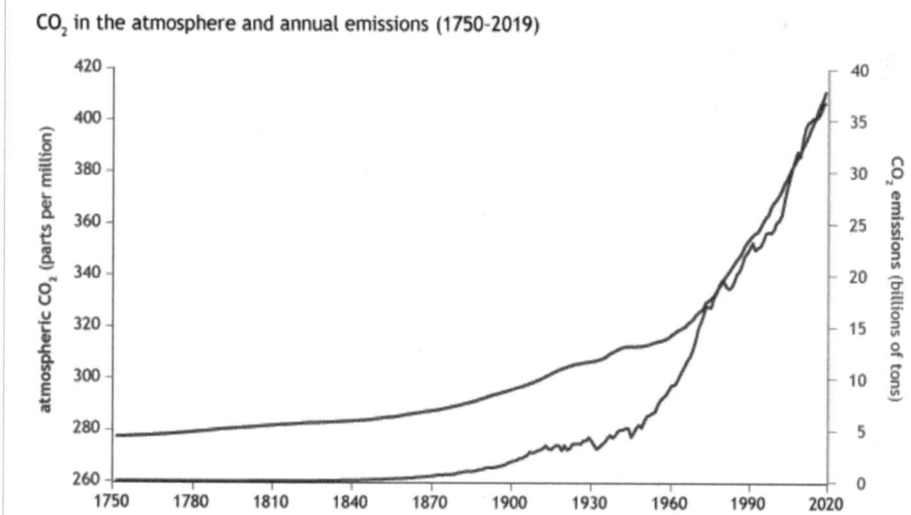

*Source:* NOAA Climate.gov.

Carbon dioxide, methane, nitrous oxides, and some chemicals used as substitutes for CFCs are the most significant substances that have an effect crudely comparable to that of the glass in a greenhouse—they allow visible light to pass through the atmosphere. Heat radiated from the Earth is transmitted in a different form, as infrared rays, and much of it is trapped by these gases, resulting in a net warming effect. Measurements of ice cores show much higher concentrations of carbon dioxide and much warmer temperatures today than in previous epochs. Further physical proof of the greenhouse effect is provided by study of other planets: Mars, with virtually no atmosphere, is a frozen wasteland, while Venus, with an atmosphere largely comprised of carbon dioxide, is as hot as an oven.

While the greenhouse effect is a part of nature, the rapid increase in the atmospheric concentrations of greenhouse gases is directly caused by human activities. The combustion of fossil fuels releases carbon dioxide; coal releases almost twice as much per unit of energy as natural gas, while oil is about halfway in between. Since trees store carbon dioxide as they grow, cutting and burning of trees (as is occurring on a vast scale in tropical rain forests) releases carbon dioxide while simultaneously reducing the amount of carbon dioxide being removed from the atmosphere by forests. Other significant greenhouse gases include methane and nitrous oxides, both of which are emitted by the use of fossil fuels and also from agriculture and other human activities. New sources of concern are the realization that some alternatives to CFCs and black soot (the pollutant produced by poorly controlled diesel engines and rural cookstoves used by the poor) also are potent greenhouse gases.

The problem of controlling emissions of greenhouse gases is exacerbated by their distribution. Western industrialized countries accounted for over two-thirds of CFC use in the mid-1980s but only about 40 percent of greenhouse gas emissions. The use of fossil fuels is increasing far more rapidly in developing countries than in industrialized nations. Developing countries are projected to account for more than 50 percent of carbon emissions from fossil fuels by 2030.

In an effort to foster international consensus on climate change, two UN agencies, the World Meteorological Organization and UNEP, organized an Intergovernmental Panel on Climate Change (IPCC) in 1988. The IPCC is composed of nearly 2,500 independent scientists from more than 100 countries who are charged with reviewing and summarizing what is known about climate change. Its reports are reviewed and approved by governments. See generally, *www.ipcc.ch.*

The magnitude and pace of global warming are difficult to predict precisely for many of the same reasons weather forecasts remain unreliable—localized climate is a chaotic system, subject to sudden and unanticipated changes. Moreover, year-to-year variations in temperatures can mask long-term trends. However, in recent years the Intergovernmental Panel on Climate Change has observed that what once were worst-case scenarios it posited are being realized more rapidly than anticipated.

In November 2014, the IPCC completed its Fifth Assessment Report (FAR). IPCC, Climate Change 2014: Synthesis Report, *https://www.ipcc.ch/report/ar5/.* It concluded that "[h]uman influence on the climate system is clear, and recent anthropogenic emissions of greenhouse gases are the highest in history. Recent climate changes have had widespread impacts on human and natural systems." The "atmosphere and ocean have warmed, the amounts of snow and ice have diminished, and sea level has risen. . . ."

**Figure 11.3    Global Land-Ocean Temperature Index**

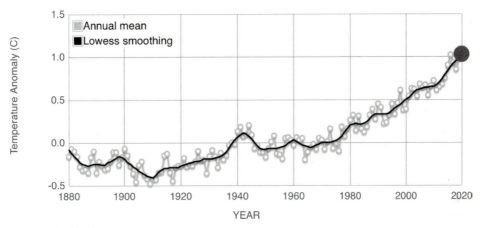

*Source:* NASA/GISS.

A sharp increase in catastrophic weather events, devastating flooding, enormous wildfires, and even fire tornadoes are becoming our new reality. Although
the IPCC is not scheduled to release its Sixth Assessment Report until June 2022, in
October 2018 it issued a Special Report warning that without "rapid, far-reaching
and unprecedented changes in all aspects of society," the 1.5-degree Celsius goal is
unachievable. The Special Report warned that there may be only 12 years left for
such actions to be taken before the effects of climate change became irreversible.

## NOTES AND QUESTIONS

1. Hurricane Katrina, which devastated New Orleans in August 2005, caused
more than 1,800 deaths and $125 billion in damage. This fueled concerns about
the impact of climate change on the intensity of storms. Early research found that
the total power released by storms had increased dramatically, even if hurricanes
had not increased in frequency. Hurricane Sandy, which caused more than $65
billion in damage in the United States, focused further attention on the consequences of climate change and sea level rise on coastal flooding.

2. In 2007, the IPCC and former Vice President Al Gore, whose documentary
film, *An Inconvenient Truth*, publicized the climate change problem, won the Nobel
Peace Prize "for their efforts to build up and disseminate greater knowledge about
man-made climate change, and to lay the foundations for the measures that are
needed to counteract such change." In 2017, Gore released a new film, *An Inconvenient Sequel: Truth to Power*. In the film he notes that *An Inconvenient Truth* had been
criticized as alarmist because of an animation suggesting that lower Manhattan and

the 9/11 Memorial could be flooded due to sea level rise and storm surges. *An Inconvenient Sequel* then shows actual footage of that happening in 2012 when Hurricane Sandy struck New York.

3. Hurricane Harvey's devastating flooding of Houston in August 2017, Hurricane Maria's destruction of much of Puerto Rico in October 2017, and vast wildfires in Australia and California focused public attention on the potentially catastrophic consequences of climate change. In 2020, the United States experienced a record 22 weather and climate disaster events that each caused more than $1 billion in damage. The year 2020 was the sixth consecutive year in which ten or more separate billion-dollar disaster events occurred in the United States. NOAA, Billion-Dollar Weather and Climate Disasters: Overview, Jan. 2021, *https://www.ncdc.noaa. gov/billions/*. A senior scientist at the National Center for Atmospheric Research, Dr. Kevin Trenberth, observes that the "answer to the oft-asked question of whether an event is caused by climate change is that it is the wrong question. All weather events are affected by climate change because the environment in which they occur is warmer and moister than it used to be. . . ."

4. Other striking empirical developments supporting climate change include a precipitous decline in summer Arctic sea ice and extreme heat waves in various parts of the world. NASA reports that global average temperatures in 2020 tied with 2016 for the warmest year ever. The year 2019 was the second warmest on record and 18 of the 19 warmest years on record have occurred since 2001. For the first time ever, temperatures reached more than 100 degrees Fahrenheit above the Arctic Circle. Extreme heat in Australia convinced Australia's Bureau of Meteorology to add additional color codes to its temperature maps for temperatures between 52 and 54 degrees Celsius (125.6 to 129.2 degrees Fahrenheit) and above 54 Celsius.

5. Achieving sharp reductions in global GHG emissions will require an unprecedented degree of international cooperation between the industrialized countries and the largest, most rapidly growing developing countries—particularly China and India, both of which have been heavily dependent on coal as a locally available, low-cost fuel for electricity. We now review the history of efforts to establish a coordinated, global response to climate change.

## B.   Legal and Policy Responses to Climate Change

### UN Framework Convention on Climate Change

An international response to the global warming problem began with a UN General Assembly resolution in December 1988 declaring climate change a "common concern of mankind" and calling for global action to combat the problem. In 1989, the European Community stated its support for an international agreement on global warming. At the end of 1990, the General Assembly adopted a resolution entitled Protection of Global Climate for Present and Future Generations of Mankind that established a process for negotiating an international framework convention on climate change. In response, the UN Secretary General established an ad hoc secretariat in Geneva with the goal of signing an agreement in time for the 1992 Rio Conference on Environment and Development. During the contentious negotiations that followed, most European nations pushed for "targets and timetables" while the United States insisted on a more cautious approach. However, agreement was reached in time for signing in Rio.

On June 12, 1992, the United States and 153 other nations attending the Rio Earth Summit signed the U.N. Framework Convention on Climate Change (UNFCC). U.S. President George H.W. Bush, who attended the summit despite being in the middle of a campaign for reelection, signed on behalf of the United States. On September 8, 1992, President Bush submitted the Convention to the U.S. Senate for ratification. On October 7, 1992, the Convention was ratified by the U.S. Senate without a dissenting vote, and it entered into force on March 21, 1994, 90 days after having been ratified by 50 signatories. The Framework Convention endorsed the principle of stabilizing emissions of greenhouse gases in order to prevent dangerous interference with the global climate system. However, the U.S. delegation achieved its goal of ensuring that the UNFCC did not establish any specific numeric limits or timetables for reducing emissions.

In subsequent negotiations, the parties to the Climate Convention ultimately agreed to establish an ad hoc process for negotiating a protocol or other legal instrument to set quantified limits and emissions reduction objectives, but only for developed countries, for the years 2005, 2010, and 2020. This agreement, subsequently coined "the Berlin Mandate," took on added importance as U.S. opposition to further action to limit emissions focused on the absence of developing country commitments.

### Kyoto Protocol to the Convention on Climate Change

During the Rio Earth Summit the United States had succeeded in keeping specific emission limits out of the UNFCC. However, the parties ultimately agreed that such limits were needed and that they should be applied first only to developed countries. This made sense because the vast majority of historic GHG emissions had come from them. This produced a backlash in the United States that resulted in the U.S. Senate adopting S.Res. 98 on July 25, 1997 by a vote of 95-0. Known as the "Byrd-Hagel Resolution" it directed the president to sign a climate treaty that includes new commitments to limit greenhouse gas emissions only if it also "mandates new specific scheduled commitments to limit or reduce greenhouse gas emissions for Developing Country Parties within the same compliance period."

In December 1997 at the Third Conference of the Parties to the UNFCC in Kyoto, Japan, the major industrialized nations adopted the Kyoto Protocol. It required developed countries to reduce their GHG emissions to a level 5 percent below their 1990 levels during the period 2008 to 2012. Nations negotiated differing obligations reflecting differing circumstances — reductions of 6 percent by Japan, 7 percent by the United States, and 8 percent by the European Union. A few nations were allowed increased emissions, including Australia, Iceland, and Norway. Developing nations rejected any commitments to reduce their GHG emissions and only reluctantly agreed in principle to allow emission trading between developed nations. As a consequence, several Senate Republicans immediately pronounced the Protocol "dead on arrival" in the U.S. Senate. While the United States signed the protocol, President Clinton never submitted it to the Senate for ratification, knowing that it would not be approved by the necessary two-thirds vote.

During the 2000 U.S. presidential election campaign, candidate George W. Bush acknowledged that climate change was a serious problem and he pledged, if elected president, to support new legislation to establish legally binding controls on U.S. emissions of $CO_2$. George W. Bush speech on energy issues, Saginaw, Michigan, Sept. 29, 2000. However, shortly after taking office as president, he repudiated that promise on March 13, 2001, and announced that he no longer would support such legislation. This greatly embarrassed his new EPA administrator Christine Todd Whitman, who had just returned from a global meeting of environment ministers in Trieste where she had emphasized that while Bush did not support the Kyoto Protocol, he was committed to controlling U.S. emissions of $CO_2$.

The Protocol became effective on February 16, 2005, as a result of ratification by the Russian Federation and without the United States. Australia was the only other developed country that initially rejected the Kyoto Protocol, though it subsequently reversed course and ratified it in 2007 after Kevin Rudd was elected Prime Minister. The text of the Protocol is available online at *https://unfccc.int/resource/docs/convkp/kpeng.pdf.*

At the time the Kyoto Protocol was adopted, it was well known that for any long-term, global response to climate change to be effective, measures would have to be taken to control the rapidly rising emissions of large developing countries. At the G8 Summit at Gleneagles in July 2005, representatives of China, India, Brazil, Mexico, and South Africa, as well as the heads of the International Energy Agency, United Nations, World Bank, and WTO discussed climate issues. The Summit joint statement included recognition that human activity is contributing to climate change, and it announced a new dialogue between the G8 nations and major developing nations to promote clean energy technologies.

Arguably the most innovative and controversial feature of the Kyoto Protocol was the Clean Development Mechanism (CDM) authorized by Article 12, which allowed developed countries to receive credit for funding projects to reduce GHG emissions in developing countries. Environmentalists were divided in their view of the CDM, with some embracing the opportunity for more efficient reductions while others worrying about the potential for creating loopholes and removing incentives for technological innovation.

### The Copenhagen Accord

In December 2007, the Thirteenth Conference of the Parties (COP-13) to the UN Framework Convention on Climate Change (UNFCC) was held in Bali. After sometimes contentious debate, all participants in the conference, including the United States, agreed upon a "Bali Action Plan" for negotiating a post-Kyoto regime to control global GHG emissions. The Bali Action Plan provided for an ambitious schedule of negotiations with the aim of an agreement by the Fifteenth Conference of the Parties (COP-15), to be held in Copenhagen in December 2009. The significance of a goal by end 2009 was to allow for sufficient time for governments to ratify and prepare for a new regime to begin at the end of the Kyoto commitment period in 2012. A dedicated working group was established to focus on the elements of such an agreement.

When President Barack Obama took office in January 2009, he pledged to "work tirelessly" to "roll back the specter of a warming planet." The president appointed former EPA administrator Carol Browner to be his "climate czar," and he told congressional leaders that he wanted legislation adopted to establish a comprehensive GHG emission control regime before the Copenhagen conference in December 2009. Mark Peters, White House Seeks Bill on Climate by December, Wall St. J., Apr. 13, 2009.

In June 2009, the U.S. House of Representatives narrowly approved the American Clean Energy and Security Act of 2009, comprehensive legislation to establish binding controls on emissions of GHGs. The legislation would have established a cap-and-trade program to reduce total U.S. emissions of GHGs by 15 percent below 2005 levels by the year 2020 and 75 percent below 2005 levels by 2050. The legislation died when the Senate failed to act on it. Due to the failure of Congress to act, EPA has launched its own program to control GHG emissions under the Clean Air Act, as discussed in Chapter 5.

The Kyoto Protocol only required emission reductions from developed countries because these countries had caused most of the climate change problem through their historic emissions. Thus, it made sense that they should be the first to control their emissions. But it was well understood that without the eventual adoption of controls on emissions from China and other rapidly growing developing countries, any reductions achieved by developed countries would be more than offset by emission increases from developing countries. In 2007, China had passed the United States as the country emitting the most GHGs. However, as climate negotiators prepared for COP-15 in Copenhagen, the Chinese government continued to fiercely resist suggestions that it should agree to cap its emissions of GHGs. Seizing on the "common but differentiated responsibilities" language in Article 3 of the Framework Convention on Climate Change and Article 10 of the Kyoto Protocol, Chinese officials argued that as a developing country China should not have to control its rapidly growing emissions. They noted that China's per capita emissions were still less than a third the level of the United States and only a little more than half the level of the EU.

In December 2009, representatives of 193 countries including 119 heads of state gathered in Copenhagen for the Fifteenth Conference of the Parties (COP-15) to the Framework Convention on Climate Change. President Obama, who stopped in Copenhagen on his way to Oslo to accept the Nobel Peace Prize, inserted himself into a last-minute meeting with the leaders of China, Brazil, India, and South Africa. The result was what has been dubbed "the Copenhagen Accord," an agreement between the United States and leaders of these rapidly developing countries that was applauded by most, but not all, other countries. The accord recognized as a "long term goal" keeping global temperature rise to 2 degrees Celsius, while calling for later consideration of an even more ambitious goal of 1.5 degrees. It committed developed countries to implement economy-wide emissions targets for 2020 while stating that developing countries "will implement mitigation measures." To assist developing countries in controlling their GHG emissions, the Accord pledged the creation of a "Green Climate Fund" to be funded by developed countries at the rate of $30 billion annually until 2012 and eventually $100 billion annually by 2020. In the face of objections from Venezuela, Cuba, Bolivia, Nicaragua, and Sudan, the Conference of the Parties simply agreed to "take note" of the Copenhagen Accord, rather than adopting it. A summary of the Copenhagen Accord is online at *https://unfccc.int/sites/default/files/resource/docs/2009/cop15/eng/11.pdf*.

The Copenhagen Accord asked both developed and developing countries to submit their own voluntary commitments for measures to control GHG emissions by the end of January 2010. In response, the United States promised a 17 percent reduction in its GHG emissions from 2005 levels by the year 2020 (only a 4 percent reduction from Kyoto's 1990 baseline). The EU pledged to reduce its GHG emissions by 20 percent below 1990 levels by 2020. China announced as a "voluntary goal" a reduction in the carbon intensity of its economy (GHG emissions per unit of gross domestic product) by 40 percent from 2005 levels by 2020, a commitment it incorporated into its Five Year Plan. India announced what it described as an "aspirational target": reducing the carbon intensity of its economy by 20 percent below 2005 levels by 2020.

At COP-17 in Durban, South Africa, Canada, Russia, and Japan stated that they would not accept a second Kyoto commitment period, and Canada became the first Party to the Protocol to withdraw from it. But the resistance of developing countries, led by China, to the adoption of a new global agreement requiring all countries to control their GHG emissions collapsed. Chinese officials were stung by the criticism they had received for their intransigence at COP-15, and they were beginning to discover that green energy represented an economic opportunity for China, which had advanced solar, wind, and electric car technology. Chinese GHG emissions had increased so rapidly that they nearly equaled those of the EU on a per capita basis (7.2 tons per person in China compared to 7.5 tons/person in the EU). The Parties at COP-17 eventually agreed to what they called the "Durban Platform." Essentially an "agreement to agree," the Durban Platform called for negotiating by 2015 a comprehensive new agreement to take effect in 2020. The Durban Platform called for "a protocol, another legal instrument or an agreed outcome with legal force" that would include all nations and seek to limit global temperature rise to 2 degrees Celsius.

The Kyoto Protocol required 38 developed countries to reduce their average annual GHG emissions by 5 percent (or 1 gigatonne of $CO_2$) below 1990 levels during the period from 2008 to 2012. Overall global emissions of GHGs increased, but emissions from the 38 developed countries were 2.2 gigatonnes (2 Gt $CO_2$) per year lower than in 1990 during the 2008-2012 period. Only 9 of the 36 developed countries that ratified Kyoto (Austria, Denmark, Iceland, Japan, Lichtenstein, Luxembourg, Norway, Spain, and Switzerland) emitted greater levels of GHG emissions than they promised, but these countries missed by only a small amount (1 percent on average), and they actually complied with the Protocol on paper by using its flexibility mechanisms to obtain carbon credits. The 2.2 Gt reduction from developed countries was largely due to the economic downturn following the collapse of the Soviet Union in 1991, which occurred even before the Protocol was signed (often referred to as the "hot air" in the Protocol). If that reduction were excluded, the 38 developed countries did not meet Kyoto targets. However, if emissions from Canada and the United States, countries that signed the deal but later rejected it, were excluded, the other 36 countries met their targets. But much of these reductions likely were the result of the global economic downturn that occurred in 2008.

### The Road to Paris

The negotiations in Cancún (2010) and Durban (2011) launched an effort to develop a broader global agreement to replace the Kyoto Protocol after the end of its commitment period in 2012. The Copenhagen Accord suggested a new model of voluntary, bottom-up individual national commitments. The global economic downturn that began in 2008 made it harder for countries to make expansive financial pledges, but it also contributed to reductions in GHG emissions as economic activity slowed. Due to the economic downturn, the price of carbon allowances in the EU plunged from more than 30 €/ton in July 2008 to only 3.3 €/ton in May 2013. Energy-related emissions of $CO_2$ in the United States actually declined from 6 billion metric tons in 2007 to 5.3 billion in 2012, the lowest level since 1994. This decline occurred in large part due to the rapid growth of hydraulic fracturing, which greatly expanded the U.S. natural gas supply, lowered prices, and accelerated utilities' shift away from coal-fired power plants.

In June 2013, President Obama announced the President's Climate Action Plan, an ambitious effort to reduce carbon emissions from power plants, accelerate investment in renewable energy and green transportation, and to improve the energy efficiency of homes, businesses, and factories. President Obama also pledged that the United States would resume leadership on international efforts to address global climate change. At COP-19 in Warsaw in December 2013, countries agreed to submit in advance of COP-21 in Paris "intended nationally determined contributions" (INDCs) outlining what they would agree to do to reduce their GHG emissions. The Parties also created the Warsaw International Mechanism for Loss and Damage Associated with Climate Change Impacts to explore possible compensation for the victims of climate change.

Because the United States and China are the two largest emitters of GHGs, see Figure 11.4, some scholars proposed that they should work together on bilateral measures to respond to the climate change problem. See, e.g., Jun Bi et al., Same Dream, Different Beds: Can America and China Learn How to Solve the Climate Problem?, 24 Global Envtl. Change 2 (Jan. 2014). They did not know that the United States and China already were conducting secret bilateral negotiations on these issues. At a Climate Summit held at the UN General Assembly in New York

**Figure 11.4   Absolute GHG Emissions of the Top Six Emitters (left) and Per Capita Emissions of the Top Six Emitters and the Global Average (right)**

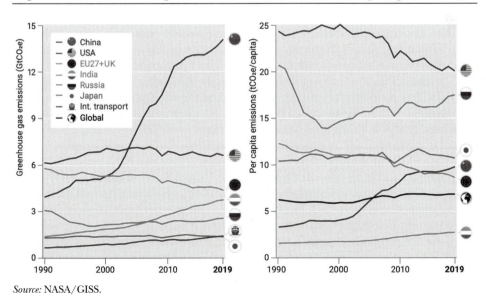

*Source:* NASA/GISS.

in September 2014, President Obama challenged China's leadership to agree to control the country's greenhouse emissions. Seven weeks later at an Asia-Pacific Economic Cooperation (APEC) summit in Beijing, President Obama and Chinese President Xi Jinping stunned the world by issuing a "Joint Announcement on Climate Change." In the announcement, China pledged for the first time to halt the increase in its GHG emissions by 2030, if not earlier. U.S.-China Joint Announcement on Climate Change, Nov. 12, 2014. Both countries also pledged to work together on a broad array of projects to share and develop improved technology for green energy production and carbon capture, utilization, and storage.

The U.S.-China Joint Announcement provided momentum for further progress at COP-20, which was held in Peru in December 2014. In March 2015, Mexico surprised the world by announcing a detailed climate action plan to cap its emissions by 2026 and to reduce them by 22 percent by 2030, contingent on substantial foreign assistance. In June 2015, the Vatican released a papal encyclical, *Laudato Si: On Care for Our Common Home*, in which Pope Francis urged the nations of the world to adopt a strong new global agreement to respond to climate change. As discussed in Chapter 1, the pope argued that the poor are the greatest victims of climate change and framed the urgency of a global agreement as an issue of environmental justice.

### COP-21 and the Paris Agreement

The Twenty-first Conference of the Parties to the UN Framework Convention on Climate Change (COP-21) was held in Paris from November 30-December 12, 2015. Prior to the conference, 184 countries submitted INDCs outlining what they pledged to do to control their emissions of GHGs from 2020 onward. The principal issues to be decided at Paris included the new agreement's ultimate goal in terms of global temperature rise, whether developed and developing countries would have different obligations, the degree of transparency to monitor countries' progress in meeting their INDCs, the status of the Green Climate Fund, whether compensation for "loss and damage" would be required, and whether the new agreement would be legally binding.

On December 12, 2015, 195 nations unanimously endorsed a new global climate agreement. Although the agreement had been widely anticipated, it was a historic achievement because it commits virtually every country in the world for the first time to take action to control emissions of GHGs. Although it is well recognized that the INDCs each country submitted will not, taken together, be sufficient to meet the global target of keeping the rise in global temperatures well below 2 degrees Celsius, countries intend to strengthen their commitments every five years and a robust system of transparency and monitoring will be established to measure progress.

One of the most important factors in the success of the Paris negotiations was the bilateral climate agreement China and the United States announced in November 2014. The two countries, the largest emitters of GHGs, coordinated their negotiating stances, and when they briefly differed, a phone call from President Obama to Xi Jinping helped smooth things out. When a last-minute flap occurred over what the United States insisted was a translation error (translating "should" as "shall"), China's chief negotiator took the lead in explaining to representatives of developing countries that the United States was right and not seeking to gain an unfair advantage.

The world knew that with opponents of climate action in control of the U.S. Congress, the Obama administration could not make any commitment that would require Senate ratification of a treaty. As a result, the Paris Agreement was carefully crafted so that the United States could accede to it as an executive agreement without seeking any new legislation from Congress. Below is an excerpt from the text of the Paris Agreement.

## Paris Agreement

(2015)

### Article 2

1. This Agreement, in enhancing the implementation of the [Framework] Convention [on Climate Change], including its objective, aims to strengthen the global response to the threat of climate change, in the context of sustainable development and efforts to eradicate poverty, including by:

(a) Holding the increase in the global average temperature to well below 2°C above pre-industrial levels and pursuing efforts to limit the temperature increase to 1.5°C above pre-industrial levels, recognizing that this would significantly reduce the risks and impacts of climate change;

(b) Increasing the ability to adapt to the adverse impacts of climate change and foster climate resilience and low greenhouse gas emissions development, in a manner that does not threaten food production; and

(c) Making finance flows consistent with a pathway towards low greenhouse gas emissions and climate-resilient development.

2. This Agreement will be implemented to reflect equity and the principle of common but differentiated responsibilities and respective capabilities, in the light of different national circumstances.

### Article 3

As nationally determined contributions to the global response to climate change, all Parties are to undertake and communicate ambitious efforts as defined in Articles 4, 7, 9, 10, 11 and 13 with the view to achieving the purpose of this Agreement as set out in Article 2. The efforts of all Parties will represent a progression over time, while recognizing the need to support developing country Parties for the effective implementation of this Agreement.

### Article 4

1. In order to achieve the long-term temperature goal set out in Article 2, Parties aim to reach global peaking of greenhouse gas emissions as soon as possible, recognizing that peaking will take longer for developing country Parties, and to undertake rapid reductions thereafter in accordance with best available science, so as to achieve a balance between anthropogenic emissions by sources and removals by sinks of greenhouse gases in the second half of this century, on the basis of equity, and in the context of sustainable development and efforts to eradicate poverty.

2. Each Party shall prepare, communicate and maintain successive nationally determined contributions that it intends to achieve. Parties shall pursue

domestic mitigation measures, with the aim of achieving the objectives of such contributions.

3. Each Party's successive nationally determined contribution will represent a progression beyond the Party's then current nationally determined contribution and reflect its highest possible ambition, reflecting its common but differentiated responsibilities and respective capabilities, in the light of different national circumstances.

4. Developed country Parties should continue taking the lead by undertaking economy-wide absolute emission reduction targets. Developing country Parties should continue enhancing their mitigation efforts, and are encouraged to move over time towards economy-wide emission reduction or limitation targets in the light of different national circumstances.

5. Support shall be provided to developing country Parties for the implementation of this Article, in accordance with Articles 9, 10 and 11, recognizing that enhanced support for developing country Parties will allow for higher ambition in their actions.

6. The least developed countries and small island developing States may prepare and communicate strategies, plans and actions for low greenhouse gas emissions development reflecting their special circumstances.

7. Mitigation co-benefits resulting from Parties' adaptation actions and/or economic diversification plans can contribute to mitigation outcomes under this Article.

8. In communicating their nationally determined contributions, all Parties shall provide the information necessary for clarity, transparency and understanding in accordance with decision 1/CP.21 and any relevant decisions of the Conference of the Parties serving as the meeting of the Parties to this Agreement.

9. Each Party shall communicate a nationally determined contribution every five years in accordance with decision 1/CP21 and any relevant decisions of the Conference of the Parties serving as the meeting of the Parties to this Agreement and be informed by the outcomes of the global stocktake referred to in Article 14.

10. The Conference of the Parties serving as the meeting of the Parties to this Agreement shall consider common time frames for nationally determined contributions at its first session.

11. A Party may at any time adjust its existing nationally determined contribution with a view to enhancing its level of ambition, in accordance with guidance adopted by the Conference of the Parties serving as the meeting of the Parties to this Agreement.

12. Nationally determined contributions communicated by Parties shall be recorded in a public registry maintained by the secretariat.

13. Parties shall account for their nationally determined contributions. In accounting for anthropogenic emissions and removals corresponding to their nationally determined contributions, Parties shall promote environmental integrity, transparency, accuracy, completeness, comparability and consistency, and ensure the avoidance of double counting, in accordance with guidance adopted by the Conference of the Parties serving as the meeting of the Parties to this Agreement. . . .

19. All Parties should strive to formulate and communicate long-term low greenhouse gas emission development strategies, mindful of Article 2 taking into account their common but differentiated responsibilities and respective capabilities, in the light of different national circumstances. . . .

## Article 14

1. The Conference of the Parties serving as the meeting of the Parties to this Agreement shall periodically take stock of the implementation of this Agreement to assess the collective progress towards achieving the purpose of this Agreement and its long-term goals (referred to as the "global stocktake"). It shall do so in a comprehensive and facilitative manner, considering mitigation, adaptation and the means of implementation and support, and in the light of equity and the best available science.

2. The Conference of the Parties serving as the meeting of the Parties to this Agreement shall undertake its first global stocktake in 2023 and every five years thereafter unless otherwise decided by the Conference of the Parties serving as the meeting of the Parties to this Agreement.

3. The outcome of the global stocktake shall inform Parties in updating and enhancing, in a nationally determined manner, their actions and support in accordance with the relevant provisions of this Agreement, as well as in enhancing international cooperation for climate action.

## Article 21

1. This Agreement shall enter into force on the thirtieth day after the date on which at least 55 Parties to the Convention accounting in total for at least an estimated 55 per cent of the total global greenhouse gas emissions have deposited their instruments of ratification, acceptance, approval or accession.

2. Solely for the limited purpose of paragraph 1 of this Article, "total global greenhouse gas emissions" means the most up-to-date amount communicated on or before the date of adoption of this Agreement by the Parties to the Convention.

3. For each State or regional economic integration organization that ratifies, accepts or approves this Agreement or accedes thereto after the conditions set out in paragraph 1 of this Article for entry into force have been fulfilled, this Agreement shall enter into force on the thirtieth day after the date of deposit by such State or regional economic integration organization of its instrument of ratification, acceptance, approval or accession. . . .

## Article 23

1. At any time after three years from the date on which this Agreement has entered into force for a Party, that Party may withdraw from this Agreement by giving written notification to the Depositary.

2. Any such withdrawal shall take effect upon expiry of one year from the date of receipt by the Depositary of the notification of withdrawal, or on such later date as may be specified in the notification of withdrawal.

3. Any Party that withdraws from the Convention shall be considered as also having withdrawn from this Agreement.

## NOTES AND QUESTIONS

1. The Paris Agreement creates the first regular process for systematically evaluating progress in controlling GHG emissions at regular intervals and enhancing nations' voluntary commitments. Perhaps the most remarkable thing about the Agreement is the support it has received from virtually every country in the world. Prior to President Trump's June 2017 decision to announce his intent to withdraw from the Agreement, only Syria and Nicaragua had announced their opposition to the Agreement. Nicaragua's problem with the Agreement is that it was not strong enough. As of September 2017, a total of 161 INDCs covering 188 countries have been submitted to the UN. A fascinating paper by one of the top negotiators for the United States at Paris is Susan Biniaz, Comma but Differentiated Responsibilities: Punctuation and 30 Other Ways Negotiators Have Resolved Issues in the International Climate Change Regime, 6 Mich. J. Envtl. & Admin. L. 37 (2016). It provides examples of how changes in textual language and punctuation have been used to resolve differences among negotiators.

2. On September 3, 2016, the United States and China both deposited their instruments of acceptance of the Paris Agreement with the UN. Pursuant to Article 21, the Paris Agreement entered into force on November 4, 2016, 30 days after the date on which 55 parties to the UNFCCC accounting for at least 55 percent of global GHG emissions deposited their instruments of ratification, acceptance, approval, or accession. This requirement was achieved on October 5, 2017, when Austria, Bolivia, Canada, France, Germany, Hungary, Malta, Nepal, Portugal, and Slovakia, as well as the European Union, deposited instruments confirming their formal approval of the Agreement. As of November 2017, a total of 197 countries had accepted the Paris Agreement (although the United States had indicated its intent to withdraw, see Note 7 below), and 170 countries had ratified it.

3. One surprise during the negotiations was the influence of "High Ambition" countries, a coalition of 35 rich and poor countries including small island nations, the EU, Colombia, Mexico, and some African countries that pressed to make the Agreement stronger. They succeeded in having Article 2's statement of goals refer to holding the rise in global temperatures to "well below" 2 degrees Celsius, while pursuing 1.5 degrees. It is estimated that if all the INDCs submitted by countries were achieved, it would only limit global temperature rise to 3 degrees above pre-industrial levels.

4. Supporters of the Agreement maintained that it is only the start and that countries will strengthen the commitments in their INDCs after the "stocktake" that will occur beginning in 2023 and every five years thereafter. See Article 14. Article 4.11 of the Agreement allows any country to revise its INDC at any time "with a view to enhancing its level of ambition." Is this "review and ratchet" approach a one-way ratchet to strengthen commitments, or can a country relax its INDC? The INDCs are not legally binding, and some argue that revisions in either direction should be permitted to avoid deterring countries from making ambitious initial commitments. Article 4.3 provides that a "Party's successive nationally determined contribution will represent a progression beyond the Party's then current nationally determined contribution and reflect its highest possible ambition." Does this mean that INDCs can only be made stronger?

5. A major effort was made in Paris to reduce differentiation between developed and developing countries. This is reflected in the fact that the Agreement does not mention Annex I and Annex II countries, though it does mention "common but differentiated responsibilities" in several places. While INDCs are not legally binding, the reporting and transparency requirements are, despite China's efforts to have the Agreement simply repeat two cryptic sentences in its September 2015 Joint Statement with the United States.

6. The Agreement does not specifically mention Copenhagen's promise of a $100 billion per year contribution from developed countries to the Green Climate Fund, although this is referenced in the separate COP decision document. This document extends the time frame for raising the $100 billion annually from 2020 to 2025 and pledges a higher funding target thereafter. Nicaragua wanted the Agreement to include language promising that the developed world would indemnify developing countries for "loss and damage" due to climate change. However, the Agreement simply refers to the Warsaw Mechanism with no mention of "loss and damage."

7. On June 1, 2017, President Donald Trump announced that he intended to withdraw the United States from the Paris Agreement. Following Trump's announcement, Nicaragua and Syria, the only two countries not to accept the Paris Agreement, reversed their positions and ratified it. Under the terms of the Paris Agreement, the United States could not submit its withdrawal until November 4, 2019, three years after the Agreement entered into forced. It then had to wait one year until the withdrawal would become effective. Thus, on November 4, 2020, the day after the 2020 U.S. presidential election, the U.S. withdrawal became effective, making the United States the only country in the world not to be part of the Paris Agreement. However, because President Trump was defeated in the 2020 presidential election, the U.S. withdrawal only lasted 107 days. On the day he took office on January 20, 2021, President Biden announced that the United States would rejoin the Paris Agreement, which became effective 30 days later on February 19, 2021. On April 22-23, 2021 President Biden hosted a virtual global climate summit at which he announced that the U.S. would reduce its GHG emissions by 50-52 percent by 2030.

### Regulation of GHG Emissions from Aviation

Emissions of greenhouse gases from aviation, which account for more than 2 percent of total global emissions, have been rising rapidly. If airlines were a country, they would be among the top ten global emitters of GHGs. On November 19, 2008, the European Parliament approved Directive 2008/101/EC that included emissions from aviation in the EU's cap-and-trade program that had been adopted in 2003. Directive 2003/87. Under the EU program, airlines were allocated a limited number of emissions allowances that had to be used to offset emissions for all flights that took off from or landed in EU member states. The amount of allowances that had to be surrendered for each flight were determined on the basis of calculations of the GHG emissions for the entire flight. Airlines could buy extra allowances if needed or sell surplus allowances. If a flight took off from or landed in another nation that imposed its own emissions charge on the flight, this charge could be deducted from the allowances owed the EU.

Foreign airlines and their governments, including the United States, China, India, and Russia, fiercely opposed the EU's efforts to collect emissions charges from airlines. The Chinese government directed its airlines not to pay the EU charges, and it threatened to cancel an Airbus order. Arguing that the program violated international treaties and principles of customary international law by applying regulation extraterritorially to airlines of non-member states, airlines and their trade associations brought suit. Considering a referral from a UK court, the European Court of Justice in December 2011 issued the following ruling.

## Air Transportation Association of America v. Secretary of State for Energy and Climate Change

ECLI:EU:C:2011:864 (2011)

111. [T]he answer to the first question is that the only principles and provisions of international law, from among those mentioned by the referring court, that can be relied upon, in circumstances such as those of the main proceedings and for the purpose of assessing the validity of Directive 2008/101, are:

— first, within the limits of review as to a manifest error of assessment attributable to the European Union regarding its competence, in the light of those principles, to adopt that directive:
— the principle that each State has complete and exclusive sovereignty over its airspace,
— the principle that no State may validly purport to subject any part of the high seas to its sovereignty, and
— the principle which guarantees freedom to fly over the high seas,
— and second:
— Articles 7 and 11(1) and (2)(c) of the Open Skies Agreement, and
— Article 15(3) of that agreement read in conjunction with Articles 2 and 3(4) thereof. . . .

125. In laying down a criterion for Directive 2008/101 to be applicable to operators of aircraft registered in a Member State or in a third State that is founded on the fact that those aircraft perform a flight which departs from or arrives at an aerodrome situated in the territory of one of the Member States, Directive 2008/101, inasmuch as it extends application of the [EU cap-and-trade] scheme laid down by Directive 2003/87 to aviation, does not infringe the principle of territoriality or the sovereignty which the third States from or to which such flights are performed have over the airspace above their territory, since those aircraft are physically in the territory of one of the Member States of the European Union and are thus subject on that basis to the unlimited jurisdiction of the European Union.

126. Nor can such application of European Union law affect the principle of freedom to fly over the high seas since an aircraft flying over the high seas is not subject, in so far as it does so, to the allowance trading scheme. Moreover, such an aircraft can, in certain circumstances, cross the airspace of one of the Member States without its operator thereby being subject to that scheme.

127. It is only if the operator of such an aircraft has chosen to operate a commercial air route arriving at or departing from an aerodrome situated in the

territory of a Member State that the operator, because its aircraft is in the territory of that Member State, will be subject to the allowance trading scheme.

128. As for the fact that the operator of an aircraft in such a situation is required to surrender allowances calculated in the light of the whole of the international flight that its aircraft has performed or is going to perform from or to such an aerodrome, it must be pointed out that, as European Union policy on the environment seeks to ensure a high level of protection in accordance with Article 191(2) [of the Treaty on the Functioning of the European Union], the European Union legislature may in principle choose to permit a commercial activity, in this instance air transport, to be carried out in the territory of the European Union only on condition that operators comply with the criteria that have been established by the European Union and are designed to fulfil the environmental protection objectives which it has set for itself, in particular where those objectives follow on from an international agreement to which the European Union is a signatory, such as the Framework Convention and the Kyoto Protocol.

129. Furthermore, the fact that, in the context of applying European Union environmental legislation, certain matters contributing to the pollution of the air, sea or land territory of the Member States originate in an event which occurs partly outside that territory is not such as to call into question, in the light of the principles of customary international law capable of being relied upon in the main proceedings, the full applicability of European Union law in that territory.

130. It follows that the European Union had competence, in the light of the principles of customary international law capable of being relied upon in the context of the main proceedings, to adopt Directive 2008/101, in so far as the latter extends the allowance trading scheme laid down by Directive 2003/87 to all flights which arrive at or depart from an aerodrome situated in the territory of a Member State.

131. ATA and others contend, in essence, that Directive 2008/101 infringes Article 7 of the Open Skies Agreement since, so far as it concerns them, Article 7 requires aircraft engaged in international navigation to comply with the laws and regulations of the European Union only when the aircraft enter or depart from the territory of the Member States or, in the case of its laws and regulations relating to the operation and navigation of such aircraft, when their aircraft are within that territory. They maintain that Directive 2008/101 seeks to apply the allowance trading scheme laid down by Directive 2003/87 not only upon the entry of aircraft into the territory of the Member States or on their departure from that territory, but also to those parts of flights that are carried out above the high seas and the territory of third States.

132. In that regard, it need only be recalled that Directive 2008/101 does not render Directive 2003/87 applicable as such to aircraft registered in third States that are flying over third States or the high seas.

133. It is only if the operators of such aircraft choose to operate commercial air routes arriving at or departing from aerodromes situated in the territory of the Member States that, because their aircraft use such aerodromes, those operators are subject to the allowance trading scheme.

134. Directive 2008/101 provides that Directive 2003/87 is to apply to flights which arrive at or depart from an aerodrome situated in the territory of a Member State. Thus, since that legislation relates to the admission to or departure from the territory of the Member States of aircraft engaged in international air navigation,

both European and transatlantic, it is clear from the very wording of Article 7(1) of the Open Skies Agreement that such legislation applies to any aircraft utilised by the airlines of the other party to that agreement and that such aircraft are required to comply with that legislation. . . .

152. As regards the validity of Directive 2008/101 in the light of the second sentence of Article 15(3) of the Open Skies Agreement, it must be stated that that provision, read in conjunction with Article 3(4) of the agreement, does not prevent the parties thereto from adopting measures that would limit the volume of traffic, frequency or regularity of service, or the aircraft type operated by the airlines established in the territory of those parties, when such measures are linked to protection of the environment.

153. Article 3(4) of the Open Skies Agreement expressly provides that neither of the parties to the agreement may impose such limitations "except as may be required for . . . environmental . . . reasons." Furthermore, it is to be noted that in any event, the allowance trading scheme does not set any limit on the emissions of aircraft which depart from or arrive at an aerodrome situated in the territory of a Member State and also does not limit frequency or regularity of service, as the fundamental obligation owed by aircraft operators is solely to surrender allowances corresponding to their actual emissions. Nor, for the reasons set out in paragraphs 141 to 147 of the present judgment, can such an obligation be regarded as an airport charge.

154. Article 15(3) of the Open Skies Agreement, read in conjunction with Articles 2 and 3(4) thereof, provides however that, when the parties to the Open Skies Agreement adopt such environmental measures, they must, as is apparent from paragraph 99 of the present judgment, be applied in a non-discriminatory manner to the airlines concerned.

155. In that regard, it must be stated that, as is indeed apparent from the express terms of recital 21 in the preamble to Directive 2008/101, the European Union has expressly provided for uniform application of the allowance trading scheme to all aircraft operators on routes which depart from or arrive at an aerodrome situated in the territory of a Member State and, in particular, it has sought to comply strictly with the non-discrimination provisions of bilateral air service agreements with third States, like the provisions in Articles 2 and 3(4) of the Open Skies Agreement.

156. Therefore, Directive 2008/101, inasmuch as it provides in particular for application of the allowance trading scheme in a non-discriminatory manner to aircraft operators established both in the European Union and in third States, is not invalid in the light of Article 15(3) of the Open Skies Agreement, read in conjunction with Articles 2 and 3(4) thereof.

157. Having regard to all of the foregoing, it must be concluded that examination of Directive 2008/101 has disclosed no factor of such a kind as to affect its validity.

## NOTES AND QUESTIONS

1. As a result of the court's decision, the EU's emissions trading scheme became applicable to all airlines beginning on January 1, 2012. However, after strong protests from the United States, China, India, and Russia, the EU agreed to suspend enforcement of the emissions charges owed by non-EU airlines in order to

give the International Civil Aviation Organization (ICAO) an opportunity to nego-tiate a global agreement. Although the ICAO previously had rebuffed efforts to address GHG emissions from aviation, it announced that it would consider three options: (1) an international emissions trading regime, (2) mandatory emissions offsets, and (3) offsets with a revenue-raising mechanism. Which approach would be best for controlling GHG emissions from aviation?

2.  On November 27, 2012, President Obama signed the EU Emissions Trad-ing Scheme Prohibition Act, Pub. L. No. 112-200, which passed both houses of the U.S. Congress by large majorities. The law provides that the U.S. Secretary of Trans-portation shall prohibit U.S. airlines from participating in the EU emissions trad-ing scheme if he or she determines that it is in the "public interest" considering impacts on U.S. consumers; U.S. economic, energy, and environmental security; and foreign relations. President Obama signed the legislation, repeating his oppo-sition to including foreign airlines in the EU cap-and-trade scheme and arguing that a better approach would be a global agreement negotiated through the ICAO.

3.  On October 6, 2016, a plenary session of the Thirty-ninth Assembly of the ICAO, meeting in Montreal, approved a Carbon Offsetting and Reduction Scheme for International Aviation (CORSIA). Implementation of the CORSIA is to begin with a pilot phase from 2021 to 2023, followed by a first phase from 2024 to 2026. Partici-pation in these first two phases will be voluntary until 2027, when all non-exempted states must participate in the scheme to control aviation emissions. Exemptions were agreed to for least developed countries, small island developing states, landlocked developing countries, and states with very low levels of international aviation activity. CORSIA has an aspirational goal of carbon neutral growth from 2020 on.

# C.   INTERNATIONAL TRADE AND THE ENVIRONMENT

## 1.   Overview

The rapid expansion and increased integration of the global economy has been one of the most important developments of the last half of the twentieth cen-tury and the first years of the twenty-first. The World Bank estimates that the size of the world economy (measured as the sum of countries' gross domestic products) increased from $33.6 trillion in 2000 to $88 trillion in 2019. Increased global trade, spurred by a relaxation of trade barriers, has played a major role in this expansion, despite a global economic downturn in 2008-2009.

Many authorities attribute the rapid expansion of world trade prior to 2008 to the successful evolution of the General Agreement on Tariffs and Trade (GATT), first drafted in 1947 and transformed into the World Trade Organization in 1994. The aim of the GATT treaty "is the moderation of national foreign trade policies to ensure, as much as possible, the unencumbered flow of international commerce." M. Janis, An Introduction to International Law 296 (2003). Toward this end, a pro-cess is created for parties to challenge, through WTO review, national measures (including environmental regulations) that constitute unjustified nontariff trade barriers. Environmental criticism of the GATT regime has been on both procedural and substantive grounds, reflecting its intentionally narrow focus and insular style. As Professor Esty argues, these characteristics arguably had much to do with the success of the system but needed to evolve in response to societal concerns. D. Esty, Greening the GATT 52-54 (1994).

Trade liberalization has long generated political controversy as countries fear job losses from increased foreign competition. The birth of NAFTA in 1992 spurred a national debate over the environmental consequences of trade liberalization. Herman Daly, an environmental economist formerly with the World Bank, harshly criticized NAFTA. He maintained that there is a clear conflict between free trade and national efforts to internalize environmental costs.

> If one nation internalizes environmental and social costs to a high degree, . . . and then enters into free trade with a country that does not force its producers to internalize those costs, then the result will be that firms in the second country will have lower prices and will drive the competing firms in the first country out of business. [Daly, From Adjustment to Sustainable Development: The Obstacle of Free Trade, 15 Loy. L.A. Int'l & Comp. L.J. 33, 36 (1992).]

Daly maintained that environmental externalities have become so important that this conflict should be resolved in favor of "tariffs to protect, not an inefficient industry, but an efficient national policy of internalizing external costs into prices."

Daly argued that international free trade is in fundamental conflict with five important domestic policies: (1) getting prices right (by making it more difficult for a country to use regulation to internalize the external costs of pollution), (2) moving toward a more just distribution of income between labor and capital (by reducing returns to domestic labor), (3) fostering community (by forcing greater labor mobility and further separating ownership from the community as foreign investment occurs), (4) controlling the macroeconomy (by creating huge international payment imbalances), and (5) keeping scale within ecological limits (as more nations seek to live in excess of a sustainable development path by importing carrying capacity from others).

In contrast to Daly, a report prepared by the GATT Secretariat for the 1992 Rio Summit not surprisingly adopted the view that trade makes countries richer and less polluting. GATT Secretariat, Trade and the Environment (Feb. 1992). This argument echoes what has come to be known as the "environmental Kuznets curve," named after economist Simon Kuznets who argued in the 1950s and 1960s that as economies grew income inequality first increases and then decreases when a certain level of GDP per capita is reached. Studying time series data on pollution levels in different countries, economists Gene Grossman and Alan Krueger concluded:

> [W]e find little evidence that environmental quality deteriorates steadily with economic growth. Rather we find for most indicators that economic growth brings an initial phase of deterioration followed by a subsequent phase of improvement. We suspect that the eventual improvement reflects, in part, an increased demand for (and supply of) environmental protection at higher levels of national income. The turning points for the different pollutants vary, but in most cases they occur before a country reaches a per capita income of $8,000. [G. Grossman & Alan Krueger, Economic Growth and the Environment, 110 Q.J. Econ. 353, 369 (1995).]

Because trade liberalization is thought to spur faster economic growth, the argument is made that it will hasten the day when "dirty" economies start to become "green," as wealthier citizens press for improved pollution control.

The case that trade does not—or at least need not—result inevitably in harm to the environment continues to receive general support from economists. See, e.g., Martin Wolf, Why Globalization Works 194 (2004) ("The alleged link between trade liberalization and environmental damage is wholly unsupported by the evidence. What is true, however, is that the management of environmental externalities requires well-targeted measures aimed at making decision makers aware of the costs."); Douglas Irwin, Free Trade Under Fire 59 (2d ed. 2005) ("[F]ree trade and a cleaner environment are not incompatible. Because free trade in itself is not a driving force behind pollution, a policy of free trade rarely detracts from such goals, in many instances may help.").

As the preceding discussion suggests, much of the early debate on trade and the environment was based on theoretical and political perspectives. What had been largely missing during the NAFTA debate was empirical evidence evaluating the environmental consequences of free trade policies. Empirical work that followed explored three types of effects that increased trade could have on the environment. These are described in the excerpt below.

P.G. Fredriksson

## Trade, Global Policy, and the Environment: New Evidence and Issues

(1999)

Although many issues in the trade and environment debate are contentious, a consensus appears to be emerging on a few matters. Many participants in the debate now agree that (a) more open trade improves growth and economic welfare, and (b) increased trade and growth without appropriate environmental policies in place may have unwanted effects on the environment. However, in some situations more open trade may also reduce pressure on the environment. This ambiguity occurs because trade policy and trade flows have several conflicting effects on both the environment and resource use. It has proven useful to view the various effects of trade liberalization in three categories: *scale, composition,* and *technique effects.* This is now a standard way of thinking about the problem and a helpful tool for analyzing the issues involved. . . .

### SCALE EFFECT

The *scale* effect refers to the fact that more open trade creates greater economic activity, thus raising the demand for inputs such as raw materials, transportation services, and energy. If output is produced and delivered using unchanged technologies, an increase in emissions and resource depletion must follow.

### COMPOSITION EFFECT

The *composition* effect stems from changes in the relative size of the economic sectors following a reduction in trade barriers. Lowering trade barriers changes the relative prices between goods produced in different sectors, so that producers and consumers face new trade-offs. Countries tend to specialize production in sectors in which they have a comparative advantage; this tendency becomes more pronounced with freer trade. If the difference between abatement costs and the price of resource extraction is sufficiently large—making environmental regulations more important in the determination of comparative advantage—countries with lax regulations are likely to shift away from relatively clean sectors and specialize in more polluting or resource-dependent sectors, thus damaging the environment.

If, on the other hand, the base for international comparative advantage is differences in the supply of labor and capital or in the efficiency of technologies, then the impact of changing sector composition (in response to trade liberalization) on environmental quality and resource extraction will be ambiguous. . . .

## TECHNIQUE EFFECT

The *technique* effect refers to changes in production methods that follow trade liberalization. Pollution emissions per unit of output do not necessarily stay constant; final intensity depends on a number of subcomponents:

- Since trade liberalization generates increased income levels, demand for environmental quality is also likely to increase. Assuming that this leads to political pressure for more stringent environmental policies and enforcement, the per-unit pollution load will be lower.
- If investment liberalization also takes place, foreign investment may bring modern technologies which are likely to be cleaner than older versions.
- As the relative price of intermediate inputs changes when tariffs are lowered, the input mix chosen by firms is adjusted; the new mix may be more or less pollution-intensive.
- Governments may begin competing for investment and jobs by setting lower environmental standards—a "race to the bottom." However, if foreign consumers demand goods produced with cleaner methods, international trade could reduce pollution intensities, instead stimulating a "race to the top."
- Closely related to the previous point, incentives for lobby groups to pressure governments for more favorable environmental legislation may shift as a result of liberalization. If the sectoral composition effect (discussed above) implies a shift into more pollution-intensive sectors, both industry and environmental interests can be expected to intensify their efforts to receive favors from environmental policy-makers—at higher output levels more is at stake, both in terms of profits and environmental degradation.

In sum, the technique effect has an ambiguous effect on pollution and resource extraction, but is generally believed to be positive for environmental quality. In addition, seen from a global perspective, free trade results in a more efficient use of resources; thus fewer raw materials and inputs are used to produce a given amount of output. As noted above, however, the amount of output produced is not constant.

The three main effects described above often have both local and global environmental implications, and their relative importance differs among countries. The final impact of trade liberalization on the environment is therefore ambiguous. A quantification of the relative magnitude of these effects, and their final result, is therefore useful to understand the range of the relative significance of the three effects in different countries.

The country-specific effects point to a need to identify and forecast the effects of existing and future trade and environmental policies—which puts great pressure on policy-making institutions. Sufficient institutional capacity is not always in place to permit environmental problems to be prevented or handled as they arise, underscoring the need for a thorough analysis of future environmental effects as foreign trade continues to open up.

## NOTES AND QUESTIONS

1. Fredriksson identifies three avenues—the scale, composition, and technique effects—by which trade liberalization may affect environmental conditions. To what extent does his analysis support or contradict Daly's views?

2. In discussing the composition effect, Fredriksson notes that freer trade will enhance the ability of countries to specialize in production sectors in which they have a comparative advantage. Where environmental regulations are a more important factor in determining a country's comparative advantage, trade liberalization should enable countries with lax regulations to increase specialization in more polluting or resource-dependent sectors, thus damaging the environment (the "pollution haven" hypothesis). But if a country's international comparative advantage is differences in the supply of labor and capital or in the efficiency of technologies, then the impact of trade liberalization can be positive for the environment (the "factor endowment" hypothesis). An empirical study reviewing pollution data from numerous countries tried to assess the relative strength of the pollution haven and factor endowment hypotheses. The researchers' "results give support to the pollution haven hypothesis. Trade liberalization will increase emissions in poorer countries (low- and middle-income economies), while it will decrease emissions in rich countries (high income)." But no significant relationship was found for $SO_2$ emissions. Nicolas Korves, Immaculada Martinez-Zarzoso & Anca Monika Voicu, Is Free Trade Good or Bad for the Environment? New Empirical Evidence (2011).

3. Can an international agreement expand foreigners' standing to seek redress in the U.S. courts? In Corrosion Proof Fittings v. EPA, 947 F.2d 1201 (5th Cir. 1991), Canadian asbestos producers argued that they had standing to challenge EPA's asbestos ban because GATT gives them the right to challenge another country's environmental standards as de facto trade barriers. Noting that GATT establishes its own procedures for solving trade disputes, the court rejected this argument. The Fifth Circuit held that the Canadians did not fall within the zone of interests protected by U.S. law because TSCA does not require EPA to consider the extraterritorial effect of domestic regulation. The court noted that section 6(c)(1)(D) of TSCA expressly requires EPA to consider "the effect [of a rule] on the *national* economy," 15 U.S.C. §2605(c)(1)(D) (emphasis supplied), and that "[i]nternational concerns are conspicuously absent from the statute." 947 F.2d at 1209.

4. The Montreal Protocol's restrictions on international trade in CFCs initially were opposed by the EC as a possible violation of GATT. Under the Protocol,

parties are prohibited from importing CFCs or halons from nonparties and, beginning in January 1993, developing countries were precluded from exporting them to nonparties. These restrictions were included in the Montreal Protocol after a GATT representative explained that they qualified for exceptions provided in Article XX(b) & (g) for standards "necessary to protect human, animal, or plant life or health" or "relating to the conservation or exhaustion of exhaustible natural resources." Benedick, Ozone Diplomacy 91 (1991). See also Frankel, Climate and Trade: Links Between the Kyoto Protocol and the WTO, 47 Environment 8 (2005).

## 2.  *The GATT and WTO*

The World Trade Organization (WTO) is a product of the Marrakesh Agreement that completed the Uruguay Round of negotiations under the old General Agreement on Tariffs and Trade (GATT) in December 1993. United States membership in the WTO was approved by Congress in December 1994, and the WTO came into being on January 1, 1995. The principles established under GATT still remain the centerpiece of the international trading system, which now has been integrated into a new, unified system under the WTO. Unlike GATT's "contracting parties," the WTO has "Members" who are required to attend the organization's ministerial conferences. The WTO's General Council, which reports to the ministerial conference, is responsible for running the day-to-day business of the WTO. Its subsidiary, the General Council on Trade and Goods administers existing trade agreements, the role GATT used to play. The WTO has dispute settlement provisions that are more developed than GATT's by making the formation of dispute settlement panels and the adoption of their decisions automatic, subject to appeal to an Appellate Body of seven members.

GATT insulates health and environmental regulations from attacks as trade restrictions as long as they "are not applied in a manner which would constitute a means of arbitrary or unjustifiable discrimination between countries where the same conditions prevail, or a disguised restriction on international trade." GATT, art. XX. Thus, trade disputes often turn on whether a regulation discriminates against foreign products. While a GATT panel rejected a challenge to CERCLA's feedstock tax because it applied equally to foreign and domestic chemical products, more difficult issues arise when ostensibly nondiscriminatory measures have a disproportionate impact on imported products, as with the EU's ban on hormone-treated beef and the U.S. effort to ban asbestos, nearly all of which is imported. D. Esty, Greening the GATT (1994).

Conflicts over the trade implications of environmental standards may be avoided when the standards are themselves a product of international agreement. Several existing treaties, such as the Montreal Protocol, which regulates trade in CFCs, impose trade restrictions to protect the environment. The Convention on International Trade in Endangered Species of Wild Fauna and Flora (CITES) has been highly effective because it imposes strict controls on trade in endangered species.

Trade disputes have been spawned by U.S. environmental laws that use trade sanctions to promote environmental protection outside U.S. borders. The most prominent example is the Marine Mammal Protection Act of 1972 (MMPA). Designed to reduce the incidental kill of marine mammals in the course of commercial fishing, the MMPA requires the government to "ban the importation of commercial fish or products from fish which have been caught with commercial fishing technology which results in the incidental kill or incidental serious injury of ocean mammals in excess of United States standards." 16 U.S.C. §1371(a)(2). In order to import yellowfin tuna caught in a certain area of the Pacific Ocean, a country had to demonstrate that the average incidental taking rate (in terms of dolphins killed each time the purse seine nets are set) for its tuna fleet was no more than 1.25 times the average taking rate of U.S. vessels in the same period. While seemingly nondiscriminatory, these regulations spawned international trade disputes because they represented a unilateral effort to promote extraterritorial environmental protection. In 1991, the United States imposed a ban on tuna imports from Mexico and four other countries after environmentalists won a judgment holding that such an embargo was required by the MMPA. Earth Island Institute v. Mosbacher, 929 F.2d 1449 (9th Cir. 1991). Arguing that the embargo was inconsistent with GATT, the Mexican government then asked the GATT Council to convene a panel to hear its complaint. The panel rendered the following decision.

## GATT Council, United States

## Restrictions on Imports of Tuna: Report of the Panel 1991

[After describing the tuna embargo, the panel noted that MMPA also provides for an embargo of tuna products from any "intermediary nation" that fails within 90 days to prove that it has acted to ban tuna imports from the target country. Six months after the initial ban, the Pelly Amendment authorized the president to ban imports of all fish and wildlife products from the target country "for such duration as the President determines appropriate and to the extent that such prohibition is sanctioned by the General Agreement on Tariffs and Trade."]

The Panel proceeded to examine whether Article XX(b) or Article XX(g) could justify the MMPA provisions on imports of certain yellowfin tuna and yellowfin tuna products, and the import ban imposed under these provisions. The Panel noted that Article XX provides that:

"Subject to the requirement that such measures are not applied in a manner which would constitute a means of arbitrary or unjustifiable discrimination between countries where the same conditions prevail, or a disguised restriction on international trade, nothing in this Agreement shall be construed to prevent the adoption or enforcement by any contracting party of measures . . .

(b) necessary to protect human, animal or plant life or health; . . .

(g) relating to the conservation of exhaustible natural resources if such measures are made effective in conjunction with restrictions on domestic production or consumption; . . . "

The Panel noted that the United States considered the prohibition of imports of certain yellowfin tuna and certain yellowfin tuna products from Mexico, and the provisions of the MMPA on which this prohibition is based, to be justified by Article XX(b) because they served solely the purpose of protecting dolphin life and health and were "necessary" within the meaning of that provision because, in respect of the protection of dolphin life and health outside its jurisdiction, there was no alternative measure reasonably available to the United States to achieve this objective. Mexico considered that Article XX(b) was not applicable to a measure imposed to protect the life or health of animals outside the jurisdiction of the contracting party taking it and that the import prohibition imposed by the United States was not necessary because alternative means consistent with the General Agreement were available to it to protect dolphin lives or health, namely international co-operation between the countries concerned.

The Panel noted that the basic question raised by these arguments, namely whether Article XX(b) covers measures necessary to protect human, animal or plant life or health outside the jurisdiction of the contracting party taking the measure, is not clearly answered by the text of that provision. It refers to life and health protection generally without expressly limiting that protection to the jurisdiction of the contracting party concerned. The Panel therefore decided to analyze this issue in the light of the drafting history of Article XX(b), the purpose of this provision, and the consequences that the interpretations proposed by the parties would have for the operation of the General Agreement as a whole.

The Panel noted that the proposal for Article XX(b) dated from the Draft Charter of the International Trade Organization (ITO) proposed by the United States, which stated in Article 32, "Nothing in Chapter IV [on commercial policy] of this Charter shall be construed to prevent the adoption or enforcement by any Member of measures . . . (b) necessary to protect human, animal or plant life or health." In the New York Draft of the ITO Charter, the preamble had been revised to read as it does at present, and exception (b) read: "For the purpose of protecting human, animal or plant life or health, if corresponding domestic safeguards under similar conditions exist in the importing country." This added proviso reflected concerns regarding the abuse of sanitary regulations by importing countries. Later, Commission A of the Second Session of the Preparatory Committee in Geneva agreed to drop this proviso as unnecessary. Thus, the record indicates that the concerns of the drafters of Article XX(b) focused on the use of sanitary measures to safeguard life or health of humans, animals, or plants within the jurisdiction of the importing country.

The Panel further noted that Article XX(b) allows each contracting party to set its human, animal or plant life or health standards. The conditions set out in Article XX(b) which limit resort to this exception, namely that the measure taken must be "necessary" and not "constitute a means of arbitrary or unjustifiable discrimination or a disguised restriction on international trade," refer to the trade measure requiring justification under Article XX(b), not, however, to the life or health standard chosen by the contracting party. The Panel recalled the finding of a previous panel that this paragraph of Article XX was intended to allow contracting parties to impose trade restrictive measures inconsistent with the General Agreement to pursue overriding public policy goals to the extent that such inconsistencies were unavoidable. The Panel considered that if the broad interpretation of Article XX(b) suggested by the United States were accepted, each contracting party could unilaterally determine the life or health protection policies from which other contracting parties could not deviate without jeopardizing their rights under the General Agreement. The General Agreement would then no longer constitute a multilateral framework for trade among all contracting parties but would provide legal security only in respect of trade between a limited number of contracting parties with identical internal regulations.

The Panel considered that the United States' measures, even if Article XX(b) were interpreted to permit extrajurisdictional protection of life and health, would not meet the requirement of necessity set out in that provision. The United States had not demonstrated to the Panel—as required of the party invoking an Article XX exception—that it had exhausted all options reasonably available to it to pursue its dolphin protection objectives through measures consistent with the General Agreement, in particular through the negotiation of international cooperative arrangements, which would seem to be desirable in view of the fact that dolphins roam the waters of many states and the high seas. Moreover, even assuming that an import prohibition were the only resort reasonably available to the United States, the particular measure chosen could in the Panel's view not be considered to be necessary within the meaning of Article XX(b). The United States linked the maximum incidental dolphin taking rate which Mexico had to meet during a particular period in order to be able to export tuna to the United States to the taking rate actually recorded for United States fishermen during the same period. Consequently, the Mexican authorities could not know whether, at a given point of time, their policies conformed to the United States' dolphin protection standards. The Panel considered that a limitation on trade based on such unpredictable conditions could not be regarded as necessary to protect the health or life of dolphins.

On the basis of the above considerations, the Panel found that the United States' direct import prohibition imposed on certain yellowfin tuna and certain yellowfin tuna products of Mexico and the provisions of the MMPA under which it is imposed could not be justified under the exception in Article XX(b).

The Panel proceeded to examine whether the prohibition . . . could be justified under the exception in Article XX(g). The Panel noted the United States, in invoking Article XX(g) with respect to its direct import prohibition under the MMPA, had argued that the measures taken under the MMPA are measures primarily aimed at the conservation of dolphin, and that the import restrictions on certain tuna and tuna products under the MMPA are "primarily aimed at rendering effective restrictions on domestic production or consumption" of dolphin. The Panel also noted that Mexico had argued that the United States measures were not justified under the exception in Article XX(g) because, inter alia, this provision could not be applied extrajurisdictionally.

The Panel noted that Article XX(g) required that the measures relating to the conservation of exhaustible natural resources be taken "in conjunction with restrictions on domestic production or consumption." A previous panel had found that a measure could only be considered to have been taken "in conjunction with" production restrictions "if it was primarily aimed at rendering effective these restrictions." A country can effectively control the production or consumption of an exhaustible natural resource only to the extent that the production or consumption is under its jurisdiction. This suggests that Article XX(g) was intended to permit contracting parties to take trade measures primarily aimed at rendering effective restrictions on production or consumption within their jurisdiction.

The Panel further noted that Article XX(g) allows each contracting party to adopt its own conservation policies. The conditions set out in Article XX(g) which limit resort to this exception, namely that the measures taken must be related to the conservation of exhaustible natural resources, and that they not "constitute a means of arbitrary or unjustifiable discrimination . . . or a disguised restriction on international trade" refer to the trade measure requiring justification under Article XX(g), not, however, to the conservation policies adopted by the contracting party. The Panel considered that if the extrajurisdictional interpretation of Article XX(g) suggested by the United States were accepted, each contracting party could unilaterally determine the conservation policies from which other contracting parties could not deviate without jeopardizing their rights under the General Agreement. The considerations that led the Panel to reject an extrajurisdictional application of Article XX(b) therefore apply also to Article XX(g).

The Panel did not consider that the United States measures, even if Article XX(g) could be applied extrajurisdictionally, would meet the conditions set out in that provision. A previous panel found that a measure could be considered as "relating to the conservation of exhaustible natural resources" within the meaning of Article XX(g) only if it was primarily aimed at such conservation. The Panel recalled that the United States linked the maximum incidental dolphin-taking rate which Mexico had to meet during a particular period in order to be able to export tuna to the United States to the taking rate actually recorded for United States fishermen during the same period. Consequently, the Mexican authorities could not know whether, at a given point in time, their conservation policies conformed to the United States conservation standards. The Panel considered that a limitation on trade based on such unpredictable conditions could not be regarded as being primarily aimed at the conservation of dolphins.

On the basis of the above considerations, the Panel found that the United States' direct import prohibition on certain yellowfin tuna products of Mexico directly imported from Mexico, and the provisions of the MMPA under which it is imposed, could not be justified under Article XX(g).

## NOTES AND QUESTIONS

1. Does the panel's decision mean that the Article XX(b) exemption extends only to measures designed to protect resources within a nation's boundaries? If other countries choose to harm their own environment, does the United States have a legitimate interest in not trading with them? The UNCED Declaration endorses GATT's approach and states that "[u]nilateral actions to deal with environmental challenges outside the jurisdiction of the importing country should be avoided." Could restrictions designed solely to protect resources in another country ever be justified? What if the harm spills over into the global commons? Are there any circumstances in which import restrictions validly could be imposed under GATT solely to protect resources in the global commons?

2. The panel found that the United States failed to meet the "necessity" requirement of Article XX(b) because it had not first exhausted all options to pursue dolphin protection consistent with GATT. What other options were open to the United States? Is the panel saying, in effect, that unilateral import restrictions will presumptively be invalid?

3. Why did the panel reject the U.S. claim that the tuna embargo was a valid conservation measure under Article XX(g)? Could the MMPA regulations be amended to satisfy these objections? In the first dispute involving the Canada-U.S. Free Trade Agreement (the precursor to NAFTA), a trade panel found that regulations under Canada's Fisheries Act that required biological sampling of fish prior to export were invalid because their primary goal was not conservation. The panel indicated that regulations restricting trade would be upheld only if their *sole* purpose was conservation and only if there was no available alternative that was less restrictive. McKeith, The Environment and Free Trade, 10 Pac. Basin L.J. 183, 207 (1991).

4. Could this problem be resolved by implementing a "dolphin-safe" labeling scheme, as discussed in Chapter 2? Would such a scheme essentially let U.S. consumers decide whether they are willing to pay more to protect the global commons? In 1990, Congress enacted the Dolphin Consumer Protection Information Act, 16 U.S.C. §1385 (1990), which provides penalties for companies that use "dolphin safe" labels falsely. The GATT tuna panel went on to hold that this legislation was not inconsistent with U.S. obligations under GATT.

5. Hardly any U.S. tuna boats fish in the waters of the eastern tropical Pacific Ocean. If the United States had little or no tuna industry of its own that was competing directly with the Mexican fleet, should this fact make it more likely or less likely that the tuna embargo would be deemed a protectionist measure?

6. How is the methodology used to assess the validity of import restrictions under GATT similar to, or different from, the Supreme Court's formula for assessing the constitutionality of state restrictions on waste imports? Recall *Philadelphia v. New Jersey* and its progeny, discussed in Chapter 4E. Note the importance of the principle of nondiscrimination for both. Is the Article XX(b) exception for health and safety measures equivalent to the "nuisance exception" to dormant Commerce Clause doctrine? Is GATT's provision for measures to conserve natural resources in Article XX(g) the equivalent of the conservation cases (*Baldwin v. Fish & Game Commission* and *Hughes v. Oklahoma*) discussed above in Chapter 4E?

7. Despite this ruling in its favor, Mexico announced that it would strengthen its dolphin protections by requiring internationally certified observers on all tuna boats and by seeking legislation authorizing prison sentences for violators of its dolphin protection laws.

### The *Tuna/Dolphin II* Decision

Although the Mexican government sought to delay enforcing the GATT decision pending negotiations with the United States, a U.S. district court directed that the tuna embargo be broadened, under the provisions of the Pelly Amendment, to prevent "tuna laundering" by 30 countries that purchased tuna from Mexico. Earth Island Institute v. Mosbacher, 785 F. Supp. 826 (N.D. Cal. 1992). The United States then negotiated a compromise to defuse the tuna-dolphin dispute with Mexico. In June 1992, the United States came to an agreement with Mexico, Vanuatu, and Venezuela to ban the practice of setting purse seine nets around schools of tuna swimming with dolphins. The Earth Island Institute, the group that initiated the lawsuit that required the embargo, supported the compromise, Pro-Dolphin Accord Made, N.Y. Times, June 16, 1992, at D9, which was implemented through amendments to the MMPA approved by Congress in October 1992. The International Dolphin

Conservation Act of 1992, 16 U.S.C.A. §§952 et seq., authorizes the Secretary of State to negotiate a five-year moratorium on the use of purse seine nets that encircle dolphins or other marine mammals during the harvesting of tuna. The amendments also banned the sale of any tuna product that is not "dolphin safe." Does the ban on the sale of such tuna indicate that the labeling approach was a failure? Does the settlement of the tuna-dolphin dispute indicate that, GATT notwithstanding, for certain countries and certain products trade with the United States is so important that unilateral trade sanctions by the United States can be effective in changing how other countries use the global commons?

Several European nations remained dissatisfied with Mexico's settlement with the United States. They decided to file their own GATT complaint based on their status as "intermediary nations" under MMPA—importers of yellowfin tuna that also export tuna to the United States. Under the Act, these nations must certify that they have not imported products subject to prohibition from import into the United States within the preceding six months. As GATT panel decisions are not binding on subsequent proceedings, the second panel addressed issues similar to those considered in the first. General Agreement on Tariffs and Trade: Dispute Settlement Panel Report on United States Restrictions on Imports of Tuna, 33 I.L.M. 839 (1994).

In its review of Article XX(g), the *Tuna/Dolphin II* panel rejected arguments that the exhaustible natural resource to be conserved could not be located outside the territorial jurisdiction of the country taking the measure. Noting that the text of the provision is silent and the drafting history ambiguous on the location of resources covered, the Panel cited the fact that Article XX(g) has been applied to migratory species of fish in two previous decisions and that no distinction had been made on the basis of where the fish had been caught. The Panel further observed that other measures of Article XX applied to actions occurring outside the territory of the party taking the measure (e.g., Article XX(e), which relates to products of prison labor). Finally, the Panel made reference to general principles of international law that permit states to regulate conduct outside their territory, especially with respect to fishermen and vessels on the high seas.

The United States was, however, again unsuccessful in defending the legality under GATT of measures that required changes in the policies of other countries in order to be effective. Noting that the bias of GATT decisions has been to interpret Article XX exceptions narrowly, the Panel concluded:

> If however Article XX were interpreted to permit contracting parties to take trade measures so as to force other contracting parties to change their policies within their jurisdiction, including their conservation policies, the balance of rights and obligations among contracting parties, in particular the right of access to markets, would be seriously impaired. Under such an interpretation the General Agreement could no longer serve as a multilateral framework for trade among contracting parties.

The United States also lost with respect to assertions that the MMPA was justified by Article XX(b) as a measure necessary to protect the life and health of dolphins. Based on the same logic that led to its narrow interpretation of Article XX(g), the Panel concluded that allowing trade embargoes to force other countries to protect living things would also seriously impair the objectives of the General Agreement. In a paragraph labeled Concluding Observations, the Panel added that the importance of sustainable development and efforts to protect dolphins was not in dispute: "The issue was whether, in the pursuit of its environmental objectives, the United States could impose trade embargoes to secure changes in the policies which other contracting parties pursued within their own jurisdiction." Specifically, the Panel had to resolve whether the intent in Article XX was to accord parties the right to impose trade embargoes as a means for promoting conservation. "The Panel had examined this issue in the light of the recognized methods of interpretation and had found that none of them lent any support to the view that such an agreement was reflected in Article XX."

## NOTES AND QUESTIONS

1. Unlike the panel in *Tuna/Dolphin I*, the *Tuna/Dolphin II* panel suggests that the resources covered by Article XX(g)'s exemption of measures to conserve exhaustible natural resources do not have to be located within the jurisdiction of the country adopting the conservation measure. Why did the panels reach a different conclusion in this regard?

2. While the United States believed that the embargo on intermediary nations was necessary to prevent "tuna laundering" from undermining the effectiveness of its sanctions, the *Tuna/Dolphin II* panel finds it objectionable because it seeks to encourage other governments to adopt trade policies similar to those of the United States. Can you think of any circumstances under which an embargo on intermediary nations could be upheld in light of the decision in *Tuna/Dolphin II*?

3. In September 1994, another GATT panel upheld key provisions of U.S. fuel economy measures that had been challenged by the European Union as violative of GATT. General Agreement on Tariffs and Trade: Dispute Settlement Panel Report on United States—Taxes on Automobiles (Sept. 29, 1994). The panel held that U.S. Corporate Average Fuel Economy (CAFE) requirements, a "gas guzzler" tax, and a luxury tax on expensive cars did not discriminate against Mercedes and BMW. However, the panel did strike down one aspect of the regulations—CAFE accounting rules that establish separate "domestic" and "import" fleets for determining overall fuel economy. This panel decision is noteworthy because it may suggest latitude within GATT principles for regulations on imports based on more than differences in their physical characteristics or end uses. The two previous panel decisions finding U.S. regulations on the importation of tuna designed to protect dolphins inconsistent with GATT caused significant concern that nations could not regulate imports based on the manner in which they were produced, a potentially serious obstacle to environmental regulation. (Note that none of these panel decisions has been formally adopted, and that there is no *stare decisis* in GATT or WTO decisions.)

The *Auto Taxes* panel was still concerned that any discrimination due to an environmental regulation be "based on factors directly relating to the product as such." Differential taxes based on fuel economy passed the test, but the CAFE accounting regulations did not. "Thus, the Auto Taxes Panel seems to have expanded the leeway for measures that are closely related to, but do not strictly affect, the product; however, it is impossible to say just how broad or narrow that expansion is." R. Housman et al., The Use of Trade Measures in Select Multilateral Environmental Agreements (paper prepared for the United Nations Environment Programme, 1995). See Lee, Process and Product: Making the Link Between Trade and the Environment, 6 Int'l Envtl. Aff. 320 (1994).

4. The *Auto Taxes* and *Tuna/Dolphin* decisions all concerned the GATT consistency of unilateral legislative acts. The issue might have been very different if presented in conjunction with a bilateral or multilateral environmental agreement. With the increasing number and importance of such agreements, the application of GATT rules to actions taken pursuant to multilateral agreements is of considerable importance. R. Housman and colleagues argue that *Tuna/Dolphin I* implied that measures operating under the authority of an international agreement would be covered by the Article XX exceptions to the GATT. Id. The *Tuna/Dolphin II* panel employed a three-part test for determining the applicability of Article XX, which subsequently was followed by the *Auto Taxes* panel.

> First, the *policy* upon which the measure is based must fall within the range of policies covered by the relevant article XX provisions.
>
> Second, the *measure* must be either "necessary" to protect human, animal or plant life or health under XX(b), or "related to" the conservation of exhaustible natural resources, and made effective "in conjunction" with restrictions on domestic production or consumption under XX(g).
>
> Third, the measure must be applied in a manner consistent with the requirements of article XX's preamble; specifically, the measure cannot be applied in a manner that would constitute a means of arbitrary or unjustifiable discrimination between countries where the same conditions prevail or in a manner that would constitute a disguised restriction on international trade.

Measures taken to protect the environment outside of a country's territorial jurisdiction were acceptable to the *Tuna/Dolphin II* panel. However, measures to change the policies of other countries, acting within their own jurisdiction, were not acceptable if such measures would achieve their intended effect only if they were followed by such changes. The *Tuna/Dolphin II* panel stated that such measures would "seriously impair the objectives of the GATT" and, thus, could neither be considered "necessary" as required by the Article XX(b) exception nor "primarily aimed at" legitimate conservation goals as required by Article XX(g). Multilateral environmental agreements that seek to alter the policies of other countries, acting within their own jurisdiction, thus could be vulnerable under the reasoning of the *Tuna/Dolphin II* panel.

Housman and colleagues argue that both the history of GATT and strong policy arguments support treating multilateral protections differently than unilateral protections. They maintain that "broad-based multilateral protections are the only effective means of addressing problems that spill over borders, affect the global commons, or are global in nature" and that they "serve to harmonize measures within their purview," thus reducing trade barriers. Id.

5. Fears that the WTO could threaten domestic environmental regulations were reinforced in January 1996 when the organization ruled against the United

States in response to a complaint by Venezuela. The WTO ruled that a regulation governing reformulated gasoline in the Clean Air Act unfairly discriminated against some foreign refiners because it based standards for domestic refiners on the quality of gasoline they actually produced in 1990, while holding foreign refiners to a standard based on the overall average quality of gasoline in the United States. Sanger, World Trade Group Orders U.S. to Alter Clean Air Act, N.Y. Times, Jan. 18, 1996, at D1. Because the provision of the Clean Air Act applied in differential fashion only until 1998, the decision itself was not of great concern, but the potential implications of allowing the WTO to authorize trade sanctions against the United States because of its environmental regulations was worrisome to many.

6. The United States has sometimes availed itself of the WTO to attack regulations motivated by environmental concerns, most notably in response to an EU regulation restricting imports of meat products derived from cattle given growth hormones. Because the United States, but not the EU, produces most of its meat with these hormones, the effect fell disproportionately on U.S. beef exports. The United States based its challenge on the Agreement on the Application of Sanitary and Phytosanitary Measures, relying particularly on Article 5.1, which requires that food safety measures be "based on an assessment, as appropriate to the circumstances, of the risks to human, animal or plant life or health, taking into account risk assessment techniques developed by the relevant international organizations." In reviewing the basis for the EU policy, a WTO appellate body considered the scientific basis for the import restriction and, more particularly, whether the EU had used a risk assessment within the meaning of Article 5.1. The body found against the EU on both counts, noting a lack of scientific evidence supporting the conclusion that use of the hormones is unsafe, even assuming abusive use.

The EU unsuccessfully sought to rely on the precautionary principle as further support for its measures. The United States refused to accept that the precautionary principle represents customary international law and suggested it is more "approach" than "principle." The appellate body found more narrowly that the principle (whether or not accepted) would not change their interpretation of the provisions of the SPS agreement. WTO, EC Measures Concerning Meat and Meat Products (Hormones), WT/DS26/AB/R, Jan. 16, 1998.

### The *Shrimp/Turtle* Decision

On April 6, 1998, a World Trade Organization dispute settlement panel ruled that U.S. enforcement of section 609 of Pub. L. No. 101-162 was inconsistent with U.S. obligations under the WTO Agreement. This law, enacted in 1989, bans the import of shrimp harvested with technology that may adversely affect sea turtles on the endangered species list. Shrimp fishers in the United States are required to use "turtle excluder devices" (TEDs) when trawling for shrimp. These devices prevent sea turtles from drowning when caught in shrimp nets, which had been estimated to kill 150,000 turtles a year. Although the United States initially applied section 609 only to countries in the Caribbean/Western Atlantic, the U.S. Court of International Trade ruled in December 1995 that it was illegal to so limit the geographical scope of the import ban. After the U.S. Department of State published guidelines broadening the ban to apply to "all shrimp products harvested in the wild by citizens or vessels of nations which have not been certified" as using turtle-safe harvesting methods, Thailand, Malaysia, India, and Pakistan filed a complaint with the WTO.

The WTO panel's decision focused on Article XX(g) and issues similar to those raised in *Tuna/Dolphin I* with the addition of evidence that the law was designed to protect a highly migratory species identified as endangered under the Convention on International Trade in Endangered Species. In defending the law, the United States had noted that the law applied equally to American fishers and that the TEDs are both inexpensive and effective. Yet the panel refused to interpret Article XX to permit such measures. The panel stated:

> In our view, if an interpretation of the chapeau of Article XX were to be followed which would allow a Member to adopt measures conditioning access to its market for a given product upon the adoption by the exporting Members of certain policies, including conservation policies, GATT 1994 and the WTO Agreement could no longer serve as a multilateral framework for trade among Members as security and predictability of trade relations under those agreements would be threatened. This follows because, if one WTO Member were allowed to adopt such measures, then other Members would also have the right to adopt similar measures on the same subject but with differing, or even conflicting requirements. If that happened, it would be impossible for exporting Members to comply at the same time with multiple conflicting policy requirements. Indeed, as each of these requirements would necessitate the adoption of a policy applicable not only to export production (such as specific standards applicable only to goods exported to the country requiring them) but also to domestic production, it would be impossible for a country to adopt one of those policies without running the risk of breaching other Members' conflicting policy requirements for the same product and being refused access to these other markets. We note that, in the present case, there would not even be the possibility of adapting one's export production to the respective requirements of the different Members. Market access for goods could become subject to an increasing number of conflicting policy requirements for the same product and this would rapidly lead to the end of the WTO multilateral trading system.

The panel emphasized that it was not dealing with measures undertaken to implement any international agreement and that it did not challenge any nation's right to ban products that it believes are dangerous. It stressed that the key defect of the law was that it "condition[ed] access to the U.S. market for a given product on the adoption by the exporting Member of certain conservation policies." While stating that the United States could require "that U.S. norms regarding the characteristics of a given product be met for that product to be allowed on the U.S. market," the panel explained that "requiring that other Members adopt policies comparable to the U.S. policy for their domestic markets and all other markets represents a threat to the WTO multilateral trading system." The panel concluded by recognizing that protection of sea turtles was an important goal, but it stated that the goal could best be pursued by reaching "cooperative agreements on integrated conservation strategies," rather than through trade sanctions.

The United States decided to appeal the panel's decision, which had reinforced concerns of environmentalists that the WTO always will rule against the use of trade sanctions to promote environmental goals, no matter how small the restraint on trade.

An appeal produced a similar result, although based on somewhat narrower reasoning. WTO, United States — Import Prohibition of Certain Shrimp and Shrimp Products, WT/DS58/AB/R, Oct. 12, 1998. The Appellate Body emphasized that the application of the law effectively required a regulatory program "essentially the same" as that applied to American vessels. This was unacceptable without taking into account differences in conditions in other territories. In addition, the U.S. scheme excluded imports of shrimp from waters of countries not certified under the regulatory program whether or not caught using methods identical to those required in the United States. Finally, the United States was found at fault for failing to negotiate seriously with some shrimp-exporting parties and, ironically, for failing to avail itself of potentially relevant mechanisms in international agreements, including several conventions it had failed to ratify.

## NOTES AND QUESTIONS

1. Does the *Shrimp/Turtle* decision represent a threat to domestic environmental regulation, or is it largely a product of U.S. failure to apply a legitimate regulation in a manner that does not discriminate against imports from other nations?

2. The U.S. General Accounting Office issued a report in June 2000 that examined the impact of the WTO's dispute settlement procedures on U.S. laws and regulations. GAO, World Trade Organization: U.S. Experience to Date in Dispute Settlement System (June 2000). The report found that as of April 2000 the United States had initiated 25 cases at the WTO and had been a defendant in 17 cases brought against it by other countries. In 13 of the 25 cases initiated by the United States, the United States prevailed in a final WTO dispute settlement ruling; 10 cases were resolved without a rule, and the United States did not prevail in the other 2. Of the 17 cases brought against the United States, 10 were resolved without a ruling, the United States lost 6 cases and prevailed in only one. A total of 187 complaints had been filed with the WTO during the first five years of its existence, with the United States and the European Union being the most active participants in the system. The GAO concluded "that the United States has gained more than it has lost in the WTO dispute settlement system to date. WTO cases have resulted in a substantial number of changes in foreign trade practices, while their effect on U.S. laws and regulations has been minimal." Id. at 4.

3. While the *Corrosion Proof Fittings* decision, discussed in Chapter 3, derailed EPA's efforts to ban asbestos in the United States, in September 2000, a WTO panel rejected a challenge by Canada to France's 1996 ban on imports of chrysotile asbestos. World Trade Organization, European Communities — Measures Affecting Asbestos and Asbestos-Containing Products (WT/DS135/R, Sept. 18, 2000). Although the panel found that an import ban normally would violate WTO rules promoting free trade, it concluded that a ban on asbestos imports was justified under Article XX(b), the GATT's provision exempting measures necessary to protect life or health. This decision is highly significant because it represents the first time that a measure restricting trade has been upheld on environmental grounds. Throughout the dispute, Canada argued that France's asbestos ban was not based on adequate scientific research and that it was contrary to international trade rules. The Canadian government claimed that chrysotile asbestos is safer than many alternative products, and that it is perfectly safe to use and install if adequate safety

measures are taken. France, supported by the European Union, maintained that asbestos kills approximately 2,000 people in France each year. All five scientific experts consulted by the WTO panel agreed that chrysotile asbestos is carcinogenic and dangerous to human health. Canada appealed the panel's decision to the WTO's Appellate Body, which upheld the decision in March 2001. As of July 2019, 67 countries have banned asbestos, Laurie Kazan-Allen, Current Asbestos Bans and Restrictions (July 15, 2019).

4. An analysis of the implications of WTO decisions for the environment after the *Shrimp/Turtle* ruling identifies three factors that seem most important to the determination whether environmental measures are being applied in an unacceptably arbitrary manner: the measures must be flexible in allowing how the environmental objective is to be achieved; the enacting state must make good faith efforts to negotiate a multilateral agreement; and there must be reasonable phase-in times for those affected to come into compliance. While noting that numerous questions remain, they conclude: "At the end of the day, though, the new state of trade law in the area of PPMs and ET (extraterritoriality) is a much more balanced and nuanced approach — one that stems directly from the integration of sustainable development into the fabric of WTO law through its preamble." Mann & Porter, The State of Trade and Environmental Law 2003: Implications for Doha & Beyond vii (2003).

5. Douglas Irwin argues that WTO rulings have not weakened U.S. environmental protections. He notes that by 2004, "fewer than 10 of the 140 disputes brought before the WTO had dealt with environmental and health issues" and the "few environmental cases have mainly focused on whether the regulation in question has been implemented in a nondiscriminatory way, not whether the regulation is justifiable." Douglas Irwin, Free Trade Under Fire 231 (2005). Irwin draws three lessons from the WTO decisions: (1) world trade rules are not anti-environmental, (2) there are sound reasons for not allowing any and all process regulations because this could open the door to the imposition of standards that developing countries cannot afford, and (3) unilateral trade sanctions are a poor instrument for achieving environmental objectives because keeping foreign goods out of the U.S. market does not solve the underlying problem to which the sanctions are directed.

6. WTO Director-General Pascal Lamy, in a speech on October 27, 2007, declared that the environmentalists' fear that the WTO would become a "GATT-ZILLA" had proven unfounded. He noted that the *Shrimp/Turtle* decision pushed WTO members toward greater environmental collaboration, including a cooperative solution between the parties to the conflict that was reflected in a Memorandum of Understanding on the Conservation and Management of Marine Turtles and Their Habitats in the Indian Ocean. He also cited WTO's upholding of France's asbestos ban. Lamy noted that public hearings are now being held in many cases to increase transparency of the WTO dispute settlement process and that the "WTO has consulted environmental experts in nearly all of the environmental disputes that were brought to it for settlement since its creation."

7. The linkage between trade and environmental services has been of increasing interest in the context of climate change. A World Bank study found that removal of tariff and non-tariff trade barriers can increase the diffusion of clean technologies significantly, with trade gains of up to 13 percent in 18 of the highest

GHG emitting developing countries. However, the report also notes that the use of trade barriers to restrict imports of products from countries without carbon regulations could run afoul of GATT rules. World Bank, International Trade and Climate Change (2008). Other legal researchers maintain that, with certain constraints, carbon tariffs are generally permissible under WTO law. Paul-Erik Veel, Carbon Tariffs and the WTO: An Evaluation of Feasible Policies, 12 J. Int'l Econ. L. 749 (2009). On March 1, 2021, the Biden administration's Office of U.S. Trade Representative said that it is exploring the use of carbon tariffs as a means for developing market approaches to reduce GHG emissions.

### 3. NAFTA, the U.S.- Mexico-Canada Agreement, and the Environment

Some opponents of global free trade, including Herman Daly, distinguish regional trade agreements as more likely to achieve the benefits of trade based on comparative advantage. On the other hand, the economic disparity between the United States and Mexico has been the source of its own unique environmental concerns. Beginning in 1965, the Mexican government created a free-trade zone in a 60-mile strip along the 2,000-mile border with the United States. In this area, *maquiladoras* owned jointly by U.S. and Mexican companies operate tariff-free, importing raw materials or components and shipping finished products or components back to the United States. More than 2,500 factories operate in this free-trade zone, until relatively recently largely without environmental regulation. See generally P. Johnson & A. Beaulieu, The Environment and NAFTA (1996); Hunter, Salzman & Zaelke, International Environmental Law and Policy 1220-1274 (1998).

The initial proposal to create a North American Free Trade Agreement was opposed by many environmentalists, who feared it would undermine environmental standards in the United States and foster relocation of pollution-intensive industries on the Mexican side of the border, where they could benefit from lax regulation. In response, President Clinton negotiated an environmental side agreement, the North American Agreement on Environmental Cooperation (Sept. 8, 1993), 32 I.L.M. 1480. The side agreement created the North American Commission for Environmental Cooperation (CEC) and endowed it with authority to investigate allegations by citizens that a party is failing to enforce its environmental laws and regulations.

The environmental problems of the border zone were the subject of a separate bilateral agreement that created two new institutions, the Border Environment Cooperation Commission (BECC) and the North American Development Bank (NADB). The BECC assists border communities with environmental projects, while the NADB uses public and private funding to invest in projects.

NAFTA itself made only sparse reference to environmental protection measures. Under Article 712.2, each country reserved the right to establish the "appropriate level of protection" for life or health within its territory "notwithstanding any other provision" of NAFTA. However, the countries were directed to "avoid arbitrary or unjustifiable distinctions" in levels of health or environmental protection that would cause "unjustifiable discrimination" against goods from another country or that would "constitute a disguised restriction on trade." The Trump administration renegotiated NAFTA, replacing it with the U.S.-Mexico-Canada Agreement (USMCA) that entered into force on July 1, 2020.

Chapter 24 of the USMCA requires all three countries to maintain their levels of environmental protection and to enforce their environmental laws, while promoting transparency and public participation. The Agreement also includes specific provisions relating to fisheries, alien invasive species, and sustainable forestry and encourages countries to promote "corporate social responsibility" relating to the environment. In 2018 the three countries reached an Environmental Cooperation Agreement (ECA) that became effective when the USMCA entered into force. The ECA retains the CEC and authorizes citizen submissions that must be "aimed at promoting enforcement rather than at harassing industry."

The first complaint to the CEC under NAFTA, made by the National Audubon Society and two Mexican groups, cited the deaths of more than 40,000 migratory birds at the Silva Reservoir in central Mexico. The CEC determined that the deaths were caused by exposure to raw sewage and recommended that a new agency be created to monitor the health of wildlife. U.S. environmentalists complained to the CEC about the appropriations rider that lifted legal restrictions on "timber salvage" operations on public lands. This claim was rejected on the ground that it reflected a relaxation of the environmental laws, rather than a failure to enforce them. The CEC concluded that "enactment of legislation which specifically alters the operation of pre-existing environmental law in essence becomes a part of the greater body of laws and statutes on the books." Trade-Environment: NAFTA Environment Commission Disappoints, Inter-Press Service, Dec. 15, 1995.

In 1997, the CEC for the first time directed the United States to respond to a complaint charging it with violating NAFTA by failing to enforce its own environmental laws. The complaint, filed by two citizen groups in the United States, charged that the U.S. Defense Department violated NEPA by failing to prepare an EIS for its decision to relocate 2,000 new army personnel to a fort in Arizona. A NEPA lawsuit filed by the citizen groups previously had been dismissed because the statute of limitations had expired.

In 1997, the CEC released the results of its investigation into complaints filed in 1996 by three NGOs concerning an alleged failure by Mexican authorities to enforce their environmental laws when approving a new cruise ship pier in Cozumel. Final Factual Record of the Cruise Ship Pier Project in Cozumel, Quintana Roo (1997). The 55-page report summarized the facts concerning the submission, the response of the Mexican government, and other relevant factual information gathered by Secretariat of the CEC. However, the report made no conclusions and provided no remedies, apparently leaving it to the political process in each country to determine the appropriate response.

There is some evidence that NAFTA increased environmental awareness in Mexico, contributing to a growing environmental movement there. See Pollution Fight Takes Root in Courtrooms of Mexico, San Jose Mercury News, Apr. 30, 2001, at A11. As of February 2021, a total of 94 submissions had been made to the CEC. More than half of the submissions (50) complained about conditions in Mexico. Nearly a third of the complaints (29) involved Canada, 13 involved the United

States, and 2 involved both the United States and Canada. Over the 25-year life of the CEC, submissions have averaged less than four per year, but since 2010 there have only been an average of two submissions per year. CEC, Registry of Submissions, *http://www.cec.org/sem-submissions/registry-of-submissions.*

One of the most controversial elements of trade agreements has been the special procedures they often create for investor-state dispute resolution. Because these provisions are designed to protect foreign investors against arbitrary action by governments, they enable companies to bypass normal domestic legal processes. For example, Chapter 11 of NAFTA allowed the Metalclad Corporation, a U.S. company, to convene an arbitral panel to hear its claim that Mexico had effectively expropriated a hazardous waste landfill it was building in Mexico when local officials refused to grant it an operating license. The company argued that it had received assurances from the Mexican government that the landfill would be allowed to operate. Mexico argued that the permit denial was the result of a change of plans by Metalclad, which had decided to significantly expand its site despite public opposition. The tribunal awarded Metalclad $16.68 million after finding that the locality had exceeded its authority and that a decree by the region's governor declaring the site a protected natural area was tantamount to expropriation without compensation. Anthony DePalma, NAFTA's Powerful Little Secret, N.Y. Times, Mar. 11, 2001, at C2.

A study reviewing the first decade of experience with NAFTA provides some empirical analysis of its environmental consequences and, by analogy, the larger consequences of trade liberalization. Its primary finding is that "on a national level, a number of environmental conditions worsened in Mexico despite rising incomes, but not because dirty industry in the United States flocked there. Rather, environmental degradation worsened because the Mexican and U.S. governments did not instate effective environmental policies that would have brought the desired benefits from economic integration." Kevin Gallagher, Free Trade and the Environment 7 (2004). He further concludes:

- While Mexico reached $5,000 GDP per capita in 1985, a level of income associated with environmental improvements by the Kuznets Curve, the country has yet to reach a general turning point and may not "for decades to come." Id. at 8.
- The marginal costs of pollution abatement in the United States are too small to justify relocation to Mexico (the "pollution haven hypothesis"), and the composition of Mexican industry became less pollution-intensive with growth. Id. at 8-9.
- Increases in pollution due to growth in manufacturing exceeded reductions due to declines in pollution intensity, and total criteria air pollution in manufacturing nearly doubled. Id. at 9.
- The impact of transfer of technology (the "technique effect") was evident in the steel and cement industries, which are less polluting than firms in the United States; but in general "the share of those industries in Mexico that are cleaner than their U.S. counterparts has been shrinking by every measure." Id.
- "Since 1993, the year after NAFTA was signed, real spending and plant-level environmental inspections have both fallen by 45 percent. On an international level, the environmental side accords of NAFTA, with some exceptions have done little fill this gap." Id.

Gallagher's work represents an important middle ground in discussions about the environmental consequences of free trade and leads to several important conclusions. First, policies associated with trade liberalization can lead to environmental problems if they are used to justify dismantling or not enforcing domestic environmental regulations, as has unfortunately sometimes been the case. Second, effective environmental policies are not likely to discourage foreign investment and can avoid substantial costs from pollution. And third, Mexico and other developing nations require much greater assistance to develop and implement effective environmental policies simultaneously with the development of the laws and institutions required for economic growth. While economists have widely recognized the general importance of laws and institutions as a fundamental condition for economic growth, few recognize the analogous importance of the same for environmental policies.

Reviewing the first 20 years of experience with NAFTA, the Sierra Club, which had opposed NAFTA from the start, reported in 2014 that NAFTA had:

- facilitated the expansion of large-scale, export-oriented farming that relies heavily on fossil fuels, pesticides, and genetically modified organisms;
- encouraged a boom in environmentally destructive mining activities in Mexico;
- undermined Canada's ability to regulate its tar sands industry and locked the country into shipping large quantities of fossil fuels to the United States;
- catalyzed economic growth in North American industries and manufacturing sectors while simultaneously failing to safeguard against the increase in air and water pollution associated with this growth; and
- weakened domestic environmental safeguards by providing corporations with new legal avenues to challenge environmental policymaking. [Sierra Club, NAFTA: 20 Years of Costs to Communities and the Environment (2014).]

The report notes that although NAFTA has an environmental side agreement that created the North American CEC, it was "never given the funding or legal mandate needed to prevent environmental damage." But the side agreement did set a precedent for including environmental provisions in virtually all subsequent trade agreements the United States negotiated with other countries.

## 4. *International Trade in Hazardous Substances*

International trade in hazardous substances has exacerbated tensions between developing nations and the industrialized world. As industrialized countries adopted increasingly stringent environmental standards, countries without such standards became inviting targets for the marketing and disposal of hazardous substances. Three types of activities—exports of hazardous waste, marketing of products banned in industrialized nations, and trade in other hazardous substances—raise environmental concerns explored below.

### A.  Policy Issues

Exports of hazardous waste from industrialized nations have created international incidents when developing nations have discovered that they were the intended dumping grounds for toxic residue. When 8,000 drums of toxic waste, including 150 tons of PCBs, were dumped in a small Nigerian fishing village by an Italian firm, Nigeria recalled its ambassador to Italy and forced the firm to reclaim the waste. The waste, aboard the *Karin B.*, was then refused by five countries before being returned to Italy. Guinea jailed a Norwegian diplomat after a Norwegian ship dumped toxic waste there. After Panama refused a shipment of incinerator ash on board the *Khian Sea*, the shipper tried to dump it on a Haitian beach but was stopped after unloading 3,000 tons. The *Khian Sea* then roamed the oceans for 18 months, unable to find a willing recipient for its cargo. After visiting five continents and changing its name three times the boat reappeared, without its cargo, which probably was dumped in the Indian Ocean. French, A Most Deadly Trade, World-Watch 11 (July-Aug. 1990).

It is not difficult to understand the economic incentive for exporting hazardous waste to developing countries that prevailed in the early 1990s. Wendy Grieder of EPA's Office of International Activities then noted that some developing countries charged as little as $40 per ton for disposal of wastes that could cost $250 to $300 per ton for disposal in the United States. Chepesiuk, From Ash to Cash: The International Trade in Toxic Waste, 31, 35 (July-Aug. 1991). While data on the volume of waste exports are sketchy, it is estimated that industrialized nations shipped three million tons of toxic waste to less developed countries between 1986 and 1988. Obstler, Toward a Working Solution to Global Pollution: Importing CERCLA to Regulate the Export of Hazardous Waste, 16 Yale J. Int'l L. 73, 76 (1991). But see Montgomery, Reassessing the Waste Trade Crisis: What Do We Really Know?, 4 J. Env't & Dev. 1 (1995) (arguing that the data do not support the conclusion that the problem is serious).

The export of hazardous substances also expanded. As regulation and increased consumer awareness reduced the domestic demand for such substances, producers of hazardous substances intensified marketing efforts in developing countries. Products that are banned for use in the United States legally can be, and are, manufactured here for export. Other pesticides that have not been approved by EPA also are manufactured for export. Exports of such pesticides and other hazardous materials place workers at risk in developing countries, where regulatory standards are far less strict than in the United States. U.S. consumers may continue to be exposed to pesticides banned as unreasonably dangerous under FIFRA when residues of such pesticides are present on imported fruits and vegetables, a phenomenon called the "circle of poison." See D. Weir & M. Shapiro, Circle of Poison: Pesticides and People in a Hungry World (1982).

Export markets have been aggressively pursued for products whose use was phased out or discouraged to protect health in the United States. For example, after the United States prohibited use of lead additives in gasoline to prevent lead poisoning, manufacturers of lead additives expanded their sales to developing countries. In 1991, the Ethyl Corporation of Richmond, Virginia, applied for permission to double production of lead additives at a plant in Sarnia, Canada, to facilitate greater exports to South America. Although Canada also had banned lead additives in gasoline, fuel additives manufactured for export are exempt from the 1988 Canadian Environmental Protection Act's prohibition on the export of products banned domestically. Gorrie, Groups Oppose Canada's Export of Lead Additive, Toronto Star, Mar. 25, 1991, at D8. By 2017, the use of leaded gasoline was banned in every country in the world except for Algeria, Iraq, Myanmar, North Korea, and Afghanistan.

U.S. exports of cigarettes to developing countries have soared, even as domestic demand has plummeted. Between 2012 and 2016, U.S. exports of cigarettes increased by 166.5 percent, the largest increase of any country. In 1990, the American Medical Association charged that the dramatic increase in smoking in foreign countries was a result of U.S. trade policies that ignored the hazards of U.S. products sold abroad. Arguing that the United States has no business dictating how American companies should respond to foreign demand, the U.S. Cigarette Export Association opposed efforts to require foreign-language health warning labels on cigarettes exported from the United States. A.M.A. Assails Nation's Export Policy on Tobacco, N.Y. Times, June 27, 1990, at A12. When Thailand sought to ban cigarette imports, the United States invoked GATT, and the ban was struck down because it did not apply to Thai cigarettes. When it was revealed that tobacco companies were aggressively targeting women and youth in Asia, Congress was so outraged that in 1997 it passed the Doggett Amendment as an appropriations rider banning employees of the Justice, Commerce, and State Departments from promoting tobacco use abroad. On January 18, 2001, President Clinton issued Executive Order 13,193, which banned all U.S. agencies from promoting tobacco use. In 2016, the Trans-Pacific Partnership (TPP) became the first trade agreement expressly to exclude anti-smoking measures from its investor-state dispute resolution procedures.

Critics of international trade in hazardous substances argue that it is unfair or immoral for industrialized nations to export risks they are unwilling to bear to poor countries that are ill-prepared to handle them. Because "[m]ost developing countries have neither the technical capability nor the regulatory infrastructure to ensure safe handling and destruction of toxic waste," environmentalists argue that exports to such countries are "economically, environmentally, morally, and technically indefensible." Uva & Bloom, Exporting Pollution: The International Waste Trade, 31 Environment 4 (June 1989). Critics argue that the absence of effective controls on hazardous substance exports also promotes environmental damage, poisons relations between industrialized and developing countries, and puts U.S. consumers at risk through the "circle of poison."

Opponents of stricter regulation argue that it is paternalistic for the industrialized world to dictate environmental standards to less developed countries. They argue that it may be more efficient for developing countries to adopt less stringent environmental standards to promote development. As noted in Chapter 1, in 1991 Lawrence Summers, then the World Bank's chief economist, wrote that "the economic logic behind dumping a load of toxic waste in the lowest wage country is impeccable" because lost earnings caused by a given amount of health damage would be lower there. Arguing that "underpopulated countries in Africa are vastly *under* polluted," the memo maintained that cancer risks should be of less concern there because life expectancy already is low. Weisskopf, World Bank Official's Irony Backfires, Wash. Post, Feb. 10, 1992, at A9. Brazil's environmental minister dubbed this reasoning "perfectly logical but totally insane." Cockburn, "Earth Summit" Is in Thrall to the Marketeers, L.A. Times, Mar. 1, 1992, at M5.

## B. Regulation of International Trade in Hazardous Substances

One approach to the problems raised by international trade in hazardous substances is to emphasize the principle of informed consent in a manner similar to the informational approaches to regulation explored in Chapter 4. This is the approach most existing U.S. laws follow, as indicated in Figure 11.5 below. Section 3017 of RCRA requires persons seeking to export hazardous waste to notify EPA at least 60 days prior to shipment of the waste. The Secretary of State is then required to notify the government of the intended recipient and those of any countries through which the waste will pass in transit. Waste may not be exported until written consent has been obtained from the recipient's government, and copies of such consent must be attached to a manifest accompanying such shipments. Waste shipped pursuant to a bilateral agreement, such as the existing agreement between the United States and Canada (the largest recipient of U.S. hazardous waste exports), is exempt from the prior notification and consent requirements on the theory that the agreement already constitutes blanket consent to such shipments.

TSCA and FIFRA require that other countries be notified when regulatory action is taken against a chemical substance or when a pesticide's registration is canceled or suspended. Both statutes, however, permit products banned in the United States to be exported. Indeed, they actually insulate products manufactured solely for export from most domestic regulation. Under section 12(a) of TSCA, EPA can only regulate such products if it determines the risks they present *within the United States* are unreasonable, without considering their impact in countries importing them.

Signed in 1989, the Basel Convention on the Control of Transboundary Movement of Hazardous Wastes sought to establish a framework for controlling hazardous waste exports. It banned hazardous waste exports unless the receiving country and any transit countries have consented in writing to such shipments. While the U.S. Senate ratified the Basel Convention in 1992, the United States has not become a formal party because Congress has not been willing to amend RCRA to conform to Basel requirements. In 1991, African nations signed the Bamako Convention, prohibiting hazardous waste imports into Africa. In 1994, the Basel COP agreed to prohibit exports of hazardous waste from OECD to non-OECD countries. In 1999, the parties to the Basel Convention agreed to impose strict liability on exporting states for damages caused by waste shipments. The Basel and Bamako Conventions have not entirely solved the problem of hazardous waste dumping in developing countries as considerable quantities of electronic waste are exported under the guise of being recyclable materials rather than waste.

### Tort Litigation in the United States for Actions Abroad by U.S. Multinationals

One possible strategy for holding multinational companies accountable for damage caused by the export of hazardous substances is tort litigation by foreigners injured due to exposure to such substances. In addition to the usual difficulties of

**Figure 11.5    Provisions in U.S. Environmental Statutes Addressing International Trade in Hazardous Substances**

| Statutory Provision | Activities or Substances Covered | Requirements |
| --- | --- | --- |
| RCRA §3017 | Export of hazardous wastes | Prohibited unless notification is provided and the receiving country agrees to accept the waste or unless shipped in conformance with agreement between the United States and the receiving country |
| TSCA §12(a) | Chemical substances intended for export and so labeled unless found to present an unreasonable risk of injury to health or the environment within the United States | Exempt from all provisions of TSCA except for recordkeeping and reporting requirements imposed under §8 |
| TSCA §12(b) | Chemical substances intended for export for which a data Submission has been required under §4 or §5(b) or for which restrictions have been proposed or promulgated under §5 or §6 | Notification of government of importing country of availability of data required to be submitted or of the existence of restrictions |
| FIFRA §17(a) | Unregistered pesticides produced solely for export to a foreign country | Exempt from most regulation when prepared and packed according to the specifications of a foreign purchaser when accompanied by a signed Statement filed by the purchaser acknowledging that the pesticide is not registered in the United States |
| FIFRA §17(b) | Pesticides whose registration is canceled or suspended | Notification of governments of other countries and of appropriate international agencies of cancellation or Suspension of registration |

proving causation in toxic tort cases, foreign plaintiffs face other formidable obstacles. American courts may refuse to hear cases brought by plaintiffs injured in foreign countries by invoking the doctrine of *forum non conveniens,* as illustrated by the litigation over the Bhopal tragedy, which was rejected by American courts. In re Union Carbide Corp. Gas Plant Disaster, 809 F.2d 195 (2d Cir. 1987). See Arthaud,

Environmental Destruction in the Amazon: Can U.S. Courts Provide a Forum for the Claims of Indigenous Peoples?, 7 Geo. Int'l Envtl. L. Rev. 195 (1994). Because American tort law is perceived to be more generous to plaintiffs than the law in most foreign countries, the choice of forum can have a substantial impact on the amount of damages recoverable. In Dow Chemical Co. v. Alfaro, 786 S.W.2d 674 (Tex. 1990), banana workers in Costa Rica claimed that they had been injured by a pesticide that EPA had banned within the United States, but which continued to be produced in the United States for export abroad. The workers brought a tort action in Texas state court against the U.S. company that manufactured the pesticide. After the trial court dismissed the action, the plaintiffs appealed to the Texas Supreme Court. The court's 5-4 decision produced sharp disagreement among the justices, with the majority ruling that the case must be heard in Texas. In a concurring opinion, Justice Doggett explained why:

> Shell Oil Company is a multinational corporation with its world headquarters in Houston, Texas. Dow Chemical Company, though headquartered in Midland, Michigan, conducts extensive operations from its Dow Chemical USA building located in Houston. Dow operates this country's largest chemical manufacturing plant within 60 miles of Houston in Freeport, Texas. The district court where this lawsuit was filed is three blocks away from Shell's world headquarters, One Shell Plaza in downtown Houston.
>
> Shell has stipulated that all of its more than 100,000 documents relating to DBCP are located or will be produced in Houston. Shell's medical and scientific witnesses are in Houston. The majority of Dow's documents and witnesses are located in Michigan, which is far closer to Houston (both in terms of geography and communications linkages) than to Costa Rica. The respondents have agreed to be available in Houston for independent medical examinations, for depositions and for trial. Most of the respondents' treating doctors and co-workers have agreed to testify in Houston. Conversely, Shell and Dow have purportedly refused to make their witnesses available in Costa Rica.
>
> The banana plantation workers allegedly injured by DBCP were employed by an American company on American-owned land and grew Dole bananas for export solely to American tables. The chemical allegedly rendering the workers sterile was researched, formulated, tested, manufactured, labeled and shipped by an American company in the United States to another American company. The decision to manufacture DBCP for distribution and use in the third world was made by these two American companies in their corporate offices in the United States. Yet now Shell and Dow argue that the one part of this equation that should not be American is the legal consequences of their actions. . . .
>
> Comity—deference shown to the interests of the foreign forum—is a consideration best achieved by rejecting forum non conveniens. Comity is not achieved when the United States allows its multinational corporations to adhere to a double standard when operating abroad and subsequently refuses to hold them accountable for those actions. . . .
>
> The doctrine of forum non conveniens is obsolete in a world in which markets are global and in which ecologists have documented the delicate

balance of all life on this planet. The parochial perspective embodied in the doctrine of *forum non conveniens* enables corporations to evade legal control merely because they are transnational. This perspective ignores the reality that actions of our corporations affecting those abroad will also affect Texans. Although DBCP is banned from use within the United States, it and other similarly banned chemicals have been consumed by Texans eating foods imported from Costa Rica and elsewhere. See D. Weir & M. Schapiro, Circle of Poison 28-30, 77, 82-83 (1981). In the absence of meaningful tort liability in the United States for their actions, some multinational corporations will continue to operate without adequate regard for the human and environmental costs of their actions. This result cannot be allowed to repeat itself for decades to come. [786 S.W.2d at 681, 687, 689.]

In response, Justice Gonzalez argued in dissent:

Under the guise of statutory construction, the court today abolishes the doctrine of forum non conveniens in suits brought pursuant to section 71.032 of the Civil Practice and Remedies Code. This decision makes us one of the few states in the Union without such a procedural tool, and if the legislature fails to reinstate this doctrine, Texas will become an irresistible forum for all mass disaster lawsuits. See generally, Note, Foreign Plaintiffs and Forum Non Conveniens: Going Beyond *Reyno*, 64 Tex. L. Rev. 193 (1985). "Bhopal"-type litigation, with little or no connection to Texas, will *add* to our already crowded dockets, forcing our residents to wait in the corridors of our courthouses while foreign causes of action are tried. I would hold that section 71.031 of the Texas Civil Practice and Remedies Code *does not* confer upon foreign litigants an *absolute right* to bring suit in Texas. Because I believe that trial courts have the inherent power to apply forum non conveniens in appropriate cases, I would provide guidelines and set parameters for its use. I would thus modify the judgment of the court of appeals and remand the cause to the trial court for further proceedings.

   This cause of action arose in Costa Rica where certain Costa Rican agricultural workers suffered injuries allegedly as a result of exposure to a pesticide manufactured by the defendants. The injured workers are seeking to enforce in Texas courts claims for personal injuries that occurred in Costa Rica. Several suits involving many of the same plaintiffs and essentially the same defendants have previously been filed in the United States and then dismissed on forum non conveniens grounds. . . .

   In conclusion, I have no intent, much less "zeal," to implement social policy as Justice Doggett charges. That is not our role. It is clear that if anybody is trying to advance a particular social policy, it is Justice Doggett. I admire his altruism, and I too sympathize with the plight of the plaintiffs. However, the powers of this court are well-defined, and the sweeping implementations of social welfare policy Justice Doggett seeks to achieve by abolishing the doctrine of forum non conveniens are the exclusive domain of the legislature. [786 S.W.2d at 690, 697.]

## NOTES AND QUESTIONS

1. The pesticide DBCP to which the plaintiffs were exposed had been banned in the United States since 1977. The history behind this ban is told in Davis, When Smoke Ran Like Water 195-200 (2002).

2. Do you agree with Justice Doggett's claim that forum non conveniens is an obsolete doctrine in a world of global markets? A court's decision to invoke the doctrine to avoid hearing a case is often determinative of the outcome. In a portion of his concurring opinion not reproduced here, Justice Doggett cited a study that concluded that fewer than 4 percent of cases dismissed by American courts pursuant to the doctrine of forum non conveniens ever are litigated in foreign courts. Robertson, Forum Non Conveniens in America and England: "A Rather Fantastic Fiction," 103 Law Q. Rev. 398, 419 (1987). After the Bhopal litigation was rejected by courts in the United States, the Supreme Court of India approved a settlement in 1989 that barred all actions against Union Carbide, the owner of the plant involved in the Bhopal tragedy, in return for a payment of $470 million to compensate the victims. Efforts to overturn the settlement have not been successful. More than 3,000 people were killed and more than 100,000 were injured by the gas leak.

3. It is easy to understand why the Costa Rican plaintiffs preferred a U.S. forum for their claims. Under Costa Rican law they would have been limited to recoveries of no more than $1,500 each. Developments in the Law—International Environmental Law, 104 Harv. L. Rev. 1484, 1618 (1991). The *Alfaro* decision may have opened the door to similar lawsuits on behalf of foreigners allegedly injured by U.S. corporations. In October 1991, a toxic tort suit was filed against a company in Brownsville, Texas, on behalf of a group of more than 60 Mexican children who are deformed or developmentally disabled. McClintock, In Matamoros, Residents' Rage at Polluting U.S.-Owned Companies Is Growing, Baltimore Sun, Jan. 19, 1992, at A8.

4. The *Alfaro* case was settled shortly before it was scheduled to go to trial in Texas state court in August 1992. Terms of the settlement were not disclosed, but plaintiffs are thought to have received close to $50 million. One factor leading to the settlement was the plaintiffs' concern that the Texas legislature would overturn *Alfaro* by statute and reinstate the forum non conveniens doctrine in Texas. The business community expected a change in the membership of the Texas Supreme Court to reinstate the doctrine. When that did not occur, overturning *Alfaro* through legislation became the business lobby's top priority for the 1993 legislative session. In February 1993, the Texas legislature passed a bill reinstating the forum non conveniens doctrine. The legislation took effect on September 1, 1993. Ironically, after *Alfaro* was decided by the Texas Supreme Court, but before the new legislation was enacted, Exxon moved its corporate headquarters from New York to Texas.

5. The *Alfaro* case was not the end of tort suits against U.S. chemical companies by foreign banana workers exposed to DBCP. In May 1997, Shell, Dow Chemical Co., and Occidental Chemical Corp. settled a class action filed on behalf of 13,000 banana workers in the Philippines, Honduras, Nicaragua, Ecuador, Guatemala, and Costa Rica who allegedly became sterile or suffered other health problems as a result of exposure to DBCP. Although the companies maintained that any

harm to the workers was caused by misuse of the pesticide, they agreed to create a $41.5 million fund to compensate the workers. The first payments from the fund were received by the workers in December 1997. Filipino Workers Receive Compensation from Banana Pesticide Settlement Fund, Wall St. J., Dec. 12, 1997, at B9C. Workers who suffered health problems received between $800 and $5,000, depending on the seriousness of their problems. Workers unable to document health problems but who could show they were exposed to DBCP were to receive $100 each. In 2009, a state superior court judge in Los Angeles dismissed similar claims against Dole Food Company on the ground that the plaintiffs had engaged in fraud by lying about working in Dole's banana plantations and being exposed to DBCP. Steve Stecklow, Fraud by Trial Lawyers Taints Wave of Pesticide Lawsuits, Wall St. J., Aug. 19, 2009.

6. Several other lawsuits have been brought against U.S. corporations for alleged environmental torts committed in other countries. In Beanal v. Freeport-McMoran, Inc., 197 F.3d 161 (5th Cir. 1999), a resident of Indonesia sued mining companies that allegedly discharged 100,000 tons of tailings per day in several rivers, rendering them unusable for bathing and drinking. The Fifth Circuit held that the plaintiffs had failed to show that environmental abuses by the mining company were so egregious as to violate "the law of nations" that would allow them to bring suit under the Alien Tort Statute. Following the Fifth Circuit's decision, the very kind of harm feared by plaintiffs in the *Beanal* litigation occurred. The plaintiffs had alleged that overburden dumped by the company's Grasberg mining operation created a risk of landslides that threatened them. On May 4, 2000, a rock-waste containment for the overburden collapsed, causing an adjoining water basin to overflow, killing four workers and spilling waste and water into the Wanagon Valley. Jay Solomon, U.S. Mining Firm, Indonesia at Odds over Latest Spill, Wall St. J., May 8, 2000, at A30. The Indonesian Ministry of Environmental Affairs stated that it had "warned Freeport a long time ago" about the dangers of its waste containment, but that the company had not acted to correct the problem. On May 24, 2000, Freeport agreed not to continue placing overburden in the Wanagon basin and to temporarily limit production at its Grasberg open pit to an average of no more than 200,000 metric tons of ore per day pending completion of studies concerning how to prevent future spills.

7. In Flores v. Southern Peru Copper Corp., 414 F.3d 233 (2d Cir. 2003), the Second Circuit affirmed the dismissal of a lawsuit brought by residents of Peru under the ATS against a U.S. company operating a copper smelter in their neighborhood. The court held that the plaintiffs' allegations that uncontrolled emissions from the smelter injured their health and threatened their lives did not rise to the level of a violation of the "law of nations," as required to state a case under the ATS, because it only involved "intranational pollution."

8. Some ATS cases have generated favorable settlements. In *Doe v. Unocal*, 15 Burmese villagers filed a class action under the ATS against the Unocal Corporation. The lawsuit alleged that the company had been complicit with the Burmese government in the use of forced labor, murder, rape, and torture in order to aid construction of a pipeline. The villagers sought damages for past injuries, slave trading practices, and gross human rights violations inflicted upon them and asked the court to stop further pipeline development in the region. After the

district court dismissed the lawsuits, the plaintiffs appealed to the Ninth Circuit. In September 2002, a panel of the Ninth Circuit held that Unocal could be found liable under the ATS for aiding and abetting the military's actions if the plaintiffs' allegations were found to be true at trial. In February 2003, the Ninth Circuit vacated the panel's decision and agreed to rehear the case en banc. While the U.S. government supported dismissal of the lawsuits, shortly after the oral argument before the en banc court, a settlement was announced. While the amount of the settlement is confidential, Unocal announced that it "will compensate plaintiffs and provide funds enabling plaintiffs and their representatives to develop programs to improve living conditions, health care and education and protect the rights of people from the pipeline region." In June 2009, Shell Oil Company agreed to pay $15.5 million to settle a lawsuit about to go to trial under the ATS alleging the company collaborated in human rights abuses against the Ogoni people in Nigeria to counter their protests of environmental destruction caused by oil development. Plaintiffs included the survivors of environmental activist Ken Saro-wiwa who was executed by the Nigerian military in 1995. The suit had been dismissed by a district court, but the Court of Appeals for the Second Circuit reversed and allowed the case to go forward. The settlement ended a 13-year legal battle. Shell Settles with Nigerian Tribe, L.A. Times, June 13, 2009.

9. The Ninth Circuit had held off on hearing *Doe v. Unocal* en banc pending the U.S. Supreme Court's decision in Sosa v. Alvarez-Machain, 542 U.S. 692 (2004). In *Sosa*, the Supreme Court rejected an effort by a Mexican national to recover against the federal government and agents of the U.S. Drug Enforcement Agency for abducting him and forcibly taking him to the United States for trial on charges of murdering a DEA agent, a crime for which he later was acquitted. The Court held that the U.S. government was immune from liability under the "foreign country" exception to the Federal Tort Claims Act. It also held that a single illegal detention of less than one day prior to transferring the Mexican citizen to lawful authorities in the United States did not violate any norm of customary international law that is so well defined as to give rise to a cause of action under the ATS. The Court's decision narrowed the range of cases that may be brought under the ATS, while not entirely foreclosing them. The Court interpreted the ATS as a jurisdictional statute that creates no new causes of action, but it noted that courts could recognize private causes of action for certain torts in violation of the law of nations. However, it cautioned that courts should exercise caution in allowing such actions by not recognizing claims under federal common law for violations of any international law norm with less definite content and acceptance among civilized nations than those familiar when the ATS was enacted in 1789.

### The Chevron/Ecuador Litigation, *Kiobel,* and the Alien Tort Statute

In 1964, Texaco began oil exploration in the Oriente region of eastern Ecuador pursuant to a concession agreement with the government of Ecuador. Texaco discovered oil there in 1967 and, beginning in 1972, it was transported by pipeline over the Andes to the Pacific coast where it was shipped to California for refining. Texaco disposed of its drilling waste in unlined earthen pits and discharged polluted water into rivers. A senior Texaco official ordered workers not to keep records of the pollution and to destroy previous reports concerning it. In 1992, the government of Ecuador bought out Texaco's share of the concession on behalf of Petroecuador, the state-owned oil company. Texaco ceased operations in Ecuador while promising the government that it would clean up contamination.

In 1993, a group of residents of Ecuador who alleged that they were harmed by Texaco's pollution filed suit in federal district court in New York under the Alien Tort Statute, which authorizes civil suits by aliens for torts "committed in violation of the law of nations." Texaco argued that the case should be dismissed on grounds of forum non conveniens because nearly all of the evidence was in Ecuador and because the plaintiffs failed to join the government of Ecuador, who filed an amicus brief in support of Texaco, as a co-defendant. The company praised Ecuador's judiciary as fair. In April 1994, federal district judge Vincent Broderick in a preliminary ruling stated that the case would not be dismissed on forum non conveniens grounds unless Texaco agreed to "a binding acceptance of personal jurisdiction over it in Ecuadoran courts" or the filing of a bond adequate "to cover any liability imposed by the Ecuadoran courts." Before he could issue a ruling, Judge Broderick was stricken with cancer and died on March 3, 1995. The case was then re-assigned to Judge Jed Rakoff, who on November 12, 1996 dismissed the case on grounds of international comity, foreign non conveniens, and failure to join the government of Ecuador, which cannot be sued due to sovereign immunity, as an indispensable party. Aguinda v. Texaco, Inc., 945 F. Supp. 625 (S.D.N.Y. 1996). After a change in government in Ecuador, the new government and Petroecuador moved to intervene in the case and, switching sides, to support the plaintiffs, but Judge Rakoff denied the motion as untimely, 175 F.R.D. 50 (1997).

In 1998, yet another new government of Ecuador certified that Texaco performed the cleanup it had promised. It signed a release absolving the company of any liability to the government for oil contamination. In 1999, the *Aguinda* plaintiffs offered to settle their case against Texaco for $140 million. Texaco rejected the proposal and did not make any counteroffer.

On appeal from Judge Rakoff's ruling, the Second Circuit ruled that it was erroneous for the judge to dismiss the case without requiring Texaco to submit to the jurisdiction of the courts in Ecuador. Jota v. Texaco, Inc., 157 F.3d 153 (2d Cir. 1998). On remand from the Second Circuit, Judge Rakoff in January 2000 asked for more briefing on the quality of the judiciary in Ecuador, noting that there had been an ultimately abortive military coup in Ecuador the week before and that the State Department did not believe the Ecuadoran judiciary was impartial. 2000 WL 122143 (S.D.N.Y. 2000). The plaintiffs then lost a motion seeking Judge Rakoff's recusal in both the district court, 139 F. Supp. 438 (S.D.N.Y. 2000), and the Second Circuit, Aguinda v. Texaco, 241 F.3d 194 (2d Cir. 2001).

On October 15, 2000, Chevron announced that it was acquiring Texaco for $45 billion, creating the second largest oil company in the United States and the fourth largest publicly traded oil company in the world. After approval by shareholders, the merger closed on October 9, 2001. After initially being known as ChevronTexaco, the combined company dropped Texaco from its name and returned to being known as Chevron in 2005.

On May 30, 2001, Judge Rakoff dismissed the suit on forum non conveniens grounds after Texaco agreed to consent to be sued in Ecuador. Aguinda v. Texaco, Inc., 142 F. Supp. 2d 534 (S.D.N.Y. 2001). In his decision, Judge Rakoff found that

Ecuador was an adequate alternate forum, as Texaco had argued. He observed that "[w]hile no one claims the Ecuadorian judiciary is wholly immune to corruption, inefficiency, or outside pressure, the present Government of Ecuador, headed by a former law school dean, has taken vigorous steps to further the independence and impartiality of the judiciary." 142 F. Supp. 2d at 545. Noting the high level of public scrutiny the case was receiving in Ecuador, Judge Rakoff concluded that "even the possibility that corruption or undue influence might be brought to bear if this litigation were pursued in Ecuador seems exceedingly remote." Id. While it did not specifically appear in Judge Rakoff's decision, Texaco also had promised in its briefs to satisfy any judgments in plaintiffs' favor, reserving only its rights to contest them in the limited circumstances permitted by New York's Recognition of Foreign Country Money Judgments Act. On August 16, 2002, the Second Circuit affirmed Judge Rakoff's decision conditioned on Texaco waiving any statute of limitation defenses in Ecuador. Aguinda v. Texaco, 303 F.3d 470 (2d Cir. 2002).

In 2003, the *Aguinda* plaintiffs refiled their litigation in Lago Agria, Ecuador. The plaintiffs asked the Ecuadoran court to require Chevron to pay $6 billion to clean up oil contamination in the Oriente. Chevron argued that it already had cleaned up any pollution for which it was responsible and that any remaining pollution was the responsibility of Petroecuador. Evidence gathering with inspection of contaminated sites continued for the next several years. In 2009, Chevron tried to arrange for a freelance journalist to spy on the plaintiffs' legal team, but she backed out at the last minute. Chevron then released a heavily edited video of a sting operation that it claims shows the judge hearing the case to be open to receiving a bribe. While denying that he was corrupt, the judge stepped down from the case and was replaced by a new judge, further delaying the case.

On February 1, 2011, realizing that it was about to lose the case in Ecuador, Chevron took an extraordinarily bold step by filing suit against all of the plaintiffs and all of their lawyers in federal district court in New York under the Racketeer Influenced and Corrupt Organizations (RICO) Act. The RICO suit alleged that the lawsuit in Ecuador was part of a corrupt conspiracy to extort money from Chevron. Less than two weeks later, on February 14, 2011, the court in Ecuador issued a $8.6 billion judgment against Chevron. Maria Aguinda y Otros v. Chevron Corp., No. 002-2003 (Provincial Court of Justice of Sucumbios 2011). The court stated that it did not consider the supposedly ghostwritten expert's report in reaching its decision. The judgment included a bizarre provision, later struck down by the National Court of Justice of Ecuador, that the judgment would double to more than $17 billion if Chevron did not apologize to the people of Ecuador within ten days.

On February 16, 2011, the *Wall Street Journal* denounced the Ecuadoran court's judgment in an editorial entitled "Shakedown in Ecuador." Without mentioning that the case had been transferred to Ecuador at the oil company's insistence, the editorial claimed that "[t]he Ecuador suit is a form of global forum shopping, with U.S. trial lawyers and NGOs trying to hold American companies hostage in the world's least accountable and transparent legal systems." The *Journal* warned that "[i]f the plaintiffs prevail, the result could be a global free-for-all against U.S. multinationals in foreign jurisdiction."

Alleging that the judicial decision in Ecuador was the product of fraud by the plaintiffs, Chevron, in its RICO suit in New York, persuaded federal district judge

Lewis Kaplan to issue an injunction barring enforcement of the Ecuador judgment in any court in the world. Chevron Corp. v. Donziger, 786 F. Supp. 2d 581 (S.D.N.Y. 2011). In September 2011, the injunction was vacated by the U.S. Court of Appeals for the Second Circuit, which held that the court did not have authority to bar enforcement of the judgment outside of the United States. Chevron Corp. v. Naranjo, 2011 WL 4375022 (2d Cir. 2011), 667 F.3d 232 (2d Cir. 2012). Shortly before Chevron's RICO suit went to trial in 2013, the company dropped its demand for damages from the defendants in order to avoid having the case heard by a jury.

On November 12, 2013, while the RICO trial was underway in New York, Ecuador's highest court, the National Court of Justice, affirmed the trial court's judgment, while cutting it in half to $8.646 billion by striking the provision that the judgment doubled because of Chevron's failure to apologize. On March 4, 2014, Judge Kaplan issued a devastating ruling against the plaintiffs in the RICO case. In an exhaustive, book-length opinion, he found that the judgment of the court in Ecuador had been procured by fraud and thus was unenforceable. Chevron Corp. v. Donziger, 974 F. Supp. 2d 362 (S.D.N.Y. 2014). Judge Kaplan found that the plaintiffs bribed the judge in Ecuador to permit them to write his judgment. With respect to Texaco's prior assertions that the courts in Ecuador were fair, the premise of the forum non conveniens dismissal in 2001, Judge Kaplan found that they "pertained to an entirely different time period and entirely different circumstances and thus could not be controlling here." 974 F. Supp. 2d at 629. He also held that because its acquisition of Texaco had been executed through "a reverse triangular merger," Chevron was not responsible for any statements made by Texaco in the initial *Aguinda* litigation. Id. at 630. Finally Judge Kaplan noted that Texaco's commitment to satisfy any judgment appeared only in briefs in *Aguinda* and reserved the right to assert defenses under New York's Recognition of Foreign Country Money Judgments Act, which would permit contesting a judgment on the grounds that it had been obtained fraudulently. Id. at 631.

Judge Kaplan enjoined Donziger and two other representatives of the plaintiffs from taking any action to enforce the Ecuadoran judgment in the United States, and he required them to turn over to Chevron any money they receive from enforcement of the judgment in a foreign country. Judge Kaplan's decision was affirmed by the Second Circuit on appeal. Chevron Corp. v. Donziger, 833 F.3d 74 (2d Cir. 2016). The court noted that the relief granted to Chevron "does not invalidate the Ecuadorian judgment and does not prohibit any of the [plaintiffs] from seeking enforcement of that judgment anywhere outside of the United States. What it does is prohibit Donziger and [two plaintiffs'] Representatives from profiting from the corrupt conduct that led to the entry of the Judgment against Chevron, by imposing on them a constructive trust for the benefit of Chevron." 833 F.3d at 150.

Because Chevron had pulled all of its assets out of Ecuador, the plaintiffs have sought to collect the judgment in the courts of Argentina, Brazil, and Canada. Courts in Argentina and Brazil held that the judgment cannot be collected because Chevron's subsidiaries there are not responsible for the acts of the parent corporation. However, on September 4, 2015, the Supreme Court of Canada unanimously held that it was error to dismiss a similar collection action without first hearing evidence. On remand, the Ontario Superior Court of Justice in Yaigua v. Chevron, No. 12-9808 (Jan. 20, 2017), held that the assets of Chevron Canada Ltd. could not be seized to satisfy the Ecuadoran judgment.

The Chevron/Ecuador litigation brings to mind the fictional lawsuit of Jarndyce v. Jarndyce from Charles Dickens's *Bleak House*. Dickens described the lawsuit as one that has "become so complicated that no man alive knows what it means. The parties to it understand it least, but it has been observed that no two Chancery lawyers can talk about it for five minutes without coming to a total disagreement as to all the premises. . . . Scores of persons have deliriously found themselves made parties in Jarndyce and Jarndyce without knowing how or why; whole families have inherited legendary hatreds with the suit." A former reporter for the *Wall Street Journal* has written an excellent book reviewing the history of this litigation. Paul M. Barrett, Law of the Jungle: The $19 Billion Legal Battle over Oil in the Rain Forest and the Lawyer Who'd Stop at Nothing to Win (2014).

Ironically, if the *Aguinda* case initially had not been dismissed from U.S. courts on forum non conveniens grounds, it would have been vulnerable to reversal on appeal because it was premised on the Alien Tort Statute. On April 17, 2013, the U.S. Supreme Court issued a major decision sharply narrowing the reach of the ATS. In Kiobel v. Royal Dutch Petroleum Co., 569 U.S. 108 (2013), the Court affirmed the dismissal of a lawsuit brought by survivors of environmental activists killed by the Nigerian military in Nigeria. They sued Royal Dutch Shell, a Dutch corporation, in federal district court in New York. The plaintiffs alleged that the company conspired with the Nigerian military to kill their relatives to silence their complaints about Shell's oil pollution in Nigeria. The case involved review of a September 2010 decision by the U.S. Court of Appeals for the Second Circuit holding that corporations cannot be held liable under the ATS because corporations cannot violate international law. The five-Justice majority applied the presumption against extraterritorial application of U.S. law to the ATS to find that the *Kiobel* litigation could not be brought because it alleged torts occurring entirely outside the United States. In his majority opinion, Chief Justice Roberts concluded that "all the relevant conduct took place outside the United States. And even where the claims touch and concern the territory of the United States, they must do so with sufficient force to displace the presumption against extraterritorial application." 569 U.S. at 124-125. But the Chief Justice had a difficult time explaining why the presumption against extraterritorial application of U.S. law, a doctrine that had not even been developed at the time the ATS was enacted, should apply. He noted that the doctrine is designed to avoid conflicts with foreign sovereigns by not applying U.S. norms to foreign conduct unless Congress so specifies. But the ATS does not seek to apply U.S. norms abroad, but rather only to create jurisdiction to redress egregious violations of international law. The Chief Justice conceded that the ATS permits actions against those who commit piracy on the high seas, but he concluded that the presumption against extraterritorial application bars suits for other international law violations committed within the territory of another country. It was widely expected that the decisive vote in the case would come from Justice Kennedy. Kennedy joined the Court's four most conservative members in providing the fifth vote for the Chief Justice's majority opinion. In a classic Kennedy concurring opinion, he tried to soften the harsh implications of the decision for human rights litigation. Kennedy noted that in future cases alleging "serious violations of international law principles protecting persons, the proper implementation of the presumption against extraterritorial application [of the ATS] may require some further elaboration and explanation." Id. (Kennedy, J., concurring).

Four Justices rejected Chief Justice Roberts's view that the ATS cannot apply to conduct that occurs in another country. In an opinion by Justice Breyer, they concurred in the judgment on other grounds. These four Justices argued that the majority's use of the presumption against extraterritoriality is particularly inappropriate because the ATS was enacted to deal with foreign matters. The four interpreted the ATS to provide jurisdiction if any of the three following conditions are met: "(1) the alleged tort occurs on American soil, (2) the defendant is an American national, or (3) the defendant's conduct substantially and adversely affects an important American national interest." Id. at 127 (Breyer, J., dissenting). Justice Breyer noted that the third condition could be met to prevent the United States "from becoming a safe harbor (free of civil as well as criminal liability) for a torturer or other common enemy of mankind." Id. The four agreed that *Kiobel* should be dismissed because it involves the acts of a foreign corporation (Shell) that occurred outside the United States without affecting an important U.S. interest. What impact will the *Kiobel* decision have on environmental cases? No environmental plaintiff ever has successfully litigated an ATS case to judgment, though some cases have been settled on terms favorable to plaintiffs (see the *Unocal* and *Saro-wiwa* cases discussed above). Ironically, the decision means that Chevron would have prevailed in the litigation against it for polluting Ecuador had it not fought and won dismissal from the U.S. courts on the grounds that Ecuador was a more convenient forum.

## D.   INTERNATIONAL DEVELOPMENT POLICY AND THE ENVIRONMENT

Environmentalists have been urging international development policy to shift to a model of "sustainable development" that respects the absorptive and regenerative capacities of ecosystems. Sustainable development is development that occurs on a scale that does not exceed the carrying capacity of the biosphere. While it is difficult to define, the concept has been valuable as a broad goal for shaping environmental policy debates. See The Role of Law in Defining Sustainable Development, 3 Widener L. Symp. J. 1 (1998). Efforts to move development policy toward sustainability have focused on influencing federal agencies and international financial institutions.

### 1.   Multilateral Development Banks

The World Bank Group made more than $61 billion in loans in FY 2016. While much smaller than private financial flows, the influence of the World Bank and the smaller regional development banks on the financing of international development projects greatly exceeds their direct lending, which serves as a catalyst for attracting funding from other sources. These projects have historically included construction of large dams, clearing of large forest areas, and other activities with major environmental impact. Until the early 1990s, lending was done with minimal environmental review and even less public input.

The multilateral development banks (MDBs) are run by boards of governors composed of representatives from member countries with voting power based on each country's respective financial contribution to the bank. A board of executive directors has substantial delegated authority over significant policy decisions subject to approval of the board of governors. The MDBs are becoming aware of environmental concerns, in part because environmental organizations in the United States and Europe have been able to focus greater public attention on the disparity between environmental requirements in developing countries and those established by European and U.S. law.

With the dramatic increase in private financing directed to developing nations, the role of the World Bank has increasingly been questioned. Countries with open markets and attractive policy environments can obtain private financing on terms as attractive as those from the Bank, and without being subjected to politically sensitive policy dialogues or public scrutiny. Countries without open markets and supportive policies may not be good candidates for Bank loans. In response, the Bank has attempted to demonstrate its continued relevance to global needs in numerous ways, not all necessarily compatible. For example, in its 1999 Annual Report, the Bank emphasized that its core mission is not generalized growth but poverty alleviation. To achieve this goal, more attention was given to the "software" of development — training, technical assistance, and institution building more often associated with UN agencies. Other priorities included combating corruption, working with NGOs, and in general responding more directly to country priorities (which rarely include climate change and other global environmental concerns).

In the late 1980s, environmental NGOs started paying attention to the World Bank, and they were not impressed with what they saw, blaming the Bank for funding mega-projects that had severe environmental consequences. In *Mortgaging the Earth: The World Bank, Environmental Impoverishment, and the Crisis of Development* (Island Press 1994), Environmental Defense Fund lawyer Bruce Rich sharply criticized the Bank for failing to make protection of the environment a top priority. In subsequent years, the Bank has elevated environmental concerns to an important priority. The World Bank's environmental experts rose from a handful in 1990 to more than 300 in 1999, and environment was made the subject of its own department. Summarizing these changes, an article in an environmental newspaper was aptly headlined "The Kinder, Softer, Leaner, Tougher, More Transparent, Environmentally Sensitive, Corruption-Busting World Bank." Earth Times, Sept. 16-30, 1999, at 13. Environmental initiatives at the World Bank were reported annually from 1995-2009 and again in 2012 in the publication Environment Matters, which is available online at the World Bank's website at *http://www.worldbank.org/en/topic/environment/publication/environment-matters*.

Although it has declined dramatically relative to total financial flows, multilateral and nationally supported lending to developing countries still exerts significant influence on the economies of most developing nations. The United States and other industrialized nations provide insurance and guarantees through agencies like the Export-Import Bank to facilitate exports. By some estimates, such policies support about 10 percent of foreign investment in developing nations, including some of the most controversial projects like the Three Gorges Dam in China.

Miller, Environmental Policy in the New World Economy, 3 Widener L. Symp. J. 287, 306 (1998). The indirect stimulus to investment created by such programs may be even greater as the presence of multilateral banks and export credit agencies legitimizes projects for other investors.

The World Bank is governed by a Board of Governors consisting of one Governor and one Alternate Governor appointed by each member country. The World Bank Group is managed by four separate boards of directors for the International Bank for Reconstruction and Development (IBRD), the International Development Agency (IDA), the International Finance Corporation (IFC), and the Multilateral Investment Guarantee Agency (MIGA). Each board manages its respective organization. Voting power of each member country is roughly proportional to its financial contribution, though shares are allocated differently in each organization within the group. As a consequence, no country or small group of countries has a veto; this effectively insulates the Bank from short-term political intervention, but it also impedes attempts at reform. The Bank was also traditionally very restrictive about disclosures of project and loan information. Although it is not subject to the Freedom of Information Act or similar requirements of U.S. law, the Bank has made itself more accessible to public scrutiny, as noted above. These actions responded in part to environmentalists' criticisms, as articulated in Wirth, Legitimacy, Accountability, and Partnership: A Model for Advocacy on Third World Environmental Issues, 100 Yale L.J. 2645, 2664 (1991); and Rodgers, Looking a Gift Horse in the Mouth: The World Bank and Environmental Accountability, 3 Geo. Int'l Envtl. L. Rev. 457 (1990).

In December 1989, the International Development and Finance Act, 103 Stat. 2492 (1989), was enacted by Congress. The Act requires U.S. executive directors of MDBs to refrain from voting in favor of projects with a major effect on the environment unless an environmental assessment has been performed at least 120 days in advance of the vote. This legislation and other amendments to foreign aid laws require the U.S. representatives to the MDBs to promote the hiring of trained environmental staff, to develop and implement management plans to ensure environmental review of projects, to involve citizens' and indigenous peoples' organizations in project planning, and to increase the proportion of lending to environmental projects, including integrated pest management, solar energy, and small-scale mixed farming. 22 U.S.C. §§2621(a), (k). The Agency for International Development (AID) is further directed to analyze environmental impacts of proposed multilateral development loans and, where substantial adverse impacts are found, to ensure a public investigation. 22 U.S.C. §262(m)(2)(A). Since 1989, the World Bank has required that an environmental assessment be prepared for virtually all major projects. World Bank Operational Directive 4.00 (1989). In 1991, the Bank broadened this directive to require consultation with nongovernmental organizations and the public in preparation of such assessments. World Bank Operational Directive 4.01 (1991). See Scott, Making a Bank Turn, 1992 Envtl. Forum 21 (Mar.-Apr. 1992). Are these provisions enforceable through litigation by environmental groups? Do they provide any assurance that the U.S. position will prevail? Critics of these provisions argue that they inject politics into World Bank decision making in violation of Article IV of the Bank's Articles of Agreement, which states that "[o]nly economic considerations shall be relevant" to such decisions.

The World Bank and other international financial institutions must walk a narrow line in supporting resource development in poor countries with significant financial needs but weak governance, a combination frequently associated with mining and resource extraction in Africa. The World Bank attempted to create a model for transparency and effective oversight of resource revenues, including prohibitions on redirecting funds to military purposes, in support for an oil pipeline through Chad and Cameroon. In September 2008, the Bank withdrew from the project after the government of Chad breached its agreement to allocate oil revenue for poverty-reducing projects. Another loan for mining in Ghana was described by Bank managers as "expected to become a demonstration for how to handle environmental, social and community development issues." According to a Bank official, the mining company did not need the loan but wanted the stamp of approval that went with meeting the Bank's environmental and social standards. Duggar, Loan for Foreign Mining in Ghana Approved, N.Y. Times, Feb. 1, 2006.

In *Foreclosing the Future: The World Bank and the Politics of Environmental Destruction* (Island Press 2013), Bruce Rich updates the critique of the Bank's environmental policies that he had made in *Mortgaging the Earth* two decades earlier. He argues that failures of governance and corruption have undermined the ability of the Bank effectively to carry out President Jim Yong Kim's vow that the Bank will fight poverty and climate change.

The International Finance Corporation (IFC) is an IDB headquartered in Washington, D.C. that is charged with furthering economic development, particularly in less developed countries. Unlike the World Bank, which lends to governments, the IFC finances private sector development projects. The IFC has its own set of Performance Standards on Environment and Social Sustainability, dating from 2012, that it expects its borrowers to comply with as part of its loan agreements. In 2008 IFC loaned $450 million to Coastal Gujarat Power Limited, a company in India, to construct a coal-fired power plant. Under the terms of the loan the plant was required to comply with an environmental and social action plan in constructing and operating the plant to protect against environmental damage. The IFC's own internal audit found that the company had failed to comply with the plan and that the IFC had failed to supervise the project adequately. In 2015 a group of farmers and fishermen sued the IFC in federal district court in Washington, D.C., claiming that it should be held responsible for environmental contamination from the plant. Both the district court and the D.C. Circuit held that the IFC was immune from suit under the International Organizations Immunities Act of 1945, 22 U.S.C. §§288a(c), 288c. The U.S. Supreme Court then agreed to review the case and reached the following decision.

## Jam v. International Finance Corporation

139 S.Ct. 759 (2019)

ROBERTS, C. J., delivered the opinion of the Court, in which THOMAS, GINSBURG, ALITO, SOTOMAYOR, KAGAN, and GORSUCH, JJ., joined. BREYER, J., filed a dissenting opinion. KAVANAUGH, J., took no part in the consideration or decision of the case.

CHIEF JUSTICE ROBERTS delivered the opinion of the Court.

The International Organizations Immunities Act of 1945 grants international organizations such as the World Bank and the World Health Organization the "same immunity from suit . . . as is enjoyed by foreign governments." 22 U.S.C. §288a(b). At the time the IOIA was enacted, foreign governments enjoyed virtually absolute immunity from suit. Today that immunity is more limited. Most significantly, foreign governments are not immune from actions based upon certain kinds of commercial activity in which they engage. This case requires us to determine whether the IOIA grants international organizations the virtually absolute immunity foreign governments enjoyed when the IOIA was enacted, or the more limited immunity they enjoy today. . . .

The IFC contends that the IOIA grants international organizations the "same immunity" from suit that foreign governments enjoyed in 1945. Petitioners argue that it instead grants international organizations the "same immunity" from suit that foreign governments enjoy today. We think petitioners have the better reading of the statute.

### A

The language of the IOIA more naturally lends itself to petitioners' reading. In granting international organizations the "same immunity" from suit "as is enjoyed by foreign governments," the Act seems to continuously link the immunity of international organizations to that of foreign governments, so as to ensure ongoing parity be- tween the two. The statute could otherwise have simply stated that international organizations "shall enjoy absolute immunity from suit," or specified some other fixed level of immunity. Other provisions of the IOIA, such as the one making the property and assets of international organizations "immune from search," use such noncomparative language to define immunities in a static way. Or the statute could have specified that it was incorporating the law of foreign sovereign immunity as it existed on a particular date. Because the IOIA does neither of those things, we think the "same as" formulation is best understood to make international organization immunity and foreign sovereign immunity continuously equivalent. . . .

The IFC objects that the IOIA is different because the purpose of international organization immunity is entirely distinct from the purpose of foreign sovereign immunity. Foreign sovereign immunity, the IFC argues, is grounded in the mutual respect of sovereigns and serves the ends of international comity and reciprocity. The purpose of international organization immunity, on the other hand, is to allow such organizations to freely pursue the collective goals of member countries without undue interference from the courts of any one member country. The IFC therefore urges that the IOIA should not be read to tether international organization immunity to changing foreign sovereign immunity.

But that gets the inquiry backward. We ordinarily assume, "absent a clearly expressed legislative intention to the contrary," that "the legislative purpose is expressed by the ordinary meaning of the words used." Whatever the ultimate purpose of international organization immunity may be—the IOIA does not address that question—the immediate purpose of the immunity provision is expressed in language that Congress typically uses to make one thing continuously equivalent to another.

## B

The more natural reading of the IOIA is confirmed by a canon of statutory interpretation that was well established when the IOIA was drafted. According to the "reference" canon, when a statute refers to a general subject, the statute adopts the law on that subject as it exists whenever a question under the statute arises. 2 J. Sutherland, Statutory Construction §§5207–5208 (3d ed. 1943). . . .

Federal courts have often relied on the reference canon, explicitly or implicitly, to harmonize a statute with an external body of law that the statute refers to generally. Thus, for instance, a statute that exempts from disclosure agency documents that "would not be *available by law* to a party . . . in litigation with the agency" incorporates the general law governing attorney work-product privilege as it exists when the statute is applied. Likewise, a general reference to federal discovery rules incorporates those rules "as they are found on any given day, today included," and a general reference to "the crime of piracy as defined by the law of nations" incorporates a definition of piracy "that changes with advancements in the law of nations."

The same logic applies here. The IOIA's reference to the immunity enjoyed by foreign governments is a general rather than specific reference. The reference is to an external body of potentially evolving law—the law of foreign sovereign immunity—not to a specific provision of another statute. The IOIA should therefore be understood to link the law of international organization immunity to the law of foreign sovereign immunity, so that the one develops in tandem with the other.

The IFC contends that the IOIA's reference to the immunity enjoyed by foreign governments is not a general reference to an external body of law, but is instead specific reference to a common law concept that had a fixed meaning when the IOIA was enacted in 1945. And because we ordinarily presume that "Congress intends to incorporate the well-settled meaning of the common-law terms it uses," the IFC argues that we should read the IOIA to incorporate what the IFC maintains was the then-settled meaning of the "immunity enjoyed by foreign governments": virtually absolute immunity.

But in 1945, the "immunity enjoyed by foreign governments" did not *mean* "virtually absolute immunity." The phrase is not a term of art with substantive content, such as "fraud" or "forgery." It is rather a concept that can be given scope and content only by reference to the rules governing foreign sovereign immunity. It is true that under the rules applicable in 1945, the *extent* of immunity from suit was virtually absolute, while under the rules applicable today, it is more limited. But in 1945, as today, the IOIA's instruction to grant international organizations the immunity "enjoyed by foreign governments" is an instruction to look up the applicable rules of foreign sovereign immunity, wherever those rules may be found—the common law, the law of nations, or a statute. In other words, it is a general reference to an external body of (potentially evolving) law. . . .

## D

The IFC argues that interpreting the IOIA's immunity provision to grant anything less than absolute immunity would lead to a number of undesirable results.

The IFC first contends that affording international organizations only restrictive immunity would defeat the purpose of granting them immunity in the first place. Allowing international organizations to be sued in one member country's courts would in effect allow that member to second-guess the collective decisions of the others. It would also expose international organizations to money damages, which would in turn make it more difficult and expensive for them to fulfill their missions. The IFC argues that this problem is especially acute for international development banks. Because those banks use the tools of commerce to achieve their objectives, they may be subject to suit under the FSIA's commercial activity exception for most or all of their core activities, unlike foreign sovereigns. According to the IFC, allowing such suits would bring a flood of foreign-plaintiff litigation into U. S. courts, raising many of the same foreign-relations concerns that we identified when considering similar litigation under the Alien Tort Statute.

The IFC's concerns are inflated. To begin, the privileges and immunities accorded by the IOIA are only default rules. If the work of a given international organization would be impaired by restrictive immunity, the organization's charter can always specify a different level of immunity. The charters of many international organizations do just that. Notably, the IFC's own charter does not state that the IFC is absolutely immune from suit.

Nor is there good reason to think that restrictive immunity would expose international development banks to excessive liability. As an initial matter, it is not clear that the lending activity of all development banks qualifies as commercial activity within the meaning of the FSIA. To be considered "commercial," an activity must be "the *type*" of activity "by which a private party engages in" trade or commerce. See 28 U.S.C. §1603(d). As the Government suggested at oral argument, the lending activity of at least some development banks, such as those that make conditional loans to governments, may not qualify as "commercial" under the FSIA.

And even if an international development bank's lending activity does qualify as commercial, that does not mean the organization is automatically subject to suit. The FSIA includes other requirements that must also be met. For one thing, the commercial activity must have a sufficient nexus to the United States. See 28 U.S.C. §§1603, 1605(a)(2). For another, a lawsuit must be "based upon" either the commercial activity itself or acts performed in connection with the commercial activity. See §1605(a)(2). Thus, if the "gravamen" of a lawsuit is tortious activity abroad, the suit is not "based upon" commercial activity within the meaning of the FSIA's commercial activity exception. At oral argument in this case, the Government stated that it has "serious doubts" whether petitioners' suit, which largely concerns allegedly tortious conduct in India, would satisfy the "based upon" requirement. In short, restrictive immunity hardly means unlimited exposure to suit for international organizations.

\* \* \*

The International Organizations Immunities Act grants international organizations the "same immunity" from suit "as is enjoyed by foreign governments" at any given time. Today, that means that the Foreign Sovereign Immunities Act governs the immunity of international organizations. The International Finance Corporation is therefore not absolutely immune from suit.

The judgment of the United States Court of Appeals for the D. C. Circuit is reversed, and the case is remanded for further proceedings consistent with this opinion.

*It is so ordered.*

## NOTES AND QUESTIONS

1. Although it surprised some observers, the Trump administration supported the position of the Indian farmers and fishermen in this case and argued that the IFC was not automatically immune from suit. However, although the *Jam* decision was a victory for the plaintiffs in India, Chief Justice Roberts noted that the government had "serious doubts" about whether the suit could survive trial because most of the allegedly tortious conduct occurred in India. On remand, the case was dismissed for precisely this reason. Thus, it may not have as broad an impact as hoped in providing a mechanism for holding multilateral development banks accountable for failing to enforce environmental terms in their loans.

2. Writing alone in dissent, Justice Breyer argued that the IFC should be immune from suit based on the purposes of the IOIA. He argued that "international organizations, unlike foreign nations, are multilateral, with members from many different nations. That multilateralism is threatened if one nation alone, through application of its own liability rules (by nonexpert judges), can shape the policy choices or actions that an international organization believes it must take or refrain from taking. Yet that is the effect of the majority's interpretation."

## 2. *The Global Environment Facility*

The Global Environment Facility (GEF) was initially created as a pilot program by the World Bank in November 1990. H. Sjöberg, From Idea to Reality: The Creation of the Global Environment Facility (1994). The GEF seeks to promote multilateral funding for environmentally desirable projects. The Fund, which was established with contributions of more than $1.5 billion, is designed to enhance the attractiveness of investments with environmental benefits that fail to meet traditional lending criteria. Loans are available for projects that address biological diversity, forestry, global warming (including energy efficiency), land degradation and persistent organic pollutants, and ozone depletion (where necessary to supplement the ozone fund).

After completing its initial three-year pilot phase, the GEF was the subject of a detailed and highly critical assessment prepared by an independent evaluation committee to inform decisions about restructuring and further financing. UN Development Programme, UN Environment Programme, and the World Bank, Global Environmental Facility: Independent Evaluation of the Pilot Phase (1994). See also I. Bowles & G. Prickett, Reframing the Green Window: An Analysis of the GEF Pilot Phase Approach to Biodiversity and Global Warming and Recommendations for the Operational Phase (1994); Wells, The Global Environment Facility and Prospects for Biodiversity Conservation, 6 Int'l Envtl. Aff. 69 (1994).

Based on the evaluation, participating governments agreed in March 1994 to restructure the GEF. Twenty-six countries pledged to provide $2 billion for three years. Decisions were to be supervised by a council of 32 nations—18 from recipients and 14 from developed countries. Voting was by a "double majority" system that requires a 60 percent majority of both the participating governments and GEF "shareholders" (with shares awarded in proportion to each country's financial contribution). The future of the GEF grows increasingly important, as it becomes the financial mechanism of choice for implementing environmental agreements including the climate and biodiversity conventions. H. French, Partnership for the Planet 24-28 (1995). H. Sjöberg, Restructuring the Global Environment Facility (1999). In 2002, the donors agreed to further replenish the GEF with an additional $3 billion for four years.

Korinna Horta

## In Focus: Global Environment Facility

Foreign Policy in Focus 1-3 (Dec. 1998)

The establishment of the GEF prior to the 1992 United Nations Conference on Environment and Development (UNCED), commonly known as the Rio Earth Summit, effectively preempted alternative proposals for a green fund which some Southern governments were expected to present in Rio. Because they had no role in its creation, many Southern governments now feel ambivalent about the GEF, although they will accept whatever financial resources may be made available through the facility. At the Rio summit, Southern nations were presented with an already established GEF with a $1 billion core fund, which donor governments promised to make available in addition to their ongoing development assistance programs.

The Rio summit produced a global action plan called Agenda 21. This ambitious plan to make development environmentally, socially, and economically sustainable stipulated that Northern nations had to increase their aid flow to the South. According to the plan, the North would provide $141 billion annually in grants and low-interest loans in the 1993-2000 period to foster sustainable development. This aid would, among other things, facilitate the North-South transfer of environmental technologies. But the promise of Agenda 21, though initially hailed as a major advance in international environmental cooperation, has fallen short—mainly because it never received the backing of the United States. Other donor countries, pointing to the failure of the U.S. to take the lead and meet its share of Agenda 21 obligations, have also failed to increase their assistance to the South.

The creation of the GEF prior to the Rio Earth Summit allowed the U.S. and its G-7 partners to define global environmental problems as they perceived them and to establish the limits and scope of their responsibilities in assisting developing countries. Furthermore, the existence of the GEF has proved a convenient way for the G-7 nations to sidestep the more ambitious North-South funding plan outlined in Agenda 21.

### PROBLEMS WITH CURRENT U.S. POLICY . . .

Numerous problems beset Washington's policy with respect to the GEF. These include the U.S. failure: (1) to pay its assessed contribution, (2) to insist on the implementation of environmental reforms by the World Bank and the GEF's Implementing Agencies (primarily the World Bank), and (3) to ratify the Kyoto Protocol of the UN Biodiversity Conservation Convention and the Kyoto Protocol of the Climate Change Convention.

With support from its German counterparts, the French government launched the GEF proposal as a way of responding to growing domestic pressure to do something about the global environment. With less of a domestic constituency for international environmental efforts, the U.S. government was initially reluctant to accept the Franco-German proposal. The U.S. government knew that making a financial commitment to a new international entity would be fraught with difficulties given congressional reluctance to authorize funding to cover U.S. arrears with the UN. In addition, the administration was aware that any attempt to obtain replenishment funds for international financial institutions like the World Bank would be subject to extensive congressional questioning and delays.

Several key congressional members with seats on important oversight committees together with a few administration officials with years of experience trying to promote environmental reforms in World Bank operations believed that entrusting the World Bank with the management of a fund intended to protect the global environment was tantamount to putting the proverbial fox in charge of the chicken coop. In their view, the World Bank's massive lending to promote the energy sector and forestry without adequate environmental safeguards made the institution part of the problem in both the climate change and biodiversity areas. Consequently, these congressional members and administration officials felt that the World Bank should first demonstrate the ability to implement environmental reforms in its own operations before undertaking new environmental responsibilities.

But the initial U.S. reluctance to support the GEF was quickly overcome. With preparations for the 1992 UNCED event fully under way and more than one hundred heads of state expected at Rio, endorsement of the GEF was a convenient way of demonstrating environmental leadership. Because the size of the contributions of donor governments to the GEF is based on the size of a country's economy—a principle known as "burden-sharing"—the U.S. became the GEF's largest donor followed by Japan and Germany.

Congressional conditions on U.S. funding have helped bring about some reforms in the GEF, such as greater public access to information and broader participation by NGOs in both GEF policy discussions and project implementation. But the accumulation of arrears of the U.S. contribution has hampered determined action on the part of the U.S. to obtain more fundamental reforms. When other donor governments threaten to withhold their funding unless the U.S. pays its share, U.S. credibility is hurt. But to achieve further GEF reforms, Washington will need to fulfill its financial obligations.

The greatest problem thus far has been the failure of the implementing agencies (and especially the World Bank) to meet their promises of mainstreaming global environmental goals into their overall programs. The World Bank's annual lending portfolio of more than $20 billion finances development projects that contribute to the very problems that the GEF seeks to address. What is more, the proposals advocated in the Country Assistance Strategies reports, which are the World Bank's blueprints for its development financing programs in individual borrowing countries, do not reflect any systematic consideration of the environmental implications of these strategies.

An additional problem for U.S. foreign policy—and a major irony—is that the GEF has been adopted, at least on an interim basis, as the financial mechanism for both the UN Biodiversity Conservation and Climate Change conventions (not yet ratified by the U.S.). As such, one of its principal tasks is to assist countries in implementing their obligations under the conventions.

Finally, U.S. foreign policy with regard to the GEF elicits charges of hypocrisy due to U.S. failure to take determined action at home to reduce the use of fossil fuels and to protect its old-growth forests. Meanwhile, the United States uses the GEF to call on other countries to prevent climate change and conserve biodiversity.

## NOTES AND QUESTIONS

1. As of 2021, the GEF had committed $21.1 billion for more than 5,000 projects in 170 countries. Global Environmental Facility (*www.thegef.org/about-us*). An independent evaluation of the GEF is prepared every four years as an input to the negotiation of the GEF replenishment. This "Overall Performance Study" is available at the GEF website.

2. Financial contributions to the GEF are made on the basis of a burden-sharing formula proportional to GDP, with the United States responsible for a little less than 21 percent of the total. When the United States was in arrears due to its failure to make certain payments, the GEF Instrument allowed other parties to reduce their payments pro rata such that total resources available to the GEF were further reduced.

3. GEF support continues to be an important source of incentives for renewable energy and energy efficiency projects. The World Bank implements many clean energy projects using GEF funds. In addition to the GEF Trust Fund, the GEF administers a Special Climate Change Fund, a Least Developed Countries Fund, a Capacity-Building Initiative for Transparency, a Climate Adaptation Fund, and a Nagoya Protocol Implementation Fund.

4. The scope of GEF support for global environmental programs has expanded beyond the original strategies for climate change mitigation and biodiversity. Programs have been added for adaptation to climate change and rehabilitation of coal-burning power plants, and commitments have been made to support the Convention to Combat Desertification and the Stockholm Convention on Persistent Organic Pollutants. The demand for GEF resources has thus increased considerably, while donor commitment of resources has increased only modestly.

### Climate Financing

The GEF is funded ("replenished") by donors on a four-year cycle. The Seventh GEF Replenishment for the period 2018-2022 amounted to $4.1 billion. As a condition for its continued financial support, the United States successfully pushed for the adoption of a Resource Allocation Framework (RAF), a system of allocating funds to countries based on expected impact and some measure of prior performance. Initially, the RAF applied only to climate change and biodiversity projects, although the intent was to gradually extend it to all GEF focal areas. The key result is that the bulk of funds were allocated to a relatively small subset of countries—in the case of climate change, fewer than 20—essentially the largest GHG emitters. The rest were able to apply for less than a total of a few million dollars over four years, barely enough to do a single meaningful project. A more popular feature of the RAF has been to vest greater authority in country focal points, who are now given a sense of the total amount they will receive over four years and the power to prioritize and approve how the funds are used. (This too has a downside, which is that private sector–initiated projects have much less chance of obtaining approval.)

The first Board approval of a World Bank approach to addressing climate change occurred in October 2008—Development and Climate Change: A Strategic Framework for the World Bank Group. Some of the measures discussed include measuring and reporting the carbon footprint of investments; supporting climate vulnerability studies as a basis for climate proofing investments; and developing a program to support the commercialization of new clean energy technologies applicable to developing countries. In fiscal year 2019, the Bank Group provided $17.8 billion in financing for climate investments in developing countries. The World Bank's Climate Change Action Plan for 2021-2025, which took effect in July 2020, focuses on increasing adaptation, leveraging private sector finance, and supporting increased systemic climate action at the country level. The plan supports finance ministers to share best practices and experience on macro, fiscal, and public financial management policies for low-carbon and climate-resilient growth.

## E. COMPLIANCE AND ENFORCEMENT

As in domestic environmental law, success in international law requires more than agreement on a legal framework; it also requires compliance. In an international regime, the question of compliance presents yet another challenge due to the absence of a centralized enforcement regime. How to respond to this challenge has become the subject of a growing body of investigation. "[A]fter an exciting period of treaty-making and institution-building, international environmental lawyers have now turned to the even more difficult task of building compliance with good laws already made and good institutions already in place." M. Janis, An Introduction to International Law 234 (1999).

Weiss & Jacobson

### Getting Countries to Comply with International Agreements

Environment (July/Aug. 1999)

An essential first step in the analysis is to distinguish between implementation, compliance, and effectiveness. *Implementation* refers to measures that countries take to effectuate international treaties in their domestic law. Most treaties are not self-executing and require national legislation or regulations. *Compliance* goes beyond implementation. It refers to whether countries in fact adhere to the agreement's provisions and to the implementing measures that they have instituted.

Some obligations are procedural (such as national reporting); others are substantive (such as reducing or phasing out ozone-depleting substances). Moreover, even if the formal obligations are complied with, there may be a question of compliance with the spirit of the convention. *Effectiveness* is related to compliance, but is not identical. A country may comply with an agreement but the agreement may nonetheless be ineffective at achieving its objectives. . . .

The research confirmed the conventional wisdom that the smaller the number of participants involved, the easier and less expensive it is to regulate and to monitor activity. The striking contrast between the limited number of facilities that produced ozone-depleting substances regulated under the Montreal Protocol and the millions of individuals who could engage in illicit trade in endangered species helps to explain why CITES is much more difficult to enforce than the Montreal Protocol.

The characteristics of an accord, such as the perceived equity of the obligations, the precision of the obligations, provisions for obtaining scientific and technical advice, monitoring and reporting requirements, implementation and noncompliance procedures, incentives, and sanctions, are important to compliance.

Not surprisingly, for parties to comply with treaties, they must regard the obligations imposed as equitable. The Montreal Protocol's differentiated obligations for industrialized and for developing countries as well as the Montreal Protocol Multilateral Fund to help the latter are essential in convincing developing countries to join the protocol. . . .

Although it is difficult to assess whether a country has complied with an agreement when the obligations are imprecise, stating obligations precisely cannot always override factors that run against compliance. For example, even though the CITES obligations are relatively precise, customs officers find it difficult to identify the subtle differences between species. . . .

### Zaelke, Stilwell & Young

### What Reason Demands: Making Laws Work for Sustainable Development, in Making Law Work: Environmental Compliance & Sustainable Development

(Zaelke, Kaniaru & Kruzikova eds., 2005)

The efforts of various governments and institutions . . . are helping advance the rule of law and good governance. However, these efforts must be further strengthened by increasing the focus on compliance and enforcement. The need to strengthen enforcement and compliance has received some attention at international meetings, but more is required to convert words into action. Many States still lack a sound foundation for the rule of law, and many judicial and legal systems still function poorly. Despite a growing body of environmental law both at the national and international levels, environmental quality and some important social indicators have been declining around the world. One reason for these trends is the inadequate investment in assuring effective compliance and enforcement, at both the national and international levels. International and national donor agencies should expand their efforts on good governance and rule of law to include an explicit focus on compliance and enforcement.

While the challenges across these levels differ, some notable commonalities exist. Among other things, enhancing compliance requires:

**Strengthening the empirical foundations of compliance.** Effective policies, including those relating to compliance, must be based on a sound empirical foundation. More empirical research is required about the behavior of different actors — states, firms and individuals — in different circumstances. It has been said of compliance at the national level that, "20 percent of the regulated population will automatically comply with any regulation, 5 percent will attempt to evade it, and the remaining 75 percent will comply as long as they think that the 5 percent will be caught and punished."

Understanding the spectrum of actors in practice, and how to change their behavior, is a key task in conducting empirical research and in enforcing compliance. . . .

**Applying new analytical tools.** New analytic techniques need to be applied to problems of compliance, including systems approaches, simulation and modeling techniques, configurational comparisons and meta-analyses, case studies, counterfactuals and narratives, and structured stakeholder interviews, all of which provide a toolkit for understanding the broader human-environment interactions.

**Strengthening the theoretical foundations of compliance.** Empirical data is interpreted and given meaning through theories, and theories generate testable hypotheses. Theories about compliance provide accounts of why different actors comply or do not comply with international and domestic laws. . . . To be effective, policymakers must understand the various theories and when they will be useful, make their own theoretical assumptions explicit, measure these assumptions against the evolving empirical results to ensure they are sound, and make adjustments as required.

**Diagnosing specific problems.** Reliable empirical data and sound theory can help diagnose underlying problems of non-compliance accurately. Why are some problems harder to address than others? What specifically is the source of non-compliance? Given the limited and fixed budgets of most enforcement and compliance agencies, they need to find the most cost effective means to ensure compliance. . . .

**Understanding and empowering key actors.** When diagnosing problems, policymakers at all levels should take an expansive, system-wide view of the actors in the universe they are attempting to regulate. Several of the more recent theories of compliance tend to recognize that States and firms are not unitary actors, but rather are made up of numerous entities and are influenced by various forces that all contribute to compliance behavior. Actors such as scientists, the media, NGOs, and financial institutions, in addition to the individuals and departments that comprise States and firms, all have important roles to play in promoting compliance, the rule of law, and sustainable development. Policymakers should consider how these actors could best be empowered, in order to most efficiently and effectively generate the desired behavioral changes in the regulated community.

**Strengthening the role of civil society.** Enhancing compliance requires tools that empower citizens to participate in governance, including through access to justice, with opportunities to apply pressure on and through the judicial and legal systems. The international community is moving in this direction. The Aarhus Convention guarantees the rights of access to information, public participation in decision-making, and access to justice in environmental matters. These rights empower citizens to ensure that environmental laws are properly enforced and complied with, as well as foster norms that complement and support the rule of law and good governance.

**Building capacity of regulators and those they regulate.** Strengthening efforts to build capacity is essential, to enhance both the ability of those in the regulated community to comply and the knowledge and capability of those seeking to secure compliance—judges, policymakers, and other governmental officials. . . .

**Building political will and expanding funding.** It is increasingly recognized that the fundamental changes needed to promote the rule of law and sustainable development require the support and commitment of the key decision-makers within the system—whether in government or civil society—and this core group needs to be given enabling assistance to help build the essential internal political will these reforms require. Donor assistance is critical, but so is the will to reform, which must be fostered from within.

**Strengthening the norms that complement and support compliance and the rule of law.** Efforts to strengthen compliance and the rule of law must be complemented by broader efforts to replace cultures of non-compliance and corruption with cultures of compliance. Institutions built on cultures of non-compliance, like buildings erected on sand, are likely to founder. Consequently, additional efforts must be made to promote social norms that complement and support the rule of law and that support legal and judicial reform. This includes general norms such as the norms of good governance; rule of law; and compliance, obedience, and law-abidingness. More specific environmental norms also should be considered.

## NOTES AND QUESTIONS

1. The study of compliance has become a major topic within comparative law. See Victor & Skolnikoff, Translating Intent into Action: Implementing Environmental Commitments, 41 Environment 16 (March 1999); Young, Hitting the Mark, 41 Environment 20 (Oct. 1999); and P. Haas, R. Keohane & M. Levy, eds., Institutions for the Earth: Sources of Effective International Environmental Protection (1993). A robust conclusion from the work to date is the absence of a "smoking gun" in the sense of one mechanism or type of mechanism that will provide an explanation as to why some international environmental agreements are more successful than others. Young, Hitting the Mark, 41 Environment 27-28 (Oct. 1999).

2. The question of compliance should not be viewed as necessarily synonymous with effectiveness in achieving the objectives of an international convention; it is possible to have compliance while failing to achieve larger goals. For example, this may be the case with the Convention on International Trade in Endangered Species (CITES), which has not stopped the extinction of many species due to habitat loss despite high rates of compliance with restrictions on trade. Is the opposite possible; that is, can a Convention achieve its goals without high rates of compliance?

3. Compare the role of citizens as agents for domestic enforcement with the role of citizen organizations in promoting compliance with international agreements. In what ways are they similar, and in what ways do they differ?

4. The Paris Agreement incorporates what essentially are voluntary commitments by its parties to reduce their emissions of GHGs. Through transparency mechanisms, each country's progress in meeting its nationally determined contribution will be assessed and countries will be asked to strengthen their commitments after each stocktake. How likely is it that the Paris Agreement will achieve its goals? What could be done to enhance its effectiveness in achieving compliance?

# CHAPTER 12

# ENVIRONMENTAL PROGRESS AND PROSPECTS

Late in life, reflecting on where EPA stood and what the future held, [Bill Ruckelshaus] remarked that the future of EPA rested on the strength of our democracy. "Could a free society," he wondered, "meet the existential challenges the environment presents us?" It was, to him, an open question. Ruckelshaus lamented the fact that fewer and fewer Americans have any memory of the threats to our environment and health fifty years ago and how much has been accomplished in response to public demand for action. A sense of that history would better prepare us, he thought, for future environmental problems, ones that would be more complex and international in scope.

*— Phil Angell, Chief of Staff to former EPA Administrator William Ruckelshaus*[*]

We believe corporations should lead by example, support sound public policies and drive the innovation needed to address climate change, which is why we have called for action to meet the Paris climate treaty goals. A comprehensive, coordinated and market-based approach to reduce emissions, together with U.S. technology and innovation, must lead the way in reducing greenhouse gases from fossil fuel-based energy while also ensuring that a diverse spectrum of clean fuels and energy sources is available to meet global growth. President Biden's efforts to stand up a National Climate Task Force and streamline permitting processes are important steps to support the energy transition to a lower carbon future, and we welcome his Administration's engagement on these issues.

*— Business Roundtable*[**]

This book has provided a whirlwind tour of the complex maze that environmental law has become. Today, more than a half century after the rise of the modern environmental movement, environmental protection has grown from a national concern to a global imperative. By the time of its 50th anniversary in 2020, Earth Day had become the world's largest civic event, celebrated in hundreds of cities throughout the world. However, in 2020 Earth Day celebrations were forced to go entirely digital due to the global COVID-19 pandemic. The pandemic has

---

[*] Fifty Years at the U.S. Environmental Protection Agency xii (2021).
[**] Statement on Biden Administration's Engagement on Climate Policy, Jan. 28, 2021.

demonstrated how interconnected the world is today as it killed millions, devastated the global economy, and exacerbated racial and economic inequalities.

The year 2021 dawned with the rule of law being severely tested by the first U.S. president to refuse to accept his electoral defeat. Yet, ultimately, the rule of law prevailed, and a new president committed to environmental protection was inaugurated. President Biden immediately announced that the U.S. would rejoin the Paris Climate Agreement, which is now embraced by every country in the world. Yet at the same time the world knows that it will not be adequate to combat the ravages of climate change that already are becoming evident throughout the planet. This chapter reviews what environmental law has accomplished to date, its prospects for future improvement, and the growing influence of private environmental governance.

## A.   *ENVIRONMENTAL PROGRESS*

Clearly, much progress has been made, but it is equally clear that most environmental laws have failed to live up to the lofty expectations that accompanied their enactment. Looking back to the First Annual Report of the Council on Environmental Quality, one cannot help but be struck by how similar the problems outlined in the report are to today's environmental concerns. CEQ, Environmental Quality—1970, at 93 (1970). Although the ozone hole had not yet been discovered, the CEQ report devoted an entire chapter to concern that atmospheric pollution might cause global warming and climate change. New concerns, such as environmental justice, pollution from nonpoint sources, and the environmental impact of hydraulic fracturing, have been added to the environmental agenda. But with the possible exception of noise pollution, none of the environmental concerns outlined by CEQ in 1970 has vanished from the national agenda.

The CEQ was prescient in forecasting not only the significance of the policy changes launched in 1970, but also that environmental problems were bound to get worse before they got better. In the opening paragraphs of its first annual report, CEQ noted that:

> Historians may one day call 1970 the year of the environment. They may not be able to say that 1970 actually marked a significant change for the better in the quality of life; in the polluting and the fouling of the land, the water, and the air; or in health, working conditions, and recreational opportunity. Indeed, they are almost certain to see evidence of worsening environmental conditions in many parts of the country.
>
> Yet 1970 marks the beginning of a new emphasis on the environment—a turning point, a year when the quality of life has become more than a phrase; environment and pollution have become everyday words; and ecology has become almost a religion to some of the young. Environmental problems, standing for many years on the threshold of national prominence, are now at the center of nationwide concern. Action to improve the environment has been launched by government at all levels. And private groups, industry, and individuals have joined the attack. [CEQ, Environmental Quality—1970, at 5 (1970).]

What progress has been made? What have been the success stories and the failures, and what can be learned from them to help shape the development of better policy in the future? Many of the greatest successes of U.S. environmental law were made in its first quarter-century, as reflected in the following assessment by the Council on Environmental Quality.

*Council on Environmental Quality*

## Environmental Quality, 25th Anniversary Report

(1996)

Over the past 25 years, Americans have witnessed remarkable changes in policy and perspectives about the environment.

It was not so long ago that most environmental problems were thought to be largely local in nature and to have short-term, benign effects. Even when the effects were neither short-term nor benign, as in the case of coal mine workers' exposure to coal dust, there was in some quarters a willingness to accept such conditions as an unalterable part of life. In this 25-year period, we have learned that environmental problems can be local, regional, or global in scale, and that many effects are both long-term and life-threatening. Furthermore, we have learned that some environmental problems actually threaten the most fundamental global systems and cycles. In response, we have taken action on numerous fronts. For example, in just 25 years, we have:

- substantially reduced most conventional air and water pollution;
- taken international action to phase out chlorofluorocarbons (CFCs), after learning they could deplete the stratospheric ozone layer;
- made significant progress in reducing children's average blood lead levels, after learning that lead can have devastating impacts on children's intellectual development.

. . . [C]ommand-and-control approaches, with the help of a strong monitoring and enforcement effort, have been successful in controlling large point sources of pollution such as industrial facilities or mass-produced products such as cars. They have been somewhat less successful when the targets are more numerous and diverse and there are many more control options. . . .

Overall, between 1970 and 1994 the combined emissions of the six principal [air] pollutants declined 24 percent. . . . Since passage of the Clean Water Act in 1972, most of the conspicuous water pollution from point sources has been eliminated. More than 57,000 industrial facilities now operate under a pollution control permit. . . . Direct industrial discharges of toxic pollutants are down dramatically since 1972. . . .

Despite the progress that has been made on some fronts, many challenges remain. In some cases, the pressures posed by population growth have been difficult to overcome. Partly as a result of the growth in the number of automobiles on the road, total emissions of nitrogen oxides (NOx) have increased since 1970, which has contributed to a continuing problem with ground-level ozone in many cities. Population and development have played a role in the continuing degradation of coastal zones and estuaries and the wide-scale destruction of critical habitats, though in many cases creative policymaking and careful management can at least partially overcome such conflicts.

In addition, about 40 percent of the nation's rivers, lakes and estuaries still don't meet basic clean water standards; wetlands losses on nonfederal lands were about 70,000-90,000 acres per year during the early 1990s; and localized cases of waterborne disease continue to threaten drinking water safety.

A few problems escaped attention under the early command-and-control approaches. The most notable was non-point source water pollution, such as pesticide and fertilizer runoff from farms and stormwater runoff in urban areas.

A few problems were late-bloomers, including the realization that indoor air pollutants such as environmental tobacco smoke and radon pose significant human health risks.

Finally, there was a growing realization that human activities could be affecting the global environment. In this realm, the emerging issues have included stratospheric ozone depletion, deforestation, declining marine fishery resources in some species and regions, and new evidence that some air emissions were affecting global climate. Since 1972, for example, worldwide generation of carbon dioxide, a common "greenhouse" gas, has increased by 8 percent. Most scientists now believe that such emissions have contributed to an increase in global temperature.

Over the past 25 years a great deal has been learned about environmental problems and strategies to deal with them. Though a number of residual problems remain, the effort was generally successful and has almost certainly provided benefits well in excess of the costs.

## NOTES AND QUESTIONS

1. Why has environmental policy been more successful in some areas than in others? In its 1990 report, the Council on Environmental Quality suggests that problems with diverse and widely dispersed sources and problems that emerged slowly have been particularly difficult to control. Council on Environmental Quality, Environmental Quality: Twentieth Annual Report 11 (1990). Is this an accurate assessment of progress to date? What examples of specific problems support or contradict this assessment?

2. Dr. Barry Commoner, an outspoken environmental scientist who has been a persistent critic of the current regulatory system, is far less sanguine about environmental law's accomplishments. He argues that

> changes in the technology of production are the *root cause* of modern environmental pollution. . . . Only in the few instances in which the technology of production has been changed—by eliminating lead from gasoline, mercury from chlorine production, DDT from agriculture, PCB from the electrical industry, and atmospheric nuclear explosions from the military enterprise—has the environment been substantially improved. [B. Commoner, Failure of the Environmental Effort, 18 Envtl. L. Rep. 10195, 10196 (1988).]

Commoner maintains that rather than focusing on defining "acceptable" levels of pollution, the environmental laws should focus on changing production technology to prevent pollutants from being generated. Do you agree that changes in technology are the "root cause" of contemporary environmental problems? Even if this is true, does the solution necessarily require that the government intervene in the production process?

3. Note that the prohibition of lead additives in gasoline and the phaseout of the production of CFCs are two prominent examples cited by CEQ as environmental success stories. To what extent were these initiatives the product of idiosyncratic factors, rather than the result of the routine application of existing laws? The gasoline lead additive phaseout has now gone global and is widely considered one of the greatest achievements in the history of global environmental law. Robert V. Percival, Getting the Lead Out: The Phaseout of Gasoline Lead Additives—A Global Environmental Success Story, in The Impact of Environmental Law: Stories of the World We Want (Eisma-Osorio, Kirk & Albin, eds. 2018).

4. Visions of the future world environment are many and varied. Many believe that changes in technology offer the best hope for defusing some of the political difficulties of regulating smaller and more diffuse sources of pollution and for overcoming the daunting global challenges posed by population growth and increasing resource consumption. Consider the following reflections from the editors of the New York Times, discussing the fundamental changes that occurred in humankind's attitude toward nature during the twentieth century.

## A New Way of Living with Nature

N.Y. Times, Dec. 19, 1999, at 12

A century that will be remembered for material and scientific progress may also be remembered for something more modest—as a moment when mankind, realizing that the earth's resources were not infinite and perhaps seeking expiation for years of predatory behavior, struck a truce with nature.

Early in this century, for example, federal sharpshooters hunted wolves for bounty. Today, the federal Fish and Wildlife Service is orchestrating the wolf's revival. Sixty-five years ago the Hoover Dam, rising 70 stories above the bed of the Colorado River, was hailed as the greatest engineering feat in American history. Today, dams are increasingly seen as enemies of the natural order and are actually being dismantled. Only 30 years ago the Hudson River, once among America's most majestic waterways, was little more than a 350-mile sewer stretching from the Adirondacks to Manhattan, choked with untreated municipal waste, industrial chemicals and agricultural runoff. Today, the Hudson pulses with life.

Wolves, dams, wilderness, forests, lakes, rivers, estuaries—all are seen differently now than they were less than 50 years ago. . . .

It was thus fitting that this same century would eventually produce a citizens' revolt against environmental degradation. This revolt—symbolized by the first Earth Day in 1970, and defined by the creation of an astonishing body of environmental laws—not only gave the nation the tools with which to heal itself but conferred upon ordinary citizens the indispensable right to take even the government to court if it failed to carry out these laws.

## NOTES AND QUESTIONS

1. In August 2020, the Environmental Protection Network, a group of more than 500 former EPA career employees, released a report "Resetting the Course of EPA," *https://www.environmentalprotectionnetwork.org/wp-content/uploads/2020/08/Resetting-the-Course-of-EPA-Report.pdf.* The report was dedicated to William Ruckelshaus, EPA's first administrator, who died in November 2019, thirteen months short of the 50th anniversary of EPA's creation in December 1970. The report noted that EPA spending had been cut in half since 1980, while the U.S. population had increased by 40 percent and discretionary federal spending had increased by 48 percent. Six former EPA administrators, three who served in Republican administrations (William Reilly, Lee Thomas, and Christine Whitman) and three who served in Democratic administrations (Carol Browner, Lisa Jackson, and Gina McCarthy) endorsed the recommendations in the report.

2. December 2020 marked the 50th anniversary of the U.S. Environmental Protection Agency. In honor of this event, the *Case Western Law Review* published a symposium issue, "The Environmental Protection Agency Turns 50," which includes a keynote address from then-Administrator Andrew Wheeler. 70 Case Western L. Rev. 871 (2020). The book, *Fifty Years at the U.S. Environmental Protection Agency: Progress, Retrenchment and Opportunities* (Barnes, Graham & Konisky, eds. 2021), provides an excellent assessment of environmental progress made during the agency's first half-century. Bill Ruckelshaus's former chief of staff writes that late in life Ruckelshaus "lamented the fact that fewer and fewer Americans have any memory of the threats to our environment and health fifty years ago and how much has been accomplished in response to public demand for action. A sense of that history would better prepare us, he thought, for future environmental problems, ones that would be more complex and international in scope." Id., at xii.

## B.  ENVIRONMENTAL PROSPECTS

Environmentalists sometimes have been accused of being alarmists who exaggerate the urgency of various environmental problems in order to provoke a response from the public. In 1968, ecologist Paul Ehrlich attracted national attention with his book *The Population Bomb*, which forecast mass starvation and mineral shortages because population growth soon would overwhelm the Earth's carrying capacity. Calling Ehrlich a Malthusian, economist Julian Simon argued in *The Ultimate Resource* that "[n]atural resources are not finite" because human ingenuity continually finds more efficient ways to use them. In 1980, the two agreed to test their theories by betting $1,000 on whether the prices of five metals—chrome, copper, nickel, tin, and tungsten—would be higher or lower in the year 1990. Ehrlich argued that prices would rise with increased demand for a finite supply of the metals. Simon bet that prices would fall. In 1990, Simon won the bet when the prices of all five metals had declined in real terms due in part to the development of substitutes (such as plastics). Tierney, A Bet on the Planet Earth, N.Y. Times Mag., Dec. 2, 1990, at 52. Prior to Simon's death in 1998, Simon and Ehrlich had been sparring over terms for another bet. Ehrlich offered "15 separate bets, totaling $1,000 each, that 15 environmental indicators—things like greenhouse gases, biodiversity, fishery stocks—will get worse over the next decade." Simon rejected the proposal. McCoy, When the Boomster Slams the Doomster, Bet on a New Wager, Wall St. J., June 5, 1995, at A1.

The Earth now has 7.77 billion people, but population growth has slowly slipped from the forefront of environmental concerns. As countries develop, birth rates consistently have fallen, and the rate of overall population growth has slowed. Today Ehrlich believes that a collapse of global civilization can be avoided "because modern society has shown some capacity to deal with long-term threats, at least if they are obvious or continuously brought to attention (think of the risks of nuclear conflict)." Paul R. Ehrlich and Anne H. Ehrlich, Can a Collapse of Global Civilization Be Avoided?, 280 Proceedings of the Royal Society, December 2012, available at *http://dx.doi.org/10.1098/rspb.2012.2845*. However, Ehrlich has not yet become a full-fledged optimist. He is skeptical of how well environmental concerns will fare in the political process because "the risks are clearly not obvious to most people" and the costs of preventing them are incurred up front, while the benefits accrue to unknown future generations.

Two prominent critics of the environmental movement have been journalist Gregg Easterbrook and statistician Bjorn Lomborg. In his 1995 book *A Moment on the Earth: The Coming Age of Environmental Optimism*, Easterbrook argued:

- That in the Western world pollution will end within our lifetimes, with society almost painlessly adopting a zero-emissions philosophy.
- That several categories of pollution have already ended.
- That the environments of Western countries have been growing cleaner during the very period the public has come to believe they are growing more polluted.
- That First World industrial countries, considered the scourge of the global environment, are by most measures much cleaner than developing nations.
- That most feared environmental catastrophes, such as runaway global warming, are almost certain to be avoided.
- That far from becoming a new source of global discord, environmentalism, which binds nations to a common concern, will be the best thing that's ever happened to international relations.
- That nearly all technical trends are toward new devices and modes of production that are more efficient, use fewer resources, produce less waste, and cause less ecological disruption than technology of the past.
- That there exists no fundamental conflict between the artificial and the natural.
- That artificial forces which today harm nature can be converted into allies of nature in an incredibly short time by natural standards.
- Most important, that humankind, even a growing human population of many billions, can take a constructive place in the natural order.

Advocating for an approach he calls "ecorealism," Easterbrook proclaims "a law of environmental affairs: Whenever all respectable commentators believe a problem cannot be solved, it is about to be solved." Thus, he maintains that the problem of global warming is about to be solved, and he predicts that "the end of the fossil-fuel economy is near at hand."

Not surprisingly, Easterbrook's views generated considerable controversy. Environmentalists maintained that he did not fully appreciate that many of the positive environmental trends he cites are due to hard-fought battles waged by them. As one reviewer wrote, "He wants it both ways—to condemn professional enviros and other doomsayers and at the same time to champion nature. This amounts to ecosophistry and ignores the fact that what are often perceived as extreme positions effect moderate, positive gains in any field." Conaway, Mother Nature's Prospects, Wash. Post Book World, Apr. 23, 1995, at 5. The Environmental Defense Fund (EDF) observed that Easterbrook "repeatedly criticizes scientists whose dire predictions have not come to pass, without fully acknowledging that their forecasts catalyzed changes in laws and policies that forestalled the predictions themselves." Environmental Defense Fund, A Moment of Truth: Correcting the Scientific Errors in Gregg Easterbrook's A Moment on the Earth (1995).

Five years after the publication of Easterbrook's book, Bjorn Lomborg, then an associate professor of statistics from Denmark's University of Aarhus, received considerable attention by making claims remarkably similar to those of Gregg Easterbrook in Lomborg's book *The Skeptical Environmentalist* (2001). Lomborg writes:

> We will not lose our forests; we will not run out of energy, raw materials, or water. We have reduced atmospheric pollution in the cities of the developed world and have good reason to believe that this will also be achieved in the developing world. Our oceans have not been defiled, our rivers have become cleaner and support more life. . . . Nor is waste a particularly big problem. . . . The problem of the ozone layer has been more or less solved. The current outlook on the development of global warming does not indicate a catastrophe. . . . And, finally, our chemical worries and fear of pesticides are misplaced and counterproductive.

Lomborg claimed to have been a committed environmentalist until encountering the work of Julian Simon. He charged that the reason this good news is not more widely accepted is that environmental groups have engaged in a pattern and practice of exaggeration and statistical manipulation to mislead the media. Not surprisingly, critics of environmental regulation were quick to acclaim Lomborg's work. See, e.g., Alex Kozinski, Gore Wars, 100 Mich. L. Rev. 1742 (2002) (book review).

Surprisingly, Lomborg never cited Easterbrook's work, nor does it appear in Lomborg's extensive bibliography. Despite the striking similarity of their theme that environmental conditions are improving more than most environmentalists acknowledge, Easterbrook's work is more nuanced than Lomborg's. Although making the same optimistic claims Lomborg does, Easterbrook recognizes that not all environmental trends are moving in a positive direction, and he gives more credit to environmental regulation as a source of environmental progress. While both decry doom and gloom forecasts by environmentalists, Lomborg puts a different "spin" on his argument. Lomborg claims that fear mongering by environmentalists has led society to put too much emphasis on environmental protection, and he suggests that resources should be shifted to other priorities. Lomborg denies the possibility that much of the environmental progress he trumpets is the product of existing environmental protection policies.

If the state of the environment is improving because environmental policies are working, this progress provides no basis for Lomborg's claim that environmental protection efforts should be relaxed. As one reviewer has noted, "[t]he ultimate irony is that Lomborg could have presented his mass of data as a tribute to the effectiveness of environmental policy. That he chooses to do the opposite says far more about him than about any claimed objectivity of his statistical analysis." Michael Grubb, Relying on Manna from Heaven?, 294 Science 1285, 1286 (Nov. 9, 2001). See also Douglas A. Kysar, Some Realism About Environmental Skepticism: The Implications of Bjorn Lomborg's The Skeptical Environmentalist for Environmental Law and Policy, 30 Ecology L.Q. 223 (2003); Robert V. Percival, Skeptical Environmentalist or Statistical Spin-Doctor? Bjorn Lomborg and the Relationship Between Environmental Law and Environmental Progress, 53 Case W. Res. L. Rev. 263 (2002).

## NOTES AND QUESTIONS

1. Were the successes of past policies due in part to public response to "doom and gloom" forecasts by environmentalists? Paul Ehrlich, who lost the bet with the late Julian Simon, had been highly popular with the public, while Simon, who won, had few followers. Does the outcome of Ehrlich's bet with Simon prove that Ehrlich's ideas were wrong, or just that he is a poor gambler? Does Simon's argument imply that no action needed to be taken to avert environmental crises, or just that we need not get too worried about the future because we can and will act to avert crises? The more people agreed with Ehrlich, the more likely it was that society would impose stringent environmental protection measures. Was Simon's optimism more likely to prove correct if more people believed that Ehrlich was right and acted to prevent environmental damage?

2. More than a decade after his book was published, Easterbrook announced that he had modified his position concerning global warming in light of mounting scientific evidence. "As an environmental commentator, I have a long record of opposing alarmism. But based on the data I'm now switching sides regarding global warming, from skeptic to convert." Easterbrook proclaimed that "[t]he science has changed from ambiguous to near-unanimous concerning the 'greenhouse effect' and that greenhouse gas emissions must be curbed." Steven Milloy, Global Warming Skeptic Claims Environmental Conversion, Fox News.com, May 25, 2006, *http://www.foxnews.com/story/2006/05/25/global-warming-skeptic-claims-environmental -conversion/* (last visited Apr. 29, 2013).

3. Some of Lomborg's predictions proved to be wildly optimistic. For example, Lomborg predicted that oil prices would remain below $27/barrel until 2020. Instead, they soared to more than $140 per barrel in mid-2008 before plunging to $40/barrel after the global financial crisis and then rising to current levels, which are significantly higher than Lomborg's forecast. Lomborg's rosy view of the impact of climate change also has been contradicted by subsequent events. In 2010, Lomborg conceded that global warming is "undoubtedly one of the chief concerns facing the world today" and "a challenge that humanity must confront." Matthew

Moore, Climate "Sceptic" Bjørn Lomborg Now Believes Global Warming Is One of
World's Greatest Threats, The Telegraph, Aug. 31, 2010.

4. Gus Speth, former Dean of the Yale School of Forestry and Environmental
Studies, expresses frustration that "[e]lectoral politics and mobilizing a green political movement have played second fiddle to lobbying, litigating, and working with
government agencies and corporations." James Gustave Speth, The Case for a New
American Environmentalism, 39 Envtl. L. Rep. 10066 (2009). Speth calls for "a new
environmental politics" that will pursue an expanded agenda "to embrace a profound challenge to consumerism and commercialism and the lifestyles they offer,
a healthy skepticism of growthmania and a redefinition of what society should be
striving to grow, a challenge to corporate dominance and a redefinition of the corporation and its goals, a commitment to deep change in both the functioning and
the reach of the market, and a powerful assault on the anthropocentric and con-
tempocentric values that currently dominate." Id. at 10068.

Consider the following modest predictions for the future of environmental
law by one of the authors of this casebook.


Robert V. Percival

## Looking Backward, Looking Forward: The Next 40 Years of Environmental Law

43 Envtl. L. Rep. 10492 (June 2013)

The one thing we know about predictions for the future of environmental law
is that most of them are likely to be wrong. . . . In an edition of *The Weekly Standard*
that went to press on April 16, 2010—four days before the *Deepwater Horizon* offshore oil platform exploded, precipitating the worst oil spill in U.S. history, a fellow
at the American Enterprise Institute wrote: "Improvements in drilling technology
have greatly reduced the risk of the kind of offshore [oil] spill that occurred off
Santa Barbara in 1969. . . . To fear oil spills from offshore rigs is analogous to fearing air travel now because of prop plane crashes in the 1950s." Steven F. Hayward,
*The Energy Policy Morass*, The Weekly Standard, Apr. 26, 2010. Oops. . . .

### II. LEGAL RESPONSES TO ENVIRONMENTAL RISKS

. . . It now seems clear that the bipartisan consensus that spawned ambitious
U.S. environmental legislation during the 1970s and 1980s has disappeared. . . .
Despite all-time record temperatures and hurricanes that caused unprecedented devastation to coastal areas, climate change nearly disappeared from U.S. political discourse during the 2012 U.S. presidential campaign. Climate change was never once
mentioned during three 90-minute debates between the presidential candidates. . . .

Predicting future federal law and policy is difficult because it depends in large
part on the country's future political leadership, who will be determined based
largely on factors exogenous to the environment. Environmental issues played virtually no role in pivotal presidential campaigns in 1980 and 2000, both of which
resulted in leaders who pursued sharp changes in federal environmental policy.

## III. LOOKING FORWARD: CONTEMPORARY PREDICTIONS OF THE ENVIRONMENTAL FUTURE

Contemporary predictions for the fate of the planet seem to be shaped in large part by forecasts concerning the future of technology.

### A. *Al Gore's* The Future

In a book entitled *The Future: Six Drivers of Global Change* (2013) former Vice President Al Gore identifies six emerging trends that will pose challenges crucial to the future health of the planet. These include a more deeply interconnected global economy; planet-wide electronic communications; a new balance of global political, economic and military power that has shifted influence from states to private actors and from political systems to markets; rapid unsustainable growth; a revolutionary new set of powerful genetic and materials sciences technology; and a radically new relationship between the aggregate power of human civilization and the Earth's ecological systems.

Gore notes that there has been substantial progress on many fronts, including the fact that global poverty is declining and wars seem to be on the decline. In March 2012 the United Nations announced that the world already had achieved the Millennium Development Goal of cutting in half the proportion of people who lack sustainable access to safe drinking water in advance of a 2015 deadline. However, the goal of having 75% of the world's population with access to improved sanitation is unlikely to be met by 2015, when it is projected that only 67% will have such access. . . .

While Gore calls himself "an optimist," he founds such optimism on a belief that Americans eventually will be able to restore the United States to a leadership role on global environmental issues by overcoming a political system that has been "hacked" by special interests. "As more of the power to make decisions about the future flows from political systems to markets, and as ever more powerful technologies magnify the strength of the invisible hand, the muscles of self-government have atrophied." The vast majority of members of Congress "now represent the people and corporations who donate money, not the people who actually vote in their congressional districts."

### B. The 2052 Project

The most detailed forecasts concerning the environmental future come from . . . Jørgen Randars, a Norwegian professor who was one of the authors of *The Limits to Growth*. [H]e has authored a new report for the Club of Rome predicting the future of the planet in 2052. *2052: A Global Forecast for the Next 40 Years* (2012). Randars incorporated 35 predictions from experts in various fields to help guide his predictions.

He concludes that nearly four decades from now the world will no longer have an expanding population. The *2052 Report* forecasts that global population will reach a peak of 8.1 billion in the early 2040s before declining to 7 billion people by the year 2075. By 2052 80% of the world population will be living in large urban cities (10-40 million people) or smaller cities (1-5 million) surrounding megacities, shifting political focus onto water, noise, and air pollution as well as traffic.

The report forecasts that by 2052 the world economy will be 2.2 times larger than it is today, meaning that 120% more goods and services will be produced. Average consumption rates will increase, making for a larger "human ecological footprint" that will only be softened by increased efficiency in the use of natural resources and energy. . . . China will pass the United States in the size of its economy, and India's economy will come close to the size of the U.S. economy by the year 2050. But China still is forecast to have a per capita gross domestic product that trails both the United States ($56,000 per capita versus a U.S. GDP of $73,000 per capita) and the non-U.S. Organization for Economic Cooperation and Development (OECD) ($63,000).

The *2052 Report* forecasts that substantial additional investments will need to be made in the development and implementation of (1) scarce resources to substitute for oil, gas, and phosphorus, (2) measures to control dangerous emissions, (3) replacement of formerly free ecological services such as fresh water and fish protein, (4) repair of accumulated environmental damage from nuclear plants and offshore drilling, (5) measures to protect against future threats such as rising sea levels, (6) measures to rebuild infrastructure damaged by extreme weather, and (7) maintenance of military forces to defend resources, fight off immigration, and to provide manpower during emergencies. Forced investments from adaptation and disaster costs will increase by 1-10% as the weather gets wilder, crowded locations require expensive new infrastructure investments to be made in exposed locations, and the expected lifetime of existing infrastructure decreases.

Growing economies will correlate with increased emissions and rising global temperatures. By 2052, global energy use will increase by 50% and more than half of world energy use will involve fossil fuels. Energy use will remain high but more of it will be used wisely and sustainably with the sun either directly (through solar heat or electricity) or indirectly (wind, hydro, or biomass) providing an increased share. The greatest uncertainty in this forecast is the speed at which a transition to sustainable energy sources will occur. This transition already is underway, but it will encounter serious difficulties before and after the year 2052. Energy use is forecast to peak in the 2030s before declining as a proportion of GDP by 30% in light of growing incentives, and increased ability to conserve energy. . . .

## IV. CONCLUSION: THE FUTURE OF GLOBAL ENVIRONMENTAL LAW

Some environmental challenges that will command the attention of future policymakers already are well known. Conflicts over water resources are a significant problem that is likely to become even more challenging over time. The most widely forecast environmental challenge—anthropogenic climate change—now has become a contemporary reality as its effects become more apparent each year. . . .

Future technological advances . . . raise both new challenges and opportunities for improvement in the global environment. During the last few years, technological changes have affected U.S. energy production in a manner that few could have foreseen. The widespread use of hydraulic fracturing has significantly increased domestic production of natural gas and oil. China's oil imports are growing by 8%

annually, while U.S. oil imports are declining by 8% per year. As a result China will soon pass the United States as the world's largest oil importer. In November 2012 the International Energy Agency predicted that the United States will become the world's largest oil producer by 2020 and that by 2030 the United States will become a net exporter of oil.

Accidents and natural disasters have posed unexpected challenges to environmental policy. The *Deepwater Horizon* oil spill demonstrated the dangers of extracting oil at ever-increasing depths and Shell's ill-fated efforts to drill in the Arctic have shown the difficulties of drilling in that harsh environment. Just as a new generation of nuclear power plants were about to be launched, the tsunami and Fukushima Daiichi disaster caused countries around the world to rethink their policies toward nuclear power.

One cannot be confident that new technology will largely solve future environmental problems, leading to the dawn of the zero-emissions society. . . . Indeed, the history of environmental law demonstrates that innovations in pollution control technology are highly correlated with increases in the stringency of emissions controls. If federal regulators continue to demand cleaner and more efficient production processes and means of transportation, as illustrated by significant increases in fuel economy standards, further progress can be expected in the transition towards a green society. It is less likely that technological progress will occur with respect to environmental problems that are not the focus of regulatory pressure. This is illustrated by the finding of the President's Oil Spill Commission that virtually no progress has been made in oil spill cleanup technologies in the decades since the [1989] *Exxon Valdez* oil spill. Non-point source pollution is one of the top problems that federal regulatory policy has failed to address effectively and agricultural interests that strongly oppose actions to redress this problem remain politically powerful.

When environmental problems become so bad as to become politically salient, regulation has produced notable successes. In the developed world, air pollution standards have been an unbridled success story. In 2011 EPA released a study finding that air pollution controls mandated by the CAA Amendments of 1990 are saving so many lives that they will produce net benefits of $1.935 trillion by 2020. The phaseout of leaded gasoline in the United States has now been adopted throughout the world, producing dramatic reductions in levels of lead in children's blood.

Horrendous levels of pollution in parts of the developing world are generating pressure to upgrade environmental standards. . . .

Initially environmental law responded to polluting industries by encouraging them to locate away from populated areas. This "zoning function" performed by the early common law eventually was replaced by a "technology-forcing" one as fear of liability inspired industry to develop new pollution control technology. Responding to new controls on various environmental risks in developed countries, industry exported some of those risks to developing countries. Today, this pattern is rapidly changing as developing countries upgrade their environmental standards and nongovernmental organizations (NGOs) shine the spotlight of international publicity on companies who degrade the environment in any part of the world, even if such degradation is legal under domestic law.

Due to the growth of NGO networks throughout the world, no corporation can damage the environment in some remote corner of the planet without fear of protests at its far away corporate headquarters. NGOs in the developing world are using creative information disclosure strategies to promote environmental protection. In China Ma Jun's Institute of Public and Environmental Affairs (IPEA) has made major strides in improving environmental and working conditions in the supply chains of major multinational electronics companies. Faced with audits by the IPEA and other NGOs revealing environmental and labor violations in its suppliers, Apple Corporation has agreed to employ regular independent auditors to police its supply chain. . . .

While environmental concerns continue to command broad popular support, it has now become virtually impossible to shepherd new environmental legislation through the U.S. Congress. Proponents of environmental progress need to work on building creative, bipartisan coalitions to win the political battles of the future. For example, economic conservatives who oppose federal subsidies could be strong supporters of efforts to eliminate some of the most environmentally destructive subsidy programs. The received political wisdom is that new energy taxes are political suicide, following the ill-fated effort in the early days of the first Clinton Administration to persuade Congress to adopt a British thermal unit (BTU) tax. Yet it makes enormous sense to consider shifting much of the tax burden away from productive labor and toward discouraging environmentally damaging production and consumption decisions. Energy taxes can create powerful incentives to improve energy efficiency and to reduce overall energy consumption, and they need not increase the overall tax burden if they are rebated in a proper manner.

Great progress has been made in controlling air and water pollution in the developed world, but climate change is creating substantial new environmental challenges to countries throughout the world. It would be comforting to be able confidently to predict a future of unbroken progress in environmental protection, but such progress is not inevitable. The notion that globalization would result in an unstoppable and beneficial spread of democracy, capitalism, and innovation is now being openly questioned [by some].

Until bipartisanship returns to environmental politics, the future of environmental policy will depend largely on who controls the White House and Congress, which usually is determined by factors divorced from voters' environmental values. The global financial collapse in 2008 created an opportunity for opponents of environmental regulation to erect a deceptive narrative blaming it for unrelated economic troubles. This narrative seeks to depict environmental regulation as excessive and economically damaging. It seeks to exploit high levels of unemployment to demonize regulation as "job killing," even though "life saving" usually would be a more appropriate description. The narrative is founded on a false dichotomy between environmental regulation and a robust economy. Economic history demonstrates that strong environmental protection measures can coexist with a strong economy, but political history shows that a weak economy can be a threat to environmental protection. Thus, promotion of a strong economy is crucial for improving the future of environmental policy and, in turn, the kind of planet our progeny will inherit.

## NOTES AND QUESTIONS

1. The author concludes that although the future of environmental law will depend largely on the future of U.S. political leadership, environmental issues have not played a significant role in most U.S. presidential campaigns. This was not the case in 2020 when presidential candidate Joe Biden campaigned on a platform that promised muscular executive action to combat climate change. The author also notes that technological changes, such as oil spill remediation technology, seem to be correlated with regulatory pressures. What can be done to encourage the development of greener technology in the future?

2. In *Beyond Environmental Law: Policy Proposals for a Better Environmental Future* (Alyson C. Flournoy & David M. Driesen eds., 2010), a group of environmental law scholars led by Professors Flournoy and Driesen unveil proposals for launching what they call the "third generation" of environmental law. They propose the enactment of a National Environmental Legacy Act and an Environmental Competition Statute. The former would apply to resources under public ownership or management or protected by the public trust doctrine. It would impose "a clear and enforceable conservation mandate that focuses on sustainability and constrains resource use." Id. at 5. The latter would try to create a "race to the top" for improvements in environmental technology by providing that innovators may collect the cost of making such improvements plus a premium preset by statute from competitors who pollute more. They argue that this approach would make "the achievements of the most environmentally capable firms rather than the timid actions of government bureaucrats the driver of environmental improvement."

3. Yale's "Next Generation" project published its vision for the future in a book entitled *Thinking Ecologically: The Next Generation of Environmental Policy* (M. Chertow & D. Esty eds., 1997). Cautioning that "the devil lies in the details," Marian Chertow and Dan Esty warn that "reforms" in environmental policy must "not become an excuse for shifting pollution costs onto the public or for inattention to the risk of environmental disasters." Id. at 233. Chertow and Esty sketch their vision for the future by attempting to describe how the world would look in 2020 if policies incorporating the ideas of the "Next Generation" project were implemented.

*Daniel C. Esty & Marian R. Chertow*

## A Vision for the Future, in Thinking Ecologically: The Next Generation of Environmental Policy

(Chertow & Esty eds., 1997)

- Environmental policy has become more ecological—comprehensive in focus and attentive to linkages across problems. Systems thinking in the form of both industrial ecology and ecosystem management has emerged as the analytic core of ecological policy. Fragmented regulatory approaches derived from individual laws separately governing air and water pollution and waste management have, over time, been reassembled, omitting some parts, adding others, into a more coherent and unified set of obligations. . . .

- In the land use context, this new policy approach provides a mechanism to address the cumulative impacts of many small harms and thus to ensure that environmental goals are better connected to development decisions. With an emphasis on comprehensive analysis and data-driven decisionmaking, new procedures gauge the air, water, and habitat impacts of proposed land uses. This process supports local priority setting and helps to guarantee that any environmental burdens created are not unfairly imposed on those in the next town, in the next state, or even thousands of miles away. . . .

- While responsibility for some policy matters has been decentralized, the "spirit of regulatory devolution" from the 1990s has given way to a recognition that the diversity of environmental and resource use issues requires a diversity of responses. Some problems are known to be best dealt with at a community or company level; other issues require a national or even global response. . . .

- Environmental rights — the entitlement of every person to be free from pollution harms — have been firmly established, actually reestablished, building on the tradition of nuisance law. The property rights of the public have similarly been clarified, and landowners recognize that they must pay for harms that spill beyond their property boundaries or for any scarce common resources such as air or water that they consume or pollute.

- A carefully structured system of fees for emissions has been established. Payment is required for discharges that cause adverse ecological or public health effects above established thresholds. After a phase-in period that extended twenty years in some sectors, companies from multinational giants to mom-and-pop enterprises pay emissions fees.

## NOTES AND QUESTIONS

1. To what extent could the changes described above be accomplished without changing the environmental laws? What would be required to bring these changes about? Could a carbon tax or a carbon cap-and-trade program help stimulate the development of new renewable energy technologies?

2. Esty and Chertow endorse making environmental law more ecological in focus and the establishment of environmental rights for individuals, building on the tradition of nuisance law introduced in Chapter 2. Some visions for the future of environmental law are centered around the creation of "ecological law," "earth rights," or rights for nature. See Katherine Bleu, Ecological Law: A New Era for the Environment, Nat. Res. & Env't (Spring 2021). The Earth Law Center is an NGO dedicated to promoting an "ecocentric" approach to law that recognizes nature's inherent rights to exist, thrive, and evolve. Although some countries, including New Zealand, Bolivia, Ecuador, and India, have granted legal personality to certain natural resources, "[a]t this stage, ecological law is largely conceptual." But just as accepted wisdom about environmental policy has changed over time, it is fair to anticipate that environmental law also will do so.

3. In October 2019 Yale University Press published a book entitled *A Better Planet: 40 Big Ideas for a Sustainable Future*. Dan Esty, the editor, argues in the book that "environmental law and policy cannot be all about 'red lights' and 'stop signs'

that tell people what not to do; we need an equal measure of 'green lights' that incentivize creative individuals and entrepreneurial businesses to bring innovation to bear on pollution control, renewable power generation, and other environmental breakthroughs that society needs." Id. at 5. The book includes 40 essays arguing in favor of new approaches to environmental law and policy.

4. Gus Speth has been among the most influential environmental voices in the United States since the 1970s — a founder of the Natural Resources Defense Council, chair of the Council on Environmental Quality, founder and president of the World Resources Institute, head of the UNDP, and dean of the Yale School of Forestry and the Environment. Much of his career was based on the effective use of existing legal and policy instruments to effectuate change. However, Speth now argues that the problems of the United States are now so deeply rooted that only more fundamental change — a social movement — can bring about the necessary change.

> [W]e environmentalists have been too wonkish and too focused on technical fixes. We have not developed well the capacity to speak in a language that goes straight to the American heart, resonates with both core moral values and common aspirations, and projects a positive and compelling vision. Throughout my forty-odd years in the environmental community, public discourse on environment has been dominated by lawyers, scientists, and economists — people like me. Now we need to hear a lot more from the preachers, the poets, the psychologists, and the philosophers. And our message must be one that is founded on hope and honest possibility. [James Gustave Speth, America the Possible: A Manifesto (2012).]

## C.  PRIVATE ENVIRONMENTAL GOVERNANCE

Corporate environmentalism once would have been considered an oxymoron. When the McDonald's Corporation and the Environmental Defense Fund agreed in 1989 to work together to develop strategies to reduce solid waste, skeptics and critics abounded. But the project proved enormously successful. A key discovery it made was that McDonald's had sufficient market power to dictate to suppliers the environmental characteristics of the packaging materials the company used. McDonald's succeeded in significantly reducing the solid waste it generated while saving considerable money. Environmental Defense Fund and McDonald's, Waste Reduction Task Force Final Report (1991).

In 1989 the Coalition for Environmentally Responsible Economies (CERES) was founded by an investment fund manager who worked with environmentalists to formulate a set of principles for responsible environmental behavior by corporations. Initially named the Valdez Principles, they were renamed the CERES Principles after pushback from companies who did not appreciate being reminded of the *Exxon Valdez* oil spill. Investors and consumers increasingly have become attracted to corporations that address environmental, social, and governance (ESG) issues in their corporate policies.

Many companies now file annual reports that specifically address their environmental performance. Initially, many of these reports lacked any common scope or content, making comparison and interpretation difficult. CERES launched the Global Reporting Initiative (GRI) in 1997 to address this need. The GRI is an international initiative that includes UN agencies as well as business and environmental interests. It seeks to achieve some standardization and encompasses criteria for sustainability that transcend narrow environmental, health, and safety concerns. Surveying thousands of companies operating around the world, the accounting firm KPMG found that by 2015 including corporate environmental responsibility data in annual reports had become "a firmly established global trend." In its December 2020 report KPMG found that 90 percent of corporations in North America and 80 percent worldwide now report on sustainability and that "GRI remains the dominant global standard for sustainability reporting." KPMG, The Time Has Come (2020). Third-party assurance of sustainability information in corporate reports is now a majority business practice worldwide.

One source of incentives for voluntary improvements in the environmental behavior of private companies is through private standards developed by national and international standard-setting agencies. The growth in global trade added to interest in this approach because trading companies have an interest in standardized measures of the quality of products purchased from foreign suppliers. Much of this effort is coordinated by the International Organization for Standardization (ISO), an international association of standard-setting agencies founded in 1947. See generally ISO 14001 and Beyond: Environmental Management Systems in the Real World (1997); Miller, Environmental Policy in the New World Economy, 3 Widener Symp. L.J. 287, 297-301 (1998); D. Hunter, J. Salzman & D. Zaelke, International Environmental Law and Policy 1396-1409 (1998).

Historically, ISO standards have mostly focused on technical issues of product manufacture and performance (e.g., procedures for measuring the strength or elasticity of a material). However, in the last decade ISO began to develop standards for quality management systems, including internal audit procedures. Compliance with these standards, ISO 9000 and 10011, has become a condition for doing business in many nations, especially in Europe. More and more, compliance must also be certified by an independent third party. ISO 9000/10011 touched on environmental issues as one element of overall quality control and generated interest in a more formal examination of the potential for an environmental focus. This led to the development of the ISO 14000 environmental standards governing management systems, audits, labeling, environmental performance evaluation, and lifecycle assessment.

Many corporations opposed the Trump administration's efforts to roll back environmental regulations. Several automakers opposed the administration's rollback of national fuel economy standards, and most utilities opposed repeal of limits on mercury emissions by power plants. In August 2019, the Business Roundtable stunned the corporate world by issuing a new Statement on the Purpose of a Corporation. In a dramatic shift in its 22-year-old policy, the group endorsed the notion that corporations have obligations that extend beyond creating value for their shareholders. The statement recognizes that corporations have duties to their customers, their employees, their communities, and to "protect the environment by embracing sustainable practices across our businesses." A total of 181 chief executives of the 193 major corporations that were members of the Business Roundtable signed the statement.

Business Roundtable

## Statement on the Purpose of a Corporation

(2019)

Americans deserve an economy that allows each person to succeed through hard work and creativity and to lead a life of meaning and dignity. We believe the free-market system is the best means of generating good jobs, a strong and sustainable economy, innovation, a healthy environment and economic opportunity for all.

Businesses play a vital role in the economy by creating jobs, fostering innovation and providing essential goods and services. Businesses make and sell consumer products; manufacture equipment and vehicles; support the national defense; grow and produce food; provide health care; generate and deliver energy; and offer financial, communications and other services that underpin economic growth.

While each of our individual companies serves its own corporate purpose, we share a fundamental commitment to all of our stakeholders. We commit to:

- Delivering value to our customers. We will further the tradition of American companies leading the way in meeting or exceeding customer expectations.
- Investing in our employees. This starts with compensating them fairly and providing important benefits. It also includes supporting them through training and education that help develop new skills for a rapidly changing world. We foster diversity and inclusion, dignity and respect.
- Dealing fairly and ethically with our suppliers. We are dedicated to serving as good partners to the other companies, large and small, that help us meet our missions.
- Supporting the communities in which we work. We respect the people in our communities and protect the environment by embracing sustainable practices across our businesses.
- Generating long-term value for shareholders, who provide the capital that allows companies to invest, grow and innovate. We are committed to transparency and effective engagement with shareholders.

Each of our stakeholders is essential. We commit to deliver value to all of them, for the future success of our companies, our communities and our country.

## NOTES AND QUESTIONS

1. Should corporations owe obligations to any stakeholders other than their shareholders? In 1970 economist Milton Friedman argued that the sole purpose of a corporation should be to increase its profits. Critics of the Business Roundtable's statement maintain that any focus that extends beyond creating shareholder value through maximizing profits is likely to disadvantage shareholders who are the actual owners of the corporation.

2. Jamie Dimon, CEO of JP Morgan Chase, who was chairman of the Business Roundtable when the statement was issued, stated that the Statement on the Purpose of a Corporation "more accurately reflects how our CEOs and their companies operate" and that it "will help to set a new standard for corporate leadership."

3. Disclosure strategies are being used to improve the performance of multinational supply chains. A coalition of Chinese environmental groups led by Ma Jun from Beijing's Institute of Public and Environmental Affairs persuaded Apple Inc. to hire independent auditors who now conduct annual inspections of the company's Chinese suppliers. The audits assess how well these suppliers are complying with China's labor, worker health, and environmental laws. Apple discloses the results of these audits in annual Supplier Responsibility Progress Reports available online at *https://www.apple.com/supplier-responsibility/*.

### Disclosure of Environmental Liabilities and Climate Risks

Enactment of the Sarbanes-Oxley Act of 2002 placed increased attention on disclosure of environmental liabilities by corporations. The Act requires a company's chief executive officer and chief financial officer to certify that the company has an adequate internal management system consisting of "disclosure controls and procedures" encompassing environmental matters required to be reported in filings with the Securities and Exchange Commission (SEC). While the SEC's role in environmental matters has been relatively minor, both environmental groups and advocates for improved corporate governance have been pushing companies to make greater environmental disclosures.

The application of requirements for corporate disclosure of "material risks" to concerns about climate change has become an important trend. See, e.g., R. Repetto & D. Austin, Coming Clean: Corporate Disclosure of Financially Significant Environmental Risks (2000). The financial risks of climate change are most often discussed in relation to the potential consequences of future regulatory policies and therefore are of most relevance to firms, such as electric utilities, who use fossil fuels to generate significant emissions of greenhouse gases (GHG). This risk may be indirect, such as with respect to automobile companies, insofar as regulatory policies may differentially favor companies producing more energy-efficient models. Firms such as insurance companies may also be at risk from exposure to the impacts of climate change. Large emitters also arguably share a risk of future litigation or liability (equivalent to the positions of companies with Superfund sites). Without reporting requirements, the existence of such risks has been compared to investor ignorance of toxic assets owned by financial institutions. As then–Vice President Gore told an audience of investors, "[i]f you really take a fine-tooth comb and go through your portfolios, many of you are going to find them chock-full of subprime carbon assets." H. Fernando, Sub-Prime Carbon: Preparing for the Dangers of Hidden Carbon Risk (2008).

Pension funds and other large investors have been pushing for corporate disclosure of climate risks for several years through organizations such as the Carbon Disclosure Project (*www.cdp.net*) and CERES (*www.ceres.org*). The power of a survey sent on behalf of a substantial aggregation of global investors (collectively $87 trillion in 2013) is such that many of the world's largest corporations now annually respond voluntarily to questionnaires soliciting information on their emissions and analysis of risks from climate change. However, the level of detail varies considerably; most of those responding report on climate change risks and GHG emissions, but fewer report on lifetime emissions from products they sell and still fewer report on emissions from suppliers. Nevertheless, the information provided is sufficient to indicate that the risks within industrial categories vary considerably—particularly for utilities, which vary greatly in their carbon intensity.

In addition to voluntary reporting, several efforts have been initiated to require disclosure of climate change risks based on requirements of the Securities and Exchange Commission and state laws. In September 2007, a coalition of investors, state officials, and environmental organizations filed a petition with the SEC arguing that the risks of climate change are "material" and thus should be disclosed in corporate annual reports. S. Mufson, SEC Pressed to Require Climate-Risk Disclosures, Wash. Post, Sept. 18, 2007, at D1. Courts have concluded that an omitted fact is "material" if there is "a substantial likelihood that a reasonable shareholder would consider it important in deciding how to vote."

On January 27, 2010, the SEC voted to publish Commission Guidance Regarding Disclosure Related to Climate Change. This document clarifies how existing SEC disclosure rules should be applied by publicly traded corporations to reveal information concerning the risks climate change poses to their businesses. SEC, Commission Guidance Regarding Disclosure Related to Climate Change: Securities and Exchange Commission, Feb. 2, 2010, available at *http://www.sec.gov/rules/interp/2010/33-9106.pdf*. See also Congressional Research Service, SEC Climate Change Guidance: An Overview and Congressional Concerns, May 24, 2012.

In February 2012, a federal judge refused to dismiss a lawsuit against BP by shareholders who allege that the company made misleading statements concerning its preparedness for an oil spill in filings it made in 2009. In re BP P.L.C. Securities Litigation, 852 F. Supp. 2d 767 (S.D. Tex. 2012). In November 2012, the SEC charged BP with misleading investors in reports it filed concerning the rate at which oil was being released into the Gulf of Mexico from the *Deepwater Horizon* spill. BP settled the charges by agreeing to pay $525 million, the third largest penalty in SEC history.

The SEC has been criticized for lax enforcement of its climate change guidance. David Gelles, S.E.C. Is Criticized for Lax Enforcement of Climate Risk Disclosure, N.Y. Times, Jan. 23, 2016. Some state attorneys general have been active in questioning the adequacy of disclosure of climate risks by companies in the fossil fuel industry. In November 2015, Peabody Energy, the world's largest private coal company, settled claims by the New York Attorney General that it had failed adequately to disclose the impact of climate risks on its business prospects.

In August 2020, the SEC voted to change its rules for risk factor disclosures that registrants must make pursuant to Regulation S-K, but it declined to include anything specific regarding the disclosure of climate-related risks. Senator Elizabeth Warren (D-Mass.) criticized the SEC for failing to enact a "mandatory, uniform standard for reporting on climate risk," given the seriousness of the "climate crisis." SEC chairman Jay Clayton defended the decision on the grounds that environmental risks "are very company-specific and sector-specific issues."

## NOTES AND QUESTIONS

1. In January 2020, BlackRock, an investment management company that manages more than $7 trillion in assets, declared, "We believe that sustainability should be our new standard for investing." The company justified this new focus as a matter of minimizing financial risk to investors rather than embracing broader ethical considerations, noting that "sustainability-related factors can affect economic growth, asset values, and financial markets as a whole." It observed that climate change presents not only "physical risk associated with rising global temperatures, but also transition risk—namely, how the global transition to a low-carbon economy could affect a company's long-term profitability."

2. How can consumers determine if corporations' environmental pledges are genuine or simply "greenwashing" to convince consumers to view them favorably? Countries, corporations, universities, and others are making pledges to achieve "carbon neutrality" by dates decades into the future. In most cases the leaders of these entities are unlikely to still be in power when the pledges are due. How can one determine if these pledges are realistic?

3. In May 2021, ExxonMobil CEO Darren Woods was asked if his company would follow other oil companies in making pledges of future carbon neutrality. "Woods refused, arguing that oil companies making such pledges had no real plans to achieve them." Christopher M. Matthews, Exxon v. Activists: Battle Over Future of Oil and Gas Reaches Showdown, Wall St. Journal, May 25, 2021. Is he right? On May 26, 2021, the company's shareholders defied management by electing three new board members supported by environmental activists, stunning the financial community.

4. In February 2020 the Earth Island Institute sued ten companies for their claims that their plastic products are recyclable. Earth Island Institute v. Crystal Geyser Water Co., No. 20CIV01213 (Superior Ct. San Mateo County, Calif). Earth Island argues that the claims are deceptive and contribute to a public nuisance because, in reality, the vast majority of plastics labeled as recyclable will never be recycled. Of the estimated 8.3 billion metric tons of plastic produced since 1950, only 9 percent has been recycled. Instead, what is not recycled is either incinerated, causing air pollution, or becomes waste, contributing to the global burden of plastic waste pollution.

### Environmental Certification Programs

Many corporations also are involved in voluntary product certification programs that allow them to approach consumers with independent certification that they engage in best environmental practices in their global operations. Professor Michael Vandenbergh reports that by 2016 there were more than 400 eco-labels, many of them developed by private corporations. M. Vandenbergh, The Future of Environmental Enforcement, 47 Envtl. L. Rep. 10206 (March 2017). For example, all of Chiquita's banana farms have been certified by the Rainforest Alliance as complying with a Better Banana program, a set of environmental and social best practices that involves significant reductions in pesticide use and water pollution and improved waste management practices. In April 2001, officials of the Canadian timber industry agreed with a coalition of environmental groups to protect from logging 1.5 million acres of coastal rainforest in British Columbia. Jim Carlton,

Canada, Timber Firms Agree on Rainforest Pact, Wall St. J., Apr. 4, 2001, at A2. The agreement follows successful efforts by environmental groups to get large retailers like Home Depot to agree to phase out selling products using wood from old growth forests. A representative of the Natural Resources Defense Council explained: "The basic goal is for the consumer to ask, 'Where does my wood come from?'" Id. Other environmentalists predicted that the agreement represented "the beginning of the end for old-growth logging." Id.

Given the current partisan gridlock blocking governments from acting decisively on pressing environmental problems, many experts, including Vandenbergh, believe that "[p]rivate sector action provides one of the most promising opportunities to reduce the risks of climate change, buying time while governments move slowly or even oppose climate mitigation." All over the world, companies are pursuing voluntary initiatives to address environmental problems. For example, Microsoft, Google, and other major companies have committed to becoming carbon neutral. Walmart and EDF are working together to cut one billion tons of emissions from Walmart's supply chain by 2030. Despite his enthusiasm for private initiatives, Vandenbergh concedes that private initiatives "cannot keep global emissions on track to achieve the most widely adopted climate target, but they can achieve a private governance wedge: they can reduce emissions by roughly 1,000 million tons (a gigaton) of $CO_2$ per year between 2016 and 2025. When combined with other efforts, this private governance wedge offers a reasonable chance of buying a decade to resolve the current government gridlock."

### Environmentally Responsible Financing

Beginning in the early 1990s, project finance has become an increasingly common means of financing large infrastructure projects in developing countries. Typically, such financing is based on the creation of a legally independent company with financing secured solely by project assets (e.g., power plants, mines, and toll roads). Private banks frequently help structure project finance as well as acting as lenders. The size and potential environmental consequences of such projects have made private banks an increasing target for environmental critics. In 2002, several large private banks approached the International Finance Corporation (IFC), the private sector arm of the World Bank, to discuss the Bank's approach to sustainable development. The banks were interested in identifying common standards that would be both practical and credible, and they quickly settled on the World Bank and IFC policies as the most relevant to private practice.

On June 4, 2003, a group of ten large banks announced the adoption of the Equator Principles. By November 2005, the list of participating banks and financial institutions had grown to 36, including institutions accounting for a substantial percentage of all privately funded project finance in developing countries. See Esty, Knop & Sesia, The Equator Principles: An Industry Approach to Managing Environmental and Social Risks (Harv. Bus. Sch., June 2005). By 2021, a total of 116 financial institutions in 37 countries covering more than 70 percent of international project finance debt have officially adopted the Equator Principles. *www. equator-principles.com.*

The Equator Principles commit participating institutions to follow IFC safeguard policies and World Bank Pollution Prevention and Abatement guidelines. The basic approach requires categorization of the risks associated with each project and analysis of mitigation measures. Projects with higher levels of risk are required to have an environmental management plan outlining risk mitigation measures that must be included in the loan agreements; failure to comply means a borrower can be declared in default.

Why have so many banks (particularly large banks) signed on to the Equator Principles? Several factors presumably are at work. One is the need for evaluating environmental risks that may threaten the financial performance of an investment, a potentially serious concern with large infrastructure projects. For example, a large, highly profitable gold mine in Peru has been endangered by public uprisings. Perlez & Bergman, Tangled Strands in Fight over Peru Gold Mine, N.Y. Times, Oct. 25, 2005. While the banks individually define their environmental review procedures, following practices of public institutions provides added credibility; the fact that the IFC and World Bank use them provides some confidence in their practicality.

The environmentalist reaction to the Equator Principles has been mixed. NGOs are suspicious that private banks will not follow the same disclosure and transparency requirements that apply to the IFC and World Bank, and they also worry that the Principles apply only to project finance and not to the much wider range of corporate lending practices. The Principles also do not include "no-go" zones. When the IFC was revising its safeguards, some NGOs worried about the potential for downgrading to satisfy the private banks.

Similar issues have been raised with respect to World Bank funding of commercial banks and with respect to the environmental practices of export credit agencies. Curmally, Sohn & Wright, Multilateral Development Bank Lending Through Financial Intermediaries (WRI Issue Brief 2005); Harmon, Maurer, Sohn & Carbonell, Diverging Paths: What Future for Export Credit Agencies in Development Finance? (2005). In an article in the January 2009 issue of the Environmental Forum ("A Test Case for Export Finance"), Bruce Rich sharply criticized the involvement of export credit agencies (ECAs) in the financing of the Ilisu Dam project. The dam, which would be built on the Tigris River in southeastern Turkey, would forcibly displace nearly 65,000 ethnic Kurds while flooding archeological treasures in Anatolia.

An effort by a consortium of companies in Germany, Switzerland, and the United Kingdom to obtain financing for the project collapsed in 2002 after an international outcry. However, the project later was revived when ECAs from Austria, Germany, and Switzerland approved nearly $600 million in loan guarantees for the project. Arguing that this represents an important test of the OECD's "Common Approaches on Environment" for export credit agencies, Rich notes that the three ECAs involved in the project required the Turkish government to meet 153 conditions dealing with the environment, resettlement, and cultural heritage. After independent monitoring committees determined in March and August 2008 that the Turkish government had failed to meet these conditions, the ECAs in October 2008 sent an official Environmental Failure Notice. This notice gave the Turkish government 60 days to remedy these deficiencies or face withdrawal of ECA support. On December 23, 2008, the three ECAs ordered work on the project suspended for 180 days due to the failure to live up to the environmental conditions. The dam ultimately was completed despite withdrawal of the foreign funding.

In February 2009, a landmark settlement was announced of a National Environmental Policy Act (NEPA) lawsuit brought by Friends of the Earth (FOE), Greenpeace, Boulder, Colorado, and three California cities against the U.S. Export-Import Bank and the Overseas Private Investment Corporation (OPIC). The lawsuit charged that these ECAs had failed to consider the impact on global warming and climate change of their actions financing fossil fuel power projects in violation of NEPA. In the settlement, the agencies agreed to provide $500 million in financing for renewable energy projects over the next ten years. The Export-Import Bank agreed to develop, in consultation with plaintiffs, a carbon policy with financial incentives for reducing GHG emissions. It also agreed to evaluate GHG emissions when assessing fossil fuel project investments. OPIC agreed to set a goal of reducing by 20 percent the GHG emissions associated with the projects it funds over the next ten years. It also agreed to include climate change impacts in the environmental assessment it performs of any projects it funds that emit more than 100,000 tons of carbon dioxide equivalents per year.

## NOTES AND QUESTIONS

1. Some environmental certification programs are more demanding than others. How can a consumer assess the accuracy and value of information provided by certification programs?

2. The definition of "material" arguably has a self-fulfilling quality insofar as the more petitions and requests for information are made, the more apparent it is that "a reasonable shareholder" would consider such information relevant to their vote. Another means by which shareholders can request information is through shareholder resolutions, which have been used increasingly to raise concerns about climate change. The 2008 annual meeting of Exxon shareholders proved noteworthy when several members of the Rockefeller family, the original owners of Standard Oil and Exxon, came out in favor of several climate change–related resolutions. None were approved. Krauss, Exxon Rejects Proposals Backed by Rockefellers, N.Y. Times, May 29, 2008. CERES reports that in 2012 environmental and social responsibility proposals by shareholders comprised 45 percent of all corporate proxy ballots, an increase from 30 percent in 2010 and 40 percent in 2011. In 2020 a total of 16 shareholders ESG resolutions won approval, an increase from 14 approved in 2019.

3. The Carbon Disclosure Project (CDP) began as an effort focused on companies based in Europe, the United States, and other industrialized countries, but in recent years it has gradually begun extending its inquiry to large industrial firms in China, India, Brazil, and South Africa. What response rate would you expect from companies in these countries? For more information, see the CDP website, *www.cdp.net.*

4. A major question about the CDP is the extent to which the information it provides is subsequently used by the sponsoring investment funds in their financial decisions. Some large pension funds, notably those of public employees in California, are increasingly linking their investment strategies to environmental concerns. However, many institutional investors (including most universities and private foundations) have resisted this trend. Why?

5. Another approach is based on providing consumers with information that allows them to make informed choices and in turn to influence the products offered, much as disclosure of nutritional information on grocery products and in fast food restaurants has been promoted as a way to influence diet. The UK retailer Marks & Spencer has attempted to implement carbon reporting on its products in addition to reporting its corporate GHG emissions. It reported that by April 2012 this had helped the company reduce its GHG emissions by 22 percent from 2007 levels and by 34 percent using the retail industry's standard carbon intensity ratio of emissions per square foot. But the retailer cautions that comparisons can be difficult: "The most carbon efficient retailer is one that does nothing other than retailing, only operates big stores, sells no fresh food and closes at 6pm." Comparison between companies can be difficult because the extent of outsourcing will affect a company's reported carbon footprint. And "some important carbon conversion rates also vary by country, so a store operating off a mainly nuclear-powered electricity grid in France will have a fraction of the reported emissions of a similar store in the UK." Rowland Hill, Comparing Apples and Petticoats, Environmental Finance, Jan. 15, 2013.

## D.   CONCLUDING THOUGHTS

Because environmental regulation raises many fundamental policy dilemmas for which there are no clear answers, it is hardly surprising that it has been such a persistent source of controversy. As we saw at the outset of this book, beneath the veneer of consensus on environmental values that permits politicians to declare the environment a "moral issue," lie deep divisions over policy. The characteristics of modern environmental problems—uncertainty of mechanism and effect, the collective nature of risk, irreversibility, and potentially catastrophic effects—help explain why. Even as some believed that these challenges are so daunting that environmental protection should become "the central organizing principle for civilization," A. Gore, Earth in the Balance: Ecology and the Human Spirit 269 (1992), others depicted environmentalists as power-hungry alarmists bent on destroying jobs. See, e.g., Will, Earth Day's Hidden Agenda, Wash. Post, Apr. 19, 1990, at A27.

These divisions are not simply the product of different interpretations of environmental "facts"; they also turn largely on differences in values concerning how much environmental risk society should tolerate, how that risk should be distributed, and how cautious society should be in the face of uncertainty. The difficulty of resolving such questions of value is reflected in the common law's long struggle between utilitarian and rights-based approaches to environmental problems. This tension persists today, even as public law has taken center stage in environmental protection efforts, in the fierce debate over competing approaches to regulatory policy.

While public law has overcome many of the common law's limitations, it faces difficulties of its own in designing and implementing regulatory policies that will affect human behavior in predictable ways. Over four decades of experience with federal regulation has generated considerable knowledge that can be used to improve future regulatory policy. We have learned that regulation can affect human behavior in unintended and counterproductive ways, but that it also can stimulate technological innovation, expanding our capability to control environmental problems and reducing the costs of such controls. As the limitations of policies that emphasized command-and-control regulation become more evident, environmental law is becoming increasingly receptive to approaches that use economic incentives to affect behavior.

Improved scientific understanding of environmental problems has made us more acutely aware of the limits of our knowledge even as our desire to know more intensifies. We have come to realize that even small changes in human behavior can have an enormous impact on our environment, even if we still cannot trace micro-level impacts with precision. This understanding is contributing to expanded notions of social responsibility embodied in laws that extend liability to parties more remotely connected to environmental damage or that seek to regulate increasingly smaller entities.

As legal responsibility for environmental protection expands, conflicts between environmental regulation and individual autonomy may arise more frequently. In such circumstances, environmentalists may become the cool analysts while their opponents seek to muster moral outrage against perceived threats to their property. Recognition that concern for fairness and respect for individual autonomy are at the root of much environmental regulation should provide some common ground for resolving these controversies as society decides how to control environmental risks and how to distribute the costs of regulation.

Many of the same policy dilemmas that have confronted national environmental policy making are now appearing on a global scale as the international community seeks to develop a coordinated response to global environmental problems, including the global climate crisis. How effectively the world community addresses these issues will have a profound effect not only on what sort of planet we leave our children, but also on the values they will hold and their ability to fulfill their aspirations.

# GLOSSARY

This glossary and the acronym list in Appendix B are adapted from various EPA publications, including Terms of Environment (1997), and EPA, Glossary of Climate Change Terms. Some of them have been modified by the casebook authors to improve their clarity or accuracy. The definitions are intended to acquaint you with the basic concepts; they do not represent legal definitions of the terms.

**Acid deposition.** Particulates and gases deposited onto soil and surface waters after emissions of sulfur and nitrogen compounds are transformed by chemical processes in the atmosphere. The wet forms, popularly called "acid rain," can fall as rain, snow, or fog.

**Action level.** The level of a pollutant or contaminant that, when detected, triggers a requirement for some form of further action.

**Active ingredient.** In any pesticide product, the component that kills, or otherwise controls, target pests. Pesticides are regulated primarily on the basis of their active ingredients.

**Adaptation.** Adjustment in natural or human systems to a new or changing environment. Adaptation to climate change refers to adjustment in natural or human systems in response to actual or expected climatic stimuli or their effects, which moderates harm or exploits beneficial opportunities.

**Administrative order.** A directive requiring an individual, business, or other entity to take action or to refrain from an activity. It can be enforced in court and may be issued as a result of an administrative complaint ordering payment of a penalty for violations of a statute.

**Advanced waste water treatment.** Treatment of sewage that goes beyond the secondary or biological water treatment stage by removing nutrients such as phosphorus and nitrogen and a high percentage of suspended solids.

**Advisory.** A non-regulatory document that communicates risk information to persons.

**Air quality criteria.** Documents summarizing what is known about adverse health and welfare effects associated with various levels of air pollution.

**Air quality standards.** Regulations limiting levels of pollutants in the ambient air that may not be exceeded during a specified time in a defined area.

**Airborne particulates.** Total suspended particulate matter found in the atmosphere as solid particles or liquid droplets, including windblown dust, emissions from industrial processes, smoke from the burning of wood and coal, and the exhaust of motor vehicles.

**Anthropocene.** A proposed geological epoch that dates from the beginning of significant human impact on the earth's geology and ecosystems.

**Anthropogenic.** Caused by or relating to the impact of human activity on the environment.

**Antidegradation policy.** A policy that restricts activities that would cause air or water quality to deteriorate in areas that currently meet applicable air or water quality standards.

**Aquifer.** An underground layer of permeable rock, sand, or gravel containing groundwater that can supply wells and springs.

**Asbestos.** A family of fibrous silicate minerals with electrical and thermal insulating properties that can cause lung cancer, mesothelioma, or asbestosis when inhaled.

**Asbestosis.** A disease associated with chronic exposure to and inhalation of asbestos fibers that makes breathing progressively more difficult and can lead to death.

**Ash.** The mineral content of a product remaining after complete combustion.

**Assimilative capacity.** The ability of a body of air or water to receive pollutants without causing significant environmental damage.

**Attainment area.** An area where air quality is in compliance with the national ambient air quality standards established under the Clean Air Act. An area may be an attainment area for one pollutant and a nonattainment area for others.

**Background level.** The naturally occurring level of a chemical substance found in air, water, or soil in the absence of a source of pollution.

**Banking.** A system for recording credits for qualified emissions reductions for later use in bubble, offset, or netting transactions.

**BEN.** EPA's computer model for analyzing a violator's economic gain from not complying with the law.

**Benthic organism (Benthos).** A form of aquatic plant or animal life that is found on or near the bottom of a stream, lake, or ocean.

**Benthic region.** The bottom layer of a body of water.

**Best available control technology (BACT).** An emission limitation based on the maximum degree of emission reduction achievable through application of production processes and available methods, systems, and techniques. Use of the BACT concept is allowable on a case-by-case basis for major new or modified emissions sources in attainment areas, and it applies to each regulated pollutant.

**Best demonstrated available technology (BDAT).** As identified by EPA, the most effective commercially available means of treating specific types of hazardous waste. The BDATs may change with advances in treatment technologies.

**Best management practices (BMP).** Methods that have been determined to be the most effective, practical means of preventing or reducing pollution from nonpoint sources.

**Bioaccumulative.** The propensity of substances to increase in concentration in living organisms as they are ingested because they are very slowly metabolized or excreted.

**Bioassay.** A test used to evaluate the effects of a chemical substance by exposing living organisms (*in vivo*) or isolated tissue (*in vitro*) to it.

**Biochemical oxygen demand (BOD).** A measure of the amount of oxygen consumed in the biological processes that break down organic matter in water.

**Biodegradable.** Having the ability to break down or decompose rapidly under natural conditions and processes.

**Biodiversity.** Refers to the variety and variability among living organisms and the ecological complexes in which they occur. Diversity can be defined as the number of different items and their relative frequencies. For biological diversity, these items are organized at many levels, ranging from complete ecosystems to the biochemical structures that are the molecular basis of heredity. Thus, the term encompasses different ecosystems, species, and genes.

**Biofuels.** Fuels produced from living organisms or from metabolic by-products of such organisms (organic or food waste products) as distinguished from fossil fuels, which are fuels derived from long dead biological material.

**Biological assessment.** A document prepared for the consultation process under section 7 of the Endangered Species Act to assist in the determination whether a proposed major activity under the authority of a federal agency is likely to adversely affect listed species, proposed species, or designated critical habitat.

**Biological opinion.** A document that is the product of formal consultation under section 7 of the Endangered Species Act that expresses the opinion of the Fish and Wildlife Service or the National Marine Fisheries Service on whether or not a federal action is likely to jeopardize the continued existence of a listed species or result in the destruction or adverse modification of critical habitat.

**Biological treatment.** A treatment technology that uses bacteria to consume waste by breaking down organic materials.

**Biomass.** All of the living material in a given area; often refers to vegetation. Also called "biota."

**Biomimicry.** A design strategy that seeks to observe nature and emulate its best ideas, especially when it comes to waste reduction and limiting environmental impact.

**Biomonitoring.** (1) The use of living organisms to test the effects of effluent discharges. (2) Analysis of blood, urine, and tissues to measure chemical exposure in humans.

**Biosphere.** The portion of Earth and its atmosphere that can support life.

**Black carbon.** Operationally defined matter based on measurement of light absorption and chemical reactivity and/or thermal stability; consists of soot, charcoal, and/or possible light-absorbing refractory organic matter.

**BlueGreen Alliance.** A national partnership of labor unions and environmental organizations dedicated to expanding the number and quality of jobs in the green economy.

**BOD5.** The amount of dissolved oxygen consumed in five days by biological processes breaking down organic matter.

**Brownfields.** Real estate with some degree of environmental contamination, usually due to previous industrial use, which may deter redevelopment because of fears of environmental liability.

**Bubble policy.** An EPA policy that allows a plant complex with several facilities to decrease pollution from some facilities while increasing it from others, so long as total results are equal to or better than those required by previous limits. Facilities where this is done are treated as if they exist in a bubble in which total emissions are averaged out.

**Cancellation.** Refers to revoking the registration of a pesticide under section 6(b) of the Federal Insecticide, Fungicide and Rodenticide Act (FIFRA) if unreasonable adverse effects to the environment and public health develop when a product is used according to widespread and commonly recognized practice, or if its labeling or other material required to be submitted does not comply with FIFRA provisions.

**Cap.** A layer of clay or other highly impermeable material installed over the top of a closed landfill to prevent entry of rainwater and to minimize production of leachate, or a limit on the total amount of emissions from a group of pollution sources covered by a particular control regime.

**Cap-and-trade.** Technique for controlling pollution by setting a limit on the total emissions from a group of sources while allowing the sources to trade emissions allowances to reduce the overall cost of complying with the cap.

**Carbon dioxide ($CO_2$).** A colorless, odorless gas that results from fossil-fuel combustion and is normally a part of the ambient air. Increasing levels of carbon dioxide in the atmosphere are contributing to the greenhouse effect.

**Carbon dioxide equivalent ($CO_2$e).** A metric measure used to compare the emissions from various greenhouse gases based upon their global warming potential (GWP). Carbon dioxide equivalents are commonly expressed as "million metric tons of carbon dioxide equivalents (MMTCO2Eq)." The carbon dioxide equivalent for a gas is derived by multiplying the tons of the gas by the associated GWP. MMTCO2Eq = (million metric tons of a gas)×(GWP of the gas).

**Carbon footprint.** The amount of greenhouse gases and specifically carbon dioxide emitted by a person's activities or a product's manufacture and transport during a particular period.

**Carbon monoxide (CO).** A colorless, odorless, poisonous gas produced by incomplete fossil fuel combustion.

**Carbon neutral.** Actions that result in no net increase in carbon dioxide ($CO_2$) in the atmosphere because they offset additions of $CO_2$ with equivalent reductions.

**Carbon sequestration.** The uptake or storage of carbon, such as by trees and plants, or the process of capturing and storing carbon that otherwise would be emitted into the atmosphere and storing it deep underground to reduce emissions of greenhouse gases that contribute to global warming and climate change.

**Carbon sink.** Any process, activity, or mechanism that removes a greenhouse gas, an aerosol, or a precursor of a greenhouse gas or aerosol from the atmosphere.

**Carcinogen.** Any substance that can cause or contribute to the production of cancer.

**Carrying capacity.** The amount of use a natural area can sustain without deterioration of its integrity.

**Catalytic converter.** An air pollution abatement device that removes pollutants from motor vehicle exhaust, either by oxidizing them into carbon dioxide and water or reducing them to nitrogen and oxygen.

**Categorical exclusion.** A class of actions that does not require preparation of an environmental assessment or environmental impact statement under the National Environmental Policy Act (NEPA) because they are deemed not to have a significant effect on the environment.

**Categorical pretreatment standard.** A technology-based effluent limitation for an industrial facility that discharges into a municipal sewer system.

**Characteristic hazardous waste.** A waste deemed hazardous because it exhibits any one of four hazardous characteristics: ignitability, corrosivity, reactivity, or toxicity.

**Chlorinated hydrocarbons.** A class of compounds consisting of chlorine, hydrogen, and carbon that are very persistent in the environment and that tend to bioaccumulate in living organisms. Examples include polychlorinated and polybrominated biphenyls and pesticides such as DDT, aldrin, dieldrin, heptachlor, chlordane, lindane, endrin, mirex, and toxaphene.

**Chlorination.** The application of chlorine to drinking water, sewage, or industrial waste to disinfect it or to oxidize undesirable compounds.

**Chlorofluorocarbons (CFCs).** A family of inert, nontoxic, and easily liquified chemicals formerly used widely in refrigeration, air conditioning, packaging, and insulation or as solvents and aerosol propellants. Because CFCs are very stable in the troposphere, they move to the stratosphere and are broken down by strong ultraviolet (UV) light, where they release chlorine atoms that then deplete the Earth's protective ozone layer.

**Chronic toxicity.** The capacity of a substance to cause adverse health effects due to exposure for an extended period of time, usually at least one-tenth of an organism's lifetime.

**Clean Development Mechanism (CDM).** Established by Article 12 of the Kyoto Protocol, the CDM allows a country with an emission-reduction or emission-limitation commitment under the Protocol (Annex B Party) to implement an emission-reduction project in developing countries. Such projects can earn saleable certified emission reduction (CER) credits, each equivalent to one ton of $CO_2$, which can be counted toward meeting Kyoto targets.

**Clean Power Plan.** Regulations issued by EPA during the Obama administration to limit emissions of greenhouse gases from existing power plants under §111(d) of the Clean Air Act.

**Climate change.** Changes in worldwide climate and weather patterns of anthropogenic origin, including changes in precipitation patterns and storm activity, induced by global warming.

**Closed-loop recycling.** Reclaiming or reusing materials in an enclosed process.

**Coastal zone.** An area adjacent to a seacoast whose use can affect the sea and coastal ecosystems.

**Co-benefits.** Benefits produced by an action that accrue as side effects of the action (e.g., the benefits of reducing particulates that occur when measures to control mercury emissions are employed).

**Coefficient of haze.** A measurement of atmospheric interference with visibility.

**Coliform index.** A rating of the purity of water based on a count of fecal bacteria.

**Combined sewers.** A sewer system that carries both sewage and stormwater runoff. Normally its entire flow goes to a waste treatment plant, but during a heavy storm, the stormwater volume may be so great as to cause overflows, releasing untreated mixtures of stormwater and sewage into receiving waters.

**Comment period.** Time provided for the public to review and comment on a proposed federal agency action after the proposal is published in the Federal Register.

**Community water system.** Under the Safe Drinking Water Act, a system for providing the public with water that has at least 15 service connections or that regularly serves at least 25 individuals.

**Compact fluorescents.** Fluorescent light bulbs small enough to fit into standard light sockets, which are much more energy-efficient than standard incandescent bulbs.

**Compliance schedule.** An agreement between a regulated entity and a government agency that specifies a schedule of actions to be taken by certain dates to bring the entity into compliance with a regulation.

**Concentrated animal feeding operation.** Agricultural operations where large numbers of animals are kept and raised in confined situations with feed being brought to the animals rather than the animals grazing or otherwise seeking feed in pastures. These operations are subject to regulation under the Clean Water Act because the animal waste and wastewater they generate can enter water bodies from spills or breaks of waste storage structures (due to accidents or excessive rain), and from non-agricultural application of manure to crop land.

**Consent decree.** A legal document, approved by a judge, that formalizes an agreement reached to settle litigation between opposing parties.

**Conservation biology.** An interdisciplinary approach to the problems of biological conservation emphasizing the maintenance of biodiversity at the genetic, species, and ecosystem levels.

**Contaminant.** Any physical, chemical, biological, or radiological substance or matter that has an adverse effect on air, water, or soil.

**Contingency plan.** A document outlining a planned course of action to be followed in case of an accident that releases materials that threaten human health or the environment.

**Conventional pollutants.** Water pollutants other than those listed as toxic or non-conventional. These include suspended solids, fecal coliform, and oxygen-demanding nutrients.

**Corrosive.** A chemical agent that reacts with the surface of a material, causing it to deteriorate or wear away.

**Cost-effectiveness analysis.** Analysis that compares alternative means to achieve a given objective in order to determine which is the least costly.

**Cost recovery.** A legal process by which potentially responsible parties who contributed to contamination at a Superfund site can be required to reimburse the government for money it spent during cleanup actions.

**Criteria air pollutants.** Six air pollutants for which national ambient air quality standards have been established by EPA: ozone, carbon monoxide, total suspended particulates, sulfur dioxide, lead, and nitrogen oxide. The term derives from the requirement that EPA issue air quality criteria describing the characteristics and potential health and welfare effects of these pollutants.

**Critical areas.** Environmentally sensitive lands, often located adjacent to shorelines, that may be subject to particular restrictions on development to protect the environment.

**Critical habitat.** A region where physical and biological features essential to the survival of an endangered or threatened species are found.

**Data call-in.** A request that pesticide manufacturers provide EPA with test data on the effects of existing pesticides to expedite re-registration or cancellation.

**DDT.** The first chlorinated hydrocarbon insecticide (chemical name: dichloro-di-phenyl-trichloroethane). It has a half-life of 15 years and can collect in fatty tissues of certain animals. EPA banned registration and interstate sale of DDT for virtually all but emergency uses in the United States in 1972 because of its persistence in the environment and accumulation in the food chain.

**Decommissioning.** Process of closing, dismantling, and rendering safe abandoned nuclear power plants after the end of their operating lives.

**Decomposition or degradation.** The breakdown of matter by bacteria, enzymes, erosion, and fungi to transform a complex substance into simpler compounds or its constituent elements.

**Delegated program.** A federal program that a state (or other government entity) has applied for and received authority to administer within its territory, subject to federal supervision.

**Delisting.** A decision to exclude a waste generated at a particular facility from listing as hazardous under RCRA subtitle C in response to a petition demonstrating that site-specific factors render the waste nonhazardous.

**Demand side management (DSM).** Strategies used by electric utilities to reduce customers' demand for electricity or energy by promoting improvements in the energy efficiency of appliances and other devices that use electricity or by shifting consumption to off-peak times.

**Desertification.** Land degradation in arid, semi-arid, and dry sub-humid areas resulting from various factors that results in the reduction or loss of the biological or economic productivity and complexity of the area.

**Designated uses.** The purposes for which individual water segments are to be protected as identified by state authorities under the Clean Water Act (e.g., cold water fisheries, public water supply, or agriculture).

**Dioxin.** Any of a family of compounds known chemically as dibenzo-p-dioxins that are a by-product or contaminant of herbicides, paper mill emissions, and combustion processes. Concern about them arises from their persistence and bioaccumulative capacity, their adverse effects on the immune system, and their association with cancer and birth defects in certain animal species.

**Direct discharger.** A municipal or industrial facility that introduces pollution directly into surface waters.

**Dissolved oxygen (DO).** The level of oxygen available in water, an important indicator of a water body's ability to support aquatic life.

**Dissolved solids.** Disintegrated organic and inorganic material contained in water. Excessive amounts make water unfit to drink or use in industrial processes.

**Ecological economics.** Movement that promotes the integration of economics and ecology into a transdiscipline that promotes sustainable development by properly valuing natural resources and the environmental services they provide.

**Ecological impact.** The effect that an action or activity has on living organisms and their nonliving (abiotic) environment.

**Ecology.** Study of the relationship of living things to one another and their environment.

**Ecosystem.** The interacting system of a biological community and its environmental surroundings.

**Ecosystem services.** Benefits produced by ecosystems through natural processes including filtration of pollutants, flood control, pollination, nutrient cycling, and other services.

**Effluent.** Waste material discharged into surface waters.

**Effluent limitation.** A regulation restricting the quantities, rates, or concentrations of pollutants in wastewater discharges.

**Effluent trading.** The purchase, sale, or exchange of allowances to discharge effluents or runoff into particular watersheds.

**Electrostatic precipitator.** An air pollution control device that removes particles from the gas stream (smoke) after combustion occurs by imparting an electrical charge to the particles, causing them to adhere to metal plates inside the precipitator.

**Eminent domain.** Government acquisition of private land for public use, with compensation paid to the landowner.

**Emission standard.** A regulation limiting the amount of pollutants that legally may be discharged from a source.

**Emissions trading.** The buying and selling of allowances to emit pollution in order to enable pollutant sources to reduce the cost of pollution control.

**Endangered species.** An animal, bird, fish, plant, or other species that is in danger of extinction throughout all or a significant portion of its range.

**Endocrine disruptors.** Substances that stop the production or block the transmission of hormones in the body.

**Environment.** The sum of all external conditions affecting the life, development, and survival of an organism.

**Environmental assessment.** A written analysis prepared pursuant to the National Environmental Policy Act to determine whether a federal action would significantly affect the environment and thus require preparation of a more detailed environmental impact statement.

**Environmental audit.** A systematic assessment of an entity's compliance with applicable environmental requirements which may include evaluation of compliance policies, practices, and controls.

**Environmental impact statement.** A document the National Environmental Policy Act requires federal agencies to prepare before undertaking major projects or legislative proposals significantly affecting the environment. It provides a detailed assessment of the environmental consequences of the proposed action and it must include an analysis of alternative actions.

**Environmental management system.** Corporate management system for ensuring compliance with environmental regulations and for incorporating environmental concerns into corporate decisions.

**Epidemiology.** Study of the health effects of environmental exposures to a substance based on systematic comparisons of the incidence of diseases in population groups that differ primarily in their levels of exposure to the substance.

**Equator Principles.** Set of principles established in 2003 by private banks to govern environmental assessment of development projects they fund and the mitigation of their adverse environmental impacts.

**Estuary.** Regions of interaction between rivers and near-shore ocean waters where tidal action and river flow create a mixing of fresh and salt water.

**Eutrophication.** The process by which shallow bodies of water receive increased amounts of dissolved nutrients such as nitrogen and phosphorus that encourage excessive plant growth and result in oxygen depletion.

**E-waste.** Refuse created by discarded electronic equipment and components.

**Exceedance.** Violation of environmental protection standards by exceeding allowable limits or concentration levels.

**Extremely hazardous substances.** Any of hundreds of chemicals identified by EPA on the basis of their toxicity and listed as extremely hazardous under the Emergency Planning and Community Right-to-Know Act.

**Feasibility study.** Analysis of the practicability of alternative means for remediating environmental contamination, a study that usually starts as soon as a remedial investigation is underway; together, they are commonly referred to as the "RI/FS."

**Fenceline community.** A community located adjacent to a locally undesirable land use such as a plant that emits pollutants, odors, noise, and traffic.

**Filtration.** A treatment process for removing solid (particulate) matter from water by passing the water through porous media such as sand or a man-made filter.

**Finding of no significant impact.** A decision, based upon the results of an environmental assessment, finding that a proposed action would not have a significant impact on the environment and thus would not require preparation of an environmental impact statement.

**Flue gas desulfurization.** A technology that uses a sorbent, usually lime or limestone, to remove sulfur dioxide from the gases produced by burning fossil fuels.

**Fly ash.** Noncombustible residual particles from the combustion process carried by flue gas.

**Food chain.** A sequence of organisms, each of which uses the next lower member of the sequence as a food source.

**Forum non conveniens.** A legal doctrine that gives courts discretionary power to dismiss a case if a court in another jurisdiction is better suited to hearing it.

**Fracking.** See "Hydraulic Fracturing."

**Fuel economy standard.** The Corporate Average Fuel Economy (CAFE) standard imposes financial penalties on motor vehicle manufacturers whose vehicles fail to meet certain average levels of fuel economy (as measured in miles per gallon).

**Fugitive emissions.** Emissions not caught by a capture system.

**Fungicide.** A pesticide used to control, prevent, or destroy fungi.

**General permit.** A permit automatically applicable to a class or category of dischargers that does not require processing of individual permit applications.

**Genetically modified organism (GMO).** An organism or microorganism whose genetic material has been altered as a result of genetic engineering.

**Geoengineering.** The deliberate large-scale manipulation of an environmental process that affects the earth's climate, done in an attempt to counteract the effects of global warming.

**Global warming.** An increase in worldwide temperature due to increased atmospheric concentrations of carbon dioxide and other gases that contribute to the greenhouse effect.

**Global warming potential (GWP).** The GWP is the ratio of the warming caused by a substance to the warming caused by a similar mass of carbon dioxide. Thus, the GWP of $CO_2$ is defined to be 1.0. CFC-12 has a GWP of 8,500, while CFC-11 has a GWP of 5,000.

**Green building.** A building designed to reduce overall environmental impact of the built environment by efficiently using energy, water, and other resources and reducing waste, pollution, and environmental degradation.

**Green growth.** Ecologically sustainable economic development.

**Greenhouse effect.** The accumulation of carbon dioxide and other greenhouse gases in the upper atmosphere that allows sunlight to raise the surface temperature of the Earth while preventing the escape of heat.

**Greenhouse gas.** A gas whose presence in the upper atmosphere contributes to the greenhouse effect by allowing visible light to pass through the atmosphere while preventing heat radiating back from the Earth from escaping. Greenhouse gases from anthropogenic sources include carbon dioxide, nitrous oxide, methane, and CFCs. There also are even larger quantities of naturally occurring greenhouse gases, notably ozone and water vapor, whose concentrations may be affected by interactions with atmospheric pollutants.

**Greenwashing.** The practice of making misleading or unsubstantiated claims about the environmental benefits of a product or service.

**Groundwater.** The supply of fresh water found beneath the Earth's surface, usually in aquifers, which is often used for supplying wells and springs.

**Habitat.** The place where a population (e.g., human, animal, plant, microorganism) lives and its surroundings, both living and nonliving.

**Habitat conservation plan.** A plan for minimizing and mitigating the impact of activities that otherwise would harm endangered species that must be approved as a condition for receiving a permit authorizing activities that would result in the incidental taking of such species pursuant to section 10 of the Endangered Species Act.

**Hazard identification.** A determination of whether or not a substance is capable of causing some form of adverse effect (e.g., determining if a substance is a carcinogen or reproductive toxin).

**Hazardous air pollutants.** Air pollutants that may cause death, serious irreversible, or incapacitating reversible illness and that are not covered by ambient air quality standards. Since the 1990 Clean Air Act Amendments these include an initial list of 189 chemicals designated by Congress that is subject to revision by EPA.

**Hazardous substance.** Any material that poses a threat to human health or the environment. CERCLA makes broad classes of parties strictly liable for the costs of remediating releases of hazardous substances which it broadly defines to include any toxic water pollutant, hazardous waste, hazardous air pollutant, imminently hazardous chemical, or any substance designated by EPA to be reported if a designated quantity of the substance is released into the environment.

**Hazardous waste.** A solid waste regulated under subtitle C of RCRA because it may pose a substantial present or potential hazard to human health or the environment when improperly managed either because it exhibits at least one of four hazardous characteristics (ignitability, corrosivity, reactivity, or toxicity) or because it has been specifically listed by EPA as hazardous.

**Hazard ranking system.** The principal screening tool used by EPA to evaluate risks to public health and the environment associated with abandoned or uncontrolled hazardous waste sites. Based on assessment of the potential for hazardous substances to cause harm to human health or the environment, the HRS calculates a score that is the primary factor in deciding if the site should be on the National Priorities List for cleanup under the Superfund program.

**Heavy metals.** Metallic elements with high atomic weights (for example, mercury, cadmium, and lead), which can damage living things and can be stored in tissues for long periods of time.

**Herbicide.** A chemical agent designed to control or destroy unwanted vegetation.

**High-level radioactive waste.** Highly radioactive waste generated by the fuel of a nuclear reactor, found primarily at nuclear power plants. This waste will remain highly radioactive, and thus dangerous, for thousands of years.

**High priority substances.** Chemicals identified for risk evaluation under the Toxic Substances Control Act because of their hazard and exposure potential to determine if they pose an unreasonable risk.

**Homeostasis.** The tendency of an organism or ecosystem to maintain equilibrium usually through feedback mechanisms that adjust to external changes in a manner that stabilizes their health and functioning.

**Hydraulic fracturing ("Fracking").** A method of extracting natural gas or oil by drilling deep into the ground and injecting a mixture of water, sand, and chemicals at high pressures to break apart shale formations.

**Hydrocarbons (HC).** Chemical compounds that consist entirely of carbon and hydrogen.

**Hydrocholorofluorocarbons (HCFCs).** The HCFCs are a class of chemicals initially used to replace CFCs because their potential to deplete stratospheric ozone is much less than that of CFCs. However, because HCFCs are potent greenhouse gases their use also is being phased out.

**Hydrofluorocarbons (HFCs).** The HFCs are a class of replacements for CFCs because they initially were not thought to deplete the ozone layer. However, because they are potent greenhouse gases with high Global Warming Potentials (GWPs), their use is being phased out.

**Hydrogeology.** Study of geological formations that contain groundwater, with particular emphasis on its fate and transport.

**Hydrology.** The science dealing with the properties, distribution, and circulation of water.

**Hypoxia.** The depletion of dissolved oxygen in water, a condition resulting from an overabundance of nutrients of human or natural origin that stimulates the growth of algae, which in turn die and require large amounts of oxygen as the algae decompose.

**Ignitable.** Capable of burning or causing a fire.

**Impoundment.** A body of water or sludge confined by a dam, dike, floodgate, or other barrier.

**Indicator species.** A species whose condition is thought to reflect the health of a larger ecosystem.

**Indirect discharger.** Commercial or industrial facilities that discharge wastes into local sewers.

**Indoor air pollution.** Chemical, physical, or biological contaminants in the air inside a home, building, or other habitable structure.

**Inert ingredient.** Pesticide components such as solvents, carriers, and surfactants that are not active against target pests.

**Injection well.** A well into which fluids are injected for purposes such as waste disposal, improving the recovery of crude oil, or solution mining.

**Injection zone.** A geological formation, group of formations, or part of a formation receiving fluids through a well.

**Inorganic chemicals.** Chemical compounds that do not contain carbon.

**Insecticide.** An agent that destroys or controls the growth of insects.

**Inspection and maintenance.** Programs to ensure proper operation of emission control systems on automobiles.

**Integrated pest management.** Pest control practices that emphasize the use of natural predators to control pests.

**Intended Nationally Determined Contribution.** An individual country's pledge of what it will do to mitigate emissions of greenhouse gases pursuant to the Paris Agreement. These pledges are to be reviewed every five years.

**Intergovernmental Panel on Climate Change (IPCC).** Panel established by the United Nations Environment Programme and the World Meteorological Organization in 1988 to assess information in the scientific and technical literature related to all significant components of the issue of climate change.

**Interim status.** Regulatory status that allowed treatment, storage, and disposal facilities for hazardous waste to continue to operate temporarily after the enactment of RCRA in 1980 pending denial or issuance of a permit.

**Interstitial monitoring.** The continuous surveillance of the space between the walls of an underground storage tank.

**Inversion.** An atmospheric condition that occurs when a layer of warm air prevents the rise of cooler air trapped beneath it, causing pollutants that might otherwise be dispersed to become more concentrated.

**In vitro.** (1) "In glass"; a test-tube culture. (2) Any laboratory test using living cells taken from an organism.

**In vivo.** In the living body of a plant or animal. In vivo tests are those laboratory experiments carried out on whole animals or human volunteers.

**Ionizing radiation.** Radiation with enough energy to penetrate matter and eject electrons or protons, producing charged ion pairs.

**ISO.** A series of voluntary standards relating to environmental management systems for corporations drafted by the International Organization for Standardization, named "ISO" after the Greek prefix for "equal."

**Joint and several liability.** A concept employed in CERCLA and derived from the common law of torts that permits any or all joint tortfeasors to be held for the full amount of damage they cause in the absence of proof of divisibility of the harm.

**Land disposal restrictions.** Rules issued under RCRA that require hazardous wastes to be treated before disposal on land to destroy or immobilize hazardous constituents that otherwise might migrate into soil or groundwater.

**Landfills.** Sites where wastes are disposed by being buried and covered with soil.

**Leachate.** The liquid that results from water collecting contaminants as it trickles through a landfill, which may result in the entry of hazardous substances into surface water, groundwater, or soil.

**Leachate collection system.** A system that gathers leachate and pumps it to the surface for treatment.

**Leaching.** The process by which soluble constituents are dissolved and carried down through the soil by a percolating fluid.

**Lead (Pb).** A heavy metal that exerts toxic effects on the nervous, reproductive, renal, and immune systems, and that is associated with increases in blood pressure.

**Leadership in Energy and Environmental Design (LEED).** A "green building" rating system designed by the U.S. Green Building Council.

**Light-emitting diode.** A semiconductor light source that is a far more efficient source of light than incandescent lighting.

**Light pollution.** Environmental pollution consisting of harmful or annoying light.

**Liner.** A relatively impermeable barrier, usually of plastic or clay, that is designed to prevent leachate from leaking from a landfill.

**Listed hazardous waste.** Waste expressly listed as hazardous under subtitle C of RCRA because it is part of a waste stream that may pose a substantial threat to human health or the environment when managed improperly.

**Local emergency planning committee.** A committee appointed by a state's emergency response commission, as required by section 301 of the Emergency Planning and Community Right-to-Know Act, to formulate a comprehensive emergency response plan.

**Lowest achievable emission rate (LAER).** Under the Clean Air Act, this is the rate of emissions that reflects (a) the most stringent emission limitation contained in the implementation plan of any state for such source unless the owner or operator of the proposed source demonstrates such limitations are not achievable; or (b) the most stringent emissions limitation achieved in practice, whichever is more stringent.

**Low-level radioactive waste.** Radioactive wastes generated by hospitals, research laboratories, and certain industries that contain lower levels of radioactivity than those generated by a nuclear reactor.

**Major modification.** Any nonroutine physical or operational change in a stationary source that will result in a significant net increase in emissions that may subject the source to PSD or new source review requirements under the Clean Air Act.

**Major stationary source.** Any stationary source that emits or has the potential to emit certain threshold levels of emissions to which PSD and new source requirements of the Clean Air Act are applicable.

**Material safety data sheet.** A compilation of information OSHA requires certain employers to provide to workers to inform them of the identities of hazardous chemicals, health and physical hazards, exposure limits, and precautions.

**Maximum contaminant level (MCL).** The maximum permissible level of a contaminant in water delivered to any user of a public water system established pursuant to the Safe Drinking Water Act.

**Maximum contaminant level goal (MCLG).** The maximum level of a contaminant in water at which no known or anticipated adverse effects on health occur and which includes an adequate margin of safety.

**Methane.** A greenhouse gas that is colorless, odorless, and flammable which is produced by the decomposition of organic matter.

**Metropolitan planning organization.** Metropolitan-wide planning organization that is responsible for developing regional transportation plans under the Urban Mass Transportation Act.

**Mitigation.** Measures taken to reduce the adverse environmental effects of an activity.

**Mixing zone.** Area in which effluent discharges mix with receiving waters to be diluted prior to assessing compliance with water quality standards.

**Mobile source.** A source of air pollution that moves, such as cars, trucks, motorcycles, and airplanes.

**Modeling.** Efforts to predict the fate and transport of pollutants or the environmental effects of human activities by using a mathematical or physical representation of a system to test the effect of changes in system components.

**Monitoring.** Periodic or continuous surveillance or testing to determine the level of compliance with statutory requirements or to assess pollutant levels in various media or in humans, animals, and other living things.

**Monitoring wells.** Wells drilled to collect groundwater samples for the purpose of determining the amounts, types, and distribution of contaminants in the groundwater.

**Municipal solid waste (MSW).** Residential solid waste and some non-hazardous commercial, institutional, and industrial wastes. This material is generally sent to municipal landfills for disposal.

**Mutagen/Mutagenicity.** Any chemical or physical agent capable of causing a permanent genetic change in a cell other than that which occurs during normal growth. Mutagenicity is the capacity of any agent to cause such changes.

**National Ambient Air Quality Standards (NAAQSs).** Uniform, national air quality standards established by EPA that restrict ambient levels of certain pollutants to protect public health (primary standards) or public welfare (secondary standards).

**National Contingency Plan (NCP).** The federal plan that outlines procedures and standards for responding to releases of oil and hazardous substances including responses to sites designated for cleanup under the Superfund program.

**National Emissions Standards for Hazardous Air Pollutants (NESHAPS).** National standards established by EPA that limit emissions of hazardous air pollutants.

**National Pollutant Discharge Elimination System (NPDES).** The Clean Water Act's national permit program that regulates the discharge of pollutants into waters of the United States.

**National Priorities List (NPL).** EPA's list of sites identified as priorities for remedial action under CERCLA.

**National Response Center.** Operations center run by the U.S. Coast Guard and open 24 hours per day that receives notifications of releases of oil and hazardous substances into the environment, evaluates the reports, and notifies the appropriate agency for responding to the releases.

**National Response Team.** Representatives of various federal agencies who coordinate federal responses to nationally significant incidents of pollution and provide advice and technical assistance to the responding agency or agencies before and during a response action.

**Navigable waters.** Initially, waters sufficiently deep and wide for navigation but now including waters adjacent to or connected to waters navigable in fact.

**New source.** Any stationary source built or modified after publication of final or proposed regulations that prescribe a standard of performance intended to apply to that type of emissions source.

**New Source Performance Standards (NSPSs).** Uniform national EPA air emissions and water effluent standards that limit the amount of pollution allowed from new sources or from existing sources that have been modified.

**Nitrate.** A form of nitrogen that can exist in the atmosphere or as a dissolved gas in water and that can have harmful effects on humans and animals.

**Nitric oxide (NO).** A gas formed by the oxidation of nitrogen or ammonia, whose primary source is the combustion pressure in an internal combustion engine. It can change into nitrogen dioxide in the ambient air, contributing to photochemical smog.

**Nitrogen dioxide ($NO_2$).** A major component of photochemical smog formed when nitric oxide combines with oxygen in the atmosphere.

**Nitrogen oxide ($NO_x$).** A product of combustion by mobile and stationary sources and a major contributor to acid deposition and the formation of ozone in the troposphere.

**No Observable Adverse Effect Level (NOAEL).** Greatest concentration or amount of a substance at which there are no statistically or biologically significant increases in the frequency or severity of adverse effects between the exposed population and its appropriate control.

**Nonattainment area.** A geographic area that is not in compliance with the National Ambient Air Quality Standard for a criteria air pollutant under the Clean Air Act.

**Nonconventional pollutant.** Water pollutants that are not listed as toxic pollutants or conventional pollutants, including color, nitrates, iron, ammonia, and chlorides.

**Nonpoint source pollution.** Pollution from sources that are diffuse and that do not have any single point of origin or discharge, such as pollutants generally carried off land by runoff.

**Nutrient.** Any substance assimilated by living things that promotes growth. Contaminant of water resources by excessive inputs of nutrients causes excess algal production.

**Oncogenic.** Capable of causing tumors, whether benign or malignant.

**Opacity.** A measure of the amount of light obscured by particulate pollution in the air; clear window glass has a zero opacity, a brick wall has 100 percent opacity.

**Open dump.** A site where solid waste is disposed of without satisfying the criteria established by EPA under section 4004 of RCRA.

**Organic.** (1) Derived from or relating to living organisms. (2) In chemistry, any compound containing carbon.

**Organic matter.** Carbonaceous waste contained in plant or animal matter and originating from domestic or industrial sources.

**Organism.** Any living thing.

**Organophosphates.** Relatively nonpersistent insecticides that contain phosphorus.

**Organotins.** Chemical compounds used to kill bacteria, algae, molluscs, fungi, and insects, which are known to be toxic to the immune system.

**Outfall.** The place where effluent is discharged into receiving waters.

**Overburden.** The rock and soil cleared away before mining.

**Overfiling.** Filing of federal enforcement actions in cases where states with delegated enforcement authority either have failed to act or have pursued actions deemed insufficient by federal authorities.

**Ozone ($O_3$).** A substance found in the stratosphere and the troposphere. In the stratosphere (the atmospheric layer beginning 7 to 10 miles above the Earth's surface), ozone is a form of oxygen found naturally that provides a protective layer shielding the Earth from ultraviolet radiation. In the troposphere (the layer extending up 7 to 10 miles from the Earth's surface), ozone is a chemical oxidant and a major component of photochemical smog.

**Ozone depletion.** Destruction of the stratospheric ozone layer caused by the breakdown of certain chlorine- and/or bromine-containing compounds (chlorofluorocarbons or halons), which catalytically destroy ozone molecules.

**Ozone depletion potential (ODP).** A number that refers to the amount of ozone-depletion caused by a substance. The ODP is the ratio of the impact on ozone of a chemical compared to the impact of a similar mass of CFC-11. Thus, the ODP of CFC-11 is defined to be 1.0. Other CFCs and HCFCs have ODPs that range from 0.01 to 1.0. The halons have ODPs ranging up to 10.

**Pandemic.** A disease that spreads across several countries and infects a large number of people.

**Particulates.** Fine liquid or solid particles found in air, such as dust, smoke, mist, fumes, or smog.

**Pathogenic.** Capable of causing disease.

**Pathogens.** Microorganisms (such as bacteria, viruses, or parasites) that can cause disease in other organisms, including humans, animals, and plants.

**PCBs.** A group of toxic, persistent chemicals (polychlorinated biphenyls) formerly used in electrical transformers and capacitators for insulating purposes and in gas pipeline systems as a lubricant.

**Percolation.** The movement of water downward and radially through subsurface soil layers, usually continuing downward to groundwater.

**Perfluoroalkyl and polyfluoroaklyl substances (PFAS).** A group of man-made chemical substances that include chains of linked carbon and fluorine atoms that often are called "forever chemicals" because they do not easily degrade in the environment. The most studied PFAS include perfluorooctanoic acid (PFOA) and perfluorooctanesulfonic acid (PFOS) that have been linked to kidney cancer, testicular cancer, thyroid disease, high cholesterol, and other adverse health effects in humans. Thousands of chemical variants of these chemicals, including GenX, are now widely used in a variety of products.

**Permit.** An authorization, license, or equivalent control document issued by a government agency.

**Persistence.** The length of time a compound, once introduced into the environment, stays there.

**Pesticide.** A general term for any agent that destroys, injures, inhibits, or prevents the growth of rodents, insects, plants, algae, or fungi.

**Pesticide tolerance.** The amount of pesticide residue allowed by law to remain in or on a harvested crop.

**pH.** A measure of the acidity or alkalinity of a liquid or solid material.

**Phosphates.** Organic compounds of phosphoric acid physiologically important for acid-base balance in the blood. Produced in the environment by decaying organic matter and used as a component of detergents and fertilizers, phosphates have been a major cause of the eutrophication of water bodies by serving as nutrients for algae blooms.

**Photochemical air pollution.** Also called photochemical smog, a type of oxidizing pollution characterized by hydrocarbons, nitrogen oxides, and photochemical oxidants. Results from photochemical reactions of sunlight, automobile exhaust, and other oxidant pollutants.

**Photochemical oxidants.** Air pollutants formed by the action of sunlight on oxides of nitrogen and hydrocarbons.

**Point source.** A stationary location or fixed facility from which pollutants are discharged or emitted such as a pipe, ditch, or smokestack.

**Pollutant.** Generally, any substance introduced into the environment that adversely affects the usefulness of a resource.

**Pollution.** Generally, the presence of matter or energy whose nature, location, or quantity produces undesired environmental effects.

**Polychlorinated Biphenyls (PCBs).** A group of toxic, persistent chemicals used in electrical transformers and capacitors for insulating purposes, and in gas pipeline systems as lubricants, the sale and new use of which were banned in 1979.

**Post-closure period.** The time period following the shutdown of a waste management facility during which the site must be monitored.

**Potentially responsible party.** Any individual or company potentially liable under section 107 of CERCLA for the costs of responding to releases of hazardous substances.

**Preliminary assessment.** The process of collecting and reviewing available information about a known or suspected waste site or release.

**Pretreatment.** Processes used to reduce, eliminate, or alter the toxicity of pollutants in wastewater from nondomestic sources before it is discharged into a sewer system.

**Prevention of significant deterioration.** An EPA program in which state or federal permits are required to restrict emissions from new or modified stationary sources in places where air quality is already better than required to meet primary and secondary ambient air quality standards.

**Primary waste treatment.** The first steps in wastewater treatment, which typically use screens and sedimentation tanks to remove most materials that float or will settle.

**Prompt letter.** Letter from the administrator of OMB's Office of Information and Regulatory Affairs requesting an agency to consider taking some regulatory action.

**Publicly owned treatment works.** A waste-treatment works owned by a state, unit of local government, or Indian tribe, usually designed to treat domestic wastewaters.

**Public water system.** Under the Safe Drinking Water Act, a system that provides piped water for human consumption to at least 15 service connections or that regularly serves at least 25 individuals.

**Radiation.** A general term for radiant energy emitted in the form of particles or electromagnetic waves from radioactive elements, fluorescent substances, or luminous bodies.

**Radiative forcing.** The change in the net vertical irradiance (expressed in Watts per square meter: Wm-2) at the tropopause due to an internal change or a change in the external forcing of the climate system, such as, for example, a change in the concentration of carbon dioxide or the output of the Sun.

**Radio frequency radiation.** Non-ionizing electromagnetic radiation that does not change the structure of atoms but does heat tissue and may cause harmful biological effects. This radiation is emitted by microwaves, radio waves, and low-frequency electromagnetic fields from high-voltage transmission lines.

**Radionuclide.** Isotopes of elements that spontaneously emit radiation by disintegration (decay) of their unstable nuclei. Can be man-made or naturally occurring.

**Radon.** A colorless, naturally occurring, radioactive, inert gaseous element formed by decay of radium atoms in soil or rocks.

**Reasonably available control technology (RACT).** Control technology that is reasonably available and both technologically and economically feasible. Usually it is applied to existing sources of air pollution in nonattainment areas.

**Recharge.** The process by which water is added to a zone of saturation, usually by percolation from the soil surface, for example, the recharge of an aquifer.

**Recharge area.** A land area in which water reaches to the zone of saturation from surface infiltration, for example, an area where rainwater soaks through the earth to reach an aquifer.

**Recommended maximum contaminant level.** The term formerly used for maximum contaminant level goal.

**Record of decision.** A public document that explains which cleanup alternative(s) will be used at National Priorities List sites.

**Recycling.** The process of minimizing the generation of waste by recovering usable products that might otherwise become waste. Examples are the recycling of aluminum cans, wastepaper, and bottles.

**Reference Dose (RfD).** A numerical estimate of a daily oral exposure to the human population, including sensitive subgroups such as children, for which a particular substance is not likely to cause harmful effects during a lifetime.

**Registration.** Formal listing with EPA of a new pesticide under the Federal Insecticide, Fungicide, and Rodenticide Act so that it can be sold or distributed in intrastate or interstate commerce.

**Remedial action.** The actual construction or implementation phase of a Superfund site cleanup that follows remedial design.

**Remedial design.** A stage of the Superfund cleanup process that follows the remedial investigation feasibility study and includes development of engineering drawings and specifications for a site cleanup.

**Remedial investigation.** An in-depth study designed to gather the data necessary to determine the nature and extent of contamination at a Superfund site, establish criteria for cleaning up the site, identify preliminary alternatives for remedial actions, and support the technical and cost analyses of the alternatives. The remedial investigation is usually done with the feasibility study. Together they are referred to as the "RI/FS."

**Removal actions.** Short-term actions taken to address releases of hazardous substances (e.g., removal of chemical drums).

**Reportable quantity.** The quantity of a hazardous substance that triggers reporting requirements under CERCLA. If a substance is released in amounts exceeding this quantity, the release must be reported to the National Response Center, state authorities, and community emergency coordinators for areas likely to be affected.

**Re-registration.** The reevaluation and relicensing of existing pesticides originally registered prior to the implementation of current scientific and regulatory standards.

**Resource recovery.** The process of obtaining matter or energy from materials formerly discarded.

**Response action.** A CERCLA-authorized action involving either a removal action or a remedial action.

**Restricted use.** A pesticide whose uses have been restricted because it requires special handling due to its toxicity. Restricted-use pesticides may be applied only by trained, certified applicators or those under their direct supervision.

**Return letter.** A letter from the Administrator of the Office of Information and Regulatory Affairs (OIRA) in OMB returning proposed or final regulations to an agency for reconsideration.

**Riparian rights.** Entitlement of a land-owner to the water on or bordering his or her property, including the right to prevent diversion or misuse of upstream waters.

**Risk assessment.** The process of identifying and characterizing the nature and magnitude of the adverse effects of a substance or activity.

**Risk communication.** The exchange of information about the nature and magnitude of health or environmental risks between risk assessors, risk managers, and the general public.

**Risk management.** The process of evaluating and selecting among alternative strategies for managing environmental risks.

**Rodenticide.** An agent that kills, repels, or controls rodents to prevent the spread of disease and consumption or contamination of food.

**Rolling easements.** Legal arrangements that transfer property rights through options, easements, covenants, or defeasible estates as shorelines migrate.

**Runoff.** Precipitation that the ground does not absorb and that ultimately reaches rivers, lakes, or oceans.

**Saturated zone.** A subsurface area in which all pores and cracks are filled with water under pressure equal to or greater than that of the atmosphere.

**Scrubber.** An air pollution device that uses a spray of water or reactant or a dry process to trap pollutants in emissions.

**Secondary treatment.** The second step in most publicly owned waste treatment systems, in which bacteria consume the organic parts of the waste. It is accomplished by bringing together waste, bacteria, and oxygen in trickling filters or in an activated sludge process.

**Sedimentation.** Letting solids settle out of wastewater by gravity during wastewater treatment.

**Sedimentation tanks.** Holding areas for wastewater where floating wastes are skimmed off and settled solids are removed for disposal.

**Sediments.** Soil, sand, and minerals washed from land into water, usually after rain.

**Selective catalytic reduction.** A process for reducing emissions of nitrogen oxides from electricity generators.

**Service line.** The pipe that carries tap water from the public water main to a building.

**Settling tank.** A holding area for wastewater where heavier particles sink to the bottom for removal and disposal.

**Sewage.** The waste and wastewater produced by residential and commercial establishments and discharged into sewers.

**Sewage sludge.** Waste produced by sewage treatment processes at a publicly owned treatment works, the disposal of which is regulated under the Clean Water Act.

**Sewer.** A channel or conduit that carries wastewater or stormwater runoff from the source to a treatment plant or receiving stream.

**Silviculture.** Management of forest land for timber.

**Site inspection.** The collection of data concerning the extent and severity of hazards posed by a site where hazardous substances have been released to gather information necessary to score the site, using the Hazard Ranking System, and to determine if the site presents an immediate threat that requires prompt removal action.

**Siting.** The process of choosing a location for a facility.

**Sludge.** A semisolid residue from any of a number of air or water treatment processes.

**Slurry.** A watery mixture of insoluble matter that results from some pollution control techniques.

**Smart growth.** Policies that seek to encourage residential, commercial and industrial development that is environmentally sound and fiscally smart by channeling new development to areas with existing infrastructure.

**Smelter.** A facility that melts or fuses ore, often with an accompanying chemical change, to separate the metal.

**Smog.** Air pollution associated with oxidants.

**Social cost of carbon.** A dollar estimate of the value of environmental and economic damage from emitting an additional ton of greenhouse gases into the atmosphere.

**Sole source aquifer.** An aquifer that supplies 50 percent or more of the drinking water of an area.

**Solid waste.** Defined by RCRA to include "any garbage, refuse, sludge from a waste treatment plant, water supply treatment plant, or air pollution control facility and other discarded material, including solid, liquid, semisolid, or contained gaseous materials resulting from industrial, commercial, mining, and agricultural activities."

**Solvent.** A substance (usually liquid) capable of dissolving or dispersing one or more other substances.

**Sorption.** The action of soaking up or attracting substances.

**Special review.** A regulatory process through which existing pesticides suspected of posing unreasonable risk to human health, nontarget organisms, or the environment are referred for review by EPA.

**Species.** A reproductively isolated aggregate of interbreeding populations of organisms.

**Spoil.** Dirt or rock that has been removed from its original location, destroying the composition of the soil in the process, as with strip-mining or dredging.

**Stabilization.** Conversion of the active organic matter in sludge into inert, harmless material.

**State emergency response commission (SERC).** A commission appointed by each governor according to the requirements of the Emergency Planning and Community Right-to-Know Act. The SERCs designate emergency planning districts, appoint local emergency planning committees, and supervise and coordinate their activities.

**State implementation plans.** State plans, for which EPA approval is required, for controlling air pollution in order to attain national ambient air quality standards.

**Stationary sources.** Fixed, nonmoving producers of pollution, including power plants and other facilities using industrial combustion processes.

**Storm sewer.** A system of pipes that carry only water runoff from building and land surfaces.

**Stratosphere.** The uppermost portion of the atmosphere that is 10 to 25 miles above the Earth's surface.

**Strip-mining.** A process that uses machines to scrape soil or rock away from mineral deposits just under the Earth's surface.

**Sulfur dioxide (SO$_2$).** A heavy, pungent, colorless, gaseous air pollutant formed primarily by the combustion of fossil fuels, which causes respiratory problems in humans and contributes to acid deposition.

**Superfund.** A trust fund established by the Comprehensive Environmental Response, Compensation, and Liability Act (CERCLA) to help pay for cleanup of hazardous waste sites and for legal action to force those responsible for the sites to clean them up. Also is used to refer to the program operated under the legislative authority of CERCLA that carries out EPA response activities.

**Surface impoundment.** A facility for the treatment, storage, or disposal of liquid wastes in ponds.

**Surface water.** All water naturally open to the atmosphere (rivers, lakes, reservoirs, streams, impoundments, seas, estuaries, and so on) and all springs, wells, or other collectors that are directly influenced by surface water.

**Suspended solids.** Small particles of solid pollutants that float on the surface of, or are suspended in, sewage or other liquids.

**Sustainable development.** Development that meets the needs of the present without compromising the ability of future generations to meet their own needs.

**Synthetic organic chemicals.** Man-made organic chemicals.

**Tailings.** Residue of raw materials or waste separated out during the processing of crops or mineral ores.

**Technology-based standards.** Emission limits that are established on the basis of what levels of pollution control certain types or levels of technology can achieve.

**Teratogen.** A substance that causes malformation or abnormal development of embryos and fetuses.

**Tertiary treatment.** Advanced cleaning of wastewater that goes beyond the secondary or biological treatment stage to remove nutrients such as phosphorus and nitrogen and most suspended solids.

**Threatened species.** Species of flora or fauna likely to become endangered within the foreseeable future.

**Thermal pollution.** Discharge of heat from industrial processes that can affect the environment adversely.

**Threshold limit value.** The maximum air concentrations of chemical substances to which it is believed that workers may be exposed on a daily basis without adverse effect.

**Threshold planning quantity.** A quantity designated for each chemical on the list of extremely hazardous substances that triggers EPCRA notification to state emergency response commissions.

**Tolerances.** Permissible residue levels for pesticides in raw agricultural produce and processed foods.

**Total maximum daily loading (TMDL).** The maximum amount of a pollutant that can be discharged into a water segment each day by all sources without causing violation of a water quality standard.

**Total suspended solids.** A measure of the suspended solids in wastewater, effluent, or water bodies.

**Toxicity.** The degree of danger posed by a substance to living organisms. Acute toxicity involves harmful effects in an organism through a single or short-term exposure. Chronic toxicity is the ability of a substance or mixture of substances to cause harmful effects over an extended period, usually upon repeated or continuous exposure sometimes lasting for the entire life of the exposed organism. Subchronic toxicity is the ability of the substance to cause effects for more than one year but less than the lifetime of the exposed organism.

**Toxicology.** The study of adverse effects of chemicals on living organisms.

**Toxic pollutant.** A pollutant that is capable of causing adverse effects on living organisms.

**Toxics Release Inventory (TRI).** The national inventory of the quantities of toxic substances released into different environmental media annually by facilities that manufacture, process, or use (in quantities above a specific amount) chemicals listed under the Emergency Planning and Community Right-to-Know Act.

**Transferable development rights.** Development rights sometimes allocated to property owners unable to develop a specific property that can be sold or used to qualify to develop another property in a more suitable location.

**Treatment, storage, or disposal facility.** A site where hazardous wastes are treated, stored, or disposed.

**Trichloroethylene (TCE).** A stable, low-boiling, colorless liquid, toxic by inhalation. TCE is used as a solvent and as a metal degreasing agent and in other industrial applications.

**Troposphere.** The lowermost portion of the atmosphere up to 10 kilometers from the Earth's surface, where clouds are formed.

**Tundra.** A type of ecosystem dominated by lichens, mosses, grasses, and woody plants, which is found at high latitudes (arctic tundra) and high altitudes (alpine tundra).

**Turbidity.** (1) Haziness in air caused by the presence of particles and pollutants. (2) A similar cloudy condition in water due to suspended silt or organic matter.

**Ultraviolet rays.** Radiation from the sun to which humans are exposed that can cause skin cancer or other tissue damage.

**Underground injection control.** The program under the Safe Drinking Water Act that regulates the use of underground injection wells to pump fluids into the ground.

**Underground storage tank.** A tank located totally or partially underground that is designed to hold gasoline or other petroleum products or chemical solutions.

**Unsaturated zone.** The area above the water table where the soil pores are not fully saturated, although some water may be present.

**Urban growth boundary.** Growth management device that seeks to channel future urban growth inside a boundary drawn around an existing urban area generally by prohibiting or discouraging urban development outside the boundary.

**Urban runoff.** Stormwater from city streets and adjacent domestic or commercial properties that may carry pollutants of various kinds into the sewer systems or receiving waters.

**Vaporization.** The change of a substance from a liquid to a gas.

**Variance.** Government permission for a delay or exception in the application of a given law, ordinance, or regulation.

**Virus.** A minute organism comprised of either one strand of DNA or RNA, which is dependent on nutrients inside cells in order to live and to reproduce intracellularly.

**Volatile.** Capable of evaporating readily.

**Volatile organic compound.** An organic compound that participates in atmospheric photochemical reactions.

**Waste load allocation.** The maximum load of pollutants each discharger of waste is allowed to release into a particular waterway.

**Waste minimization.** Measures or techniques that reduce the amount of wastes generated during industrial production processes; term also is applied to recycling and other efforts to reduce the amount of waste going into the waste stream.

**Wastewater treatment plant.** A facility containing a series of tanks, screens, niters, and other processes by which pollutants are removed from water.

**Water quality criteria.** Specific levels of water quality that, if reached, are expected to render a body of water suitable for certain designated uses.

**Water quality standards.** State-adopted and EPA-approved ambient standards for water bodies that specify the water quality that must be met to protect designated uses.

**Watershed.** The land area that drains into a stream or other water body.

**Water table.** The level of groundwater.

**Wetlands.** An ecosystem that depends on constant or recurrent shallow inundation or saturation at or near the surface. Wetlands commonly feature hydric soils and hydrophytic vegetation, except where specific factors have removed them or prevented their development.

**Xenobiotic.** A chemical substance that is not normally a constitutive component of a biological system (i.e., non-naturally occurring man-made substances found in the environment, such as synthetic material solvents or plastics).

**Zero-Emission Vehicles (ZEVs).** Cars or trucks that generate no tailpipe emissions of any pollutant throughout their lifetimes. ZEVs are powered by electricity.

**Zoonosis.** A disease that can be transmitted from animals to humans.

# LIST OF ACRONYMS

**AA** Assistant Administrator or Associate Administrator
**ACC** American Chemistry Council
**ACE** Affordable Clean Energy rule
**ACGIH** American Council of Government Industrial Hygienists
**ACL** alternate concentration limit
**ACO** administrative compliance order
**ADI** acceptable daily intake
**ADR** alternative dispute resolution
**AEA** Atomic Energy Act
**AFFF** aqueous film-forming foam
**AFO** animal feeding operation
**AHERA** Asbestos Hazard Emergency Response Act
**AID** Agency for International Development
**ALJ** administrative law judge
**ANPR** advance notice of proposed rulemaking
**ANSI** American National Standards Institute
**ANWR** Arctic National Wildlife Refuge
**APA** Administrative Procedure Act
**ARAR** applicable or relevant and appropriate standards, limitations, criteria, and requirements
**ASLB** Atomic Safety and Licensing Board
**ATS** Alien Tort Statute
**ATSDR** Agency for Toxic Substances and Disease Registry (HHS)
**BACT** best available control technology
**BADT** best available demonstrated technology
**BART** best available retrofit technology
**BAT** best available technology
**BATEA** best available treatment economically achievable
**BCT** best control technology
**BDAT** best demonstrated achievable technology
**BDT** best demonstrated technology
**BLM** Bureau of Land Management
**BMPs** best management practices
**BOD** biochemical oxygen demand
**BPJ** best professional judgment
**BPT** best practicable technology, or best practicable treatment
**BTU** British thermal unit
**CAA** Clean Air Act

**CAFE** corporate average fuel economy
**CAFO** concentrated animal feeding operation
**CAG** Carcinogen Assessment Group
**CAIR** Clean Air Interstate Rule
**CARB** California Air Resources Board
**CAS** Chemical Abstract Service
**CASAC** Clean Air Scientific Advisory Committee
**CBA** cost-benefit analysis
**CBF** Chesapeake Bay Foundation
**CBO** Congressional Budget Office
**CCR** coal combustion residuals (coal ash)
**CDC** Centers for Disease Control (HHS)
**CDM** Clean Development Mechanism
**CDP** Carbon Disclosure Project
**CEC** Commission for Environmental Cooperation
**CEQ** Council on Environmental Quality
**CEQA** California Environmental Quality Act
**CER** certified emission reduction
**CERCLA** Comprehensive Environmental Response, Compensation, and Liability Act
**CERCLIS** Comprehensive Environmental Response, Compensation, and Liability Information System
**CERES** Coalition for Environmentally Responsible Economies
**CFCs** chlorofluorocarbons
**CFR** Code of Federal Regulations
**CITES** Convention on International Trade in Endangered Species
**CO$_2$** carbon dioxide
**CO$_2$e** carbon dioxide equivalent
**COP** Conference of the Parties
**CORSIA** Carbon Offsetting and Reduction Scheme for International Aviation
**COVID-19** coronavirus disease
**CPP** Clean Power Plan
**CPSC** Consumer Product Safety Commission
**CRA** Congressional Review Act
**CRP** Conservation Reserve Program
**CRS** Congressional Research Service
**CSAPR** Cross-State Air Pollution Rule
**CSO** combined sewer overflow
**CVRA** Crime Victims Rights Act
**CWA** Clean Water Act (also known as FWPCA)
**CZMA** Coastal Zone Management Act
**DAPL** Dakota Access Pipeline
**DBCP** 1,2-Dibromo-3-chloropropane
**DDT** dichloro-diphenyl-trichloroethane
**DMR** discharge monitoring report
**DO** dissolved oxygen
**DOD** Department of Defense

**DOE**  Department of Energy
**DOI**  Department of the Interior
**DOJ**  Department of Justice
**DOL**  Department of Labor
**DOT**  Department of Transportation
**DPA**  Deepwater Ports Act
**DPS**  distinct population segment
**DSAP**  data self-auditing program
**DSM**  demand side management
**EA**  environmental assessment
**EC**  European Commission
**ECA**  export credit agency
**ECJ**  European Court of Justice
**ECOS**  Environmental Council of the States
**ECRA**  Environmental Cleanup Responsibility Act (New Jersey)
**ECT**  environmental courts and tribunals
**EDF**  Environmental Defense Fund
**EEC**  European Economic Commission
**EHS**  extremely hazardous substance
**EIS**  environmental impact statement
**EISA**  Energy Independence and Security Act of 2007
**EJ**  environmental justice
**ELI**  Environmental Law Institute
**EMF**  electromagnetic frequency radiation
**EMS**  environmental management system
**EO**  executive order
**EPA**  U.S. Environmental Protection Agency
**EPCA**  Energy Policy and Conservation Act
**EPCRA**  Emergency Planning and Community Right-to-Know Act
**ESA**  Endangered Species Act
**ESG**  environmental, social, and governance
**ESU**  evolutionary significant unit
**ETS**  emergency temporary standard, Emissions Trading System (EU),
    environmental tobacco smoke
**EU**  European Union
**FACA**  Federal Advisory Committee Act
**FAST**  Fixing America's Surface Transportation Act
**FDA**  Food and Drug Administration
**FDF**  fundamentally different factors
**FEMA**  Federal Emergency Management Agency
**FERC**  Federal Energy Regulatory Commission
**FFA**  federal facility agreement
**FFDCA**  Federal Food, Drug, and Cosmetic Act
**FHWA**  Federal Highway Administration
**FIFRA**  Federal Insecticide, Fungicide, and Rodenticide Act
**FIP**  federal implementation plan
**FLPMA**  Federal Land Policy and Management Act

**FMCSA** Federal Motor Carrier Safety Administration
**FOIA** Freedom of Information Act
**FONSI** finding of no significant impact
**FQPA** Food Quality Protection Act
**FR** Federal Register
**FS** Forest Service (U.S.)
**FSIA** Foreign Sovereign Immunities Act
**FTC** Federal Trade Commission
**FWPCA** Federal Water Pollution Control Act (Clean Water Act)
**FWS** Fish and Wildlife Service (U.S.)
**GAO** Government Accountability Office
**GATT** General Agreement on Tariffs and Trade
**GEF** Global Environment Facility
**GEMI** Global Environmental Management Initiative
**GHG** greenhouse gas
**GMO** genetically modified organism
**GPRA** Government Performance and Results Act
**GRI** Global Reporting Initiative
**GWP** global warming potential
**HCFC** hydrochlorofluorocarbon
**HCP** habitat conservation plan
**HFC** hydrofluorocarbon
**HHS** Department of Health and Human Services
**HLRW** high-level radioactive waste
**HMTA** Hazardous Materials Transportation Act
**HPV** high production volume
**HRS** hazard ranking system
**HSWA** Hazardous and Solid Waste Amendments of 1984
**HWIR** Hazardous Waste Identification Rule
**IARC** International Agency for Research on Cancer
**ICAO** International Civil Aviation Organization
**ICJ** International Court of Justice
**ICS** individual control strategy
**IFC** International Finance Corporation
**IG** inspector general
**I/M** inspection/maintenance
**INDC** Intended nationally determined contribution
**IOAI** International Organizations Immunities Act
**IPCC** Intergovernmental Panel on Climate Change
**IPM** integrated pest management
**IQA** Information Quality Act
**ISC** Interagency Scientific Committee
**ISTEA** Intermodal Surface Transportation Efficiency Act
**IUCN** International Union for the Conservation of Nature
**IWC** International Whaling Commission
**JI** joint implementation
**LAER** lowest achievable emission rate

**LEED** Leadership in Energy and Environmental Design
**LEV** low-emission vehicle
**LLRWPA** Low-Level Radioactive Waste Policy Act
**LULU** locally undesirable land use
**MACT** maximum achievable control technology
**MAER** maximum allowable emission rate
**MCL** maximum contaminant level
**MCLG** maximum contaminant level goal
**MDB** multilateral development bank
**MEE** Ministry of Ecology and Environment (China)
**MIR** maximum individual risk
**MMPA** Marine Mammal Protection Act
**MOA** memorandum of agreement
**MOU** memorandum of understanding
**MPO** metropolitan planning organization
**MPRSA** Marine Protection, Research, and Sanctuaries Act (Ocean Dumping Act)
**MSHA** Mine Safety and Health Administration (DOL)
**MSW** municipal solid waste
**MTBE** methyl tertiary butyl ether
**MTD** maximum tolerated dose
**NAACP** National Association for the Advancement of Colored People
**NAAEC** North American Agreement on Environmental Cooperation
**NAAQS** national ambient air quality standards
**NAFTA** North American Free Trade Agreement
**NAPA** National Academy of Public Administration
**NAPAP** National Acid Precipitation Assessment Program
**NAS** National Academy of Sciences
**NBAR** non-binding allocation of responsibility
**NCP** National Contingency Plan
**NEJAC** National Environmental Justice Advisory Council
**NEPA** National Environmental Policy Act
**NEPPS** National Environmental Performance Partnership System
**NESHAP** national emissions standard for hazardous air pollutants
**NFMA** National Forest Management Act
**NGO** nongovernmental organization
**NHANES** National Health and Nutrition Examination Survey
**NHTSA** National Highway Traffic Safety Administration
**NIEHS** National Institute of Environmental Health Sciences
**NIH** National Institutes of Health
**NIMBY** not in my backyard
**NIOSH** National Institute of Occupational Safety and Health
**NMFS** National Marine Fisheries Service
**NO** nitric oxide
**NO$_2$** nitrogen dioxide
**NOAA** National Oceanic and Atmospheric Administration
**NO$_x$** nitrogen oxide
**NPDES** National Pollutant Discharge Elimination System

**NPL** National Priority List
**NPRM** notice of proposed rulemaking
**NPS** National Park Service
**NRC** National Research Council, National Response Center, or Nuclear
     Regulatory Commission
**NRDC** Natural Resources Defense Council
**NSF** National Science Foundation
**NSO** nonferrous smelter orders
**NSPS** new source performance standards
**NSR** new source review
**NTP** National Toxicology Program
**NWF** National Wildlife Federation
**NWPA** Nuclear Waste Policy Act
**NWPR** Navigable Waters Protection Rule
**OCS** outer continental shelf
**OCSLA** Outer Continental Shelf Lands Act
**ODP** ozone depletion potential
**OECD** Organization for Economic Cooperation and Development
**OIRA** Office of Information and Regulatory Affairs (OMB)
**OLC** Office of Legal Counsel
**OMB** Office of Management and Budget
**OPA 90** Oil Pollution Prevention, Response, Liability, and Compensation Act
**OPIC** Overseas Private Investment Corporation
**ORV** off-road vehicle
**OSHA** Occupational Safety and Health Administration
**OSH Act** Occupational Safety and Health Act
**OSM** Office of Surface Mining
**OTAG** Ozone Transport Assessment Group
**OTC** Ozone Transport Commission
**OTR** ozone transport region
**PA** preliminary assessment
**PCBs** polychlorinated biphenyls
**PEL** permissible exposure limit
**PFAS** per- and polyfluorinated substances
**PFOA** perfluorooctanoic acid
**PFOS** perfluorooctanesulfonic acid
**PIC** prior informed consent
**PM$_{2.5}$** particulate matter smaller than 2.5 micrometers in diameter
**PM$_{10}$** particulate matter smaller than 10 micrometers
**PMN** premanufacture notification
**POM** polycyclic organic matter
**POP** persistent organic pollutant
**POTW** publicly owned treatment works
**PPA** Pollution Prevention Act
**ppm** parts per million
**PRA** Paperwork Reduction Act
**PRP** potentially responsible party

**PSD**  prevention of significant deterioration
**PTE**  potential to emit
**PVC**  polyvinyl chloride
**QA/QC**  quality assurance/quality control
**QRA**  quantitative risk assessment
**RA**  regulatory analysis, remedial action, or risk assessment
**RACM**  reasonably available control measures
**RACT**  reasonably available control technology
**RARG**  Regulatory Analysis Review Group
**RCRA**  Resource Conservation and Recovery Act
**RD**  remedial design
**REACH**  Registration, Evaluation, and Authorisation of Chemicals (EU)
**R&D**  research and development
**RECLAIM**  Regional Clean Air Incentives Market
**RFA**  Regulatory Flexibility Act
**RfD**  reference dose
**RFP**  reasonable further progress
**RGGI**  Regional Greenhouse Gas Initiative
**RIA**  regulatory impact analysis
**RI/FS**  remedial investigation/feasibility study
**RMRR**  routine maintenance, repair, or replacement
**ROD**  record of decision
**RPA**  reasonable and prudent alternative
**RPAR**  rebuttable presumption against registration
**RQ**  reportable quantities
**SAB**  Science Advisory Board
**SAFE**  Safer Affordable Fuel Efficient vehicle rule
**SAR**  structure activity relationship
**SARA**  Superfund Amendments and Reauthorization Act of 1986
**SBLRBRA**  Small Business Liability Relief and Brownfields Revitalization Act
**SBREFA**  Small Business Regulatory Enforcement Fairness Act
**SCAQMD**  South Coast Air Quality Management District (California)
**SCC**  social cost of carbon
**SCR**  selective catalytic reduction
**SCS**  Soil Conservation Service
**SDG**  Sustainable Development Goals
**SDWA**  Safe Drinking Water Act
**SEP**  supplemental environmental project
**SERC**  state emergency response commission
**SEQRA**  State Environmental Quality Review Act (New York)
**SIP**  state implementation plan
**SMCRA**  Surface Mining Control and Reclamation Act
**SNUR**  significant new use rule
**SO$_2$**  sulfur dioxide
**SPR**  significant portion of its range
**SQG**  small quantity generator
**STEL**  short-term exposure limit

**SUWA** Southern Utah Wilderness Alliance
**SWDA** Solid Waste Disposal Act
**SWMU** solid waste management unit
**TCE** trichloroethylene
**TCDD** dioxin (tetrachlorodibenzo-p-dioxin)
**TCDF** tetrachlorodibenzofurans
**TCLP** toxicity characteristic leachate procedure
**TCP** transportation control plan
**TDR** transferable development right
**TDS** total dissolved solids
**TEL** tetraethyl lead
**TKN** total kjeldahl nitrogen
**TLV** threshold limit value
**TMDL** total maximum daily loading
**TQM** total quality management
**TRI** Toxics Release Inventory
**TRPA** Tahoe Regional Planning Agency
**TSCA** Toxic Substances Control Act
**TSD** treatment, storage, and disposal facility
**TVA** Tennessee Valley Authority
**UAO** unilateral administrative order
**UGB** urban growth boundary
**UIC** underground injection control
**ULEV** ultra low-emission vehicle
**UMTRCA** Uranium Mill Tailings Radiation Control Act
**UN** United Nations
**UNCED** United Nations Conference on Environment and Development
**UNCLOS** United Nations Convention on the Law of the Sea
**UNEP** United Nations Environment Programme
**UNFCC** United Nations Framework Convention on Climate Change
**USMCA** United States-Mexico-Canada Agreement
**UST** underground storage tank
**UV** ultraviolet
**VOC** volatile organic compound
**WARS** Wilderness Attribute Rating System
**WCED** World Commission on Environment and Development
**WHO** World Health Organization
**WOTUS** waters of the United States
**WSA** wilderness study area
**WSSD** World Summit on Sustainable Development
**WTO** World Trade Organization
**WWF** World Wildlife Fund
**ZEV** zero-emission vehicle